"Appreciating human diversity" was rated the *most important* outcome of an introductory anthropology course.

appreciating DIVERSITY

Culture Clash: Makah Seek Return to Whaling Past

Cultures are diverse but not isolated. Throughout human history links between groups have been provided by cultural practices such as marriage, kinship, religion, trade, travel, exploration, and conquest. For centuries, indigenous peoples have been exposed to a world system. Contemporary forces and events make even the illusion of autonomy hard to maintain. Nowadays, as is described here, members of local cultures and communities must heed not only their own customs but also agencies, laws, and lawsuits operating at the national and international levels.

As you read this account and this chapter on culture, pay attention to the various kinds of rights being asserted—animal rights, cultural rights, economic rights, legal rights, and human rights—and how those rights might clash. Also consider the different levels of culture and of political representation (local, re-

On May 17, 1999, a week into the hunt, the Makah killed a 30-ton gray whale, striking it with harpoons and then killing it with a gunshot to the back of the head.

That rainy spring day remains etched in the minds of many Makah as a defining moment in their efforts to reach back to their cultural and historical roots. It was their first kill in seven decades, and it was their last since they were stopped by court rulings. They have asked the federal government for permission to resume hunting. . . .

The Makah, a tribe of about 1,500 near the mouth of the Strait of Juan de Fuca on the Olympic Peninsula, see themselves as whalers and continue to identify themselves spiritually with whales.

"Everybody felt like it was a part of making history," Micah L. McCarty, a tribal council member, said of the 1999 hunt. "It's inspired a

By the time they were ready, none of the Makah had witnessed a whale hunt or even tasted the meat, hearing only stories passed down through the generations. They learned that the whale was a touchstone of Makah culture—the tribe's logo today pictures an eagle perched on a whale—and that the tribe's economy was built around the lucrative trade with Europeans in whale oil, used for heating and lighting, during the 18th and early 19th centuries.

For a year before the 1999 hunt, the new Makah whale hunters prepared for their sacramental pursuit, training in canoes on the cold and choppy waters of the Pacific Ocean, praying on the beach in the mornings and at the dock in the evenings.

Animal rights groups were preparing, too. When the hunt began, the small reservation and its surrounding waters were teeming with

> "Appreciating Diversity" boxes explore the rich diversity of cultures (past and present) that anthropologists study. These boxes supplement the extensive discussions of cultures around the world presented throughout the text.

→ These are just some of the reasons why **three out of four** Kottak adopters report that they will continue to use the text.

anthropology APPRECIATING HUMAN DIVERSITY

FIFTEENTH EDITION

Conrad Phillip Kottak

University of Michigan

Mc Graw Hill

Connect
Learn
Succeed™

To my mother, Mariana Kottak Roberts

ANTHROPOLOGY: APPRECIATING HUMAN DIVERSITY, FIFTEENTH EDITION

Published by McGraw-Hill, a business unit of The McGraw-Hill Companies, Inc., 1221 Avenue of the Americas, New York, NY 10020. Copyright © 2013 by The McGraw-Hill Companies, Inc. All rights reserved. Printed in the United States of America. Previous editions © 2011, 2009, and 2008. No part of this publication may be reproduced or distributed in any form or by any means, or stored in a database or retrieval system, without the prior written consent of The McGraw-Hill Companies, Inc., including, but not limited to, in any network or other electronic storage or transmission, or broadcast for distance learning.

Some ancillaries, including electronic and print components, may not be available to customers outside the United States.

This book is printed on acid-free paper.

2 3 4 5 6 7 8 9 0 DOW/DOW 1 0 9 8 7 6 5 4 3

ISBN 978-0-07-803501-2
MHID 0-07-803501-5

Senior Vice President, Products & Markets: *Kurt L. Strand*
Vice President, General Manager, Products & Markets: *Michael Ryan*
Vice President, Content Production & Technology Services: *Kimberly Meriwether David*
Managing Director: *Gina Boedeker*
Director of Development: *Dawn Groundwater*
Development Manager: *Barbara A. Heinssen*
Development Editor: *Craig Leonard*
Marketing Manager: *Josh Zlatkus*
Content Project Manager: *Jennifer Gehl*
Buyer: *Susan K. Culbertson*
Designer: *Tara McDermott*
Cover/Interior Designer: *Maureen McCutcheon*
Cover Image: © *Agustinus Wibowo/OnAsia*
Senior Content Licensing Specialist: *Keri Johnson*
Photo Research: *Barbara Salz*
Compositor: *Aptara®, Inc.*
Typeface: *10/11 Minion Pro*
Printer: *R. R. Donnelley*

All credits appearing on page or at the end of the book are considered to be an extension of the copyright page.

Library of Congress Cataloging-in-Publication Data

Kottak, Conrad Phillip.
   Anthropology: appreciating human diversity / Conrad Phillip Kottak. — 15th ed.
      p. cm.
   Includes index.
   ISBN 978-0-07-803501-2 (hard copy: alk. paper)
   ISBN 0-07-803501-5 (hard copy: alk. paper)
   1. Ethnology.   2. Anthropology.   I. Title.
   GN316.K638 2013
   301—dc23

                                                2012020777

www.mhhe.com

contents in brief

contents

1 What Is Anthropology? 3

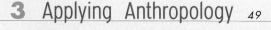

4 Doing Archaeology and Physical Anthropology 71

5 Evolution and Genetics 91

6 Human Variation and Adaptation 113

7 The Primates 133

8 Early Hominins *157*

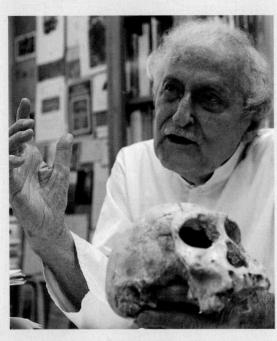

9 Archaic *Homo* 179

10 The Origin and Spread of Modern Humans 199

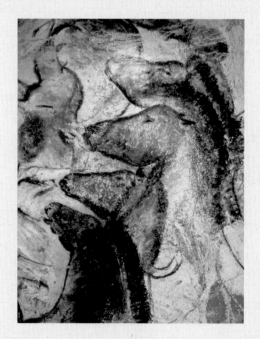

13 Method and Theory in Cultural Anthropology 273

16 Making a Living 349

17 Political Systems 377

18 Gender 403

19 Families, Kinship, and Descent 427

20 Marriage *449*

21 Religion *471*

22 Arts, Media, and Sports 495

list of boxes

appreciating ANTHROPOLOGY

appreciating DIVERSITY

living anthropology VIDEOS

focus on GLOBALIZATION

RECAP

about the author

Conrad Phillip Kottak

Conrad Phillip Kottak (A.B. Columbia College, Ph.D. Columbia University) is the Julian H. Steward Collegiate Professor Emeritus of Anthropology at the University of Michigan, where he served as anthropology department chair from 1996 to 2006. He has been honored for his teaching by the university and the state of Michigan. In 1999 the American Anthropological Association (AAA) awarded Professor Kottak the AAA/Mayfield Award for Excellence in the Undergraduate Teaching of Anthropology. In 2005 he was elected to the American Academy of Arts and Sciences, and in 2008 to the National Academy of Sciences, where he chairs Section 51, Anthropology.

Professor Kottak has done ethnographic fieldwork in Brazil, Madagascar, and the United States. His general interests are in the processes by which local cultures are incorporated—and resist incorporation—into larger systems. This interest links his earlier work on ecology and state formation in Africa and Madagascar to his more recent research on globalization, national and international culture, and the mass media.

The fourth edition of Kottak's popular case study *Assault on Paradise: The Globalization of a Little Community in Brazil*, based on his continuing fieldwork in Arembepe, Bahia, Brazil, was published in 2006 by McGraw-Hill. Professor Kottak and his students and associates (Brazilian and American) have combined ethnography and survey research to study "Television's Behavioral Effects in Brazil." That research is the basis of Kottak's book *Prime-Time Society: An Anthropological Analysis of Television and Culture* (updated edition published by Left Coast Press in 2009)—a comparative study of the nature and impact of television in Brazil and the United States.

Kottak's other books include *The Past in the Present: History, Ecology and Cultural Variation in Highland Madagascar* (1980), *Researching American Culture: A Guide for Student Anthropologists* (edited 1982) (both University of Michigan Press), and *Madagascar: Society and History* (edited 1986) (Carolina Academic Press). The most recent editions (15th) of his texts *Anthropology: Appreciating Human Diversity* (this book) and *Cultural Anthropology: Appreciating Cultural Diversity* were published by McGraw-Hill in 2013. He also is the author of *Mirror for Humanity: A Concise Introduction to Cultural Anthropology* (8th ed., McGraw-Hill, 2012) and *Window on Humanity: A Concise Introduction to Anthropology* (5th ed., McGraw-Hill, 2012). With Kathryn A. Kozaitis, he wrote *On Being Different: Diversity and Multiculturalism in the North American Mainstream* (4th ed., McGraw-Hill, 2012).

Conrad Kottak's articles have appeared in academic journals, including *American Anthropologist, Journal of Anthropological Research, American Ethnologist, Ethnology, Human Organization,* and *Luso-Brazilian Review.* He also has written for more popular journals, including *Transaction/SOCIETY, Natural History, Psychology Today,* and *General Anthropology.*

Kottak and his colleagues also have researched the emergence of ecological awareness in Brazil, the social context of deforestation and biodiversity conservation in Madagascar, and popular participation in economic development planning in northeastern Brazil. Professor Kottak has been active in the University of Michigan's Center for the Ethnography of Everyday Life, supported by the Alfred P. Sloan Foundation. In that capacity, for a research project titled "Media, Family, and Work in a Middle-Class Midwestern Town," Kottak and his colleague Lara Descartes investigated how middle-class families draw on various media in planning, managing, and evaluating their choices and solutions with respect to the competing demands of work and family. That research is the basis of their book *Media and Middle Class Moms: Images and Realties of Work and Family* (Descartes and Kottak 2009, Routledge/Taylor and Francis).

Conrad Kottak appreciates comments about his books from professors and students. He can be reached by e-mail at the following Internet address: **ckottak@ bellsouth.net.**

a letter from the author

Welcome to the 15th edition of *Anthropology: Appreciating Human Diversity!*

I wrote the first edition of this book at a time of rapid change in my favorite academic discipline—anthropology. My colleagues and I were excited about new discoveries and directions in all four of anthropology's subfields—biological anthropology, anthropological archaeology, sociocultural anthropology, and linguistic anthropology. My goal was to write a book that would capture that excitement, that would address key changes in the field of anthropology, while also providing a solid foundation of core concepts and the basics.

Anthropology has never stopped being an exciting and dynamic field. "Fascinating" is one of the most common words used to describe its subject matter. New discoveries are reported all the time (including in this book)! Profound changes—many associated with globalization—have affected the people and societies that anthropologists study. While any competent text must present anthropology's core, it must also demonstrate anthropology's relevance to the 21st-century world we inhabit. Accordingly, I've added a new feature titled "Focus on Globalization" to many chapters. Focusing on an increasingly interconnected world, these essays examine topics as diverse as tourism in the ancient and modern worlds, global disease pandemics, world events (including the Olympics and the World Cup), and the expansion of international finance and branding.

Each chapter of this book begins with a discussion titled "Understanding Ourselves." Drawing on students' own experience, these introductions use familiar examples to show how anthropology relates to everyday life, and to set the stage for the content that follows. One way I keep this book current after multiple editions is to follow changes not only in anthropology, but also in American culture. Use of popular culture examples can help students understand and appreciate anthropological concepts and approaches. To cite just a few examples, the anthropology of *Star Wars*, *The Wizard of Oz*, *The Hunger Games*, and even *Jersey Shore* are explored in this book, along with more traditional aspects of American culture.

No academic field has a stronger commitment to, or respect for, human diversity than anthropology does. In this text, boxes titled "Appreciating Diversity" focus on various forms and expressions of human biological and cultural diversity that make anthropology so fascinating. Some of these explorations of diversity, for example, the recent popularity of hugging in U.S. high schools, will likely be familiar to students. Others, like the story of a Turkish man with five wives and fifty-five children, will prompt them to consider human societies very different from their own.

My overarching goal for this textbook is to help students appreciate the field of anthropology and the various kinds of diversity it studies. How do anthropologists think and work? Where do we go, and how do we interpret what we see? How do we step back, compare, and analyze? How does anthropology contribute to our understanding of the world? To answer these questions, chapters contain boxed sections titled "Appreciating Anthropology," which focus on the value and usefulness of anthropological research and approaches.

I chose anthropology, first as my undergraduate major, then as my profession, because I appreciated its breadth, its approaches, and its content. I know that most students who read this book will not go on to become anthropologists, or even anthropology majors. For those who do, this book should provide a solid foundation to build on. For those who don't—that is, for most of my readers—my goal is to instill a sense of appreciation: of human diversity, of anthropology as a field, and of how anthropology can build on, and help make sense of, the experience that students bring to the classroom. May this course and this text help students think differently about, and achieve greater understanding of, their own culture and its place within our globalizing world.

Conrad Phillip Kottak

Appreciating Human Diversity

"Appreciating Diversity" Boxes

These boxes explore the rich diversity of cultures—past and present—that anthropologists study. Hugging in U.S. high schools, Googling in different languages, and art created more than 100,000 years ago in South Africa are just a few of the topics explored in these sections.

appreciating DIVERSITY

Australian Aborigine Hair Tells a Story of Human Migration

Before the 17th century, Native Australians, aka Australian Aborigines, lived on the world's most isolated inhabited continent. The recent analysis of one sample of Aboriginal DNA suggests that ancestral Australians branched off from ancestral Europeans and Asians between 70,000 and 50,000 years ago and had little contact with outsiders until the formation of the modern world system. Tropical Australians retained the dark skin color of their African forebears because they never left the tropics during their gradual migration from Africa to Australia.

A lock of hair, collected by a British anthropologist a century ago, has yielded the first genome of an Australian Aborigine, along with insights into the earliest migration from the ancestral human homeland somewhere in northeast Africa.

The Aboriginal genome bolsters earlier genetic evidence showing that once the Aborigines' ancestors arrived in Australia, some 50,000 years ago, they somehow kept the whole continent to themselves without admitting any outsiders.

The Aborigines are thus direct descendants of the first modern humans to leave Africa, without any genetic mixture from other races so far as can be seen at present. Their dark skin reflects an African origin and a migration and residence in latitudes near the equator, unlike Europeans and Asians whose ancestors gained the paler skin necessary for living in northern latitudes.

"Aboriginal Australians likely have one of the oldest continuous population histories outside sub-Saharan Africa today," say the researchers who analyzed the hair, a group led by Eske Willerslev of the Natural History Museum of Denmark.

Dr. Willerslev is an expert at working with ancient DNA, which is usually highly fragmented. Use of the ancient hair reduced the possibility of mixture with European genes and sidestepped the political difficulties of obtaining DNA from living Aborigines.

The DNA in the Aboriginal genome, when compared with DNA from other peoples around the world, shows that when modern humans first migrated out of Africa the ancestors of the Aborigines split away from the main group very early, and before Europeans and East Asians split from each other....

Based on the rate of mutation in DNA, the geneticists estimate that the Aborigines split from the ancestors of all Eurasians some 70,000 years ago, and that the ancestors of Europeans and East Asians split from each other about 30,000 years ago.

But the genetic data offers no information as to where these population splits may have occurred, whether in India or even earlier, before the migratory group had left Africa.... Genetic dates are based on a mixture of statistics and best guesses, but the split times calculated by the Danish team are compatible with the more reliable archaeological dates, which record the earliest known human presence in Australia at 44,000 years ago. The Aborigines' ancestors could have arrived several thousand years before this date....

The first inhabitants of Australia must have possessed advanced boat-building technology to cross from the nearest point in Asia to Sahul, the ancient continent that included Australia, New Guinea and Tasmania until the rise of sea level that occurred at the end of the last ice age, 10,000 years ago. But there is no archaeological evidence for boats....

Despite the Aborigines' genetic isolation, there is evidence of some profound cultural exchange that occurred around 6,000 years ago. The stone tools become more sophisticated, and the population increased. The Aborigines did not domesticate plants or animals, but a wild dog, the dingo, first appears in the archaeological record at this time....

Most of Australia is a forbidding desert, and this barrier may have been the downfall of most invasions, whether of people or of animals.... The ancestors of the Aborigines were lucky enough to find their way south, where there is more vegetation, and the dingo is a skillful hunter, able to look after itself....

Indigenous Australians in ceremonial dress on Tiwi Island, Northern Territory, Australia. Northern Australia is in the tropics.

"Appreciating Anthropology" Boxes

These accounts explore ways in which anthropologists are actively engaged in some of our most urgent 21st-century concerns. From studying the culture of Hurricane Katrina survivors to observing the habitats and habits of endangered primates, these boxes demonstrate that topics raised in every chapter can be found in today's headlines.

appreciating ANTHROPOLO

Remote and Poked, Anthropology's Dream Tribe

Anthropology, remember, is a four-subfield discipline that is comparative, cross-cultural, and biocultural. Anthropologists are known for their close observation of human behavior in natural settings and their focus on human biological and cultural diversity in time and space. It is typical of the anthropological approach to go right to—and live with—the local people, whether in northern Kenya, as described here, or in middle-class America (see Descartes and Kottak 2009).

Anthropologists study human biology and culture in varied times and places and in a rapidly changing world. This account focuses on a remote population, the Ariaal of northern Kenya, whom anthropologists have been studying since the 1970s. In the account we learn about the multifaceted research interests that anthropologists have. Among the Ariaal, anthropologists have studied a range of topics, including kinship and marriage customs, conflict, and even biomedical issues such as illness and body type and function. As you read this account, consider, too, what anthropologists get from the people being studied and vice versa.

The Ariaal, a nomadic community of about 10,000 people in northern Kenya, have been seized on by researchers since the 1970s, after one anthropologist, Elliot Fratkin—stumbled upon them and began publishing his accounts of their lives....

Other researchers have done studies on everything from their cultural practices to their testosterone levels. National Geographic focused on the Ariaal in 1999, in an article on vanishing cultures.

But over the years, more and more Ariaal—like the Masai and the Turkana in Kenya and the Tuaregs and Bedouins elsewhere in Africa—are settling down. Many have emigrated closer to Marsabit, the nearest town, which has cellphone reception and even sporadic Internet access.

The scientists continue to arrive in Ariaal country, with their notebooks, tents, and bizarre queries, but now they document a semi-isolated people straddling modern life and more traditional ways.

For Benjamin C. Campbell, a biological anthropologist at Boston University who was introduced to the Ariaal by Dr. Fratkin, their way of life, diet, and cultural practices make them worthy of study.

Other academics agree. Local residents say they have been asked over the years how many livestock they own (many), how many times they have had diarrhea in the last month (often) and what they ate the day before yesterday (usually meat, milk or blood).

Ariaal women have been asked about the work they do, which seems to exceed that of the men, and about local marriage customs, which compel their prospective husbands to hand over livestock to their parents before the ceremony can take place....

The researchers may not know this, but the Ariaal have been studying them all these years as well.

The Ariaal wear toothbrushes made of wood, and the research does not cease....

"I was young when Elliot first arrived," recalled an Ariaal elder known as Lenampere in Lewogoso Lukumai, a settlement that moves from time to time to a new patch of sand. "He came here and lived with us. He drank milk and blood with us. After him, so many others came."...

Not all African tribes are as welcoming to researchers, even those with the necessary permits from government bureaucrats. But the Ariaal have a reputation for cooperating—in exchange, that is, for pocket money. "They think I'm stupid for asking dumb questions," said Daniel Lemoille, headmaster of the school in Songa, a village outside of Marsabit for Ariaal nomads who have settled down, and a frequent research assistant for visiting professors. "You have to try to explain that these same questions are asked to people all over the world and that their answers will help advance science."...

The Ariaal have no major gripes about the studies, although the local chief in Songa, Stephen Lesseren, who wore a Boston University T-shirt the other day, said he wished their work would lead to more tangible benefits for his people.

"We didn't mind helping people get their Ph.D.'s," he said. "But once they get their Ph.D.'s, many of them go away. They don't send us their reports... We want feedback. We want development."

Even when conflicts break out in the area, as happened this year as members of rival tribes slaughtered each other, victimizing the Ariaal, the research does not cease. With tensions still high, John G. Galaty, an anthropologist at McGill University in Montreal who studies ethnic conflicts, arrived in northern Kenya to question them.

In a study in The International Journal of Impotence Research, Dr. Campbell found that Ariaal men with many wives showed less erectile dysfunction than did men of the same age with fewer spouses.

Dr. Campbell's body image study, published in the Journal of Cross-Cultural Psychology this year, also found that Ariaal men are much more consistent than men in other parts of the world in their views of the average man's body (one like their own) and what they think women want (one like their own).

Dr. Campbell came across no billboards or international magazines in Ariaal country and only one television in a local restaurant that played CNN, leading him to contend that Ariaal men's views of their bodies were less affected by media images of burly male models with six-pack stomachs and rippling chests.

To test his theories, a nonresearcher without a Ph.D. showed a group of Ariaal men a copy of Men's Health magazine full of pictures of impossibly well-sculpted men and women. The men looked on with rapt attention and admired the chiseled forms.

"That one, I like," said one nomad who was up in his years, pointing at a photo of a curvy woman who was clearly a regular at the gym. Another old-timer gazed at the bulging pectoral muscles of a male bodybuilder in the magazine and posed a question that got everybody talking. Was it a man, he asked, or a very, very strong woman?

Kobolon Garawale (left) is amused by questions posed by researcher Daniel Lemoille in Songa, Kenya. The Ariaal, a nomadic community of about 10,000 people in northern Kenya, have been studied since the 1970s by Elliot Fratkin and other anthropologists, representing various subfields.

focus on **GLOBALIZATION**

A Devastating Encounter in the Columbian Exchange

The Columbian exchange (named for Christopher Columbus) was a key early form of globalization, because it forever linked our globe's western and eastern hemispheres. The term refers to the exchange of products, populations, and pathogens between the Old World and the New World that occurred after Columbus reached the Americas in 1492.

One devastating aspect of the Columbian exchange was the global spread of diseases previously confined to the Old World. Having lived with these pathogens for generations, Old World populations had developed various forms of immunity to many of them. Native Americans had no such resistance to Old World diseases, which included smallpox, chicken pox, measles, malaria, yellow fever, cholera, typhoid, bubonic plague, influenza, and the common cold. Only syphilis, as we learned in Chapter 5, moved the other way—from the New World to the Old.

By debilitating and decimating the Aztecs of Mexico and the Inca of Peru, severe smallpox epidemics helped the Spanish conquer those peoples and their territories. Up to 90 percent of the population of the New World may have perished from Old World pathogens between 1500 and 1650 (Nunn and Qian 2010).

The African slave trade emerged in the context of Native American depopulation and the demand for human labor to produce commodities on New World plantations. Plantation economies outside the southern United States (where cotton was a New World domesticate) were based mainly on Old World crops (especially sugar and tobacco) introduced to the Americas and the Caribbean as part of the Columbian exchange. About twelve million human beings were involuntarily transported from Africa to the New World during the centuries of the Atlantic slave trade—the 16th through the 19th centuries.

Europeans from Spain, Portugal, the Netherlands, England, and France extended their colonial empires from the Americas to Africa and Asia. Europeans had a degree of genetic resistance to many Old World pathogens, but not to malaria—the scourge of the tropics. Quinine was a New World product that—again through the Columbian exchange—eventually offered Europeans a degree of protection against malaria. Europeans might never have been able to maintain colonial empires in the tropics of Africa, Asia, and South America without quinine (Nunn and Qian 2010). This is yet another way in which western expansion, and ultimately the formation of the modern world system, depended on the Columbian exchange.

Globalization remains an important factor in the spread of diseases today, as anyone knows who has seen the movie *Contagion*. In real life, as described in Chapter 5, the H1N1 virus, known originally as swine flu, gained attention as a pandemic in 2009–2010. The spread of pathogens from animals (like pigs, or swine) to humans became more common after people began living in close proximity to domesticated pigs, poultry, sheep, and cattle. These animals, originally domesticated in the Old World, now have a global distribution. How have humans adapted to the diseases their animals transmit?

Other facial features also illustrate adaptation to selective forces. Among contemporary humans, average tooth size is largest among Native Australian hunters and gatherers, for whom large teeth had an adaptive advantage, given a diet based on foods with a considerable amount of sand and grit. People with small teeth—if false teeth and sand-free foods are unavailable—can't feed themselves as effectively as people with more massive dentition can (see Brace 2005).

Size and Body Build

Certain body builds have adaptive advantages for particular environments. In 1847, the German biologist Karl Christian Bergmann observed that within the same species of warm-blooded animals, populations with smaller individuals are more often found in warm climates, while those with greater bulk, or mass, are found in colder regions. The relation between body weight and temperature is summarized in **Bergmann's rule**: The smaller of two bodies similar in shape has more surface area per unit of weight. Therefore, it sheds heat more efficiently. (Heat loss occurs on the body's surface—the skin perspires.) Average body size tends to increase in cold areas and to decrease in hot ones because big bodies hold heat better than small ones do. To be more precise, in a large sample of native populations, average adult male weight increased by 0.66 pound (0.3 kilogram) for every 1 degree Fahrenheit fall in mean annual temperature (Roberts 1953; Steegman 1975). The "pygmies" and the San, who live in hot climates and weigh only 90 pounds on the average, illustrate this relation in reverse.

Body shape differences also reflect adaptation to temperature through natural selection. The relationship between temperature and body shape in animals and birds was first recognized in 1877 by the zoologist J. A. Allen. **Allen's rule** states that the relative size of protruding body parts—ears, tails, bills, fingers, toes, limbs, and so on—increases with temperature. Among humans, slender bodies with long digits and limbs are advantageous in tropical climates. Such bodies increase body surface relative to mass and allow for more efficient heat dissipation. Among the cold-adapted Eskimos or Inuit, the opposite phenotype is found. Short limbs and stocky bodies serve to conserve heat. Cold-area populations tend to have larger chests and shorter arms than do people from warm areas (Roberts 1953).

This discussion of adaptive relationships between climate and body size and shape illustrates that natural selection may achieve the same effect in different ways. East African Nilotes, who live in a hot area, have tall, linear bodies with elongated extremities that increase surface area relative to mass and thus maximize heat dissipation (illustrating Allen's rule). Among the "pygmies," the reduction of body size

Focus on Globalization

New "Focus on Globalization" boxes examine topics as diverse as tourism in the ancient and modern worlds, global disease pandemics, world events (including the Olympics and the World Cup), and the expansion of international finance and branding that anthropologists study. These boxes supplement the extensive discussions of cultures around the world presented throughout the text.

cultural rights
Rights vested in religious and ethnic minorities and indigenous societies.

cultural relativism
Idea that behavior should be evaluated not by outside standards but in the context of the culture in which it occurs.

IPR
Intellectual property rights; an indigenous group's collective knowledge and its applications.

anthropology **ATLAS**
http://www.mhhe.com/anthromaps Map 10 locates classic ethnographic field sites—"cultures" or societies already studied by 1950.

human rights
Rights based on justice and morality beyond and superior to particular countries, cultures, and religions.

Several societies in Africa and the Middle East have customs requiring female genital modification. *Clitoridectomy* is the removal of a girl's clitoris. *Infibulation* involves sewing the lips (labia) of the vagina to constrict the vaginal opening. Both procedures reduce female sexual pleasure and, it is believed in some societies, the likelihood of adultery. Although traditional in the societies where they occur, such practices, characterized as female genital mutilation (FGM), have been opposed by human rights advocates, especially women's rights groups. The idea is that the custom infringes on a basic human right: disposition over one's body and one's sexuality. Indeed, such practices are fading as a result of worldwide attention to the problem and changing sex/gender roles. Some African countries have banned or otherwise discouraged the procedures, as have Western nations that receive immigration from such cultures. Similar issues arise with circumcision and other male genital operations. Is it right to require adolescent boys to undergo collective circumcision to fulfill cultural traditions, as has been done traditionally in parts of Africa and Australia? Is it right for a baby boy to be circumcised without his permission, as has been done routinely in the United States and as is customary among Jews and Muslims? (A 2011 initiative aimed at banning circumcision in San Francisco, California, failed to make it to the ballot.)

According to an idea known as **cultural relativism,** it is inappropriate to use outside standards to judge behavior in a given society; such behavior should be evaluated in the context of the culture in which it occurs. Anthropologists employ cultural relativism not as a moral belief but as a methodological position: In order to understand another culture fully, we must try to understand how the people in that culture see things. What motivates them—what are they thinking—when they do those things? Such an approach does not preclude making moral judgments. In the FGM example, one can understand the motivations for the practice only by looking at things from the point of view of the people who engage in it. Having done this, one then faces the moral question of what, if anything, to do about it.

We also should recognize that different people and groups within the same society—for example, women versus men or old versus young—can have very different opinions about what is proper, necessary, and moral. When there are power differentials in a society, a particular practice may be supported by some people more than others (e.g., old men versus young women). In trying to understand the meaning of a practice or belief within any cultural context, we should ask who is relatively advantaged and disadvantaged by that custom.

The idea of **human rights** invokes a realm of justice and morality beyond and superior to particular countries, cultures, and religions. Human rights, usually seen as vested in individuals, include the right to speak freely, to hold religious beliefs without persecution, and not to be murdered, injured, enslaved, or imprisoned without charge. These rights are not ordinary laws that particular governments make and enforce. Human rights are seen as *inalienable* (nations cannot abridge or terminate them) and international (larger than and superior to individual nations and cultures). Four United Nations documents describe nearly all the human rights that have been internationally recognized. Those documents are the UN Charter; the Universal Declaration of Human Rights; the Covenant on Economic, Social and Cultural Rights; and the Covenant on Civil and Political Rights.

Alongside the human rights movement has arisen an awareness of the need to preserve cultural rights. Unlike human rights, **cultural rights** are vested not in individuals but in groups, including indigenous peoples and religious and ethnic minorities. Cultural rights include a group's ability to raise its children in the ways of its forebears, to continue its language, and not to be deprived of its economic base by the nation in which it is located (Greaves 1995). Many countries have signed pacts endorsing, for cultural minorities within nations, such rights as self-determination; some degree of home rule; and the right to practice the group's religion, culture, and language. The related notion of indigenous intellectual property rights (**IPR**) has arisen in an attempt to conserve each society's cultural base—its core beliefs and principles. IPR are claimed as a cultural right, allowing indigenous groups to control who may know and use their collective knowledge and its applications. Much traditional cultural knowledge has commercial value. Examples include ethnomedicine (traditional medical knowledge and techniques), cosmetics, cultivated plants, foods, folklore, arts, crafts, songs, dances, costumes, and rituals. According to the IPR concept, a particular group may determine how its indigenous knowledge and the products of that knowledge are used and distributed, and the level of compensation required. (This chapter's "Appreciating Diversity" discusses how notions of human, cultural, and animal rights may come into conflict.)

The notion of cultural rights recalls the previous discussion of cultural relativism, and the issue raised there arises again. What does one do about cultural rights that interfere with human rights? I believe that anthropology, as the scientific study of human diversity, should strive to present accurate accounts and explanations of cultural phenomena. Most ethnographers try to be objective, accurate, and sensitive in their accounts of other cultures. However, objectivity, sensitivity, and a cross-cultural perspective don't mean that anthropologists have to ignore international standards of justice and morality. The anthropologist doesn't have to approve customs

Anthrology Atlas

Located online at www.mhhe.com/anthromaps, the Anthropology Atlas is comprised of 18 maps that present a global view of issues important to anthropologists and to the people they study, such as world forest loss, the origin and spread of food production, and ancient civilizations. Cross references in the text tie the maps to relevant chapter discussions.

Highlights of the 15th Edition

CHAPTER 1
- New focus on globalization—what world events capture and retain global attention

CHAPTER 2
- Major new discussion of globalization as fact and process versus globalization as ideology and contested policy
- Revised content on culture as instrumental, adaptive, and maladaptive and on cultural universals and generalities

CHAPTER 3
- New focus on globalization—HIV/AIDS as the deadliest pandemic of our time
- New content on forensic anthropology

CHAPTER 4
- Complete reorganized and retitled chapter, with archaeology now preceding physical/biological anthropology
- New content on ethical issues, including those raised by NAGPRA and Kennewick Man

CHAPTER 5
- Updated throughout, especially in discussion of intelligent design versus evolutionary theory

CHAPTER 6
- New content on globalization—the worldwide spread of diseases as part of the Columbian Exchange
- New discussion of the AAA race project
- New material on how humans reached Australia and on lactose tolerance

CHAPTER 7
- New material on global threats to primates, especially orangutans
- New content on ape diversity past and present and on the *Rise of the Planet of the Apes*

CHAPTER 8
- New material on the *Australopithecus sediba* find
- New coverage of "Lucy's baby," the world's most ancient fossil child

CHAPTER 9
- Thorough updating, with the latest fossil and archaeological discoveries
- New material on Neandertal cannibalism and social life

CHAPTER 10
- New focus on globalization—the global spread of anatomically modern humans
- New material on the Denisovans, Asiatic cousins of the Neandertals, who apparently mated with ancestral Melanesians
- New material on how fossil teeth put humans in Europe earlier than thought
- New evidence for early art and symbolic expression in South African caves

CHAPTER 11
- Updated discussion of domestication and the spread of farming and herding

CHAPTER 12
- New content on globalization—the seven wonders of the ancient and modern world
- New material on the urban revolution
- New content on pseudo-archaeology and debunking of fantastic claims

CHAPTER 13
- Significantly revised discussion of recent theory in anthropology
- New discussions of ethics and of anthropologists studying war and terrorism

CHAPTER 14
- Added discussion of new media, including texting, Facebook, and Twitter
- Expanded coverage of sociolinguistics, including linguistic stratification
- New material on the recent reconstruction of ancient syntax, which may be ancestral to all languages

CHAPTER 15
- New discussion of the growing opposition between older Americans, who tend to be white, and younger Americans, who are much more diverse
- New discussion of ethnic diversity within countries, by global region
- New material on minority group poverty rates, and updating based on 2010 census data

CHAPTER 16
- New focus on globalization—interconnectedness in today's global economy

CHAPTER 17
- New focus on globalization—the political role of new media
- Major new section on social (versus governmental) control, with discussions of hegemony and resistance, weapons of the weak, shame and gossip, and the Igbo women's war

CHAPTER 18
- New focus on globalization—the Global Gender Gap Index, by country
- New major section, "Beyond Male and Female," discussing transgender and chromosomal anomalies creating sex-gender differences
- New discussion of work and happiness, exposing a correlation between a national happiness index and female extradomestic employment
- New information on the feminization of poverty

CHAPTER 19
- Thoroughly updated with latest statistics available

CHAPTER 20
- Thoroughly revised discussions of exogamy, incest, and incest avoidance
- Revised discussion of gifts and exchanges surrounding marriage
- New material on pair bonding, extended kinship, and group alliance

CHAPTER 21
- New focus on globalization—the spread of Evangelical Protestantism and Islam
- New discussion of problems in defining religion
- Expanded discussion of secular rituals

CHAPTER 22
- Updated coverage and new illustrations

CHAPTER 23
- New focus on globalization—where in the world jobs are located
- New discussion of the 99 percent versus the 1 percent and the Occupy movement

CHAPTER 24
- Expanded discussion of the globalization of risk

Support for Students and Instructors

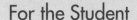

With the CourseSmart eTextbook version of this title, students can save up to 50 percent off the cost of a print book, reduce their impact on the environment, and access powerful Web tools for learning. Faculty can also review and compare the full text online without having to wait for a print desk copy. CourseSmart is an online eTextbook, which means users need to be connected to the Internet in order to access it. Students can also print sections of the book for maximum portability.

For the Student

The Student Online Learning Center website (www.mhhe.com/kottak15e) is a free Web-based student supplement featuring video clips, self-quizzes, interactive exercises and activities, anthropology Web links, and other useful tools. Designed specifically to complement individual chapters of the 15th edition, the Online Learning Center gives students access to material such as the following:

- "Living Anthropology" Video Icons

These icons reference a set of videos that show practicing anthropologists at work and that can be viewed on the open-access online learning center (www.mhhe.com/kottak15e). Students hear anthropologists describe the research they are doing and are given a glimpse of the many sites and peoples that anthropologists study.

- Online "Through the Eyes of Others" Essays: Written by students raised outside the United States, these essays contrast aspects of life in contemporary American culture with similar aspects in the authors' cultures of origin. The observations within these essays show students how cultural practices that seem familiar and natural are not seen as such by others.

- Anthropology Atlas: Comprising 18 maps, this online atlas presents a global view of issues important to anthropologists and to the people they study, such as world forest loss, the origin and spread of food production, and ancient civilizations. Cross references in the text tie the maps to relevant chapter discussions. These maps can be found at http://www.mhhe.com/anthromaps.

- An electronic version of the in-text Anthropology Atlas
- Student Self-Quizzes
- Virtual Exploration Activities
- Interactive Exercises
- Chapter Outlines and Objectives
- Vocabulary Flash Cards
- FAQs

For the Instructor

The Instructor Online Learning Center website (www.mhhe.com/kottak15e) is a password-protected instructor-only site, which includes the following materials:

- Instructor's Manual
- PowerPoint Lecture Slides
- Computerized Test Bank
- Question Bank for the Classroom Performance System (CPS)
- Image Bank
- Links to Professional Resources
- *Faces of Culture* Video Correlation Guide

Acknowledgments

As always, I'm grateful to many colleagues at McGraw-Hill. Thanks to Gina Boedeker, McGraw-Hill's Managing Director for anthropology (along with sociology, women's studies, and criminal justice). Thanks as well to Ryan Viviani, editorial coordinator for anthropology (as well as sociology and women's studies). I'm also grateful to Barbara Heinssen and especially to Craig Leonard for their work as developmental editors. Craig summarized the comments and suggestions made by reviewers of the 14th edition. He also helped me tremendously in submitting everything needed by the production team that I did not supply, including preparation of the visual manuscript. Thanks to Barbara and Craig for inspiring me to write, and for reviewing, the new "Focus on Globalization" boxes in this 15th edition. I thank marketing manager Josh Zlatkus and McGraw-Hill's entire team of sales reps and regional managers for the work they do in helping professors and students gain access to my books.

I'm delighted to have Jennifer Gehl as project manager for this edition. She and Christine Demma Foushi have helped me so much with the K4 system I'm now using to input—rather than simply review—what I've written. Thanks, Jennifer, for your willingness to oversee the production process for this edition from start to finish. Sue Culbertson, production supervisor, worked with the printer to make sure everything came out right. It's always a pleasure to plan and choose photos with Barbara Salz, freelance photo researcher, with whom I've worked for over 20 years. Sincere thanks to Beth Bulger for her amazing job of copyediting; and Carey Lange for proofreading. I am grateful to Tara McDermott and Maureen McCutcheon for their work on the design of this edition.

Keri Johnson, photo research coordinator, also deserves thanks. For creating and updating the attractive maps in the online Anthropology Atlas, I would like to acknowledge the work of Mapping Specialists.

Thanks, as well, to Mahalakshmi Rengarajan, media project manager, for creating the OLC with video clips and all the other supplements. Once again I thank Wesley Hall, who has handled the literary permissions.

I'm especially indebted to the professors who reviewed the 14th edition of this book and of my *Cultural Anthropology* text in preparation for the 15th edition. They suggested changes I've implemented here in the 15th edition—and others I'll work on for subsequent editions. Alejandro Lugo of the University of Illinois, a long-time adopter, took the time to write me with several useful suggestions, some of which I've implemented here, some of which I'll work on later. Michael McCrath of the Seattle Community Colleges made an excellent suggestion for the chapter on marriage, which I discussed with him at length and have implemented in this edition. Robin Huffman of Butte Community College in Oroville, California, also wrote independently with useful suggestions, especially for the last chapter of the book.

The names and schools of the reviewers contracted by McGraw-Hill to review the 14th edition are as follows:

Lisa Gezon, *University of West Georgia*

Maria Altemara, *West Virginia University*

Jennifer Chase, *University of North Texas–Denton*

James Derrick Lemons, *The University of Georgia*

Bernard K. Means, *Virginia Commonwealth University*

Holly Peters-Golden, *University of Michigan*

Mariella Squire, *University of Maine at Fort Kent*

I'm also grateful to the valued reviewers of previous editions of this book and of my *Cultural Anthropology* text. Their names are as follows:

Julianna Acheson, *Green Mountain College*

Stephanie W. Alemán, *Iowa State University*

Mohamad Al-Madani, *Seattle Central Community College*

Douglas J. Anderson, *Front Range Community College*

E. F. Aranyosi, *University of Washington*

Robert Bee, *University of Connecticut*

Joy A. Bilharz, *SUNY at Fredonia*

James R. Bindon, *University of Alabama*

Kira Blaisdell-Sloan, *Louisiana State University*

Kathleen T. Blue, *Minnesota State University*

Daniel Boxberger, *Western Washington University*

Vicki Bradley, *University of Houston*

Lisa Kaye Brandt, *North Dakota State University*

Ethan M. Braunstein, *Northern Arizona University*

Ned Breschel, *Morehead State University*

Peter J. Brown, *Emory University*

Margaret S. Bruchez, *Blinn College*

Vaughn M. Bryant, *Texas A&M University*

Andrew Buckser, *Purdue University*

Richard H. Buonforte, *Brigham Young University*

Karen Burns, *University of Georgia*

Richard Burns, *Arkansas State University*

Mary Cameron, *Auburn University*

Joseph L. Chartkoff, *Michigan State University*

Dianne Chidester, *University of South Dakota*

Stephen Childs, *Valdosta State University*

Inne Choi, *California Polytechnic State University–San Luis Obispo*

Wanda Clark, *South Plains College*

Jeffrey Cohen, *Penn State University*

Fred Conquest, *Community College of Southern Nevada*

Barbara Cook, *California Polytechnic State University–San Luis Obispo*

Maia Greenwell Cunningham, *Citrus College*

Sean M. Daley, *Johnson County Community College*

Karen Dalke, *University of Wisconsin–Green Bay*

Norbert Dannhaeuser, *Texas A&M University*

Michael Davis, *Truman State University*

Hillary DelPrete, *Wagner College*

Paul Demers, *University of Nebraska–Lincoln*

Darryl de Ruiter, *Texas A&M University*

Robert Dirks, *Illinois State University*

William W. Donner, *Kutztown University*

Mary Durocher, *Wayne State University*

Paul Durrenberger, *Pennsylvania State University*

George Esber, *Miami University of Ohio*

Les W. Field, *University of New Mexico*

Grace Fraser, *Plymouth State College*

Todd Jeffrey French, *University of New Hampshire, Durham*

Richard H. Furlow, *College of DuPage*

Vance Geiger, *University of Central Florida*

Laurie Godfrey, *University of Massachusetts–Amherst*

Bob Goodby, *Franklin Pierce College*

Gloria Gozdzik, *West Virginia University*

Tom Greaves, *Bucknell University*

Mark Grey, *University of Northern Iowa*

Sharon Gursky, *Texas A&M University*

John Dwight Hines, *University of California, Santa Barbara*

Brian A. Hoey, *Marshall University*

Homes Hogue, *Mississippi State University*

Kara C. Hoover, *Georgia State University*

Charles W. Houck, *University of North Carolina–Charlotte*

Stevan R. Jackson, *Virginia Tech*

Alice James, *Shippensburg University of Pennsylvania*

Cara Roure Johnson, *University of Connecticut*

Richard King, *Drake University*

Christine Kray, *Rochester Institute of Technology*

Eric Lassiter, *Ball State University*

Jill Leonard, *University of Illinois—Urbana–Champaign*

Kenneth Lewis, *Michigan State University*

David Lipset, *University of Minnesota*

Walter E. Little, *University at Albany, SUNY*

Jon K. Loessin, *Wharton County Junior College*

Brian Malley, *University of Michigan*

Jonathan Marks, *University of North Carolina–Charlotte*

H. Lyn Miles, *University of Tennessee at Chattanooga*

Barbara Miller, *George Washington University*

Richard G. Milo, *Chicago State University*

John Nass, Jr., *California University of Pennsylvania*

Frank Ng, *California State University–Fresno*

Constanza Ocampo-Raeder, *University of Maine (Orono)*

Divinity B. O'Connor DLR-Roberts, *Des Moines Area Community College*

Martin Ottenheimer, *Kansas State University*

De Ann Pendry, *University of Tennessee–Knoxville*

Leonard Plotnicov, *University of Pittsburgh*

Janet Pollak, *William Patterson College*

Christina Nicole Pomianek, *University of Missouri–Columbia*

Geoffrey G. Pope, *William Patterson University*

Howard Prince, *CUNY–Borough of Manhattan Community College*

Frances E. Purifoy, *University of Louisville*

Asa Randall, *University of Florida*

Mark A. Rees, *University of Louisiana at Lafayette*

Bruce D. Roberts, *Minnesota State University Moorhead*

Rita C. Rodabaugh, *Central Piedmont Community College*

Steven Rubenstein, *Ohio University*

Robert Rubinstein, *Syracuse University*

Richard A. Sattler, *University of Montana*

Richard Scaglion, *University of Pittsburgh*

Mary Scott, *San Francisco State University*

James Sewastynowicz, *Jacksonville State University*

Brian Siegel, *Furman University*

Michael Simonton, *Northern Kentucky University*

Megan Sinnott, *University of Colorado–Boulder*

Esther Skirboll, *Slippery Rock University of Pennsylvania*

Alexia Smith, *University of Connecticut*

Gregory Starrett, *University of North Carolina–Charlotte*

Karl Steinen, *University of West Georgia*

Noelle Stout, *Foothill and Skyline Colleges*

Merrily Stover, *University of Maryland–University College*

Elizabeth A. Throop, *Eastern Kentucky University*

Ruth Toulson, *Brigham Young University*

Susan Trencher, *George Mason University*

Mark Tromans, *Broward Community College*

Christina Turner, *Virginia Commonwealth University*

Donald Tyler, *University of Idaho*

Daniel Varisco, *Hofstra University*

Albert Wahrhaftig, *Sonoma State University*

Joe Watkins, *University of New Mexico*

David Webb, *Kutztown University of Pennsylvania*

George Westermark, *Santa Clara University*

Donald A. Whatley, *Blinn College*

Nancy White, *University of South Florida*

Katharine Wiegle, *Northern Illinois University*

Mary S. Willis, *University of Nebraska–Lincoln*

Brent Woodfill, *University of Louisiana at Lafayette*

I'm grateful to all these reviewers and professors for their enthusiasm and their suggestions for changes, additions, and deletions (sometimes in very different directions!).

Students, too, regularly share their insights about this and my other texts via e-mail and so have contributed to this book. Anyone—student or instructor—with access to e-mail can reach me at **ckottak@ bellsouth.net.**

As usual, my family has offered me understanding, support, and inspiration during the preparation of this book. Dr. Nicholas Kottak, who like me holds a doctorate in anthropology, regularly shares his insights with me, as does my daughter, Dr. Juliet Kottak Mavromatis, and my wife, Isabel Wagley Kottak. Isabel has been my companion in the field and in life during my entire career in anthropology, and I can't imagine being without her. I renew my dedication of this book to the memory of my mother, Mariana Kottak Roberts, for kindling my interest in the human condition, for reading and commenting on my writing, and for the insights about people and society she provided.

I've benefited from the knowledge, help, and advice of so many friends, colleagues, teaching assistants, graduate student instructors, and students that I can no longer fit their names into a short preface. I hope they know who they are and accept my thanks. I do especially thank my co-authors of other books: Kathryn Kozaitis (*On Being Different*), Lara Descartes (*Media and Middle Class Moms*), and most recently Lisa Gezon (*Culture*). Kathryn, Lara, and Lisa are prized former students of mine. Today they all are accomplished anthropologists in their own right, and they continue to share their wisdom with me.

I'm very grateful to my Michigan colleagues who share their insights and have suggested ways of making my books better. Thanks especially to a 101 team that includes Tom Fricke, Stuart Kirsch, Holly Peters-Golden, and Andrew Shryock. Special thanks as well to Joyce Marcus and Kent Flannery for continuing to nurture the archaeologist in me.

Over my many years of teaching introductory anthropology, feedback from undergraduates and graduate students has kept me up to date on the interests, needs, and views of the people for whom this book is written, as does my ongoing participation in workshops on the teaching of anthropology. I continue to believe that effective textbooks are based in the enthusiastic practice of teaching. I hope this product of my experience will be helpful to others.

Conrad Phillip Kottak
Seabrook Island, SC and Decatur, Georgia
ckottak@bellsouth.net

anthropology APPRECIATING HUMAN DIVERSITY

What Is Anthropology?

What distinguishes anthropology from other fields that study human beings?

How do anthropologists study human diversity in time and space?

Why is anthropology both scientific and humanistic?

◀ In Karachi, Pakistan, a bus gathers passengers next to watermelon stalls at the edge of a roadside market.

understanding OURSELVES

When you grew up, which sport did you appreciate the most—soccer, swimming, football, baseball, tennis, golf, or some other sport (or perhaps none at all)? Is this because of "who you are" or because of the opportunities you had as a child to practice and participate in this particular activity? Think about the phrases and sentences you would use to describe yourself in a personal ad or on a networking site—your likes and dislikes, hobbies, and habits. How many of these descriptors would be the same if you had been born in a different place or time?

When you were young, your parents might have told you that drinking milk and eating vegetables would help you grow up "big and strong." They probably didn't as readily recognize the role that *culture* plays in shaping bodies, personalities, and personal health. If nutrition matters in growth, so, too, do cultural guidelines. What is proper behavior for boys and girls? What kinds of work should men and women do? Where should people live? What are proper uses of their leisure time? What role should religion play? How should people relate to their family, friends, and neighbors? Although our genetic attributes provide a foundation for our growth and development, human biology is fairly plastic—that is, it is malleable. Culture is an environmental force that affects our development as much as do nutrition, heat, cold, and altitude. Culture also guides our emotional and cognitive growth and helps determine the kinds of personalities we have as adults.

Among scholarly disciplines, anthropology stands out as the field that provides the cross-cultural test. How much would we know about human behavior, thought, and feeling if we studied only our own kind? What if our entire understanding of human behavior were based on analysis of questionnaires filled out by college students in Oregon? That is a radical question, but one that should make you think about the basis for statements about what humans are like, individually or as a group. A primary reason why anthropology can uncover so much about what it means to be human is that the discipline is based on the cross-cultural perspective. One culture can't tell us everything we need to know about what it means to be human. Often culture is "invisible" (assumed to be normal, or just the way things are) until it is placed in comparison to another culture. For example, to appreciate how watching television affects us, as human beings, we need to study not just North America today but some other place—and perhaps also some other time (such as Brazil in the 1980s; see Kottak 1990*b*). The cross-cultural test is fundamental to the anthropological approach, which orients this textbook.

HUMAN DIVERSITY

Anthropologists study human beings and their products wherever and whenever they find them—in rural Kenya, a Turkish café, a Mesopotamian tomb, or a North American shopping mall. Anthropology explores human diversity across time and space, seeking to understand as much as possible about the human condition. Of particular interest is the diversity that comes through human adaptability.

Humans are among the world's most adaptable animals. In the Andes of South America, people wake up in villages 16,000 feet above sea level and then trek 1,500 feet higher to work in tin mines. Tribes in the Australian desert worship animals and discuss philosophy. People survive malaria in the tropics. Men have walked on the moon. The model of the *USS Enterprise* in Washington's Smithsonian Institution symbolizes the desire to "seek out new life and civilizations, to boldly go where no one has gone before." Wishes to know the unknown, control the uncontrollable, and create order out of chaos find expression among all peoples. Creativity, adaptability, and flexibility are basic human attributes, and human diversity is the subject matter of anthropology.

Students often are surprised by the breadth of **anthropology,** which is the study of the human species and its immediate ancestors. Anthropology is a uniquely comparative and **holistic** science. Holism refers to the study of the whole of the human condition: past, present, and future; biology, society, language, and culture. Most people think that anthropologists study fossils and nonindustrial, non-Western cultures, and many of them do. But anthropology is much more than the study of nonindustrial peoples: It is a comparative field that examines all societies, ancient and modern, simple and complex, local and global. The other social sciences tend to focus on a single society, usually an industrial nation like the United States or Canada. Anthropology, however, offers a unique cross-cultural perspective by constantly comparing the customs of one society with those of others.

People share society—organized life in groups—with other animals, including baboons, wolves, mole rats, and even ants. Culture, however, is more distinctly human. **Cultures** are traditions and customs, transmitted through learning, that form and guide the beliefs and behavior of the people exposed to them. Children learn such a tradition by growing up in a particular society, through a process called enculturation. Cultural traditions include customs and opinions, developed over the generations, about proper and improper behavior. These traditions

answer such questions as these: How should we do things? How do we make sense of the world? How do we tell right from wrong? What is right, and what is wrong? A culture produces a degree of consistency in behavior and thought among the people who live in a particular society. (This chapter's "Appreciating Diversity" box on pp. 6–7 discusses how attitudes about displays of affection, which are transmitted culturally, can also change.)

The most critical element of cultural traditions is their transmission through learning rather than through biological inheritance. Culture is not itself biological, but it rests on certain features of human biology. For more than a million years, humans have possessed at least some of the biological capacities on which culture depends. These abilities are to learn, to think symbolically, to use language, and to make and use tools.

Anthropology confronts and ponders major questions about past and present human existence. By examining ancient bones and tools, we unravel the mysteries of human origins. When did our ancestors separate from those remote great-aunts and great-uncles whose descendants are the apes? Where and when did *Homo sapiens* originate? How has our species changed? What are we now, and where are we going? How have changes in culture and society influenced biological change? Our genus, *Homo,* has been changing for more than one million years. Humans continue to adapt and change both biologically and culturally.

Adaptation, Variation, and Change

Adaptation refers to the processes by which organisms cope with environmental forces and stresses. How do organisms change to fit their environments, such as dry climates or high mountain altitudes? Like other animals, humans have biological means of adaptation. But humans also habitually rely on cultural means of adaptation. Recap 1.1 summarizes

anthropology
The study of the human species and its immediate ancestors.

holistic
Encompassing past, present, and future; biology, society, language, and culture.

culture
Traditions and customs transmitted through learning.

RECAP 1.1 Forms of Cultural and Biological Adaptation (to High Altitude)

FORM OF ADAPTATION	TYPE OF ADAPTATION	EXAMPLE
Technology	Cultural	Pressurized airplane cabin with oxygen masks
Genetic adaptation (occurs over generations)	Biological	Larger "barrel chests" of native highlanders
Long-term physiological adaptation (occurs during growth and development of the individual organism)	Biological	More efficient respiratory system, to extract oxygen from "thin air"
Short-term physiological adaptation (occurs spontaneously when the individual organism enters a new environment)	Biological	Increased heart rate, hyperventilation

"Give Me a Hug"

A few years ago I created and taught a course called "Experiencing Culture" to American college students in Italy. Students wrote bi-weekly journals reflecting on the cultural differences they observed between Europeans and Americans. One thing that really impressed them was the greater frequency and intensity of PDAs—public displays of affection—between romantic couples in Italy, compared with the U.S.

The world's nations and cultures have strikingly different notions about displays of affection and personal space. Cocktail parties in international meeting places such as the United Nations can resemble an elaborate insect mating ritual as diplomats from different countries advance, withdraw, and sidestep. When Americans talk, walk, and dance, they maintain a certain distance from others. Italians or Brazilians, who need less personal space, may interpret such "standoffishness" as a sign of coldness. In conversational pairs, the Italian or Brazilian typically moves in, while the American "instinctively" retreats from a "close talker."

Such bodily movements illustrate not instinct, but culture—behavior programmed by years of exposure to a particular cultural tradition. Culture, however, is not static, as is suggested by this recent account of hugging

behavior in American schools. Appreciate as well that any nation usually contains diverse and even conflicting cultural values. One example is generational diversity, which the famed anthropologist Margaret Mead, one of my teachers, referred to as "the generation gap." Americans (in this case parents and school officials versus teenagers) exhibit

Does high school hugging as described in this news story seem strange to you?

generational differences involving the propriety of PDAs and concerns about sexual harassment.

There is so much hugging at Pascack Hills High School in Montvale, N.J., that students have broken down the hugs by type:

There is the basic friend hug, probably the most popular, and the bear hug, of course.

But now there is also the bear claw, when a boy embraces a girl awkwardly with his elbows poking out.

There is the hug that starts with a high-five, then moves into a fist bump, followed by a slap on the back and an embrace.

There's the shake and lean; the hug from behind; and, the newest addition, the triple— any combination of three girls and boys hugging at once.

"We're not afraid, we just get in and hug," said Danny Schneider, a junior at the school, where hallway hugging began shortly after 7 A.M. on a recent morning as students arrived. "The guy friends, we don't care. You just get right in there and jump in."

There are romantic hugs, too, but that is not what these teenagers are talking about.

Girls embracing girls, girls embracing boys, boys embracing each other—the hug has

the cultural and biological means that humans use to adapt to high altitudes.

Mountainous terrains pose particular challenges, those associated with altitude and oxygen deprivation. Consider four ways (one cultural and three biological) in which humans may cope with low oxygen pressure at high altitudes. Illustrating cultural (technological) adaptation would be a pressurized airplane cabin equipped with oxygen masks. There are three ways of adapting biologically to high altitudes: genetic adaptation, long-term physiological adaptation, and short-term physiological adaptation. First, native populations of high-altitude areas, such as the Andes of Peru and the Himalayas of

Tibet and Nepal, seem to have acquired certain genetic advantages for life at very high altitudes. The Andean tendency to develop a voluminous chest and lungs probably has a genetic basis. Second, regardless of their genes, people who grow up at a high altitude become physiologically more efficient there than genetically similar people who have grown up at sea level would be. This illustrates long-term physiological adaptation during the body's growth and development. Third, humans also have the capacity for short-term or immediate physiological adaptation. Thus, when lowlanders arrive in the highlands, they immediately increase their breathing and heart rates. Hyperventilation increases the oxygen in their

become the favorite social greeting when teenagers meet or part these days. . . .

A measure of how rapidly the ritual is spreading is that some students complain of peer pressure to hug to fit in. And schools from Hillsdale, N.J., to Bend, Ore., wary in a litigious era about sexual harassment or improper touching—or citing hallway clogging and late arrivals to class—have banned hugging or imposed a three-second rule.

Parents, who grew up in a generation more likely to use the handshake, the low-five or the high-five, are often baffled by the close physical contact. "It's a wordless custom, from what I've observed," wrote Beth J. Harpaz, the mother of two boys, 11 and 16, and a parenting columnist for The Associated Press, in a new book, "13 Is the New 18." . . .

"Witnessing this interaction always makes me feel like I am a tourist in a country where I do not know the customs and cannot speak the language." For teenagers, though, hugging is hip. And not hugging?

"If somebody were to not hug someone, to never hug anybody, people might be just a little wary of them and think they are weird or peculiar," said Gabrielle Brown, a freshman at Fiorello H. LaGuardia High School in Manhattan.

Comforting as the hug may be, principals across the country have clamped down.

"Touching and physical contact is very dangerous territory," said Noreen Hajinlian, the principal of George G. White School, a junior high school in Hillsdale, N.J., who banned hugging two years ago. . . .

Schools that have limited hugging invoked longstanding rules against public displays of affection, meant to maintain an atmosphere of academic seriousness and prevent unwanted touching, or even groping.

But pro-hugging students say it is not a romantic or sexual gesture, simply the "hello" of their generation. . . .

Amy L. Best, a sociologist at George Mason University, said the teenage embrace is more a reflection of the overall evolution of the American greeting, which has become less formal since the 1970s. "Without question, the boundaries of touch have changed in American culture," she said. "We display bodies more readily, there are fewer rules governing body touch and a lot more permissible access to other people's bodies."

Hugging appears to be a grassroots phenomenon and not an imitation of a character or custom on TV or in movies. The prevalence of boys' nonromantic hugging (especially of other boys) is most striking to adults. Experts say that over the last generation, boys have become more comfortable expressing emotion, as embodied by the MTV show "Bromance," which is now a widely used term for affection between straight male friends. . . .

African American boys and men have been hugging as part of their greeting for decades, using the word "dap" to describe a ritual involving handshakes, slaps on the shoulders and, more recently, a hug, also sometimes called the gangsta hug among urban youth. . . .

Some parents find it paradoxical that a generation so steeped in hands-off virtual communication would be so eager to hug.

"Maybe it's because all these kids do is text and go on Facebook so they don't even have human contact anymore," said Dona Eichner, the mother of freshman and junior girls at the high school in Montvale. . . .

Carrie Osbourne, a sixth-grade teacher at Claire Lilienthal Alternative School, said hugging was a powerful and positive sign that children are inclined to nurture one another, breaking down barriers. "And it gets to that core that every person wants to feel cared for, regardless of your age or how cool you are or how cool you think you are," she said.

As much as hugging is a physical gesture, it has migrated online as well. Facebook applications allowing friends to send hugs have tens of thousands of fans.

lungs and arteries. As the pulse also increases, blood reaches their tissues more rapidly. These varied adaptive responses—cultural and biological—all fulfill the need to supply an adequate supply of oxygen to the body.

As human history has unfolded, the social and cultural means of adaptation have become increasingly important. In this process, humans have devised diverse ways of coping with the range of environments they have occupied in time and space. The rate of cultural adaptation and change has accelerated, particularly during the last ten thousand years. For millions of years, hunting and gathering of nature's bounty—*foraging*—was the sole basis of human subsistence. However, it took only a few thousand years for **food production** (the cultivation of plants and domestication of animals), which originated some 12,000–10,000 years ago, to replace foraging in most areas. Between 6000 and 5000 B.P. (before the present), the first civilizations arose. These were large, powerful, and complex societies, such as ancient Egypt, that conquered and governed large geographic areas.

Much more recently, the spread of industrial production has profoundly affected human life. Throughout human history, major innovations have spread at the expense of earlier ones. Each economic revolution has had social and cultural repercussions.

food production
An economy based on plant cultivation and/or animal domestication.

Today's global economy and communications link all contemporary people, directly or indirectly, in the modern world system. Nowadays, even remote villagers experience world forces and events. (See "Focus on Globalization" on p. 10.) The study of how local people adapt to global forces poses new challenges for anthropology: "The cultures of world peoples need to be constantly rediscovered as these people reinvent them in changing historical circumstances" (Marcus and Fischer 1986, p. 24).

GENERAL ANTHROPOLOGY

general anthropology
Anthropology as a whole: cultural, archaeological, biological, and linguistic anthropology.

The academic discipline of anthropology, also known as **general anthropology** or "four-field" anthropology, includes four main subdisciplines or subfields. They are sociocultural, archaeological, biological, and linguistic anthropology. (From here on, the shorter term *cultural anthropology* will be used as a synonym for "sociocultural anthropology.") Of the subfields, cultural anthropology has the largest membership. Most departments of anthropology teach courses in all four subfields.

anthropology ATLAS

http://www.mhhe.com/anthromaps
See Maps 8 and 9. Map 8 shows the origin and spread of agriculture (food production). Map 9 shows ancient civilizations.

There are historical reasons for the inclusion of four subfields in a single discipline. The origin of anthropology as a scientific field, and of American anthropology in particular, can be traced back to the 19th century. Early American anthropologists were concerned especially with the history and cultures of the native peoples of North America. Interest in the origins and diversity of Native Americans brought together studies of customs, social life, language, and physical traits. Anthropologists still are pondering such questions as these: Where did Native Americans come from? How many waves of migration brought them to the New World? What are the linguistic, cultural, and biological links among Native Americans and between them and Asia?

biocultural
Combining biological and cultural approaches to a given problem.

Another reason for anthropology's inclusion of four subfields was an interest in the relation between biology (e.g., "race") and culture. More than sixty years ago, the anthropologist Ruth Benedict realized that "in World history, those who have helped to build the same culture are not necessarily of one race, and those of the same race have not all participated in one culture. In scientific language, culture is not a function of race" (Benedict 1940, chap. 2). (Note that a unified four-field anthropology did not develop in Europe, where the subdisciplines tend to exist separately.)

There also are logical reasons for the unity of American anthropology. Each subfield considers variation in

Early American anthropology was especially concerned with the history and cultures of Native North Americans. Ely S. Parker, or Ha-sa-noan-da, was a Seneca Indian who made important contributions to early anthropology. Parker also served as Commissioner of Indian Affairs for the United States.

time and space (that is, in different geographic areas). Cultural and archaeological anthropologists study (among many other topics) changes in social life and customs. Archaeologists have used studies of living societies and behavior patterns to imagine what life might have been like in the past. Biological anthropologists examine evolutionary changes in physical form, for example, anatomical changes that might have been associated with the origin of tool use or language. Linguistic anthropologists may reconstruct the basics of ancient languages by studying modern ones.

The subdisciplines influence each other as anthropologists talk to each other, share books and journals, and associate at professional meetings. General anthropology explores the basics of human biology, society, and culture and considers their interrelations. Anthropologists share certain key assumptions. Perhaps the most fundamental is the idea that sound conclusions about "human nature" cannot be derived from studying a single nation, society, or cultural tradition. A comparative, cross-cultural approach is essential.

Cultural Forces Shape Human Biology

For example, anthropology's comparative, biocultural perspective recognizes that cultural forces constantly mold human biology. (**Biocultural** refers to using and combining both biological and cultural perspectives and approaches to analyze and understand a particular issue or problem.) As we saw in "Understanding Ourselves," culture is a key environmental force in determining how human bodies grow and develop. Cultural traditions promote certain activities and abilities, discourage others, and set standards of physical well-being and attractiveness. Physical activities, including sports, which are influenced by culture, help build the body. For example, North American girls are encouraged to pursue, and therefore do well in, competition involving figure skating, gymnastics, track and field, swimming, diving, and many other sports. Brazilian girls, although excelling in the team sports of basketball and volleyball, haven't fared nearly as well in individual sports as have their American and Canadian counterparts. Why are people encouraged to excel as athletes in some nations but not others? Why do people in some countries invest so much time and effort in competitive sports that their bodies change significantly as a result?

Cultural standards of attractiveness and propriety influence participation and achievement in sports. Americans run or swim not just to compete but to keep

U.S. swimmers Natalie Coughlin, Kara-Lynn Joyce, Lacey Nymeyer, and Dara Torres await their swim in the Women's 4 × 100M Freestyle Relay Final in Beijing, China, during the 2008 Olympics. How might years of competitive swimming affect phenotype?

trim and fit. Brazil's beauty standards traditionally have accepted more fat, especially in female buttocks and hips. Brazilian men have had significant international success in swimming and running, but Brazil rarely sends female swimmers or runners to the Olympics. One reason Brazilian women avoid competitive swimming in particular may be that sport's effects on the body. Years of swimming sculpt a distinctive physique: an enlarged upper torso, a massive neck, and powerful shoulders and back. Successful female swimmers tend to be big, strong, and bulky. The countries that have produced them most consistently are the United States, Canada, Australia, Germany, the Scandinavian nations, the Netherlands, and the former Soviet Union, where this body type isn't as stigmatized as it is in Latin countries. For women, Brazilian culture prefers ample hips and buttocks to a muscled upper body. Many young female swimmers in Brazil choose to abandon the sport rather than their culture's "feminine" body ideal.

THE SUBDISCIPLINES OF ANTHROPOLOGY

Cultural Anthropology

Cultural anthropology, the study of human society and culture, is the subfield that describes, analyzes, interprets, and explains social and cultural similarities and differences. To study and interpret cultural diversity, cultural anthropologists engage in two kinds of activity: ethnography (based on fieldwork) and ethnology (based on cross-cultural comparison). **Ethnography** provides an account of a particular group, community, society, or culture. During ethnographic field work, the ethnographer gathers data that he or she organizes, describes, analyzes, and interprets to build and present that account, which may be in the form of a book, article, or film. Traditionally, ethnographers lived in small communities, where they studied local behavior, beliefs, customs, social life, economic activities, politics, and religion. Today, any ethnographer will recognize that such settings are increasingly exposed to and influenced by external forces and events.

An anthropological perspective derived from ethnographic fieldwork often differs radically from that of economics or political science. Those fields focus on national and official organizations and policies and often on elites. However, the groups that anthropologists traditionally have studied usually have been relatively poor and powerless. Ethnographers often observe discriminatory practices directed toward such people, who experience food and water shortages, dietary deficiencies, and other aspects of poverty. Political scientists tend to study programs that national planners develop, while anthropologists discover how these programs work on the local level.

Communities and cultures are less isolated today than ever before. In fact, as the anthropologist Franz Boas (1940–1966) noted many years ago, contact

ethnography
Fieldwork in a particular cultural setting.

cultural anthropology
The comparative, cross-cultural study of human society and culture.

World Events

People everywhere–even remote villagers—now participate in world events–especially through the mass media. The study of global-local linkages is an increasingly prominent part of modern anthropology. What kinds of events generate global interest? As many as 600 million people may have watched the first (Apollo 11) moon landing in 1969–a huge audience in the early days of global television. Up to a billion people tuned in for the opening ceremony of the 2008 Beijing Summer Olympics. Another billion may have seen part of the dramatic 2010 rescue of a group of Chilean miners who spent 69 days trapped underground.

The world can't seem to get enough of royals, especially photogenic ones. The wedding of England's Prince William and Catherine Middleton attracted 161 million viewers–twice the population of the United Kingdom. A generation earlier, millions of people watched Lady Diana Spencer marry England's Prince Charles. Princess Diana's funeral attracted a global audience, as did the memorial service for Michael Jackson, the "King of Pop."

Major international sports events consistently attract global audiences. Consider the World Cup (soccer) final, held every four years. In 2006, an estimated 320 million people tuned in; this figure more than doubled to 700 million viewers in 2010 (see photo below). The World Cup generates huge global interest because it truly is a "world series," with 32 countries and five continents competing. Even a match between just two countries can attract a huge viewership if the countries are populous and the sport is played internationally. The 2011 Cricket World Cup semifinal between India and Pakistan, for example, may have attracted one billion viewers.

It seems rather arrogant to call American baseball's ultimate championship "The World Series" when the Toronto Blue Jays are the only non-American team ever to win it. The title dates back to 1903, a time of less globalization and more American provincialism. Just how global is baseball, and how well does it represent the world? Baseball is popular in the United States (including Puerto Rico), Canada, Japan, Cuba, Mexico, Venezuela, and the Dominican Republic. South Korea, Taiwan, and China all have professional leagues. Elsewhere the sport has little mass appeal.

On the other hand, when we focus on the players in American baseball we see a multiethnic world in miniature. With its prominent Latino and Japanese players, American baseball appears to be more ethnically diverse than American football or basketball. Consider the finalists for the 2011 American League MVP (Most Valuable Player) award, won by Justin Verlander, a non-Hispanic white man playing for a team with an Asian totem (the Detroit Tigers). Second place went to Boston's Jacoby Ellsbury, one of three registered Native American major league players. Next came Jose Bautista, a Dominican who plays in Canada, followed by Curtis Granderson, an African-American New York Yankee. In fifth place was Venezuelan Miguel Cabrera, Verlander's Tiger teammate. Can you think of a sport as ethnically diverse as baseball? What's the last world event that drew your attention?

between neighboring tribes has always existed and has extended over enormous areas. "Human populations construct their cultures in interaction with one another, and not in isolation" (Wolf 1982, p. ix). Villagers increasingly participate in regional, national, and world events. Exposure to external forces comes through the mass media, migration, and modern transportation. City, nation, and world increasingly invade local communities with the arrival of tourists, development agents, government and religious officials, and political candidates. Such linkages are prominent components of regional, national, and global systems of politics, economics, and information. These larger systems increasingly affect the people and places anthropology traditionally has studied. The study of such linkages and systems is part of the subject matter of modern anthropology. (See "Focus on Globalization: World Events" for a discussion of world events familiar to millions of people.)

Ethnology examines, interprets, and analyzes the results of ethnography—the data gathered in different societies. It uses such data to compare and contrast and to make generalizations about society and culture. Looking beyond the particular to the more general, ethnologists attempt to identify and explain cultural differences and similarities, to test hypotheses, and to build theory to enhance our understanding of how social and cultural systems work. (See the section "The Scientific Method" at the end of this chapter.) Ethnology gets its data for comparison not just from ethnography but also from the other subfields, particularly from archaeology, which reconstructs social systems of the past. (Recap 1.2 summarizes the main contrasts between ethnography and ethnology.)

Archaeological Anthropology

Archaeological anthropology (also known as anthropological archaeology or, most simply, "archaeology") reconstructs, describes, and interprets human behavior and cultural patterns through material remains. At sites where people live or have lived, archaeologists find artifacts, material items that humans have made, used, or modified, such as tools, weapons, campsites, buildings, and garbage. Plant and animal remains and garbage tell stories about consumption and activities. Wild and domesticated grains have different characteristics, which

The closing ceremony of the 2010 World Cup in Soweto, suburban Johannesburg, South Africa.

ETHNOGRAPHY	ETHNOLOGY
Requires field work to collect data	Uses data collected by a series of researchers
Often descriptive	Usually synthetic
Group/community specific	Comparative/cross-cultural

allow archaeologists to distinguish between gathering and cultivation. Examination of animal bones reveals the ages of slaughtered animals and provides other information useful in determining whether species were wild or domesticated.

Analyzing such data, archaeologists answer several questions about ancient economies. Did the group get its meat from hunting, or did it domesticate and breed animals, killing only those of a certain age and sex? Did plant food come from wild plants or from sowing, tending, and harvesting crops? Did the residents make, trade for, or buy particular items? Were raw materials available locally? If not, where did they come from? From such information, archaeologists reconstruct patterns of production, trade, and consumption.

Archaeologists have spent much time studying potsherds, fragments of earthenware. Potsherds are more durable than many other artifacts, such as textiles and wood. The quantity of pottery fragments allows estimates of population size and density. The discovery that potters used materials unavailable locally suggests systems of trade. Similarities in manufacture and decoration at different sites may be proof of cultural connections. Groups with similar pots might be historically related. Perhaps they shared common cultural ancestors, traded with each other, or belonged to the same political system.

Many archaeologists examine paleoecology. *Ecology* is the study of interrelations among living things in an environment. The organisms and environment together constitute an ecosystem, a patterned arrangement of energy flows and exchanges. Human ecology studies ecosystems that include people, focusing on the ways in which human use "of nature influences and is influenced by social organization and cultural values" (Bennett 1969, pp. 10–11). *Paleoecology* looks at the ecosystems of the past.

 living anthropology **VIDEOS**

"New" Knowledge among the Batak, www.mhhe.com/kottak

This clip shows Batak women, men, and children at work, making a living. It describes how they grow rice in an environmentally friendly way, unlike the destructive farming techniques of the lowlanders who have invaded their homeland. How have the Batak and conservation agencies worked together to reduce deforestation? Based on the clip, name several ways in which the Batak are influenced by forces beyond their homeland.

In addition to reconstructing ecological patterns, archaeologists may infer cultural transformations, for example, by observing changes in the size and type of sites and the distance between them. A city develops in a region where only towns, villages, and hamlets existed a few centuries earlier. The number of settlement levels (city, town, village, hamlet) in a society is a measure of social complexity. Buildings offer clues about political and religious features. Temples and pyramids suggest that an ancient society had an authority structure capable of marshaling the labor needed to build such monuments. The presence or absence of certain structures, like the pyramids of ancient Egypt and Mexico, reveals differences in function between settlements. For example, some towns were places where people came to attend ceremonies. Others were burial sites; still others were farming communities.

Archaeologists also reconstruct behavior patterns and lifestyles of the past by excavating. This involves digging through a succession of levels at a particular site. In a given area, through time, settlements may change in form and purpose, as may the connections between settlements. Excavation can document changes in economic, social, and political activities.

Although archaeologists are best known for studying prehistory, that is, the period before the invention of writing, they also study the cultures of historical and even living peoples. Studying sunken ships off the Florida coast, underwater archaeologists have been able to verify the living conditions on the vessels that brought ancestral African Americans to the New World as enslaved people. In a research project begun in 1973 in Tucson, Arizona, archaeologist William Rathje has learned about contemporary life by studying modern garbage. The value of "garbology," as Rathje calls it, is that it provides "evidence of what people did, not what they think they did, what they think they should have done, or what the interviewer thinks they should have done" (Harrison, Rathje, and Hughes 1994, p. 108). What people report may contrast strongly with their real behavior as revealed by garbology. For example, the garbologists discovered that the three Tucson neighborhoods that reported the lowest beer consumption actually had the highest number of discarded beer cans per household (Podolefsky and Brown 1992, p. 100)! Findings from garbology also have challenged common misconceptions about the kinds and quantities of trash found in landfills: While most people thought that fast-food containers and disposable diapers were

ethnology
The study of sociocultural differences and similarities.

archaeological anthropology
The study of human behavior through material remains.

major waste problems, they were actually relatively insignificant compared with paper (Rathje and Murphy 2001).

Biological, or Physical, Anthropology

The subject matter of **biological,** or **physical, anthropology** is human biological diversity in time and space. A common interest in biological variation unites five specialties within biological anthropology:

1. Human evolution as revealed by the fossil record (paleoanthropology).

2. Human genetics.

3. Human growth and development.

4. Human biological plasticity (the living body's ability to change as it copes with stresses, such as heat, cold, and altitude).

5. Primatology (the biology, evolution, behavior, and social life of monkeys, apes, and other nonhuman primates).

These interests link biological anthropology to other fields: biology, zoology, geology, anatomy, physiology, medicine, and public health. Osteology—

the study of bones—helps paleoanthropologists, who examine skulls, teeth, and bones, to identify human ancestors and to chart changes in anatomy over time. A paleontologist is a scientist who studies fossils. A paleoanthropologist is one sort of paleontologist, one who studies the fossil record of human evolution. Paleoanthropologists often collaborate with archaeologists, who study artifacts, in reconstructing biological and cultural aspects of human evolution. Fossils and tools often are found together. Different types of tools provide information about the habits, customs, and lifestyles of the ancestral humans who used them.

More than a century ago, Charles Darwin noticed that the variety that exists within any population permits some individuals (those with the favored characteristics) to do better than others at surviving and reproducing. Genetics, which developed later, enlightens us about the causes and transmission of this variety. However, it isn't just genes that cause variety. During any individual's lifetime, the environment works along with heredity to determine biological features. For example, people with a genetic tendency to be tall will be shorter if they are poorly nourished during childhood. Thus, biological anthropology also investigates the influence of environment on the body as it grows and matures. Among

Archaeology in the coastal deserts around Nazca and Ica, Peru.

biological anthropology
The study of human biological variation in time and space.

physical anthropology
Same as biological anthropology.

the environmental factors that influence the body as it develops are nutrition, altitude, temperature, and disease, as well as cultural factors, such as the standards of attractiveness that were discussed previously.

Biological anthropology (along with zoology) also includes primatology. The primates include our closest relatives—apes and monkeys. Primatologists study their biology, evolution, behavior, and social life, often in their natural environments. Primatology assists paleoanthropology, because primate behavior may shed light on early human behavior and human nature.

Linguistic Anthropology

We don't know (and we probably never will know) when our ancestors started speaking, although biological anthropologists have looked to the anatomy of the face and the skull to speculate about the origin of language. As well, primatologists have described the communication systems of monkeys and apes. We do know that well-developed, grammatically complex languages have existed for thousands of years. Linguistic anthropology offers further illustration of anthropology's interest in comparison, variation, and change. **Linguistic anthropology** studies language in its social and cultural context, across space and over time. Some linguistic anthropologists also make inferences about universal features of language, linked perhaps to uniformities in the human brain. Others reconstruct ancient languages by comparing their contemporary descendants and in so doing make discoveries about history. Still others study linguistic differences to discover varied perceptions and patterns of thought in different cultures.

Historical linguistics considers variation over time, such as the changes in sounds, grammar, and vocabulary between Middle English (spoken from approximately 1050 to 1550 C.E.) and modern English. **Sociolinguistics** investigates relationships between social and linguistic variation. No language is a homogeneous system in which everyone speaks just like everyone else. How do different speakers use a given language? How do linguistic features correlate with social factors, including class and gender differences (Tannen 1990)? One reason for variation is geography, as in regional dialects and accents. Linguistic variation also is expressed in the bilingualism of ethnic groups. Linguistic and cultural anthropologists collaborate in studying links between language and many other aspects of culture, such as how people reckon kinship and how they perceive and classify colors.

ANTHROPOLOGY AND OTHER ACADEMIC FIELDS

As mentioned previously, one of the main differences between anthropology and the other fields that study people is holism, anthropology's unique blend of biological, social, cultural, linguistic,

historical, and contemporary perspectives. Paradoxically, while distinguishing anthropology, this breadth also is what links it to many other disciplines. Techniques used to date fossils and artifacts have come to anthropology from physics, chemistry, and geology. Because plant and animal remains often are found with human bones and artifacts, anthropologists collaborate with botanists, zoologists, and paleontologists.

Anthropology is a **science**—a "systematic field of study or body of knowledge that aims, through experiment, observation, and deduction, to produce reliable explanations of phenomena, with reference to the material and physical world" (*Webster's New World Encyclopedia* 1993, p. 937). This book presents anthropology as a *humanistic science* devoted to discovering, describing, understanding, appreciating, and explaining similarities and differences in time and space among humans and our ancestors. Clyde Kluckhohn (1944) described anthropology as "the science of human similarities and differences" (p. 9). His statement of the need for such a field still stands: "Anthropology provides a scientific basis for dealing with the crucial dilemma of the world today: how can peoples of different appearance, mutually unintelligible languages, and dissimilar ways of life get along peaceably together?" (p. 9). Anthropology has compiled an impressive body of knowledge that this textbook attempts to encapsulate.

Besides its links to the natural sciences (e.g., geology, zoology) and social sciences (e.g., sociology, psychology), anthropology also has strong links to the humanities. The humanities include English, comparative literature, classics, folklore, philosophy, and the arts. These fields study languages, texts, philosophies, arts, music, performances, and other forms of creative expression. Ethnomusicology, which studies forms of musical expression on a worldwide basis, is especially closely related to anthropology. Also linked is folklore, the systematic study of tales, myths, and legends from a variety of cultures. Anthropology, it may be argued, is one of the most humanistic of all academic fields because of its fundamental respect for human diversity. Anthropologists listen to, record, and represent voices from a multitude of nations, cultures, times, and places. Anthropology values local knowledge, diverse worldviews, and alternative philosophies. Cultural anthropology and linguistic anthropology in particular bring a comparative and nonelitist perspective to forms of creative expression, including language, art, narratives, music, and dance, viewed in their social and cultural context.

Cultural Anthropology and Sociology

Cultural anthropology and sociology share an interest in social relations, organization, and behavior. However, important differences between these disciplines arose from the kinds of societies each traditionally studied. Initially sociologists focused on the

science
Field of study that seeks reliable explanations, with reference to the material and physical world.

linguistic anthropology
The study of language and linguistic diversity in time, space, and society.

sociolinguistics
The study of language in society.

FIGURE 1.1 Location of Trobriand Islands.

Anthropology and Psychology

Like sociologists, most psychologists do research in their own society. But statements about "human" psychology cannot be based solely on observations made in one society or in a single type of society. The area of cultural anthropology known as psychological anthropology studies cross-cultural variation in psychological traits. Societies instill different values by training children differently. Adult personalities reflect a culture's child-rearing practices.

Bronislaw Malinowski, an early contributor to the cross-cultural study of human psychology, is famous for his fieldwork among the Trobriand Islanders of the South Pacific (Figure 1.1). The Trobrianders reckon kinship matrilineally. They consider themselves related to the mother and her relatives, but not to the father. The relative who disciplines the child is not the father but the mother's brother, the maternal uncle. Trobrianders show a marked respect for the uncle, with whom a boy usually has a cool and distant relationship. In contrast, the Trobriand father-son relationship is friendly and affectionate.

Malinowski's work among the Trobrianders suggested modifications in Sigmund Freud's famous theory of the universality of the Oedipus complex (Malinowski 1927). According to Freud (1918/1950), boys around the age of five become sexually attracted to their mothers. The Oedipus complex is resolved, in Freud's view, when the boy overcomes his sexual jealousy of, and identifies with, his father. Freud lived in patriarchal Austria during the late 19th and early 20th centuries—a social milieu in which the father was a strong authoritarian figure. The Austrian father was the child's primary authority figure and the mother's sexual partner. In the Trobriands, the father had only the sexual role.

If, as Freud contended, the Oedipus complex always creates social distance based on jealousy toward the mother's sexual partner, this would have shown up in Trobriand society. It did not. Malinowski concluded that the authority structure did more to influence the father-son relationship than did sexual jealousy. Although Melford Spiro (1993) has critiqued Malinowski's conclusions (see also Weiner 1988), no contemporary anthropologist would dispute Malinowski's contention that individual psychology is molded in a specific cultural context. Anthropologists continue to provide cross-cultural perspectives on psychoanalytic propositions (Paul 1989) as well as on issues of developmental and cognitive psychology (Shore 1996).

APPLIED ANTHROPOLOGY

What sort of man or woman do you envision when you hear the word "anthropologist"? Although anthropologists have been portrayed as quirky and eccentric, bearded and bespectacled, anthropology is not a science of the exotic carried on by quaint scholars in ivory towers. Rather, anthropology has a

industrial West; anthropologists, on nonindustrial societies. Different methods of data collection and analysis emerged to deal with those different kinds of societies. To study large-scale, complex nations, sociologists came to rely on questionnaires and other means of gathering masses of quantifiable data. Sampling and statistical techniques are fundamental in sociology, whereas statistical training has been less common in anthropology (although this is changing as anthropologists increasingly work in modern nations).

Traditional ethnographers studied small and nonliterate (without writing) populations and relied on methods appropriate to that context. "Ethnography is a research process in which the anthropologist closely observes, records, and engages in the daily life of another culture—an experience labeled as the fieldwork method—and then writes accounts of this culture, emphasizing descriptive detail" (Marcus and Fischer 1986, p. 18). One key method described in this quote is participant observation—taking part in the events one is observing, describing, and analyzing.

In many areas and topics, anthropology and sociology now are converging. Sociologists now do research in developing countries and other places that used to be mainly within the anthropological orbit. As industrialization spreads, many anthropologists now work in industrial nations, where they study diverse topics, including rural decline, inner-city life, and the role of the mass media in creating national cultural patterns.

lot to tell the public. Anthropology's foremost professional organization, the American Anthropological Association (AAA), has formally acknowledged a public service role by recognizing that anthropology has two dimensions: (1) academic anthropology and (2) practicing or **applied anthropology.** The latter refers to the application of anthropological data, perspectives, theory, and methods to identify, assess, and solve contemporary social problems. As Erve Chambers (1987, p. 309) states, applied anthropology is "concerned with the relationships between anthropological knowledge and the uses of that knowledge in the world beyond anthropology." More and more anthropologists from the four subfields now work in such "applied" areas as public health, family planning, business, market research, economic development, and cultural resource management. (This chapter's "Appreciating Anthropology" box on pp. 16–17 discusses the career of President Barack Obama's mother, a sociocultural and applied anthropologist.)

Because of anthropology's breadth, applied anthropology has many applications. For example, applied medical anthropologists consider both the sociocultural and the biological contexts and implications of disease and illness. Perceptions of good and bad health, along with actual health threats and problems, differ among societies. Various ethnic groups recognize different illnesses, symptoms, and causes and have developed different health care systems and treatment strategies.

Applied archaeology, usually called *public archaeology,* includes such activities as cultural resource management, contract archaeology, public educational programs, and historic preservation. An important role for public archaeology has been created by legislation requiring evaluation of sites threatened by dams, highways, and other construction activities. To decide what needs saving, and to preserve significant information about the past when sites cannot be saved, is the work of **cultural resource management** (CRM). CRM involves not only preserving sites but allowing their destruction if they are not significant. The "management" part of the term refers to the evaluation and decision-making process. Cultural resource managers work for federal, state, and county agencies and other clients. Applied cultural anthropologists sometimes work with the public archaeologists, assessing the human problems generated by the proposed change and determining how they can be reduced.

THE SCIENTIFIC METHOD

Anthropology, remember, is a science, although a very humanistic one. Within sociocultural anthropology, ethnology is the comparative science that attempts to identify and explain cultural differences and similarities, test hypotheses, and build theory to enhance our understanding of how social and

Bronislaw Malinowski is famous for his fieldwork among the matrilineal Trobriand Islanders of the South Pacific. Does this Trobriand market scene suggest anything about the status of Trobriand women?

cultural systems work. The data for ethnology come from societies located in various times and places and so can come from archaeology as well as from ethnography, their more usual source. Ethnologists compare, contrast, and make generalizations about societies and cultures.

Theories, Associations, and Explanations

A **theory** is a set of ideas formulated to explain something. An effective theory offers an explanatory framework that can be applied to multiple cases. Just as ethnological theories help explain sociocultural differences and similarities, evolutionary theory is used to explain biological associations. An **association** is an observed relationship between two or more variables, such as the length of a giraffe's neck and the number of its offspring. Theories, which are more general than associations, suggest or imply multiple associations and attempt to explain them. Something, for example, the giraffe's long neck, is explained if it illustrates a general principle (a law), such as the concepts of adaptive advantage and differential fitness. In evolutionary theory, fitness is measured by reproductive success. In this case, giraffes with longer necks have a feeding advantage compared with their shorter-necked fellows; in times of food scarcity they eat better, live longer, and have more surviving offspring. The truth of a scientific statement (e.g., evolution occurs because of differential reproductive success based on variation within the population) is confirmed by repeated observations.

applied anthropology
Using anthropology to solve contemporary problems.

cultural resource management
Deciding what needs saving when entire archaeological sites cannot be saved.

theory
A set of ideas formulated to explain something.

association
An observed relationship between two or more variables.

appreciating ANTHROPOLOGY

His Mother the Anthropologist

It is widely known that President Barack Obama is the son of a Kenyan father and a white American mother. Less recognized is the fact that the 44th president of the United States is the son of an anthropologist—Dr. Stanley Ann Dunham Soetoro (usually called simply Ann Dunham). This account focuses on her life and her appreciation of human diversity, which led her to a career in anthropology. A sociocultural anthropologist by training, Dunham focused her attention on issues of microfinance and socioeconomic problems faced by Indonesian women. She used her knowledge to identify and solve contemporary problems. She was both a cultural and an applied anthropologist. A fuller account of Dr. Dunham's life appears in Janny Scott's recent book *A Singular Woman: The Untold Story of Barack Obama's Mother (2011).*

Anthropologists study humanity in varied times and places and in a rapidly changing world. By virtue of his parentage, his enculturation, and his experience abroad, Barack Obama provides an excellent symbol of the diversity and interconnections that characterize such a world.

In the capsule version of the Barack Obama story, his mother is simply the white woman from Kansas. . . . On the campaign trail, he has called her his "single mom." But neither description begins to capture the unconventional life of Stanley Ann Dunham Soetoro, the parent who most shaped Mr. Obama. . . .

In Hawaii, she married an African student at age 18. Then she married an Indonesian, moved to Jakarta, became an anthropologist, wrote an 800-page dissertation on peasant blacksmithing in Java, worked for the Ford Foundation, championed women's work and helped bring microcredit to the world's poor.

She had high expectations for her children. In Indonesia, she would wake her son at 4 A.M. for correspondence courses in English before school; she brought home recordings of Mahalia Jackson, speeches by the Rev. Dr. Martin Luther King Jr., and when Mr. Obama asked to stay in Hawaii for high school rather than return to Asia, she accepted living apart—a decision her daughter says was one of the hardest in Ms. Soetoro's life.

"She felt that somehow, wandering through uncharted territory, we might stumble upon something that will, in an instant, seem to represent who we are at the core," said Maya Soetoro-Ng, Mr. Obama's half-sister. "That was very much her philosophy of life—to not be limited by fear or narrow definitions, to not build walls around ourselves and to do our best to find kinship and beauty in unexpected places." . . .

Mr. Obama . . . barely saw his father after the age of 2. Though it is impossible to pinpoint the imprint of a parent on the life of a grown child, people who knew Ms. Soetoro well say they see her influence unmistakably in Mr. Obama. . . .

"She was a very, very big thinker," said Nancy Barry, a former president of Women's World Banking, an international network of microfinance providers, where Ms. Soetoro worked in New York City in the early 1990s. . . .

In a Russian class at the University of Hawaii, she met the college's first African student, Barack Obama. They married and had a son in August 1961, in an era when interracial marriage was rare in the United States. . . .

The marriage was brief. In 1963, Mr. Obama left for Harvard, leaving his wife and child. She then married Lolo Soetoro, an Indonesian student. When he was summoned home in 1966 after the turmoil surrounding the rise of Suharto, Ms. Soetoro and Barack followed. . . .

Her second marriage faded, too, in the 1970s. Ms. Soetoro wanted to work, one friend said, and Mr. Soetoro wanted more children. He became more American, she once said, as she became more Javanese. "There's a Javanese belief that if you're married to someone and it doesn't work, it will

---

Any science aims for reliable explanations that predict future occurrences. Accurate predictions stand up to tests designed to disprove (falsify) them. Scientific explanations rely on data, which can come from experiments, observation, and other systematic procedures. Scientific causes are material, physical, or natural (e.g., viruses) rather than supernatural (e.g., ghosts). Science is one way of understanding the world, but not the only way.

In their 1997 article "Science in Anthropology," Melvin Ember and Carol R. Ember describe how scientists strive to improve our understanding of the world by testing **hypotheses**—suggested but as yet unverified explanations. An explanation must show how and why the thing to be understood (the *explicandum* or *dependent variable*) is associated with or related to something else, a *predictor variable*. Associations require covariation; when one thing (a variable) changes, the other one varies as well. Theories provide explanations for associations (Ember and Ember 1997).

One explanation for the occurrence of an association is that it illustrates a general principle. Thus, "water freezes at 32°F" states an association between two variables: the state of the water and the air temperature. The truth of the statement is confirmed by repeated observations of freezing and the fact that water does not solidify at higher temperatures. Such

hypothesis
A suggested but as yet unverified explanation.

PART 1   Introduction to Anthropology

make you sick," said Alice G. Dewey, an anthropologist and friend. "It's just stupid to stay married." . . .

By 1974, Ms. Soetoro was back in Honolulu, a graduate student and raising Barack and Maya, nine years younger. . . . When Ms. Soetoro decided to return to Indonesia three years later for her field work, Barack chose not to go . . .

Fluent in Indonesian, Ms. Soetoro moved with Maya first to Yogyakarta, the center of Javanese handicrafts. A weaver in college, she was fascinated with what Ms. Soetoro-Ng calls "life's gorgeous minutiae." That interest inspired her study of village industries, which became the basis of her 1992 doctoral dissertation.

"She loved living in Java," said Dr. Dewey, who recalled accompanying Ms. Soetoro to a metalworking village. "People said: 'Hi! How are you?' She said: 'How's your wife? Did your daughter have the baby?' They were friends. Then she'd whip out her notebook and she'd say: 'How many of you have electricity? Are you having trouble getting iron?'"

She became a consultant for the United States Agency for International Development on setting up a village credit program, then a Ford Foundation program officer in Jakarta specializing in women's work. Later, she was a consultant in Pakistan, then joined Indonesia's oldest bank to work on what is described as the world's largest sustainable microfinance program, creating services like credit and savings for the poor.

President Barack Obama and his mother, Ann Dunham, who was a cultural and applied anthropologist, in an undated photo from the 1960s. Dunham met Obama's father, Barack Obama Sr. from Kenya, when both were students at the University of Hawaii at Manoa; they married in 1960.

Visitors flowed constantly through her Ford Foundation office in downtown Jakarta and through her house in a neighborhood to the south, where papaya and banana trees grew in the front yard and Javanese dishes . . . were served for dinner. Her guests were leaders in the Indonesian human rights movement, people from women's organizations, representatives of community groups doing grass-roots development. . . .

Ms. Soetoro-Ng . . . remembers conversations with her mother about philosophy or politics, books, esoteric Indonesian woodworking motifs. . . .

"She gave us a very broad understanding of the world," her daughter said. "She hated bigotry. She was very determined to be remembered for a life of service and thought that service was really the true measure of a life." Many of her friends see her legacy in Mr. Obama—in his self-assurance and drive, his boundary bridging, even his apparent comfort with strong women.

She died in November 1995, as Mr. Obama was starting his first campaign for public office. After a memorial service at the University of Hawaii, one friend said, a small group of friends drove to the South Shore in Oahu. With the wind whipping the waves onto the rocks, Mr. Obama and Ms. Soetoro-Ng placed their mother's ashes in the Pacific, sending them off in the direction of Indonesia.

general relationships are called laws. Explanations based on such laws allow us to understand the past and predict the future. Yesterday ice formed at 32°F, and tomorrow it will still form at 32°F.

In the social sciences, associations usually are stated in the form of probability rather than as such absolute laws. The variables of interest are likely to, but don't always, vary as predicted. They *tend* to be related in a predictable way, but there are exceptions (Ember and Ember 1997). For example, in a worldwide sample of societies, the anthropologist John Whiting (1964) found a strong (but not 100 percent) association or correlation between a sexual custom and a type of diet. A long postpartum sex taboo (a ban on sexual intercourse between husband and wife for a year or more after the birth of a child) tended to be found in societies where the diet was low in protein.

After confirming the association through cross-cultural data (ethnographic information from a sample of several societies), Whiting's job was to formulate a theory that would explain why the dependent variable (in this case the postpartum sex taboo) depended on the predictor variable (a low-protein diet). Why might societies with low-protein diets develop this taboo? Whiting's theory was that the taboo is adaptive; it helps people survive and reproduce in certain environments. (More generally, anthropologists have

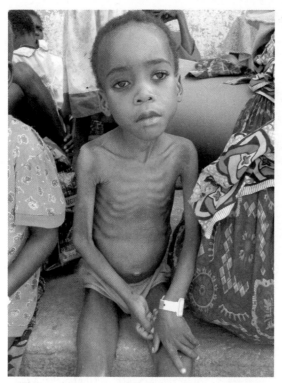

The name *kwashiorkor*, for a condition caused by severe protein deficiency, comes from a West African word meaning "one-two." Some cultures abruptly wean one infant when a second one is born. In today's world, refugees from civil wars, including the Angolan girl shown here, are among the most common victims of malnutrition.

argued that many cultural practices are adaptive.) In this case, with too little protein in their diets, babies may develop and die from a protein-deficiency disease called kwashiorkor. If the mother delays her next pregnancy, her current baby gets to breast-feed lon-

ger and is more likely to survive. Whiting suggests that parents are aware, unconsciously or consciously, that having another baby too soon would jeopardize the survival of the previous one. Thus, they avoid sex for more than a year after the birth of the first baby. When such abstinence becomes institutionalized, everyone is expected to respect the taboo.

Theories suggest patterns, connections, and relationships that may be confirmed by new research. Whiting's theory, for example, suggests hypotheses for future researchers to test. Because his theory proposes that the postpartum taboo is adaptive given certain conditions, one might hypothesize that changes in those conditions would cause the taboo to disappear. By adopting birth control, for instance, families could space births without avoiding intercourse. So, too, might the taboo disappear if babies started receiving protein supplements, which would reduce the threat of kwashiorkor.

What constitutes good evidence that a theory or explanation probably is right? Cases that have been personally selected by a researcher don't provide an acceptable test of a hypothesis or theory. Ideally, hypothesis testing should be done using a sample of cases that have been selected randomly from some statistical universe. (Whiting did this in choosing his cross-cultural sample.) The relevant variables should be measured reliably, and the strength and significance of the results should be evaluated using legitimate statistical methods (Bernard 2006). Recap 1.3 summarizes the main steps in using the scientific method, as just discussed here.

When Multiple Variables Predict

The scientific method, as shown in Recap 1.3, is not limited to ethnology but applies to any anthropological

RECAP 1.3	Steps in the Scientific Method
Have a research question	Why do some societies have long postpartum taboos?
Construct a hypothesis	Delaying marital sex reduces infant mortality when diets are low in protein.
Posit a mechanism	Babies get more protein when they nurse longer; nursing is not a reliable method of contraception.
Get data to test your hypothesis	Use a (random) sample of cross-cultural data (data from several societies; such data sets exist for cross-cultural research).
Devise a way of measuring	Code societies 1 when they have a postpartum taboo of one year or longer, 0 when they do not; code 1 when diet is low protein, 0 when it is not.
Analyze your data	Notice patterns in the data: long postpartum taboos generally are found in societies with low-protein diets, whereas societies with better diets tend to lack those taboos. Use appropriate statistical methods to evaluate the strength of these associations.
Draw a conclusion	In most cases, the hypothesis is confirmed.
Derive implications	Such taboos tend to disappear when diets get better or new reproductive technologies become available.
Contribute to larger theory	Cultural practices can have adaptive value because they can enhance the survival of offspring.

Family and friends watching a soccer game on TV in Brazil. Soccer and *telenovelas* are key features of Brazilian popular culture.

endeavor that formulates research questions and gathers or uses systematic data to test hypotheses. Nor does there have to be a single research question. Often anthropologists gather data that enable them to pose and test a number of separate hypotheses about attitudes and behavior. For example, in a research project during the 1980s, my associates and I used a combination of methods to study television's behavioral effects in Brazil (see Kottak 1990*a*).

Our most general research question was this: How has variable exposure to television affected Brazilians? We gathered data from more than one thousand Brazilians living in seven different communities to answer this question. Uniquely, our research design permitted us to distinguish between *two key measures of individual exposure to television.* First was current viewing level (average daily hours spent watching TV). Such a measure is used routinely to assess the impact of television in the United States. Our second, and far more significant, variable was *length of home TV exposure.*

Unlike us, researchers in the United States must rely solely on current viewing level to measure TV's influence, because there is little variation in length of home exposure, except for variation based on age. Americans aged 60 and younger never have known a world without TV. Some American researchers have tried to use age as an *indirect* measure of TV's long-term effects. Their assumption is that viewing has a cumulative effect, its influence increasing (up to a point) with age. However, that approach has difficulty distinguishing between the effects of years of TV exposure and other changes

associated with aging. By contrast, our Brazilian sample included people in the same age groups but exposed to TV for different lengths of time—because television had reached their towns at different times. Years of age and years of home exposure were two separate variables.

Having gathered detailed quantitative data, we could use a statistical method that measures the separate (as well as the combined) effects of several "potential predictors" on a dependent variable. To use a more general example, to predict "risk of heart attack" (the dependent variable), potential predictors would include sex (gender), age, family history, weight, blood pressure, cholesterol level, exercise, and cigarette smoking. Each one would make a separate contribution, and some would have more impact than others. However, someone with many "risk factors" (particularly the most significant ones) would have a greater risk of heart attack than someone with few predictors.

Returning to television in Brazil, we used a standard set of nine potential predictor variables and examined their effects on hundreds of dependent variables (Kottak 1990*a*). Our potential predictors included gender, age, skin color, social class, education, income, religious involvement, years of home TV exposure, and current televiewing level. We could measure the separate (as well as the combined) influence of each predictor on each dependent variable.

One of our strongest statistical measures of television's impact on attitudes was the correlation between TV exposure and liberal views on sex-gender issues. TV exposure had a stronger effect on sex-gender views than did such other predictor variables as gender, education, and income. The heavier and longer-exposed viewers were strikingly more liberal—less traditional in their opinions on such matters as whether women "belong at home," should work when their husbands have good incomes, should work when pregnant, should go to bars, should leave a husband they no longer love, should pursue men they like; whether men should cook and wash clothes; and whether parents should talk to their children about sex. All these questions produced TV-biased answers, in that Brazilian television depicts an urban-modern society in which sex-gender roles are less traditional than in small communities.

Are these effects or just correlations? That is, does Brazilian TV make people more liberal, or do already liberal people, seeking reinforcement for their views, simply watch more television? Do they look to TV and its urban-elite world for moral options that are missing, suppressed, or disapproved of in their own, more traditional, towns? We concluded that this liberalization is both a correlation and an effect. There is a strong *correlation* between liberal social views and *current* viewing hours. Liberal small-town Brazilians appear to watch more TV to validate personal views that the local setting suppresses. However, confirming that long-term TV exposure also has an *effect* on Brazilians' attitudes, there is an even stronger correlation between years of home viewing by individuals and their liberal social views.

It is difficult to separate effects of televiewing from mere correlations when we use current viewing level as a predictor variable. Questions like the following always arise: Does television create fears about the outside world—or do already fearful people tend to stay home and watch more TV? *Effects* are clearer when length of home exposure can be measured. Logically, we can compare this predictor and its influence over time to education and its effects. If the cumulative effects of formal education increase with years of schooling, then it seems reasonable to assume some similar influence as a result of years of home exposure to television.

Heavy viewers in Brazil probably are predisposed to liberal views. However, content, entering homes each day, reinforces those views over time. TV-biased and TV-reinforced attitudes spread as viewers take courage from the daily validation of their unorthodox (local) views in (national) programming. More and more townsfolk encounter nontraditional views and come to see them as normal.

In this case, we measured and confirmed an association and then offered explanations for why that association is an effect as well as a correlation. Our study suggested hypotheses for future research on how people use television and how it affects them in other ways, places, and times. Indeed, recent research in a Michigan town (Descartes and Kottak 2009) has revealed forms of use and impact similar to those we discovered in Brazil. Think about how these findings might apply to the political views of contemporary Americans who habitually watch either Fox News or MSNBC.

acing the **COURSE**

summary

1. Anthropology is the holistic and comparative study of humanity. It is the systematic exploration of human biological and cultural diversity. Examining the origins of, and changes in, human biology and culture, anthropology provides explanations for similarities and differences. The four subfields of general anthropology are sociocultural, archaeological, biological, and linguistic. All consider variation in time and space. Each also examines adaptation—the process by which organisms cope with environmental stresses.

2. Cultural forces mold human biology, including our body types and images. Societies have particu-

lar standards of physical attractiveness. They also have specific ideas about what activities—for example, various sports—are appropriate for males and females.

3. Cultural anthropology explores the cultural diversity of the present and the recent past. Archaeology reconstructs cultural patterns, often of prehistoric populations. Biological anthropology documents diversity involving fossils, genetics, growth and development, bodily responses, and nonhuman primates. Linguistic anthropology considers diversity among languages. It also studies how speech changes in social situations and over time.

4. Concerns with biology, society, culture, and language link anthropology to many other fields—sciences and humanities. Anthropologists study art, music, and literature across cultures. But their concern is more with the creative expressions of common people than with arts designed for elites. Anthropologists examine creators and products in their social context. Sociologists traditionally study urban and industrial populations, whereas anthropologists have focused on rural, nonindustrial peoples. Psychological anthropology views human psychology in the context of social and cultural variation.

5. Anthropology has two dimensions: academic and applied. Applied anthropology is the use of anthropological data, perspectives, theory, and methods to identify, assess, and solve contemporary social problems.

6. Ethnologists attempt to identify and explain cultural differences and similarities and to build theories about how social and cultural systems work. Scientists strive to improve understanding by testing hypotheses—suggested explanations. Explanations rely on associations and theories. An association is an observed relationship between variables. A theory is more general, suggesting or implying associations and attempting to explain them. The scientific method characterizes any anthropological endeavor that formulates research questions and gathers or uses systematic data to test hypotheses. Often anthropologists gather data that enable them to pose and test a number of separate hypotheses.

key terms

anthropology 5
applied anthropology 15
archaeological anthropology 11
association 15
biocultural 8
biological anthropology 12
cultural anthropology 9
cultural resource management 15
culture 5
ethnography 9

ethnology 11
food production 7
general anthropology 8
holistic 5
hypothesis 16
linguistic anthropology 13
physical anthropology 12
science 13
sociolinguistics 13
theory 15

test yourself

MULTIPLE CHOICE

1. Which of the following most characterizes anthropology among disciplines that study humans?
   a. It studies foreign places.
   b. It includes biology.
   c. It uses personal interviews of the study population.
   d. It is holistic and comparative.
   e. It studies only groups that are thought to be "dying."

2. What is the most critical element of cultural traditions?
   a. their stability due to the unchanging characteristics of human biology
   b. their tendency to radically change every fifteen years
   c. their ability to survive the challenges of modern life
   d. their transmission through learning rather than through biological inheritance
   e. their material manifestations in archaeological sites

3. Over time, how has human reliance on cultural means of adaptation changed?
   a. Humans have become less dependent on them.
   b. Humans have become entirely reliant on biological means.
   c. Humans have become more dependent on them.
   d. Humans are just beginning to depend on them.
   e. Humans no longer use them.

4. The fact that anthropology focuses on both culture and biology
   a. is unique to European anthropology.
   b. is the reason it traditionally has studied nonindustrial societies.
   c. is a product of the participant observation approach.
   d. allows it to address how culture influences biological traits and vice versa.
   e. is insignificant, since biology is studied by biological anthropologists while culture is studied by cultural anthropologists.

5. In this chapter, what is the point of describing the ways in which humans cope with low oxygen pressure in high altitudes?
    a. to illustrate human capacities of cultural and biological adaptation, variation, and change
    b. to expose the fact that "it is all in the genes"
    c. to show how culture is more important than biology
    d. to describe how humans are among the world's least adaptable animals
    e. to show how biology is more important than culture in human adaptation

6. Four-field anthropology
    a. was largely shaped by early American anthropologists' interests in Native Americans.
    b. is unique to Old World anthropology.
    c. stopped being useful when the world became dominated by nation-states.
    d. was replaced in the 1930s by the two-field approach.
    e. originally was practiced in Europe, because of a particularly British interest in military behavior.

7. The study of nonhuman primates is of special interest to which subdiscipline of anthropology?
    a. cultural anthropology
    b. archaeological anthropology
    c. linguistic anthropology
    d. developmental anthropology
    e. biological anthropology

8. Which of the following statements about applied anthropology is false?
    a. It encompasses any use of the knowledge and/or techniques of the four subfields to identify, assess, and solve practical social problems.
    b. It has been formally acknowledged by the American Anthropological Association as one of the two dimensions of the discipline.

c. It is less relevant for archaeology since archaeology typically concerns the material culture of societies that no longer exist.
    d. It is a growing aspect of the field, with more and more anthropologists developing applied components of their work.
    e. It has many applications because of anthropology's breadth.

9. Which of the following terms is defined as a suggested but yet unverified explanation for observed things and events?
    a. hypothesis
    b. theory
    c. association
    d. model
    e. law

10. The scientific method
    a. is limited to ethnology since it is the aspect of anthropology that studies sociocultural differences and similarities.
    b. is a powerful tool for understanding ourselves since it guarantees complete objectivity in research.
    c. is the best and only reliable way of understanding the world.
    d. characterizes any anthropological endeavor that formulates research questions and gathers or uses systematic data to test hypotheses.
    e. only applies to the analysis of data that leads to predictions, not associations.

FILL IN THE BLANK

1. Anthropology is unique among the social sciences in its emphasis on both _____ and _____ perspectives.

2. A _____ approach refers to the inclusion and combination of both biological and cultural perspectives and approaches to comment on or solve a particular issue or problem.

3. _____ provides an account of fieldwork in a particular community, society, or culture.

4. _____ encompasses any use of the knowledge and/or techniques of the four subfields of anthropology to identify, assess, and solve practical problems. More and more anthropologists increasingly work in this dimension of the discipline.

5. The _____ characterizes any anthropological endeavor that formulates research questions and gathers or uses systematic data to test hypotheses.

CRITICAL THINKING

1. What is culture? How is it distinct from what this chapter describes as a biocultural approach? How do these concepts help us understand the complex ways that human populations adapt to their environments?

2. What themes and interests unify the subdisciplines of anthropology? In your answer, refer to historical reasons for the unity of anthropology. Are these historical reasons similar in all places where anthropology developed as a discipline?

3. If, as Franz Boas illustrated early on in American anthropology, cultures are not isolated, how can ethnography provide an account of a particular community, society, or culture? Note: There is no easy answer to this question! Anthropologists continue to deal with it as they define their research questions and projects.

4. The American Anthropological Association has formally acknowledged a public service role by recognizing that anthropology has two dimensions: (1) academic anthropology and (2) practicing or applied anthropology. What is applied anthropology? Based on your reading of this chapter, identify examples from current events where an anthropologist could help identify, assess, and solve contemporary social problems.

5. In this chapter, we learn that anthropology is a science, although a very humanistic one. What do you think this means? What role does hypothesis testing play in structuring anthropological research? What are the differences between theories, laws, and hypotheses?

Multiple Choice: 1. (D); 2. (D); 3. (C); 4. (D); 5. (A); 6. (A); 7. (E); 8. (C); 9. (A); 10. (D); **Fill in the Blank:** 1. holistic, cross-cultural; 2. biocultural; 3. Ethnography; 4. Applied anthropology; 5. scientific method

Endicott, K. M., and R. Welsch
  2009 *Taking Sides: Clashing Views on Controversial Issues in Anthropology,* 4th ed. Guilford, CT: McGraw-Hill/Dushkin. Thirty-eight anthropologists offer opposing viewpoints on nineteen polarizing issues, including ethical dilemmas.

Fagan, B. M.
  2012 *Archeology: A Brief Introduction,* 11th ed. Upper Saddle River, NJ: Prentice Hall. Introduction to archaeological theory, techniques, and approaches, including field survey, excavation, and analysis of materials.

Geertz, C.
  1995 *After the Fact: Two Countries, Four Decades, One Anthropologist.* Cambridge, MA: Harvard University Press. A prominent cultural anthropologist reflects on his work in Morocco and Indonesia.

Harris, M.
  1989 *Our Kind: Who We Are, Where We Came From, Where We Are Going.* New York: Harper-Collins. Clearly written survey of the origins of humans, culture, and major sociopolitical institutions.

Scott, J.
  2011 *A Singular Woman: The Untold Story of Barack Obama's Mother.* New York: Riverhead Books. The life and work of a cultural/applied anthropologist.

Wolf, E. R.
  1982 *Europe and the People Without History.* Berkeley: University of California Press. Influential and award-winning study of the relation between Europe and various nonindustrial populations.

suggested additional readings

Go to our Online Learning Center website at **www.mhhe.com/kottak** for Internet exercises directly related to the content of this chapter.

internet exercises

Culture

What is culture and why do we study it?

What is the relation between culture and the individual?

How does culture change—especially with globalization?

◀ Offerings at a temple in Bali, Indonesia. People learn and share beliefs and behavior as members of cultural groups.

understanding OURSELVES

How special are you? To what extent are you "your own person" and to what extent are you a product of your particular culture? How much does, and should, your cultural background influence your actions and decisions? Americans may not fully appreciate the power of culture because of the value their culture places on "the *individual*." Americans like to regard everyone as unique in some way. Yet individualism itself is a distinctive *shared* value, a feature of American culture, transmitted constantly in our daily lives. In the media, count how many stories focus on individuals versus groups. From the late Mr. (Fred) Rogers of daytime TV to "real-life" parents, grandparents, and teachers, our enculturative agents insist we all are "someone special." That we are individuals first and members of groups second is the opposite of this chapter's lesson about culture. Certainly we have distinctive features because we are individuals, but we have other distinct attributes because we belong to cultural groups.

For example, as we saw in the "Appreciating Diversity" box in Chapter 1 (pp. 6–7), a comparison of the United States with Brazil, Italy, or virtually any Latin nation reveals striking contrasts between a national culture (American) that discourages physical affection and national cultures in which the opposite is true. Brazilians touch, embrace, and kiss one another much more frequently than North Americans do. Such behavior reflects years of exposure to particular cultural traditions. Middle-class Brazilians teach their kids—both boys and girls—to kiss (on the cheek, two or three times, coming and going) every adult relative they ever see. Given the size of Brazilian extended families, this can mean hundreds of people. Women continue kissing all those people throughout their lives. Until they are adolescents, boys kiss all adult relatives. Men typically continue to kiss female relatives and friends, as well as their fathers and uncles, throughout their lives.

Do you kiss your father? Your uncle? Your grandfather? How about your mother, aunt, or grandmother? The answer to these questions may differ between men and women, and for male and female relatives. Culture can help us to make sense of these differences. In America, a cultural homophobia (fear of homosexuality) may prevent American men from engaging in displays of affection with other men; similarly, American girls typically are encouraged to show affection, while American boys typically aren't. It's important to note that these cultural explanations rely upon example and expectation, and that no cultural trait exists because it is natural or right. *Ethnocentrism* is the error of viewing one's own culture as superior and applying one's own cultural values in judging people from other cultures. How easy is it for you to see beyond the ethnocentric blinders of your own experience? Do you have an ethnocentric position regarding displays of affection?

WHAT IS CULTURE?

The concept of culture is fundamental in anthropology. Well over a century ago, in his book *Primitive Culture,* the British anthropologist Sir Edward Tylor proposed that cultures—systems of human behavior and thought—obey natural laws and therefore can be studied scientifically. Tylor's definition of culture still offers an overview of the subject matter of anthropology and is widely quoted: "Culture . . . is that complex whole which includes knowledge, belief, arts, morals, law, custom, and any other capabilities and habits acquired by man as a member of society" (Tylor 1871/1958, p. 1). The crucial phrase here is "acquired . . . as a member of society." Tylor's definition focuses on attributes that people acquire not through biological inheritance but by growing up in a particular society where they are exposed to a specific cultural tradition. **Enculturation** is the process by which a child learns his or her culture.

Culture Is Learned

The ease with which children absorb any cultural tradition rests on the uniquely elaborated human capacity to learn. Other animals may learn from experience; for example, they avoid fire after discovering that it hurts. Social animals also learn from other members of their group. Wolves, for instance, learn hunting strategies from other pack members. Such social learning is particularly important among monkeys and apes, our closest biological relatives. But our own *cultural learning* depends on the uniquely developed human capacity to use **symbols,** signs that have no necessary or natural connection to the things they signify or for which they stand.

On the basis of cultural learning, people create, remember, and deal with ideas. They grasp and apply specific systems of symbolic meaning. Anthropologist Clifford Geertz defines culture as ideas based on cultural learning and symbols. Cultures have been characterized as sets of "control mechanisms—plans, recipes, rules, instructions, what computer engineers call programs for the governing of behavior" (Geertz 1973, p. 44). These programs are absorbed by people through enculturation in particular traditions. People gradually internalize a previously established system of meanings and symbols. They use this cultural system to define their world, express their feelings, and make their judgments. This system helps guide their behavior and perceptions throughout their lives.

Every person begins immediately, through a process of conscious and unconscious learning and interaction with others, to internalize, or incorporate, a cultural tradition through the process of enculturation. Sometimes culture is taught directly, as when parents tell their children to say "thank you" when someone gives them something or does them a favor.

Culture also is transmitted through observation. Children pay attention to the things that go on around them. They modify their behavior not just because other people tell them to but as a result of their own observations and growing awareness of what their culture considers right and wrong. Culture also is absorbed unconsciously. North Americans acquire their culture's notions about how far apart people should stand when they talk not by being told directly to maintain a certain distance but through a gradual process of observation, experience, and conscious and unconscious behavior modification. No one tells Latins to stand closer together than North Americans do, but they learn to do so anyway as part of their cultural tradition.

Anthropologists agree that cultural learning is uniquely elaborated among humans and that all humans have culture. Anthropologists also accept a doctrine named in the 19th century as "the psychic unity of man." This means that although *individuals* differ in their emotional and intellectual tendencies and capacities, all human *populations* have equivalent capacities for culture. Regardless of their genes or their physical appearance, people can learn any cultural tradition.

To understand this point, consider that contemporary Americans and Canadians are the genetically mixed descendants of people from all over the world. Our ancestors were biologically varied, lived in different countries and continents, and participated in hundreds of cultural traditions. However, early colonists, later immigrants, and their descendants have all become active participants in American and Canadian life. All now share a national culture.

Culture Is Symbolic

Symbolic thought is unique and crucial to humans and to cultural learning. Anthropologist Leslie White defined culture as

> dependent upon symbolling . . . Culture consists of tools, implements, utensils, clothing, ornaments, customs, institutions, beliefs, rituals, games, works of art, language, etc. (White 1959, p. 3)

For White, culture originated when our ancestors acquired the ability to use symbols, that is, to originate and bestow meaning on a thing or event, and, correspondingly, to grasp and appreciate such meanings (White 1959, p. 3).

A symbol is something verbal or nonverbal, within a particular language or culture, that comes to stand for something else. There is no obvious, natural, or necessary connection between the symbol and what it symbolizes. A pet that barks is no more naturally a *dog* than a *chien, Hund,* or *mbwa,* to use the words for the animal we call "dog" in French, German, and Swahili. Language is one of the distinctive possessions of *Homo sapiens.* No other animal has developed anything approaching the complexity of language.

Symbols are usually linguistic. But there are also nonverbal symbols, such as flags, that stand for countries, as arches do for a hamburger chain. Holy water is a potent symbol in Roman Catholicism. As

enculturation
The process by which culture is learned and transmitted across the generations.

symbol
Something, verbal or nonverbal, that stands for something else.

Some symbols are linguistic. Others are nonverbal, such as flags, which stand for countries. Here, colorful flags of several nations wave in front of the United Nations building in New York City.

is true of all symbols, the association between a symbol (water) and what is symbolized (holiness) is arbitrary and conventional. Water is not intrinsically holier than milk, blood, or other natural liquids. Nor is holy water chemically different from ordinary water. Holy water is a symbol within Roman Catholicism, which is part of an international cultural system. A natural thing has been arbitrarily associated with a particular meaning for Catholics, who share common beliefs and experiences that are based on learning and that are transmitted across the generations.

For hundreds of thousands of years, humans have possessed the abilities on which culture rests. These abilities are to learn, to think symbolically, to manipulate language, and to use tools and other cultural products in organizing their lives and coping with their environments. Every contemporary human population has the ability to use symbols and thus to create and maintain culture. Our nearest relatives—chimpanzees and gorillas—have rudimentary cultural abilities. No other animal, however, has elaborated cultural abilities—to learn, to communicate, and to store, process, and use information—to the extent that *Homo* has.

Culture Is Shared

Culture is an attribute not of individuals per se but of individuals as members of *groups*. Culture is transmitted in society. Don't we learn our culture by observing, listening, talking, and interacting with many other people? Shared beliefs, values, memories, and expectations link people who grow up in the same culture. Enculturation unifies people by providing us with common experiences.

Today's parents were yesterday's children. If they grew up in North America, they absorbed certain values and beliefs transmitted over the generations. People become agents in the enculturation of their children, just as their parents were for them. Although a culture constantly changes, certain fundamental beliefs, values, worldviews, and child-rearing practices endure. Consider a simple American example of enduring shared enculturation. As children, when we didn't finish a meal, our parents may have reminded us of starving children in some foreign country, just as our grandparents might have done a generation earlier. The specific locale changes (China, India, Bangladesh, Ethiopia, Somalia, Darfur—what was it in your home?). Still, American culture goes on transmitting the idea that by eating all our brussels sprouts or broccoli, we can justify our own good fortune, compared to a hungry child in an impoverished or war-ravaged country.

Despite characteristic American notions that people should "make up their own minds" and "have a right to their opinion," little of what we think is original or unique. We share our opinions and beliefs with many other people. Illustrating the power of shared cultural background, we are most likely to agree with and feel comfortable with people who are socially, economically, and culturally similar to ourselves. This is one reason why Americans abroad tend to socialize with each other, just as French and British colonials did in their overseas empires. Birds of a feather flock together, but for people, the familiar plumage is culture.

Culture and Nature

Culture takes the natural biological urges we share with other animals and teaches us how to express them in particular ways. People have to eat, but culture teaches us what, when, and how. In many cultures people have their main meal at noon, but most North Americans prefer a large dinner. English people may eat fish for breakfast, while North Americans may prefer hot cakes and cold cereals. Brazilians put hot milk into strong coffee, whereas North Americans pour cold milk into a weaker brew. Midwesterners dine at 5 or 6 P.M., Spaniards at 10 P.M.

Culture molds "human nature" in many directions. People have to eliminate wastes from their bodies. But some cultures teach people to defecate squatting, while others tell them to do it sitting down. A generation ago, in Paris and other French cities, it was customary for men to urinate almost publicly, and seemingly without embarrassment, in barely shielded *pissoirs* located on city streets. Our "bathroom" habits, including waste elimination, bathing, and dental care, are parts of cultural traditions that have converted natural acts into cultural customs.

Our culture—and cultural changes—affect the ways in which we perceive nature, human nature, and "the natural." Through science, invention, and discovery, cultural advances have overcome many "natural" limitations. We prevent and cure diseases such as polio and smallpox that felled our ancestors. We use Viagra to restore and enhance sexual potency. Through cloning, scientists have altered the way we think about biological identity and the meaning of life itself. Culture, of course, has not freed us from natural threats. Hurricanes, floods, earthquakes, and other natural forces regularly challenge our wishes to modify the environment through building, development, and expansion. Can you think of other ways in which nature strikes back at people and their products?

living anthropology **VIDEOS**

Being Raised Canela, www.mhhe.com/kottak

This clip focuses on Brazil's Canela Indians. One of the key figures in the clip is a boy, Carampei. Another is the "formal friend" of a small boy whose finger has been burned and who has been disciplined by his mother. The clip depicts enculturation among the Canela—various ways in which children learn their culture. How does the footage of Carampei show his learning of the rhythms of Canela life? The clip shows that children start doing useful work at an early age, but that the playfulness and affection of childhood are prolonged into adulthood. How does the behavior of the formal friend illustrate this playfulness? Notice how Canela culture is integrated in that songs, dances, and tales are interwoven with subsistence activity. What is the function of the hunters' dance for the Canela? Think about how the clip shows formal, informal, conscious, and unconscious aspects of enculturation.

Culture Is All-Encompassing

For anthropologists, culture includes much more than refinement, taste, sophistication, education, and appreciation of the fine arts. Not only college graduates but all people are "cultured." The most interesting and significant cultural forces are those that affect people every day of their lives, particularly those that influence children during enculturation. *Culture,* as defined anthropologically, encompasses features that are sometimes regarded as trivial or unworthy of serious study, such as "popular" culture. To understand contemporary North American culture, we must consider television, fast-food restaurants, sports, and games. As a cultural manifestation, a rock star may be as interesting as a symphony conductor, a comic book as significant as a book-award winner. (Describing the multiple ways in which anthropologists have studied the Ariaal of northern Kenya, this chapter's "Appreciating Anthropology" demonstrates how anthropology, like culture, is all encompassing.)

 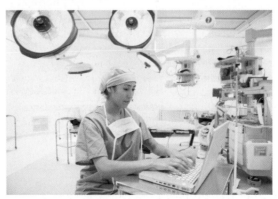

Cultures are integrated systems, so that when one behavior pattern changes, others also change. During the 1950s, most American women expected to have careers as wives, mothers, and domestic managers. As millions of women entered the workforce, attitudes toward work and family changed. Compare the 1950s mom and kids doing dishes with the contemporary physician entering data on a laptop computer. What do you imagine she will do when she gets home?

appreciating ANTHROPOLOGY

Remote and Poked, Anthropology's Dream Tribe

Anthropology, remember, is a four-subfield discipline that is comparative, cross-cultural, and biocultural. Anthropologists are known for their close observation of human behavior in natural settings and their focus on human biological and cultural diversity in time and space. It is typical of the anthropological approach to go right to—and live with—the local people, whether in northern Kenya, as described here, or in middle-class America (see Descartes and Kottak 2009).

Anthropologists study human biology and culture in varied times and places and in a rapidly changing world. This account focuses on a remote population, the Ariaal of northern Kenya, whom anthropologists have been studying since the 1970s. In the account we learn about the multifaceted research interests that anthropologists have. Among the Ariaal, anthropologists have studied a range of topics, including kinship and marriage customs, conflict, and even biomedical issues such as illness and body type and function. As you read this account, consider, too, what anthropologists get from the people being studied and vice versa.

The Ariaal, a nomadic community of about 10,000 people in northern Kenya, have been seized on by researchers since the 1970s, after one anthropologist, Elliot Fratkin—stumbled upon them and began publishing his accounts of their lives. . . .

Other researchers have done studies on everything from their cultural practices to their testosterone levels. *National Geographic* focused on the Ariaal in 1999, in an article on vanishing cultures.

But over the years, more and more Ariaal—like the Masai and the Turkana in Kenya and the Tuaregs and Bedouins elsewhere in Africa—are settling down. Many have emigrated closer to Marsabit, the nearest town, which has cellphone reception and even sporadic Internet access.

The scientists continue to arrive in Ariaal country, with their notebooks, tents, and bizarre queries, but now they document a semi-isolated people straddling modern life and more traditional ways.

For Benjamin C. Campbell, a biological anthropologist at Boston University who was introduced to the Ariaal by Dr. Fratkin, their way of life, diet, and cultural practices make them worthy of study.

Other academics agree. Local residents say they have been asked over the years how many livestock they own (many), how many times they have had diarrhea in the last month (often) and what they ate the day before yesterday (usually meat, milk or blood).

Ariaal women have been asked about the work they do, which seems to exceed that of the men, and about local marriage customs, which compel their prospective husbands to hand over livestock to their parents before the ceremony can take place. . . .

The researchers may not know this, but the Ariaal have been studying them all these years as well.

The Ariaal note that foreigners slather white liquid on their very white skin to protect them

Koitaton Garawale (left) is amused by questions posed by researcher Daniel Lemoille in Songa, Kenya. The Ariaal, a nomadic community of about 10,000 people in northern Kenya, have been studied since the 1970s by Elliot Fratkin and other anthropologists, representing various subfields.

from the sun, and that many favor short pants that show off their legs and the clunky boots on their feet. Foreigners often partake of the local food but drink water out of bottles and munch on strange food in wrappers between meals, the Ariaal observe.

The scientists leave tracks as well as memories behind. For instance, it is not uncommon to see nomads in T-shirts bearing university logos, gifts from departing academics.

In Lewogoso Lukumai, a circle of makeshift huts near the Ndoto Mountains, nomads rushed up to a visitor and asked excitedly in the Samburu language, "Where's Elliot?"

They meant Dr. Fratkin, who describes in his book "Ariaal Pastoralists of Kenya" how in 1974 he stumbled upon the Ariaal, who had been little known until then. With money from the University of London and the Smithsonian Institution, he was traveling north from Nairobi in search of isolated agro-pastoralist groups in Ethiopia. But a coup toppled Haile Selassie, then the emperor, and the border between the countries was closed. So as he sat in a bar in Marsabit, a boy approached and, mistaking him for a tourist, asked if he wanted to see the elephants in a nearby forest. When the aspiring anthropologist declined, the boy asked if he wanted to see a traditional ceremony at a local village instead. That was Dr. Fratkin's introduction to the Ariaal, who share cultural traits with the Samburu and Rendille tribes of Kenya.

Soon after, he was living with the Ariaal, learning their language and customs while fighting off mosquitoes and fleas in his hut of sticks covered with grass.

The Ariaal wear sandals made from old tires and many still rely on their cows, camels and goats to survive. Drought is a regular feature of their world, coming in regular intervals and testing their durability.

"I was young when Elliot first arrived," recalled an Ariaal elder known as Lenampere in Lewogoso Lukumai, a settlement that moves from time to time to a new patch of sand. "He came here and lived with us. He drank milk and blood with us. After him, so many others came." . . .

Not all African tribes are as welcoming to researchers, even those with the necessary permits from government bureaucrats. But the Ariaal have a reputation for cooperating—in exchange, that is, for pocket money. "They think I'm stupid for asking dumb questions," said Daniel Lemoille, headmaster of the school in Songa, a village outside of Marsabit for Ariaal nomads who have settled down, and a frequent research assistant for visiting professors. "You have to try to explain that these same questions are asked to people all over the world and that their answers will help advance science." . . .

The Ariaal have no major gripes about the studies, although the local chief in Songa, Stephen Lesseren, who wore a Boston University T-shirt the other day, said he wished their work would lead to more tangible benefits for his people.

"We don't mind helping people get their Ph.D.'s," he said. "But once they get their Ph.D.'s, many of them go away. They don't send us their reports . . . We want feedback. We want development."

Even when conflicts break out in the area, as happened this year as members of rival tribes slaughtered each other, victimizing the Ariaal, the research does not cease. With tensions still high, John G. Galaty, an anthropologist at McGill University in Montreal who studies ethnic conflicts, arrived in northern Kenya to question them.

In a study in *The International Journal of Impotence Research,* Dr. Campbell found that Ariaal men with many wives showed less erectile dysfunction than did men of the same age with fewer spouses.

Dr. Campbell's body image study, published in the *Journal of Cross-Cultural Psychology* this year, also found that Ariaal men are much more consistent than men in other parts of the world in their views of the average man's body [one like their own] and what they think women want [one like their own].

Dr. Campbell came across no billboards or international magazines in Ariaal country and only one television in a local restaurant that played CNN, leading him to contend that Ariaal men's views of their bodies were less affected by media images of burly male models with six-pack stomachs and rippling chests.

To test his theories, a nonresearcher without a Ph.D. showed a group of Ariaal men a copy of *Men's Health* magazine full of pictures of impossibly well-sculpted men and women. The men looked on with rapt attention and admired the chiseled forms.

"That one, I like," said one nomad who was up in his years, pointing at a photo of a curvy woman who was clearly a regular at the gym. Another old-timer gazed at the bulging pectoral muscles of a male bodybuilder in the magazine and posed a question that got everybody talking. Was it a man, he asked, or a very, very strong woman?

Culture Is Integrated

Cultures are not haphazard collections of customs and beliefs. Cultures are integrated, patterned systems. If one part of the system (e.g., the economy) changes, other parts change as well. For example, during the 1950s, most American women planned domestic careers as homemakers and mothers. Most of today's college women, by contrast, expect to get paid jobs when they graduate.

Economic changes have social repercussions. Attitudes and behavior about marriage, family, and children have changed. Late marriage, "living together," and divorce have become more common. Work competes with marriage and family responsibilities and reduces the time available to invest in child care.

Cultures are integrated not simply by their dominant economic activities and related social patterns but also by sets of values, ideas, symbols, and judgments. Cultures train their individual members to share certain personality traits. A set of **core values** (key, basic, or central values) integrates each culture and helps distinguish it from others. For instance, the work ethic and individualism are core values that have integrated American culture for generations. Different sets of dominant values exist in other cultures.

Culture Is Instrumental, Adaptive, and Maladaptive

Culture is the main reason for human adaptability and success. Other animals rely on biological means of adaptation (such as fur or blubber, which are adaptations to cold). Humans also adapt biologically—for example, by shivering when we get cold or sweating when we get hot. But people also have cultural ways of adapting. To cope with environmental stresses we habitually use technology, or tools. We hunt cold-adapted animals and use their fur coats as our own. We turn the thermostat up in the winter and down in the summer. Or we plan action to increase our comfort. We have a cold drink, jump in a pool, or travel to someplace cooler in the summer or warmer in the winter. People use culture instrumentally, that is, to fulfill their basic biological needs for food, drink, shelter, comfort, and reproduction.

People also use culture to fulfill psychological and emotional needs, such as friendship, companionship, approval, and being desired sexually. People seek informal support—help from people who care about them—as well as formal support from associations and institutions. To these ends, individuals cultivate ties with others on the basis of common experiences, political interests, aesthetic sensibilities, or personal attraction.

On one level, cultural traits (e.g., air conditioning) may be called adaptive if they help individuals cope with environmental stresses. But, on a different level, such traits can also be *maladaptive*. That is, they may threaten a group's continued existence. Thus chlorofluorocarbons from air conditioners deplete the ozone layer and, by doing so, can harm humans and other life. Many modern cultural patterns may be maladaptive in the long run. Some examples of maladaptive aspects of culture are policies that encourage overpopulation, poor food-distribution systems, overconsumption, and industrial pollution of the environment.

CULTURE'S EVOLUTIONARY BASIS

The human capacity for culture has an evolutionary basis that extends back at least 2.6 million years—to early toolmakers whose products survive in the archeological record (and most probably even farther back, based on observation of tool use and manufacture by apes).

Similarities between humans and apes, our closest relatives, are evident in anatomy, brain structure, genetics, and biochemistry. Most closely related to us are the African great apes: chimpanzees and gorillas. *Hominidae* is the zoological family that includes fossil and living humans. Also included as **hominids** are chimps and gorillas. The term **hominins** is used for the group that leads to humans but not to chimps and gorillas and that encompasses all the human species that ever have existed.

Many human traits reflect the fact that our primate ancestors lived in the trees. These traits include grasping ability and manual dexterity (especially opposable thumbs), depth and color vision, learning ability based on a large brain, substantial parental investment in a limited number of offspring, and tendencies toward sociality and cooperation. Like other primates, humans have flexible, five-fingered hands and *opposable thumbs:* Each thumb can touch all the other fingers on the same hand. Like monkeys and apes, humans also have excellent depth and color vision. Our eyes are placed forward in the skull and look directly ahead, so that their fields of vision overlap. Depth perception, impossible without overlapping visual fields, proved adaptive—for judging distance, for example—in the trees. Having color and depth vision also facilitates the identification of various food sources, as well as mutual grooming, picking out burrs, insects, and other small objects from hair. Such grooming is one way of forming and maintaining social bonds.

The combination of manual dexterity and depth perception allows monkeys, apes, and humans to pick up small objects, hold them in front of their eyes, and appraise them. Our ability to thread a needle reflects an intricate interplay of hands and eyes that took millions of years of primate evolution to achieve. Such dexterity, including the opposable thumb, confers a tremendous advantage in

---

core values

Key, basic, or central values that integrate a culture.

hominid

Member of hominid family; any fossil or living human, chimp, or gorilla.

hominins

Hominids excluding the African apes; all the human species that ever have existed.

manipulating objects and is essential to a major human adaptive capacity: tool making. In primates, and especially in humans, the ratio of brain size to body size exceeds that of most mammals. Even more important, the brain's outer layer—concerned with memory, association, and integration—is relatively larger. Monkeys, apes, and humans store an array of images in their memories, which permits them to learn more. Such a capacity for learning is a tremendous adaptive advantage. Like most other primates, humans usually give birth to a single offspring rather than a litter. Receiving more parental attention, that one infant has enhanced learning opportunities. The need for longer and more attentive care of offspring places a selective value on support by a social group. Humans have developed considerably the primate tendency to be social animals, living and interacting regularly with other members of their species.

What We Share with Other Primates

There is a substantial gap between primate *society* (organized life in groups) and fully developed human *culture,* which is based on symbolic thought. Nevertheless, studies of nonhuman primates reveal many similarities with humans, such as the ability to learn from experience and change behavior as a result. Apes and monkeys, like humans, learn throughout their lives. In one group of Japanese macaques (land-dwelling monkeys), for example, a three-year-old female started washing sweet potatoes before she ate them. First her mother, then her age peers, and finally the entire troop began washing sweet potatoes as well. The ability to benefit from experience confers a tremendous adaptive advantage, permitting the avoidance of fatal mistakes. Faced with environmental change, humans and other primates don't have to wait for a genetic or physiological response. They can modify learned behavior and social patterns instead.

Although humans do employ tools much more than any other animal does, tool use also turns up among several nonhuman species, including birds, beavers, sea otters, and especially apes (see Campbell 2011, Mayell 2003). Nor are humans the only animals that make tools with a specific purpose in mind. Chimpanzees living in the Tai forest of Ivory Coast make and use stone tools to break open hard, golf-ball-sized nuts (Mercader, Panger, and Boesch 2002). At specific sites, the chimps gather nuts, place them on stumps or flat rocks, which are used as anvils, and pound the nuts with heavy stones. The chimps must select hammer stones suited to smashing the nuts and carry them to where the nut trees grow. Nut cracking is a learned skill, with mothers showing their young how to do it.

In 1960, Jane Goodall (1996) began observing wild chimps—including their tool use and hunting behavior—at Gombe Stream National Park in Tanzania, East Africa. The most studied form of ape toolmaking involves "termiting," in which chimps make tools to probe termite hills. They choose twigs, which they modify by removing leaves and peeling off bark to expose the sticky surface beneath. They carry the twigs to termite hills, dig holes with their fingers, and insert the twigs. Finally, they pull out the twigs and dine on termites that were attracted to the sticky surface. Given what is known about ape tool use and manufacture, it is almost certain that early hominins shared this ability, although the first evidence for hominin stone toolmaking dates back only 2.6 million years. Upright bipedalism would have permitted the carrying and use of tools and weapons against predators and competitors.

The apes have other abilities essential to culture. Wild chimps and orangs aim and throw objects. Gorillas build nests, and they throw branches, grass, vines, and other objects. Hominins have elaborated the capacity to aim and throw, without which we never would have developed projectile technology and weaponry—or baseball.

Like toolmaking, hunting once was cited as a distinctive human activity not shared with the apes. Again, however, primate research shows that other primates, especially chimpanzees, are habitual hunters. For example, in Uganda's Kibale National Park chimps form large hunting parties, including an average of twenty-six individuals (almost always adult and adolescent males). Most hunts (78 percent) result in at least one prey item's being caught—a much higher success rate than that among lions (26 percent), hyenas (34 percent), or cheetahs (30 percent). Chimps' favored prey there is the red colobus monkey (Mitani and Watts 1999).

Archaeological evidence suggests that humans were hunting by at least 2.6 million years ago, based on stone meat-cutting tools found at Olduvai Gorge in Tanzania. Given our current understanding of chimp hunting and toolmaking, we can infer that hominids may have been hunting much earlier than the first archaeological evidence attests. Because chimps typically devour the monkeys they kill, leaving few remains, we may never find archaeological evidence for the first hominin hunt, especially if it was done without stone tools.

Primates have five-digited feet and hands, well suited for grasping. Flexible hands and feet that could encircle branches were important features in the early primates' arboreal life. In adapting to bipedal (two-footed) locomotion, hominids eliminated most of the foot's grasping ability—illustrated here by the chimpanzee.

anthropology **ATLAS**

http://www.mhhe.com/anthromaps Map 2 locates major primate groups, including monkeys and apes.

Tool use by chimps. These chimps in Liberia are using stone tools to crack palm nuts, as described in the text.

How We Differ from Other Primates

Although chimps often share meat from a hunt, apes and monkeys (except for nursing infants) tend to feed themselves individually. Cooperation and sharing are much more developed among humans. Until fairly recently (twelve thousand to ten thousand years ago), all humans were hunter-gatherers who lived in small groups called bands. In some world areas, the hunter-gatherer way of life persisted into recent times, permitting study by ethnographers. In such societies, men and women bring resources back to the camp and share them. Everyone shares the meat from a large animal. Nourished and protected by younger band members, elders live past reproductive age and are respected for their knowledge and experience. Humans are among the most cooperative of the primates—in the food quest and other social activities. In addition, the amount of information stored in a human band is far greater than that in any other primate group.

Another difference between humans and other primates involves mating. Among baboons and chimps, most mating occurs when females enter estrus, during which they ovulate. In estrus, the vaginal area swells and reddens, and receptive females form temporary bonds with, and mate with, males. Human females, by contrast, lack a visible estrus cycle, and their ovulation is concealed. Not knowing when ovulation is occurring, humans maximize their reproductive success by mating throughout the year. Human pair bonds for mating are more exclusive and more durable than are those of chimps. Related to our more constant sexuality, all human societies have some form of marriage. Marriage gives mating a reliable basis and grants to each spouse special, though not always exclusive, sexual rights to the other.

Marriage creates another major contrast between humans and nonhuman primates: exogamy and kinship systems. Most cultures have rules of exogamy requiring marriage outside one's kin or local group. Coupled with the recognition of kinship, exogamy confers adaptive advantages. It creates ties between the spouses' different groups of origin. Their children have relatives, and therefore allies, in two kin groups rather than just one. The key point here is that ties of affection and mutual support between members of different local groups tend to be absent among primates other than *Homo*. Other primates tend to disperse at adolescence. Among chimps and gorillas, females tend to migrate, seeking mates in other groups. Humans also choose mates from outside the natal group, and usually at least one spouse moves. However, *humans maintain lifelong ties with sons and daughters*. The systems of kinship and marriage that preserve these links provide a major contrast between humans and other primates.

UNIVERSALITY, GENERALITY, AND PARTICULARITY

In studying human diversity in time and space, anthropologists distinguish among the universal, the generalized, and the particular. Certain biological, psychological, social, and cultural features are **universal,** found in every culture. Others are merely **generalities,** common to several but not all human groups. Still other traits are **particularities,** unique to certain cultural traditions.

Universals and Generalities

Biologically based universals include a long period of infant dependency, year-round (rather than seasonal) sexuality, and a complex brain that enables us to use symbols, languages, and tools. Among the social universals is life in groups and in some kind of family (see Brown 1991). Generalities occur in certain times and places but not in all cultures. They may be widespread, but they are not universal. One cultural generality that is present in many but not all societies is the nuclear family, a kinship group consisting of parents and children. Although many middle-class Americans ethnocentrically view the nuclear family as a proper and "natural" group, it is not universal. It was absent, for example, among the Nayars, who live on the Malabar Coast of India. Traditionally, the Nayars lived in female-headed households, and husbands and wives did not live together. In many other societies, the nuclear family is

universal
Something that exists in every culture.

generality
Culture pattern or trait that exists in some but not all societies.

particularity
Distinctive or unique culture trait, pattern, or integration.

submerged in larger kin groups, such as extended families, lineages, and clans.

Societies can share the same beliefs and customs because of borrowing or through (cultural) inheritance from a common cultural ancestor. Speaking English is a generality shared by North Americans and Australians because both countries had English settlers. Another reason for generalities is domination, as in colonial rule, when customs and procedures are imposed on one culture by another one that is more powerful. In many countries, use of the English language reflects colonial history. More recently, English has spread through diffusion (cultural borrowing) to many other countries, as it has become the world's foremost language for business and travel.

Particularity: Patterns of Culture

A cultural particularity is a trait or feature of culture that is not generalized or widespread; rather, it is confined to a single place, culture, or society. Yet because of cultural borrowing, which has accelerated through modern transportation and communication systems, traits that once were limited in their distribution have become more widespread. Traits that are useful, that have the capacity to please large audiences, and that don't clash with the cultural values of potential adopters are more likely to spread than others are. Still, certain cultural particularities persist. One example would be a particular food dish (e.g., pork barbeque with a mustard-based sauce available only in South Carolina, or the pastie—beef stew baked in pie dough—characteristic of Michigan's upper peninsula). Besides diffusion, which, for example, has spread McDonald's food outlets, once confined to San Bernardino, California, across the globe, there are other reasons why cultural particularities are increasingly rare. Many cultural traits are shared as cultural universals and as a result of independent invention. Facing similar problems, people in different places have come up with similar solutions. Again and again, similar cultural causes have produced similar cultural results.

At the level of the individual cultural trait or element (e.g., bow and arrow, hot dog, MTV), particularities may be getting rarer. But at a higher level, particularity is more obvious. Different cultures emphasize different things. *Cultures are integrated and patterned differently and display tremendous variation and diversity.* When cultural traits are borrowed, they are modified to fit the culture that adopts them. They are reintegrated—patterned anew—to fit their new setting. MTV in Germany or Brazil isn't at all the same thing as MTV in the United States. As was stated in the earlier section "Culture Is Integrated," patterned beliefs, customs, and practices lend distinctiveness to particular cultural traditions.

Consider universal life-cycle events, such as birth, puberty, marriage, parenthood, and death, which many cultures observe and celebrate. The

Cultures use rituals to mark such universal life-cycle events as birth, puberty, marriage, parenthood, and death. But particular cultures differ as to which events merit special celebration and in the emotions expressed during their rituals. Compare the wedding party (top) in Bali, Indonesia, with the funeral (bottom) among the Tanala of eastern Madagascar. How would you describe the emotions suggested by the photos?

occasions (e.g., marriage, death) may be the same and universal, but the patterns of ceremonial observance may be dramatically different. Cultures vary in just which events merit special celebration. Americans, for example, regard expensive weddings as more socially appropriate than lavish funerals. However, the Betsileo of Madagascar take the opposite view. The marriage ceremony is a minor event that brings together just the couple and a few close relatives. However, a funeral is a measure of the deceased person's social position and lifetime

anthropology **ATLAS**

http://www.mhhe.com/anthromaps Map 12 shows patterns of world land use around 500 years ago. The different economic types are examples of cultural generalities.

achievement, and it may attract a thousand people. Why use money on a house, the Betsileo say, when one can use it on the tomb where one will spend eternity in the company of dead relatives? How unlike contemporary Americans' dreams of home ownership and preference for quick and inexpensive funerals. Cremation, an increasingly common option in the United States (see Sack 2011), would horrify the Betsileo, for whom ancestral bones and relics are important ritual objects.

Cultures vary tremendously in their beliefs, practices, integration, and patterning. By focusing on and trying to explain alternative customs, anthropology forces us to reappraise our familiar ways of thinking. In a world full of cultural diversity, contemporary American culture is just one cultural variant, more powerful perhaps, but no more natural, than the others.

CULTURE AND THE INDIVIDUAL: AGENCY AND PRACTICE

Generations of anthropologists have theorized about the relationship between the "system," on the one hand, and the "person" or "individual," on the other. The "system" can refer to various concepts, including culture, society, social relations, and social structure. Individual human beings always make up, or constitute, the system. But, living within that system, humans also are constrained (to some extent, at least) by its rules and by the actions of other individuals. Cultural rules provide guidance about what to do and how to do it, but people don't always do what the rules say should be done. People use their culture actively and creatively, rather than blindly following its dictates. Humans aren't passive beings who are doomed to follow their cultural traditions like programmed robots. Instead, people learn, interpret, and manipulate the same rules in different ways—or they emphasize different rules that better suit their interests. Culture is *contested:* Different groups in society struggle with one another over whose ideas, values, goals, and beliefs will prevail. Even common symbols may have radically different *meanings* to different individuals and groups in the same culture. Golden arches may cause one person to salivate, while another person plots a vegetarian protest. The same flag may be waved to support or oppose a given war.

Even when they agree about what should and shouldn't be done, people don't always do as their culture directs or as other people expect. Many rules are violated, some very often (e.g., automobile speed limits). Some anthropologists find it useful to distinguish between ideal culture and real culture. The *ideal culture* consists of what people say they should do and what they say they do. *Real culture* refers to their actual behavior as observed by the anthropologist.

Culture is both public and individual, both in the world and in people's minds. Anthropologists are interested not only in public and collective behavior but also in how *individuals* think, feel, and act. The individual and culture are linked because human social life is a process in which individuals internalize the meanings of *public* (i.e., cultural) messages. Then, alone and in groups, people influence culture by converting their private (and often divergent) understandings into public expressions (D'Andrade 1984).

Conventionally, culture has been seen as social glue transmitted across the generations, binding people through their common past, rather than as something being continually created and reworked in the present. The tendency to view culture as an entity rather than a process is changing. Contemporary anthropologists now emphasize how day-to-day action, practice, or resistance can make and remake culture (Gupta and Ferguson, eds. 1997b). *Agency* refers to the actions that individuals take, both alone and in groups, in forming and transforming cultural identities.

The approach to culture known as *practice theory* (Ortner 1984) recognizes that individuals within a society or culture have diverse motives and intentions and different degrees of power and influence. Such contrasts may be associated with gender, age, ethnicity, class, and other social variables. Practice theory focuses on how such varied individuals—through their ordinary and extraordinary actions and practices—manage to influence, create, and transform the world they live in. Practice theory appropriately recognizes a reciprocal relation between culture (the system—see above) and the individual. The system shapes the way individuals experience and respond to external events, but individuals also play an active role in the way society functions and changes. Practice theory recognizes both constraints on individuals and the flexibility and changeability of cultures and social systems.

Levels of Culture

We can distinguish levels of culture, which vary in their membership and geographic extent. **National culture** refers to those beliefs, learned behavior patterns, values, and institutions that are shared by citizens of the same nation. **International culture** is the term for cultural traditions that extend beyond and across national boundaries. Because culture is transmitted through learning rather than genetically, cultural traits can spread through borrowing or *diffusion* from one group to another.

Because of borrowing, colonialism, migration, and multinational organizations, many cultural traits and patterns have international scope. For example, Roman Catholics in many different countries share beliefs, symbols, experiences, and values transmitted by their church. The contemporary United States, Canada, Great Britain, and Australia share

national culture
Cultural features shared by citizens of the same nation.

international culture
Cultural traditions that extend beyond national boundaries.

cultural traits they have inherited from their common linguistic and cultural ancestors in Great Britain. The World Cup has become an international cultural event, as people in many countries know the rules of, play, and follow soccer.

Cultures also can be smaller than nations (see Jenks 2004). Although people who live in the same country share a national cultural tradition, all cultures also contain diversity. Individuals, families, communities, regions, classes, and other groups within a culture have different learning experiences as well as shared ones. **Subcultures** are different symbol-based patterns and traditions associated with particular groups in the same complex society. In a large nation like the United States or Canada, subcultures originate in region, ethnicity, language, class, and religion. The religious backgrounds of Jews, Baptists, and Roman Catholics create subcultural differences between them. While sharing a common national culture, U.S. northerners and southerners also differ in aspects of their beliefs, values, and customary behavior as a result of regional variation. French-speaking Canadians contrast with English-speaking people in the same country. Italian Americans have ethnic traditions different from those of Irish, Polish, and African Americans. Using sports and foods, Table 2.1 gives some examples of international culture, national culture, and subculture. Soccer and basketball are played internationally. Monster-truck rallies are held throughout the United States. Bocci is a bowling-like sport from Italy still played in some Italian American neighborhoods.

Nowadays, many anthropologists are reluctant to use the term *subculture*. They feel that the prefix "sub-" is offensive because it means "below." "Subcultures" may thus be perceived as "less than" or somehow inferior to a dominant, elite, or national culture. In this discussion of levels of culture, I intend no such implication. My point is simply that nations may contain many different culturally defined groups. As mentioned earlier, culture is contested. Various groups may strive to promote the correctness and value of their own practices, values, and beliefs in comparison with those of other groups or of the nation as a whole. (This chapter's "Appreciating Diversity" demonstrates how contemporary indigenous groups have to grapple with multiple levels of culture, contestation, and political regulation.)

Ethnocentrism, Cultural Relativism, and Human Rights

Ethnocentrism is the tendency to view one's own culture as superior and to use one's own standards and values in judging outsiders. We witness ethno-

Illustrating the international level of culture, Roman Catholics in different nations share knowledge, symbols, beliefs, and behavior associated with their religion. Shown here, Chinese Catholics at an Easter mass in Beijing. In China, worship is allowed only in government-controlled churches, but an estimated 12 million Chinese Catholics belong to unofficial congregations loyal to Rome.

centrism when people consider their own cultural beliefs to be truer, more proper, or more moral than those of other groups. However, fundamental to anthropology, as the study of human diversity, is the fact that what is alien (even disgusting) to us may be normal, proper, and prized elsewhere (see the previous discussion of cultural particularities, including burial customs). The fact of cultural diversity calls ethnocentrism into question, as anthropologists have shown all kinds of reasons for unfamiliar practices. During a course like this, anthropology students often reexamine their own ethnocentric beliefs. Sometimes as the strange becomes familiar, the familiar seems a bit stranger and less comfortable. One goal of anthropology is to show the value in the lives of others. But how far is too far? What happens when cultural practices, values, and rights come into conflict with human rights?

subcultures
Different cultural traditions associated with subgroups in the same nation.

TABLE 2.1 Levels of Culture, with Examples from Sports and Foods

LEVEL OF CULTURE	SPORTS EXAMPLES	FOOD EXAMPLES
International	Soccer, basketball	Pizza
National	Monster-truck rallies	Apple pie
Subculture	Bocci	Big Joe Pork Barbeque (South Carolina)

ethnocentrism
Judging other cultures using one's own cultural standards.

appreciating **DIVERSITY**

Culture Clash: Makah Seek Return to Whaling Past

Cultures are diverse but not isolated. Throughout human history links between groups have been provided by cultural practices such as marriage, kinship, religion, trade, travel, exploration, and conquest. For centuries, indigenous peoples have been exposed to a world system. Contemporary forces and events make even the illusion of autonomy hard to maintain. Nowadays, as is described here, members of local cultures and communities must heed not only their own customs but also agencies, laws, and lawsuits operating at the national and international levels.

As you read this account and this chapter on culture, pay attention to the various kinds of rights being asserted—animal rights, cultural rights, economic rights, legal rights, and human rights—and how those rights might clash. Also consider the different levels of culture and of political representation (local, regional, national, and global) that determine how contemporary people such as the Makah live their lives and maintain their traditions. Think, too, about the minimal impact on whale populations of the Makah hunt compared with commercial whaling. Today, cultural connections come increasingly through the Internet, as indigenous groups, including the Makah, maintain their own websites—forums for discussions of whaling and other issues of interest to them. Check out http://www.makah. com for the latest on the issues discussed here.

The whaling canoes are stored in a wooden shed, idle for [several] years. They were last used when the Makah Indians were allowed to take their harpoons and a .50-caliber rifle and set out on their first whale hunt since the late 1920s.

There were eight young men in a canoe with a red hummingbird, a symbol of speed, painted on the tip. There were motorboats ferrying other hunters, news helicopters, and animal rights activists in speedboats and even a submarine.

On May 17, 1999, a week into the hunt, the Makah killed a 30-ton gray whale, striking it with harpoons and then killing it with a gunshot to the back of the head.

That rainy spring day remains etched in the minds of many Makah as a defining moment in their efforts to reach back to their cultural and historical roots. It was their first kill in seven decades, and it was their last since they were stopped by court rulings. They have asked the federal government for permission to resume hunting. . . .

The Makah, a tribe of about 1,500 near the mouth of the Strait of Juan de Fuca on the Olympic Peninsula, see themselves as whalers and continue to identify themselves spiritually with whales.

"Everybody felt like it was a part of making history," Micah L. McCarty, a tribal council member, said of the 1999 hunt. "It's inspired a cultural renaissance, so to speak. It inspired a lot of people to learn artwork and become more active in building canoes; the younger generation took a more keen interest in singing and dancing."

The Makah, a tribe of mostly fishermen that faces serious poverty and high unemployment, were guaranteed the right to hunt whales in an 1855 treaty with the United States, the only tribe with such a treaty provision. Whaling had been the tribe's mainstay for thousands of years.

But the tribe decided to stop hunting whales early in the 20th century, when commercial harvesting had depleted the species. Whale hunting was later strictly regulated nationally and internationally, and the United States listed the Northern Pacific gray whale, the one most available to the Makah, as endangered.

The protections helped the whales rebound, and they were taken off the endangered list in 1994. Several years later, the Makah won permission to hunt again, along with a $100,000 federal grant to set up a whaling commission.

By the time they were ready, none of the Makah had witnessed a whale hunt or even tasted the meat, hearing only stories passed down through the generations. They learned that the whale was a touchstone of Makah culture—the tribe's logo today pictures an eagle perched on a whale—and that the tribe's economy was built around the lucrative trade with Europeans in whale oil, used for heating and lighting, during the 18th and early 19th centuries.

For a year before the 1999 hunt, the new Makah whale hunters prepared for their sacramental pursuit, training in canoes on the cold and choppy waters of the Pacific Ocean, praying on the beach in the mornings and at the dock in the evenings.

Animal rights groups were preparing, too. When the hunt began, the small reservation and its surrounding waters were teeming with news helicopters and protest groups. On that May afternoon, when the protesters were somewhere off the reservation, the Makah killed their whale. They held a huge celebration on the beach, where 15 men were waiting to butcher the animal, its meat later kippered and stewed.

But the protests and the television cameras "took a lot of the spirituality out of it," said Dave Sones, vice chairman of the tribal council.

Mr. McCarty said, "I equate it with interrupting High Mass."

The Makah went whale hunting, largely unnoticed, again in 2000, paddling out on a 32-foot cedar whaling canoe, but they did not catch anything. Soon after, animal rights groups, including the Humane Society of the United States, sued to stop the hunting. In 2002, an appeals court declared the hunting illegal, saying the National Oceanic and Atmospheric Administration had not adequately studied the impact of Makah hunting on the survival of the whale species.

Despite the strict national and international regulations on whale hunting, several tribes of Alaska Natives, subsistence whale hunters for centuries, are exempt from provisions of the 1972 Marine Mammal Protection Act, allowing them to hunt the bowhead whale. That species, unlike the gray whale, is listed as endangered, said Brian Gorman, a spokesman for the oceanic agency.

Despite their treaty rights, the Makah were not granted an exemption under the 1972 act. The tribe [has requested] a waiver that would grant them permanent rights to kill up to 20 gray whales in any five-year period, which they insist they already have under their 1855 treaty.

The Makah's request is "setting a dangerous precedent," said Naomi Rose, a marine mammal scientist for the Humane Society.

The Alaska hunting, Ms. Rose said, "is a true subsistence hunt," whereas the Makah . . . are pursuing "cultural whaling" that is not essential to their diet. . . .

The Makah "have a treaty right, but we're asking them not to exercise it," she said. But other environmental groups, including Greenpeace, which is adamantly opposed to the commercial harvesting of whales, have remained neutral on the Makah's quest.

"No indigenous hunt has ever destroyed whale populations," said John Hocevar, an oceans specialist with Greenpeace. "And looking at the enormous other threats to whales and putting the Makah whaling in context, it's pretty different."

Mr. Gorman, of the federal fisheries agency, said: "They have a treaty right that the U.S. government signed. It doesn't take an international lawyer to figure out that they do have this treaty."

2012 Update: The situation remains unresolved. The Makah petition to resume whaling continues to be considered by the Marine Fisheries division of NOAA—the National Oceanic and Atmospheric Administration.

Dewey Johnson and his son Michael (top) show their support for fellow Makah tribe members at Neah Bay, Washington, in their quest to hunt gray whales for the first time in seventy years. *Sea Shepherd* captain Paul Watson stands at Neah Bay beside a 25-foot submarine painted to look like an orca whale (below). This ship emits orca sounds that can scare away gray whales. Watson leads the opposition against Makah whaling, which was declared illegal in 2002.

SOURCE: Sarah Kershaw, "In Petition to Government, Tribe Hopes for Return to Whaling Past." From *The New York Times*, September 19, 2005. © 2005 The New York Times. All rights reserved. Used by permission and protected by the Copyright Laws of the United States. The printing, copying, redistribution, or retransmission of this Content without express written permission is prohibited. www.nytimes.com

Several societies in Africa and the Middle East have customs requiring female genital modification. *Clitoridectomy* is the removal of a girl's clitoris. *Infibulation* involves sewing the lips (labia) of the vagina to constrict the vaginal opening. Both procedures reduce female sexual pleasure and, it is believed in some societies, the likelihood of adultery. Although traditional in the societies where they occur, such practices, characterized as female genital mutilation (FGM), have been opposed by human rights advocates, especially women's rights groups. The idea is that the custom infringes on a basic human right: disposition over one's body and one's sexuality. Indeed, such practices are fading as a result of worldwide attention to the problem and changing sex/gender roles. Some African countries have banned or otherwise discouraged the procedures, as have Western nations that receive immigration from such cultures. Similar issues arise with circumcision and other male genital operations. Is it right to require adolescent boys to undergo collective circumcision to fulfill cultural traditions, as has been done traditionally in parts of Africa and Australia? Is it right for a baby boy to be circumcised without his permission, as has been done routinely in the United States and as is customary among Jews and Muslims? (A 2011 initiative aimed at banning circumcision in San Francisco, California, failed to make it to the ballot.)

According to an idea known as **cultural relativism,** it is inappropriate to use outside standards to judge behavior in a given society; such behavior should be evaluated in the context of the culture in which it occurs. Anthropologists employ cultural relativism not as a moral belief but as a methodological position: In order to understand another culture fully, we must try to understand how the people in that culture see things. What motivates them—what are they thinking—when they do those things? Such an approach does not preclude making moral judgments. In the FGM example, one can understand the motivations for the practice only by looking at things from the point of view of the people who engage in it. Having done this, one then faces the moral question of what, if anything, to do about it.

We also should recognize that different people and groups within the same society—for example, women versus men or old versus young—can have very different opinions about what is proper, necessary, and moral. When there are power differentials in a society, a particular practice may be supported by some people more than others (e.g., old men versus young women). In trying to understand the meaning of a practice or belief within any cultural context, we should ask who is relatively advantaged and disadvantaged by that custom.

The idea of **human rights** invokes a realm of justice and morality beyond and superior to particular countries, cultures, and religions. Human rights, usually seen as vested in individuals, include the right to speak freely, to hold religious beliefs without persecution, and not to be murdered, injured, enslaved, or imprisoned without charge. These rights are not ordinary laws that particular governments make and enforce. Human rights are seen as *inalienable* (nations cannot abridge or terminate them) and international (larger than and superior to individual nations and cultures). Four United Nations documents describe nearly all the human rights that have been internationally recognized. Those documents are the UN Charter; the Universal Declaration of Human Rights; the Covenant on Economic, Social and Cultural Rights; and the Covenant on Civil and Political Rights.

Alongside the human rights movement has arisen an awareness of the need to preserve cultural rights. Unlike human rights, **cultural rights** are vested not in individuals but in groups, including indigenous peoples and religious and ethnic minorities. Cultural rights include a group's ability to raise its children in the ways of its forebears, to continue its language, and not to be deprived of its economic base by the nation in which it is located (Greaves 1995). Many countries have signed pacts endorsing, for cultural minorities within nations, such rights as self-determination; some degree of home rule; and the right to practice the group's religion, culture, and language. The related notion of indigenous intellectual property rights (**IPR**) has arisen in an attempt to conserve each society's cultural base—its core beliefs and principles. IPR are claimed as a cultural right, allowing indigenous groups to control who may know and use their collective knowledge and its applications. Much traditional cultural knowledge has commercial value. Examples include ethnomedicine (traditional medical knowledge and techniques), cosmetics, cultivated plants, foods, folklore, arts, crafts, songs, dances, costumes, and rituals. According to the IPR concept, a particular group may determine how its indigenous knowledge and the products of that knowledge are used and distributed, and the level of compensation required. (This chapter's "Appreciating Diversity" discusses how notions of human, cultural, and animal rights may come into conflict.)

The notion of cultural rights recalls the previous discussion of cultural relativism, and the issue raised there arises again. What does one do about cultural rights that interfere with human rights? I believe that anthropology, as the scientific study of human diversity, should strive to present accurate accounts and explanations of cultural phenomena. Most ethnographers try to be objective, accurate, and sensitive in their accounts of other cultures. However, objectivity, sensitivity, and a cross-cultural perspective don't mean that anthropologists have to ignore international standards of justice and morality. The anthropologist doesn't have to approve customs

cultural rights
Rights vested in religious and ethnic minorities and indigenous societies.

cultural relativism
Idea that behavior should be evaluated not by outside standards but in the context of the culture in which it occurs.

IPR
Intellectual property rights; an indigenous group's collective knowledge and its applications.

anthropology **ATLAS**

http://www.mhhe.com/anthromaps Map 10 locates classic ethnographic field sites—"cultures" or societies already studied by 1950.

human rights
Rights based on justice and morality beyond and superior to particular countries, cultures, and religions.

such as infanticide, cannibalism, and torture to record their existence and determine their causes and the motivations behind them. Each anthropologist has a choice about where he or she will do fieldwork. Some anthropologists choose not to study a particular culture because they discover in advance or early in fieldwork that behavior they consider morally repugnant is practiced there. When confronted with such behavior, each anthropologist must make a judgment about what, if anything, to do about it. What do you think?

MECHANISMS OF CULTURAL CHANGE

Why and how do cultures change? One way is **diffusion,** or borrowing of traits between cultures. Such exchange of information and products has gone on throughout human history because cultures never have been truly isolated. Contact between neighboring groups has always existed and has extended over vast areas (Boas 1940/1966). Diffusion is *direct* when two cultures trade, intermarry, or wage war on one another. Diffusion is *forced* when one culture subjugates another and imposes its customs on the dominated group. Diffusion is *indirect* when items move from group A to group C via group B without any firsthand contact between A and C. In this case, group B might consist of traders or merchants who take products from a variety of places to new markets. Or group B might be geographically situated between A and C, so that what it gets from A eventually winds up in C, and vice versa. In today's world, much transnational diffusion is due to the spread of the mass media and advanced information technology.

Acculturation, a second mechanism of cultural change, is the exchange of cultural features that results when groups have continuous firsthand contact. The cultures of either group or both groups may be changed by this contact (Redfield, Linton, and Herskovits 1936). With acculturation, parts of the cultures change, but each group remains distinct. In situations of continuous contact, cultures may exchange and blend foods, recipes, music, dances, clothing, tools, technologies, and languages.

One example of acculturation is a *pidgin,* a mixed language that develops to ease communication between members of different societies in contact. This usually happens in situations of trade or colonialism. Pidgin English, for example, is a simplified form of English. It blends English grammar with the grammar of a native language. Pidgin English was first used for commerce in Chinese ports. Similar pidgins developed later in Papua New Guinea and West Africa.

Independent invention—the process by which humans innovate, creatively finding solutions to problems—is a third mechanism of cultural change. Faced with comparable problems and challenges, people in different societies have innovated and changed in similar ways, which is one reason cultural generalities exist. One example is the independent invention of

acculturation
An exchange of cultural features between groups in firsthand contact.

diffusion
Borrowing of cultural traits between societies.

independent invention
The independent development of a cultural feature in different societies.

The notion of indigenous intellectual property rights (IPR) has arisen in an attempt to conserve each society's cultural base, including its medicinal plants, which may have commercial value. Shown here is the hoodia plant, a cactus that grows in the Kalahari Desert of southern Africa. Hoodia, which traditionally is used by the San people to stave off hunger, is used now in diet pills marketed on the Internet.

agriculture in the Middle East and Mexico. Over the course of human history, major innovations have spread at the expense of earlier ones. Often a major invention, such as agriculture, triggers a series of subsequent interrelated changes. These economic revolutions have social and cultural repercussions. Thus, in both Mexico and the Middle East, agriculture led to many social, political, and legal changes, including notions of property and distinctions in wealth, class, and power.

GLOBALIZATION

globalization
The accelerating interdependence of nations in the world system today.

Globalization describes a series of processes that work transnationally to promote change in a world in which nations and people increasingly are interlinked and mutually dependent. Promoting globalization are economic and political forces, along with modern systems of transportation and communication. The forces of globalization include international commerce and finance, travel and tourism, and transnational migration. Equally important are the mass media, including the Internet and other high-tech information flows (see Appadurai 2001; Friedman and Friedman 2008; Haugurud, Stone, and Little 2011; Kjaerulff 2010; Scholte 2000).

Long-distance communication is faster and easier than ever, and now covers most of the globe. I can e-mail or call families in Arembepe, Brazil,

which lacked phones and even postal service when I first began to study that community decades ago. Information about Arembepe is now available to anyone, including potential tourists, on hundreds of websites. Anything can be Googled. The media fuel a transnational culture of consumption as they spread information about products, services, and lifestyles. Emigrants transmit information and resources transnationally, as they maintain their ties with home (phoning, Skyping, videoconferencing, texting, e-mailing, making visits, sending money). In a sense such people live multilocally—in different places and cultures at once. They learn to play various social roles and to change behavior and identity depending on the situation (see Cresswell 2006).

The effects of globalization are broad and not always welcome. Local people must cope increasingly with forces generated by larger systems. An army of outsiders and potential change agents now intrudes on people everywhere. Tourism has become the world's number one industry (see Holden 2005). Economic development agents and the media promote the idea that work should be for cash rather than mainly for subsistence. Indigenous peoples and traditional societies have devised various strategies to deal with threats to their autonomy, identity, and livelihood (Maybury-Lewis 2002). New forms of cultural expression and political mobilization, including the rights movements discussed previously, have emerged from the interplay of local, regional, national, international, and global, cultural forces (see Ong and Collier 2005).

Globalization: Its Meaning and Its Nature

Mark Smith and Michele Doyle (2002) draw an important distinction between two meanings of globalization:

1. Globalization as fact: the spread and connectedness of production, communication, and technologies across the world. As used in this book, this is the primary meaning of globalization.

2. Globalization as contested ideology and policy: efforts by the International Monetary Fund (IMF), the World Bank, the World Trade Organization (WTO), and other international financial powers to create a global free market for goods and services.

For those who advocate free trade, globalization in this second sense is the way the world should go. For their opponents—antiglobalization activists—it's the way the world should not go (Lewellen 2010). This second sense of globalization—

Globalization in its current form would not exist without the Internet. Shown here, Chinese youth in an Internet café in Beijing. Using cameras and ID card scanners, the Chinese government monitors activity in each of Beijing's more than 1,500 Internet cafés. Users must be 18 or older. Who monitors Internet use in your country?.

as something to be promoted by deregulating markets—has generated considerable opposition.

Protesters regularly surround the meetings of agencies concerned with international trade. One of the largest rallies took place in December 1999 in Seattle. This was a massive and violent demonstration against the WTO, which was meeting there. Opponents continue to show their disapproval of the WTO, the IMF, and the World Bank. In November 2009 there were clashes with police during a march by demonstrators protesting the opening of a WTO meeting in Geneva, Switzerland. The WTO had called that meeting of its 153 members to find ways to revive world trade and get the global economy out of recession (*Huffington Post* 2010).

WTO opponents claim that its policies favor multinational corporations at the expense of farmers, workers, and poor people. Human rights groups contend that international development policies help only big business. Trade unionists advocate for global labor standards. Are such protests valid, and are they likely to halt globalization?

Let's return to the first—more neutral—meaning of globalization. The fact of globalization as systemic connectedness reflects the relentless and ongoing growth of the world system. Although that system has existed for centuries, it has some radical new aspects. Three are especially noteworthy: (1) the speed of global communication, (2) the scale (complexity and size) of global networks, and (3) the volume of international transactions.

Russia and the other former Soviet-bloc countries opened to world capitalism with the fall of the Soviet Union in 1989–90. Once that happened a new and truly global economy could emerge (Lewellen 2010). According to Manuel Castells (2001), this economy has three key features: (1) It is based on knowledge and information; (2) its networks are transnational, and (3) its core activities, even if dispersed, can proceed as a unit in real time (Castells 2001).

By the year 2000, multinational corporations accounted for one-third of global output, and two-thirds of world trade (Gray 1999, p. 62). Seeking to maximize profit, multinationals move production, sales, and services to areas where labor and materials are cheap. This globalization of labor creates unemployment "back home" as industries relocate and outsource abroad.

Multinationals also seek out new markets, striving to create new needs, especially in the youth market. Young people increasingly construct their identities around consumption, especially of brand name products. Such successful multinationals as Nike, Coca Cola, Apple, and McDonald's invest huge sums in promoting their brands. The goal is to make a particular brand an integral part of the way people see themselves. Savvy branders try to "get them young" (Klein 2001; Smith and Doyle 2002). A

Advertizing Coca Cola, a powerful global brand, in Xi'an, China. *Savvy branders try to "get them young."*

brand can become part of one's social and cultural identity.

Multinational corporations increasingly influence national policy. They attempt to forge beneficial alliances with politicians and government officials. The influence of multinationals extends to key transnational players, such as the European Union and banks that have been called "too big to fail." With the globalization of financial markets, nations have less control over their own economies. Can you think of examples? The World Bank, the International Monetary Fund, the European Union, and the European Central Bank routinely constrain and dictate national economic policy.

With the global spread of capitalism, the gap between rich and poor has widened both within and between nations. In the United States the gap has widened considerably in recent years, especially since 2000. In 2011, growing North American inequality—between the top 1 percent and everyone else—spurred the Occupy movement, which quickly spread from Wall Street to other American (and Canadian) cities. David Landes (1999) calculated the difference in per capita income between the world's richest nation (he cited Switzerland) and the poorest nation (Mozambique) as 400 to 1. This compares with a mere 5 to 1 when the Industrial Revolution began.

The preeminent value of knowledge, which tends to be concentrated in wealthy countries, has deepened the gap between rich and poor. Knowledge capitalism describes the commercial value of generating new ideas and converting them into brands, products, and services that consumers want (Leadbeater 1999). How much do brands figure in your own identity and relationships? Do you, for example, love your iPhone?

acing the COURSE

summary

1. Culture, which is distinctive to humanity, refers to customary behavior and beliefs that are passed on through enculturation. Culture rests on the human capacity for cultural learning. Culture encompasses rules for conduct internalized in human beings, which lead them to think and act in characteristic ways.

2. Although other animals learn, only humans have cultural learning, dependent on symbols. Humans think symbolically—arbitrarily bestowing meaning on things and events. By convention, a symbol stands for something with which it has no necessary or natural relation. Symbols have special meaning for people who share memories, values, and beliefs because of common enculturation. People absorb cultural lessons consciously and unconsciously.

3. Cultural traditions mold biologically based desires and needs in particular directions. Everyone is cultured, not just people with elite educations. Cultures may be integrated and patterned through economic and social forces, key symbols, and core values. Cultural rules don't rigidly dictate our behavior. There is room for creativity, flexibility, diversity, and disagreement within societies. Cultural means of adaptation have been crucial in human evolution. Aspects of culture also can be maladaptive.

4. The human capacity for culture has an evolutionary basis that extends back at least 2.6 million years—to early toolmakers whose products survive in the archaeological record (and most probably even farther back—based on observation of tool use and manufacture by apes). Humans share with monkeys and apes such traits as manual dexterity (especially opposable thumbs), depth and color vision, learning ability based on a large brain, substantial parental investment in a limited number of offspring, and tendencies toward sociality and cooperation.

5. Many hominin traits are foreshadowed in other primates, particularly in the African apes, which, like us, belong to the hominid family. The ability to learn, basic to culture, is an adaptive advantage available to monkeys and apes. Chimpanzees make tools for several purposes. They also hunt and share meat. Sharing and cooperation are more developed among humans than among the apes, and only humans have systems of kinship and marriage that permit us to maintain lifelong ties with relatives in different local groups.

6. Using a comparative perspective, anthropology examines biological, psychological, social, and cultural universals and generalities. There also are unique and distinctive aspects of the human condition (cultural particularities). North American cultural traditions are no more natural than any others. Levels of culture can be larger or smaller than a nation. Cultural traits may be shared across national boundaries. Nations also include cultural differences associated with ethnicity, region, and social class.

7. Ethnocentrism describes judging other cultures by using one's own cultural standards. Cultural relativism, which anthropologists may use as a methodological position rather than a moral stance, is the idea of avoiding the use of outside standards to judge behavior in a given society. Human rights are those based on justice and morality beyond and superior to particular countries, cultures, and religions. Cultural rights are vested in religious and ethnic minorities and indigenous societies, and IPR, or intellectual property rights, apply to an indigenous group's collective knowledge and its applications.

8. Diffusion, migration, and colonialism have carried cultural traits and patterns to different world areas. Mechanisms of cultural change include diffusion, acculturation, and independent invention.

9. Globalization describes a series of processes that promote change in a world in which nations and people are interlinked and mutually dependent. There is a distinction between globalization as fact (the primary meaning of globalization in this book) and globalization as contested ideology and policy (international efforts to create a global free market for goods and services).

key terms

test yourself

MULTIPLE CHOICE

1. Which of the following is *not* one of the ways in which individuals acquire the culture?
   a. genetic transmission
   b. unconscious acquisition
   c. observation
   d. direct instruction
   e. conscious acquisition

2. The "psychic unity" of humans, a doctrine that most anthropologists accept, states that
   a. psychology is the exclusive domain of the academic discipline of psychology.
   b. all humans share the same spiritual ethos.
   c. although individuals differ in their emotional and intellectual tendencies and capacities, all human populations have equivalent capacities for culture.
   d. psychological attributes are determined by our genes.
   e. even psychological attributes must be analyzed through the lens of cultural relativism.

3. Which of the following statements about cultural traits, patterns, and inventions is false?
   a. They mostly are determined genetically.
   b. They can be disadvantageous in the long run.
   c. They can be disadvantageous in the short run.
   d. They can be maladaptive.
   e. They are transmitted through learning.

4. This chapter's description of the similarities and differences between humans and apes, our closest relatives,
   a. explains why all hominids have evolved the same capacities for culture.
   b. emphasizes the need to expand the definition of cultural rights to include not just human individuals but also chimps and gorillas.
   c. explains why genetics has been more important than culture in determining our particular evolutionary path.

   d. illustrates how human females' lack of a visible estrus cycle determined our unique capacity for culture.
   e. emphasizes culture's evolutionary basis, stressing the interaction between biology and culture.

5. Certain biological, psychological, social, and cultural features are universal, found in every culture. All of the following are examples of universal features *except*
   a. a long period of infant dependency.
   b. seasonal (rather than year-round) sexuality.
   c. common ways in which humans think, feel, and process information.
   d. life in groups and in some kind of family.
   e. exogamy and the incest taboo (prohibition against marrying or mating with a close relative).

6. Which of the following statements about culture is *not* true?
   a. All human groups have culture.
   b. Culture is the major reason for human adaptability.
   c. Human groups differ in their capacities for culture.
   d. The capacity for culture is shared by all humans.
   e. Cultural learning is uniquely elaborated among humans.

7. In explaining how anthropologists have theorized the relationship between "system" and "person," this chapter notes that culture is contested. This means that
   a. different groups in a society struggle with one another over whose ideas, values, goods, and beliefs will prevail.
   b. while symbols can have different meanings, most common symbols are agreed upon by everyone in a culture.
   c. humans are passive beings who have little choice but to follow their cultural traditions.

    d. genes have programmed humans to manipulate the meanings and cultural symbols to increase our reproductive process.

    e. culture doesn't exist.

8. In anthropology, methodological cultural relativism

    a. is not a moral position, but a methodological one.

    b. is both a moral and a methodological stance toward other cultures.

    c. is synonymous with moral relativism.

    d. is another version of ethnocentrism.

    e. is a political position that argues for the defense of human rights, regardless of culture.

9. There were at least seven different regions where plant cultivation developed. Therefore,

agriculture is an example of which of the following mechanisms of cultural change?

    a. acculturation

    b. enculturation

    c. independent invention

    d. colonization

    e. diffusion

10. What is the term for the processes that are making nations and people increasingly interlinked and mutually dependent?

    a. acculturation

    b. independent invention

    c. diffusion

    d. globalization

    e. enculturation

FILL IN THE BLANK

1. Although humans continue to adapt _____, reliance on _____ means of adaptation has increased during human evolution.

2. Cultural traits, patterns, and inventions also can be _____, threatening the group's continued existence (survival and reproduction).

3. According to Leslie White, culture, and therefore humanity, came into existence when humans began to use _____.

4. The term _____ refers to any fossil or living human, chimp, or gorilla, while the term _____ refers only to any fossil or living human.

5. Unlike human rights, _____ are vested not in individuals but in groups, including indigenous peoples and religious and ethnic minorities.

CRITICAL THINKING

1. This chapter includes various authors' definitions of culture (e.g., those of Tylor, Geertz, and Kottak). How are these definitions similar? How are they different? How has reading this chapter altered your own understanding of what culture is?

2. Our culture—and cultural changes—affect how we perceive nature, human nature, and "the natural." This theme continues to fascinate science fiction writers. Recall a recent science fiction book, movie, or TV program that creatively explores the boundaries between nature and culture. How does the story develop the tension between nature and culture to craft a plot?

3. In American culture today, the term *diversity* is used in many contexts, usually referring to some positive attribute of our human experience, something to appreciate, to maintain, and even to increase. In what contexts have you heard the term used? To what precisely does the term refer?

4. What are some issues about which you find it hard to be culturally relativistic? If you were an anthropologist with the task of investigating these issues in real life, can you think of a series of steps that you would take to design a project that would, to the best of your ability, practice methodological cultural relativism? (You may want to review the use of the scientific method in an anthropological project presented in Chapter 1.)

5. What are the mechanisms of cultural change described in this chapter? Can you come up with additional examples of each mechanism? Also, recall the relationship between culture and the individual. Can individuals be agents of cultural change?

Multiple Choice: 1. (A); 2. (C); 3. (A); 4. (E); 5. (B); 6. (C); 7. (A); 8. (A); 9. (C); 10. (D); **Fill in the Blank:** 1. biologically, culturally; 2. maladaptive; 3. symbols; 4. hominid, hominin; 5. cultural rights

Appadurai, A., ed.
2001   *Globalization.* Durham, NC: Duke University Press. An anthropological approach to globalization and international relations.
Brown, D.
1991   *Human Universals.* New York: McGraw-Hill. Surveys the evidence for "human nature" and explores the roles of culture and biology in human variation.
Geertz, C.
1973   *The Interpretation of Cultures.* New York: Basic Books. Essays about culture viewed as a system of symbols and meaning.
Handwerker, P.
2009   *The Origins of Cultures: How Individual Choices Make Cultures Change.* Walnut Grove, CA: Left Coast Press. How culture influences choices that individuals make, and how those choices change cultures.
Lewellen, T. C.
2002   *The Anthropology of Globalization: Cultural Anthropology Enters the 21st Century.* Westport, CT: Bergin and Garvey. How anthropology is changing in relation to globalization.
Van der Elst, D., and P. Bohannan
2003   *Culture as Given, Culture as Choice,* 2nd ed. Prospect Heights, IL: Waveland. Culture and individual choices.

suggested additional readings

Go to our Online Learning Center website at **www.mhhe.com/kottak** for Internet exercises directly related to the content of this chapter.

internet exercises

3

Applying Anthropology

How can change be bad?

How can anthropology be applied to medicine, education, and business?

How does the study of anthropology fit into a career path?

◀ In Bangladesh, a health worker (dressed in teal) explains how to give oral rehydration fluids to treat childhood diarrhea. Smart planners, including those in public health, pay attention to locally based demand—what the people want—such as ways to reduce infant mortality.

understanding OURSELVES

Is change good? The idea that innovation is desirable is almost axiomatic and unquestioned in American culture—especially in advertising. "New and improved" is a slogan we hear all the time—a lot more often than "old reliable." Which do you think is best—change or the status quo?

That "new" isn't always "improved" is a painful lesson learned by the Coca-Cola Company (TCCC) in 1985 when it changed the formula of its premier soft drink and introduced "New Coke." After a national brouhaha, with hordes of customers protesting, TCCC brought back old, familiar, reliable Coke under the name "Coca-Cola Classic," which thrives today. New Coke, now history, offers a classic case of how not to treat consumers. TCCC tried a *top-down change* (a change initiated at the top of a hierarchy rather than inspired by the people most affected by the change). Customers didn't ask TCCC to change its product; executives made that decision.

Business executives, like public policy makers, run organizations that provide goods and services to people. The field of market research, which employs a good number of anthropologists, is based on the need to appreciate what actual and potential customers do, think, and want. Smart planners study and listen to people to try to determine *locally based demand*. In general, what's working well (assuming it's not discriminatory or illegal) should be maintained, encouraged, tweaked, and strengthened. If something's wrong, how can it best be fixed? What changes do the people—and which people—want? How can conflicting wishes and needs be accommodated? Applied anthropologists help answer these questions, which are crucial in understanding whether change is needed, and how it will work.

Innovation succeeds best when it is culturally appropriate. This axiom of applied anthropology could guide the international spread of programs aimed at social and economic change as well as of businesses. Each time an organization expands to a new nation, it must devise a culturally appropriate strategy for fitting into the new setting. In their international expansion, companies as diverse as McDonald's, Starbucks, and Ford have learned that more money can be made by fitting in with, rather than trying to Americanize, local habits.

Recall from Chapter 1 that anthropology has two dimensions: academic and applied. **Applied anthropology** is the use of anthropological data, perspectives, theory, and methods to identify, assess, and solve contemporary problems (see Ervin 2005). Applied anthropologists help make anthropology relevant and useful to the world beyond anthropology. Medical anthropologists, for example, have worked as cultural interpreters in public health programs, helping such programs fit into local culture. Development anthropologists work for or with international development agencies, such as the World Bank and the U.S. Agency for International Development (USAID). The findings of garbology, the archaeological study of waste, are relevant to the Environmental Protection Agency, the paper industry, and packaging and trade associations. Archaeology also is applied in cultural resource management and historic

ANTHROPOLOGY'S SUBFIELDS (ACADEMIC ANTHROPOLOGY)	EXAMPLES OF APPLICATION (APPLIED ANTHROPOLOGY)
Cultural anthropology	Development anthropology
Archaeological anthropology	Cultural resource management (CRM)
Biological or physical anthropology	Forensic anthropology
Linguistic anthropology	Study of linguistic diversity in classrooms

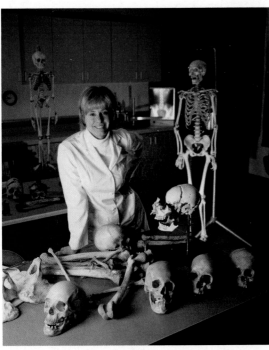

Like other forensic anthropologists, Dr. Kathy Reichs (shown here) and her alter ego, Temperance Brennan (played on the TV show *Bones* by Emily Deschanel), work with the police, medical examiners, the courts, and international organizations to identify victims of crimes, accidents, wars, terrorism, and genocide.

The ethnographic method is a particularly valuable tool in applying anthropology. Remember that ethnographers study societies firsthand, living with, observing, and learning from ordinary people. Nonanthropologists working in social-change programs often are content to converse with officials, read reports, and copy statistics. However, the applied anthropologist's likely early request is some variant of "take me to the local people." Anthropologists know that people must play an active role in the changes that affect them and that "the people" have information that "the experts" lack.

Anthropological theory, the body of findings and generalizations of the four subfields, also guides applied anthropology. Just as theory aids practice, application fuels theory (see Rylko-Bauer, Singer, and Van Willigen 2006). As we compare social-change programs, our understanding of cause and effect increases. We add new generalizations about culture change to those discovered in traditional and ancient cultures.

applied anthropology
Using anthropology to solve contemporary problems.

 living anthropology **VIDEOS**

Unearthing Evil: Archaeology in the Cause of Justice, www.mhhe.com/kottak

This clip features archaeologist Richard Wright and his team of fifteen forensic archaeologists and anthropologists working "in the cause of justice" in Bosnia. The focus of the clip is the excavation of a site of mass burial or reburial of the bodies of some 660 civilians who were murdered during the conflict that followed the dissolution of Yugoslavia. Wright and his colleagues worked with the international community to provide evidence of war crimes. This evidence has led to the convictions of war criminals. Why was Wright nervous about this work? Compare the forensic work shown here with the discussion of forensic anthropology in this chapter's "Appreciating Anthropology."

preservation. Biological anthropologists apply their expertise in programs aimed at public health, nutrition, genetic counseling, aging, substance abuse, and mental health. As described in this chapter's "Appreciating Anthropology," forensic anthropologists work with the police, medical examiners, the courts, and international organizations to identify victims of crimes, accidents, wars, and terrorism. Linguistic anthropologists study physician–patient communication and show how dialect differences influence classroom learning. Most applied anthropologists seek humane and effective ways of helping local people.

What Bones Can Tell

The television series *Bones,* along with the books of anthropologist and fiction writer Kathy Reichs, have dramatized, and to some extent, glamorized the field of forensic anthropology. This form of applied anthropology entails work with the police, medical examiners, the courts, and international organizations to identify victims of crimes, accidents, wars, terrorism, and genocide. *Bones* does not deal much with the human anguish associated with forensic anthropology–the horrors of crimes against humanity and the efforts of families to learn the fate of their missing loved ones. Described here is the forensic work of Dr. Eric Stover and his colleagues, who have helped identify victims of persecution and genocide in several parts of the world.

Bones are life's records. The forces of a lifetime—diet, accidents, age—are inscribed upon them. Forensics experts use bones to interpret these stories, . . . which can identify a person's identity and cause of death.

Eric Stover helps piece together the narratives left behind in the bones of war crime victims. Currently director of the Human Rights Center at the University of California, Berkeley, Dr. Stover's work has taken him to Guatemala, Iraq, Rwanda and other sites of human rights atrocities. The evidence he uncovers can be used to prosecute crimes against humanity and return victims' remains to their families . . .

Dr. Stover's first involvement with war crime forensics was in Argentina. During the so-called dirty war waged by the military against suspected leftists from 1976 to 1983, between 9,000 and 30,000 people disappeared. After the military junta fell in 1983, families began pressuring the new civilian government to find their loved ones. But even as remains were unearthed from mass graves, many bodies could not be identified.

In 1984, three Argentinean women who said they were relatives of missing Argentinean

A forensic anthropologist holds a blind-folded skull exhumed from the grave of a student leader in Irbil, Iraq. The student was executed during Saddam Hussein's "Anfal Campaign" against Iraq's Kurdish population in the late 1980s.

children showed up at Dr. Stover's office in Berkeley. They explained that during military rule, pregnant women were kidnapped and then executed after giving birth so their babies could be given to childless military or police couples. The women pleaded with Dr. Stover to help find their missing children and grandchildren. Over the coming months, he put together a team of forensic anthropologists, pathologists, radiologists, and odontologists, then recruited and trained Argentine medical students to help identify remains. . . .

The means of killing is often easy to identify, whether by machete or rifle. And evidence of execution is often readily apparent as well: bound hands, blindfolded skulls and wounds from point-blank gunshots are usually tell-tale signs. . . .

Victims' names also must be found so they can be returned to their families. Age, gender and even left-versus-right handedness are told

through their bones, while identity can be revealed through dental records and X-rays. . . .

Liliana Carmen Pereyra was one victim identified by Dr. Stover's team in Argentina. A 21-year old law student, she disappeared in October 1977, when she was five months pregnant. In 1985, officials told Liliana's mother, Coqui Pereyra, that her daughter had died in a shoot-out with the police, but Ms. Pereyra doubted their story, Dr. Stover said.

The site where Ms. Pereyra thought Liliana was buried contained three graves. Two of the bodies were young women and either could have been Liliana. . . . Vertebrae X-rays taken in life matched one of the exhumed bodies. The forensics team had found Liliana. Her skull was reconstructed to show an execution-style wound made with an Ithaca shotgun—a weapon commonly used by military forces. Liliana's remains were returned to her mother, and in September 2010, Liliana's son, now in his 30s, was found living in Argentina. . . .

The sheer magnitude of genocidal killing in some places—Rwanda or Cambodia, for instance—can make it exceedingly difficult to identify remains. But in Bosnia, Dr. Stover says, "There's no question that families wanted the remains returned."

Though individually identified bodies from every grave are not needed when it comes to prosecuting crimes against humanity, Dr. Stover and his team try to fulfill families' wishes first, and in the process they also gather evidence for court.

"There's not closure here," he said. "But this chapter in a way is closed, and people can better move on with their lives."

SOURCE: Rachel Nuwer, "Reading Bones to Identify Genocide Victims." From *The New York Times,* November 18, 2011. © 2011 The New York Times. All rights reserved. Used by permission and protected by the Copyright Laws of the United States. The printing, copying, redistribution, or retransmission of this Content without express written permission is prohibited. www.nytimes.com

THE ROLE OF THE APPLIED ANTHROPOLOGIST

Early Applications

Application was a central concern of early anthropology in Great Britain (in the context of colonialism) and the United States (in the context of Native American policy). Before turning to the new, we should consider some deficiencies and dangers of the old. For the British empire, specifically its African colonies, Bronislaw Malinowski (1929a) proposed that "practical anthropology" (his term for colonial applied anthropology) should focus on Westernization, the diffusion of European culture into tribal societies. Malinowski questioned neither the legitimacy of colonialism nor the anthropologist's role in making it work. He saw nothing wrong with aiding colonial regimes by studying land tenure and land use, to recommend how much of their land local people should be allowed to keep and how much Europeans should be permitted to take. Malinowski's views exemplify a historical association between early anthropology, particularly in Europe (especially England, France, and Portugal), and colonialism (see also Duffield and Hewitt 2009; Lange 2009; Maquet 1964; Rylko-Bauer, Singer, and Van Willigen 2006).

During World War II, American anthropologists studied Japanese and German "culture at a distance" in an attempt to predict the behavior of the enemies of the United States. After that war, applied anthropologists worked on Pacific islands to promote local-level cooperation with American policies in various trust territories. The American Anthropological Association (AAA) has raised strong ethical objections to applying anthropology in war zones and for military intelligence. Such concerns were voiced during the Vietnam War. More recently they have emerged in criticisms of anthropologists' participation in the Human Terrain System (HTS) project in Iraq and Afghanistan, as will be discussed in Chapter 13. Anthropological research should not be applied to the potential detriment of the people anthropologists study.

Academic and Applied Anthropology

After World War II, the baby boom, which began in 1946 and peaked in 1957, fueled a tremendous expansion of the American educational system. New junior, community, and four-year colleges opened, and anthropology became a standard part of the college curriculum. During the 1950s and 1960s, most American anthropologists were college professors, although some still worked in agencies and museums.

The growth of academic anthropology continued through the early 1970s. Especially during the Vietnam

During the Vietnam War, many anthropologists protested the superpowers' disregard for the values, customs, social systems, and lives of indigenous peoples. Several anthropologists (including the author) attended this all-night Columbia University teach-in against the war in 1965.

War, undergraduates flocked to anthropology classes to learn about other cultures. Students were especially interested in Southeast Asia, whose indigenous societies were being disrupted by war. Many anthropologists protested the superpowers' apparent disregard for non-Western lives, values, customs, and social systems.

Most anthropologists still worked in colleges and museums during the 1970s and 1980s. However, an increasing number of anthropologists were employed by international organizations, governments, businesses, hospitals, and schools. The AAA estimates that nowadays more than half of anthropology Ph.D.s seek nonacademic employment. This shift toward application has benefited the profession. It has forced anthropologists to consider the wider social value and implications of their research.

Applied Anthropology Today

Most contemporary applied anthropologists see their work as radically removed from the colonial enterprise. Modern applied anthropology usually is seen as a helping profession, devoted to assisting local people, as anthropologists speak up for the disenfranchised. However, applied anthropologists also have clients that are neither poor nor powerless. An applied anthropologist working as a market researcher for a business is concerned with discovering how to expand profits for his or her employer or client. Such goals can pose ethical dilemmas, as can work in cultural resource management (CRM). The CRM anthropologist helps decide how to preserve significant remains when

Supervised by archaeologists from India, with funding from the United Nations, these workers are cleaning and restoring the front facade of Cambodia's historic Angkor Wat temple. To decide what needs saving, and to preserve significant information about the past even when sites cannot be saved, is the work of cultural resource management (CRM).

development anthropology
Field that examines the sociocultural dimensions of economic development.

sites are threatened by development or public works. A CRM firm typically is hired by someone seeking to build a road or a factory. That client may have a strong interest in an outcome in which no sites are found that need protecting. Even if they don't work for colonial powers or the military, applied anthropologists still face ethical questions: To whom does the researcher owe loyalty? What problems are involved in holding firm to the truth? What happens when applied anthropologists don't make the policies they have to implement? How does one criticize programs in which one has participated (see Escobar 1991, 1994)? Anthropology's professional organizations have addressed such questions by establishing codes of ethics and ethics committees. As Karen Tice (1997) notes, attention to ethical issues has become paramount in the teaching of applied anthropology today.

Anthropologists are experts on human problems and social change who study, understand, and respect diverse cultural values. Given this background, anthropologists are highly qualified to suggest, plan, and implement social policy affecting people. Proper roles for applied anthropologists include (1) identifying needs for change that local people perceive, (2) working with those people to design culturally appropriate and socially sensitive change, and (3) protecting local people from harmful policies and projects that may threaten them.

increased equity
Reduction in absolute poverty, with a more even distribution of wealth.

DEVELOPMENT ANTHROPOLOGY

Development anthropology is the branch of applied anthropology that focuses on social issues in, and the cultural dimension of, economic development. Development anthropologists don't just carry out development policies planned by others; they also plan and guide policy. (For more detailed discussions of issues in development anthropology, see Edelman and Haugerud 2005; Escobar 1995; Ferguson 1995; Nolan 2002.)

Still, ethical dilemmas often confront development anthropologists (Escobar 1991, 1995). Foreign aid, including funds for economic development, usually doesn't go where need and suffering are greatest. Rather, such funds are spent on political, economic, and strategic priorities as international donors, political leaders, and powerful interest groups perceive them. Planners' interests don't always coincide with the best interests of the local people. Although the stated aim of most development projects is to enhance the quality of life, living standards often decline in the affected area (Bodley 1988).

Equity

A commonly stated goal of recent development policy is to promote equity. **Increased equity** means reduced poverty and a more even distribution of wealth. However, if projects are to increase equity, they must have the support of reform-minded governments. Wealthy and powerful people typically resist projects that threaten their vested interests.

Some development projects actually widen wealth disparities; that is, they have a negative equity impact. An initial uneven distribution of resources often becomes the basis for even greater socioeconomic inequality after the project. In Bahia, Brazil (Kottak 2006), for example, sailboat owners (but not nonowners) got loans to buy motors for their boats. To repay the loans, the owners increased the percentage of the catch they took from the men who fished in their boats. Over the years, they used their rising profits to buy larger and more expensive boats. The result was stratification—the creation of a group of wealthy people within a formerly more egalitarian community. These events hampered individual initiative and interfered with further development of the fishing industry. New boats became so expensive that ambitious young men, who once would have sought careers in fishing, no longer could afford to buy a boat of their own. They sought wage labor on land instead. To avoid such results, credit-granting agencies must seek out and invest in enterprising young fishers, rather than giving loans only to owners and established businesspeople.

STRATEGIES FOR INNOVATION

Development anthropologists should work closely with local people to assess, and help them realize, their own wishes and needs for change. Too many true local needs cry out for a solution to waste money funding development projects in area A that are inappropriate there but needed in area B, or that are unnecessary anywhere. Development anthropology can help sort out the needs of the As and Bs and fit projects accordingly. Projects that put people first by consulting with them and responding to their expressed needs must be identified (Cernea 1991). Thereafter, development anthropologists can work to ensure socially compatible ways of implementing a good project.

In a comparative study of 68 rural development projects from all around the world, I found the culturally compatible economic development projects to be twice as successful financially as the incompatible ones (Kottak 1990b, 1991). This finding suggests that using anthropological expertise in planning, to ensure cultural compatibility, is cost effective. To maximize social and economic benefits, projects must (1) be culturally compatible, (2) respond to locally perceived needs, (3) involve men and women in planning and carrying out the changes that affect them, (4) harness traditional organizations, and (5) be flexible.

Consider a recent example of a development initiative that failed because it ignored local culture. Working in Afghanistan after the fall of the Taliban,

A mix of boats harbored in Pucasana, a fishing village in Peru. A boat owner gets a loan to buy a motor. To repay it, he increases the share of the catch he takes from his crew. Later, he uses his rising profits to buy a more expensive boat and takes even more from his crew. Can a more equitable solution be found?

ethnographer Noah Coburn (2011) studied Istalif, a village of potters. During his fieldwork there Coburn discovered that an NGO had spent $20,000 on an electric kiln that could have greatly enhanced the productivity of local potters. The only problem was that the kiln was donated to a women's center that men could not enter. The misguided donors ignored the fact that Istalif's men did the work—pot-making and firing—that a kiln could facilitate. Women's role in pottery came later—in glazing and decorating.

Overinnovation

In my comparative study, the compatible and successful projects avoided the fallacy of **overinnovation** (too much change). People usually are willing to change just enough to maintain, or slightly improve on, what they already have. Motives for modifying behavior come from the traditional culture and the small concerns of ordinary life. Peasants' values are not such abstract ones as "learning a better way," "progressing," "increasing technical know-how," "improving efficiency," or "adopting modern techniques." (Those phrases exemplify intervention philosophy.)

Instead, their objectives are down-to-earth and specific. People want to guarantee the productivity of their crops, amass resources for a ceremony, get a child through school, or have enough cash to pay the tax bill. The goals and values of subsistence producers differ from those of people who work for cash, just as they differ from the intervention philosophy of development planners. Different value systems must be considered during planning.

Development projects that fail usually are either economically or culturally incompatible (or both).

overinnovation
Trying to achieve too much change.

For example, one South Asian project promoted the cultivation of onions and peppers, expecting this practice to fit into a preexisting labor-intensive system of rice growing. Cultivation of these cash crops wasn't traditional in the area. It conflicted with existing crop priorities and other interests of farmers. Also, the labor peaks for pepper and onion production coincided with those for rice, to which the farmers gave priority.

Another naive and incompatible project was an overinnovative scheme in Ethiopia. Its major fallacy was to try to convert free-ranging nomadic herders into farm workers. Outsiders—commercial farmers—were to get much of the herders' territory, to convert to commercial farmland—plantations. The pastoralists were expected to settle down and start working on those plantations. The planners naively expected the herders to give up a generations-old way of life to work three times harder growing rice and picking cotton for bosses.

Underdifferentiation

The fallacy of **underdifferentiation** is planners' tendency to view "the less-developed countries" as more alike than they are. Often development agencies have ignored huge cultural contrasts (e.g., between Brazil and Burundi) and adopted a uniform approach to deal with very different sets of people. Planners also have tried to impose incompatible property concepts and social units. Most often, the faulty social design assumes either (1) individualistic productive units that are privately owned by an individual or couple and worked by a nuclear family or (2) cooperatives that are at least partially based on models from the former Eastern bloc and Socialist countries.

One example of using an inappropriate First World model (the individual and the nuclear family) was a West African project designed for an area where the extended family was the basic social unit. The project succeeded despite its faulty social design because the participants used their traditional extended family networks to attract additional settlers. Eventually, twice as many people as planned benefited as extended family members flocked to the project area. Here, settlers modified the project design that had been imposed on them by following the principles of their traditional society.

The second dubious foreign social model that is common in development planning is the cooperative. In the comparative study of rural development projects, new cooperatives fared badly. Cooperatives succeeded only when they harnessed preexisting local-level communal institutions. This is a corollary of a more general rule: Participants' groups are most effective when they are based on traditional social organization or on a socioeconomic similarity among members.

An alternative to such foreign models is needed: greater use of indigenous social models in economic development. These are traditional social units, such as the clans, lineages, and other extended kin groups of Africa, Oceania, and many other nations, with their communally held estates and resources. The most humane and productive strategy for change is to base the social design for innovation on traditional social forms in each target area.

Indigenous Models

Many governments are not genuinely, or realistically, committed to improving the lives of their citizens. Interference by major powers also has kept governments from enacting needed reforms. Occasionally, however, a government does act as an agent of and for its people. One historic example is Madagascar, whose people, the Malagasy, were organized into descent groups prior to indigenous state formation in the 18th century. The Merina, creators of the major precolonial state of Madagascar, wove descent groups into its structure, making members of important groups advisers to the king and thus giving them authority in government. The Merina state made provisions for the people it ruled. It collected taxes and organized labor for public works projects. In return, it redistributed resources to peasants in need. It also granted them some protection against war and slave raids and allowed them to cultivate their rice fields in peace. The government maintained the water works for rice cultivation. It opened to ambitious peasant boys the chance of becoming, through hard work and study, state bureaucrats.

Throughout the history of the Merina state—and continuing to some extent in postcolonial

To maximize benefits, development projects should respond to locally perceived needs. Shown here (foreground) is the president of a Nicaraguan cooperative that makes and markets hammocks. This cooperative has been assisted by a nongovernmental organization (NGO) whose goals include increasing the benefits that women derive from economic development.

Madagascar—there have been strong relationships between the individual, the descent group, and the state. Local Malagasy communities, where residence is based on descent, are more cohesive and homogeneous than are communities in Latin America or North America. Madagascar gained political independence from France in 1960. Its new government had an economic development policy aimed at increasing the ability of the Malagasy to feed themselves. Government policy emphasized increased production of rice, a subsistence crop, rather than cash crops. Furthermore, local communities, with their traditional cooperative patterns and solidarity based on kinship and descent, were treated as partners in, not obstacles to, the development process.

In a sense, the descent group is preadapted to equitable national development. In Madagascar, descent groups pooled their resources to educate their most ambitious members. Once educated, these men and women gained economically secure positions in the nation. They then shared the advantages of their new positions with their kin. For example, they gave room and board to rural cousins attending school and helped them find jobs.

A teacher displays flashcards to students in a Spanish language class. In educational anthropology, fieldwork occurs not only in schools and classrooms but also in communities. Educational anthropologists study the backgrounds, behavior, beliefs, and attitudes of teachers, students, parents, and families in their cultural context.

This Madagascar example suggests that when government officials are of "the people" (rather than the elites) and have strong personal ties to common folk, they are more likely to promote democratic economic development. In Latin America, by contrast, leaders and followers too often have been from different socioeconomic strata, with no connections based on kinship, descent, marriage, or common background. When elites rule, elites usually prosper. Recently, however, Latin America has elected some non-elite leaders. Brazil's lower class (indeed the entire nation) benefited socioeconomically when one of its own was elected president. Luis Inácio da Silva, aka Lula, a former factory worker with only a fourth-grade education, served two terms (ending in 2011) as one of the Western Hemisphere's most popular leaders.

Realistic development policies promote change but not overinnovation. Many changes are possible if the aim is to preserve things while making them work better. Successful economic development projects respect, or at least don't attack, local cultural patterns. Effective development draws on indigenous cultural practices and social structures. As nations become more tied to the world capitalist economy, it is not inevitable that indigenous forms of social organization will break down into nuclear family organization, impersonality, and alienation. Descent groups, with their traditional communalism and solidarity, have important roles to play in economic development.

ANTHROPOLOGY AND EDUCATION

Attention to culture also is fundamental to **anthropology and education,** a field whose research extends from classrooms into homes, neighborhoods, and communities (see Levinson and Pollock 2011; Spindler 2000; Spindler and Hammond 2006). In classrooms, anthropologists have observed interactions among teachers, students, parents, and visitors. Jules Henry's classic account of the American elementary school classroom (1955) shows how students learn to conform to and compete with their peers. Anthropologists view children as total cultural creatures whose enculturation and attitudes toward education belong to a context that includes family and peers.

Sociolinguists and cultural anthropologists have worked side by side in education research. In one classic study of Puerto Rican seventh-graders in the urban Midwest (Hill-Burnett 1978), anthropologists uncovered some key misconceptions held by teachers. The teachers mistakenly had assumed that Puerto Rican parents valued education less than did non-Hispanics, but in-depth interviews revealed that the Puerto Rican parents valued it more. The anthropologists also identified certain practices that were preventing Hispanics

anthropology and education
Study of students in the context of their family, peers, and enculturation.

from being adequately educated. For example, the teachers' union and the board of education had agreed to teach "English as a foreign language." However, they had provided no bilingual teachers to work with Spanish-speaking students. The school was assigning all students (including non-Hispanics) with low reading scores and behavior problems to the English-as-a-foreign-language classroom. This educational disaster brought together in the classroom a teacher who spoke no Spanish, children who barely spoke English, and a group of English-speaking students with reading and behavior problems. The Spanish speakers were falling behind not just in reading but in all subjects. They could at least have kept up in the other subjects if a Spanish speaker had been teaching them science, social studies, and math until they were ready for English-language instruction in those areas.

urban anthropology
Anthropological study of cities and urban life.

URBAN ANTHROPOLOGY

For centuries, cities have been influenced by global forces, including world capitalism and colonialism (Smart and Smart 2003). However, the roles of cities in the world system have changed recently because of the time-space compression made possible by modern transportation and communication systems. That is, everything appears closer today because contact and movement are so much easier.

In the context of globalization, the mass media have joined local factors in guiding people's routines, dreams, and aspirations. Although people live in particular places, their imaginations are not locally confined (Appadurai 1996). Media-transmitted images and information help draw people to cities. People migrate partly for economic reasons, but also to be where the action is. Rural Brazilians routinely cite *movimento*, urban activity and excitement, as something to be valued. International migrants tend to settle in large cities, where a lot is going on, and where they can feel at home in ethnic enclaves. Consider Canada, which, after Australia, is the country with the highest percentage of foreign-born population; 71 percent of immigrants to Canada settle in Toronto, Vancouver, or Montreal. Nearly half of Toronto's citizens were born outside Canada (Smart and Smart 2003).

Urban living has increased steadily since the Industrial Revolution. The percentage of the world's population living in cities surpassed 50 percent for the first time in 2008 and is projected to rise to 70 percent by 2050 (Handwerk 2008). Only about 3 percent of people were city dwellers in 1800, compared with 13 percent in 1900, over 40 percent in 1980, and over 50 percent today (see Handwerk 2008; Smart and Smart 2003). The More Developed Countries (MDCs) were 76 percent urbanized in 1999, compared with 39 percent for the Less Developed Countries (LDCs). However, the urbanization growth rate is much faster in the LDCs (Smart and Smart 2003). In Africa and Asia alone, a million people a week migrate to cities (Handwerk 2008). The world had only 16 cities with more than a million people in 1900, versus 314 such cities in 2005 (Butler 2005; Stevens 1992).

One billion people now live in urban slums, mostly without reliable water, sanitation, public services, and legal security (Handwerk 2008; Vidal 2003). If current trends continue, urban population increase and the concentration of people in slums will be accompanied by rising rates of crime, along with water, air, and noise pollution. These problems will be most severe in the LDCs.

As industrialization and urbanization spread globally, anthropologists increasingly study these processes and the social problems they create. **Urban anthropology,** which has theoretical (basic research) and applied dimensions, is the cross-cultural and ethnographic study of urbanization and life in cities (see Gmelch and Zenner 2002; Smart and Smart 2003; Stevenson 2003). The United States and Canada have become popular arenas for urban anthropological research on topics such as immigration, ethnicity, poverty, class, and urban violence (Vigil 2003, 2010).

Urban versus Rural

An early student of urbanization, the anthropologist Robert Redfield, contrasted rural communities, whose social relations are on a face-to-face basis, with cities, where impersonality reigns. Redfield (1941) proposed that urbanization be studied along a rural–urban continuum. He described differences in values and social relations in four sites that spanned such a continuum. In Mexico's Yucatán Peninsula, Redfield compared an isolated Maya-speaking Indian community, a rural peasant village, a small provincial city, and a large capital. Several studies in Africa (Little 1971) and Asia were influenced by Redfield's view that cities are centers through which cultural innovations spread to rural and tribal areas.

In any nation, urban and rural represent different social systems. However, cultural diffusion or borrowing occurs as people, products, images, and messages move from one to the other. Migrants bring rural practices and beliefs to cities and take urban patterns back home. The experiences and social forms of the rural area affect adaptation to city life. City folk also develop new institutions to meet specific urban needs (Mitchell 1966).

An applied anthropology approach to urban planning starts by identifying key social groups in specific urban contexts—avoiding the fallacy of underdifferentiation. After identifying those groups, the anthropologist might elicit their wishes for change, convey those needs to funding agencies, and work with agencies and local people to realize those goals. In Africa relevant groups might include ethnic associations, occupational groups, social clubs, religious groups, and burial societies. Through membership in such groups, urban Africans maintain wide networks of personal contacts and support. The groups provide cash support and urban lodging for their rural relatives. Sometimes such groups think of themselves as a gigantic kin group, a clan that includes urban and rural members. Members may call one another "brother" and "sister." As in an extended family, richer members help their poorer relatives. A member's improper behavior, however, can lead to expulsion—an unhappy fate for a migrant in a large ethnically heterogeneous city.

One role for the urban applied anthropologist is to help people deal with urban institutions, such as legal and social services, with which recent migrants may be unfamiliar. In certain North American cities, as in Africa, ethnic associations are relevant urban groups. One example comes from Los Angeles, which has the largest Samoan immigrant community in the United States (over fifty thousand people). Samoans in Los Angeles draw on their traditional system of matai (matai means "chief"; the matai system now refers to respect for elders) to deal with modern urban problems. One example: a white police officer once shot and killed two unarmed Samoan brothers. When a judge dismissed charges against the officer, local leaders used the matai system to calm angry youths (who have formed gangs, like other ethnic groups in the Los Angeles area). Clan leaders and elders organized a well-attended community meeting, in which they urged young members to be patient. The Samoans then used the American judicial system. They brought a civil case against the officer in question and pressed the U.S. Justice Department to initiate a civil rights case in the matter (Mydans 1992b). Not all conflicts involving gangs and law enforcement end so peacefully.

James Vigil (2003, 2010) examines gang violence in the context of large-scale immigrant adaptation to American cities. He notes that most gangs prior to the 1970s were located in white ethnic enclaves in eastern and midwestern cities. Back then, gang incidents typically were brawls involving fists, sticks, and knives. Today, gangs more often are composed of nonwhite ethnic groups, and handguns have replaced less lethal weapons. Gangs still consist mostly of male adolescents who have grown up together, usually in a low-income neighborhood, where it's estimated that about 10 percent of young men join gangs. Female gang members are much rarer. With gangs organized hierarchically by age, older members push younger ones (usually 14- to 18-year-olds) to carry out violent acts against rivals (Vigil 2003, 2010).

The populations that include most of today's gang members settled originally in poor urban areas. On the East Coast these usually were rundown neighborhoods where a criminal lifestyle already was

Anthropologists have noted the significance of urban youth groups, including gangs, which now have transnational scope. This 29-year-old man, lodged in the Denver County jail, was one of several jailed gang members who discussed their lives on a 2010 History Channel special. Members look to gangs for social support and physical protection. How might this man's tatoos have social significance.

present. Around Los Angeles, urban migrants created squatterlike settlements in previously empty spaces. Immigrants tend to reside in neighborhoods apart from middle-class people, thus limiting their opportunities for integration (Vigil 2003). As well, many industries and jobs have moved from American cities to distant suburbs and foreign nations. Given their limited access to entry-level jobs, many urban minority youth pursue informal and illegal economic arrangements, of which drug trafficking in particular has heightened gang violence (Singer 2008; Vigil 2003, 2010). How might an applied anthropologist approach the problem of urban violence? Which groups would have to be involved in the study (see Vigil 2010)?

MEDICAL ANTHROPOLOGY

Medical anthropology is both academic and applied and includes anthropologists from all four subfields (see Anderson 1996; Briggs 2005; Brown and Barrett 2010: Dressler et al. 2005; Joralemon 2010; Singer and Baer 2007; Trevathan, Smith, and McKenna 2008). Medical anthropologists examine such questions as which diseases and health conditions affect particular populations (and why) and how illness is socially constructed, diagnosed, managed, and treated in various societies.

Disease refers to a scientifically identified health threat caused genetically or by a bacterium, virus, fungus, parasite, or other pathogen. **Illness** is a condition of poor health perceived or felt by an individual (Inhorn and Brown 1990). Perceptions of

medical anthropology
The comparative, biocultural study of disease, health problems, and health care systems.

disease
A scientifically identified health threat caused by a known pathogen.

illness
A condition of poor health perceived or felt by an individual.

good and bad health are culturally constructed. Various cultures and ethnic groups recognize different illnesses, symptoms, and causes and have developed different health care systems and treatment strategies.

The incidence and severity of disease vary as well (see Baer, Singer, and Susser 2003; Barnes 2005). Group differences are evident in the United States. Keppel, Pearch, and Wagener (2002) examined data between 1990 and 1998 using ten health status indicators in relation to categories used in the U.S. census: non-Hispanic white, non-Hispanic black, Hispanic, American Indian or Alaska Native, and Asian or Pacific Islander. Black Americans' rates for six measures (total mortality, heart disease, lung cancer, breast cancer, stroke, and homicide) exceeded those of other groups by a factor ranging from 2.5 to almost 10. Other ethnic groups had higher rates for suicide (white Americans) and motor vehicle accidents (American Indians and Alaskan Natives). Overall, Asians had the longest life spans (see Dressler et al. 2005).

Hurtado and colleagues (2005) note the unusually high rates of early mortality among South America's indigenous populations, whose life expectancy at birth is at least twenty years shorter than that of other South Americans. The life expectancy of indigenous peoples in Brazil and Venezuela was lower than that in Sierra Leone, which had the world's lowest reported national life expectancy (Hurtado et al. 2005). What can applied anthropologists do to help improve health conditions among indigenous peoples? Hurtado and colleagues (2005)

health care systems
Beliefs, customs, and specialists concerned with preventing and curing illness.

suggest three steps: (1) Identify the most pressing health problems that indigenous communities face; (2) gather information on solutions to those problems; and (3) implement solutions in partnership with the agencies that are in charge of public health programs for indigenous populations.

In many areas, the world system and colonialism worsened the health of indigenous peoples by spreading diseases, warfare, servitude, and other stressors. Traditionally and in ancient times, hunter-gatherers, because of their small numbers, mobility, and relative isolation from other groups, lacked most of the epidemic infectious diseases that affect agrarian and urban societies (Cohen and Armelagos 1984; Inhorn and Brown 1990). Epidemic diseases such as cholera, typhoid, and bubonic plague thrive in dense populations, and thus among farmers and city dwellers. The spread of malaria has been linked to population growth and deforestation associated with food production.

Certain diseases, and physical conditions such as obesity, have spread with economic development and globalization (Ulijaszek and Lofink 2006). Schistosomiasis or bilharzia (liver flukes) is probably the fastest-spreading and most dangerous parasitic infection now known. It is propagated by snails that live in ponds, lakes, and waterways, usually ones created by irrigation projects. The applied anthropology approach to reducing such diseases is to see if local people perceive a connection between the vector (e.g., snails in the water) and the disease. If not, such information may be provided by enlisting active local groups, schools, and the media.

The highest global rates of HIV infection and AIDS-related deaths are in Africa, especially southern Africa. As it kills productive adults, AIDS leaves behind dependent children and seniors (Baro and Deubel 2006). In southern and eastern Africa, AIDS and other sexually transmitted diseases (STDs) have spread along highways, via encounters between truckers and prostitutes. STDs also are spread through prostitution as young men from rural areas seek wage work in cities, labor camps, and mines. When the men return home, they infect their wives (Larson 1989; Miller and Rockwell 1988). Cities also are prime sites of STD transmission in Europe, Asia, and North and South America (see Baer, Singer, and Susser 2003; French 2002). Cultural factors affect the spread of HIV, which is less likely to be transmitted when men are circumcised. (For more on the AIDS pandemic, see this chapter's "Focus on Globalization.")

The kinds of and incidence of disease vary among societies, and cultures perceive and treat illness differently. Health standards are cultural constructions that vary in time and space (Martin 1992). Still, all societies have what George Foster and Barbara Anderson call "disease-theory systems" to identify, classify, and explain illness. Foster and Anderson (1978) identified three basic theories about the causes of illness: personalistic,

Merina women plant paddy rice in the highlands south of Antsirabe, Madagascar. Schistosomiasis, of which all known varieties are found in Madagascar, is among the fastest-spreading and most dangerous parasitic infections now known. It is propagated by snails that live in ponds, lakes, and waterways (often ones created by irrigation systems, such as those associated with paddy rice cultivation).

naturalistic, and emotionalistic. Personalistic disease theories blame illness on agents, such as sorcerers, witches, ghosts, or ancestral spirits.

Naturalistic disease theories explain illness in impersonal terms. One example is Western medicine or biomedicine, which aims to link illness to scientifically demonstrated agents that bear no personal malice toward their victims. Thus Western medicine attributes illness to organisms (e.g., bacteria, viruses, fungi, or parasites), accidents, toxic materials, or genes. Other naturalistic systems blame poor health on unbalanced body fluids. Many Latin cultures classify food, drink, and environmental conditions as "hot" or "cold." People believe their health suffers when they eat or drink hot or cold substances together or under inappropriate conditions. For example, one shouldn't drink something cold after a hot bath or eat a pineapple (a "cold" fruit) when one is menstruating (a "hot" condition).

Emotionalistic disease theories assume that emotional experiences cause illness. For example, Latin Americans may develop susto, an illness caused by anxiety or fright (Bolton 1981; Finkler 1985). Its symptoms (lethargy, vagueness, distraction) are similar to those of "soul loss," a diagnosis of similar symptoms made by people in Madagascar. Modern psychoanalysis also focuses on the role of the emotions in physical and psychological well-being.

All societies have **health care systems** consisting of beliefs, customs, specialists, and techniques aimed at ensuring health and diagnosing and curing illness. A society's illness-causation theory is important for treatment. When illness has a personalistic cause, magicoreligious specialists may be good curers. They draw on varied techniques (occult and practical), which comprise their special expertise. A shaman may cure soul loss by enticing the spirit back into the body. Shamans may ease difficult childbirths by asking spirits to travel up the birth canal to guide the baby out (Lévi-Strauss 1967). A shaman may cure a cough by counteracting a curse or removing a substance introduced by a sorcerer.

This tapestry by South African artist Jane Makhubele promotes condom use as a method of AIDS prevention.

The Deadliest Global Pandemic of Our Time

A pandemic is an infectious disease that crosses national boundaries and affects millions. In the case of HIV/AIDS, the pandemic has been global. HIV is the virus that causes the disease known as AIDS, which has killed about 25 million people since its discovery in 1981. Globally the number of people living with HIV has risen from about 8 million in 1990 to over 33 million today. In many countries, however, the number of new HIV infections and AIDS cases has declined because millions of people now take antiretroviral drugs. (HIV is classified as a retrovirus—a virus whose genes are encoded in RNA instead of DNA). As Bono of U2 fame, a prominent campaigner against AIDS, notes, it's amazing what a difference "two little pills a day" can make (see Bono 2011).

Although HIV/AIDS is a global threat, some world areas are more infected than others are. About 68 percent of all HIV infections are in Africa, especially southern Africa. The following indicate the percentage of adults (ages 15–49) living with HIV in the nine contiguous southern Africa countries of Swaziland (26.1 percent), Botswana (23.9), Lesotho (23.2), South Africa (18.1), Namibia (15.3), Zimbabwe (15.3), Zambia (15.2), Mozambique (12.5), and Malawi (11.9). These are the highest rates in the world; in no other country does the figure rise above 10 percent. In these countries, HIV has spread through prostitution (mainly involving female sex workers and their clients). The infection rate is especially high among truckers, miners, and young rural men seeking wage work in cities and labor camps. Returning to their villages, these men infect their wives and the babies they bear.

Overall in Africa the adult infection rate is 5 percent. This is significantly higher than the rates of 1 percent in the Caribbean, 0.8 percent in Eastern Europe, 0.5 percent in North, Central, and South America, and 0.2 percent in Western and Central Europe, North Africa, and the Middle East. The rate in East Asia is minuscule—less than 0.1 percent. The HIV infection rates are below 1 percent in these populous countries: United States, 0.6 percent; Brazil, 0.4 percent; India, 0.3 percent; and China, 0.1 percent (Avert.org 2010).

American foreign aid has been instrumental in slowing the AIDS pandemic. Progress against HIV/AIDS is considered a signature accomplishment of the George W. Bush administration (2001–2009). In 2002, only fifty thousand people in sub-Saharan Africa were being treated for HIV/AIDS. In 2003, President Bush launched a five-year program aimed at fighting HIV/AIDS (and tuberculosis) in fifteen high-risk countries. Congress extended the program in 2008, and it continued under President Obama. American funding for HIV/AIDS increased from $2.3 billion in 2003 to $6 billion in 2008, and to $6.8 billion in 2011 (Ezekiel 2011).

U.S. foreign aid enabled the treatment of almost 4 million people globally in 2011, compared with 1.7 million in 2008. Although the United States was spending only 12 percent more on fighting HIV in 2011 than in 2008, twice as many people were benefiting because of reduced drug costs and streamlined program management (Ezekiel 2011).

Cultural practices play a clear role in HIV transmission. Sexual abstinence and condom use slow the spread of HIV. Infection rates are lower when men are circumcised (as is customary among Muslims) and there is little prostitution. It's estimated that male circumcision cuts HIV transmission by 60 percent. Since 2007, a million men worldwide have been circumcised; three-fourths of those procedures were paid for by the U.S. government.

If there is a "world's oldest profession" besides hunter and gatherer, it is **curer,** often a shaman. The curer's role has some universal features (Foster and Anderson 1978). Thus a curer emerges through a culturally defined process of selection (parental prodding, inheritance of the role, visions, dream instructions) and training (apprentice shamanship, medical school). Eventually, the curer is certified by older practitioners and acquires a professional image. Patients believe in the skills of the curer, whom they consult and compensate.

We should not lose sight, ethnocentrically, of

A traditional healer at work in Malaysia. Shown here, mugwort, a small, spongy herb, is burned to facilitate healing. The healer lights one end of a moxa stick, roughly the shape and size of a cigar, and attaches it, or holds it close, to the area being treated for several minutes until the area turns red. The purpose of moxibustion is to strengthen the blood, stimulate spiritual energy, and maintain general health.

expected to regulate their behavior and shape themselves in keeping with new medical knowledge. Those who do so acquire the status of sanitary citizens—people with modern understanding of the body, health, and illness. Such citizens practice hygiene and look to health care professionals when they are sick. People who act differently (e.g., smokers, overeaters, those who avoid doctors) are stigmatized as unsanitary and blamed for their own health problems (Briggs 2005; Foucault 1990).

the difference between **scientific medicine** and Western medicine per se. To be sure, there have been scientific advances in technology, genomics, molecular biology, pathology, surgery, diagnostics, and applications. However, many Western medical procedures have little justification in science, logic, or fact. Overprescription of drugs, unnecessary surgery, and the impersonality and inequality of the physician–patient relationship are questionable features of Western medical systems (see Briggs 2005 for linguistic aspects of this inequality). Also, overuse of antibiotics, not just for people but also in animal feed, seems to be triggering an explosion of resistant microorganisms, which may pose a long-term global public health hazard.

Still, biomedicine surpasses tribal treatment in many ways. Although medicines such as quinine, coca, opium, ephedrine, and rauwolfia were discovered in nonindustrial societies, thousands of effective drugs are available today to treat myriad diseases. Today's surgical procedures are much safer and more effective than those of traditional societies.

But industrialization and globalization have spawned their own health problems. Modern stressors include poor nutrition, dangerous machinery, impersonal work, isolation, poverty, homelessness, substance abuse, and noise, air, and water pollution (see McElroy and Townsend 2009). Health problems in industrial nations are caused as much by economic, social, political, and cultural factors as by pathogens. In modern North America, for example, poverty contributes to many illnesses, including arthritis, heart conditions, back problems, and hearing and vision impairment (see Bailey 2000). Poverty also is a factor in the differential spread of infectious diseases.

In the United States and other developed countries, good health has become something of an ethical imperative (Foucault 1990). Individuals are

Even getting an epidemic disease such as cholera may be interpreted today as a moral failure. It's assumed that people who act rationally can avoid "preventable" diseases. Individuals are expected to follow scientifically based imperatives (e.g., "boil water," "don't smoke"). People (e.g., gay men, smokers, veterans) can become objects of avoidance and discrimination simply by belonging to a group seen as having a greater risk of disease or poor health (Briggs 2005).

Health interventions always have to fit into local cultures and be accepted by local people. When Western medicine is introduced, people usually retain many of their old methods while also accepting new ones (see Green 1987/1992). Native curers may go on treating certain conditions (spirit possession), while physicians deal with others. When patients are cured, the native curer may get as much credit as the physician, or more.

A more personal treatment of illness that emulates the non-Western curer-patient-community relationship might benefit Western systems. Western medicine tends to draw a rigid line between biomedical and psychological causation. Non-Western theories usually lack this sharp distinction, recognizing that poor health has intertwined physical, emotional, and social causes. The mind-body opposition is part of Western folk taxonomy, not of science (see also Brown and Barrett 2010; Helman 2007; Joralemon 2010; Strathern and Stewart 2010).

Medical anthropology also considers the impact of new scientific and medical techniques on ideas about life, death, and personhood (what it means to be a person). For decades, disagreements about personhood—e.g., about when life begins and ends—have been part of political and religious discussions of contraception, abortion, assisted suicide, and euthanasia (mercy killing). More recent additions to such discussions include stem cells, "harvested" embryos, assisted reproduction, genetic screening, cloning, and life-prolonging medical treatments.

Culturally Appropriate Marketing

Innovation succeeds best when it is culturally appropriate. This axiom of applied anthropology could guide the international spread not only of development projects but also of businesses, including fast food. Each time McDonald's or Burger King expands to a new nation, it must devise a culturally appropriate strategy for fitting into the new setting.

McDonald's has been very successful internationally. Over 60 percent of its current annual revenue comes from sales outside the United States. One place where McDonald's has expanded successfully is Brazil, where 90 million middle-class people, most living in densely packed cities, provide a concentrated market for a fast-food chain. Still, it took McDonald's some time to find the right marketing strategy for Brazil.

In 1980 when I visited Brazil after a seven-year absence, I first noticed, as a manifestation of Brazil's growing participation in the world economy, the appearance of two McDonald's restaurants in Rio de Janeiro. There wasn't much difference between Brazilian and North American McDonald's. The restaurants looked alike. The menus were more or less the same, as was the taste of the quarter-pounders. I picked up an artifact, a white paper bag with yellow lettering, exactly like the take-out bags then used in American McDonald's. An advertising device, it carried several messages about how Brazilians could bring McDonald's into their lives. However, it seemed to me that McDonald's Brazilian ad campaign was missing some important points about how fast food should be marketed in a culture that values large, leisurely lunches.

The bag proclaimed, "You're going to enjoy the [McDonald's] difference," and listed several "favorite places where you can enjoy McDonald's products." This list confirmed that the marketing people were trying to adapt to Brazilian middle-class culture, but they were making some mistakes. "When you go out in the car with the kids" transferred the uniquely developed North American cultural combination of highways, affordable cars, and suburban living to the very different context of urban Brazil. A similar suggestion was "traveling to the country place." Even Brazilians who owned country places could not find McDonald's, still confined to the cities, on the road. The ad creator had apparently never attempted to drive up to a fast-food restaurant in a neighborhood with no parking spaces.

Several other suggestions pointed customers toward the beach, where *cariocas* (Rio natives) do spend much of their leisure time. One could eat McDonald's products "after a dip in the ocean," "at a picnic at the beach," or "watching the surfers." These suggestions ignored the Brazilian custom of consuming cold things, such as beer, soft drinks, ice cream, and ham and cheese sandwiches, at the beach. Brazilians don't consider a hot, greasy hamburger proper beach food. They view the sea as "cold" and hamburgers as "hot"; they avoid "hot" foods at the beach.

Also culturally dubious was the suggestion to eat McDonald's hamburgers "lunching at the office." Brazilians prefer their main meal at midday, often eating at a leisurely pace with business associates. Many firms serve ample lunches to their employees. Other workers take advantage of a two-hour lunch break to go home to eat with the spouse and children. Nor did it make sense to suggest that children should eat hamburgers for lunch, since most kids attend school for half-day sessions and have lunch at home. Two other suggestions—"waiting for the bus" and "in the beauty parlor"—did describe common aspects of daily life in a Brazilian city. However, these settings have not proved especially inviting to hamburgers or fish filets.

The homes of Brazilians who can afford McDonald's products have cooks and maids to do many of the things that fast-food restaurants do in the United States. The suggestion that McDonald's products be eaten "while watching your favorite television program" is culturally appropriate, because Brazilians watch TV a lot. However, Brazil's consuming classes can ask the cook to make a snack when hunger strikes. Indeed, much televiewing occurs during the light dinner served when the husband gets home from the office.

Most appropriate to the Brazilian lifestyle was the suggestion to enjoy McDonald's "on the cook's day off." Throughout Brazil, Sunday is that day. The Sunday pattern for middle-class families who live on the coast is a trip to the beach, liters of beer, a full midday meal around 3 P.M., and a light evening snack. McDonald's found its niche in the Sunday evening meal, when families flock to the fast-food restaurant.

McDonald's has expanded rapidly in Brazil, where, as in North America, teenage appetites have fueled the fast-food explosion. As McDonald's outlets appeared in urban neighborhoods, Brazilian teenagers used them for after-school snacks, while families had evening meals there. As an anthropologist could have predicted, the fast-food industry has not revolutionized Brazilian food and meal customs. Rather, McDonald's is succeeding because it has adapted to preexisting Brazilian cultural patterns.

The main contrast with North America is that the Brazilian evening meal is lighter. McDonald's now caters to the evening meal rather than to lunch. Once McDonald's realized that more money could be made by fitting in with, rather than trying to Americanize, Brazilian meal habits, it started aiming its advertising at that goal.

Dr. Genevieve Bell, an Australian-born anthropologist, is the director of User Interaction and Experience at Intel. Her interdisciplinary team helps create new Intel technologies and products designed around people's needs and desires. Anthropologists like Bell help make products more culturally appropriate.

How long should a human body be kept alive if there is no hope of recovery?

Kaufman and Morgan (2005) emphasize the contrast between what they call low-tech and high-tech births and deaths. A desperately poor young mother dies of AIDS in Africa while half a world away an American child of privilege is born as the result of a $50,000 in-vitro fertilization procedure. Medical anthropologists increasingly are concerned with how the boundaries of life and death are being questioned and negotiated in the 21st century.

ANTHROPOLOGY AND BUSINESS

For decades anthropologists have used ethnography to understand business settings (Arensberg 1987; Jordan 2003). Ethnographic research in an auto factory, for example, may view workers, managers, and executives as different social categories participating in a common system. Each group has characteristic attitudes and behavior patterns. These are transmitted through microenculturation, the process by which people learn particular roles within a limited social system. The free-ranging nature of ethnography takes the anthropologist back and forth from worker to executive. Each employee is both an individual with a personal viewpoint and a cultural creature whose perspective is, to some extent, shared with other members of his or her group. Applied anthropologists have acted as "cultural brokers," translating managers' goals or workers' concerns to the other group (see Ferraro 2010).

Carol Taylor (1987) stresses the value of an "anthropologist-in-residence" in a large, complex organization, such as a hospital or corporation. A free-ranging ethnographer can be a perceptive oddball when information and decisions typically move through a rigid hierarchy. If allowed to observe and converse freely with all types and levels of personnel, the anthropologist may acquire a unique perspective on organizational conditions and problems. Such high-tech companies as Xerox, IBM, and Apple have employed anthropologists in various roles. Closely observing how people actually use computer products, anthropologists have worked with engineers to design products that are more user friendly.

Key features of anthropology that are of value to business include (1) ethnography and observation as ways of gathering data, (2) a focus on diversity, and (3) cross-cultural expertise. Businesses have heard that anthropologists are specialists on cultural diversity and observing behavior in natural settings, including home and office. Hallmark Cards has hired anthropologists to observe parties, holidays, and celebrations of ethnic groups to improve its ability to design cards for targeted audiences. Applied anthropologists routinely go into people's homes to see how they actually use products (see Sunderland and Denny 2007).

CAREERS AND ANTHROPOLOGY

Many college students find anthropology interesting and consider majoring in it. However, their parents or friends may discourage them by asking, "What kind of job are you going to get with an anthropology degree?" The first step in answering that question is to consider the more general question, "What do you do with any college major?" The answer is, "Not much, without a good bit of effort, thought, and planning." A survey of graduates of the University of Michigan's literary college showed that few had jobs that were clearly linked to their majors. Most professions, including medicine and law, require advanced degrees. Although many colleges offer bachelor's degrees in engineering, business, accounting, and social work, master's degrees often are needed to get the best jobs in those fields. Anthropologists, too, need an advanced degree, almost always a Ph.D., to find gainful employment in academic, museum, or applied anthropology.

A broad college education, and even a major in anthropology, can be an excellent foundation for success in many fields. One survey of women executives showed that most had majored not in business but in the social sciences or humanities. Only after graduating from college did they study business, leading to an M.B.A., a master's degree in business administration. These executives felt that the breadth of their college educations had contributed to their business careers. Anthropology majors go on to medical, law, and business schools and find success in many professions that often have little explicit connection to anthropology.

Anthropology's breadth provides knowledge and an outlook on the world that are useful in many kinds of work. For example, an anthropology major combined with a master's degree in business is excellent preparation for work in international business. Breadth is anthropology's hallmark. Anthropologists study people biologically, culturally, socially, and linguistically, across time and space, in various countries, in simple and complex settings. Most colleges offer anthropology courses that compare cultures, along with others that focus on particular world areas, such as Latin America, Asia, and Native North America. The knowledge of foreign areas acquired in such courses can be useful in many jobs. Anthropology's comparative outlook and its focus on diverse lifestyles combine to provide an excellent foundation for overseas employment (see Omohundro 2001).

For work in modern North America, anthropology's focus on culture is increasingly relevant. Every day we hear about cultural differences and about problems whose solutions require a multicultural viewpoint—an ability to recognize and reconcile ethnic differences. Government, schools, hospitals, and businesses constantly deal with people from different social classes, ethnic groups, and cultural backgrounds. Physicians, attorneys, social workers, police officers, judges, teachers, and students can all do a better job if they understand cultural differences in a nation that is one of the most ethnically diverse in history.

Knowledge of the traditions and beliefs of the groups that make up a modern nation is important in planning and carrying out programs that affect those groups. Experience in planned social change—whether community organization in North America or economic development overseas—shows that a proper social study should be done before a project or policy is implemented. When local people want the change and it fits their lifestyle and traditions, it has a better chance of being successful, beneficial, and cost effective.

People with anthropology backgrounds do well in many fields. Even if one's job has little or nothing to do with anthropology in a formal or obvious sense, a background in anthropology provides a useful orientation when we work with our fellow human beings. For most of us, this means every day of our lives.

acing the COURSE

summary

1. Anthropology has two dimensions: academic and applied. Applied anthropology uses anthropological perspectives, theory, methods, and data to identify, assess, and solve problems. Applied anthropologists have a range of employers. Examples are government agencies; development organizations; NGOs; tribal, ethnic, and interest groups; businesses; social service and educational agencies. Applied anthropologists come from all four subfields. Ethnography is one of applied anthropology's most valuable research tools. A systemic perspective recognizes that changes have multiple consequences, some unintended.

2. Development anthropology focuses on social issues in, and the cultural dimension of, economic development. Development projects typically promote cash employment and new technology at the expense of subsistence economies. Not all governments seek to increase equality and end poverty. Resistance by elites to reform is typical and hard to combat. At the same time, local people rarely cooperate with projects requiring major and risky changes in their daily lives. Many projects seek to impose inappropriate property notions and incompatible social units on their intended beneficiaries. The best strategy for change is to base the social design for innovation on traditional social forms in each target area.

3. Anthropology and education researchers work in classrooms, homes, and other settings relevant to education. Such studies may lead to policy recommendations. Both academic and applied anthropologists study migration from rural areas to cities and across national boundaries. North America has become a popular arena for urban anthropological research on migration, ethnicity, poverty, and related topics. Although rural and urban are different social systems, there is cultural diffusion from one to the other.

4. Medical anthropology is the cross-cultural, biocultural study of health problems and conditions, disease, illness, disease theories, and health care systems. Medical anthropology includes anthropologists

from all four subfields and has theoretical (academic) and applied dimensions. In a given setting, the characteristic diseases reflect diet, population density, the economy, and social complexity. Native theories of illness may be personalistic, naturalistic, or emotionalistic. In applying anthropology to business, the key features are (1) ethnography and observation as ways of gathering data, (2) cross-cultural expertise, and (3) a focus on cultural diversity.

5. A broad college education, including anthropology and foreign-area courses, offers excellent background for many fields. Anthropology's comparative outlook and cultural relativism provide an excellent basis for overseas employment. Even for work in North America, a focus on culture and cultural diversity is valuable. Anthropology majors attend medical, law, and business schools and succeed in many fields, some of which have little explicit connection with anthropology.

key terms

anthropology and education 57

applied anthropology 50

curer 62

development anthropology 54

disease 59

health care systems 61

illness 59

increased equity 54

medical anthropology 59

overinnovation 55

scientific medicine 62

underdifferentiation 56

urban anthropology 58

test yourself

MULTIPLE CHOICE

1. The use of anthropological data, perspectives, theory, and methods to identify, assess, and solve contemporary social problems is known as
   a. economic anthropology.
   b. conceptual anthropology.
   c. applied anthropology.
   d. sociobiology.
   e. participant observation.

2. What is one of the most valuable and distinctive tools of the applied anthropologist?
   a. knowledge of genetics
   b. familiarity with farming techniques
   c. statistical expertise
   d. teaching ability
   e. the ethnographic research method

3. Which of the following is an example of cultural resource management?
   a. any archaeological work done in an urban setting
   b. any archaeology implemented by the World Bank
   c. the emergency excavation and cataloging of a site that is about to be destroyed by a new highway

   d. archaeology sponsored by indigenous peoples
   e. a museum returning archaeological finds to the indigenous peoples whose ancestors produced the artifacts

4. What case does this chapter use to illustrate some of the dangers of the old applied anthropology?
   a. anthropologists' collaboration with NGOs in the 1920s
   b. the American Anthropological Association's drafting of the ethics guidelines
   c. Robert Redfield's work on the contrasts between urban and rural communities
   d. Malinowski's view that anthropologists should focus on Westernization and aid colonial regimes in their expansion
   e. the correlation between the increase of undergraduates interested in anthropology and the Vietnam War

5. Which of the following should *not* be one of the goals of an applied anthropological approach to urban programs?
   a. work with the community to ensure that the change is implemented correctly

b. create a single universal policy to be applied to all urban communities

c. identify key social groups in the urban context

d. translate the needs and desires of the community to funding agencies

e. elicit wishes from the target community

6. In 1992 a Los Angeles policeman shot and killed two unarmed Samoan brothers. When a judge dismissed charges against the officer, local Samoan leaders used the traditional matai system to calm angry youths and organize community meetings that eventually led to a just resolution. This example illustrates

   a. how an immigrant community can draw from its traditions (in this case kin-based ethnic associations) to adapt to urban life.

   b. that anthropology has little application in urban settings.

   c. that non-Western immigrants have difficulty adjusting to modern city life, unless they give up their traditions.

   d. how some traditional systems contribute disproportionately to homelessness.

   e. that "clan mentality" is excessively violent in urban settings.

7. What is medical anthropology?

   a. the field that has proved that indigenous peoples do not give up their indigenous ways, even in modern cities with technologically advanced health care programs

   b. the application of non-Western health knowledge to a troubled industrialized medical system

   c. a growing field that considers the biocultural context and implications of disease and illness

   d. typically in cooperation with pharmaceutical companies, a field that does market research on the use of health products around the world

   e. the application of Western medicine to solve health problems around the world

8. What term refers most generally to beliefs, customs, specialists, and techniques aimed at ensuring health and curing illness?

   a. a disease theory

   b. medical anthropology

   c. shamanism

   d. health care system

   e. overinnovation

9. Why would companies designing and marketing products hire an anthropologist?

   a. to pretend they care about customers' cultural preferences

   b. to provide jobs for the growing number of unemployed academics

   c. to make sure that they are abiding by the American Anthropological Association's code of ethics

   d. to gain a better understanding of their customers in an increasingly multicultural world

   e. to fulfill the requirements to become a non-profit organization

10. What best describes the breadth of applied anthropology?

   a. any use of the knowledge and/or techniques of the four subfields, with a special emphasis on forensics and biological anthropology, given the rise of deaths due to the so-called War on Terror

   b. the use of anthropological knowledge to increase the size of anthropology departments nationwide

   c. the hiring of anthropologists by the armed forces interested in improving secret intelligence

   d. any use of the knowledge and/or techniques of the four subfields to identify, assess, and solve practical problems

   e. the hiring practices of nongovernmental organizations interested in culture

FILL IN THE BLANK

1. _____ examines the sociocultural dimensions of economic development.

2. The term _____ describes the consequence of development programs that try to achieve too much change.

3. Increased _____ describes the goal of reducing absolute poverty, with a more even distribution of wealth.

4. Medical anthropologists use the term _____ to refer to a scientifically identified health threat caused by a known pathogen, while the term _____ refers to a condition of poor health perceived or felt by an individual.

5. A _____ is one who diagnoses and treats illness.

CRITICAL THINKING

1. This chapter uses the association between early anthropology and colonialism to illustrate some of the dangers of early applied anthropology. We also learn how American anthropologists studied Japanese and German "culture at a distance" in an attempt to predict the behavior of the enemies of the United States during World War II. Political and military conflicts with other nations and cultures continue today. What role, if any, could and/or should applied anthropologists play in these conflicts?

2. What roles could applied anthropologists play in the design and implementation of development projects? Based on past experience and research on this topic, what could an applied anthropologist focus on avoiding and/or promoting?

3. This chapter describes some of the applications of anthropology in educational settings. Think back to your grade school or high school classroom. Were there any social issues that might have interested an anthropologist? Were there any problems that an applied anthropologist might have been able to solve? How so?

4. In Chapter 2 we learned how our culture—and cultural changes—affect how we perceive nature, human nature, and the "natural." Give examples of how medical anthropologists examine the shifting boundaries between culture and nature.

5. Indicate your career plans, if known, and describe how you might apply the knowledge learned through introductory anthropology in your future vocation. If you have not yet chosen a career, pick one of the following: economist, engineer, diplomat, architect, or elementary schoolteacher. Why is it important to understand the culture and social organization of the people who will be affected by your work?

Multiple Choice: 1. (C); 2. (E); 3. (C); 4. (D); 5. (B); 6. (A); 7. (C); 8. (D); 9. (D); 10. (D); **Fill in the Blank:** 1. Development anthropology; 2. overinnovation; 3. equity; 4. disease, illness; 5. curer

Anderson-Levitt, K. M., ed.
2012   *Anthropologies of Education: A Global Guide to Ethnographic Studies of Learning and Schooling.* New York: Berghahn Books. Anthropological studies of education in several countries.

Coburn, N.
2011   *Bazaar Politics: Power and Pottery in an Afghan Market Town.* Stanford, CA: Stanford University Press. Local politics, NGOs, and development in Afghanistan after the Taliban.

Ervin, A. M.
2005   *Applied Anthropology: Tools and Perspectives for Contemporary Practice,* 2nd ed. Boston: Pearson/ Allyn & Bacon. Up-to-date treatment of applied anthropology.

Ferraro, G. P.
2010   *The Cultural Dimension of International Business,* 6th ed. Upper Saddle River, NJ: Prentice Hall. How the theory and insights of cultural anthropology can influence the conduct of international business.

Joralemon, D.
2010   *Exploring Medical Anthropology,* 3rd ed. Boston: Pearson. Recent introduction to a growing field.

Omohundro, J. T.
2001   *Careers in Anthropology,* 2nd ed. Boston: McGraw-Hill. Offers some vocational guidance.

suggested additional readings

Go to our Online Learning Center website at **www.mhhe.com/kottak** for Internet exercises directly related to the content of this chapter.

internet exercises

Doing Archaeology and Physical Anthropology

How do physical anthropologists and archaeologists study the past?

How do anthropologists determine the dates of sites, remains, and evolutionary events?

What ethical concerns and issues affect physical anthropology and archaeology?

◀ Excavations at Gran Dolina, Atapuerca, Spain, where hominin fossils and stone tools date back 800,000 years. Physical anthropologists and archeologists often collaborate as members of the same field team.

understanding OURSELVES

Take a quiz on Facebook, a *social* networking website that "helps you connect and share with the people in your life." Notice the many questions that get at how social (or not) you are. For example, do you prefer to: chill with friends, attend family events, take a nature hike, or be alone and concentrate on work or study? Anthropology studies people as members of groups—societies and cultures. Compared with our primate relatives, humans are unusually social. Even chimpanzees, our closest relatives, don't cooperate nearly as much as we do. There's reason to believe our urge to cooperate emerged early in human evolution. We'll never know all the causes of human sociality, and there is substantial cross-cultural variation in preferences for social contact versus solitude. In some societies sick people say, "I want to be alone" while in others it's "Please don't leave me." Which would it be for you?

Regardless of cultural variation, a human appreciation of the social appears to be based in features of human anatomy—from the brain to the pelvis. Consider the female pelvis, whose evolution has been guided by these facts: (1) Humans walk upright; (2) babies are born with big brains; and (3) babies have to negotiate a complicated birth canal during childbirth. There are striking contrasts between humans and other primates in anatomy and in the birthing process. Nonhuman primates aren't bipedal; they use four limbs rather than two to move about. Compared with humans, they have smaller brains, simpler birth canals, and more independent infants.

Human babies, in moving through the birth canal, must make several turns. Their heads and shoulders, the two body parts with the largest dimensions, must be aligned consistently with the widest parts of that canal. Monkeys and apes don't have this problem; their birth canals have a constant shape. Also, the primate infant emerges facing forward. The mother can grasp it, even pull it straight to her nipple. Human babies are born facing backward, away from the mother, so she has trouble assisting in the birth. The presence of someone else (e.g., a midwife or doctor) to help with delivery reduces the mortality risk for human infants and their mothers.

Birthing assistance is almost universal among human societies. The characteristic human wish to have supportive, familiar people around at childbirth probably goes way back. Based on pelvic openings and estimated infant skull sizes of fossilized human precursors, anthropologists Karen Rosenberg and Wenda Trevathan (2001) surmise that such assistance may date back millions of years. Nonhuman primate mothers seek seclusion when they give birth and act as their own midwives in the birthing process. Not so humans, who are as social as ever. Midwives, obstetricians, baby showers are all manifestations of human sociality. The next time you encounter one, appreciate that such manifestations of human sociality have deep evolutionary roots.

"Been on any digs lately?" Ask your professor how many times she or he has been asked this question. Then ask how often he or she actually has been on a dig. Remember that anthropology has four subfields, only two of which (archaeology and biological anthropology) require much digging—in the ground at least. Even among biological anthropologists it's mainly paleoanthropologists (those concerned with the hominin fossil record) who must dig. Students of primate behavior in the wild, such as Jane Goodall, don't do it. Nor, most of the time, is it done by forensic anthropologists, such as the title character in the TV series *Bones*.

Before this course, did you know the names of any anthropologists? If so, which ones—real or fictional? For the general public, biological anthropologists and archaeologists tend to be better known than cultural anthropologists because of what they study and discover—making them attractive subjects for the Discovery Channel. You're more likely to have watched *Bones* or seen a film of Jane Goodall with chimps or a paleoanthropologist holding a skull than to have seen a linguistic or cultural anthropologist at work. Archaeologists occasionally appear in the media to describe a new discovery or to debunk pseudo-archaeological arguments about how visitors from space have left traces on Earth.

This chapter (like Chapter 13 later in the book) is about what anthropologists do. It focuses on archaeology and biological anthropology. Sociocultural and linguistic methods are discussed in Chapters 13 and 14. (Given space limitations, only some of the diverse methods and techniques employed by anthropological archaeologists and biological anthropologists can be covered here.)

RESEARCH METHODS IN ARCHAEOLOGY AND PHYSICAL ANTHROPOLOGY

Recall from Chapter 1 that archaeology and biological or physical anthropology are two of anthropology's four subfields. Anthropological archaeology reconstructs human behavior, social patterns, and cultural features through the analysis of material remains (and other sources, including written records, if available). Biological anthropologists study living and recent humans (e.g., their genetics, growth, development, and physiological adaptation) and primates (e.g., their behavior and social organization) as well as deceased and ancient ones. Paleoanthropologists study human evolution through skeletal material and related material remains, such as biological traces (e.g., pollens, animal bones) and artifacts. Doing so, and as they attempt to date ancient human remains, physical anthropologists share many research interests and techniques with archaeologists. Members of both subfields must collaborate with many other kinds of scientists to do their work effectively.

Multidisciplinary Approaches

Scientists from diverse fields—for example, soil science and **paleontology** (the study of ancient life through the fossil record)—collaborate with archaeologists and physical anthropologists in the study of sites where artifacts or fossils have been found. **Palynology,** the study of ancient plants through pollen samples, can be used to determine a site's environment at the time of occupation. Physicists and chemists help archaeologists and physical anthropologists with dating techniques. Bioarchaeologists may form a picture of ancient life at a particular site by examining human skeletons to reconstruct their physical traits, health status, and diet (Larsen 2000). Evidence for social status may endure in hard materials—bones, jewels, buildings—through the ages. During life, bone growth and stature are influenced by diet. Genetic differences aside, taller people often are that way because they eat better than shorter people do. Differences in the chemical composition of groups of bones at a site may help distinguish privileged nobles from less fortunate commoners.

To reconstruct ancient human biological and cultural features, anthropologists and their collaborators analyze the remains of humans, plants, and animals, as well as such artifacts (manufactured items) as ceramics, casts, and metals. Visible remains found at archaeological sites include animal and human bones, charcoal from ancient fires, remains in burials and storage pits, and worked stone and bone. Archaeologists today also can draw on microscopic evidence, such as fossil pollen, phytoliths (plant crystals), and starch grains. A phytolith ("plant stone") is a microscopic crystal found in many plants, including wheat, maize, rice, beans, squash, manioc (cassava), and other early domesticates. Because phytoliths are inorganic and don't decay, they can reveal which plants were present at a given site even when no other plant remains survive. Phytoliths can be recovered from teeth, tools, containers, ritual objects, and garden plots.

Starch grain analysis, another useful technique, recovers microfossils of food plants from the stone tools used to process them. Starch grains preserve well in areas—for example, the humid tropics—where other organic remains typically decay. These grains have been recovered from stone tools, pottery fragments, and basketry, and in human coprolites (ancient feces) (Bryant 2003, 2007a, 2007b). Vaughn Bryant (2007b) presents a strong case for the importance of such microscopic evidence in studying the past. As one example, he cites Bonnie Williamson's analysis of Middle to Late Stone Age tools from a cave site in South Africa. Examining hundreds of stone tools, Williamson found that many still had residues stuck to their cutting edges. Contradicting the prevailing assumption that such tools were used mainly to hunt and butcher game animals, Williamson found that over 50 percent of all the residues were from plants. Williamson's analysis

paleontology
Study of ancient life through the fossil record.

palynology
Study of ancient plants and environments through pollen samples.

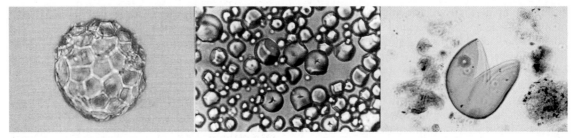

These photos illustrate three kinds of microscopic evidence of plant characteristics, including domestication. The photo on the left shows a phytolith from domesticated squash, dated to 10,000 B.P., found in the soil at Ecuador's Vegas site. The middle photo shows reserve starch grains from the root of a modern manioc plant. The photo on the right shows maize pollen grain dated to 5,000 B.P. from the Kob site in Belize.

suggested an important role for women (in gathering and processing plant foods) in early cultures.

Anthropologists also work with geologists, geographers, and other scientists in using satellite images to find ancient footpaths, roads, canals, and irrigation systems, which can then be investigated on the ground. Aerial photos (taken from airplanes) and satellite images are forms of **remote sensing** used in site location. For example, remote sensing enabled archaeologists to discover and study ancient footpaths in Costa Rica around a volcano called Arenal (Scott 2002). Volcanic ash, sediment, and vegetation had hidden the paths, which were up to 2,500 years old. A NASA aircraft discovered them in 1984 using instruments that could "see" in a spectrum invisible to the naked human eye. In 2001 a commercial satellite took additional images. The ancient trails showed up as thin red lines, reflecting the dense vegetation growing over them. The paths were dated on the basis of the stratigraphy (layers of geological deposits) formed by multiple eruptions of the nearby Arenal volcano.

Village life arose in this area about 4,000 years ago and lasted through the Spanish Conquest around 500 years ago. Villagers periodically fled volcanic eruptions, returning when it was safe to resume farming in the rich volcanic soil. According to team leader Payson Sheets of the University of Colorado, "they inhabited a very large region and seemed to avoid conflict, conquest and serious disease. . . . They led comfortable lives, relying on an abundance of natural resources and a stable culture" (quoted in Scott 2002).

When archaeologists excavated the footpaths, they found stone tools, pottery, and floors of ancient houses. The paths once connected a cemetery, a spring, and quarries where construction stone was mined. A goal of Sheets's field team was to understand ancient activities at the cemetery, where bodies were buried in stone coffins. Ceramics, vessels, and cooking stones confirmed that people had camped, cooked, and feasted at the cemetery (Scott 2002).

Anthropologists and other scientists also can use remote sensing to discover and understand events of the more recent past. Satellite images reveal, for example, patterns and sites of flooding and deforestation. By comparing a time series of satellite images of forest cover, scientists can identify regions where deforestation has been especially severe. Anthropologists can then travel to these areas to see what is happening on the ground—where people and biodiversity (including nonhuman primates) may be at risk. Working with anthropologist Lisa Gezon and geologist Glen Green, I did just this to understand the causes of deforestation in Madagascar (see Green and Sussman 1990; Kottak 1999b; Kottak, Gezon, and Green 1994).

remote sensing
Use of aerial photos and satellite images to locate sites on the ground.

Many archaeological sites are visible from the air. Shown here, El Candelabro (the candelabra) is a giant ground drawing within the Paracas Natural Reserve, Peru. This drawing, located on the coast, can be seen from 12 miles out at sea. El Candelabro has been compared to Peru's Nazca lines, visible only from the air.

Studying the Past

Archaeologists and physical anthropologists share interests and techniques that enable them to reconstruct the human past. Paleoanthropologists continue to compile the fossil record of human evolution. **Fossils** are remains (e.g., bones), traces, or impressions (e.g., footprints) of ancient life forms. Typically, a team composed of scientists, students, and local workers participates in a paleoanthropological or archaeological study. Such teams may include physical anthropologists, archaeologists, paleontologists, geologists, palynologists, paleoecologists, physicists, and chemists. Paleontologists help locate fossil beds containing remains of animals that can be dated and that are known to have coexisted with hominins at various time periods. Good preservation of faunal (animal) remains may suggest that hominin fossils have survived as well. Sometimes it's impossible to date the hominin fossils and artifacts found at a given site by using the most accurate and direct (radiometric) methods. In this case, comparison of the faunal remains at that site with similar, but more securely dated, fauna at another site may suggest a date for those animal fossils and the hominins and artifacts associated with them (see Gugliotta 2005b).

Once potential sites have been identified, more intensive surveying begins. Archaeologists take over and search for hominin traces—bones or tools (see Watzman 2006). Some early hominin sites are strewn with thousands of tools. If a site is shown to be a hominin site, much more concentrated work begins. Financial support may come from private donations and government agencies. The research project usually is headed by an archaeologist or a physical anthropologist. The field crew will continue to survey and map the area and start searching carefully for bones and artifacts eroding out of the soil. Also, they will take pollen and soil samples for ecological analysis and rock samples for use in various dating techniques. Analysis is done in laboratories, where specimens are cleaned, sorted, labeled, and identified.

Consideration of the animal habitats suggested by the site (e.g., forest, woodland, or open country) will assist in the reconstruction of the paleoecological settings in which early hominins lived. Pollen samples help reveal diet. Sediments and other geological samples will suggest climatic conditions at the time of deposition. Sometimes fossils are embedded in rock, from which they must be extracted carefully. Once recovered and cleaned, fossils may be made into casts to permit wider study.

Survey and Excavation

Archaeologists and paleoanthropologists typically work in teams and across time and space. Typically, archaeologists, paleoanthropologists, and paleontologists combine both local (e.g., excavation) and regional (e.g., survey) perspectives. The most common local approach is to excavate, or dig, through layers in a site. Regional approaches include remote sensing—for example, the discovery of ancient Costa Rican footpaths from space, as described earlier, and systematic survey on the ground. Archaeologists recognize that sites aren't usually discrete and isolated but are parts of larger (regional) social systems. One example of such systems might be a series of villages that offered tribute to the same chief. Another example might be a few bands of hunter-gatherers that once got together for annual ceremonies at a particular place.

Let's examine some of the main techniques that archaeologists use to study patterns of behavior in ancient societies, based on their material remains. Archaeologists recover remains from a series of contexts, such as pits, sites, and regions. The archaeologist also integrates data about different social units of the past, such as the household, the band, the village, and the regional system.

Systematic Survey

Archaeologists and paleoanthropologists have two key fieldwork strategies: systematic survey and excavation. **Systematic survey** provides a regional perspective by gathering information on settlement patterns over a large area. Settlement pattern refers to the distribution of sites within a region—how people grouped themselves and interacted spatially. (See this chapter's "Appreciating Diversity" for more on the human urge to cooperate that underlies group formation and that has been basic to human adaptation and survival.) Regional surveys reconstruct settlement patterns by addressing several questions: Where were sites located? How big were they? What kinds of buildings did they have? How old are the sites? Ideally, a systematic survey involves walking over the entire survey area and recording the location and size of all sites. From artifacts found on the surface, the surveyor estimates when each site was occupied. A full-coverage survey isn't always possible. The ground cover may be impenetrable (e.g., thick jungle); certain parts of the survey area may be inaccessible. Landowners may deny permission to survey on their property. Archaeologists may have to rely on remote sensing to help locate and map sites.

With regional data, archaeologists can address many questions about the prehistoric communities that lived in a given area. Archaeologists use settlement pattern information to make population estimates and to assess levels of social complexity. Among hunter-gatherers and simple farmers, there are generally low numbers of people living in small campsites or hamlets with little variation in the architecture. Such sites are scattered fairly evenly across the landscape. With increasing social complexity, the settlement patterns become more elaborate.

fossils
Remains of ancient life.

systematic survey
Study of settlement patterns over a large area.

anthropology ATLAS

http://www.mhhe.com/anthromaps
Map 1 documents deforestation by showing annual percent of forest loss worldwide, 1990–2000.

Urge to Cooperate Appears to Be Innate and Basic to Human Society and Culture

The study of ancient human, or hominin, diversity involves reconstructions based on collecting, analyzing, and dating physical and archaeological remains. Actual human behavior does not fossilize, except in the form of its material products—such as tools. Students of the human past use varied approaches to reconstruct how early apes lived. Archaeologists examine settlement sites and patterns to see how ancient humans grouped themselves. Anthropologists have approached the evolution of human cooperation, which is basic to group formation, society, and culture, in several ways, including comparative studies of nonhuman primates. Although cooperation is more valued in some cultures than in others, the urge to cooperate appears to be, to some extent at least, innate among humans—lodged in the human brain. Anthropologists generally assume that it took teamwork and altruism for our ancestors to hunt large game, share food, and engage in other social activities, including raising children. A neural tendency to cooperate and to share would have conferred a survival advantage on our ancestors.

Using a novel method of scanning neural activity in people playing games, scientists have discovered that cooperation triggers pleasure in the brain.

Anthropologist James Rilling and five other scientists monitored brain activity in young women playing a laboratory game called Prisoner's Dilemma. Players select greedy or cooperative strategies as they pursue financial gain. The researchers found that the choice to cooperate stimulated areas of the brain associated with pleasure and reward-seeking behavior—the same areas that respond to desserts, pictures of pretty faces, money, and cocaine (Angier 2002;

Rilling et al. 2002). According to coauthor Gregory S. Berns, "In some ways, it says that we're wired to cooperate with each other" (quoted in Angier 2002).

The researchers studied 36 women age 20 to 60. Why women? Some previous studies had found male–male pairs to be more cooperative than female–female pairs, and others had found the opposite. Rilling and his colleagues didn't want to mix more cooperative and less cooperative pairs, and so they restricted their sample to one gender to control for possible differences in tendencies toward cooperation. The choice to use women rather than men was an arbitrary one.

In the experiment two women would meet each other briefly ahead of time. One was then placed in the scanner, while the other remained outside the scanning room. The two interacted by computer, playing about 20 rounds of the game. In every round, each player pressed a button to indicate whether she would "cooperate" or "defect." Her answer would be shown on-screen to the other player. Money was awarded after each round. When one player defected and the other cooperated, the defector earned $3, and the cooperator earned nothing. When both cooperated, each earned $2. If both defected, each earned $1. Mutual cooperation from start to finish was a more profitable strategy, at $40 a woman, than complete mutual defection, which yielded only $20 to each woman.

If one woman got greedy, she took the risk that the cooperative strategy might fall apart and that both players would lose money as a result. Most of the time, the women cooperated. Even occasional defections weren't always fatal to an alliance, although the woman who had been "betrayed" once might be suspicious after that. Because of occasional defections, the average per-experiment take for the participants was in the range of $30.

The scans showed that two broad areas of the brain were activated by cooperation. Both areas are rich in neurons that respond to dopamine, a brain chemical that plays a well-known role in addictive behaviors. One is the antero-ventral striatum in the midbrain, just above the spinal cord. Experiments have shown that when electrodes are placed in this area, rats will repeatedly press a bar to stimulate the electrodes. They apparently receive such pleasurable feedback that they will starve to death rather than stop pressing the bar (Angier 2002).

Another brain region activated during cooperation was the orbitofrontal cortex, just above the eyes. Besides being part of the reward-processing system, this area is involved in impulse control. According to Rilling, "Every round, you're confronted with the possibility of getting an extra dollar by defecting. The choice to cooperate requires impulse control" (quoted in Angier 2002).

In some cases, the woman in the scanner played a computer and knew her partner was a machine. In other tests, women played a computer but thought it was a human. The reward circuitry of the women was considerably less responsive when they knew they were playing against a computer. The thought of a human bond, not mere monetary gain, was the source of contentment. Also, the women were asked afterward to summarize their feelings during the games. They often described feeling good when they cooperated and expressed feelings of camaraderie toward their playing partners.

SOURCE: Information from N. Angier, "Why We're So Nice: We're Wired to Cooperate," *New York Times*, July 23, 2002. http://www.nytimes.com/2002/07/23/health/psychology/23COOP.html; J. K. Rilling et al., "A Neural Basis for Social Cooperation," *Neuron* 35:395–405; J. K. Rilling, personal communication.

Population levels rise. Such social factors as trade and warfare have played a more important role in determining the location of sites (on hilltops, waterways, trade routes). In complex societies, a settlement hierarchy of sites emerges. Certain sites are larger than others, with greater architectural differentiation. Large sites with specialized architecture (elite residences, temples, administrative buildings, meeting places) are generally interpreted as regional centers that exerted control over the smaller sites with less architectural differentiation.

Excavation

During an **excavation,** scientists dig through the layers of deposits that make up a site. These layers or strata are used to establish the time order of materials. This relative chronology is based on the principle of superposition: In an undisturbed sequence of strata, the oldest layer is on the bottom. Each successive layer above is younger than the one below. Thus, remains from lower strata are older than those recovered from higher strata in the same deposit. This relative time ordering of material remains lies at the heart of archaeological, paleoanthropological, and paleontological research.

The archaeological and fossil records are so rich, and excavation is so labor-intensive and expensive, that nobody digs a site without a good reason. Sites are excavated because they are endangered, or because they answer specific research questions (see Sabloff 2008). Cultural resource management (CRM) focuses on managing the preservation of archaeological sites that are threatened by modern development. Many countries require archaeological impact studies before construction can take place. If a site is at risk and the development cannot be stopped, CRM archaeologists are called in to salvage what information they can from the site.

Another reason for choosing a particular site to excavate is that it is well suited to answer specific research questions. An archaeologist studying the origins of agriculture wouldn't want to excavate a large, fortified hilltop city with a series of buildings dating to a period well after the first appearance of farming communities. Rather, he or she would look for a small hamlet-size site located near good farmland and a water source. Such a site would have evidence of an early occupation dating to the period when farming communities first appeared in that region.

Before a site is excavated, it is surface collected and mapped so that the researchers can make an informed decision about where exactly to dig. The collecting of surface materials at a given site is similar to what is done over a much larger area in a regional survey. A grid is drawn to subdivide the site. Then collection units, which are equal-size sections of the grid, are marked off on the actual site (see photo). This grid enables the researchers to record the exact location of any artifact, fossil, or feature found at the site. By examining all the materials on the surface of the site,

archaeologists can direct their excavations toward those areas of the site most likely to yield information that will address their research interests. Once an area is selected, digging begins, and the location of every artifact or feature is recorded in three dimensions.

Digging may be done according to arbitrary levels. Thus, starting from the surface, consistent amounts of soil (usually 4 to 8 feet [1.2 to 2.4 meters]) are removed systematically from the excavation unit. This technique of excavation is a quick way of digging, since everything within a certain depth is removed at once. This kind of excavation usually is done in test pits, which are used to determine how deep the deposits of a site go and to establish a rough chronology for that site.

A more labor-intensive and refined way of excavating is to dig through the stratigraphy one layer at a time. The strata, which are separated by differences in color and texture, are studied one by one. This technique provides more information about the context of the artifacts, fossils, or features because the scientist works more slowly and in meaningful layers. A given 4-foot (1.2-meter) level may include within it a series of successive house floors, each with artifacts. If this deposit is excavated according to arbitrary levels, all the artifacts are mixed together. But if it is excavated according to the natural stratigraphy, with each house floor excavated separately, the resulting picture is much more detailed. The procedure here is for the archaeologist to remove and bag all the artifacts from each house floor before proceeding to the level below that one.

Any excavation recovers varied material remains, such as ceramics, stone artifacts (lithics),

excavation
Digging through layers at a site.

An archaeologist drives in another stake for a large grid at an excavation site in Teotihuacán, Mexico. Such a grid enables the researchers to record the exact location of any artifact or feature found at the site.

appreciating ANTHROPOLOGY

Archaeologist in New Orleans Finds a Way to Help the Living

One role for anthropologists is to help communities preserve their culture in the face of threat or disaster. The following account describes the work of an anthropologist doing public archaeology in New Orleans in the wake of Hurricane Katrina.

"That's a finger bone."

Shannon Lee Dawdy kneeled in the forlorn Holt graveyard to touch a thimble-size bone poking up out of the cracked dirt. She examined it without revulsion, with the fascination of a scientist and with the sadness of someone who loves New Orleans.

Dr. Dawdy, a 38-year-old assistant professor of anthropology at the University of Chicago, is one of the more unusual relief workers among the thousands who have come to the devastated expanses of Louisiana, Mississippi and Texas in the aftermath of Hurricanes Katrina and Rita. She is officially embedded with the Federal Emergency Management Agency [FEMA] as a liaison to the state's historic preservation office.

Her mission is to try to keep the rebuilding of New Orleans from destroying what is left of its past treasures and current culture.

While much of the restoration of the battered Gulf Coast is the effort of engineers and machines, the work of Dr. Dawdy, trained as an archaeologist, an anthropologist and a historian,

shows that the social sciences have a role to play as well. "It's a way that archaeology can contribute back to the living," she said, "which it doesn't often get to do."

Holt cemetery, a final resting place for the city's poor, is just one example of what she wants to preserve and protect.

Other New Orleans graveyards have gleaming mausoleums that keep the coffins above the marshy soil. But the coffins of Holt are buried, and the ground covering many of them is bordered with wooden frames marked with makeshift headstones.

Mourners decorate the graves with votive objects: teddy bears for children and an agglomeration of objects, including ice chests, plastic jack-o'-lanterns and chairs, on the graves of adults. There is the occasional liquor bottle....

Many of the objects on the graves were washed away by the storm, or shifted from one part of the graveyard to another. Dr. Dawdy has proposed treating the site as archaeologists would an ancient site in which objects have been exposed on the surface by erosion.

Before the hurricanes, the cemetery was often busy, a hub of activity on All Soul's Day, when people came to freshen the grave decorations.

"The saddest thing to me now was how few people we see," she said, looking at the empty

expanse and the scarred live oaks. "I realize we're having enough trouble taking care of the living," she added, but the lack of activity in a city normally so close to the spirits of the past "drove home how far out of whack things are." . . .

Treating Holt as an archaeological site means the government should not treat the votive artifacts as debris, she said, but as the religious artifacts that they are, with some effort to restore the damaged site, to find the objects and at least record where they came from.

FEMA simply tries to clean up damaged areas, and its Disaster Mortuary Operational Response Teams—called Dmort—deal with the bodies of the dead and address problems in cemeteries that might lead to disease.

If such places are destroyed, Dr. Dawdy said, "then people don't feel as connected there." She added that they might be more willing to come back to a damaged city if they felt they were returning to a recognizable home.

Though she has deep emotional ties to New Orleans, Dr. Dawdy was born in Northern California. She came here in 1994 to write her master's thesis for the College of William & Mary, and, "I wrote it all day," she said. "If I had written a minimum of five pages, I could come out for a parade at night." Over the eight weeks it took to finish the project, she said: "I fell in love with New Orleans. I really consider it the home of my heart."

---

human and animal bones, and plant remains. Such remains may be small and fragmented. To increase the likelihood that small remains will be recovered, the soil is passed through screens. To recover very small remains, such as fish bones and carbonized plant remains, archaeologists use a technique called flotation. Soil samples are sorted using water and a series of very fine meshes. When the water dissolves the soil, the carbonized plant remains float to the top. The fish bones and other heavier remains sink to the bottom. Flotation requires considerable time and labor. This makes it inappropriate to use on all the soil that is excavated from a site. Flotation samples are taken from

a limited number of deposits, such as house floors, trash pits, and hearths.

KINDS OF ARCHAEOLOGY

Archaeologists pursue diverse research topics, using a wide variety of methods (see Renfrew and Bahn 2010). Experimental archaeologists try to replicate ancient techniques and processes (e.g., toolmaking) under controlled conditions. Historical archaeologists use written records as guides and supplements to archaeological research. They work with remains more recent—often much more recent—than the advent of writing. (See this chapter's

78   PART 2   Physical Anthropology and Archaeology

Archaeologist Shannon Lee Dawdy of the University of Chicago at work in New Orleans, post-Katrina.

It went on: "Gentlemen may here rely upon finding attentive Servants. The bar will be supplied with genuine good Liquors; and at the Table, the fare will be of the best the market or the season will afford." . . .

New Orleans, she noted, has always been known for its libertine lifestyle. The French all but abandoned the city as its colony around 1735 as being unworthy of the nation's support as a colony. Novels like "Manon Lescaut" portrayed the city as a den of iniquity and corruption, and across Europe, "they thought the locals were basically a bunch of rogues, immoral and corrupt," Dr. Dawdy said.

She added that she saw parallels to today, as some skepticism emerges about rebuilding the city. Dr. Dawdy characterized that posture as, "Those people in New Orleans aren't worth saving, because they're all criminals anyway." But even if the devastation makes it hard to envision the road back, the city, she said, is worth fighting for.

"The thing about New Orleans that gives me hope is they are so tied to family, place, history," Dr. Dawdy said. "If anyone is going to stick it out, out of a sense of history, out of a sense of tradition, it is New Orleans."

She started a pilot program at the University of New Orleans, working with city planners and grants for research projects that involved excavation, oral history and hands-on work with the city to safeguard its buried treasures.

She left that job to earn a double doctorate at the University of Michigan in anthropology and history that focused on French colonial times in New Orleans, then landed a coveted faculty position at the University of Chicago. . . .

Even before Hurricane Katrina, Dr. Dawdy had found ways to return to New Orleans.

In 2004, she made an intriguing discovery while researching a possible archaeological site under an old French Quarter parking garage slated for demolition. Property records and advertisements from the 1820s said that the site had been the location of a hotel with an enticing name: the Rising Sun Hotel.

Dr. Dawdy found a January 1821 newspaper advertisement for the hotel in which its owners promised to "maintain the character of giving the best entertainment, which this house has enjoyed for twenty years past."

"Appreciating Anthropology.") Colonial archaeologists are historical archaeologists who use written records as guides to locate and excavate postcontact sites in North and South America, and to verify or question the written accounts. Classical archaeologists usually are affiliated with university departments of classics or the history of art, rather than with anthropology departments. These classical scholars tend to focus on the literate civilizations of the Old World, such as Greece, Rome, and Egypt. Classical archaeologists often are more interested in styles of architecture and sculpture than in the social, economic, and political features that typically interest anthropological archaeologists.

Underwater archaeology is a growing field that investigates submerged sites, most often shipwrecks. Special techniques, including remotely operated vehicles like the one shown in the movie *Titanic*, are used, but divers also do underwater survey and excavation.

In Chapter 3, cultural resource management (CRM) was discussed as a form of applied (or public) anthropology. In CRM, archaeological techniques are applied in assessing sites that are threatened by development, public works, and road building. Some CRM archaeologists are contract archaeologists, who typically negotiate specific contracts (rather than applying for research grants) for

taphonomy
Study of processes affecting remains of dead animals.

paleoanthropology
Study of hominid, hominin, and human life through the fossil record.

their studies. CRM often must be done rapidly, for example, when an immediate threat to archaeological materials becomes known. Based on a membership study done for the Society of American Archaeology, Melinda Zeder (1997) found that 40 percent of the respondents worked as contract archaeologists. Their employers included firms in the private sector, state and federal agencies, and educational institutions. An equivalent 40 percent held academic positions.

This diver holds a ceramic vessel uncovered from a ship wrecked in 1025 A.D., in Turkey's Serce Liman Bay, Mugla province. Graduate degrees in underwater, or nautical, archaeology are available at East Carolina University, Florida State University, and Texas A&M University. This growing field of study investigates submerged sites, most often shipwrecks.

DATING THE PAST

The archaeological record hasn't revealed every ancient society that has existed on Earth; nor is the fossil record a representative sample of all the plants and animals that ever have lived. Some species and body parts are better represented than others are, for many reasons. Hard parts, such as bones and teeth, preserve better than do soft parts, such as flesh and skin. The chances of fossilization increase when remains are buried in silt, gravel, or sand. Good places for bone preservation include swamps, floodplains, river deltas, lakes, and caves. The species that live in such areas have a better chance to be preserved than do animals that live in other habitats. Fossilization also is favored in areas with volcanic ash. Once remains do get buried, chemical conditions must be right for fossilization to occur. If the sediment is too acidic, even bones and teeth will dissolve. The study of the processes that affect the remains of dead animals is called **taphonomy**, from the Greek *taphos*, which means "tomb." Such processes include scattering by carnivores and scavengers, distortion by various forces, and the possible fossilization of the remains.

The conditions under which fossils are found also influence the fossil record. For example, fossils are more likely to be uncovered through erosion in arid areas than in wet areas. Sparse vegetation allows wind to scour the landscape and uncover fossils. The fossil record has been accumulating longer and is more extensive in Europe than in Africa because civil engineering projects and fossil hunting have been going on longer in Europe than in Africa. A world map showing where fossils have been found does not indicate the true range of ancient animals. Such a map tells us more about ancient geological activity, modern erosion, or recent human activity—such as paleontological research or road building. In considering the primate and hominin fossil records in later chapters, we'll see that certain areas provide more abundant fossil evidence for particular time periods. This doesn't necessarily mean that primates or hominins were living only in that area at that time. Nor does failure to find a fossil species in a particular place always mean the species didn't live there. In the words of paleoanthropologist Christopher Stringer, "absence of evidence does not necessarily prove evidence of absence" (quoted in Gugliotta 2005b).

We've seen that paleontology is the study of ancient life through the fossil record and that **paleoanthropology** is the study of ancient humans and their immediate ancestors. These fields have established a time frame, or chronology, for the evolution of life. Scientists use several techniques to date fossils. These methods offer different degrees of precision and are applicable to different periods of the past.

Relative Dating

Chronology is established by assigning dates to geologic layers (strata) and to the material remains—the fossils and artifacts—within them. Dating may be relative or absolute. **Relative dating** establishes a time frame in relation to other strata or materials rather than absolute dates in numbers. Many dating methods are based on the geological study of **stratigraphy,** the science that examines the ways in which earth sediments accumulate in layers known as strata (singular, *stratum*). As was noted previously, in an undisturbed sequence of strata, age increases with depth. Soil that erodes from a hillside into a valley covers, and is younger than, the soil deposited there previously.

Stratigraphy permits relative dating. That is, the fossils in a given stratum are younger than those in the layers below and older than those in the layers above. We may not know the exact or absolute dates of the fossils, but we can place them in time relative to remains in other layers. Changing environmental forces, such as volcanic eruptions, or the alternation of land and sea, cause different materials to be deposited in a given sequence of strata; this allows scientists to distinguish between the strata.

Remains of animals and plants that lived at the same time are found in the same stratum. When fossils are found within a stratigraphic sequence, scientists know their dates relative to fossils in other strata; this is relative dating. When fossils are found in a particular stratum, the associated geological features (such as frost patterning) and remains of particular plants and animals offer clues about the climate at the time of deposition.

Besides stratigraphic placement, another technique of relative dating is fluorine absorption analysis. Bones fossilizing in the same ground for the same length of time absorb the same proportion of fluorine from the local groundwater. Fluorine analysis uncovered a famous hoax involving the so-called Piltdown man, once considered an unusual and perplexing human ancestor (Winslow and Meyer 1983). The Piltdown "find," from England, turned out to be the jaw of a young orangutan attached to the skull of a modern human. Fluorine analysis showed the association to be false. The skull had much more fluorine than the jaw—impossible if they had come from the same individual and had been deposited in the same place at the same time. Someone had fabricated Piltdown man in an attempt to muddle the interpretation of the fossil record. (The attempt was partially successful—it did fool some scientists.)

Absolute Dating: Radiometric Techniques

Fossils can be dated more precisely, with dates in numbers (**absolute dating**), by using several methods.

A swamp is a good place for bones to be buried in sediments. Here a female mammoth is represented sinking into the La Brea Tar Pits in Los Angeles, California. What other locales and conditions favor fossilization?

For example, the ^{14}C, or carbon-14, technique is used to date organic remains. This is a radiometric technique (so called because it measures radioactive decay). ^{14}C is an unstable radioactive isotope of normal carbon, ^{12}C. Cosmic radiation entering the Earth's atmosphere produces ^{14}C, and plants take in ^{14}C as they absorb carbon dioxide. ^{14}C moves up the food chain as animals eat plants and as predators eat other animals.

With death, the absorption of ^{14}C stops. This unstable isotope starts to break down into nitrogen (^{14}N). It takes 5,730 years for half the ^{14}C to change to nitrogen; this is the half-life of ^{14}C. After another 5,730 years only one-quarter of the original ^{14}C will

Many dating methods rely on stratigraphy, the science that studies how sediments accumulate in layers, or *strata*. Labels make the strata evident as Professor Christopher Henshilwood excavates the south section of Blombos Cave, South Africa.

relative dating
Establishing a time frame in relation to other strata or materials.

stratigraphy
Study of earth sediments deposited in demarcated layers (strata).

absolute dating
Establishing dates in numbers or ranges of numbers.

Early hominin fossils abound in Africa's Great Rift Valley, a vista of which is shown on the left. Past volcanic activity permits K/A dating in the Valley, including at Olduvai Gorge, Tanzania, whose centerpiece is the rock formation on the right. Note the stratigraphy in the rock formation.

remain. After yet another 5,730 years only one-eighth will be left. By measuring the proportion of ^{14}C in organic material, scientists can determine a fossil's date of death, or the date of an ancient campfire. However, because the half-life of ^{14}C is short, this dating technique is less dependable for specimens older than 40,000 years than it is for more recent remains.

Fortunately, other radiometric dating techniques are available for earlier periods. One of the most widely used is the potassium-argon (K/A) technique. ^{40}K is a radioactive isotope of potassium that breaks down into argon-40, a gas. The half-life of ^{40}K is far longer than that of ^{14}C—1.3 billion years. With this method, the older the specimen, the more reliable the dating. Furthermore, whereas ^{14}C dating can be done only on organic remains, K/A dating can be used only for inorganic substances: rocks and minerals. ^{40}K in rocks gradually breaks down into argon-40. That gas is trapped in the rock until the rock is heated intensely (as with volcanic activity), at which point it may escape. When the rock cools, the breakdown of potassium into argon resumes. Dating is done by reheating the rock and measuring the escaping gas.

In Africa's Great Rift Valley, which runs down eastern Africa and in which early hominin fossils abound, past volcanic activity permits K/A dating. In studies of strata containing fossils, scientists find out how much argon has accumulated in rocks since they were last heated. They then determine, using the standard ^{40}K deterioration rate (half-life), the date of that heating. Considering volcanic rocks at the top of a stratum with fossil remains, scientists establish that the fossils are older than, say, 1.8 million years. By dating the volcanic rocks below the fossil remains,

they determine that the fossils are younger than, say, 2 million years. Thus, the age of the fossils is set at between 2 million and 1.8 million years. Note that absolute dating is that in name only; it may give ranges of numbers rather than exact dates.

Many fossils were discovered before the advent of modern stratigraphy. Often we can no longer determine their original stratigraphic placement. Furthermore, fossils aren't always discovered in volcanic layers. Like ^{14}C dating, the K/A technique applies to a limited period of the fossil record. Because the half-life of ^{40}K is so long, the technique cannot be used with materials less than 500,000 years old.

Other radiometric dating techniques can be used to cross-check K/A dates, again by using minerals surrounding the fossils. One such method, uranium series dating, measures fission tracks produced during the decay of radioactive uranium (^{238}U) into lead. Two other radiometric techniques are especially useful for fossils that can't be dated by ^{14}C (up to 40,000 before the present, or B.P.) or ^{40}K (more than 500,000 B.P.). These methods are thermoluminescence (TL) and electron spin resonance (ESR). Both TL and ESR measure the electrons that are constantly being trapped in rocks and minerals (Shreeve 1992). Once a date is obtained for a rock found associated with a fossil, that date also can be applied to that fossil. The time spans for which the various absolute dating techniques are applicable are summarized in Recap 4.1.

Absolute Dating: Dendrochronology

Dendrochronology, or tree-ring dating, is a method of absolute dating based on the study and comparison

anthropology **ATLAS**

http://www.mhhe.com/anthromaps
See Map 4 for the locations of sites in the Great Rift Valley.

dendrochronology
Tree-ring dating; a form of absolute dating.

TECHNIQUE	ABBREVIATION	MATERIALS DATED	EFFECTIVE TIME RANGE
Carbon-14	^{14}C	Organic materials	Up to 40,000 years
Potassium-argon	K/A and ^{40}K	Volcanic rock	Older than 500,000 years
Uranium series	^{238}U	Minerals	Between 1,000 and 1,000,000 years
Thermoluminescence	TL	Rocks and minerals	Between 5,000 and 1,000,000 years
Electron spin resonance	ESR	Rocks and minerals	Between 1,000 and 1,000,000 years
Dendrochronology	Dendro	Wood and charcoal	Up to 11,000 years

of patterns of tree-ring growth. Because trees grow by adding one ring every year, counting the rings reveals the age of a tree. Around 1920, A. E. Douglass of the University of Arizona noticed that wide rings grew during wet years, while narrow rings grew during dry years. Climatic variation, for example, moisture, cold, or drought, produces a distinctive year-by-year ring pattern—observable in all the trees that have grown over the same time period in the same region. Ring patterns of trees can be compared and matched ring for ring. Charting such patterns back through time, scientists can compare wood from ancient buildings to known tree-ring chronologies, match the ring patterns, and determine precisely—to the year—the age of the wood used by the historic or prehistoric builder (see Kuniholm 1995; Miller 2004; Schweingruber 1988).

Crossdating is the process of matching ring patterns among trees and assigning rings to specific calendar years. Both visual and statistical techniques are used to make the matches. Wood or charcoal samples from buildings and archaeological sites are crossdated with each other and with wood from living trees to extend the tree-ring chronology beyond the date of the oldest ring of the oldest living tree in the region (Kuniholm 1995).

Tree-ring dating was first used in the southwestern United States for Native American communities and historical settlements. The bristlecone pine chronology of the American Southwest now exceeds 8,500 years (see Miller 2004). A northern European chronology based on the study of oak and pine is over 11,000 years long. The objective of Cornell University's Aegean dendrochronology project (www.arts.cornell.edu/dendro/), directed by Peter Kuniholm, is to build a master chronology for the region of the Aegean Sea and the Middle East. So far this project has established over 6,000 years of tree-ring chronologies covering much of the period back to about 9,500 years ago. The project encompasses portions of the Aegean, the Balkans, and the Middle East, including Turkey, Cyprus, Greece, parts of Bulgaria and the former Yugoslavia, and some of Italy. (There is one major gap, for which matches have not yet been made,

between about 1,500 and 2,500 years ago.) Scientists hope eventually to extend the chronology back to the period in which prehistoric peoples first started using significant amounts of wood in construction (Kuniholm 1995, 2004).

Dendrochronology is limited to certain tree species—those growing in a climate with marked seasons. The technique works with oak, pine, juniper, fir, boxwood, yew, spruce, and occasionally chestnut. Trees that can't be used include olive, willow, poplar, fruit trees, and cypress. The trees always have to come from the same region—thus having been exposed to the same environmental patterns—and long ring sequences are needed. Some charcoal fragments from the Neolithic site of Çatal Hüyük in Turkey (see Chapter 12), where dendrochronology has established a 700-year sequence, have as many as 250 rings preserved (Kuniholm 1995). Not only do tree rings permit absolute dating; they also provide information about climatic patterns in specific regions.

Dr. Tom Sweatnam of the University of Arizona displays tree samples from a giant sequoia. What kinds of information can you get from studying tree rings?

Molecular Anthropology

Molecular anthropology uses genetic analysis (of DNA sequences) to date, and to estimate evolutionary distance between, species. Molecular studies have been used to assess and date the origins of modern humans and to examine their relation to extinct human groups such as the Neandertals, which lived in Europe between 130,000 and 28,000 years ago.

Molecular anthropologists examine relationships among ancient and contemporary populations and among species. It's well established, for example, that humans and chimpanzees have more than 98 percent of their DNA in common. Molecular anthropologists also reconstruct waves and patterns of migration and settlement. A haplogroup is a biological lineage (a large group of related people) defined by a specific cluster of genetic traits that occur together. Native Americans have four major haplogroups, which also are linked to East Asia. Molecular anthropologists also use "genetic clocks" to estimate divergence time (date of most recent common ancestry) among species (e.g., humans, chimps, and gorillas—5 million to 8 million years ago) and of various human groups (e.g., Neandertals and modern humans).

 **anthropology ATLAS**

http://www.mhhe.com/anthromaps Map 8 shows the spread of agriculture during and after the Neolithic, in the Aegean region and elsewhere.

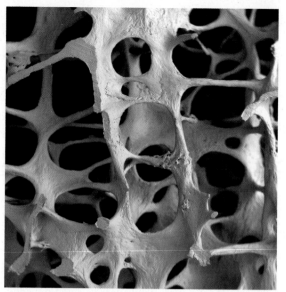

Bone biology studies such conditions as osteoporosis (shown here in an 89-year-old woman), a disease in which bones become extremely porous. They fracture more easily and heal more slowly than firmer bones.

KINDS OF PHYSICAL ANTHROPOLOGY

The past grades into the present when archaeologists do garbology—using garbage to interpret behavior among contemporary humans—or when physical anthropologists study patterns of movement or growth and development among living people. The interests of biological anthropologists are varied and encompass recent and living as well as ancient and deceased humans and other primates. Described in this chapter are many, but far from all, of the topics and methods within contemporary biological anthropology.

Bone Biology

Central to biological or physical anthropology is **bone biology** (aka skeletal biology)—the study of bone as a biological tissue, including its genetics; cell structure; growth, development, and decay; and patterns of movement (biomechanics) (White, Black, and Folkens 2012). Bone biologists study skeletal characteristics of living and deceased humans and hominins. Any scientific interpretation of fossil remains relies on understanding the structure and function of the skeleton. **Paleopathology** is the study of disease and injury in skeletons from archaeological sites. Some forms of cancer leave evidence in the bone. Breast cancer, for example, may spread (metastasize) skeletally, leaving holes or lesions in bones and skull. Certain infectious diseases (e.g., syphilis and tuberculosis) also mark bone, as do injuries and nutritional deficiencies (e.g., rickets, a vitamin D deficiency that deforms the bones).

In forensic anthropology, physical anthropologists work in a legal context, assisting coroners, medical examiners, and law enforcement agencies in recovering, analyzing, and identifying human remains and determining the cause of death (Blau and Ubelaker 2008; Komar and Buikstra 2008; Nafte 2009). The television series *Bones* offers a view of such work through the character Temperance Brennan (aka "Bones" by her partner FBI agent Seeley Booth), whose creator is physical/forensic anthropologist Kathy Reichs.

Anthropometry

Physical anthropologists use various techniques to study nutrition, growth, and development. **Anthropometry** is the measurement of human body parts and dimensions, including skeletal parts (osteometry). Anthropometry is done on living people as well as on skeletal remains from sites. Body mass and composition provide measures of nutritional status in living people. Body mass is calculated from height and weight. The body mass index (kg/m^2) is the ratio of weight in kilograms divided by height in meters squared. An adult body mass above 30 is considered at risk of overweight, while one below 18 is at risk of underweight or malnutrition.

Primatology

Primatology is considered a subfield of biological anthropology, although primate studies also are useful to archaeologists who are attempting to understand the behavior and social life of ancient hominins. Primatology also links with sociocultural anthropology (especially ethnography) through its focus on behavior and social life. Primate behavior has been observed in zoos (e.g., de Waal 1998) and through experimentation (e.g., Harlow 1971), but the most significant studies have been done in natural settings, among free-ranging apes, monkeys, and lemurs. Since the 1950s, when primatologists began their shift from zoos to natural settings, numerous studies have been done of apes (chimps, gorillas, orangutans, and gibbons), monkeys (e.g., baboons, macaques), and lemurs (e.g., Madagascar's indrii, sifaka, and ring-tailed lemurs). Arboreal primates (those that spend most of their time in the trees) are difficult to see and follow, but they typically make a lot of noise. Their howls and calls can be studied and teach us about how primates communicate. Studies of primate social systems and behavior, including their mating patterns, infant care, and patterns of contact and dispersal, suggest hypotheses about behavior that humans do or do not share with our nearest relatives—and also with our hominin ancestors.

DOING ANTHROPOLOGY RIGHT AND WRONG: ETHICAL ISSUES

Science exists in society and in the context of law and ethics. Anthropologists can't study things simply because they happen to be interesting or of value to science. Ethical issues must be considered as well. Anthropologists typically have worked abroad, outside their own society. In the context of international contacts and cultural diversity, different ethical codes and value systems will meet, and often compete.

Archaeologists and physical anthropologists, in particular, often work as members of international teams (see Dalton 2006). These teams typically include researchers from several countries, including the host country—the place (e.g., Ethiopia) where the research takes place. Anthropologists must inform officials and colleagues in the host country about the purpose, funding, and likely results, products, and impacts of their research. They need to negotiate the matter of where the materials produced by the research will be analyzed and stored—in the host country or in the anthropologists' country—and for how long. To whom do research materials such as bones, artifacts, and blood samples belong? What kinds of restrictions will apply to their use?

Contemporary anthropologists recognize that **informed consent** (agreement to take part in the

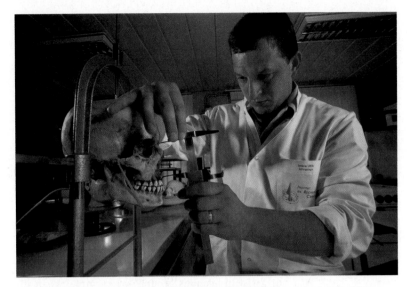

Anthropometry, being done here by a French anthropologist, is the measurement of human body parts and dimensions, including skulls and skeletal parts. Anthropometry is done on remains from sites as well as on living people. Has anyone done anthropometry on you?

research—after having been informed about its nature, procedures, and possible impacts) should be obtained from anyone who provides information or who might be affected by the research. Although nonhuman primates can't give informed consent, primatologists still must take steps to ensure that their research doesn't endanger the animals they study. Either government agencies or nongovernmental organizations (NGOs) may be entrusted with protecting primates. If this is the case, the anthropologist will need their permission and informed consent to conduct research.

With living humans, informed consent is a necessity, not only in gathering information, but especially in obtaining biological samples such as blood or urine. The research subjects must be told how the samples will be collected, used, and identified, and about the potential costs and benefits to them. Informed consent is needed from anyone providing data or information, owning materials being studied, or otherwise having an interest that might be affected by the research.

It is appropriate for North American anthropologists working in another country to (1) include host country colleagues in their research planning and requests for funding, (2) establish truly collaborative relationships with those colleagues and their institutions before, during, and after fieldwork, (3) include host country colleagues in dissemination, including publication, of the research results, and (4) ensure that something is "given back" to host country colleagues. For example, research equipment and technology are allowed to remain in the host country. Or funding is provided for host country colleagues to do research, attend international meetings, or visit foreign institutions—especially those where their international collaborators work.

informed consent
Agreement to take part in research, after being fully informed about it.

Even with broad efforts to respect diverse value systems and acknowledge the contributions of the host country and its colleagues, ethical issues continue to arise. Lawsuits against museums by groups seeking the repatriation of remains and artifacts have become common (see Rothstein 2006). Peru, for instance, sued Yale University to recover objects removed during the exploration of Machu Picchu (an important Peruvian archaeological and tourist site) by Yale explorer Hiram Bingham in 1912. Native Australians have argued that images of native Australian fauna, such as the emu and kangaroo, belong exclusively to the Aboriginal people (Brown 2003). Michael F. Brown (2003) describes efforts by Hopi Indians to control and restrict historic photos of secret religious ceremonies.

Many anthropologists have worked to represent or assist indigenous groups, for example, when disasters strike or when disputes arise with external agents. Sometimes, however, issues involving access to, or ownership of, physical and archaeological remains place anthropologists and indigenous people in opposed camps. The Native American Graves Protection and Repatriation Act (NAGPRA) gives ownership of Native American remains to Native Americans. Hundreds of thousands of Native American remains are said to be in American museums. NAGPRA requires museums to return remains and artifacts to any tribe that requests them and can prove a "cultural affiliation" between itself and the remains or artifact.

The 1996 discovery in Washington State (on federal land) of a skeleton dubbed "Kennewick Man" led to a legal case between anthropologists and five Native American tribes (aka nations) with ancestral homelands in the area where Kennewick Man was discovered. The anthropologists wanted to conduct a thorough scientific study of the 9,000-year-old skeleton—one of the oldest and best preserved human remains ever discovered in North America. What might its anatomy and DNA reveal about the early settlement of the Americas? The Umatilla Indians and their allies in four other Native American nations believe they have always occupied the region where the skeleton was found. In their view, Kennewick Man was an ancestor, whom they wanted to rebury with dignity and without contamination from scientific testing.

In 2002, U.S. Magistrate Judge John Jelderks ruled that the Kennewick remains could be subjected to scientific study. The judge found little evidence linking the Kennewick find to any identifiable contemporary group or culture. He suggested that the culture to which Kennewick belonged may have ended thousands of years ago. The ruling, later backed by a federal appeals court, cleared the way for the scientists to begin their ongoing study (see Egan 2005).

The Code of Ethics

To guide its members in making decisions involving ethics and values, the American Anthropological Association (AAA) offers a Code of Ethics. The most recent code, approved in 2009, points out that anthropologists have obligations to their scholarly field, to the wider society and culture, and to the human species, other species, and the environment. Like physicians who take the Hippocratic oath, the anthropologist's first concern should be to do no harm to the people, animals, or artifacts being studied. The stated aim of the AAA code is to offer guidelines and to promote discussion and education, rather than to investigate possible misconduct. The code addresses several contexts in which anthropologists work. Some of its main points may be highlighted.

 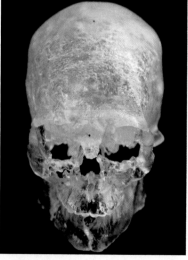

A Seattle radio reporter examines plastic recreations of Kennewick Man's pelvis and skull made using CT scans of the bones (left). At right is a clear image of the skull reconstruction.

Anthropologists should be open and honest about their research projects with all parties affected by the research. These parties should be informed about the nature, procedures, purpose(s), potential impacts, and source(s) of support for the research. Researchers should pay attention to proper relations between themselves as guests and the host nations and communities where they work. The AAA does not advise anthropologists to avoid taking stands on issues.

Indeed, seeking to shape actions and policies may be as ethically justifiable as inaction. The full Code of Ethics is available at the AAA website http://www.aaanet.org/issues/policy-advocacy/Code-of-Ethics.cfm.

acing the COURSE

summary

1. As they study the past, archaeologists and physical anthropologists may share research topics and methods, and work together in multidisciplinary teams. Remote sensing may be used to locate ancient footpaths, roads, canals, and irrigation systems, which can then be investigated on the ground. Archaeologists combine both local (excavation) and regional (systematic survey) perspectives. Sites are excavated because they are in danger of being destroyed or because they address specific research interests. There are many kinds of archaeology, such as historical, classical, and underwater archaeology.

2. The fossil record is not a representative sample of all the plants and animals that have ever lived. Hard parts, such as bones and teeth, preserve better than soft parts, such as flesh and skin. Stratigraphy and radiometric techniques are used to date fossils. Carbon-14 (^{14}C) dating is most effective with fossils less than 40,000 years old. Potassium-argon (K/A) dating can be used for fossils older than 500,000 years. Dendrochronology provides absolute dates by counting and matching tree rings. Molecular anthropology uses genetic analysis (of DNA sequences) to assess and date evolutionary relationships.

3. Within physical anthropology, bone biology is the study of bone genetics; cell structure; growth, development, and decay; and patterns of movement. Paleopathology is the study of disease and injury in skeletons from archaeological sites. Anthropometry, the measurement of human body parts and dimensions, is done on living people and on skeletal remains from sites. Studies of primates suggest hypotheses about behavior that humans do or do not share with our nearest relatives—and also with our hominid ancestors.

4. Because science exists in society, and in the context of law and ethics, anthropologists can't study things simply because they happen to be interesting or of scientific value. Anthropologists have obligations to their scholarly field, to the wider society and culture (including that of the host country), and to the human species, other species, and the environment. The AAA Code of Ethics offers ethical guidelines for anthropologists.

key terms

absolute dating 81
anthropometry 84
bone biology 84
dendrochronology 82
excavation 77
fossils 75
informed consent 85
molecular anthropology 84
paleoanthropology 80

paleontology 73
paleopathology 84
palynology 73
relative dating 81
remote sensing 74
stratigraphy 81
systematic survey 75
taphonomy 80

test yourself

MULTIPLE CHOICE

1. Fossil pollen, phytoliths, and starch grains are all examples of
   a. microscopic evidence that archaeologists increasingly use to study the past.
   b. palynology.
   c. remote sensing techniques.
   d. taphonomic processes.
   e. dendrochronological techniques used to study agricultural remains.

2. In this chapter, what is the main point of describing the University of Colorado and NASA archaeological research project in Costa Rica?

a. to illustrate how scientists from diverse fields work as a team, often with technologically sophisticated tools, to make sense of the human past

b. to criticize collaborative efforts between universities and governmental agencies that impose their will on Latin American countries

c. to illustrate the use of remote sensing when stratigraphic methods cannot be used

d. to show the impact of the downsizing of NASA

e. to emphasize the fact that the U.S. government supports anthropological research

3. What are the two major components of fieldwork in archaeological anthropology?

a. the genealogical method and excavation

b. excavation and participant observation

c. systematic survey and geothermal analysis

d. systematic survey and excavation

e. stratigraphy and taphonomy

4. What does the principle of superposition state?

a. In an undisturbed sequence of strata, the oldest layer is on the top.

b. In an undisturbed sequence of strata, the youngest layer is on the bottom.

c. In an undisturbed sequence of strata, the youngest layer is the deepest in the sequence.

d. In an undisturbed sequence of strata, the oldest layer is the shallowest in the sequence.

e. In an undisturbed sequence of strata, the oldest layer is on the bottom.

5. Why do archaeologists use relative dating?

a. to create precise dates in numbers

b. to create a relative chronology for the materials uncovered during excavation

c. to overlay various maps of a site to produce a composite map

d. to superimpose motifs from one site onto designs found at another site

e. to locate sites during a systematic survey

6. What point is this chapter emphasizing when quoting paleoanthropologist Christopher Stringer, stating that "absence of evidence does not necessarily prove evidence of absence"?

a. that taphonomy is not a true science because it lacks accuracy

b. that the fields of paleontology and paleoanthropology have established a chronology of the evolution of life

c. that even paleontology and paleoanthropology are humanistic disciplines

d. that the failure to find a fossil species in a particular place does not necessarily mean that it did not live there

e. that the fossil record is a representative sample of all the plants and animals that ever have lived

7. What do molecular anthropologists study?

a. human body size and dimensions, using an extensive series of measurements of the human form

b. the relationships among ancient and contemporary populations and among species using DNA comparisons

c. the biological and geological processes by which dead animals become fossils

d. the diffusion of languages between communities

e. how prestige is passed between generations

8. What is anthropometry?

a. the measurement of human linguistic variability

b. the use of remote sensing to measure the carrying capacity of human populations in a given region

c. the measurement of human body parts and dimensions

d. the study of ancient plants used by humans through pollen samples collected from archaeological sites

e. the study of the ways in which cultural sediments accumulate over time

9. The American Anthropological Association's Code of Ethics is

a. designed to protect anthropologists who conduct fieldwork in remote places and are subject to potentially hazardous working conditions.

b. designed to ensure that anthropologists are aware of their obligations to the field of anthropology, to the host communities that allow them to conduct their research, and to society in general.

c. applicable only to research being conducted in the United States.

d. irrelevant today, because most researchers tend to disregard its main points.

e. too broad and too encompassing for most anthropologists to find it useful.

10. All of the following are true about informed consent *except* that

a. it refers to people's agreement to take part in research, after they have been fully informed about its purpose, nature, procedures, and potential impact on them.

b. it is required when working with living humans.

c. it is consistent with the American Anthropological Association's Code of Ethics concern that anthropologists should not exploit individuals.

d. it must be obtained from anyone providing information or data.

e. it is applicable only to research being conducted in the United States.

FILL IN THE BLANK

1. _____ are microscopic crystals found in many plants. Because they are inorganic and do not decay, they can be a great source of information for archaeologists studying sites in which the plants were present.

2. _____ are remains (e.g., bones), traces, or impressions (e.g., footprints) of ancient life.

3. Many dating methods are based on the geological study of _____, the science that examines the ways in which earth sediments accumulate in layers known as strata.

4. _____ is the study of disease and injury in skeletons from archaeological sites.

5. _____ refers to people's agreement to take part in research after they have been fully informed about its purpose, nature, funding, procedures, and potential impact on them.

CRITICAL THINKING

1. Imagine yourself to be an archaeologist researching early farming communities somewhere in the world. What guidelines might you use in choosing sites to investigate? What methods and techniques might you use in your study? What kinds of problems might you encounter during your research?

2. Imagine yourself to be a physical anthropologist working as part of an international team at an African site where early human fossils have been found. What other academic disciplines might be represented on your team? What kinds of jobs would there be for team members, and where would the members be recruited? What might happen to the fossils and other materials that were recovered? Who would be the authors of the scientific papers describing any discovery made by the team?

3. How can fossils be dated when radiometric dating is impossible?

4. This chapter is about how physical anthropologists and archaeologists conduct scientific studies of the past. Science, however, exists in society and also in the context of law, values, and ethics. What are some examples of how this fact affects the work of physical anthropologists and archaeologists?

5. As this chapter illustrates, many of the ethical issues that affect the work of anthropologists have some legal dimension, whether in their own country, in another country, or even among several nations. Have you thought about law as a possible future career? (If not, think of a friend who has!) Write a convincing argument about why anthropology could be a valuable tool for a lawyer.

Multiple Choice: 1. (A); 2. (C); 3. (D); 4. (E); 5. (B); 6. (D); 7. (B); 8. (C); 9. (C); 10. (E); **Fill in the Blank:** 1. Phyroliths; 2. Fossils; 3. stratigraphy; 4. Paleopathology; 5. Informed consent

Feder, K. L.
   2011   *The Past in Perspective: An Introduction to Human Prehistory,* 5th ed. New York: Oxford University Press. Includes a discussion of field methods in archaeology.

Lewis, B., R. Jurmain, and L. Kilgore
   2007   *Understanding Physical Anthropology and Archaeology,* 9th ed. Belmont, CA: Thomson. Introduction to these two subfields, with a discussion of methods in each.

Nafte, M.
   2009   *Flesh and Bone: An Introduction to Forensic Anthropology,* 2nd ed. Durham, NC: Carolina Academic Press. Methods and procedures, avoiding technical terminology.

Park, M. A.
   2010   *Biological Anthropology,* 6th ed. Boston: McGraw-Hill. A concise introduction, with a focus on scientific inquiry.

Renfrew, C., and P. Bahn
   2010   *Archaeology Essentials: Theories, Methods, and Practice,* 2nd ed. London: Thames and Hudson. Most useful treatment of methods in archaeological anthropology.

White, T. D., M. T. Black, and P. A. Folkens
   2012   *Human Osteology,* 3rd ed. San Diego: Academic Press. Includes case studies and discussion of molecular osteology, with life-size photos of skeletal parts.

suggested additional readings

Go to our Online Learning Center website at **www.mhhe.com/kottak** for Internet exercises directly related to the content of this chapter.

internet exercises

Evolution and Genetics

What is evolution, and how does it occur?

How does heredity work, and how is it studied?

What forces contribute to genetic evolution?

◀ Famed biologist E.O. Wilson enjoys a Darwin exhibition in New York's American Museum of Natural History. Wilson has been an effective defender of Darwinian evolution against attacks by nonscientists. In science, evolution is both a theory—that is, an interpretive framework—and a fact.

understanding OURSELVES

H ey, it's all in the genes." We routinely use assumptions about genetic determination to explain, say, why tall parents have tall kids or why obesity runs in families. But just how much do genes really influence our bodies? The genetics behind some physical traits (e.g., blood types) are clear, but the genetic roots of other traits are less so. For example, can you crease or fold your tongue by raising its sides? (See the photo below.) Some people easily can; some people never can; some people who never thought they could can after practicing. An apparent genetic limitation turns out to be more plastic.

Human biology is plastic, but only to a degree. If you're born with blood group O, you've got it for life. The same is true for hemophilia and sickle-cell anemia. Fortunately, cultural (medical) solutions now exist for many genetic disorders. Can you appreciate in yourself or your family any genetic condition for which there has been a cultural (e.g., medical) intervention? Although modern medical advances usually are viewed favorably, some people worry that culture may be intervening too much with intrinsic biological features. Some members of the hearing-impaired community, for example, spurn cochlear implants, viewing them as a threat to a deaf subculture that they hold dear. Plastic surgery, genetic screening, and the possibility of genetic engineering of infants (e.g., "designer babies") concern those who imagine a future in which physical "perfection" might reduce human diversity and increase socioeconomic inequality.

Even as our culture struggles with issues of medically manipulated biological plasticity, many people still question the long-term plasticity of the human genome, a process known as evolution. Most basically, evolution is the idea that all living organisms come from ancestors that were different in some way. The oft-heard statement "evolution is only a theory" suggests to the nonscientist that evolution hasn't been proven. Scientists, however, use the

Tongue rolling—a genetic trait, at least partially, which this dad has transmitted to his son.

term *theory* differently—to refer to an interpretive framework that helps us understand the natural world. In science, evolution is both a theory and a fact. As a *scientific theory*, evolution is a central organizing principle of modern biology and anthropology. Evolution also is a fact. The following are examples of evolutionary facts: (1) All living forms come from older or previous living forms. (2) Birds arose from nonbirds; humans arose from nonhumans; and neither birds nor humans existed 250 million years ago. (3) Major ancient life forms (e.g., dinosaurs) are no longer around. (4) New life forms, such as viruses, are evolving right now. (5) Natural processes help us understand the origins and history of plants and animals, including humans and diseases.

What alternatives to evolution have you heard about? Are those scientific theories? Should they be taught in science classes? Do viruses mutate? Should people who reject evolution still get flu shots?

EVOLUTION

Compared with other animals, humans have uniquely varied ways—cultural and biological—of adapting to environmental stresses. Exemplifying cultural adaptation, we manipulate our artifacts and behavior in response to environmental conditions. Contemporary North Americans turn up thermostats or travel to Florida in the winter. We turn on fire hydrants, swim, or ride in air-conditioned cars from New York City to Maine to escape the summer's heat. Although such reliance on culture has increased in the course of human evolution, people haven't stopped adapting biologically. As in other species, human populations adapt genetically in response to environmental forces, and individuals react physiologically to stresses. Thus, when we work in the midday sun, sweating occurs spontaneously, cooling the skin and reducing the temperature of subsurface blood vessels.

We are ready now for a more detailed look at the principles that determine human biological adaptation, variation, and change.

During the 18th century, many scholars became interested in biological diversity, human origins, and our position within the classification of plants and animals. At that time, the commonly accepted explanation for the origin of species came from Genesis, the first book of the Bible: God had created all life during six days of Creation. According to *creationism*, biological similarities and differences originated at the Creation. Characteristics of life forms were seen as immutable; they could not change. Through calculations based on genealogies in the Bible, the biblical scholars James Ussher and John Lightfoot even claimed to trace the Creation to a very specific time: October 23, 4004 B.C., at 9 A.M.

Carolus Linnaeus (1707–1778) developed the first comprehensive and still influential classification, or taxonomy, of plants and animals. He grouped life forms on the basis of similarities and differences in their physical characteristics. He used traits such as the presence of a backbone to distinguish vertebrates from invertebrates and the presence of mammary glands to distinguish mammals from birds. Linnaeus viewed the differences between life forms as part of the Creator's orderly plan. Biological similarities and differences, he thought, had been established at the time of Creation and had not changed.

Fossil discoveries during the 18th and 19th centuries raised doubts about creationism. Fossils showed that different kinds of life had once existed. If all life had originated at the same time, why weren't ancient species still around? Why weren't contemporary plants and animals found in the fossil record? A modified explanation combining creationism with *catastrophism* arose to replace the original doctrine. In this view, fires, floods, and other catastrophes, including the biblical flood involving Noah's ark, had destroyed ancient species. After each destructive event, God had created again, leading to contemporary species. How did the catastrophists explain certain clear similarities between fossils and modern animals?

According to creationism, all life originated during the six days of Creation described in the Bible. Catastrophism proposed that fires and floods, including the biblical deluge involving Noah's ark (depicted in this painting by the American artist Edward Hicks), destroyed certain species. Note that creationism is not a scientific theory.

They argued that some ancient species had managed to survive in isolated areas. For example, after the biblical flood, the progeny of the animals saved on Noah's ark spread throughout the world. (This chapter's "Appreciating Diversity" discusses a recent approach called "intelligent design," which has been judged to be a secular repackaging of old-time "creationism.")

Theory and Fact

The alternative to creationism and catastrophism was *transformism,* also called **evolution.** Evolutionists believe that species arise from others through a long and gradual process of transformation, or descent with modification. Charles Darwin became the best known of the evolutionists. However, he was influenced by earlier scholars, including his own grandfather. In a book called *Zoonomia* published in 1794, Erasmus Darwin had proclaimed the common ancestry of all animal species.

Charles Darwin also was influenced by Sir Charles Lyell, the father of geology (see Eldredge and Pearson 2010). During Darwin's famous voyage to South America aboard the *Beagle,* he read Lyell's influential book *Principles of Geology* (1837/1969), which exposed him to Lyell's principle of **uniformitarianism.** Uniformitarianism states that the present is the key to the past. Explanations for past events should be sought in the long-term action of ordinary forces that still operate today. Thus, natural forces (rainfall, soil deposition, earthquakes, and volcanic action) gradually have built and modified geological features such as mountain ranges. The Earth's structure has been transformed gradually through natural forces operating for millions of years.

Uniformitarianism was a necessary building block for evolutionary theory. It cast serious doubt on the belief that the world was only six thousand years old. It would take much longer than that for such ordinary forces as rain and wind to produce major geological changes. The longer time span also allowed enough time for the biological changes that fossil discoveries were revealing. Darwin applied the ideas of uniformitarianism and long-term transformation to living things. He argued that all life forms are related and that the number of species has increased over time. (For more on science, evolution, and creationism, see Gould 1999 and Wilson 2002.)

Charles Darwin provided a theoretical framework for understanding evolution. He offered natural selection as a powerful evolutionary mechanism that could explain the origin of species, biological diversity, and similarities among related life forms. Darwin proposed a *theory of evolution* in the strict sense. A *theory* is a set of ideas formulated (by reasoning from known facts) to explain something. The main value of a theory is to promote new understanding. A theory suggests patterns, connections, and relationships that may be confirmed by new research. The *fact* of evolution (that evolution has

occurred) was known earlier, for example, by Erasmus Darwin. The *theory* of evolution, through natural selection (*how* evolution occurred), was Darwin's major contribution. Actually, natural selection wasn't Darwin's unique discovery. Working independently, the naturalist Alfred Russel Wallace had reached a similar conclusion (Shermer 2002). In a joint paper read to London's Linnaean Society in 1858, Darwin and Wallace made their discovery public. Darwin's book *On the Origin of Species* (1859/2009) offered much fuller documentation.

Natural selection is the process by which the forms most fit to survive and reproduce in a given environment do so in greater numbers than others in the same population. More than survival of the fittest, natural selection is differential reproductive success. Natural selection is a natural process that leads to a result. Natural selection operates when there is competition for strategic resources (those necessary for life) such as food and space between members of the population. There is also the matter of finding mates. You can win the competition for food and space and have no mate and thus have no impact on the future of the species. For natural selection to work on a particular population, there must be variety within that population, as there always is.

The giraffe's neck can illustrate how natural selection works on variety within a population. In any group of giraffes, there always is variation in neck length. When food is adequate, the animals have no problem feeding themselves. But when there is pressure on strategic resources, so that dietary foliage is not as abundant as usual, giraffes with longer necks have an advantage. They can feed off the higher branches. If this ability permits longer-necked giraffes to survive and reproduce even slightly more effectively than shorter-necked ones, giraffes with longer necks will transmit more of their genetic material to future generations than will giraffes with shorter necks.

 living anthropology **VIDEOS**

Theory of Evolution and Darwin, www.mhhe.com/kottak

Charles Darwin introduced the ideas of natural selection and survival of the fittest to explain evolution. Fossils offer one line of evidence for evolutionary changes. Observation of differences and similarities among living species provides additional support. The variety Darwin observed among domestic birds (English pigeons) and wild birds (finches in the Galápagos Islands) led him to believe that comparable processes of selection were at work. In the first case the selection was artificial, the result of animal domestication and breeding experiments. In the second case the selection was natural, having to do with impersonal environmental forces. For scientists, what is a "theory"?

Contrast the speckled (peppered) moth on the left with the darker one on the right. Which environment would favor each of these variants?

An incorrect alternative to this (Darwinian) explanation would be the inheritance of acquired characteristics. That is the idea that in each generation, individual giraffes strain their necks to reach just a bit higher. This straining somehow modifies their genetic material. Over generations of strain, the average neck gradually gets longer through the accumulation of small increments of neck length acquired during the lifetime of each generation of giraffes. This is not how evolution works. If it did work in this way, weight lifters could expect to produce especially muscular babies. Workouts that promise no gain without the pain apply to the physical development of individuals, not species. Instead, evolution works as the process of natural selection takes advantage of the variety that is already present in a population. That's how giraffes got their necks.

Evolution through natural selection continues today. For example, in human populations there is differential resistance to disease, as we'll see in the discussion of sickle-cell anemia below. One classic recent example of natural selection is the peppered moth, which can be light or dark (in either case with black speckles, thus the name "peppered"). A change in this species illustrates recent natural selection (in our own industrial age) through what has been called *industrial melanism*. Great Britain's industrialization changed the environment to favor darker moths (those with more melanin) rather than the lighter-colored ones that were favored previously. During the 1800s industrial pollution increased; soot coated buildings and trees, turning them a darker color. The previously typical peppered moth, which had a light color, now stood out against the dark backgrounds of sooty buildings and trees. Such light-colored moths were easily visible to their predators. Through mutations a new strain of peppered moth, with a darker phenotype, was favored. Because these darker moths were fitter—that is, harder to detect—in polluted environments, they survived and reproduced in greater numbers than lighter moths did. We see how natural selection may favor darker moths in polluted environments and lighter-colored moths in nonindustrial or less polluted environments because of their variant abilities to merge in with their environmental colors and thus avoid predators.

Evolutionary theory is used to explain. Remember from Chapter 1 that the goal of science is to increase understanding by *explaining* things. A scientific explanation shows how and why the thing (or class of things) to be understood (e.g., the variation within species) depends on other things. Explanations rely on associations and theories. An association is an observed relationship between two or more variables, such as the length of a giraffe's neck and the number of its offspring, or an increase in the frequency of dark moths as industrial pollution spreads. A theory is more general, suggesting or implying associations and attempting to explain them. A thing or event— for example, the giraffe's long neck—is explained if it illustrates a general principle or association, such as the concept of adaptive advantage. The truth of a scientific statement (e.g., evolution occurs because of differential reproductive success due to variation within the population) is confirmed by repeated observations. (See "Appreciating Diversity" for a discussion of differences between evolutionary theory and intelligent design.)

Charles Darwin (1809–1882).

appreciating DIVERSITY

Intelligent Design versus Evolutionary Theory

Evolutionary theory is basic to understanding and appreciating human diversity. Contemporary humans, members of the species *Homo sapiens,* represent one branch in the tree of life. Scientists, who seek natural rather than supernatural explanations, use evolutionary theory to explain how humans evolved from ancestors that were not human. Evolutionary theory also is used to explain biological diversity among contemporary and recent human beings. One proposed alternative to evolution known as "intelligent design" (ID) is not a scientific theory. In a 2005 ruling (the most recent definitive one on this issue), a federal district judge ruled that ID no longer could be taught in biology classes in Pennsylvania's Dover public school district. The judge found that Dover school board members had violated the Constitution by requiring their schools' biology curriculum to include the notion that life on earth was produced by an unspecified intelligent designer.

Before this ruling, administrators had been required to read a statement in biology classes asserting that evolution was a theory, not a fact; that the evidence for evolution had gaps; and that ID offered an alternative explanation laid out in a book (purchased by church funds) in the school library. According to the judge (a Republican appointed by President George W. Bush), that statement amounted to an endorsement of religion. It could cause students to doubt a well-established scientific theory by presenting a religious alternative masquerading as a scientific theory (see *New York Times* 2005, p. A32).

The Dover school board policy, adopted in October 2004, was believed to have been the first of its kind in the United States. Their attorneys claimed that school board members were seeking to improve science education by exposing students to alternatives to Charles Darwin's theory that evolution occurs through natural

selection. ID proponents argued that evolutionary theory can't fully explain complex life forms. Their opponents contended that ID amounts to a secular repackaging of creationism, which courts have ruled cannot be taught in public schools. The Pennsylvania judge agreed: The secular purposes claimed by the board were a pretext for the board's real purpose—to promote religion in public schools.

ID advocates have since been voted off the Dover school board. Although the new board planned to remove ID from science classes, interested students could still learn about ID in an elective course on comparative religion. ID did not belong in the *science* curriculum, the judge ruled, because it is "a religious view, a mere relabeling of creationism and not a scientific theory" (*New York Times* 2005, p. A32).

The ID movement asserts that life forms are too complex to have been formed by natural processes and must have been created by a

---

population genetics
Field that studies genetics of breeding populations.

dominant
Term describing an allele that masks another allele in a heterozygote.

recessive
Term describing a genetic trait masked by a dominant trait.

chromosomes
Paired lengths of DNA, composed of multiple genes.

gene
Place (locus) on a chromosome that determines a particular trait.

GENETICS

Charles Darwin recognized that for natural selection to operate, there must be variety in the population undergoing selection. Documenting and explaining such variety among humans—human biological diversity—is one of anthropology's major concerns (see Relethford 2012). Genetics, a science that emerged after Darwin, helps us understand the causes of biological variation. We now know that DNA (deoxyribonucleic acid) molecules make up genes and chromosomes, which are basic hereditary units. Biochemical changes (mutations) in DNA provide much of the variety on which natural selection operates. Through sexual reproduction, recombination of the genetic traits of mother and father in each generation leads to new arrangements of the hereditary units received from each parent. Such genetic recombination also adds variety on which natural selection may operate.

Mendelian genetics studies the ways in which chromosomes transmit genes across the generations. *Biochemical genetics* examines structure, function, and changes in DNA. **Population genetics**

investigates natural selection and other causes of genetic variation, stability, and change in breeding populations.

Mendel's Experiments

In 1856, in a monastery garden, the Austrian monk Gregor Mendel began a series of experiments that were to reveal the basic principles of genetics. Mendel studied the inheritance of seven contrasting traits in pea plants. For each trait there were only two forms. For example, plants were either tall (6 to 7 feet [1.8 to 2.1 meters]) or short (9 to 18 inches [23 to 46 centimeters]), with no intermediate forms. The ripe seeds could be either smooth and round or wrinkled. The peas could be either yellow or green, again with no intermediate colors.

When Mendel began his experiments, one of the prevailing beliefs about heredity was what has been called the "paint-pot" theory. According to this theory, the traits of the two parents blended in their children much as two pigments are blended in a can of paint. Children were therefore a unique mixture of their parents, and when these children married

higher intelligence. The fundamental claim of intelligent design proponents, such as William A. Dembski, is that "there are natural systems that cannot be adequately explained in terms of undirected natural forces and that exhibit features which in any other circumstance we would attribute to intelligence" (Dembski 2004). The source of this intelligence never is identified officially. But since the naturalness of the design is denied, its supernaturalness would seem to be assumed. By injecting ID into the science curriculum, the judge ruled, Dover's board was unconstitutionally endorsing a religious view that advances "a particular version of Christianity" (*New York Times* 2005, p. A32).

The Pennsylvania court case thoroughly examined the claim that ID was science. After a six-week trial featuring hours of expert testimony, that claim was rejected. Echoing the overwhelming majority of scientists, the judge found that ID violated the ground rules of science. It relied on supernatural, rather than natural, causation and made assertions that could not be tested or proved wrong (falsified).

Evolution as a *scientific theory* (as defined in the text) is a central organizing principle of modern biology and anthropology. Evolution also is a *fact*. There is absolutely no doubt that biological evolution has occurred and still occurs. To be sure, biologists and anthropologists do debate details involving evolutionary processes and the relative importance of different evolutionary mechanisms. But they accept certain facts: "It is a *fact* that the earth with liquid water is more than 3.6 billion years old. It is a *fact* that cellular life has been around for at least half of that period and that organized multicellular life is at least 800 million years old. It is a *fact* that major life forms now on earth were not at all represented in the past. There were no birds or mammals 250 million years ago. It is a *fact* that major life forms of the past are no longer living. There used to be dinosaurs . . . and there are none now. It is a *fact* that all living forms come from previous living forms. Therefore, all present forms of life arose from ancestral forms that were different. Birds arose from nonbirds and humans from nonhumans. No person who pretends to any understanding of the natural world can deny these facts any more than she or he can deny that the earth is round, rotates on its axis, and revolves around the sun" (Lewontin 1981, quoted in Moran 1993).

One key feature of science, as we saw in Chapter 1, is to recognize the tentativeness and uncertainty of knowledge and understanding, which scientists try to improve. As they work to refine theories and to provide accurate explanations, scientists strive for objectivity and impartiality (trying to reduce the influence of the scientist, including his or her personal beliefs and actions). Science has many limitations and is not the only way we have of understanding things. Certainly, the study of religion is another path to understanding. But the goals of objectivity and impartiality do help distinguish science from ways of knowing that are more biased, more rigid, and more dogmatic.

and reproduced, their traits would inextricably blend with those of their mates. However, prevailing notions about heredity also recognized that occasionally the traits of one parent might swamp those of the other. If children looked far more like their mother than their father, people might say that her "blood" was stronger than his. Occasionally, too, there would be a "throwback," a child who was the image of his or her grandparent or who possessed a distinctive chin or nose characteristic of a whole line of descent.

Through his experiments with pea plants, Mendel discovered that heredity is determined by discrete particles or units. Although traits could disappear in one generation, they reemerged in their original form in later generations. For example, Mendel crossbred pure strains of tall and short plants. Their offspring were all tall. This was the first descending, or first filial, generation, designated F_1. Mendel then interbred the plants of the F_1 generation to produce a generation of grandchildren, the F_2 generation (Figure 5.1). In this generation, short plants reappeared. Among thousands of plants in the F_2 generation, there was ap-

proximately one short plant for every three tall ones.

From similar results with the other six traits, Mendel concluded that although a **dominant** form could mask the other form in *hybrid,* or mixed, individuals, the dominated trait—the **recessive**—was not destroyed; it wasn't even changed. Recessive traits would appear in unaltered form in later generations because genetic traits were inherited as discrete units.

These basic genetic units that Mendel described were factors (now called genes or alleles) located on **chromosomes.** Chromosomes are arranged in matching (homologous) pairs. Humans have 46 chromosomes, arranged in 23 pairs, one in each pair from the father and the other from the mother.

For simplicity, a chromosome may be pictured as a surface (see Figure 5.2) with several positions, to each of which we assign a lowercase letter. Each position is a **gene.** Each gene

Gregor Mendel, the father of genetics.

Trait Exhibited by F₁ Hybrids	F₂ Generation (produced by crossbreeding F₁ hybrids)	
	Exhibit Dominant Trait	Exhibit Recessive Trait
Smooth seed shape	Smooth 3	Wrinkled 1
Yellow seed interior	Yellow 3	Green 1
Gray seed coat	Gray 3	White 1
Inflated pod	Inflated 3	Pinched 1
Green pod	Green 3	Yellow 1
Axial pod	Axial 3	Terminal 1
Tall stem	Tall 3	Short 1
	Offspring exhibit dominant or recessive traits in ratio of 3:1.	

FIGURE 5.1 Mendel's Second Set of Experiments with Pea Plants. Dominant colors are shown unless otherwise indicated.

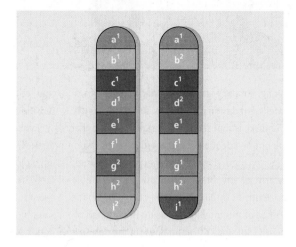

FIGURE 5.2 Simplified Representation of a Normal Chromosome Pair. Letters indicate genes; superscripts indicate alleles.

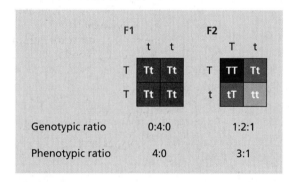

FIGURE 5.3 Punnett Squares of a Homozygous Cross and a Heterozygous Cross. These squares show how phenotypic ratios of the F₁ and F₂ generations are generated. Colors show genotypes.

allele
A variant of a particular gene.

heterozygous
Having dissimilar alleles of a given gene.

homozygous
Having identical alleles of a given gene.

genotype
An organism's hereditary makeup.

phenotype
An organism's evident biological traits.

determines, wholly or partially, a particular biological trait, such as whether one's blood is A, B, or O. **Alleles** (for example, b¹ and b² in Figure 5.2) are biochemically different forms of a given gene. In humans, A, B, AB, and O blood types reflect different combinations of alleles of a particular gene.

In Mendel's experiments, the seven contrasting traits were determined by genes on seven different pairs of chromosomes. The gene for height occurred in one of the seven pairs. When Mendel crossbred pure tall and pure short plants to produce his F₁ generation, each of the offspring received an allele for tallness (T) from one parent and one for shortness (t) from the other. These offspring were mixed, or **heterozygous,** with respect to height; each had two dissimilar alleles of that gene. Their parents, in contrast, had been **homozygous,** possessing two identical alleles of that gene (see Hartl and Jones 2011).

In the next generation (F₂), after the mixed plants were interbred, short plants reappeared in the ratio of one short to three talls. Knowing that shorts only

produced shorts, Mendel could assume that they were genetically pure. Another fourth of the F₂ plants produced only talls. The remaining half, like the F₁ generation, were heterozygous; when interbred, they produced three talls for each short. (See Figure 5.3.)

Dominance produces a distinction between **genotype,** or hereditary makeup, and **phenotype,** or expressed physical characteristics. Genotype is what you really are genetically; phenotype is what you appear as. Mendel's peas had three genotypes—TT, Tt, and tt—but only two phenotypes—tall and short. Because of dominance, the heterozygous plants were just as tall as the genetically pure tall ones. How do Mendel's discoveries apply to humans? Although some of our genetic traits follow Mendelian laws, with only two forms—dominant and recessive—other traits are determined differently. For instance, three alleles determine whether our blood type is A, B, AB, or O. People with two alleles for type O have that blood type. However, if they

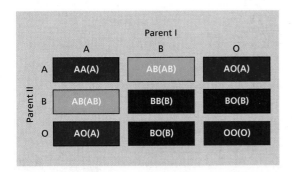

FIGURE 5.4 Determinants of Phenotypes (Blood Groups) in the ABO System.
The four phenotypes—A, B, AB, and O—are indicated in parentheses and by color.

received a gene for either A or B from one parent and one for O from the other, they will have blood type A or B. In other words, A and B are both dominant over O. A and B are said to be *codominant.* If people inherit a gene for A from one parent and one for B from the other, they will have type AB blood, which is chemically different from the other varieties, A, B, and O.

These three alleles produce four phenotypes—A, B, AB, and O—and six different genotypes—OO, AO, BO, AA, BB, and AB (Figure 5.4). There are fewer phenotypes than genotypes because O is recessive to both A and B.

Independent Assortment and Recombination

Through additional experiments, Mendel also formulated his law of **independent assortment.** He discovered that traits are inherited independently of one another. For example, he bred pure round yellow peas with pure wrinkled green ones. All the F_1 generation peas were round and yellow, the dominant forms. But when Mendel interbred the F_1 generation to produce the F_2, four phenotypes turned up. Round greens and wrinkled yellows had been added to the original round yellows and wrinkled greens.

The independent assortment and recombination of genetic traits provide one of the main ways by which variety is produced in any population. *Recombination* is important in biological evolution because it creates new types on which natural selection can operate.

BIOCHEMICAL, OR MOLECULAR, GENETICS

If, as in Mendel's experiments, the same genetic traits always appeared in predictable ratios across the generations, there would be continuity rather than change. There would be no evolution. Various kinds of mutations produce the variety on which natural selection depends. Since Mendel's time, scientists have learned about **mutations**—changes in the DNA molecules of which genes and chromosomes are built. Mendel demonstrated that variety is produced by genetic recombination. Mutation, however, is even more important as a source of new biochemical forms on which natural selection may operate.

DNA does several things basic to life. DNA can copy itself, forming new cells, replacing old ones, and producing the sex cells, or *gametes,* that make new generations. DNA's chemical structure also guides the body's production of proteins—enzymes, antigens, antibodies, hormones, and hundreds of others.

The DNA molecule is a double helix (Crick 1962/1968; Watson 1970). Imagine it as a small rubber ladder that you can twist into a spiral. Its sides are held together by chemical bonds between four bases: thymine (T), adenine (A), cytosine (C), and guanine (G). DNA's duplication leads to ordinary cell division, as shown in Figure 5.5.

In protein building, another molecule, RNA, carries DNA's message from the cell's nucleus to its

mutation
Change in DNA molecules.

independent assortment
Chromosomes inherited independently of one another.

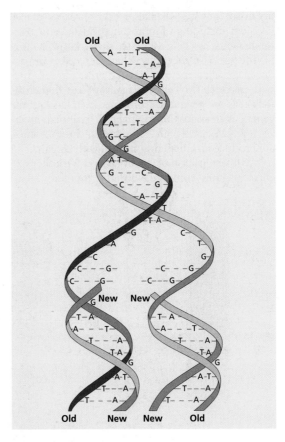

FIGURE 5.5 DNA Replication.
A double-stranded DNA molecule "unzips," and a new strand forms on each of the old ones, producing two molecules, and eventually two cells, each identical to the first.

cytoplasm (outer area). The structure of RNA, with paired bases, matches that of DNA. This permits RNA to carry a message from DNA in the cell nucleus to guide the construction of proteins in the cytoplasm. A protein, which is a chain of amino acids, is constructed by "reading" a length of RNA. RNA's bases are read as three-letter "words," called *triplets*—for example, AAG. (Because DNA and RNA have four bases, which can occur anywhere in the "word," there are $4 \times 4 \times 4 = 64$ possible triplets.) Each triplet "calls" a particular amino acid, although there is some redundancy; for example, AAA and AAG both call for the amino acid lysine. A protein is made as amino acids are assembled in the proper sequence.

Thus proteins are built following instructions sent by DNA, with RNA's assistance. In this way, DNA, the basic *hereditary* material, also initiates and guides the construction of hundreds of proteins necessary for bodily growth, maintenance, and repair.

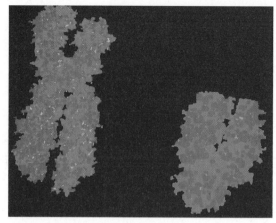

The chromosomes that determine sex in humans. The X chromosome (left) is clearly larger than the Y chromosome (right). What are the genotypes of males and females in terms of these chromosomes?

Cell Division

An organism develops from a fertilized egg, or *zygote,* created by the union of two sex cells (gametes), a sperm from the father and an egg (ovum) from the mother. The zygote grows rapidly through **mitosis,** or ordinary cell division, which continues as the organism grows. Mistakes in this process of cell division, including chromosomal breaks and rearrangements, can cause diseases such as cancer.

The special process by which sex cells are produced is called **meiosis.** Unlike ordinary cell division, in which two cells emerge from one, in meiosis four cells are produced from one. Each has half the genetic material of the original cell. In human meiosis, four cells, each with 23 individual chromosomes, are produced from an original cell with 23 pairs.

With fertilization of egg by sperm, the father's 23 chromosomes combine with the mother's 23 to re-create the pairs in every generation. However, the chromosomes sort independently, so that a child's genotype is a random combination of the DNA of its four grandparents. It is conceivable that one grandparent will contribute very little to his or her grandchild's heredity. Independent assortment of chromosomes is a major source of variety, because the parents' genotypes can be assorted in 2^{23}, or more than 8 million, different ways.

Crossing Over

Another source of variety is **crossing over.** Before fertilization, early in meiosis, as a sperm or egg is being formed, paired chromosomes temporarily intertwine as they duplicate themselves. As they do this, they often exchange lengths of their DNA (Figure 5.6). Crossovers are the sites where homologous

mitosis
Ordinary cell division.

meiosis
Process by which sex cells are produced.

crossing over
Homologous chromosomes intertwine and exchange DNA.

FIGURE 5.6 Crossing Over.

In the first phase of meiosis, homologous chromosomes intertwine as they duplicate themselves. As they do this, they often exchange lengths of their DNA, as shown here. This is known as crossing over. Note that the lower lengths of the original pair now differ. Each chromosome is therefore chemically different from either member of the original pair.

chromosomes have exchanged segments by breakage and recombination.

Because of crossing over, each new chromosome is partially different from either member of the original pair. As a person produces sex cells, replacing, say, part of a chromosome one has received from one's mother with a corresponding section of the homologous chromosome from one's father, crossing over partially contradicts Mendel's law of independent assortment and makes a new combination of genetic material available to the offspring. Because crossing over can occur with any chromosome pair, it is an important source of variety.

Mutation

Mutations are the most important source of variety on which natural selection depends and operates. The simplest mutation results from substitution of just one base in a triplet by another. (This is called a *base substitution mutation.*) If such a mutation occurs in a sex cell that joins with another in a fertilized egg, the new organism will carry the mutation in every cell. As DNA directs protein building, a protein different from that produced by the nonmutant parent *may* be produced in the child. The child's protein building will differ from the parent's only if the new base codes for a different amino acid. Because the same amino acid can be coded by more than one triplet, a base substitution mutation doesn't always produce a different protein. However, the abnormal protein associated with the hereditary disease sickle-cell anemia, described in "Stabilizing Selection" in this chapter, is caused by just such a difference in a single base between normal individuals and those afflicted with the disease.

Another form of mutation is *chromosomal rearrangement.* Pieces of a chromosome can break off, turn around and reattach, or migrate someplace else on that chromosome. This can occur in the sex cell, or in the fertilized egg or the growing organism, during mitosis. A mismatch of chromosomes resulting from rearrangement can lead to speciation (the formation of new species). Scientists often find that separate but closely related species living in overlapping ranges cannot interbreed because their chromosomes, due to rearrangement, no longer match. Chromosome rearrangements in a fertilized egg can lead to congenital disorders. Cancer cells undergo large-scale chromosome rearrangements. Chromosomes also may fuse. When the ancestors of humans split off from those of chimpanzees around six million years ago, two ancestral chromosomes fused together in the human line. Humans have 23 chromosome pairs, versus 24 for chimps.

Mutation rates vary, but for base substitution mutations, the likely average is 10^{-9} mutations per DNA base per generation. This means that approximately three mutations will occur in every sex cell (Strachan and Read 2004). Many geneticists believe that most

mutations are neutral, conferring neither advantage nor disadvantage. Others argue that most mutations are harmful and will be weeded out because they deviate from types that have been selected over the generations. However, if the selective forces affecting a population change, mutations in its gene pool may acquire an adaptive advantage they lacked in the old environment.

Evolution depends on mutations as a major source of genetically transmitted variety, raw material on which natural selection can work. (Crossing over, independent assortment, and chromosomal recombination are other sources.) Alterations in genes and chromosomes may result in entirely new types of organisms, which may demonstrate some new selective advantage. Variants produced through mutation can be especially significant if there is a change in the environment. They may prove to have an advantage they lacked in the old environment. The spread of the allele that determines sickle-cell anemia, to be examined in "Stabilizing Selection" later in this chapter, provides one example.

POPULATION GENETICS AND MECHANISMS OF GENETIC EVOLUTION

Population genetics studies the stable and changing populations in which most breeding normally takes place (see Gillespie 2004; Hartl and Jones 2011). The term **gene pool** refers to all the alleles, genes, chromosomes, and genotypes within a breeding population—the "pool" of genetic material available. When population geneticists use the term *evolution,* they have a more specific definition in mind than the one given earlier ("descent with modification over the generations"). For geneticists, **genetic evolution** is defined as a change in gene frequency—that is, in the frequency of alleles in a breeding population from generation to generation. Any factor that contributes to such a change can be considered a mechanism of genetic evolution. Those mechanisms include natural selection, mutation (already examined), random genetic drift, and gene flow (see Mayr 2001; Relethford 2012).

Natural Selection

Natural selection remains the best explanation for (genetic) evolution. Essential to understanding evolution through natural selection is the distinction between genotype and phenotype. Genotype refers just to hereditary factors—genes and chromosomes. Phenotype—the organism's evident biological characteristics—develops over the years as the organism is influenced by particular environmental forces. (See the photo of the identical twins. Identical twins have exactly the same genotype, but their actual biology, their phenotypes, may differ as a result

gene pool
All the genetic material in a breeding population.

genetic evolution
Change in gene (allele) frequency in a breeding population.

Twins Day is an annual event in Twinsburg, Ohio. This photo was taken on August 7, 2011, when about 1,700 sets of twins attended. At the festival, twins can compete in look-a-like and not-look-alike competitions. Are identical twins always identical? Why or why not?

adaptive
Favored by natural selection.

of variation in the environments in which they have been raised.) Also, because of dominance, individuals with different genotypes may have identical phenotypes (like Mendel's tall pea plants). Natural selection can operate only on phenotype—on what is exposed, not on what is hidden. For example, a harmful recessive gene can't be eliminated from the gene pool if it is masked by a favored dominant.

Phenotype includes not only outward physical appearance but also internal organs, tissues and cells, and physiological processes and systems. Many biological reactions to foods, disease, heat, cold, sunlight, and other environmental factors are not automatic, genetically programmed responses but the product of years of exposure to particular environmental stresses. Human biology is not set at birth but has considerable *plasticity*. That is, it is changeable, being affected by the environmental forces, such as diet and altitude, that we experience as we grow up (see Bogin 2001).

The environment works on the genotype to build the phenotype, and certain phenotypes do better in some environments than other phenotypes do. However, remember that favored phenotypes can be produced by different genotypes. Because natural selection works only on genes that are expressed, maladaptive recessives can be removed only when they occur in homozygous form. When a heterozygote carries a maladaptive recessive, its effects are masked by the favored dominant. The process of perfecting the fit between organisms and their environment is gradual.

Directional Selection

After several generations of selection, gene frequencies will change. Adaptation through natural selection will have occurred. Once that happens, those traits that have proved to be the most **adaptive** (favored by natural selection) in that environment will be selected again and again from generation to generation. Given such *directional selection,* or long-term selection of the same trait(s), maladaptive recessive alleles will be removed from the gene pool.

Directional selection will continue as long as environmental forces stay the same. However, if the environment changes, new selective forces start working, favoring different phenotypes. This also happens when part of the population colonizes a new environment. Selection in the changed, or new, environment continues until a new equilibrium is reached. Then there is directional selection until another environmental change or migration takes place. Over millions of years, such a process of successive adaptation to a series of environments has led to biological modification and branching. The process of natural selection has led to the tremendous array of plant and animal forms found in the world today.

Selection operates *only* on traits that are present in a population. A favorable mutation *may* occur, but a population doesn't normally come up with a new genotype or phenotype just because one is needed or desirable. Many species have become extinct because they weren't sufficiently varied to adapt to environmental shifts.

There are also differences in the amount of environmental stress that organisms' genetic potential enables them to tolerate. Some species are adapted to a narrow range of environments. They are especially endangered by environmental fluctuation. Others—*Homo sapiens* among them—tolerate much more environmental variation because their genetic potential permits many adaptive possibilities. Humans can adapt rapidly to changing conditions by modifying both biological responses and learned behavior. We don't have to delay adaptation until a favorable mutation appears.

Sexual Selection

Selection also operates through competition for mates in a breeding population. Males may openly compete for females, or females may choose to mate with particular males because they have desirable traits. Obviously, such traits vary from species to species. Familiar examples include color in birds; male birds, such as cardinals, tend to be more brightly colored than females are. Colorful males have a selective advantage because females like them better. As, over the generations, females have opted for colorful mates, the alleles responsible for color have built up in the species. **Sexual selection,** based on differential success in mating, is the term for this process in which certain traits of one sex are selected because of advantages they confer in winning mates.

Stabilizing Selection

We have seen that natural selection reduces variety in a population through directional selection—by favoring one trait or allele over another. Selective forces can also work to *maintain* variety through *stabilizing selection,* by favoring a **balanced polymorphism,** in which the frequencies of two or more alleles of a gene remain constant from generation to generation. This may be because the phenotypes they produce are neutral, or equally favored, or equally opposed by selective forces. Sometimes a particular force favors (or opposes) one allele while a different but equally effective force favors (or opposes) the other allele.

One well-studied example of a balanced polymorphism involves two alleles, Hb^A and Hb^S, that affect the production of the beta strain (Hb) of human hemoglobin. Hemoglobin, which is located in our red blood cells, carries oxygen from the lungs to the rest of the body via the circulatory system. The allele that produces normal hemoglobin is Hb^A. Another allele, Hb^S, produces a different hemoglobin. Individuals who are homozygous for Hb^S suffer from *sickle-cell anemia.* Such anemia, in which the red blood cells are shaped like crescents or sickles, is associated with a disease that usually is fatal. This condition interferes with the blood's ability to store oxygen. It increases the heart's burden by clogging the small blood vessels.

Sexual selection: In many bird species, colorful males have a selective advantage because females are more likely to mate with them than with less colorful males. The male in this pair of painted buntings (how accurate and sexist is that name?), photographed in Texas, is much brighter than the female.

Given the fatal disease associated with Hb^S, geneticists were surprised to discover that certain populations in Africa, India, and the Mediterranean had very high frequencies of Hb^S (Figure 5.7). In some West African populations, that frequency is around 20 percent. Researchers eventually discovered that both Hb^A and Hb^S are maintained because selective

sexual selection
Selection of traits that enhance mating success.

balanced polymorphism
Alleles maintain a constant frequency in a population over time.

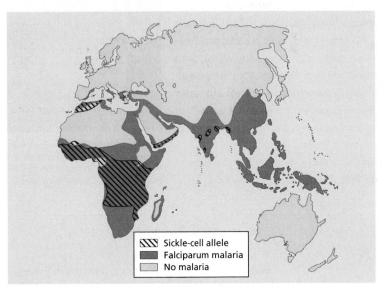

FIGURE 5.7 Distribution of Sickle-Cell Allele and Falciparum Malaria in the Old World.

SOURCE: Adapted from Joseph B. Birdsell, *Human Evolution: An Introduction to the New Physical Anthropology,* 3rd ed., © 1981. Reprinted and electronically reproduced by permission of Pearson Education, Inc., Upper Saddle River, New Jersey.

H1N1 Anyone?

Anthropology is noteworthy for its holistic and biocultural approaches and its relevance to understanding historic as well as contemporary processes and events. The anthropologists described below view the evolution of disease not just biologically but in the context of social and political history.

Known to us as a dreaded venereal—aka sexually transmitted—disease (STD), syphilis apparently originated in the Americas as a nonvenereal bacterium. After it reached Europe, the bacterium mutated into venereal syphilis, which became a major killer during the Renaissance. The same evolutionary principles and mechanisms (e.g., adaptation to new environments and mutation) that operate in the evolution of life in general also apply specifically to the evolution of pathogens that cause disease.

Globalization is an important factor in the spread and mutation of diseases in today's world. The title above suggests one example, the H1N1 virus, which gained attention as a pandemic in 2009–2010, and which continues to mutate today. Also known as swine flu, the virus illustrates the spread of pathogens from animals to humans (and vice versa). Such transmission became much more common after humans domesticated animals and began to live in close proximity to such animals as pigs, poultry, sheep, and cattle.

Columbus, it seems, made another discovery of something that he was not looking for.

In a comprehensive genetic study, scientists have found what they say is the strongest evidence yet linking the first European explorers of the New World to the origin of sexually transmitted syphilis.

The research, they say, supports the hypothesis that returning explorers introduced organisms leading, in probably modified forms, to the first recorded syphilis epidemic, beginning in Europe in 1493.

The so-called Columbus hypothesis had previously rested on circumstantial evidence, mainly the timing of the epidemic. . . .

Earlier traces of syphilis or related diseases had been few and inconclusive in Europe. Yet nonvenereal forms of the diseases were widespread in the American tropics.

Leaders of the new study said the most telling results were that the bacterium causing sexually transmitted syphilis arose relatively recently in humans and was closely related to a strain responsible for the nonvenereal infection known as yaws. The similarity was especially evident, the researchers said, in a variation of the yaws pathogen isolated recently among

Like earlier diseases, the H1N1 virus spread (rapidly) within the world system. In spring-summer 2009, people in Mexico bought masks and used hand sanitizers to fend off the flu. About eight thousand foreigners live in the Mexican town of San Miguel Allende, shown here. In this photo two expatriate women carefully purchase items in a local pharmacy. What precautions do they appear to be taking?

forces in certain environments favor the heterozygote over either homozygote.

Initially, scientists wondered why, if most Hb^S homozygotes died before they reached reproductive age, the harmful allele hadn't been eliminated. Why was its frequency so high? The answer turned out to lie in the *heterozygote's* greater fitness. Only

people who were homozygous for Hb^S died from sickle-cell anemia. Heterozygotes suffered very mild anemia, if any. On the other hand, although people homozygous for Hb^A did not suffer from anemia, they were much more susceptible to *malaria*—a killer disease that continues to plague *Homo sapiens* in the tropics.

afflicted children in a remote region of Guyana in South America. . . .

The findings suggested Columbus and his men could have carried the nonvenereal tropical bacteria home, where the organisms may have mutated into a more deadly form in the different conditions of Europe.

In the New World, the infecting organisms for nonvenereal syphilis, known as bejel, and yaws were transmitted by skin-to-skin and oral contact, more often in children. The symptoms are lesions primarily on the legs, not on or near the genitals.

Kristin N. Harper, a researcher in molecular genetics at Emory University who was the principal investigator in the study, said the findings supported "the hypothesis that syphilis, or some progenitor, came from the New World.". . . Her co-authors included George J. Armelagos, an Emory anthropologist who has studied the origins of syphilis for more than 30 years, and Dr. Michael S. Silverman, a Canadian infectious diseases physician who collected and tested specimens from yaws lesions in Guyana, the only known site today of yaws infections in the Western Hemisphere. The researchers said their study "represents the first attempt to address the problem of the origin of syphilis using molecular genetics, as well as the first source of information regarding the genetic makeup of nonvenereal strains from the Western Hemisphere."

They applied phylogenetics, the study of evolutionary relationships between organisms, in examining 26 geographically disparate strains in the family of Treponema bacteria. Treponema

pallidum subspecies pallidum is the agent for the scourge of venereal syphilis. The subspecies endemicum causes bejel, usually in hot, arid climates. . . .

John W. Verano, an anthropologist at Tulane, said the findings would "probably not settle the debate" over the origins of venereal syphilis, though most scientists had become convinced that the disease was not transmitted sexually before Europeans made contact with the New World.

Donald J. Ortner, an anthropologist at the Smithsonian Institution, questioned whether the organisms causing the first European epidemic were actually distinct from others in the treponemal family. "What we are seeing is an organism with a long history, and it is very adaptable to different modes of transmission that produce different manifestations," Dr. Ortner said. . . .

Paleopathologists . . . have for years analyzed skeletons for the bone scars from lesions produced by treponemal diseases, except for the mild form called pinta. In this way, they traced the existence of these infections in the New World back at least 7,000 years. But it has often been difficult to determine the age of the bones and distinguish the different diseases that share symptoms but have different modes of transmission. . . .

In her investigation, Ms. Harper studied 22 human Treponemal pallidum strains. The DNA in their genes was sequenced in nearly all cases, examined for changes and eventually used in constructing phylogenetic trees incorporating all variations in the strains.

An Old World yaws subspecies was found to occupy the base of the tree, indicating its ancestral position in the treponemal family, she said. The terminal position of the venereal syphilis subspecies on the tree showed it had diverged most recently from the rest of the bacterial family.

Specimens from two Guyana yaws cases were included in the study, after they were collected and processed by Dr. Silverman. Genetic analysis showed that this yaws strain was the closest known relative to venereal syphilis.

If this seemed to solidify the Columbus hypothesis, the researchers cautioned that a "transfer agent between humans and nonhuman primates cannot be ruled out."

Dr. Armelagos said research into the origins of syphilis would continue, because "understanding its evolution is important not just for biology, but for understanding social and political history."

Noting that the disease was a major killer in Renaissance Europe, he said, "It could be argued that syphilis is one of the important early examples of globalization and disease, and globalization remains an important factor in emerging diseases."

The heterozygote, with one sickle-cell allele and one normal one, was the fittest phenotype for a malarial environment. Heterozygotes have enough abnormal hemoglobin, in which malaria parasites cannot thrive, to protect against malaria. They also have enough normal hemoglobin to fend off sickle-cell anemia. The Hb^S allele has been maintained in these populations because the heterozygotes survived and reproduced in greater numbers than did people with any other phenotype.

The example of the sickle-cell allele demonstrates the relativity of evolution through natural selection: Adaptation and fitness are in relation to specific environments. Traits are not adaptive or

NETSFORLIFE is a nongovernmental organization (NGO) that combats the spread of malaria through education and the distribution of mosquito nets, such as these in the maternity ward of a government hospital in Katanga, Democratic Republic of Congo.

random genetic drift
Genetic change due to chance.

gene flow
Exchange of genetic material through interbreeding.

maladaptive for all times and places. Even harmful alleles can be selected if heterozygotes have an advantage. Moreover, as the environment changes, favored phenotypes and gene frequencies can change. In malaria-free environments, normal-hemoglobin homozygotes reproduce more effectively than heterozygotes do. With no malaria, the frequency of Hb^S declines because Hb^S homozygotes can't compete in survival and reproduction with the other types. This has happened in areas of West Africa where malaria has been reduced through drainage programs and insecticides. Selection against Hb^S also has occurred in the United States among Americans descended from West Africans (Diamond 1997).

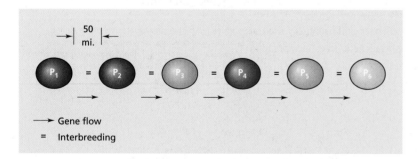

FIGURE 5.8 Gene Flow between Local Populations.

P$_1$–P$_6$ are six local populations of the same species. Each interbreeds (=) only with its neighbor(s). Although members of P$_6$ never interbreed with P$_1$, P$_6$ and P$_1$ are linked through gene flow. Genetic material that originates in P$_1$ eventually will reach P$_6$, and vice versa, as it is passed from one neighboring population to the next. Because they share genetic material in this way, P$_1$–P$_6$ remain members of the same species. In many species, local populations distributed throughout a larger territory than the 250 miles depicted here are linked through gene flow.

Random Genetic Drift

A second mechanism of genetic evolution is **random genetic drift.** This is a change in allele frequency that results not from natural selection but from chance. To understand why, compare the sorting of alleles to a game involving a bag of 12 marbles, 6 red and 6 blue. In step 1, you draw 6 marbles from the bag. Statistically, your chances of drawing 3 reds and 3 blues are less than those of getting 4 of one color and 2 of the other. Step 2 is to fill a new bag with 12 marbles on the basis of the ratio of marbles you drew in step 1. Assume that you drew 4 reds and 2 blues: The new bag will have 8 red marbles and 4 blue ones. Step 3 is to draw 6 marbles from the new bag. Your chances of drawing blues in step 3 are lower than they were in step 1, and the probability of drawing all reds increases. If you do draw all reds, the next bag (step 4) will have only red marbles.

This game is analogous to random genetic drift operating over the generations. The blue marbles were lost purely by chance. Alleles, too, can be lost by chance rather than because of any disadvantage they confer. Lost alleles can reappear in a gene pool only through mutation.

Although genetic drift can operate in any population, large or small, *fixation* due to drift is more rapid in small populations. Fixation refers to the total replacement of blue marbles by red marbles—or, to use a human example, of blue eyes by brown eyes. The history of the human line is characterized by a series of small populations, migrations, and fixation due to genetic drift. One cannot understand human origins, human genetic variation, and a host of other important anthropological topics without recognizing the importance of genetic drift.

Gene Flow

A third mechanism of genetic evolution is **gene flow,** the exchange of genetic material between populations of the same species. Gene flow, like mutation, works in conjunction with natural selection by providing variety on which selection can work. Gene flow may consist of direct interbreeding between formerly separated populations of the same species (e.g., Europeans, Africans, and Native Americans in the United States), or it may be indirect.

Consider the following hypothetical case (Figure 5.8). In a certain part of the world live six local populations of a certain species. P$_1$ is the westernmost of these populations. P$_2$, which interbreeds with P$_1$, is located 50 miles to the east. P$_2$ also interbreeds with P$_3$, located 50 miles east of P$_2$. Assume that each population interbreeds with, and only with, the adjacent populations. P$_6$ is located 250 miles from P$_1$ and does not directly interbreed with P$_1$, but it is tied to P$_1$ through the chain of interbreeding that ultimately links all six populations.

Assume further that some allele exists in P$_1$ that isn't particularly advantageous in its environment.

Because of gene flow, this allele may be passed on to P_2, by it to P_3, and so on, until it eventually reaches P_6. In P_6 or along the way, the allele may encounter an environment in which it does have a selective advantage. If this happens, it may serve, like a new mutation, as raw material on which natural selection can operate.

Alleles are spread through gene flow even when selection is not operating on the allele. In the long run, natural selection works on the variety within a population, whatever its source. Selection and gene flow have worked together to spread the Hb^S allele in Central Africa. Frequencies of Hb^S in Africa reflect not only the intensity of malaria but also the length of time gene flow has been going on (Livingstone 1969).

Gene flow is important in the study of the origin of species. A **species** is a group of related organisms whose members can interbreed to produce offspring that can live and reproduce. A species has to be able to reproduce itself through time. We know that horses and donkeys belong to different species because their offspring cannot meet the test of long-term survival. A horse and a donkey may breed to produce a mule, but mules are sterile. So are the offspring of lions with tigers. Gene flow tends to prevent **speciation**—the formation of new species—unless subgroups of the same species are separated for a sufficient length of time.

When gene flow is interrupted, and isolated subgroups are maintained, new species may arise. Imagine that an environmental barrier arises between P_3 and P_4, so that they no longer interbreed. If over time, as a result of isolation, P_1, P_2, and P_3 become incapable of interbreeding with the other three populations, speciation will have occurred.

THE MODERN SYNTHESIS

The currently accepted view of evolution is known as the "modern synthesis." This refers to the synthesis or combination of Darwin's theory of evolution by natural selection and Mendel's genetic discoveries. The modern synthesis also explains what Mendel could not—the inheritance of multifactorial or complex traits (e.g., height; see the next chapter). According to the modern synthesis, speciation (the formation of new species) occurs when they become reproductively isolated from one another. How does genetic evolution lead, or not, to new species?

Microevolution refers to genetic changes in a population or species over a few, several, or many generations, but without speciation. *Macroevolution* refers to larger-scale or more significant genetic changes in a population or species, usually over a longer time period, which result in speciation. Indeed, macroevolution is defined as speciation, the divergence of one ancestral species into two (or more) descendant species. Most biologists assume that species develop gradually as successive muta-

tions accumulate in isolated populations, so that eventually the populations are too different to interbreed. But the time and the number of generations required for microevolution to become macroevolution are highly variable.

Modern-day creationists sometimes use a misunderstanding of the contrast between microevolution and macroevolution to comment on evolution. They may say they accept microevolution, such as a change in a species' size or coloring, or as demonstrated in the laboratory or through studies of such traits as the sickle-cell allele. Macroevolution, they claim, by contrast, can't be demonstrated, only inferred from the fossil record.

Note, however, that no degree of phenotypical difference is implied by the term *macroevolution*. A simple chromosomal rearrangement can be sufficient to separate two closely related species whose ranges overlap. They belong to different species not because they are isolated from each other in space but because they cannot hybridize. Although no phenotypic difference is visible between these reproductively isolated species, this is a case of macroevolution rather than microevolution.

To exaggerate the contrast between microevolution and macroevolution would imply, incorrectly, that there are two fundamentally distinct evolutionary processes. Scientists see no such contrast: Microevolution and macroevolution happen in the same way and for the same reasons, reflecting the mechanisms of genetic evolution discussed in this chapter. The modern synthesis recognizes that microevolutionary processes are sufficient to explain macroevolution.

Punctuated Equilibrium

Charles Darwin saw species as arising from others over time, in a gradual and orderly fashion. Microevolutionary changes would accumulate over the generations to eventually produce macroevolution. In other words, minor alterations in the gene pool, accumulating generation after generation, would add up to major changes, including speciation, after thousands of years.

The **punctuated equilibrium** model of evolution (see Eldredge 1985; Gould 2002) points to the fact that long periods of stasis (stability), during which species change little, may be interrupted (punctuated) by evolutionary leaps. One reason for such apparent jumps (which are revealed by the fossil record) may be extinction of one species followed by invasion by a closely related species. For example, a sea species may die out when a shallow body of water dries up, while a closely related species survives in deeper waters. Later, when the sea reinvades the first locale, the protected species will extend its range to the first area. Another possibility is that when barriers are removed, a group may replace, rather than succeed, a related one because it has a trait that makes it adaptively fitter in the environment they now share.

species
Population whose members can interbreed to produce offspring that live and reproduce.

speciation
Formation of new species.

punctuated equilibrium
Long periods of stability, with occasional evolutionary leaps.

When there is a sudden environmental change, rather than such extinction and replacement, another possibility is for the pace of evolution to speed up. Some highly significant mutation(s) or combination of genetic changes may permit the survival of a radically altered species in a new and very different environmental niche. Many scientists believe that the evolution of our hominin ancestors was marked by one or more such evolutionary leaps.

Although species can survive radical environmental shifts, a more common fate is extinction. The Earth has witnessed several mass extinctions—worldwide catastrophes affecting multiple species. The biggest one divided the era of "ancient life" (the Paleozoic) from the era of "middle life" (the Mesozoic). This mass extinction occurred 245 million years ago, when 4.5 million of the Earth's estimated 5 million species (mostly inverte-

brates) were wiped out. The second-biggest extinction, around 65 million years ago, destroyed the dinosaurs. One explanation for the extinction of the dinosaurs is that a massive, long-lasting cloud of gas and dust arose from the impact of a giant meteorite at the end of the Mesozoic. The cloud blocked solar radiation and therefore photosynthesis, ultimately destroying most plants and the chain of animals that fed on them.

From the fossil record, including the hominin fossil record to be discussed in Chapters 8 to 10, we know there are periods of more intense evolutionary change. At the end of the Mesozoic, the extinction of the dinosaurs was accompanied by the rapid spread and speciation of mammals and birds. Speciation responds to many factors, including the rate of environmental change, the speed with which geographic barriers rise or fall, the degree of competition with other species, and the effectiveness of the group's adaptive response.

acing the COURSE

summary

1. In the 18th century, Carolus Linnaeus developed biological taxonomy. He viewed differences and similarities among organisms as part of God's orderly plan rather than as evidence for evolution. Charles Darwin and Alfred Russel Wallace proposed that natural selection could explain the origin of species, biological diversity, and similarities among related life forms. Natural selection requires variety in the population undergoing selection.

2. Through breeding experiments with peas in 1856, Gregor Mendel discovered that genetic traits pass on as units. These are now known to be chromosomes, which occur in homologous pairs. Alleles, some dominant, some recessive, are the chemically different forms that occur at a given genetic locus. Mendel also formulated the law of independent assortment. Each of the seven traits he studied in peas was inherited independently of all the others. Independent assortment of chromosomes and their recombination provide some of the variety needed for natural selection. But the major source of such variety is mutation, an alteration in the DNA molecules of which genes are made.

3. Biochemical, or molecular, genetics studies structure, function, and changes in genetic material—DNA. Genetic changes that provide variety within a population include base substitution mutations, chromosomal rearrangements, and genetic recombination. Population genetics studies gene frequencies in stable and changing populations. Natural selection is the most important mechanism of evolutionary change. Others include random genetic drift and gene flow. Natural selection works with traits already present in the population. If variety is insufficient to permit adaptation to environmental change, extinction is likely. New types don't appear just because they are needed.

4. One well-documented case of natural selection in contemporary human populations is that of the sickle-cell allele. In homozygous form, the sickle-cell allele, Hb^S, produces an abnormal hemoglobin. This clogs the small blood vessels, impairing the blood's capacity to store oxygen. The result is sickle-cell anemia, which usually is fatal. The distribution of Hb^S has been linked to that of malaria. Homozygotes for normal hemoglobin are susceptible to malaria and die in great numbers. Homozygotes for

the sickle-cell allele die from anemia. Heterozygotes get only mild anemia and are resistant to malaria. In a malarial environment, the heterozygote has the advantage. This explains why an apparently mal-adaptive allele is preserved. The preservation of Hb^A and Hb^S alleles within a breeding population is an example of a balanced polymorphism, in which the heterozygote has greater fitness than does either homozygote.

5. Other mechanisms of genetic evolution comple-ment natural selection. Random genetic drift oper-ates most obviously in small populations, where pure chance can easily change allele frequencies. Gene flow and interbreeding keep subgroups of the same species genetically connected and thus im-pede speciation.

6. The modern synthetic theory of evolution (the modern synthesis) blends the Darwin and Wallace theory of evolution through natural selection with Mendel's discovery of the gene. Microevolution and macroevolution are two ends (short-term and long-term) of a continuum of evolutionary change in which gradually changing allele frequencies in a population eventually can lead to the formation of new species. Punctuated equilibrium theory states that long periods of stasis (stability), during which species change little, are interrupted (punctuated) by evolutionary leaps.

key terms

adaptive 102
allele 98
balanced polymorphism 103
chromosomes 96
crossing over 100
dominant 96
evolution 94
gene 96
gene flow 106
gene pool 101
genetic evolution 101
genotype 98
heterozygous 98
homozygous 98

independent assortment 99
meiosis 100
mitosis 100
mutation 99
natural selection 94
phenotype 98
population genetics 96
punctuated equilibrium 107
random genetic drift 106
recessive 96
sexual selection 103
speciation 107
species 107
uniformitarianism 94

test yourself

MULTIPLE CHOICE

1. The *fact* of evolution was known prior to Charles Darwin. The *theory* of evolution, through natural selection (*how* evolution occurred), was
   a. Linnaeus's major contribution.
   b. actually the idea of Darwin's grandfather, Erasmus Darwin.
   c. Charles Darwin's major contribution.
   d. compatible with theories of biblical scholars.
   e. at odds with the fossil record.

2. Which of the following is *not* part of Darwin's theory of evolution?
   a. competition for resources
   b. variety in a population
   c. change in form over generations
   d. natural selection
   e. catastrophism

3. Sir Charles Lyell, the father of geology, influenced Darwin with which principle?
   a. catastrophism, the view that extinct species were destroyed by fires, floods, and other catastrophes
   b. uniformitarianism, the view that the present is the key to the past
   c. culpability, the view that the soul is a victim of the flesh
   d. creationism, the explanation for the origin of species given in Genesis
   e. macroevolution, the explanation of large-scale changes in allele frequencies in a population over a long time period

4. What are the two other mechanisms of genetic evolution that complement natural selection?
   a. random genetic drift and gene flow
   b. mutation and Lamarckism

c. directed genetic drift and genetic engineering

d. microdrift and macrodrift

e. mutation and drift

5. Mutations
   a. were discovered by Mendel.
   b. only occur during the development of an individual.
   c. always result in phenotypic change.
   d. occur in 50 percent of sex cells.
   e. are the major source of genetic variation.

6. Evolution can be defined most simply as
   a. natural selection.
   b. mutations in a breeding population.
   c. the process of achieving a perfect fit to the environment.
   d. descent with modification.
   e. competition over strategic resources.

7. Natural selection
   a. is unique to flowering plants.
   b. remains the best explanation for genetic evolution.
   c. is the driving principle behind creationism.
   d. was discovered by Gregor Mendel.
   e. operates only on single-celled animals, since their genotypes are readily accessible to specific environments.

8. What does natural selection directly act on?
   a. heterozygous individuals
   b. the genotypes of organisms
   c. the phenotypes of organisms
   d. DNA
   e. mitochondrial DNA

9. The allele Hb^S, which codes for the type of hemoglobin associated with sickle-cell anemia,
   a. is evenly distributed throughout all human populations.
   b. is always lethal.
   c. has no effect on the viability of a population.
   d. is never expressed in the phenotype when present in a heterozygous state.
   e. confers resistance to malaria.

10. What is the term for the exchange of genetic material between populations of the same species through direct or indirect interbreeding?
    a. gene pool
    b. gene flow
    c. mutation
    d. genetic drift
    e. genetic evolution

FILL IN THE BLANK

1. _____ (1707–1778) developed the first comprehensive and still influential classification, or taxonomy, of plants and animals. He believed, as did many scholars at the time, that biological similarities and differences had been established at the time of Creation and had not changed.

2. A _____ occurs when alleles maintain a constant frequency in a population over time.

3. Mendel discovered that traits are inherited independently of one another. This is called _____.

4. Gene _____ refers to the exchange of genetic material through interbreeding, while gene _____ refers to all the genetic material in a breeding population.

5. The term _____ refers to long periods of stability, with occasional evolutionary steps.

CRITICAL THINKING

1. During the 18th century, many scholars became interested in biological diversity, human origins, and our position within the classification of plants and animals. Why do you think that this interest arose at this time, at least in Europe? Think of historical events that led to the realization that the world is much larger and also much more diverse than previously thought.

2. In the context of understanding evolution, why is it important to distinguish between a theory and a fact?

3. Also in the context of understanding evolution, why is it important to distinguish between phenotype and genotype?

4. The strange consequences of mutations have been featured in science fiction books and movies. What is a mutation? What role do they play in evolution? Are they always bad?

Darwin, C.

2009   (orig. 1859) *On the Origin of Species,* ed. J. Endersby. New York: Cambridge University Press. Very useful annotated edition published on the 100th anniversary of Darwin's birth.

Eldredge, N., and S. Pearson

2010   *Charles Darwin and the Mystery of Mysteries.* New York: Rb Flash Point/Roaring Brook Press. Follows Darwin on his journey aboard the HMS *Beagle* and presents the thinking that led him to the theory of evolution.

Hartl, D. L., and E. W. Jones

2011   *Essential Genetics: A Genomics Perspective,* 5th ed. Boston: Jones and Bartlett. Up-to-date introduction to genetics.

Mayr, E.

2001   *What Evolution Is.* New York: Basic Books. A master scholar sums it all up.

Relethford, J.

2012   *Human Population Genetics.* Hoboken, NJ: Wiley-Blackwell. Population genetics in general and applied to humans.

Weiner, J.

1994   *The Beak of the Finch: A Story of Evolution in Our Time.* New York: Alfred A. Knopf. An excellent introduction to Darwin and to evolutionary theory.

suggested additional readings

Go to our Online Learning Center website at **www.mhhe.com/kottak** for Internet exercises directly related to the content of this chapter.

internet exercises

Human Variation and Adaptation

What is the race concept, and why have anthropologists rejected it?

How does natural selection work on contemporary and recent human populations?

Does biological adaptation occur during an individual's lifetime?

◀ A father gives a piggyback ride to his son and daughter. Physical contrasts are evident to anyone. Anthropology's job is to explain them.

understanding OURSELVES

How do you imagine human "diversity"? Maybe you associate that word with "race" or "ethnicity." Perhaps you think of differences in skin or eye color, or something like height, which can be observed by the naked eye. In fact, human biological diversity encompasses much more than observable physical differences. It includes our abilities to digest various foods. It also includes our innate resistance or susceptibility to particular diseases. Consider smallpox, a virus that once plagued humankind. When I was a child, everyone was vaccinated against smallpox. Were you? Probably not, because smallpox has been eradicated in nature since 1979. The virus is preserved only in labs. In the context of the anthrax scare following the September 11, 2001, attacks, fears arose that evildoers might find a way to access lab samples and unleash a smallpox epidemic. In anticipation of such an attack, the government planned to increase the supply and availability of smallpox vaccine. Who, however, would and should receive that vaccine, a highly effective but potentially lethal one? At one time, when smallpox was nearing extinction, more people were dying from the cure than from the disease. Anthropologists know that people with certain blood types seem to be more at risk from smallpox and its vaccine than are people with other blood types.

This type of knowledge about biological diversity can help us make important decisions about public policy and public safety in a society as diverse as our own.

Contemporary North America is strikingly rich in human biological diversity. The photos in this chapter and throughout this book illustrate just a fraction of the world's biological variation. Additional illustration comes from your own experience. Look around you in your classroom or at the mall or multiplex. Inevitably you'll see people whose ancestors lived in many lands. The first (Native) Americans had to cross a land bridge that once linked Siberia to North America. For later immigrants, perhaps including your own parents or grandparents, the voyage may have been across the sea, or overland from nations to the south. They came for many reasons; some came voluntarily, while others were brought in chains. The scale of migration in today's world is so vast that millions of people routinely cross national borders or live far from the homelands of their grandparents. Now meeting every day are diverse human beings whose biological features reflect adaptation to a wide range of environments other than the ones they now inhabit. Physical contrasts are evident to anyone. Anthropology's job is to explain them.

RACE: A DISCREDITED CONCEPT IN BIOLOGY

Historically, scientists have approached the study of human biological diversity in two main ways: (1) racial classification (now largely abandoned) versus (2) the current explanatory approach, which focuses on understanding specific differences. First we'll consider problems with **racial classification** (the attempt to assign humans to discrete categories [purportedly] based on common ancestry). Then we'll offer some explanations for specific aspects of human biological diversity. *Biological differences are real, important, and apparent to us all.* Modern scientists find it most productive to seek explanations for this diversity, rather than trying to pigeonhole people into categories called races. Certainly, human groups do vary biologically—for example, in their genetic attributes. But often we observe gradual, rather than abrupt, shifts in gene frequencies between neighboring groups. Such gradual genetic shifts are called **clines,** and they are incompatible with discrete and separate races.

What is race anyway? In theory, a biological race would be a geographically isolated subdivision of a species. Such a *subspecies* would be capable of interbreeding with other subspecies of the same species, but it would not actually do so because of its geographic isolation. Some biologists also use "race" to refer to "breeds," as of dogs or roses. Thus, a pit bull and a chihuahua would be different races of dogs. Such domesticated "races" have been bred by humans for generations. Humanity (*Homo sapiens*) lacks such races because human populations have not been isolated enough from one another to develop into such discrete groups. Nor have humans experienced controlled breeding like that which has created the various kinds of dogs and roses.

A race is supposed to reflect shared genetic material (inherited from a common ancestor), but early scholars instead used phenotypical traits (usually skin color) for racial classification. Phenotype refers to an organism's evident traits, its "manifest biology"—anatomy and physiology. Humans display hundreds of evident (detectable) physical traits. They range from skin color, hair form, eye color, and facial features (which are visible) to blood groups, color blindness, and enzyme production (which become evident through testing).

Racial classifications based on phenotype raise the problem of deciding which trait(s) should be primary. Should races be defined by height, weight, body shape, facial features, teeth, skull form, or skin color? Like their fellow citizens, early European and

The photos in this chapter illustrate only a small part of the range of human biological diversity. Shown here is a Bai minority woman, from Shapin, in China's Yunnan province.

living anthropology **VIDEOS**

Origins of the Modern Concepts of Race,
www.mhhe.com/kottak

This clip features Dr. Jonathan Marks, a prominent biological anthropologist, discussing the origin and development of the problematic concept of race. As Marks points out, racial classification rests on the universal human tendency to classify. According to the clip, what historical political development also contributed to the race concept? Besides arbitrary physical characteristics, what are other ways of classifying human beings? How many human races did Linnaeus recognize? What, according to the clip, is the proper number of races into which humans should be categorized?

American scientists gave priority to skin color. Many schoolbooks and encyclopedias still proclaim the existence of three great races: the white, the black, and the yellow. This overly simplistic classification was compatible with the political use of race during the colonial period of the late 19th and early 20th centuries. Such a tripartite scheme kept white Europeans neatly separate from their African, Asian, and Native American subjects. Colonial empires began to break up, and scientists began to question established racial categories, after World War II.

racial classification
Assigning organisms to categories (purportedly) based on common ancestry.

cline
Gradual shift in gene (allele) frequencies between neighboring populations.

Races Are Not Biologically Distinct

History and politics aside, one obvious problem with "color-based" racial labels is that the terms don't accurately describe skin color. "White" people are more pink, beige, or tan than white. "Black" people are various shades of brown, and "yellow" people are tan or beige. But these terms have been dignified by more scientific-*sounding* synonyms: Caucasoid, Negroid, and Mongoloid.

Another problem with the tripartite scheme is that many populations don't fit neatly into any one of the three "great races." For example, where would one put the Polynesians? *Polynesia* is a triangle of South Pacific islands formed by Hawaii to the north, Easter Island to the east, and New Zealand to the southwest. Does the "bronze" skin color of Polynesians connect them to the Caucasoids or to the

A Native American: a Chiquitanos Indian woman from Bolivia.

A palace guard in Mysore, Tamil Nadu, southern India.

A young man from the Marquesas Islands in Polynesia.

Mongoloids? Some scientists, recognizing this problem, enlarged the original tripartite scheme to include the Polynesian "race." Native Americans presented a similar problem. Were they red or yellow? Some scientists added a fifth race—the "red," or Amerindian—to the major racial groups.

Many people in southern India have dark skins, but scientists have been reluctant to classify them with "black" Africans because of their Caucasoid facial features and hair form. Some, therefore, have created a separate race for these people. What about the Australian aborigines, hunters and gatherers native to what has been, throughout human history, the most isolated continent? By skin color, one might place some Native Australians in the same race as tropical Africans. However, similarities to Europeans in hair color (light or reddish) and facial features have led some scientists to classify them as Caucasoids. But there is no evidence that Australians are closer genetically to either of these groups than they are to Asians. Recognizing this problem, scientists often regard Native Australians as a separate race.

Finally, consider the San ("Bushmen") of the Kalahari Desert in southern Africa. Scientists have perceived their skin color as varying from brown to yellow. Some who regard San skin as "yellow" have placed them in the same category as Asians. In theory, people of the same race share more recent common ancestry with each other than they do with anyone else. But there is no evidence for recent common ancestry between San and Asians. Somewhat more reasonably, some scholars assign the San to the Capoid race (from the Cape of Good Hope), which is seen as being different from other groups inhabiting tropical Africa.

Similar problems arise when any single trait is used for racial classification. An attempt to use facial features, height, weight, or any other phenotypical trait is fraught with difficulties. For example, consider the *Nilotes,* natives of the upper Nile region of

Uganda and South Sudan. Nilotes tend to be tall and to have long, narrow noses. Certain Scandinavians also are tall, with similar noses. Given the distance between their homelands, however, there is no reason to assume that Nilotes and Scandinavians are more closely related to each other than either is to shorter and nearer populations with different kinds of noses.

Would it be better to base racial classifications on a combination of physical traits? This would avoid some of the problems just mentioned, but others would arise. First, skin color, stature, skull form, and facial features (nose form, eye shape, lip thickness) don't go together as a unit. For example, people with dark skin may be tall or short and have hair ranging from straight to very curly. Dark-haired populations may have light or dark skin, along with various skull forms, facial features, and body sizes and shapes. The number of combinations is very large, and the amount that heredity (versus environment) contributes to such phenotypical traits is often unclear (see also Anemone 2011).

Genetic Markers Don't Correlate with Phenotype

The analysis of human DNA indicates that fully 94 percent of human genetic variation occurs within so-called "races." Considering conventional geographic "racial" groupings such as Africans, Asians, and Europeans, there is only about 6 percent variation in genes from one group to the other. In other words, there is much greater variation within each of the traditional "races" than between them. Humans are much more alike genetically than are other hominoids (the living apes). This suggests a recently shared common ancestor (perhaps as recent as 70,000 to 50,000 years) for all members of modern *Homo sapiens*. Sampling the mitochondrial DNA (mtDNA) of various populations, Rebecca Cann, Mark Stoneking, and Allan C. Wilson (1987) concluded that humans are genetically uniform overall, suggesting recent common ancestry. The fact that African populations are the most diverse genetically provides evidence that Africa was the site where the human diaspora originated.

Contemporary work in genomics has allowed scientists to construct regional and global phylogenetic trees based on shared genetic markers. Such trees are based on mitochondrial DNA (mtDNA) (sampling females) and the Y chromosome (sampling males). As the human genome becomes better known,

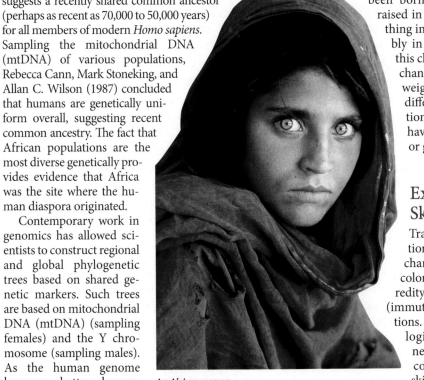
An Afghan woman.

molecular anthropologists refine their models of genetic relationships among humans and how they dispersed. A **haplogroup** is a lineage or branch of such a genetic tree marked by one or more specific genetic mutations. For example, the global mtDNA tree includes branches known as M and N (among others). The Y chromosome tree includes branches known as C and F (among others). Those four branches (either M or N for mtDNA and either C or F for the Y chromosome) are known to be associated with the spread of modern humans out of Africa between 70,000 and 50,000 B.P. (see this chapter's "Appreciating Diversity"). Because Native Australians share those four branches, they are known to be part of that diaspora. The Americas were settled (from Asia) much later than Australia by multiple haplogroups, which reached North America at different times and came by different routes.

Although long-term genetic markers do exist, they don't correlate neatly with phenotype. Phenotypical similarities and differences aren't precisely or even necessarily correlated with genetic relationships. Because of changes in the environment that affect individuals during growth and development, the range of phenotypes characteristic of a population may change without any genetic change whatsoever. There are several examples. In the early 20th century, the anthropologist Franz Boas (1940/1966) described changes in skull form (e.g., toward rounder heads) among the children of Europeans who had migrated to North America. The reason for this was not a change in genes, for the European immigrants tended to marry among themselves. Also, some of their children had been born in Europe and merely raised in the United States. Something in the environment, probably in the diet, was producing this change. We know now that changes in average height and weight produced by dietary differences in a few generations are common and may have nothing to do with race or genetics.

Explaining Skin Color

Traditional racial classification assumed that biological characteristics such as skin color were determined by heredity and that they were stable (immutable) over many generations. We now know that a biological similarity doesn't necessarily indicate recent common ancestry. Dark skin color, for example, can

haplogroup
Lineage or branch of a genetic tree marked by one or more specific genetic mutations.

Australian Aborigine Hair Tells a Story of Human Migration

Before the 17th century, Native Australians, aka Australian Aborigines, lived on the world's most isolated inhabited continent. The recent analysis of one sample of Aboriginal DNA suggests that ancestral Australians branched off from ancestral Europeans and Asians between 70,000 and 50,000 years ago and had little contact with outsiders until the formation of the modern world system. Tropical Australians retained the dark skin color of their African forebears because they never left the tropics during their gradual migration from Africa to Australia.

A lock of hair, collected by a British anthropologist a century ago, has yielded the first genome of an Australian Aborigine, along with insights into the earliest migration from the ancestral human homeland somewhere in northeast Africa.

Indigenous Australians in ceremonial dress on Tiwi Island, Northern Territory, Australia. Northern Australia is in the tropics.

The Aboriginal genome bolsters earlier genetic evidence showing that once the Aborigines' ancestors arrived in Australia, some 50,000 years ago, they somehow kept the whole continent to themselves without admitting any outsiders.

The Aborigines are thus direct descendants of the first modern humans to leave Africa, without any genetic mixture from other races so far as can be seen at present. Their dark skin reflects an African origin and a migration and residence in latitudes near the equator, unlike Europeans and Asians whose ancestors gained the paler skin necessary for living in northern latitudes.

"Aboriginal Australians likely have one of the oldest continuous population histories outside sub-Saharan Africa today," say the researchers who analyzed the hair, a group led by Eske Willerslev of the Natural History Museum of Denmark.

Dr. Willerslev is an expert at working with ancient DNA, which is usually highly fragmented. Use of the ancient hair reduced the possibility of mixture with European genes and sidestepped the political difficulties of obtaining DNA from living Aborigines.

The DNA in the Aboriginal genome, when compared with DNA from other peoples around the world, shows that when modern humans first migrated out of Africa the ancestors of the Aborigines split away from the main group very early, and before Europeans and East Asians split from each other. . . .

Based on the rate of mutation in DNA, the geneticists estimate that the Aborigines split from the ancestors of all Eurasians some 70,000 years ago, and that the ancestors of Europeans and East Asians split from each other about 30,000 years ago.

But the genetic data offers no information as to where these population splits may have occurred, whether in India or even earlier, before the migratory group had left Africa. . . . Genetic dates are based on a mixture of statistics and best guesses, but the split times calculated by the Danish team are compatible with the more reliable archaeological dates, which record the earliest known human presence in Australia at 44,000 years ago. The Aborigines' ancestors could have arrived several thousand years before this date. . . .

The first inhabitants of Australia must have possessed advanced boat-building technology to cross from the nearest point in Asia to Sahul, the ancient continent that included Australia, New Guinea and Tasmania until the rise of sea level that occurred at the end of the last ice age, 10,000 years ago. But there is no archaeological evidence for boats. . . .

Despite the Aborigines' genetic isolation, there is evidence of some profound cultural exchange that occurred around 6,000 years ago. The stone tools become more sophisticated, and the population increased. The Aborigines did not domesticate plants or animals, but a wild dog, the dingo, first appears in the archaeological record at this time. . . .

Most of Australia is a forbidding desert, and this barrier may have been the downfall of most invasions, whether of people or of animals. . . . The ancestors of the Aborigines were lucky enough to find their way south, where there is more vegetation, and the dingo is a skillful hunter, able to look after itself. . . .

be shared by tropical Africans and Australians for reasons other than common heredity. Scientists have made considerable progress in explaining variation in human skin color, along with many other features of human biological diversity. We shift now from racial classification to explanation, in which natural selection plays a key role.

Natural selection, remember, is the process by which the forms most fit to survive and reproduce in a given environment do so. Over the generations, the less fit organisms die out, and the favored types survive by producing more offspring. The role of natural selection in producing variation in skin color will illustrate the explanatory approach to human biological diversity. Comparable explanations have been provided for many other aspects of human biological variation, as we'll see later in this chapter.

Skin color is a complex biological trait—influenced by several genes (see Jablonski 2006). Just how many genes is not known. **Melanin,** the primary determinant of human skin color, is a chemical substance manufactured in the epidermis, or outer skin layer. The melanin cells of darker-skinned people produce more and larger granules of melanin than do those of lighter-skinned people. By screening out ultraviolet (UV) radiation from the sun, melanin offers protection against a variety of maladies, including sunburn and skin cancer.

Before the 16th century, most of the world's very dark-skinned peoples lived in the **tropics,** a belt extending about 23 degrees north and south of the equator, between the Tropic of Cancer and the Tropic of Capricorn. The association between dark skin color and a tropical habitat existed throughout the Old World, where humans and their ancestors have lived for millions of years. The darkest populations of Africa evolved not in shady equatorial forests but in sunny open grassland, or savanna, country.

Outside the tropics, skin color tends to be lighter. Moving north in Africa, for example, there is a gradual transition from dark brown to medium brown. Average skin color continues to lighten as one moves through the Middle East, into southern Europe, through central Europe, and to the north. South of the tropics skin color also is lighter. In the Americas, by contrast, tropical populations don't have very dark skin. This is the case because the settlement of the New World by light-skinned Asian ancestors of Native Americans was relatively recent, probably dating back no more than twenty thousand years.

How, aside from migrations, can we explain the geographic distribution of human skin color? Natural selection provides an answer. In the tropics, intense UV radiation poses a series of threats, including severe sunburn, that make light skin color an adaptive disadvantage (Recap 6.1 summarizes those threats). By damaging sweat glands, sunburn reduces the body's ability to perspire and thus to regulate its own temperature (thermoregulation). Sunburn also can increase susceptibility to disease. Melanin, nature's own sunscreen, confers a selective advantage

(i.e., a better chance to survive and reproduce) on darker-skinned people living in the tropics. (Today, light-skinned people manage to survive in the tropics by staying indoors and by using cultural products, such as umbrellas and lotions, to screen sunlight). Yet another disadvantage of having light skin color in the tropics is that exposure to UV radiation can cause skin cancer (Blum 1961).

Many years ago, W. F. Loomis (1967) focused on the role of UV radiation in stimulating the manufacture (synthesis) of vitamin D by the human body. The unclothed human body can produce its own vitamin D when exposed to sufficient sunlight. However, in a cloudy environment that also is so cold that people have to clothe themselves much of the year (such as northern Europe, where very light skin color evolved), clothing interferes with the body's manufacture of vitamin D. The ensuing shortage of vitamin D diminishes the absorption of calcium in the intestines. A nutritional disease known as **rickets,** which softens and deforms the bones, may develop. In women, deformation of the pelvic bones from rickets can interfere with childbirth. In cold northern areas, light skin color maximizes the absorption of UV radiation and the synthesis of vitamin D by the few parts of the body that are exposed to direct sunlight during northern winters. There has been selection against dark skin color in northern areas because melanin screens out UV radiation.

This natural selection continues today: East Asians who have migrated recently from India and Pakistan to northern areas of the United Kingdom have a higher incidence of rickets and osteoporosis (also related to vitamin D and calcium deficiency) than the general British population. A related illustration involves Eskimos (Inuit) and other indigenous inhabitants of northern Alaska and northern Canada. According to Nina Jablonski (quoted in Iqbal 2002), "Looking at Alaska, one would think that the native people should be pale as ghosts." One reason they aren't is that they haven't inhabited this region very long in terms of geological time. Even more important, their traditional diet, rich in fish oils, supplied sufficient vitamin D so as to make a reduction in pigmentation unnecessary. However, and again illustrating natural selection at work today, "when these people don't eat their aboriginal diets of fish and marine mammals, they suffer tremendously high rates of vitamin D–deficiency diseases such as rickets in children and osteoporosis in adults" (Jablonski quoted in Iqbal 2002). Far from being immutable, skin color can become an evolutionary liability very quickly.

According to Jablonski and George Chaplin (2000; see also Jablonski 2006), another key factor explaining the geographic distribution of skin color involves the effects of UV on folate, an essential nutrient that the human body manufactures from folic acid. Folate is needed for cell division and to

melanin
"Natural sunscreen" produced by skin cells responsible for pigmentation.

tropics
Zone between 23 degrees north (Tropic of Cancer) and 23 degrees south (Tropic of Capricorn) of the equator.

rickets
Vitamin D deficiency marked by bone deformation.

anthropology **ATLAS**

http://www.mhhe.com/anthromaps Map 7 plots the distribution of human skin color in relation to ultraviolet variation from the sun.

Also shown are cultural alternatives that can make up for biological disadvantages and examples of natural selection (NS) operating today in relation to skin color.

		CULTURAL ALTERNATIVES	NS IN ACTION TODAY
DARK SKIN COLOR	Melanin is natural sunscreen		
Advantage	In tropics: Screens out UV radiation		
	Reduces susceptibility to folate destruction and thus to NTDs, including spina bifida		
	Prevents sunburn and thus enhances sweating and thermoregulation		
	Reduces disease susceptibility		
	Reduces risk of skin cancer		
Disadvantage	Outside tropics: Reduces UV absorption		
	Increases susceptibility to rickets, osteoporosis	Foods, vitamin D supplements	East Asians in northern UK Inuit with modern diets
LIGHT SKIN COLOR	No natural sunscreen		
Advantage	Outside tropics: Admits UV		
	Body manufactures vitamin D and thus prevents rickets and osteoporosis		
Disadvantage	Increases susceptibility to folate destruction and thus to NTDs, including spina bifida	Folic acid/folate supplements	Whites still have more NTDs
	Impaired spermatogenesis		
	Increases susceptibility to sunburn and thus to impaired sweating and poor thermoregulation	Shelter, sunscreens, lotions, etc.	
	Increases disease susceptibility		
	Increases susceptibility to skin cancer		

produce new DNA. Pregnant women require large amounts of folate to support rapid cell division in the embryo, and there is a direct connection between folate and individual reproductive success. Folate deficiency causes neural tube defects (NTDs) in human embryos. NTDs are marked by the incomplete closure of the neural tube, so the spine and spinal cord fail to develop completely. One NTD, anencephaly (with the brain an exposed mass), results in stillbirth or death soon after delivery. With spina bifida, another NTD, survival rates are higher, but babies have severe disabilities, including paralysis. NTDs are the second-most-common human birth defect after cardiac abnormalities. Today, women of reproductive age are advised to take folate supplements to prevent serious birth defects such as spina bifida.

Dark skin color, as we have seen, is adaptive in the tropics because it protects against such UV hazards as sunburn and its consequences. UV radiation also destroys folate in the human body. Preventing this destruction, melanin has the additional adaptive advantage of conserving folate and thus protecting against NTDs, which are much more common in light-skinned than in darker-skinned populations (Jablonski and Chaplin 2000). Studies confirm that Africans and African Americans have a low incidence of severe folate deficiency, even among individuals with marginal nutritional status. Folate also plays a role in another process that is central to reproduction, spermatogenesis—the production of sperm. In mice and rats, folate deficiency can cause male sterility; it may well play a similar role in humans.

Today, of course, cultural alternatives to biological adaptation permit light-skinned people to survive in the tropics and darker-skinned people to live in the far north. People can clothe themselves and seek shelter from the sun; they can use artificial sunscreens if they lack the natural protection that melanin provides. Dark-skinned people living in the north can, indeed must, get vitamin D from their diet or take supplements. Today, pregnant women are routinely advised to take folic acid or folate supplements as a hedge against NTDs. Even so, light skin color still is correlated with a higher incidence of spina bifida.

Jablonski and Chaplin (2000) explain variation in human skin color as resulting from a balancing act

Spina bifida, a congenital (birth) disorder that leaves a portion of the spinal cord exposed, can be treated with surgery and physiotherapy. Shown here, an outing, including fishing, for children with spina bifida in Lee's Summit, Missouri. Why is light skin color correlated with a higher incidence of spina bifida?

experience. It explains how human variation differs from race, when and why the idea of race was invented, and how race and racism affects our everyday lives. The program's three key messages are that (1) race is a recent human invention, (2) race is about culture, not biology, and (3) race and racism are embedded in institutions and everyday life. For more on anthropological approaches to race and ethnicity, see Chapter 15, "Ethnicity and Race," in this book.

HUMAN BIOLOGICAL ADAPTATION

This section considers several additional examples of human biological diversity that reflect adaptation to environmental stresses, such as disease, diet, and climate. There is abundant evidence for human genetic adaptation and thus for evolution (change in gene frequency) through selection working in specific environments. One example is the adaptive value of the Hb^S heterozygote and its spread in malarial environments, which was discussed in Chapter 5. Adaptation and evolution go on in specific environments. There is no generally or ideally adaptive allele and no perfect phenotype. Nor can an allele be assumed to be maladaptive for all times and all places. We've seen that even Hb^S, which produces a lethal anemia, has a selective advantage in the heterozygous form in malarial environments.

Also, alleles that once were maladaptive may lose their disadvantage if the environment shifts. Color blindness (disadvantageous for hunters and forest dwellers) and a form of genetically determined diabetes are examples. Today's environment contains medical techniques that allow people with such conditions to live fairly normal lives. Alelles that once were maladaptive have thereby become neutral with respect to selection. With thousands of human genes now known, new genetic traits are discovered almost every day. Such discoveries tend to focus on genetic abnormalities, because of their medical and treatment implications.

between the evolutionary needs to (1) protect against all UV hazards (thus favoring dark skin in the tropics) and (2) have an adequate supply of vitamin D (thus favoring lighter skin outside the tropics). This discussion of skin color shows that common ancestry, the presumed basis of race, is not the only reason for biological similarities. Natural selection, still at work today, makes a major contribution to variations in human skin color, as well as to many other human biological differences and similarities.

The AAA RACE Project

To broaden public understanding of race and human variation, the American Anthropological Association (AAA) offers its RACE Project. A key component of this project is the award-winning public education program titled "RACE Are We So Different?" The program, which is geared at middle school–aged children through adults, includes an interactive website and a traveling museum exhibit. You can visit the interactive website right now at www.understandingrace.org/home.html. The museum exhibit may be showing somewhere near you. For its touring schedule visit this website: http://www.understandingrace.org/about/tour.html.

"RACE Are We So Different?" examines race through the eyes of history, science, and lived

Genes and Disease

The World Health Organization (WHO), based in Geneva, Switzerland, reports that about one billion people worldwide are affected by one or more neglected tropical diseases. These diseases are named "neglected" because they persist exclusively in the poorest and the most marginalized populations. WHO's most recent annual World Malaria Report (2011) reported 216 million cases of malaria worldwide. Schistosomiasis (snail fever), a waterborne parasitic disease, affects more than 200 million people. Over 120 million people have filariasis, which causes elephantiasis—lymphatic obstruction leading to the enlargement of body parts, particularly the

Before the 16th century, almost all the very dark-skinned populations of the world lived in the tropics, as does this Samburu woman from Kenya.

Very light skin color, illustrated in this photo of Prince Harry, maximizes absorption of ultraviolet radiation by those few parts of the body exposed to direct sunlight during northern winters. This helps prevent rickets.

After food production emerged around ten thousand years ago, infectious diseases posed a mounting risk and eventually became the foremost cause of human mortality. Food production favors infection for several reasons. Cultivation sustains larger, denser populations and a more sedentary lifestyle than does hunting and gathering. People live closer to each other and to their own wastes, making it easier for microbes to survive and to find hosts. Domesticated animals also transmit diseases to people.

Until 1977, when the last case of smallpox was reported, smallpox had been a major threat to humans and a determinant of blood group frequencies (Diamond 1990, 1997). The smallpox virus is a mutation from one of the pox viruses that plague such domesticated animals as cows, sheep, goats, horses, and pigs. Smallpox appeared in human beings after people and animals started living together. Smallpox epidemics have played important roles in world history, often killing one-fourth to one-half of the affected populations. Smallpox contributed to Sparta's defeat of Athens in 430 B.C.E. and to the decline of the Roman empire after C.E. 160.

The ABO blood groups have figured in human resistance to smallpox. Blood is typed according to the protein and sugar compounds on the surface of the red blood cells. Different substances (compounds) distinguish between type A and type B blood. Type A cells trigger the production of *antibodies* in B blood, so that A cells clot in B blood. The different substances work like chemical passwords; they help us distinguish our own cells from invading cells, including microbes we ought to destroy. The surfaces of some microbes have substances similar to ABO blood group substances. We don't produce antibodies to substances similar to those on our own blood cells. We can think of this as a clever evolutionary trick by the microbes to deceive their hosts, because we don't normally develop antibodies against our own biochemistry.

People with A or AB blood are more susceptible to smallpox than are people with type B or type O. Presumably this is because a substance on the smallpox virus mimics the type A substance, permitting the virus to slip by the defenses of the type A individual. By contrast, type B and type O individuals produce antibodies against smallpox because they recognize it as a foreign substance.

The relation between type A blood and susceptibility to smallpox was first suggested by the low frequencies of the A allele in areas of India and Africa where smallpox had been endemic. A comparative study done in rural India in 1965–1966, during a virulent smallpox epidemic, did much to confirm this relationship. Drs. F. Vogel and M. R. Chakravartti analyzed blood samples from smallpox victims and their uninfected siblings (Diamond 1990). The researchers focused on 415 infected children, none ever vaccinated against smallpox. All but eight of these children had an uninfected (also unvaccinated) sibling.

legs and scrotum (check out the website of the World Health Organization at www.who.int/home/).

Microbes have been major selective agents for humans, particularly before the arrival of modern medicine. Some people are genetically more susceptible to certain diseases than others are, and the distribution of human blood types continues to change in response to natural selection.

The results of the study were clear: Susceptibility to smallpox varied with ABO type. Of the 415 infected children, 261 had the A allele; 154 lacked it. Among their 407 uninfected siblings, the ratio was reversed. Only 80 had the A allele; 327 lacked it. The researchers calculated that a type A or type AB person had a seven times greater chance of getting smallpox than did an O or B person.

In most human populations, the O allele is more common than A and B combined. A is most common in Europe; B frequencies are highest in Asia. Since smallpox was once widespread in the Old World, we might wonder why natural selection didn't eliminate the A allele entirely. The answer appears to be this: Other diseases spared the type A people and penalized those with other blood groups.

For example, type O people seem to be especially susceptible to the bubonic plague—the "Black Death" that killed a third of the population of medieval Europe. Type O people also are more likely to get cholera, which has killed as many people in India as smallpox has. On the other hand, the O allele may protect against syphilis, which originated in the New World. Frequencies of type O blood are very high among the native populations of Central and South America. The distribution of human blood groups appears to represent a compromise among the selective effects of many diseases.

Associations between ABO blood type and noninfectious disorders also have been noted. Type O individuals are most susceptible to duodenal and gastric ulcers. Type A individuals seem most prone to stomach and cervical cancer and ovarian tumors. However, since these noninfectious disorders tend to occur after reproduction has ended, their relevance to adaptation and evolution through natural selection is doubtful.

In the case of diseases for which there are no cures, genetic resistance maintains its significance. There is genetic variation in susceptibility to the HIV virus, for example. Longitudinal studies have shown that people exposed to HIV vary in their risk of developing AIDS and in the rate at which the disease progresses. Genetic variation no doubt will help determine differential resistance and susceptibility to microbes that may emerge or mutate in the future. (This chapter's "Focus on Globalization" discusses the global spread of infectious diseases.)

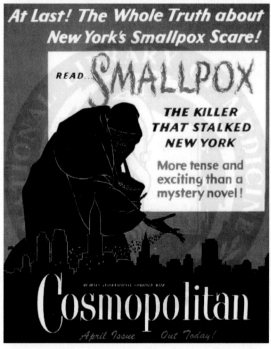

In New York City in 1947, the appearance of nine cases of smallpox, including two deaths, spurred a very successful mass vaccination program. Shown here, lines of people wait to be vaccinated at the New York Health Department on April 14, 1947. The threat made the cover of *Cosmopolitan* magazine.

Facial Features

Natural selection also affects facial features. For instance, long noses seem to be adaptive in arid areas (Brace 2005; Weiner 1954), because membranes and blood vessels inside the nose moisten the air as it is breathed in. Long noses also are adaptive in cold environments, because blood vessels warm the air as it is breathed in. This nose form distances the brain, which is sensitive to bitter cold, from raw outer air. These were adaptive biological features for humans who lived in cold climates before the invention of central heating.

The association between nose form and temperature is recognized as **Thomson's nose rule** (Thomson and Buxton 1923), which shows up statistically. In plotting the geographic distribution of nose length among human populations who have lived for many generations in the areas they now inhabit, the average nose does tend to be longer in areas with lower mean annual temperatures.

Thomson's nose rule Average nose length increases in cold areas.

focus on GLOBALIZATION

A Devastating Encounter in the Columbian Exchange

The Columbian exchange (named for Christopher Columbus) was a key early form of globalization, because it forever linked our globe's western and eastern hemispheres. The term refers to the exchange of products, populations, and pathogens between the Old World and the New World that occurred after Columbus reached the Americas in 1492.

One devastating aspect of the Columbian exchange was the global spread of diseases previously confined to the Old World. Having lived with these pathogens for generations, Old World populations had developed various forms of immunity to many of them. Native Americans had no such resistance to Old World diseases, which included smallpox, chicken pox, measles, malaria, yellow fever, cholera, typhoid, bubonic plague, influenza, and the common cold. Only syphilis, as we learned in Chapter 5, moved the other way—from the New World to the Old.

By debilitating and decimating the Aztecs of Mexico and the Inca of Peru, severe smallpox epidemics helped the Spanish conquer those peoples and their territories. Up to 90 percent of the population of the New World may have perished from Old World pathogens between 1500 and 1650 (Nunn and Qian 2010).

The African slave trade emerged in the context of Native American depopulation and the demand for human labor to produce commodities on New World plantations. Plantation economies outside the southern United States (where cotton was a New World domesticate) were based mainly on Old World crops (especially sugar and tobacco) introduced to the Americas and the Caribbean as part of the Columbian exchange. About twelve million human beings were involuntarily transported from Africa to the New World during the centuries of the Atlantic slave trade—the 16th through the 19th centuries.

Europeans from Spain, Portugal, the Netherlands, England, and France extended their colonial empires from the Americas to Africa and Asia. Europeans had a degree of genetic resistance to many Old World pathogens, but not to malaria—the scourge of the tropics. Quinine was a New World product that—again through the Columbian exchange—eventually offered Europeans a degree of protection against malaria. Europeans might never have been able to maintain colonial empires in the tropics of Africa, Asia, and South America without quinine (Nunn and Qian 2010). This is yet another way in which western expansion, and ultimately the formation of the modern world system, depended on the Columbian exchange.

Globalization remains an important factor in the spread of diseases today, as anyone knows who has seen the movie *Contagion*. In real life, as described in Chapter 5, the H1N1 virus, known originally as swine flu, gained attention as a pandemic in 2009–2010. The spread of pathogens from animals (like pigs, or swine) to humans became more common after people began living in close proximity to domesticated pigs, poultry, sheep, and cattle. These animals, originally domesticated in the Old World, now have a global distribution. How have humans adapted to the diseases their animals transmit?

Other facial features also illustrate adaptation to selective forces. Among contemporary humans, average tooth size is largest among Native Australian hunters and gatherers, for whom large teeth had an adaptive advantage, given a diet based on foods with a considerable amount of sand and grit. People with small teeth—if false teeth and sand-free foods are unavailable—can't feed themselves as effectively as people with more massive dentition can (see Brace 2005).

Size and Body Build

Certain body builds have adaptive advantages for particular environments. In 1847, the German biologist Karl Christian Bergmann observed that within the same species of warm-blooded animals, populations with smaller individuals are more often found in warm climates, while those with greater bulk, or mass, are found in colder regions. The relation between body weight and temperature is summarized in **Bergmann's rule**: The smaller of two bodies similar in shape has more surface area per unit of weight. Therefore, it sheds heat more efficiently. (Heat loss occurs on the body's surface—the skin perspires.) Average body size tends to increase in cold areas and to decrease in hot ones because big bodies hold heat better than small ones do. To be more precise, in a large sample of native populations, average adult male weight increased by 0.66 pound (0.3 kilogram) for every 1 degree Fahrenheit fall in mean annual temperature (Roberts 1953; Steegman 1975). The "pygmies" and the San, who live in hot climates and weigh only 90 pounds on the average, illustrate this relation in reverse.

Body shape differences also reflect adaptation to temperature through natural selection. The relationship between temperature and body shape in animals and birds was first recognized in 1877 by the zoologist J. A. Allen. **Allen's rule** states that the relative size of protruding body parts—ears, tails, bills, fingers, toes, limbs, and so on—increases with temperature. Among humans, slender bodies with long digits and limbs are advantageous in tropical climates. Such bodies increase body surface relative to mass and allow for more efficient heat dissipation. Among the cold-adapted Eskimos or Inuit, the opposite phenotype is found. Short limbs and stocky bodies serve to conserve heat. Cold-area populations tend to have larger chests and shorter arms than do people from warm areas (Roberts 1953).

This discussion of adaptive relationships between climate and body size and shape illustrates that natural selection may achieve the same effect in different ways. East African Nilotes, who live in a hot area, have tall, linear bodies with elongated extremities that increase surface area relative to mass and thus maximize heat dissipation (illustrating Allen's rule). Among the "pygmies," the reduction of body size achieves the same result (illustrating Bergmann's rule). Similarly, the large bodies of northern Europeans and the compact stockiness of the Inuit serve the same function of heat conservation.

Similarly, as we see in "Appreciating Anthropology," human populations use different, but equally effective, biological means of adapting to the environmental stresses associated with high altitudes. Andeans have adapted to thin air by developing the ability to carry more oxygen in each red blood cell, compared with people who live at sea level. Having more hemoglobin to carry oxygen counterbalances the effects of hypoxia. Tibetans, in contrast, increase their oxygen intake by taking more breaths per minute than do people who live at sea level. Also, their lungs synthesize large amounts of nitric oxide from the air they breathe. The nitric oxide works to expand the diameter of their blood vessels, so that Tibetans offset low oxygen content in their blood with increased blood flow. Ethiopian highlanders, by contrast, use none of these mechanisms. Compared with sea-level peoples, they don't breathe more rapidly, synthesize nitric oxide more effectively, or have a higher hemoglobin count. The exact biological mechanisms that enable Ethiopians to survive at high altitudes are being investigated.

Lactose Tolerance

Many biological traits that illustrate human adaptation are not under simple genetic control. Genetic determination of such traits may be only partial, or several genes may interact to influence the trait in question. Sometimes there is a known genetic component, but the trait also responds to stresses encountered during growth. We speak of **phenotypical adaptation** when adaptive changes occur during an individual's lifetime. Phenotypical adaptation is made possible by biological plasticity—our ability to change in response to the environments we encounter as we grow (see Bogin 2001; Frisancho 1993).

One genetically determined biochemical difference among human groups involves the ability to digest large amounts of milk—an adaptive advantage when other foods are scarce and milk is available, as it is in dairying societies. All milk, whatever its source, contains a complex sugar called *lactose*. The digestion of milk depends on an enzyme called *lactase*, which works in the small intestine. Among all mammals except humans and some of their pets, lactase production ceases after weaning, so that these animals can no longer digest milk.

Lactase production and the ability to tolerate milk vary between populations. About 90 percent of northern Europeans and their descendants are lactose tolerant; they can digest several glasses of milk with no difficulty. Similarly, about 80 percent of two African populations, the Tutsi of Rwanda and Burundi in East Africa and the Fulani of Nigeria in West Africa, produce lactase and digest milk easily. Both of these groups traditionally have been herders.

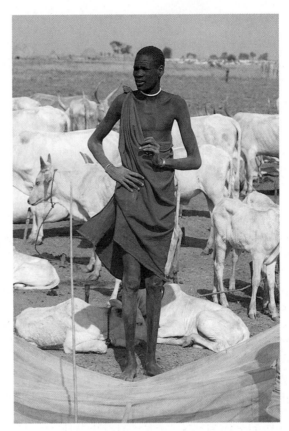

This Nilotic man, a Nuer herder from Sudan, has a tall linear body with elongated extremities (note his fingers). Such proportioning increases the surface area relative to mass and thus dissipates heat (Allen's rule). What other body form can achieve the same result?

Bergmann's rule Larger bodies are found in colder areas and smaller bodies in warmer ones.

Allen's rule Protruding body parts are bigger in warmer areas.

phenotypical adaptation Adaptive biological changes during an individual's lifetime.

Tatigat, an Inuk man, shown inside his home at Igloolik, Nunavut, Canada. Compact stockiness, fur coats, well-sealed dwellings, and indoor heating systems are biological and cultural ways of adapting to a very cold environment.

Adapting to Thin Air

Anthropologists study the varied ways in which humans adapt, biologically and culturally, to environmental stresses, including disease, temperature, humidity, sunlight, and altitude—as described here. This account describes how anthropologists are studying the dramatically different ways in which three populations have adapted to high altitudes. Working with these populations, in Tibet, Ethiopia, and the Andes, anthropologists follow many lines of evidence—archaeological, biological, and climatological—to answer questions about social, cultural, and biological adaptations. Anthropologists know that the biological diversity we observe among contemporary and prehistoric humans has many causes. This chapter examines those causes, while rejecting attempts to pigeonhole humans into discrete biological categories called races.

Prehistoric and contemporary human populations living at altitudes of at least 8,000 feet (2,500 meters) above sea level may provide unique insights into human evolution, reports an interdisciplinary group of scientists.

Indigenous highlanders living in the Andean Altiplano in South America, in the Tibetan Plateau in Asia, and at the highest elevations of the Ethiopian Highlands in east Africa have evolved three distinctly different biological adaptations for surviving in the oxygen-thin air found at high altitude.

"To have examples of three geographically dispersed populations adapting in different ways to the same stress is very unusual," said Cynthia Beall, a physical anthropologist at Case Western Reserve University in Cleveland, Ohio.

"From an evolutionary standpoint the question becomes, Why do these differences exist? . . ."

"High-altitude populations offer a unique natural lab that allows us to follow [many] lines of evidence—archaeological, biological, climatological—to answer intriguing questions about social, cultural, and biological adaptations," said Mark Aldenderfer, an archaeologist at the University of California, Santa Barbara. . . .

The Andean and Tibetan plateaus rise some 13,000 feet (4 kilometers) above sea level. As prehistoric hunter-gatherers moved into these environments, they . . . likely suffered acute hypoxia, a condition created by a diminished supply of oxygen to body tissues. At high altitudes the air is much thinner than at sea level. As a result, a person inhales fewer oxygen molecules with each breath. Symptoms of hypoxia, sometimes known as mountain sickness, include headaches, vomiting, sleeplessness, impaired thinking, and an inability to sustain long periods of physical activity. At elevations above 25,000 feet (7,600 meters), hypoxia can kill.

The Andeans adapted to the thin air by developing an ability to carry more oxygen in each red blood cell. That is: They breathe at the same rate as people who live at sea level, but the Andeans have the ability to deliver oxygen throughout their bodies more effectively than people at sea level do.

"Andeans counter having less oxygen in every breath by having higher hemoglobin concentrations in their blood," Beall said. Hemoglobin is the protein in red blood cells that ferries oxygen through the blood system. Having more hemoglobin to carry oxygen through the blood system than people at sea level counterbalances the effects of hypoxia.

Tibetans compensate for low oxygen content much differently. They increase their oxygen intake by taking more breaths per minute than people who live at sea level.

"Andeans go the hematological route, Tibetans the respiratory route," Beall said.

In addition, Tibetans may have a second biological adaptation, which expands their blood vessels, allowing them to deliver oxygen throughout their bodies more effectively than sea-level people do.

Tibetans' lungs synthesize larger amounts of a gas called nitric oxide from the air they breathe. "One effect of nitric oxide is to increase the diameter of blood vessels, which suggests that Tibetans may offset low oxygen content in their blood with increased blood flow," Beall said.

A pilot study Beall conducted of Ethiopian highlanders living at 11,580 feet (3,530 meters) suggests that—unlike the Tibetans—they don't breathe more rapidly than people at sea level and aren't able to more effectively synthesize nitric oxide. Nor do the Ethiopians have higher hemoglobin counts than sea-level people, as the Andeans do.

Yet despite living at elevations with low oxygen content, "the Ethiopian highlanders were hardly hypoxic at all," Beall said. "I was genuinely surprised."

So what adaptation have the Ethiopian highlanders' bodies evolved to survive at high altitude? "Right now we have no clue how they do it," Beall said. . . .

Knowing how long the populations have been living at the top of the world is crucial to answering the evolutionary question of whether these adaptations are the result of differences in

the founding populations, random genetic mutations, or the passage of time.

Archaeologists, paleontologists, and climatologists are pooling their knowledge to pinpoint when some of these early migrations to the high plateaus occurred.

Aldenderfer . . . says cultural adaptations would have to occur first.

"The ability to survive in such harsh environments required control of fire, an expanded tool kit that included bone needles to make complicated clothing that protected the body in a significant way, and the cultural flexibility to change subsistence practices," he said.

Climatologists' changing understanding of the nature of the last ice age is contributing to archaeological efforts.

Ice-core and other evidence show that, rather than being a monolithic period lasting 100,000 years with frigid temperatures and glacial landscapes, the Ice Age included long periods of relatively mild weather.

"Through most of the 20th century it was thought that the Tibetan Plateau was covered by a monstrous ice sheet during the last glacial maximum, about 21,000 years ago," Aldenderfer said. "People couldn't live on an ice sheet. So archaeologists wouldn't even bother to look for sites from that time period."

[Now] knowing the Tibetan Plateau more closely resembled Arctic tundra has led to the discovery of new sites. Archaeological evidence suggests hunter-gatherers occupied the Tibetan Plateau some 25,000 to 20,000 years ago. People began moving into the Andean Altiplano around 11,500 to 11,000 years ago.

What motivated prehistoric people to move into the harsh and challenging conditions presented by high altitude?

Natives of the Himalayas, like this man (a Nepalese Sherpa), adapt biologically to their high altitude by breathing more rapidly than people who live at sea level. In addition, their lungs synthesize larger amounts of nitric oxide from the air they breathe, which increases the diameter of their blood vessels. People have lived in the Himalayas for more than 20,000 years.

"The highlands offered an attractive option with a landscape that was open and pristine," Aldenderfer said. "People probably started out moving up and down for short terms, and then gradually settled at the higher elevations."

Changing environmental conditions also created "new opportunities and new constraints," he said.

In South America, for example, the maritime environment began transforming as temperatures warmed, glaciers retreated, and sea levels rose. Large mammals such as mammoths and mastodons gradually went extinct, as did other herbivores. Warmer temperatures allowed plants and animals to move to higher elevations, creating resource-rich patches of habitat in highland areas. . . .

Similar processes likely occurred in Tibet. Prehistoric people occupied the landscape during the interglacial process, when conditions were relatively benign and hunting was plentiful, Aldenderfer said.

"Suddenly [thereafter] it gets really cold. Biomass declined precipitously. It becomes very arid because of wind-flow patterns. The landscape becomes one of very patchy vegetation, rocky. And the huge herds of gazelle, antelope, and sheep wax and wane," Aldenderfer said. "What happens? . . . Finding biological differences suggests they toughed it out and adapted."

SOURCE: Hillary Mayell, "Three High-Altitude Peoples, Three Adaptations to Thin Air," *National Geographic News*, February 25, 2004. http://news.nationalgeographic.com. © 2004 National Geographic Society. Reprinted with permission.

However, such nonherders as the Yoruba and the Igbo in Nigeria, the Baganda in Uganda, the Japanese and other Asians, Inuit, South American Indians, and many Israelis cannot digest lactose (Kretchmer 1972/1975).

Recent genetic studies have helped clarify when and how humans developed lactose tolerance. An allele known to favor adult lactose tolerance existed, but still was uncommon, in Central and Eastern Europe as recently as 3,800 years ago (Burger et al. 2007). Sarah Tishkoff and her associates found that the alleles behind lactose tolerance in East African differ from those of lactose-tolerant Europeans. Her genetic studies of forty-three East African groups suggested that three different mutations favoring lactose tolerance arose in Africa between 6,800 and 2,700 years ago (Tishkoff et al. 2007). Again we see that the same phenotype—in this case lactose tolerance—can be produced by different genotypes. As with the high altitude adaptations

described in "Appreciating Anthropology," natural selection has resulted in different selective solutions to the same environmental challenge. It also should be noted that the variable human ability to digest milk seems to be a difference of degree. Some populations can tolerate very little or no milk, but others are able to metabolize much greater quantities. People who move from no-milk or low-milk diets to high-milk diets can increase their lactose tolerance; this suggests some phenotypical adaptation.

Human biology changes constantly, even without genetic change. In this chapter we've considered ways in which humans adapt biologically to their environments, and the effects of such adaptation on human biological diversity. Modern biological anthropology seeks to explain specific aspects of human biological variation. The explanatory framework encompasses the same mechanisms—selection, mutation, drift, gene flow, and plasticity—that govern adaptation, variation, and evolution among other life forms (see Mayr 2001).

acing the COURSE

summary

1. Humans have access to varied ways—biological and cultural—of adapting to environmental stresses, such as disease, heat, cold, humidity, sunlight, and altitude. Biological diversity among contemporary and prehistoric humans has many causes. This chapter examines those causes, while rejecting attempts to pigeonhole humans into discrete biological categories called races.

2. How do scientists approach the study of human biological diversity? Because of a range of problems involved in classifying humans into racial categories,

contemporary biologists focus on specific differences and try to explain them. Because of extensive gene flow and interbreeding, *Homo sapiens* has not evolved subspecies or distinct races. The genetic breaks that do exist among human populations have not led to the formation of discrete races.

3. Biological similarities between groups may reflect—rather than common ancestry—similar but independent adaptations to similar natural selective forces, such as degrees of ultraviolet radiation from the sun in the case of skin color.

4. Differential resistance to infectious diseases such as smallpox has influenced the distribution of human blood groups. There are genetic antimalarials, such as the sickle-cell allele discussed in Chapter 5. Natural selection also has operated on facial features and body size and shape.

5. Phenotypical adaptation refers to adaptive changes that occur in an individual's lifetime in response to the environment the organism encounters as it grows. Biological similarities between geographically distant populations may be due to similar but independent genetic changes, rather than to common ancestry. Or they may reflect similar physiological responses to common stresses during growth. Also, human populations have developed different but equally effective ways of adapting to environmental conditions such as heat, cold, and high altitudes.

key terms

Allen's rule 124
Bergmann's rule 124
cline 115
haplogroup 117
melanin 119

phenotypical adaptation 125
racial classification 114
rickets 119
Thomson's nose rule 123
tropics 119

test yourself

MULTIPLE CHOICE

1. It is important to understand that human racial categories are based upon *perceptions* of phenotypic features, and not on genotypes, because
   a. racial categories are internationally standardized.
   b. race should be determined by skeletal measurements, especially cranial capacity.
   c. you are in a place that does not use genealogy.
   d. racial categories are socially defined, not biologically determined.
   e. racial genotypes are more accurate.

2. Which of the following statements about human racial categories is true?
   a. They are applied to endogamous breeding populations.
   b. They are culturally arbitrary, even though most people assume them to be based in biology.
   c. They are biologically valid.
   d. They are based on global racial categories that vary little among societies.
   e. They are only valid when defined by haplogroups.

3. Some biologists use "race" to refer to "breeds," as of dogs or roses. Such domesticated "races" have been bred by humans for generations. Humanity (*Homo sapiens*) lacks such races because
   a. they are politically incorrect.
   b. humans are superior to dogs and roses.
   c. human populations have experienced a type of controlled breeding distinct from that experienced by dogs and roses.
   d. humans are less genetically predictable than dogs and roses.
   e. human populations have not been isolated enough from one another to develop such discrete groups.

4. Rather than attempting to classify humans into racial categories, biologists and anthropologists are
   a. increasingly focusing their attention on explaining why specific biological variations occur.
   b. denying the existence of any biological variation among humankind.
   c. attempting to create new categories based on blood type only.
   d. confident that earlier notions of racial categories are valid.
   e. trying to verify the anthropometric data from the turn of the century.

5. Which of the following has played an evolutionary role in determining skin color?
   a. Hb^S allele
   b. Allen's rule
   c. Bergmann's rule
   d. Thompson's rule
   e. ultraviolet radiation

6. Which of the following is the most likely reason for the dark skin color shared by tropical Africans and southern Indians?
   a. dietary adaptation
   b. UV radiation hazards
   c. reducing the frequency of rickets
   d. recent common ancestry
   e. malarial resistance

7. By acting as a natural sunscreen, melanin confers a selective advantage on darker-skinned people living in the tropics. In this part of the world, darker skin
   a. reduces the susceptibility to folate destruction, and thus helps prevent folate deficiencies such as neural tube defects (in the case of pregnant women).
   b. diminishes the production of sperm.
   c. confers an advantage by increasing human mating success.
   d. stimulates the production of folic acid in pregnant women, and thus helps prevent premature births.
   e. limits sweat production and helps keep the body cool.

8. In the early 20th century, anthropologist Franz Boas described changes in skull form among the children of Europeans who had migrated to North America. He found that these changes could not be explained by genetics. His findings underscore the fact that
   a. although the environment influences phenotype, genetics are a more powerful determinant of racial differences.
   b. the politics of migration only get worse with the input of science.
   c. describing changes in skull form is the most accurate way to study the impact of migration on traveling populations.
   d. phenotypical similarities and differences don't necessarily have a genetic basis.
   e. even well-intentioned science can be used for racist ends.

9. What is the term for adaptive biological changes that take place during an individual's lifetime?
   a. genotypical adaptation
   b. cultural adaptation
   c. linguistic adaptation
   d. species-level adaptation
   e. phenotypical adaptation

10. What does Thomson's nose rule state?
    a. Short noses are adaptive in cold environments.
    b. Nose size is causally linked to skin color.
    c. Long noses are adaptive in cold environments.
    d. Nose size is causally linked to cranial capacity.
    e. Long noses are adaptive in hot environments.

FILL IN THE BLANK

1. Modern scientists find it most productive to use an _____ approach to studying human biological diversity.
2. A _____ is a gradual shift in gene frequencies between neighboring populations.
3. One vitamin D deficiency marked by bone deformation is called _____.
4. _____ refers to an organism's evident traits, its "manifest biology."
5. Considering conventional geographic "racial" groupings such as Africans, Asians, and Europeans, there is only about a _____ percent variation in genes from one group to another. This means that there is much greater variation _____ each of the traditional "races" than _____ them.

CRITICAL THINKING

1. Describe three problems with human racial classification.
2. What explains skin color in humans? Are the processes that determined skin color in humans still continuing today? If so, what are some examples of this?
3. Read the "American Anthropological Association Statement on 'Race'" (http://www.aaanet.org/stmts/racepp.htm). What is its main argument? Why was such a public statement by this institution necessary?
4. If "race" is a discredited concept when applied to humans, what has replaced it?
5. Choose five people in your classroom who illustrate a range of phenotypical diversity. Which of their features vary most evidently? How do you explain this variation? Is some of the variation due to culture rather than to biology?

Multiple Choice: 1. (D); 2. (B); 3. (E); 4. (A); 5. (A); 6. (E); 7. (B); 8. (D); 9. (E); 10. (C); **Fill in the Blank:** 1. explanatory; 2. cline; 3. rickets; 4. Phenotype; 5, 6. within, between

Anemone, R. L.

   2011   *Race and Human Diversity: A Biocultural Approach.* Upper Saddle River, NJ: Prentice Hall/Pearson. Biological and cultural dimensions of human variation and the race concept.

Brace, C. L.

   2005   *"Race" Is a Four-Letter Word.* New York: Oxford University Press. Perceptions of human variation before and since the emergence of the race concept.

Fluehr-Lobban, C.

   2005   *Race and Racism: An Introduction.* Walnut Creek, CA: Altamira. Ideas about, and discrimination based on, race.

Jablonski, N. G.

   2006   *Skin: A Natural History.* Berkeley: University of California Press. Explaining human skin color.

Molnar, S.

   2006   *Human Variation: Races, Types, and Ethnic Groups,* 6th ed. Upper Saddle River, NJ: Prentice Hall. Links between biological and social diversity.

Mukhopadhyay, C. C., R. Henze, and Y. T. Moses

   2007   *How Real Is Race? A Sourcebook on Race, Culture, and Biology.* Lanham, MD: AltaMira. A broad consideration of the issues raised in this chapter and Chapter 15.

The following website has a detailed, annotated bibliography on race and racism: http://www.understandingrace.org/resources/pdf/annotated_bibliography.pdf

suggested additional readings

Go to our Online Learning Center website at **www.mhhe.com/kottak** for Internet exercises directly related to the content of this chapter.

internet exercises

The Primates

How and why are monkeys and apes similar to humans?

When, where, and how did the first primates, monkeys, apes, and hominids evolve?

How did diversity among Miocene proto-apes figure in hominid origins?

◀ An infant mountain gorilla shows affection to a silverback male. Apes fascinate us because of their humanlike qualities. Zoo gorillas are especially popular when they are displayed in "family" groups.

understanding OURSELVES

Think about our senses—vision, hearing, touch, taste, and smell. Which are you using right now? Which do you most depend upon to navigate the world? Like almost all other anthropoids—a group that includes monkeys, humans, and apes—humans are diurnal, active during the day. As animals, we are programmed to rise at dawn and to sleep when the sun goes down. As cultural creatures, we venture into the night with torches, lanterns, and flashlights, and shut the dark out of our dwellings with artificial light. If we were night animals, we'd sense things differently. Our eyes might be bigger, like those of an owl or a tarsier. Maybe we'd have biological radar systems, as bats do. Perhaps we'd develop a more acute sense of hearing or smell to penetrate the dark.

Many animals rely upon scents and odors to help them interpret the world. Humans, by contrast, use an array of products to cover up or eliminate even the faint odors our limited olfactory apparatus permits us to smell. *Blindness* and *deafness* are common words that indicate the senses whose loss we deem most significant. The rarity of the word *anosmia,* the inability to smell, tells us something about our senses and our values. The sensory shifts that occurred in primate evolution, especially the one from smell to sight, explain something fundamental about ourselves.

How different are we from other primates? No human looks much like a lemur or a tarsier. That's understandable; our ancestries diverged maybe 50 million years ago. We're much more closely related to, and look more like, our fellow anthropoids—monkeys and apes. Within this group, we are much more similar to apes than to monkeys. Likewise, apes are more similar to humans than to monkeys. Still, in the popular imagination, humans group apes with monkeys, rather than with themselves. At zoos human parents say to their kids "look at the monkey" when they are seeing a chimp, gorilla, or orangantun. The national tabloids use phrases like "monkeying around" or "monkey see, monkey do" when reporting on stories that involve apes. We easily appreciate the monkey in the ape but not the ape in ourselves.

Still, the apes do fascinate us to some degree because of their humanlike qualities. Zoo gorillas are especially popular when they are displayed in "family" groups. The antics of orangutans and especially of chimps have been featured in movies and TV shows. The *Planet of the Apes* movies recognize both that apes are not monkeys, and that apes are quite similar to us. Imagine a live-action film called *Planet of the Monkeys.* Where could a director find human actors who could locomote on four legs for an entire movie?

Primatology is the study of nonhuman primates—fossil and living apes, monkeys, and prosimians—including behavior and social life. Fascinating in itself, primatology also helps anthropologists make inferences about the early social organization of *hominids* (members of the family that includes fossil and living humans). Of particular relevance are two kinds of primates:

1. Those whose ecological adaptations are similar to our own: **terrestrial** monkeys and apes—that is, primates that live on the ground rather than in the trees.

2. Those that are most closely related to us: the great apes, specifically the chimpanzees and gorillas.

OUR PLACE AMONG PRIMATES

Similarities between humans and apes are evident in anatomy, brain structure, genetics, and biochemistry. The physical similarities between humans and apes are recognized in zoological **taxonomy**—the assignment of organisms to categories (*taxa*; singular, *taxon*) according to their relationship and resemblance. Many similarities between organisms reflect their common *phylogeny*—their genetic relatedness based on common ancestry. In other words, organisms share features they have inherited from the same ancestor. Humans and apes belong to the same taxonomic superfamily Hominoidea (hominoids). Monkeys are placed in two others (Ceboidea and Cercopithecoidea). This means that humans and apes are more closely related to each other than either is to monkeys.

Figure 7.1 summarizes the various levels of classification used in zoological taxonomy. Each lower-level unit belongs to the higher-level unit above it. Thus, looking toward the bottom of Figure 7.1, similar species belong to the same genus (plural, *genera*). Similar genera make up the same family, and so on through the top of Figure 7.1, where similar phyla (plural of *phylum*) are included in the same kingdom. The highest (most inclusive) taxonomic level is the *kingdom*. At that level, animals are distinguished from plants.

At the lowest level of taxonomy, a species may have subspecies. These are its more or less—but not yet totally—isolated subgroups. Subspecies can coexist in time and space. For example, the Neandertals, who lived between 130,000 and 28,000 years ago, often are assigned not to a separate species but merely to a different subspecies of *Homo sapiens*. Just one subspecies of *Homo sapiens* survives today.

The similarities used to assign organisms to the same taxon are called **homologies,** similarities they have jointly inherited from a common ancestor. Table 7.1 summarizes the place of humans in zoological taxonomy. We see in Table 7.1 that we are mammals, members of the class Mammalia. This is

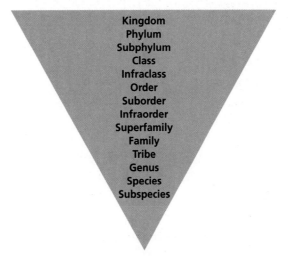

FIGURE 7.1 The Principal Classificatory Units of Zoological Taxonomy.

Moving down the figure, the classificatory units become more exclusive, so that "Kingdom" at the top is the most inclusive unit and "Subspecies" at the bottom is the most exclusive.

primatology
The study of apes, monkeys, and prosimians.

terrestrial
Ground-dwelling.

taxonomy
Classification scheme; assignment to categories (*taxa*; singular, *taxon*).

homologies
Traits inherited from a common ancestor.

TABLE 7.1 The Place of Humans (*Homo sapiens*) in Zoological Taxonomy

Homo sapiens *is an Animal, Chordate, Vertebrate, Mammal, Eutherian, Primate, Anthropoid, Catarrhine, Hominoid, Hominid, and Hominin. (Table 7.2 shows the taxonomic placement of the other primates.)*

TAXON	SCIENTIFIC (LATIN) NAME	COMMON (ENGLISH) NAME
Kingdom	Animalia	Animals
Phylum	Chordata	Chordates
Subphylum	Vertebrata	Vertebrates
Class	Mammalia	Mammals
Infraclass	Eutheria	Eutherians
Order	Primates	Primates
Suborder	Anthropoidea	Anthropoids
Infraorder	Catarrhini	Catarrhines
Superfamily	Hominoidea	Hominoids
Family	Hominidae	Hominids
Tribe	Hominini	Hominins
Genus	*Homo*	Humans
Species	*Homo sapiens*	Recent humans
Subspecies	*Homo sapiens sapiens*	Anatomically modern humans

TABLE 7.2 Primate Taxonomy

Major subdivisions of the two primate suborders: Prosimii and Anthropoidea. Humans are anthropoids who belong to the superfamily Hominoidea, along with the apes.

SUBORDER	INFRAORDER	SUPERFAMILY	FAMILY
Prosimii (Prosimians)	Lemuriformes (Lemurs)	Lemuroidea	Daubentoniidae (Aye-ayes), Indridae (Indri), Lemuridae (Lemurs)
	Lorisiformes (Lorises)	Lorisoidea	Lorisidae
	Tarsiiformes (Tarsiers)	Tarsioidea	Tarsiidae
Anthropoidea (Anthropoids)	Platyrrhini (Platyrrhines—New World monkeys)	Ceboidea	Callitrichidae (Tamarins and marmosets), Cebidae
	Catarrhini (Catarrhines—Old World monkeys, apes, and humans)	Cercopithecoidea	Cercopithecidae (Old World monkeys)
		Hominoidea) (Hominoids)	Hylobatidae (Gibbons and siamangs), Pongidae (Pongids—orangutans), Hominidae (Hominids—gorillas, chimpanzees, and humans)

SOURCE: Adapted from Robert Martin, "Classification of Primates," in Steve Jones, Robert Martin, and David Pilbeam, eds., *The Cambridge Encyclopedia of Human Evolution*, pp. 20–21. © Cambridge University Press, 1992. Reprinted with permission of Cambridge University Press.

analogies
Adaptive traits due to convergent evolution.

convergent evolution
Similar selective forces produce similar adaptive traits.

anthropology ATLAS

http://www.mhhe.com/anthromaps Map 2 locates the major primate groups. Orangutans and the African apes are part of the primate group most closely related to us: the great apes.

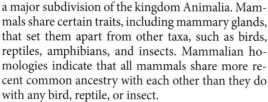

a major subdivision of the kingdom Animalia. Mammals share certain traits, including mammary glands, that set them apart from other taxa, such as birds, reptiles, amphibians, and insects. Mammalian homologies indicate that all mammals share more recent common ancestry with each other than they do with any bird, reptile, or insect.

Humans are mammals that, at a lower taxonomic level, belong to the *order* Primates. Another mammalian order is Carnivora: the carnivores (dogs, cats, foxes, wolves, badgers, weasels). Rodentia (rats, mice, beavers, squirrels) form yet another mammalian order. The primates share structural and biochemical homologies that distinguish them from other mammals. These resemblances were inherited from their common early primate ancestors after those early primates became reproductively isolated from the ancestors of the other mammals.

HOMOLOGIES AND ANALOGIES

Organisms should be assigned to the same taxon on the basis of homologies. The extensive biochemical homologies between apes and humans confirm our common ancestry and support our traditional joint classification as hominoids (see Table 7.2). For example, it is estimated that humans, chimpanzees, and gorillas have more than 97 percent of their DNA in common.

However, common ancestry isn't the only reason for similarities between species. Similar traits also can arise if species experience similar selective forces and adapt to them in similar ways. We call such similarities **analogies.** The process by which analogies are produced is called **convergent evolution.** For example, fish and porpoises share many analogies resulting from convergent evolution to life in the water. Like fish, porpoises, which are mammals, have fins. They are also hairless and streamlined for efficient locomotion. Analogies between birds and bats (wings, small size, light bones) illustrate convergent evolution to flying (see Angier 1998).

In theory, only homologies should be used in taxonomy. With reference to the hominoids, there is no doubt that humans, gorillas, and chimpanzees are more closely related to each other than any of the three is to orangutans, which are Asiatic apes (Ciochon 1983). *Hominidae* is the name of the zoological family that includes hominids—fossil and living humans. Because chimps and gorillas share a more recent common ancestor with humans than they do with the orangutan, many scientists now also place gorillas and chimps in the hominid family. *Hominid* would then refer to the zoological family that includes fossil and living humans, chimpanzees, gorillas,

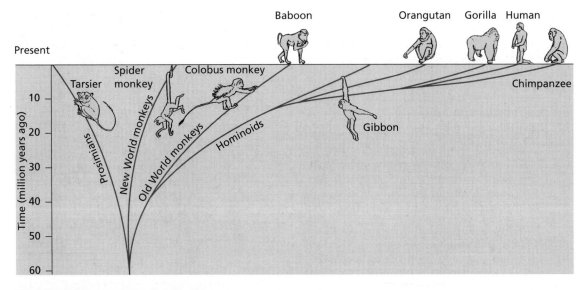

FIGURE 7.2 Primate Family Tree.

When did the common ancestors of all the primates live?

SOURCE: From Roger Lewin, *Human Evolution: An Illustrated Introduction*, 3rd ed., p. 44. Copyright © 1993 by Blackwell Publishing Ltd. Reprinted by permission of Blackwell Publishing Ltd., Oxford, UK.

and their common ancestors. This leaves the orangutan (genus *Pongo*) as the only member of the pongid family (*Pongidae*). If chimps and gorillas are classified as hominids, what do we call the group that leads to humans but not to chimps and gorillas? For that, some scientists insert a taxonomic level called *tribe* between family and genus. The tribe *hominini* describes all the human species that ever have existed (including the extinct ones) and excludes chimps and gorillas. When scientists use the word *hominin* today, they mean pretty much the same thing as when they used the word *hominid* twenty years ago (Greiner 2003). Table 7.2 and Figure 7.2 illustrate our degree of relatedness to other primates.

PRIMATE TENDENCIES

Primates are varied because they have adapted to diverse ecological niches. Some primates are active during the day; others, at night. Some eat insects; others, fruits; others, shoots, leaves, and bulk vegetation; and others, seeds or roots. Some primates live on the ground, others live in trees, and there are intermediate adaptations. However, because the earliest primates were tree dwellers, modern primates share homologies reflecting their common **arboreal** heritage (see also Nystrom and Ashmore 2008)

Many trends in primate evolution are best exemplified by the **anthropoids:** monkeys, apes, and humans, which constitute the suborder *Anthropoidea*. The other primate suborder, *Prosimii*, includes lemurs, lorises, and tarsiers. These **prosimians** are more distant relatives of humans than are monkeys and apes. The primate trends—most developed in the anthropoids—can be summarized briefly. Together they constitute an anthropoid heritage that humans share with monkeys and apes.

1. **Grasping.** Primates have five-digited feet and hands that are suited for grasping. Certain features of hands and feet that were originally adaptive for arboreal life have been transmitted across the generations to contemporary primates. Flexible hands and feet that could encircle branches were important features in the early primates' arboreal life. Thumb opposability might have been favored by the inclusion of insects in the early primate diet. Manual dexterity makes it easier to catch insects attracted to abundant arboreal flowers and fruits. Humans and many other primates have **opposable thumbs:** The thumb can touch the other fingers. Some primates also have grasping feet. However, in adapting to **bipedal** (two-footed) locomotion, humans eliminated most of the foot's grasping ability.

2. **Smell to Sight.** Several anatomical changes reflect the shift from smell to sight as the primates' most important means of obtaining information. Monkeys, apes, and humans have excellent *stereoscopic* (able to see in depth) and color vision. The portion of the brain devoted to vision expanded, while the area concerned with smell shrank.

3. **Nose to Hand.** Sensations of touch, conveyed by *tactile organs,* also provide information. The tactile skin on a dog's or cat's nose transmits information. Cats' tactile hairs, or whiskers, also serve this function. In primates, however, the main touch organ is the hand,

arboreal
Living in the trees.

anthropoids
Monkeys, apes, and humans.

prosimians
The primate suborder that includes lemurs, lorises, and tarsiers.

opposable thumb
A thumb that can touch all the other fingers.

bipedal
Two-footed; upright locomotion (of hominins).

specifically the sensitive pads of the "finger-print" region.

4. **Brain Complexity.** The proportion of brain tissue concerned with memory, thought, and association has increased in primates. The primate ratio of brain size to body size exceeds that of most mammals.

5. **Parental Investment.** Most primates give birth to a single offspring rather than a litter. Because of this, growing primates receive more attention and have more learning opportunities than do other mammals. Learned behavior is an important part of primate adaptation.

6. **Sociality.** Primates tend to be social animals that live with others of their species. The need for longer and more attentive care of offspring places a selective value on support by a social group.

PROSIMIANS

The primate order has two suborders: prosimians and anthropoids. The early history of the primates is limited to prosimian-like animals known through the fossil record. The first anthropoids, ancestral to monkeys, apes, and humans, appeared around 50 million years ago. Some prosimians managed to survive in Africa and Asia because they were adapted to nocturnal life. As such, they did not compete with anthropoids, which are active during the day. Prosimians (lemurs) in Madagascar had no anthropoid competitors until people colonized that island some 1,500 years ago.

In their behavior and biology, Madagascar's *lemurs*, with 33 species, show adaptations to an array of environments or ecological niches. Their diets and times of activity differ. Lemurs eat fruits, other plant foods, eggs, and insects. Some are nocturnal; others are active during the day. Some are totally arboreal; others spend some time in the trees and some on the ground. Another kind of prosimian is the *tarsier,* today confined to Indonesia, Malaysia, and the Philippines. From the fossil record, we know that 50 million years ago, several genera of tarsierlike prosimians lived in North America and Europe, which were much warmer then than they are now (Boaz 1997). The one genus of tarsier that survived is totally nocturnal. Active at night, tarsiers don't directly compete with anthropoids, which are active during the day. Lorises are other nocturnal prosimians found in Africa and Asia.

MONKEYS

All anthropoids share resemblances that can be considered trends in primate evolution in the sense that these traits are fully developed neither in the fossils of primates that lived prior to 50 million years ago nor among contemporary prosimians.

Compare this line drawing reconstruction of Shoshonius, a tarsierlike Eocene primate, with a modern tarsier from Mindanao in the Philippines. What similarities and differences do you notice?

The anthropoid suborder has two infraorders: *platyrrhines* (New World monkeys) and *catarrhines* (Old World monkeys, apes, and humans). The catarrhines (sharp-nosed) and platyrrhines (flat-nosed) take their names from Latin terms that describe the placement of the nostrils (see Figure 7.3). Old World monkeys, apes, and humans are all catarrhines. Being placed in the same taxon (infraorder in this case) means that Old World monkeys, apes, and humans are more closely related to each other than to New World monkeys. In other words, one kind of monkey (Old World) is more like a human than it is like another kind of monkey (New World). The New World monkeys were reproductively isolated from the catarrhines before the latter diverged into the Old World monkeys, apes, and humans. This is why New World monkeys are assigned to a different infraorder.

All New World monkeys and many Old World monkeys are arboreal. Whether in the trees or on the

FIGURE 7.3 Nostril Structure of Catarrhines and Platyrrhines.
Above: narrow septum and "sharp nose" of a guenon, a catarrhine (Old World monkey). Below: broad septum and "flat nose" of Humboldt's woolly monkey, a platyrrhine (New World monkey). Which nose is more like your own? What does that similarity suggest?

A woolly spider monkey, aka *muriqui,* from Monte Clares, Brazil. The long arms and elongated prehensile tail create a spiderlike image for this New World monkey.

tactile skin, which permits it to work like a hand, for instance, in conveying food to the mouth. Old World monkeys, however, have developed their own characteristic anatomic specializations. They have rough patches of skin on the buttocks, adapted to sitting on hard rocky ground and rough branches. If the primate you see in the zoo has such patches, it's from the Old World. If it has a prehensile tail, it's a New World monkey. Among the anthropoids, there's only one nocturnal animal, a New World monkey called the night monkey or owl monkey. All other monkeys and apes, and humans, too, of course, are diurnal—active during the day.

Old World Monkeys

The Old World monkeys have both terrestrial and arboreal species. Baboons and many macaques are terrestrial monkeys. Certain traits differentiate terrestrial and arboreal primates. Arboreal primates tend to be smaller. Smaller animals can reach a greater variety of foods in shrubs and trees, where the most abundant foods are located at the ends of branches. Arboreal monkeys typically are lithe and agile. They escape from the few predators in their environment—snakes and monkey-eating eagles—through alertness and speed. Large size, by contrast, is advantageous for terrestrial primates in dealing with their predators, which are more numerous on the ground.

Another contrast between arboreal and terrestrial primates is in **sexual dimorphism**—marked differences in male and female anatomy and temperament. Sexual dimorphism tends to be more

ground, however, monkeys move differently from apes and humans. Their arms and legs move parallel to one another, as dogs' legs do. This contrasts with the tendency toward *orthograde posture,* the straight and upright stance of apes and humans. Unlike apes, which have longer arms than legs, and humans, who have longer legs than arms, monkeys have arms and legs of about the same length. Most monkeys also have tails, which help them maintain balance in the trees. Apes and humans lack tails. The apes' tendency toward orthograde posture is most evident when they sit down. When they move about, chimps, gorillas, and orangutans habitually use all four limbs.

New World Monkeys

New World monkeys live in the forests of Central and South America. Unlike Old World monkeys, many New World monkeys have *prehensile,* or grasping, tails. Sometimes the prehensile tail has

sexual dimorphism
Marked differences in male and female anatomy and temperament.

This mandrill (*Papio sphinx*) is a brightly colored terrestrial Old World (African) monkey. Related to the baboon, which shares the same genus name (*Papio*), mandrills live in family groups consisting of an adult male, several females, and their young. Illustrating sexual dimorphism, female color is drabber and size smaller than in the male.

gibbons
Small, arboreal, Asiatic apes.

brachiation
Under-the-branch swinging.

marked in terrestrial than in arboreal species. Baboon and macaque males are larger and fiercer than are females of the same species. However, it's hard to tell, without close inspection, the sex of an arboreal monkey.

Of the terrestrial monkeys, the baboons of Africa and the (mainly Asiatic) macaques have been the subjects of many studies. Terrestrial monkeys have specializations in anatomy, psychology, and social behavior that enable them to cope with terrestrial life. Adult male baboons, for example, are fierce-looking animals that can weigh 100 pounds (45 kilograms). They display their long, projecting canines to intimidate predators and when confronting other baboons. Faced with a predator, a male baboon can puff up his ample mane of shoulder hair, so that the would-be aggressor perceives the baboon as larger than he actually is.

Longitudinal field research shows that, near the time of puberty, baboon and macaque males typically leave their home troop for another. Because males move in and out, females form the stable core of the terrestrial monkey troop (Cheney and Seyfarth 1990). By contrast, among chimpanzees and gorillas, females are more likely to emigrate and seek mates outside their natal social groups (Bradley et al. 2004; Wilson and Wrangham 2003). Among terrestrial monkeys, then, the core group consists of females; among apes it is made up of males.

APES

The Old World monkeys have their own separate superfamily (Cercopithecoidea), while humans and the apes together compose the hominoid superfamily (Hominoidea). Among the hominoids, the so-

called great apes are orangutans, gorillas, and chimpanzees (see Raffaele 2010). Humans could be included here, too; sometimes we are called "the third African ape." The lesser (smaller) apes are the gibbons and siamangs of Southeast Asia and Indonesia.

Several traits are shared by apes (and humans) as distinct from monkeys and other primates. Body size tends to be larger. The life span is longer. There is a longer interval between births of infants, which depend longer on their parent(s). There is a tendency toward upright posture, although habitual upright bipedalism only is characteristic of hominins. The brain is larger, the muzzle or face is shorter and less projecting, and no hominoid has a tail.

Apes live in forests and woodlands, and almost all apes are threatened or endangered today because of human encroachment (see "Appreciating Diversity" on p. 150). The light and agile **gibbons,** which are skilled brachiators, are completely arboreal. (**Brachiation** is hand-over-hand movement through the trees.) The heavier gorillas, chimpanzees, and adult male orangutans spend considerable time on the ground. Nevertheless, ape behavior and anatomy reveal past and present adaptation to arboreal life. For example, apes still build nests to sleep in trees. Apes have longer arms than legs, which is adaptive for brachiation (see Figure 7.4). The structure of the shoulder and clavicle (collarbone) of the apes and humans suggests that we had a brachiating ancestor. In fact, young apes still do brachiate. Adult apes tend to be too heavy to brachiate safely. Their weight is more than many branches can withstand. Gorillas and chimps now use the long arms they have inherited from their more arboreal ancestors for life on the ground. The terrestrial locomotion of chimps and gorillas is called *knuckle-walking*. In it, long arms and callused knuckles support the trunk as the apes amble around, leaning forward.

Gibbons

Gibbons are found in the forests of Southeast Asia, especially in Malaysia. Smallest of the apes, male and female gibbons have about the same average height (3 feet, or 1 meter) and weight (12–25 pounds, or 5–10 kilograms). Gibbons spend most of their time just below the forest canopy (treetops). For efficient brachiation, gibbons have long arms and fingers, with short thumbs. Slenderly built, gibbons are the most agile apes. They use their long arms for balance when they occasionally walk erect on the ground or along a branch. Gibbons are the preeminent arboreal specialists among the apes. They subsist on a diet mainly of fruits, with occasional insects and small animals. Gibbons and siamangs, their slightly larger relatives, tend to live in *primary groups,* which are composed of a permanently bonded male and female and their preadolescent offspring.

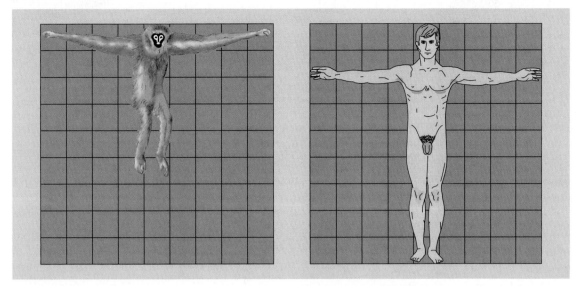

FIGURE 7.4 The Limb Ratio of the Arboreal Gibbon and Terrestrial *Homo*.
How does this anatomical difference fit the modes of locomotion used by gibbons and humans?

Orangutans

There are two existing species of orangutan, Asiatic apes that belong to the genus *Pongo*. Highly endangered (see this chapter's "Appreciating Anthropology"), contemporary orangs are confined to two Indonesian islands—Borneo and Sumatra (Mayell 2004a). Orangutans once were found throughout Southeast Asia, but today 90 percent of them live in Indonesia. Borneo has between 40,000 and 50,000 orangutans, while a mere 7,000 survive on Sumatra (Isaacson 2012).

The degree of sexual dimorphism in orangs is striking. Adult males weigh more than twice as much as females. The orangutan male, like his human counterpart, is intermediate in size between chimps and gorillas. Orang males can weigh up to 300 pounds (135 kilograms), but usually they weigh around 200 pounds (90 kilograms). Less bulky than gorillas, male orangs can be more arboreal, although they typically climb, rather than swing through, the trees. The smaller size of females and young permits them to make fuller use of the trees. Orangutans have a varied diet of fruit, bark, leaves, and insects. Because orangutans live in jungles and feed in trees, they are especially difficult to study. However, field reports about orangutans in their natural setting (MacKinnon 1974; Schaik 2004) have clarified their behavior and social organization. Orangs are the least sociable of the great apes (see Schaik 2004, Isaacson 2012). Often they are solitary, with their tightest social units formed by females and preadolescent young, and males foraging alone.

Gorillas

With just one species, *Gorilla gorilla,* there are three subspecies of gorillas. The western lowland gorilla is

With long arms and fingers, the gibbon is the most agile of the apes. As we see here, gibbons occasionally walk upright on the ground, using their long arms as balancers.

the animal you normally see in zoos. This, the smallest subspecies of gorilla, lives mainly in forests in the Central African Republic, Congo, Cameroon, Gabon, Equatorial Guinea, and Nigeria. The eastern lowland

Global Economy Threatens Orangutans

Read this poignant account by Biruté Mary Galdikas, who since 1971 has studied wild orangs in central Borneo. Galdikas is one of three prominent primatologists—all women—encouraged by Louis B. Leakey to study and protect the great apes. The others are Jane Goodall (working with chimpanzees) and the late Dian Fossey (working with mountain gorillas). Galdikas describes how global economic forces, including demand for palm oil, pulp, paper, and precious metals, fuel destruction of Indonesia's once vast forests, threatening Asia's only great ape.

Once again, I am driving, under the blazing equatorial sun . . . into the interior of central Borneo. . . . The landscape is bleak, no trees, no shade. . . . Our mission is to confiscate orangutan orphans whose mothers have been killed as a result of the sweeping forest clearance taking place throughout Borneo. . . .

Without forests, orangutans cannot survive. They spend more than 95 percent of their time in the trees, which, along with vines and termites, provide more than 99 percent of their food. Two forests form their only habitat, and they are the tropical rain forests of Borneo and Sumatra.

Sumatra is exclusively Indonesian, as is the two thirds of the island of Borneo known as Kalimantan. That places 80 to 90 percent of the orangutan population, which numbers only 40,000 to 50,000, in Indonesia, with the remainder in Malaysian Borneo. . . .

When I first arrived in Central Kalimantan in 1971, orangutans were already endangered because of poaching (for the pet trade and for the cooking pot) and deforestation (by loggers and by villagers making way for gardens and rice fields).

But it was all relatively small-time. . . . People still used axes and saws to cut down trees and traveled by dugout canoes or small boats with inboard engines.

I went straight to work, beginning a wild orangutan study that continues to this day, and establishing an orangutan rehabilitation program, the first in Kalimantan, which has returned more than 300 ex-captive orangutans to the wild.

But the wild is increasingly difficult to find. In the late 1980s, as it entered the global economy, Indonesia decided to become a major producer and exporter of palm oil, pulp and paper. Before this, the government had endorsed selective logging. Now vast areas of forest were slated for conversion to plantations to grow trees for palm oil and paper production. Monster-sized bulldozers . . . tore up the forests. At the same time, the price of wood, particularly the valuable hardwoods that grow in the rain forests . . . increased. Illegal logging became rampant. . . .

Forest-clearing leaves huge amounts of dry branches and other wood litter on forest floors; a small spark can ignite enormous forest fires, particularly in times of drought. During the 1997 El Niño drought, approximately 25 million acres, an area about half the size of Oklahoma, burned in Indonesia. Thousands of orangutans died.

Indonesia has achieved its goal of becoming one of the two largest palm-oil producers and exporters in the world. But at what cost? At least half of the world's wild orangutans have

gorilla, of which there are only four in captivity, is slightly larger and lives in eastern Congo. There are no mountain gorillas, the third subspecies, in captivity, and it's estimated that no more than 650 of these animals survive in the wild. These are the largest gorillas with the longest hair (to keep them warm in their mountainous habitat). They also are the rarest gorillas, which Dian Fossey (1983) and other scientists have studied in Rwanda, Uganda, and eastern Congo.

Full-grown male gorillas may weigh 400 pounds (180 kilograms) and stand 6 feet tall (183 centimeters). Like most terrestrial primates, gorillas show marked sexual dimorphism. The average adult female weighs half as much as the male. Gorillas spend little time in the trees. It's hard for an adult male to move his bulk about in a tree. When gorillas sleep in trees, they build nests, which are usually no more than 10 feet (3 meters) off the ground. By contrast, the nests of chimps and female orangs may be 100 feet (30 meters) above the ground.

Most of the gorilla's day is spent feeding. Gorillas move through jungle undergrowth eating ground plants, leaves, bark, fruits, and other vegetation (see Rothman, Raubenheimer, and Chapman 2011). Like most primates, gorillas live in social groups. The troop is a common unit of primate social organization, consisting of multiple males and females and their offspring. Although troops with up to thirty gorillas have been observed, most gorillas live in groups of from ten to twenty. Gorilla troops tend to have fairly stable memberships, with little shifting between troops (Fossey 1983). Each troop has a silverback male, so designated because of the strip of white hair that extends down his back. This is the physical sign of full maturity

disappeared in the last 20 years . . . and 80 percent of the orangutan habitat has either been depopulated or totally destroyed. The trend shows no sign of abating. . . .

Indonesia is a vast, densely populated country where millions live in or near poverty. The temptation to exploit natural resources to feed people today, never mind tomorrow, and to expand the economy, is great. And the plantations are but one example. Surface-mining of gold . . . has been practiced for two decades, leaving virtual moonscapes near the National Park where I work. . . .

The international community must recognize that it has some responsibility for what happens to the great rain forests of Indonesian Borneo. Foreign investment in local development programs needs to be expanded. . . .

Indonesia could also impose a special tax on companies that profit from rain forest destruction, with the revenues dedicated to forest and orangutan conservation. Proper labeling of palm oil content could allow a consumer boycott of soap, crackers, cookies and other products that contain it. Finally, Indonesia needs to be more vigorous in enforcing the excellent laws it already has to protect its forests.

SOURCE: Biruté Mary Galdikas, "The Vanishing Man of the Forest." From *The New York Times*, January 6, 2007. © 2007 The New York Times. All rights reserved. Used by permission and protected by the Copyright Laws of the United States. The printing, copying, redistribution, or retransmission of this Content without express written permission is prohibited. www.nytimes.com

Dr. Biruté Galdikas has studied orangutans in Indonesia for decades. Here she carries an orangutan named Isabel, soon to be released into the wild at Tanjung Puting National Park on the Indonesian island of Borneo.

among male gorillas. The silverback is usually the only breeding male in the troop, which is why gorilla troops are sometimes called "one-male groups." However, a few younger, subordinate males may also adhere to such a one-male group (Harcourt, Fossey, and Sabater-Pi 1981).

Chimpanzees

Chimpanzees belong to the genus *Pan,* which has two species: *Pan troglodytes* (the common chimpanzee) and *Pan paniscus* (the bonobo or "pygmy" chimpanzee) (de Waal 1997, 2007; Susman 1987). Like humans, chimps are closely related to the gorilla, although there are some obvious differences. Like gorillas, chimps live in tropical Africa, but they range over a larger area and more varied environments than gorillas do. The common chimp, *Pan troglodytes,* lives in western central Africa (Gabon, Congo, Cameroon), as well as in western Africa (Ivory Coast, Sierra Leone, Liberia, Gambia) and eastern Africa (Congo, Uganda, and Tanzania). Bonobos live in remote and densely forested areas of just one country—the Democratic Republic of Congo (DRC). Common chimps live mainly in tropical rain forests but also in woodlands and mixed forest–woodland-grassland areas, such as the Gombe Stream National Park, Tanzania, where Jane Goodall and other researchers began to study them in 1960 (see Goodall 2009, 2010).

There are dietary differences between chimps and gorillas. Gorillas eat large quantities of green bulk vegetation, but chimps, like orangutans and gibbons, prefer fruits. Chimps are actually omnivorous, adding animal protein to their diet by capturing small mammals, birds' eggs, and insects.

Mountain gorillas are the rarest and most endangered kind of gorilla. Dian Fossey and other scientists have studied them in Rwanda, Uganda, and eastern Congo. Shown here, Fossey (now deceased) plays with a group of young gorillas in Rwanda's Virunga Mountains.

Chimps are lighter and more arboreal than gorillas are. The adult male's weight—between 100 and 200 pounds (45–90 kilograms)—is about a third that of the male gorilla. There is much less sexual dimorphism among chimps than among gorillas.

Females approximate 88 percent of the average male height. This is similar to the ratio of sexual dimorphism in *Homo sapiens*.

Several scientists have studied wild chimps, and we know more about the full range of their behavior

Chimpanzees live mainly in tropical rain forests but also in woodlands and mixed forest-woodland-grassland areas, such as the Gombe Stream National Park, Tanzania, where Jane Goodall began to study them in 1960. Shown here 30 years after her first visit to Gombe, Goodall continues her lifelong commitment to these endangered animals.

and social organization than we do about the other apes (see Wilson and Wrangham 2003, Goodall 2009). The long-term research of Jane Goodall (2010) and others at Gombe provides especially useful information. Approximately 150 chimpanzees range over Gombe's 30 square miles (80 square kilometers). Goodall (2009, 2010) has described communities of about 50 chimps, all of which know one another and interact from time to time. Communities regularly split up into smaller groups: a mother and her offspring; a few males; males, females, and young; and occasionally solitary animals. The social networks of males are more closed than are those of females, which are more likely to migrate and mate outside their natal group than males are (Wrangham et al., 1994).

When chimps, which are very vocal, meet, they greet one another with gestures, facial expressions, and calls. They hoot to maintain contact during their daily rounds. Like baboons and macaques, chimps exhibit dominance relationships through attacks and displacement. Some adult females outrank younger males, although females do not display as strong dominance relationships among themselves as males do. Males occasionally cooperate in hunting parties.

Bonobos

Ancestral chimps, and especially hominins, eventually spread out of the forests and into woodlands and more open habitats (see Choi 2011). Bonobos, which belong to the species *Pan paniscus,* apparently never left the protection of the trees. Up to 10,000 bonobos survive in the humid forests south of the Zaire River, in the Democratic Republic of Congo. Despite their common name—the *pygmy* chimpanzee—bonobos can't be distinguished from chimpanzees by size. Adult males of the smallest subspecies of chimpanzee average 95 pounds (43 kilograms), and females average 73 pounds (33 kilograms). These figures are about the same for bonobos (de Waal 1995, 1997).

 living anthropology **VIDEOS**

Apes Make Tools, www.mhhe.com/kottak

For decades primatologists have known that chimpanzees make and use tools. Wild chimps in the Tai forest of Ivory Coast make and use stone tools to break open hard, golf ball–size nuts. Nut cracking is a learned skill, with mothers showing their young how to do it. Chimps in Tanzania peel the bark off sticks to make tools to probe termite hills. In this clip, a captive chimp uses a tool (a large wooden stick) to knock leaves from a tree, and captive bonobos use small sticks to extract honey from wooden posts. How does learning proceed in this clip?

This photo was taken at a bonobo sanctuary in the Democratic Republic of Congo. Are bonobos (aka pygmy chimpanzees) smaller than chimps?

Although much smaller than the males, female bonobos seem to rule. De Waal (1995, 1997) characterizes bonobo communities as female-centered, peace-loving, and egalitarian. The strongest social bonds are among females, although females also bond with males. The male bonobo's status reflects that of his mother, to whom he remains closely bonded for life.

The frequency with which bonobos have sex—and use it to avoid conflict—makes them exceptional among the primates (De Waal 1997). Despite frequent sex, the bonobo reproductive rate doesn't exceed that of the chimpanzee. A female bonobo gives birth every 5 or 6 years. Then, like chimps, female bonobos nurse and carry around their young for up to 5 years. Bonobos reach adolescence around 7 years of age. Females, which first give birth at age 13 or 14, are full grown by 15 years.

BEHAVIORAL ECOLOGY AND FITNESS

According to evolutionary theory, when the environment changes, natural selection starts to modify the *population's* pool of genetic material. Natural selection has another key feature: the differential reproductive success of *individuals* within the population. **Behavioral ecology** studies the evolutionary

behavioral ecology
Study of the evolutionary basis of social behavior.

basis of social behavior. It assumes that the genetic features of any species reflect a long history of differential reproductive success (that is, natural selection). In other words, biological traits of contemporary organisms have been transmitted across the generations because those traits enabled their ancestors to survive and reproduce more effectively than their competition.

Natural selection is based on *differential* reproduction. Members of the same species may compete to maximize their reproductive fitness—their genetic contribution to future generations. *Individual fitness* is measured by the number of direct descendants an individual has. Illustrating a primate strategy that may enhance individual fitness are cases in which male monkeys kill infants after entering a new troop. Destroying the offspring of other males, they clear a place for their own progeny (Hausfater and Hrdy 1984).

Besides competition, one's genetic contribution to future generations also can be enhanced by cooperation, sharing, and other apparently unselfish behavior. This is because of *inclusive fitness*—reproductive success measured by the genes one shares with relatives. By sacrificing for their kin—even if this means limiting their own direct reproduction—individuals actually may increase their genetic contributions (their shared genes) to the future. Inclusive fitness helps us understand why a female might invest in her sister's offspring, or why a male might risk his life to defend his brothers. If self-sacrifice perpetuates more of their genes than direct reproduction does, it makes sense in terms of behavioral ecology. Such a view can help us understand aspects of primate behavior and social organization (for application to humans see Chapais 2008 and Hill, Walker, et al. 2011).

Maternal care always makes sense in terms of reproductive fitness theory because females know their offspring are their own. But it's harder for males to be sure about paternity. Inclusive fitness theory predicts that males will invest most in offspring when they are surest the offspring are theirs. Gibbons, for example, have strict male–female pair bonding, which makes it almost certain that the offspring are those of both members of the pair. Thus we expect male gibbons to offer care and protection to their young, and they do. However, among species and in situations in which a male can't be sure about his paternity, it may make more sense to invest in a sister's offspring than in a mate's because the niece or nephew definitely shares some of that male's genes.

PRIMATE EVOLUTION

The fossil record offers evidence for no more than 5 percent of extinct types of primates. Such small numbers provide the merest glimpse of the diverse

m.y.a.
Million years ago.

bioforms—living beings—that have existed on earth.

With reference to the primate fossil record, we'll see that different geographic areas provide more abundant fossil evidence for different time periods. This doesn't necessarily mean that primates were not living elsewhere at the same time. Discussions of primate and human evolution must be tentative because the fossil record is limited and spotty. Much is subject to change as knowledge increases. A key feature of science is to recognize the tentativeness and uncertainty of knowledge. Scientists, including fossil hunters, constantly seek out new evidence and devise new methods, such as DNA comparison, to improve their understanding, in this case of primate and human evolution.

CHRONOLOGY

We learned in Chapter 4 that the remains of organisms that lived at the same time are found in the same stratum. Based on fossils found in stratigraphic sequences, the history of vertebrate life has been divided into three main eras. The *Paleozoic* (544–245 **m.y.a.**—million years ago) was the era of ancient life—fishes, amphibians, and primitive reptiles. The *Mesozoic* (245–65 m.y.a.) was the era of middle life—reptiles, including the dinosaurs. The *Cenozoic* (65 m.y.a.–present) is the era of recent life—birds and mammals. Each era is divided into periods; and the periods, into epochs.

Anthropologists are concerned with the Cenozoic *era* (Figure 7.5), which includes two *periods:* Tertiary and Quaternary. Each of these periods is subdivided into *epochs*. The Tertiary had five epochs: Paleocene, Eocene, Oligocene, Miocene, and Pliocene. The Quaternary includes just two epochs: Pleistocene and Holocene, or Recent. Figure 7.5b gives the approximate dates of these epochs. Sediments from the Paleocene epoch (65–54 m.y.a.) have yielded fossil remains of diverse small mammals, some probably ancestral to the primates. Prosimianlike fossils abound in strata dating from the Eocene (54–34 m.y.a.). Anthropoid fossils date to the Eocene and become more abundant in the ensuing Oligocene (34–23 m.y.a.). Hominoids became widespread during the Miocene (23–5 m.y.a.). Hominins first appeared in the late Miocene, just before the Pliocene (5–2 m.y.a.).

EARLY PRIMATES

When the Mesozoic era ended, and the Cenozoic era began, around 65 million years ago, North America was connected to Europe but not to South America. (The Americas joined around 20 million years ago.) Over millions of years, the continents have "drifted" to their present locations, carried along by the gradually shifting plates of the Earth's surface (Figure 7.6).

Era	Period	Epoch		Climate and Life Forms
Cenozoic	Quaternary	Holocene	10,000 B.P.	Transition to agriculture; emergence of states
		Pleistocene	2 m.y.a.	Climatic fluctuations, glaciation; *Homo*, *A. boisei*, *A. robustus*
	Tertiary	Pliocene	5 m.y.a.	*A. africanus*, *A. afarensis*, *A. anamensis*, *Ardipithecus*
		Miocene	23 m.y.a.	Cooler and drier grasslands spread in middle latitudes; Africa collides with Eurasia (16 m.y.a.)
		Oligocene	34 m.y.a.	Cooler and drier in the north; anthropoids in Africa (Fayum); separation of catarrhines and platyrrhines; separation of hylobatids (gibbons) from pongids and hominids
		Eocene	54 m.y.a	Warm tropical climates become widespread; modern orders of mammals appear; prosimian-like primates abundant; anthropoids appear
		Paleocene	65 m.y.a	First major mammal radiation

FIGURE 7.5 Periods and Epochs of the Cenozoic Era.
The geological time scale is based on stratigraphy. Eras are subdivided into periods, and periods into epochs. In what era, period, and epoch did *Homo* originate?

During the Cenozoic, most landmasses had tropical or subtropical climates. The Mesozoic era had ended with a massive worldwide extinction of plants and animals, including the dinosaurs. Thereafter, mammals replaced reptiles as the dominant large land animals. Trees and flowering plants soon proliferated, supplying arboreal foods for the primates that eventually evolved to fill the new niches.

According to the *arboreal theory*, primates became primates by adapting to arboreal life. The primate traits and trends discussed previously developed as adaptations to life high up in the trees. A key feature was the importance of sight over smell. Changes in the visual apparatus were adaptive in the trees, where depth perception facilitated leaping. Grasping hands and feet were used to crawl along slender branches. Grasping feet anchored the body as the primate reached for foods at the ends of branches. Early primates probably had omnivorous diets based on foods available in the trees, such as flowers, fruits, berries, gums, leaves, and insects. The early Cenozoic era witnessed a proliferation of flowering plants, attracting insects that were to figure prominently in many primate diets.

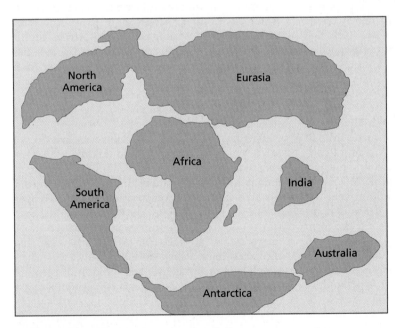

FIGURE 7.6 Placement of Continents at the End of the Mesozoic.
When the Mesozoic era ended and the Cenozoic began, some 65 million years ago, North America was connected to Europe but not to South America.

Smilodectes was a lemurlike primate that lived during the Eocene. Compare this drawing reconstructing a *Smilodectes* from Wyoming (left) with a modern black lemur (*Eulemur macaco*) from Madagascar.

Early Cenozoic Primates

There is considerable fossil evidence that a diversified group of primates lived, mainly in Europe and North America, during the second epoch of the Cenozoic, the Eocene. On that basis it is likely that the earliest primates lived during the first epoch of the Cenozoic, the Paleocene (65–54 m.y.a.). The status of several fossils as possible Paleocene primates has been debated. Because there is no consensus on this matter, such fossils are not discussed here.

A tiny primate skull from China (Malkin 2004; Ni et al. 2004) confirms that early primates lived in Asia near the start of the Eocene. A team of Chinese paleontologists led by Xijun Ni found the new primate species, *Teilhardina asiatica*, in China's Hunan Province. The tiny 55-million-year-old skull, with most of its teeth intact, is the most complete skull ever found of a euprimate. (The term *euprimate* refers to the first mammals that shared characteristics such as forward-facing eyes and a relatively large braincase with modern primates.) Fragments of euprimates, all dating to around 55 m.y.a., have been found in Europe and North America. The discovery of a euprimate in Asia means that primates were already widespread by then and that their common ancestor must have evolved even earlier.

In primate evolution, the Eocene (54–34 m.y.a.) was the age of the prosimians, with at least sixty genera in two main families. They lived in North America, Europe, Africa, and Asia. Ancestral lemurs reached Madagascar from Africa late in the Eocene. They must have traveled across the Mozambique Channel, which was narrower then than it is now, on thick mats of vegetation. Such naturally formed "rafts" have been observed forming in East African rivers, then floating out to sea.

During the Eocene—perhaps as early as 52 m.y.a. (see Schultz, Opie, and Atkinson 2011)—ancestral anthropoids branched off from the prosimians by becoming more diurnal (active during the day). In this new niche, vision was favored over smell. The brain and eyes got bigger, and the snout was reduced. Anthropoid eyes are rotated more forward than are those of prosimians. Also, anthropoids have a fully enclosed bony eye socket, which lemurs and lorises lack. And unlike lemurs and lorises, anthropoids lack a rhinarium, a moist nose continuous with the upper lip. Anthropoids have a dry nose, separate from the upper lip. By the end of the Eocene, many prosimian species had become extinct, reflecting competition from the first anthropoids.

Oligocene Anthropoids

During the Oligocene epoch (34–23 m.y.a.), anthropoids became the most numerous primates. Most of our knowledge of early anthropoids is based on fossils from Egypt's Fayum deposits. This area is a desert today, but 34–31 million years ago it was a tropical rain forest.

The anthropoids of the Fayum lived in trees and ate fruits and seeds. Compared with prosimians, they had fewer teeth, reduced snouts, larger brains, and increasingly forward-looking eyes. Of the Fayum anthropoid fossils, one group is the more primitive and perhaps is ancestral to the New World monkeys. These protomonkeys were very small (2–3 pounds, 0.9–1.4 kilograms), with similarities to living marmosets and tamarins, small South American monkeys.

Another Fayum group seems ancestral to the catarrhines—Old World monkeys, apes, and humans. This group shares with the later catarrhines a distinctive dental formula: 2.1.2.3, meaning two incisors, one canine, two premolars, and three molars. (The formula is based on one-fourth of the mouth, either the right or left side of the upper or lower jaw.) The more primitive primate dental formula is 2.1.3.3. Most other primates, including prosimians and New World monkeys, have the second formula, with three premolars instead of two. Besides the Fayum, Oligocene deposits with primate bones have been found in North and West Africa, southern Arabia, China, Southeast Asia, and North and South America.

The Oligocene was a time of major geological and climatic change: North America and Europe separated and became distinct continents; the Great Rift Valley system of East Africa formed; India drifted into Asia; and a cooling trend began, especially in the Northern Hemisphere, where primates disappeared.

MIOCENE HOMINOIDS

The earliest hominoid fossils date to the Miocene epoch (23–5 m.y.a.), which is divided into three parts: lower, middle, and upper or late. The early Miocene (23–16 m.y.a.) was a warm and wet period, when forests covered East Africa. Recall that Hominoidea is the superfamily that includes fossil and living apes and humans. For simplicity's sake, the earliest **hominoids** are here called *proto-apes*, or simply *apes*. Although some of these may be ancestral to living apes, none is identical, or often even very similar, to modern apes.

Proconsul

The *Proconsul* group represents the most abundant and successful anthropoids of the early Miocene.

A reconstruction of *Gigantopithecus* by Russell Ciochon and Bill Munns. Munns is shown here with "Giganto." What would be the likely environmental effects of a population of such large apes?

This group lived in Africa and includes three species. These early Miocene proto-apes had teeth with similarities to those of living apes. But their skeleton below the neck was more monkeylike. Some *Proconsul* species were the size of a small monkey; others, the size of a chimpanzee, usually with marked sexual dimorphism. Their dentition suggests they ate fruits and leaves. *Proconsul* probably contained the last common ancestor shared by the Old World monkeys and the apes. By the middle Miocene, *Proconsul* had been replaced by Old World monkeys and apes.

Later Miocene Apes

During the early Miocene (23–16 m.y.a.), Africa had been cut off by water from Europe and Asia. But during the middle Miocene, Arabia drifted into Eurasia, providing a land connection between Africa, Europe, and Asia. Migrating both ways—out of and into Africa—about 16 m.y.a. were various animals, including hominoids. Proto-apes were the most

hominoid
Zoological superfamily that includes extinct and living apes and hominins.

A Planet Without Apes

In the past—and continuing today on a global scale—human activity has threatened and reduced diversity among primates. My colleague John Mitani, a Professor of Anthropology at the University of Michigan, writes here about global threats to the (barely) surviving apes. He appeals to the U.S. Congress to reauthorize the Great Apes Conservation Fund, which can help preserve the diversity represented by our closest relatives. As of this writing (2012), Congress has not acted on this matter.

VIEWERS of . . . [the 2011 film] "Rise of the Planet of the Apes" may be surprised to learn that before our earliest ancestors arrived on the scene roughly seven million years ago, apes really did rule the planet. As many as 40 kinds roamed Eurasia and Africa between 10 and 25 million years ago. Only five types remain. Two live in Asia, the gibbon and orangutan; another three, the chimpanzee, bonobo and gorilla, dwell in Africa. All five are endangered, several critically so. All may face extinction.

A decade ago, Congress stepped forward with a relatively cheap but vitally important effort to protect these apes through innovative conservation programs . . . But attempts to reauthorize the Great Apes Conservation Fund have gotten stuck in Congress and may become a victim of the larger debate over the national debt.

Hollywood's depiction of apes as cunning—if not conniving—creatures comes close to reality. Fifty years ago, Jane Goodall's observations of chimpanzees' using tools and eating meat demonstrated just how similar apes are to humans. Subsequent fieldwork has underscored this point. . . .

Orangutans fashion tools to extract seeds that are otherwise difficult to obtain. Gorillas engage in conversational vocal exchanges. Bonobos appear to have sex not only to reproduce but also to relieve stress. Male chimpanzees form coalitions to kill their neighbors and take over their territory. . . .

Apes . . . are prime attractions at zoos, and scientists from disciplines ranging from anthropology to biology and psychology study them closely in captivity and in the wild. As our first cousins in the primate family, apes help us to understand what makes us human.

I have been lucky to study all five kinds of apes during 33 years of fieldwork in Africa and Asia. When I look into the eyes of an ape, something stares back at me that seems familiar. Perhaps it is a shock of recognition, or a thoughtfulness not seen in the eyes of a frog, bird or cat. The penetrating stare makes me wonder, "What is this individual thinking?"

But as the human population expands, ape numbers continue to dwindle. In previous versions of the "Planet of the Apes" films, greed and consumption by humanlike apes threatened the world. In reality, it is these all-too-human traits that imperil apes.

Habitat destruction because of human activity, including logging, oil exploration and subsistence farming, is the biggest concern. Hunting is another major problem, especially in West and Central Africa, where a thriving "bush meat" trade severely threatens African apes. Poachers are now entering once-impenetrable forests on roads built for loggers and miners. Recently, periodic outbreaks of deadly diseases that can infect humans and apes, like Ebola, have begun to ravage populations of chimpanzees and gorillas.

The Great Apes Conservation Act, enacted in 2000, authorized the spending of $5 million annually over five years to help protect apes in the wild. The act was re-authorized in 2005 for another five years. The program matches public with private dollars to maximize the impact. Since 2006, for example, $21 million in federal dollars spent by the Great Ape Conservation Fund generated an additional $25 million in private grants and support from other governments. . . . The money pays for protecting habitat, battling poachers and educating local populations about the importance of these apes.

For instance, in Indonesia . . . money has been earmarked to block the conversion of forests to commercial oil palm and rubber plantations. In Congo, home to the extremely rare mountain gorilla, alternative fuels have been introduced to discourage the cutting of forests for charcoal production. In Gabon, the program has paid for law enforcement training for park rangers battling poachers. . . . In all, [in 2010], the Great Apes Conservation Fund helped to underwrite more than 50 programs in 7 Asian and 12 African countries. . . .

A planet without apes is not sci-fi fantasy. If we do not take action [to reauthorize] now, sometime in the future . . . our children and our children's children will ask with wonder, and perhaps a certain amount of anger, why we stood by idly while these remarkable creatures were driven to extinction.

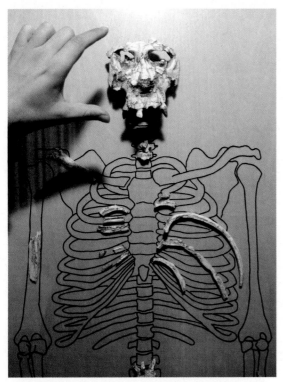

Pierolapithecus catalaunicus. The *Pierolapithecus* bones discovered so far include much of the skull, hand, and foot bones, including toe and finger fragments, three vertebrae, two complete ribs, and large pieces of a dozen others. This Miocene ape, first described in 2004, may be the last common ancestor of all the world's living great apes, including the human family.

common primates of the middle Miocene (16–10 m.y.a.). Over twenty species have been discovered in Europe, Africa, and Asia.

Perhaps the most remarkable Miocene ape was *Gigantopithecus*—almost certainly the largest primate that ever lived. Confined to Asia, it persisted for millions of years, from the Miocene until 400,000 years ago, when it coexisted with members of our own genus, *Homo erectus*. Some people think *Gigantopithecus* is not extinct yet, and that we know it today as the yeti and Bigfoot (Sasquatch).

With a fossil record consisting of nothing more than jawbones and teeth, it is difficult to say for sure just how big *Gigantopithecus* was. Based on ratios of jaw and tooth size to body size in other apes, various reconstructions have been made. One has *Gigantopithecus* weighing 1,200 pounds (544 kilograms) and standing 10 feet (3 meters)

tall (Ciochon, Olsen, and James 1990). Another puts the height at 9 feet (2.7 meters) and cuts the weight in half (Simons and Ettel 1970). All agree, however, that *Gigantopithecus* was the largest ape that ever lived. There have been at least two species of *Gigantopithecus*: one coexisted with *H. erectus* in China and Vietnam, and the other, much earlier (5 m.y.a.), lived in northern India.

Pierolapithecus catalaunicus

In 2004, Spanish anthropologists announced their discovery of what may be the last common ancestor of humans, chimpanzees, gorillas, and orangutans (Moyà-Solà et al. 2004). The new ape species, named *Pierolapithecus catalaunicus*, lived around 13 million years ago, during the middle Miocene. The find comes from a rich fossil site near the village of Hostalets de Pierola in Catalonia, Spain. The name *Pierolapithecus* combines part of the village's name with the Greek word for "ape," while *catalaunicus* commemorates Catalonia, the province where both the village and Barcelona are located.

The *Pierolapithecus* bones include much of the skull, hand and foot bones, three vertebrae, two complete ribs, and large pieces of a dozen others. The find appears to represent a single adult male that weighed about 75 pounds (34 kilograms). Like chimps and gorillas, *Pierolapithecus* was well adapted for tree climbing and knuckle-walking on the ground. Based on the shape of the single surviving tooth, it was probably a fruit eater. Several features distinguished *Pierolapithecus* from the lesser apes (gibbons and siamangs) and monkeys. Its rib cage, lower spine, and wrist suggest it climbed the way modern great apes do. The ape's chest, or thorax, is wider and flatter than that of monkeys and is the earliest modern apelike thorax yet found in the fossil record.

In the current timetable of primate evolution, the lineage of monkeys split off some 25 m.y.a. from the hominoid line, which led to apes and humans. The ancestors of the lesser apes separated from those of the great apes some 16–14 m.y.a. Then, around 11–10 m.y.a., the orangutan line diverged from that leading to the African apes and humans. Yet another split took place when the gorilla line branched off from the line leading to chimpanzees and hominins. Around 7–6 m.y.a., another split in the lineage led to the various early hominins, to be examined in the next chapter. Some intriguing fossils dating from that critical time period have been discovered recently.

summary

1. Humans, apes, monkeys, and prosimians are primates. The primate order is subdivided into suborders, superfamilies, families, tribes, genera, species, and subspecies. Organisms in any subdivision (taxon) of a taxonomy are assumed to share more recent ancestry with each other than they do with organisms in other taxa. But it's sometimes hard to tell the difference between homologies, which reflect common ancestry, and analogies, biological similarities that develop through convergent evolution.

2. Prosimians are the older of the two primate suborders. Around 50 million years ago, anthropoids (the other suborder) arose by adapting to a diurnal (daytime) ecological niche. Tarsiers and lorises are prosimians that survived by adapting to nocturnal life. Lemurs survived on the island of Madagascar.

3. Anthropoids include humans, apes, and monkeys. All share fully developed primate trends, such as depth and color vision. Other anthropoid traits include a shift in tactile areas to the fingers. All New World monkeys are arboreal. Old World monkeys include both terrestrial species (e.g., baboons and macaques) and arboreal ones. The great apes are orangutans, gorillas, chimpanzees, and bonobos. The lesser apes are gibbons and siamangs.

4. Gibbons and siamangs live in Southeast Asian forests. These apes are slight, arboreal animals whose mode of locomotion is brachiation. Sexual dimorphism, slight among gibbons, is marked among orangutans, which are confined to two Indonesian islands. Sexually dimorphic gorillas, the most terrestrial apes, are vegetarians confined to equatorial Africa. Two species of chimpanzees live in the forests and woodlands of tropical Africa. Chimps are less sexually dimorphic, more numerous, and more omnivorous than gorillas.

5. From the perspective of behavioral ecology, individuals in a population compete to increase their genetic contribution to future generations. Maternal care makes sense from this perspective because females can be sure their offspring are their own. Because it's harder for males to be sure about paternity, evolutionary theory predicts they will invest most in offspring when they are surest the offspring are theirs.

6. Primates have lived during the past 65 million years, the Cenozoic era, with seven epochs: Paleocene, Eocene, Oligocene, Miocene, Pliocene, Pleistocene, and Holocene, or Recent. The arboreal theory states that primates evolved by adapting to life high up in the trees.

7. The first (prosimian-like) primates lived during (and probably before) the Eocene (54–34 m.y.a.), mainly in North America and Europe. During the Oligocene (34–23 m.y.a.), anthropoids became the most numerous primates. The split between ancestral platyrrhines (New World monkeys) and catarrhines (Old World monkeys, apes, and humans) occurred during the Oligocene.

8. The earliest hominoid (proto-ape) fossils are from the Miocene (23–5 m.y.a.). Africa's *Proconsul* group contained the last common ancestor shared by the Old World monkeys and the apes. Since the middle Miocene (16–10 m.y.a.), Africa, Europe, and Asia have been connected. Proto-apes spread beyond Africa and became the most common primates of the middle Miocene. Asia's *Gigantopithecus,* the largest primate ever to live, persisted for millions of years, finally coexisting with *Homo erectus. Pierolapithecus catalaunicus,* which lived around 13 million years ago, could be the last common ancestor of humans, chimpanzees, gorillas, and orangutans.

152   PART 2 Physical Anthropology and Archaeology

key terms

MULTIPLE CHOICE

test yourself

1. What is the relevance of primatology to anthropology?
   a. Primatology is relevant only to applied anthropologists concerned about deforestation and poaching.
   b. It is central to anthropologists who work in forensics.
   c. It provides evidence for a newly revised description of the Great Chain of Being.
   d. It helps anthropologists make inferences about the early social organization of hominins and untangle issues of human nature and the origins of culture.
   e. Primatology no longer is relevant to anthropology because the most important research in the field was done when there were still wild primates.

2. Which of the following is (are) used for putting organisms in the same taxon (zoological category)?
   a. homologies
   b. anthropometrics
   c. only similarities that have evolved since the time of their common ancestor
   d. analogies
   e. all phenotypic similarities

3. What is the term for the evolutionary process by which organisms as unrelated as birds and butterflies develop similar characteristics because of adaptations to similar environments?
   a. inclusive fitness
   b. convergent evolution
   c. brachiation
   d. genetic drift
   e. gene flow

4. If chimps and gorillas are classified as hominids, what do some scientists call the group that leads to humans but not to chimps and gorillas?
   a. the tribe *humanity*
   b. the subtaxa *hominoid*

   c. siamang *humanoids*
   d. the tribe *hominini*
   e. no scientist makes this taxonomic distinction

5. What do the trends that *all* primates share (five fingers, opposable thumbs, stereoscopic vision) suggest?
   a. a common ancestral terrestrial heritage
   b. an ancestral culturally complex environment
   c. a common ancestral arboreal heritage
   d. the primitive "sexual division of labor," in which females gathered seeds while males hunted insects and small animals
   e. a common ancestral frugivorous heritage

6. Which of the following traits is *not* associated with primates?
   a. stereoscopic vision
   b. social groupings
   c. grasping adaptations
   d. reliance on smell as the main sense
   e. brain complexity

7. According to behavioral ecologists, what is inclusive fitness?
   a. reproductive success measured by the representation of genes one shares with other, related individuals
   b. the number of direct descendants an individual organism has
   c. the idea that human behavior is unconnected to genetics because of the existence of culture
   d. the degree to which anaerobic fitness is included in certain behaviors
   e. the ability of an individual to reproduce

8. Rough patches of skin on the buttocks and nonprehensile tails are characteristic traits of
   a. pongids.
   b. prosimians.
   c. Old World monkeys.
   d. New World monkeys.
   e. tarsiers.

9. Sexual dimorphism refers to
   a. marked differences between terrestrial and arboreal mating patterns.
   b. marked differences in male and female anatomy and temperament.
   c. marked differences between Old World and New World monkeys.
   d. continued sexual discrimination in anthropology departments.
   e. sexual maturation rates of prosimians.

10. What makes bonobos exceptional among primates?
   a. their ability to withstand the pressures of deforestation
   b. their degree of sociality
   c. their marked sexual dimorphism
   d. the frequency with which they have sex, a behavior associated with conflict avoidance
   e. their cannibalism

FILL IN THE BLANK

1. A _____ is a trait that organisms have jointly inherited from a common ancestor.
2. Based on primate taxonomy, lemurs, lorises, and tarsiers are part of the _____ primate suborder.
3. The process by which analogies are produced (resulting, for example, in fins in both fish and porpoises) is called _____.
4. The first anthropoids, ancestral to monkeys, apes, and humans, appeared around _____ million years ago, which, according to the geological time scale, corresponds to the _____ period and the _____ era.
5. The _____ group represents most abundant and successful anthropoids of the early Miocene. It also probably contained the last common ancestor shared by the Old World monkeys and apes.

CRITICAL THINKING

1. How does social organization vary among primates?
2. What is behavioral ecology? How would a behavioral ecologist explain parental investment in their offspring? Can you think of any other theoretical frameworks that could be used to explain these cases?
3. What are some unanswered questions about early primate evolution? What kinds of information would help provide answers? What are some of the difficulties that investigators face in solving these questions?
4. There have been reported sightings of "Bigfoot" in the Pacific Northwest of North America and of the yeti (abominable snowman) in the Himalayas. What facts about apes lead you to question such reports?
5. In Chapter 2 you were introduced to how our culture—and cultural changes—affect the ways in which we perceive nature, human nature, and "the natural." Can you think of aspects of your culture that have affected the way you think about humans' relationship to other primates?

Multiple Choice: 1. (D); 2. (A); 3. (B); 4. (D); 5. (C); 6. (C); 7. (A); 8. (A); 9. (C); 10. (D); **Fill in the Blank:** 1. homology; 2. prosimian; 3. convergent evolution; 4. 40, Tertiary, Cenozoic; 5. *Proconsul*

Cachel, S.

2006 *Primate and Human Evolution.* New York: Cambridge University Press. Human and primate evolution, behavior, and the fossil record.

De Waal, F. B. M.

2007 *Chimpanzee Politics: Power and Sex among Apes,* 25th anniversary ed. Baltimore, MD: Johns Hopkins University Press. Updating of classic study.

Hart, D., and R. W. Sussman

2009 *Man the Hunted: Primates, Predators, and Human Evolution,* expanded ed. Boulder, CO: Westview. The role of predation in human evolution; unique and readable examination of humans not as hunters but as prey.

Montgomery, S.

1991 *Walking with the Great Apes: Jane Goodall, Dian Fossey, Biruté Galdikas.* Boston: Houghton Mifflin. The stories of three primatologists who have worked with, and to preserve, chimpanzees, gorillas, and orangutans.

Nystrom, P., and P. Ashmore

2008 *The Life of Primates.* Boston: Pearson Prentice Hall. Survey of primates, their behavior, and social organization.

Strier, K. B.

2011 *Primate Behavioral Ecology,* 4th ed. Upper Saddle River, NJ: Prentice Hall. Behavior and reproductive strategies among primates.

Go to our Online Learning Center website at **www.mhhe.com/kottak** for Internet exercises directly related to the content of this chapter.

CHAPTER 8

Early Hominins

What key traits make us human, and when and how are they revealed in the fossil record?

Who were the australopithecines, and what role did they play in human evolution?

When and where did hominins first make tools?

◀ South African paleoanthropologist Phillip Tobias, who died in 2012 at the age of 86. Tobias was well known for his excavations at Sterkfontein, which yielded significant australopithecine remains.

understanding OURSELVES

Do you remember the "monkey bars" in your playground? How did you use them? It sure wasn't like a monkey. The human shoulder bone, like that of the apes, is adapted for brachiation—swinging hand over hand through the trees. Monkeys, by contrast, move about on four limbs. Apes can stand and walk on two feet, as humans habitually do, but in the trees, and otherwise when climbing, apes and humans don't leap around as monkeys do. In climbing we extend our arms and pull up. When we use "monkey bars," we hang and move hand over hand rather than getting on top and running across, as a monkey would do. For most contemporary humans, the ability to use "monkey bars" declines long before our ability to walk. Humans have the shoulder of a brachiator because we share a distant brachiating ancestor with the apes. Bipedal locomotion, on the other hand, is the most ancient trait that makes us truly human.

Only when we lose it do we appreciate fully the supreme significance of bipedalism. I know this from personal experience. On the day before her 99th birthday, my mother broke her hip. She survived a hip replacement operation, spent a week in the hospital, then entered a rehab center, where she had to rely on staff for much of what previously she had done on her own. She couldn't climb in and out of bed, nor could she bathe herself or attend to personal functions.

Watching my mother endure weeks of indignity, I became acutely aware of what bipedalism means to humans. Younger people with greater upper body strength often can move about independently without using their legs. Not so a very old woman who over the years had developed osteoporosis and suffered several fractures (along with arthritis) affecting wrists, arms, and shoulders. All those had been painful reminders of the aging process. None, however, was as devastating as her hip break. Unable to walk and debilitated by an infection she contracted in the hospital, my mother gradually lost her interests and her will to live. She stopped following the news, abandoning TV and any attempt to read. Her rehabilitation wasn't succeeding; she hated relying on others for her personal functions. She died less than two months after her fall. My mother's longevity illustrates how cultural advances (e.g., medicine, nutrition, operations) have extended the human lifespan—but only to a point. Certainly no Ice Age hominin lived for a century; however, images of the future in the movie *Wall-E* notwithstanding, humans today are no less bipedal than our ancestors were five million years ago. Bipedalism is an integral and enduring feature of human adaptation.

WHAT MAKES US HUMAN?

In trying to determine whether a fossil is a human ancestor, should we look for traits that make us human today? Sometimes yes; sometimes no. We do look for similarities in DNA, including mutations shared by certain lineages but not others. But what about such key human attributes as bipedal locomotion, a long period of childhood dependency, big brains, and the use of tools and language? Some of these key markers of humanity are fairly recent—or have origins that are impossible to date. And ironically, some of the physical markers that have led scientists to identify certain fossils as early hominins rather than apes are features that have been lost during subsequent human evolution.

Bipedalism

As is true of all subsequent hominins, postcranial material from **Ardipithecus,** the earliest widely accepted hominin genus (5.8–4.4 m.y.a.), indicates a capacity—albeit an imperfect one—for upright bipedal locomotion. The *Ardipithecus* pelvis appears to be transitional between one suited for arboreal climbing and one modified for bipedalism. Reliance on bipedalism—upright two-legged locomotion—is the key feature differentiating early hominins from the apes. This way of moving around eventually led to the distinctive hominin way of life. Based on African fossil discoveries, such as Ethiopia's *Ardipithecus,* hominin bipedalism is more than five million years old. Some scientists see even earlier evidence of bipedalism in two other fossil finds described below—one from Chad (*Sahelanthropus tchadensis*) and one from Kenya (*Orrorin tugenensis*).

Bipedalism traditionally has been viewed as an adaptation to open grassland or savanna country, although *Ardipithecus* lived in a humid woodland habitat. Perhaps bipedalism developed in the woodlands but became even more adaptive in a savanna habitat (see Choi 2011). Scientists have suggested several advantages of bipedalism: the abilities to see over long grass and scrub, to carry items back to a home base, and to reduce the body's exposure to solar radiation. Studies with scale models of primates suggest that quadrupedalism exposes the body to 60 percent more solar radiation than does bipedalism. The fossil and archaeological records confirm that upright bipedal locomotion preceded stone tool manufacture and the expansion of the hominin brain. However, although early hominins could move bipedally on the ground, they also preserved enough of an apelike anatomy to make them good climbers (see the description of *Ardipithecus* on pp. 162–163). They could take to the trees to sleep and to escape terrestrial predators.

Brains, Skulls, and Childhood Dependency

Compared with contemporary humans, early hominins had very small brains. *Australopithecus afarensis,* a bipedal hominin that lived more than three million years ago, had a cranial capacity (430 cm³—cubic centimeters) that barely surpassed the chimp average (390 cm³). The form of the *afarensis* skull also is like that of the chimpanzee, although the brain-to-body size ratio may have been larger. Brain size has increased during hominin evolution, especially with the advent of the genus *Homo*. But this increase had to overcome some obstacles. Compared with the young of other primates, human children have a long period of childhood dependency,

Reconstruction of *Australopithecus* running bipedally with a pebble tool in hand. Along with tool use and manufacture, bipedalism is a key part of being human.

Ardipithecus
Earliest recognized hominin genus (5.8–4.4 m.y.a.), Ethiopia.

during which their brains and skulls grow dramatically. Larger skulls demand larger birth canals, but the requirements of upright bipedalism impose limits on the expansion of the human pelvic opening. If the opening is too large, the pelvis doesn't provide sufficient support for the trunk. Locomotion suffers, and posture problems develop. If, by contrast, the birth canal is too narrow, mother and child (without the modern option of Caesarean section) may die. Natural selection has struck a balance between the structural demands of upright posture and the tendency toward increased brain size—the birth of immature and dependent children whose brains and skulls grow dramatically after birth.

Tools

Given what is known (see Chapter 2) about tool use and manufacture by the great apes, it is likely that early hominins shared this ability as a homology with the apes. We'll see later that the first evidence for hominin stone tool manufacture is dated to 2.6 m.y.a. Upright bipedalism would have permitted the use of tools and weapons against predators and competitors. Bipedal locomotion also allowed early hominins to carry things, perhaps including scavenged parts of carnivore kills. We know that primates have generalized abilities to adapt through learning. It would be amazing if early hominins, who are much more closely related to us than the apes are, didn't have even greater cultural abilities than contemporary apes have.

Teeth

One example of an early hominin trait that has been lost during subsequent human evolution is big back teeth. (Indeed, a pattern of overall dental reduction has characterized human evolution.) Once they adapted to the savanna, with its gritty, tough, and fibrous vegetation, it was adaptively advantageous for early hominins to have large back teeth and thick tooth enamel. This permitted thorough chewing of tough, fibrous vegetation and mixture with salivary enzymes to permit digestion of foods that otherwise would not have been digestible. The churning, rotary motion associated with such chewing also favored reduction of the canines and first premolars (bicuspids). These front teeth are much sharper and longer in the apes than in early hominins. The apes use their sharp self-honing teeth to pierce fruits. Males also flash their big, sharp canines to intimidate and impress others, including potential mates. Although bipedalism seems to have characterized the human lineage since it split from the line leading to the African apes, many other "human" features came later. Yet other early hominin features, such as large back teeth and thick enamel—which we don't have now—offer clues about who was a human ancestor back then.

CHRONOLOGY OF HOMININ EVOLUTION

Recall that the term *hominin* is used to designate the human line after its split from ancestral chimps. *Hominid* refers to the taxonomic family that includes humans and the African apes and their immediate ancestors. In this book *hominid* is used when there is doubt about the hominin status of the fossil. Although recent fossil discoveries have pushed the hominin lineage back to almost six million years ago, humans actually haven't been around too long when the age of the Earth is considered. If we compare Earth's history to a 24-hour day (with one second equaling 50,000 years),

Earth originated at midnight.

The earliest fossils were deposited at 5:45 A.M.

The first vertebrates appeared at 9:02 P.M.

The earliest mammals, at 10:45 P.M.

The earliest primates, at 11:43 P.M.

The earliest hominins, at 11:57 P.M.

And *Homo sapiens* arrived 36 seconds before midnight. (Wolpoff 1999, p. 10)

Although the first hominins appeared late in the Miocene epoch, for the study of hominin evolution, the Pliocene (5–2 m.y.a.), Pleistocene (2 m.y.a.–10,000 B.P.), and Recent (10,000 B.P.–present) epochs are most important. Until the end of the Pliocene, the main hominin genus was *Australopithecus,* which lived in sub-Saharan Africa. By the start of the Pleistocene, *Australopithecus* had evolved into *Homo.*

WHO WERE THE EARLIEST HOMININS?

Recent discoveries of fossils and tools have increased our knowledge of hominid and hominin evolution. The most significant recent discoveries have been made in Africa—Kenya, Tanzania, Ethiopia, South Africa, and Chad. These finds come from different sites and may be the remains of individuals that lived hundreds of thousands of years apart. Furthermore, geological processes operating over thousands or millions of years inevitably distort fossil remains. Table 8.1 summarizes the major events in hominid and hominin evolution. You should consult it throughout this chapter and the next one.

Sahelanthropus tchadensis

In July 2001 anthropologists working in Central Africa—in northern Chad's Djurab Desert—unearthed the 6- to 7-million-year-old skull of the oldest possible human ancestor yet found. This discovery consists of a nearly complete skull, two lower jaw fragments, and three teeth. It dates to the time period when humans and chimps would have been diverging from a common ancestor. "It takes us into another world, of creatures that include the common ancestor, the ancestral human and the ancestral chimp," George Washington University paleobiologist Bernard Wood said (quoted in Gugliotta 2002). The discovery

French paleoanthropologist Michel Brunet holds *Sahelanthropus tchadensis,* nicknamed "Toumai" (on the left), and a modern chimpanzee skull (on the right). If Toumai isn't a human ancestor, what else might it be?

TABLE 8.1 Dates and Geographic Distribution of Major Hominoid, Hominid, and Hominin Fossil Groups

FOSSIL GROUP	DATES, m.y.a.	KNOWN DISTRIBUTION
Hominoid		
Pierolapithecus catalaunicus	13	Spain
Hominid		
Common ancestor of hominids	8?	East Africa
Sahelanthropus tchadensis	7–6	Chad
Orrorin tugenensis	6	Kenya
Hominins		
Ardipithecus kadabba	5.8–5.5	Ethiopia
Ardipithecus ramidus	4.4	Ethiopia
Kenyanthropus platyops	3.5	Kenya
Australopithecines		
A. anamensis	4.2–3.9	Kenya
A. afarensis	3.8–3.0	East Africa (Laetoli, Hadar)
A. garhi	2.5	Ethiopia
A. sediba	1.98	South Africa
Robusts	2.6–1.2	East and South Africa
A. robustus (aka *Paranthropus*)	2.0?–1.0?	South Africa
A. boisei	2.6?–1.2	East Africa
Graciles		
A. africanus	3.0?–2.0?	South Africa
Homo		
H. habilis/H. rudolfensis	2.4?–1.4?	East Africa
H. erectus	1.9?–0.3?	Africa, Asia, Europe
Homo sapiens	0.3–present	
Archaic H. sapiens	0.3–0.28 (300,000–28,000)	Africa, Asia, Europe
Neandertals	0.13–0.28 (130,000–28,000)	Europe, Middle East, North Africa
Anatomically modern humans (AMHs)	0.15?–present (150,000–present)	Worldwide (after 20,000 B.P.)

was made by a forty-member multinational team led by the French paleoanthropologist Michel Brunet. The actual discoverer was the university undergraduate Ahounta Djimdoumalbaye, who spied the skull embedded in sandstone. The new fossil was dubbed *Sahelanthropus tchadensis*, referring to the northern Sahel region of Chad where it was found. The fossil also is known as "Toumai," a local name meaning "hope of life."

The discovery team identified the skull as that of an adult male with a chimp-sized brain (320–380 cm³), heavy brow ridges, and a relatively flat, humanlike face. Toumai's habitat included savanna, forests, rivers, and lakes—and abundant animal life such as elephants, antelope, horses, giraffes, hyenas, hippopotamuses, wild boars, crocodiles, fish, and rodents. The animal species enabled the team to date the site where Toumai was found (by comparison with radiometrically dated sites with similar fauna).

The discovery of Toumai moves scientists close to the time when humans and the African apes diverged from a common ancestor (see Weiss 2005, Wood 2011). As we would expect in a fossil so close to the common ancestor, Toumai blends apelike and

human characteristics. Although the brain was chimp-sized, the tooth enamel was thicker than a chimp's enamel, suggesting a diet that included not just fruits but also tougher vegetation of a sort typically found in the savanna. Also, Toumai's snout did not protrude as far as a chimp's, making it more humanlike, and the canine tooth was shorter than those of other apes. "The fossil is showing the first glimmerings of evolution in our direction," according to University of California at Berkeley anthropologist Tim White (quoted in Gugliotta 2002).

Toumai is a nearly complete, although distorted, skull. The placement of its *foramen magnum* (the "big hole" through which the spinal cord joins the brain) farther forward than in apes suggests that *Sahelanthropus* moved bipedally. Its discovery in Chad indicates that early hominin evolution was not confined to East Africa's Rift Valley. The Rift Valley's abundant fossil record may well reflect geology, preservation, and modern exposure of fossils rather than the actual geographic distribution of species in the past. If *Sahelanthropus* was indeed a hominin, its discovery in Chad is the first proof of a more widespread distribution of early hominins.

Orrorin tugenensis

In January 2001 Brigitte Senut, Martin Pickford, and others reported the discovery, near the village of Tugen in Kenya's Baringo district, of possible early hominin fossils they called *Orrorin tugenensis* (Aiello and Collard 2001; Senut et al. 2001). The find consisted of thirteen fossils from at least five individuals. The fossils include pieces of jaw with teeth, isolated upper and lower teeth, arm bones, and a finger bone. *Orrorin* appears to have been a chimp-sized creature that climbed easily and walked on two legs when on the ground. Its date of 6 million years is close to the time of the common ancestor of humans and chimps. The fossilized left femur (thigh bone) suggests upright bipedalism, while the thick right humerus (upper arm bone) suggests tree-climbing skills. Animal fossils found in the same rocks indicate *Orrorin* lived in a wooded environment.

Orrorin's upper incisor, upper canine, and lower premolar are more like the teeth of a female chimpanzee than like human teeth. But other dental and skeletal features, especially bipedalism, led the discoverers to assign *Orrorin* to the hominin lineage. *Orrorin* lived after *Sahelanthropus tchadensis* but before *Ardipithecus kadabba*, discovered in Ethiopia, also in 2001, and dated to 5.8–5.5 m.y.a. The hominin status of *Ardipithecus* is more generally accepted than is that of either *Sahelanthropus tchadensis* or *Orrorin tugenensis*.

Ardipithecus

Early hominins assigned to *Ardipithecus kadabba* lived during the late Miocene, between 5.8 and 5.5 million years ago. *Ardipithecus* (*ramidus*) fossils were first discovered at Aramis in Ethiopia by Berhane Asfaw, Gen Suwa, and Tim White. Dating to 4.4 m.y.a., these *Ardipithecus ramidus* fossils consisted of the remains of some seventeen individuals, with cranial, facial, dental, and upper limb bones. Subsequently, much older *Ardipithecus* (*kadabba*) fossils, dating back to 5.8 m.y.a., were found in Ethiopia. The *kadabba* find consists of eleven specimens, including a jawbone with teeth, hand and foot bones, fragments of arm bones, and a piece of collarbone. At least five individuals are represented. These creatures were apelike in size, anatomy, and habitat. They lived in a wooded area rather than the open grassland or savanna habitat where later hominins proliferated. As of this writing, because of its probable bipedalism, *Ardipithecus kadabba* is recognized as the earliest known hominin, with the *Sahelanthropus tchadensis* find from Chad, dated to 7–6 m.y.a., and *Orrorin tugenensis* from Kenya, dated to 6 m.y.a., as possibly even older hominins.

In October 2009, a newly reported *Ardipithecus* find—a fairly complete skeleton of *Ardipithecus ramidus,* dubbed "Ardi"—was heralded on the front page of the *New York Times* and throughout the media (Wilford 2009a). Ardi (4.4 m.y.a.) replaces Lucy

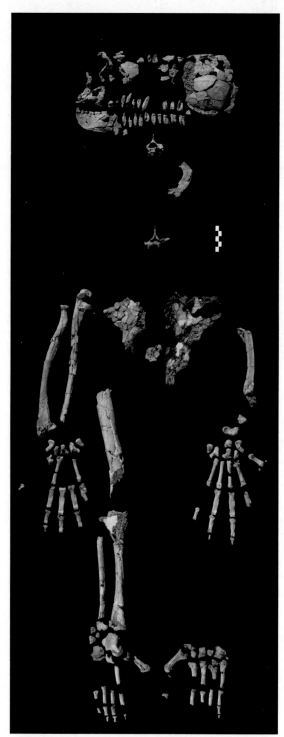

In October 2009, a newly reported *Ardipithecus* find—a fairly complete skeleton of *Ardipithecus ramidus,* dubbed "Ardi," was heralded throughout the media.

(3.2 m.y.a.—see below) as the earliest known hominin skeleton. The Ethiopian discovery site lies on what is now an arid floodplain of the Awash River, 45 miles south of Hadar, where Lucy was found. Scientists infer that Ardi was female, based on its small and lightly built (gracile) skull and its small canine teeth compared with others at the site. At four feet

Shown here are three members of the international team responsible for Ardi's discovery and reconstruction. Above is American Tim White. Below are Ethiopians Johannes Haile-Selassie and Berhane Asfaw.

tall and 120 pounds, Ardi stood about a foot taller than and weighed twice as much as Lucy.

The *Ardipithecus* pelvis appears to be transitional between one suited for arboreal climbing and one modified for bipedal locomotion. The pelvis of later hominins such as Lucy shows nearly all the adaptations needed for full bipedalism. Although Ardi's lower pelvis remains primitive, the structure of her upper pelvis allowed her to walk on two legs with a straightened hip. Still, she probably could neither walk nor run as well as later hominins. Her feet lacked the archlike structure of later hominin feet (see Ward, Kimbel, and Johanson 2011). Ardi's apelike lower pelvis indicates retention of powerful hamstring muscles for climbing. Her hands, very long arms, and short legs all recall those of extinct apes, and her brain was no larger than that of a modern chimp.

Based on associated animal and plant remains, *Ardipithecus* lived in a humid woodland habitat. More than 145 hominin teeth have been collected at the site. Their size, shape, and wear patterns suggest an omnivorous diet of plants, nuts, and small mammals. Although *Ardipithecus* probably fed both in trees and on the ground, the canines suggest less of a fruit diet than is characteristic of living apes. With reduced sexual dimorphism, *Ardipithecus* canines resemble modern human canines more than the tusklike piercing upper canines of chimps and gorillas.

The first comprehensive reports describing Ardi and related findings, the result of seventeen years of study, were published on October 2, 2009, in the journal *Science,* including eleven papers by forty-seven authors from ten countries. They analyzed

more than 110 *Ardipithecus* specimens from at least 36 different individuals, including Ardi. The ancestral relationship of *Ardipithecus* to *Australopithecus* has not been determined, but Ardi has been called a plausible ancestor for *Australopithecus* (see Wilford 2009a).

Kenyanthropus

Complicating the picture is another discovery, which Maeve Leakey has named *Kenyanthropus platyops,* or

Maeve Leakey and *Kenyanthropus platyops,* which she discovered in 1999 by Lake Turkana in northern Kenya. What's the significance of *Kenyanthropus*?

THE VARIED AUSTRALOPITHECINES

Some Miocene hominins eventually evolved into a varied group of Pliocene-Pleistocene hominins known as the **australopithecines**—for which we have an abundant fossil record. This term reflects their one-time classification as members of a distinct taxonomic subfamily, the "Australopithecinae." We now know that the various species of *Australopithecus* discussed in this chapter do not form a distinct subfamily within the order Primates, but the name "australopithecine" has stuck to describe them. Today the distinction between the australopithecines and later hominins is made on the genus level. The australopithecines are assigned to the genus *Australopithecus (A.);* later humans, to *Homo (H.).*

In the scheme followed here, *Australopithecus* had at least seven species:

1. *A. anamensis* (4.2–3.9 m.y.a.)
2. *A. afarensis* (3.8–3.0 m.y.a.)
3. *A. africanus* (3.0?–2.0? m.y.a.)
4. *A. garhi* (2.5 m.y.a.)
5. *A. robustus* (2.0?–1.0? m.y.a.)
6. *A. boisei* (2.6?–1.2 m.y.a.)
7. *A. sediba* (1.98–1.78 m.y.a.)

The date ranges given for these species are approximate because an organism isn't a member of one species one day and a member of another species the next day. Nor could the same dating techniques be used for all the finds. The earliest South African australopithecine fossils (*A. africanus* and *A. robustus*), for example, come from a nonvolcanic area where radiometric dating could not be done. Dating of those fossils has been based mainly on stratigraphy. The hominin fossils from the volcanic regions of East Africa usually have radiometric dates.

Australopithecus anamensis

Ardipithecus ramidus may (or may not) have evolved into *A. anamensis,* a bipedal hominin from northern Kenya, whose fossil remains were reported first by Maeve Leakey and Alan Walker in 1995 (Leakey et al. 1995; Rice 2002). **A. anamensis** consists of seventy-eight fragments from two sites: Kanapoi and Allia Bay. The fossils include upper and lower jaws, cranial fragments, and the upper and lower parts of a leg bone (tibia). The Kanapoi fossils date to 4.2 m.y.a., and those at Allia Bay to 3.9 m.y.a. The molars have thick enamel, and the apelike canines are large. Based on the tibia (shinbone), *anamensis* weighed about 110 pounds (50 kg). This would have made it larger than either the earlier *Ardipithecus* or the later *A. afarensis.* Its anatomy implies that anamensis was bipedal. Because of its date and its location in the East African Rift Valley, *A. anamensis* may be

australopithecines
Common term for all members of the genus *Australopithecus.*

A. anamensis
Earliest known *Australopithecus* species (4.2–3.9 m.y.a.), Kenya.

flat-faced "man" of Kenya. (Actually, the sex hasn't been determined.) This 1999 fossil find—of a nearly complete skull and partial jawbone—was made by a research team led by Leakey, excavating on the western side of Lake Turkana in northern Kenya. They consider this 3.5-million-year-old find to represent an entirely new branch of the early human family tree.

Leakey views *Kenyanthropus* as showing that at least two hominin lineages existed as far back as 3.5 million years. One was the well-established fossil species *Australopithecus afarensis* (see below), best known from the celebrated Lucy skeleton. With the discovery of *Kenyanthropus* it would seem that Lucy and her kind weren't alone on the African plain. The hominin family tree, once drawn with a straight trunk, now looks more like a bush, with branches leading in many directions (Wilford 2001*a*).

Kenyanthropus has a flattened face and small molars that are strikingly different from those of *afarensis.* Ever since its discovery in Ethiopia in 1974 by Donald Johanson, *afarensis* has been regarded as the most likely common ancestor of all subsequent hominins, including humans (see Johanson and Wong 2009). With no other hominin fossils dated to the period between 3.8 and 3.0 m.y.a., this was the most reasonable conclusion scientists could draw. As a result of the *Kenyanthropus* discovery, however, the place of *afarensis* in human ancestry has been and will be debated. Taxonomic "splitters" (those who stress diversity and divergence) will focus on the differences between *afarensis* and *Kenyanthropus* and see it as representing a new taxon (genus and/or species), as Maeve Leakey has done. Taxonomic "lumpers" will focus on the similarities between *Kenyanthropus* and *afarensis* and may try to place them both in the same taxon—probably *Australopithecus,* which is well established.

ancestral to *A. afarensis* (3.8–3.0 m.y.a.), which usually is considered ancestral to all the later australopithecines (*garhi, africanus, robustus,* and *boisei*) as well as to *Homo* (Figure 8.1).

Australopithecus afarensis

The hominin species known as **A. afarensis** includes fossils found at two sites, Laetoli in northern Tanzania and Hadar in the Afar region of Ethiopia. Laetoli is earlier (3.8–3.6 m.y.a.). The Hadar fossils probably date to between 3.3 and 3.0 m.y.a. Thus, based on the current evidence, *A. afarensis* lived between about 3.8 and 3.0 m.y.a. Research directed by Mary Leakey was responsible for the Laetoli finds. The Hadar discoveries resulted from an international expedition directed by D. C. Johanson and M. Taieb. The two sites have yielded significant samples of early hominin fossils. There are two dozen specimens from Laetoli, and the Hadar finds include the remains of between thirty-five and sixty-five individuals. The Laetoli remains are mainly teeth and jaw fragments, along with some very informative fossilized footprints. The Hadar sample includes skull fragments and postcranial material, most notably 40 percent of the complete skeleton of a tiny hominin female, dubbed "Lucy," who lived around 3 m.y.a.

Although the hominin remains at Laetoli and Hadar were deposited half a million years apart, their many resemblances explain their placement in the same species, *A. afarensis.* These fossils forced a reinterpretation of the early hominin fossil record. *A. afarensis,* although clearly a hominin, was so similar in many ways to chimps and gorillas that our common ancestry with the African apes had to be very recent, certainly no more than 8 m.y.a. *Ardipithecus* and *A. anamensis* are even more apelike. These discoveries showed that hominins are much closer to the apes than the previously known fossil record had suggested. Studies of the learning abilities, biochemistry, and DNA of chimps and gorillas have taught a valuable lesson about homologies that the fossil record is now confirming.

The *A. afarensis* finds make this clear. The many apelike features are surprising in definite hominins

A. afarensis
Early *Australopithecus* species (3.8–3.0 m.y.a.), Ethiopia ("Lucy"), Tanzania.

An ancient trail of hominin footprints fossilized in volcanic ash. Mary Leakey found this 230-foot (70-meter) trail at Laetoli, Tanzania, in 1979. It dates from 3.6 m.y.a. and confirms that *A. afarensis* was a striding biped.

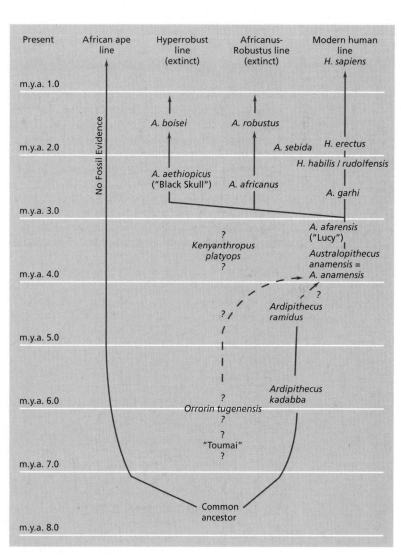

FIGURE 8.1 Phylogenetic Tree for African Apes, Hominids, and Hominins.

The presumed divergence date for ancestral chimps and hominins was between 6 and 8 m.y.a. Branching in later hominin evolution is also shown. For more exact dates, see the text and Table 8.1.

that lived as recently as 3 m.y.a. Discussion of hominin fossils requires a brief review of dentition. Moving from front to back, on either side of the upper or lower jaw, humans (and apes) have two incisors, one canine, two premolars, and three molars. Our dental formula is 2.1.2.3, for a total of 8 teeth on each side, upper and lower—32 teeth in all—if we have all our "wisdom teeth" (our third molars). Now back to the australopithecines.

From the same general area of northern Ethiopia as Lucy comes another important member of *A. afarensis* (Owen 2006). This toddler, the world's oldest fossil child, soon was dubbed "Lucy's Baby"—despite having lived a hundred thousand years before Lucy (3.3 m.y.a. for the child versus 3.2 for Lucy). The child is an amazingly complete find, with a more intact skull and much more skeletal material than exists for Lucy. Not surprisingly, given what we already know about *A. afarensis,* the skull and upper body are apelike, while the lower body confirms bipedalism. Despite bipedalism, the skeleton's upper body includes two complete shoulder blades similar to a gorilla's, so it probably was better at climbing than humans are.

Unearthed in 2000, the child probably was female and about three years old when she died. The remains include a well-preserved skull, baby teeth, tiny fingers, a torso, a foot, and a kneecap. Although Lucy doesn't have much of a head, her "baby" has a complete skull, a mandible (jaw bone), and a monkey-sized face with a smooth brow.

Lucy's baby sheds light on the growth process in early humans. A prolonged, dependent childhood allowed later human species to grow larger brains, which need several years to develop after birth. Such a long period of brain growth apparently did not characterize *A. afarensis*. While the adult *A. afarensis* brain is thought to have been slightly larger than a chimp's, Lucy's "baby's" brain was smaller than that of a chimp of comparable age.

Compared with *Homo, A. afarensis* had larger and sharper canine teeth that projected beyond the other teeth. The canines, however, were reduced compared with an ape's tusklike canines. The *afarensis* lower premolar was pointed and projecting to sharpen the upper canine. It had one long cusp and one tiny bump that hints at the bicuspid premolar that eventually developed in hominin evolution.

There is, however, evidence that powerful chewing associated with savanna vegetation was entering the *A. afarensis* feeding pattern. When the coarse, gritty, fibrous vegetation of grasslands and semidesert enters the diet, the back teeth change to accommodate heavy chewing stresses. Massive back teeth, jaws, and facial and cranial structures suggest a diet demanding extensive grinding and powerful crushing. *A. afarensis* molars are large (see Figure 8.2). The lower jaw (mandible) is thick and is buttressed with a bony ridge behind the front teeth. The cheekbones are large and flare out to the side for the attachment of powerful chewing muscles.

The skull of *A. afarensis* contrasts with those of later hominins. The cranial capacity of 430 cm^3 barely surpasses the chimp average (390 cm^3). Below the neck, however—particularly in regard to locomotion—*A. afarensis* was unquestionably human. Early evidence of striding bipedalism comes from Laetoli, where volcanic ash, which can be directly dated by the K/A technique, covered a trail of footprints of two or three hominins walking to a water

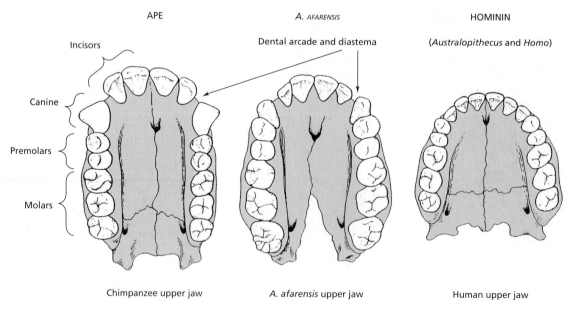

FIGURE 8.2 Comparison of Dentition in Ape, Human, and *A. afarensis* Palates.

SOURCE: © 1981 Luba Dmytryk Gudz/Brill Atlanta.

SPECIES	DATES (m.y.a.)	KNOWN DISTRIBUTION	IMPORTANT SITES	BODY WEIGHT (MID-SEX)	BRAIN SIZE (MID-SEX) (cm³)
Anatomically modern humans (AMHs)	195,000–present			132 lb/60 kg	1,350
Pan troglodytes (chimpanzee)	Modern			93 lb/42 kg	390
A. sediba	1.98–1.78	S. Africa	Malapa	Insufficient data	420
A. boisei	2.6?–1.2	E. Africa	Olduvai, East Turkana	86 lb/39 kg	490
A. robustus	2.0?–1.0?	S. Africa	Kromdraai, Swartkrans	81 lb/37 kg	540
A. africanus	3.0?–2.0?	S. Africa	Taung, Sterkfontein, Makapansqat	79 lb/36 kg	490
A. afarensis	3.8–3.0	E. Africa	Hadar, Laetoli	77 lb/35 kg	430
A. anamensis	4.2–3.9	Kenya	Kanapoi Allia Bay	Insufficient data	No published skulls
Ardipithecus	5.8–4.4	Ethiopia	Aramis	Insufficient data	No published skulls

hole. These prints leave no doubt that a small striding biped lived in Tanzania by 3.6 m.y.a. The structure of the pelvic, hip, leg, and foot bones also confirms that upright bipedalism was *A. afarensis*'s mode of locomotion (see Ward, Kimbel, and Johanson 2011).

Although bidepal, *A. afarensis* still contrasts in many ways with later hominins. Sexual dimorphism is especially marked. *A. afarensis* females, such as Lucy, stood between 3 and 4 feet (0.9 and 1.2 meters) tall; males might have reached 5 feet (1.5 meters). Adult males weighed perhaps twice as much as the females did (Wolpoff 1999). Recap 8.1 summarizes data on the various australopithecines, including mid-sex body weight and brain size. Mid-sex means midway between the male average and the female average.

Lucy and her kind were far from dainty. Her muscle-engraved bones are much more robust than ours are. With only rudimentary tools and weapons, early hominins needed powerful and resistant bones and muscles. Lucy's arms are longer relative to her legs than are those of later hominins. Here again her proportions are more apelike than ours are. Lucy was probably a much better climber than modern people are, and she spent some of her day in the trees.

The *A. afarensis* fossils show that as recently as 3 m.y.a., our ancestors had a mixture of apelike and hominin features. Canines, premolars, and skulls were more apelike than most scholars had imagined would exist in such a recent ancestor. On the other hand, the molars, chewing apparatus, and cheekbones foreshadowed later hominin trends, and the

Illustration of female *Australopithecus afarensis* "Lucy," discovered in Ethiopia's Omo Valley in 1974.

pelvic and limb bones were indisputably hominin (Figure 8.3 on page 168). The hominin pattern was being built from the ground up.

The pelvis, the lower spine, the hip joint, and the thigh bone changed in accordance with the stresses

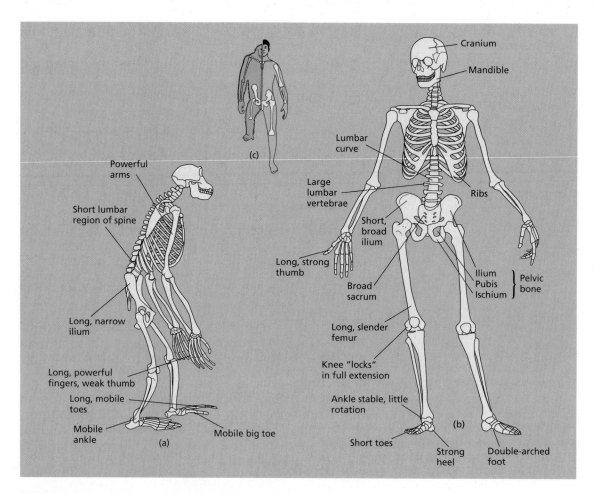

FIGURE 8.3 Comparison of *Homo sapiens* and *Pan troglodytes* (the Common Chimp).
(a) Skeleton of chimpanzee in bipedal position; (b) skeleton of modern human; (c) chimpanzee and human "bisected" and drawn to the same trunk length for comparison of limb proportions. The contrast in leg length is largely responsible for the proportional difference between humans and apes.

of bipedal locomotion. Australopithecine pelvises are much more similar (although far from identical) to *Homo*'s than to apes' and show adaptation to bipedalism (Figure 8.4). The blades of the australopithecine pelvis (iliac blades) are shorter and broader than are those of the ape. The sacrum, which anchors the pelvis's two side bones, is larger, as in *Homo*. With bipedalism, the pelvis forms a sort of basket that balances the weight of the trunk and supports this weight with less stress. The australopithecine spine had the lower spine (lumbar) curve characteristic of *Homo*. This curvature helps transmit the weight of the upper body to the pelvis and the legs. Placement of the *foramen magnum* (the "big hole" through which the spinal cord joins the brain) farther forward in *Australopithecus* and *Homo* than in the ape also represents an adaptation to upright bipedalism (Figure 8.5).

In apes, the thigh bone (femur) extends straight down from the hip to the knees. In *Australopithecus* and *Homo*, however, the thigh bone angles into the hip, permitting the space between the knees to be narrower than the pelvis during walking. The pelvises

living anthropology **VIDEOS**

Lucy, www.mhhe.com/kottak

This clip describes the discovery and characteristics of Lucy, the first member of *Australopithecus afarensis* to enter the fossil record. On her discovery in 1974, Lucy became the most ancient hominin and hominid in the fossil record at that time. Today that record includes several older probable or possible hominin ancestors, identified as such—like Lucy—by their upright bipedalism. The clip supplies answers to the following questions: Which of Lucy's anatomical traits were similar to those of chimpanzees? Which were similar to those of modern humans? How did Lucy's pelvis differ from an ape's pelvis? What is the explanation for this difference?

of the australopithecines were similar but not identical to those of *Homo*. The most significant contrast is a narrower australopithecine birth canal (Tague and Lovejoy 1986).

Expansion of the birth canal is a trend in hominin evolution. The width of the birth canal is related to the size of the skull and brain. *A. afarensis* had a small cranial capacity. Even in later australopithecines, brain size did not exceed 600 cm³. Undoubtedly, the australopithecine skull grew after birth to accommodate a growing brain, as it does (much more) in *Homo*. However, the brains of the australopithecines expanded less than ours do. In the australopithecines, the cranial sutures (the lines where the bones of the skull eventually come together) fused relatively earlier in life.

Young australopithecines must have depended on their parents and kin for nurturance and protection. Those years of childhood dependency would have provided time for observation, teaching, and learning. This may provide indirect evidence for a rudimentary cultural life.

Gracile and Robust Australopithecines

The fossils of *A. africanus* and *A. robustus* come from South Africa. In 1924, the anatomist Raymond Dart coined the term **A. (Australopithecus) africanus** to describe the first fossil representative of this species, the skull of a juvenile that was found accidentally in a quarry at Taung, South Africa. Radiometric dates are lacking for this nonvolcanic region, but the fossil hominins found at five main South African sites appear (from stratigraphy) to have lived between 3 and 1 m.y.a. The most recent South African *Australopithecus* find, *A. sediba*, described in this chapter's "Appreciating Anthropology," has been dated more precisely, to 1.98 m.y.a.

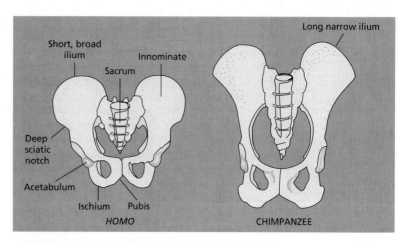

FIGURE 8.4 A Comparison of Human and Chimpanzee Pelvises. The human pelvis has been modified to meet the demands of upright bipedalism. The blades (*ilia*; singular, *ilium*) of the human pelvis are shorter and broader than those of the ape. The sacrum, which anchors the side bones, is wider. The australopithecine pelvis is far more similar to that of *Homo* than to that of the chimpanzee, as we would expect in an upright biped.

The South African australopithecines fall into two groups: **gracile** (*A. africanus*) and **robust** (*A. robustus*). "Gracile" indicates that members of *A. africanus* were smaller and slighter, less robust, than were members of **A. robustus.** In addition, very robust—*hyperrobust*—australopithecines have been found in East Africa. In the classification scheme followed here, the hyperrobust australopothecines are assigned to **A. boisei.** However, some scholars consider *A. robustus* and *A. boisei* to be regional variants of just one species, usually called *A. robustus* (sometimes given its own genus name as well— *Paranthropus robustus*).

A. (Australopithecus) africanus
Gracile *Australopithecus* species (3.0?–2.0? m.y.a.), South Africa.

gracile
e.g., *A. africanus*; less robust, i.e., smaller and slighter, than *A. robustus*.

robust
e.g., *A. robustus* and *A. boisei*; having large, strong, sturdy bones, muscles, and teeth.

A. robustus
aka *Paranthropus*; robust *Australopithecus* species (2.0?–1.0? m.y.a.), South Africa.

A. boisei
Late, hyperrobust *Australopithecus* species (2.6–1.2 m.y.a.), East Africa.

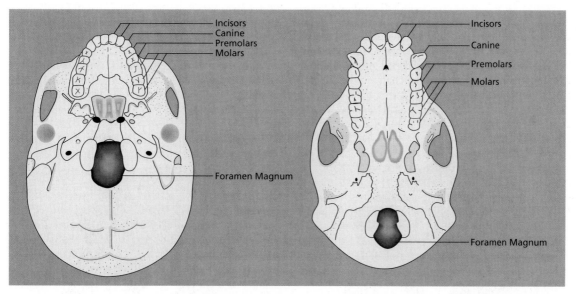

FIGURE 8.5 A Comparison of the Skull and Dentition (Upper Jaw) of *Homo* and the Chimpanzee. The foramen magnum, through which the spinal cord joins the brain, is located farther forward in *Homo* than in the ape. This permits the head to balance atop the spine with upright bipedalism. The molars and premolars of the ape form parallel rows. Human teeth, by contrast, are arranged in rounded, parabolic form. What differences do you note between human and ape canines? Canine reduction has been an important trend in hominin evolution.

The relationship between the graciles and the robusts has been debated for generations but has not been resolved. Graciles and robusts probably descend from *A. afarensis,* which itself was gracile in form, or from a South African version of *A. afarensis.* Some scholars have argued that the graciles lived before (3–2? m.y.a.) and were ancestral to the robusts (2?–1? m.y.a.). Others contend that the graciles and the robusts were separate species that may have overlapped in time. (Classifying them as members of different species implies they were reproductively isolated from each other in time or space.)

The trend toward enlarged back teeth, chewing muscles, and facial buttressing, which already is noticeable in *A. afarensis,* continues in the South African australopithecines. However, the canines are reduced, and the premolars are fully bicuspid. Dental form and function changed as dietary needs shifted from cutting and slashing to chewing and grinding.

The mainstay of the australopithecine diet was the vegetation of the savanna, although these early hominins also might have hunted small and slow-moving game. As well, they may have scavenged, bringing home parts of kills made by large cats and other carnivores. The ability to hunt large animals was probably an achievement of *Homo* and is discussed in the next chapter.

The skulls, jaws, and teeth of the australopithecines leave no doubt that their diet was mainly vegetarian. Natural selection modifies the teeth to conform to the stresses associated with a particular diet. Massive back teeth, jaws, and associated facial and cranial structures confirm that the australopithecine diet required extensive grinding and powerful crushing.

In the South African australopithecines, both deciduous ("baby") and permanent molars and premolars are massive, with multiple cusps. The later australopithecines had bigger back teeth than did the earlier ones. However, this evolutionary trend ended with early *Homo,* which had much smaller back teeth, reflecting a dietary change that will be described later.

Contrasts with *Homo* in the front teeth are less marked. But they are still of interest because of what they tell us about sexual dimorphism. *A. africanus*'s canines were more pointed, with larger roots, than *Homo*'s are. Still, the *A. africanus* canines were only 75 percent the size of the canines of *A. afarensis.* Despite this canine reduction, there was just as much canine sexual dimorphism in *A. africanus* as there had been in *A. afarensis* (Wolpoff 1999). Sexual dimorphism in general was much more pronounced among early hominins than it is among *Homo sapiens. A. africanus* females were about 4 feet (1.2 meters), and males 5 feet (1.5 meters), tall. The average female probably had no more than 60 percent the weight of the average male (Wolpoff 1980a). (That figure contrasts with today's average female-to-male weight ratio of about 88 percent.)

Teeth, jaw, face, and skull changed to fit a diet based on tough, gritty, fibrous grasslands vegetation. A massive face housed large upper teeth and provided a base for the attachment of powerful chewing muscles. Australopithecine cheekbones were elongated and massive structures (Figure 8.6) that anchored large chewing muscles running up the jaw. Another set of robust chewing muscles extended from the back of the jaw to the sides of the skull.

In the more robust australopithecines (*A. robustus* in South Africa and *A. boisei* in East Africa), these muscles were strong enough to produce a *sagittal crest,* a bony ridge on the top of the skull. Such a crest forms as the bone grows. It develops from the pull of the chewing muscles as they meet at the midline of the skull.

In 1985, the paleoanthropologist Alan Walker made a significant find near Lake Turkana in northern Kenya. Called the "black skull" because of the blue-black sheen it bore from the minerals surrounding it, the fossil displayed a "baffling combination of features" (Fisher 1988a). The jaw was apelike and the brain was small (as in *A. afarensis*), but there was a massive bony crest atop the skull (as in *A. boisei*). Walker and Richard Leakey (Walker's associate on the 1985 expedition) view the black skull (dated

(Left) Profile view of an *A. boisei* skull—Olduvai Hominid (OH) 5, originally called *Zinjanthropus boisei.* This skull of a young male, discovered by Mary Leakey in 1959 at Olduvai Gorge, Tanzania, dates back 1.8 million years. (Right) Profile view of an *A. africanus* (gracile) skull (Sterkfontein 5). The cranium, discovered by Dr. Robert Broom and J. T. Robinson in April 1947, dates back to 2.4–2.9 m.y.a.

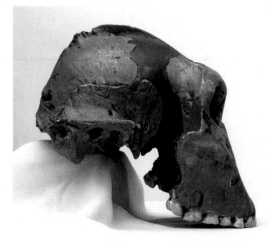

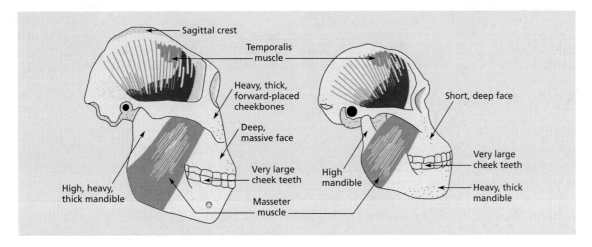

FIGURE 8.6 Skulls of Robust (Left) and Gracile (Right) Australopithecines, Showing Chewing Muscles.

Flaring cheek arches and, in some robusts, a sagittal crest supported this massive musculature. The early hominin diet—coarse, gritty vegetation of the savanna—demanded such structures. These features were most pronounced in *A. boisei.*

to 2.6 m.y.a.) as a very early hyperrobust *A. boisei.* Others (e.g., Jolly and White 1995) assign the black skull to its own species, *A. aethiopicus.* The black skull shows that some of the anatomical features of the hyperrobust australopithecines (2.6?–1.0 m.y.a.) did not change very much during more than one million years.

A. boisei survived through 1.2 m.y.a in East Africa. Compared with their predecessors, the later australopithecines tended to have larger overall size, skulls, and back teeth. They also had thicker faces, more prominent crests, and more rugged muscle markings on the skeleton. By contrast, the front teeth stayed the same size.

Brain size (measured as cranial capacity, in cubic centimeters—cm^3) increased only slightly between *A. afarensis* (430 cm^3), *A. africanus* (490 cm^3), and *A. robustus* (540 cm^3) (Wolpoff 1999). These figures can be compared with an average cranial capacity of 1,350 cm^3 in *Homo sapiens.* The modern range goes from less than 1,000 cm^3 to more than 2,000 cm^3 in normal adults. The cranial capacity of chimps (*Pan troglodytes*) averages 390 cm^3 (see Recap 8.1). The brains of gorillas *(Gorilla gorilla)* average around 500 cm^3, which is within the australopithecine range, but gorilla body weight is much greater.

THE AUSTRALOPITHECINES AND EARLY *HOMO*

By 2 m.y.a., the ancestors of *Homo* had become reproductively isolated from the later australopithecines, such as *A. robustus* and *A. boisei.* The earliest (very fragmentary) evidence for the genus *Homo* (2.5 m.y.a.) comes from the Chemeron formation in Kenya's Baringo Basin (Sherwood, Ward, and Hill 2002). This is a skull fragment, an isolated right temporal bone, known as the Chemeron temporal. By 2 m.y.a. the fossil sample of hominin teeth from East Africa has two clearly different sizes. One set is huge, the largest molars and premolars in hominin evolution; those teeth belonged to *A. boisei.* The other group of (smaller) teeth belonged to members of the genus *Homo.* The status of a recent find, *A. sediba,* as a possible human ancestor is debated in this chapter's "Appreciating Anthropology."

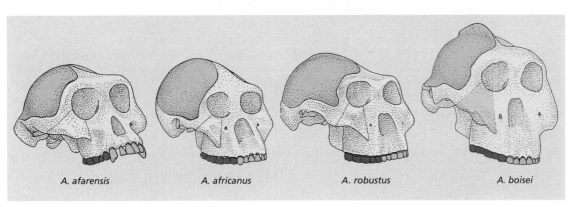

A. afarensis   A. africanus   A. robustus   A. boisei

Shown from left to right are *A. afarensis, A. africanus, A. robustus,* and *A. boisei.* What are the main differences you notice among these four types of early hominins?

appreciating ANTHROPOLOGY

New Fossils (*A. sediba*) May Redraw Human Ancestry

Named by *Smithsonian* magazine as the number one hominid (and hominin) fossil discovery of 2011, *Australopithecus sediba* (actually discovered between 2008 and 2010 but fully described in 2011), has generated a new debate about human origins. The original find is an almost complete skull and partial skeleton of an 11- to 12-year-old boy who stood 4'3" (1.3 m.) tall. Is this australopithecine a plausible human ancestor, as is claimed by its discoverer, paleoanthropologist Lee Berger? Most experts have been skeptical about that claim, while appreciating the fossil for its unique blend of hominin features. What do you think—could *A. sediba* be your ancestor?

An apelike creature with human features, whose fossil bones were discovered recently in a South African cave, is being greeted by paleoanthropologists as a likely watershed in the understanding of human evolution.

The discoverer of the fossils, Lee Berger of the University of Witwatersrand in Johannesburg, says the new species, known as *Australopithecus sediba*,

is the most plausible known ancestor of archaic and modern humans. Several other paleoanthropologists, while disagreeing with that interpretation, say the fossils are of great importance anyway, because they elucidate the mix-and-match process by which human evolution was shaped.

Dr. Berger's claim, if accepted, would radically redraw the present version of the human family tree, placing the new fossils in the center. The new species, in his view, should dislodge *Homo habilis*, the famous tool-making fossil found by Louis and Mary Leakey, as the most likely bridge between the australopithecenes and the human lineage. . . .

The principal significance of the new fossils is not that *Australopithecus sediba* is necessarily the direct ancestor of the human genus, other scientists said, but rather that the fossils emphasize the richness of evolutionary experimentation within the australopithecine group. . . .

Besides two skulls reported [in 2010], researchers led by Dr. Berger have since retrieved an almost complete right hand, a foot and a pelvis. The bones are especially well preserved because their owners apparently fell into a deep

cave and a few weeks later were swept into a sediment that quickly fossilized their bones. The rocks above the cave have gradually eroded away, bringing the fossils to the surface, where one was found by Dr. Berger's 9-year-old son, Matthew, in 2008, while chasing his dog.

That fall into the cave happened 1.977 million years ago, according to dating based on the rate of decay of uranium in the rock layer that holds the fossils. . . .

In articles in [the magazine] *Science*, Dr. Berger's team describes novel combinations of apelike and humanlike features in the hand, foot and pelvis of the new species. The hand, for instance, is apelike because it has long, strong fingers suitable for climbing trees, yet is also humanlike in having a long thumb that in combination with the fingers could have held tools in a precision grip. A cast of the inside of the skull shows an apelike brain, but one that had taken the first step toward being reorganized on human lines.

This mixture of apelike and humanlike features suggests that the new species was transitional between the australopithecines and humans, the

Palates of *Homo sapiens* (left) and *A. boisei* (right), a late, hyperrobust australopithecine. In comparing them, note the australopithecine's huge molars and premolars. What other contrasts do you notice? The large back teeth represent an extreme adaptation to a diet based on coarse, gritty savanna vegetation. Reduction in tooth size during human evolution applied to the back teeth much more than to the front.

researchers said. . . . Given its age, *Australopithecus sediba* is just old enough to be the ancestor of *Homo erectus*, the first species that paleoanthropologists agree belonged to the human ancestry and which existed 1.9 million years ago.

But the fossils are significant even if sediba is not a direct human ancestor. They are evidence

Lee Berger with his son, Matthew, and fossils of *Australopithecus sediba*. Matthew found one of the fossils while chasing his dog.

that a ferment of evolutionary experimentation was going on at the time, out of which the human lineage somehow emerged. . . .

Bernard Wood, a paleoanthropologist at George Washington University . . . gave little credence to Dr. Berger's arguments that *Australopithecus* is a direct ancestor of the human group,

saying there was too little time for the small-brained, tree-climbing ape to evolve into the large-brained *Homo erectus*. More interesting, in his view, are the strange combinations of apelike and humanlike features that Dr. Berger's team has described. . . .

In arguing that *Australopithecus* is the ancestor of the human lineage, Dr. Berger dismisses all earlier fossils held to be human, including a jawbone 2.33 million years old discovered in 1994 in Hadar, Ethiopia, by the paleoanthropologist Donald Johanson. The jawbone has some human-like features, Dr. Berger and colleagues write, yet that does not mean the owner of the jawbone was necessarily human. But Dr. Johanson said in an e-mail that the Hadar jawbone "possesses all the hallmarks of Homo," the human lineage, and "places the origins of Homo firmly in eastern Africa, at least 400,000 years prior to the dating of *A. sediba*."

By 1.9 m.y.a., there is clear fossil evidence that different hominin groups occupied different ecological niches in Africa. One of them, Homo—by then *Homo erectus*—had a larger brain and a reproportioned skull; it had increased the areas of the brain that regulate higher mental functions. These were our ancestors, hominins with greater capacities for culture than the australopithecines had. *H. erectus* hunted and gathered, made sophisticated tools, and eventually displaced its cousin species, *A. boisei*.

A. boisei of East Africa, the hyperrobust australopithecines, had mammoth back teeth. Their females had bigger back teeth than did earlier australopithecine males. *A. boisei* became ever more specialized with respect to one part of the traditional australopithecine diet, concentrating on coarse vegetation with a high grit content.

We still don't know why, how, and exactly when the split between *Australopithecus* and *Homo* took place. Scholars have defended many different models, or theoretical schemes, to interpret the early hominin

fossil record. Because new finds so often have forced reappraisals, most scientists are willing to modify their interpretation when given new evidence.

The model of Johanson and White (1979), who coined the term *A. afarensis*, proposes that *A. afarensis* split into two groups. One group, the ancestors of *Homo*, became reproductively isolated from the australopithecines between 3 and 2 m.y.a. This group eventually gave rise to **Homo habilis,** a term coined by L. S. B. and Mary Leakey to describe the earliest members of the genus *Homo*. Another form of early Homo was *H. erectus*, which appears to have lived contemporaneously with *H. habilis* between around 1.9 and 1.4 m.y.a. (Spoor et al. 2007, Wood 2011). Other members of *A. afarensis* evolved into the various kinds of later australopithecines (*A. africanus*, *A. robustus*, and hyperrobust *A. boisei*, the last member to become extinct).

There is good fossil evidence that *Homo* and *A. boisei* coexisted in East Africa. *A. boisei* seems to have lived in very arid areas, feeding on harder-to-chew

Homo habilis
Earliest (2.4?–1.4? m.y.a.) member of genus *Homo*.

vegetation than had any previous hominin. This diet would explain the hyperrobusts' huge back teeth, jaws, and associated areas of the face and skull.

OLDOWAN TOOLS

The simplest obviously manufactured tools were discovered in 1931 by L. S. B. and Mary Leakey at Olduvai Gorge, Tanzania. That locale gave the tools their name—Oldowan pebble tools. The oldest tools from Olduvai are about 1.8 million years old. Still older (2.6–2.0 m.y.a.) Oldowan implements have been found in Ethiopia, Congo, and Malawi.

Stone tools consist of flakes and cores. The *core* is the piece of rock, in the Oldowan case about the size of a tennis ball, from which flakes are struck. Once flakes have been removed, the core can become a tool itself. A *chopper* is a tool made by flaking the edge of such a core on one side and thus forming a cutting edge.

Oldowan pebble tools represent the world's oldest formally recognized stone tools. Core tools are not the most common Oldowan tools; flakes are. The purpose of flaking stone in the Oldowan tradition was not to create pebble tools or choppers but to create the sharp stone flakes that made up the mainstay of the Oldowan tool kit (Toth 1985). Choppers were a convenient by-product of flaking and were used as

well. However, hominins most likely did not have a preconceived tool form in mind while making them.

Oldowan choppers could have been used for food processing—by pounding, breaking, or bashing. Flakes probably were used mainly as cutters, for example, to dismember game carcasses. Crushed fossil animal bones indicate that stones were used to break open marrow cavities. Also, Oldowan deposits include pieces of bone or horn with scratch marks suggesting they were used to dig up tubers or insects. Oldowan core and flake tools are shown in the photos on this page. The flake tool in the lower photo is made of chert. Most Oldowan tools at Olduvai Gorge were made from basalt, which is locally more common and coarser.

For decades anthropologists have debated the identity of the earliest stone toolmakers. The first *Homo habilis* find got its name (*habilis* is Latin for "able") for its presumed status as the first hominin toolmaker. Recently the story has grown more complicated, with a discovery making it very likely that at least one kind of australopithecine also made and habitually used stone tools.

A. garhi and Early Stone Tools

In 1999 an international team reported the discovery, in Ethiopia, of a new species of hominin, along with the earliest traces of animal butchery (Asfaw, White, and Lovejoy 1999). These new fossils, dating to 2.5 m.y.a., may be the remains of a direct human ancestor and an evolutionary link between *Australopithecus* and the genus *Homo*. At the same site was evidence that antelopes and horses had been butchered with the world's earliest stone tools. When scientists excavated these hominin fossils, they were shocked to find a combination of unforeseen skeletal and dental features. They named the specimen *Australopithecus garhi* (**A. garhi**). The word *garhi* means "surprise" in the Afar language.

Tim White, coleader of the research team, viewed the discoveries as important for three reasons. First, they add a new potential ancestor to the human family tree. Second, they show that the thigh bone (femur) had elongated by 2.5 million years ago, a million years before the forearm shortened—to create our current human limb proportions. Third, evidence that large mammals were being butchered shows that early stone technologies were aimed at getting meat and marrow from big game. This signals a dietary revolution that eventually may have allowed an invasion of new habitats and continents (*Berkeleyan* 1999).

In 1997 the Ethiopian archaeologist Sileshi Semaw announced he had found the world's earliest stone tools, dating to 2.6 m.y.a., at the nearby Ethiopian site of Gona. But which human ancestor had made these tools, he wondered, and what were they used for? The 1999 discoveries by Asfaw, White, and their colleagues provided answers, identifying *A. garhi* as the best candidate for toolmaker (*Berkeleyan* 1999).

Oldowan
Earliest (2.6–1.2 m.y.a.) stone tools; sharp flakes struck from cores (choppers).

A. garhi
Toolmaking *Australopithecus* species (2.6 m.y.a.), Ethiopia.

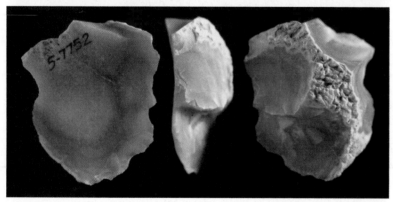

Above, an Oldowan chopper core; below, an Oldowan flake tool. The purpose of flaking stone in the Oldowan tradition was not to create pebble tools or choppers but to create the sharp stone flakes that made up the mainstay of the Oldowan tool kit.

The association, in the same area at the same time, of *A. garhi,* animal butchery, and the earliest stone tools suggests that the australopithecines were toolmakers, with some capacity for culture. Nevertheless, cultural abilities developed exponentially with *Homo*'s appearance and expansion. With increasing reliance on hunting, toolmaking, and other cultural abilities, *Homo* eventually became the most efficient exploiter of the savanna niche. The last surviving members of *A. boisei* may have been forced into ever-more-marginal areas. They eventually became extinct. By 1 m.y.a., a single species of hominin, *H. erectus,* not only had rendered other hominin forms extinct but also had expanded the hominin range to Asia and Europe. An essentially human strategy of adaptation, incorporating hunting as a fundamental ingredient of a generalized foraging economy, had emerged. Despite regional variation, it was to be the basic economy for our genus until 11,000 years ago. The next chapter describes the fossils, tools, and life patterns of the various forms of *Homo.*

acing the COURSE

summary

1. A skull found in 2001 in northern Chad, dated at 6–7 million years old, officially named *Sahelanthropus tchadensis,* more commonly called "Toumai," may or may not be the earliest hominin yet known, as may the somewhat less ancient *Orrorin tugenensis,* found in Kenya in 2001.

2. Hominins lived during the late Miocene, Pliocene (5.0–2.0 m.y.a.), and Pleistocene (2.0 m.y.a–10,000 B.P.) epochs. The australopithecines had appeared by 4.2 m.y.a. The seven species of *Australopithecus* were *A. anamensis* (4.2–3.9 m.y.a.), *A. afarensis* (3.8–3.0 m.y.a.), *A. africanus* (3.0?–2.0? m.y.a.), *A. garhi* (2.5 m.y.a.), *A. robustus* (2.0?–1.0? m.y.a.), *A. boisei* (2.6?–1.2 m.y.a.), and *A. sediba* (1.98–1.78 m.y.a.). The earliest definite hominin remains, from Ethiopia, are classified as *Ardipithecus kadabba* (5.8–5.5 m.y.a.) and *ramidus* (4.4 m.y.a.). Next comes *A. anamensis,* then a group of fossils from Hadar, Ethiopia, and Laetoli, Tanzania, classified as *A. afarensis.*

3. These earliest hominins shared many primitive features, including slashing canines, elongated premolars, a small apelike skull, and marked sexual dimorphism. Still, *A. afarensis* and its recently discovered predecessors were definite hominins. In *A. afarensis* this is confirmed by large molars and, more important, by skeletal evidence (e.g., in Lucy) for upright bipedalism.

4. Remains of two later groups, *A. africanus* (graciles) and *A. robustus* (robusts), were found in South Africa. Both groups show the australopithecine trend toward a powerful chewing apparatus. They had large molars and premolars and large and robust faces, skulls, and muscle markings. All these features are more pronounced in the robusts than they are in the graciles. The basis of the australopithecine diet was savanna vegetation.

5. By 2.0 m.y.a. there is ample evidence for two distinct hominin groups: early *Homo* and *A. boisei,* the hyperrobust australopithecines. The latter eventually became extinct around 1.2 m.y.a. *A. boisei* became increasingly specialized, dependent on tough, coarse, gritty, fibrous savanna vegetation. The australopithecine trend toward dental, facial, and cranial robustness continued with *A. boisei,* but these structures were reduced in *H. habilis* (2.4?–1.4? m.y.a.) and *H. erectus* (1.9–0.3? m.y.a).

6. Pebble tools dating to between 2.6 and 2.0 m.y.a. have been found in Ethiopia, Congo, and Malawi. Scientists have disagreed about their maker, some arguing that only early *Homo* could have made them. Evidence has been presented that *A. garhi* made pebble tools around 2.6 m.y.a. Cultural abilities developed exponentially with *Homo*'s appearance and evolution.

test yourself

MULTIPLE CHOICE

1. Bipedalism traditionally has been viewed as an adaptation to open grassland or savanna country. However,
   a. the fossils of *Sahelanthropus tchadensis* and *Orrorin tugenensis* establish beyond doubt that bipedalism emerged over 7 million years ago, while these hominins still lived in trees.
   b. the recent Ardi find suggests that bipedalism was an adaptation to mountain trekking.
   c. adaptation to the savanna probably occurred later in hominin evolution, after the emergence of bipedalism, as the evidence of *Ardipithecus,* which lived in a humid woodland habitat, suggests.
   d. recent DNA evidence suggests that the main cause of bipedalism was a mutation that occurred 7 million years ago.
   e. the fossils of *Orrorin tugenensis* suggest that bipedalism was an adaptation to river wading, an activity that provided key nutrients from fish.

2. The term *hominin* is used to refer to the human line after its split from ancestral chimps. *Hominid* is used
   a. to refer to the taxonomic family that includes humans and the African apes and their immediate ancestors.
   b. in cases where the brain cavity of fossils equals or exceeds that of anatomically modern humans.
   c. by scientists who do not view "Ardi" as a hominin.
   d. by Asian scientists who disagree with the rest of the scientific community's use of the term *hominin.*
   e. to refer to the human line after its split from ancestral tarsiers.

3. If we compare Earth's history to a 24-hour day (with 1 second equaling 50,000 years),
   a. the first vertebrates arrive 36 seconds before midnight.
   b. the latest dinosaurs die out at midnight.
   c. the ocean levels increase twofold at 1 A.M.
   d. *Homo sapiens* arrives 36 seconds before midnight.
   e. the earliest hominins arrive at midday.

4. What do researchers know about *Ardipithecus ramidus*?
   a. It was a knuckle-walking proto chimpanzee.
   b. It was really a male *Australopithecus anamensis.*
   c. It evolved into *Ardipithecus kadabba.*
   d. It is ancestral to Neandertals, but not to anatomically modern humans.
   e. It was a bipedal hominin with strongly apelike characteristics.

5. As a result of the *Kenyanthropus* discovery in 1999,
   a. the debate over the place of *afarensis* in human ancestry has been won by the taxonomic "splitters."
   b. the place of *afarensis* in human ancestry has been and will be debated between taxonomic "splitters" and "lumpers."
   c. Oldowan stone tools are no longer considered the oldest tools.
   d. the hominin family tree, once drawn with branches leading in many directions, now looks more like it has a straight trunk.
   e. the chronology of the emergence of human culture is no longer debated.

6. "Lucy" is the nickname of
   a. a small female member of *A. anamensis.*
   b. Mary Leakey
   c. an *Ardipithecus ramidus* found in Ethiopia.
   d. a small female member of *A. afarensis.*
   e. a large female *A. tugenensis* from Kenya.

7. Which of the following most clearly identifies *Australopithecus afarensis* as a hominin?
   a. pointed canines that project beyond the other teeth
   b. stereoscopic vision
   c. postcranial (below the head) remains that confirm upright bipedalism
   d. a curved or parabolic dental arcade
   e. molars larger than those of later *Australopithecus* remains

8. The presence of very large molars and a sagittal crest on the top of the skull is evidence of
   a. the more robust australopithecines' adaptation to food sources dominated by hard-shelled seeds and grasses.
   b. a probable adaptation to a cold weather climate exhibited by Neandertals.
   c. the earliest hominin use of domesticated plants.
   d. the earliest australopithecine evidence of humanlike brain organization.
   e. the dramatic increase in hunting activity starting with the earliest members of the genus *Homo.*

9. What is the significance of the discovery of *Australopithecus afarensis*?
   a. It showed that humans evolved in Asia rather than in Africa.
   b. It is the oldest hominin fossil yet found in the New World.
   c. *Afarensis* remains are the oldest to be found in association with evidence of both stone tools and fire use.
   d. It shows that the gracile australopithecines were not hominins after all.
   e. It provided fossil evidence that bipedalism preceded the evolution of a humanlike brain.

10. How were Oldowan tools, the oldest recognized stone tools, manufactured?
    a. by chipping blades off a metal core
    b. using deer antlers to pressure flake a chert core
    c. by chipping flakes, the mainstay of the Oldowan tool kit, off a core
    d. by striking steel against a stone core
    e. by grinding a coarser stone against a softer one

FILL IN THE BLANK

1. _____ refers to upright two-legged locomotion, and it is considered the key feature differentiating early hominins from the apes.

2. The fossil and archaeological records confirm that upright bipedal locomotion _____ stone tool manufacture and the expansion of the hominin brain.

3. The average cranial capacity in *Homo sapiens* is _____ cm^3. The cranial capacity of chimps (*Pan troglodytes*) averages _____ cm^3. The brains of gorillas (*Gorilla gorilla*) average _____ cm^3, which is within the australopithecine range.

4. Between 3 and 2 m.y.a., the ancestors of *Homo* became reproductively isolated from the later australopithecines, such as *A. robustus* and *A. boisei*, the latter of which coexisted with *Homo* until around _____ m.y.a.

5. _____ pebble tools represent the world's oldest formally recognized stone tools.

CRITICAL THINKING

1. If you found a new hominid fossil in East Africa, dated to five million years ago, would it most likely be an ape ancestor or a human ancestor? How would you tell the difference?

2. In trying to determine whether a fossil is a human ancestor, researchers sometimes look for traits that have been lost during subsequent human evolution. What is an example of this? How could humans come to lose a trait that is used to determine ancestry in the past?

3. In human evolution, what is the relationship between brains, skulls, and childhood dependency? Thinking back to Chapter 1, how does the study of this relationship illustrate anthropology's biocultural approach?

4. In October 2009, a newly reported *Ardipithecus* fossil was heralded in the news as a very important find. What new light did it shed on the understanding of human evolution?

5. The fossil remains found in Laetoli and Hadar forced a reinterpretation of the early hominin record. How so? What does this reinterpretation suggest about hominins' relation to apes?

Multiple Choice: 1. (C); 2. (A); 3. (D); 4. (E); 5. (B); 6. (D); 7. (C); 8. (A); 9. (E); 10. (C); **Fill in the Blank:** 1. Bipedalism; 2. preceded; 3. 1,350, 390, 500; 4. 1.2; 5. Oldowan

Campbell, B. G., J. D. Loy, and K. Cruz-Uribe
 2006 *Humankind Emerging,* 9th ed. Boston: Pearson Allyn & Bacon. Well-illustrated survey of physical anthropology, particularly the fossil record.

Johanson, D. C., and K. Wong
 2009 *Lucy's Legacy: The Quest for Human Origins.* New York: Harmony Books. Popular account of Lucy and subsequent fossil discoveries.

Larsen, C. S.
 2011 *Our Origins: Discovering Physical Anthropology,* 2nd ed. New York: W. W. Norton. Excellent introduction to the subfield, including human evolution.

Park, M. A.
 2010 *Biological Anthropology,* 6th ed. New York: McGraw-Hill. A concise introduction, with a focus on scientific inquiry.

Relethford, J. H.
 2010 *The Human Species: An Introduction to Biological Anthropology,* 8th ed. New York: McGraw-Hill. Up-to-date text in biological anthropology.

Wood, B.
 2011 *Human Evolution.* New York: Sterling. Covers the entire span of human evolution.

suggested additional readings

Go to our Online Learning Center website at **www.mhhe.com/kottak** for Internet exercises directly related to the content of this chapter.

internet exercises

Archaic *Homo*

What were the earliest forms of *Homo,* and where did they originate and eventually migrate?

What were the major toolmaking traditions and adaptive strategies of archaic *Homo*?

What were the Neandertals like, and how did they differ from earlier and later forms of *Homo*?

◀ A Neandertal skeleton (right) and a modern human skeleton (left and behind) displayed at New York's American Museum of Natural History. The Neandertal skeleton, reconstructed from casts of more than 200 fossil bones, was part of an exhibit titled "The First Europeans: Treasures from the Hills of Atapuerca" (Spain).

understanding OURSELVES

Fred Flintstone was the only caveman (the only cave person, for that matter) to appear on a VH1 list of the "200 Greatest Pop Culture Icons." He ranked number 42, between Cher and Martha Stewart. The Flintstones and their neighbors the Rubbles don't look much like Neanderthals (which anthropologists spell Neandertal, without the *h*). Real Neandertals had heavy brow ridges and slanting foreheads and lacked chins. The Flintstones and the Rubbles didn't act much like Neandertals either. *The Flintstones* transposed a 20th-century American blue-collar lifestyle back to prehistoric times—Fred and Barney worked in factories, "drove" stone cars, and used dinosaurs as construction cranes and can openers. While it is certainly ridiculous to imagine that Neandertals used dinosaurs as tools, it is equally ridiculous to imagine dinosaurs and Neandertals coexisting at all. Dinosaurs were extinct long before humans, hominins, or hominids ever walked the earth. Just as American popular culture never tires of calling apes "monkeys," it can't seem to resist mixing dinosaurs and ancient humans.

Decades after Fred first appeared on TV, Geico commercials introduced new cavemen, along with the slogan "So easy a caveman can do it." Geico's cavemen live in a modern world of bowling alleys, cell phones, airports, and tennis courts. They have another modern trait—a sense of outrage over the insult implied in Geico's slogan. Should it be insulting to call someone "a Neandertal"? Their average cranial capacity, exceeding 1,400 cubic centimeters, actually was larger than the modern average. What that says about intelligence isn't clear. One fossil in particular helped create the enduring popular stereotype of the slouching, inferior Neandertal caveman. This was the skeleton discovered a century ago at La Chapelle-aux-Saints in southwestern France. The original assessment of this fossil created an inaccurate image of Neandertals as apelike brutes who had trouble walking upright. Closer analysis revealed that La Chapelle was an aging man whose bones were distorted by osteoarthritis. This illustrates the danger of attempting to reach broad conclusions based upon a small sample size.

Actually, as one would expect, Neandertals were a variable population. Some fossil hominins even combine Neandertal robustness with modern features. For example, the remains of a four-year-old boy found in Portugal, dating back some 24,000 years, show mixed Neandertal and modern features. This find and others have raised the question as to whether Neandertals and anatomically modern humans could have mated. Another modern activity in which the Geico cavemen engage is dating anatomically modern women. Whether similar attractions are part of history, or are as unrealistic as Fred using a dinosaur to open a can of creamed corn, is one more subject for scientific debate.

Meet two kinds of early *Homo.* On the left, KNM-ER 1813. On the right, KNM-ER 1470. The latter (1470) has been classified as *H. rudolfensis.* What's the classification of 1813?

EARLY *HOMO*

As we saw in Chapter 8, at two million years ago, there is African evidence for two distinct hominin groups: early *Homo* and *A. boisei,* the hyperrobust australopithecines, which became extinct around 1.2 m.y.a. *A. boisei* became increasingly specialized, dependent on tough, coarse, gritty, fibrous savanna vegetation. The australopithecine trend toward dental, facial, and cranial robustness continued with *A. boisei.* However, these structures were reduced as early forms of *Homo* evolved into early *H. erectus* by 1.9 m.y.a. By that date *Homo* was generalizing the subsistence quest to the hunting of large animals to supplement the gathering of vegetation and scavenging.

H. rudolfensis and *H. habilis*

In 1972, in an expedition led by Richard Leakey, Bernard Ngeneo unearthed a skull designated KNM-ER 1470. The name comes from its catalog number in the Kenya National Museum (KNM) and its discovery location (East Rudolph—ER)—east of Lake Rudolph, at a site called Koobi Fora, in Kenya. The 1470 skull attracted immediate attention because of its unusual combination of a large brain (775 cm³) and very large molars. Its brain size was more human than that of the australopithecines, but its molars recalled those of the hyperrobust australopithecines. Some paleoanthropologists attributed the large skull and teeth to a very large body, assuming that this had been one *big hominin.* But no postcranial remains were found with 1470, nor have they been found with any later discovery of a 1470-like specimen.

How to interpret KNM-ER 1470? On the basis of its brain size, it seemed to belong in *Homo.* On the basis of its back teeth, it seemed more like *Australopithecus.* There also are problems with dating. The best dating guess is 1.8 m.y.a., but another estimate suggests that 1470 may be as old as 2.4 m.y.a. Originally, some paleoanthropologists assigned 1470 to *H. habilis,* while others saw it as an unusual australopithecine. In 1986, it received its own species name, *Homo rudolfensis,* from the lake near which it was found. This label has stuck—although it isn't accepted by all paleoanthropologists. Those who find *H. rudolfensis* to be a valid species emphasize its contrasts with *H. habilis.* Note the contrasts in the two skulls in the photo above. KNM-ER 1813, on the left, is considered *H. habilis;* KNM-ER 1470, on the right, is *H. rudolfensis.* The *habilis* skull has a more marked brow ridge and a depression behind it, whereas 1470 has a less pronounced brow ridge and a longer, flatter face. Some think that *rudolfensis* lived earlier than and is ancestral to *habilis.* Some think that *rudolfensis* and *habilis* are simply male and female members of the same species—*H. habilis.* Some think they are separate species that coexisted in time and space (from about 2.4 m.y.a. to about 1.7 m.y.a.). Some think that one or the other gave rise to *H. erectus.* The debate continues. The only sure conclusion is that several different kinds of hominin lived in Africa before and after the advent of *Homo.*

H. habilis and *H. erectus*

A team headed by L. S. B. and Mary Leakey found the first representative of *Homo habilis* (OH7—Olduvai Hominid 7) at Olduvai Gorge in Tanzania in 1960. Olduvai's oldest layer, Bed I, dates to 1.8 m.y.a. This layer has yielded both small-brained *A. boisei* (average 490 cm³) fossils and *H. habilis* skulls, with cranial capacities between 600 and 700 cm³.

Another important *habilis* find was made in 1986 by Tim White of the University of California, Berkeley. OH62 is the partial skeleton of a female *H. habilis* from Olduvai Bed I. This was the first find of an *H. habilis* skull with a significant amount of skeletal material. OH62, dating to 1.8 m.y.a., consists of parts of the skull, the right arm, and both legs. Because scientists had assumed that *H. habilis* would be taller than tiny Lucy (*A. afarensis*), OH62 was surprising because of its small size and apelike limb bones. Not only was OH62 just as tiny as Lucy (3 feet, or 0.9 meter), its arms were longer and more apelike than expected. The limb proportions suggested greater tree-climbing ability than later hominins had. *H. habilis* may still have sought occasional refuge in the trees.

The small size and primitive proportions of *H. habilis* were unexpected given what was known about early *H. erectus* in East Africa. In deposits near Lake Turkana, Kenya, Richard Leakey had uncovered two *H. erectus* skulls dating to 1.6 m.y.a. By that date, *H. erectus* (males at least) had already attained a cranial capacity of 900 cm^3, along with a modern body shape and height. An amazingly complete young male *H. erectus* fossil (WT15,000) found at West Turkana in 1984 by Kimoya Kimeu, a collaborator of the Leakeys, has confirmed this. WT15,000, also known as the Nariokotome boy, was a twelve-year-old male who had already reached 5 feet 5 inches (1.67 meters). He might have grown to 6 feet had he lived.

Sister Species

Two recent hominin fossil finds from Ileret, Kenya (east of Lake Turkana), are very significant for two main reasons: they show that (1) *H. habilis* and *H. erectus* overlapped in time rather than being ancestor and descendant, as had been thought; (2) sexual dimorphism in *H. erectus* was much greater than expected (see Spoor et al. 2007; Wilford 2007*a*).

One of these finds (KNM-ER 42703) is the upper jawbone of a 1.44-million-year-old *H. habilis*. The other (KNM-ER 42700) is the almost complete but faceless skull of a 1.55-million-year-old *H. erectus*. Their names come from their catalog numbers in the Kenya National Museum–East Rudolph, and their dates were determined from volcanic ash deposits.

These Ileret finds negated the conventional view (held since the Leakeys described the first *habilis* in 1960) that *habilis* and then *erectus* evolved one after the other. Instead, they apparently split from a common ancestor prior to 2 m.y.a. Then they lived side by side in eastern Africa for perhaps half a million years. According to Maeve Leakey, one of the authors of the report (Spoor et al. 2007), the fact that they remained separate species for so long "suggests that they had their own ecological niche, thus avoiding direct competition" (quoted in Wilford 2007*a*, p. A6). They lived in the same general area (an ancient lake basin), much as gorillas and chimpanzees do today.

Given these finds, the fossil record for early *Homo* in East Africa can be revised as follows: *H. habilis* (1.9–1.44 m.y.a) and *H. erectus* (1.9–0.3? m.y.a). The oldest definite *H. habilis* (OH24) dates to 1.9 m.y.a., although some fossil fragments with *habilis* attributes have been dated as early as 2.33 m.y.a. The oldest *erectus* may date back to 1.9 m.y.a. as well.

What about sexual dimorphism in *H. erectus*? As the smallest *erectus* find ever, KNM-ER 42700 also may be the first female *erectus* yet found, most probably a young adult or late subadult. The small skull suggests that the range in overall body size among *H. erectus* was much greater than previously had been imagined, with greater sexual dimorphism than among chimps or contemporary humans. Human and chimp males are about 15 percent larger than females, but dimorphism is much greater in gorillas, and apparently also in *erectus*. Another possibility is that the (as yet undiscovered) *H. erectus* males that inhabited this lake basin along with this female at that time also were smaller than the typical *erectus* male.

The Significance of Hunting

The ecological niche that separated *H. erectus* from both *H. habilis* and *A. boisei* probably involved greater reliance on hunting, along with improved cultural means of adaptation, including better tools. Significant changes in technology occurred during the 200,000-year period between Bed I (1.8 m.y.a.) and Lower Bed II (1.6 m.y.a) at Olduvai. Toolmaking got more sophisticated soon after the advent of *H. erectus*. Out of the crude tools in Bed I evolved better-made and more varied tools. The earliest (1.76 m.y.a.) tools of the *Acheulean* type (see the following section) associated with *H. erectus* come from

A. boisei (left) and *H. habilis* (right). Both OH5 (L) and OH24 (R) were found in Bed I at Olduvai Gorge, Tanzania, and were probable contemporaries.

the site of Kokiselei near Lake Turkana in Kenya (Wilford 2011). These tools show signs of symmetry, uniformity, and planning. Edges are straighter than with Oldowan tools, and differences in form suggest functional differentiation—that is, the tools were being made and used for different jobs, such as smashing bones or digging for tubers. The more sophisticated tools aided in hunting and gathering. With such tools, *Homo* could obtain meat on a more regular basis and dig and process tubers, roots, nuts, and seeds more efficiently. New tools that could batter, crush, and pulp coarse vegetation also reduced chewing demands.

With changes in the types of foods consumed, the burden on the chewing apparatus eased. Chewing muscles developed less, and supporting structures, such as jaws and cranial crests, also were reduced. With less chewing, jaws developed less, and so there was no place to put large teeth. The size of teeth, which form before they erupt, is under stricter genetic control than jaw size and bone size are (see von Cramon-Taubadel 2011). Natural selection began to operate against the genes that caused large teeth. In smaller jaws, large teeth now caused dental crowding, impaction, pain, sickness, fever, and sometimes death (there were no dentists). *H. erectus* back teeth are smaller, and the front teeth are relatively larger than australopithecine teeth. *H. erectus* used its front teeth to pull, twist, and grip objects. A massive ridge over the eyebrows (a superorbital torus) provided buttressing against the forces exerted in these activities. It also provided protection, as we see in "Appreciating Diversity" on p. 184.

As hunting became more important, encounters with large animals increased. Individuals with stronger skulls had better-protected brains and better survival rates. Given the dangers associated with larger prey, and without sophisticated spear or arrow technology, which developed later, natural selection favored the thickening of certain areas for better protection against blows and falls. The base of the skull expanded dramatically, with a ridge of spongy bone (an occipital bun) across the back, for the attachment of massive neck muscles. The frontal and parietal (side) areas of the skull also increased, indicating expansion in those areas of the brain. Finally, average cranial capacity expanded from about 500 cm^3 in the australopithecines to 1,000 cm^3 in *H. erectus*, which is within the modern range of variation.

OUT OF AFRICA I: *H. ERECTUS*

Biological and cultural changes enabled *H. erectus* to exploit a new adaptive strategy—gathering and hunting. *H. erectus* pushed the hominin range beyond Africa—to Asia and Europe. Small groups broke off from larger ones and moved a few miles

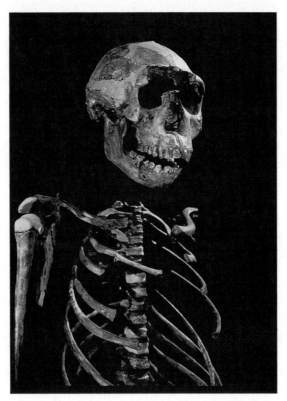

This photo shows the early (1.6 m.y.a) *Homo erectus* WT15,000, or Nariokotome boy, found in 1984 near Lake Turkana, Kenya. This is the most complete *Homo erectus* ever found.

away. They foraged new tracts of edible vegetation and carved out new hunting territories. Through population growth and dispersal, *H. erectus* gradually spread and changed. Hominins were following an essentially human lifestyle based on hunting and gathering. This basic pattern survived until recently in marginal areas of the world, although it is now fading rapidly. We focus in this chapter on the biological and cultural changes that led from early *Homo*, through intermediate forms, to anatomically modern humans (AMHs).

Paleolithic Tools

The stone toolmaking techniques that evolved out of the Oldowan, or pebble tool, tradition and that lasted until about 15,000 years ago are described by the term **Paleolithic** (from Greek roots meaning "old" and "stone"). The Paleolithic has three divisions: Lower (early), Middle, and Upper (late). Each part is roughly associated with a particular stage in human evolution. The Lower Paleolithic is roughly associated with *H. erectus*; the Middle Paleolithic, with archaic *H. sapiens,* including the Neandertals of Western Europe and the Middle East; and the Upper Paleolithic, with anatomically modern humans.

The best stone tools are made from rocks such as flint that fracture sharply and in predictable ways when hammered. Quartz, quartzite, chert, and obsidian also are suitable. Each of the three main divisions of the Paleolithic had its typical *toolmaking*

Paleolithic
Old Stone Age, including Lower (early), Middle, and Upper (late).

Headstrong Hominins

On the evolutionary timeline of hominin biological diversity, the anatomical contrasts between *Homo erectus* and modern humans are clear. There must have been behavioral differences as well. How did anatomy and behavior fit together in *H. erectus* populations? Noel Boaz and Russell Ciochon (2004) proposed that several protective features of the *H. erectus* skull evolved in response to behavior, specifically interpersonal violence—fighting among those thick-skulled hominins. Ever since the discovery of the first *H. erectus* skull, scholars have been struck by the unusual cranial anatomy. The top and sides of the skull have thick, bony walls (see the photos). The *H. erectus* skullcap resembles a cyclist's helmet—low and streamlined, so as to protect the brain, ears, and eyes from impact. "In contrast, we modern humans hold our enormous, easily injured, semiliquid brains in relatively thin-walled bony globes. We have to buy our bicycle helmets" (Boaz and Ciochon 2004, p. 29). In other words, a cultural adaptation (plastic) has replaced a biological one (bone).

Based on these and other cranial features, Boaz and Ciochon speculate that *H. erectus* needed sturdy anatomical headgear to protect against life-threatening breaks. Even today, with

modern medicine, skull fractures can be fatal. An apparently minor fracture can rip blood vessels inside the skull. Blood builds up under the skull. Such a hematoma pushing on the brain can cause a coma and, eventually, death.

For *H. erectus* this bleeding would have been much more problematic than for people with access to modern medicine. The neurological damage caused by such a hematoma can lead to partial paralysis, locomotion problems, poor hand-eye coordination, difficulties in speaking, and cognitive disruptions. Boaz and Ciochon note that "any traits that reduced the chances of cranial fracture would have given a substantial evolutionary advantage to the individuals who possessed them" (Boaz and Ciochon 2004, p. 30).

The authors contend that the blows delivered in a fight are more likely to land at eye level than on the top of the head. Although modern human skulls have some degree of eye-level bony armor, the thicker ring of bone in the *H. erectus* skull would have provided much more protection. The thick brow ridge protected the eye sockets, while bony bulges on each side of the skull shielded the sinus where blood flows into the internal jugular vein. This buttressing also protected the ear region. Finally, the bony ridge at the back of the

skull protected several sinuses that carried blood within the rearmost brain lobes.

The thick jaws of *H. erectus* also would have been adaptive. Today, a broken jaw makes it painful, difficult, and sometimes impossible to chew. Surgical wiring of the broken sections is required. For *H. erectus*, such a break could have been life-threatening. There was an inside thickening of the jaw, just behind the chin, to protect against breaks.

Among the dozens of *H. erectus* fossils found near Beijing, China, the anthropologist/anatomist Franz Weidenreich detected several fractures that had subsequently healed. The fact that the trauma victims survived offers confirmation of the protective value of their skulls. Boaz and Ciochon believe that the thick skulls and healed fractures of *H. erectus* provide a record of violence within the species.

This defensive armor—the anatomical headgear—was reduced once *H. sapiens* evolved a larger, more globular, thin-walled skull. Although human violence didn't end, other means of protection, or avoidance of conflict, or both, evolved among the descendants of *H. erectus*. Boaz and Ciochon think those new protective mechanisms belong to the realm of cultural rather than biological diversity.

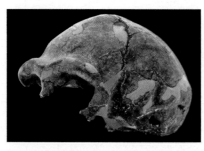

Homo erectus skullcaps have been likened to a bicycle helmet because of their protective properties. These three skulls show dramatic similarities despite different ages. The skull shown at the left is a cast of skull XII from the "Peking Man" collection and dates to 670,000 to 410,000 years ago. The two other skulls are much older. Sangiran 2 from Java (middle photo) may be as old as 1.6 m.y.a., while OH9 from Olduvai Gorge, Tanzania (right), may date back 1.4 million years. What similarities do you note among the three skulls?

traditions—coherent patterns of tool manufacture. The main Lower Paleolithic toolmaking tradition used by *H. erectus* was the **Acheulean,** named after the French village of St. Acheul, where it was first identified.

As we saw in Chapter 8, Oldowan flaking wasn't done to make choppers (according to a predetermined form). It was done simply to produce sharp flakes. A fundamental difference shows up in the Acheulean toolmaking tradition. The Acheulean technique involved chipping the core bilaterally and symmetrically. The core was converted from a round piece of rock into a flattish oval hand ax about 6 inches (15 centimeters) long. Its cutting edge was far superior to that of the Oldowan chopper (see Figure 9.1). The Acheulean hand ax, shaped like a teardrop, represents a predetermined shape based on a template in the mind of the toolmaker. Evidence for such a mental template in the archaeological record suggests a cognitive leap between earlier hominins and *H. erectus*.

Acheulean hand axes, routinely carried over long distances, were used in various cutting and butchering tasks, including gutting, skinning, and dismembering animals. Analysis of their wear patterns suggests that hand axes were versatile tools used for many tasks, including woodworking and vegetable preparation. Cleavers—core tools with a straight edge at one end—were used for heavy chopping and hacking at the sinews of larger animals. Stone picks, which were heavier than the hand ax, probably were used for digging. Hand axes, cleavers, and picks were heavy-duty tools, used for cutting and digging. Acheulean toolmakers also used flakes, with finer edges, for light-duty tools—to make incisions and for finer work. Flakes became progressively more important in human evolution, particularly in Middle and Upper Paleolithic toolmaking.

Dating back at least 1.76 m.y.a., the Acheulean tradition illustrates trends in the evolution of technology: greater efficiency, manufacture of tools with predetermined forms and for specific tasks, and an increasingly complex technology. These trends became even more obvious with the advent of *H. sapiens.*

Adaptive Strategies of *H. erectus*

Interrelated changes in biology and culture have increased human adaptability—the capacity to live in and modify an ever-wider range of environments. Improved tools helped *H. erectus* increase its range. Biological changes also increased hunting efficiency. *H. erectus* had a rugged but essentially modern skeleton that permitted long-distance stalking and endurance during the hunt. The *H. erectus* body was much larger and longer-legged than those of previous hominins, permitting longer-distance hunting of large prey. There is archaeological evidence of *H.*

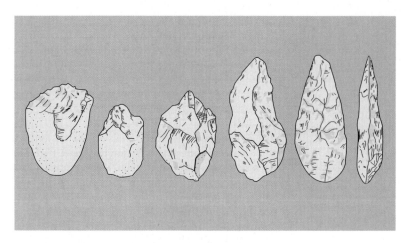

FIGURE 9.1 Evolution in Toolmaking.

Finds at Olduvai Gorge and elsewhere show how pebble tools (the first tool at the left) evolved into the Acheulean hand ax of *H. erectus*. This drawing begins with an Oldowan pebble tool and moves through crude hand axes to fully developed Acheulean tools associated with *H. erectus*.

erectus's success in hunting elephants, horses, rhinos, and giant baboons.

An increase in cranial capacity has been a trend in human evolution. The average *H. erectus* brain (about 1,000 cm^3) doubled the australopithecine average. The capacities of *H. erectus* skulls range from 800 to 1,250 cm^3, well above the modern minimum.

H. erectus had an essentially modern, though very robust, skeleton with a brain and body closer in size to *H. sapiens* than to *Australopithecus*. Still, several anatomical contrasts, particularly in the

Acheulean
Lower Paleolithic tool tradition associated with *H. erectus*.

An Acheulean hand ax from Gesher Benot Ya'aqov, Israel, Jordan River. This site, shown here under excavation, dates back to 750,000 B.P. Which hominin might have made the ax?

cranium, distinguish *H. erectus* from modern humans. Compared with moderns, *H. erectus* had a lower and more sloping forehead accentuated by a large brow ridge above the eyes (see "Appreciating Diversity" on p. 184). Skull bones were thicker, and, as noted, average cranial capacity was smaller. The braincase was lower and flatter than in *H. sapiens,* with spongy bone development at the lower rear of the skull. Seen from behind, the *H. erectus* skull has a broad-based angular shape that has been compared to a half-inflated football and to a hamburger bun (Figure 9.2). The *H. erectus* face, teeth, and jaws were larger than those in contemporary humans but smaller than those in *Australopithecus*. The front teeth were especially large, but molar size was well below the australopithecine average. Presumably, this reduction reflected changes in diet or food processing.

Taken together, the *H. erectus* skeleton and chewing apparatus provide biological evidence of a fuller commitment to hunting and gathering, which was *Homo*'s only adaptive strategy until plant cultivation and animal domestication emerged some 10,000 to 12,000 years ago. Archaeologists have found and studied several sites of *H. erectus* activity, including cooperative hunting.

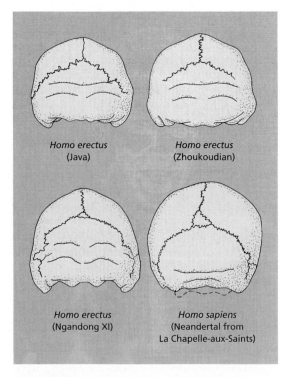

FIGURE 9.2 Rear Views of Three Skulls of *H. erectus* and One of "Archaic" *Homo sapiens* (a Neandertal).

Note the more angular shape of the *H. erectus* skulls, with the maximum breadth low down, near the base.

SOURCE: Clifford J. Jolly and Randall White, *Physical Anthropology and Archaeology*, 5th ed., p. 271. Copyright © 1995 by The McGraw-Hill Companies, Inc. Reprinted with permission.

Hearths at various sites confirm that fire was part of the human adaptive kit by this time. Earlier evidence for human control over fire has been found in Israel, dating back to almost 800,000 years ago (Gugliotta 2004). Sites with even earlier claims for fire (around 1.5 m.y.a.) include Koobi Fora, Kenya; Baringo, Kenya; and Middle Awash, Ethiopia. However, none of these early claims has unequivocal evidence for the controlled use of fire. Definitive evidence of human control of fire by 500,000 B.P. has been demonstrated at Cave of Hearths, South Africa; Montagu Cave, South Africa; Kalambo Falls, Zambia; and Kabwe in Zimbabwe. Fire provided protection against cave bears and saber-toothed tigers. It permitted *H. erectus* to occupy cave sites, including Zhoukoudian, near Beijing, in China, which has yielded the remains of more than forty specimens of *H. erectus*. Fire widened the range of climates open to human colonization. It may have played a role in the expansion out of Africa. Its warmth enabled people to survive winter cold in temperate regions. Human control over fire offered other advantages, such as cooking, which breaks down vegetable fibers and tenderizes meat. Cooking kills parasites and makes meat more digestible, thus reducing strain on the chewing apparatus.

Could language (fireside chats, perhaps) have been an additional advantage available to *H. erectus*? Archaeological evidence confirms the cooperative hunting of large animals and the manufacture of complicated tools. These activities might have been too complex to have gone on without some kind of language. Speech would have aided coordination, cooperation, and the learning of traditions, including toolmaking. Words, of course, aren't preserved until the advent of writing. However, given the potential for language-based communication—which even chimps and gorillas share with *H. sapiens*—and given brain size within the low *H. sapiens* range, it seems plausible to assume that *H. erectus* had rudimentary speech. For contrary views, see Binford (1981), Fisher (1988*b*), and Wade (2002).

The Evolution and Expansion of *H. erectus*

The archaeological record of *H. erectus* activities can be combined with the fossil evidence to provide a more complete picture of our Lower Paleolithic ancestors. We now consider some of the fossil data, whose geographic distribution is shown in Figure 9.3. Early *H. erectus* remains, found by Richard Leakey's team at East and West Turkana, Kenya, and dated to around 1.6 m.y.a., including the Nariokotome boy, were discussed previously.

One fairly complete skull, one large mandible, and two partial skulls—one of a young adult male (780 cm^3) and one of an adolescent female (650 cm^3)—were found in the 1990s at the Dmanisi site in the former Soviet Republic of Georgia. They have been assigned a date of 1.7–1.77 m.y.a. There are notable similarities between the two partial skulls and that of the Nariokotome boy from Kenya (1.6 m.y.a.). Chopping tools of comparable age associated with the Kenyan and Georgian fossils also are similar. (Chopping tools, found alongside Acheulean tools at the Kokiselei site in Kenya, date back to 1.76 m.y.a.) The fairly complete Dmanisi skull is more primitive than the two partial skulls, and looks somewhat like *H. habilis*. Primitive characteristics include its large canine teeth and small cranial capacity (Vekua, Lordkipanidze, and Rightmire 2002). This specimen may be that of a teenage girl whose skull had not yet reached full size, but whose canines had. The simplest explanation for the anatomical diversity observed at Dmanisi is that *H. erectus* was at least as variable a species as is *H. sapiens*. The Dmanisi finds suggest a rapid spread, by 1.77 m.y.a., of early *Homo* out of Africa and into Eurasia (see Figure 9.3).

The Dmanisi fossils are the most ancient undisputed hominin finds outside Africa. How did they get to Georgia? The most probable answer is in pursuit of meat. As hominins became more carnivorous, they expanded their home ranges in accordance with those of the animals they hunted. Meat-rich diets provided higher-quality protein as fuel. The australopithecines, with smaller bodies and brains, could survive mainly on plants and had smaller home ranges. Once hominins developed stronger bodies and high-protein meat diets, they could—indeed had to—spread out. They ranged farther to find meat, and this expansion eventually led them out of Africa, into Eurasia (Georgia) and eventually Asia (see Wilford 2000).

More recent skeletal finds from Dmanisi suggest how this expansion might have taken place (Wilford 2007*b*). (Previously only skulls had been found there.) Four new fossil skeletons show that the ancient Dmanisi population combined primitive skulls and upper bodies with more advanced spines and lower limbs for greater mobility. These evolved limb proportions enabled early *Homo* to expand beyond Africa.

In 1891, the Indonesian island of Java yielded the first *H. erectus* fossil find, popularly known as "Java man." Eugene Dubois, a Dutch army surgeon, had gone to Java to discover a transitional form between apes and humans. Of course, we now know that the transition to hominin had taken place much earlier than the *H. erectus* period and occurred in Africa. However, Dubois's good luck did lead him to the most ancient human fossils discovered at that time. Excavating near the village of Trinil, Dubois found parts of an

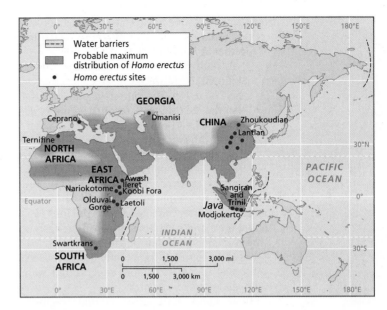

FIGURE 9.3 The Sites of Discovery of *Homo erectus* and Its Probable Maximum Distribution.

SOURCE: Clifford J. Jolly and Randall White, *Physical Anthropology and Archaeology*, 5th ed., p. 268. Copyright © 1995 by The McGraw-Hill Companies, Inc. Reprinted with permission.

H. erectus skull and a thigh bone. During the 1930s and 1940s, excavations in Java uncovered additional remains. The various Indonesian *H. erectus* fossils date back at least 700,000, and perhaps as much as 1.6 million, years. Fragments of a skull and a lower jaw found in northern China at Lantian may be as old as the oldest Indonesian fossils. Other *H. erectus* remains, of uncertain date, have been found in Algeria and Morocco in North Africa.

H. erectus remains also have been found in Upper Bed II at Olduvai, Tanzania, in association with Acheulean tools. In "Appreciating Diversity" on p. 184, you will find a photo of one such find, OH9, which dates back perhaps 1.4 million years, along with a photo of a Javanese find, Sangiran 2, which may be a bit older. African *H. erectus* fossils also have been found in Ethiopia, Eritrea, and South Africa (in addition to Kenya and Tanzania). The time span of *H. erectus* in East Africa was long. *H. erectus* fossils have been found in Bed IV at Olduvai, dating to 500,000 B.P., about the same age as the Beijing fossils, described below as well as in "Appreciating Diversity."

The largest group of *H. erectus* fossils was found in the Zhoukoudian cave in China. The Zhoukoudian ("Peking"—now Beijing—"man") site, excavated from the late 1920s to the late 1930s, was a major find for the human fossil record. Zhoukoudian yielded remains of tools, hearths, animal bones, and more than forty hominins, including five skulls. The analysis of these remains led to the conclusion that the Java and Zhoukoudian fossils were examples of the same broad stage of human evolution. Today they are commonly classified together as *H. erectus.*

A skull of one of these Beijing fossils, Skull XII, is shown in "Appreciating Diversity" on p. 184. The four-stage photo spread (to the left) shows a reconstruction of *H. erectus* based on the Javanese find Sangiran 17, the most complete *H. erectus* skull found in Indonesia. The Zhoukoudian individuals lived more recently than did the Javanese *H. erectus,* between 670,000 and 410,000 years ago, when the climate in China was colder and moister than it is today. The inference about the climate has been made on the basis of the animal remains found with the human fossils. The people at Zhoukoudian ate venison, and seed and plant remains suggest they were both gatherers and hunters.

What about Europe? A cranial fragment found at Ceprano, near Rome, Italy, in 1994, has been assigned a date of 400,000 B.P. (see Mounier, Condemi, and Manzi 2011). Other possible *H. erectus* remains have been found in Europe, but their dates are uncertain. They usually are classified as late *H. erectus,* or transitional between *H. erectus* and early *H. sapiens.*

ARCHAIC *H. SAPIENS*

Africa, which was center stage during the australopithecine period, is joined by Asia and Europe during the *H. erectus* and *H. sapiens* periods of hominin evolution. European fossils and tools have contributed disproportionately to our knowledge and interpretation of early (archaic) *H. sapiens.* This doesn't mean that *H. sapiens* evolved in Europe or that most early *H. sapiens* lived in Europe. Indeed, the fossil evidence suggests that *H. sapiens,* like *H. erectus* before it, originated in Africa. *H. sapiens* lived in Africa for more than 100,000 years before reaching Europe around 45,000 B.P. (Benazzi 2011, Higham 2011). There probably were many more humans in the tropics than in Europe during the ice ages. We merely *know more* about recent human evolution in Europe because archaeology and fossil hunting—not human evolution—have been going on longer there than in Africa and Asia.

Recent discoveries, along with reinterpretation of the dating and the anatomical relevance of some earlier finds, are

filling in the gap between *H. erectus* and archaic *H. sapiens.* **Archaic *H. sapiens*** (300,000?–28,000 B.P.) encompasses the earliest members of our species, along with the **Neandertals** (*H. sapiens neanderthalensis*—130,000–28,000 B.P.) of Europe and the Middle East and their Neandertal-like contemporaries in Africa and Asia. (See Recap 9.1 and Figure 9.4 for a summary and timeline of species within the genus *Homo.*) Brain size in archaic *H. sapiens* was within the modern human range. (The modern average, remember, is about 1,350 cm^3.) A rounding out of the braincase was associated with the increased brain size. As Jolly and White (1995) put it, evolution was pumping more brain into the *H. sapiens* cranium—like filling a football with air.

Ice Ages of the Pleistocene

Traditionally and correctly, the geological epoch known as the **Pleistocene** has been considered the epoch of early human life. Its subdivisions are the Lower Pleistocene (2–1 m.y.a.), the Middle Pleistocene (1 m.y.a.–130,000 B.P.), and the Upper Pleistocene (130,000–11,000 B.P.). These subdivisions refer to the placement of geological strata containing, respectively, older, intermediate, and younger fossils. The Lower Pleistocene extends from the start of the Pleistocene to the advent of the ice ages in the Northern Hemisphere around one million years ago.

Each subdivision of the Pleistocene is associated with a particular group of hominins. Late *Australopithecus* and early *Homo* lived during the Lower Pleistocene. *Homo erectus* spanned most of the Middle Pleistocene. *Homo sapiens* appeared late in the Middle Pleistocene and was the sole hominin of the Upper Pleistocene.

During the second million years of the Pleistocene, there were several ice ages, or **glacials,** major advances of continental ice sheets in Europe and North America. These periods were separated by **interglacials,** long warm periods between the major glacials. (Scientists used to think there were four main glacial advances, but the picture has grown more complex.) With each advance, the world climate cooled and continental ice sheets—massive glaciers—covered the northern parts of Europe and North America. Climates that are temperate today were arctic during the glacials.

During the interglacials, the climate warmed up and the *tundra*—the cold, treeless plain—retreated north with the ice sheets. Forests returned to areas, such as southwestern France, that once had tundra vegetation. The ice sheets advanced and receded several times during the last glacial, the *Würm* (75,000–12,000 B.P.). Brief periods of relative warmth during the Würm (and other glacials) are called *interstadials,* in contrast to the longer interglacials. Hominin fossils found in association with animals known to occur in cold or warm climates, respectively, permit us to date them to glacial or interglacial (or interstadial) periods.

Meet *Homo erectus.* Sangiran 17 is the most complete *H. erectus* skull from Java. In this process of reconstruction, a cast of the fossil (a) was rounded out with teeth, lower jaw, and chewing muscles (b). Additional soft tissues (c) and then the skin (d) were added. Given the robust features of this fossil, it is assumed to be male.

Fossil representatives of the genus Homo, *compared with anatomically modern humans (AMHs) and chimps* (Pan troglodytes).

SPECIES	DATES	KNOWN DISTRIBUTION	IMPORTANT SITES	BRAIN SIZE (IN cm³)
Anatomically modern humans (AMHs)	195,000 B.P. to present	Worldwide	Omo Kibish, Herto, Border Cave, Klasies River, Skhūl, Qafzeh, Cro-Magnon	1,350
Neandertals	130,000 to 28,000 B.P.	Europe, southwestern Asia	La Chapelle-aux-Saints	1,430
Archaic *Homo sapiens*	300,000 to 28,000 B.P.	Africa, Europe, Asia	Kabwe, Arago, Dali, Mount Carmel caves	1,135
Homo erectus	1.9 m.y.a. to 300,000 B.P.	Africa, Asia, Europe	East, West Turkana, Olduvai, Ileret, Dmanisi, Zhoukoudian, Java, Ceprano	900
Pan troglodytes	Modern	Central Africa	Gombe, Mahale	390

archaic *H. sapiens*
Early *H. sapiens* (300,000 to 28,000 B.P.); includes Neandertals.

Neandertals
Archaic *H. sapiens* group inhabiting Europe and the Middle East from 130,000 to 28,000 B.P.

Pleistocene
Main epoch (1.8 m.y.a.–11,000 B.P.) of evolution of *Homo*.

glacials
Major advances of continental ice sheets in Europe and North America.

interglacials
Extended warm periods between glacials.

H. antecessor and *H. heidelbergensis*

In northern Spain's Atapuerca Mountains, the site of Gran Dolina has yielded the remains of 780,000-year-old hominins that Spanish researchers call *H. antecessor* and see as a possible common ancestor of the Neandertals and anatomically modern humans. The nearby cave of Sima dos Huesos has yielded thousands of fossils representing at least thirty-three hominins. Almost 300,000 years old, they may represent an early stage of Neandertal evolution (Lemonick and Dorfman 1999). Northern Spain also is home to the El Sidrón cave, where scientists have found over 1,800 Neanderthal bone fragments, some of which have yielded snippets of DNA. (See "Appreciating Anthropology" on p. 193 for evidence of cannibalism at El Sidrón.)

A massive hominin jaw was discovered in 1907 in a gravel pit at Mauer near Heidelberg, Germany. Originally called "Heidelberg man" or *Homo heidelbergensis,* the jaw appears to be around 500,000 years old. The deposits that yielded this jaw also contained fossil remains of several animals, including bear, bison, deer, elephant, horse, and rhinoceros. Some anthropologists have revived the species name *H. heidelbergensis* to refer to a group of fossil hominins, including the Ceprano fragment described on p. 188, that in this text are described as either late *H. erectus* or archaic *H. sapiens.* This group would include hominins dated (very roughly) between 700,000 and 200,000 years ago and found in Europe, Africa, and Asia. Such fossils, here assigned to either *H. erectus* or archaic *H. sapiens,* would be transitional between *H. erectus* and later hominin forms such as the Neandertals and anatomi-

cally modern humans (see Mounier, Condemi, and Manzi 2011).

Besides the hominin *fossils* found in Europe, there is archaeological—including abundant stone tool—evidence for the presence and behavior of late *H. erectus* and then archaic *H. sapiens* in Europe. A chance discovery on England's Suffolk seacoast shows that humans reached northern Europe 700,000 years ago (Gugliotta 2005b). Several stone flakes were recovered from seashore sediment bordering the North Sea. These archaic humans crossed the Alps into northern Europe more than 200,000

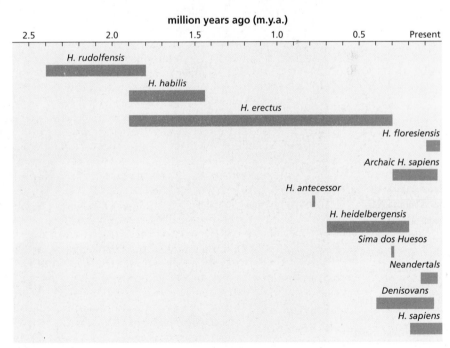

FIGURE 9.4 Timeline of Species within the Genus *Homo* in Increments of 100,000 Years, from 2.5 m.y.a. through the Present.
Some scientists include *H. heidelbergensis* and the Neandertals within archaic *H. sapiens.*

years earlier than previously imagined—during an interglacial period. At that time, the fertile lowlands they inhabited were part of a land bridge connecting what is now Britain to the rest of Europe. They lived in a large delta with several rivers and a dry, mild Mediterranean climate. Various animals were among its abundant resources. It is not known whether the descendants of these settlers remained in England. The next glacial period may have been too extreme for human habitation so far back.

At the site of Terra Amata, which overlooks Nice in southern France, archaeologists have documented human activity dating back some 300,000 years. Small bands of hunters and gatherers consisting of fifteen to twenty-five people made regular visits during the late spring and early summer to Terra Amata, a sandy cove on the coast of the Mediterranean. Archaeologists determined the season of occupation by examining fossilized human excrement, which contained pollen from flowers that are known to bloom in late spring. There is evidence for twenty-one such visits. Four groups camped on a sand bar, six on the beach, and eleven on a sand dune. Archaeologists surmise that the eleven dune sites represent that number of annual visits by the same band (deLumley 1969/1976).

From a camp atop the dune, these people looked down on a river valley where animals were abundant. Bones found at Terra Amata show that their diet included red deer, young elephants, wild boars, wild mountain goats, an extinct variety of rhinoc-eros, and wild oxen. The Terra Amata people also hunted turtles and birds and collected oysters and mussels. Fish bones also were found at the site. The arrangement of postholes shows that these people used saplings to support temporary huts. There were hearths—sunken pits and piled stone fireplaces—within the shelters. Stone chips inside the borders of the huts show that tools were made from locally available rocks and beach pebbles. Thus, at Terra Amata, hundreds of thousands of years ago, people were already pursuing an essentially human lifestyle, one that survived in certain coastal regions into the 20th century.

Archaic *H. sapiens* lived during the last part of the *Middle Pleistocene*—during the *Mindel* (second) glacial, the interglacial that followed it, and the following *Riss* (third) glacial. The distribution of the fossils and tools of archaic *H. sapiens,* which have been found in Europe, Africa, and Asia, shows that *Homo*'s tolerance of environmental diversity had increased. For example, the Neandertals and their immediate ancestors managed to survive extreme cold in Europe. Archaic *H. sapiens* occupied the Arago cave in southeastern France at a time when Europe was bitterly cold. The only Riss glacial site with facial material, Arago, was excavated in 1971. It produced a partially intact skull, two jawbones, and teeth from a dozen individuals. With an apparent date of about 200,000 B.P., the Arago fossils have mixed features that seem transitional between *H. erectus* and the Neandertals.

Reconstruction of a hut made from saplings about 300,000 years ago at the Terra Amata site in Nice, France. The Terra Amata Museum, whose diorama is shown here, was built on the archaeological site, which was visited annually by ancient foragers. What foods did they eat?

THE NEANDERTALS

Neandertals were first discovered in Western Europe. The first one was found in 1856 in a German valley called Neander Valley—*tal* is the German word for "valley." Scientists had trouble interpreting the discovery. It was clearly human and similar to modern Europeans in many ways, yet different enough to be considered strange and abnormal. This was, after all, thirty-five years before Dubois discovered the first *H. erectus* fossils in Java and almost seventy years before the first australopithecine was found in South Africa. Darwin's *On the Origin of Species,* published in 1859, had not yet appeared to offer a theory of evolution through natural selection. There was no framework for understanding human evolution. Over time, the fossil record filled in, along with evolutionary theory. There have been numerous subsequent discoveries of Neandertals in Europe and the Middle East and of archaic human fossils with similar features in Africa and Asia. The similarities and differences between Neandertals and other relatively recent hominins have become clearer.

Fossils that are not Neandertals but that have similar features (such as large faces and brow ridges) have been found in Africa and Asia. The Kabwe skull from Zambia (130,000 B.P.) is an archaic *H. sapiens* with a Neandertal-like brow ridge. Archaic Chinese fossils with Neandertal-like features have been found at Maba and Dali. Neandertals have been found in Central Europe and the Middle East. For example, Neandertal fossils found at the Shanidar cave in northern Iraq date to around 60,000 B.P., as does a Neandertal skeleton found at Israel's Kebara cave (Shreeve 1992). At the Israeli site of Tabun on Mount Carmel, a Neandertal female skeleton was excavated in 1932. She was a contemporary of the Shanidar Neandertals, and her brow ridges, face, and teeth show typical Neandertal robustness.

In 2007 Svante Pääbo and his colleagues at Germany's Max Planck Institute for Evolutionary Anthropology announced their identification of Neandertal mitochondrial DNA (mtDNA) in bones found at two sites in central Asia and Siberia. One of them, Teshik Tash, in Uzbekistan, previously had been seen as the easternmost limit of Neandertal territory. However, bones from the second site, the Okladnikov cave in the Altai mountains, place the Neandertals much farther (1,250 miles) east, in southern Siberia. The mtDNA sequence at these sites differs only slightly from that of European Neandertals. The Neandertals may have reached these areas around 127,000 years ago, when a warm period made Siberia more accessible than it is today (see Wade 2007).

Cold-Adapted Neandertals

By 75,000 B.P., after an interglacial interlude, Western Europe's hominins (Neandertals, by then) again faced extreme cold as the Würm glacial began. To

Neandertal technology, a Middle Paleolithic tradition called Mousterian, improved considerably during the Würm glacial. These Mousterian flake tools were found at Gorham's Cave, Gibraltar.

deal with this environment, they wore clothes, made more elaborate tools (see the photo above), and hunted reindeer, mammoths, and woolly rhinos (see Conard 2011).

The Neandertals were stocky, with large trunks relative to limb length—a phenotype that minimizes surface area and thus conserves heat. Another adaptation to extreme cold was the Neandertal face, which has been likened to a *H. erectus* face that has been pulled forward by the nose. Illustrating Thomson's rule (see Chapter 6), this extension increased the distance between outside air and the arteries that carry blood to the brain and was adaptive in a cold climate. The brain is sensitive to temperature changes and must be kept warm. The massive nasal cavities of Neandertal fossils suggest long, broad noses. This would expand the area for warming and moistening air.

Neandertal characteristics also include huge front teeth, broad faces, and large brow ridges, and ruggedness of the skeleton and musculature. What activities were associated with these anatomical traits? Neandertal teeth probably did many jobs later done by tools (Brace 1995; Rak 1986). The front teeth show heavy wear, suggesting that they

Reconstruction of a Neandertal woman from skull and skeletal evidence found at Tabun in Israel. She lived about 100,000 years ago.

were used for varied purposes, including chewing animal hides to make soft winter clothing out of them. The massive Neandertal face showed the stresses of constantly using the front teeth for holding and pulling.

Comparison of early and later Neandertals shows a trend toward reduction of their robust features. Neandertal technology, a Middle Paleolithic tradition called **Mousterian**, improved considerably during the Würm glacial. Although the Neandertals are remembered more for their physiques than for their manufacturing abilities, their tool kits were sophisticated. Mousterian technology included at least fourteen categories of tools designed for different jobs. The Neandertals elaborated on a revolutionary technique of flake-tool manufacture (the *Levallois* technique) invented in southern Africa around 200,000 years ago, which spread widely throughout the Old World. Uniform flakes were chipped off a specially prepared core of rock. Additional work on the flakes produced such special-purpose tools as those shown in Figure 9.5. Scrapers were used to prepare animal hides for clothing. And special tools also were designed for sawing, gouging, and piercing (Binford and Binford 1979, Conard 2011). See this chapter's "Appreciating Anthropology" for a description of some less pleasant uses of Mousterian blades.)

Tools assumed many burdens formerly placed on the anatomy. For example, tools took over jobs once done by the front teeth. Through a still imperfectly understood mechanism, facial muscles and supporting structures developed less. Smaller front teeth—

perhaps because of dental crowding—were favored. The projecting face reduced, as did the brow ridge, which had provided buttressing against the forces generated when the large front teeth were used for environmental manipulation.

The Neandertals and Modern People

Generations of scientists have debated whether the Neandertals were ancestral to modern Europeans. The current prevailing view, denying this ancestry, proposes that *H. erectus* split into separate groups, one ancestral to the Neandertals, the other ancestral to *anatomically modern humans* (**AMHs**), who first reached Europe around 45,000 B.P. (Early AMHs in Western Europe often are referred to as *Cro Magnon*, after the earliest fossil find of an anatomically modern human, in France's Les Eyzies region, Dordogne Valley, in 1868.) The current predominant view is that modern humans evolved in Africa and eventually colonized Europe, displacing the Neandertals there.

Consider the contrasts between the Neandertals and AMHs. Like *H. erectus* before them, the Neandertals had heavy brow ridges and slanting foreheads. However, average Neandertal cranial capacity (more than 1,400 cm^3) exceeded the modern average. Neandertal jaws were large, providing support for huge front teeth, and their faces were massive. The bones and skull were generally more rugged and had greater sexual dimorphism—particularly in the face and skull—than do those of AMHs. In some

Mousterian
Middle Paleolithic tool tradition associated with Neandertals.

AMHs
Anatomically modern humans; e.g., Cro Magnon, Skhūl, Qafzeh, Herto.

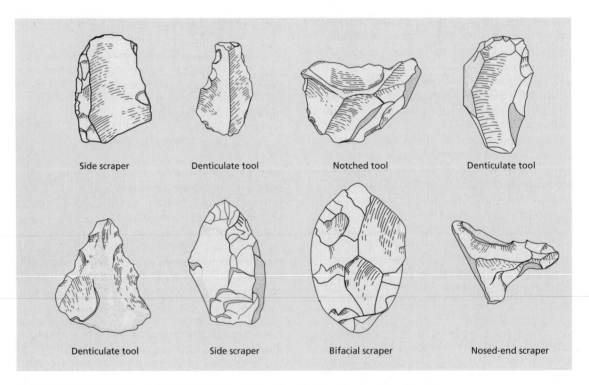

Side scraper   Denticulate tool   Notched tool   Denticulate tool

Denticulate tool   Side scraper   Bifacial scraper   Nosed-end scraper

FIGURE 9.5 Middle Paleolithic Tools of the Mousterian Toolmaking Tradition.
The manufacture of diverse tool types for special purposes confirms Neandertal sophistication.

Neannibalism?

Described here is a Spanish cave site where remains of Neandertal bones and tools have allowed scientists to reconstruct ancient social structure and behavior—including cannibalism. This discovery illustrates how anthropologists use a combination of fossil, archaeological, and DNA evidence to unravel the mysteries of the hominin past.

Deep in a cave in the forests of northern Spain are the remains of a gruesome massacre. The first clues came to light in 1994, when explorers came across a pair of what they thought were human jawbones in the cave, called El Sidrón.... The police discovered more bone fragments . . . which they sent to forensic scientists, who determined that the bones . . . were the remains of Neanderthals who died 50,000 years ago.

Today, El Sidrón is one of the most important sites on Earth for learning about Neanderthals.... Scientists have found 1,800 more Neanderthal bone fragments in the cave, some of which have yielded snippets of DNA.

But the mystery has lingered on for sixteen years. What happened to the El Sidrón victims? ... Spanish scientists who analyzed the bones and DNA report the gruesome answer. The victims

were a dozen members of an extended family, slaughtered by cannibals.

"It's an amazing find," said Todd Disotell, an anthropologist at New York University. Chris Stringer of the Natural History Museum of London said the report "gives us the first glimpse of Neanderthal social structures."

All of the bones were located in a room-size space the scientists dubbed the Tunnel of Bones. They were mixed into a jumble of gravel and mud, which suggests that the Neanderthals did not die in the chamber. Instead, they died on the surface above the cave....

"The bones haven't been scavenged or worn out by erosion," said Carles Lalueza-Fox of Pompeu Fabra University in Barcelona, a co-author of the new paper. Part of the ceiling . . . most likely collapsed during a storm, and the bones fell into the cave....

The only other things scientists have found there are fragments of Neanderthal stone blades. And when the scientists closely examined the Neanderthal bones, they found cut marks—signs that the blades had been used to slice muscle from bone. The long bones had been snapped open. From these clues, the scientists concluded that the Neanderthals were

victims of cannibalism. Scientists have found hints of cannibalism among Neanderthals at other sites, but El Sidrón is exceptional for the scale of evidence....

Dr. Lalueza-Fox and his colleagues could identify twelve individuals. The shape of the bones allowed the scientists to estimate their age and sex. The bones belonged to three men, three women, three teenage boys and three children, including one infant.

Once the scientists knew who they were dealing with, they looked for DNA in the bones. The cold, damp darkness of El Sidrón has made it an excellent storehouse for ancient DNA. . . . In two individuals . . . they found a gene variant that may have given them red hair.... They were able to identify a Y chromosome in four [individuals]. The scientists had already identified all four of them as males—the three men and one teenage boy—based on their bones.

Western European fossils, these contrasts between Neandertals and AMHs are accentuated—giving a stereotyped, or *classic Neandertal,* appearance. The interpretation of one fossil in particular helped create the popular stereotype of the slouching cave dweller. This was the complete human skeleton discovered in 1908 at La Chapelle-aux-Saints in southwestern France, in a layer containing the characteristic Mousterian tools made by Neandertals. It was the first Neandertal to be discovered with the whole skull, including the face, preserved.

The La Chapelle skeleton was given for study to the French paleontologist Marcellin Boule. His analysis of the fossil helped create an inaccurate stereotype of Neandertals as brutes who had trouble walking upright. Boule argued that La Chapelle's brain, although larger than the modern average, was

inferior to modern brains. Further, he suggested that the Neandertal head was slung forward like an ape's. To round out the primitive image, Boule proclaimed that the Neandertals were incapable of straightening their legs for fully erect locomotion. However, later fossil finds show that the La Chapelle fossil wasn't a typical Neandertal but an extreme one. Also, this much-publicized "classic" Neandertal turned out to be an aging man whose skeleton had been distorted by osteoarthritis. Hominins, after all, have been erect bipeds for millions of years. European Neandertals were a variable population. Other Neandertal finds lack La Chapelle's combination of extreme features and are more acceptable ancestors for AMHs.

Those scientists who still believe that Neandertals could have contributed to the ancestry of modern Europeans cite certain fossils to support their view. For example, the Central European site of Mladeč (31,000 to 33,000 B.P.) has yielded remains of several hominins that combine Neandertal robustness with modern features. Wolpoff (1999) also notes modern features in the late Neandertals found at l'Hortus in France and Vindija in Croatia. The fossil remains of a four-year-old boy discovered at Largo Velho in Portugal in 1999 and dated to 24,000 B.P. also shows mixed Neandertal and modern features.

HOMO FLORESIENSIS

In 2004 news reports trumpeted the discovery of bones and tools of a group of tiny humans who inhabited Flores, an Indonesian island 370 miles east of Bali, until fairly recent times (see Wade 2004; Roach 2007). Early in hominin evolution, as we saw in the last chapter, it wasn't unusual for different species, even genera, of hominins, to live at the same time. But until the 2003–2004 discoveries on Flores, few scientists imagined that a different human species had survived through 12,000 B.P., and possibly even later. These tiny people lived, hunted, and gathered on Flores from about 95,000 B.P. until at least 13,000 B.P. One of their most surprising features is the very small skull, about 370 cm³—slightly smaller than the chimpanzee average.

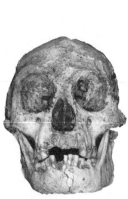

A skull and several skeletons of these miniature people were found in a limestone cave on Flores by a team of Australian and Indonesian archaeologists, who assigned them to a new human species, *H. floresiensis.* (Additional specimens have been

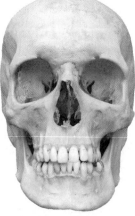

A cast of the anatomically extreme classic Neandertal skull found at La Chapelle-aux-Saints, France.

The skull of *Homo floresiensis* (left; modern human, right), a miniature hominid that inhabited Middle Earth, or at least the Indonesian island of Flores, between 95,000 and 13,000 years ago.

found and described subsequently; see Gugliotta 2005a; Roach 2007.) The discovery of *H. floresiensis,* described as a downsized version of *H. erectus,* shows that archaic humans survived much later than had been thought. Before modern people reached Flores, which is very isolated, the island was inhabited only by a select group of animals that had managed to reach it. These animals, including *H. floresiensis,* faced unusual evolutionary forces that pushed some toward gigantism and some toward dwarfism. The carnivorous lizards that reached Flores, perhaps on natural rafts, became giants. These Komodo dragons now are confined mainly to the nearby island of Komodo. Elephants, which are excellent swimmers, reached Flores, where they evolved to a dwarf form the size of an ox.

Previous excavations by Michael Morwood, one of the discoverers of *H. floresiensis,* estimated that *H. erectus* had reached Flores by 840,000 years ago, based on crude stone tools found there. This *H. erectus* population and its descendants are assumed to have been influenced by the same evolutionary forces that reduced the size of the elephants. The first specimen of *H. floresiensis,* an adult female, was uncovered in 2003, from beneath 20 feet (6.1 meters) of silt coating the floor of the Liang Bua cave. Paleoanthropologists identified her as a very small but otherwise normal individual—a diminutive version of *H. erectus.* Because the downsizing was so extreme, smaller than that in modern human pygmies, she and her fellows were assigned to a new species. Her skeleton is estimated to date back some 18,000 years. Remains of six additional individuals found in the cave date from 95,000 to 13,000 B.P. The cave also has yielded bones of giant lizards, giant rats, pygmy elephants, fish, and birds.

H. floresiensis apparently controlled fire, and the stone tools found with them are more sophisticated than any known to have been made by *H. erectus.* Among the tools were small blades that might have been mounted on wooden shafts. Hunting elephants—probably cooperatively—and making complex tools, the Floresians may (or may not) have had some form of language. The suggestion of such cultural abilities is surprising for a hominin with a chimplike brain. The small cranium has raised some doubt that *H. floresiensis* actually made the tools. The ancestors of the anatomically modern people who colonized Australia might have traveled through this area, and it is possible that they made the stone tools. On the other hand, there is no evidence that modern humans reached Flores prior to 11,000 years ago.

The *H. floresiensis* population of the Liang Bua cave region appears to have been wiped out by a volcanic eruption around 12,000 B.P., but they may have survived until much later elsewhere on Flores. The Ngadha people of central Flores and the Manggarai people of West Flores still tell stories about little people who lived in caves until the arrival of the Dutch traders in the 16th century (Wade 2004).

As reported in 2009, an analysis of the lower limbs and especially an almost complete left foot and parts of the right shows that *H. floresiensis* walked upright, but possessed apelike features (Wilford 2009b). The big toe, for example, was stubby, like a chimp's. The feet were large, more than $7\frac{1}{2}$ inches long, out of proportion to the short lower limbs. These proportions, similar to those of some African apes, have never before been seen in hominins. The feet were flat. The navicular bone, which helps form the arch in modern human feet, was more like one in the great apes. Without a strong arch *H. floresiensis* could have walked but not run like humans.

William Jungers, the anthropologist who led the analytic team, raised the possibility that the ancestor of *H. floresiensis* was not *H. erectus*, as originally had been assumed, but possibly another, more primitive, hominin ancestor (see Wilford 2009).

acing the **COURSE**

summary

1. Compared with late *Australopithecus,* dental, facial, and cranial robustness was reduced in early *Homo—habilis* (1.9–1.44 m.y.a.) and *erectus* (1.9–0.3 m.y.a.). *H. erectus* extended the hominin food quest to the hunting of large animals. *H. erectus,* with a much larger body, had smaller back teeth than *Australopithecus* but larger front teeth and supporting structures, including a massive eyebrow ridge. The Lower Paleolithic Acheulean tradition provided *H. erectus* with better tools. *H. erectus*'s average cranial capacity doubled the australopithecine average. Tool complexity and archaeological evidence for cooperative hunting suggest a long period of enculturation and learning. *H. erectus* extended the hominin range beyond Africa to Asia and Europe.

2. Ancient *H. erectus* skulls have been found in Kenya and Georgia (in Eurasia), dating back some 1.77–1.6 million years. At Olduvai Gorge, Tanzania, geological strata spanning more than a million years demonstrate a transition from Oldowan tools to the Acheulean implements of *H. erectus*. *H. erectus* persisted for more than a million years, evolving into archaic *H. sapiens* by the Middle Pleistocene epoch, some 300,000 years ago. Fire allowed *H. erectus* to expand into cooler areas, to cook, and to live in caves.

3. The classic Neandertals, who inhabited Western Europe during the early part of the Würm glacial, were among the first hominin fossils found. With no examples of *Australopithecus* or *H. erectus* yet discovered, the differences between them and modern humans were accentuated. Even today, anthropologists tend to exclude the classic Neandertals from the ancestry of Western Europeans.

4. The classic Neandertals adapted physically and culturally to bitter cold. Their tool kits were much more complex than those of preceding humans. Their front teeth were among the largest to appear in human evolution. The Neandertals manufactured Mousterian flake tools. Neandertals may have persisted in Western Europe through 28,000 B.P.

5. In 2004 and 2005 scientists reported discoveries of bones and tools of a new hominin species they called *H. floresiensis*. This population of tiny humans lived on the isolated island of Flores in Indonesia. A probable descendant of *H. erectus,* which had settled Flores by 840,000 B.P., *H. floresiensis* is marked by the unusually small size of its body and its chimp-sized skull. There is debate about whether *H. floresiensis* was smart enough to have made the stone tools found in association with the skeletal remains, though there is no evidence that AMHs reached Flores before 11,000 B.P. The *H. floresiensis* remains have been assigned dates ranging from 95,000 to 13,000 B.P.

key terms

test yourself

MULTIPLE CHOICE

1. Despite the continued debate surrounding *H. rudolfensis* and *H. habilis*, there is a sure conclusion:
   a. that a seafood diet made *Homo*'s success in Africa possible.
   b. that several different kinds of hominins lived in Africa before and after the advent of *Homo*.
   c. that *rudolfensis* and *habilis* are simply male and female members of the same species.
   d. that *H. erectus* descended from one of the two.
   e. that the debate will probably never be settled because all of the potential fossil sites in Africa have been dug.

2. Which of the following factors definitely is *not* related to the development of larger brains among *H. erectus* populations?
   a. environmental challenges
   b. greater reliance on hunting
   c. more complex social environment
   d. animal domestication
   e. bipedalism

3. Which of the following is a trend in hominin evolution since the australopithecines?
   a. Sexual dimorphism has disappeared.
   b. Population numbers have remained stable.
   c. Bipedalism has appeared.
   d. The geographic range of the hominins has decreased.
   e. Molar size has decreased.

4. Which of the following traits did *not* contribute to the increasing adaptability of *H. erectus*?
   a. a varied tool kit that facilitated cooperative hunting
   b. microlithic stone tools
   c. an essentially modern postcranial skeleton, permitting long-distance stalking and endurance during a hunt
   d. an average brain size that was double that of the australopithecines
   e. a period of childhood dependency that exceeded that of the australopithecines

5. What is the most likely explanation for why early *Homo* left Africa and spread into Eurasia?
   a. the hyperspecialization on vegetarian diets
   b. *Homo*'s smaller bodies, in relation to australopithecines', making them more nimble and fit for long-distance travel
   c. the need to find meat
   d. overpopulation in Africa
   e. the maladaptation to a more energy-inefficient system of locomotion

6. What species is associated with Zhoukoudian, a site in China that has yielded the most specimens of this species?
   a. *H. habilis*
   b. archaic *Homo sapiens*
   c. Neandertals
   d. *H. erectus*
   e. anatomically modern humans

7. The Dmanisi fossils (1.77–1.7 m.y.a.) found in the former Soviet Republic of Georgia
   a. suggest a very slow spread of early *Homo* out of Africa and into Eurasia.
   b. exhibit no anatomical diversity, unlike the variable anatomically modern humans.
   c. establish the undisputed new species, *H. ergaster*.
   d. are younger than the fossils of the Nariokotome boy found in Kenya.
   e. are the most ancient undisputed hominin fossils found outside of Africa.

8. Why do so many archaic *H. sapiens* finds come from Europe?
   a. because anatomically modern humans evolved in France
   b. because of the richness of data from the Zhoukoudian site
   c. because archaic *H. sapiens* were driven there by the more aggressive Cro Magnons
   d. because there is a long history of Paleolithic archaeology in Europe compared with other world areas
   e. because glaciers caused stratigraphic disturbances

9. What does the debate about Neandertals' relation to anatomically modern humans focus on?
   a. whether Neandertals are directly in anatomically modern humans' evolutionary line, or whether they constitute an extinct offshoot
   b. whether Neandertals were human or a *H. erectus* hybrid
   c. whether Neandertals made microlithic tools
   d. whether Neandertals are the isolated ancestors of the Caucasian race or more general ancestors
   e. whether Neandertals are the founders of the Native American population

10. What is one of the most surprising aspects of the recent discovery of *H. floresiensis?*
    a. the suggestion that this species had developed capacities for language despite their small brains, as is evidenced in their cave art
    b. the suggestion of sophisticated cultural abilities typically associated with anatomically modern humans, and not with a hominin with a chimplike brain
    c. the evidence that this new species may have replace Neandertals in the Middle East later than expected
    d. the clear evidence that this species evolved from *H. erectus*
    e. the suggestion that anatomically modern humans may have reached the Americas much earlier than expected

FILL IN THE BLANK

1. ________ toolmaking evolved out of the Oldowan, or pebble tool, tradition and lasted until about 15,000 years ago.
2. Two hominin fossil finds from Ileret, Kenya, are very significant because they show that *H.* ________ and *H.* ________ overlapped in time rather than being ancestor and descendant, as had been thought.
3. The ________, shaped like a teardrop, represents a predetermined shape based on a template in the mind of the toolmaker. Evidence for such a mental template in the archaeological record suggests a cognitive leap between earlier hominins and *H. erectus*.
4. Although there are African sites with early claims for fire (around 1.5 m.y.a.), definitive evidence of human control of fire dates to ________.
5. Although the Neandertals are remembered more for their physiques than for their manufacturing abilities, their tool kits were sophisticated. Their technology, a Middle Paleolithic tradition, is called ________.

CRITICAL THINKING

1. As anatomically modern humans we make up a variable population and yet we are all one species. When looking at the fossil record, how have scientists confronted the issue of variability and speciation?
2. *H. erectus* persisted for more than a million years. What were its key adaptation strategies? In particular, what do its toolmaking abilities suggest about its evolving cognitive capacities?
3. The classic Neandertals, who inhabited Western Europe during the early part of the Würm glacial, were among the first hominin fossils found. Why did scientists have trouble interpreting these early discoveries? How have early misinterpretations of Neandertals persisted in our culture? Do these persistent misinterpretations matter?
4. Paleoanthropology is an exciting and constantly changing field! What is the significance of two recent hominin fossil finds from Ileret, Kenya? Also, what are some explanations that researchers have recently offered to explain the surprising *Homo floresiensis* discoveries in Indonesia?

Multiple Choice: 1. (B); 2. (D); 3. (E); 4. (B); 5. (C); 6. (D); 7. (E); 8. (D); 9. (A); 10. (B); **Fill in the Blank:** 1. Paleolithic; 2. *habilis, erectus*; 3. Acheulean hand ax; 4. 500,000 B.P.; 5. Mousterian

suggested additional readings

Chazan, M.
2011 *World Prehistory and Archaeology,* 2nd ed. Upper Saddle River, NJ: Prentice Hall. Early hominins through ancient civilizations.

Conard, N. J.
2011 *Neanderthal Lifeways, Subsistence, and Technology*. New York: Springer. Focus on Neandertal cultural adaptations.

Fagan, B. M.
2010 *People of the Earth: A Brief Introduction to World Prehistory,* 13th ed. Upper Saddle River, NJ: Prentice Hall. Prehistoric peoples and civilizations.
2011 *World Prehistory: A Brief Introduction,* 8th ed. Boston: Prentice Hall. From the Paleolithic to the Neolithic around the world.

Reader, J.
2011 *Missing Links: In Search of Human Origins.* New York: Oxford University Press. The search for human origins, from the Middle Ages through the latest fossil and genetic discoveries.

Wenke, R. J., and D. I. Olszewski
2007 *Patterns in Prehistory: Mankind's First Three Million Years,* 5th ed. New York: Oxford University Press. Very thorough survey of fossil and archaeological reconstruction of human evolution.

internet exercises

Go to our Online Learning Center website at **www.mhhe.com/kottak** for Internet exercises directly related to the content of this chapter.

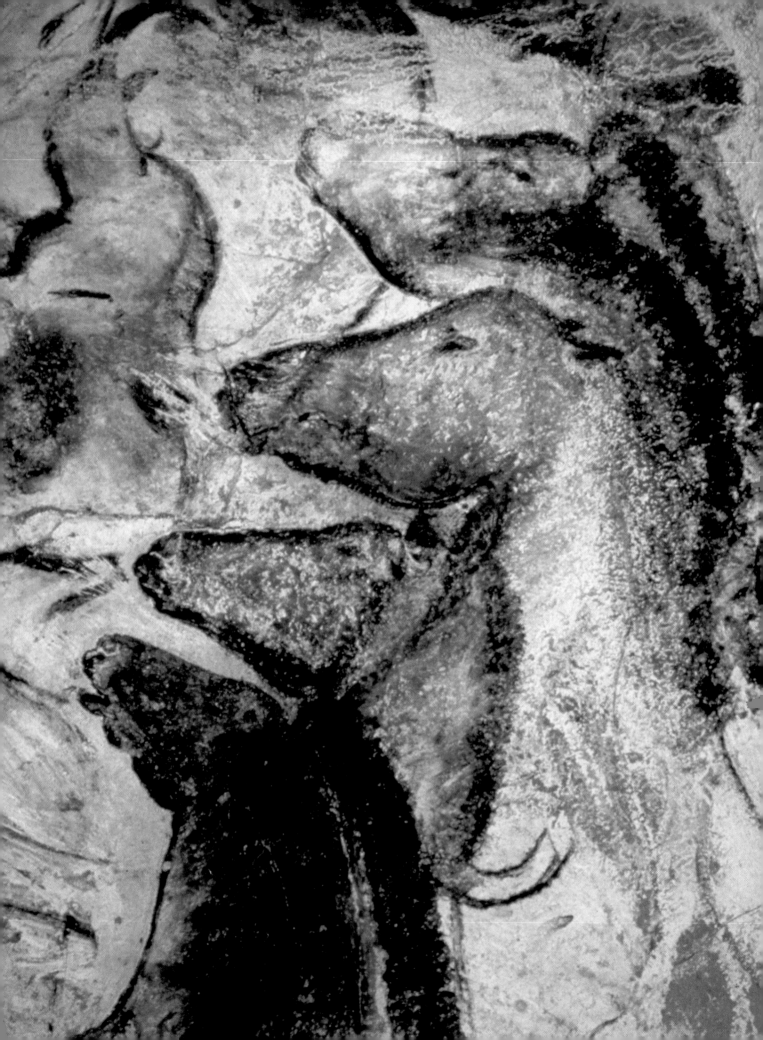

The Origin and Spread of Modern Humans

When and where did modern human anatomy and behavior originate?

What major changes took place in human lifestyles and adaptive strategies as the Ice Age ended?

When and how did modern humans settle Australia, the Americas, and the Pacific?

◄ Murals in Chauvet Cave at Vallon Pont-d'Arc in southern France date back 20,000 years.

understanding OURSELVES

Our choices about how, and to whom, we display aspects of ourselves say something about us not only as individuals but also as social and cultural beings. Think about your appearance right now. What does your clothing say about you—implicitly or explicitly, intentionally or unintentionally? Does your cap, shirt, or jacket display the name of your school, a brand, or a favorite sports team? Do or don't you—and why do you or don't you—have tattoos or piercings? What does facial hair, or its absence, say about you or someone else? Why is your hair long or short? Why did you choose any makeup you are wearing? How about any jewelry? If you're male, why are you, or are you not, circumcised? The way that we present our bodies reflects both on (1) who and what we're trying to look like and (2) what sort of person we're trying *not* to resemble.

Body decoration is a cultural universal, as are other forms of creative expression, including the arts and language, and all say something about us. Expressive culture rests on symbolic thought. As is true generally of symbols (remember Chapter 2), the relation between a symbol and what it stands for is arbitrary. Nike shoes are no more intrinsically swooshlike than Adidas are. Michigan Wolverines are no more like wolverines than Florida Gators are, and vice versa. For archaeologists, evidence for symbolic thought, as manifested materially in patterned or decorated artifacts, strongly suggests modern behavior. Consider the pigment red ochre, a natural iron oxide that modern hunter-gatherers use to create body paint for ritual occasions. Archaeologists suspect that ochre was used similarly in the past. Evidence for the manufacture of red ochre dates back 100,000 years, at South Africa's Blombos Cave. An artifact also discovered in that cave has a carved crosshatch design—three straight lines with another set of three at a diagonal to them—offering the world's earliest evidence for intentional patterning with symbolic meaning.

There is abundant evidence for expressive culture, including art and music, in Europe by 35,000 years ago. At this point, humans were decorating themselves with paints and jewelry and making flutes and figurines. It's likely that linguistic ability was part of this expressive package. As we see in this chapter's "Living Anthropology Videos" clip, linguist Merritt Ruhlen (1994) speculates that all the world's languages descend from a common one spoken 40,000 to 50,000 years ago by anatomically modern humans who originated in Africa. Did a "creative" gene emerge in Africa and fuel human colonization of the rest of the world? Although anthropologists don't have a definitive answer to this question, we do agree about the key role that expressive culture plays in human life.

MODERN HUMANS

Anatomically modern humans (AMHs) evolved from an archaic *H. sapiens* African ancestor. Eventually, AMHs spread to other areas, including Europe, where they replaced, or interbred with, the Neandertals, whose robust traits eventually disappeared (see Barton et al. 2011).

Out of Africa II

Recent Fossil and Archaeological Evidence

Fossil and archaeological evidence has been accumulating to support the African origin of AMHs. A major find was announced in 2003: the 1997 discovery in an Ethiopian valley of three anatomically modern skulls—those of two adults and a child. When found, the fossils had been fragmented so badly that their reconstruction took several years. Tim White and Berhane Asfaw were coleaders of the international team that made the find near the village of Herto, 140 miles northeast of Addis Ababa. All three skulls were missing the lower jaw. The skulls showed evidence of cutting and handling, suggesting they had been detached from their bodies and used—perhaps ritually—after death. A few teeth, but no other bones, were found with the skulls, again suggesting their deliberate removal from the body. Layers of volcanic ash allowed geologists to date them to 154,000–160,000 B.P. The people represented by the skulls had lived on the shore of an ancient lake, where they hunted and fished. The skulls were found along with hippopotamus and antelope bones and some 600 tools, including blades and hand axes.

Except for a few archaic characteristics, the **Herto** skulls are anatomically modern—long with broad midfaces, featuring tall, narrow nasal bones. The cranial vaults are high, falling within modern dimensions. These finds offered important support for the view that modern humans originated in Africa.

Omo Kibish is one of several sites along the Omo River in southwestern Ethiopia. Between 1967 and 1974 Richard Leakey and his colleagues from the Kenya National Museum recovered AMH remains

originally considered to be about 125,000 years old. The specimens now appear to be much older. Indeed, with an estimated date of 195,000 B.P., they appear to be the earliest AMH fossils yet found (McDougall, Brown, and Fleagle 2005). The Omo remains include two partial skulls (Omo 1 and Omo 2), four jaws, a leg bone, about 200 teeth, and several other parts. One site, Omo Kibish I, contained a nearly complete skeleton of an adult male. Middle Stone Age tools have been found in the same stratigraphic layers. Studies of the Omo 1 skull and skeleton indicate an overall modern human morphology with some primitive features. The Omo 2 skull is more archaic. (See the illustration for cranial contrasts between *H. erectus*, archaic *H. sapiens*, Neandertals, and AMHs.)

From sites in South Africa comes further evidence of early African AMHs. At Border Cave, a remote rock shelter in South Africa, fossil remains dating back perhaps 150,000 years are believed to be those of early modern humans. The remains of at least five AMHs have been discovered, including the nearly complete skeleton of a 4- to 6-month-old infant buried in a shallow grave. Excavations at Border Cave also have produced some 70,000 stone tools, along with the remains of several mammal species, including elephants, believed to have been hunted by the ancient people who lived there. Middle Stone Age tools and

Herto
Very early (160,000–154,000 B.P.) AMHs found in Ethiopia.

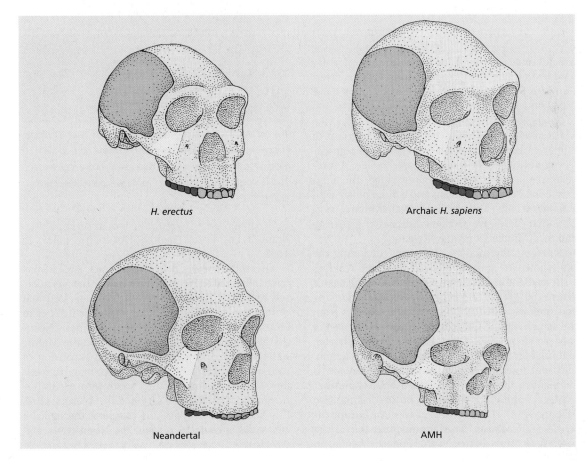

H. erectus

Archaic *H. sapiens*

Neandertal

AMH

Compare these drawings of *H. erectus*, archaic *H. sapiens*, Neandertal, and AMH. What are the main differences you notice? Is the Neandertal more like *H. erectus* or AMH?

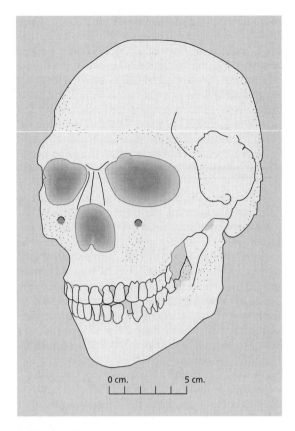

FIGURE 10.1 Skhūl V.

This anatomically modern human with some archaic features dates to 100,000 B.P. This is one of several fossils found at Skhūl, Israel.

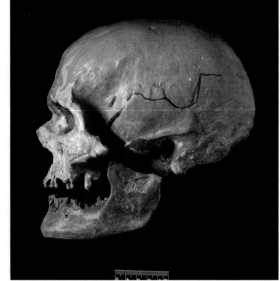

Cro Magnon I, the skull of a 45-year-old anatomically modern human, discovered in 1868 near Les Eyzies in France's Dordogne region. Note the distinct chin.

The Cro Magnon rock shelter near Les Eyzies-de-Tayac, Dordogne, France. Remains of anatomically modern humans, such as the famous fossil found here in 1868, have been found in rock shelters from France to South Africa. The Cro Magnon people lived here around 31,000 years ago.

considerable evidence for behavioral modernity have been found at two other South African caves: Pinnacle Point (164,000 B.P.) and Blombos Cave (100,000 B.P.).

A complex of South African caves near the Klasies River Mouth was occupied by a group of hunter-gatherers some 120,000 years ago. Fragmentary bones suggest how those people looked. A forehead fragment has a modern brow ridge. There is a thin-boned cranial fragment and a piece of jaw with a modern chin. The archaeological evidence suggests that these cave dwellers did coastal gathering and used Middle Stone Age stone tools.

Anatomically modern specimens, including the skull shown in Figure 10.1, have been found at Skhūl, a site on Mount Carmel in Israel. The Skhūl fossils date to 100,000 B.P. Another group of modern-looking and similarly dated (92,000 B.P.) skulls comes from the Israeli site of Qafzeh. All these skulls have a modern shape; their braincases are higher, shorter, and rounder than Neandertal skulls. There is a more filled-out forehead region, which rises more vertically above the brows. A marked chin is another modern feature (see the photo of the original Cro Magnon find). (Early AMHs in western Europe often are referred to as **Cro Magnons,** after the earliest fossil find of an anatomically modern human, in

France's Les Eyzies region, Dordogne Valley, in 1868.)

Given these early dates from Israel, AMHs may have inhabited the Middle East before the Neandertals did. Ofer Bar-Yosef (1987) has suggested that during the last (Würm) glacial period, which began around 75,000 years ago, Western European Neandertals spread east and south (and into the Middle East) as part of a general southward expansion of cold-adapted fauna. AMHs, in turn, may have followed warmer-climate fauna south into Africa, returning to the Middle East once the Würm ended. (The illustration on page 201 compares the skulls of *H. erectus,* archaic *H. sapiens,* the Neandertals, and AMHs.)

Cro Magnon
The first fossil find (1868) of an AMH, from France's Dordogne Valley.

Genetic Evidence for Out of Africa II

In 1987 a group of molecular geneticists at the University of California at Berkeley offered support for the idea that modern humans (AMHs) arose fairly recently in Africa, then spread out and colonized the world. Rebecca Cann, Mark Stoneking, and Allan C. Wilson (1987) analyzed genetic markers in placentas donated by 147 women whose ancestors came from Africa, Europe, the Middle East, Asia, New Guinea, and Australia.

The researchers focused on mitochondrial DNA (mtDNA). This genetic material is located in the cytoplasm (the outer part of a cell—not the nucleus) of cells. Ordinary DNA, which makes up the genes that determine most physical traits, is found in the nucleus and comes from both parents. But only the mother contributes mitochondrial DNA to the fertilized egg. The father plays no part in mtDNA transmission, just as the mother has nothing to do with the transmission of the Y chromosome, which comes from the father and determines the sex of the child.

living anthropology **VIDEOS**

Origins of the World's Languages, www.mhhe.com/kottak

Linguist Merritt Ruhlen attempts to uncover "fossil words" that have been passed down from a single original language to the 5,000 or so languages of today. Ruhlen reduces those 5,000 languages to 420 families, then to 12 groups, and finally into universal word roots such as those for "one" and "water." He speculates that all the world's languages descend from a common language spoken perhaps 40,000 to 50,000 years ago by anatomically modern humans who originated in Africa, eventually spreading out to colonize the world.

To establish a "genetic clock," the Berkeley researchers measured the variation in mtDNA in their 147 tissue samples. They cut each sample into segments to compare with the others. By estimating the number of mutations that had taken place in each sample since its common origin with the 146 others, the researchers drew an evolutionary tree with the help of a computer.

That tree started in Africa and then branched in two. One group remained in Africa, while the other one split off, carrying its mtDNA to the rest of the world. The variation in mtDNA was greatest among Africans. This suggests they have been evolving the longest. The Berkeley researchers concluded that everyone alive today has mtDNA that descends from a woman (dubbed "Eve") who lived in sub-Saharan Africa around 200,000 years ago. Eve was not the only woman alive then; she was just the only one whose descendants have included a daughter in each generation up to the present. Because mtDNA passes exclusively through females, mtDNA lines disappear whenever a woman has no children or has only sons. The details of the Eve theory suggest that her descendants left Africa no more than 135,000 years ago. They eventually displaced the Neandertals in Europe and went on to colonize the rest of the world.

In 1997, ancient DNA was extracted from one of the Neandertal bones originally found in Germany's Neander Valley in 1856. This DNA, from an upper arm bone (humerus), has been compared with the DNA of modern humans. The kinds of matches we would expect in closely related humans did not occur. Thus, there were 27 differences between the Neandertal DNA and a reference sample of modern DNA. By contrast, samples of DNA from modern populations worldwide show only five to eight differences with the reference sample. This was the first time that DNA of a premodern human had been recovered. The original analysis was done by Svante Pääbo. The findings then were duplicated by Mark Stoneking and Anne Stone at Pennsylvania State University.

In 2006, Pääbo reported on the first sequencing of nuclear DNA (in addition to mtDNA) extracted from a Neandertal. This genetic material came from a 45,000-year-old Neandertal fossil from Vindija Cave, outside Zagreb, Croatia. As of 2006, Pääbo and his colleagues (Green et al. 2006) had sequenced about a million base-pairs, constituting 0.03 percent of the Neandertal genome. One particularly interesting finding was that the Neandertal Y chromosome differs significantly from that of modern humans. This may mean there was little interbreeding between the two groups.

The Neandertals may (or may not) have coexisted with modern humans in the Middle East for thousands of years. The overlap in Europe apparently spanned the period between 45,000 B.P. and Neandertal extinction around 28,000 B.P. (see Benazzi et al. 2011, Higham et al. 2011, and this chapter's "Appreciating Anthropology"). At the Israeli and African sites discussed previously, modern humans date back 100,000 years or more. Middle Eastern Neandertals date back 40,000 to 60,000 years. In Western Europe, Neandertals may have survived until about 28,000 years ago.

To what extent did Neandertals and AMHs interact? Did they trade or interbreed? Were the Neandertals outcompeted by modern humans or killed off by them? Future discoveries will continue to provide answers to such questions, which have engaged paleoanthropologists for decades.

The Denisovans

In late 2010, based on ancient DNA evidence, scientists identified a hominin group known as the Denisovans as distant cousins to Neandertals (Callaway

Fossil Teeth Put Humans in Europe Earlier Than Thought

For over a century anthropologists have known of the overlap between archaic (Neandertal) and anatomically modern humans (AMHs) in Europe. But how long did it last? This account describes the recent redating of a piece of jawbone with three teeth from England and the redating and reinterpretation of two baby teeth from Italy. The results reveal the oldest known skeletal remains of anatomically modern humans in Europe. Modern anthropology is exciting not only because of its new discoveries but also because of improvements in our understanding of human evolution that come through the application of new and improved techniques. Confirmation that modern humans reached Europe by 45,000 years ago provides more time for contacts with Neandertals before the latter became extinct.

The fossils seemed hardly worth a second look. The one from England was only a piece of jawbone with three teeth, and the other, from southern Italy, was nothing more than two infant teeth. But scientists went ahead, re-examining them with refined techniques, and found that one specimen's age had previously been significantly underestimated and that the other's dating and identity had been misinterpreted.

They had in fact discovered the oldest known skeletal remains of anatomically modern humans in the whole of Europe, two international research teams reported Wednesday.

The scientists who made the discovery and others who study human origins say they expect the findings to reignite debate over the relative capabilities of the immigrant modern humans

and the indigenous Neanderthals, their closest hominid relatives; the extent of their interactions; and perhaps the reasons behind the Neanderthal extinction. The findings have already prompted speculation that the *Homo sapiens* migrations into Europe may have come in at least two separate waves, rather than just one.

In tests conducted at the Oxford Radiocarbon Accelerator Unit in England, the baby teeth from Italy were dated at 43,000 to 45,000 years old. Other analysis showed the teeth to be those of a modern human, not a Neanderthal, as previously thought when the fossil was unearthed in 1964 from the Grotta del Cavallo. Similar tests at Oxford established that the age of the jawbone, from Kents Cavern near Torquay, Devon, had been significantly underestimated. . . . The age is now set at 41,500 to 44,200 years old, making this the oldest known modern human fossil from northwestern Europe.

These dates are remarkable on several counts, scientists said. The earliest reliably dated European modern human specimen, up to now, came from . . . Romania. . . . [and its] age is estimated at 37,800 to 42,000 years old. . . .

And in the absence of early fossils, archaeologists had not been sure who made some of the stone tools they were uncovering, the arriving humans or the Neanderthals. It had been generally assumed that modern humans probably entered Europe at least as early as 45,000 years ago, based on changing patterns of artifacts that soon followed. . . .

The lead author of the jawbone report was Thomas Higham of the University of Oxford. The principal author of the report on the baby teeth

from Cavallo was Stefano Benazzi of the University of Vienna.

Not only does the jawbone indicate "the wide and rapid dispersal of the earliest moderns across Europe" during the last ice age, more than 40,000 years ago, Dr. Higham's team wrote, it was also found in cave layers associated with a technology that archaeologists call the Aurignacian culture. . . .

The confirmed early appearance of modern humans in Europe gave them more time for contacts with Neanderthals before the latter's extinction about 30,000 years ago. Although recent genetic research shows some evidence of interbreeding between the species, there was uncertainty as to how much contact the two had in Europe. . . .

Determining the age for any samples more than 40,000 years old was no sure thing. At that age, levels of remaining radiocarbon are low, and contamination can be a serious problem. As an alternative, Katerina Douka of Oxford, a member of the team examining the Italian specimen, focused on the dating of marine shell beads found in the same archaeological levels as the teeth. . . .

The Kents Cavern fossil might represent an early dispersal through Central Europe that crossed into Britain on a land bridge where the North Sea is now. The Cavallo remains might represent a possibly even earlier migration along the Southern European coasts.

2011; Zimmer 2010). The research was led by Svante Paabo, who in May 2010 had published a complete Neandertal genome (see Green et al. 2010). Analyzing that genome, Paabo and his colleagues concluded that humans and Neandertals descend from common ancestors that lived in Africa 600,000 years ago. They also found 2.5 percent of the Neandertal genome to be more similar to the DNA of living Europeans and Asians than to African DNA. This finding suggests that Neandertals interbred with AMHs soon after the latter emerged from Africa around 50,000 years ago.

The Denisovans get their name from Denisova, a cave in southern Siberia where their traces (so far only a finger fragment and a wisdom tooth) were found. The Denisovans apparently lived in Asia from roughly 400,000 to 50,000 years ago. Remarkably, scientists have managed to extract the entire Denisovan genome from the finger and the tooth. The common ancestors of Neandertals and Denisovans may have left Africa around half a million years ago. The DNA suggests that the split between ancestral Neandertals and Denisovans happened around 400,000 years ago. The Neandertals spread to the west, eventually reaching the Middle East and Europe. The Denisovans headed east.

Comparison of the Denisovan genome with a spectrum of modern human populations revealed a striking relationship. Melanesians, who inhabit Papua New Guinea and islands northeast of Australia, have inherited about one-twentieth of their DNA from Denisovan roots. This suggests that after the ancestors of today's Papuans split from other AMHs and migrated east, they interbred with Denisovans (see Callaway 2011). Precisely when, where, and to what extent is unclear.

If the Denisovan range extended from Siberia to South Asia, they must have been a very successful kind of hominin. The wisdom tooth offers the only clues as to what they looked like. It resembles the teeth of neither AMHs nor Neandertals. It has bulging sides and large, flaring roots. Only when someone finds the same kind of tooth in a fossil skull, or perhaps even a complete skeleton, will we be able to see what the Denisovans really looked like.

THE ADVENT OF BEHAVIORAL MODERNITY

Scientists agree that (1) around 6 million years ago, our hominin ancestors originated in Africa, and as apelike creatures they became habitual bipeds; (2) by 2.6 million years ago, still in Africa, hominins were making crude stone tools; (3) by 1.7 million years ago, hominins had spread from Africa to Asia and eventually Europe; and (4) sometime around 200,000 years ago, anatomically modern humans (AMHs) evolved from ancestors who had remained in Africa. Like earlier hominins (*H. erectus*), AMHs spread out from Africa. Eventually they replaced nonmodern human types, such as the Neandertals in Europe and the successors of *H. erectus* in the Far East.

There is disagreement, however, about when, where, and how early AMHs achieved **behavioral modernity**—relying on symbolic thought, elaborating cultural creativity, and as a result becoming fully human in behavior as well as in anatomy. Was it as much as 165,000 or as little as 45,000 years ago? Was it in Africa, the Middle East, or Europe? What triggered the change: a genetic mutation,

population increase, competition with nonmodern humans, or some other cause? The traditional view has been that modern behavior originated fairly recently, perhaps 45,000 years ago, and only after *Homo sapiens* pushed into Europe. This theory of a "creative explosion" is based on finds such as the impressive cave paintings at Lascaux, Chauvet Cave, and other sites in France and Spain (Wilford 2002*b*). However, recent discoveries outside Europe suggest a much older, more gradual evolution of modern behavior.

Anthropologist Richard G. Klein of Stanford University is a leading advocate for the idea that human creativity dawned suddenly, in Europe around 45,000 years ago. Prior to this time, Klein thinks *Homo* had changed very slowly in anatomy and behavior. After this "dawn of culture," human anatomy changed little, but behavior started changing dramatically (Klein with Edgar 2002). Indeed, by 40,000 years ago AMHs in Europe were making varied tools that display a pattern of abstract and symbolic thought. Their modern behavior included burying their dead with ceremonies, adorning their bodies with paints and jewelry, and making figurine images of fertile females. Their cave paintings displayed images from their minds, as they remembered the hunt, and events and symbols associated with it.

To explain such a flowering of creativity, Klein proposes a neurological hypothesis. About 50,000 years ago, he thinks, a genetic mutation acted to rewire the human brain, possibly allowing for an advance in language. Improved communication, in Klein's view, could have given people "the fully modern ability to invent and manipulate culture" (quoted in Wilford 2002*b*). Klein thinks this genetic change probably happened in Africa and then allowed "human populations to colonize new and challenging environments" (quoted in Wilford 2002*b*). Reaching Europe, the rewired modern humans met and replaced the resident Neandertals. Klein recognizes that his genetic hypothesis "fails one important measure of a proper scientific hypothesis—it cannot be tested or falsified by experiment or by examination of relevant human fossils" (quoted in Wilford 2002*b*). AMH skulls from the time period in question show no change at all in brain size or function.

Challenging Klein's views are discoveries made in Africa and the Middle East that provide substantial evidence for earlier (than in Europe) modern behavior. These finds include finely made stone and bone tools, self-ornamentation, and abstract carvings. Surveying African archaeological sites dating to between 300,000 and 30,000 years ago, Sally McBrearty and Alison Brooks (2000) conclude that what might appear to be a sudden event in Europe actually rested on a slow process of cultural accumulation within Africa, where *Homo sapiens* became fully human long before 40,000 years ago. At South Africa's Blombos Cave, for example, an archaeological team

behavioral modernity Fully human behavior based on symbolic thought and cultural creativity.

led by Christopher Henshilwood found evidence that AMHs were making bone awls and weapon points more than 70,000 years ago. Three points had been shaped with a stone blade and then finely polished. Henshilwood thinks these artifacts indicate symbolic behavior and artistic creativity; their makers were trying to create beautiful objects (Wilford 2002*b*). This chapter's "Appreciating Diversity" describes even older (100,000 B.P.) evidence for behavioral modernity at Blombos Cave.

Earlier excavations in Congo's Katanda region had uncovered barbed bone harpoon points dating back 90,000 to 80,000 years (Yellen, Brooks, and Cornelissen 1995). Anthropologists Brooks and John Yellen contend that these ancient people "not only possessed considerable technological capabilities at this time, but also incorporated symbolic or stylistic content into their projectile forms" (quoted in Wilford 2002*b*).

In 2007 anthropologists reported the discovery of even earlier evidence (dating back to 164,000 B.P.) for behavioral modernity in a cave site at Pinnacle Point, South Africa. The cave yielded small stone bladelets, which could be attached to wood to make spears, as well as red ochre, a pigment often used for body paint. Also significant is the ancient diet revealed by remains from this seaside site. For the first time, we see early representatives of *H. sapiens* subsisting on a variety of shellfish and other marine resources. According to paleoanthropologist Curtis Marean

(2007), who led the discovery team, once early humans knew how to make a living from the sea, they could use coastlines as productive home ranges and move long distances (see also Guyot and Hughes 2007, McBrearty and Stringer 2007).

Cultural advances would have facilitated the spread of AMHs out of Africa. Such advances had reached the Middle East by 43,000 years ago, where, in Turkey and Lebanon, Steven Kuhn, Mary Stiner, and David Reese (2001) found evidence that coastal people made and wore beads and shell ornaments (see also Mayell 2004*b*). Some of the shells were rare varieties, white or brightly colored. These authors suggest that population increase could have caused changes in the living conditions of these AMHs—putting pressure on their resources and forcing experimentation with new strategies for survival (Kuhn, Stiner, and Reese 2001).

Even a modest increase in the population growth rate could double or triple the numbers and populations of small AMH bands. People would be living nearer to one another with more opportunities to interact. Body ornaments could have been part of a system of communication, signaling group identity and social status. Such communication through ornamentation implies "the existence of certain [modern] cognitive capacities" (Stiner and Kuhn, quoted in Wilford 2002*b*; Kuhn, Stiner, and Reese 2001).

Clive Gamble attributes the rise of modern human behavior more to increasing social competition

Body ornamentation, a sign of behavioral modernity. On the left, a man from Irian Jaya, Indonesia (island of New Guinea). On the right, a man photographed at Finsbury Park, England. What are the social functions of such ornamentation?

appreciating DIVERSITY

Ancient Paint Factory Found in South African Cave

Cultural variation is based on diversity in behavior patterns and beliefs. Recent discoveries in Africa suggest that modern behavior and symbolic thought (as well as anatomically modern bodies) are much older than anthropologists imagined just a generation ago. Described here is the recent discovery of early evidence for behavioral modernity—a 100,000-year-old paint factory—in Blombos Cave, a rich and important site in South Africa.

Digging deeper in a South African cave that had already yielded surprises from the Middle Stone Age, archaeologists have uncovered a 100,000-year-old workshop holding the tools and ingredients with which early modern humans apparently mixed some of the first known paint.

These cave artisans had stones for pounding and grinding colorful dirt . . . to a powder, known as ocher. This was blended with the binding fat of mammal-bone marrow and a dash of charcoal. Traces of ocher were left on the tools, and samples of the reddish compound were collected in large abalone shells, where the paint was liquefied, stirred and scooped out with a bone spatula.

Archaeologists said that . . . they were seeing the earliest example yet of how emergent *Homo sapiens* processed ocher . . . its red color apparently rich in symbolic significance. The early humans may have applied the concoction to their skin for protection or simply decoration. . . . Perhaps it was their way of making social and artistic statements on their bodies or their artifacts. . . .

The ocher workshop showed that early humans, whose anatomy was modern, had also begun thinking like us. . . .

Previously, no workshop older than 60,000 years had come to light, and the earliest cave and rock art began appearing about 40,000 years ago. The exuberant flowering among the Cro-Magnon artists in the caves of Europe would come even later; the parade of animals on the walls of Lascaux in France, for example, was executed 17,000 years ago. . . .

The discovery was made at Blombos Cave, 200 miles east of Cape Town, on a high cliff facing the Indian Ocean at the tip of South Africa. Christopher S. Henshilwood, of the University of Bergen in Norway and the University of Witwatersrand in Johannesburg, led the team of researchers from Australia, France, Norway and South Africa. . . .

Alison S. Brooks, an archaeologist at George Washington University who studies the Middle Stone Age in Africa but was not involved in this research, said, "This is another spectacular discovery from Blombos."

Archaeologists and other scholars have come to expect the unexpected from Blombos Cave. In the past decade, Dr. Henshilwood's teams have shaken conventional wisdom by finding persuasive evidence that people living in the cave were taking important strides toward modern behavior.

The researchers reported in 2001 finding tools there made from animal bones and finely worked stone weapon points. They gathered hundreds of pieces of ocher stone, including two inscribed with crisscrossed triangles and horizontal lines. This was occurring 75,000 years ago. . . .

Dr. Brooks noted . . . that large quantities of ocher had been found elsewhere in Africa even before the 100,000-year-old workshop.

Recent research has also documented ocher's early use in Africa as an adhesive to haft small points onto weapon shafts.

"But the Blombos discovery, not only of elaborate ocher processing but also of its mixture with marrow fat to produce a paint . . . argues strongly for its symbolic function," Dr. Brooks said. . . .

The assumed symbolic role of red ocher, Dr. Henshilwood said, comes from the large amounts

An engraved stone fragment decorated with red ocher from Blombos Cave, South Africa. The fragment, which is 77,000 years old, suggests early human creativity and symbolic thought.

of the predominantly red material found at a number of African sites as old as 160,000 years.

It is supposed that the color red relates to blood's being associated with life and death or menstruation and fertility.

Based on the absence of scattered animal and seafood bones, hearths and other evidence of typical living quarters, the archaeologists said that the ocher artisans did not occupy the cave for long periods.

They came only to work, collecting their hammer stones and grindstones nearby and the chunks of ocher from perhaps as far away as 12 miles.

Inside the cave, the artisans chipped and crushed the soft ocher stones. They may have heated the mammal bones before crushing them, to enhance the extraction of the marrow fat. Then the [ingredients] were gently stirred in the shells from the abalone they may have feasted on the day before.

Over the years, windblown sand enveloped the workshop, preserving its tools in hardened sediments. . . .

SOURCE: John Noble Wilford, "In African Cave, Signs of an Ancient Paint Factory." From *The New York Times*, October 13, 2011. © 2011 The New York Times. All rights reserved. Used by permission and protected by the Copyright Laws of the United States. The printing, copying, redistribution, or retransmission of this Content without express written permission is prohibited. www.nytimes.com

The Venus of Willendorf (left), carved from limestone, was discovered in Austria and is displayed in Vienna's Natural History Museum. It dates to about 25,000 years ago. The roughly contemporaneous Venus of Lespurge (right), carved from tusk ivory, was discovered in the foothills of the French Pyrenees and now resides at the Musée de l'Homme in Paris. Notice the apparent fertility symbolism in both figures.

than to population increase. Competition with neighboring populations, including the Neandertals in Europe, could have produced new subsistence strategies along with new ways of sharing ideas and organizing society. Such innovations would have advantaged AMH bands as they occupied new lands and faced new circumstances, including contact with nonmodern humans (see Barton et al. 2011).

According to archaeologist Randall White, early personal adornment in Africa and the Middle East shows that human creativity capacity existed among AMHs long before they reached Europe (Wilford 2002*b*). Facing new circumstances, including competition, AMHs honed their cultural abilities, which enabled them to maintain a common identity, communicate ideas, and organize their societies into "stable, enduring regional groups" (quoted in Wilford 2002*b*). Symbolic thought and cultural advances, expressed most enduringly in artifacts, ornamentation, and art, gave them the edge over the Neandertals, whom they eventually replaced in Europe.

The origin of behavioral modernity continues to be debated. We see, however, that archaeological work in many world areas suggests strongly that neither anatomical modernity nor behavioral modernity was a European invention. Africa's role in the origin and development of humanity has been prominent for millions of years of hominin evolution.

Upper Paleolithic
Blade-toolmaking traditions of early AMHs.

blade tool
Basic Upper Paleolithic tool, hammered off a prepared core.

ADVANCES IN TECHNOLOGY

In Europe, Upper Paleolithic toolmaking is associated with AMHs. In Africa, earlier AMHs made varied tools. The terms *Lower, Middle*, and *Upper Paleolithic* are applied to stone tools from Europe. The terms *Early, Middle*, and *Late Stone Age* are applied to materials from Africa. The people who lived at the Klasies River Mouth cave sites in South Africa made Middle Stone Age tools. However, some of the early African tool finds at Blombos Cave and in Katanda are reminiscent of the European Upper Paleolithic. AMHs in Europe made tools in a variety of traditions, collectively known as Upper Paleolithic because of the tools' location in the upper, or more recent, layers of sedimentary deposits. Some cave deposits have Middle Paleolithic Mousterian tools (made by Neandertals) at lower levels and increasing numbers of Upper Paleolithic tools at higher levels.

The **Upper Paleolithic** traditions all emphasized **blade tools.** Blades were hammered off a prepared core, as in Mousterian technology, but a blade is longer than a flake—its length is more than twice its width. Blades were chipped off cores 4 to 6 inches (10 to 15 centimeters) high by hitting a punch made of bone or antler with a hammerstone (Figure 10.2). Blades were then modified to produce a variety of special-purpose implements. Some were composite tools that were made by joining reworked blades to other materials.

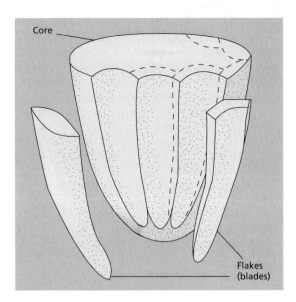

Core

Flakes
(blades)

FIGURE 10.2 Upper Paleolithic
Blade-Toolmaking.
Blades are flakes that are detached from a specially prepared core.
A punch (usually a piece of bone or antler) and a hammerstone
(not shown here) were used to knock the blade off the core.

The blade-core method was faster than the Mousterian and produced 15 times as much cutting edge from the same amount of material. More efficient tool production might have been especially valued by people whose economy depended on cooperative hunting of mammoths, woolly rhinoceroses, bison, wild horses, bears, wild cattle, wild boars, and—principally—reindeer. It has been estimated that approximately 90 percent of the meat eaten by Western Europeans between 25,000 and 15,000 B.P. came from reindeer.

We see certain trends when we compare Upper Paleolithic tools with the earlier Mousterian tradition. First, the number of distinct tool types increased. This trend reflected functional specialization—the manufacture of special tools for particular jobs. A second trend was increasing standardization in tool manufacture. The form and inventory of tools reflect several factors: the jobs tools are intended to perform, the physical properties of the raw materials from which they are made, and distinctive cultural traditions about how to make tools. Furthermore, accidental or random factors also influenced tool forms and the proportions of particular tool types (Isaac 1972). However, Mousterian and Upper Paleolithic tools were more standardized than those of *H. erectus* were.

Other trends include growth in *Homo*'s total population and geographic range and increasing local cultural diversity as people specialized in particular economic activities. Illustrating increasing economic diversity are the varied special-purpose tools made by Upper Paleolithic people. Scrapers were used to hollow out wood and bone, scrape animal hides, and remove bark from trees. Burins, the first chisels, were used to make slots in bone and wood

and to engrave designs on bone. Awls, which were drills with sharp points, were used to make holes in wood, bone, shell, and skin.

Upper Paleolithic bone tools have survived: knives, pins, needles with eyes, and fishhooks. The needles suggest clothing sewn with thread, probably from the sinews of animals. Fishhooks and harpoons confirm an increased emphasis on fishing. (As described by Marean et al. [2007], South Africa's Pinnacle Point Cave provides the earliest evidence, at 164,000 B.P., for a diet based on marine resources, along with small stone blade tools and red ochre used as body paint.)

Different tool types may represent culturally distinct populations that made their tools differently because of different ancestral traditions. Archaeological sites also may represent different activities carried out at different times of the year by a single population. Some sites, for example, are obviously butchering stations, where prehistoric people hunted, made their kills, and carved them up. Others are residential sites, where a wider range of activities was carried out.

With increasing technological differentiation, specialization, and efficiency, humans have become increasingly adaptable. Through heavy reliance on cultural means of adaptation, *Homo* has become (in numbers and range) the most successful primate by far. The hominin range expanded significantly in Upper Paleolithic times (See "Focus on Globalization" on p. 210).

GLACIAL RETREAT

Consider now one regional example, Western Europe, of the consequences of glacial retreat. The Würm glacial ended in Europe between 17,000 and 12,000 years ago, with the melting of the ice sheet in northern Europe (Scotland, Scandinavia, northern Germany, and Russia). As the ice retreated, the tundra and steppe vegetation grazed by reindeer and other large herbivores gradually moved north. Some people moved north, too, following their prey.

Shrubs, forests, and more solitary animals appeared in southwestern Europe. With most of the big-game animals gone, Western Europeans were forced to use a greater variety of foods. To replace specialized economies based on big game, more generalized adaptations developed during the 5,000 years of glacial retreat.

As water flowed from melting glacial ice, sea levels all over the world started rising. Today, off most coasts, there is a shallow-water zone called the *continental shelf,* over which the sea gradually deepens until the abrupt fall to deep water, which is known as the *continental slope.* During the ice ages, so much water was frozen in glaciers that most continental shelves were exposed. Dry land extended right up to the slope's edge. The waters right offshore were deep, cold, and dark. Few species of marine life could thrive in this environment.

How did people adapt to the postglacial environment? As seas rose, conditions more encouraging to

focus on GLOBALIZATION

Giant Steps Toward Globalization

Among academic disciplines, anthropology is uniquely qualified to study the succession of necessary giant steps along the road to globalization. Those prerequisites to globalization may be summarized as follows: (1) settlement of the six continents by anatomically modern humans; (2) the Neolithic revolution, which fueled the growth and expansion of human populations; (3) the rise of cities, states, civilizations, and empires; (4) the European Age of Discovery, which established the Columbian exchange and gave rise to (5) the world capitalist economy, the Industrial Revolution, and the modern world system.

For a global system to form, humans needed to settle all the habitable continents, and the hemispheres needed to be linked. The latter didn't happen until 1492, when Columbus reached the Americas. But global forces—most notably an early form of global climate change known as the Ice Age—did influence the human migrations that led to the settlement of the six continents. The Ice Age, with its ebb and flow of continental glaciers, had a strong impact on Paleolithic humans, including their livelihoods, their settlement patterns, and their opportunities to spread out. During the major glacial phases, with so much water frozen in ice, land bridges over areas that now are under water aided human colonization of vast new areas, especially Australia and North America.

Scientists can follow human migrations of the past by constructing global phylogenetic trees (as well as through fossil and archaeological evidence). Branches of such trees, aka human genetic lineages or haplogroups, show how the peoples of today's world are related to one another. One key global genetic tree is based on mtDNA—mitochondrial DNA, which is transmitted only through the female line. (A son cannot transmit his mother's mtDNA; only daughters can.) Another tree, based on the Y chromosome tree, is based on transmission from fathers to sons. Only sons receive their father's Y chromosome and get to pass it on. (Girls get their dad's X chromosome.) The global phylogenetic tree based on mtDNA and the one based on the Y chromosome have known branches whose global distribution can be plotted to show relationships and human migratory paths. Certain branches, for example, are known to be associated with the spread of modern humans out of Africa between 70,000 and 50,000 B.P. Other (smaller) branches show that the Americas were settled not by a single ancestral population but by multiple haplogroups. In other words, there were waves of migration into North, and eventually South, America.

This chapter examines the human settlement of most of the globe, as anatomically modern humans spread from Africa into Australia, Europe, Asia, the Americas, and the Pacific. Chapter 11 focuses on a major economic transformation—the emergence of food production (i.e., farming and animal domestication)—sometimes called the Neolithic Revolution. Neolithic economies spread rapidly because they were more productive and reliable than Paleolithic economies based on hunting, gathering, and collecting. The eventual rise of ancient cities and states was fueled by the population growth and economic complexity associated with food production. For thousands of years after the first cities and states appeared (see Chapter 12), empires rose and fell. None of them, however, was an empire on which "the sun never set." What was necessary before such an empire (of which the British empire is the best-known example) could form?

marine life developed in the shallower, warmer offshore waters. The quantity and variety of edible species increased tremendously in waters over the shelf. Furthermore, because rivers now flowed more gently into the oceans, fish such as salmon could ascend rivers to spawn. Flocks of birds that nested in seaside marshes migrated across Europe during the winter. Even inland Europeans could take advantage of new resources, such as migratory birds and springtime fish runs, which filled the rivers of southwestern France.

Although hunting remained important, southwestern European economies became less specialized. A wider range, or broader spectrum, of plant and animal life was being hunted, gathered, collected, caught, and fished. This was the beginning of what anthropologist Kent Flannery (1969) has called the *broad-spectrum revolution*. It was revolutionary because, in the Middle East, it led to food production—human control over the reproduction of plants and animals, a process to be examined in Chapter 11. In a mere 10,000 years—after more than a million years during which hominins had subsisted by foraging for natural resources—food production based on plant cultivation and animal domestication replaced hunting and gathering in most areas.

CAVE ART

It isn't the tools or the skeletons of Upper Paleolithic people but their art that has made them most familiar to us. Most extraordinary are the cave paintings, the earliest of which dates back some 36,000 years. More than a hundred cave painting sites are known, mainly from a limited area of southwestern France and adjacent northeastern Spain. The most famous site is Lascaux, found in 1940 in southwestern France by a dog and his young human companions.

The paintings adorn limestone walls of caves located deep in the earth. Over time, the paintings have been absorbed by the limestone and thus preserved. Prehistoric big-game hunters painted their prey: woolly mammoths, wild cattle and horses, deer, and reindeer. The largest animal image is 18 feet (5.5 meters) long.

Most interpretations associate cave painting with magic and ritual surrounding the hunt. For example, because animals sometimes are depicted with spears in their bodies, the paintings might have been attempts to ensure success in hunting. Artists might have believed that by capturing the animal's image in paint and predicting the kill, they could influence the hunt's outcome.

Another interpretation sees cave painting as a magical human attempt to control animal reproduction. Something analogous was done by Native Australian (Australian aboriginal) hunters and gatherers, who held annual *ceremonies of increase* to honor and to promote, magically, the fertility of the

Vivid Upper Paleolithic cave paintings from Lascaux, Dordogne, France. How might you explain what you see depicted here?

plants and animals that shared their homeland. Australians believed that ceremonies were necessary to perpetuate the species on which humans depended. Similarly, cave paintings might have been part of annual ceremonies of increase. Some of the animals in the cave murals are pregnant, and some are copulating. Did Upper Paleolithic people believe they could influence the sexual behavior or reproduction of their prey by drawing them? Or did they perhaps think that animals would return each year to the place where their souls had been captured pictorially?

Paintings often occur in clusters. In some caves, as many as three paintings have been drawn over the original, yet next to these superimposed paintings stand blank walls never used for painting. It seems reasonable to speculate that an event in the outside world sometimes reinforced a painter's choice of a given spot. Perhaps there was an especially successful hunt soon after the painting had been done. Perhaps members of a social subdivision significant in Upper Paleolithic society customarily used a given area of wall for their drawings.

Cave paintings also might have been a kind of pictorial history. Perhaps Upper Paleolithic people, through their drawings, were reenacting the hunt after it took place, as hunters of the Kalahari Desert in southern Africa still do today. Designs and markings on animal bones may indicate that Upper Paleolithic people had developed a calendar based on the phases of the moon (Marshack 1972). If this is so, it seems possible that Upper Paleolithic hunters,

who were certainly as intelligent as we are, would have been interested in recording important events in their lives.

It is worth noting that the *late* Upper Paleolithic, when many of the most spectacular multicolored cave paintings were done and Paleolithic artistic techniques were perfected, coincides with the period of glacial retreat. An intensification of cave painting for any of the reasons connected with hunting magic could have been caused by concern about decreases in herds as the open lands of southwestern Europe were being replaced by forests.

THE SETTLING OF AUSTRALIA

As continental glaciers ebbed and flowed, modern humans took advantage of global climate change to expand their range. During the major glacial phases, with so much water frozen in ice, land bridges formed, aiding human colonization of new areas. People spread from Africa into Europe and Asia, eventually reaching Australia and, much later, the Americas and the Pacific islands.

When and how was Australia settled? At times of major glacial advance, such as 50,000 years ago, dry land connected Australia, New Guinea, and Tasmania. *Sahul* is the name for the larger continent thus formed (O'Connell and Allen 2004). At its largest, Sahul was separated from Asia only by narrow straits (Figure 10.3). Humans somehow made the crossing, perhaps in primitive watercraft, from Asia into

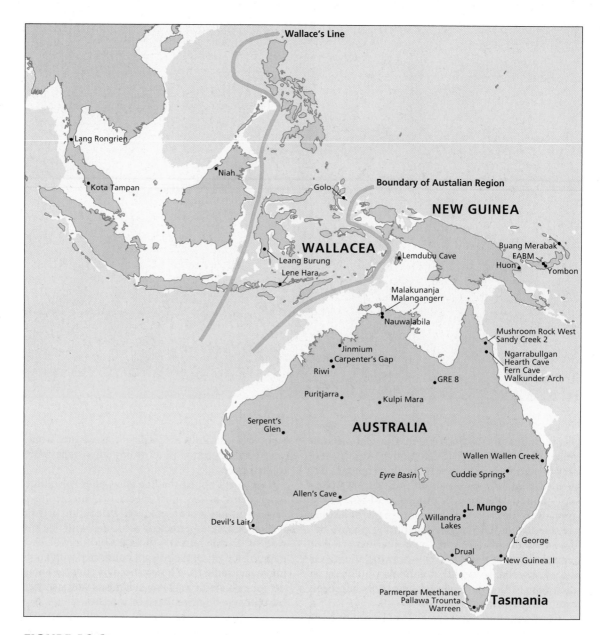

FIGURE 10.3

At times of major glacial advance, such as 50,000 years ago, dry land connected Australia, New Guinea, and Tasmania. Sahul is the name for the larger continent thus formed. At its largest, Sahul was separated from Asia only by narrow straits. Shaded on this map is the continent formed by a 200-meter fall in sea level. Wallacea is a transitional zoogeographic zone between Asia and Australia. The map also locates major archaeological sites, including Lake Mungo.

SOURCE: Reprinted from *Journal of Archaeological Science,* Vol. 31, No. 6, O'Connell, J. F., and J. Allen, "Dating the Colonization of Sahul (Pleistocene Australia–New Guinea): A Review of Recent Research," pp. 835–853, copyright 2004, with permission from Elsevier. http://www.sciencedirect.com/science/journal03054403

Sahul, perhaps around 50,000 B.P. Genetic markers, fossils, and archaeological sites help us understand that settlement.

Georgi Hudjashov and his colleagues (2007) analyzed genetic samples from Native Australians and New Guineans/Melanesians. They looked at both mitochondrial DNA (mtDNA) (n = 172 samples) and Y chromosomes (n = 522). They compared those samples with known branches of global phylo-genetic trees. The global mtDNA tree includes branches known as M and N (among others). The Y chromosome tree includes branches known as C and F (among others). All the Australian/New Guinean samples fit into one of those four branches (either M or N for mtDNA and either C or F for the Y chromosome). Those four branches are known to be associated with the spread of modern humans out of Africa between 70,000 and 50,000 B.P.

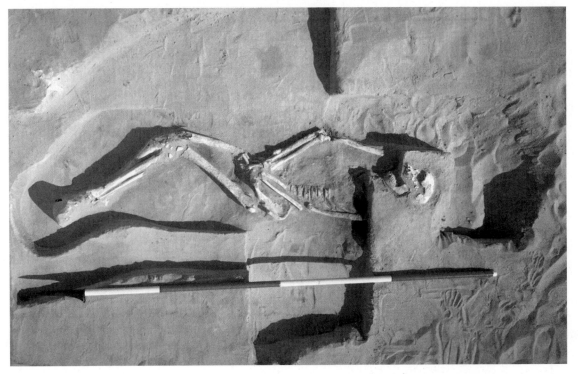

The earliest Australian skeletons, including this one, come from Lake Mungo in New South Wales. The world's oldest human mtDNA (dating back 46,000 years) has been extracted from this fossil. When was Australia first settled?

Not surprisingly (given their geographical proximity), Native Australians are closely related to New Guineans and Melanesians. This close genetic relationship suggested that there was only one initial colonization of Sahul. Genetic dating (ca. 50,000 B.P.) agrees more or less with archaeological evidence for early Australian settlement by 46,000 B.P. After that, prehistoric Australia and New Guinea appear to have been cut off genetically from the rest of the world. Between them, however, there was some gene flow until the land bridge that once connected Australia and New Guinea was submerged around 8,000 B.P. Long-time isolation explains the marked genetic contrasts between Australia/New Guinea, on the one hand, and Eurasia on the other.

In terms of the fossil record, Australia has given us a few of the oldest (ca. 46,000 B.P.) modern human skeletons known outside Africa. The earliest Australian skeletons come from Lake Mungo in New South Wales (Figure 10.3). One of these finds (Mungo III) is of the world's oldest ritual ochre burial. The body was intentionally buried and decorated with ochre, a natural pigment (Bowler et al. 2003). The world's oldest human mtDNA was extracted from this fossil. The same stratum at Mungo contains evidence for the first recorded cremation of a human being (Mungo I). Radiometric dating places humans, including these specimens, at Lake Mungo by 46,000 B.P. O'Connell and Allen (2004) reviewed data from more than thirty Australian archaeological sites older than 20,000 B.P. They concluded that Australia was occupied by 46,000 B.P.— but not much earlier. Dating based on genetic markers, on the other hand, has not ruled out earlier colonization. Northern and western Australia, closer to the rest of Sahul, may have been settled by 50,000 years ago.

SETTLING THE AMERICAS

Another effect of continental glaciation was to expose—during several periods of glacial advance—*Beringia,* the Bering land bridge that once connected North America and Siberia. Submerged today under the Bering Sea, Beringia once was a vast area of dry land, several hundred miles wide. The original settlers of the Americas came from northeast Asia. Living in Beringia thousands of years ago, these ancestors of Native Americans didn't realize they were embarking on the colonization of a new continent. They were merely biggame hunters who, over the generations, moved gradually eastward as they spread their camps and followed their prey—woolly mammoths and other tundra-adapted herbivores. Other ancient foragers entered North America along the shore by boat, fishing, and hunting sea animals.

This was truly a "new world" to its earliest colonists, as it would be to the European voyagers who rediscovered it thousands of years later. Its natural resources, particularly its big game, never before had been exploited by humans. Early bands followed the game south. Although ice sheets covered most of what is now Canada, colonization gradually penetrated the heartland of what is now the United States.

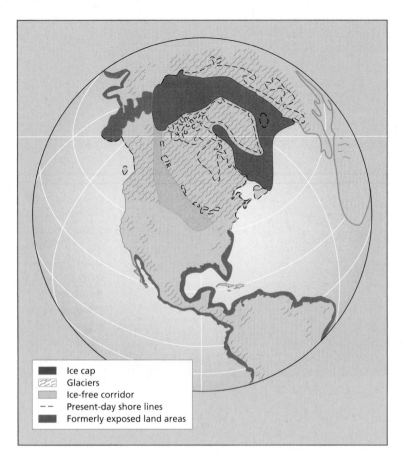

FIGURE 10.4 The Ancestors of Native Americans Came to North America as Migrants from Asia.

They followed big-game herds across Beringia, an immense stretch of land exposed during the ice ages. Was their settlement of the Americas intentional? When did it probably happen? Other migrants reached North America along the shore by boat, fishing and hunting sea animals.

Legend:
- Ice cap
- Glaciers
- Ice-free corridor
- – – Present-day shore lines
- Formerly exposed land areas

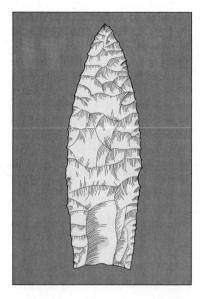

FIGURE 10.5 A Clovis Spear Point.

Such points were attached to spears used by Paleoindians of the North American plains between 13,250 and 12,800 B.P. Are there sites with comparable ages or older in South America?

Clovis

Early American tool tradition; projectile point attached to hunting spear.

haplogroup

A lineage marked by one or more specific genetic mutations.

Successive generations of hunters followed game through unglaciated corridors, breaks in the continental ice sheets (see Figure 10.4). Other colonists spread by boat down the Pacific coast.

On North America's grasslands, early American Indians, *Paleoindians,* hunted horses, camels, bison, elephants, mammoths, and giant sloths. The **Clovis** tradition—a sophisticated stone technology based on a point that was fastened to the end of a hunting spear (Figure 10.5)—flourished, widely but very briefly, in the Central Plains, on their western margins, and in what is now the eastern United States (Green 2006; Largent 2007*a*, 2007*b*). Non-Clovis sites dating to the Clovis period also exist, in both North and South America.

Using C^{14} (radiocarbon) dates, where available, for all known Clovis sites, Michael Waters and Thomas Stafford (2007) conclude that the Clovis tradition lasted no more than 450 years (13,250–12,800 B.P.) and perhaps only 200 years (13,125–12,925 B.P.). During this short time span, Clovis technology originated and spread throughout North America. Unknown is whether this spread involved the actual movement of big-game hunters, or the very rapid

diffusion of a superior technology from group to group (Largent 2007*b*). Waters and Stafford (2007) also calculate that it would have taken from 600 to 1,000 years for the first Americans and their descendants to spread by land from the southern part of the Canadian ice-free corridor to Tierra del Fuego at the southern tip of South America—a distance of more than 8,680 miles (14,000 km). At least four sites in southern South America have C^{14} dates about the same as the Clovis C^{14} dates.

Waters and Stafford conclude there must have been people in the Americas before Clovis. Indeed, an emerging archaeological record supports a pre-Clovis occupation of the New World. One pre-Clovis find is a bone projectile point found embedded in a mastodon rib at the Manis site in Washington state, dated to 13,800 B.P. (Waters et al. 2011). The oldest pre-Clovis site is in South America, at the northern Patagonia settlement of Monte Verde, Chile, dating to 14,800 B.P. In Oregon's Paisley Caves, scientists uncovered 14,300-year-old human feces (Largent 2007*a*, Pappas 2011). Non-Clovis tools and butchered mammoth remains dating to 13,500 B.P. and 12,500 B.P. have been found at sites in Wisconsin.

Thus, the Clovis people were not the first or only early settlers of the Americas. Evidence for the early occupation of Monte Verde in southern South America (along with other lines of evidence) suggests that the first migration(s) of people into the Americas may date back 18,000 years. Analysis of DNA—bolstered, some anthropologists believe, by anatomical evidence—suggests that the Americas were settled by more than one **haplogroup**—a lineage marked by one or more specific genetic mutations. The various early colonists (as many as four or five

This mural of early Americans crossing over Beringia is from the National Museum of Anthropology in Mexico City. Beringia was a vast stretch of land exposed during the ice ages. The settlement of North America was not as intentional as this mural suggests.

haplogroups, according to some anthropologists) came at different times, perhaps by different routes, and had different physiques and genetic markers, which continue to be discovered and debated (see Bonnichsen and Schneider 2000).

THE PEOPLING OF THE PACIFIC

Who settled the vast Pacific? Today, when archaeologists dig in Australia, Papua New Guinea, and the neighboring islands of the southwest Pacific (consult the map in Figure 10.6 throughout this discussion), they find traces of humankind more than 30,000 years old. Humans reached northern Australia around 50,000 years ago. People even reached the islands north of Australia, as far as the Solomon Islands, more than 30,000 years ago (Terrell 1998).

And there they stayed. Based on current evidence, people waited thousands of years before they risked sailing farther eastward on the open sea. Until 3000 B.P., the Solomon Islands formed the eastern edge of the inhabited Pacific. The deep-sea crossings and colonization that began around 3000 B.P. were linked to the rapid spread of the earliest pottery found in Oceania, an ornately decorated ware with geometric designs called Lapita.

The first Lapita potsherds were excavated in 1952. The name comes from the discovery site on the Melanesian island of New Caledonia. (Locate New Caledonia on the map [Figure 10.6] on page 216.) Many scholars see this ornate ware as the product of an ethnically distinct people, and think the Lapita "cultural complex" was carried into the Pacific by a migration of racially distinct newcomers from Asia.

No one knows why people with Lapita pottery left home and risked sailing in deeper waters. Was it for reasons of wanderlust, a pioneering spirit, or improvements in canoe building and navigation? Some experts think the domestication of certain plants and animals thought to be of Asian origin—such as dogs, pigs, and chickens—somehow fueled Lapita's expansion (Terrell 1998).

Lapita pottery fragments from the Solomon Islands, dated to 3000 B.P.

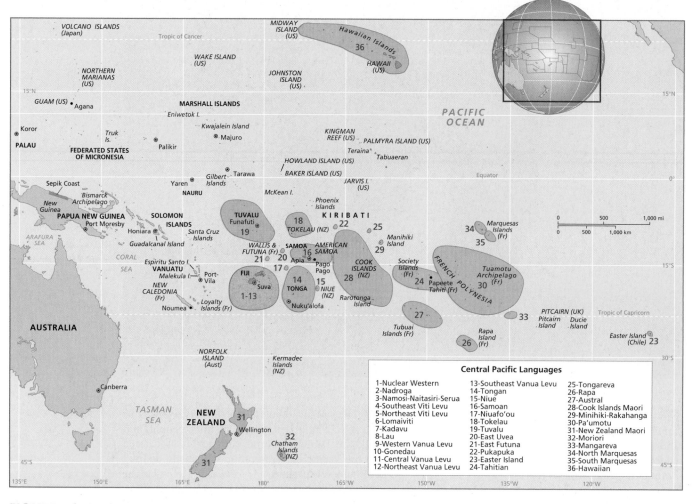

FIGURE 10.6 Oceania.

Polynesian islands are shaded khaki. Other Central Pacific languages outside of Polynesia are spoken in the area shaded orange, which includes Fiji.

Archaeologist John Terrell has excavated a site dated to 3000 B.P. on the Sepik (midnorthern) coast of Papua New Guinea. At that time, according to Terrell (1998), newly stabilized coastal lagoons were producing an abundance of (mainly wild) foods, fueling human population growth. The resource base of the early Lapita pottery makers included diverse foods, some wild and some domesticated (e.g., yams, taro, pigs, chickens).

Archaeologist David Burley uncovered early Lapita shards (potsherds) at Fanga'uta lagoon on the island of Tongatapu in the Polynesian kingdom of Tonga. Early outrigger canoes reached that lagoon after traveling hundreds, and perhaps more than a thousand, miles from the west. Radiocarbon dating of charcoal among the shards showed that seafarers reached Tonga between 2,950 and 2,850 years ago. *This is the earliest known settlement in Polynesia.* Burley thinks that Tongatapu "probably served as the initial staging point for population expansion" to other islands of Tonga, then to Samoa, and then on to the rest of Polynesia (quoted in Wilford 2002*a*).

Improvements in their outrigger canoes allowed Lapita navigators to sail across large stretches of open sea, thus propelling the Polynesian diaspora. The larger canoes could have carried dozens of people, plus pigs and other cargo. Polynesian seafarers eventually reached Tahiti to the east, and Hawaii—located more than 2,500 miles northeast of Tonga and Samoa. Later voyages carried the Polynesian diaspora south to New Zealand, and farther east to Easter Island. Covering one-fourth of the Pacific, Polynesia became the last large area of the world to be settled by humans.

The Lapita pottery found at Tongatapu offered clues about where the seafarers originated. Analyzing bits of the shards, William Dickinson, a University of Arizona geologist, found sandy minerals from outside Tonga. Some of the pots had been brought there from elsewhere. It turned out that the artifacts were made of minerals found only on the Santa Cruz Islands in Melanesia, some 1,200 miles to the west of Tonga, and just east of the Solomon Islands (Burley and Dickinson 2001).

This print from 1811 shows a traditional (New Zealand) Maori war canoe. Earlier, the Lapita people had reached and colonized vast areas of the Pacific, including New Zealand, in their outrigger canoes.

The shards from Tongatapu provided the first physical evidence linking the voyages of the Lapita people between the western and eastern parts of the Pacific. This evidence may mean that Tonga was first settled by people who came directly from central Melanesia (Wilford 2002*a*).

Anthropologists from all four subfields—archaeologists and physical, cultural, and linguistic anthropologists—have considered questions about Polynesian origins. Who made Lapita pottery, along with the distinctive stone tools, beads, rings, and shell ornaments often found with it? Did the Lapita complex originate with indigenous dark-skinned Melanesians, assumed to descend from the first settlers of the Pacific? Or was it introduced by new, lighter-skinned arrivals from southeast Asia? Did lighter- and darker-skinned groups intermarry in Melanesia, forming a hybrid population that created the Lapita complex and eventually colonized Polynesia?

In the 18th century, the explorer Captain James Cook was struck by how similar were the appearance and customs of light-skinned Polynesians living on islands thousands of miles apart, such as Tonga, Hawaii, New Zealand, and Easter Island. Cook thought that the Polynesians originally had come from Malaysia. French navigators stressed the physical and cultural differences between the Polynesians and the darker-skinned Melanesians who lived near New Guinea, and who resembled the indigenous peoples of Papua New Guinea.

Until recently, anthropologists supposed that the ancestors of the Polynesians originated in mainland China and/or Taiwan, which they left between 3,600 and 6,000 years ago. They were seen as spreading rapidly through the Pacific, largely bypassing Melanesia. This would explain why the Polynesians are not dark-skinned and why they speak Austronesian languages, rooted in Taiwan, rather than Papuan languages, spoken in parts of Melanesia. This view now seems discredited by the fact that nothing resembling Lapita pottery has ever been found in Taiwan or southern China. Lapita features first show up in Melanesia, on islands of the Bismarck Archipelago. Recent genetic studies also suggest that ancestral Polynesians stopped off in Melanesia. Interbreeding between early Polynesians and Melanesians has left clear genetic markers in today's Polynesians, The debate now focuses on where the interbreeding took place and how extensive it was.

DNA evidence has convinced Mark Stoneking, a molecular anthropologist, that the ancestors of the Polynesians were indeed Austronesians. (The Austronesian, or Malayo-Polynesian, language family covers a large area of the world. Austronesian languages are the main languages of Polynesia [e.g., Hawaiian], Indonesia, and Malaysia, and even of Madagascar, located just

On the left, a Polynesian woman from Tahiti, Society Islands, French Polynesia. On the right, a Melanesian woman from Madang, Papua New Guinea. What differences and similarities do you notice between these two women?

off the African coast.) Stoneking thinks that the ancestral Polynesians left southeast Asia and sailed to, then expanded along, the coast of New Guinea. They intermingled with Melanesians there and then started voyaging eastward into the Pacific. Interacting with other human groups, ancestral Polynesians exchanged genes and cultural traits (Gibbons 2001; Wilford 2002a).

Excavating in Melanesia's Bismarck Archipelago, archaeologist Patrick Kirch found evidence that newcomers from the islands of southeast Asia had reached Melanesia by 3500 B.P. They built their houses on stilts, as in houses still found in southeast Asia. They sailed in outrigger canoes and brought agricultural plants along with them. There was mixing between the newcomers and the Melanesians. *Out of their contact and interaction emerged the Lapita pottery style* (see Kirch 2000).

Why don't Polynesians resemble their presumed Melanesian cousins? Can we explain the physical differences between Polynesians and Melanesians? Might the Polynesian population have originated in what geneticists call a founder event? In such an event, just a few people, whose physical traits do not randomly sample the larger population from which they came, happen to give rise to a very large diaspora. A very small number of people, say, a few canoeloads, reaching Tonga's Fanga'uta lagoon, may have given rise to the entire, geographically dispersed Polynesian population. The physical traits of such a small founding group could not fully represent the population from which they came. Whatever traits the founders happened to have, such as light skin color, would be transmitted to their descendants. This may explain why the Polynesians look so different from Melanesians, even though they have DNA in common.

By 2000 B.P., according to Patrick Kirch (2000), the people of Tonga had developed a significant new technology: the double-hull sailing canoe. Even though they could not spot other islands on the distant horizon, as their ancestors had been able to do in the southwestern Pacific, the notion that the ocean was full of islands endured. Once they could more securely travel long distances—with the new canoe—they set forth. These weren't all accidental voyages and discoveries, as once was thought. These ancient sailors tacked against the prevailing east-to-west winds, knowing that, if necessary, they could ride a following wind back home.

Long ago, the anthropologist Alexander Lesser disputed what he saw as the "myth of the primitive isolate" (quoted in Terrell 1998)—the idea that ancient peoples lived in closed societies, each one out of contact with others. It is doubtful that the human world has ever been one of distinct societies, sealed cultures, or isolated ethnic groups. Even on the small islands and atolls of the vast Pacific Ocean lived societies that contradicted the "primitive isolate." The adventurous and interconnected peoples of the Pacific and their prehistoric past reveal that human diversity is as much a product of contact as of isolation (Terrell 1998).

acing the COURSE

summary

1. The ancestors of AMHs (anatomically modern humans) were archaic *H. sapiens* groups, most probably those in Africa. Early AMH fossil finds include Skhūl (100,000 B.P.), Qafzeh (92,000 B.P.), Herto (160,000–154,000 B.P.), Omo Kibish (195,000 B.P.), and various South African sites. The Neandertals (130,000–28,000 B.P.) and AMHs were contemporaries, rather than ancestor and descendant. AMHs made Upper Paleolithic blade tools in Europe and Middle and Late Stone Age flake tools in Africa.

2. As glacial ice melted, foraging patterns were generalized, adding fish, fowl, and plant foods to the diminishing big-game supply. The beginning of a broad-spectrum economy in western Europe coincided with an intensification of Upper Paleolithic cave art. On limestone cave walls, prehistoric hunters painted images of animals important in their lives. Explanations of cave paintings link them to hunting magic, ceremonies of increase, and initiation rites.

3. During the major glacial phases, land bridges formed, aiding human colonization of new areas, including Australia and the Americas. Around 50,000 years ago, dry land connected Australia, New Guinea, and Tasmania, forming the large continent of Sahul, separated from Asia only by narrow straits, which humans somehow crossed. The close genetic relationship between Native Australians, New Guineans, and Melanesians suggests a single initial colonization of Sahul from Asia. Genetic dating (ca. 50,000 B.P.) agrees more or less with archaeological evidence for early Australian settlement by 46,000 B.P. Australia has yielded a few of the oldest (ca. 46,000 B.P.) modern human skeletons known outside Africa, including the Lake Mungo finds.

4. Humans probably entered the Americas no more than 18,000 years ago. Pursuing big game or moving by boat along the North Pacific Coast, they gradually moved into North America. Adapting to different environments, Native Americans developed a variety of cultures. Some continued to rely on big game. Others became broad-spectrum foragers.

5. Papua New Guinea and the neighboring islands of the southwest Pacific have been settled for at least 30,000 years. Only around 3,000 B.P. did people start sailing farther eastward, carrying the earliest Oceanian pottery, called Lapita. Seafarers reached Tonga between 2,950 and 2,850 years ago—the earliest known settlement in Polynesia. Tonga appears to have served as the initial point of expansion, via outrigger canoe, to Samoa and eventually to Tahiti, Hawaii, New Zealand, and Easter Island. The ancestral Polynesians probably left southeast Asia, sailed to, and then expanded along the coast of New Guinea. They intermingled with Melanesians there, then started voyaging eastward. The light skin color of Polynesians, which contrasts with the darker skin color of Melanesians, may have originated as an instance of the founder effect.

behavioral modernity 205
blade tool 208
Clovis 214
Cro Magnon 202

haplogroup 214
Herto 201
Upper Paleolithic 208

key terms

MULTIPLE CHOICE

1. Fossil and archaeological evidence has been accumulating to support the African origin of anatomically modern humans. Sometimes this evidence results from reanalyzing fossils years after their discovery, as in the case of
   a. the Herto remains found in South Africa's Blombos Cave, which have an estimated date of 100,000 B.P.
   b. the Omo remains from southwestern Ethiopia, which now appear to be the earliest AMH fossils yet found, with an estimated date of 195,000 B.P.
   c. Neandertal remains found in 1967 in the Neader Valley, Kenya, now believed to be twice as old as originally estimated.
   d. the Skhūl remains found in South Africa's Pinnacle Point Cave, dating back to 200,000 B.P.
   e. *H. erectus* fossils found in southern Ethiopia, which were originally thought to date to 150,000 B.P. and are now believed to be twice as old.

2. All of the following are characteristic of AMH skulls *except*
   a. narrow nasal bones.
   b. a long skull with broad midface.
   c. a more filled-out forehead region, which rises more vertically above the brows.

   d. a marked chin.
   e. a pronounced occipital bun.

3. What does the Eve theory suggest?
   a. Everyone alive today has the mtDNA from a woman (dubbed "Eve") who lived in Australia around 40,000 years ago.
   b. There are serious limits to the use of genetic evidence in studies of human evolution.
   c. "Eve's" descendants left Africa no more than 135,000 years ago, and eventually displaced the Neandertals in Europe, and went on to colonize the rest of the world.
   d. There is more than one "Eden," with AMHs originating simultaneously in Africa, Australia, and Europe.
   e. Fossils of a woman named "Eve" show that AMHs left Africa no earlier than 50,000 years ago, and eventually colonized Europe.

4. Scientists disagree most about
   a. when, where, and how early anatomically modern humans achieved behavioral modernity.
   b. when and where our hominin ancestors became habitual bipeds.
   c. when and where hominins began making crude stone tools.

test yourself

d. when anatomically modern humans evolved from ancestors who remained in Africa.

e. when hominins spread from Africa to Asia and eventually Europe.

5. Evidence of behavioral modernity dating back to 164,000 B.P. has been found in a cave site at Pinnacle Point, South Africa. Among the finds at this site was evidence of an ancient diet containing a variety of shellfish and other marine sources. Why might this be significant?

   a. It suggests early humans' capacity to make a living from the sea, and to expand along coastlines.

   b. It suggests humans' capacity to make fire used to soften the shells of crustaceans.

   c. Such foods point to a diet rich in essential fatty acids.

   d. It suggests early humans' difficulty digesting red meats.

   e. It confirms early humans' capacity to share food.

6. All of the following are trends that mark the changeover from the Mousterian to the Upper Paleolithic *except*

   a. an increase in the number of distinct tool types, reflecting functional specialization.

   b. increasing standardization in tool manufacture.

   c. growth in *Homo*'s total population and geographic range.

   d. rudimentary cultivation techniques to grow medicinal herbs.

   e. increasing local cultural diversity as people specialized in particular economic activities.

7. The broad-spectrum revolution was a significant event in human evolution because

   a. it led to the extinction of the Neandertals, who had survived by eating big-game animals.

   b. it marked the sudden advent of behavioral modernity.

   c. it brought about a new tool tradition based on flaked tools.

   d. it provided new environmental circumstances that made important sociocultural adaptations, like the development of plant cultivation, more likely.

   e. it made possible AMHs' colonization of Africa.

8. The geographic expansion of the hominin range

   a. reached its territorial maximum by 50,000 B.P.

   b. reflects the evolutionary success of increasing reliance on tools, language, and culture.

   c. is limited to Europe and Africa prior to the anatomically modern human's stage of human evolution.

   d. usually involved large migrations over long distances, triggered by natural disasters like flood and drought.

   e. was completed when Neandertal foragers entered the New World.

9. The spread of AMHs to Australia by 46,000 B.P. and into the Americas perhaps by 18,000 B.P. illustrate

   a. AMHs' capacity to cross, directly from southern Africa, large and deep bodies of water with rudimentary sailing rafts.

   b. the problem of overpopulation and disease that pushed AMHs to unpopulated regions.

   c. the role of mutations that predisposed some groups of AMHs to take greater risks and explore the unknown.

   d. the impact that the discovery of the wheel had on human mobility.

   e. the importance of understanding the effects of major glacial phases on the reduction of water levels and the narrowing of straits and the exposure of land bridges connecting otherwise separate land masses.

10. All of the following are true about the peopling of the Pacific *except*

    a. humans may have reached as far as the Solomon Islands more than 30,000 years ago.

    b. once humans reached the Pacific, they did not settle there but moved on to the western coast of South America.

    c. the earliest known settlement in Polynesia occurred sometime between 2,950 and 2,850 years ago.

    d. navigation skills played an important role in the peopling of the Pacific.

    e. Tonga appears to have served as an initial point of expansion, via outrigger canoe, to Samoa and eventually to Tahiti, Hawaii, New Zealand, and Easter Island.

FILL IN THE BLANK

1. Hominins burying their dead with ceremonies, adorning their bodies with paints and jewelry, and making figurine images of fertile females are all evidence of _____, fully human behavior based on symbolic thought and cultural activity.

2. The _____ traditions, associated with AMHs in Europe, all emphasized _____ tools.

3. _____ are the hominins associated with cave paintings, among the earliest evidence of human art.

4. At times of major glacial advance, such as 50,000 years ago, dry land connected Australia, New Guinea, and Tasmania, thus forming the _____ continent.

5. The _____ tradition—a sophisticated stone technology based on a point that was fastened to the end of a hunting spear—flourished in the Central Plains, on their western margins, and in what is now the eastern United States, approximately 13,000 B.P.

CRITICAL THINKING

1. In 1997, ancient DNA was extracted from one of the Neandertal bones originally found in Germany in 1856. This was the first time that DNA of a premodern human had been recovered. What does the analysis of this DNA suggest about Neandertals' relation to AMHs? What other evidence have scientists presented regarding Neandertals' place in the modern human's evolutionary line?

2. What does behavioral modernity mean? What are the competing theories that attempt to explain the advent of behavioral modernity in AMHs? Is behavioral modernity a quality of individual humans or humans as part of a social group? (Perhaps the answer is not one or the other but an interaction between the two, which some anthropologists might argue are inseparable.)

3. What cultural advances facilitated the spread of AMHs out of Africa?

4. What cultural changes accompanied glacial retreat in Europe during the late Upper Paleolithic?

5. It isn't the tools or the skeletons of Upper Paleolithic people but their art that has made them most familiar to us. What are some of the interpretations of cave art that researchers have proposed?

Multiple Choice: 1. (B); 2. (E); 3. (C); 4. (A); 5. (A); 6. (D); 7. (D); 8. (B); 9. (E); 10. (B); **Fill in the Blank:** 1. behavioral modernity; 2. Upper Paleolithic, blade; 3. Anatomically modern humans; 4. Sahul; 5. Clovis

Fagan, B. M.
    2010   *People of the Earth: A Brief Introduction to World Prehistory*, 13th ed. Upper Saddle River, NJ: Prentice Hall. Prehistoric peoples and civilizations.
    2011   *World Prehistory: A Brief Introduction*, 8th ed. New York: Longman. From the Paleolithic to the Neolithic around the world.
Gamble, C.
    1999   *The Palaeolithic Societies of Europe*. New York: Cambridge University Press. Survey mainly of the Middle and Upper Paleolithic in Europe.

Klein, R. G., with B. Edgar
    2002   *The Dawn of Human Culture*. New York: Wiley. Becoming modern, physically and culturally.
Larsen, C. S.
    2011   *Our Origins: Discovering Physical Anthropology*. New York: W. W. Norton. Includes good coverage of recent human evolution.
Wood, B.
    2011   *Human Evolution*. New York: Sterling Books. Very thorough survey of fossil and archaeological reconstruction of human evolution.

suggested additional readings

Go to our Online Learning Center website at **www.mhhe.com/kottak** for Internet exercises directly related to the content of this chapter.

internet exercises

CHAPTER 11

The First Farmers

When and where did the Neolithic originate, and what were its main features?

What similarities and differences marked the Neolithic economies of the Old World and the New World?

What costs and benefits are associated with food production?

◀ A farmer holds rice stalks on Mindanao island, the Philippines. Rice was domesticated in China more than 8,000 years ago.

understanding OURSELVES

What could be more American than McDonald's, hamburgers, hot dogs, or apple pie? More American, in other words, than a now global fast-food chain, a sandwich and sausage named for German cities, or a fruit first grown in the Middle East baked in a pastry crust from wheat, domesticated there as well. What we think of as truly American usually has foreign roots. Consider just McDonald's Big Mac as a world system in miniature. It consists of two all-beef patties (from cattle, an Old World domesticate), special sauce (similar to mayonnaise, invented in France), lettuce (Egypt), cheese (from cow's milk—Old World), pickles (India), onions (Iran and West Pakistan), and it comes on a sesame-seed (India) bun (wheat—Middle East). The breakfast Egg McMuffin is only slightly less cosmopolitan. Eggs are from chickens, domesticated in southeast Asia. Cheese comes from cow's milk (cows were domesticated in India, the Middle East, and Africa's eastern Sahara). Canadian bacon is from pork (western Asia), and the muffin is made of wheat (Middle East). If you crave "real American," that is, New World origin, food, have some turkey or beans on a taco or tortilla (from maize or corn) and chocolate for dessert.

The domestication of plants and animals for food occurred, independently, in both the Old World and the Americas around 11,000 years ago. Animals and crops thrived together in the Middle East, Africa, Europe, and Asia. Not so in the Americas, where wild oxen, horses, pigs, and camels went extinct long before crops were ever cultivated. Key differences in early food production between the hemispheres help us to understand their subsequent histories. A mutually supportive relationship developed between farming and herding in the Old World, where crops sustained sheep, goats, and eventually cattle, pigs, horses, and donkeys.

What, again deceptively, could be more American than the habit of using your own wheels to get you to your favorite restaurant? Wheels? Only in Old World prehistory were animals harnessed to pull wheeled vehicles. Ancient Mexicans did also invent the wheel, but only for toys. Their homeland lacked the appropriate animals to pull plows, oxcarts, chariots, and carriages. How could a dog, turkey, or duck match a horse, donkey, or ox as a beast of burden? The absence of large-animal domestication in ancient Mexico is a key factor in world history, helping us understand the divergent development of societies on different sides of the oceans. Wheels fueled the growth of transport, trade, and travel in the Old World. Thousands of years after the origin of food production, advantages in transport would fuel an "age of discovery" and enable the European conquest of the Americas. Again, a key feature of contemporary American life turns out to have foreign roots.

In Chapter 10, we considered some of the economic implications of the end of the Ice Age in Europe. With glacial retreat, foragers pursued a more generalized economy, focusing less on large animals. This was the beginning of what Kent Flannery (1969) has called the **broad-spectrum revolution.** This refers to the period beginning around 15,000 B.P. in the Middle East and 12,000 B.P. in Europe, during which a wider range, or broader spectrum, of plant and animal life was hunted, gathered, collected, caught, and fished. It was revolutionary because in the Middle East it led to food production—human control over the reproduction of plants and animals.

THE MESOLITHIC

The broad-spectrum revolution in Europe includes the late Upper Paleolithic and the **Mesolithic,** which followed it. Again, because of the long history of European archaeology, our knowledge of the Mesolithic (particularly in southwestern Europe and the British Isles) is extensive. The Mesolithic had a characteristic tool type—the *microlith* (Greek for "small stone"). Of interest to us is what an abundant inventory of small and delicately shaped stone tools can tell us about the total economy and way of life of the people who made them.

By 12,000 B.P., subarctic animals no longer lived in southwestern Europe. By 10,000 B.P. the glaciers had retreated to such an extent that the range of hunting, gathering, and fishing populations in Europe extended to the formerly glaciated British Isles and Scandinavia. The reindeer herds had gradually retreated to the far north, with some human groups following (and ultimately domesticating) them. Europe around 10,000 B.P. was forest rather than treeless steppe and tundra—as it had been during the Ice Age. Europeans were exploiting a wider variety of resources and gearing their lives to the seasonal appearance of particular plants and animals.

People still hunted, but their prey were solitary forest animals, such as the roe deer, the wild ox, and the wild pig, rather than herd species. This led to new hunting techniques: solitary stalking and trapping. The coasts and lakes of Europe and the Middle East were fished intensively. Some important Mesolithic sites are Scandinavian shell mounds—the garbage dumps of prehistoric oyster collectors. Microliths were used as fishhooks and in harpoons. Dugout canoes facilitated fishing and travel. The process of preserving meat and fish by smoking and salting grew increasingly important. (Meat preservation had been less of a problem in a subarctic environment since winter snow and ice, often on the ground nine months of the year, offered convenient refrigeration.) The bow and arrow became essential for hunting waterfowl in swamps and marshes. Dogs were domesticated as retrievers by Mesolithic people (Champion and Gamble 1984). Woodworking was important in the forested environment of northern and western Europe. Tools used by Mesolithic carpenters appear in the archaeological record: new kinds of axes, chisels, and gouges.

Big-game hunting and, thereafter, Mesolithic hunting and fishing were important in Europe, but

Evidence of the Mesolithic occupation of Italy. Displayed here are a beaver jaw, ochre, stone tools, and assorted bones, just as they were found (in situ) at a Mesolithic cave burial in Arene Candide grotto, near Savona, Italian Riviera.

other foraging strategies were used by prehistoric people in Africa and Asia. Among contemporary foragers in the tropics, gathering is the dietary mainstay (Lee 1968/1974). Although herds of big-game animals were more abundant in the tropics in prehistory than they are today, gathering probably always has been at least as important as hunting for tropical foragers (Draper 1975; Mercader 2009).

Generalized, broad-spectrum economies lasted about 5,000 years longer in Europe than in the Middle East. Whereas Middle Easterners had begun to cultivate plants and breed animals by 10,000 B.P., food production reached western Europe only around 5000 B.P. (3000 B.C.E.) and northern Europe 500 years later.

After 15,000 B.P., throughout the inhabited world, as the big-game supply dwindled, foragers had to pursue new resources. Human attention shifted from large-bodied, slow reproducers (such as mammoths) to species such as fish, mollusks, and rabbits that reproduce quickly and prolifically (Hayden 1981). This happened with the European Mesolithic. It also happened at the Japanese site of Nittano (Akazawa 1980), located on an inlet near Tokyo. Nittano was occupied several times between 6000 and 5000 B.P. by members of the *Jomon* culture, for which 30,000 sites are known in Japan. These broad-spectrum foragers hunted deer, pigs, bears, and antelope. They also ate fish, shellfish, and plants. Jomon sites have yielded the remains of 300 species of shellfish and 180 species of edible plants (including berries, nuts, and tubers) (Akazawa and Aikens 1986).

broad-spectrum revolution
Foraging of varied plant and animal foods at end of Ice Age; prelude to Neolithic.

Mesolithic
Stone toolmaking, emphasizing microliths within broad-spectrum economies.

THE NEOLITHIC

The archaeologist V. Gordon Childe (1951) used the term *Neolithic Revolution* to describe the origin and impact of food production—plant cultivation and animal domestication. **Neolithic** was coined to refer to new techniques of grinding and polishing stone tools. However, the primary significance of the Neolithic was the new total economy rather than just its characteristic artifacts, which also included pottery (see Simmons 2007).

The transition from Mesolithic to Neolithic occurs when groups become dependent on domesticated foods (for more than 50 percent of their diet). Usually this happens after a very long period of experimenting with and using domesticates as supplements to broad-spectrum foraging. The archaeological signature of Neolithic cultures (which are called *Formative* in the Americas) includes dependence on cultivation, sedentary (settled) life, and the use of ceramic vessels.

Neolithic economies based on food production were associated with substantial changes in human lifestyles. By 12,000 B.P., the shift toward the Neo-lithic was under way in the Middle East (Turkey, Iraq, Iran, Syria, Jordan, and Israel). People started intervening in the reproductive cycles of plants and animals. No longer simply harvesting nature's bounty, they grew their own food and modified the biological characteristics of the plants and animals in their diet. By 10,000 B.P., domesticated plants and animals were part of the broad spectrum of resources used by Middle Easterners. By 7500 B.P., most Middle Easterners had moved away from the broad-spectrum foraging pattern toward more specialized, Neolithic, economies based on fewer species, which were domesticates.

They had become committed farmers and herders. Kent Flannery (1969) has proposed a series of eras during which the Middle Eastern transition to farming and herding took place. The era of seminomadic hunting and gathering (12,000–10,000 B.P.) encompasses the last stages of broad-spectrum foraging. This was the period just before the first domesticated plants (wheat and barley) and animals (goats and sheep) were added to the diet. Next came the era of early dry farming (of wheat and barley) and caprine domestication (10,000–7500 B.P.). *Dry farming* refers to farming without irrigation; such farming depended on rainfall. *Caprine* (from *capra*, Latin for "goat") refers to goats and sheep, which were domesticated during this era.

During the era of increased specialization in food production (7500–5500 B.P.), new crops were added to the diet, along with more productive varieties of wheat and barley. Cattle and pigs were domesticated. By 5500 B.P., agriculture extended to the alluvial plain of the Tigris and Euphrates rivers (Figure 11.1), where early Mesopotamians lived in walled towns, some of which grew into cities. (Recap 11.1 highlights these stages or eras in the transition to food production in the ancient Middle East.) After two million years of stone-tool-making, *H. sapiens* was living in the Bronze Age, when metallurgy and the wheel were invented.

THE FIRST FARMERS AND HERDERS IN THE MIDDLE EAST

Middle Eastern food production arose in the context of four environmental zones. From highest to lowest, they are high plateau (5,000 feet, or 1,500 meters), Hilly Flanks, piedmont steppe (treeless plain),

Neolithic was coined to refer to techniques of grinding and polishing stone tools, like these axes and hammers from Austria, Hungary, and the Czech Republic. Was the new toolmaking style the most significant thing about the Neolithic?

RECAP 11.1	The Transition to Food Production in the Middle East

ERA	DATES (B.P.)
Origin of state (Sumer)	5500 B.P.
Increased specialization in food production	7500–5500 B.P.
Early dry farming and caprine domestication	10,000–7500 B.P.
Seminomadic hunting and gathering (e.g., Natufians)	12,000–10,000 B.P.

and alluvial desert. The last zone is the area watered by the Tigris and Euphrates rivers (100–500 feet, or 30–150 meters). The **Hilly Flanks** is a subtropical woodland zone that flanks those rivers to the north (see Figure 11.1).

It once was thought that food production began in oases in the alluvial desert. (*Alluvial* describes rich, fertile soil deposited by rivers and streams.) This arid region was where Mesopotamian civilization arose later. Today, we know that although the world's first civilization (Mesopotamian) did indeed develop in this zone, irrigation, a late (7000 B.P.) invention, was necessary to farm the alluvial desert. Plant cultivation and animal domestication started not in the dry river zone but in areas with reliable rainfall.

The archaeologist Robert J. Braidwood (1975) proposed instead that food production started in the Hilly Flanks, or subtropical woodland zone, where wild wheat and barley would have been most abundant (see Figure 11.1). In 1948, a team headed by Braidwood started excavations at Jarmo, an early farming village inhabited between 9000 and 8500 B.P., located in the Hilly Flanks. We now know that there were farming villages earlier than Jarmo in zones adjacent to the Hilly Flanks. One example is Ali Kosh (see Figure 11.1), a village in the foothills (piedmont steppe) of the Zagros mountains. By 9000 B.P., the people of Ali Kosh were herding goats, intensively collecting various wild plants, and harvesting wheat during the late winter and early spring (Hole, Flannery, and Neely 1969).

Climate change played a role in the origin of food production (Smith 1995). The end of the Ice Age brought greater regional and local variation in climatic conditions. Lewis Binford (1968) proposed that in certain areas of the Middle East (such as the Hilly Flanks), local environments were so rich in resources that foragers could adopt **sedentism**— sedentary (settled) life in villages. Binford's prime example is the widespread Natufian culture (12,500–10,500 B.P.), based on broad-spectrum foraging. The **Natufians,** who collected wild cereals and hunted gazelles, had year-round villages. They were able to stay in the same place (early villages) because they could harvest nearby wild cereals for six months.

Donald Henry (1989, 1995) documented a climate change toward warmer, more humid conditions just before the Natufian period. This expanded the altitude range of wild wheat and barley, thus enlarging the available foraging area and allowing a longer harvest season. Wheat and barley ripened in the spring at low altitudes, in the summer at middle altitudes, and in the fall at high altitudes. As locations for their villages, the Natufians chose central places where they could harvest wild cereals in all three zones.

Around 11,000 B.P., this favorable foraging pattern was threatened by a second climate change— to drier conditions. As many wild cereal habitats dried up, the optimal zone for foraging shrank.

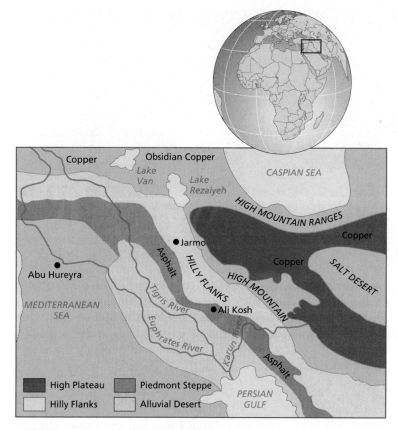

FIGURE 11.1 The Vertical Economy of the Ancient Middle East. Geographically close but contrasting environments were linked by seasonal movements and trade among broad-spectrum foragers. As people traveled and traded, they removed plants from the zones where they grew wild in the Hilly Flanks into adjacent zones where humans became agents of selection. Food production emerged on the margins of the Hilly Flanks, at places such as Ali Kosh, rather than within that area, at places such as Jarmo.

Natufian villages were now restricted to areas with permanent water. As population continued to grow, some Natufians attempted to maintain productivity by transferring wild cereals to well-watered areas, where they started cultivating those cereals.

In the view of many scholars, the people most likely to adopt a new subsistence strategy, such as food production, would be those having the most trouble in following their traditional subsistence strategy (Binford 1968; Flannery 1973; Wenke and Olszewski 2007). Thus, those ancient Middle Easterners living outside the area where wild foods were most abundant would be the most likely to experiment and to adopt new subsistence strategies. This would have been especially true as the climate dried up. Recent archaeological finds support this hypothesis that food production began in *marginal areas,* such as the piedmont steppe, rather than in the optimal zones, such as the Hilly Flanks, where traditional foods were most abundant.

Even today, wild wheat grows so densely in the Hilly Flanks that one person working just an hour with Neolithic tools can easily harvest a kilogram of wheat (Harlan and Zohary 1966). People would have

Hilly Flanks
Woodland zone just north of Tigris and Euphrates rivers.

sedentism
Settled (sedentary) life.

Natufians
Widespread Middle Eastern foraging culture (12,500–10,500 B.P.).

Some 12,000 to 10,000 years ago, ancient Middle Easterners followed the availability of plants and animals, from lower to higher zones. With domestication, this pattern evolved into nomadic herding (pastoralism). Contemporary Middle Eastern herders, like this Bedouin shepherd in Syria, still take their flocks to grazing areas at different elevations.

Mesoamerica
Middle America, including Mexico, Guatemala, and Belize.

had no reason to invent cultivation when wild grain was ample to feed them. Wild wheat ripens rapidly and can be harvested over a three-week period. According to Flannery, over that time period, a family of experienced plant collectors could harvest enough grain—2,200 pounds (1,000 kilograms)—to feed themselves for a year. But after harvesting all that wheat, they'd need a place to put it. They could no longer maintain a nomadic lifestyle, since they'd need to stay close to their wheat.

Sedentary village life thus developed before farming and herding in the Middle East. The Natufians and other Hilly Flanks foragers had no choice but to build villages near the densest stands of wild grains. They needed a place to keep their grain. Furthermore, sheep and goats came to graze on the stubble that remained after humans had harvested the grain. The fact that basic plants and animals were available in the same area also favored village life. Hilly Flanks foragers built houses, dug storage pits for grain, and made ovens to roast it.

Natufian settlements, occupied year round, show permanent architectural features and evidence for the processing and storage of wild grains. One such site is Abu Hureyra, Syria (see Figure 11.1), which was initially occupied by Natufian foragers around 11,000 to 10,500 B.P. Then it was abandoned—to be reoccupied later by food producers, between 9500 and 8000 B.P.

Prior to domestication, the favored Hilly Flanks zone had the densest human population. Eventually, its excess population started to spill over into adjacent areas. Colonists from the Flanks tried to maintain their traditional broad-spectrum foraging in these marginal zones. But with sparser wild foods available, they had to experiment with new

subsistence strategies. Eventually, population pressure on more limited resources forced people in the marginal zones to become the first food producers (Binford 1968; Flannery 1969). *Early cultivation began as an attempt to copy, in a less favorable environment, the dense stands of wheat and barley that grew wild in the Hilly Flanks.*

The Middle East, along with certain other world areas where food production originated, is a region that for thousands of years has had a *vertical economy.* (Other examples include Peru and **Mesoamerica**—Middle America, including Mexico, Guatemala, and Belize.) A vertical economy exploits environmental zones that, although close together in space, contrast with one another in altitude, rainfall, overall climate, and vegetation (see Figure 11.1). Such a close juxtaposition of varied environments allowed broad-spectrum foragers to use different resources in different seasons.

Early seminomadic foragers in the Middle East had followed game from zone to zone. In winter they hunted in the piedmont steppe region, which had winter rains rather than snow and provided winter pasture for game animals 12,000 years ago. (Indeed it still is used for winter grazing by herders today.) When winter ended, the steppe dried up. Game moved up to the Hilly Flanks and high plateau country as the snow melted. Pastureland became available at higher elevations. Foragers gathered as they climbed, harvesting wild grains that ripened later at higher altitudes. Sheep and goats followed the stubble in the wheat and barley fields after people had harvested the grain.

The four Middle Eastern environmental zones shown in Figure 11.1 also were tied together through trade. Certain resources were confined to specific zones. Asphalt, used as an adhesive in the manufacture of sickles, came from the steppe. Copper and turquoise sources were located in the high plateau. Contrasting environments were linked in two ways: by foragers' seasonal migration and by trade.

The movement of people, animals, and products between zones—plus population increase supported by highly productive broad-spectrum foraging—was a precondition for the emergence of food production. As they traveled between zones, people carried seeds into new habitats. Mutations, genetic recombinations, and human selection led to new kinds of wheat and barley. Some of the new varieties were better adapted to the steppe and, eventually, the alluvial desert than the wild forms had been.

Genetic Changes and Domestication

What are the main differences between wild and domesticated plants? The seeds of domesticated cereals, and often the entire plant, are larger. Compared with wild plants, crops produce a higher yield per unit of area. Domesticated plants also lose their natural seed dispersal mechanisms. Cultivated beans, for example, have pods that hold together, rather than shattering as they do in the wild. Domesticated cereals have tougher connective tissue holding the seedpods to the stem.

Grains of wheat, barley, and other cereals occur in bunches at the end of a stalk (Figure 11.2). The grains are attached to the stalk by an *axis* (plural *axes*). In wild cereals, this axis is brittle. Sections of the axis break off one by one, and a seed attached to each section falls to the ground. This is how wild cereals spread their seeds and propagate their species. But a brittle axis is a problem for people. Imagine the annoyance experienced by broad-spectrum foragers as they tried to harvest wild wheat, only to have the grain fall off or be blown away.

In very dry weather, wild wheat and barley ripen—their axes totally disintegrating—in just three days (Flannery 1973). The brittle axis must have been even more irritating to people who planted the seeds and waited for the harvest. But fortunately, certain stalks of wild wheat and barley happened to have tough axes. These were the ones whose seeds people saved to plant the following year.

Another problem with wild cereals is that the edible portion is enclosed in a tough husk. This husk was too tough to remove with a pounding stone. Foragers had to roast the grain to make the husk brittle enough to come off. However, some wild plants happened to have genes for brittle husks. Humans chose the seeds of these plants (which would have germinated prematurely in nature) because they could be more effectively prepared for eating.

People also selected certain features in animals (Smith 1995). Some time after sheep were domesti-

cated, advantageous new phenotypes arose. Wild sheep aren't woolly; wool coats were products of domestication. Although it's hard to imagine, a wool coat offers protection against extreme heat. Skin temperatures of sheep living in very hot areas are much lower than temperatures on the surface of their wool. Woolly sheep, but not their wild ancestors, could survive in hot, dry alluvial lowlands. Wool had an additional advantage: its use for clothing.

Plants got larger with domestication, while animals got smaller, probably because smaller animals are easier to control. We've seen that sheep and goats were the first animals to be domesticated in the Middle East, where the domestication of cattle, pigs, and other animals came later. Domestication was an ongoing process, as people kept refining and changing the traits they considered desirable in plants and animals—as they still do today through bioengineering. Different animals were domesticated at different times and in different regions. The factors that govern animal domestication are discussed further in the section "Explaining the Neolithic" later in this chapter.

Food Production and the State

The shift from foraging to food production was gradual. The knowledge of how to grow crops and breed livestock didn't immediately convert Middle Easterners into full-time farmers and herders. Domesticated plants and animals began as minor parts of a broad-spectrum economy. Foraging for fruits, nuts, grasses, grains, snails, and insects continued.

Over time, Middle Eastern economies grew more specialized, geared more exclusively toward crops and herds. The former marginal zones became centers of the new economy and of population increase and emigration. Some of the increasing population spilled back into the Hilly Flanks, where people eventually had to intensify production by cultivating. Domesticated crops could now provide a bigger harvest than could the grains that grew wild there. Thus, in the Hilly Flanks, too, farming eventually replaced foraging as the economic mainstay.

Farming colonies spread down into drier areas. By 7000 B.P., simple irrigation systems had developed, tapping springs in the foothills. By 6000 B.P., more complex irrigation techniques made agriculture possible in the arid lowlands of southern Mesopotamia. In the alluvial desert plain of the Tigris and Euphrates rivers, a new economy based on irrigation and trade fueled the growth of an entirely new form of society. This was the *state*, a social and political unit featuring a central government, extreme contrasts of wealth, and social classes. The process of state formation is examined in the next chapter.

We now understand why the first farmers lived neither in the alluvial lowlands, where the Mesopotamian state arose around 5500 B.P., nor in the Hilly Flanks, where wild plants and animals abounded.

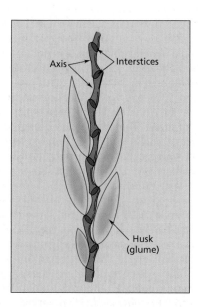

FIGURE 11.2 A Head of Wheat or Barley.

In the wild, the axis comes apart as its parts fall off one by one. The connecting parts (interstices) are tough and don't come apart in domesticated grains. In wild grains, the husks are hard. In domestic plants, they are brittle, which permits easy access to the grain. How did people deal with hard husks before domestication?

Simple irrigation systems were being used in the Middle East by 7000 B.P. By 6000 B.P., complex irrigation techniques made agriculture possible in the arid lowlands of southern Mesopotamia. Simple irrigation systems continue to be used in many world areas, including the rural area shown here near Cairo, Egypt.

Food production began in marginal zones, such as the piedmont steppe, where people experimented at reproducing, artificially, the dense grain stands that grew wild in the Hilly Flanks. As seeds were taken to new environments, new phenotypes were favored by a combination of natural and human selection. The spread of cereal grains outside their natural habitats was part of a system of migration and trade between zones, which had developed in the Middle East during the broad-spectrum period. Food production also owed its origin to the need to intensify production to feed an increasing human population—the legacy of thousands of years of productive foraging (see Bocquet-Appel and Bar Yosef 2008).

OTHER OLD WORLD FOOD PRODUCERS

The path from foraging to food production was one that people followed independently in at least seven world areas. As we'll see later in this chapter, at least three were in the Americas. At least four were in the Old World. In each of these centers, people independently invented domestication, although of different sets of crops and animals.

As we'll see in more detail later in this chapter, food production also spread from the Middle East. This happened through trade; through diffusion of plants, animals, products, and information; and through the actual migration of farmers. Middle Eastern domesticates spread westward to northern Africa, including Egypt's Nile Valley, and eventually into Europe. Trade also extended eastward to India and Pakistan. In Egypt, an agricultural economy based on plants and animals originally domesticated in the Middle East led to a pharaonic civilization.

The African Neolithic

Excavations in southern Egypt have revealed considerable complexity in its Neolithic economy and social system, along with very early pottery and cattle, which may have been domesticated locally. Located in the eastern Sahara and southern Egypt, Nabta Playa is a basin that, during prehistoric summers, filled with water. Over several millennia this temporary lake attracted people who used it for social and ceremonial activities (Wendorf and Schild 2000). Nabta Playa was first occupied around 12,000 B.P., as Africa's summer rains moved northward, providing moisture for grasses, trees, bushes, hares, and gazelle, along with humans. The earliest settlements (11,000–9300 B.P.) at Nabta were small seasonal camps of herders of domesticated cattle. (Note the very early, and perhaps independent, domestication of cattle here.) According to Wendorf and Schild (2000), Nabta Playa provides early evidence for what anthropologists have called the "African cattle complex," in which cattle are used economically for their milk and blood, rather than killed for their meat (except on ceremonial occasions). Nabta was occupied only seasonally, as people came over from the Nile or from better-watered areas to the south. They returned to those areas in the fall.

By 9000 B.P. people were living at Nabta Playa year round. To survive in the desert, they dug large, deep wells and lived in well-organized villages, with small huts arranged in straight lines. Plant remains show they collected sorghum, millet, legumes (peas and beans), tubers, and fruits. These were wild plants, and so the economy was not fully Neolithic. By 8800 B.P. these people were making their own pottery, possibly the earliest pottery in Egypt. By 8100 B.P. sheep and goats had diffused in from the Middle East.

Around 7500 B.P. new settlers occupied Nabta, whose previous inhabitants had been forced away by a major drought. The newcomers brought a more sophisticated social and ceremonial system. They sacrificed young cattle, which they buried in clay-lined chambers covered with rough stone slabs. They lined up large, unshaped stones. They also built Egypt's earliest astronomical measuring device: a "calendar circle" used to mark the summer solstice. Nabta Playa had become a regional ceremonial center: a place where various groups gathered seasonally or occasionally to conduct ceremonies and to socialize. The existence of such centers, as well as their religious, political, and social functions, is familiar to ethnographers who have worked in Africa. Nabta probably began to function as a regional ceremonial center around 8100–7600 B.P., when various groups gathered there for ceremonial and other purposes during the summer wet season.

Gathering on the northwestern shores of the summer lake, those ancient people left debris, including numerous cattle bones. At other African Neolithic sites (Edwards 2004), cattle bones are rarely numerous, which suggests that the cattle were being tapped "on the hoof" for their milk and blood, rather than being slaughtered and eaten. The numerous cattle bones at Nabta Playa, however, suggest that its people killed cattle seasonally for ceremonial purposes. Among modern African herders, cattle, which represent wealth and political power, are rarely killed except on important ceremonial or social occasions.

Nabta's role as a regional ceremonial center is also suggested by an alignment of nine large upright stone slabs near the place where people gathered, along the northwest margin of the seasonal lake. This formation, probably dating between 7500 and 5500 B.P., recalls similar large stone alignments, such as Stonehenge, found in western Europe, that were built during the late Neolithic and early Bronze Age.

Construction of large, complex megalithic structures requires well-organized work parties and a major effort. This suggests that some authority (religious or civil) may have been managing resources and human labor over time. The findings at Nabta Playa represent an elaborate and previously unsuspected ceremonialism, as well as social complexity, during the African Neolithic (see also Sadig 2010).

The Neolithic in Europe and Asia

Around 8000 B.P., communities on Europe's Mediterranean shores, in Greece, Italy, and France, started shifting from foraging to farming, using imported species. By 7000 B.P., there were fully sedentary farming villages in Greece and Italy. By 6000 B.P., there were thousands of farming villages as far east as Russia and as far west as northern France (see Bogaard 2004).

Domestication and Neolithic economies spread rapidly across Eurasia. Archaeological research confirms the early (8000 B.P.) presence of domesticated goats, sheep, cattle, wheat, and barley in Pakistan (Meadow 1991). In that country's Indus River Valley, ancient cities (Harappa and Mohenjo-daro) emerged slightly later than did the first Mesopotamian city-states. Domestication and state formation in the Indus Valley were influenced by developments in, and trade with, the Middle East.

China was also one of the first world areas to develop farming, based on millet and rice. Millet is a tall, coarse cereal grass still grown in northern China. This grain, which today feeds a third of the world's population, is used in contemporary North America mainly as birdseed. By 7500 B.P., two varieties of millet supported early farming communities in northern China, along the Yellow River. Millet cultivation paved the way for widespread village life and eventually for Shang dynasty civilization, based on irrigated agriculture, between 3600 and 3100 B.P. (See Chapter 12.) The northern Chinese also had

Nepalese women harvest in a millet field at sunset. Millet was grown in China's Hwang-He (Yellow River) Valley by 7000 B.P. This grain supported early farming communities in northern China. What was being grown in southern China at the same time?

domesticated dogs, pigs, and possibly cattle, goats, and sheep by 7000 B.P. (Chang 1977).

Discoveries by Chinese archaeologists suggest that rice was domesticated in the Yangtze River corridor of southern China as early as 8400 B.P. (Smith 1995; Jiao 2007). Other early rice comes from the 7,000-year-old site Hemudu, on Lake Dongting in southern China. The people of Hemudu used both wild and domesticated rice, along with domesticated water buffalo, dogs, and pigs. They also hunted wild game (Jolly and White 1995).

China seems to have been the scene of two independent transitions to food production, based on different crops grown in strikingly different climates. Southern Chinese farming was rice aquaculture in

 living anthropology **VIDEOS**

Agriculture and Change, www.mhhe.com/kottak

This clip focuses on early food production and its implications. According to the clip, humans started managing the reproduction of plants and animals around 12,000 years ago. The clip suggests that food production enabled nomadic humans to settle down and live in permanent villages near their fields and water sources. Food production eventually led to towns, cities, and states. Compare the discussion of sedentism in the ancient Middle East in the text with the contention that food production caused sedentary life in the clip. Did food production in the Middle East precede or follow sedentism? According to the clip, what role did women play in the origin of food production?

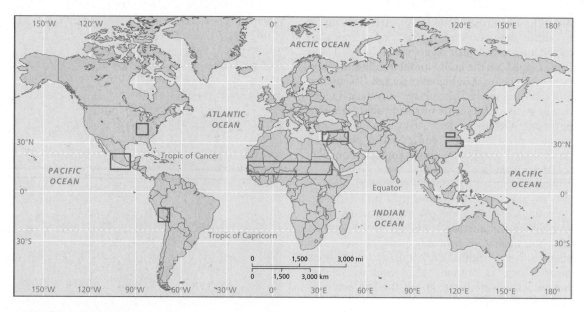

FIGURE 11.3 Seven World Areas Where Food Production Was Independently Invented.
Do any of these areas surprise you?

SOURCE: Bruce D. Smith, *The Emergence of Agriculture* (New York: Scientific American Library, 1995), p. 12. Reprinted by permission of the author. smith.bruce@nmnh.si.edu

rich subtropical wetlands. Southern winters were mild, and summer rains, reliable. Northern China, by contrast, had harsh winters, with unreliable rainfall during the summer growing season. This was an area of grasslands and temperate forests. Still, in both areas by 7500 B.P., food production supported large and stable villages. Based on the archaeological evidence, early Chinese villagers lived in substantial houses, made elaborate ceramic vessels, and had rich burials.

At Nok Nok Tha in central Thailand, pottery made more than 5,000 years ago has imprints of husks and grains of domesticated rice (Solheim 1972/1976). Animal bones show that the people of Nok Nok Tha also had humped zebu cattle similar to those of contemporary India. Rice might have been cultivated at about the same time in the Indus River Valley of Pakistan and adjacent western India.

It appears that food production arose independently at least seven times in different world areas. Figure 11.3 is a map highlighting those seven areas: the Middle East, northern China, southern China, sub-Saharan Africa, central Mexico, the south central Andes, and the eastern United States. A different set of major foods was domesticated, at different times, in each area, as is shown in Recap 11.2. Some grains, such as millet and rice, were domesticated more than once. Millet grows wild in China and Africa, where it became an important food crop, as well as in Mexico, where it did not. Indigenous

RECAP 11.2	Seven World Areas Where Food Production Was Independently Invented	
WORLD AREA	**MAJOR DOMESTICATED PLANTS/ANIMALS**	**EARLIEST DATE (B.P.)**
Middle East	Wheat, barley Sheep, goats, cattle, pigs	10,000
Andean region	Squash, potato, quinoa, beans Camelids (llama, alpaca), guinea pigs	10,000–5000
Southern China (Yangtze River corridor)	Rice Water buffalo, dogs, pigs	8500–6500
Mesoamerica	Maize, beans, squash Dogs, turkeys	8000–4700
Northern China (Yellow River)	Millet Dogs, pigs, chickens	7500
Sub-Saharan Africa	Sorghum, pearl millet, African rice	4000
Eastern United States	Goosefoot, marsh elder, sunflower, squash	4500

SOURCE: Data compiled from Bruce D. Smith, *The Emergence of Agriculture* (New York: Scientific American Library, W. H. Freeman, 1995).

African rice, grown only in West Africa, belongs to the same genus as Asian rice. Pigs and probably cattle were independently domesticated in the Middle East, China, and sub-Saharan Africa. Independent domestication of the dog was virtually a worldwide phenomenon, including the Western Hemisphere. We turn now to archaeological sequences in the Americas.

THE FIRST AMERICAN FARMERS

As hunters benefiting from the abundance of big game, bands of foragers gradually spread through the Americas. As they moved, these early Americans learned to cope with a great diversity of environments. Eventually their descendants would independently invent food production, paving the way for the emergence of states based on agriculture and trade in Mexico and Peru.

The most significant contrast between Old and New World food production involved animal domestication, which was much more important in the Old World than in the New World. The animals that had been hunted during the early American big-game tradition either became extinct before people could domesticate them or were not domesticable. The largest animal ever domesticated in the New World (in Peru, around 4500 B.P.) was the llama. Early Peruvians and Bolivians ate llama meat and used that animal as a beast of burden (Flannery, Marcus, and Reynolds 1989). They bred the llama's relative, the alpaca, for its wool. Peruvians also added animal protein to their diet by raising and eating guinea pigs and ducks.

The turkey was domesticated in Mesoamerica and in the southwestern United States. Lowland South Americans domesticated a type of duck. The dog is the only animal that was domesticated throughout the New World. There were no cattle, sheep, or goats in the areas where food production arose. As a result, neither herding nor the kinds of relationships that developed between herders and farmers in many parts of the Middle East, Europe, Asia, and Africa emerged in the precolonial Americas. The New World crops were different, although staples as nutritious as those of the Old World were domesticated from native wild plants.

Three key caloric staples, major sources of carbohydrates, were domesticated by Native American farmers. **Maize**, or corn, first domesticated in the tropical lowlands of southwestern Mexico, became the caloric staple in Mesoamerica and Central America and eventually reached coastal Peru. The other two staples were root crops: white ("Irish") potatoes, first domesticated in the Andes, and **manioc,** or cassava, a tuber first cultivated in the South American lowlands, where other root crops such as yams and sweet potatoes also were important. Other crops added variety to New World diets and made them nutritious. Beans and squash provided essential proteins, vitamins, and minerals. Maize, beans, and squash were the basis of the Mesoamerican diet. This chapter's "Appreciating Anthropology" discusses how anthropologists recently have confirmed

maize
Corn; first domesticated in tropical southwestern Mexico around 8000 B.P.

manioc
Cassava; tuber domesticated in the South American lowlands.

Early Peruvians and Bolivians ate llama meat, harnessed llamas as beasts of burden, and used llama dung to fertilize their fields. What was the largest animal domesticated in the New World?

The Early Origin of New World Domestication

New dating techniques applied to plant remains found in northern Peru have pushed back the origin of domestication in the New World to about the same time that food production arose in the Old World. Previously anthropologists had believed that Old World (Middle Eastern) farming predated the earliest cultivation in the Americas by three or four millennia. Peruvian squash seeds dating back 10,000 years show there was no such time lag between the first farming in the New World and that in the Old. Other sites and dates discussed in this chapter support this finding.

Seeds of domesticated squash found by scientists on the western slopes of the Andes in northern Peru are almost 10,000 years old, about twice the age of previously discovered cultivated crops in the region, new, more precise dating techniques have revealed.

The findings about Peru and recent research in Mexico, anthropologists say, are evidence that some farming developed in parts of the Americas nearly as early as in the Middle East, which is considered the birthplace of the earliest agriculture.

Digging under house floors and grinding stones and in stone-lined storage bins, the archaeologist Tom D. Dillehay of Vanderbilt University, in Nashville, uncovered the squash seeds at several places in the Ñanchoc Valley, near the Pacific coast about 400 miles north of Lima. The excavations also yielded peanut hulls and cotton fibers—about 8,500 and 6,000 years old, respectively.

The new, more precise dating of the plant remains, some of which were collected two decades ago, is being reported by Dr. Dillehay and colleagues in today's issue of the journal *Science*.

Their research also turned up traces of other domesticated plants, including a grain, manioc and unidentified fruits, and stone hoes, furrowed garden plots and small-scale irrigation canals from approximately the same period of time.

The researchers concluded that these beginnings in plant domestication "served as catalysts for rapid social changes that eventually contributed to the development of intensified agriculture, institutionalized political power and towns in both the Andean highlands and on the coast between 5,000 and 4,000 years ago."

The evidence at Ñanchoc, Dr. Dillehay's team wrote, indicated that "agriculture played a more important and earlier role in the development of Andean civilization than previously understood."

In an accompanying article on early agriculture, Eve Emshwiller, an ethnobotanist at the University of Wisconsin, Madison, was quoted as saying that the reports of early dates for plant domestication in the New World were remarkable because this appeared to have occurred not long after humans colonized the Americas, now thought to be at least 13,000 years ago. . . .

In the Fertile Crescent of the Middle East, an arc from modern-day Israel through Syria and Turkey to Iraq, wheat and barley were domesticated by 10,000 years ago. . . .

Dr. Dillehay has devoted several decades of research to ancient cultures in South America. His most notable previous achievement was the discovery of a campsite of [very early] hunter-gatherers at Monte Verde, in Chile. Most archaeologists recognize this as the earliest well-documented human occupation site uncovered so far in the New World.

By diffusion, manioc or cassava, originally domesticated in lowland South America, has become a caloric staple in the tropics worldwide. This young Thai farmer displays his manioc crop.

that the earliest domesticates, including squash, in the Americas are about as old as the first Old World domesticates.

Food production was independently invented in at least three areas of the Americas: Mesoamerica, the eastern United States, and the south central Andes. (Mesoamerica is discussed in detail below.) Food plants known as goosefoot and marsh elder, along with the sunflower and a species of squash, were domesticated by Native Americans in the eastern United States by 4500 B.P. Those crops supplemented a diet based mainly on hunting and gathering. They never became caloric staples like maize, wheat, rice, millet, manioc, and potatoes. Eventually, maize diffused from Mesoamerica into what is now the United States, reaching both the Southwest and the eastern area just mentioned. Maize provided a more reliable caloric staple for native North American farming. Domestication of several food species was underway in the south

Other explorations in recent years have yielded increasing evidence of settlements and organized political societies that flourished in the coastal valleys of northern Peru possibly as early as 5,000 years ago. Until recently, the record of earlier farming in the region had been sparse.

Initial radiocarbon dating of the plant remains from Ñanchoc was based on wood charcoal buried at the sites, but the results varied widely and were considered unreliable. More recent radiocarbon dating, with a technique called accelerator mass spectrometry, relied on measurements from undisturbed buried charcoal and an analysis of the actual plant remains.

The distribution of building structures, canals and furrowed fields, Dr. Dillehay said, indicated that the Andean culture was moving beyond cultivation limited to individual households toward an organized agricultural society. Botanists studying the squash, peanut, and cotton remains determined that the specific strains did not grow naturally in the Ñanchoc area. The peanut, in particular, was thought to be better suited to cultivation in tropical forests and savannas elsewhere in South America.

On May 29, 2007, in Huancavelica, Peru, farmers harvest native potatoes at the International Potato Centre (CIP) experimental station in the Andean highlands. The CIP conserves genetic samples of most of the potatoes native to Peru, the birthplace of the potato with more than three thousand varieties. New dating techniques applied to plant remains (squash seeds) found in Peru have pushed back the origin of domestication in the New World to about the same time that food production arose in the Old World, around 10,000 years ago.

SOURCE: John Noble Wilford, "Squash Seeds Show Andean Cultivation Is 10,000 Years Old, Twice as Old as Thought." From *The New York Times*, June 29, 2007. © 2007 The New York Times. All rights reserved. Used by permission and protected by the Copyright Laws of the United States. The printing, copying, redistribution, or retransmission of this Content without express written permission is prohibited. www.nytimes.com

central Andes of Peru and Bolivia by 5,000 B.P. They were the potato, quinoa (a cereal grain), beans, llamas, alpacas, and guinea pigs (Smith 1995). This chapter's "Appreciating Anthropology" discusses how anthropologists recently have confirmed the very early domestication of squash, cotton, and peanuts in Peru.

The Tropical Origins of New World Domestication

Based on microscopic evidence from early cultivated plants, New World farming began in the lowlands of South America and then spread to Central America, Mexico, and the Caribbean islands. In Chapter 4 we learned about new techniques that allow archaeologists and botanists to recover and analyze microscopic evidence from pollens, starch grains, and phytoliths (plant crystals) (Bryant 2003, 2007a). This evidence has forced revision of old assumptions, most prominently the idea that New World farming originated in upland areas, such as the highlands of Mexico and Peru. This chapter's "Appreciating Anthropology" reports that domesticated squash seeds from Peru date back 10,000 years. Although found in the highlands (western Andes), those seeds, along with other domesticates from that site, were not domesticated there originally. Domestication must have occurred even earlier, most probably in South America's tropical lowlands.

Dolores Piperno and Karen Stothert (2003) found that phytoliths from cultivated squashes and gourds are substantially larger than those from wild species. They then used phytolith size to confirm that domesticated squash and gourds (*Cucurbita*) were grown in coastal Ecuador between 9,000 and 10,000 years ago.

According to Piperno and Deborah Pearsall (1998), farming in the tropical lowlands of Central and South America began at about the same time as food production arose in the Middle East—around 10,000 years ago. By that time, cultural groups in Panama, Peru, Ecuador, and Colombia were cultivating plants in garden plots near their homes. Between 9000 and 8000 B.P., changes in seed form and phytolith size suggest that farmers were selecting certain characteristics in their cultivated plants. By 7,000 years ago, farmers had expanded their plots into nearby forests, which they cleared using slash-and-burn techniques. By that time also, early farming ideas and techniques were diffusing from tropical lowlands into drier regions at higher elevations (Piperno and Pearsall 1998; Bryant 1999, 2003).

What about maize (corn), a major New World crop, long thought to have been domesticated in the Mexican highlands? Recent molecular and genetic studies indicate that maize domestication actually took place in the lowlands of southwestern Mexico. The wild ancestor of maize is a species of **teosinte** (a wild grain) native to the Rio Balsas watershed of tropical southwestern Mexico (Holst, Moreno, and Piperno 2007). Evidence for the evolution of maize from its wild ancestor has yet to be found in that poorly studied region. Still, we can infer some of the likely steps in maize domestication.

Such a process would have included increases in the number of kernels per cob, cob size, and the

teosinte
Wild ancestor of maize; grows wild in southwestern Mexico.

Two different types of corn (maize) from among the many varieties grown in Oaxaca, Mexico, where archaeologists have studied early highland maize cultivation. Do the earliest Mesoamerican domesticates come from the Mexican highlands?

number of cobs per stalk. These changes would make it increasingly profitable to collect wild teosinte and eventually to plant maize. Undoubtedly, some of the mutations necessary for domesticated maize had occurred in wild teosinte before people started growing it. However, since teosinte was well adapted to its natural niche, the mutations offered no advantage and didn't spread. But once people started harvesting wild maize intensively, they became selective agents, taking back to camp a greater proportion of plants with tough axes and cobs. These were the plants most likely to hold together during harvesting and least likely to disintegrate on the way back home. Eventually, teosinte became dependent on humans for its survival because maize lacks a natural means of dispersal—a brittle axis or cob. If humans chose plants with tough axes inadvertently, their selection of plants with soft husks must have been intentional, as was their selection of larger cobs, more kernels per cob, and more cobs per plant.

A phytolith analysis of sediments from San Andrés, in the Mexican state of Tabasco, confirms the spread of maize cultivation eastward to the tropical Mexican Gulf Coast by 7300 B.P. Data from many sites now confirm that maize spread rapidly from its domestication cradle in tropical southwestern Mexico during the eighth millennium B.P. (8000–7000) (Bryant 2007b; Piperno 2001; Pohl et al. 2007). For example, analysis of starch grains from stone tools in Panama's tropical lowlands confirms that maize was grown there by 7800–7000 B.P. (Dickau, Ranere, and Cooke 2007).

During the last century, for reasons enumerated by Vaughn Bryant (2003), archaeologists tended to seek evidence for early New World farming in the highlands of Mexico and Peru. These upland areas were easy to reach and had caves and rock shelters with preserved plant remains. They also were in the vicinity of the centers of major civilizations that would eventually develop in the Mexican highlands (see Chapter 12). Decades ago, excavations in the Mexican Valleys of Tehuacan and Oaxaca (see the next section) yielded well-preserved seeds and fruits, maize kernels and cobs, fibers, and rinds. Few archaeologists sought the origin of domestication in lowland and jungle regions, which were wrongly assumed to be infertile and where plants did not preserve well (Bryant 2003). Today, the microscopic evidence says otherwise and reveals the key role of tropical lowland regions in early New World farming.

The Mexican Highlands

Long before Mexican highlanders developed a taste for maize, beans, and squash, they hunted as part of a pattern of broad-spectrum foraging. Mammoth remains dated to 11,000 B.P. have been found along with spear points in the basin that surrounds Mexico City. However, small animals were more important than big game, as were the grains, pods, fruits, and leaves of wild plants.

In the Valley of Oaxaca, in Mexico's southern highlands, between 10,000 and 4000 B.P., foragers concentrated on certain wild animals—deer and rabbits—and plants—cactus leaves and fruits, and tree pods, especially mesquite (Flannery 1986). Those early Oaxacans dispersed to hunt and gather in fall and winter. But they came together in late spring and summer, forming larger groups to harvest seasonally available plants. Cactus fruits appeared in the spring. Since summer rains would reduce the fruits to mush and since birds, bats, and rodents competed for them, cactus collection required hard work by large groups of people. The edible pods of the mesquite, available in June, also required intensive gathering.

Eventually, people started planting maize in the alluvial soils of valley floors. This was the zone where foragers traditionally had congregated for the annual spring/summer harvest of cactus fruits and mesquite pods. By 4000 B.P., a type of maize was available that provided more food than the mesquite pods did. Once that happened, people started cutting down mesquite trees and replacing them with corn fields.

By 3500 B.P. in the Valley of Oaxaca, where winter frosts are absent, simple irrigation permitted the establishment of permanent villages based on maize farming. Water close to the surface allowed early farmers to dig wells right in their corn fields. Using pots, they dipped water out of these wells and poured it on their growing plants, a technique known as pot irrigation. Early permanent villages supported by farming appeared in areas of Mesoamerica where there was reliable rainfall, pot irrigation, or access to humid river bottomlands.

The spread of maize farming resulted in further genetic changes, higher yields, higher human populations, and more intensive farming. Pressures to intensify cultivation led to improvements in water-control systems. New varieties of fast-growing maize eventually appeared, expanding the range of areas that could be cultivated. Increasing population and irrigation also helped spread maize farming. The advent of intensive cultivation laid the foundation for the emergence of the state in Mesoamerica—some 3,000 years later than in the Middle East, a process examined in the next chapter.

EXPLAINING THE NEOLITHIC

This section focuses on the factors that influenced the origin and spread of Neolithic economies in various world areas. (Much of this section is based on observations in Chapters 8 through 10 of Jared Diamond's influential book *Guns, Germs, and Steel: The Fates of Human Societies* [2005].)

Several factors had to converge to make domestication happen and to promote its spread. Most plants, and especially animals, aren't easy—or particularly valuable—to domesticate. Thus, of some 148 large animal species that seem potentially domesticable, only 14

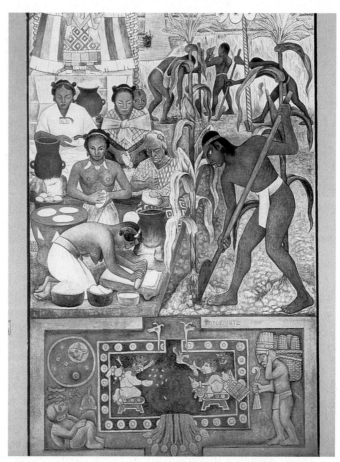

As maize cultivation spread, genetic changes led to higher yields and more productive farming. Pressures to intensify cultivation helped improve water-control systems, such as the canal irrigation shown in this mural by Diego Rivera.

actually have been domesticated. And a mere dozen among 200,000 known plant species account for 80 percent of the world's farm production. Those twelve caloric staples are wheat, corn (maize), rice, barley, sorghum (millet), soybeans, potatoes, cassava (manioc), sweet potatoes, sugarcane, sugar beets, and bananas.

Domestication rested on a combination of conditions and resources that had not come together previously. The development of a full-fledged Neolithic economy required settling down. Sedentism, such as that adopted by ancient Natufian hunter-gatherers, was especially attractive when several species of plants and animals were available locally for foraging and eventual domestication. The Fertile Crescent area of the Middle East had such species, along with a Mediterranean climate favorable to the origin and spread of the Neolithic economy. Among those species were several self-pollinating plants, the easiest wild plants to domesticate, including wheat, which required few genetic changes for domestication. We've seen that the Natufians adopted sedentism prior to farming. They lived off abundant wild grain and the animals attracted to the stubble left after the harvest. Eventually, with climate change, population growth, and the need for people to sustain themselves in the marginal zones, hunter-gatherers started cultivating (see Bocquet-Appel and Bar-Yosef 2008).

Compared with other world areas, the Fertile Crescent region had the largest area with a Mediterranean climate, with the highest species diversity. As we saw previously, this was an area of vertical economy and closely packed microenvironments. Such diverse terrains and habitats concentrated in a limited area offered a multiplicity of plant species, as well as goats, sheep, pigs, and cattle. The first farmers eventually domesticated several crops: two kinds of wheat, barley, lentils, peas, and chickpeas (garbanzo beans). As in Mesoamerica, where corn (supplying carbohydrate) was supplemented by squash and beans (supplying protein), the Neolithic diet of the Middle East combined caloric staples such as wheat and barley with protein-rich pulses such as lentils, peas, and chickpeas.

Anthropologists once thought, erroneously, that domestication would happen almost automatically once people gained sufficient knowledge of plants and animals and their reproductive habits to figure out how to make domestication work. Anthropologists now realize that foragers have an excellent knowledge of plants, animals, and their reproductive characteristics, and that some other trigger is needed to start and sustain the process of domestication. A full-fledged Neolithic economy requires a minimal set of nutritious domesticates. Some world areas, for example, North America (north of Mesoamerica), managed independently to invent domestication, but the inventory of available plants and animals was too meager to sustain a Neolithic economy. The early North American domesticates—squash, sunflower, marsh elder, and goosefoot—had to be supplemented by hunting and gathering. A full Neolithic economy and sedentism did not develop in the east, southeast, and southwest of what is now the United States until maize diffused in from Mesoamerica— more than 3,000 years after the first domestication in the eastern United States.

We've seen how the presence or absence of domesticable animals helps explain the divergent trajectories of the Eastern and Western hemispheres in that the mixed economies that developed in Eurasia and Africa never emerged in Mesoamerica. Of the world's fourteen large (over 100 pounds) successful domesticated animal species, thirteen are from Eurasia, and only one (the llama) is from South America. Ancient Mexicans domesticated dogs and turkeys and created toy wheels, but they lacked sheep, goats, and pigs as well as the oxen or horses needed to make the wheel a viable transport option. Once the big five Eurasian animal domesticates (cow, sheep, goat, pig, horse) were introduced into Africa and the Americas, they spread rapidly.

We've seen that detailed knowledge of plants and their reproduction is not a sufficient condition for domestication to occur. Similarly, the knowledge that animals can be tamed or kept as pets isn't enough to produce animal domestication, because not all tamed animals can be domesticated. Just as some plants (e.g., self-pollinating annuals) are easier to domesticate than others are, so are some animals. Cattle, dogs, and pigs were so easy to domesticate that they were domesticated independently in multiple world areas.

Consider some reasons why most large animal species (134 out of 148 big species) have not been domesticated. Some are finicky eaters (e.g., koalas). Others refuse to breed in captivity (e.g., vicunas). Some animals are just too nasty to domesticate (e.g., grizzly bears), and others have a tendency to panic (e.g., deer and gazelles).

Perhaps the key factor in domestication is animal social structure. The easiest wild animals to domesticate live in hierarchical herds. Accustomed to dominance relations, they allow humans to assume superior positions in the hierarchy. Herd animals are easier to domesticate than solitary ones are. Among the latter, only cats and ferrets have been domesticated, and there's some question about the completeness of domestication of those animals (hence the expression "It's like herding cats"). A final factor in ease of domestication is whether a wild animal typically shares its range with others. Animals with exclusive territories (e.g., rhinoceros, African antelope) are harder to pen up with others than are animals that share their territories with other species.

Geography and the Spread of Food Production

As Jared Diamond (2005, Chapter 10) observes convincingly, the geography of the Old World facilitated the diffusion of plants, animals, technology (e.g., wheels and vehicles), and information (e.g., writing) (see also Ramachandran and Rosenberg 2011). Most crops in Eurasia were domesticated just once and spread rapidly in an east-west direction. The first domesticates spread from the Middle East to Egypt, Northern Africa, Europe, India, and eventually China (which, however, also had its own domesticates, as we have seen). By contrast, there was less diffusion of American domesticates.

Look at Figure 11.4 to see that Eurasia has a much broader east-west spread than does Africa or than does either of the Americas, which are arranged north-south. This is important because climates are more likely to be similar moving across thousands of miles east-west than doing so north-south. In Eurasia, plants and animals could spread more easily east-west than north-south because of common day lengths and similar seasonal variations. More radical climatic contrasts have hindered north-south diffusion. In the Americas, for example, although the distance between the cool Mexican highlands and the South American highlands is just 1,200 miles, those two similar zones are separated by a low, hot, tropical

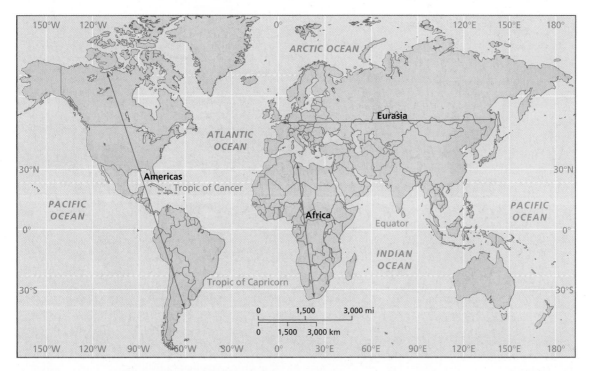

FIGURE 11.4 Major Axes of the Continents.

Note the breadth of the east-west axis in Eurasia, compared with the much narrower east-west spreads in Africa, North America, and South America. Those three continents have north-south as their major axes.

SOURCE: "Figure 10.1: Major Axes of the Continents" from *Guns, Germs, and Steel: The Fates of Human Societies* by Jared Diamond. Published by W. W. Norton & Company, Inc., and Jonathan Cape. Copyright © 1997 by Jared Diamond. Used by permission of W. W. Norton & Company, Inc., The Random House Group Ltd., and the author.

region, which supports very different plant species than the highlands. Such environmental barriers to diffusion kept the Neolithic societies of Mesoamerica and South America more separate and independent in the Americas than they were in Eurasia. It took some 3,000 years for maize to reach what is now the United States, where productive Neolithic economies eventually did develop. They were based on the cultivation of new varieties of maize adapted to a colder climate and different day lengths.

In the Old World, the spread of Middle Eastern crops southward into Africa eventually was halted by climatic contrasts as well. Certain tropical crops did spread west-east in Africa, but they did not reach southern Africa because of climatic barriers. Again and again, the geographic and climatic barriers posed by high mountains and broad deserts have slowed the spread of domesticates. In what is now the United States, for example, the east-west spread of farming from the southeast to the southwest was slowed by the dry climates of Texas and the southern Great Plains.

This section has examined the factors that favored or retarded the origin and spread of Neolithic economies in various world areas. Several factors combined to promote early domestication in the ancient Middle East. The first domesticates spread rapidly across Eurasia, facilitated by climatic simi-larities across a broad territorial expanse. In the Americas, food production spread less rapidly because of north-south contrasts. Another factor that slowed the Neolithic transition in the Americas was the lack of large animals suitable for domestication. Factors that explain the origin and diffusion of food production involve climate, economic adaptation, demography, and the specific attributes of plants and animals.

COSTS AND BENEFITS

Food production brought advantages and disadvantages. Among the advantages were discoveries and inventions. People eventually learned to spin and weave; to make pottery, bricks, and arched masonry; and to smelt and cast metals. They developed trade and commerce by land and sea. By 5500 B.P., Middle Easterners were living in vibrant cities with markets, streets, temples, and palaces. They created sculpture, mural art, writing systems, weights, measures, mathematics, and new forms of political and social organization.

Because it increased economic production and led to new social, scientific, and creative forms, food production often is considered an evolutionary advance. But the new economy also brought hardships. For example, food producers typically work harder

The labor demands of food production far exceed those associated with foraging. Here, in Timbuktu, Mali, a Songhai family pounds grain. Such processing of food is just one step in getting the grain from the fields into people's mouths. What are some of the other steps?

than foragers do—and for a less adequate diet. Because of their extensive leisure time, foragers have been characterized as living in "the original affluent society" (Sahlins 1972). Certain foragers have survived into recent times and have been studied by anthropologists. Among foragers living in the Kalahari Desert of southern Africa, for example, only part of the group needed to hunt and gather, maybe twenty hours a week, to provide an adequate diet for the entire group. Women gathered, and adult men hunted. Their labor supported older people and children. Early retirement from the food quest was possible, and forced child labor was unknown.

With food production, yields are more reliable, but people work much harder. Herds, fields, and irrigation systems need care. Weeding can require hours of arduous bending. No one has to worry about where to keep a giraffe or a gazelle, but pens and corrals are built and maintained for livestock. Trade takes men, and sometimes women, away from home, leaving burdens for those who stay behind. For several reasons, food producers tend to have more children than foragers do. This means greater child care demands, but child labor also tends to be more needed and valued than it is among foragers. Many tasks in farming and herding can be done by children. The division of economic labor grows more complex, so that children and older people have assigned economic roles.

And public health declines. Diets based on crops and dairy products tend to be less varied, less nutritious, and less healthful than foragers' diets, which usually are higher in proteins and lower in fats and carbohydrates. With the shift to food production, the physical well-being of the population often declines. Communicable diseases, protein deficiency, and dental caries increase (Cohen and Armelagos 1984). Greater exposure to pathogens comes with food production.

Compared with a seminomadic foraging band, food producers tend to be sedentary. Their populations are denser, which makes it easier to transmit and maintain diseases. Malaria, sickle-cell anemia, and smallpox all spread along with food production. Population concentrations, especially cities, are breeding grounds for epidemic diseases. People live nearer to other people and animals and their wastes, which also affect public health (Diamond 2005). Compared with farmers, herders, and city dwellers, foragers were relatively disease free, stress free, and well nourished.

Other hardships and stresses accompanied food production and the state. Social inequality and poverty increased. Elaborate systems of social stratification eventually replaced the egalitarianism of the past. Resources were no longer common goods, open to all, as they tend to be among foragers. Property distinctions proliferated. Slavery and other forms of human bondage eventually were invented. Crime, war, and human sacrifice became widespread.

The rate at which human beings degraded their environments also increased with food production. The environmental degradation in today's world,

DO THE COSTS OUTWEIGH THE BENEFITS?	
BENEFITS	**COSTS**
Discoveries and inventions	Harder work
New social, political, scientific, and creative forms (e.g., spinning, weaving, pottery, bricks, metallurgy)	Less nutritious diets
	Child labor and child care demands
Monumental architecture, arched masonry, sculpture	Taxes and military drafts
	Public health declines (e.g., more exposure to pathogens, including communicable and epidemic diseases)
Writing	
Mathematics, weights, and measures	Rise in protein deficiency and dental caries
Trade and markets	Greater stress
	Social inequality and poverty
Urban life	Slavery and other forms of human bondage
Increased economic production	Rise in crime, war, and human sacrifice
More reliable crop yields	Increased environmental degradation (e.g., air and water pollution, deforestation)

including air and water pollution and deforestation, is on a much larger scale, compared with early villages and cities, but modern trends are foreshadowed. After food production, population increase and the need to expand farming led to deforestation in the Middle East. Even today, many farmers think of trees as giant weeds to be cut down to make way for productive fields. Previously, we saw how early Mesoamerican farmers cut down mesquite trees for maize cultivation in the Valley of Oaxaca.

Many farmers and herders burn trees, brush, and pasture. Farmers burn to remove weeds; they also use the ashes for fertilizer. Herders burn to promote the growth of new tender shoots for their livestock. But such practices do have environmental costs, including air pollution. Smelting and other chemical

processes basic to the manufacture of metal tools also have environmental costs. As modern industrial pollution has harmful effluents, early chemical processes had by-products that polluted air, soils, and waters. Salts, chemicals, and microorganisms accumulate in irrigated fields. Pathogens and pollutants that were nonissues during the Paleolithic endanger growing human populations. To be sure, food production had benefits. But its costs are just as evident. Recap 11.3 summarizes the costs and benefits of food production. We see that *progress* is much too optimistic a word to describe food production, the state, and many other aspects of the evolution of society.

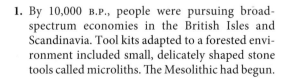

acing the COURSE

1. By 10,000 B.P., people were pursuing broad-spectrum economies in the British Isles and Scandinavia. Tool kits adapted to a forested environment included small, delicately shaped stone tools called microliths. The Mesolithic had begun.

The broad-spectrum revolution, based on a wide variety of dietary resources, began in the Middle East somewhat earlier than in Europe. It culminated in the first food-producing economies in the Middle East around 10,000 B.P.

summary

2. By 10,000 B.P., domesticated plants and animals were part of a broad spectrum of resources used by Middle Easterners. By 7500 B.P., most Middle Easterners were moving away from broad-spectrum foraging toward more specialized food-producing economies. *Neolithic* refers to the period when the first signs of domestication appeared.

3. Braidwood proposed that food production started in the Hilly Flanks zone, where wheat and barley grew wild. Others questioned this: The wild grain supply in that zone already provided an excellent diet for the Natufians and other ancient Middle Easterners. There would have been no incentive to domesticate. Other scholars view the origin of food production in the context of increasing population and climate changes.

4. Ancient Middle Eastern foragers migrated seasonally in pursuit of game. They also collected wild plant foods as the plants ripened at different altitudes. As they moved about, these foragers took grains from the Hilly Flanks zone, where they grew wild, to adjacent areas. Population spilled over from the Hilly Flanks into areas like the piedmont steppe. In such marginal zones, people started cultivating plants. They were trying to duplicate the dense wild grains of the Hilly Flanks.

5. After the harvest, sheep and goats fed off the stubble of these wild plants. Animal domestication occurred as people started selecting certain features and behavior and guiding the reproduction of goats, sheep, cattle, and pigs. Gradually, food production spread into the Hilly Flanks. Later, with irrigation it spread down into Mesopotamia's alluvial desert, where the first cities, states, and civilizations developed by 5500 B.P. Food production then spread west from the Middle East into North Africa and Europe and east to India and Pakistan.

6. There were at least seven independent inventions of food production: in the Middle East, sub-Saharan Africa, northern and southern China, Mesoamerica, the south central Andes, and the eastern United States. Millet was domesticated by 7000 B.P. in northern China; and rice, by 8000 B.P. in southern China.

7. In the New World the most important domesticates were maize, potatoes, and manioc. The llama of the central Andes was the largest animal domesticated in the New World, where herding traditions analogous to those of the Old World did not develop. Economic similarities between the hemispheres must be sought in foraging and farming.

8. New World farming started in the lowlands of South America, then spread to Central America, Mexico, and the Caribbean islands. Tropical lowland cultivation in Central and South America began at about the same time as food production arose in the Middle East—around 10,000 years ago. By 7000 B.P., farming was diffusing from tropical lowlands into drier regions at higher elevations. The specific ancestor of maize, teosinte, grows wild in tropical southwestern Mexico, where maize probably was domesticated around 8000 B.P. At Oaxaca, in Mexico's southern highlands, maize was gradually added to a broad-spectrum diet by 4000 B.P. Early permanent villages supported by maize cultivation arose in the lowlands and in a few frost-free areas of the highlands.

9. Several factors, including a diversity of useful plant and animal species and early sedentism, combined to promote domestication in the ancient Middle East. Domesticates spread rapidly across Eurasia, facilitated by climatic similarities across a broad territorial expanse. In the Americas, food production spread less rapidly because of north-south contrasts. Another factor that slowed the Neolithic transition in the Americas was the lack of large animals suitable for domestication. Factors that explain the origin and diffusion of food production involve climate, economic adaptation, demography, and the specific attributes of plants and animals.

10. Food production and the social and political system it supported brought advantages and disadvantages. The advantages included discoveries and inventions. The disadvantages included harder work, poorer health, crime, war, social inequality, and environmental degradation.

key terms

broad-spectrum revolution 224
Hilly Flanks 227
maize 233
manioc 233
Mesoamerica 228

Mesolithic 225
Natufians 227
Neolithic 226
sedentism 227
teosinte 236

MULTIPLE CHOICE

1. The Mesolithic refers to
   a. stone toolmaking emphasizing microliths within broad-spectrum economies.
   b. the period between 15,000 B.P. in the Middle East and 12,000 B.P. in Europe, during which foragers focused on hunting a limited range of big game.
   c. the technique of cutting and smoking meats to preserve them through the long winters.
   d. the last major glaciation that covered most of Europe with ice.
   e. Scandinavian shell mounds—the garbage dumps of prehistoric oyster collectors.

2. With glacial retreat, foragers pursued a more generalized economy, focusing less on large animals. This was the beginning of what Kent Flannery (1969) has called the
   a. Upper Paleolithic.
   b. Jomon revolution.
   c. vertical economy revolution.
   d. Neolithic revolution.
   e. broad-spectrum revolution.

3. Why were the Natufians able to live in year-round villages prior to the emergence of domestication?
   a. Because their diet became hyperspecialized in the locally grown foods
   b. Because they could exploit their rich local environment with broad-spectrum foraging
   c. Because they had a low-calorie diet relative to the average caloric intake of foragers
   d. Because they traded with nearby populations that did develop domestication
   e. Because they reduced the population size of their villages

4. Early cultivation in the Middle East began as an attempt to
   a. improve, in a more favorable environment, the foraging techniques of villagers living in the Hilly Flanks.
   b. improve the supply of animal feed for the already domesticated cattle.
   c. win a war against nomads encroaching on Natufian territory.
   d. copy, in a less favorable environment, the dense stands of wheat and barley that grew wild in the Hilly Flanks.
   e. impose a social hierarchy among the Natufian commoners.

5. Why do most domesticated grains (such as wheat and barley) have a tougher axis and more brittle husk than wild grains?
   a. Grains with a weak axis and tough husk could not survive in the wild.
   b. They yield better nutrients through being domesticated.
   c. The practices of harvesting and processing grain gradually selected for these features.
   d. The first domesticated grains were from the alluvial plains, where caprine influences strengthened the axis and husk.
   e. B and D only

6. In the alluvial desert plain of the Tigris and Euphrates rivers, a new economy based on irrigation and trade fueled the growth of an entirely new form of society:
   a. the Jomon, a social and political unit with roots in East Asia.
   b. the state, a social and political unit featuring a central government, extreme contrasts of wealth, and social classes.
   c. the city-state, a social and political unit featuring egalitarianism.
   d. the state, featuring what Marshall Sahlins called "the original affluent society."
   e. the village.

7. Food production spread out from the Middle East through trade, diffusion of domesticated species, and actual migration of farmers, to northern Africa, Europe, India, and Pakistan. However, archeological evidence suggests that
   a. in southern Egypt, cattle may have been domesticated locally rather than imported from the Fertile Crescent.
   b. in Oaxaca, llamas may have been domesticated locally rather than imported from the Fertile Crescent.
   c. in certain regions of Pakistan sheep may have been domesticated independently.
   d. in southern France barley may have been domesticated locally rather than imported from the Fertile Crescent.
   e. in northern India wheat may have been domesticated earlier than in the Fertile Crescent.

8. The findings at Nabta Playa, located in the eastern Sahara and southern Egypt,
   a. represent an elaborate and previously unsuspected ceremonialism, as well as social complexity during the African Neolithic.

test yourself

b. suggest that it was a ceremonial site where the economy was fully Neolithic by 10,000 B.P.

c. provide evidence for the "African sheep complex."

d. suggest it was entirely isolated from Middle Eastern influence until 5,000 B.P.

e. represent a case of sheep and goat domestication unlike the one that occurred in the Middle East.

9. Which of the following statements about life in the Valley of Oaxaca prior to cultivation is *not* true?

a. People ate cactus fruits, tree pods, deer, and rabbit.

b. The populations shifted seasonally between bands and microbands.

c. People lived in sedentary villages.

d. The people periodically harvested the wild grass, teosinte.

e. The inhabitants were foragers.

10. Which of the following is correct about the food-producing traditions of Mesopotamia and Mesoamerica?

a. Food production occurred as a gradual process in Mesoamerica but was revolutionary in Mesopotamia.

b. In Mesoamerica, goats, sheep, and pigs were domesticated, while in Mesopotamia, only dogs were domesticated.

c. Food production emerged in Mesoamerica thousands of years prior to that in Mesopotamia.

d. Maize was the staple grain in Mesopotamia, while the primary grain in Mesoamerica was wheat.

e. Large domesticated animals played an important role in Mesopotamia, but were absent from Mesoamerica.

FILL IN THE BLANK

1. _____ refers to the first cultural period in a given region in which the first signs of domestication are present.

2. A _____ is a system that exploits environmental zones that contrast with one another in altitude, rainfall, overall climate, and vegetation.

3. The practice of using cattle for their milk and blood rather than killing them for their meat (except on ceremonial occasions) is called _____.

4. In contrast to the sequence of events in Mesopotamia, food production *led* to the early village farming community (around 3500 B.P.) in _____.

5. Recent evidence has forced the revision of old assumptions in archaeology, most prominently the idea that New World farming originated in upland areas, such as the highlands of Mexico and Peru. Researchers now suggest that farming in the tropical lowlands of Central and South America began around _____ years ago, about the same time as food production in _____.

CRITICAL THINKING

1. What is revolutionary about what Kent Flannery (1969) called the "broad-spectrum revolution"? What other more recent events in history do you consider revolutionary? Why?

2. Why is the lack of animal domestication in Mesoamerica considered a key factor in world history?

3. Previously anthropologists had believed that Old World (Middle Eastern) farming predated the earliest cultivation in the Americas by three or four millennia. How have new dating techniques pushed back the origin or domestication in the New World?

4. In this chapter, what are some examples of the role geography plays in key events in human history? Geography also affects how we come to know about the past. How so?

5. Was the origin of food production good or bad? Why?

Bellwood, P. S.

2005　*First Farmers: Origins of Agricultural Societies.* Malden, MA: Blackwell. Origins and spread of agriculture in various world areas.

Diamond, J. M.

2005　*Guns, Germs, and Steel: The Fates of Human Societies.* New York: W. W. Norton. Disease, tools, and environmental forces and effects throughout human history.

Gamble, C.

2008　*Archaeology, the Basics,* 2nd ed. New York: Routledge. The title says it all.

Price, T. D., and G. M. Feinman

2010　*Images of the Past,* 6th ed. Boston: McGraw-Hill. Introduction to prehistory, including the origin of food production.

Renfrew, C., and P. Bahn

2010　*Archaeology: Theories, Methods, and Practice,* 5th ed. London: Thames and Hudson. Basic text.

Wenke, R. J., and D. I. Olszewski

2007　*Patterns in Prehistory: Humankind's First Three Million Years,* 5th ed. New York: Oxford University Press. Rise of food production and the state throughout the world; thorough, useful text.

Go to our Online Learning Center website at **www.mhhe.com/kottak** for Internet exercises directly related to the content of this chapter.

suggested additional readings

internet exercises

CHAPTER 12

The First Cities and States

When, where, and why did early states originate, and what were their key attributes?

How do archaeologists distinguish between chiefdoms and states?

What similarities and differences marked the origin of early states in the Old World and the New World?

◀ Overview of terraced royal Inca ruins at Machu Picchu, Peru, which has been designated one of the Seven Wonders of today's world.

understanding OURSELVES

"Y**ou're not the boss of me."** Have you ever heard or uttered those words? Who might say them to whom? Certainly you would not be likely to say this to a real employer, or to a police officer who just pulled you over, or to someone judging you in a court of law. We resent it when our siblings, cousins, or friends tell us what to do. But we learn to call judges "Your Honor," police officers "Officer," "Detective," "Lieutenant," "Captain," or "Chief," and employers "Ms." or "Mr." (as in "Mr. Trump"). Such titles (honorifics) mark differences in status and authority. Generally, we learn to respect and obey such people ("the authorities"). That is, we follow their orders or instructions, as people in the military routinely do with their superiors.

Marked contrasts in status, power, wealth, and privilege distinguish cities and states from the societies that came before them. Everyone reading this book lives in a state-organized society. Our lives differ dramatically from those of our Paleolithic ancestors, or those of more recent foragers. The state has a lot to do with these differences. The demand for labor (human, animal, etc.) increased in Neolithic economies compared with Paleolithic times. This trend continued in states, whose economies and political systems have placed even greater demands on ordinary people.

Perhaps you've seen a museum display depicting an early state society (e.g., Egypt, Mesopotamia, Maya). Such exhibits tend to highlight the artistic, architectural, literary, and scientific achievements of those civilizations. Ancient Sumerians (in Mesopotamia), Egyptians, Mexicans, and Peruvians had their artists, architects, mathematicians, astronomers, priests, and rulers—just as we do. However (but depicted more rarely), their ordinary citizens had to sweat in the fields to grow food for landlords, specialists, and elites. Unlike hunter-gatherers, residents of states must deal with bosses, despots, and commanders. The elites of ancient states could summon involuntary labor to build temples and pyramids, and to move stone for enduring monuments. In all states, people must pay taxes; in many states, citizens are drafted for work or war. Ordinary people no longer set their own priorities.

How do modern state-organized societies mirror those of the past? Ordinary people no longer may be drafted for work or war, but we do have to work to pay the taxes that pay for wars and public works. Our society is still stratified. Perks still go with wealth, fame, and power. Most of us still work much harder (usually for bosses) than foragers ever did. It's a myth that leisure time has increased with civilization. For a few, there is leisure and privilege; for most, there is work and obligation. And that's not because of human nature; it's because of the state.

THE ORIGIN OF THE STATE

As food-producing economies spread and became more productive, chiefdoms, and eventually states, developed in many parts of the world. A **state** is a form of social and political organization that has a formal, central government and a division of society into classes. The first states developed in Mesopotamia by 5500 B.P. and in Mesoamerica some 3,000 years later. Chiefdoms were precursors to states, with privileged and effective leaders—chiefs—but lacking the sharp class divisions that characterize states. By 7000 B.P. in the Middle East and 3200 B.P. in Mesoamerica, there is evidence for what archaeologists call the elite level, indicating a chiefdom or a state.

How and why did chiefdoms and states originate? Compared with foraging, food production could support larger and denser populations. Also, the complexity of the division of social and economic labor tended to grow as food production spread and intensified. Systems of political authority and control typically develop to handle regulatory problems encountered as the population grows and/or the economy increases in scale and diversity. Competition, including warfare, among chiefdoms for territory and resources also can stimulate state formation. Anthropologists have identified the causes of state formation and reconstructed the rise of several states. A *systemic* perspective recognizes that multiple factors always contribute to state formation, with the effects of one magnifying those of the others. Although some contributing factors have appeared again and again, no single one is always present. In other words, state formation has generalized rather than universal causes.

Furthermore, because state formation may take centuries, people experiencing the process at any time rarely perceive the significance of the long-term changes. Later generations find themselves dependent on government institutions that took generations to develop.

Hydraulic Systems

One suggested cause of state formation is the need to regulate *hydraulic* (water-based) agricultural economies (Wittfogel 1957). In certain arid areas, such as ancient Egypt and Mesopotamia, states have emerged to manage systems of irrigation, drainage, and flood control. However, hydraulic agriculture is neither a sufficient nor a necessary condition for the rise of the state. That is, many societies with irrigation never experienced state formation, and states have developed without hydraulic systems.

But hydraulic agriculture does have certain implications for state formation. Water control increases production in arid lands. Because of its labor demands and its ability to feed more people, irrigated agriculture fuels population growth. This in turn leads to enlargement of the system. The expanding hydraulic system supports larger and denser concentrations of people. Interpersonal tensions increase, and conflicts over access to water and irrigated land become more frequent. Political authorities may arise to regulate production as well as interpersonal and intergroup relations.

Large hydraulic works can sustain towns and cities and become essential to their subsistence. Regulators protect the economy by mobilizing crews to maintain and repair the hydraulic system. These life-and-death functions enhance the authority of state officials. Thus, growth in hydraulic systems is often (as in Mesopotamia, Egypt, and the Valley of Mexico), but not always, associated with state formation.

Long-Distance Trade Routes

Another theory is that states arise at strategic locations in regional trade networks. These sites include points of supply or exchange, such as crossroads of caravan routes, and places (e.g., mountain passes and river narrows) situated so as to threaten or halt trade between centers. Here again, however, the cause is generalized but neither necessary nor sufficient. Long-distance trade has been important in the evolution of many states, including those in Mesopotamia and Mesoamerica. Such exchange does eventually develop in all states, but it can follow rather than precede state formation. Furthermore, long-distance trade also occurs in societies such as those of Papua New Guinea, where no states developed.

Population, War, and Circumscription

Robert Carneiro (1970) proposed an influential theory that incorporates three factors working together instead of a single cause of state formation. (We call a theory involving multiple factors or variables a **multivariate** theory.) Wherever and whenever *environmental circumscription (or resource concentration), increasing population, and warfare exist,* suggested Carneiro, state formation will begin (Figure 12.1). Environmental circumscription may be physical or social. Physically circumscribed environments include small islands and, in arid areas, river plains, oases, and valleys with streams. Social circumscription exists when neighboring societies block expansion, emigration, or access to resources. When strategic resources are concentrated in limited areas—even when no obstacles to migration exist—the effects are similar to those of circumscription.

Coastal Peru, one of the world's most arid areas, illustrates the interaction of environmental circumscription, warfare, and population increase. The earliest cultivation there was limited to valleys with springs. Each valley was circumscribed by the Andes Mountains to the east, the Pacific Ocean to the west, and desert regions to the north and south. The advent of food production triggered a population increase. In each valley, villages got bigger. Colonists split off from the old villages and founded new ones. With more villages and people, a scarcity of land developed. Rivalries and raiding developed between villages in the same valley.

Population pressure and land shortages were developing in all the valleys. Because the valleys were circumscribed, when one village conquered another, the losers had to submit to the winners—they

state
Society with central government, administrative specialization, and social classes.

multivariate
Involving multiple factors, causes, or variables.

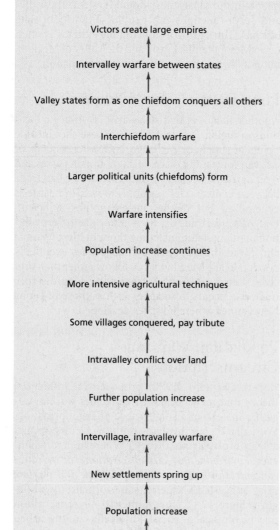

empire

Mature state that is large, multiethnic, militaristic, and expansive.

FIGURE 12.1 Carneiro's Multivariate Approach to the Origin of the State as Applied to Coastal Peru.

In this very arid area, food production developed in narrow river valleys where water for cultivation was available (resource concentration). With cultivation, the population increased. Population pressure on land led to warfare, and some villages conquered others. Physical circumscription meant that the losers had no way to escape. The process accelerated as the population grew and as warfare and cultivation intensified. Chiefdoms, states, and empires eventually developed.

had nowhere else to go. Conquered villagers could keep their land only if they agreed to pay tribute to their conquerors. To do this, they had to intensify production, using new techniques to produce more food. By working harder, they managed to pay tribute while meeting their own subsistence needs. Villagers brought new areas under cultivation by means of irrigation and terracing.

Those early inhabitants of the Andes didn't work harder because they chose to do so. They were *forced* to pay tribute, accept political domination, and intensify production by factors beyond their control. Once established, all these trends accelerated. Population grew, warfare intensified, and villages eventually were united in chiefdoms. The first states developed when one chiefdom in a valley conquered the others (Carneiro 1990). Eventually, different valleys began to fight. The winners brought the losers into growing states and **empires**—mature, territorially larger, and expansive systems—which eventually expanded from the coast to the highlands. By the 16th century, from their capital, Cuzco, in the high Andes, the Inca ruled one of the major empires in the tropics.

Carneiro's theory is very useful, but again, the association between population density and state organization is generalized rather than universal. States do tend to have large and dense populations (Stevenson 1968). However, population increase and warfare within a circumscribed environment did not trigger state formation in highland Papua New Guinea. Certain valleys there are socially or physically circumscribed and have population densities similar to those of many states. Warfare also was present, but no states emerged. Again, we are dealing with an important theory that explains many but not all cases of state formation.

Whatever their faults may be, all these theories properly look to environmental, demographic, economic, and other down-to-earth factors in particular areas to explain the origin of early states and civilizations. Some theories for the origin of the state are not nearly as plausible. This chapter's "Appreciating Anthropology" examines the false claims of certain pseudo-archaeological theories about ancient civilizations.

Early states arose in different places, and for many reasons. In each case, interacting causes (often comparable ones) magnified each other's effects. To explain any instance of state formation, we must search for the specific changes in access to resources and in regulatory problems that fostered stratification and state machinery. We also must remember that chiefdoms and states don't inevitably arise from food production. Anthropologists know of, and have studied, many societies that maintained Neolithic economies without ever developing chiefdoms or states. Similarly, there are chiefdoms that never developed into states, just as there are foragers who never adopted food production, even when they knew about it. Recall from the previous chapter those early food producers in what is now the eastern United States who had to keep hunting and gathering for the bulk of their subsistence because the foods they had domesticated (e.g., sunflower, marsh elder) could not supply a complete diet.

THE URBAN REVOLUTION

The previous chapter cited V. Gordon Childe's (1951) phrase "Neolithic Revolution" to describe the origin and impact of food production. Childe, probably the most influential archaeologist of the 20th century, chose the term "revolution" deliberately. He wanted to compare the major social transformations of prehistory (food production and the state) to the Industrial Revolution (Smith 2009). He used the term "Urban Revolution" (1950) to describe the major transformation of human life and social institutions examined in this chapter. Key features were that institutions of government, including rulers with real power, emerged for the first time, along with social stratification. As a result of the Urban Revolution, economic activity of all sorts expanded greatly, and the first cities were built. On the downside, former freedoms and independence were replaced by servitude, taxes, rules, and regulations (Smith 2009).

Childe listed ten key attributes of early cities and states—all revealed by archaeological evidence. They may be paraphrased as follows:

1. The first cities were larger, more extensive, and more densely populated than any previous settlements.

2. Early cities differed from villages in composition and function; within the city were full-time specialist craftsmen, transport workers, merchants, officials, and priests.

3. Each primary producer (e.g., farmer) had to pay a tithe or tax to a deity or a divine king, who concentrated these contributions in a central place (e.g., temple or treasury).

4. Monumental buildings distinguished cities from villages, while also symbolizing the right of rulers to draw on the treasury and to command a labor force.

5. Supported by the treasury, priests, civil officials, and military leaders made up a ruling class.

6. Writing was used for record keeping.

7. Predictive sciences developed, including arithmetic, geometry, and astronomy.

8. Sophisticated art styles developed, expressed in sculpture, painting, and architecture.

9. There was long-distance and foreign trade.

10. Society was reorganized on the basis of territorial divisions (where one lived) rather than kinship groups.

Cities and writing were key features of Childe's Urban Revolution. In and after the 1960s, however, anthropologists shifted to such phrases as "the origin of the state," "the rise of the state," and "state formation" for this process. Use of such terms, which continues today, recognizes that some instances of state formation lack writing and significant urbanism (see Spencer and Redmond, 2004; Peregrine et al. 2007).

Early states had hereditary rulers and a military, with the rulers often playing a military role. Rulers stayed in power by combining personal ability, religious authority, economic control, and the privileged use of force. Shown here is a detail from the painted casket of Egypt's Tutankhamun, the famous "King Tut," who ruled between 1347 and 1337 B.C.E.

focus on GLOBALIZATION

The Seven Wonders of the World

States are precursors to empires, which are precursors to the world system and globalization. The state is an expansive form of human social organization that wields considerable power. Many states have developed into empires that cover huge territories and rule large numbers of people. Some historic examples include the Persian Empire, the empire created by Alexander the Great, the Roman and Byzantine empires, the Ottoman Empire, and most recently the British and French empires. The Inca (Peru) and Aztec (Mexico) empires are New World examples.

States clearly mark their environments. They build; they create a "built environment"—architecture that lasts and that archaeologists can study to determine the spread and influence of ancient states. Early states erected imposing public buildings and monumental architecture, including temples, palaces, and storehouses.

Occasionally a feature of a state's "built environment" is impressive enough to earn it the status of "wonder of the world." The "Seven Wonders of the Ancient World" were renowned among ancient Greeks and other Mediterranean tourists, particularly in the 1st and 2nd centuries B.C.E. Those sites worth seeing were close to, or on, the eastern rim of the Mediterranean Sea. Of them, only the Great Pyramid of Giza, the oldest of the seven wonders, is still standing after all those years.

Listed in order from oldest to youngest, the seven wonders of the ancient world are as follows: the Great Pyramid of Giza (constructed by ancient Egyptians), the Hanging Gardens of Babylon (Babylonians), the Temple of Artemis at Ephesus (Lydians, Persians, and Greeks), the Statue of Zeus at Olympia (Greeks), the Mausoleum of Halicarnassus (Carians, Persians, and Greeks), the Colossos of Rhodes (Greeks), and the Lighthouse of Alexandria (Ptolemaic Egyptians, Greeks).

Today's world has its own seven wonders, selected through a worldwide popular vote and announced in 2007. The New Seven Wonders of the World (2001–2007) was an initiative launched in 2001 by a Swiss corporation to choose new Wonders from a selection of 200 existing monuments through a popularity poll. The winners—from oldest to youngest (based on when construction began)—were Petra (Jordan), the Great Wall of China (Beijing), the Colosseum (Rome, Italy), Chichén Itzá (Yucatan, Mexico), Machu Picchu (Peru), the Taj Mahal (Agra, India), and the Christ the Redeemer statue (Corcovado) (Rio de Janeiro, Brazil).

Common to all these wonders—ancient and modern—is that they were erected by states, often for political or religious reasons, and eventually they became sites that people wanted to visit to marvel at these creations. Sightseeing tourism certainly existed in the ancient world, but on a much more limited scale than today. Nowadays, in the context of global tourism, the world's most popular attractions still include monuments named for people (e.g., Washington, Lincoln, Eiffel, Disney) and structures built for religious reasons (e.g., St. Peter's in Rome, Notre Dame de Paris, Hagia Sofia in Istanbul). No doubt the seven wonders of today's world are "must sees" for anyone doing tourism in a given country. I've seen four of the seven. How about you?

ATTRIBUTES OF STATES

Childe's list of ten defining attributes of the Urban Revolution aptly describes the first states in Mesopotamia and Egypt. Something a bit less specific, however, is needed to characterize all states, including those without writing. Most anthropologists today probably would agree that the following attributes (some shared with Childe's list) distinguished states from earlier forms of society:

1. A state controls a specific regional territory, such as the Nile Valley or the Valley of Mexico. The regional expanse of a state contrasts with the much smaller territories controlled by kin groups and villages in prestate societies. Early states were expansionist; they arose from competition among chiefdoms, as the most powerful chiefdom conquered others, extended its rule over a larger territory, and managed to hold on to, and rule, the land and people acquired through conquest.

2. Early states had productive farming economies, supporting dense populations, often in cities. The agricultural economies of early states usually involved some form of water control or irrigation.

3. Early states used tribute and taxation to accumulate, at a central place, resources needed to support hundreds, or thousands, of specialists. These states had rulers, a military, and control over human labor.

4. States are stratified into social classes. In the first states, the non-food-producing population consisted of a tiny elite, plus artisans, officials, priests, and other specialists. Most people were commoners. Slaves and prisoners constituted the lowest rung of the social ladder. Rulers stayed

"Egypt's renowned Sphinx, with the Great Pyramid behind it at Giza."

in power by combining personal ability, religious authority, economic control, and force.

5. Early states had imposing public buildings and monumental architecture, including temples, palaces, and storehouses. (See this chapter's "Focus on Globalization" for some of the most impressive examples of monumental architecture.)

6. Early states developed some form of record-keeping system, usually a written script (Fagan 1996).

STATE FORMATION IN THE MIDDLE EAST

In the last chapter we saw that food production arose in the ancient Middle East around 10,000 B.P. In the ensuing process of change, the center of population growth shifted from the zone where wheat and barley grew wild (Hilly Flanks) to adjacent areas (piedmont steppe) where those grains were first domesticated. By 6000 B.P., population was increasing most rapidly in the alluvial plain of southern Mesopotamia. (**Mesopotamia** refers to the area between the Tigris and Euphrates rivers in what is now southern Iraq and southwestern Iran.) This growing population supported itself through irrigation and intensive river valley agriculture. By 5500 B.P. towns had grown into cities (Gates 2003). The earliest city-states were Sumer (southern Iraq) and Elam (southwestern Iran), with their capitals at Uruk (Warka) and Susa, respectively.

Urban Life

The first towns arose around 10,000 years ago in the Middle East. Over the generations houses of mud brick were built and rebuilt in the same place. Substantial tells, or mounds, arose from the debris of a succession of such houses. The Middle East and Asia have hundreds or thousands of such mounds, only a few of which have been excavated. These sites have yielded remains of ancient community life, including streets, buildings, terraces, courtyards, wells, and other artifacts.

The earliest known town was Jericho, located in what is now Israel, below sea level at a well-watered oasis a few miles northwest of the Dead Sea (Figure 12.2). From the lowest (oldest) level, we know that

Mesopotamia Area where earliest states developed, between Tigris and Euphrates rivers.

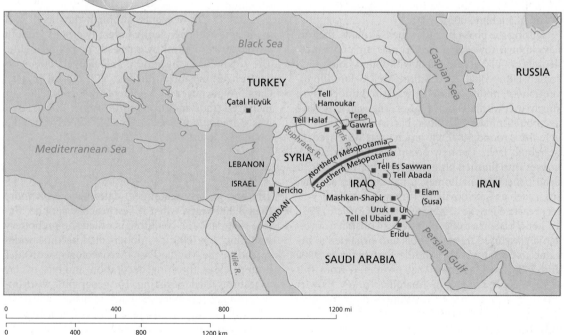

FIGURE 12.2 Sites in Middle Eastern State Formation.

The world's earliest known town was Jericho, located in what is now Israel. Jericho was first settled by Natufian foragers around 11,000 B.P. This round tower dates back 8,000 years.

animals, and was harnessed for irrigation by 7000 B.P. Over the mound's 32 acres (12.9 hectares), up to 10,000 people once lived in crowded mud-brick houses packed so tightly that residents entered from their roofs.

Shielded by a defensive wall, Çatalhöyük flourished between 8000 and 7000 B.P. Its individual mud-brick dwellings, rarely larger than a suburban American bedroom, had separate areas reserved for ritual and secular uses. In a given house, the ritual images (wall paintings) were placed along the walls that faced north, east, or west, but never south. That area was reserved for cooking and other domestic tasks.

The ritual spaces were decorated with wall paintings, sculpted ox heads, bull horns, and relief models of bulls and rams. The paintings showed bulls surrounded by stick figures running, dancing, and sometimes throwing stones. Vultures attacked headless humans. One frieze had human handprints painted below mounted bull horns. These images and their placement are reminiscent of Paleolithic cave art. The dwellings at Çatalhöyük were entered through the roof, and people had to crawl through holes from room to room, somewhat like moving between chambers in a cave. The deeper down one went, the richer the art became. The town's spiritual life seems to have revolved around a preoccupation with animals, danger, and death, perhaps related to the site's recent hunter-gatherer past.

Two or three generations of a family were buried beneath their homes. In one dwelling, archaeologists found remains of seventeen individuals, mostly children. After two or three generations of family burials, the dwelling was burned. The site was then covered with fine dirt, and a floor laid for a new dwelling.

Çatalhöyük's residents, although they lived in a town, acted independently in family groups without any apparent control by a priestly or political elite. The town never became a full-fledged city with centralized organization. Just as it lacked priests, Çatalhöyük never had leaders who controlled or managed trade and production (Fagan 1996). Food was stored and processed not collectively but on a smaller, domestic scale (DeMarco 1997).

The Elite Level

The first pottery (ceramics) dates back a bit more than 8,000 years, when it first reached Jericho. Before that date, the Neolithic is called the prepottery Neolithic. By 7000 B.P., pottery had become widespread in the Middle East. Archaeologists consider pottery shape, finishing, decoration, and type of clay as features used for dating. The geographic distribution of a given pottery style may indicate trade or an alliance spanning a large area at a particular time.

An early and widespread pottery style, the **Halafian,** was first found at Tell Halaf in the mountains of northern Syria. Halafian (7500–6500 B.P.)

around 11,000 years ago, Jericho was first settled by Natufian foragers. Occupation continued thereafter, through and beyond biblical times, when "Joshua fit the battle of Jericho, and the walls came tumbling down" (Laughlin 2006).

During the phase just after the Natufians, the earliest known town appeared. It was an unplanned, densely populated settlement with round houses and some 2,000 people. At this time, well before the invention of pottery, Jericho was surrounded by a sturdy wall with a massive tower. The wall may have been built initially as a flood barrier rather than for defense. Around 9000 B.P. Jericho was destroyed, to be rebuilt later. The new occupants lived in square houses with finished plaster floors. They buried their dead beneath their homes, a pattern seen at other sites, such as Çatalhöyük in Turkey (see below). Pottery reached Jericho around 8000 B.P. (Gowlett 1993).

Long-distance trade, especially of obsidian, a volcanic glass used to make tools and ornaments, became important in the Middle East between 9500 and 7000 B.P. One town that prospered from this trade was Çatalhöyük in Anatolia, Turkey (Fowler 2011; Hodder 2006). A grassy mound 65 feet high holds the remains of this 9,000-year-old town, probably the largest settlement of the Neolithic age. Çatalhöyük was located on a river, which deposited rich soil for crops, created a lush environment for

Halafian
Early (7500–6500 B.P.), widespread Mesopotamian pottery style.

refs to a delicate ceramic style. It also describes the period during which the elite level and the first chiefdoms emerged. The low number of Halafian ceramics suggests they were luxury goods associated with a social hierarchy.

By 7000 B.P. chiefdoms had emerged in the Middle East. The Ubaid period (7000–6000 B.P.) is named for a southern Mesopotamian pottery type first discovered at a small site, Tell el-Ubaid, located near the major city of Ur in southern Iraq. Similar pottery has been discovered in the deep levels of the Mesopotamian cities of Ur, Uruk, and Eridu. Ubaid pottery is associated with advanced chiefdoms and perhaps the earliest states. It diffused rapidly over a large area, becoming more widespread than earlier ceramic styles such as the Halafian.

Social Ranking and Chiefdoms

It is easy for archaeologists to identify early states. Evidence for state organization includes monumental architecture, central storehouses, irrigation systems, and written records. In Mesoamerica, even chiefdoms are easy to detect archaeologically. Ancient Mexican chiefdoms left behind stone works, such as temple complexes and the huge carved Olmec heads (see page 262). Mesoamericans also had a penchant for distinguishing their elites with durable ornaments and prestige goods, including those buried with chiefs and their families. Early Middle Eastern chiefs were less ostentatious in their use of material markers of prestige, making their chiefdoms somewhat harder to detect archaeologically (Flannery 1999).

Considering the degrees =of status differentiation within a society, the anthropologist Morton Fried (1960) divided societies into three types: egalitarian, ranked, and stratified. An **egalitarian society,** most typically found among foragers, lacks status distinctions except for those based on age, gender, and individual qualities, talents, and achievements. Thus, depending on the society, adult men, elder women, talented musicians, or ritual specialists might receive special respect for their activities or knowledge. In egalitarian societies, status distinctions are not usually inherited. The child of a respected person will not receive special recognition because of his or her parent but must earn such respect.

Ranked societies, in contrast, do have hereditary inequality. But they lack **stratification** (sharp social divisions—*strata*—based on unequal access to wealth and power) into noble and commoner classes. In ranked societies, individuals tend to be ranked in terms of their genealogical distance from the chief. Closer relatives of the chief have higher rank or social status than more distant ones do. But there is a continuum of status, with many individuals and kin groups ranked about equally, which can lead to competition for positions of leadership. Recap 12.1 lists key features and examples of egalitarian, ranked, and stratified societies.

Not all ranked societies are chiefdoms. Robert Carneiro (1991) has distinguished between two kinds of ranked societies, only the second of which is a chiefdom. In the first type, exemplified by some Native Americans of the Pacific Northwest, there were hereditary differences in rank among individuals, but

egalitarian society
Society with rudimentary status distinctions.

ranked society
Society with hereditary inequality but lacking social stratification.

stratification
Presence of social divisions—*strata*—with unequal wealth and power.

Unlike states such as Cameroon, whose King Njoya is shown here, egalitarian societies lack inherited wealth and status and succession to political office. How are inherited status distinctions marked in your society?

KIND OF STATUS DISTINCTION	NATURE OF STATUS	COMMON FORM OF SUBSISTENCE ECONOMY	COMMON FORMS OF SOCIAL ORGANIZATION	EXAMPLES
Egalitarian	Status differences are not inherited. All status is based on age, gender, and individual qualities, talents, and achievements.	Foraging	Bands and tribes	Inuit, Ju/'hoansi San, and Yanomami
Ranked	Status differences are inherited and distributed along a continuum from the highest-ranking member (chief) to the lowest without any breaks.	Horticulture, pastoralism, and some foraging groups	Chiefdoms and some tribes	Native American groups of the Pacific Northwest (e.g., Salish and Kwakiutl), Natchez, Halaf and Ubaid period polities, Olmec
Stratified	Status differences are inherited and divided sharply between distinct noble and commoner classes.	Agriculture	States	Teotihuacán, Uruk period states, Inca, Shang dynasty, Rome, United States, Great Britain

chiefdom
Ranked society with two- or three-level settlement hierarchy.

primary states
States arising through competition among chiefdoms.

villages were independent of one another and not ranked in relation to one another. Exemplifying the second type were the Cauca of Colombia and the Natchez of the eastern United States. These ranked societies had become **chiefdoms,** societies in which relations among villages as well as among individuals were unequal. The smaller villages had lost their autonomy and were under the authority of leaders who lived at larger villages. According to Kent Flannery (1999), *only those ranked societies with such loss of village autonomy should be called chiefdoms.* In chiefdoms, there is always inequality—differences in rank—among both individuals and communities.

In Mesopotamia, Mesoamerica, and Peru, chiefdoms were precursors to **primary states** (states that arose on their own, not through contact with other state societies—see Wright 1994). Primary states emerged from competition among chiefdoms, as one chiefdom managed to conquer its neighbors and to make them part of a larger political unit (Flannery 1995).

Archaeological evidence for chiefdoms in Mesoamerica dates back more than 3,000 years. Mesoamerican chiefdoms are easy to detect archaeologically because they were flamboyant in the way they marked their aristocracy. High-status families deformed the heads of their infants and buried them with special symbols and grave goods. In burials, prestige goods show a continuum in numbers of precious minerals, such as jade and turquoise, from graves—some have many; some, fewer; and some, none at all (Flannery 1999).

The first Middle Eastern states developed between 6000 and 5500 B.P. The first societies based on rank, including the first chiefdoms, emerged during the preceding 1,500 years. In the Middle East, the

archaeological record after 7300 B.P. reveals behavior typical of chiefdoms, including exotic goods used as markers of status, along with raiding and political instability. Early Middle Eastern chiefdoms included both the Halafian culture of northern Iraq and the Ubaid culture of southern Iraq, which eventually spread north.

As in Mesoamerica, ancient Middle Eastern chiefdoms had cemeteries where high-status people were buried with distinctive items: vessels, statuettes, necklaces, and high-quality ceramics. Such goods were buried with children too young to have earned prestige on their own, who happened to be born into elite families. In the ancient village of Tell es-Sawwan, infant graves show a continuum of richness from six statuettes, to three statuettes, to one statuette, to none. Such signs of slight gradations in social status are exactly what one expects in ranked societies (Flannery 1999).

Such burials convince Flannery (1999) that hereditary status differences were present in the Middle East by 7000 B.P. But had the leaders of large villages extended their authority to the smaller villages nearby? Is there evidence for the loss of village autonomy, converting simple ranked societies into chiefdoms? One clue that villages were linked in political units is the use of a common canal to irrigate several villages. This suggests a way of resolving disputes among farmers over access to water, for example, by appeal to a strong leader. By later Halafian times in northern Mesopotamia, there is evidence for such multivillage alliances (Flannery 1999). Another clue to the loss of village autonomy is the emergence of a two-tier settlement hierarchy, with small villages clustering around a large village, especially one with public buildings. There is evidence for this pattern in northern Mesopotamia during the Halafian (Watson 1983).

Advanced Chiefdoms

In northeastern Syria, near the border with Iraq, archaeologists have been excavating an ancient settlement that once lay on a major trade route. This large site, Tell Hamoukar, dates back more than 5,500 years (Wilford 2000). Its remains suggest that advanced chiefdoms arose in northern areas of the Middle East independently of the better-known city-states of southern Mesopotamia, in southern Iraq (Wilford 2000).

The oldest layer yet uncovered at Tell Hamoukar contains traces of villages dating back 6,000 years. By 5700 B.P. the settlement was a prosperous town of 32 acres, enclosed by a defensive wall 10 feet (3 meters) high and 13 feet (3.9 meters) wide. The site had fine pottery and large ovens—evidence of food preparation on an institutional scale. The site has yielded pieces of large cooking pots, animal bones, and traces of wheat, barley, and oats for baking and brewing. The archaeologist McGuire Gibson, one of the excavators, believes that food preparation on this scale is evidence of a ranked society in which elites were organizing people and resources (Wilford 2000). Most likely they were hosting and entertaining in a chiefly manner.

Also providing evidence for social ranking are the seals used to mark containers of food and other goods. Some of the seals are small, with only simple incisions or cross-hatching. Others are larger and more elaborate, presumably for higher officials to stamp more valuable goods. Gibson suspects the larger seals with figurative scenes were held by the few people who had greater authority. The smaller, simply incised seals were used by many more people with less authority (Wilford 2000). (Visit the Tell Hamoukar project website at https://oi.uchicago.edu/research/projects/ham/.)

living anthropology **VIDEOS**

The First States, www.mhhe.com/kottak

The clip offers brief views of Mesopotamia and Egypt, plus commentary by a Canadian professor. The clip poses the contrast between the "city-states" of Mesopotamia and the Egyptian "empire," implying a difference in the scale of political organization, with the Egyptian state controlling a much larger territory than did the rulers of Mesopotamia. What was the key factor in Egyptian territorial expansion? Besides the pharaoh, ancient Egypt had a vizier, who administered state officials and oversaw the royal treasury. What kind of role did rulers and temple officials play, according to the clip and the text, in the Mesopotamian city-states? Based on the clip and the text, what kind of association existed between religion and political control in the two areas?

At El Cano, Pana, archaeologists have recently uncovered rich funerary offerings, including golden implements and carvings and black beads. In chiefdoms and states, high-status families often bury their dead with distinctive symbols and grave goods.

The Rise of the State

In southern Mesopotamia at this time (5700 B.P.), an expanding population and increased food production from irrigation were changing the social landscape even more drastically than in the north. Irrigation had allowed Ubaid communities to spread along the Euphrates River. Travel and trade were expanding, with water serving as the highway system. Such raw materials as hardwood and stone, which southern Mesopotamia lacked, were imported via river routes. Population density increased as new settlements appeared. Social and economic networks now linked communities on the rivers in the south and in the foothills to the north. Settlements spread north into what is now Syria. Social differentials also increased. Priests and political leaders joined expert potters and other specialists. These non-food-producers were supported by the larger population of farmers and herders (Gilmore-Lehne 2000).

Economies were being managed by central leadership. Agricultural villages had grown into cities, some of which were ruled by local kings. The Uruk period (6000–5200 B.P.), which succeeded the Ubaid period, takes its name from a prominent southern city-state located more than 400 miles south of Tell Hamoukar (Recap 12.2). The Uruk period established Mesopotamia as "the cradle of civilization" (see Pollock 1999). Recap 12.2 highlights archaeological periods in the process of state formation in the ancient Middle East.

There is no evidence of Uruk influence at Tell Hamoukar until 5200 B.P., when some Uruk pottery showed up. When southern Mesopotamians expanded north, they found advanced chiefdoms, which were not yet states. The fact that writing

DATES	PERIOD	AGE
3000–2539 B.P.	Neo-Babylonian	Iron Age
3600–3000 B.P.	Kassite	
4000–3600 B.P.	Old Babylonian	Bronze Age
4150–4000 B.P.	Third Dynasty of Ur	
4350–4150 B.P.	Akkadian	
4600–4350 B.P.	Early Dynastic III	
4750–4600 B.P.	Early Dynastic II	
5000–4750 B.P.	Early Dynastic I	
5200–5000 B.P.	Jemdet Nasr	
6000–5200 B.P.	Uruk	Chalcolithic (Copper/Stone)
7500–6000 B.P.	Ubaid (southern Mesopotamia)–Halaf (northern Mesopotamia)	
10,000–7000 B.P.		Neolithic

originated in Sumer, in southern Mesopotamia, indicates a more advanced, state-organized society there. The first writing presumably developed to handle record keeping for a centralized economy.

Initially writing was used to keep accounts, reflecting the needs of trade. Rulers, nobles, priests, and merchants were the first to benefit from it. Writing had reached Egypt by 5200 B.P., probably from Mesopotamia. The earliest writing was pictographic, for example, with pictorial symbols of horses used to represent them.

Early Mesopotamian scribes used a stylus (writing implement) to scrawl symbols on raw clay. This writing, called **cuneiform** writing, from the Latin word for "wedge," left a wedge-shaped impression on the clay. Both the Sumerian (southern Mesopotamia) and the Akkadian (northern Mesopotamia) languages were written in cuneiform (Gowlett 1993).

Writing and temples played key roles in the Mesopotamian economy. For the historic period after 5600 B.P., when writing was invented, there are temple records of economic activities. States can exist

cuneiform
Early Mesopotamian wedge-shaped writing, using stylus on clay.

Early Mesopotamian scribes used a stylus to scrawl symbols on raw clay. This writing, called *cuneiform*, left a wedge-shaped impression on the clay. What languages were written in cuneiform?

Illustrating pictographic writing is this limestone tablet from the proto-urban period of lower Mesopotamia. This Sumerian script records proper names, including that of a landowner—symbolized by the hand—who commissioned the tablet.

without writing, but literacy facilitates the flow and storage of information. We know that Mesopotamian priests managed herding, farming, manufacture, and trade. Temple officials allotted fodder and pastureland for cattle and donkeys, which were used as plow and cart animals. As the economy expanded, trade, manufacture, and grain storage were centrally managed. Temples collected and distributed meat, dairy products, crops, fish, clothing, tools, and trade items. Potters, metalworkers, weavers, sculptors, and other artisans perfected their crafts.

Prior to the invention of **metallurgy** (knowledge of the properties of metals, including their extraction and processing and the manufacture of metal tools), raw copper was shaped by hammering. If copper is hammered too long, it hardens and becomes brittle, with a risk of cracking. But once heated (annealed) in a fire, copper becomes malleable again. Such annealing of copper was an early form of metallurgy. A vital step for metallurgy was the discovery of **smelting,** the high-temperature process by which pure metal is produced from an ore. Ores, including copper ore, have a much wider distribution than does native copper, which was initially traded as a luxury good because of its rarity (Gowlett 1993).

When and how smelting was discovered is unknown. But after 5000 B.P., metallurgy evolved rapidly. The Bronze Age began when alloys of arsenic and copper, or tin and copper (in both cases known as **bronze**), became common and greatly extended the use of metals. Bronze flows more easily than copper does when heated to a similar temperature, so bronze was more convenient for metal casting. Early molds were carved in stone, as shaped depressions to be filled with molten metal. A copper ax cast from such a mold has been found in northern Mesopotamia and predates 5000 B.P. Thereafter, other metals came into common use. By 4500 B.P., golden objects were found in royal burials at Ur.

Iron ore is distributed more widely than is copper ore. Iron, when smelted, can be used on its own; there is no need for tin or arsenic to make a metal alloy (bronze). The Iron Age began once high-temperature iron smelting was mastered. In the Old World after 3200 B.P., iron spread rapidly. Formerly valued as highly as gold, iron crashed in value when it became plentiful (Gowlett 1993).

The Mesopotamian economy, based on craft production, trade, and agriculture, spurred population growth and increased urbanism. Sumerian cities were protected by a fortress wall and surrounded by a farming area. By 4800 B.P., Uruk, the largest early Mesopotamian city, had a population of 50,000. As irrigation and the population expanded, communities fought over water. People sought protection in the fortified cities (Adams 1981, 2008) when neighbors or invaders threatened.

By 4600 B.P., secular authority had replaced temple rule. The office of military coordinator developed into kingship. This change shows up architecturally

This ziggurat, or temple tower, at Ur, Iraq, dates back to 4100 B.P. (2100 B.C.E.). Temples and their officials played key roles in the Mesopotamian economy. Who handles such duties in our society?

in palaces and royal tombs. The palace raised armies and supplied them with armor, chariots, and metal armaments. At Ur's royal cemetery, by 4600 B.P. monarchs were being buried with soldiers, charioteers, and ladies in waiting. These subordinates were killed at the time of a royal burial to accompany the monarch to the afterworld.

Agricultural intensification made it possible for the number of people supported by a given area to increase. Population pressure on irrigated fields helped create a stratified society. Land became scarce private property that was bought and sold. The wealth of people with large estates set them off from ordinary farmers. These landlords joined the urban elite, while sharecroppers and serfs toiled in the fields. By 4600 B.P., Mesopotamia had a well-defined class structure, with complex stratification into nobles, commoners, and slaves.

OTHER EARLY STATES

In northwestern India and Pakistan, the Indus River Valley (or *Harappan)* state, with major cities at Harappa and Mohenjo-daro, takes its name from the river valley along which it extended. (Figure 12.3 maps the four great early river valley states of the Old World: Mesopotamia, Egypt, India/Pakistan, and northern China.) Trade and the spread of writing from Mesopotamia may have played a role in the emergence of the Harappan state around 4600 B.P. Located in Pakistan's Punjab Province, the ruins of Harappa were the first to be identified as part of the Indus River Valley civilization. At its peak, the Indus River Valley state incorporated 1,000 cities, towns, and villages, spanning 280,000 square miles (725,000 square kilometers). This state, which

metallurgy
Extraction and processing of metals to make tools.

smelting
High-temperature extraction of metal from ore.

bronze
Alloy of copper and arsenic or tin.

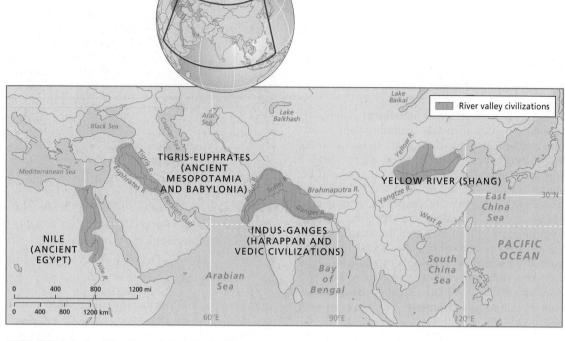

FIGURE 12.3 The Four Great Early River Valley States of the Old World.

By approximately 4000 B.P., urban life had been established along the Tigris and Euphrates rivers in Mesopotamia, the Nile River in Egypt, the Indus and Ganges rivers in India/Pakistan, and the Yellow River in China.

SOURCE: Based on Map 1-1 from Craig, Albert M.; Graham, William A.; Kagan, Donald; Ozment, Steven; Turner, Frank M., *Heritage of World Civilizations: Volume I to 1650*, 4th ed. © 1997. Reprinted and electronically reproduced by permission of Pearson Education, Inc., Upper Saddle River, New Jersey.

flourished between 4600 and 3900 B.P., featured urban planning, social stratification, and an early writing system, which remains undeciphered. The Harappans maintained a uniform system of weights. Their cities had carefully planned residential areas with wastewater systems. An array of products from sophisticated craft industries included ceramic vessels made on potter's wheels (Meadow and Kenoyer 2000).

The Indus River Valley state collapsed, apparently through warfare, around 3900 B.P. Its cities became largely depopulated. Skeletons of massacre victims have been found in the streets of Mohenjo-daro. Harappa continued to be occupied, but on a much smaller scale than previously (Meadow and Kenoyer 2000). (For more on the ongoing Harappa Archaeological Research Project, visit http://www.harappa.com.)

The first Chinese state, dating to 3750 B.P., was that of the Shang dynasty. It arose in the Huang He (Yellow) River area of northern China, with wheat as its dietary staple. This state was characterized by urbanism, palatial (as well as domestic) architecture, human sacrifice, and a sharp division between social classes. Burials of the aristocracy were marked by ornaments of stone, including jade. The Shang had bronze metallurgy and an elaborate writing system. In warfare they used chariots and took prisoners (Gowlett 1993).

Like Mesopotamia and China, many early civilizations came to rely on metallurgy. At Nok Nok Tha in northern Thailand, metalworking goes back 6,000 years. In Peru's Andes metalworking appeared around 4000 B.P. Ancient Andeans were skilled in working with bronze, copper, and gold. They are well known, too, for their techniques of pottery manufacture. Their arts, crafts, and agricultural knowledge compared well with those of Mesoamerica at its height, to which we turn after a discussion of African states. Note that both Mesoamerican and Andean state formation were truncated by Spanish conquest. The Aztecs of Mexico were conquered in 1519 C.E., and the Inca of Peru in 1532 C.E.

African States

Egypt, a major ancient civilization, developed in northern Africa, as one of the world's first states (Morkot 2005). Egyptian influence extended southward along the Nile into what is now Sudan. Sub-Saharan Africa witnessed the emergence of several states (Hooker 1996), only a few of which will be described here.

As in the states just discussed, metallurgy (especially iron and gold) played a role in the eventual rise of African states (Connah 2004). About 2,000 years ago, iron smelting began to diffuse rapidly throughout Africa. That spread was aided by the migrations of Bantu speakers. (Bantu is Africa's largest linguistic family.) The Bantu migrations, launched from northcentral Africa around 2100 B.P., continued for more than a thousand years. Bantu speakers migrated south into the rain forests of the Congo River and east into the African highlands. Along with their language and iron-smelting techniques, they also spread farming, particularly of high-yielding crops such as yams, bananas, and plantains.

One crowning achievement of the Bantu migrations was the Mwenemutapa empire. The southeast-moving ancestors of the Mwenemutapa brought iron smelting and farming to the region called Zimbabwe, south of the Zambezi River and located

A 16th-century bronze statue of a royal messenger from Benin. An important precolonial state in what is now southern Nigeria, Benin, which thrived in the 15th–16th century C.E., is known for its artistic creativity. Benin art became one of the most influential African art traditions.

within the contemporary nation of the same name. This area was rich in gold, which the Mwenemutapa mined and traded with cities on the Indian Ocean, starting around 1000 C.E. (1000 B.P.). The Mwenemutapa developed a powerful kingdom based on trade. The first centralized state there was Great Zimbabwe (*zimbabwe* means "stone enclosure"—the capital was protected by huge stone walls), which arose around 1300 C.E. (700 B.P.). By 1500, Great Zimbabwe dominated the Zambezi Valley militarily and commercially as the seat of the Mwenemutapa empire.

Another African region where states arose, also abetted by trade, was the Sahel, the area just south of the Sahara in western Africa. Farming towns started appearing in the Sahel around 2600 B.P. One such town, Kumbi Saleh, eventually became the capital of the ancient kingdom of Ghana. West Africa was rich in gold, precious metals, ivory, and other resources, which after 750 C.E. (1250 B.P.) were traded (thanks to the camel) across the Sahara to North Africa, Egypt, and the Middle East. Cities in the Sahel served as southern terminal points for the trans-Saharan trade (e.g., of gold for salt). Several kingdoms developed in this area: Ghana, Mali, Songhay, and Kanem-Bornu, together known as the Sahelian kingdoms, of which Ghana was the first. By 1000 B.P. Ghana's economic vitality, based on the trans-Saharan trade, was supporting an empire formed through the conquest of local chiefdoms, from which tribute was extracted.

States also arose in the forested region of western Africa south of the Sahel. Between 1000 and 1500 C.E., local farming villages started consolidating into larger units, which eventually became centralized states. The largest and most enduring of these states was Benin, in what is now southern Nigeria. Benin, which thrived in the 15th century C.E. (600–500 B.P.), is known for its artistic creativity, expressed in terra-cotta, ivory, and brass sculpture. Benin art became one of the most influential African art traditions.

STATE FORMATION IN MESOAMERICA

In the last chapter we examined the independent inventions of farming in the Middle East and Mesoamerica. The processes of state formation that took place in these areas were also comparable, beginning with ranked societies and chiefdoms, and ending with fully formed states and empires.

The first monumental buildings (temple complexes) in the Western Hemisphere were constructed by Mesoamerican chiefdoms in many areas, from the Valley of Mexico to Guatemala. These chiefdoms influenced one another as they traded materials, such as obsidian, shells, jade, and

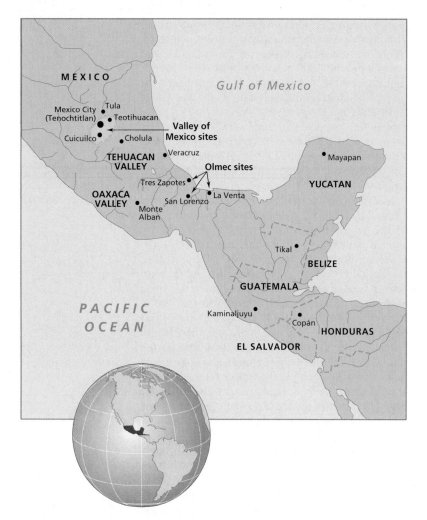

FIGURE 12.4 Major Sites in the Emergence of Food Production and the State in Mesoamerica.

SOURCE: From Clifford J. Jolly and Fred Plog, *Physical Anthropology and Archaeology,* 4th ed., p. 115. Copyright © 1986 by The McGraw-Hill Companies, Inc. Reprinted with permission.

This colossal Olmec head, carved from basalt, is displayed at the La Venta Archaeology Museum in Tabasco state, Mexico, in a setting designed to recall its original site. What is the significance of such a massive artifact?

pottery. (Figure 12.4 maps major sites in the emergence of Mesoamerican food production, chiefdoms, and states.)

Early Chiefdoms and Elites

The Olmec built a series of ritual centers on Mexico's southern Gulf Coast between 3,200 and 2,500 years ago. Three of these centers, each from a different century, are known. Earthen mounds were grouped into plaza complexes, presumably for religious use. Such centers show that Olmec chiefs could marshal human labor to construct such mounds. The Olmec were also master sculptors; they carved massive stone heads, perhaps as images of their chiefs or their ancestors.

There is evidence, too, that trade routes linked the Olmec with other parts of Mesoamerica, such as the Oaxaca Valley in the southern highlands and the Valley of Mexico (see Figure 12.4). By 3000 B.P. a ruling elite had emerged in Oaxaca. The items traded at that time between Oaxaca and the Olmec were for elite consumption. High-status Oaxacans wore mussel shell ornaments from the coast. In return the Olmec elites got mirrors and jade made by Oaxacan artisans. Chiefdoms in Oaxaca developed canal and well irrigation, exported magnetite mirrors, and were precocious in their use of adobes (mud bricks), stucco, stone masonry, and architecture. Chiefdoms in the Olmec area farmed river levees, built mounds of earth, and carved colossal stone heads.

The Olmec are famous for their huge carved stone heads, but other early Mexican chiefdoms also had skilled artists and builders, using adobes and lime plaster and constructing stone buildings, precisely oriented 8 degrees north of east.

The period between 3200 and 3000 B.P. was one of rapid social change in Mexico. All or almost all of Mesoamerica's chiefdoms were linked by trade and exchange. Many competing chiefly centers were concentrating labor power, intensifying agriculture, exchanging trade goods, and borrowing ideas, including art motifs and styles, from each other. Archaeologists now believe it was the *intensity of competitive interaction*—rather than the supremacy of any one chiefdom—that made social change so rapid. The social and political landscape of Mexico around 3000 B.P. was one in which twenty-five or so chiefly centers were (1) sufficiently separate and autonomous to adapt to local zones and conditions and (2) sufficiently interactive and competitive to borrow and incorporate new ideas and innovations as they arose in other regions (Flannery and Marcus 2000).

It used to be thought that a single chiefdom could become a state on its own. Archaeologists know now that state formation involves one chiefdom's incorporating several others into the emerging state it controls, and making changes in its own infrastructure as it acquires and holds on to new territories, followers, and goods. Warfare and attracting followers are two key elements in state formation. (This chapter's "Appreciating Anthropology" debunks popular pseudo-archaeological theories about the origin of Mesoamerican civilization.)

Many chiefdoms have dense populations, intensive agriculture, and settlement hierarchies that include hamlets, villages, and perhaps towns. These factors pave the way for greater social and political complexity. Political leaders emerge, and military success often solidifies their position. Such figures attract lots of followers, who are loyal to their leader. Conquest warfare brings in new territories and subjects. States, in contrast to chiefdoms, can acquire labor and land and hold on to them. States have armies, warfare, developed political hierarchies, law codes, and military force, which can be used in fact or as a threat.

Olmec and Oaxaca were just two among many flamboyant early Mexican chiefdoms that once thrived in the area from the Valley of Mexico to Guatemala. Oaxaca went on to develop a state a bit earlier than the Teotihuacán state of the Valley of Mexico. Oaxaca and other highland areas came to overshadow the Olmec area and the Mesoamerican lowlands in general. By 2500 B.P., Oaxaca's Zapotec people had developed a distinctive art style, perfected at their capital city of Monte Albán (see Blanton 1999; Marcus and Flannery 1996).

Three of more than 300 carved stones depicting slain war captives at the important archaeological site of Monte Albán, Oaxaca, Mexico. Dated to 500–400 B.C.E., these images originally were set in the Prisoner Gallery of Monte Albán's Building L. This huge display of slain enemies was a form of political and military propaganda. The carved stones warned potential rivals what would happen if they defied Monte Albán.

Warfare and State Formation: The Zapotec Case

Warfare can play a key role in primary state formation. The first Mesoamerican state, **Zapotec state** had developed in Mexico's Valley of Oaxaca by the start of the Common Era (C.E.—formerly A.D.). The city of Monte Albán served as capital of this Zapotec *polity* (political unit, such as a chiefdom or a state) for *twelve hundred years*, between 500 B.C.E. and 700 C.E. (The Zapotec polity was a chiefdom from ca. 500 B.C.E. to 100 B.C.E., and after that a state.) Kent Flannery and Joyce Marcus (2003b) describe the archaeological evidence for changing warfare patterns in Oaxaca—from early raiding among sedentary villages to warfare aimed at conquest between 330 and 20 B.C.E. (formerly B.C.).

The oldest defensive palisade in the Valley of Oaxaca dates to 3260–3160 B.P., just a few centuries after village life was established there (see Chapter 11). Over the next millennium, raiding evolved into war, with homes and temples burned, captives killed, and populations relocating to defensible hills. A monument from the site of San José Mogote, dating no later than 2510 B.P. (560 B.C.E.), is the earliest reliably dated monument with writing in Mesoamerica. It depicts a named, sacrificed captive, likely a rival chief and a probable victim of intervillage raiding. Armed conflict in Oaxaca began as raiding, with killing, burning, and captive taking but

no permanent acquisition of territory. By the time the Spanish conquistadors arrived in the 16th century, the Zapotec-speaking inhabitants of the Valley of Oaxaca had armies with noble officers and commoner foot soldiers. They waged wars and exacted tribute from conquered territories (Flannery and Marcus 2003b).

The shift from intervillage raiding to warfare aimed at territorial conquest occurred prior to 300 B.C.E. This shift is documented not only by hieroglyphs but also by survey and excavation in areas that were targets of Monte Albán's expansionistic designs. As Charles Spencer (2003) notes of Oaxaca, evidence for the earliest conquest warfare occurs simultaneously with evidence for emerging state organization. This correlation supports the idea of a causal link between conquest warfare and state formation.

Long ago, Henry Wright (1977) described the state as a society with not only a centralized but also an internally specialized, administrative organization—a bureaucracy. Chiefdoms, by contrast, lack administrative specialization. States have at least four levels of decision making (Wright 1977). The center or capital establishes subsidiary administrative centers (Elson 2007). Population size tends to follow this administrative structure: States typically have at least a four-level hierarchy of settlements according to both administrative functions and population size. Chiefdoms have no more than three levels (Spencer 2003).

Zapotec state
First Mesoamerican state, in the Valley of Oaxaca.

The Fantastic Claims of Pseudo-Archaeology

Interest in prehistory has spawned numerous popular-culture creations, including movies, TV programs, and books. In fictional works, the anthropologists don't bear much resemblance to their real-life counterparts. Unlike Indiana Jones, normal and reputable archaeologists don't go around fighting Nazis, lashing whips, or seizing antiquities. The archaeologist's profession isn't a matter of raiding lost arks, going on crusades, or finding crystal skulls, but of reconstructing ancient lifeways through the careful and systematic analysis of material remains.

Over the generations the media have exposed us to the pseudoscientific theories of such popular writers as Thor Heyerdahl (1971), Erich von Daniken (1971), and Graham Hancock (2011)—none of them a professional archaeologist. Heyerdahl argued that developments in one world area (e.g., Mesoamerica) were based on ideas borrowed from somewhere else (e.g., Egypt). Von Daniken carried diffusionism several steps further, proposing that major human achievements were created or assisted by extraterrestrials. These writers share a degree of contempt for human inventiveness. They assume that major features of the ancient human landscape were beyond the capabilities of people actually living in the places where the achievements occurred.

In *The Ra Expeditions,* world traveler and adventurer Heyerdahl (1971) argued that his voyage in a papyrus boat from the Mediterranean to the Caribbean demonstrated that ancient Egyptians could have navigated to the New World. (The boat was modeled on an ancient Egyptian vessel, but Heyerdahl and his crew had with them such modern conveniences as a radio and canned goods.) Heyerdahl maintained that given the possibility of ancient trans-Atlantic travel, Old World people could have influenced the emergence of civilization in the Americas. In *Fingerprints of the Gods* (2011) and other books aimed at popular audiences, writer-journalist Graham Hancock has advanced a series of fantastic claims, including that Africans influenced the Olmecs (because of, in his opinion, African-looking faces in Olmec sculpture).

The University of Michigan offers a popular undergraduate class titled "Frauds and Fantastic Claims in Archaeology." The course examines and debunks popular media theories that archaeologists view as fringe or "pseudoscientific." Especially problematic are claims that cultural achievements by indigenous peoples result from contact with superior beings. The course exposes the logical flaws and questionable evidence used to support such claims. Its textbook

is Kenneth L. Feder's *Frauds, Myths, and Mysteries: Science and Pseudoscience in Archaeology* (2011)—a must for any reader wanting to pursue this topic further.

Pseudo-archaeologists often have trouble with chronology. We've seen in this chapter that around 2,000 years ago, states fully comparable to those of Mesopotamia and Egypt began to rise and fall in the Mexican highlands. This occurred about 1,500 years after the major period of Egyptian pyramid building. If Egypt did contribute to Mesoamerican civilization, we would expect this influence to have been exerted during Egypt's heyday as an ancient power—not 1,500 years later. There is, however, no archaeological evidence for trans-Atlantic contact at either time.

There is, on the other hand, abundant archaeological evidence for the gradual emergence of food production and the state in the Middle East, in Mesoamerica, and in Peru. This evidence effectively counters the diffusionist theories and other fantastic claims about how and why human achievements, including farming and the state, began. Popular theories to the contrary, changes, advances, and setbacks in ancient American social life were the products of the ideas and activities of Native Americans themselves.

To expand, a state must send delegates, such as soldiers, governors, and other officials, to subjugate and rule in distant territories. Lacking a group of bureaucrats, chiefdoms can't do this, which means that the geographic range of chiefly authority is smaller than in a state. According to Spencer (2003), the limit of a chiefdom's range is half a day's travel from its center. States, however, can transcend such limits and carry out long-distance conquests.

Subjugation of polities in other regions, coupled with regularized tribute exaction, can bring about a transition from chiefdom to state (Spencer 2003). For such a strategy to succeed (especially when the conquered polities lie more than a half-day's trip away), the leadership will have to dispatch agents

to the conquered areas. Generals and bureaucrats are needed not only to carry out the subjugation but also to maintain long-term control and to manage tribute collection. The central leadership promotes internal administrative specialization and loyalty. Tribute provides new resources to support this administrative transformation. Archaeological data from Oaxaca confirm that the conquest of distant polities and bureaucratic growth were integral parts of the process of Zapotec primary state formation.

Typically, state bureaucracies occupy a group of administrative buildings, especially at the capital. Surrounding the Main Plaza at Monte Albán were specialized buildings, including palaces, temples,

Neither Mexico nor Peru has yielded a shred of accepted archaeological evidence for Old World interference prior to the European Age of Discovery, which began late in the 15th century. Francisco Pizarro conquered Peru's Inca state in 1532, eleven years after its Mesoamerican counterpart, Tenochtitlán, the Aztec capital, fell to Spanish conquistadores. (We do have abundant archaeological, as well as written, evidence for this contact between Europeans and Native Americans.)

The archaeological record also casts doubt on contentions that the advances of earthlings came with extraterrestrial help. Abundant, well-

analyzed archaeological data from the Middle East, Mesoamerica, and Peru tell a clear story. Food production and the state were not brilliant secrets, discoveries, or inventions that humans needed to learn or borrow from outsiders. They were long-term developments, gradual processes with down-to-earth causes and effects. They required thousands of years of orderly change, not some chance meeting in the high Andes between an ancient Inca chief and a beneficent Johnny Appleseed from Aldebaran.

Occasionally, fantastic claims about prehistory exaggerate, rather than deny, the abilities of ancient humans. One example is when pseudo-archaeologists claim that Paleolithic societies could have constructed monumental structures. Writer-journalist Graham Hancock, for example, has suggested that an Upper Paleolithic civilization, rather than ancient Egyptians, built Egypt's great Sphinx, some 7,000 years earlier than its actual construction date (Hancock and Bauval 1996). Semir Osmanagic is a Bosnian amateur archaeologist who has been dubbed the Indiana Jones of the Balkans because of his favored flat-crowned Navajo hat. Osmanagic claims to have identified in Bosnia the world's largest ancient pyramid,

which he thinks is "older than the last ice age" (Smith 2006). Archaeologists and geologists, however, say that his "pyramid" is actually a large symmetrical hill formed by buckling of the earth's crust millions of years ago. Zilka Kujundzic-Vejzagic, a trained prehistoric archaeologist at Bosnia's National Museum, points out the lack of any evidence for a Paleolithic civilization in Bosnia. (Were there Paleolithic civilizations anywhere in the world?) Indeed, archaeologists working in Bosnia have found little more than flint tools from the end of the last ice age and only simple Neolithic settlements that appeared thousands of years after that. The country's most substantial ancient monument is a modest stone city in southern Bosnia built during the third century B.C.E. Nevertheless, uncritical media coverage has popularized Osmanagic's theories, and volunteers have flocked to the site to help him excavate (Smith 2006).

Responding to his claims, the European Association of Archaeologists issued an official statement signed by the heads of the official archaeological organizations of seven European countries (Parzinger et al. 2006). Their statement called Osmanagic's so-called "pyramid" project "a cruel hoax on an unsuspecting public" that "has no place in the world of genuine science" (Parzinger et al. 2006). When and where have you heard a fantastic claim about prehistory?

Sarajevo-born American Semir Osmanagic claims to have discovered a giant pyramid built by an ancient civilization under Visocica Hill, Bosnia. Most scientists doubt his claim.

and ball courts. Of these, the palace is an especially useful diagnostic of state organization. Hieroglyphs on a building in Monte Albán's Main Plaza record the bringing of outlying areas under Monte Albán's control, often by conquest. There is archaeological evidence at Cañada de Cuicatlán (a two-day walk north of Monte Albán) for Zapotec conquest around 300 B.C.E. Evidence of outright colonization has been found in the Sola Valley, a two-day walk southwest of Monte Albán. The Zapotec also claimed control of the Tututepec area on Oaxaca's Pacific coast.

Evidence for co-occurrence of Monte Albán's conquest strategy with the emerging Zapotec state offers strong support for the expansionist model of primary state formation. That state had formed by 30–20 B.C.E., with a four-tier, site-size settlement hierarchy. After 700 C.E., the Zapotec state dissolved into a series of smaller centers or principalities—alternately vying for supremacy through continued warfare and forming peaceful alliances through marriage (Flannery and Marcus 2003a; Marcus 1989). (Figure 12.5 locates the Valley of Oaxaca and the sites discussed here.)

States in the Valley of Mexico

During the first century C.E., the Valley of Mexico, located in the highlands where Mexico City now stands, came to prominence in Mesoamerican

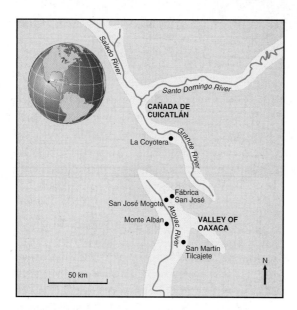

FIGURE 12.5 The Oaxaca Region, Mexico, Showing Places Mentioned.

state formation. In this large valley, **Teotihuacán** flourished between 1900 and 1300 B.P. (100 and 700 C.E.).

The Valley of Mexico is a large basin surrounded by mountains. The valley has rich volcanic soils, but rainfall isn't always reliable. The northern part of the valley, where the huge city and state of Teotihuacán eventually arose, is colder and drier than the south. Frosts there limited farming until quick-growing varieties of maize were developed. Until 2500 B.P., most people lived in the warmer and wetter southern part of the valley, where rainfall made farming possible. After 2500 B.P., new maize varieties and small-scale irrigation appeared. Population increased and began to spread north.

The Pyramid of the Sun, Teotihuacán's largest structure, is shown in the upper part of the photo. At its height around A.D. 500, Teotihuacán was larger than imperial Rome. The mobilization of manual labor to build such structures is one of the costs of state organization.

By 1 C.E. Teotihuacán was a town of 10,000 people. It governed a territory of a few thousand square kilometers and perhaps 50,000 people (Parsons 1974). Teotihuacán's growth reflected its agricultural potential. Perpetual springs permitted irrigation of a large alluvial plain. Rural farmers supplied food for the growing urban population.

By this time, a clear **settlement hierarchy** had emerged. This is a ranked series of communities that differ in size, function, and building types. The settlements at the top of the hierarchy were political and religious centers. Those at the bottom were rural villages. We have seen that a four-level settlement hierarchy provides archaeological evidence for state organization (Wright and Johnson 1975).

Along with state organization at Teotihuacán went large-scale irrigation, status differentiation, and complex architecture. Teotihuacán thrived between 100 and 700 C.E. It grew as a planned city built on a grid pattern, with the Pyramid of the Sun at its center. By 500 C.E. the population of Teotihuacán had reached 130,000, making it larger than imperial Rome. Farmers were one of its diverse specialized groups, along with artisans, merchants, and political, religious, and military personnel.

After 700 C.E. Teotihuacán declined in size and power. By 900 C.E. its population had shrunk to 30,000. Between 900 and 1200 C.E., the Toltec period, the population scattered, and small cities and towns sprang up throughout the valley. People also left the Valley of Mexico to live in larger cities—like Tula, the Toltec capital—on its edge (see Figure 12.4).

Population increase (including immigration by the ancestors of the Aztecs) and urban growth returned to the Valley of Mexico between 1200 and 1520 C.E. During the **Aztec** period (1325–1520 C.E.) there were several cities, the largest of which—Tenochtitlán, the capital—may have surpassed Teotihuacán at its height. A dozen Aztec towns had more than 10,000 people. Fueling this population growth was intensification of agriculture, particularly in the southern part of the valley, where the drainage of lake bottoms and swamps added new cultivable land (Parsons 1976).

Another factor in the renaissance of the Valley of Mexico was trade. Local manufacture created products for a series of markets. The major towns and markets were located on the lakeshores, with easy access to canoe traffic. The Aztec capital stood on an island in the lake. In Tenochtitlán, the production of luxury goods was more prestigious and more highly organized than that of pottery making, basket making, and weaving. Luxury producers, such as stone workers, feather workers, and gold- and silversmiths, occupied a special position in Aztec society. The manufacture of luxury goods for export was an important part of the economy of the Aztec capital (Hassig 1985; Santley 1985).

Ruins at Copán, a center of classic Maya royalty in western Honduras.

WHY STATES COLLAPSE

States can disintegrate along the same cleavage lines (e.g., regional political units) that were forged together to form the state originally. Various factors, such as invasion, disease, famine, or prolonged drought, could threaten their economies and political institutions. Citizens might degrade the environment, usually with economic costs. For example, farmers and smelters might cut down trees. Such deforestation promotes erosion and leads to a decline in the water supply. Overuse of land may deplete the soil of the nutrients needed to grow crops.

If factors such as irrigation help create states to begin with, does their decline or failure explain the fall of the state? Irrigation does have costs as well as benefits. In ancient Mesopotamia, irrigation water came from the Tigris and Euphrates rivers. Because sediment (silt) had accumulated in those rivers, their beds were higher than the alluvial plain and fields they irrigated. Canals channeled river water as it flowed down into the fields by gravity. As the water evaporated, water-borne mineral salts remained in the fields. This accumulation eventually created a poisonous environment for crops, forcing abandonment of the fields.

The Maya Decline

Generations of scholars have debated the decline of classic Maya civilization around 900 C.E. Classic Maya culture, featuring several competing states, flourished between 300 and 900 C.E. (1700–1100 B.P.) in parts of what are now Mexico, Honduras, El Salvador, Guatemala, and Belize. The ancient Maya are known for their monuments (temples and pyramids), calendars, mathematics, and hieroglyphic writing.

Archaeological clues to Maya decline have been found at Copán, in western Honduras. This classic Maya royal center, the largest site in the southeastern part of the Maya area, covered 29 acres (11.7 hectares). It was built on an artificial terrace overlooking the Copán River. Its rulers inscribed their monuments with accounts of their coronation, their lineage history, and reports of important battles. The Maya dated their monuments with the names of kings and when they reigned. One monument at Copán was intended to be the ruler's throne platform, but only one side had been finished. The monument bears a date, 822 C.E., in a section of unfinished text. Copán has no monuments with later dates. The site probably was abandoned by 830 C.E.

The environmental factors behind Copán's collapse may have included deforestation, erosion, and soil exhaustion due to overpopulation and overfarming. Hillside farmhouses in particular had debris from erosion—probably caused by overfarming of the hillsides. This erosion began as early as 750 C.E.—until these farm sites were abandoned, with some eventually buried by erosion debris.

Food stress and malnutrition were clearly present at Copán, where 80 percent of the buried skeletons display signs of anemia, due to iron deficiency. One skull shows anemia severe enough to have been the cause of death. Even the nobility were malnourished. One noble skull, known to be such from its carved teeth and cosmetic deformation, also has telltale signs of anemia: spongy areas at its rear (Annenberg/CPB Exhibits 2000).

Just as the origins of states, and their causes, are diverse, so are the reasons for state decline. The Maya state was not as powerful as was once assumed; it was fragile and vulnerable. Increased warfare and political competition destabilized many of its dynasties and governments. Archaeologists now stress the role of warfare in Maya state decline. Hieroglyphic texts document increased warfare among many Maya cities. From the period just before the collapse, there is archaeological evidence for increased concern with fortifications and moving to defensible locations. Archaeologists have evidence of the burning of structures, the projectile points from spears, and some of the bodies of those killed. Some sites were abandoned, with the people fleeing into the forests to occupy perishable huts. (Copán, as we have seen, was depopulated after 822 C.E.) Archaeologists now believe that social, political, and military upheaval and competition had as much as or more to do with the

Maya decline and abandonment of cities as did natural environmental factors (Marcus, personal communication).

Formerly archaeologists tended to explain state origin and decline mainly in terms of natural environmental factors, such as climate change, habitat destruction, and demographic pressure (see Weiss 2005). Archaeologists now see state origins and declines more fully—in social and political terms—because we can read the texts. And the Maya texts document competition and warfare between dynasties jockeying for position and power. Warfare was indeed a creator and a destroyer of ancient chiefdoms and states. What's its role in our own?

acing the COURSE

summary

1. States develop to handle regulatory problems as the population grows and the economy gets more complex. Multiple factors contribute to state formation. Some appear repeatedly, but no single factor is always present. Among the most important factors are irrigation and long-distance trade. Coastal Peru, a very arid area, illustrates how environmental circumscription, population growth, and warfare may contribute to state formation.

2. A state is a society with a formal, central government and a division of society into classes. The first cities and states, supported by irrigated farming, developed in southern Mesopotamia between 6000 and 5500 B.P. Evidence for early state organization includes monumental architecture, central storehouses, irrigation systems, and written records.

3. Towns predate pottery in the Middle East. The first towns grew up 10,000 to 9,000 years ago. The first pottery dates back just over 8,000 years. Halafian (7500–6500 B.P.) refers to a pottery style and to the period when the first chiefdoms emerged. Ubaid pottery (7000–6000 B.P.) is associated with advanced chiefdoms and perhaps the earliest states. Most state formation occurred during the Uruk period (6100–5100 B.P.).

4. Based on the status distinctions they include, societies may be divided into egalitarian, ranked, and stratified types. In egalitarian societies, status distinctions are not usually inherited. Ranked societies have hereditary inequality, but they lack stratification. Stratified societies have sharp social divisions—social classes or *strata*—based on unequal access to wealth and power. Ranked societies with loss of village autonomy are chiefdoms.

5. Mesopotamia's economy was based on craft production, trade, and intensive agriculture. Writing, invented by 5600 B.P., was first used to keep accounts for trade. With the invention of smelting, the Bronze Age began just after 5000 B.P.

6. In northwestern India and Pakistan, the Indus River Valley state flourished from 4600 to 3900 B.P. The first Chinese state, dating to 3750 B.P., was that of the Shang dynasty in northern China. Various states developed in sub-Saharan Africa. The major early states of the Western Hemisphere were in Mesoamerica and Peru.

7. Between 3200 and 3000 B.P., intense competitive interaction among many chiefdoms in Mesoamerica fueled rapid social change. Some chiefdoms would develop into states (e.g., Oaxaca, Valley of Mexico). Others (e.g., Olmec) would not. In the Valley of Oaxaca, changing military patterns—from village raiding to conquest warfare—played a prominent role in the formation of Mesoamerica's

earliest state, the Zapotec state, whose capital was Monte Albán. This city served as the Zapotec capital for one thousand years, from 300 B.C.E. to 700 C.E. After that, the Zapotec state continued, but in the form of small principalities that fought among themselves until Spanish conquest in the early 16th century C.E. By 1 C.E. (2000 B.P.), the Valley of Mexico had come to prominence. In this large valley in the highlands, Teotihuacán thrived between 100 and 700 C.E. Tenochtitlán, the capital of the Aztec state (1325 to 1520 C.E.), may have surpassed Teotihuacán at its height.

8. Early states faced various threats: invasion, disease, famine, drought, soil exhaustion, erosion, and the buildup of irrigation salts. States may collapse when they fail to keep social and economic order or to protect themselves against outsiders. The Maya state fell in the face of increased warfare among competing dynasties.

test yourself

MULTIPLE CHOICE

1. Chiefdoms
   a. are rarely sedentary.
   b. inevitably develop into states.
   c. require elaborate hydraulic systems if they are to grow into states.
   d. are the most common social arrangement of human populations.
   e. were precursors to states, with privileged and effective leaders—chiefs—but lacking the sharp class divisions that characterize states.

2. Which variable does *not* enter into Carneiro's multivariate theory of state formation?
   a. warfare
   b. population growth
   c. long-distance trade
   d. environmental circumscription
   e. resource concentration

3. Which of the following did *not* distinguish states from earlier forms of society?
   a. control over a specific regional territory
   b. productive farming, supporting dense populations
   c. social stratification
   d. the development of some form of record-keeping system
   e. burials

4. Which of the following statements about egalitarian society is *not* true?
   a. They often are found among foragers.
   b. Everybody has equal status.
   c. There are no social classes.
   d. There is no hereditary inequality.
   e. A person's status is based on his or her age, gender, and individual qualities, talents, and achievements.

5. Which term refers to a ranked society in which villages are *not* autonomous?
   a. chiefdom
   b. primary state
   c. archaic state
   d. tribe
   e. band

6. Which of the following did *not* accompany primary state formation in southern Mesopotamia?
   a. an expanding population
   b. increasing specialization
   c. a growing central leadership
   d. increasing isolation of communities
   e. increasing trade

7. Which of the following statements about the earliest writing is *not* true?
   a. It was syllabic.
   b. It was developed as a form of record keeping.

c. It spread from Mesopotamia to Egypt.

d. It played no role in the development of Mesoamerican writing systems.

e. It was scrawled on wet clay with a stylus.

8. What was the vital step for the development of metallurgy and the wider and rapid distribution of metals evident after 5000 B.P.?

   a. smelting

   b. copper hammering

   c. heating copper at low temperatures

   d. finding richer veins of copper

   e. investing more labor into mining

9. Which of the following is true about the emergence of states in Africa?

   a. Egypt was the only place in Africa where states arose.

   b. Iron smelting was unknown in Africa until European colonial expansion.

c. States arose only along the Nile Valley.

d. Southward Bantu migrations resulted in the emergence of the Mwenemutapa empire.

e. No early states emerged in Africa.

10. Which of the following statements about the collapse of Copán is *not* true?

   a. It led to its abandonment around 830 C.E.

   b. It was linked to soil exhaustion.

   c. It was linked to overpopulation and malnutrition.

   d. It was linked to erosion.

   e. It was precipitated by an Olmec invasion.

FILL IN THE BLANK

1. A(n) _____ is a society with hereditary inequality but lacking social stratification.

2. A(n) _____ society lacks status distinctions except those based on age, gender, and individual qualities, talents, and achievements.

3. _____ is the name for the early writing in Mesopotamia.

4. _____ was the capital of the first state to develop in the Valley of Mexico (100–700 C.E.).

5. First settled by Natufian foragers in what is now Israel, _____ is considered the earliest known town.

CRITICAL THINKING

1. This chapter describes Robert Carneiro's (1970) multivariate theory of state formation. What does it state? How is it representative of a systemic perspective?

2. Imagine yourself an archaeologist trying to identify ancient chiefdoms in the Middle East after excavating Mesoamerican chiefdom sites. What similar and different lines of evidence for ranking and political alliance might you find in the two contexts?

3. How could reviewing the history of state formation prompt us to reexamine our assumptions about what is natural or universal about social organization?

4. Only those ranked societies with loss of village autonomy should be called chiefdoms. What kinds of evidence could archaeologists search for as clues of this loss of autonomy?

5. Based on the evidence from coastal Peru (near the beginning of the chapter) and Oaxaca (near the end of the chapter), what role did warfare play in early state formation?

Fagan, B. M.

2011 *World Prehistory: A Brief Introduction*, 8th ed. Upper Saddle River, NJ: Pearson/Prentice Hall. Major events in human prehistory, including the emergence of the state in various locales.

Feder, K. L.

2011 *Frauds, Myths, and Mysteries: Science and Pseudoscience in Archaeology*. New York: McGraw-Hill. Debunks the fantastic claims of pseudoarchaeology.

Feinman, G. M., and J. Marcus, eds.

1998 *Archaic States*. Santa Fe, NM: School of American Research Press. Features of early states, in general and in particular world areas.

Joyce, R. A.

2008 *Ancient Bodies, Ancient Lives: Sex, Gender, and Archaeology*. New York: Thames and Hudson. What archaeology can tell us about ancient sex/gender roles.

Trigger, B. G.

2003 *Understanding Early Civilizations: A Comparative Study*. Cambridge, England: Cambridge University Press. A comparative study of seven archaic states: ancient Egypt and Mesopotamia, Shang dynasty China, Aztec, Maya, Inca, and Yoruba.

Wenke, R., and D. I. Olszewski

2007 *Patterns in Prehistory: Humankind's First Three Million Years,* 5th ed. New York: Oxford University Press. Rise of food production and the state throughout the world; thorough, useful text.

suggested additional readings

Go to our Online Learning Center website **www.mhhe.com/kottak** for Internet exercises directly related to the content of this chapter.

internet exercises

13

Method and Theory in Cultural Anthropology

Where and how do cultural anthropologists do fieldwork?

What are some ways of studying modern societies?

What theories have guided anthropologists over the years?

◀ In Mozambique's Gaza province, the Dutch ethnographer Janine van Vugt (red hair) sits on mats near reed houses, talking to local women.

understanding OURSELVES

"**B**een on any digs lately?" Ask your professor how many times she or he has been asked this question. Then ask how often he or she actually has been on a dig. Remember that anthropology has four subfields, only two of which (archaeology and biological anthropology) require much digging—in the ground at least. Even among biological anthropologists it's mainly paleoanthropologists (those concerned with the hominid fossil record) who must dig. Students of primate behavior in the wild, such as Jane Goodall, don't do it. Nor, most of the time, is it done by forensic anthropologists, including the title character in the TV show *Bones*.

To be sure, cultural anthropologists "dig out" information about varied lifestyles, as linguistic anthropologists do about the features of unwritten languages. Traditionally cultural anthropologists have done a variant on the *Star Trek* theme of seeking out, if not new, at least different "life" and "civilizations," sometimes boldly going where no scientist has gone before.

Despite globalization, the cultural diversity under anthropological scrutiny right now may be as great as ever before, because the anthropological universe has expanded to modern nations. Today's cultural anthropologists are as likely to be studying artists in Miami or bankers in Beirut as Trobriand sailors in the South Pacific. Still, we can't forget that anthropology did originate in non-Western, nonindustrial societies. Its research techniques, especially those subsumed under the label "ethnography," were developed to deal with small populations. Even when working in modern nations, anthropologists still consider ethnography with small groups to be an excellent way of learning about how people live their lives and make decisions.

Before this course, did you know the names of any anthropologists? If so, which ones? For the general public, biological anthropologists tend to be better known than cultural anthropologists because of what they study. You're more likely to have seen a film of Jane Goodall with chimps or a paleoanthropologist holding a skull than one of a linguistic or cultural anthropologist at work. Archaeologists occasionally appear in the media to describe a new discovery or to debunk pseudo-archaeological arguments about how visitors from space have left traces on earth. One cultural anthropologist was an important public figure when (and before and after) I was in college. Margaret Mead, famed for her work on teen sexuality in Samoa and gender roles in New Guinea, may well be the most famous anthropologist who ever lived. Mead, one of my own professors at Columbia University, appeared regularly on NBC's *Tonight Show*. In all her venues, including teaching, museum work, TV, anthropological films, popular books, and magazines, Mead helped Americans appreciate the relevance of anthropology to understanding their daily lives. Her work is featured here and elsewhere in this book.

ETHNOGRAPHY: ANTHROPOLOGY'S DISTINCTIVE STRATEGY

Anthropology emerged as a distinctive field of inquiry as early scholars worked on Native American reservations and traveled to distant lands to study small groups of foragers (hunters and gatherers) and cultivators. Traditionally, the process of becoming a cultural anthropologist has required a field experience in another society. Early ethnographers lived in small-scale, relatively isolated societies with simple technologies and economies.

Ethnography thus emerged as a research strategy in societies with greater cultural uniformity and less social differentiation than are found in large, modern, industrial nations (see Moore 2009). Traditionally, ethnographers have tried to understand the whole of a particular culture (or, more realistically, as much as they can, given limitations of time and perception). To pursue this goal, ethnographers adopt a free-ranging strategy for gathering information. In a given society or community, the ethnographer moves from setting to setting, place to place, and subject to subject to discover the totality and interconnectedness of social life. By expanding our knowledge of the range of human diversity, ethnography provides a foundation for generalizations about human behavior and social life. Ethnographers draw on varied techniques to piece together a picture of otherwise alien lifestyles. Anthropologists usually employ several (but rarely all) of the techniques discussed next (see also Bernard 2011).

ETHNOGRAPHIC TECHNIQUES

The characteristic *field techniques* of the ethnographer include the following:

1. Direct, firsthand observation of behavior, including *participant observation.*

2. Conversation with varying degrees of formality, from the daily chitchat that helps maintain rapport and provides knowledge about what is going on, to prolonged *interviews,* which can be unstructured or structured.

3. The *genealogical method.*

4. Detailed work with *key consultants,* or *informants,* about particular areas of community life.

5. In-depth interviewing, often leading to the collection of *life histories* of particular people (narrators).

6. Discovery of local (native) beliefs and perceptions, which may be compared with the ethnographer's own observations and conclusions.

7. Problem-oriented research of many sorts.

8. Longitudinal research—the continuous long-term study of an area or site.

9. Team research—coordinated research by multiple ethnographers.

Observation and Participant Observation

Ethnographers must pay attention to hundreds of details of daily life, seasonal events, and unusual happenings. They should record what they see as they see it. Things never again will seem quite as strange as they do during the first few weeks in the field. Often anthropologists experience culture shock—a creepy and profound feeling of alienation—on arrival at a new field site. Although anthropologists study human diversity, the actual field experience of diversity takes some getting used to, as we see in this chapter's "Appreciating Diversity." The ethnographer eventually grows accustomed to, and accepts as normal, cultural patterns that initially were alien. Staying a bit more than a year in the field allows the ethnographer to repeat the season of his or her arrival, when certain events and processes may have been missed because of initial unfamiliarity and culture shock.

Many ethnographers record their impressions in a personal *diary,* which is kept separate from more formal *field notes.* Later, this record of early impressions will help point out some of the most basic aspects of cultural diversity. Such aspects include distinctive smells, noises people make, how they cover their mouths when they eat, and how they gaze at others. These patterns, which are so basic as to seem almost trivial, are part of what Bronislaw Malinowski called "the imponderabilia of native life and of typical behavior" (Malinowski 1922/1961, p. 20). These aspects of culture are so fundamental that natives take them for granted. They are too basic even to talk about, but the unaccustomed eye of the fledgling ethnographer picks them up. Thereafter, becoming familiar, they fade to the edge of consciousness. I mention my initial impressions of some such imponderabilia of northeastern Brazilian culture in this chapter's "Appreciating Diversity." Initial impressions are valuable and should be recorded.

Ethnographers strive to establish *rapport,* a good, friendly working relationship based on personal contact, with their hosts. One of ethnography's most characteristic procedures is participant observation, which means that we take part in community life as we study it. As human beings living among others, we cannot be totally impartial and detached observers. We take part in many events and processes we are observing and trying to comprehend. By participating, we may learn why people find such events meaningful, as we see how they are organized and conducted.

Even Anthropologists Get Culture Shock

My first field experience in Arembepe (Brazil) took place between my junior and senior years at New York City's Columbia College, where I was majoring in anthropology. I went to Arembepe as a participant in a now defunct program designed to provide undergraduates with experience doing ethnography—firsthand study of an alien society's culture and social life.

Brought up in one culture, intensely curious about others, anthropologists nevertheless experience culture shock, particularly on their first field trip. Culture shock refers to the whole set of feelings about being in an alien setting, and the ensuing reactions. It is a chilly, creepy feeling of alienation, of being without some of the most ordinary, trivial (and therefore basic) cues of one's culture of origin.

As I planned my departure for Brazil that year, I could not know just how naked I would feel without the cloak of my own language and culture. My sojourn in Arembepe would be my first trip outside the United States. I was an urban boy who had grown up in Atlanta, Georgia, and New York City. I had little experience with rural life in my own country, none with Latin America, and I had received only minimal training in the Portuguese language.

New York City direct to Salvador, Bahia, Brazil. Just a brief stopover in Rio de Janeiro; a longer visit would be a reward at the end of fieldwork.

As our prop jet approached tropical Salvador, I couldn't believe the whiteness of the sand. "That's not snow, is it?" I remarked to a fellow field team member....

My first impressions of Bahia were of smells— alien odors of ripe and decaying mangoes, bananas, and passion fruit—and of swatting the ubiquitous fruit flies I had never seen before,

although I had read extensively about their reproductive behavior in genetics classes. There were strange concoctions of rice, black beans, and gelatinous gobs of unidentifiable meats and floating pieces of skin. Coffee was strong and sugar crude, and every tabletop had containers for toothpicks and for manioc (cassava) flour to sprinkle, like Parmesan cheese, on anything one

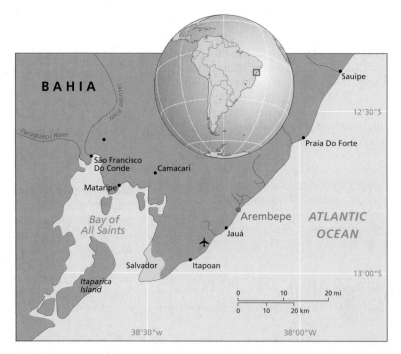

FIGURE 13.1 Location of Arembepe, Bahia, Brazil.

In Arembepe, Brazil, I learned about fishing by sailing on the Atlantic with local fishers. I gave Jeep rides to malnourished babies, to pregnant mothers, and once to a teenage girl possessed by a spirit. All those people needed to consult specialists outside the village. I danced on Arembepe's festive occasions, drank libations commemorating new births, and became a godfather to a village girl. Most anthropologists have similar field experiences. The common humanity of the student and the studied, the ethnographer and the research community, makes participant observation inevitable.

Conversation, Interviewing, and Interview Schedules

Participating in local life means that ethnographers constantly talk to people and ask questions. As their knowledge of the local language and culture increases, they understand more. There are several stages in learning a field language. First is the naming phase—asking name after name of the objects around us. Later we are able to pose more complex questions and understand the replies. We begin to understand simple conversations between two villagers. If our language expertise proceeds far enough,

might eat. I remember oatmeal soup and a slimy stew of beef tongue in tomatoes. At one meal a disintegrating fish head, eyes still attached, but barely, stared up at me as the rest of its body floated in a bowl of bright orange palm oil. . . .

I only vaguely remember my first day in Arembepe (Figure 13.1). Unlike ethnographers who have studied remote tribes in the tropical forests of interior South America or the highlands of Papua New Guinea, I did not have to hike or ride a canoe for days to arrive at my field site. Arembepe was not isolated relative to such places, only relative to every other place I had ever been. . . .

I do recall what happened when we arrived. There was no formal road into the village. Entering through southern Arembepe, vehicles simply threaded their way around coconut trees, following tracks left by automobiles that had passed previously. A crowd of children had heard us coming, and they pursued our car through the village streets until we parked in front of our house, near the central square. Our first few days in Arembepe were spent with children following us everywhere. For weeks we had few moments of privacy. Children watched our every move through our living room window. Occasionally one made an incomprehensible remark. Usually they just stood there . . . .

The sounds, sensations, sights, smells, and tastes of life in northeastern Brazil, and in Arembepe, slowly grew familiar. . . . I grew accustomed to this world without Kleenex, in which globs of mucus habitually drooped from the noses of village children whenever a cold passed through Arembepe. A world where, seemingly without effort, women . . . carried 18-liter kerosene cans of water on their heads, where boys sailed kites and sported at catching houseflies in their bare hands, where old women smoked pipes, storekeepers offered cachaça (common rum) at nine in the morning, and men played dominoes on lazy afternoons when there was no fishing. I was visiting a world where human life was oriented toward water—the sea, where men fished, and the lagoon, where women communally washed clothing, dishes, and their own bodies.

Conrad Kottak, with his Brazilian nephew Guilherme Roxo, on a revisit to Arembepe in 2004.

This description is adapted from my ethnographic study *Assault on Paradise: The Globalization of a Little Community in Brazil*, 4th ed. (New York: McGraw-Hill, 2006).

we eventually become able to comprehend rapid-fire public discussions and group conversations.

One data-gathering technique I have used in both Arembepe and Madagascar involves an ethnographic survey that includes an interview schedule. During my second summer of fieldwork in Arembepe, my fellow field-workers and I attempted to complete an interview schedule in each of that community's 160 households. We entered almost every household (fewer than 5 percent refused to participate) to ask a set of questions on a printed form. Our results provided us with a census and basic information about the village. We wrote down the name, age, and gender of each household member. We gathered data on family type, religion, present and previous jobs, income, expenditures, diet, possessions, and many other items on our eight-page form.

Although we were doing a survey, our approach differed from the survey research done by sociologists and other social scientists working in large, industrial nations. That survey research, discussed on pp. 282–283, involves sampling (choosing a small, manageable study group from a larger population). We did not select a partial sample from Arembepe's total population. Instead, we tried to interview in all households (i.e., to have a total sample). We used an

interview schedule
Form (guide) used to structure a formal, but personal, interview.

questionnaire
Form used by sociologists to obtain comparable information from respondents.

genealogical method
Using diagrams and symbols to record kin connections.

key cultural consultant
Expert on a particular aspect of local life.

life history
Of a key consultant; a personal portrait of someone's life in a culture.

interview schedule rather than a questionnaire. With the **interview schedule,** the ethnographer talks face-to-face with people, asks the questions, and writes down the answers. **Questionnaire** procedures tend to be more indirect and impersonal; often the respondent fills in the form.

Our goal of getting a total sample allowed us to meet almost everyone in the village and helped us establish rapport. Decades later, Arembepeiros still talk warmly about how we were interested enough in them to visit their homes and ask them questions. We stood in sharp contrast to the other outsiders the villagers had known, who considered them too poor and backward to be taken seriously.

Like other survey research, however, our interview schedule did gather comparable quantifiable information. It gave us a basis for assessing patterns and exceptions in village life. Our schedules included a core set of questions that were posed to everyone. However, some interesting side issues often came up during the interview, which we would pursue then or later. We followed such leads into many dimensions of village life. One woman, for instance, a midwife, became the key cultural consultant we sought out later when we wanted detailed information about local childbirth. Another woman had done an internship in an Afro-Brazilian cult (*candomblé*) in the city. She still went there regularly to study, dance, and get possessed. She became our candomblé expert.

Thus, our interview schedule provided a structure that *directed but did not confine* us as researchers. It enabled our ethnography to be both quantitative and qualitative. The quantitative part consisted of the basic information we gathered and later analyzed

statistically. The qualitative dimension came from our follow-up questions, open-ended discussions, pauses for gossip, and work with key consultants.

The Genealogical Method

As ordinary people, many of us learn about our own ancestry and relatives by tracing our genealogies. Various computer programs and websites now allow us to trace our "family tree" and degrees of relationship. The **genealogical method** is a well-established ethnographic technique. Extended kinship is a prominent building block in the social organization of nonindustrial societies, where people live and work each day with their close kin. Anthropologists need to collect genealogical data to understand current social relations and to reconstruct history. In many nonindustrial societies, links through kinship and marriage form the core of social life. Anthropologists even call such cultures "kin-based societies." Everyone is related and spends most of his or her time with relatives. Rules of behavior associated with particular kin relations are basic to everyday life (see Carsten 2004). Marriage also is crucial in organizing such societies because strategic marriages between villages, tribes, and clans create political alliances.

Key Cultural Consultants

Every community has people who by accident, experience, talent, or training can provide the most complete or useful information about particular aspects of life. These people are **key cultural consultants,** also called *key informants.* In Ivato, the Betsileo village in Madagascar where I spent most of my time, a man named Rakoto was particularly knowledgeable about village history. However, when I asked him to work with me on a genealogy of the fifty to sixty people buried in the village tomb, he called in his cousin Tuesdaysfather, who knew more about that subject. Tuesdaysfather had survived an epidemic of influenza that ravaged Madagascar, along with much of the world, around 1919. Immune to the disease himself, Tuesdaysfather had the grim job of burying his kin as they died. He kept track of everyone buried in the tomb. Tuesdaysfather helped me with the tomb genealogy. Rakoto joined him in telling me personal details about the deceased villagers.

Life Histories

In nonindustrial societies as in our own, individual personalities, interests, and abilities vary. Some villagers prove to be more interested in the ethnographer's work and are more helpful, interesting, and pleasant than others are. Anthropologists develop likes and dislikes in the field as we do at home. Often, when we find someone unusually interesting, we collect his or her **life history.** This recollection of a lifetime of experiences provides a more intimate

Kinship and descent are vital social building blocks in nonindustrial cultures. Without writing, genealogical information may be preserved in material culture, such as this totem pole being raised in Metlakatla, Alaska.

and personal cultural portrait than would be possible otherwise. Life histories, which may be recorded or videotaped for later review and analysis, reveal how specific people perceive, react to, and contribute to changes that affect their lives. Such accounts can illustrate diversity, which exists within any community, since the focus is on how different people interpret and deal with some of the same problems. Many ethnographers include the collection of life histories as an important part of their research strategy.

Local Beliefs and Perceptions, and the Ethnographer's

One goal of ethnography is to discover local (native) views, beliefs, and perceptions, which may be compared with the ethnographer's own observations and conclusions. In the field, ethnographers typically combine two research strategies, the emic (native-oriented) and the etic (scientist-oriented). These terms, derived from linguistics, have been applied to ethnography by various anthropologists. Marvin Harris (1968/2001) popularized the following meanings of the terms: An **emic** approach investigates how local people think. How do they perceive, categorize, and explain things? What are their rules for behavior? What has meaning for them? Operating emically, the ethnographer seeks the "native viewpoint," relying on local people to explain things and to say whether something is significant or not. The term **cultural consultant,** or *informant,* refers to individuals the ethnographer gets to know in the field, the people who teach him or her about their culture, who provide the emic perspective.

The **etic** (scientist-oriented) approach shifts the focus from local observations, categories, explanations, and interpretations to those of the anthropologist. The etic approach realizes that members of a culture often are too involved in what they are doing to interpret their cultures impartially. Operating etically, the ethnographer emphasizes what he or she (the observer) notices and considers important. As a trained scientist, the ethnographer should try to bring an objective and comprehensive viewpoint to the study of other cultures. Of course, the ethnographer, like any other scientist, is also a human being with cultural blinders that prevent complete objectivity. As in other sciences, proper training can reduce, but not totally eliminate, the observer's bias. But anthropologists do have special training to compare behavior in different societies.

What are some examples of emic versus etic perspectives? Consider our holidays. For North Americans, Thanksgiving Day has special significance. In our view (emically) it is a unique cultural celebration that commemorates particular historical themes. But a wider, etic, perspective sees Thanksgiving as just one more example of the postharvest festivals held in many societies. Another example: Local people (including many Americans) may believe

Anthropologists such as Christie Kiefer typically form personal relationships with their cultural consultants, such as this Guatemalan weaver.

that chills and drafts cause colds, which scientists know are caused by germs. In cultures that lack the germ theory of disease, illnesses are emically explained by various causes, ranging from spirits to ancestors to witches. *Illness* refers to a culture's (emic) perception and explanation of bad health, whereas *disease* refers to the scientific (etic) explanation of poor health, involving known pathogens.

Ethnographers typically combine emic and etic strategies in their fieldwork. The statements, perceptions, categories, and opinions of local people help ethnographers understand how cultures work. Local beliefs also are interesting and valuable in themselves. However, people often fail to admit, or even recognize, certain causes and consequences of their behavior. This is as true of North Americans as it is of people in other societies.

Problem-Oriented Ethnography

Although anthropologists are interested in the whole context of human behavior, it is impossible to study everything. Most ethnographers now enter the field with a specific problem to investigate, and they collect data relevant to that problem (see Chiseri-Strater and Sunstein 2007; Murchison 2010). Local people's answers to questions are not the only data source. Anthropologists also gather information on factors such as population density, climate, diet, and land use. Sometimes this involves direct measurement—of rainfall, temperature, fields, yields, dietary quantities, or time allocation (Bailey 1990; Johnson 1978). Often it means that we consult government records or archives.

The information of interest to ethnographers is not limited to what local people can and do tell us. In an increasingly interconnected and complicated

emic
Research strategy focusing on local explanations and meanings.

cultural consultants
People who teach an ethnographer about their culture.

etic
Research strategy emphasizing the ethnographer's explanations and categories.

world, local people lack knowledge about many factors that affect their lives. Our local consultants may be as mystified as we are by the exercise of power from regional, national, and international centers.

Longitudinal Research

Geography limits anthropologists less now than in the past, when it could take months to reach a field site and return visits were rare. New systems of transportation allow anthropologists to widen the area of their research and to return repeatedly. Ethnographic reports now routinely include data from two or more field stays. **Longitudinal research** is the long-term study of a community, region, society, culture, or other unit, usually based on repeated visits.

One example of such research is the longitudinal study of Gwembe District, Zambia (see Figure 13.2). This study, planned in 1956 as a longitudinal project by Elizabeth Colson and Thayer Scudder, continues with Colson, Scudder, and their associates of various nationalities. Thus, as is often the case with longitudinal research, the Gwembe study also illustrates team research—coordinated research by multiple ethnographers (Colson and Scudder 1975; Scudder and Colson 1980). The researchers have studied four villages, in different areas, for over fifty years. Periodic village censuses provide basic data on population, economy, kinship, and religious behavior. Censused people who have moved are traced and interviewed to see how their lives compare with those of people who have stayed in the villages.

A series of different research questions has emerged, while basic data on communities and individuals continue to be collected. The first focus of study was the impact of a large hydroelectric dam, which subjected the Gwembe people to forced resettlement. The dam also spurred road building and other activities that brought the people of Gwembe more closely in touch with the rest of Zambia. In subsequent research Scudder and Colson (1980) examined how education provided access to new opportunities as it also widened a social gap between people with different educational levels. A third study then examined a change in brewing and drinking patterns, including a rise in alcoholism, in relation to changing markets, transportation, and exposure to town values (Colson and Scudder 1988).

Team Research

As mentioned, longitudinal research often is team research. My own field site of Arembepe, Brazil, for example, first entered the world of anthropology as a field-team village in the 1960s. It was one of four sites for the now defunct Columbia-Cornell-Harvard-Illinois Summer Field Studies Program in Anthropology. For at least three years, that program sent a total of about twenty undergraduates annually, the author included, to do brief summer research abroad. We were stationed in rural communities in

living anthropology **VIDEOS**

Adoption into the Canela, www.mhhe.com/kottak

The anthropologist Bill Crocker, as shown in this clip, began studying the Canela Indians of Brazil in 1957. The clip interweaves photos and footage from his various visits to the field. Crocker's research could be longitudinal and continuous because the limitations on travel and communication are much less severe now than they were in the past. Compare the time it took to reach the field in 1957 with the more recent trip shown in the clip. The clip shows that the Canela live in a kin-based society. Crocker gained an entry to Canela society by assuming a kinship status. What was it? Did this status turn out to be a good thing? Why did Crocker hesitate when this connection was first proposed?

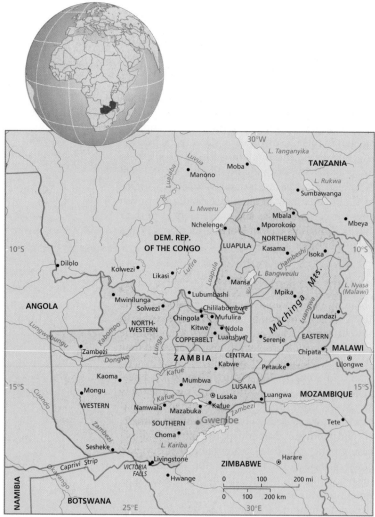

FIGURE 13.2 Location of Gwembe in Zambia.

Janet Dunn, one of many anthropologists who have worked in Arembepe. Her study focused on family planning and female reproductive strategies. Where is Arembepe, and what kinds of research have been done there?

four countries: Brazil, Ecuador, Mexico, and Peru. See this chapter's "Appreciating Diversity" on pp. 276–277 for information on how a novice undergraduate ethnographer perceived Arembepe.

Since my wife, Isabel Wagley Kottak, and I first studied it in the 1960s, Arembepe has become a longitudinal field site. Multiple researchers have monitored various aspects of change and development there. Arembepe, now a small city, illustrates the process of globalization at the local level. Its economy, religion, and social life have been transformed (see Kottak 2006).

Brazilian and American researchers worked with us on team projects during the 1980s (on television's impact) and the 1990s (on ecological awareness and environmental risk perception). Arembepe will be part of a new team project being planned right now. Students from several universities have drawn on our baseline information from the 1960s in studying various topics: standards of physical attractiveness, reproductive strategies, religious change, and dietary responses to globalization. Arembepe has become a site where various field-workers have worked as members of a longitudinal team. The more recent researchers have built on prior contacts and findings to increase knowledge about how local people meet and manage new circumstances.

Culture, Space, and Scale

The previous sections on longitudinal and team research illustrate an important shift in cultural anthropology. Traditional ethnographic research focused on a single community or "culture," which was treated as more or less isolated and unique in

time and space. The shift has been toward recognition of ongoing and inescapable flows of people, technology, images, and information. The study of such flows and linkages is now part of the anthropological analysis. And, reflecting today's world—in which people, images, and information move about as never before—fieldwork must be more flexible and on a larger scale. Ethnography is increasingly multitimed and multisited. Malinowski could focus on Trobriand culture and spend most of his field time in a particular community. Nowadays we cannot afford to ignore, as Malinowski did, the "outsiders" who increasingly impinge on the places we study (e.g., migrants, refugees, terrorists, warriors, tourists, developers). Integral to our analyses now are the external organizations and forces (e.g., governments, businesses, nongovernmental organizations) laying claim to land, people, and resources throughout the world. Also important is increased recognition of power differentials and how they affect cultures, and of the importance of diversity within culture and societies.

The anthropologist Clyde Kluckhohn (1944) saw a key public service role for anthropology. It could provide a "scientific basis for dealing with the crucial dilemma of the world today: how can peoples of different appearance, mutually unintelligible languages, and dissimilar ways of life get along peaceably together." Many anthropologists never would have chosen their profession had they doubted that anthropology had the capacity to enhance human welfare. Because we live in a world full of failed states, war, and terrorism, we must consider the proper role of anthropologists in studying such phenomena. (See the section on ethical issues on pp. 283–285.)

Like many other topics addressed by contemporary anthropology, war and terrorism would require multiple levels of analysis—local, regional, and international. It is virtually impossible in today's world to find local phenomena that are isolated from global forces.

In two volumes of essays edited by Akhil Gupta and James Ferguson (1997a and 1997b), several anthropologists describe problems in trying to locate cultures in bounded spaces. John Durham Peters (1997), for example, notes that, particularly because of the mass media, contemporary people simultaneously experience the local and the global. He describes those people as culturally "bifocal"—both "near-sighted" (seeing local events) and "far-sighted" (seeing images from far away). Given their "bifocality," their interpretations of the local are always influenced by information from outside. Thus, their attitude about a clear blue sky at home is tinged by their knowledge, through weather reports, that a hurricane may be approaching.

The mass media, which anthropologists increasingly study, are oddities in terms of culture and space. What culture or community do they represent? They certainly aren't local. Media images and messages flow electronically. TV brings them right to you. The Internet lets you discover new cultural possibilities at the click of a mouse. The Internet takes us to virtual places, but in truth, the electronic mass media are placeless phenomena, which are global in scope and play a role in forming and maintaining cultural identities.

Anthropological research today may take us traveling along with the people we study, as they move from village to city, cross the border, or migrate internationally. As fieldwork changes, with less and less of a spatially set field, what can we take from traditional ethnography? Gupta and Ferguson correctly cite the "characteristically anthropological emphasis on daily routine and lived experience" (1997*a*, p. 5). The treatment of communities as discrete entities may be a thing of the past. However, "anthropology's traditional attention to the close observation of particular lives in particular places" (Gupta and Ferguson 1997*b*, p. 25) has an enduring importance. The method of close observation helps distinguish cultural anthropology from sociology and survey research, to which we now turn.

SURVEY RESEARCH

As anthropologists work increasingly in large-scale societies, they have developed innovative ways of blending ethnography and survey research (Fricke 1994). Before examining such combinations of field methods, let's consider survey research and the main differences between survey research and ethnography. Working mainly in large, populous nations,

sociologists, political scientists, and economists have developed and refined the **survey research** design, which involves sampling, impersonal data collection, and statistical analysis. Survey research usually draws a **sample** (a manageable study group) from a much larger population. By studying a properly selected and representative sample, social scientists can make accurate inferences, or at least good guesses, about the larger population.

In smaller-scale societies and communities, ethnographers get to know most of the people. Given the greater size and complexity of nations, survey research cannot help being more impersonal. Survey researchers call the people they study *respondents*. These are people who respond to questions during a survey. Sometimes survey researchers interview their respondents directly—in person or by phone. Respondents may be asked to fill out a questionnaire, written or online. A survey may be mailed or e-mailed to randomly selected sample members. In a **random sample,** all members of the population have an equal statistical chance of being chosen for inclusion. A random sample is selected by randomizing procedures, such as tables of random numbers, which are found in many statistics textbooks.

Probably the most familiar example of sampling is the polling used to predict political races. The media hire agencies to estimate outcomes and do exit polls to find out what kinds of people voted for which candidates. During sampling, researchers gather information about age, gender, religion, occupation, income, and political party preference. These characteristics (**variables**—attributes that vary among members of a sample or population) are known to influence political decisions.

Many more variables affect social identities, experiences, and activities in a modern nation than in the small communities where ethnography grew up. In contemporary North America hundreds of factors influence our behavior and attitudes. These social predictors include our religion; the region of the country we grew up in; whether we come from a town, suburb, or city; and our parents' professions, ethnic origins, and income levels.

Ethnography can be used to supplement and fine-tune survey research. Anthropologists can transfer the personal, firsthand techniques of ethnography to virtually any setting that includes human beings. A combination of survey research and ethnography can provide new perspectives on life in **complex societies** (large and populous societies with social stratification and central governments). Preliminary ethnography also can help develop culturally appropriate questions for inclusion in surveys. Recap 13.1 contrasts traditional ethnography with elements of survey research.

In any complex society, many predictor variables (*social indicators*) influence behavior and opinions. Because we must be able to detect, measure, and compare the influence of social indicators, many contemporary anthropological studies have a statistical

On November 1, 2010, in China's Shandong Province, census takers gather personal information from a family during the Sixth National Population Census. From November 1 to November 10, more than six million census takers visited over 400 million households across the country.

ETHNOGRAPHY (TRADITIONAL)	SURVEY RESEARCH
Studies whole, functioning communities	Studies a small sample of a larger population
Usually is based on firsthand fieldwork, during which information is collected after rapport, based on personal contact, is established between researcher and hosts	Often is conducted with little or no personal contact between study subjects and researchers, as interviews are frequently conducted by assistants over the phone or in printed form
Traditionally is interested in all aspects of local life (holistic)	Usually focuses on a small number of variables (e.g., factors that influence voting) rather than on the totality of people's lives
Traditionally has been conducted in nonindustrial, small-scale societies, where people often do not read and write	Normally is carried out in modern nations, where most people are literate, permitting respondents to fill in their own questionnaires
Makes little use of statistics, because the communities being studied tend to be small, with little diversity besides that based on age, gender, and individual personality variation	Depends heavily on statistical analyses to make inferences regarding a large and diverse population, based on data collected from a small subset of that population

foundation. Even in rural fieldwork, anthropologists increasingly use samples, gather quantitative data, and use statistics to interpret them (see Bernard 2011; Bernard 1998). Quantifiable information may permit a more precise assessment of similarities and differences among communities. Statistical analysis can support and round out an ethnographic account of local social life.

However, in the best studies, the hallmark of ethnography remains: Anthropologists enter the community and get to know the people. They participate in local activities, networks, and associations. They watch the effects of national and international policies on local life. The ethnographic method and the emphasis on personal relationships in social research are valuable gifts that cultural anthropology brings to the study of any society.

DOING ANTHROPOLOGY RIGHT AND WRONG: ETHICAL ISSUES

Anthropologists can't study things simply because they happen to be interesting or of value to science. Ethical issues must be considered as well. Working internationally and in the context of cultural diversity, different ethical codes and value systems will meet, and often challenge one another (see Whiteford and Trotter 2008).

Anthropologists must be sensitive to cultural differences and aware of procedures and standards in the host country (the place where the research takes place). Researchers must inform officials and colleagues about the purpose, funding, and likely results, products, and impacts of their research. **Informed consent** should be obtained from anyone who provides information or who might be affected by the research.

Anthropologists should try to (1) include host country colleagues in their research planning, (2) establish collaborative relationships with host country institutions, (3) include host country colleagues in dissemination, including publication, of the research results, and (4) ensure that something is "given back" to the host country. For example, research equipment stays in the host country, or funding is sought for host country colleagues to do research, attend international meetings, or visit foreign institutions.

The Code of Ethics

The Code of Ethics of the American Anthropological Association (AAA) recognizes that anthropologists have obligations to their scholarly field, to the wider society, and to the human species, other species, and the environment. The anthropologist's primary obligation is to *do no harm* to the people being studied. The stated aim of the AAA code is to offer guidelines and to promote discussion and education, rather than to investigate possible misconduct. Some of the code's main points may be reviewed.

Anthropologists should inform all parties affected by their research about its nature, goals, procedures, potential impacts, and source(s) of funding. Researchers should establish proper relationships with the countries and communities where they work. The AAA does not advise anthropologists to avoid taking stands on issues. Indeed, seeking to shape actions and policies may be as ethically justifiable as inaction. The full Code of Ethics can be found on the AAA website http://www.aaanet.org/issues/policy-advocacy/Code-of-Ethics.cfm. Resources to assist anthropologists when dealing with ethical issues are available at the following website: http://www.aaanet.org/committees/ethics/ethics.htm

Informed consent
Agreement to take part in research—after having been informed about its nature, procedures, and possible impacts.

Anthropologists and Terrorism

The AAA has deemed it of "paramount importance" that anthropologists study the roots of terrorism and violence. How should such studies be conducted? What ethical issues might arise?

Consider a Pentagon program, Project Minerva, initiated late in the (George W.) Bush administration, designed to draw on social science expertise in dealing with national security threats. Project Minerva sought scholars to translate original documents captured in Iraq, study China's shift to a more open political system, and explain the resurgence of the Taliban in Afghanistan (Cohen 2008). Project Minerva and related programs have raised serious concerns among anthropologists. Scholars worry that governments will use anthropological knowledge for goals, and in ways, that are ethically problematic. Government policies and military operations have the potential to harm the people anthropologists study.

Social scientists also object to the notion that the military should determine which research projects are worthy of funding. Rather, scholars favor a (peer review) system in which panels of their professional peers (other social scientists) judge the value and propriety of proposed research, including research that might help identify and deter threats to national security. One proposal was to have the National Science Foundation (because of its long experience with social science research), rather than the Pentagon, distribute Minerva money.

Anthropologists have been especially outspoken about the Pentagon's Human Terrain System (HTS)

program. Launched in February 2007, HTS has embedded anthropologists and other social scientists in military teams in Iraq and Afghanistan. The multimillion-dollar project planned to operate as many as twenty-six teams in those countries.

On October 31, 2007, the AAA Executive Board issued a statement of disapproval of HTS—outlining how HTS violates the AAA Code of Ethics. (See http://www.aaanet.org/about/Policies/statements/Human-Terrain-System-Statement.cfm.) The Board noted that HTS places anthropologists, as contractors with the U.S. military, in war zones, where they are charged with collecting cultural and social data for use by the military. The ethical concerns raised by these activities include the following:

1. It may be impossible for anthropologists in war zones to identify themselves as anthropologists, as distinct from military personnel. This constrains their ethical responsibility as anthropologists to disclose who they are and what they are doing.

2. HTS anthropologists are asked to negotiate relations among several groups, including local populations and the military units in which they are embedded. Their responsibilities to their units may conflict with their obligations to the local people they study or consult. This may interfere with the obligation, stipulated in the AAA Code of Ethics, to do no harm.

3. In an active war zone, it is difficult for local people to give informed consent without feeling

In Afghanistan in 2009, an American anthropologist and HTT (Human Terrain Team) member talks with villagers about a tribal dispute. The HTT System is a U.S. Army program that embeds civilian social scientists with combat units to provide the military with sociocultural information. How have anthropologists reacted to the HTT operation?

coerced to provide information. As a result, "voluntary informed consent" (as stipulated by the AAA Code of Ethics, section III, A, 4) is compromised.

4. Information supplied by HTS anthropologists to military field commanders could help target specific groups for military action. Such use of fieldwork-derived information would violate the AAA Code of Ethics stipulation to do no harm to people.

5. The identification of anthropology and anthropologists with the U.S. military may indirectly (through suspicion of guilt by association) endanger the research, and even the personal safety, of other anthropologists and their consultants throughout the world.

What do you think about anthropologists' proper role in studying terrorism and war?

THEORY IN ANTHROPOLOGY OVER TIME

Anthropology has various fathers and mothers. The fathers include Lewis Henry Morgan, Sir Edward Burnett Tylor, Franz Boas, and Bronislaw Malinowski. The mothers include Ruth Benedict and especially Margaret Mead. Some of the fathers might be classified better as grandfathers, since one, Franz Boas, was the intellectual father of Mead and Benedict, and since what is known now as Boasian anthropology arose mainly in opposition to the 19th-century evolutionism of Morgan and Tylor.

My goal in the remainder of this chapter is to survey the major theoretical perspectives that have characterized anthropology since its emergence in the second half of the 19th century (see also Erickson and Murphy 2008; McGee and Warms 2012; Moore 2009). Evolutionary perspectives, especially those associated with Morgan and Tylor, dominated 19th-century anthropology. The early 20th century witnessed various reactions to 19th-century evolutionism. In Great Britain, functionalists such as Malinowski and Alfred Reginald Radcliffe-Brown abandoned the speculative historicism of the evolutionists in favor of studies of present-day living societies. In the United States, Boas and his followers rejected the search for evolutionary stages in favor of a historical approach that traced borrowing between cultures and the spread of culture traits across geographic areas. Functionalists and Boasians alike saw cultures as integrated and patterned. The functionalists especially viewed societies as systems in which various parts worked together to maintain the whole.

By the mid-20th century, following World War II and the collapse of colonialism, there was a revived interest in change, including new evolutionary approaches. Other anthropologists focused on the symbolic basis of culture, seeking to interpret patterned symbols and meanings. By the 1980s anthropologists had grown more interested in the relation between culture and the individual, and the role of human action (agency) in transforming culture. There also was a resurgence of historical approaches, including those that viewed local cultures in the context of colonialism and the world system. Contemporary anthropology features increasing specialization, based on special topics and identities. Reflecting this specialization, some universities have moved away from the holistic, biocultural view of anthropology that is reflected in this book. However, the Boasian view of anthropology as a four-subfield discipline—including biological, archaeological, cultural, and linguistic anthropology—continues to thrive at many universities as well.

Evolutionism

Both Tylor and Morgan wrote classic books during the 19th century. Tylor (1871/1958) offered a definition of culture and proposed it as a topic that could be studied scientifically. Morgan's influential books included *Ancient Society* (1877/1963), *The League of the Ho-dé-no-sau-nee or Iroquois* (1851/1966), and *Systems of Consanguinity and Affinity of the Human Family* (1870/1997). The first was a key work in cultural evolution. The second was an early ethnography. The third was the first systematic compendium of cross-cultural data on systems of kinship terminology.

Ancient Society is a key example of 19th-century evolutionism applied to society. Morgan assumed that human society had evolved through a series of stages, which he called savagery, barbarism, and civilization. He subdivided savagery and barbarism into

Ernest Smith's 1936 watercolor depicts a bitterly fought game between Native American rivals. The early American anthropologist Lewis Henry Morgan described lacrosse (shown here) as one of the six games played by the tribes of the Iroquois nation, whose League he described in a famous book (1851).

three substages each: lower, middle, and upper savagery and lower, middle, and upper barbarism. In Morgan's scheme, the earliest humans lived in lower savagery, with a subsistence based on fruits and nuts. In middle savagery people started fishing and gained control over fire. The invention of the bow and arrow ushered in upper savagery. Lower barbarism began when humans started making pottery. Middle barbarism in the Old World depended on the domestication of plants and animals, and in the Americas on irrigated agriculture. Iron smelting and the use of iron tools ushered in upper barbarism. Civilization, finally, came about with the invention of writing.

Morgan's brand of evolutionism is known as **unilinear evolutionism,** because he assumed there was one line or path through which all societies evolved. Any society in upper barbarism, for example, had to include in its history, in order, periods of lower, middle, and upper savagery, and then lower and middle barbarism. Stages could not be skipped. Furthermore, Morgan believed that the societies of his time could be placed in the various stages. Some had not advanced beyond upper savagery. Others had made it to middle barbarism, while others had attained civilization.

Critics of Morgan disputed various elements of his scheme, particularly such loaded terms as "savagery" and "barbarism" and the criteria he used for progress. Thus, because Polynesians never developed pottery, they were frozen, in Morgan's scheme, in upper savagery. In fact, in sociopolitical terms, Polynesia was an advanced region, with many complex societies, including the ancient Hawaiian state. We know now, too, that Morgan was wrong in assuming that societies pursued only one evolutionary path. Societies have followed different paths to civilization, based on very different economies.

In his book *Primitive Culture* (1871/1958), Tylor took an evolutionary approach to the anthropology of religion. Like Morgan, Tylor proposed a unilinear path—from animism to polytheism, then monotheism, and finally science. In Tylor's view, religion would retreat as science provided better and better explanations. Both Tylor and Morgan were interested in *survivals*, practices that survived in contemporary society from earlier evolutionary stages. The belief in ghosts today, for example, would represent a survival from the stage of animism—the belief in spiritual beings. Survivals were taken as evidence that a particular society had passed through earlier evolutionary stages.

Morgan is well known also for *The League of the Iroquois*, anthropology's earliest ethnography. It was based on occasional rather than protracted fieldwork. Morgan, although one of anthropology's founders, was not himself a professionally trained anthropologist. He was a lawyer in upper New York State who was fond of visiting a nearby Seneca reservation and learning about their history and customs. The Seneca were one of six Iroquois tribes. Through his fieldwork, and his friendship with Ely Parker (see Chapter 1), an educated Iroquois man, Morgan was

able to describe the social, political, religious, and economic principles of Iroquois life, including the history of their confederation. He laid out the structural principles on which Iroquois society was based. Morgan also used his skills as a lawyer to help the Iroquois in their fight with the Ogden Land Company, which was attempting to seize their lands.

The Boasians
Four-Field Anthropology
Indisputably, Franz Boas is the father of American four-field anthropology. His book *Race, Language, and Culture* (1940/1966) is a collection of essays on those key topics. Boas contributed to cultural, biological, and linguistic anthropology. His biological studies of European immigrants to the United States revealed and measured phenotypical plasticity. The children of immigrants differed physically from their parents not because of genetic change but because they had grown up in a different environment. Boas showed that human biology was plastic. It could be changed by the environment, including cultural forces. Boas and his students worked hard to demonstrate that biology (including race) did not determine culture. In an important book, Ruth Benedict (1940) stressed the idea that people of many races have contributed to major historical advances.

As was mentioned in Chapter 1, the four subfields of anthropology initially formed around interests in Native Americans—their cultures, histories, languages, and physical characteristics. Boas himself studied language and culture among Native Americans, most notably the Kwakiutl of the North Pacific coast of the United States and Canada.

Historical Particularism
Boas and his many influential followers, who studied with him at Columbia University in New York City, took issue with Morgan on many counts. They disputed the criteria he used to define his stages. They disputed the idea of one evolutionary path. They argued that the same cultural result, for example, totemism, could not have a single explanation, because there were many paths to totemism. Their position was one of **historical particularism.** Because the particular histories of totemism in societies A, B, and C had all been different, those forms of totemism had different causes, which made them incomparable. They might seem to be the same, but they were really different because they had different histories. Any cultural form, from totemism to clans, could develop, they believed, for all sorts of reasons. Boasian historical particularism rejected what those scholars called the *comparative method*, which was associated not only with Morgan and Tylor but with any anthropologist interested in cross-cultural comparison. The evolutionists had compared societies in attempting to reconstruct the evolutionary history of *Homo sapiens*. Later anthropologists, such as Émile Durkheim and Claude Lévi-Strauss (see pp. 292–293), also

unilinear evolutionism
Idea (19th century) of a single line or path of cultural development.

historical particularism
Idea (Boas) that histories are not comparable; diverse paths can lead to the same cultural result.

Franz Boas, founder of American four-field anthropology, studied the Kwakwaka' wakw, or Kwakiutl, in British Columbia (BC), Canada. The photo above shows Boas posing for a museum model of a Kwakiutl dancer. The photo on the right is a still from a film by anthropologist Aaron Glass titled *In Search of the Hamat'sa: A Tale of Headhunting* (DER distributor). It shows a real Kwakiutl dancer, Marcus Alfred, performing the same Hamat'sa (or "Cannibal Dance"), which is a vital part of an important Kwakiutl ceremony. The U'mista Cultural Centre in Alert Bay, BC (www. international.gc.ca/culture/arts/ss_umista-en.asp) owns the rights to the video clip of the Hamat'sa featuring Marcus Alfred.

compared societies in attempting to explain cultural phenomena such as totemism. As is demonstrated throughout this text, cross-cultural comparison is alive and well in contemporary anthropology.

Independent Invention versus Diffusion

Remember from the chapter "Culture" that *cultural generalities* are shared by some but not all societies. To explain cultural generalities, such as totemism and the clan, the evolutionists had stressed independent invention: Eventually people in many areas (as they evolved along a preordained evolutionary path) had come up with the same cultural solution to a common problem. Agriculture, for example, was invented several times. The Boasians, while not denying independent invention, stressed the importance of diffusion, or borrowing, among cultures. The analytic units they used to study diffusion were the culture trait, the trait complex, and the culture area. A culture trait was something like a bow and arrow. A trait complex was the hunting pattern that went along with it. A culture area was based on the diffusion of traits and trait complexes across a particular geographic area, such as the Plains, the Southwest, or the North Pacific coast of North America. Such areas usually had environmental boundaries that could limit the spread of culture traits outside that area. For the Boasians, historical particularism and diffusion were complementary. As culture traits diffused, they developed their particular histories as they entered and moved through particular societies. Boasians such as Alfred Kroeber, Clark Wissler, and Melville Herskovits studied the distribution of traits and developed culture area classifications for

Native North America (Wissler and Kroeber) and Africa (Herskovits).

Historical particularism was based on the idea that each element of culture, such as the culture trait or trait complex, had its own distinctive history and that social forms (such as totemism in different societies) that might look similar were far from identical because of their different histories. Historical particularism rejected comparison and generalization in favor of an individuating historical approach. In this rejection, historical particularism stands in contrast to most of the approaches that have followed it.

Functionalism

Another challenge to evolutionism (and to historical particularism) came from Great Britain. *Functionalism* postponed the search for origins (whether through evolution or through diffusion) and instead focused on the role of culture traits and practices in contemporary society. The two main strands of **functionalism** are associated with Alfred Reginald Radcliffe-Brown and Bronislaw Malinowski, a Polish anthropologist who taught mainly in Great Britain.

Malinowski

Both Malinowski and Radcliffe-Brown focused on the present rather than on historical reconstruction. Malinowski did pioneering fieldwork among living people. Usually considered the father of ethnography by virtue of his years of fieldwork in the Trobriand Islands, Malinowski was a functionalist in two senses. In the first, rooted in his ethnography, he believed

functionalism
Approach focusing on the role (function) of sociocultural practices in social systems.

Bronislaw Malinowski (1884–1942), who was born in Poland but spent most of his professional life in England, did fieldwork in the Trobriand Islands from 1914 to 1918. Malinowski is generally considered to be the father of ethnography. Does this photo suggest anything about his relationship with Trobriand villagers?

satisfying those universal biological needs, such as the need for food, sex, shelter, and so on.

Conjectural History

According to Radcliffe-Brown (1962/1965), although history is important, social anthropology could never hope to discover the histories of people without writing. (*Social anthropology* is what cultural anthropology is called in Great Britain.) He trusted neither evolutionary nor diffusionist reconstructions. Viewing all historical statements about nonliterate peoples as merely conjectural, Radcliffe-Brown urged anthropologists to focus on the role that particular practices play in the life of societies today. In a famous essay Radcliffe-Brown (1962/1965) examined the prominent role of the mother's brother among the Ba Thonga of Mozambique. An evolutionist priest previously had explained the special role of the mother's brother in this patrilineal society as a survival from a time when the descent rule had been matrilineal. (In a patrilineal society, people belong to their father's group, whereas in a matrilineal society they belong to their mother's group. The unilinear evolutionists believed all human societies had passed through a matrilineal stage before becoming patrilineal.) Since Radcliffe-Brown believed that the history of Ba Thonga society could only be conjectural, he explained the special role of the mother's brother with reference to the institutions of present rather than past Ba Thonga society. Radcliffe-Brown advocated that social anthropology be a **synchronic** rather than a **diachronic** science, that is, that it study societies as they exist today (synchronic, at one time) rather than across time (diachronic).

Structural Functionalism

The term *structural functionalism* is associated with Radcliffe-Brown and Edward Evan Evans-Pritchard, another prominent British social anthropologist. The latter is famous for many books, including *The Nuer* (1940), an ethnographic classic that laid out very clearly the structural principles that organized Nuer society in what is now South Sudan. According to functionalism and structural functionalism, customs (social practices) function to preserve the social structure. In Radcliffe-Brown's view, the *function* of any practice is what it does to maintain the system of which it is a part. That system has a structure whose parts work or function to maintain the whole. Radcliffe-Brown saw social systems as comparable to anatomical and physiological systems. The function of organs and physiological processes is their role in keeping the body running smoothly. So, too, he thought, did customs, practices, social roles, and behavior function to keep the social system running smoothly.

synchronic
(Studying societies) at one time.

diachronic
(Studying societies) across time.

that all customs and institutions in society were integrated and interrelated, so that if one changed, others would change as well. Each, then, was a *function* of the others. A corollary of this belief was that the ethnography could begin anywhere and eventually get at the rest of the culture. Thus, a study of Trobriand fishing eventually would lead the ethnographer to study the entire economic system, the role of magic and religion, myth, trade, and kinship. The second strand of Malinowski's functionalism is known as *needs functionalism*. Malinowski (1944) believed that humans had a set of universal biological needs, and that customs developed to fulfill those needs. The function of any practice was the role it played in

The University of Manchester was developed by bringing together the Victoria University of Manchester (shown here) and the University of Manchester Institute of Science and Technology. Max Gluckman, one of the founders of anthropology's "Manchester school," taught here from 1949 until his death in 1975.

Dr. Pangloss versus Conflict

Given this suggestion of harmony, some functionalist models have been criticized as Panglossian, after Dr. Pangloss, a character in Voltaire's *Candide* who was fond of proclaiming this "the best of all possible worlds." Panglossian functionalism means a tendency to see things as functioning not just to maintain the system but to do so in the most optimal way possible, so that any deviation from the norm would only damage the system. A group of British social anthropologists working at the University of Manchester, dubbed the Manchester school, are well known for their research in African societies and their departure from a Panglossian view of social harmony. Manchester anthropologists Max Gluckman and Victor Turner made conflict an important part of their analysis, such as when Gluckman wrote about rituals of rebellion. However, the Manchester school did not abandon functionalism totally. Its members examined how rebellion and conflict were regulated and dissipated, thus maintaining the system.

Functionalism Persists

A form of functionalism persists in the widely accepted view that there are social and cultural systems and that their elements, or constituent parts, are functionally related (are functions of each other) so that they covary: when one part changes, others also change. Also enduring is the idea that some elements—often the economic ones—are more important than others are. Few would deny, for example, that significant economic changes, such as the increasing cash employment of women, have led to changes in family and household organization and in related variables such as age at marriage and frequency of divorce. Changes in work and family arrangements then affect other variables, such as frequency of church attendance, which has declined in the United States and Canada.

Configurationalism

Two of Boas's students, Benedict and Mead, developed an approach to culture that has been called **configura-**

tionalism. This is related to functionalism in the sense that culture is seen as integrated. We've seen that the Boasians traced the geographic distribution of culture traits. But Boas recognized that diffusion wasn't automatic. Traits might not spread if they met environmental barriers, or if they were not accepted by a particular culture. There had to be a fit between the culture and the trait diffusing in, and borrowed traits would be indigenized—modified to fit the culture adopting them. Although traits may diffuse in from various directions, Benedict stressed that culture traits—indeed, whole cultures—are uniquely patterned or integrated. Her best-selling book *Patterns of Culture* (1934/1959) described such culture patterns.

Mead also found patterns in the cultures she studied, including Samoa, Bali, and Papua New Guinea. Mead was particularly interested in how cultures varied in their patterns of enculturation. Stressing the plasticity of human nature, she saw culture as a powerful force that created almost endless possibilities. Even among neighboring societies, different enculturation patterns could produce very different personality types and cultural configurations. Mead's best-known—albeit controversial—book is *Coming of Age in Samoa* (1928/1961). Mead traveled to Samoa to study female adolescence there in order to compare it with the same period of life in the United States. Suspicious of biologically determined universals, she assumed that Samoan adolescence would differ from the same period in the United States and that this would affect adult personality. Using her Samoan ethnographic findings, Mead contrasted the apparent sexual freedom there with the repression of adolescent sexuality in the United States. Her findings supported the Boasian view that culture, not biology, determines variation

configurationalism
View of culture as integrated and patterned.

Two U.S. stamps commemorating anthropologists. The 46-cent stamp, issued in 1995, honors Ruth Fulton Benedict (1887–1948), best known for her widely read book *Patterns of Culture.* In 1998, the U.S. Post Office Service issued this 32-cent Margaret Mead (1901–1978) stamp as part of its "Celebrate the Century" commemorative series. The stamp shows a young Dr. Mead against a Samoan background.

Margaret Mead in the field in Bali, Indonesia, in 1957.

in human behavior and personality. Mead's later fieldwork among the Arapesh, Mundugumor, and Tchambuli of New Guinea resulted in *Sex and Temperament in Three Primitive Societies* (1935/1950). That book documented variation in male and female personality traits and behavior across cultures. She offered it as further support for cultural determinism. Like Benedict, Mead was more interested in describing how cultures were uniquely patterned or configured than in explaining how they got to be that way.

Neoevolutionism

cultural materialism
Idea (Harris) that cultural infrastructure determines structure and superstructure.

Around 1950, with the end of World War II and a growing anticolonial movement, anthropologists renewed their interest in culture change and even evolution. The American anthropologists Leslie White

Marvin Harris (1927–2001), chief advocate of the approach known as cultural materialism. Harris taught anthropology at Columbia University and the University of Florida.

and Julian Steward complained that the Boasians had thrown the baby (evolution) out with the bath water (the particular flaws of 19th-century evolutionary schemes). There was a need, the neoevolutionists contended, to reintroduce within the study of culture a powerful concept—evolution itself. This concept, after all, remains basic to biology. Why should it not apply to culture as well?

In his book *The Evolution of Culture* (1959), White claimed to be returning to the same concept of cultural evolution used by Tylor and Morgan, but now better informed by a century of archaeological discoveries and a much larger ethnographic record. White's approach has been called *general evolution*, the idea that over time and through the archaeological, historical, and ethnographic records, we can see the evolution of culture as a whole. For example, human economies have evolved from Paleolithic foraging, through early farming and herding, to intensive forms of agriculture, and to industrialism. Sociopolitically, too, there has been evolution, from bands and tribes to chiefdoms and states. There can be no doubt, White argued, that culture has evolved. But unlike the unilinear evolutionists of the 19th century, White realized that particular cultures might not evolve in the same direction.

Julian Steward, in his influential book *Theory of Culture Change* (1955), proposed a different evolutionary model, which he called *multilinear evolution*. He showed how cultures had evolved along several different lines. For example, he recognized different paths to statehood (e.g., those followed by irrigated versus nonirrigated societies). Steward was also a pioneer in a field of anthropology he called *cultural ecology*, today generally known as *ecological anthropology*, which considers the relationships between cultures and environmental variables.

Unlike Mead and Benedict, who were not interested in causes, White and Steward were. For White, energy capture was the main measure and cause of cultural advance: Cultures advanced in proportion to the amount of energy harnessed per capita per year. In this view, the United States is one of the world's most advanced societies because of all the energy it harnesses and uses. White's formulation is ironic in viewing societies that deplete nature's bounty as being more advanced than those that conserve it.

Steward was equally interested in causality, and he looked to technology and the environment as the main causes of culture change. The environment and the technology available to exploit it were seen as part of what he called the *culture core*—the combination of environmental and economic factors that determined the social order and the configuration of that culture in general.

Cultural Materialism

In proposing **cultural materialism** as a theoretical paradigm, Marvin Harris adapted multilayered models of determinism associated with White and Steward. For Harris (1979/2001) all societies had an *infrastructure*, corresponding to Steward's culture core, consisting of technology, economics, and demography—the systems of production and reproduction without which societies could not survive. Growing out of infrastructure was *structure*—social relations, forms of kinship and descent, patterns of distribution and consumption. The third layer was *superstructure*: religion, ideology, play—aspects of culture farthest away from the meat and bones that enable cultures to survive. Harris's key belief, shared with White, Steward, and Karl Marx, was that in the final analysis infrastructure determines structure and superstructure.

Harris therefore took issue with theorists (he called them "idealists") such as Max Weber who argued for the prominent role of religion (the Protestant ethic, as discussed in the chapter "Religion") in changing society. Weber didn't argue that Protestantism had caused capitalism. He merely contended that individualism and other character traits associated with early Protestantism were especially compatible with capitalism and therefore aided its spread. One could infer from Weber's argument that without Protestantism, the rise and spread of capitalism would have been much slower. Harris probably would counter that given the change in economy, some new religion compatible with the new economy would inevitably appear and spread with that economy, since infrastructure always determines in the final analysis.

Science and Determinism

Harris's influential books include *The Rise of Anthropological Theory* (1968/2001) and *Cultural Materialism: The Struggle for a Science of Culture* (1979/2001). Like most of the anthropologists discussed so far, Harris insisted that anthropology is a *science*; that science is based on explanation, which uncovers relations of cause and effect; and that the role of science is to discover causes, to find determinants. One of White's two influential books was *The Science of Culture* (1949). Malinowski set forth his theory of needs functionalism in a book titled *A Scientific Theory of Culture, and Other Essays* (1944). Mead viewed anthropology as a humanistic science of unique value in understanding and improving the human condition.

Like Harris, White, and Steward, all of whom looked to infrastructural factors as determinants, Mead was a determinist, but of a very different sort. Mead's cultural determinism viewed human nature as more or less a blank slate on which culture could write almost any lesson. Culture was so powerful that it could change drastically the expression of a biological stage—adolescence—in Samoa and the United States. Mead stressed the role of culture rather than economy, environment, or material factors in this difference.

Culture and the Individual
Culturology

Interestingly, Leslie White, the avowed evolutionist and champion of energy as a measure of cultural progress, was, like Mead, a strong advocate of the importance of culture. White saw cultural anthropology as a science, and he named that science *culturology*. Cultural forces, which rested on the unique human capacity for symbolic thought, were so powerful, White believed, that individuals made little difference. White disputed what was then called the "great man theory of history," the idea that particular individuals were responsible for great discoveries and epochal changes. White looked instead to the constellation of cultural forces that produced great individuals. During certain historical periods, such as the Renaissance, conditions were right for the expression of creativity and greatness, and individual genius blossomed. At other times and places, there may have been just as many great minds, but the culture did not encourage their expression. As proof of this theory, White pointed to the simultaneity of discovery. Several times in human history, when culture was ready, people working independently in different places have come up with the same revolutionary idea or achievement at the same time. Examples include the formulation of the theory of evolution through natural selection by Charles Darwin and Alfred Russel Wallace, the independent rediscovery of Mendelian genetics by three separate scientists in 1917, and the independent invention of flight by the Wright brothers in the United States and Santos Dumont in Brazil.

The Superorganic

Much of the history of anthropology has been about the roles and relative prominence of culture and the individual. Like White, the prolific Boasian anthropologist Alfred Kroeber stressed the power of culture. Kroeber (1952/1987) called the cultural realm, whose origin converted an ape into an early hominin, the **superorganic.** The superorganic opened up a new domain of analysis separable from, but comparable in importance to, the organic (life—without which there could be no superorganic) and the inorganic (chemistry and physics—the basis of the organic). Like White (and long before him Tylor, who first proposed a science of culture), Kroeber saw culture as the basis of a new science, which became cultural anthropology. Kroeber (1923) laid out the basis of this science in anthropology's first textbook. He attempted to demonstrate the power of culture over the individual by focusing on the rise and fall of particular styles and fashions, such as those involving women's hem lengths. Kroeber (1944) thought that individuals had little choice but to follow the trends of their times. Unlike White, Steward, and Harris, Kroeber did not attempt to explain cultural forces; he simply used them to show the power of culture over the individual. Like Mead, he was a cultural determinist.

superorganic (Kroeber) The special domain of culture, beyond the organic and inorganic realms.

Durkheim

In France, Émile Durkheim had taken a similar approach, calling for a new social science to be based in what he called, in French, the *conscience collectif.* The usual translation of this as "collective consciousness" does not convey adequately the similarity of this notion to Kroeber's superorganic and White's culturology. This new science, Durkheim proposed, would be based on the study of *social facts,* analytically distinct from the individuals from whose behavior those facts were inferred. Many anthropologists agree with the central premise that the role of the anthropologist is to study something larger than the individual. Psychologists study individuals; anthropologists study individuals as representative of something more. It is those larger systems, which consist of social positions—statuses and roles—and which are perpetuated across the generations through enculturation, that anthropologists should study.

Of course sociologists also study such systems, and Durkheim was a prominent early figure in both anthropology and sociology. Durkheim wrote of religion in Native Australia as readily as of suicide rates in modern societies. As analyzed by Durkheim, suicide rates (1897/1951) and religion (1912/2001) are collective phenomena. Individuals commit suicide for all sorts of reasons, but the variation in rates (which apply only to collectivities) can and should

be linked to social phenomena, such as a sense of anomie, malaise, or alienation at particular times and in particular places.

Symbolic and Interpretive Anthropology

Victor Turner was a colleague of Max Gluckman in the Department of Social Anthropology at the University of Manchester, and thus a member of the Manchester school, previously described, before moving to the United States, where he taught at the University of Chicago and the University of Virginia. Turner wrote several important books and essays on ritual and symbols. His monograph *Schism and Continuity in an African Society* (1957/1996) illustrates the interest in conflict and its resolution previously mentioned as characteristic of the Manchester school. *The Forest of Symbols* (1967) is a collection of essays about symbols and rituals among the Nbembu of Zambia, where Turner did his major fieldwork. In *The Forest of Symbols* Turner examines how symbols and rituals are used to redress, regulate, anticipate, and avoid conflict. He also examines a hierarchy of meanings of symbols, from their social meanings and functions to their internalization within individuals.

Turner recognized links between **symbolic anthropology** (the study of symbols in their social and cultural context), a school he pioneered along with Mary Douglas (1970), and such other fields as social psychology, psychology, and psychoanalysis. The study of symbols is all-important in psychoanalysis, whose founder, Sigmund Freud, also recognized a hierarchy of symbols, from potentially universal ones to those that had meaning for particular individuals and emerged during the analysis and interpretation of their dreams. Turner's symbolic anthropology flourished at the University of Chicago, where another major advocate, David Schneider (1968), developed a symbolic approach to American culture in his book *American Kinship: A Cultural Account* (1968).

Related to symbolic anthropology, and also associated with the University of Chicago (and later with Princeton University), is **interpretive anthropology,** whose main advocate has been Clifford Geertz. As mentioned in the chapter "Culture," Geertz defined culture as ideas based on cultural learning and symbols. During enculturation, individuals internalize a previously established system of meanings and symbols. They use this cultural system to define their world, express their feelings, and make their judgments.

Interpretive anthropology (Geertz 1973, 1983) approaches cultures as texts whose forms and, especially, meanings must be deciphered in particular cultural and historical contexts. Geertz's approach recalls Malinowski's belief that the ethnographer's primary task is "to grasp the native's point of view, his relation to life, to realize *his* vision of *his* world" (1922/1961, p. 25—Malinowski's

symbolic anthropology
The study of symbols in their social and cultural context.

interpretive anthropology
(Geertz) The study of a culture as a system of meaning.

Mary Douglas (1921–2007), a prominent symbolic anthropologist, who taught at University College, London, England; and Northwestern University, Evanston, Illinois. This photo shows her at an awards ceremony celebrating her receipt in 2003 of an honorary degree from Oxford.

(a)

(b)

italics). Since the 1970s, interpretive anthropology has considered the task of describing and interpreting that which is meaningful to natives. Cultures are texts that natives constantly "read" and ethnographers must decipher. According to Geertz (1973), anthropologists may choose anything in a culture that interests or engages them (such as a Balinese cockfight he interprets in a famous essay), fill in details, and elaborate to inform their readers about meanings in that culture. Meanings are carried by public symbolic forms, including words, rituals, and customs.

Structuralism

In anthropology, structuralism mainly is associated with Claude Lévi-Strauss, a renowned and prolific French anthropologist, who died in 2009 at the age of 100. Lévi-Strauss's structuralism evolved over time, from his early interest in the structures of kinship and marriage systems to his later interest in the structure of the human mind. In this latter sense, Lévi-Straussian structuralism (1967) aims not at explaining relations, themes, and connections among aspects of culture but at discovering them.

Structuralism rests on Lévi-Strauss's belief that human minds have certain universal characteristics, which originate in common features of the *Homo sapiens* brain. These common mental structures lead people everywhere to think similarly regardless of their society or cultural background. Among these universal mental characteristics are the need to classify: to impose order on aspects of nature, on people's relation to nature, and on relations between people.

According to Lévi-Strauss, a universal aspect of classification is opposition, or contrast. Although many phenomena are continuous rather than discrete, the mind, because of its need to impose order, treats them as being more different than they are. One of the most common means of classifying is by using binary opposition. Good and evil, white and black, old and young, high and low are oppositions that, according to Lévi-Strauss, reflect the universal human need to convert differences of degree into differences of kind.

Lévi-Strauss applied his assumptions about classification and binary opposition to myths and folk tales. He showed that these narratives have simple building blocks—elementary structures or "my-themes." Examining the myths of different cultures, Lévi-Strauss shows that one tale can be converted into another through a series of simple operations, for example, by doing the following:

1. Converting the positive element of a myth into its negative

2. Reversing the order of the elements

3. Replacing a male hero with a female hero

4. Preserving or repeating certain key elements

Through such operations, two apparently dissimilar myths can be shown to be variations on a common structure—that is, to be transformations of each other. One example is Lévi-Strauss's (1967) analysis of "Cinderella," a widespread tale whose elements vary between neighboring cultures. Through reversals, oppositions, and negations, as the tale is told, retold, diffused, and incorporated within the traditions of successive societies, "Cinderella" becomes "Ash Boy," along with a series of other oppositions (e.g., stepfather versus stepmother) related to the change in gender from female to male.

Processual Approaches

Agency

Structuralism has been faulted for being overly formal and for ignoring social process. We saw in the chapter "Culture" that culture conventionally has been seen as social glue transmitted across the generations, binding people through their common past. More recently, anthropologists have come to see culture as something continually created and reworked in the present. The tendency to view culture as an entity rather than a process is changing. Contemporary anthropologists now emphasize how day-to-day action, practice, or resistance can make and remake culture (Gupta and Ferguson 1997b). **Agency** refers to the actions that individuals take, both alone and in groups, in forming and transforming cultural identities.

agency
The actions of individuals, alone and in groups, that create and transform culture.

Practice Theory

The approach to culture known as *practice theory* (Ortner 1984) recognizes that individuals within a society vary in their motives and intentions and in the amount of power and influence they have. Such contrasts may be associated with gender, age, ethnicity, class, and other social variables. Practice theory focuses on how such varied individuals—through their actions and practices—influence and transform the world they live in. Practice theory appropriately recognizes a reciprocal relation between culture and the individual. Culture shapes how individuals experience and respond to events, but individuals also play an active role in how society functions and changes. Practice theory recognizes both constraints on individuals and the flexibility and changeability of cultures and social systems. Well-known practice theorists include Sherry Ortner, an American anthropologist, and Pierre Bourdieu and Anthony Giddens, French and British social theorists, respectively.

Leach

Some of the germs of practice theory, sometimes also called action theory (Vincent 1990), can be traced to the British anthropologist Edmund Leach, who wrote the influential book *Political Systems of Highland Burma* (1954/1970). Influenced by the Italian social theorist Vilfredo Pareto, Leach focused on how individuals work to achieve power and how their actions can transform society. In the Kachin Hills of Burma, now Myanmar, Leach identified three forms of sociopolitical organization, which he called *gumlao*, *gumsa*, and Shan. Leach made a tremendously important point by taking a regional rather than a local perspective. The Kachins participated in a regional system that included all three forms of organization. Leach showed how they coexist and interact, as forms and possibilities known to everyone, in the same region. He also showed how Kachins creatively use power struggles, for example, to convert *gumlao* into *gumsa* organization, and how they negotiate their own identities within the regional system. Leach brought process into the formal models of structural functionalism. By focusing on power and how individuals get and use it, he showed the creative role of the individual in transforming culture.

World-System Theory and Political Economy

Leach's regional perspective was not all that different from another development at the same time. Julian Steward, discussed previously as a neoevolutionist, joined the faculty of Columbia University in 1946, where he worked with several graduate students, including Eric Wolf and Sidney Mintz. Steward, Mintz, Wolf, and others planned and conducted a team research project in Puerto Rico, described in Steward's volume *The People of Puerto Rico* (1956). This project exemplified a post–World War II turn of anthropology away from "primitive" and nonindustrial societies, assumed to be somewhat isolated and autonomous, to contemporary societies recognized as forged by colonialism and participating fully in the modern world system. The team studied communities in different parts of Puerto Rico. The field sites were chosen to sample major events and adaptations, such as the sugar plantation, in the island's history. The approach emphasized economics, politics, and history.

Wolf and Mintz retained their interest in history throughout their careers. Wolf wrote the modern classic *Europe and the People without History* (1982), which viewed local people, such as Native Americans, in the context of world-system events, such as the fur trade in North America. Wolf focused on how such "people without history"—that is, nonliterate people, those who lacked written histories of their own—participated in and were transformed by the world system and the spread of capitalism. Mintz's *Sweetness and Power* (1985) is another example of historical anthropology focusing on **political economy** (the web of interrelated economic and power relations). Mintz traces the domestication and spread of sugar, its transformative role in England, and its impact on the New World, where it became the basis for slave-based plantation economies in the Caribbean and Brazil. Such works in political economy illustrate a movement of anthropology toward interdisciplinarity, drawing on other academic fields, such as history and sociology. Any world-system approach in anthropology would have to pay attention to sociologist Immanuel Wallerstein's writing (1974, 2004b) on world-system theory, including his model of core, periphery, and semiperiphery, as discussed in the chapter "The World System and Colonialism" in this text. However, world-system approaches in anthropology have been criticized for overstressing the influence of outsiders, and for paying insufficient attention to the transformative actions of "the people without history" themselves. Recap 13.2 summarizes this and other major theoretical perspectives and identifies the key works associated with them.

Culture, History, Power

More recent approaches in historical anthropology, while sharing an interest in power with the world-system theorists, have focused more on local agency, the transformative actions of individuals and groups within colonized societies. Archival work has been prominent in recent historical anthropology, particularly in areas, such as Indonesia, for which colonial and postcolonial archives contain valuable information on relations between colonizers and colonized and the actions of various actors in the colonial context. Studies of culture, history, and power have drawn heavily on the work of European social theorists such as Antonio Gramsci and Michel Foucault.

political economy
The web of interrelated economic and power relations in society.

THEORETICAL APPROACH	KEY AUTHORS AND WORKS
Culture, history, power	Ann Stoler, *Carnal Knowledge and Imperial Power* (2002); Frederick Cooper and Ann Stoler, *Tensions of Empire* (1997)
Crisis of representation/ postmodernism	Jean François Lyotard, *The Postmodern Explained* (1993); George Marcus and Michael Fischer, *Anthropology as Cultural Critique* (1986)
Practice theory	Sherry Ortner, "Theory in Anthropology since the Sixties" (1984); Pierre Bourdieu, *Outline of a Theory of Practice* (1977)
World-system theory/ political economy	Sidney Mintz, *Sweetness and Power* (1985); Eric Wolf, *Europe and the People Without History* (1982)
Feminist anthropology (see the chapter "Gender")	Rayna Reiter, *Toward an Anthropology of Women* (1975); Michelle Rosaldo and Louise Lamphere, *Women, Culture, and Society* (1974)
Cultural materialism	Marvin Harris, *Cultural Materialism* (1979), *Rise of Anthropological Theory* (1968)
Interpretive anthropology	Clifford Geertz, *Interpretation of Cultures* (1973)*
Symbolic anthropology	Mary Douglas, *Purity and Danger* (1970); Victor Turner, *Forest of Symbols* (1967)*
Structuralism	Claude Lévi-Strauss, *Structural Anthropology* (1967)*
Neoevolutionism	Leslie White, *Evolution of Culture* (1959); Julian Steward, *Theory of Culture Change* (1955)
Manchester school and Leach	Victor Turner, *Schism and Continuity in an African Society* (1957); Edmund Leach, *Political Systems of Highland Burma* (1954)
Culturology	Leslie White, *Science of Culture* (1949)*
Configurationalism	Alfred Kroeber, *Configurations of Cultural Growth* (1944); Margaret Mead, *Sex and Temperament in Three Primitive Societies* (1935); Ruth Benedict, *Patterns of Culture* (1934)
Structural functionalism	A. R. Radcliffe-Brown, *Structure and Function in Primitive Society* (1962)*; E. E. Evans-Pritchard, *The Nuer* (1940)
Functionalism	Bronislaw Malinowski, *A Scientific Theory of Culture* (1944)*, *Argonauts of the Western Pacific* (1922)
Historical particularism	Franz Boas, *Race, Language, and Culture* (1940)*
Unilinear evolutionism	Lewis Henry Morgan, *Ancient Society* (1877); Sir Edward Burnett Tylor, *Primitive Culture* (1871)

*Includes essays written at earlier dates.

Gramsci (1971) developed the concept of *hegemony* for a stratified social order in which subordinates comply with domination by internalizing their rulers' values and accepting domination as "natural." Both Pierre Bourdieu (1977) and Foucault (1979) contend that it is easier to dominate people in their minds than to try to control their bodies. Contemporary societies have devised various forms of social control in addition to physical violence. These include techniques of persuading, coercing, and managing people and of monitoring and recording their beliefs, behavior, movements, and contacts. Anthropologists interested in culture, history, and power, such as Ann Stoler (1995, 2002), have examined systems of power, domination, accommodation, and resistance in various contexts, including colonies, postcolonies, and other stratified contexts.

ANTHROPOLOGY TODAY

Early American anthropologists, such as Morgan, Boas, and Kroeber, were interested in, and made contributions to, more than a single subfield. If there has been a single dominant trend in anthropology since the 1960s, it has been one of increasing specialization. During the 1960s, when this author attended graduate school at Columbia University, one had to study and take qualifying exams in all four subfields. This has changed. There are still strong four-field anthropology departments, but many excellent departments lack one or more of the subfields. Four-field departments such as the University of Michigan's still require courses and teaching expertise across the subfields, but graduate students must choose to specialize in a particular subfield and take qualifying exams only in that subfield. In Boasian anthropology, all four subfields shared a single theoretical assumption about human plasticity. Today, following specialization, the theories that guide the subfields differ. Evolutionary paradigms of various sorts still dominate biological anthropology and remain strong in archaeology as well. Within cultural anthropology, it has been decades since evolutionary approaches thrived.

Ethnography, too, has grown more specialized. Cultural anthropologists now head for the field with a specific problem in mind, rather than with the goal of producing a holistic ethnography—a complete account of a given culture—as Morgan and Malinowski intended when they studied, respectively, the Iroquois and the Trobriand Islanders. Boas, Malinowski, and Mead went somewhere and stayed there for a while, studying the local culture. Today "the field" that anthropologists study has expanded—inevitably and appropriately—to include regional and national systems and the movement of people, such as immigrants and diasporas, across national boundaries. Many anthropologists now follow the flows of people, information, finance, and media to multiple sites. Such movement—and the anthropologist's ability to study it—has been made possible by advances in transportation and communication.

Reflecting the trend toward specialization, the AAA (American Anthropological Association) now has all sorts of active and vital subgroups. In its early years, there were just anthropologists within the AAA. Now there are groups based on specialization in biological anthropology, archaeology, and linguistic, cultural, and applied anthropology. The AAA includes dozens of groups formed around particular interests (e.g., psychological anthropology, urban anthropology, culture and agriculture) and identities (e.g., midwestern or southeastern anthropologists, anthropologists in community colleges or small programs). The AAA also includes units representing senior anthropologists, LGBT anthropologists, Latino/a anthropologists, and so on.

Anthropology also has witnessed a crisis in representation, including questions about the ethnographer's impartiality and the validity of ethnographic accounts. Science itself may be challenged, because all scientists come from particular individual and cultural backgrounds that prevent complete and absolute objectivity. What are we to do if we, as I do, continue to share Mead's view of anthropology as a humanistic science of unique value in understanding and improving the human condition? We must try, I think, to stay aware of our biases and our inability totally to escape them. The best scientific choice would seem to be to combine the perpetual goal of objectivity with skepticism about our capacity to achieve it.

acing the COURSE

summary

1. Ethnographic methods include observation, rapport building, participant observation, interviewing, genealogies, work with key consultants, life histories, and longitudinal research. Ethnographers do not systematically manipulate their subjects or conduct experiments. Rather, they work in actual communities and form personal relationships with local people as they study their lives.

2. An interview schedule is a form that an ethnographer completes as he or she visits a series of households. The schedule organizes and guides each interview, ensuring that comparable information is collected from everyone. Key cultural consultants teach about particular areas of local life. Life histories dramatize the fact that culture bearers are individuals. Such case studies document personal experiences with culture and culture change. Genealogical information is particularly useful in societies in which principles of kinship and marriage organize social and political life. Emic approaches focus on native perceptions and explanations. Etic approaches give priority to the ethnographer's own observations and conclusions. Longitudinal research is the systematic study of an area or site over time. Anthropological research may be done by teams and at multiple sites. Outsiders, flows, linkages, and people in motion are now included in ethnographic analyses.

3. Traditionally, anthropologists worked in small-scale societies; sociologists, in modern nations. Different techniques were developed to study such different kinds of societies. Social scientists working in complex societies use survey research to sample variation.

Anthropologists do their fieldwork in communities and study the totality of social life. Sociologists study samples to make inferences about a larger population. The diversity of social life in modern nations and cities requires social survey procedures. However, anthropologists add the intimacy and direct investigation characteristic of ethnography.

4. Because science exists in society, and in the context of law and ethics, anthropologists can't study things simply because they happen to be interesting or of scientific value. Anthropologists have obligations to their scholarly field, to the wider society and culture (including that of the host country), and to the human species, other species, and the environment. The AAA Code of Ethics offers ethical guidelines for anthropologists. Ethical problems often arise when anthropologists work for governments, especially the military.

5. Evolutionary perspectives, especially those of Morgan and Tylor, dominated early anthropology, which emerged during the latter half of the 19th century. The early 20th century witnessed various reactions to 19th-century evolutionism. In the United States, Boas and his followers rejected the search for evolutionary stages in favor of a historical approach that traced borrowing between cultures and the spread of culture traits across geographic areas. In Great Britain, functionalists such as Malinowski and Radcliffe-Brown abandoned conjectural history in favor of studies of present-day living societies. Functionalists and Boasians alike saw cultures as integrated and patterned. The functionalists especially viewed societies as systems in which various parts worked together to maintain the whole. A form of functionalism persists in the widely accepted view that there are social and cultural systems whose constituent parts are functionally related, so that when one part changes, others change as well.

6. In the mid-20th century, following World War II and as colonialism was ending, there was a revived interest in change, including new evolutionary approaches. Some anthropologists developed symbolic and interpretive approaches to uncover patterned symbols and meanings within cultures. By the 1980s, anthropologists had grown more interested in the relation between culture and the individual, and the role of human action (agency) in transforming culture. There also was a resurgence of historical approaches, including those that viewed local cultures in relation to colonialism and the world system.

7. Contemporary anthropology is marked by increasing specialization, based on special topics and identities. Reflecting this specialization, some universities have moved away from the holistic, biocultural view of anthropology that is reflected in this book. However, this Boasian view of anthropology as a four-subfield discipline—including biological, archaeological, cultural, and linguistic anthropology—continues to thrive at many universities as well.

key terms

agency 293

complex societies 282

configurationalism 289

cultural materialism 290

cultural consultants 279

diachronic 288

emic 279

etic 279

functionalism 287

genealogical method 278

historical particularism 286

informed consent 283

interpretive anthropology 292

interview schedule 278

key cultural consultant 278

life history 278

longitudinal research 280

political economy 294

questionnaire 278

random sample 282

sample 282

superorganic 291

survey research 282

symbolic anthropology 292

synchronic 288

unilinear evolutionism 286

variables 282

test yourself

MULTIPLE CHOICE

1. Which of the following statements about ethnography is *not* true?
   a. It may involve participant observation and survey research.
   b. Bronislaw Malinowski was one of its earliest influential practitioners.
   c. It was traditionally practiced in non-Western and small-scale societies.
   d. Contemporary anthropologists have rejected it as overly formal and for ignoring social process.
   e. It is anthropology's distinctive strategy.

2. In the field, ethnographers strive to establish rapport,
   a. and if that fails, the next option is to pay people so they will talk about their culture.
   b. which is a timeline that states when every member of the community will be interviewed.

c. which is a respectful and formal working relationship with the political leaders of the community.

d. which is also known as a cultural relativist attitude.

e. which is a good, friendly working relationship based on personal contact.

3. Which influential anthropologist referred to everyday cultural patterns as "the imponderabilia of native life and of typical behavior"?
   a. Franz Boas
   b. Marvin Harris
   c. Clifford Geertz
   d. Bronislaw Malinowski
   e. Margaret Mead

4. Which of the following techniques was developed specifically because of the importance of kinship and marriage relationships in nonindustrial societies?
   a. the life history
   b. participant observation
   c. the interview schedule
   d. network analysis
   e. the genealogical method

5. Which of the following is a significant change in the history of ethnography?
   a. Larger numbers of ethnographies are being done about people in Western, industrialized nations.
   b. Ethnographers now use only quantitative techniques.
   c. Ethnographers have begun to work for colonial governments.
   d. Ethnographers have stopped using the standard four-member format, because it disturbs the informants.
   e. There are now fewer native ethnographers.

6. All of the following are true about ethnography *except* this statement:
   a. It traditionally studies entire communities.
   b. It usually focuses on a small number of variables within a sample population.
   c. It is based on firsthand fieldwork.
   d. It is more personal than survey research.
   e. It traditionally has been conducted in nonindustrial, small-scale societies.

7. Which of the following is one of the advantages an interview schedule has over a questionnaire-based survey?
   a. Interview schedules rely on very short responses, and therefore are more useful when you have less time.

b. Questionnaires are completely unstructured, so your informants might deviate from the subject you want them to talk about.

c. Interview schedules give informants more of a chance to bring up things *they* see as important.

d. Interview schedules are better suited to urban, complex societies where most people can read.

e. Questionnaires are emic, and interview schedules are etic.

8. Reflecting today's world in which people, images, and information move as never before, ethnography is
   a. becoming increasingly difficult for anthropologists concerned with salvaging isolated and untouched cultures around the world.
   b. becoming less useful and valuable to understanding culture.
   c. becoming more traditional, returning to evolutionary models first proposed during the 19th century.
   d. requiring that researchers stay in the same site for over three years.
   e. increasingly multisited and multitimed, integrating analyses of external organizations and forces to understand local phenomena.

9. All of the following are true about anthropology's four-field approach *except* this statement:
   a. Boas is the father of four-field American anthropology.
   b. It initially formed around interests in Native Americans—their cultures, histories, languages, and physical characteristics.
   c. There are many strong four-field anthropology departments in the United States, but some respected programs lack one or more of the subfields.
   d. Four-field anthropology has become substantially less historically oriented.
   e. It has rejected the idea of unilinear evolution, which assumed that there was one line or path through which all societies had to evolve.

10. In anthropology, the crisis in representation refers to
    a. the study of symbols in their social and cultural context.
    b. questions about the role of the ethnographer and the nature of ethnographic authority.
    c. Durkheim's critique of symbolic anthropology.
    d. the ethnographic technique that Malinowski developed during his fieldwork in the Trobriand Islands.
    e. the discipline's branding problem that has made it less popular among college students.

FILL IN THE BLANK

1. A _____ is an expert who teaches an ethnographer about a particular aspect of local life.

2. As one of the ethnographer's characteristic field research methods, the _____ method is a technique that focuses on kin connections.

3. A _____ approach studies societies as they exist at one point in time, while a _____ approach studies societies across time.

4. At the beginning of the 20th century, the influential French sociologist _____ proposed a new social science that would be based on the study of _____, analytically distinct from the individuals from whose behavior those facts were inferred.

5. _____, a theoretical approach that aims to discover relations, themes, and connections among aspects of culture, has been faulted for being overly formal and for ignoring social process. Contemporary anthropologists now emphasize how day-to-day action, practice, or resistance can make and remake culture. _____ refers to the actions that individuals take, both alone and in groups, in forming and transforming cultural identities.

CRITICAL THINKING

1. What do you see as the strengths and weaknesses of ethnography compared with survey research? Which provides more accurate data? Might one be better for finding questions, while the other is better for finding answers? Or does it depend on the context of research?

2. In what sense is anthropological research comparative? How have anthropologists approached the issue of comparison? What do they compare (what are their units of analysis)?

3. In your view, is anthropology a science? How have anthropologists historically addressed this question? Should anthropology be a science?

4. Historically, how have anthropologists studied culture? What are some contemporary trends in the study of culture, and how have they changed the way anthropologists carry out their research?

5. Do the theories examined in this chapter relate to ones you have studied in other courses? Which courses and theories? Are those theories more scientific or humanistic, or somewhere in between?

Multiple Choice: 1. (D); 2. (E); 3. (D); 4. (E); 5. (A); 6. (B); 7. (C); 8. (E); 9. (D); 10. (B); **Fill in the Blank:** 1. key cultural consultant; 2. genealogical; 3. synchronic, diachronic; 4. Emile Durkheim, social facts; 5. Structuralism, Agency

Bernard, H. R.
    2011   *Research Methods in Anthropology: Qualitative and Quantitative Methods,* 5th ed. Lanham, MD: AltaMira. Expansion of a classic text on research methods in cultural anthropology.
Chiseri-Strater, E., and B. S. Sunstein
    2007   *Fieldworking: Reading and Writing Research,* 3rd ed. Upper Saddle River, NJ: Prentice Hall. Ways of evaluating and presenting research data.
McGee, R. J., and R. L. Warms
    2012   *Anthropological Theory: An Introductory History,* 5th ed. New York: McGraw-Hill. Compiles classic articles on anthropological theory since the 19th century.
Moore, J. D.
    2009   *Visions of Culture: An Introduction to Anthropological Theory and Theorists,* 3rd ed. Lanham, MD:

AltaMira. Major anthropological theorists examined in the context of the biographical and fieldwork experiences that shaped their theories.
Murchison, J. M.
    2010   *Ethnography Essentials: Designing, Conducting, and Presenting Your Research.* San Francisco: Jossey-Bass. Excellent guide to ethnographic procedures; very useful for undergraduate research.
Whiteford, L. M., and R. T. Trotter II
    2008   *Ethics for Anthropological Research and Practice.* Long Grove, IL: Waveland. Useful guide for ethical work in anthropology.

suggested additional readings

Go to our Online Learning Center website at **www.mhhe.com/kottak** for Internet exercises directly related to the content of this chapter.

internet exercises

14

Language and Communication

What makes language different from other forms of communication?

How do anthropologists and linguists study language in general and specific languages in particular?

How does language change over short and long time periods?

◀ School girls wearing traditional Punjabi attire laugh as they wait to take part in a national celebration in the northern Indian city of Amritsar. Republic Day, celebrated annually on January 26, commemorates the transition of India from a British domination to a republic on January 26, 1950.

understanding OURSELVES

Can you appreciate anything distinctive or unusual in the way you talk? If you're from Canada, Virginia, or Savannah, you may say "oot" instead of "out." A southerner may request a "soft drink" rather than the New Yorker's "soda." How might a "Valley Girl" or "surfer dude" talk? Usually when we pay attention to how we talk, it's because someone comments on our speech. It may be only when students move from one state or region to another that they appreciate how much of a regional accent they have. I moved as a teenager from Atlanta to New York City. Previously I hadn't realized I had a southern accent, but some guardian of linguistic correctness in my new high school did. They put me in a speech class, pointing out linguistic flaws I never knew I had. One was my "dull s," particularly in terminal consonant clusters, as in the words "tusks" and "breakfasts." Apparently I didn't pronounce all three consonants at the ends of those words. Later it occurred to me that these weren't words I used very often. As far as I know, I've never conversed about tusks or proclaimed "I ate seven breakfasts last week."

Unlike grammarians, linguists and anthropologists are interested in what people do say, rather than what they should say. Speech differences are associated with, and tell us a lot about, social variation, such as region, education, ethnic background, and gender. Men and women talk differently. I'm sure you can think of examples based on your own experience, although you probably never realized that women tend to peripheralize their vowels (think of "aiiee"), whereas men tend to centralize them (think of "uh" and "ugh"). Men are more likely to speak "ungrammatically" than women are. Men and women also show differences in their sports and color terminologies. Men typically know more terms related to sports, make more distinctions among them (e.g., "runs" versus "points"), and try to use the terms more precisely than women do. Correspondingly, influenced more by the fashion and cosmetics industries than men are, women use more color terms and attempt to use them more specifically than men do. To make this point when I lecture, I bring an off-purple shirt to class. Holding it up, I first ask women to say aloud what color the shirt is. The women rarely answer with a uniform voice, as they try to distinguish the actual shade (mauve, lilac, lavender, wisteria, or some other purplish hue). I then ask the men, who consistently answer as one, "PURPLE." Rare is the man who on the spur of the moment can imagine the difference between fuchsia and magenta or grape and aubergine.

WHAT IS LANGUAGE?

Language, which may be spoken (*speech*) or written (*writing*), is our primary means of communication. Writing has existed for about 6,000 years. Language originated thousands of years before that, but no one can say exactly when. Like culture in general, of which language is a part, language is transmitted through learning, as part of enculturation. Language is based on arbitrary, learned associations between words and the things for which they stand. The complexity of language—absent in the communication systems of other animals—allows humans to conjure up elaborate images, to discuss the past and the future, to share our experiences with others, and to benefit from their experiences.

Anthropologists study language in its social and cultural context. Linguistic anthropology illustrates anthropology's characteristic interest in comparison, variation, and change (see Bonvillain 2012; Salzmann, Stanlaw, and Adachi 2011). A key feature of language is that it is always changing. Some linguistic anthropologists reconstruct ancient languages by comparing their contemporary descendants and in so doing make discoveries about history. Others study linguistic differences to discover the varied worldviews and patterns of thought in a multitude of cultures. Sociolinguists examine linguistic diversity in nation-states, ranging from multilingualism to the varied dialects and styles used in a single language, to show how speech reflects social differences (Fasold and Connor-Linton 2006; Labov 1972a, 2006). Linguistic anthropologists also explore the role of language in colonization and in the expansion of the world economy (Geis 1987; Trudgill 2010).

NONHUMAN PRIMATE COMMUNICATION

Call Systems

Only humans speak. No other animal has anything approaching the complexity of language. The natural communication systems of other primates (monkeys and apes) are **call systems.** These vocal systems consist of a limited number of sounds—*calls*—that are produced only when particular environmental stimuli are encountered. Such calls may be varied in intensity and duration, but they are much less flexible than language because they are automatic and can't be combined. When primates encounter food and danger simultaneously, they can make only one call. They can't combine the calls for food and danger into a single utterance, indicating that both are present. At some point in human evolution, however, our ancestors began to combine calls and to understand the combinations. The number of calls also expanded, eventually becoming too great to be transmitted even partly through the genes. Communication came to rely almost totally on learning.

Although wild primates use call systems, the vocal tract of apes is not suitable for speech. Until the 1960s, attempts to teach spoken language to apes suggested that they lack linguistic abilities. In the 1950s, a couple raised a chimpanzee, Viki, as a member of their family and systematically tried to teach her to speak. However, Viki learned only four words ("mama," "papa," "up," and "cup").

Sign Language

More recent experiments have shown that apes can learn to use, if not speak, true language. Several apes have learned to converse with people through means other than speech. One such communica-

Apes, such as these Congo chimpanzees, use call systems to communicate in the wild. Their vocal systems consist of a limited number of sounds—*calls*—that are produced only when particular environmental stimuli are encountered.

tion system is American Sign Language, or ASL, which is widely used by hearing-impaired Americans. ASL employs a limited number of basic gesture units that are analogous to sounds in spoken language. These units combine to form words and larger units of meaning.

The first chimpanzee to learn ASL was Washoe, a female who died in 2007 at the age of 42. Captured in West Africa, Washoe was acquired by R. Allen Gardner and Beatrice Gardner, scientists at the University of Nevada in Reno, in 1966, when she was a year old. Four years later, she moved to Norman, Oklahoma, to a converted farm that had become the Institute for Primate Studies. Washoe revolutionized the discussion of the language-learning abilities of apes (Carey 2007). At first she lived in a trailer and heard no spoken language. The researchers always used ASL to communicate with each other in her presence. The chimp gradually acquired a vocabulary of more than 100 signs representing English words (Gardner, Gardner, and Van Cantfort 1989). At the age of two, Washoe began to combine as many as five signs into rudimentary sentences such as "you, me, go out, hurry."

The second chimp to learn ASL was Lucy, Washoe's junior by one year. Lucy died, or was murdered by poachers, in 1986, after having been introduced

language
Primary means of human communication, spoken and written.

call systems
Communication systems of nonhuman primates.

to "the wild" in Africa in 1979 (Carter 1988). From her second day of life until her move to Africa, Lucy lived with a family in Norman, Oklahoma. Roger Fouts, a researcher from the nearby Institute for Primate Studies, came two days a week to test and improve Lucy's knowledge of ASL. During the rest of the week, Lucy used ASL to converse with her foster parents. After acquiring language, Washoe and Lucy exhibited several human traits: swearing, joking, telling lies, and trying to teach language to others (Fouts 1997).

When irritated, Washoe called her monkey neighbors at the institute "dirty monkeys." Lucy insulted her "dirty cat." On arrival at Lucy's place, Fouts once found a pile of excrement on the floor. When he asked the chimp what it was, she replied, "dirty, dirty," her expression for feces. Asked whose "dirty, dirty" it was, Lucy named Fouts's coworker, Sue. When Fouts refused to believe her about Sue, the chimp blamed the excrement on Fouts himself.

Cultural transmission of a communication system through learning is a fundamental attribute of language. Washoe, Lucy, and other chimps have tried to teach ASL to other animals. Washoe taught gestures to other institute chimps, including her son Sequoia, who died in infancy (Fouts, Fouts, and Van Cantfort 1989).

Because of their size and strength as adults, gorillas are less likely subjects than chimps for such experiments. Lean adult male gorillas in the wild weigh 400 pounds (180 kilograms), and full-grown females can easily reach 250 pounds (110 kilograms). Because of this, psychologist Penny Patterson's work with gorillas at Stanford University seems more daring than the chimp experiments. Patterson raised her now full-grown female gorilla, Koko, in a trailer next to a Stanford museum. Koko's vocabulary surpasses that of any chimp. She regularly employs 400 ASL signs and has used about 700 at least once.

Koko and the chimps also show that apes share still another linguistic ability with humans: **productivity.** Speakers routinely use the rules of their language to produce entirely new expressions that are comprehensible to other native speakers. I can, for example, create "baboonlet" to refer to a baboon infant. I do this by analogy with English words in which the suffix -*let* designates the young of a species. Anyone who speaks English immediately understands the meaning of my new word. Koko, Washoe, Lucy, and others have shown that apes also are able to use language productively. Lucy used gestures she already knew to create "drinkfruit" for watermelon. Washoe, seeing a swan for the first time, coined "waterbird." Koko, who knew the gestures for "finger" and "bracelet," formed "finger bracelet" when she was given a ring.

Chimps and gorillas have a rudimentary capacity for language. They may never have invented a meaningful gesture system in the wild. However, given such a system, they can learn and use it. Of course, language use by apes is a product of human intervention and teaching. The experiments mentioned here do not suggest that apes can invent language (nor are human children ever faced with that task). However, young apes have managed to learn the basics of gestural language. They can employ it productively and creatively, although not with the sophistication of human ASL users.

Apes, like humans, also may try to teach their language to others. Lucy, not fully realizing the difference between primate hands and feline paws, once tried to mold her pet cat's paw into ASL signs. Koko taught gestures to Michael, a male gorilla six years her junior.

Apes also have demonstrated linguistic **displacement.** Absent in call systems, this is a key ingredient in language. Normally, a call is tied to a particular environmental stimulus and is uttered only when that stimulus is present. Displacement means that humans can talk about things that are not present. We can discuss the past and future, share our experiences with others, and benefit from theirs.

Patterson has described several examples of Koko's capacity for displacement (Patterson 1978, 1999). The gorilla once expressed sorrow about having bitten Penny three days earlier. Koko has used the sign "later" to postpone doing things she doesn't want to do. Recap 14.1 summarizes the contrasts between language, whether sign or spoken, and the call systems that primates use in the wild.

Certain scholars doubt the linguistic abilities of chimps and gorillas (Hess 2008; Sebeok and

cultural transmission
Transmission through learning, basic to language.

productivity
Creating new expressions that are comprehensible to other speakers.

displacement
Describing things and events that are not present; basic to language.

Kanzi, a male bonobo, identifies an object he has just heard named through headphone speakers. At a young age, Kanzi learned to understand simple human speech and to communicate by using lexigrams, abstract symbols that represent objects and actions. A keyboard of lexigrams is pictured in the background.

HUMAN LANGUAGE	PRIMATE CALL SYSTEMS
Has the capacity to speak of things and events that are not present (displacement)	Are stimuli-dependent; the food call will be made only in the presence of food; it cannot be faked
Has the capacity to generate new expressions by combining other expressions (productivity)	Consist of a limited number of calls that cannot be combined to produce new calls
Is group specific in that all humans have the capacity for language, but each linguistic community has its own language, which is culturally transmitted	Tend to be species specific, with little variation among communities of the same species for each call

Umiker-Sebeok 1980; Terrace 1979). These people contend that Koko and the chimps are comparable to trained circus animals and don't really have linguistic ability. However, in defense of Patterson and the other researchers (Hill 1978; Van Cantfort and Rimpau 1982), only one of their critics has worked with an ape. This was Herbert Terrace, whose experience teaching a chimp sign language lacked the continuity and personal involvement that have contributed so much to Patterson's success with Koko (see Hess 2008).

No one denies the huge difference between human language and gorilla signs. There is a major gap between the ability to write a book or say a prayer and the few hundred gestures employed by a well-trained chimp. Apes aren't people, but they aren't just animals either. Let Koko express it: When asked by a reporter whether she was a person or an animal, Koko chose neither. Instead, she signed "fine animal gorilla" (Patterson 1978).

The Origin of Language

Although the capacity to remember and combine linguistic symbols may be latent in the apes (Miles 1983), human evolution was needed for this seed to flower into language. A mutated gene known as FOXP2 helps explain why humans speak and chimps don't (Paulson 2005). The key role of FOXP2 in speech came to light in a study of a British family, identified only as KE, half of whose members had an inherited, severe deficit in speech (Trivedi 2001). The same variant form of FOXP2 that is found in chimpanzees causes this disorder. Those who have the nonspeech version of the gene cannot make the fine tongue and lip movements that are necessary for clear speech, and their speech is unintelligible—even to other members of the KE family (Trivedi 2001). Chimps have the same (genetic) sequence as the KE family members with the speech deficit. Comparing chimp and human genomes, it appears that the speech-friendly form of FOXP2 took hold in humans around 150,000 years ago. This mutation conferred selective advantages

(linguistic and cultural abilities) that allowed those who had it to spread at the expense of those who did not (Paulson 2005).

Language offered a tremendous adaptive advantage to *Homo sapiens*. Language permits the information stored by a human society to exceed by far that of any nonhuman group. Language is a uniquely effective vehicle for learning. Because we can speak of things we have never experienced, we can anticipate responses before we encounter the stimuli. Adaptation can occur more rapidly in *Homo* than in the other primates because our adaptive means are more flexible.

NONVERBAL COMMUNICATION

Language is our principal means of communicating, but it isn't the only one we use. We communicate when we transmit information about ourselves to others and receive such information from them. Our facial expressions, bodily stances, gestures, and movements, even if unconscious, convey information and are part of our communication styles. Deborah Tannen (1990) discusses differences in the communication styles of American men and women, and her comments go beyond language. She notes that American girls and women tend to look directly at each other when they talk, whereas American boys and men do not. Males are more likely to look straight ahead rather than turn and make eye contact with someone, especially another man, seated beside them. Also, in conversational groups, American men tend to relax and sprawl out. American women may adopt a similar relaxed posture in all-female groups, but when they are with men, they tend to draw in their limbs and adopt a tighter stance.

Kinesics is the study of communication through body movements, stances, gestures, and facial expressions. Related to kinesics is the examination of cultural differences in personal space and displays of affection discussed in the chapter "Culture." Linguists

kinesics
Study of communication through body movements and facial expressions.

How do American men and women differ as they communicate and interact socially? Is this likely to be true cross-culturally? What do you notice about the interactions pictured in this open-air café in Stockholm, Sweden?

affirm; in Madagascar a similar sound is used to deny. Americans point with their fingers; the people of Madagascar point with their lips.

Body movements communicate social differences. In Japan, bowing is a regular part of social interaction, but different bows are used depending on the social status of the people who are interacting. In Madagascar and Polynesia, people of lower status should not hold their heads above those of people of higher status. When one approaches someone older or of higher status, one bends one's knees and lowers one's head as a sign of respect. In Madagascar, one always does this, for politeness, when passing between two people. Although our gestures, facial expressions, and body stances have roots in our primate heritage, and can be seen in the monkeys and the apes, they have not escaped cultural shaping. Language, which is so highly dependent on the use of symbols, is the domain of communication, in which culture plays the strongest role.

pay attention not only to what is said but to how it is said, and to features besides language itself that convey meaning. A speaker's enthusiasm is conveyed not only through words but also through facial expressions, gestures, and other signs of animation. We use gestures, such as a jab of the hand, for emphasis. We use verbal and nonverbal ways of communicating our moods: enthusiasm, sadness, joy, regret. We vary our intonation and the pitch or loudness of our voices. We communicate through strategic pauses, and even by being silent. An effective communication strategy may be to alter pitch, voice level, and grammatical forms, such as declaratives ("I am . . ."), imperatives ("Go forth . . ."), and questions ("Are you . . . ?"). Culture teaches us that certain manners and styles should accompany certain kinds of speech. Our demeanor, verbal and nonverbal, when our favorite team is winning would be out of place at a funeral.

Much of what we communicate is nonverbal and reflects our emotional states and intentions. This can create problems when we use contemporary means of communication such as texting and online messaging. People can use emoticons (☺, ☹, :~/ [confused], :~0 ['hah!' no way!]) and abbreviations (lol—laugh out loud; lmao—laugh my a** off; wtf—what the f**; omg—oh my gosh) to fill in what would otherwise be communicated by tone of voice, laughter, and facial expression (see Baron 2009).

Culture always plays a role in shaping how people communicate. Cross-culturally, nodding does not always mean affirmative, nor does head shaking from side to side always mean negative. Brazilians wag a finger to mean no. Americans say "uh huh" to

THE STRUCTURE OF LANGUAGE

The scientific study of a spoken language (*descriptive linguistics*) involves several interrelated areas of analysis: phonology, morphology, lexicon, and syntax. **Phonology,** the study of speech sounds, considers which sounds are present and significant in a given language. **Morphology** studies how sounds combine to form *morphemes*—words and their meaningful parts. Thus, the word *cats* would be analyzed as containing two morphemes: *cat,* the name for a kind of animal, and *-s,* a morpheme indicating plurality. A language's **lexicon** is a dictionary containing all its morphemes and their meanings. **Syntax** refers to the arrangement and order of words in phrases and sentences. Syntactic questions include whether nouns usually come before or after verbs, and whether adjectives normally precede or follow the nouns they modify. (See this chapter's "Appreciating Anthropology" on p. 318 for more on syntax.)

Speech Sounds

From the movies and TV, and from actually meeting foreigners, we know something about foreign accents and mispronunciations. We know that someone with a marked French accent doesn't pronounce *r* the same way an American does. But at least someone from France can distinguish between "craw" and "claw," which someone from Japan may not be able to do. The difference between *r* and *l* makes a difference in English and in French, but it doesn't in Japanese. In lin-

phonology
Study of a language's phonemics and phonetics.

morphology
(Linguistic) study of morphemes and word construction.

lexicon
Vocabulary; all the morphemes in a language and their meanings.

syntax
Arrangement of words in phrases and sentences.

guistics, we say that the difference between *r* and *l* is *phonemic* in English and French but not in Japanese; that is, *r* and *l* are phonemes in English and French but not in Japanese. A **phoneme** is a sound contrast that makes a difference, that differentiates meaning.

We find the phonemes in a given language by comparing *minimal pairs,* words that resemble each other in all but one sound. The words have totally different meanings, but they differ in just one sound. The contrasting sounds are therefore phonemes in that language. An example in English is the minimal pair *pit/bit.* These two words are distinguished by a single sound contrast between /p/ and /b/ (we enclose phonemes in slashes). Thus /p/ and /b/ are phonemes in English. Another example is the different vowel sounds of *bit* and *beat* (see Figure 14.1). This contrast serves to distinguish these two words and the two vowel phonemes written /I/ and /i/ in English.

Standard (American) English (SE), the "region-free" dialect of TV network newscasters, has about 35 phonemes: at least 11 vowels and 24 consonants. The number of phonemes varies from language to language—from 15 to 60, averaging between 30 and 40. The number of phonemes also varies between dia-

living anthropology **VIDEOS**

Language Acquisition, www.mhhe.com/kottak

This clip focuses on how babies and toddlers acquire language. It shows that language acquisition is a social and cultural process involving interaction with and learning from others. The clip hints at some universals in language acquisition, such as the common use of bilabial kin terms, for example, *mama* and *papa,* for primary caregivers. According to Professor Thomas Roeper, a linguist featured in the clip, children acquire the fundamental structure of their language by the age of two. Based on the clip, who learns lots of words faster, an adult or a two-year-old? Roeper draws an analogy between language acquisition and the growth of a seed sprinkled with water. How does this analogy address the question posed at the start of the clip: Is language inborn or learned?

phoneme
Smallest sound contrast that distinguishes meaning.

lects of a given language. In American English, for example, vowel phonemes vary noticeably from dialect to dialect. Readers should pronounce the words in Figure 14.1, paying attention to (or asking someone else) whether they distinguish each of the vowel sounds. Most Americans don't pronounce them all.

Phonetics is the study of speech sounds in general, what people actually say in various languages. **Phonemics** studies only the *significant* sound contrasts (phonemes) of a given language. In English, like /r/ and /l/ (remember *craw* and *claw*), /b/ and /v/ are also phonemes, occurring in minimal pairs like *bat* and *vat.* In Spanish, however, the contrast between [b] and [v] doesn't distinguish meaning, and they therefore are not phonemes (we enclose sounds that are not phonemic in brackets). Spanish speakers normally use the [b] sound to pronounce words spelled with either *b* or *v.*

In any language, a given phoneme extends over a phonetic range. In English, the phoneme /p/ ignores the phonetic contrast between the [pʰ] in *pin* and the [p] in *spin.* Most English speakers don't even notice that there is a phonetic difference: [pʰ] is aspirated, so that a puff of air follows the [p]; the [p] in *spin* is not. (To see the difference, light a match, hold it in front of your mouth, and watch the flame as you pronounce the two words.) The contrast between [pʰ] and [p] is phonemic in some languages, such as Hindi (spoken in India). That is, there are words whose meaning is distinguished only by the contrast between an aspirated and an unaspirated [p].

Native speakers vary in their pronunciation of certain phonemes. This variation is important in the evolution of language. With no shifts in pronunciation, there can be no linguistic change. The section on sociolinguistics below considers phonetic variation and its relationship to social divisions and the evolution of language.

phonetics
Study of speech sounds—what people actually say.

phonemics
Study of sound contrasts (phonemes) in a language.

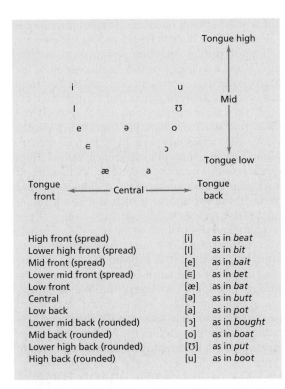

FIGURE 14.1 Vowel Phonemes in Standard American English.

The phonemes are shown according to height of tongue and tongue position at front, center, or back of mouth. Phonetic symbols are identified by English words that include them; note that most are minimal pairs.

SOURCE: Adaptation of excerpt and Figure 2-1 from Dwight Bolinger and Donald A. Sears, *Aspects of Language,* 3rd ed. © 1981 Heinle/Arts & Sciences, a part of Cengage Learning, Inc. Reproduced by permission. www.cengage.com/permissions

High front (spread)	[i]	as in *beat*
Lower high front (spread)	[I]	as in *bit*
Mid front (spread)	[e]	as in *bait*
Lower mid front (spread)	[ɛ]	as in *bet*
Low front	[æ]	as in *bat*
Central	[ə]	as in *butt*
Low back	[a]	as in *pot*
Lower mid back (rounded)	[ɔ]	as in *bought*
Mid back (rounded)	[o]	as in *boat*
Lower high back (rounded)	[ʊ]	as in *put*
High back (rounded)	[u]	as in *boot*

LANGUAGE, THOUGHT, AND CULTURE

The well-known linguist Noam Chomsky (1955) has argued that the human brain contains a limited set of rules for organizing language, so that all languages have a common structural basis. (Chomsky calls this set of rules *universal grammar.*) The fact that people can learn foreign languages and that words and ideas can be translated from one language into another tends to support Chomsky's position that all humans have similar linguistic abilities and thought processes. Another line of support comes from creole languages. Such languages develop from pidgins, languages that form in situations of acculturation, when different societies come into contact and must devise a system of communication. As mentioned in the "Culture" chapter, pidgins based on English and native languages developed in the context of trade and colonialism in China, Papua New Guinea, and West Africa. Eventually, after generations of being spoken, pidgins may develop into *creole languages.* These are more mature languages, with developed grammatical rules and native speakers (i.e., people who learn the language as their primary means of communication during enculturation). Creoles are spoken in several Caribbean societies. Gullah, which is spoken by African Americans on coastal islands in South Carolina and Georgia, is a creole language. Supporting the idea that creoles are based on universal grammar is the fact that they all share certain features. Syntactically, all creole languages use particles (e.g., will, was) to form future and past tenses and multiple negation to deny or negate (e.g., he don't got none). Also, all form questions by changing inflection rather than by changing word order. For example, "You're going home for the holidays?" (with a rising tone at the end) rather than "Are you going home for the holidays?"

The Sapir-Whorf Hypothesis

Other linguists and anthropologists take a different approach to the relation between language and thought. Rather than seeking universal linguistic structures and processes, they believe that different languages produce different ways of thinking. This position is sometimes known as the **Sapir-Whorf hypothesis** after Edward Sapir (1931) and his student Benjamin Lee Whorf (1956), its prominent early advocates. Sapir and Whorf argued that the grammatical categories of different languages lead their speakers to think about things in particular ways. For example, the third-person singular pronouns of English (*he, she; him, her; his, hers*) distinguish gender, whereas those of the Palaung, a small tribe in Burma, do not (Burling 1970). Gender exists in English, although a fully developed noun-gender and adjective-agreement system, as in French and other Romance languages (*la belle fille, le beau fils*), does not. The Sapir-Whorf hypothesis therefore might suggest that English speakers can't help paying more attention to differences between males and females than do the Palaung and less than do French or Spanish speakers.

English divides time into past, present, and future. Hopi, a language of the Pueblo region of the Native American Southwest, does not. Rather, Hopi distinguishes between events that exist or have existed (what we use present and past to discuss) and those that don't or don't yet (our future events, along with imaginary and hypothetical events). Whorf argued that this difference causes Hopi speakers to think about time and reality in different ways than English speakers do. A similar example comes from Portuguese, which employs a future subjunctive verb form, introducing a degree of uncertainty into discussions of the future. In English, we routinely use the future tense to talk about something we think will happen. We don't feel the need to qualify "The sun'll come out tomorrow" by adding "if it doesn't go supernova." We don't hesitate to proclaim "I'll see you next year," even when we can't be absolutely sure we will. The Portuguese future subjunctive qualifies the future event, recognizing that the future can't be certain. Our way of expressing the future as certain is so ingrained that we don't even think about it, just as the Hopi don't see the need to distinguish between present and past, both of which are real, while the future remains hypothetical. It would seem, however, that language does not tightly restrict thought, because cultural changes can produce changes in thought and in language, as we shall see in the next section.

Focal Vocabulary

A *lexicon* (or vocabulary) is a language's dictionary, its set of names for things, events, actions, and

Shown here is Leigh Jenkins, who was or is director of cultural preservation for the Hopi tribal council. The Hopi language would not distinguish between *was* and *is* in the previous sentence. For the Hopi, present and past are real and are expressed grammatically in the same way, while the future remains hypothetical and has a different grammatical expression.

qualities. Lexicon influences perception. Thus, Eskimos recognize, and have several distinct words for, types of snow that in English are all called *snow*. Most English speakers never notice the differences between these types of snow and might have trouble seeing them even if someone pointed them out. Similarly, the Nuer of South Sudan have an elaborate vocabulary to describe cattle. Eskimos have several words for snow and Nuer have dozens for cattle because of their particular histories, economies, and environments. When the need arises, English speakers also can elaborate their snow and cattle vocabularies. For example, skiers name varieties of snow with words that are missing from the lexicons of Florida retirees. Similarly, the cattle vocabulary of a Texas rancher is much ampler than that of a salesperson in a New York City department store. Such specialized sets of terms and distinctions that are particularly important to certain groups (those with particular foci of experience or activity) are known as **focal vocabulary.**

Vocabulary is the area of language that changes most readily. New words and distinctions, when needed, appear and spread. For example, who would have texted or e-mailed anything a generation ago? Names for items get simpler as they become common and important. A television has become a *TV,* an automobile a *car,* and a digital video disc a *DVD.*

Olives, but what kinds? Undoubtedly the olive vendor has a more elaborate focal vocabulary for what he sells than you or I do.

Language, culture, and thought are interrelated. However, and in opposition to the Sapir-Whorf hypothesis, it might be more reasonable to say that changes in culture produce changes in language and thought than the reverse. Consider differences between female and male Americans in regard to the color terms they use (Lakoff 2004). Distinctions implied by such terms as *salmon, rust, peach, beige, teal, mauve, cranberry,* and *dusky orange* aren't in the vocabularies of most American men. However, many of them weren't even in American women's lexicons fifty years ago. These changes reflect changes in American economy, society, and culture. Color terms and distinctions have increased with the growth of the fashion and cosmetic industries. A similar contrast (and growth) in Americans' lexicons shows up in football, basketball, and hockey vocabularies. Sports fans, more often males than females, use more terms in reference to, and make more elaborate distinctions between, the games they watch, such as hockey (see Table 14.1). Thus, cultural contrasts and changes affect lexical distinctions (for instance, "peach" versus "salmon") within semantic domains (for instance, color terminology). **Semantics** refers to a language's meaning system.

Meaning

Speakers of particular languages use sets of terms to organize, or categorize, their experiences and perceptions. Linguistic terms and contrasts encode (embody) differences in meaning that people perceive. **Ethnosemantics** studies such classification systems in various languages. Well-studied ethnosemantic *domains* (sets of related things, perceptions, or concepts named in a language) include kinship terminology and color terminology. When we study such domains, we are examining how those people perceive and distinguish between kin relationships or colors. Other such domains include ethnomedicine—the terminology for the causes, symptoms, and cures of disease (Frake 1961); ethnobotany—native classification of plant life (Berlin, Breedlove, and Raven 1974; Carlson and Maffi 2004; Conklin 1954); and ethnoastronomy (Goodenough 1953).

focal vocabulary
Set of words describing particular domains (foci) of experience.

semantics
A language's meaning system.

ethnosemantics
Study of lexical (vocabulary) categories and contrasts.

TABLE 14.1 Focal Vocabulary for Hockey

Insiders have special terms for the major elements of the game.

ELEMENT OF HOCKEY	INSIDERS' TERM
puck	biscuit
goal/net	pipes
penalty box	sin bin
hockey stick	twig
helmet	bucket
space between a goalie's leg pads	five hole

In the first game of the 2011 Stanley Cup playoffs, Pittsburgh Penguins goalie Marc-Andre Fleury makes a save against the Tampa Bay Lightning's Marty St. Louis (26). How might an avid fan describe this photo?

The ways in which people divide up the world—the contrasts they perceive as meaningful or significant—reflect their experiences (see Bicker, Sillitoe, and Pottier 2004). Anthropologists have discovered that certain lexical domains and vocabulary items evolve in a determined order. For example, after studying color terminology in more than 100 languages, Berlin and Kay (1991, 1999) discovered ten basic color terms: *white, black, red, yellow, blue, green, brown, pink, orange,* and *purple* (they evolved in more or less that order). The number of terms varied with cultural complexity. Representing one extreme were Papua New Guinea cultivators and Australian hunters and gatherers, who used only two basic terms, which translate as *black* and *white* or *dark* and *light*. At the other end of the continuum were European and Asian languages with all the color terms. Color terminology was most developed in areas with a history of using dyes and artificial coloring.

style shifts
Varying one's speech in different social contexts.

diglossia
Language with "high" (formal) and "low" (informal, familial) dialects.

SOCIOLINGUISTICS

No language is a uniform system in which everyone talks just like everyone else. Linguistic *performance* (what people actually say) is the concern of sociolinguists. The field of sociolinguistics investigates relationships between social and linguistic variation, or language in its social context (Eckert and Rickford 2001). How do different speakers use a given language? How do linguistic features correlate with social stratification, including class, ethnic, and gender differences (McConnell-Ginet 2010; Tannen 1990; Tannen, ed. 1993)? How is language used to gain, express, reinforce, or resist power (Geis 1987; Mooney 2011; Trudgill 2010)?

Sociolinguists don't deny that the people who speak a given language share knowledge of its basic rules. Such common knowledge is the basis of mutually intelligible communication. However, sociolinguists focus on features that vary systematically with social position and situation. To study variation, sociolinguists must do fieldwork. They must observe, define, and measure variable use of language in real-world situations. To show that linguistic features correlate with social, economic, and political differences, the social attributes of speakers also must be measured and related to speech (Fasold and Connor-Linton 2006; Labov 2006; Trudgill 2000).

Variation within a language at a given time is historic change in progress. The same forces that, working gradually, have produced large-scale linguistic change over the centuries are still at work today. Linguistic change occurs not in a vacuum but in society. When new ways of speaking are associated with social factors, they are imitated, and they spread. In this way, a language changes.

Linguistic Diversity

As an illustration of the linguistic variation that is encountered in all nations, consider the contemporary United States. Ethnic diversity is revealed by the fact that millions of Americans learn first languages other than English. Spanish is the most common. Most of those people eventually become bilinguals, adding English as a second language. In many multilingual (including colonized) nations, people use two languages on different occasions: one in the home, for example, and the other on the job or in public. This chapter's "Appreciating Diversity" focuses on India, a multilingual, formerly colonized, nation. Only about one-tenth of India's population speaks English, the colonial language. In "Appreciating Diversity" we see how even those English speakers appreciate being able to read, and to find Internet content in, their own regional languages.

Whether bilingual or not, we all vary our speech in different contexts; we engage in **style shifts** (see Eckert and Rickford 2001). In certain parts of Europe, people regularly switch dialects. This phenomenon, known as **diglossia,** applies to "high" and "low" variants of the same language, for example, in German and Flemish (spoken in Belgium). People employ the "high" variant at universities and in writing, professions, and the mass media. They use the "low" variant for ordinary conversation with family members and friends.

Just as social situations influence our speech, so do geographic, cultural, and socioeconomic differences. Many dialects coexist in the United States with Standard (American) English (SE). SE itself is a dialect that differs, say, from "BBC English," which is the preferred dialect in Great Britain. According to the principle of *linguistic relativity*, all dialects are equally effective as systems of communication, which is language's main job. Our tendency to think of particular dialects as cruder or more sophisticated than others is a social rather than a linguistic judgment. We rank certain speech patterns as better or worse because we recognize that they are used by groups that we also rank. People who say *dese, dem,* and *dere* instead of *these, them,* and *there* communicate perfectly well with anyone who recognizes that the *d* sound systematically replaces the *th* sound in their speech. However, this form of speech is stigmatized; it has become an indicator of low social rank. We call it, like the use of *ain't,* "uneducated speech." The use of *dem, dese,* and *dere* is one of many phonological differences that Americans recognize and look down on.

Gender Speech Contrasts

Comparing men and women, there are differences in phonology, grammar, and vocabulary as well as in the body stances and movements that accompany speech (Baron 1986; Eckert and McConnell-Ginet 2003; Lakoff 2004; McConnell-Ginet 2010; Tannen 1990). In public contexts, traditional Japanese women tend to adopt an artificially high voice, for the sake of politeness. In North America and Great Britain, women's speech tends to be more similar to the standard dialect than men's speech. Consider the data in Table 14.2, gathered in Detroit. In all social classes, but particularly in the working class, men were more apt to use double negatives (e.g., "I don't want none"). Women tend to be more careful about "uneducated speech." This trend shows up in both the United States and England. Men may adopt working-class speech because they associate it with masculinity. Perhaps women pay more attention to the media, where standard dialects are employed.

According to Robin Lakoff (2004), the use of certain types of words and expressions has been associated with women's traditional lesser power in American society (see also Coates 1986; Tannen 1990). For example, *Oh dear, Oh fudge,* and *Goodness!* are less forceful than *Hell* and *Damn.* Watch the lips of a disgruntled player in a football game. What's the likelihood he's saying "Phooey on you"?

Women are more likely to use such adjectives as *adorable, charming, sweet, cute, lovely,* and *divine* than men are.

Language and Status Position

Honorifics are terms used with people, often by being added to their names, to "honor" them. Such terms may convey or imply a status difference between the speaker and the person being referred to ("the good doctor") or addressed ("Professor Dumbledore"). Although Americans tend to be less formal than other nationalities, American English still has its honorifics. They include such terms as *Mr., Mrs., Ms., Dr., Professor, Dean, Senator, Reverend, Honorable,* and *President.* Often these terms are attached to names, as in "Dr. Wilson," "President Obama," and "Senator McConnell," but some of them can be used to address someone without using his or her name, such as "Dr.," "Mr. President," "Senator," and "Miss." The British have a more developed set of honorifics, corresponding to status distinctions based in class, nobility (e.g., Lord and Lady Trumble), and special recognition (e.g., knighthood—"Sir Elton" or "Dame Maggie").

The Japanese language has several honorifics, some of which convey more respect than others do. The suffix *-sama* (added to a name), showing great respect, is used to address someone of higher social status, such as a lord or a respected teacher. Women can use it to demonstrate love or respect for their husbands. The most common Japanese honorific, *-san,* attached to the last name, is respectful, but less formal than "Mr.," "Mrs.," or "Ms." in American English. Attached to a first name, *-san* denotes more familiarity. The honorific *-dono* shows more respect and is intermediate between *-san* and *-sama.* (*Free Dictionary* 2004; Loveday 1986, 2001).

Kin terms, too, can be associated with gradations in age, rank, and status. *Dad* is a more familiar, less formal kin term than *Father,* but it still shows more respect than would using the father's first name. Outranking their children, parents routinely use their kids' first names, nicknames, or baby names, rather than addressing them as "son" and "daughter." Southerners up to (and sometimes long past) a certain age routinely use "ma'am" and "sir" for older or higher-status women and men.

honorifics
Terms of respect; used to honor people.

TABLE 14.2 Multiple Negation ("I don't want none") According to Gender and Class (in Percentages)

	UPPER MIDDLE CLASS	LOWER MIDDLE CLASS	UPPER WORKING CLASS	LOWER WORKING CLASS
Male	6.3	32.4	40.0	90.1
Female	0.0	1.4	35.6	58.9

SOURCE: Peter Trudgill, *Sociolinguistics: An Introduction to Language and Society,* 4th ed. (London: Penguin Books, 1974, revised editions 1983, 1995, 2000), p. 70. Copyright © Peter Trudgill, 1974, 1983, 1995, 2000. Reproduced by permission of Penguin Books Ltd.

Googling Locally

Despite globalization, linguistic diversity is alive, well, and thriving in many countries, including India, as described here. Despite that nation's colonial history, only about a tenth of the Indian population speaks English. However, even many of those English speakers appreciate being able to read, and to seek out Internet content in, their own regional languages. In this account we see how local entrepreneurs and global companies including Google, Yahoo, and Microsoft are rushing to meet the demand for Web content in local languages. This example illustrates one of the main lessons of applied anthropology, that external inputs, including global brands, fit in best when they are tailored properly to local settings.

Asia already has [three times] as many Internet users as North America. . . . More than half of the search queries on Google come from outside the United States.

The globalization of the Web has inspired entrepreneurs like Ram Prakash Hanumanthappa, an engineer from outside Bangalore, India. Mr. Ram Prakash learned English as a teenager, but he still prefers to express himself to friends and family members in his native Kannada. But using Kannada on the Web involves computer key-

board maps that even Mr. Ram Prakash finds challenging to learn.

So in 2006 he developed Quillpad, an online service for typing in 10 South Asian languages. Users spell out words of local languages phonetically in Roman letters, and Quillpad's predictive engine converts them into local-language script. Bloggers and authors rave about the service, which has attracted interest from the cellphone maker Nokia and the attention of Google Inc., which has since introduced its own transliteration tool.

Mr. Ram Prakash said Western technology companies have misunderstood the linguistic landscape of India, where English is spoken proficiently by only about a tenth of the population and even many college-educated Indians prefer the contours of their native tongues for everyday speech. "You've got to give them an opportunity to express themselves correctly, rather than make a fool out of themselves and forcing them to use English," he said.

Only there is a shortage of non-English content and applications. So, American technology giants are spending hundreds of millions of dollars each year to build and develop foreign-language Web sites and services—before local companies like Quillpad beat them to the punch and the profits. . . .

Nowhere are the obstacles, or the potential rewards, more apparent than in India. . . . Indians may speak one language to their boss, another to their spouse and a third to a parent. In casual speech, words can be drawn from a grab bag of tongues. . . .

Yahoo and Google have introduced more than a dozen services to encourage India's Web users to search, blog, chat and learn in their mother tongues. Microsoft has built its Windows Live bundle of online consumer services in seven Indian languages. Facebook has enlisted hundreds of volunteers to translate its social networking site into Hindi and other regional languages, and Wikipedia now has more entries in Indian local languages than in Korean. Google's search service has lagged behind the local competition in China, and that has made providing locally flavored services a priority for the company in India. Google's initiatives in India are aimed at opening the country's historically slow-growing personal computer market, and at developing expertise that Google will be able to apply to building services for emerging markets worldwide.

"India is a microcosm of the world," said Dr. Prasad Bhaarat Ram, Google India's head of research and development. "Having 22 lan-

Stratification

We use and evaluate speech in the context of *extralinguistic* forces—social, political, and economic. Mainstream Americans evaluate the speech of low-status groups negatively, calling it "uneducated." This is not because these ways of speaking are bad in themselves but because they have come to symbolize low status. Consider variation in the pronunciation of *r*. In some parts of the United States, *r* is regularly pronounced, and in other (*r*less) areas, it is not. Originally, American *r*less speech was modeled on the fashionable speech of England. Because of its prestige, *r*lessness was adopted in many areas and continues as the norm around Boston and in the South.

New Yorkers sought prestige by dropping their *r*'s in the 19th century, after having pronounced them in the 18th. However, contemporary New Yorkers are going back to the 18th-century pattern of pronouncing *r*'s. What matters, and what governs linguistic change, is not the reverberation of a strong midwestern *r* but *social* evaluation, whether *r*'s happen to be "in" or "out."

Studies of *r* pronunciation in New York City have clarified the mechanisms of phonological change. William Labov (1972b) focused on whether *r* was pronounced after vowels in such words as *car, floor, card,* and *fourth.* To get data on how this linguistic variation correlated with social class, he used a series of rapid encounters with employees in three New York City department stores, each of whose prices

guages creates a new level of complexity in which you can't take the same approach that you would if you had one predominant language and applied it 22 times."

Global businesses are spending hundreds of millions of dollars a year working their way down a list of languages into which to translate their Web sites....

English simply will not suffice for connecting with India's growing online market, a lesson already learned by Western television producers and consumer products makers....

Even among the largely English-speaking base of around 50 million Web users in India today, nearly three-quarters prefer to read in a local language, according to a survey by JuxtConsult, an Indian market research company....

A Microsoft initiative, Project Bhasha, coordinates the efforts of Indian academics, local businesses and solo software developers to expand computing in regional languages. The project's Web site, which counts thousands of registered members, refers to language as "one of the main contributors to the digital divide" in India.

The company is also seeing growing demand from Indian government agencies and companies creating online public services in local languages.

"As many of these companies want to push their services into rural India or tier-two towns or smaller towns, then it becomes essential they communicate with their customers in the local language," said Pradeep Parappil, a Microsoft program manager.

"Localization is the key to success in countries like India," said Gopal Krishna, who oversees consumer services at Yahoo India.

SOURCE: Daniel Sorid, "Writing the Web's Future in Numerous Languages." From *The New York Times*, December 31, 2008. © 2008 The New York Times.

Dr. Prasad Ram, former head of Google's technology division in Bangalore, India. Google seeks to expand in regional languages, including Hindi, Gujarati, Tamil, and several others.

and locations attracted a different socioeconomic group. Saks Fifth Avenue (68 encounters) catered to the upper middle class, Macy's (125) attracted middle-class shoppers, and S. Klein's (71) had predominantly lower-middle-class and working-class customers. The class origins of store personnel tended to reflect those of their customers.

Having already determined that a certain department was on the fourth floor, Labov approached ground-floor salespeople and asked where that department was. After the salesperson had answered, "Fourth floor," Labov repeated his "Where?" in order to get a second response. The second reply was more formal and emphatic, the salesperson presumably thinking that Labov hadn't heard or understood the first answer. For each salesperson, therefore, Labov had two samples of /r/ pronunciation in two words.

Labov calculated the percentages of workers who pronounced /r/ at least once during the interview. These were 62 percent at Saks, 51 percent at Macy's, but only 20 percent at S. Klein's. He also found that personnel on upper floors, where he asked "What floor is this?" (and where more expensive items were sold), pronounced /r/ more often than ground-floor salespeople did (see also Labov 2006).

In Labov's study, summarized in Table 14.3, /r/ pronunciation was clearly associated with prestige. Certainly the job interviewers who had hired the salespeople never counted *r*'s before offering employment. However, they did use speech evaluations to make judgments about how effective certain people

Certain dialects are stigmatized, not because of actual linguistic deficiencies, but because of a symbolic association between a certain way of talking and low social status. In this scene from *My Fair Lady*, Professor Henry Higgins (Rex Harrison) encounters Eliza Doolittle (Audrey Hepburn), a Cockney flower girl. Higgins will teach Doolittle how to speak like an English aristocrat.

would be in selling particular kinds of merchandise. In other words, they practiced sociolinguistic discrimination, using linguistic features in deciding who got certain jobs.

Americans have stereotypes about how people from certain regions talk, and some stereotypes are more widespread than others. Most Americans think they can imitate a "Southern accent," and southern speech tends to be devalued outside the South. Americans also stereotype, without necessarily stigmatizing, speech in New York City (the pronunciation of *coffee*, for example), Boston ("I pahked the kah in Hahvahd Yahd"), and Canada ("oot" for "out").

It's sometimes asserted that midwestern Americans don't have accents. This belief stems from the fact that midwestern dialects don't have many stigmatized linguistic variants—speech patterns that people in other regions recognize and look down on,

TABLE 14.3 Pronunciation of *r* in New York City Department Stores

STORE	NUMBER OF ENCOUNTERS	% r PRONUNCIATION
Saks Fifth Avenue	68	62
Macy's	125	51
S. Klein's	71	20

such as *r*lessness and *dem, dese,* and *dere* (instead of *them, these,* and *there*).

Far from having no accents, midwesterners, even in the same high school, exhibit linguistic diversity (see Eckert 1989, 2000). One of the best examples of variable midwestern speech, involving vowels, is pronunciation of the *e* sound (the /e/ phoneme), in such words as *ten, rent, section, lecture, effect, best,* and *test*. In southeastern Michigan, there are four different ways of pronouncing this *e* sound. Speakers of Black English (see below) and immigrants from Appalachia often pronounce *ten* as "tin," just as Southerners habitually do. Some Michiganders say "ten," the correct pronunciation in Standard English. However, two other pronunciations also are common. Instead of "ten," many Michiganders say "tan," or "tun" (as though they were using the word *ton,* a unit of weight).

My students often astound me with their pronunciation. One day I met a Michigan-raised graduate student instructor in the hall. She was deliriously happy. When I asked why, she replied, "I've just had the best suction."

"What?" I said.

She finally spoke more precisely. "I've just had the best saction." She considered this a clearer pronunciation of the word *section*.

In another example of such speech, one of my students lamented, after an exam, that she had not done her "bust on the tust" (i.e., best on the test). The truth is, regional patterns affect the way we all speak.

Our speech habits help determine how others evaluate us and thus our access to employment and other material resources. Because of this, "proper language" itself becomes a strategic resource—and a path to wealth, prestige, and power (Gal 1989; Mooney 2011). Illustrating this, many ethnographers have described the importance of verbal skill and oratory in politics (Beeman 1986; Bloch 1975; Brenneis 1988; Geis 1987). Ronald Reagan, known as a "great communicator," dominated American society in the 1980s as a two-term president. Another twice-elected president, Bill Clinton, despite his southern accent, was known for his verbal skills in certain contexts (e.g., televised debates and town-hall meetings). Communications flaws may have helped doom the presidencies of Gerald Ford, Jimmy Carter, and George Bush (the elder). How do you evaluate the linguistic skills of the current president or prime minister of your country?

The French anthropologist Pierre Bourdieu views linguistic practices as *symbolic capital* that people, if trained properly, can convert into economic and social capital. The value of a dialect—its standing in a "linguistic market"—depends on the extent to which it provides access to desired positions in society. In turn, this reflects its legitimation by formal institutions: educational institutions, state, church, and prestige media. Even people who don't use the prestige dialect accept its authority and correctness, its "symbolic domination"

(Bourdieu 1982, 1984). Thus, linguistic forms, which lack power in themselves, take on the power of the groups they symbolize. The education system, however (defending its own worth), denies linguistic relativity, misrepresenting prestige speech as being inherently better. The linguistic insecurity often felt by lower-class and minority speakers is a result of this symbolic domination.

Black English Vernacular (BEV)

No one pays much attention when someone says "saction" instead of "section." But some nonstandard speech carries more of a stigma. Sometimes stigmatized speech is linked to region, class, or educational background; sometimes it is associated with ethnicity or "race."

The sociolinguist William Labov and several associates, both white and black, have conducted detailed studies of what they call **Black English Vernacular (BEV).** (*Vernacular* means ordinary, casual speech.) BEV is the "relatively uniform dialect spoken by the majority of black youth in most parts of the United States today, especially in the inner city areas of New York, Boston, Detroit, Philadelphia, Washington, Cleveland, . . . and other urban centers. It is also spoken in most rural areas and used in the casual, intimate speech of many adults" (Labov 1972a, p. xiii). This does not imply that all, or even most, African Americans speak BEV.

BEV may be a nonstandard dialect, but it is not an ungrammatical hodgepodge. Rather, BEV is a complex linguistic system with its own rules, which linguists have described. The phonology and syntax of BEV are similar to those of southern dialects. This reflects generations of contact between southern whites and blacks, with mutual influence on each other's speech patterns. Many features that distinguish BEV from SE (Standard English) also show up in southern white speech, but less frequently than in BEV.

Linguists disagree about exactly how BEV originated (Rickford 1997; Rickford and Rickford 2000). Smitherman (1986) calls it an Africanized form of English reflecting both an African heritage and the conditions of servitude, oppression, and life in America. She notes certain structural similarities between West African languages and BEV. African linguistic backgrounds no doubt influenced how early African Americans learned English. Did they restructure English to fit African linguistic patterns? Or did they quickly learn English from whites, with little continuing influence from the African linguistic heritage? Or, possibly, in acquiring English, did African slaves fuse English with African languages to make a pidgin or creole, which influenced the subsequent development of BEV? Creole speech may have been brought to the American colonies by the many slaves who were imported from the Caribbean

"Proper language" is a strategic resource, correlated with wealth, prestige, and power. How is linguistic (and social) stratification illustrated in the photo above, including the handwritten comments below it?

during the 17th and 18th centuries. Some slaves may even have learned, while still in Africa, the pidgins or creoles spoken in West African trading forts (Rickford 1997).

Origins aside, there are phonological and grammatical differences between BEV and SE. One phonological difference is that BEV speakers are less likely to pronounce *r* than SE speakers are. Actually, many SE speakers don't pronounce *r*'s that come right before a consonant (ca*r*d) or at the end of a word (ca*r*). But SE speakers do usually pronounce an *r* that comes right before a vowel, either at the end of a word (fou*r* o'clock) or within a word (Ca*r*ol). BEV speakers, by contrast, are much more likely to omit such intervocalic (between vowels) *r*'s. The result is that speakers of the two dialects have different *homonyms* (words that sound the same but have different meanings). BEV speakers who don't pronounce intervocalic *r*'s have the following homonyms: Carol/Cal; Paris/pass.

Observing different phonological rules, BEV speakers pronounce certain words differently than

Black English Vernacular (BEV)
Rule-governed dialect spoken by some African Americans.

The hip-hop group D12, from Detroit, Michigan, performs at the 2011 V Festival at Weston Park, Staffordshire, UK. Eminem and Rihanna also performed at the same event. What does hip-hop imply about race, gender, and nationality?

Also, phonological rules may lead BEV speakers to omit -*ed* as a past-tense marker and -*s* as a marker of plurality. However, other speech contexts demonstrate that BEV speakers do understand the difference between past and present verbs, and between singular and plural nouns. Confirming this are irregular verbs (e.g., *tell*, *told*) and irregular plurals (e.g., *child*, *children*), in which BEV works the same as SE.

SE is not superior to BEV as a linguistic system, but it does happen to be the prestige dialect—the one used in the mass media, in writing, and in most public and professional contexts. SE is the dialect that has the most "symbolic capital." In areas of Germany where there is diglossia, speakers of Plattdeusch (Low German) learn the High German dialect to communicate appropriately in the national context. Similarly, upwardly mobile BEV-speaking students learn SE.

HISTORICAL LINGUISTICS

Sociolinguists study contemporary variation in speech—language change in progress. **Historical linguistics** deals with longer-term change. Historical linguists can reconstruct many features of past languages by studying contemporary **daughter languages.** These are languages that descend from the same parent language and that have been changing separately for hundreds or even thousands of years. We call the original language from which they diverge the **protolanguage.** Romance languages such as French and Spanish, for example, are daughter languages of Latin, their common protolanguage. German, English, Dutch, and the Scandinavian languages are daughter languages of proto-Germanic. Latin and proto-Germanic were both Indo-European languages (see Figure 14.2). Historical linguists classify languages according to their degree of relationship (see "Appreciating Anthropology" for reconstruction of perhaps the world's oldest protolanguage).

Language changes over time. It evolves—varies, spreads, divides into **subgroups** (languages within a taxonomy of related languages that are most closely related). Dialects of a single parent language become distinct daughter languages, especially if they are isolated from one another. Some of them split, and new "granddaughter" languages develop. If people remain in the ancestral homeland, their speech patterns also change. The evolving speech in the ancestral homeland should be considered a daughter language like the others.

A close relationship between languages does not necessarily mean that their speakers are closely related biologically or culturally, because people can adopt new languages. In the equatorial forests of Africa, "pygmy" hunters have discarded their ancestral languages and now speak those of the cultivators who have migrated to the area. Immigrants to the United States and Canada spoke many different

historical linguistics
Study of languages over time.

daughter languages
Languages sharing a common parent language, e.g., Latin.

protolanguage
Language ancestral to several daughter languages.

subgroups
(Linguistic) closely related languages.

SE speakers do. Particularly in the elementary school context, the homonyms of BEV-speaking students typically differ from those of their SE-speaking teachers. To evaluate reading accuracy, teachers should determine whether students are recognizing the different meanings of such BEV homonyms as *passed*, *past*, and *pass*. Teachers need to make sure students understand what they are reading, which is probably more important than whether they are pronouncing words correctly according to the SE norm.

The phonological contrasts between BEV and SE speakers often have grammatical consequences. One of these involves *copula deletion*, which means the absence of SE forms of the copula—the verb *to be*. SE habitually uses contractions, as in "you're tired" instead of "you are tired." Where SE shortens with contractions, BEV goes one step further and deletes the copular altogether—thus "you tired." BEV's copula deletion is a grammatical result of its phonological rules, which dictate that *r*'s (as in *you're, we're,* and *they're*) and word-final *s*'s (as in *he's*) be dropped. However, BEV speakers do pronounce *m*, so that the BEV first-person singular is "I'm tired," just as in SE. In its deletion of the present tense of the verb *to be,* BEV is similar to many languages, including Russian, Hungarian, and Hebrew.

SE	SE CONTRACTION	BEV
you are tired	you're tired	you tired
he is tired	he's tired	he tired
we are tired	we're tired	we tired
they are tired	they're tired	they tired

FIGURE 14.2 PIE Family Tree.

This is a family tree of the Indo-European languages. All can be traced back to a protolanguage, Proto-Indo-European (PIE), spoken more than 6,000 years ago. PIE split into dialects that eventually evolved into separate languages, which, in turn, evolved into languages such as Latin and proto-Germanic, which are ancestral to dozens of modern daughter languages.

languages on arrival, but their descendants now speak fluent English.

Knowledge of linguistic relationships is often valuable to anthropologists interested in history, particularly events during the past 5,000 years. Cultural features may (or may not) correlate with the distribution of language families. Groups that speak related languages may (or may not) be more culturally similar to each other than they are to groups whose speech derives from different linguistic ancestors. Of course, cultural similarities aren't limited to speakers of related languages. Even groups whose members speak unrelated languages have contact through trade, intermarriage, and warfare. Ideas and inventions diffuse widely among human groups. Many items of vocabulary in contemporary English come from French. Even without written documen-

tation of France's influence after the Norman Conquest of England in 1066, linguistic evidence in contemporary English would reveal a long period of important firsthand contact with France. Similar linguistic evidence may confirm cultural contact and borrowing when written history is lacking. By considering which words have been borrowed, we also can make inferences about the nature of the contact.

Language Loss

One aspect of linguistic history is language loss. When languages disappear, cultural diversity is reduced as well. According to linguist K. David Harrison, "When we lose a language, we lose centuries of thinking about time, seasons, sea creatures, reindeer, edible flowers, mathematics, landscapes, myths, music, the unknown

Linguists Ancient Syntax Discover

The study described here has determined the likely syntax of the remote proto-language, spoken perhaps 50,000 years ago in East Africa, that is ancestral to all contemporary languages. The study examined word order, how subject (S), object (O), and verb (V) are arranged in phrases and sentences in 2,000 languages. English uses SVO (I like you), which derives from SOV (I you like), the most common word order, and, the authors contend, the oldest.

Many linguists believe all human languages derived from a single tongue spoken in East Africa around 50,000 years ago. They've found clues scattered throughout the vocabularies and grammars of the world as to how that original "proto-human language" might have sounded. New research suggests that it sounded somewhat like the speech of Yoda, the tiny green Jedi from "Star Wars."

There are various word orders used in the languages of the world. Some, like English, use subject-verb-object (SVO) ordering, as in the sentence "I like you." Others, such as Latin, use subject-object-verb (SOV) ordering, as in "I you like." In rare cases, OSV, OVS, VOS and VSO are used. In a new paper published in the Proceedings of the National Academy of Sciences, Merritt Ruhlen and Murray Gell-Mann, co-directors of the Santa Fe Institute Program on the Evolution of Human Languages, argue that the original language used SOV ordering ("I you like").

"This language would have been spoken by a small East African population who seemingly invented fully modern language and then spread around the world, replacing everyone else," Ruhlen told Life's Little Mysteries, a sister site to LiveScience.

The researchers came to their conclusion after creating a language family tree, which shows the historical relationships between all the languages of the world. For example, all the Romance languages (Italian, Rumanian, French, Spanish) derive from Latin, which was spoken in Rome 2,000 years ago; that Latin family is itself a branch of an even larger tree, whose other branches include

Syntax refers to the arrangement and order of words in phrases and sentences. A photo of Yoda from *Star Wars* (Revenge of the Sith) this is. What's odd, even primordial, about Yoda's speech?

Germanic, Slavic, Greek, Indic and others. Together, all those languages make up the Indo-European language family, which fits like a puzzle piece with all the other language families in the world. . . .

In the language family tree, Ruhlen and Gell-Mann discovered a distinct pattern in how word orders change as languages branch off from their mother tongues. "What we found was that the distribution of the six possible word orders did not vary randomly. . . . Rather, the distribution of these six types was highly structured, and the paths of linguistic change in word order were clear," Ruhlen said.

Out of the 2,000 modern languages that fit in the family tree, the researchers found that more than half are SOV languages. The ones that are SVO, OVS and OSV all derive directly from SOV languages—never the other way around. For example, French, which is SVO, derives from Latin, which is SOV.

Furthermore, languages that are VSO and VOS always derive from SVO languages. Thus, all languages descend from an original SOV word order "which leads to the conclusion that the word order in the language from which all modern languages derive must have been SOV," Ruhlen wrote.

Was it just an accident that the mother of all mother tongues was probably SOV, rather than one of the other five possibilities? The researchers think not. Predating Ruhlen's and Gell-Mann's work, Tom Givon, a linguist at the University of Oregon, argued that SOV had to have been the first word order, based on how children learn language. He found that the SOV word ordering seems to come most naturally to humans. . . .

And if that's the case, it seems strange that languages switch word orders as they evolve. Indeed, no one really knows why word orders would switch. "We have found that word order changes in very precise ways," Ruhlen said. "But the fact remains that half of the world's languages still have SOV word order because, in Murray's and my opinion, they have not changed word order at all. [Our data] shows how word order changes. . . . but it is unpredictable if word order will change, and I really don't know why."

SOURCE: Natalie Wolchover, "The Original Human Language Like Yoda Sounded," LifesLittleMysteries.com, October 13, 2011. http://www.lifeslittlemysteries.com/1836-original-human-language-yoda.html. Copyright © 2011 TechMediaNetwork.com. Reprinted with permission.

In India's remote Arunachal Pradesh, linguist Gregory Anderson, director of the Living Tongues Institute for Endangered Languages, makes one of the first ever recordings of Koro language, whose existence was announced in 2010.

and the everyday" (quoted in Maugh 2007). Harrison's book, *When Languages Die* (2007), notes that an indigenous language goes extinct every two weeks, as its last speakers die. The world's linguistic diversity has been cut in half (measured by number of distinct languages) in the past 500 years, and half of the remaining languages are predicted to disappear during this century. Colonial languages (e.g., English, Spanish, Portuguese, French, Dutch, Russian) have expanded at the expense of indigenous ones. Of approximately 7,000 remaining languages, about 20 percent are endangered, compared with 18 percent of mammals, 8 percent of plants, and 5 percent of birds (Maugh 2007).

National Geographic's Enduring Voices Project (http://languagehotspots.org) strives to preserve endangered languages by identifying the geographic areas with unique, poorly understood, or threatened languages and by documenting those languages and cultures.

The website shows various language hot spots where the endangerment rate ranges from low to severe. The rate is high in an area encompassing Oklahoma, Texas, and New Mexico, where 40 Native American languages are at risk. The top hot spot is northern Australia, where 153 Aboriginal languages are endangered (Maugh 2007). Other hot spots are in central South America, the Pacific Northwest of North America, and eastern Siberia. In all these areas indigenous tongues have yielded, either voluntarily or through coercion, to a colonial language (see Harrison 2010).

acing the COURSE

summary

1. Wild primates use call systems to communicate. Environmental stimuli trigger calls, which cannot be combined when multiple stimuli are present. Contrasts between language and call systems include displacement, productivity, and cultural transmission. Over time, our ancestral call systems grew too complex for genetic transmission, and hominid communication began to rely on learning. Humans still use nonverbal communication, such as facial expressions, gestures, and body stances and movements. But language is the main system humans use to communicate. Chimps and gorillas can understand and manipulate nonverbal symbols based on language.

2. No language uses all the sounds the human vocal tract can make. Phonology—the study of speech sounds—focuses on sound contrasts (phonemes) that distinguish meaning. The grammars and lexicons of particular languages can lead their speakers to perceive and think in certain ways. Studies of domains such as kinship, color terminologies, and pronouns show that speakers of different languages categorize their experiences differently.

3. Linguistic anthropologists share anthropology's general interest in diversity in time and space. Sociolinguistics investigates relationships between social and linguistic variation by focusing on the actual use of language. Only when features of speech acquire social meaning are they imitated. If they are valued, they will spread. People vary their speech, shifting styles, dialects, and languages. As linguistic systems, all languages and dialects are equally complex, rule-governed, and effective for communication. However, speech is used, is evaluated, and changes in the context of political, economic, and social forces. Often the linguistic traits of a low-status group are negatively evaluated. This devaluation is not because of *linguistic* features per se. Rather, it reflects the association of such features with low *social* status. One dialect, supported by the dominant institutions of the state, exercises symbolic domination over the others.

4. Historical linguistics is useful for anthropologists interested in historic relationships among populations. Cultural similarities and differences often correlate with linguistic ones. Linguistic clues can suggest past contacts between cultures. Related languages—members of the same language family—descend from an original protolanguage. Relationships between languages don't necessarily mean that there are biological ties between their speakers, because people can learn new languages.

5. One aspect of linguistic history is language loss. The world's linguistic diversity has been cut in half in the past 500 years, and half of the remaining 7,000 languages are predicted to disappear during this century.

key terms

Black English Vernacular (BEV) 315
call systems 303
cultural transmission 304
daughter languages 316
diglossia 310
displacement 304
ethnosemantics 309
focal vocabulary 309
historical linguistics 316

honorifics 311
kinesics 305
language 302
lexicon 306
morphology 306
phoneme 307
phonemics 307
phonetics 307
phonology 306

MULTIPLE CHOICE

1. Research on communication skills of nonhuman primates reveals that
   a. they, too, possess a universal grammar.
   b. they can't combine the calls for food and danger into a single utterance.
   c. female nonhuman primates are more sensitive to different shades of green than their male counterparts are.
   d. they can construct elaborate call systems, often indicating several messages simultaneously.
   e. only apes, not monkeys, use call systems.

2. When Washoe and Lucy tried to teach sign language to other chimpanzees, this was an example of
   a. displacement.
   b. call systems.
   c. productivity.
   d. cultural transmission.
   e. estrus.

3. Recent research on the origin of language suggests that
   a. the capacity to remember and combine linguistic symbols is latent in all mammals.
   b. a mutation in humans (which occurred about 150,000 years ago) may have conferred selective advantages (linguistic and cultural abilities).
   c. fine tongue and lip movements that are necessary for clear speech are passed on through enculturation.
   d. a sudden event made toolmaking possible for *Homo*.
   e. call systems evolved into complex languages 50,000 years ago.

4. What is the study of communication through body movements, stances, gestures, and facial expressions?
   a. ethnosemantics
   b. kinesics
   c. biosemantics
   d. protolinguistics
   e. diglossia

5. The scientific study of a spoken language involves several interrelated areas of analysis. Which area refers to all of a language's morphemes and their meanings?
   a. syntax
   b. ethnosemantics
   c. ethnoscience
   d. phonology
   e. lexicon

6. What does the Sapir-Whorf hypothesis state?
   a. The degree of cultural complexity is associated with the effectiveness of languages as systems of communication.
   b. The Hopi do not use three verb tenses; they have no concept of time.
   c. Different languages produce different ways of thinking.
   d. Culture and language are transmitted independently.
   e. Dialect variation is the result of toilet-training practices.

7. Studies on the differences between female and male Americans in regard to the color terms they use suggest that
   a. in opposition to the Sapir-Whorf hypothesis, it might be more reasonable to say that changes in culture produce changes in language and thought rather than the reverse.
   b. changes in American economy, society, and culture have had little impact on the use of color terms.
   c. in support of the Sapir-Whorf hypothesis, different languages produce different ways of thinking.
   d. women and men are equally sensitive to marketing tactics of the cosmetic industry.
   e. women spend more money on status goods than men do.

8. Which of the following statements about sociolinguists is *not* true?
   a. They are concerned more with performance than with competence.
   b. They look at society and at language.
   c. They are concerned with linguistic change.

test yourself

d. They quantify what people say.

e. They investigate the diffusion of genes between populations.

9. Honorifics are terms used with people, often being added to their names, to "honor" them. Why would sociolinguists be interested in studying the use of honorifics?

a. They enable sociolinguists to study language and culture outside of its context because the same honorifics are used everywhere and they mean the same thing.

b. Because honorifics always honor the person being addressed, sociolinguists can study the positive side of language and culture.

c. They may convey or imply a status difference between the speaker and the person being referred to or addressed.

d. They provide data about how different languages are related to one another, which is what sociolinguists are primarily interested in.

e. There is no reason for contemporary sociolinguists to be interested in honorifics because people don't use these terms anymore.

10. Which of the following statements about Black English Vernacular (BEV) is false?

a. It lacks the required linguistic depth to fully express thoughts.

b. Many aspects of BEV also are present in southern white speech.

c. BEV effectively conveys meaning.

d. Linguists view BEV as a dialect of SE, not a different language.

e. BEV has grammatical rules.

FILL IN THE BLANK

1. _____ refers to the ability to create new expressions by combining other expressions, while _____ is the ability to describe things and events that are not present.

2. Variation in speech in different contexts or situations is known as _____.

3. _____ refers to the existence of "high" and "low" dialects within a single language.

4. In a stratified society, even people who do not speak the prestige dialect tend to accept it as "standard" or superior. In Pierre Bourdieu's term, this is an instance of _____.

5. The world's linguistic diversity has been cut in half in the past _____ years, and half of the remaining _____ languages are predicted to disappear during this century.

CRITICAL THINKING

1. What dialects and languages do you speak? Do you tend to use different dialects, languages, or speech styles in different contexts? Why?

2. Culture always plays a role in shaping what we understand as "natural." What does this mean? Provide three examples of the relevance of this fact in the context of human language and communication.

3. Consider how changing technologies are altering the ways you communicate with family, friends, and even strangers. Suppose your best friend decides to study sociolinguistics in graduate school. What ideas about the relationship between changing technologies, language, and social relations could you suggest to him or her as worth studying?

4. List some stereotypes about how different people speak. Are those real differences, or just stereotypes? Are the stereotypes positive or negative? Why do you think those stereotypes exist?

5. What is language loss? Why are some researchers and communities worldwide so concerned by this growing phenomenon?

Multiple Choice: 1. (B); 2. (D); 3. (B); 4. (B); 5. (E); 6. (C); 7. (A); 8. (E); 9. (C); 10. (A); **Fill in the Blank:** 1. Productivity, displacement; 2. style shifting; 3. Diglossia; 4. symbolic domination; 5. 500, 7,000

Bonvillain, N.

2011 *Language, Culture, and Communication: The Meaning of Messages*, 6th ed. Upper Saddle River, NJ: Pearson Prentice Hall. Up-to-date text on language and communication in cultural context.

Harrison, K. D.

2010 *The Last Speakers: The Quest to Save the World's Most Endangered Languages*. Washington: National Geographic. Images of, and conversations with, speakers of endangered languages.

Hess, E.

2008 *Nim Chimpsky: The Chimp Who Would Be Human*. New York: Bantam Books. The troubled life of Nim Chimpsky, subject of the acclaimed 2011 documentary film "Project Nim."

McConnell-Ginet, S.

2010 *Gender, Sexuality, and Meaning: Linguistic Practice and Politics*. New York: Oxford University Press. How gender and sexuality are expressed in, and influence, language.

Mooney, A.

2011 *Language, Society, and Power*. New York: Routledge. Political dimensions and use of language.

Rickford, J. R., and R. J. Rickford

2000 *Spoken Soul: The Story of Black English*. New York: Wiley. Readable account of the history and social meaning of BEV.

suggested additional readings

Go to our Online Learning Center website at **www.mhhe.com/kottak** for Internet exercises directly related to the content of this chapter.

internet exercises

CHAPTER 15

Ethnicity and Race

What is social status, and how does it relate to ethnicity?

How are race and ethnicity socially constructed in various societies?

What are the positive and negative aspects of ethnicity?

◀ During a game in Seattle, David Ortiz (aka Big Papi) laughs as he tries to hold Ichiro Suzuki at first. How ethnically diverse is American baseball compared with other popular sports?

understanding OURSELVES

When asked "Who are you?" what first comes to mind? Think of the last person you met, or the person sitting nearest you. What labels pop into your head to describe that person? What kinds of identity cues and clues do people use to figure out the kinds of people they are dealing with, and how to act in various social situations? Part of human adaptive flexibility is our ability to shift self presentation in response to context. Italians, for example, maintain separate sets of clothing to be worn inside and outside the home. They invest much more in their outside wardrobe (thus supporting a vibrant Italian fashion industry)—and what it says about their public persona—than in indoor garb, which is for family and intimates to see. Identities and behavior change with context. "I may be a Neandertal at the office, but I'm all *Homo sapiens* at home." Many of the social statuses we occupy, the "hats" we wear, depend on the situation. A person can be both black and Hispanic, or both a father and a ballplayer. One identity is claimed or perceived in certain settings, another in different ones. Among African Americans a "Hispanic" baseball player might be black; among Hispanics, Hispanic.

When our claimed or perceived identity varies depending on the context, this is called the *situational negotiation of social identity*. Depending on the situation, the same man might declare: "I'm Jimmy's father." "I'm your boss." "I'm African American." "I'm your professor." In face-to-face encounters, other people see who we are—actually, who they perceive us to be. They may expect us to think and act in certain (stereotypical) ways based on their perception of our identity (e.g., Latina woman, older white male golfer). Although we can't know which aspect of identity they'll focus on (e.g., ethnicity, gender, age, or political affiliation), face to face it's hard to be anonymous or to be someone else entirely. That's what masks, costumes, disguises, and hiding are for. Who's that little man behind the curtain?

Unlike our early ancestors, people today don't just interact face to face. We routinely give our money and our trust to individuals and institutions we've never laid eyes on. We phone, write, and—more than ever—use the Internet, where we must choose which aspects of ourselves to reveal. The Internet allows myriad forms of cybersocial interaction, and people can create new personas by using different "handles," including fictitious names and identities. In anonymous regions of cyberspace, people can manipulate ("lie about") their ages, genders, and physical attributes and create their own cyberfantasies. In psychology, multiple personalities are abnormal, but for anthropologists, multiple identities are more and more the norm.

Ethnicity is based on cultural similarities and differences in a society or nation. The similarities are with members of the same ethnic group; the differences are between that group and others. Ethnic groups must deal with other such groups in the nation or region they inhabit, so that interethnic relations are important in the study of that nation or region. (Table 15.1 lists American ethnic groups, based on 2010 figures.)

TABLE 15.1 Racial/Ethnic Identification in the United States, 2010 (as reported by the U.S. Census Bureau from the 2010 census)

CLAIMED IDENTITY	NUMBER (MILLIONS)	PERCENTAGE
White (non-Hispanic)	196.8	63.7
Hispanic	50.5	16.3
Black	38.9	12.6
Asian	14.7	4.8
American Indian	2.9	0.9
Pacific Islander	0.5	0.2
Two or more races	9.0	2.9
Total population	308.7	100.0

SOURCE: U.S. Census Bureau, 2010, decennial census data.

ETHNIC GROUPS AND ETHNICITY

As with any culture, members of an **ethnic group** *share* certain beliefs, values, habits, customs, and norms because of their common background. They define themselves as different and special because of cultural features. This distinction may arise from language, religion, historical experience, geographic placement, kinship, or "race" (see Spickard 2004, 2012). Markers of an ethnic group may include a collective name, belief in common descent, a sense of solidarity, and an association with a specific territory, which the group may or may not hold (Ryan 1990, pp. xiii, xiv).

According to Fredrik Barth (1969), ethnicity can be said to exist when people claim a certain ethnic identity for themselves and are defined by others as having that identity. **Ethnicity** means identification with, and feeling part of, an ethnic group and exclusion from certain other groups because of this affiliation. But issues of ethnicity can be complex. Ethnic feelings and associated behavior vary in intensity within ethnic groups and countries and over time. A change in the degree of importance attached to an ethnic identity may reflect political changes (Soviet rule ends—ethnic feeling rises) or individual life-cycle changes (old people relinquish, or young people reclaim, an ethnic background).

Cultural differences may be associated with ethnicity, class, region, or religion. Individuals often have more than one group identity. People may be loyal (depending on circumstances) to their neighborhood, school, team, town, state or province, region, nation, continent, religion, ethnic group, or interest group (Ryan 1990, p. xxii). In a complex society such as the United States or Canada, people constantly negotiate their social identities. All of us "wear different hats," presenting ourselves sometimes as one thing, sometimes as another.

In daily conversation, we hear the term *status* used as a synonym for *prestige*. In this context, "She's got a lot of status" means she's got a lot of prestige; people look up to her. Among social scientists, that's not the primary meaning of "*status*." Social scientists use *status* more neutrally—for any position, no matter what the prestige, that someone occupies in society. In this sense, **status** encompasses the various positions that people occupy in society. Parent is a social status. So are professor, student, factory worker, Democrat, salesperson, homeless person, labor leader, ethnic-group member, and thousands of others. People always occupy multiple statuses (e.g., Hispanic, Catholic, infant, brother). Among the statuses we occupy, particular ones dominate in particular settings, such as son or daughter at home and student in the classroom.

Some statuses are **ascribed:** People have little or no choice about occupying them. Age is an ascribed status; we can't choose not to age. Race and gender usually are ascribed; people are born members of a certain group and remain so all their lives. **Achieved statuses,** by contrast, aren't automatic; they come through choices, actions, efforts, talents, or accomplishments and may be positive or negative (Figure 15.1). Examples of achieved statuses include physician, senator, convicted felon, salesperson, union member, father, and college student.

Status Shifting

Sometimes statuses, particularly ascribed ones, are mutually exclusive. It's hard to bridge the gap between black and white, or male and female. Sometimes, taking a status or joining a group requires a conversion experience, acquiring a new and overwhelming primary identity, such as becoming a "born again" Christian.

Some statuses aren't mutually exclusive, but contextual. A person can be both black and Hispanic, or both a mother and a senator. One identity is used in certain settings, another in different ones. We call this the *situational negotiation of social identity*. When ethnic identity is flexible and situational, it can become an achieved status (Leman 2001).

ethnic group
One among several culturally distinct groups in a society or region.

ethnicity
Identification with an ethnic group.

status
Any position that determines where someone fits in society.

ascribed status
Social status based on little or no choice.

achieved status
Social status based on choices or accomplishments.

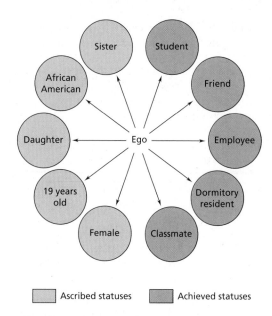

FIGURE 15.1 Social Statuses.

The person in this figure—"ego," or "I"—occupies many social statuses. The green circles indicate ascribed statuses; the purple circles represent achieved statuses.

☐ Ascribed statuses   ☐ Achieved statuses

race
Ethnic group assumed to have a biological basis.

racism
Discrimination against an ethnic group assumed to have a biological basis.

Hispanics, for example, may move through levels of culture (shifting ethnic affiliations) as they negotiate their identities. "Hispanic" is an ethnic category based mainly on language. It includes whites, blacks, and "racially" mixed Spanish speakers and their ethnically conscious descendants. (There are also "Native American," and even "Asian," Hispanics.) "Hispanic," representing the fastest-growing ethnic group in the United States, lumps together millions of people of diverse geographic origin—Puerto Rico, Mexico, Cuba, El Salvador, Guatemala, the Dominican Republic, and other Spanish-speaking countries of Central and South America and the Caribbean. "Latino" is a broader category, which can also include Brazilians (who speak Portuguese). The national origins of American Hispanics/Latinos in 2009 were as shown in Table 15.2.

Mexican Americans (Chicanos), Cuban Americans, and Puerto Ricans may mobilize to promote general Hispanic issues (e.g., opposition to "English-only"

laws) but act as three separate interest groups in other contexts. Cuban Americans are richer on average than Chicanos and Puerto Ricans are, and their class interests and voting patterns differ. Cubans are more likely to vote Republican than Puerto Ricans and Chicanos are. Some Mexican Americans whose families have lived in the United States for generations have little in common with new Hispanic immigrants, such as those from Central America. Many Americans (especially those fluent in English) claim Hispanic ethnicity in some contexts but shift to a general "American" identity in others.

In many societies an ascribed status is associated with a position in the social-political hierarchy. Certain groups, called *minority groups,* are subordinate. They have inferior power and less secure access to resources than do *majority groups* (which are superordinate, dominant, or controlling). Often ethnic groups are minorities.

Minority groups are obvious features of stratification in the United States. The 2009 poverty rate was 9.4 percent for non-Hispanic whites, 25.8 percent for blacks, and 25.3 percent for Hispanics (U.S. Census 2010). Inequality shows up consistently in unemployment figures and in median household income. The median wealth of white households is 20 times that of black households and 18 times that of Hispanic households (Kochhar, Fry, and Taylor 2011).

When an ethnic group is assumed to have a biological basis (distinctively shared "blood" or genes), it is called a **race.** Discrimination against such a group is called **racism** (Gotkowitz 2011; Kuper 2006; Scupin 2012).

RACE AND ETHNICITY

Race, like ethnicity in general, is a cultural category rather than a biological reality. That is, ethnic groups, including "races," derive from contrasts perceived and perpetuated in particular societies, rather than from scientific classifications based on common genes (see Wade 2002).

It is not possible to define human races biologically. Only cultural constructions of race are possible—even

TABLE 15.2 American Hispanics, Latinos, 2009

NATIONAL ORIGIN	PERCENTAGE
Mexican American	66.4%
Puerto Rican	8.9
Cuban	3.5
Central and South American	16.0
Other Hispanic/Latino origin	5.2
Total	100.0%

SOURCE: *Statistical Abstract of the United States 2012,* Table 37, p. 42.

though the average person conceptualizes "race" in biological terms. The belief that human races exist and are important is much more common among the public than it is among scientists. Most Americans, for example, believe that their population includes biologically based races to which various labels have been applied. These labels include "white," "black," "yellow," "red," "Caucasoid," "Negroid," "Mongoloid," "Amerindian," "Euro-American," "African American," "Asian American," and "Native American."

This chapter's "Appreciating Anthropology" is a statement on race issued by the American Anthropological Association (AAA). It discusses how races have been socially constructed, for example under colonialism. The statement also stresses that inequalities among "racial" groups are not consequences of their biological inheritance but products of social, economic, educational, and political circumstances.

We hear the words *ethnicity* and *race* frequently, but American culture doesn't draw a very clear line between them. Consider a *New York Times* article published on May 29, 1992. Discussing the changing ethnic composition of the United States, the article explained (correctly) that Hispanics "can be of any race" (Barringer 1992, p. A12). In other words, "Hispanic" is an ethnic category that crosscuts racial contrasts such as that between "black" and "white." Another *Times* article published that same day reported that during Los Angeles riots in

spring 1992, "hundreds of Hispanic residents were interrogated about their immigration status on the basis of their *race* alone [emphasis added]" (Mydans 1992a, p. A8). Use of "race" here seems inappropriate because "Hispanic" usually is perceived as referring to a linguistically based (Spanish-speaking) ethnic group, rather than a biologically based race. Since these Los Angeles residents were being interrogated because they were Hispanic, the article is actually reporting on ethnic, not racial, discrimination.

In a more recent case, consider a speech delivered by then Appeals Court Judge Sonia Sotomayor, newly nominated (in May 2009; confirmed in August 2009) for the U.S. Supreme Court by President Barack Obama. In a 2001 lecture titled "A Latina Judge's Voice," delivered at the University of California, Berkeley, School of Law, Sotomayor declared (as part of a much longer speech):

> I would hope that a wise Latina woman with the richness of her experiences would more often than not reach a better conclusion than a white male who hasn't lived that life (Sotomayor 2001/2009).

Conservatives, including Newt Gingrich and radio talk show host Rush Limbaugh, seized on this declaration as evidence that Sotomayor was a "racist" or a "reverse racist." Again, however, "Latina" is an ethnic (and gendered-female) rather

"Hispanic" and "Latino" are ethnic categories that crosscut "racial" contrasts such as that between "black" and "white." Note the physical diversity among these multiracial schoolchildren in Havana, Cuba.

appreciating ANTHROPOLOGY

What's Wrong with Race?

Anthropologists have a lot to say about the race concept. There is considerable public confusion about the meaning and relevance of "race," and false claims about biological differences among "races" continue to be advanced. Stemming from previous actions by the American Anthropological Association (AAA) designed to address public misconceptions about race and intelligence, the need was apparent for a clear AAA statement on the biology and politics of race that would be educational and informational (see also http://www.understandingrace.org/).

The following statement was adopted by the AAA Executive Board, based on a draft prepared by a committee of representative anthropologists. This statement represents the thinking and scholarly positions of most anthropologists, including me—your textbook author.

In the United States both scholars and the general public have been conditioned to viewing human races as natural and separate divisions within the human species based on visible physical differences. With the vast expansion of scientific knowledge in this century, however, it has become clear that human populations are not unambiguous, clearly demarcated, biologically distinct groups. Evidence from the analysis of genetics (e.g., DNA) indicates that most physical variation, about 94%, lies within so-called racial groups. Conventional geographic "racial"

groupings differ from one another only in about 6% of their genes. This means that there is greater variation within "racial" groups than between them. In neighboring populations there is much overlapping of genes and their phenotypic (physical) expressions. Throughout history whenever different groups have come into contact, they have interbred. The continued sharing of genetic materials has maintained all of humankind as a single species.

Physical variations in any given trait tend to occur gradually rather than abruptly over geographic areas. And because physical traits are inherited independently of one another, knowing the range of one trait does not predict the presence of others. For example, skin color varies largely from light in the temperate areas in the north to dark in the tropical areas in the south; its intensity is not related to nose shape or hair texture. Dark skin may be associated with frizzy or kinky hair or curly or wavy or straight hair, all of which are found among different indigenous peoples in tropical regions. These facts render any attempt to establish lines of division among biological populations both arbitrary and subjective.

Historical research has shown that the idea of "race" has always carried more meanings than mere physical differences; indeed, physical variations in the human species have no meaning except the social ones that humans put on them. Today scholars in many fields argue that "race" as it is understood in the United States of America

was a social mechanism invented during the 18th century to refer to those populations brought together in colonial America: the English and other European settlers, the conquered Indian (Native American) peoples, and those peoples of Africa brought in to provide slave labor.

From its inception, this modern concept of "race" was modeled after an ancient theorem of the Great Chain of Being, which posited natural categories on a hierarchy established by God or nature. Thus "race" was a mode of classification linked specifically to peoples in the colonial situation. It subsumed a growing ideology of inequality devised to rationalize European attitudes and treatment of the conquered and enslaved peoples. Proponents of slavery in particular during the 19th century used "race" to justify the retention of slavery. The ideology magnified the differences among Europeans, Africans, and Indians (Native Americans), established a rigid hierarchy of socially exclusive categories, underscored and bolstered unequal rank and status differences, and provided the rationalization that the inequality was natural or God-given. The different physical traits of African-Americans and Indians (Native Americans) became markers or symbols of their status differences.

As they were constructing US society, leaders among European-Americans fabricated the cultural/behavioral characteristics associated with each "race," linking superior traits with

than a racial category. I suspect that Sotomayor also was using "white male" as an ethnic-gender category, to refer to nonminority men. These examples from our everyday experience illustrate the difficulties in drawing a precise distinction between race and ethnicity. It probably is better to use the term *ethnic group* rather than *race* to describe *any* such social group, for example, African Americans, Asian Americans, Anglo Americans, Hispanics, Latinos, Latinas, and even non-Hispanic whites.

THE SOCIAL CONSTRUCTION OF RACE

Races are ethnic groups assumed (by members of a particular culture) to have a biological basis, but actually race is socially constructed. The "races" we hear about every day are cultural, or social, rather than biological categories. Many Americans mistakenly assume that whites and blacks, for example, are biologically distinct and that these terms stand for discrete races. But these labels, like racial terms

Europeans and negative and inferior ones to blacks and Indians (Native Americans). Numerous arbitrary and fictitious beliefs about the different peoples were institutionalized and deeply embedded in American thought....

Ultimately "race" as an ideology about human differences was subsequently spread to other areas of the world. It became a strategy for dividing, ranking, and controlling colonized people used by colonial powers everywhere. But it was not limited to the colonial situation. In the latter part of the 19th century it was employed by Europeans to rank one another and to justify social, economic, and political inequalities among their peoples. During World War II, the Nazis under Adolf Hitler enjoined the expanded ideology of "race" and "racial" differences and took them to a logical end: the extermination of 11 million people of "inferior races" (e.g., Jews, Gypsies, Africans, homosexuals, and so forth) and other unspeakable brutalities of the Holocaust.

"Race" thus evolved as a world view, a body of prejudgments that distorts our ideas about human differences and group behavior. Racial beliefs constitute myths about the diversity in the human species and about the abilities and behavior of people ho-

mogenized into "racial" categories. The myths fused behavior and physical features together in the public mind, impeding our comprehension of both biological variations and cultural behavior, implying that both are genetically determined. Racial myths bear no relationship to the reality of human capabilities or behavior....

We now understand that human cultural behavior is learned, conditioned into infants beginning at birth, and always subject to modification. No human is born with a built-in culture or language. Our temperaments, dispositions, and personalities, regardless of genetic propensities, are developed within sets of meanings and values that we call "culture"....

It is a basic tenet of anthropological knowledge that all normal human beings have the capacity to learn any cultural behavior. The American experience with immigrants from hundreds of different language and cultural backgrounds who have acquired some version of American culture traits and behavior is the clearest evidence of this fact. Moreover, people of all physical variations have learned different cultural behaviors and continue to do so as modern transportation moves millions of immigrants around the world.

How people have been accepted and treated within the context of a given society or culture has a direct impact on how they perform in that society. The "racial" world view was invented to assign some groups to perpetual low status, while others were permitted access to privilege, power, and wealth. The tragedy in the United States has been that the policies and practices stemming from this world view succeeded all too well in constructing unequal populations among Europeans, Native Americans, and peoples of African descent. Given what we know about the capacity of normal humans to achieve and function within any culture, we conclude that present-day inequalities between so-called "racial" groups are not consequences of their biological inheritance but products of historical and contemporary social, economic, educational, and political circumstances.

This photo, taken near Bucharest, Romania, shows a Rom (Gypsy) woman standing in front of another woman as she holds her baby daughter. Gypsies (Rom or Roma) have faced discrimination in many nations. During World War II, the Nazis led by Adolf Hitler murdered 11 million Jews, Gypsies, Africans, homosexuals, and others.

SOURCE: From the American Anthropological Association (AAA) Statement on "Race" (May 1998). http://www.aaanet.org/stmts/racepp.htm. Reprinted with permission of the American Anthropological Association.

used in other societies, really designate culturally perceived rather than biologically based groups.

Hypodescent: Race in the United States

How is race culturally constructed in the United States? In American culture, one acquires his or her racial identity at birth, as an ascribed status, but race isn't based on biology or on simple ancestry. Take the case of the child of a "racially mixed" marriage involving one black and one white parent. We know that 50 percent of the child's genes come from one parent and 50 percent from the other. Still, American culture overlooks heredity and classifies this child as black. This rule is arbitrary. On the basis of genotype (genetic composition), it would be just as logical to classify the child as white.

American rules for assigning racial status can be even more arbitrary. In some states, anyone known to have any black ancestor, no matter how remote, can be classified as a member of the black race. This is a rule of **descent** (it assigns social identity on the basis of

descent
Social identity based on ancestry.

A biracial American, Halle Berry, with her mother. What is Halle Berry's race?

ancestry), but of a sort that is rare outside the contemporary United States. It is called **hypodescent** (Harris and Kottak 1963) because it automatically places children of mixed marriages in the group of their minority parent (*hypo* means "lower"). Hypodescent divides American society into groups that have been unequal in their access to wealth, power, and prestige.

The following case from Louisiana is an excellent illustration of the arbitrariness of the hypodescent rule and of the role that governments (federal or, in this case, state) play in legalizing, inventing, or eradicating race and ethnicity (see Mullaney 2011; B. Williams 1989). Susie Guillory Phipps, a light-skinned woman with Caucasian features and straight black hair, discovered as an adult that she was black. When Phipps ordered a copy of her birth certificate, she found her race listed as "colored." Since she had been "brought up white and married white twice," Phipps challenged a 1970 Louisiana law declaring anyone with at least one-thirty-second "Negro blood" to be legally black. Although the state's lawyer admitted that Phipps "looks like a white person," the state of Louisiana insisted that her racial classification was proper (Yetman 1991, pp. 3–4).

Cases like Phipps's are rare because racial identity usually is ascribed at birth and doesn't change. The rule of hypodescent affects blacks, Asians, Native Americans, and Hispanics differently (see Hunter 2005). It's easier to negotiate Native American or Hispanic identity than black identity. The ascription rule isn't as definite, and the assumption of a biological basis isn't as strong.

To be considered Native American, one ancestor out of eight (great-grandparents) or out of four (grandparents) may suffice. This depends on whether the assignment is by federal or state law or by a Native American tribal council. The child of a Hispanic may (or may not, depending on context) claim Hispanic identity. Many Americans with a Native American or Latino grandparent consider themselves white and lay no claim to minority group status.

Race in the Census

The U.S. Census Bureau has gathered data by race since 1790. Initially this was done because the Constitution specified that a slave counted as three-fifths of a white person, and because Native Americans were not taxed. The racial categories included in the 1990 U.S. census were "White," "Black or Negro," "Indian (American)," "Eskimo," "Aleut or Pacific Islander," and "Other." A separate question was asked about Spanish–Hispanic heritage. Check out Figure 15.2 for the racial categories in the 2010 census.

Attempts to add a "multiracial" census category have been opposed by the National

5. **Is this person of Hispanic, Latino, or Spanish origin?**

☐ No, not of Hispanic, Latino, or Spanish origin
☐ Yes, Mexican, Mexican Am., Chicano
☐ Yes, Puerto Rican
☐ Yes, Cuban
☐ Yes, another Hispanic, Latino, or Spanish origin — *Print origin, for example, Argentinean, Colombian, Dominican, Nicaraguan, Salvadoran, Spaniard, and so on.* ⤦

☐☐☐☐☐☐☐☐☐☐☐☐☐☐☐☐☐☐

6. **What is this person's race?** *Mark* ☒ *one or more boxes.*

☐ White
☐ Black, African Am., or Negro
☐ American Indian or Alaska Native — *Print name of enrolled or principal tribe.* ⤦

☐☐☐☐☐☐☐☐☐☐☐☐☐☐☐☐☐☐

☐ Asian Indian   ☐ Japanese   ☐ Native Hawaiian
☐ Chinese   ☐ Korean   ☐ Guamanian or Chamorro
☐ Filipino   ☐ Vietnamese   ☐ Samoan
☐ Other Asian — *Print race, for example, Hmong, Laotian, Thai, Pakistani, Cambodian, and so on.* ⤦   ☐ Other Pacific Islander — *Print race, for example, Fijian, Tongan, and so on.* ⤦

☐☐☐☐☐☐☐☐☐☐☐☐☐☐☐☐☐☐

☐ Some other race — *Print race.* ⤦

☐☐☐☐☐☐☐☐☐☐☐☐☐☐☐☐☐☐

FIGURE 15.2 Reproduction of Questions on Race and Hispanic Origin from Census 2010.

SOURCE: U.S. Census Bureau, Census 2010 questionnaire.

Association for the Advancement of Colored People (NAACP) and the National Council of La Raza (a Hispanic advocacy group). Racial classification is a political issue involving access to resources, including jobs, voting districts, and programs aimed at minorities. The hypodescent rule results in all the population growth being attributed to the minority category. Minorities fear their political clout will decline if their numbers go down.

But things are changing. Choice of "some other race" in the U.S. Census tripled from 1980 (6.8 million) to 2010 (over 19 million)—suggesting imprecision in and dissatisfaction with the existing categories. In the 2000 census, 2.4 percent of Americans chose a first-ever option of identifying themselves as belonging to more than one race. That figure rose to 2.9 percent in the 2010 census. The number of interracial marriages and children is increasing, with implications for the traditional system of American racial classification. "Interracial," "biracial," or "multiracial" children undoubtedly identify with qualities of both parents. It is troubling for many of them to have so important an identity as race dictated by the arbitrary rule of hypodescent. It may be especially discordant when racial identity doesn't parallel gender identity, for instance, a boy with a white father and a black mother, or a girl with a white mother and a black father.

How does the Canadian census compare with the American census in its treatment of race? Rather than race, the Canadian census asks about "visible minorities." That country's Employment Equity Act defines such groups as "persons, other than Aboriginal peoples [aka First Nations in Canada], who are non-Caucasian in race or non-white in colour" (Statistics Canada 2001a). Figure 15.3 shows that "South Asian" and "Chinese" are Canada's largest visible minorities. Note that Canada's total visible minority population of 16.2 percent in 2006 (up from 11.2 percent in 1996) contrasts with a figure of about 25 percent for the United States in the 2000 census, rising to 36 percent in the 2010 census. In particular, Canada's black population of 2.5 percent contrasts with the American figure of 12.6 percent (2010) for African Americans, while Canada's Asian population is significantly higher than the U.S. figure of 4.8 percent (2010) on a percentage basis. Only a tiny fraction of the Canadian population (0.4 percent) claimed multiple visible minority affiliation, compared with 2.9 percent claiming more than one race in the United States in 2010.

Canada's visible minority population has been increasing steadily. In 1981, visible minorities accounted for just 4.7 percent of the population, versus 16.2 percent in 2006 (the most recent census data available as of this writing). Visible minorities are growing much faster than is Canada's overall population. Between 2001 and 2006, the total population increased 5 percent, while visible minorities rose 27 percent. If recent immigration trends

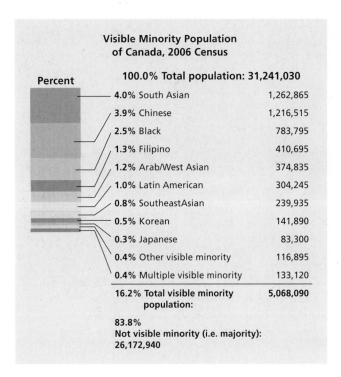

FIGURE 15.3 Visible Minority Population of Canada, 2006 Census.

SOURCE: From Statistics Canada, 2006 Census, http://www12.statcan.ca/english/census06/data/highlights/ethnic.

continue, visible minorities will soon account for 20 percent of Canada's population.

Not Us: Race in Japan

Japan is commonly viewed as a nation that is homogeneous in race, ethnicity, language, and culture—an image the Japanese themselves cultivate. Thus in 1986 Prime Minister Nakasone created an international furor by contrasting his country's supposed homogeneity (responsible, he suggested, for Japan's success at that time in international business) with the ethnically mixed United States.

Although less diverse than most countries, Japan is hardly the uniform entity Nakasone described. About 10 percent of its population consists of minorities. These include aboriginal Ainu, annexed Okinawans, outcast *burakumin*, children of mixed marriages, and immigrant nationalities, especially Koreans, who number more than 700,000 (De Vos, Wetherall, and Stearman 1983; Lie 2001; Ryang and Lie 2009).

To describe racial attitudes in Japan, Jennifer Robertson (1992) uses Kwame Anthony Appiah's (1990) term "intrinsic racism"—the belief that a (perceived) racial difference is a sufficient reason to value one person less than another. In Japan the valued group is majority ("pure") Japanese, who are believed to share "the same blood." Thus, the caption to a printed photo of a Japanese American model reads: "She was born in Japan but raised in Hawaii. Her

hypodescent
Children assigned to the same group as their minority parent.

Japan's stigmatized burakumin are physically and genetically indistinguishable from other Japanese. In response to burakumin political mobilization, Japan has dismantled the legal structure of discrimination against burakumin. This Sports Day for burakumin children is one kind of mobilization.

nationality is American but no foreign blood flows in her veins" (Robertson 1992, p. 5). Something like hypodescent also operates in Japan, but less precisely than in the United States, where mixed offspring automatically become members of the minority group. The children of mixed marriages between majority Japanese and others (including Euro-Americans) may not get the same "racial" label as their minority parent, but they are still stigmatized for their non-Japanese ancestry (De Vos and Wagatsuma 1966).

How is race culturally constructed in Japan? The (majority) Japanese define themselves by opposition to others, whether minority groups in their own nation or outsiders—anyone who is "not us." The "not us" should stay that way; assimilation generally is discouraged. Cultural mechanisms, especially residential segregation and taboos on "interracial" marriage, work to keep minorities "in their place."

In its construction of race, Japanese culture regards certain ethnic groups as having a biological basis, when there is no evidence that they do. The best example is the burakumin, a stigmatized group of at least 4 million outcasts, sometimes compared to India's untouchables. The burakumin are physically and genetically indistinguishable from other Japanese. Many of them "pass" as (and marry) majority Japanese, but a deceptive marriage can end in divorce if burakumin identity is discovered (Aoki and Dardess 1981).

Burakumin are perceived as standing apart from majority Japanese. Through ancestry or descent (and thus, it is assumed, "blood," or genetics), burakumin are "not us." Majority Japanese try to keep their lineage pure by discouraging mixing. The burakumin are residentially segregated in neighborhoods (rural or urban) called *buraku*, from which the racial label is derived. Compared with majority Japanese, the

stratified
Class-structured, with differences in wealth, prestige, and power.

burakumin are less likely to attend high school and college. When burakumin attend the same schools as majority Japanese, they face discrimination. Majority children and teachers may refuse to eat with them because burakumin are considered unclean.

In applying for university admission or a job and in dealing with the government, Japanese must list their address, which becomes part of a household or family registry. This list makes residence in a buraku, and likely burakumin social status, evident. Schools and companies use this information to discriminate. (The best way to pass is to move so often that the buraku address eventually disappears from the registry.) Majority Japanese also limit "race" mixture by hiring marriage mediators to check out the family histories of prospective spouses. They are especially careful to check for burakumin ancestry (De Vos et al. 1983).

The origin of the burakumin lies in a historical tiered system of stratification (from the Tokugawa period, 1603–1868). The top four ranked categories were warrior-administrators (*samurai*), farmers, artisans, and merchants. The ancestors of the burakumin were below this hierarchy. They did "unclean" jobs such as animal slaughter and disposal of the dead. Burakumin still do similar jobs, including work with leather and other animal products. They are more likely than majority Japanese to do manual labor (including farm work) and to belong to the national lower class. Burakumin and other Japanese minorities also are more likely to have careers in crime, prostitution, entertainment, and sports (De Vos et al. 1983).

Like blacks in the United States, the burakumin are **stratified,** or class-stratified. Because certain jobs are reserved for the burakumin, people who are successful in those occupations (e.g., shoe factory owners) can be wealthy. Burakumin also have found jobs as government bureaucrats. Financially successful burakumin can temporarily escape their stigmatized status by travel, including foreign travel.

Discrimination against the burakumin is strikingly like the discrimination that blacks have experienced in the United States. The burakumin often live in villages and neighborhoods with poor housing and sanitation. They have limited access to education, jobs, amenities, and health facilities. In response to burakumin political mobilization, Japan has dismantled the legal structure of discrimination against burakumin and has worked to improve conditions in the buraku. (The website http://blhrri.org/index_e.htm is sponsored by the Buraku Liberation and Human Rights Research Institute and includes the most recent information about the burakumin liberation movement.) However, discrimination against nonmajority Japanese is still the rule in companies. Some employers say that hiring burakumin would give their company an unclean image and thus create a disadvantage in competing with other businesses (De Vos et al. 1983).

Phenotype and Fluidity: Race in Brazil

There are more flexible, less exclusionary ways of socially constructing race than those used in the United States and Japan. Consider Brazil, which shares a history of slavery with the United States, lacks the hypodescent rule. Nor does Brazil have racial aversion of the sort found in Japan.

Brazilians use many more racial labels—over 500 were once reported (Harris 1970)—than Americans or Japanese do. In northeastern Brazil, I found 40 different racial terms in use in Arembepe, a village of only 750 people (Kottak 2006). Through their traditional classification system Brazilians recognize and attempt to describe the physical variation that exists within their population. The system used in the United States, by recognizing relatively few races, blinds Americans to an equivalent range of evident physical contrasts. The system Brazilians use to construct social race has other special features. In the United States one's race is an ascribed status; it is assigned automatically by hypodescent and usually doesn't change. In Brazil racial identity is more flexible, more of an achieved status.

Brazilian racial classification pays attention to **phenotype.** Scientists distinguish between *geno-type*, or hereditary makeup, and *phenotype*—expressed physical characteristics. Genotype is what you are genetically; phenotype is what you appear as. Identical twins and clones have the same genotype, but their phenotypes vary if they have been raised in different environments. Phenotype describes an organism's evident traits, its "manifest biology"—physiology and anatomy, including skin color, hair form, facial features, and eye color. A Brazilian's phenotype and racial label may change because of environmental factors, such as the tanning rays of the sun or the effects of humidity on the hair.

A Brazilian can change his or her "race" (say from "Indian" to "mixed") by changing his or her manner of dress, language, location (e.g., rural to urban), and even attitude (e.g., by adopting urban behavior). Two racial/ethnic labels used in Brazil are *indio* (indigenous, Native American) and *cabôclo* (someone who "looks *indio*" but wears modern clothing and participates in Brazilian culture, rather than living in an indigenous community). Similar shifts in racial/ethnic classification occur in other parts of Latin America, for example, Guatemala (see Wade 2010). The perception of biological race is influenced not just by the physical phenotype but by how one dresses and behaves.

phenotype
Expressed physical characteristics of an organism.

These photos, taken in Brazil by the author, give just a glimpse of the spectrum of phenotypical diversity encountered among contemporary Brazilians.

Furthermore, racial differences in Brazil may be so insignificant in structuring community life that people may forget the terms they have applied to others. Sometimes they even forget the ones they've used for themselves. In Arembepe, I made it a habit to ask the same person on different days to tell me the races of others in the village (and my own). In the United States I am always "white" or "Euro-American," but in Arembepe I got lots of terms besides *branco* ("white"). I could be *claro* ("light"), *louro* ("blond"), *sarará* ("light-skinned redhead"), *mulato claro* ("light mulatto"), or *mulato* ("mulatto"). The racial term used to describe me or anyone else varied from person to person, week to week, even day to day. My best informant, a man with very dark skin color, changed the term he used for himself all the time—from *escuro* ("dark") to *preto* ("black") to *moreno escuro* ("dark brunet").

The American and Japanese racial systems are creations of particular cultures, rather than scientific—or even accurate—descriptions of human biological differences. Brazilian racial classification also is a cultural construction, but Brazilians have developed a way of describing human biological diversity that is more detailed, fluid, and flexible than the systems used in most cultures. Brazil lacks Japan's racial aversion, and it also lacks a rule of descent like that which ascribes racial status in the United States (Degler 1970; Harris 1964).

For centuries the United States and Brazil have had mixed populations, with ancestors from Native America, Europe, Africa, and Asia. Although races have mixed in both countries, Brazilian and American cultures have constructed the results differently. The historical reasons for this contrast lie mainly in the different characteristics of the settlers of the two countries. The mainly English early settlers of the United States came as women, men, and families, but Brazil's Portuguese colonizers were mainly men—merchants and adventurers. Many of these Portuguese men married indigenous women and recognized their racially mixed children as their heirs. Like their North American counterparts, Brazilian plantation owners had sexual relations with their slaves. But the Brazilian landlords more often freed the children that resulted. (Sometimes these were their only children.) Freed offspring became plantation overseers and foremen and filled many intermediate positions in the emerging Brazilian economy. They were not classed with the slaves but were allowed to join a new intermediate category. No hypodescent rule developed in Brazil to ensure that whites and blacks remained separate (see Degler 1970; Harris 1964).

In today's world system, Brazil's system of racial classification is changing in the context of international identity politics and rights movements. Just as more and more Brazilians claim indigenous identities, an increasing number now assert their blackness and self-conscious membership in the African diaspora. Particularly in such northeastern Brazilian states as Bahia, where African demographic and cultural influence is strong, public universities have instituted affirmative action programs aimed at indigenous peoples and especially at blacks. Racial identities firm up in the context of international (e.g., pan-African and pan–Native American) mobilization and access to strategic resources based on race.

ETHNIC GROUPS, NATIONS, AND NATIONALITIES

The term **nation** once was synonymous with *tribe* or *ethnic group*. All three of these terms have been used to refer to a single culture sharing a single language, religion, history, territory, ancestry, and kinship. Thus one could speak interchangeably of the Seneca (Native American) nation, tribe, or ethnic group. Now *nation* has come to mean **state**—an independent, centrally organized political unit, or a government. *Nation* and *state* have become synonymous. Combined in **nation-state** they refer to an autonomous political entity, a country—like the United States, "one nation, indivisible" (see Farmen 2004; Gellner 1997).

Because of migration, conquest, and colonialism, most nation-states aren't ethnically homogeneous. A 2003 study by James Fearon found that about 70 percent of all countries have an ethnic group that forms an absolute majority of the population; the average population share of such a group is 65 percent. The average size of the second-largest group, or largest ethnic minority, is 17 percent. Only 18 percent of all countries, including Brazil and Japan, have a single ethnic group accounting for 90 percent or more of the population.

There is substantial regional variation in countries' ethnic structures. Strong states, particularly in Europe (e.g., France), have deliberately and actively worked to homogenize their diverse premodern populations to a common national identity and culture (see Beriss 2004; Gellner 1983). Although countries with no ethnic majority are fairly rare in the rest of world, this is the norm in Africa. The average African country has a plurality group of about 22 percent, with the second largest slightly less than this. Rwanda, Burundi, Lesotho, Swaziland, and Zimbabwe are exceptions; each has a large majority group and a minority that makes up almost all the rest of the population. Botswana has a large majority (the Tswana) and a set of smaller minorities (Fearon 2003).

Most Latin American and Caribbean countries have a majority group (speaking a European language, e.g., Portuguese in Brazil, Spanish in Argentina) and a single minority group—"indigenous peoples." "Indigenous peoples" is a catch-all category encompassing several small Native American tribes or remnants. Exceptions are Guatemala and the Andean countries of Bolivia, Peru, and Ecuador,

---

nation
Society sharing a language, religion, history, territory, ancestry, and kinship.

state
Stratified society with formal, central government.

nation-state
An autonomous political entity; a country.

with large indigenous populations (see Gotkowitz 2011; Wade 2010).

Most countries in Asia and the Middle East/North Africa have ethnic majorities. The Asian countries of Myanmar, Laos, Vietnam, and Thailand contain a large lowland majority edged by more fragmented mountain folk. Several oil-producing countries in the Middle East, including Saudi Arabia, Bahrain, United Arab Emirates, Oman, and Kuwait, contain an ethnically homogeneous group of citizens who form either a plurality or a bare majority; the rest of the population consists of ethnically diverse noncitizen workers. Other countries in the Middle East/North Africa contain two principal ethnic or ethnoreligious groups: Arabs and Berbers in Morocco, Algeria, Libya, and Tunisia; Muslims and Copts in Egypt; Turks and Kurds in Turkey; Greeks and Turks in Cyprus; and Palestinians and Transjordan Arabs in Jordan (Fearon 2003).

Nationalities and Imagined Communities

Ethnic groups that once had, or wish to have or regain, autonomous political status (their own country) are called **nationalities.** In the words of Benedict Anderson (1991/2006), they are "imagined communities." Even when they become nation-states, they remain imagined communities because most of their members, though feeling comradeship, will never meet (Anderson 1991, pp. 6–10). They can only imagine they all participate in the same unit.

Anderson traces Western European nationalism, which arose in imperial powers such as England, France, and Spain, back to the 18th century. He stresses that language and print played a crucial role in the growth of European national consciousness. The novel and the newspaper were "two forms of imagining" communities (consisting of all the people who read the same sources and thus witnessed the same events) that flowered in the 18th century (Anderson 1991, pp. 24–25).

Over time, political upheavals, wars, and migration have divided many imagined national communities that arose in the 18th and 19th centuries. The German and Korean homelands were artificially divided after wars, according to communist and capitalist ideologies. World War I split the Kurds, who remain an imagined community, forming a majority in no state. Kurds are a minority group in Turkey, Iran, Iraq, and Syria.

In creating multitribal and multiethnic states, **colonialism,** the foreign domination of a territory, often erected boundaries that corresponded poorly with preexisting cultural divisions. But colonial institutions also helped create new "imagined communities" beyond nations. A good example is the idea of *négritude* ("black identity") developed by African intellectuals in Franco-phone (French-speaking) West Africa. Négritude can be traced to the association and common experience in colonial times of

youths from Guinea, Mali, the Ivory Coast, and Senegal at the William Ponty school in Dakar, Senegal (Anderson 1991, pp. 123–124).

ETHNIC TOLERANCE AND ACCOMMODATION

Ethnic diversity may be associated with positive group interaction and coexistence or with conflict (discussed shortly). There are nation-states in which multiple cultural groups live together in reasonable harmony, including some Less Developed Countries.

Assimilation

Assimilation describes the process of change that a minority ethnic group may experience when it moves to a country where another culture dominates. By assimilating, the minority adopts the patterns and norms of its host culture. It is incorporated into the dominant culture to the point that it no longer exists as a separate cultural unit. Some countries, such as Brazil, are more assimilationist than others. Germans, Italians, Japanese, Middle Easterners, and Eastern Europeans started migrating to Brazil late in the 19th century. These immigrants have assimilated to a common Brazilian culture, which has Portuguese, African, and Native American roots. The descendants of these immigrants speak the national language (Portuguese) and participate in the national culture. (During World War II, Brazil, which was on the Allied side, forced assimilation by banning instruction in any language other than Portuguese—especially in German.)

The Plural Society

Assimilation isn't inevitable, and there can be ethnic harmony without it. Ethnic distinctions can persist despite generations of interethnic contact. Through a study of three ethnic groups in Swat, Pakistan, Fredrik Barth (1958/1968) challenged an old idea that interaction always leads to assimilation. He showed that ethnic groups can be in contact for generations without assimilating and can live in peaceful coexistence.

Barth (1958/1968, p. 324) defines **plural society** (an idea he extended from Pakistan to the entire Middle East) as a society combining ethnic contrasts, ecological specialization (i.e., use of different environmental resources by each ethnic group), and the economic interdependence of those groups. In Barth's view, ethnic boundaries are most stable and enduring when the groups occupy different ecological niches. That is, they make their living in different ways and don't compete. Ideally, they should depend on one another's activities and exchange with one another. When different ethnic groups exploit the *same* ecological niche, the militarily more powerful

assimilation
Absorption of minorities within a dominant culture.

nationalities
Ethnic groups that have, once had, or want their own country.

colonialism
Long-term foreign domination of a territory and its people.

plural society
Society with economically interdependent ethnic groups.

German, Italian, Japanese, Middle Eastern, and Eastern European immigrants have assimilated, culturally and linguistically, to a common Brazilian culture. More than 220,000 people of Japanese descent live in Brazil, mostly in and around the city of São Paulo, Brazil's largest. Shown here, a Sunday morning street scene in Sao Paulo's Liberdade district, home to many of that city's assimilated Japanese Brazilians.

group usually will replace the weaker one. If they exploit more or less the same niche, but the weaker group is better able to use marginal environments, they also may coexist (Barth 1958/1968, p. 331). Given niche specialization, ethnic boundaries and interdependence can be maintained, although the specific cultural features of each group may change. By shifting the analytic focus from individual cultures or ethnic groups to *relationships* between cultures or ethnic groups, Barth (1958/1968, 1969) has made important contributions to ethnic studies (see also Kamrava 2011).

Multiculturalism and Ethnic Identity

The view of cultural diversity in a country as something good and desirable is called **multiculturalism** (see Kottak and Kozaitis 2012). The multicultural model is the opposite of the assimilationist model, in which minorities are expected to abandon their cultural traditions and values, replacing them with those of the majority population. The multicultural view encourages the practice of cultural–ethnic traditions. A multicultural society socializes individuals not only into the dominant (national) culture but also into an ethnic culture. Thus in the United States millions of people speak both English and another language, eat both "American" (apple pie, steak, hamburgers) and "ethnic" foods, and celebrate both

national (July 4, Thanksgiving) and ethnic–religious holidays.

In the United States and Canada multiculturalism is of growing importance. This reflects an awareness that the number and size of ethnic groups have grown dramatically in recent years. If this trend continues, the ethnic composition of the United States will change dramatically. (See Figure 15.4.)

Even now, because of immigration and differential population growth, whites are outnumbered by minorities in many urban areas. For example, of the 8,302,659 people living in New York City in 2009, 25 percent were black, 27 percent Hispanic, 12 percent Asian, and 36 percent other—including non-Hispanic whites. The comparable figures for Los Angeles county in 2010 were 9 percent black, 48 percent Hispanic, 12 percent Asian, and 29 percent other, including non-Hispanic whites (U.S. Census Bureau 2010).

In October 2006, the population of the United States reached 300 million people, just 39 years after reaching 200 million and 91 years after reaching the 100 million mark (in 1915). The country's ethnic composition has changed dramatically in the past 40 years. The 1970 census, the first to attempt an official count of Hispanics, found they represented no more than 4.7 percent of the American population. By the 2010 census this figure had risen to 16.3 percent—over 50 million Hispanics. The number of African Americans grew from 11.1 percent in 1967 to 12.6 percent in 2010, while (non-Hispanic) whites

("Anglos") declined from 83 to 63.7 percent. In 1967 fewer than 10 million people in the United States (5 percent of the population) had been born elsewhere, compared with more than 38 million foreign born today (12.5 percent) (all data from U.S. Census Bureau). In 2011, for the first time in American history, minorities (including Hispanics, blacks, Asians, Native Americans, and those of mixed race) accounted for more than half (50.4 percent) of all births in the United States (Tavernise 2012).

In 1973, 78 percent of the students in American public schools were white, and 22 percent were minorities: blacks, Hispanics, Asians, Pacific Islanders, and "others." By 2004, only 57 percent of public school students were white, and 43 percent were minorities. If current trends continue, minority students will outnumber (non-Hispanic) white students by 2015. They already do in California, Hawaii, Mississippi, New Mexico, and Texas (Dillon 2006). (See this chapter's "Focus on Globalization.")

Immigration, mainly from southern and eastern Europe, had a similar effect on classroom diversity, at least in the largest American cities, a century ago. A study of American public schools in 1908–1909 found that only 42 percent of urban students were native born, while 58 percent were immigrants. In a very different (multicultural now versus assimilationist then) context, today's American public school classrooms have regained the ethnic diversity they contained in the early 1900s, when this author's German-speaking Austro-Hungarian-born father and grandparents migrated to the United States.

One response to ethnic diversification and awareness has been for many whites to reclaim ethnic identities (Italian, Albanian, Serbian, Lithuanian, etc.) and to joint ethnic associations (clubs, gangs). Some such groups are new. Others have existed for decades, although they lost members during the assimilationist years of the 1920s through the 1950s.

Multiculturalism seeks ways for people to understand and interact that depend not on sameness but rather on respect for differences. Multiculturalism stresses the interaction of ethnic groups and their contribution to the country. It assumes that each group has something to offer to and learn from the others. Several forces have propelled North America away from the assimilationist model toward multiculturalism. First, multiculturalism reflects the fact of recent large-scale migration, particularly from the "less developed countries" to the "developed" nations of North America and Western Europe. The global scale of modern migration introduces unparalleled ethnic variety to host nations. Multiculturalism is related to globalization: People use modern means of transportation to migrate to nations whose lifestyles they learn about through the media and from tourists who increasingly visit their own countries.

Migration also is fueled by rapid population growth, coupled with insufficient jobs (for both educated and uneducated people), in the Less Developed Countries. As traditional rural economies decline or

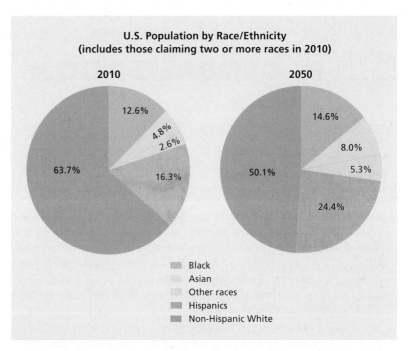

U.S. Population by Race/Ethnicity
(includes those claiming two or more races in 2010)

2010

12.6%
4.8%
2.6%
63.7%
16.3%

2050

14.6%
8.0%
5.3%
50.1%
24.4%

- Black
- Asian
- Other races
- Hispanics
- Non-Hispanic White

FIGURE 15.4 Ethnic Composition of the United States.

The proportion of the American population that is white and non-Hispanic is declining. The projection for 2050 shown here comes from a 2008 U.S. Census Bureau report. Note especially the dramatic rise in the Hispanic portion of the American population between 2010 and 2050.

SOURCE: Based on 2010 data from U.S. Census Bureau, decennial census, and a 2008 projection by the U.S. Census Bureau, http://www.census.gov/population/www/projections/analytical-document09.pdf, Table 1, p. 17.

In the United States, Canada, and western Europe, multiculturalism is of growing importance. Shown here, in the shadow of St. Vincent de Paul Roman Catholic Church, passersby reflect the ethnic diversity of Marseilles, France. Is western Europe more or less multicultural than the United States?

The Gray and the Brown

International migration, a key feature of globalization, has transformed the demographic composition of the United States, Canada, and western Europe. Drawing on a 2010 Brookings Institution report titled "State of Metropolitan America: On the Front Lines of Demographic Transformation," Ronald Brownstein (2010) analyzes an intensifying confrontation between groups he describes as "the gray and the brown." Brownstein and demographer William Frey, an author of the Brookings report, focus on two key U.S. demographic trends:

(1) Ethnic/racial diversity is increasing, especially among the young, with minorities now constituting 44 percent of all American children under 18. (2) The country is aging, and about 80% of the senior population is white.

The under-18 share of the U.S. population is projected eventually to stabilize at around 23 percent, as the senior share rises steadily from about 12 percent today to 20 percent by 2040. The U.S. working-age population is projected to shrink from about 63 percent today to 57 percent in two to three decades. Frey (in Brookings 2010, pp. 26, 63) sees these trends as creating a "cultural generation gap"—a sharp contrast in the attitudes, priorities, and political leanings of younger and older Americans. Whites now constitute 80 percent of older Americans, but only 56 percent of children—a 24-point spread, versus just 14 points in 1980.

Politically the two groups—the gray (older) and the brown (younger)—are poles apart. The aging white population appears increasingly resistant to taxes and public spending, while younger people and minorities value government support of education, health, and social welfare. In the 2008 election, young people, especially minorities, strongly supported Democrat Barack Obama. Seniors, especially white ones, voted solidly for Republican John McCain. These differences persisted thereafter in measures of approval for President Obama's job performance—consistently highest among nonwhites and young people.

The gray and the brown are actually more interdependent economically than either usually realizes. If minority children benefit disproportionately from public education today, minority workers will pay a growing share of the payroll taxes needed to sustain Social Security and Medicare—programs that most directly benefit old white people.

The history of national immigration policy helps us understand how the gap between the gray and the brown arose. Federal policies established in the 1920s had severely curtailed immigration from areas other than northern Europe. In 1965, Congress loosened restrictions—resulting in an eventual influx of immigrants from southern Europe, Asia, Africa, the Caribbean, and Latin America (see Vigil 2012).

Non-Hispanic whites comprised the overwhelming majority of Americans through the mid–20th century, including the post–World War II Baby Boom (1946–1964). Most baby boomers grew up and have lived much of their lives in white suburbs, residentially isolated from minorities (Brownstein 2010). As they age and retire, many older white Americans are reconstituting such communities in racially homogeneous enclaves in the Southeast and Southwest.

In such communities, except for their yard and construction workers and house cleaners, older white Americans live apart from the minorities who represent a growing share of

the national population. Since 1965, expanded immigration and higher fertility rates among minorities have transformed American society. As recently as 1980, minorities made up only 20 percent of the total population (versus over 35 percent today), and 25 percent of children under 18 (versus 44 percent today). Similar trends are evident in western Europe and are everyday expressions of globalization.

mechanize, displaced farmers move to cities, where they and their children often are unable to find jobs. As people in the Less Developed Countries get better educations, they seek more skilled employment. They hope to partake of an international culture of consumption that includes such modern amenities as refrigerators, televisions, computers, and automobiles (Ahmed 2004).

In a world with growing rural-urban and transnational migration, ethnic identities are used increasingly to form self-help organizations focused on enhancing a group's economic competitiveness (Williams 1989). People claim and express ethnic identities for political and economic reasons. Michel Laguerre's (1984, 1998) studies of Haitian immigrants in the United States show that they mobilize to deal with the discriminatory structure (racist in this case, since Haitians tend to be black) of American society. Ethnicity (their common Haitian French creole language and cultural background) is a basis for their mobilization. Haitian ethnicity helps distinguish them from African Americans and other ethnic groups.

In the face of globalization, much of the world, including the entire "democratic West," is experiencing an "ethnic revival." The new assertiveness of long-resident ethnic groups extends to the Basques and Catalans in Spain, the Bretons and Corsicans in France, and the Welsh and Scots in the United Kingdom. The United States and Canada are becoming increasingly multicultural, focusing on their internal diversity (see Laguerre 1999). Rather than as "melting pots," they are better described as ethnic "salads" (each ingredient remains distinct, although in the same bowl, with the same dressing).

ROOTS OF ETHNIC CONFLICT

Ethnicity, based on perceived cultural similarities and differences in a society or nation, can be expressed in peaceful multiculturalism or in discrimination or violent interethnic confrontation. Culture can be both adaptive and maladaptive. The perception of cultural differences can have disastrous effects on social interaction.

The roots of ethnic differentiation—and therefore, potentially, of ethnic conflict—can be political, economic, religious, linguistic, cultural, or racial (see Kuper 2006). Why do ethnic differences often lead to conflict and violence? The causes include a sense of injustice because of resource distribution; economic or political competition; and reaction to discrimination, prejudice, and other expressions of devalued identity (see Donham 2011; Friedman 2003; Ryan 1990, p. xxvii).

In Iraq, under the dictator Saddam Hussein, there was discrimination by one Muslim group (Sunnis) against others (Shiites and Kurds). Sunnis, although a numeric minority within Iraq's population, enjoyed privileged access to power, prestige, and position. After the elections of 2005, which many Sunnis chose to boycott, Shiites gained political control. A civil war soon developed out of "sectarian violence" (conflicts among sects of the same religion) as Sunnis (and their foreign supporters) fueled an insurgency against the new government and its foreign supporters, including the United States. Shiites retaliated against Sunni attacks and a history of Sunni privilege and perceived discrimination against Shiites. Sectarian tension in Iraq remains unresolved as of this writing.

Prejudice and Discrimination

Ethnic conflict often arises in reaction to prejudice (attitudes and judgments) or discrimination (action).

Prejudice means devaluing (looking down on) a group because of its assumed behavior, values, capabilities, or attributes. People are prejudiced when they hold stereotypes about groups and apply them to individuals. (**Stereotypes** are fixed ideas—often unfavorable—about what the members of a group are like.) Prejudiced people assume that members of the group will act as they are "supposed to act" (according to the stereotype) and interpret a wide range of individual behaviors as evidence of the stereotype. They use this behavior to confirm their stereotype (and low opinion) of the group.

Discrimination refers to policies and practices that harm a group and its members. Discrimination may be *de facto* (practiced, but not legally sanctioned) or *de jure* (part of the law). An example of de facto discrimination is the harsher treatment that American minorities (compared with other Americans) tend to get from the police and the judicial system. This unequal treatment isn't legal, but it happens anyway. Segregation in the southern United States and *apartheid* in South Africa provide two historical examples of de jure discrimination. In both systems, by law, blacks and whites once had different rights and privileges. Also, their social interaction ("mixing") was legally curtailed.

prejudice
Devaluing a group because of its assumed attributes.

stereotypes
Fixed ideas—often unfavorable—about what members of a group are like.

discrimination
Policies and practices that harm a group and its members.

Discrimination refers to policies and practices that harm a group and its members. This protest sign, hoisted in New Orleans' Lower Ninth Ward, shows that at least some community residents see ethnic and racial bias in the fact that African Americans in that city bore the brunt of Hurricane Katrina's devastation.

This clip focuses on ethnic diversity in Bosnia. The war of the early 1990s may have ended, but ethnic animosity remains. In discussing the living arrangements of Croats and Muslims, the narrator of the clip describes a "checkerboard" settlement pattern that existed before the war. What does he mean by this? The clip shows that both Muslims and Croats were displaced by the war. Was the village of Bukovica, where the clip is mainly set, originally a Muslim or a Croat village? How is ethnic difference marked in everyday life, in such routine activities as buying things, talking on the phone, and driving an automobile?

Chips in the Mosaic

Although the multicultural model is increasingly prominent in North America, ethnic competition and conflict also are evident. There is conflict between newer arrivals, for instance, Central Americans and Koreans, and longer-established ethnic groups, such as African Americans. Ethnic antago-nism flared in South-Central Los Angeles in spring 1992 in rioting that followed the acquittal of four white police officers who were tried for the video-taped beating of Rodney King (see Abelmann and Lie 1995).

Attacks against whites, Koreans, and Latinos expressed frustration by African Americans about their prospects in an increasingly multicultural society. A poll done just after the Los Angeles riots found that blacks had a bleaker outlook than whites about the effects of immigration on their lives. Only 23 percent of blacks felt they had more opportunities than recent immigrants, compared with twice that many whites (Toner 1992).

Korean stores were hard hit during the 1992 riots, and more than a third of the businesses destroyed were Latino owned. A third of those who died in the riots were Latinos. These mainly recent migrants lacked deep roots to the neighborhood and, as Spanish speakers, faced language barriers (Newman 1992). Many Koreans also had trouble with English.

Koreans interviewed on ABC's *Nightline* on May 6, 1992, recognized that blacks resented them and considered them unfriendly. One man explained, "It's not part of our culture to smile." African Americans interviewed on the same program did complain about Korean unfriendliness. "They come into our

In the Darfur region of western Sudan (shown here), Arab militias, called the *Janjaweed*, have forced black Africans off their land. The militias, equipped by the Sudanese government, are accused of killing up to 30,000 darker-skinned Africans. This campaign has been called both "ethnic cleansing" and genocide. Since the violence began in March 2003, more than one million people have fled to refugee camps in Sudan and Chad. In this photo, children play among makeshift huts in one such camp.

Two faces of ethnic difference in the former Soviet empire. A propaganda poster depicts a happy mix of nationalities that make up the population of Kyrgyzstan, Central Asia (left). The photo on the right, taken in May 2010 in Krygyzstan, shows Kyrgyz soldiers guarding a university following an attempt to storm the university during a period of ethnic violence between Kyrgyz mobs and minority Uzbeks.

neighborhoods and treat us like dirt." These comments suggest a shortcoming of the multicultural perspective: Ethnic groups (blacks here) expect other ethnic groups in the same nation-state to assimilate to some extent to a shared (national) culture. The African Americans' comments invoked a general American value system that includes friendliness, openness, mutual respect, community participation, and "fair play." Los Angeles blacks wanted their Korean neighbors to act more like generalized Americans—and good neighbors.

Aftermaths of Oppression

Forms of discrimination against ethnic groups include genocide, ethnocide, forced assimilation, and cultural colonialism. The most extreme form is **genocide,** the deliberate elimination of a group (such as Jews in Nazi Germany, Muslims in Bosnia, or Tutsi in Rwanda) through mass murder (see Hinton and O'Neill 2011). A dominant group may try to destroy the cultures of certain ethnic groups (**ethnocide**) or force them to adopt the dominant culture (*forced assimilation*). Many countries have penalized or banned the language and customs of an ethnic group (including its religious observances). One example of forced assimilation is the anti-Basque campaign that the dictator Francisco Franco (who ruled between 1939 and 1975) waged in Spain. Franco banned Basque books, journals, newspapers, signs, sermons, and tombstones and imposed fines for using the Basque language in schools. His policies led to the formation of a Basque terrorist group and spurred strong nationalist sentiment in the Basque region (Ryan 1990). A policy of *ethnic expulsion* aims at removing groups who are culturally different from a country. There are many examples, including Bosnia-Herzegovina in the 1990s. Uganda expelled 74,000 Asians in

1972. The neofascist parties of contemporary Western Europe advocate repatriation (expulsion) of immigrant workers, such as Algerians in France and Turks in Germany (see Friedman 2003; Ryan 1990, p. 9). Expulsion may create **refugees**—people who have been forced (involuntary refugees) or who have chosen (voluntary refugees) to flee a country, to escape persecution or war.

In many countries, colonial nation building left ethnic strife in its wake. Thus, over a million Hindus and Muslims were killed in the violence that accompanied the division of the Indian subcontinent into India and Pakistan. Problems between Arabs and Jews in Palestine began during the British mandate period (see Kamrava 2011).

Multiculturalism may be growing in the United States and Canada, but the opposite is happening in the former Soviet Union, where ethnic groups (nationalities) want their own nation-states. The flowering of ethnic feeling and conflict as the Soviet empire disintegrated illustrates that years of political repression and ideology provide insufficient common ground for lasting unity. **Cultural colonialism** refers to internal domination by one group and its culture or ideology over others. One example is the domination over the former Soviet empire by Russian people, language, and culture, and by communist ideology. The dominant culture makes itself the official culture. This is reflected in schools, the media, and public interaction. Under Soviet rule ethnic minorities had very limited self-rule in republics and regions controlled by Moscow. All the republics and their peoples were to be united by the oneness of "socialist internationalism." One common technique in cultural colonialism is to flood ethnic areas with members of the dominant ethnic group. Thus, in the former Soviet Union, ethnic Russian colonists were sent to many areas, to diminish the cohesion and clout of the local people.

refugees
People who flee a country to escape persecution or war.

genocide
Deliberate elimination of a group through mass murder.

ethnocide
Destruction of cultures of certain ethnic groups.

cultural colonialism
Internal domination by one group and its culture or ideology over others.

TYPE	NATURE OF INTERACTION	EXAMPLES
POSITIVE		
Assimilation	Ethnic groups absorbed within dominant culture	Brazil; United States in early, mid-20th century
Plural Society	Society or region contains economically interdependent ethnic groups	Areas of Middle East with farmers/herders; Swat, Pakistan
Multiculturalism	Cultural diversity valued; ethnic cultures coexist with dominant culture	Canada; United States in 21st century
NEGATIVE		
Prejudice	Devaluing a group based on assumed attributes	Worldwide
Discrimination De Jure	Legal policies and practices harm ethnic group	South African apartheid; former segregation in southern U.S.
Discrimination De Facto	Not legally sanctioned, but practiced	Worldwide
Genocide	Deliberate elimination of ethnic group through mass murder	Nazi Germany; Bosnia; Rwanda; Cambodia; Darfur
Ethnocide	Cultural practices attacked by dominant culture or colonial power	Spanish Basques under Franco
Ethnic Expulsion	Forcing ethnic group(s) out of a country or region	Ugandan Asians; Serbia; Bosnia; Kosovo

The Commonwealth of Independent States (CIS), founded in 1991 and headquartered in Minsk, Belarus, is what remains of the once-powerful Soviet Union (see Yurchak 2006). In Russia and other formerly Soviet nations, ethnic groups (nationalities) have sought, and continue to seek, to forge separate and viable nation-states based on cultural boundaries. This celebration of ethnic autonomy is part of an ethnic florescence that—as surely as globalization and transnationalism—is a trend of the late 20th and early 21st centuries.

Recap 15.1 summarizes the various types of ethnic interaction—positive and negative—that have been discussed.

acing the COURSE

summary

1. An ethnic group refers to members of a particular culture in a nation or region that contains others. Ethnicity is based on actual, perceived, or assumed cultural similarities (among members of the same ethnic group) and differences (between that group and others). Ethnic distinctions can be based on language, religion, history, geography, kinship, or race. A race is an ethnic group assumed to have a biological basis. Usually race and ethnicity are ascribed statuses; people are born members of a group and remain so all their lives.

2. Human races are cultural rather than biological categories. Such races derive from contrasts perceived in particular societies, rather than from scientific classifications based on common genes. In the United States, racial labels such as "white" and "black" designate socially constructed races—categories defined by American culture. American racial classification, governed by the rule of hypodescent, is based neither on phenotype nor on genes. Children of mixed unions, no matter what their appearance, are classified with the minority group parent.

3. Racial attitudes in Japan illustrate intrinsic racism—the belief that a perceived racial difference is a sufficient reason to value one person less than another. The valued group is majority (pure) Japanese, who are believed to share the same blood. Majority Japanese define themselves in opposition to others, including minority groups in Japan and outsiders—anyone who is "not us."

4. Such exclusionary racial systems are not inevitable. Although Brazil shares a history of slavery with the United States, it lacks the hypodescent rule. Brazilian racial identity is more of an achieved status. It can change during someone's lifetime, reflecting phenotypical changes.

5. The term *nation* once was synonymous with *ethnic group*. Now nation has come to mean a state—a centrally organized political unit. Because of migration, conquest, and colonialism, most nation-states are not ethnically homogeneous. Ethnic groups that seek autonomous political status (their own country) are nationalities. Political upheavals, wars, and migrations have divided many imagined national communities.

6. Assimilation describes the process of change an ethnic group may experience when it moves to a country where another culture dominates. By assimilating, the minority adopts the patterns and norms of its host culture. Assimilation isn't inevitable, and there can be ethnic harmony without it. A plural society combines ethnic contrasts and economic interdependence between ethnic groups. The view of cultural diversity in a nation-state as good and desirable is multiculturalism. A multicultural society socializes individuals not only into the dominant (national) culture but also into an ethnic one.

7. Ethnicity can be expressed in peaceful multiculturalism, or in discrimination or violent confrontation. Ethnic conflict often arises in reaction to prejudice (attitudes and judgments) or discrimination (action). The most extreme form of ethnic discrimination is genocide, the deliberate elimination of a group through mass murder. A dominant group may try to destroy certain ethnic practices (ethnocide), or to force ethnic group members to adopt the dominant culture (forced assimilation). A policy of ethnic expulsion may create refugees. Cultural colonialism refers to internal domination by one group and its culture or ideology over others.

key terms

MULTIPLE CHOICE

1. What is the term for identification with, and feeling part of, an ethnic tradition and exclusion from other ethnic traditions?
    a. culture shock
    b. cultural relativism
    c. ethnicity
    d. assimilation
    e. ethnocentrism

2. What is the term for a social status that is not automatic; that comes through choices, actions, effects, talents, or accomplishments; and that may be positive or negative?
    a. ascribed status
    b. situational status
    c. negotiated status
    d. ethnicity
    e. achieved status

test yourself

3. People may occupy a variety of different social statuses during their lives, or even during the course of a day. When claimed or perceived identity varies depending on the audience, this is called
   a. ethnic identity.
   b. racial substitution.
   c. discourse analysis.
   d. rotating core personality traits.
   e. situational negotiation of social identity.

4. Human races, like ethnicities in general, are
   a. cultural rather than biological categories.
   b. a biological reality as much as a cultural one.
   c. used by social scientists to classify humans based on genes and shared blood.
   d. key categories for biology, but not anthropology.
   e. a meaningless concept to people living day to day.

5. What is the term for the belief that a perceived racial difference is a sufficient reason to value one person less than another (such as in the case of burakumin in Japan)?
   a. extrinsic racism
   b. hypodescent
   c. intrinsic racism
   d. hyperdescent
   e. de jure discrimination

6. Which of the following best explains the differences between American and Brazilian social constructions of race?
   a. Brazilian plantation landlords had sexual relations with their slaves.
   b. There was a lack of native populations in Brazil.
   c. The Portuguese language had a greater number of intermediate color terms than the English language.
   d. Historically in Brazil, freed offspring of master and slave filled many intermediate positions in the emerging Brazilian economy.
   e. English concepts of race were very different from those of the Portuguese.

7. Which of the following statements about ethnic groups that once had, or wish to have or regain, autonomous political status is *not* true?
   a. They often are minorities in the nation in which they live.
   b. They have been called "imagined communities."
   c. They include or have included the Kurds and Germans.
   d. They are called nationalities.
   e. All or most of their members usually meet regularly face to face.

8. Which of the following statements about nation-states is true?
   a. Nation-states sometimes encourage ethnic divisions for political and economic ends.
   b. Nation-states are ethnically homogeneous.
   c. Nation-states are defined by their lack of ethnic identity.
   d. *Nation-state* is a synonym for *tribe* and *ethnic group*.
   e. Nation-states are parts of other states.

9. What does Benedict Anderson's term "imagined communities" refer to?
   a. postcolonial states, because these did not exist until colonialists thought them up
   b. communities that do not exist in real terms, but are the fictional and temporary products of the ruling intelligentsia
   c. communities composed of many different ethnic groups and subcultures, which therefore will fall apart at any moment
   d. communities in which identity is established not by direct social interaction with other members but through interaction with public media, like a national print media
   e. tribal states in which all members enjoy equal rights, regardless of their ethnicity or religion

10. What is the term for the physical destruction of an ethnic or religious group through mass murder?
   a. ethnic expulsion
   b. forced assimilation
   c. ethnocentrism
   d. racist expulsion
   e. genocide

FILL IN THE BLANK

1. Given the lack of distinction between race and ethnicity, this chapter suggests the term _____ instead of "race" to describe any such social group.

2. _____ is the term for the arbitrary rule that automatically places the children of a union between members of different socioeconomic groups in the less-privileged group.

3. _____ is the view of cultural diversity as valuable and worth maintaining.

4. _____ is the internal domination by one group and its culture/ideology over others.

5. _____ refers to the devaluing of a group because of its assumed behavior, values, abilities, or attributes.

CRITICAL THINKING

1. What's the difference between a culture and an ethnic group? In what culture(s) do you participate? To what ethnic group(s) do you belong? What is the basis of your primary cultural identity? Do others readily recognize this basis and identity? Why or why not?

2. Name five social statuses you currently occupy. Which of those statuses are ascribed, and which ones are achieved? Are any of these statuses mutually exclusive? Which are contextual?

3. In describing the recent history of the census in the United States, this chapter notes how the National Association for the Advancement of Colored People and the National Council of La Raza (a Hispanic advocacy group) have opposed adding a "multiracial" census category. What does this suggest about racial categories?

4. If *race* is a discredited concept when applied to humans, what has replaced it?

5. This chapter describes different types of ethnic interaction. What are they? Are they positive or negative? Anthropologists have made and continue to make important contributions to understanding past and ongoing cases of ethnic conflict. What are some examples of this?

Multiple Choice: 1. (C); 2. (E); 3. (E); 4. (A); 5. (C); 6. (D); 7. (E); 8. (A); 9. (D); 10. (E); **Fill in the Blank:** 1. *ethnic group;* 2. *Hypodescent;* 3. Multiculturalism; 4. Cultural colonialism; 5. Prejudice

Abraham, N., S. Howell, and A. Shryock, eds.
  2011   *Arab Detroit 9/11: Life in the Terror Decade.* Detroit: Wayne University Press. Ethnoreligious prejudice, surveillance, and scapegoating, along with political and cultural gains in Detroit's Arab communities.

Kottak, C. P., and K. A. Kozaitis
  2012   *On Being Different: Diversity and Multiculturalism in the North American Mainstream,* 4th ed. Boston: McGraw-Hill. Aspects of diversity in the United States and Canada, plus an original theory of multiculturalism.

Mukhopadhyay, C. C., R. Henze, and Y. T. Moses
  2007   *How Real Is Race: A Sourcebook on Race, Culture, and Biology.* Lanham, MD: Rowman and Littlefield Education. Valuable four-field collection of works by anthropologists on varied dimensions—biological, social, and cultural—of race, racism, and discrimination.

Schaefer, R. T.
  2013   *Race and Ethnicity in the United States,* 7th ed. Upper Saddle River, NJ: Pearson Prentice Hall. How race and ethnicity function in contemporary American society.

Scupin, R., ed.
  2012   *Race and Ethnicity: The United States and the World.* Upper Saddle River, NJ: Pearson Prentice Hall. Broad survey of race and ethnic relations.

Wade, P.
  2010   *Race and Ethnicity in Latin America,* 2nd ed. New York: Pluto Press. Race relations, ethnicity, and classification in an important region.

suggested additional readings

Go to our Online Learning Center website at **www.mhhe.com/kottak** for Internet exercises directly related to the content of this chapter.

internet exercises

CHAPTER 16

Making a Living

What are the major adaptive strategies found in nonindustrial societies?

What is an economy, and what is economizing behavior?

What principles regulate the exchange of goods and services in various societies?

◀ In Zinga, Tanzania, members of the women's group Bawodene UWAZI at the poultry farm they have established with the support of the nongovernmental organizations (NGOs) ActionAid and Bawodene Saccos.

understanding OURSELVES

The necessities of work, marriage, and raising children are fundamental. However, in the non-Western societies where the study of anthropology originated, the need to balance work (economy) and family (society) wasn't as stark as it is for us. In traditional societies, one's workmates usually were also one's kin. There was no need for a "take your child to work" day because most women did that every day. People didn't work with strangers. Home and office, society and economy, were intertwined.

The fact that subsistence and sociality are both basic human needs creates conflicts in modern society. People have to make choices about allocating their time and energy between work and family. Parents in dual-earner and single-parent households always have faced a work-family time bind, and the number of Americans living in such households has almost doubled in recent decades. Fewer than one-third of American wives worked outside the home in 1960, compared with about two-thirds today. That same year, only one-fifth of married women with children under age six were in the workforce, versus three-fifths today. With women increasingly able to make it "on their own," the economic importance of marriage has declined. In 2007, for the first time ever, the percentage of adult American women who were unmarried exceeded 50.

Think about the choices your parents have made in terms of economic versus social goals. Have their decisions maximized their incomes, their lifestyles, their individual happiness, family benefits, or what? What about you? What factors motivated you when you chose to apply to and attend college? Did you want to stay close to home, to attend college with friends, or to maintain a romantic attachment (all social reasons)? Did you seek the lowest tuition and college costs—or get a generous scholarship (economic decisions)? Did you choose prestige, or perhaps the likelihood that one day you would earn more money because of the reputation of your alma mater (maximizing prestige and future wealth)? Economists tend to assume that the profit motive rules in contemporary society. However, different individuals, like different cultures, may choose to pursue goals other than monetary gain.

Studies show that most American women now expect to join the paid labor force, just as men do. But the family remains attractive. Most young women also plan to stay home with small children and return to the workforce once their children enter school. How about you? If you have definite career plans, how do you imagine your work will fit in with your future family life—if you have one planned? What do your parents want most for you—a successful career or a happy family life with children? Probably both. Will it be easy to fulfill such expectations?

ADAPTIVE STRATEGIES

Compared with hunting and gathering (foraging), the advent of *food production* (plant cultivation and animal domestication) fueled major changes in human life, such as the formation of larger social and political systems—eventually states. The pace of cultural transformation increased enormously. This chapter provides a framework for understanding a variety of human adaptive strategies and economic systems—ranging from hunting and gathering to farming and herding.

The anthropologist Yehudi Cohen (1974b) used the term **adaptive strategy** to describe a group's system of economic production. Cohen argued that the most important reason for similarities between two (or more) unrelated societies is their possession of a similar adaptive strategy. For example, there are clear similarities among societies that have a foraging (hunting-and-gathering) strategy. Cohen developed a typology of societies based on correlations between their economies and their social features. His typology includes these five adaptive strategies: foraging, horticulture, agriculture, pastoralism, and industrialism. Industrialism is discussed in the chapter "The World System and Colonialism." The present chapter focuses on the first four adaptive strategies.

adaptive strategy
Means of making a living; productive system.

FORAGING

Until 10,000 years ago, people everywhere were foragers, also known as hunter-gatherers. However, environmental differences did create substantial contrasts among the world's foragers. Some, such as the people who lived in Europe during the ice ages, were big-game hunters. Today, hunters in the Arctic still focus on large animals and herd animals; they have much less vegetation and variety in their diets than do tropical foragers. In general, as one moves from colder to warmer areas, there is an increase in the number of species. The tropics contain tremendous biodiversity, a great variety of plant and animal species. Tropical foragers typically hunt and gather a wide range of plant and animal life. The same may be true in temperate areas, such as the North Pacific Coast of North America, where Native American foragers could draw on a rich variety of sea and land resources, including salmon, other fish species, sea mammals, berries, and mountain goats. Nevertheless, despite differences due to environmental variation, all foraging economies have shared one essential feature: People rely on available natural resources for their subsistence, rather than controlling the reproduction of plants and animals.

Such control came with the advent of animal domestication (initially of sheep and goats) and plant cultivation (of wheat and barley), which began 10,000 to 12,000 years ago in the Middle East. Cultivation based on different crops, such as maize, manioc (cassava), and potatoes, arose independently in the Americas. In both hemispheres the new economy spread rapidly. Today, almost all foragers have at least some dependence on food production or on food producers (Kent 1992).

The foraging way of life survived into modern times in certain environments (see Figure 16.1),

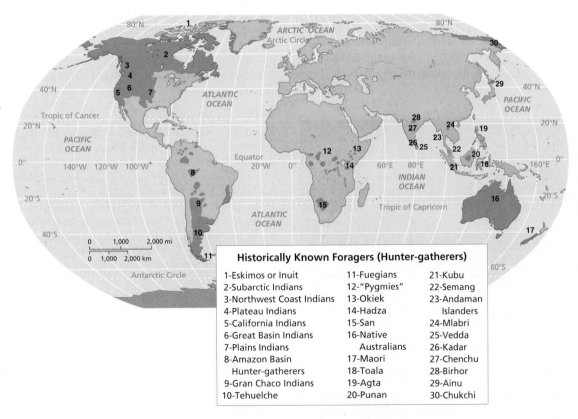

Historically Known Foragers (Hunter-gatherers)

1-Eskimos or Inuit	11-Fuegians	21-Kubu
2-Subarctic Indians	12-"Pygmies"	22-Semang
3-Northwest Coast Indians	13-Okiek	23-Andaman
4-Plateau Indians	14-Hadza	Islanders
5-California Indians	15-San	24-Mlabri
6-Great Basin Indians	16-Native	25-Vedda
7-Plains Indians	Australians	26-Kadar
8-Amazon Basin	17-Maori	27-Chenchu
Hunter-gatherers	18-Toala	28-Birhor
9-Gran Chaco Indians	19-Agta	29-Ainu
10-Tehuelche	20-Punan	30-Chukchi

FIGURE 16.1 Worldwide Distribution of Recent Hunter-Gatherers.

SOURCE: Adaptation from map and key by Ray Sim, in Göran Burenhult, ed., *Encyclopedia of Humankind: People of the Stone Age* (McMahons Point, NSW, Australia: Weldon Owen, 1993), p. 193. © Weldon Owen Pty. Ltd. Used with permission.

including a few islands and forests, along with deserts and very cold areas—places where food production was not practicable with simple technology (see Lee and Daly 1999). In many areas, foragers had been exposed to the "idea" of food production but never adopted it because their own economies provided a perfectly adequate and nutritious diet—with a lot less work. In some areas, people reverted to foraging after trying food production and abandoning it. In most areas where hunter-gatherers did survive, foraging should be described as "recent" rather than "contemporary." All foragers now live in nation-states, depend to some extent on government assistance, and have contacts with food-producing neighbors and other outsiders. We should not view contemporary foragers as isolated or pristine survivors of the Stone Age. Modern foragers are influenced by regional forces (e.g., trade and war), national and international policies, and political and economic events in the world system.

Although foraging is disappearing as a way of life, the outlines of Africa's two broad belts of recent foraging remain evident. One is the Kalahari Desert of southern Africa. This is the home of the *San* ("Bushmen"), who include the *Ju/'hoansi* (see Kent 1996; Lee 2003). The other main African foraging area is the equatorial forest of central and eastern Africa, home of the Mbuti, Efe, and other "pygmies" (Bailey et al. 1989; Turnbull 1965).

People still do, or until recently did, subsistence foraging in certain remote forests in Madagascar; in southeast Asia, including Malaysia and the Philippines; and on certain islands off the Indian coast (Lee and Daly 1999). Some of the best-known recent foragers are the aborigines of Australia. Those

Native Australians lived on their island continent for 50,000 years without developing food production.

The Western Hemisphere also had recent foragers. The Eskimos, or Inuit, of Alaska and Canada are well-known hunters. These (and other) northern foragers now use modern technology, including rifles and snowmobiles, in their subsistence activities. The native populations of California, Oregon, Washington, British Columbia, and Alaska all were foragers, as were those of inland subarctic Canada and the Great Lakes. For many Native Americans, fishing, hunting, and gathering remain important subsistence (and sometimes commercial) activities.

Coastal foragers also lived near the southern tip of South America, in Patagonia. On the grassy plains of Argentina, southern Brazil, Uruguay, and Paraguay, there were other hunter-gatherers. The contemporary Aché of Paraguay often are called "hunter-gatherers" even though they get only a third of their livelihood from foraging. The Aché also grow crops, have domesticated animals, and live in or near mission posts, where they receive food from missionaries (Hawkes, O'Connell, and Hill 1982; Hill and Hurtado 1996).

The hunter-gatherer way of life did persist in a few areas that could be cultivated, even after contact with cultivators. Those tenacious foragers, such as indigenous foragers in what is now California, Oregon, Washington, and British Columbia, did not turn to food production because they were supporting themselves very adequately by hunting and gathering (see the section on the potlatch at the end of this chapter). As the modern world system spreads, the number of foragers continues to decline. Recap 16.1 summarizes locations and attributes of foragers.

San: Then and Now

Throughout the world, foraging survived in environments that posed major obstacles to food production. (Some foragers took refuge in such areas after the rise of food production, the state, colonialism, or the modern world system.) The difficulties of cultivating at the North Pole are obvious. In southern Africa, the Dobe Ju/'hoansi San area studied by Richard Lee is surrounded by a waterless belt 45 to 125 miles (70 to 200 kilometers) in breadth. The Dobe area is hard to reach even today, and there is no evidence of occupation of this area by food producers before the 20th century (Solway and Lee 1990). However, environmental limits to other adaptive strategies aren't the only reason foragers survived. Their niches had one thing in common: their marginality. Their environments were not of immediate interest to other groups.

Most of the estimated 100,000 San who survive today live in poverty on society's fringes. Each year, more and more foragers come under the control of nation-states and are influenced by forces of globalization. As described by Motseta (2006), between 1997 and 2002, the government of Botswana in

In southwestern Madagascar, Vezo children (members of a maritime ethnic group) play in a lagoon. Is fishing a form of foraging?

GEOGRAPHIC LOCATIONS	
ARCHAEOLOGICALLY KNOWN FORAGERS	Europe: Paleolithic big-game hunters Europe, Japan, Middle East, elsewhere: Mesolithic broad-spectrum foragers Africa: Stone Age hunters and gatherers

RECENT (ETHNOGRAPHICALLY KNOWN) FORAGERS OLD WORLD	Africa:
	  Kalahari Desert, southern Africa: *San* ("Bushmen")
	  Equatorial forest, central and eastern Africa: Mbuti, Efe ("pygmies")
	Madagascar, remote forests: Mikea
	Southeast Asia—Malaysia and Philippines: Tasaday
	Islands off India's coast: Andaman Islanders
	Australia: entire continent—Native Australians ("aborigines")

WESTERN HEMISPHERE	Alaska and Canada: Eskimos, or Inuit
	N. Pacific coast: California, Oregon, Washington, British Columbia, and Alaska
	Inland subarctic Canada and U.S. Great Lakes
	South America:
	  coastal Patagonia
	  pampas: Argentina, southern Brazil, Uruguay, Paraguay

GENERALIZATIONS ABOUT FORAGERS	
	Not pristine "survivors of the Stone Age." Recent rather than contemporary. Rely on natural resources for subsistence. Don't control plant and animal reproduction. Environments posed major obstacles to food production. Live on or in islands, forests, deserts, very cold areas. Some knew about food production but rejected it. Some fled food production, states, or colonial rule.

ALL FORAGERS TODAY	Live in nation-states.
	
	Depend on outside assistance.
	
	Have significant contact with outsiders.
	
	Are influenced by:
	  food-producing economies
	  regional forces (e.g., trade and war)
	  national and international policies
	  political and economic events in the world system

southern Africa relocated about 3,000 Basarwa San Bushmen outside their ancestral territory, which was converted into a wildlife reserve. The Basarwa received some compensation for their land, along with access to schools, medical facilities, and job training in resettlement centers. However, critics claim this resettlement turned a society of free hunter-gatherers into communities dependent on food aid and government handouts (Motseta 2006).

In 2006 Botswana's High Court ruled that the Basarwa had been wrongly evicted from the "Central Kalahari Game Reserve." In the context of global political action for cultural rights, this verdict was hailed as a victory for indigenous peoples around the world (Motseta 2006). In December 2006, Botswana's attorney general recognized the court order to allow the Basarwa to return to their ancestral lands, while imposing conditions likely to prevent most of them from doing so. Only the 189 people who actually filed the lawsuit would have automatic right of return with their children, compared with some 2,000 Basarwa wishing to return. The others

On December 13, 2006, San men and women celebrate outside court in Lobatse, Botswana. The court had just ruled that the plaintiffs could return to live and hunt on their ancestral lands, which had been enclosed within a game reserve.

would have to apply for special permits. Returning Basarwa would be allowed to build only temporary structures and to use enough water for subsistence needs. Water would be a major obstacle since the government shut the main well in 2002, and water is scarce in the Kalahari. Furthermore, anyone wishing to hunt would have to apply for a permit.

Correlates of Foraging

Typologies, including Cohen's adaptive strategies, are useful because they suggest **correlations**—that is, association or covariation between two or more variables. (Correlated variables are factors that are linked and interrelated, such as food intake and body weight, such that when one increases or decreases, the other tends to change, too.) Ethnographic studies in hundreds of societies have revealed many correlations between the economy and social life. Associated (correlated) with each adaptive strategy is a bundle of particular cultural features. Correlations, however, are rarely perfect. Some foragers lacked cultural features usually associated with foraging, while some of those features were present in groups with other adaptive strategies.

What, then, are some correlates of foraging? People who subsisted by hunting, gathering, and fishing often lived in band-organized societies. Their basic social unit, the **band,** was a small group of fewer than a hundred people, all related by kinship or marriage. Band size varied among cultures and often from one season to the next in a given culture. In some foraging societies, band size stayed about the same year-round. In others, the band split up for part of the year. Families left to gather resources better exploited by just a few people. Later, they regrouped for cooperative work and ceremonies.

Several examples of seasonal splits and reunions are known from ethnography and archaeology. In southern Africa, some San aggregated around waterholes in the dry season and split up in the wet season, whereas other bands dispersed in the dry season (Barnard 1979; Kent 1992). This reflected environmental variation. San who lacked permanent water had to disperse and forage widely for moisture-filled plants. In ancient Oaxaca, Mexico, before the advent of plant cultivation, foragers assembled in large bands in summer to harvest tree pods and cactus fruits. Then, in fall, they split into much smaller family groups to hunt deer and gather grasses and plants that were effectively foraged by small teams.

One typical characteristic of the foraging life is mobility. In many San groups, as among the Mbuti of Congo, people shifted band membership several times in a lifetime. One might be born, for example, in a band where one's mother had kin. Later, one's family might move to a band where the father had relatives. Because bands were exogamous (people married outside their own band), one's parents came from two different bands, and one's grandparents might have come from four. People could join any band to which they had kinship or marriage links. A couple could live in, or shift between, the husband's band and the wife's band.

One also could affiliate with a band through fictive kinship—personal relationships modeled on kinship, such as that between godparents and godchildren. San, for example, have a limited number of personal names. People with the same name have a special relationship; they treat each other like siblings. San expected the same hospitality in bands where they had namesakes as they did in a band where a real sibling lived. Kinship, marriage, and fictive kinship thus provided entries to multiple bands. As people changed bands frequently, band membership varied substantially from year to year.

Human societies have tended to encourage a division of labor based on gender (see the chapter on gender for much more on this). Among foragers, men typically hunted and fished while women gathered and collected, but the specific nature of the work varied among cultures. Sometimes women's work contributed most to the diet. Sometimes male hunting and fishing predominated. Among foragers in tropical and semitropical areas, gathering often contributed more to the diet than hunting and fishing did—even though the labor costs of gathering were much higher than those of hunting and fishing.

All foragers have maintained social distinctions based on age. Often old people received great respect as guardians of myths, legends, stories, and traditions. Younger people valued the elders' special knowledge of ritual and practical matters. Most foraging societies were egalitarian, with contrasts in prestige minor and based on age and gender.

When considering issues of "human nature," we should remember that the egalitarian band was a basic form of human social life for most of our history. Food production has existed less than 1 percent of the time *Homo* has been on Earth. However, it has produced huge social differences. We now consider the main economic features of food-producing strategies.

CULTIVATION

The three adaptive strategies based on food production in nonindustrial societies are horticulture, agriculture, and pastoralism. In non-Western cultures, as is also true in modern nations, people carry out a variety of economic activities. Each adaptive strategy refers to the main economic activity. Pastoralists (herders), for example, consume milk, butter, blood, and meat from their animals as mainstays of their diet. However, they also add grain to the diet by doing some cultivating or by trading with neighbors. Food producers also may hunt or gather to supplement a diet based on domesticated species.

In slash-and-burn horticulture, the land is cleared by cutting down (slashing) and burning trees and bush, using simple technology. After such clearing this woman uses a digging stick to plant mountain rice in Madagascar. What might be the environmental effects of slash-and-burn cultivation?

Horticulture

Horticulture and agriculture are two types of cultivation found in nonindustrial societies. Both differ from the farming systems of industrial nations like the United States and Canada, which use large land areas, machinery, and petrochemicals. According to Cohen, **horticulture** is cultivation that makes intensive use of *none* of the factors of production: land, labor, capital, and machinery. Horticulturalists use simple tools such as hoes and digging sticks to grow their crops. Their fields are not permanently cultivated and lie fallow for varying lengths of time.

Horticulture often involves *slash-and-burn techniques*. Here, horticulturalists clear land by cutting down (slashing) and burning forest or bush or by setting fire to the grass covering a plot. The vegetation is broken down, pests are killed, and the ashes remain to fertilize the soil. Crops are then sown, tended, and harvested. Use of the plot is not continuous. Often it is cultivated for only a year. This depends, however, on soil fertility and weeds, which compete with cultivated plants for nutrients.

When horticulturalists abandon a plot because of soil exhaustion or a thick weed cover, they clear another piece of land, and the original plot reverts to forest. After several years of fallowing (the duration varies in different societies), the cultivator

horticulture
Nonindustrial plant cultivation with fallowing.

A World on Fire

Anthropologists were instrumental in pushing the Brazilian government to establish the Xingu National Park. Created in 1961, the park encompasses about 8,530 square miles. It is home to indigenous peoples representing Brazil's four major indigenous language families: Tupi, Arawak, Carib, and Gê. The people and cultures of the Xingu Park have been studied by generations of anthropologists. Now, however, the park and its people are threatened by deforestation and climate change.

XINGU NATIONAL PARK, Brazil—As the naked, painted young men of the Kamayurá tribe prepare for the ritualized war games of a festival, they end their haunting fireside chant with a blowing sound—"whoosh, whoosh"—a symbolic attempt to eliminate the scent of fish so they will not be detected by enemies. For centuries, fish from jungle lakes and rivers have been a staple of the Kamayurá diet, the tribe's primary source of protein.

But fish smells are not a problem for the warriors anymore. Deforestation and, some scientists contend, global climate change are making the Amazon region drier and hotter, decimating fish stocks in this area and imperiling the Kamayurá's very existence. Like other small indigenous cultures around the world with little money or capacity to move, they are struggling to adapt to the changes.

"Us old monkeys can take the hunger, but the little ones suffer—they're always asking for fish," said Kotok, the tribe's chief, who stood in front of a hut containing the tribe's sacred flutes on a recent evening. He wore a white T-shirt over the tribe's traditional dress, which is basically nothing.

Chief Kotok, who like all of the Kamayurá people goes by only one name, said that men can now fish all night without a bite in streams where fish used to be abundant; they safely swim in lakes previously teeming with piranhas. Responsible for 3 wives, 24 children and hundreds of other tribe members, he said his once-idyllic existence had turned into a kind of bad dream. . . .

The Intergovernmental Panel on Climate Change says that up to 30 percent of animals and plants face an increased risk of extinction if global temperatures rise 2 degrees Celsius (3.6 degrees Fahrenheit) in coming decades. But anthropologists also fear a wave of cultural extinction for dozens of small indigenous groups—the loss of their traditions, their arts, their languages. . . .

To make do without fish, Kamayurá children are eating ants on their traditional spongy flatbread, made from tropical cassava flour. "There aren't as many around because the kids have eaten them," Chief Kotok said of the ants. Sometimes members of the tribe kill monkeys for their meat, but, the chief said, "You have to eat 30 monkeys to fill your stomach."

Living deep in the forest with no transportation and little money, he noted, "We don't have a way to go to the grocery store for rice and beans to supplement what is missing."

Tacuma, the tribe's wizened senior shaman, said that the only threat he could remember rivaling climate change was a measles virus that arrived deep in the Amazon in 1954, killing more than 90 percent of the Kamayurá. . . .

Many indigenous people depend intimately on the cycles of nature and have had to adapt to climate variations—a season of drought, for example, or a hurricane that kills animals. . . .

The Kamayurá live in the middle of Xingu National Park, a vast territory that was

returns to farm the original plot again. Horticulture is also called *shifting cultivation*. Such shifts from plot to plot do not mean that whole villages must move when plots are abandoned. Horticulture can support large permanent villages. Among the Kuikuru of the South American tropical forest, for example, one village of 150 people remained in the same place for ninety years (Carneiro 1956). Kuikuru houses are large and well made. Because the work involved in building them is great, the Kuikuru would rather walk farther to their fields than construct a new village. They shift their plots rather than their settlements. On the other hand, horticulturalists in the montaña (Andean foothills) of Peru live in small villages of about thirty people (Carneiro 1961/1968). Their houses are small and simple. After a few years in one place, these people build new villages near virgin land. Because their houses are so simple, they prefer rebuilding to walking even a half-mile to their fields.

This chapter's "Appreciating Anthropology" describes "A World on Fire," the impacts of deforestation and climate change on Native Americans living in Brazil's Xingu National Park. Traditionally the Kamayurá Indians described in "Appreciating Anthropology" relied on a combination of fishing, hunting, and horticulture (mainly based on manioc or cassava) for their livelihood. The Kamayurá knew how to control their own slash-and-burn cultivation. Now, due to drier weather, forest fires are out of hand. Once too moist to ignite, the forest has become flammable. In 2007, Xingu National Park

once deep in the Amazon but is now surrounded by farms and ranches. About 5,000 square miles of Amazon forest are being cut down annually in recent years, according to the Brazilian government. And with far less foliage, there is less moisture in the regional water cycle, lending unpredictability to seasonal rains and leaving the climate drier and hotter.

That has upended the cycles of nature that long regulated Kamayurá life. They wake with the sun and have no set meals, eating whenever they are hungry. Fish stocks began to dwindle in the 1990s and "have just collapsed" since 2006, said Chief Kotok, who is considering the possibility of fish farming, in which fish would be fed in a penned area of a lake. With hotter temperatures as well as less rain and humidity in the region, water levels in rivers are extremely low. Fish cannot get to their spawning grounds. . . .

The tribe's agriculture has suffered, too. . . . Last year, families had to plant their cassava four times—it died in September, October and November because there was not enough moisture in the ground. It was not until December that the planting took. . . .

But perhaps the Kamayurá's greatest fear are the new summer forest fires. Once too moist to ignite, the forest here is now flammable because of the drier weather. In 2007, Xingu National Park burned for the first time, and thousands of acres were destroyed.

"The whole Xingu was burning—it stung our lungs and our eyes," Chief Kotok said. "We had nowhere to escape. We suffered along with the animals."

The Kamayura, including this man with two small children, face habitat endangerment from forces described in this story. The Kamayura live in the middle of Xingu National Park, a vast territory that once was deep in the Amazon forest. Today it is surrounded by farms and ranches.

burned for the first time, and thousands of acres were destroyed.

Agriculture

Agriculture is cultivation that requires more labor than horticulture does, because it uses land intensively and continuously. The greater labor demands associated with agriculture reflect its common use of domesticated animals, irrigation, or terracing.

Domesticated Animals
Many agriculturalists use animals as means of production—for transport, as cultivating machines, and for their manure. Asian farmers typically incorporate cattle and/or water buffalo into agricultural economies based on rice production. Rice farmers may use cattle to trample pretilled flooded fields, thus mixing soil and water, prior to transplanting. Many agriculturalists attach animals to plows and harrows for field preparation before planting or transplanting. Also, agriculturalists typically collect manure from their animals, using it to fertilize their plots, thus increasing yields. Animals are attached to carts for transport as well as to implements of cultivation.

Irrigation
While horticulturalists must await the rainy season, agriculturalists can schedule their planting in advance, because they control water. Like other

agriculture
Cultivation using land and labor continuously and intensively.

FIGURE 16.2 Location of the Ifugao.

cultivation continuum
Continuum of land and labor use.

An irrigated field is a capital investment that usually increases in value. It takes time for a field to start yielding; it reaches full productivity only after several years of cultivation. The Ifugao, like other irrigators, have farmed the same fields for generations. In some agricultural areas, including the Middle East, however, salts carried in the irrigation water can make fields unusable after 50 or 60 years.

Terracing

Terracing is another agricultural technique the Ifugao have mastered. Their homeland has small valleys separated by steep hillsides. Because the population is dense, people need to farm the hills. However, if they simply planted on the steep hillsides, fertile soil and crops would be washed away during the rainy season. To prevent this, the Ifugao cut into the hillside and build stage after stage of terraced fields rising above the valley floor. Springs located above the terraces supply their irrigation water. The labor necessary to build and maintain a system of terraces is great. Terrace walls crumble each year and must be partially rebuilt. The canals that bring water down through the terraces also demand attention.

Costs and Benefits of Agriculture

Agriculture requires human labor to build and maintain irrigation systems, terraces, and other works. People must feed, water, and care for their animals. Given sufficient labor input and management, agricultural land can yield one or two crops annually for years or even generations. An agricultural field does not necessarily produce a higher single-year yield than does a horticultural plot. The first crop grown by horticulturalists on long-idle land may be larger than that from an agricultural plot of the same size. Furthermore, because agriculturalists work harder than horticulturalists do, agriculture's yield relative to the labor invested also is lower. Agriculture's main advantage is that the long-term yield per area is far greater and more dependable. Because a single field sustains its owners year after year, there is no need to maintain a reserve of uncultivated land as horticulturalists do. This is why agricultural societies tend to be more densely populated than are horticultural ones.

irrigation experts in the Philippines, the Ifugao (Figure 16.2) irrigate their fields with canals from rivers, streams, springs, and ponds. Irrigation makes it possible to cultivate a plot year after year. Irrigation enriches the soil because the irrigated field is a unique ecosystem with several species of plants and animals, many of them minute organisms, whose wastes fertilize the land.

The Cultivation Continuum

Because nonindustrial economies can have features of both horticulture and agriculture, it is useful to discuss cultivators as being arranged along a **cultivation continuum**. Horticultural systems stand at one end—the "low-labor, shifting-plot" end. Agriculturalists are at the other—the "labor-intensive, permanent-plot" end.

We speak of a continuum because there are intermediate economies, combining horticultural and agricultural features—more intensive than annually shifting horticulture but less intensive than agriculture.

Agriculture requires more labor than horticulture does and uses land intensively and continuously. Labor demands associated with agriculture reflect its use of domesticated animals, irrigation, and terracing. Shown here, irrigated terraces surround the Ifugao village of Banaue on Luzon Island in the Philippines.

Unlike nonintensive horticulturalists, who farm a plot just once before fallowing it, the South American Kuikuru grow two or three crops of *manioc*, or cassava—an edible tuber—before abandoning their plots. Cultivation is even more intense in certain densely populated areas of Papua New Guinea, where plots are planted for two or three years, allowed to rest for three to five, and then recultivated. After several of these cycles, the plots are abandoned for a longer fallow period. Such a pattern is called *sectorial fallowing* (Wolf 1966). Besides Papua New Guinea, such systems occur in places as distant as West Africa and highland Mexico. Sectorial fallowing is associated with denser populations than is simple horticulture.

The key difference between horticulture and agriculture is that horticulture always has a fallow period whereas agriculture does not. The earliest cultivators in the Middle East and in Mexico were rainfall-dependent horticulturalists. Until recently, horticulture was the main form of cultivation in several areas, including parts of Africa, southeast Asia, the Pacific islands, Mexico, Central America, and the South American tropical forest.

Intensification: People and the Environment

The range of environments available for food production has widened as people have increased their control over nature. For example, in arid areas of California, where Native Americans once foraged, modern irrigation technology now sustains rich agricultural estates. Agriculturalists live in many areas that are too arid for nonirrigators or too hilly for nonterracers. Many ancient civilizations in arid lands arose on an agricultural base. Increasing labor intensity and permanent land use have major demographic, social, political, and environmental consequences.

Thus, because of their permanent fields, intensive cultivators are sedentary. People live in larger and more permanent communities located closer to other settlements. Growth in population size and density increases contact between individuals and groups. There is more need to regulate interpersonal relations, including conflicts of interest. Economies that support more people usually require more coordination in the use of land, labor, and other resources.

Intensive agriculture has significant environmental effects. Irrigation ditches and paddies (fields with irrigated rice) become repositories for organic wastes, chemicals (such as salts), and disease microorganisms. Intensive agriculture typically spreads at the expense of trees and forests, which are cut down to be replaced by fields. Accompanying such deforestation is loss of environmental diversity (see Srivastava, Smith, and Forno 1999). Agricultural economies grow increasingly specialized—focusing on one or a few caloric staples, such as rice, and on the animals that are raised and tended to aid the agricultural economy. Because tropical horticulturalists typically cultivate dozens of plant species simultaneously, a horticultural plot tends to mirror the botanical diversity that is found in a tropical forest. Agricultural plots, by contrast, reduce ecological diversity by cutting down trees and concentrating on just a few staple foods. Such crop specialization is true of agriculturalists both in the tropics (e.g., Indonesian paddy farmers) and outside the tropics (e.g., Middle Eastern irrigated farmers).

At least in the tropics, the diets of both foragers and horticulturalists are typically more diverse, although under less secure human control, than the diets of agriculturalists. Agriculturalists attempt to reduce risk in production by favoring stability in the form of a reliable annual harvest and long-term production. Tropical foragers and horticulturalists, by contrast, attempt to reduce risk by relying on multiple species and benefiting from ecological diversity. The agricultural strategy is to put all one's eggs in one big and very dependable basket. Of course, even with agriculture, there is a possibility that the single staple crop may fail, and famine may result. The strategy of tropical foragers and horticulturalists is to have several smaller baskets, a few of which may fail without endangering subsistence. The agricultural strategy makes sense when there are lots of children to raise and adults to be fed. Foraging and horticulture, of course, are associated with smaller, sparser, and more mobile populations.

Agricultural economies also pose a series of regulatory problems—which central governments often have arisen to solve. How is water to be managed—along with disputes about access to and distribution of water? With more people living closer together on more valuable land, agriculturalists are more likely to come into conflict than foragers and horticulturalists are. Agriculture paved the way for the origin of the state, and most agriculturalists live in states: complex sociopolitical systems that administer a territory and populace with substantial contrasts in occupation, wealth, prestige, and power. In such societies, cultivators play their role as one part of a differentiated, functionally specialized, and tightly integrated sociopolitical system. The social and political implications of food production and intensification are examined more fully in the next chapter, "Political Systems."

PASTORALISM

Pastoralists live in North Africa, the Middle East, Europe, Asia, and sub-Saharan Africa. These herders are people whose activities focus on such domesticated animals as cattle, sheep, goats, camels, and yak. East African pastoralists, like many others, live in symbiosis with their herds. (*Symbiosis* is an obligatory interaction between groups—here humans and animals—that is beneficial to each.) Herders attempt to protect their animals and to ensure their

pastoralists
Herders of domesticated animals.

reproduction in return for food and other products, such as leather. Herds provide dairy products, meat, and blood. Animals are killed at ceremonies, which occur throughout the year, and so meat is available regularly.

People use livestock in a variety of ways. Natives of North America's Great Plains, for example, didn't eat, but only rode, their horses. (Europeans reintroduced horses to the Western Hemisphere; the native American horse had become extinct thousands of years earlier.) For Plains Indians, horses served as "tools of the trade," means of production used to hunt buffalo, a main target of their economies. So the Plains Indians were not true pastoralists but *hunters* who used horses—as many agriculturalists use animals—as means of production.

Unlike the use of animals merely as productive machines, pastoralists typically make direct use of their herds for food. They consume their meat, blood, and milk, from which they make animals' yogurt, butter, and cheese. Although some pastoralists rely on their herds more completely than others do, it is impossible to base subsistence solely on animals. Most pastoralists therefore supplement their diet by hunting, gathering, fishing, cultivating, or trading. To get crops, pastoralists either trade with cultivators or do some cultivating or gathering themselves.

Unlike foraging and cultivation, which existed throughout the world before the Industrial Revolution, pastoralism was confined almost totally to the Old World. Before European conquest, the only pastoralists in the Americas lived in the Andean region of South America. They used their llamas and alpacas for food and wool and in agriculture and transport. Much more recently, the Navajo of the southwestern United States developed a pastoral economy based on herding domesticated sheep, which were introduced to North America by Europeans. The populous Navajo became the major pastoral society of the Western Hemisphere.

Two patterns of movement occur with pastoralism: nomadism and transhumance. Both are based on the fact that herds must move to use pasture available in particular places in different seasons. In **pastoral nomadism,** the entire group—women, men, and children—moves with the animals throughout the year. The Middle East and North Africa provide numerous examples of pastoral nomads. In Iran, for example, the Basseri and the Qashqai ethnic groups traditionally followed a nomadic route more than 300 miles (480 kilometers) long. Starting each year near the coast, they took their animals to grazing land 17,000 feet (5,400 meters) above sea level (see Salzman 2004).

nomadism (pastoral)
Annual movement of entire pastoral group with herds.

Pastoralists may be nomadic or transhumant, but they don't typically live off their herds alone. They either trade or cultivate. Above, a nomadic Afghan Koochi (also spelled Kuchi) woman, with her herd and belongings, returns to Afghanistan from a tribal area of neighboring Pakistan. Nomadic caravans like this one have followed this route for thousands of years. Below, in spring 2011, a transhumant shepherd guides sheep along a country road in Altlandsberg, Germany.

ADAPTIVE STRATEGY	ALSO KNOWN AS	KEY FEATURES/VARIETIES
Foraging	Hunting-gathering	Mobility, use of nature's resources
Horticulture	Slash-and-burn, shifting cultivation, swiddening, dry farming	Fallow period
Agriculture	Intensive farming	Continuous use of land, intensive use of labor
Pastoralism	Herding	Nomadism and transhumance
Industrialism	Industrial production	Factory production, capitalism, socialist production

With **transhumance,** part of the group moves with the herds, but most people stay in the home village. There are examples from Europe and Africa. In Europe's Alps, it is just the shepherds and goatherds—not the whole village—who accompany the flocks to highland meadows in summer. Among the Turkana of Uganda, men and boys accompany the herds to distant pastures, while much of the village stays put and does some horticultural farming. Villages tend to be located in the best-watered areas, which have the longest pasture season. This permits the village population to stay together during a large chunk of the year.

During their annual trek, pastoral nomads trade for crops and other products with more sedentary people. Transhumants don't have to trade for crops. Because only part of the population accompanies the herds, transhumants can maintain year-round villages and grow their own crops. Recap 16.2 lists the main features of Cohen's adaptive strategies.

MODES OF PRODUCTION

An **economy** is a system of production, distribution, and consumption of resources; *economics* is the study of such systems. Economists tend to focus on modern nations and capitalist systems, while anthropologists have broadened understanding of economic principles by gathering data on nonindustrial economies. Economic anthropology studies economics in a comparative perspective (see Chibnik 2011; Gudeman 1998; Hann and Hart 2011; Sahlins 1972/2004; Wilk and Cliggett 2007).

A **mode of production** is a way of organizing production—"a set of social relations through which labor is deployed to wrest energy from nature by means of tools, skills, organization, and knowledge" (Wolf 1982, p. 75). In the capitalist mode of production, money buys labor power, and there is a social gap between the people (bosses and workers) involved in the production process. By contrast, in nonindustrial societies, labor is not usually bought but is given as a social obligation. In

such a *kin-based* mode of production, mutual aid in production is one among many expressions of a larger web of social relations.

Societies representing each of the adaptive strategies just discussed (e.g., foraging) tend to have a similar mode of production. Differences in the mode of production within a given strategy may reflect differences in environments, target resources, or cultural traditions. Thus, a foraging mode of production may be based on individual hunters or teams, depending on whether the game is a solitary or a herd animal. Gathering is usually more individualistic than hunting, although collecting teams may assemble when abundant resources ripen and must be harvested quickly. Fishing may be done alone (as in ice fishing or spearfishing) or in crews (as with open-sea fishing and hunting of sea mammals).

Production in Nonindustrial Societies

Although some kind of division of economic labor related to age and gender is a cultural universal, the specific tasks assigned to each sex and to people of different ages vary. Many horticultural societies assign a major productive role to women, but some make men's work primary (see the chapter on gender for more on this). Similarly, among pastoralists, men generally tend large animals, but in some cultures women do the milking. Jobs accomplished through teamwork in some cultivating societies are done by smaller groups or individuals working over a longer period of time in others.

The Betsileo of Madagascar have two stages of teamwork in rice cultivation: transplanting and harvesting. Team size varies with the size of the field. Both transplanting and harvesting feature a traditional division of labor by age and gender that is well known to all Betsileo and is repeated across the generations. The first job in transplanting is the trampling of a previously tilled flooded field by young men driving cattle, in order to mix earth and water. They bring cattle to trample the fields just before transplanting. The young men yell at and beat the

transhumance
System in which only part of population moves seasonally with herds.

economy
System of resource production, distribution, and consumption.

mode of production
Specific set of social relations that organizes labor.

Betsileo women transplant rice seedlings in southcentral Madagascar. Transplanting and weeding are arduous tasks that especially strain the back.

cattle, striving to drive them into a frenzy so that they will trample the fields properly. Trampling breaks up clumps of earth and mixes irrigation water with soil to form a smooth mud into which women transplant seedlings. Once the tramplers leave the field, older men arrive. With their spades, they break up the clumps that the cattle missed. Meanwhile, the owner and other adults uproot rice seedlings and bring them to the field.

At harvest time, four or five months later, young men cut the rice off the stalks. Young women carry it to the clearing above the field. Older women arrange and stack it. The oldest men and women then stand on the stack, stomping and compacting it. Three days later, young men thresh the rice, beating the stalks against a rock to remove the grain. Older men then attack the stalks with sticks to make sure all the grains have fallen off.

Most of the other tasks in Betsileo rice cultivation are done by individual owners and their immediate families. All household members help weed the rice field. It's a man's job to till the fields with a spade or a plow. Individual men repair the irrigation and drainage systems and the earth walls that separate one plot from the next. Among other agriculturalists, however, repairing the irrigation system is a task involving teamwork and communal labor.

Means of Production

means (or factors) of production
Major productive resources, e.g., land, labor, technology, capital.

In nonindustrial societies, there is a more intimate relationship between the worker and the means of production than there is in industrial nations. **Means, or factors, of production** include land (territory), labor, technology, and capital.

Land

Among foragers, ties between people and land were less permanent than among food producers. Although many bands had territories, the boundaries usually were not marked, and there was no way they could be enforced. The hunter's stake in an animal being stalked or hit with a poisoned arrow was more important than where the animal finally died. A person acquired the rights to use a band's territory by being born in the band or by joining it through a tie of kinship, marriage, or fictive kinship. In Botswana in southern Africa, Ju/'hoansi San women, whose work provided over half the food, habitually used specific tracts of berry-bearing trees. However, when a woman changed bands, she immediately acquired a new gathering area.

Among food producers, rights to the means of production also come through kinship and marriage. Descent groups (groups whose members claim common ancestry) are common among nonindustrial food producers, and those who descend from the founder share the group's territory and resources. If the adaptive strategy is horticulture, the estate includes garden and fallow land for shifting cultivation. As members of a descent group, pastoralists have access to animals to start their own herds, to grazing land, to garden land, and to other means of production.

Labor, Tools, and Specialization

Like land, labor is a means of production. In nonindustrial societies, access to both land and labor comes through social links such as kinship, marriage, and descent. Mutual aid in production is merely one aspect of ongoing social relations that are expressed on many other occasions.

Nonindustrial societies contrast with industrial nations in regard to another means of production: technology. Manufacturing is often linked to age and gender. Women may weave and men may make pottery or vice versa. Most people of a particular age and gender share the technical knowledge associated with that age and gender. If married women customarily make baskets, all or most married women know how to make baskets. Neither technology nor technical knowledge is as specialized as it is in states.

However, some tribal societies do promote specialization. Among the Yanomami of Venezuela and Brazil (Figure 16.3), for instance, certain villages manufacture clay pots and others make hammocks. They don't specialize, as one might suppose, because certain raw materials happen to be available near particular villages. Clay suitable for pots is widely available. Everyone knows how to make pots, but not everybody does so. Craft specialization reflects the social and political environment rather than the natural environment. Such specialization promotes trade, which is the first step in creating an alliance with enemy villages (Chagnon 1997). Specialization contributes to keeping the

FIGURE 16.3 Location of the Yanomami.

peace, although it has not prevented intervillage warfare.

Alienation in Industrial Economies

There are some significant contrasts between industrial and nonindustrial economies. When factory workers produce for sale and for their employer's profit, rather than for their own use, they may be alienated from the items they make. Such alienation means they don't feel strong pride in or personal identification with their products. They see their product as belonging to someone else, not to the man or woman whose labor actually produced it. In nonindustrial societies, by contrast, people usually see their work through from start to finish and have a sense of accomplishment in the product. The fruits of their labor are their own, rather than someone else's. (This chapter's "Focus on Globalization" describes the increasingly impersonal nature of today's global economy.)

In nonindustrial societies, the economic relation between coworkers is just one aspect of a more general social relation. They aren't just coworkers but kin, in-laws, or celebrants in the same ritual. In industrial nations, people don't usually work with relatives and neighbors. If coworkers are friends, the personal relationship usually develops out of their common employment rather than being based on a previous association.

Thus, industrial workers have impersonal relations with their products, coworkers, and employers. People sell their labor for cash, and the economic domain stands apart from ordinary social life. Work is separate from family. In nonindustrial societies, however, the relations of production, distribution, and consumption are *social relations with economic aspects*. Economy is not a separate entity but is *embedded* in the society.

A Case of Industrial Alienation

For decades, the government of Malaysia has promoted export-oriented industry, allowing transnational companies to install labor-intensive manufacturing operations in rural Malaysia. The industrialization of Malaysia is part of a global strategy. In search of cheaper labor, corporations headquartered in Japan, western Europe, and the United States have been moving labor-intensive factories to developing countries. Malaysia has hundreds of Japanese and American subsidiaries, which produce mainly garments, foodstuffs, and electronics components. In electronics plants in rural Malaysia, thousands of young women from peasant families now assemble microchips and microcomponents for transistors and capacitors. Aihwa Ong (1987, 2010) did a study of electronics assembly workers in an area where 85 percent of the workers were young unmarried females from nearby villages.

Ong found that, unlike village women, female factory workers had to cope with a rigid work

In a garment factory in Hlaing Tharyar, Myanmar, Burmese women stitch sports clothing for a Taiwanese company. Their average wage is less than one American dollar per day. Throughout southeast Asia, hundreds of thousands of young women from peasant families now work in factories. Chances are good that you own one of their products.

focus on GLOBALIZATION

Our Global Economy

Economic systems are based on production, distribution, and consumption. All these processes now have global, and increasingly impersonal, dimensions. The products, images, and information we consume each day can come from anywhere. How likely is it that the item you last bought from a website, an outlet, or a retail store was made in the United States, rather than Canada, Mexico, Peru, or China?

The national has become international. Consider a few familiar "American" brands: Good Humor, French's mustard, Frigidaire, Adidas, Caribou Coffee, Church's Chicken, Trader Joe's, Holiday Inn, Dial soap, T-Mobile, and Toll House Cookies. All of them have foreign ownership. As well, the following iconic brands have been bought by foreign companies: Budweiser, Alka-Selzer, Hellmann's, IBM ThinkPad, Ben and Jerry's, 7-Eleven, Popsicle, Women's Day, Purina, Gerber, Vaseline, Lucky Strike, Firestone, and Car and Driver Magazine.

Also foreign owned are such American architectural icons as New York's Plaza Hotel, Flatiron Building, and Chrysler Building, along with the Indiana Toll Road and the Chicago Skyway. A Brazilian billionaire now owns a significant share in Burger King, a whopper of a chain with over 12,000 outlets worldwide.

Much of America, including about half our national debt, now belongs to outsiders. Already by the mid-1980s, 75 percent of the buildings in downtown Los Angeles were owned at least in part by foreign capital (Rouse 1991). According to Bruce Bartlett (2010), the share of the U.S. national debt owned by foreigners has swollen since the 1970s, when it was only 5 percent. Since the 1970s, oil-producing countries have invested their profits in U.S. Treasury securities, because of their liquidity and safety. By 1975 the foreign share of U.S. national debt had reached 17 percent, where it remained through the 1990s, when China started buying large amounts of Treasury bills. By 2009, foreigners were financing almost half the total publicly held U.S. national debt.

The Internet is a vital organ in our 21st-century global economy. All kinds of products—music, movies, clothing, appliances, this book, you name it—are produced, distributed, and consumed via the Internet. Economic functions that are spatially dispersed (perhaps continents apart) are coordinated online in real time. Activities that once involved face-to-face contact are now conducted impersonally, often across vast distances. When you order something via the Internet, the only actual human being you might speak to is the delivery driver (Smith and Doyle 2002). The computers that take and process your order from Amazon can be on different continents. The products you order can come from a warehouse anywhere in the world.

Transnational finance has shifted the economic control of local life to outsiders (see Kennedy 2010). Greeks blame Germans for their austerity. The European debt crisis that recently has occupied so much of the world's attention shows the fragility of the economic ties created through consolidation (of the European Union and the euro) and globalization.

How different is today's global economy from British poet Henry Wadsworth Longfellow's vision of production—noble, local, and autonomous:

> Under a spreading chestnut-tree
> The village smithy stands....
> Toiling—rejoicing—sorrowing,
> Onward through life he goes;
> Each morning sees some task begin,
> Each evening sees it close.
> (Longfellow, "The Village Blacksmith," 1839)

"A scene from an Amazon warehouse on Cyber Monday, December 5, 2011, the busiest day of the year for online shoppers. This warehouse could be in a lot of places, but it happens to be in Great Britain."

routine and constant supervision by men. The discipline that factories value was being taught in local schools, where uniforms helped prepare girls for the factory dress code. Village women wear loose, flowing tunics, sarongs, and sandals, but factory workers had to don tight overalls and heavy rubber gloves, in which they felt constrained. Assembling electronics components requires precise, concentrated labor. Demanding and depleting, labor in these factories illustrates the separation of intellectual and manual activity—the alienation that Karl Marx considered the defining feature of industrial work. One woman said about her bosses, "They exhaust us very much, as if they do not think that we too are human beings" (Ong 1987, p. 202). Nor does factory work bring women a substantial financial reward, given low wages, job uncertainty, and family claims on wages. Young women typically work just a few years. Production quotas, three daily shifts, overtime, and surveillance take their toll in mental and physical exhaustion.

One response to factory relations of production has been spirit possession (factory women are possessed by spirits). Ong interprets this phenomenon as the women's unconscious protest against labor discipline and male control of the industrial setting. Sometimes possession takes the form of mass hysteria. Spirits have simultaneously invaded as many as 120 factory workers. Weretigers (the Malay equivalent of the werewolf) arrive to avenge the construction of a factory on aboriginal burial grounds. Disturbed earth and grave spirits swarm on the shop floor. First the women see the spirits; then their bodies are invaded. The women become violent and scream abuses. The weretigers send the women into sobbing, laughing, and shrieking fits. To deal with possession, factories employ local medicine men, who sacrifice chickens and goats to fend off the spirits. This solution works only some of the time; possession still goes on. Factory women continue to act as vehicles to express their own frustrations and the anger of avenging ghosts.

Ong argues that spirit possession expresses anguish at, and resistance to, capitalist relations of production. By engaging in this form of rebellion, however, factory women avoid a direct confrontation with the source of their distress. Ong concludes that spirit possession, while expressing repressed resentment, doesn't do much to modify factory conditions. (Other tactics, such as unionization, would do more.) Spirit possession may even help maintain the current system by operating as a safety valve for accumulated tensions.

ECONOMIZING AND MAXIMIZATION

Economic anthropologists have been concerned with two main questions:

1. How are production, distribution, and consumption organized in different societies? This question focuses on *systems* of human behavior and their organization.

2. What motivates people in different cultures to produce, distribute or exchange, and consume? Here the focus is not on systems of behavior but on the motives of the *individuals* who participate in those systems.

Anthropologists view both economic systems and motivations in a cross-cultural perspective. Motivation is a concern of psychologists, but it also has been, implicitly or explicitly, a concern of economists and anthropologists. Economists tend to assume that producers and distributors make decisions rationally by using the *profit motive,* as do consumers when they shop around for the best value. Although anthropologists know that the profit motive is not universal, the assumption that individuals try to maximize profits is basic to the capitalist world economy and to much of Western economic theory. In fact, the subject matter of economics is often defined as **economizing,** or the rational allocation of scarce means (or resources) to alternative ends (or uses) (see Chibnik 2011).

What does that mean? Classical economic theory assumes that our wants are infinite and that our means are limited. Since means are limited, people must make choices about how to use their scarce resources: their time, labor, money, and capital. (This chapter's "Appreciating Diversity" disputes the idea that people always make economic choices based on scarcity.) Economists assume that when confronted with choices and decisions, people tend to make the one that maximizes profit. This is assumed to be the most rational (reasonable) choice.

The idea that individuals choose to maximize profit was a basic assumption of the classical economists of the 19th century and is one that is held by many contemporary economists. However, certain economists now recognize that individuals in Western cultures, as in others, may be motivated by many other goals. Depending on the society and the situation, people may try to maximize profit, wealth, prestige, pleasure, comfort, or social harmony. Individuals may want to realize their personal or family ambitions or those of another group to which they belong (see Chibnik 2011; Sahlins 2004).

Alternative Ends

To what uses do people in various societies put their scarce resources? Throughout the world, people devote some of their time and energy to building up a *subsistence fund* (Wolf 1966). In other words, they have to work to eat, to replace the calories they use in their daily activity. People also must invest in a *replacement fund.* They must maintain their technology and other items essential to production. If a hoe or plow breaks, they must repair or replace it. They also must obtain and replace items that are essential not to production but to everyday life, such as clothing and shelter.

People also have to invest in a *social fund.* They have to help their friends, relatives, in-laws, and neighbors. It is useful to distinguish between a social fund and a *ceremonial fund.* The latter term refers to expenditures on ceremonies or rituals. To prepare a festival honoring one's ancestors, for example, requires time and the outlay of wealth.

Citizens of nonindustrial states also must allocate scarce resources to a *rent fund.* We think of rent as payment for the use of property. However, "rent fund" has a wider meaning. It refers to resources that people must render to an individual or agency that is superior politically or economically. Tenant farmers and sharecroppers, for example, either pay rent or give some of their produce to their landlords, as peasants did under feudalism.

Peasants are small-scale agriculturalists who live in nonindustrial states and have rent fund obligations (see Kearney 1996). They produce to feed themselves, to sell their produce, and to pay rent. All peasants have two things in common:

1. They live in state-organized societies.

2. They produce food without the elaborate technology—chemical fertilizers, tractors, airplanes to spray crops, and so on—of modern farming or agribusiness.

In addition to paying rent to landlords, peasants must satisfy government obligations, paying taxes in the form of money, produce, or labor. The rent fund is not simply an *additional* obligation for peasants. Often it becomes their foremost and unavoidable

peasant
Small-scale farmer with rent fund obligations.

economizing
Allocation of scarce means among alternative ends.

Scarcity and the Betsileo

In the realm of cultural diversity, perceptions and motivations can change substantially over time. Consider some changes I've observed among the Betsileo of Madagascar during the decades I've been studying them. Initially, compared with modern consumers, the Betsileo had little perception of scarcity. Now, with population increase and the spread of a cash-oriented economy, perceived wants and needs have increased relative to means. Motivations have changed, too, as people increasingly seek profits, even if it means stealing from their neighbors or destroying ancestral farms.

In the late 1960s my wife and I lived among the Betsileo people of Madagascar, studying their economy and social life (Kottak 1980). Soon after our arrival we met two well-educated schoolteachers (first cousins) who were interested in our research. The woman's father was a congressional representative who became a cabinet minister during our stay. Their family came from a historically important and typical Betsileo village called Ivato, which they invited us to visit with them.

We had traveled to many other Betsileo villages, where often we were displeased with our reception. As we drove up, children would run away screaming. Women would hurry inside. Men would retreat to doorways, where they lurked bashfully. This behavior expressed the Betsileo's great fear of the *mpakafo*. Believed to cut out and devour his victim's heart and liver, the mpakafo is the Malagasy vampire. These cannibals are said to have fair skin and to be very tall. Because I have light skin and stand well over six feet tall, I was a natural suspect. The fact that such creatures were not known to travel with their wives offered a bit of assurance that I wasn't really a mpakafo.

When we visited Ivato, its people were different—friendly and hospitable. Our very first day there we did a brief census and found out who lived in which households. We learned people's names and their relationships to our schoolteacher friends and to each other. We met an excellent informant who knew all about the local history. In a few afternoons I learned much more than I had in the other villages in several sessions.

Ivatans were so willing to talk because we had powerful sponsors, village natives who had made it in the outside world, people the Ivatans knew would protect them. The schoolteachers vouched for us, but even more significant was the cabinet minister, who was like a grandfather and benefactor to everyone in town. The Ivatans had no reason to fear us because their more influential native son had asked them to answer our questions.

Once we moved to Ivato, the elders established a pattern of visiting us every evening. They came to talk, attracted by the inquisitive foreigners but also by the wine, tobacco, and food we offered. I asked questions about their customs and beliefs. I eventually developed interview schedules about various subjects, including rice production. I used these forms in Ivato and in two other villages I was studying less intensively. Never have I interviewed as easily as I did in Ivato.

As our stay neared its end, our Ivatan friends lamented, saying, "We'll miss you. When you leave, there won't be any more cigarettes, any more wine, or any more questions." They wondered what it would be like for us back in the United States. They knew we had an automobile and that we could afford to buy products they never would have. They commented, "When you go back to your country, you'll need a lot of money for things like cars, clothes, and food. We don't need to buy those things. We make almost everything we use. We don't need as much money as you, because we produce for ourselves."

The Betsileo weren't unusual for nonindustrial people. Strange as it may seem to an American consumer, those rice farmers actually believed *they had all they needed*. The lesson from the Betsileo of the 1960s is that scarcity, which economists view as universal, is variable. Although shortages do arise in nonindustrial societies, the concept of scarcity (insufficient means) is much less developed in stable subsistence-oriented societies than in the societies characterized by industrialism, particularly as the reliance on consumer goods increases.

---

duty. Sometimes, to meet the obligation to pay rent, their own diets suffer. The demands of paying rent may divert resources from subsistence, replacement, social, and ceremonial funds.

Motivations vary from society to society, and people often lack freedom of choice in allocating their resources. Because of obligations to pay rent, peasants may allocate their scarce means toward ends that are not their own but those of government officials. Thus, even in societies where there is a profit motive, people are often prevented from rationally maximizing self-interest by factors beyond their control.

DISTRIBUTION, EXCHANGE

The economist Karl Polanyi (1968) stimulated the comparative study of exchange, and several anthropologists followed his lead. To study exchange cross-culturally, Polanyi defined three principles orienting exchanges: the market principle, redistribution, and reciprocity. These principles can all be present in the

But, with globalization over the past few decades, significant changes have affected the Betsileo—and most nonindustrial peoples. On my last visit to Ivato, in 2006, the effects of cash and of rapid population increase were evident there—and throughout Madagascar—where the national growth rate has been about 3 percent per year. Madagascar's population doubled between 1966 and 1991—from 6 to 12 million people. Today it stands around 18 million (Kottak 2004). One result of population pressure has been agricultural intensification. In Ivato, farmers who formerly had grown only rice in their rice fields now were using the same land for cash crops, such as carrots, after the annual rice harvest. Another change affecting Ivato in recent years has been the breakdown of social and political order, fueled by increasing demand for cash.

Cattle rustling is a growing threat. Cattle thieves (sometimes from neighboring villages) have terrorized peasants who previously felt secure in their villages. Some of the rustled cattle are driven to the coasts for commercial export to nearby islands. Prominent among the rustlers are relatively well-educated young men who have studied long enough to be comfortable negotiating with outsiders, but who have been unable to find formal work, and who are unwilling to work the rice fields like their peasant ancestors. The formal education system has familiarized them with external institutions and norms, including the need for cash. The concepts of scarcity, commerce, and negative reciprocity now thrive among the Betsileo.

I've witnessed other striking evidence of the new addiction to cash during my most recent visits to Betsileo country. Near Ivato's county seat, people now sell precious stones—tourmalines, which originally were found by chance in local rice fields. We saw an amazing sight: dozens of villagers destroying an ancestral resource, digging up a large rice field, seeking tourmalines—clear evidence of the encroachment of cash on the local subsistence economy. You can't eat gemstones.

Throughout the Betsileo homeland, population growth and density are propelling emigration. Locally, land, jobs, and money are all scarce. One woman with ancestors from Ivato, herself now a resident of the national capital (Antananarivo), remarked that half the children of Ivato now lived in that city. Although she was exaggerating, a census of all the descendants of Ivato reveals a substantial emigrant and urban population.

Ivato's recent history is one of increasing participation in a cash economy. That history, combined with the pressure of a growing population on local resources, has made scarcity not just a concept but a reality for Ivatans and their neighbors.

Women hull rice in a Betsileo village. In the village of Ivato, farmers who traditionally grew only rice in their rice fields now use the same land for commercial crops, such as carrots, after the annual rice harvest.

same society, but in that case they govern different kinds of transactions. In any society, one of them usually dominates. The principle of exchange that dominates in a given society is the one that allocates the means of production (see Chibnik 2011; Hann and Hart 2011).

The Market Principle

In today's world capitalist economy, the **market principle** dominates. It governs the distribution of the means of production: land, labor, natural resources, technology, and capital. "Market exchange refers to the organizational process of purchase and sale at money price" (Dalton 1967; Hann and Hart 2009; Madra 2004). With market exchange, items are bought and sold, using money, with an eye to maximizing profit, and value is determined by the *law of supply and demand* (things cost more the scarcer they are and the more people want them).

Bargaining is characteristic of market-principle exchanges. The buyer and seller strive to maximize—to

market principle
Buying, selling, and valuation based on supply and demand.

reciprocity
Principle governing exchanges among social equals.

redistribution
Flow of goods into center, then back out; characteristic of chiefdoms.

reciprocity continuum
A continuum running from generalized reciprocity (closely related/deferred return) to negative reciprocity (strangers/immediate return).

generalized reciprocity
Exchanges among closely related individuals.

get their "money's worth." In bargaining, buyers and sellers don't need to meet personally. But their offers and counteroffers do need to be open for negotiation over a fairly short time period.

Redistribution

Redistribution operates when goods, services, or their equivalent move from the local level to a center. The center may be a capital, a regional collection point, or a storehouse near a chief's residence. Products often move through a hierarchy of officials for storage at the center. Along the way, officials and their dependents may consume some of them, but the exchange principle here is *re*distribution. The flow of goods eventually reverses direction—out from the center, down through the hierarchy, and back to the common people.

One example of a redistributive system comes from the Cherokee, the original owners of the Tennessee Valley. Productive farmers who subsisted on maize, beans, and squash, supplemented by hunting and fishing, the Cherokee had chiefs. Each of their main villages had a central plaza, where meetings of the chief's council took place, and where redistributive feasts were held. According to Cherokee custom, each family farm had an area where the family could set aside a portion of its annual harvest for the chief. This supply of corn was used to feed the needy, as well as travelers and warriors journeying through friendly territory. This store of food was available to all who needed it, with the understanding that it "belonged" to the chief and was dispersed through his generosity. The chief also hosted the redistributive feasts held in the main settlements (Harris 1978).

Reciprocity

Reciprocity is exchange between social equals, who are normally related by kinship, marriage, or another close personal tie. Because it occurs between social equals, it is dominant in the more egalitarian societies—among foragers, cultivators, and pastoralists. There are three degrees of reciprocity: generalized, balanced, and negative (Sahlins 1968, 2004; Service 1966). These may be imagined as areas of a continuum defined by these questions:

1. How closely related are the parties to the exchange?

2. How quickly and unselfishly are gifts reciprocated?

Generalized reciprocity, the purest form of reciprocity, is characteristic of exchanges between closely related people. In *balanced reciprocity,* social distance increases, as does the need to reciprocate. In *negative reciprocity,* social distance is greatest and reciprocation is most calculated. This range, from generalized to negative, is called the **reciprocity continuum.**

With **generalized reciprocity,** someone gives to another person and expects nothing concrete or immediate in return. Such exchanges (including parental gift giving in contemporary North America) are not primarily economic transactions but expressions of personal relationships. Most parents don't keep accounts of every penny they spend on their children. They merely hope that the children will respect their culture's customs involving love, honor, loyalty, and other obligations to parents.

Among foragers, generalized reciprocity has usually governed exchanges. People have routinely shared with other band members (Bird-David 1992; Kent 1992). A study of the Ju/'hoansi San (Figure 16.4) found that 40 percent of the population contributed little to the food supply (Lee 1968/1974). Children, teenagers, and people over 60 depended

 living anthropology **VIDEOS**

Insurance Policies for Hunter-Gatherers?
www.mhhe.com/kottak

This clip features Polly Wiessner, a sociocultural anthropologist who has worked among the San ("Bushmen") for over 25 years. The clip contrasts the foraging way of life with other economies in terms of storage, risk, and insurance against lean times. Industrial nations have banks, refrigerators, and insurance policies. Pastoralists have herds, which store meat and wealth on the hoof. Farmers have larders and granaries. How do the San anticipate and deal with hard times? What form of insurance do they have? What was it, according to Wiessner, that allowed *Homo sapiens* to "colonize so many niches in this world"?

Sharing the fruits of production, a keystone of many nonindustrial societies, also has been a goal of socialist nations, such as China. These workers in Yunnan province strive for an equal distribution of meat.

on other people for their food. Despite the high proportion of dependents, the average worker hunted or gathered less than half as much (12 to 19 hours a week) as the average American works. Nonetheless, there was always food because different people worked on different days.

So strong is the ethic of reciprocal sharing that most foragers have lacked an expression for "thank you." To offer thanks would be impolite because it would imply that a particular act of sharing, which is the keystone of egalitarian society, was unusual. Among the Semai, foragers of central Malaysia (Dentan 1979, 2008), to express gratitude would suggest surprise at the hunter's generosity or success.

Balanced reciprocity applies to exchanges between people who are more distantly related than are members of the same band or household. In a horticultural society, for example, a man presents a gift to someone in another village. The recipient may be a cousin, a trading partner, or a brother's fictive kinsman. The giver expects something in return. This may not come immediately, but the social relationship will be strained if there is no reciprocation.

Exchanges in nonindustrial societies also may illustrate **negative reciprocity,** mainly in dealing with people outside or on the fringes of their social systems. To people who live in a world of close personal relations, exchanges with outsiders are full of ambiguity and distrust. Exchange is one way of establishing friendly relations with outsiders, but especially when trade begins, the relationship is still tentative. Often, the initial exchange is close to being purely economic; people want to get something back immediately. Just as in market economies, but without using money, they try to get the best possible immediate return for their investment (see Clark 2010; Hann and Hart 2009).

Generalized and balanced reciprocity are based on trust and a social tie. But negative reciprocity involves the attempt to get something for as little as possible, even if it means being cagey or deceitful or cheating. Among the most extreme and "negative" examples of negative reciprocity was 19th-century horse thievery by North American Plains Indians. Men would sneak into camps and villages of neighboring tribes to steal horses. A similar pattern of cattle raiding continues today in East Africa, among tribes like the Kuria (Fleisher 2000). In these cases, the party that starts the raiding can expect reciprocity—a raid on their own village—or worse. The Kuria hunt down cattle thieves and kill them. It's still reciprocity, governed by "Do unto others as they have done unto you."

One way of reducing the tension in situations of potential negative reciprocity is to engage in "silent trade." One example is the silent trade of the Mbuti "pygmy" foragers of the African equatorial forest and their neighboring horticultural villagers. There is no personal contact during their exchanges. A Mbuti hunter leaves game, honey, or another forest product at a customary site. Villagers collect it and leave crops in exchange. Often the parties bargain silently. If one feels the return is insufficient, he or she simply leaves it at the trading site. If the other party wants to continue trade, it will be increased.

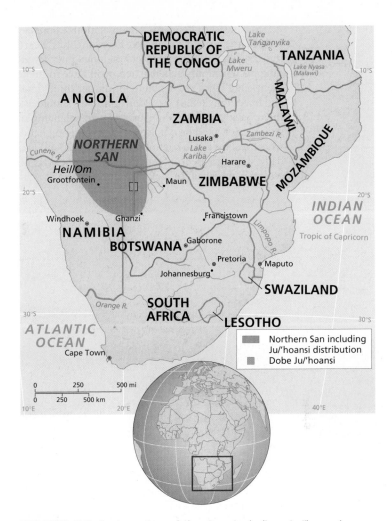

FIGURE 16.4 Location of the San, Including Ju/'hoansi.

Coexistence of Exchange Principles

In today's North America, the market principle governs most exchanges, from the sale of the means of production to the sale of consumer goods. We also have redistribution. Some of our tax money goes to support the government, but some of it also comes back to us in the form of social services, education, health care, and road building. We also have reciprocal exchanges. Generalized reciprocity characterizes the relationship between parents and children. However, even here the dominant market mentality surfaces in comments about the high cost of raising children and in the stereotypical statement of the disappointed parent: "We gave you everything money could buy."

balanced reciprocity
Midpoint on *reciprocity continuum,* between generalized and negative reciprocity.

negative reciprocity
Potentially hostile exchanges among strangers.

potlatch
Competitive feast on
North Pacific coast of
North America.

Exchanges of gifts, cards, and invitations exemplify reciprocity, usually balanced. Everyone has heard remarks like "They invited us to their daughter's wedding, so when ours gets married, we'll have to invite them" and "They've been here for dinner three times and haven't invited us yet. I don't think we should ask them back until they do." Such precise balancing of reciprocity would be out of place in a foraging band, where resources are communal (common to all) and daily sharing based on generalized reciprocity is an essential ingredient of social life and survival.

The historic photo (above) shows the amassing of blankets to be given away at a Kwakiutl potlatch. The man in the foreground is making a speech praising the generosity of the potlatch host. In the context of a modern-day potlatch, the Canoe Journey (shown below) has been incorporated as a celebration of healing, hope, happiness, and hospitality. The annual Journey began with nine canoes paddling to Seattle in 1989. It continues today with more than sixty canoes and over 40,000 participants. The Journey honors a long history of transport and trade by the Coast Salish tribes, whose potlatch is discussed in the text.

POTLATCHING

One of the most thoroughly studied cultural practices known to ethnography is the **potlatch,** a festive event within a regional exchange system among tribes of the North Pacific Coast of North America, including the Salish and Kwakiutl of Washington and British Columbia and the Tsimshian of Alaska (Figure 16.5). Some tribes still practice the potlatch, sometimes as a memorial to the dead (Kan 1986, 1989). At each such event, assisted by members of their communities, potlatch sponsors traditionally gave away food, blankets, pieces of copper, or other items. In return for this, they got prestige. To give a potlatch enhanced one's reputation. Prestige increased with the lavishness of the potlatch, the value of the goods given away in it.

The potlatching tribes were foragers, but atypical ones. They were sedentary and had chiefs. They had access to a wide variety of land and sea resources. Among their most important foods were salmon, herring, candlefish, berries, mountain goats, seals, and porpoises (Piddocke 1969).

According to classical economic theory, the profit motive is universal, with the goal of maximizing material benefits. How then does one explain the potlatch, in which substantial wealth is given away (and even destroyed—see below)? Christian missionaries considered potlatching to be wasteful and antithetical to the Protestant work ethic. By 1885, under pressure from Indian agents, missionaries, and Indian converts to Christianity, both Canada and the United States had outlawed potlatching. Between 1885 and 1951 the custom went underground. By 1951 both countries had discreetly dropped the anti-potlatching laws from the books (Miller n.d.).

Some scholars seized on this view of the potlatch as a classic case of economically wasteful behavior. The economist and social commentator Thorstein Veblen cited potlatching as an example of conspicuous consumption in his influential book *The Theory of the Leisure Class* (1934), claiming that potlatching was based on an economically irrational drive for prestige. This interpretation stressed the lavishness and supposed wastefulness, especially of the Kwakiutl displays, to support the contention that in some societies people strive to maximize prestige at the expense of their material well-being. This interpretation has been challenged.

Ecological anthropology, also known as *cultural ecology,* is a theoretical school in anthropology that attempts to interpret cultural practices, such as the potlatch, in terms of their long-term role in helping humans adapt to their environments. A different interpretation of the potlatch has been offered by the ecological anthropologists Wayne Suttles (1960) and Andrew Vayda (1961/1968). These scholars see potlatching not in terms of its apparent wastefulness but in terms of its long-term role as a cultural adaptive mechanism. This view not only helps us understand potlatching; it also has comparative value because it helps us understand similar patterns of lavish feasting in many other parts of the world. Here is the ecological interpretation: *Customs like the potlatch are cultural adaptations to alternating periods of local abundance and shortage.*

How does this work? The overall natural environment of the North Pacific Coast is favorable, but resources fluctuate from year to year and place to place. Salmon and herring aren't equally abundant every year in a given locality. One village can have a good year while another is experiencing a bad one. Later their fortunes reverse. In this context, the potlatch cycle of the Kwakiutl and Salish had adaptive value, and the potlatch was not a competitive display that brought no material benefit.

A village enjoying an especially good year had a surplus of subsistence items, which it could trade for more durable wealth items, like blankets, canoes, or pieces of copper. Wealth, in turn, by being distributed, could be converted into prestige. Members of several villages were invited to any potlatch and got to take home the resources that were given away. In this way, potlatching linked villages together in a regional economy—an exchange system that distributed food and wealth from wealthy to needy communities. In return, the potlatch sponsors and their villages got prestige. The decision to potlatch was determined by the health of the local economy. If there had been subsistence surpluses, and thus a buildup of wealth over several good years, a village could afford a potlatch to convert its food and wealth into prestige.

The long-term adaptive value of intercommunity feasting becomes clear when we consider what happened when a formerly prosperous village had a run of bad luck. Its people started accepting invitations to potlatches in villages that were doing better. The

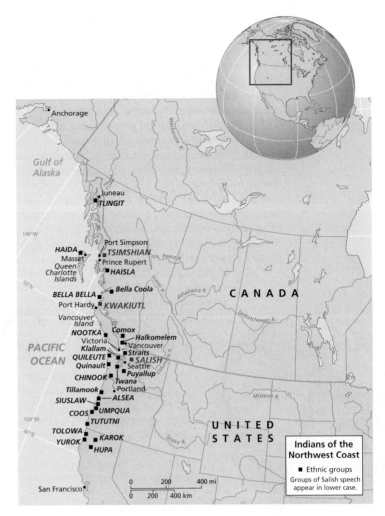

FIGURE 16.5 Location of Potlatching Groups.

At Zimbabwe's Chidamoyo Hospital, patients often barter farm products for medical treatment. How does barter fit with the exchange principles discussed here?

tables were turned as the temporarily rich became temporarily poor and vice versa. The newly needy accepted food and wealth items. They were willing to receive rather than bestow gifts and thus to relinquish some of their stored-up prestige. They hoped their luck would eventually improve so that resources could be recouped and prestige regained.

The potlatch linked local groups along the North Pacific coast into a regional alliance and exchange network. Potlatching and intervillage exchange had adaptive functions, regardless of the motivations of the individual participants. The anthropologists who stressed rivalry for prestige were not wrong. They were merely emphasizing motivations at the expense of an analysis of economic and ecological systems.

The use of feasts to enhance individual and community reputations and to redistribute wealth is not peculiar to populations of the North Pacific coast. Competitive feasting is widely characteristic of nonindustrial food producers. But among most foragers, who live, remember, in marginal areas, resources are too meager to support feasting on such a level. In such societies, sharing rather than competition prevails.

Like many other cultural practices that have attracted considerable anthropological attention, the potlatch does not, and did not, exist apart from larger world events. For example, within the spreading world capitalist economy of the 19th century, the potlatching tribes, particularly the Kwakiutl, began to trade with Europeans (fur for blankets, for example). Their wealth increased as a result. Simultaneously, a huge proportion of the Kwakiutl population died from previously unknown diseases brought by the Europeans. As a result, the increased wealth from trade flowed into a drastically reduced population. With many of the traditional sponsors dead (such as chiefs and their families), the Kwakiutl extended the right to give a potlatch to the entire population. This stimulated very intense competition for prestige. Given trade, increased wealth, and a decreased population, the Kwakiutl also started converting wealth into prestige by destroying wealth items such as blankets, pieces of copper, and houses (Vayda 1961/1968). Blankets and houses could be burned, and coppers could be buried at sea. Being rich enough to destroy wealth conveyed prestige. Here, with dramatically increased wealth and a drastically reduced population, Kwakiutl potlatching changed its nature. It became much more destructive than it had been previously and than potlatching continued to be among tribes that were less affected by trade and disease.

In any case, note that potlatching also served to prevent the development of socioeconomic stratification, a system of social classes. Wealth relinquished or destroyed was converted into a nonmaterial item: prestige. Under capitalism, we reinvest our profits (rather than burning our cash), with the hope of making an additional profit. However, the potlatching tribes were content to relinquish their surpluses rather than use them to widen the social distance between themselves and their fellow tribe members.

acing the COURSE

summary

1. Cohen's adaptive strategies include foraging (hunting and gathering), horticulture, agriculture, pastoralism, and industrialism. Foraging was the only human adaptive strategy until the advent of food production (farming and herding) 10,000 years ago. Food production eventually replaced foraging in most places. Almost all modern foragers have at least some dependence on food production or food producers.

2. Horticulture and agriculture stand at opposite ends of a continuum based on labor intensity and continuity of land use. Horticulture doesn't use land or labor intensively. Horticulturalists cultivate a plot for one or two years and then abandon it. Farther along the continuum, horticulture becomes more intensive, but there is always a fallow period. Agriculturalists farm the same plot of land continuously and use labor intensively. They use one or more of the following: irrigation, terracing, and domesticated animals as means of production and manuring.

3. The pastoral strategy is mixed. Nomadic pastoralists trade with cultivators. Part of a transhumant pastoral population cultivates while another part takes the herds to pasture. Except for some Peruvians and the Navajo, who are recent herders, the New World lacks native pastoralists.

4. Economic anthropology is the cross-cultural study of systems of production, distribution, and consumption. In nonindustrial societies, a kin-based mode of production prevails. One acquires rights to resources and labor through membership in social groups, not impersonally through purchase and

sale. Work is just one aspect of social relations expressed in varied contexts.

5. Economics has been defined as the science of allocating scarce means to alternative ends. Western economists assume that the notion of scarcity is universal—which it isn't—and that in making choices, people strive to maximize personal profit. In nonindustrial societies, indeed as in our own, people often maximize values other than individual profit.

6. In nonindustrial societies, people invest in subsistence, replacement, social, and ceremonial funds. States add a rent fund: People must share their output with social superiors. In states, the obligation to pay rent often becomes primary.

7. In addition to studying production, economic anthropologists study and compare exchange systems.

The three principles of exchange are the market principle, redistribution, and reciprocity. The market principle, based on supply and demand and the profit motive, dominates in states. With redistribution, goods are collected at a central place, but some of them are eventually given back, or redistributed, to the people. Reciprocity governs exchanges between social equals. It is the characteristic mode of exchange among foragers and horticulturists. Reciprocity, redistribution, and the market principle may coexist in a society, but the primary exchange mode is the one that allocates the means of production.

8. Patterns of feasting and exchanges of wealth among villages are common among nonindustrial food producers, as well as among the potlatching cultures of North America's North Pacific coast. Such systems help even out the availability of resources over time.

test yourself

MULTIPLE CHOICE

1. Typologies, such as Yehudi Cohen's *adaptive strategies,* are useful tools of analysis because
   a. they prove that there are causal relationships between economic and cultural variables.
   b. they suggest correlations—that is, association or covariation between two or more variables, such as economic and cultural variables.
   c. they suggest that economic systems are a better way of categorizing societies than relying on cultural patterns.
   d. they have strong predictive powers when used in computer models.
   e. they have become common language among all anthropologists.

2. Which of the following statements about foraging societies is *not* true?
   a. Foraging societies are characterized by large-scale farming.
   b. All foraging societies depend to some extent on government assistance.

   c. All modern foraging societies have contact with other, nonforaging societies.
   d. Many foragers have easily incorporated modern technology, such as rifles and snowmobiles, into their subsistence activities.
   e. All modern foragers live in nation-states.

3. Which of the following is associated with horticultural systems of cultivation?
   a. intensive use of land and human labor
   b. use of irrigation and terracing
   c. use of draft animals
   d. periodic cycles of cultivation and fallowing
   e. location in arid areas

4. Which of the following statements about horticulture is true?
   a. It typically supports life in cities.
   b. It usually leads to the destruction of the soil through overuse.
   c. It can support permanent villages.

d. It requires more labor than agriculture.

e. It is usually associated with state-level societies.

5. Which of the following is the key factor that distinguishes agriculturalists from horticulturalists? Agriculturalists

a. clear a tract of land they wish to use by cutting down trees and setting fire to the grass.

b. use their land intensively and continuously.

c. generally have much more leisure time at their disposal than do foragers.

d. must be nomadic to take full advantage of their land.

e. subsist on a more nutritious diet than do horticulturalists.

6. Which of the following is *not* one of the basic economic types found in nonindustrial societies?

a. foraging

b. agriculture

c. horticulture

d. hydroponics

e. pastoralism

7. Which of the following is found in all adaptive strategies?

a. transhumance

b. a division of labor based on gender

c. an emphasis on elaborate technology

d. domestication of animals for food

e. a strong positive correlation between the importance of kinship and complexity of subsistence technology

8. Economic alienation in industrial societies comes about as a result of

a. separation from the product of one's labor.

b. loss of land.

c. a subculture of poverty.

d. negative reciprocity.

e. discontent due to low pay.

9. Which of the following statements about generalized reciprocity is true?

a. It is characterized by the immediate return of the object exchanged.

b. It usually develops after redistribution but before the market principle.

c. It is the characteristic form of exchange in egalitarian societies.

d. It disappears with the origin of the state.

e. It is exemplified by silent trade.

10. Which of the following inhibits stratification?

a. class endogamy

b. caste notions of purity and pollution

c. monopoly on the legitimate use of force

d. ceremonial redistribution of material goods

e. control over ideology by elites

FILL IN THE BLANK

1. In nonindustrial societies, a _____ mode of production prevails.

2. The way a society's social relations are organized to produce the labor necessary for generating the society's subsistence and energy needs is known as the _____. _____ refer to society's major productive resources, such as land, labor, technology, and capital.

3. Economists tend to assume that producers and distributors make decisions rationally by using the _____ motive. Anthropologists, however, know that this motive is not universal.

4. When a farmer gives 20 percent of his crop to a landlord, he is contributing to his _____ fund.

5. The _____ is a festive event within a regional exchange system among tribes of the North Pacific coast of North America. _____ anthropologists interpret this event as a cultural adaptation to alternating periods of local abundance and shortage, rejecting the belief that it illustrates economically wasteful and irrational behavior.

CRITICAL THINKING

1. When considering issues of "human nature," why should we remember that the egalitarian band was a basic form of human social life for most of our history?

2. Intensive agriculture has significant effects on social and environmental relations. What are some of these effects? Are they good or bad?

3. What does it mean when anthropologists describe nonindustrial economic systems as "embedded" in society?

4. What are your scarce means? How do you make decisions about allocating them?

5. Give examples from your own exchanges of different degrees of reciprocity. Why are anthropologists interested in studying exchange across cultures?

Means of production, 3. profit, 4. rent, 5. potlatch, Ecological

Multiple Choice: 1. (B); 2. (A); 3. (D); 4. (C); 5. (B); 6. (D); 7. (B); 8. (A); 9. (C); 10. (D); **Fill in the Blank:** 1. kin-based; 2. mode of production,

374   PART 3   Appreciating Cultural Diversity

Chibnik, M.

    2011   *Anthropology, Economics, and Choice*. Austin: University of Texas Press. Factors that determine economic decision making.

Hann, C., and K. Hart

    2011   *Economic Anthropology: History, Ethnography, Critique*. Brooklyn, NY: Polity Press. The development of, and key issues in, economic anthropology.

Lee, R. B.

    2003   *The Dobe Ju/'hoansi*, 3rd ed. Belmont, CA: Wadsworth. Account of well-known San foragers, by one of their principal ethnographers.

Lee, R. B., and R. H. Daly

    1999   *The Cambridge Encyclopedia of Hunters and Gatherers*. New York: Cambridge University Press. Indispensable reference work on foragers.

Salzman, P. C.

    2004   *Pastoralists: Equality, Hierarchy, and the State*. Boulder, CO: Westview. What we can learn from pastoralists about equality, freedom, and democracy.

Wilk, R. R., and L. Cliggett

    2007   *Economies and Culture: Foundations of Economic Anthropology*. Boulder, CO: Westview. Useful introduction.

suggested additional readings

Go to our Online Learning Center website at **www.mhhe.com/kottak** for Internet exercises directly related to the content of this chapter.

internet exercises

Political Systems

What kinds of political systems have existed worldwide, and what are their social and economic correlates?

How does the state differ from other forms of political organization?

What is social control, and how is it established and maintained in various societies?

◀ State-organized societies have formal governmental institutions, such as the German Reichstag (Parliament) in Berlin, shown here on a typical work day.

understanding OURSELVES

You've probably heard the expression "Big Man on Campus" used to describe a collegian who is very well known and/or popular. One website (www.ehow.com/how_2112834_be-big-man-campus.html) offers advice about how to become a BMOC. According to that site, helpful attributes include lots of friends, a cool car, a hip wardrobe, a nice smile, a sports connection, and a sense of humor. "Big man" has a different but related meaning in anthropology. Many indigenous cultures of the South Pacific had a kind of political figure that anthropologists call the "big man." Such a leader achieved his status through hard work, amassing wealth in the form of pigs and other native riches. Characteristics that distinguished the big man from his fellows, enabling him to attract loyal supporters (aka lots of friends), included wealth, generosity, eloquence, physical fitness, bravery, and supernatural powers. Those who became big men did so because of their personalities rather than by inheriting their wealth or position.

Do any of the factors that make for a successful big man (or BMOC, for that matter) contribute to political success in a modern nation such as the United States? Although American politicians often use their own wealth, inherited or created, to finance campaigns, they also solicit labor and monetary contributions (rather than pigs) from supporters. And, like big men, successful American politicians try to be generous with their supporters. Payback may take the form of a night in the Lincoln bedroom, an invitation to a strategic dinner, an ambassadorship, or largesse to a particular area of the country. Tribal big men amass wealth and then give away pigs. Successful American politicians also dish out "pork."

As with the big man, eloquence and communication skills contribute to political success (e.g., Barack Obama, Bill Clinton, and Ronald Reagan), although lack of such skills isn't necessarily fatal (e.g., either President Bush). What about physical fitness? Hair, height, health (and even a nice smile) are certainly political advantages. Bravery, as demonstrated through distinguished military service, may help political careers, but it certainly isn't required. Nor does it guarantee success. Just ask John McCain, John Kerry, or Wesley Clark. Supernatural powers? Candidates who proclaim themselves atheists are as rare as self-identified witches—or not witches. Almost all political candidates claim to belong to a mainstream religion. Some even present their candidacies or policies as promoting God's will.

However, contemporary politics isn't just about personality, as big man systems are. We live in a state-organized, stratified society with inherited wealth, power, and privilege, all of which have political implications. As is typical of states, inheritance and kin connections play a role in political success. Just think of Kennedys, Bushes, Gores, Clintons, and Doles.

Anthropologists share with political scientists an interest in political systems and organization. Here again, however, the anthropological approach is global and comparative and includes nonstates, while political scientists tend to focus on contemporary and recent nation-states (see Kamrava 2008). Anthropological studies have revealed substantial variation in power, authority, and legal systems in different societies. (**Power** is the ability to exercise one's will over others; *authority* is the formal, socially approved use of power, e.g., by government officials.) (See Gledhill 2000; Kurtz 2001; Lewellen 2003; Nugent and Vincent 2004; Wolf with Silverman 2001.)

WHAT IS "THE POLITICAL"?

Morton Fried offered the following definition of political organization:

> Political organization comprises those portions of social organization that specifically relate to the individuals or groups that manage the affairs of public policy or seek to control the appointment or activities of those individuals or groups. (Fried 1967, pp. 20–21)

This definition certainly fits contemporary North America. Under "individuals or groups that manage the affairs of public policy" come various agencies and levels of government. Those who seek to influence public policy include political parties, unions, corporations, consumers, lobbyists, activists, action committees, religious groups, and nongovernmental organizations (NGOs).

Fried's definition is less applicable to nonstates, where it's often difficult to detect any "public policy." For this reason, I prefer to speak of *socio*political organization in discussing the exercise of power and the regulation of relations among groups and their representatives. Political regulation includes such processes as decision making, dispute management, and conflict resolution. The study of political regulation draws our attention to those who make decisions and resolve conflicts (are there formal leaders?).

TYPES AND TRENDS

Ethnographic and archaeological studies in hundreds of places have revealed many correlations between the economy and social and political organization. Decades ago, the anthropologist Elman Service (1962) listed four types, or levels, of political organization: band, tribe, chiefdom, and state. Today, none of the first three types can be studied as a self-contained form of political organization, because all now exist within nation-states and are subject to state control (see Ferguson 2003 and this chapter's "Appreciating Diversity"). There is archaeological evidence for early bands, tribes, and chiefdoms that existed before the first states appeared. However, because anthropology came into being long after the origin of the state, anthropologists never have been able to observe "in the flesh" a band, tribe, or chiefdom outside the influence of some state. There still may be local political leaders (e.g., village heads) and regional figures (e.g., chiefs) of the sort discussed in this chapter, but all now exist and function within the context of state organization.

A **band** is a small kin-based group (all its members are related by kinship or marriage) found among foragers. **Tribes** have economies based on

Participants in a labor rally hold up signs and posters in Santa Fe, New Mexico. As anthropologist Margaret Mead once observed about political mobilization, small groups of committed citizens have the capacity to change the world.

nonintensive food production (horticulture and pastoralism). Living in villages and organized into kin groups based on common descent (clans and lineages), tribes have no formal government and no reliable means of enforcing political decisions. *Chiefdom* refers to a form of sociopolitical organization intermediate between the tribe and the state. In chiefdoms, social relations were based mainly on kinship, marriage, descent, age, generation, and gender—just as in bands and tribes. However, although chiefdoms were kin based, they featured **differential access** to resources (some people had more wealth, prestige, and power than others did) and a permanent political structure. The *state* is a form of sociopolitical organization based on a formal government structure and socioeconomic stratification.

The four labels in Service's typology are much too simple to account for the full range of political diversity and complexity known to archaeology and ethnography. We'll see, for instance, that tribes have varied widely in their political systems and institutions. Nevertheless, Service's typology does highlight some significant contrasts in political organization, especially those between states and nonstates. For example, in bands and tribes—unlike states, which have clearly visible governments—political organization did not stand out as separate and distinct from the total social order. In bands and tribes, it was difficult to characterize an act or event as political rather than merely social.

Service's labels "band," "tribe," "chiefdom," and "state" are categories or types within a sociopolitical typology. These types are correlated with the adaptive strategies (an economic typology) discussed in the last chapter. Thus, foragers (an economic type)

power
The ability to exercise one's will over others.

differential access
Favored access to resources by superordinates over subordinates.

band
Basic (kin-based) unit of social organization among foragers.

tribe
Food-producing society with rudimentary political structure.

tended to have band organization (a sociopolitical type). Similarly, many horticulturalists and pastoralists lived in tribes. Although most chiefdoms had farming economies, herding was important in some Middle Eastern chiefdoms. Nonindustrial states usually had an agricultural base.

With food production came larger, denser populations and more complex economies than was the case among foragers. These features posed new regulatory problems, which gave rise to more complex relations and linkages. Many sociopolitical trends reflect the increased regulatory demands associated with food production. Archaeologists have studied these trends through time, and cultural anthropologists have observed them among more contemporary groups.

BANDS AND TRIBES

This chapter examines a series of societies with different political systems. A common set of questions will be addressed for each one. What kinds of social groups does the society have? How do those groups represent themselves to each other? How are their internal and external relations regulated? To answer these questions, we begin with bands and tribes and then consider chiefdoms and states.

Foraging Bands

Modern hunter-gatherers are today's remnants of foraging band societies. The strong ties they now maintain with sociopolitical groups outside the band make them markedly different from Stone Age hunter-gatherers. Modern foragers live in nation-states and an interlinked world. The pygmies of Congo, for example, have for generations shared a social world and economic exchanges with their neighbors who are cultivators. All foragers now trade

Among tropical foragers, women make an important economic contribution through gathering, as is true among the San shown here in Namibia. What evidence do you see in this photo that contemporary foragers participate in the modern world system?

with food producers. In addition, most contemporary hunter-gatherers rely on governments and on missionaries for at least part of what they consume.

The San

In the last chapter, we saw how the Basarwa San have been affected by policies of the government of Botswana, which relocated them after converting their ancestral lands into a wildlife reserve (Motseta 2006). More generally, San speakers ("Bushmen") of southern Africa have been influenced by Bantu speakers (farmers and herders) for 2,000 years and by Europeans for centuries. Edwin Wilmsen (1989) contends that many San descend from herders who were pushed into the desert by poverty or oppression. He sees the San today as a rural underclass in a larger political and economic system dominated by Europeans and Bantu food producers. Within this system, many San now tend cattle for wealthier Bantu rather than foraging independently. San also have their own domesticated animals, further illustrating their movement away from a foraging lifestyle.

Susan Kent (1992, 1996, 2002) noted a tendency to stereotype foragers, to treat them all as alike. They used to be stereotyped as isolated, primitive survivors of the Stone Age. A new, and probably more accurate, view of contemporary foragers sees them as groups forced into marginal environments by states, colonialism, and world events.

Kent (1996, 2002) stresses variation among foragers, focusing on diversity in time and space among the San. The nature of San life has changed considerably since the 1950s and 1960s, when a series of anthropologists from Harvard University, including Richard B. Lee, embarked on a systematic study of their lives. Studying the San over time, Lee and others have documented many changes (see Lee 1979, 1984, 2003; Silberbauer 1981; Tanaka 1980). Such longitudinal research monitors variation in time, and fieldwork in many San areas has revealed variation in space. One of the most important contrasts was found to be that between settled (sedentary) and nomadic groups (Kent and Vierich 1989). Although sedentism has increased substantially in recent years, some San groups (along rivers) have been sedentary for generations. Others, including the Dobe Ju/'hoansi San studied by Lee (1984, 2003) and the Kutse San whom Kent studied, have retained more of the hunter-gatherer lifestyle.

To the extent that foraging continues to be their subsistence base, groups like the San can illustrate links between a foraging economy and other aspects of band society and culture. For example, San groups that still are mobile, or that were so until recently, emphasize social, political, and gender equality, which are traditional band characteristics. A social system based on kinship, reciprocity, and sharing is appropriate for an economy with few people and limited resources. People have to share meat when they get it; otherwise it rots. The nomadic pursuit of wild plants and animals tends to discourage permanent settlement, wealth accumulation, and status distinctions.

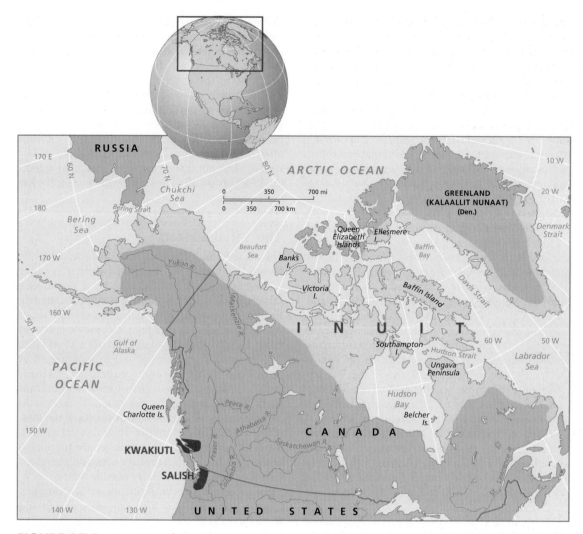

FIGURE 17.1 Location of the Inuit.

In the past, foraging bands—small nomadic or seminomadic social units—formed seasonally when component nuclear families got together. The particular families might vary from year to year. Marriage and kinship created ties between members of different bands. Trade and visiting also linked them. Band leaders were leaders in name only. In such an egalitarian society, they were first among equals (see Solway 2006). Sometimes they gave advice or made decisions, but they had no way to enforce those decisions. Because of the spread of states and the modern world system, it is increasingly difficult for ethnographers to find and observe such patterns of band organization.

The Inuit

The aboriginal Inuit (Hoebel 1954, 1954/1968), another group of foragers, provide a good example of methods of settling disputes—**conflict resolution**—in stateless societies. All societies have ways of settling disputes (of variable effectiveness) along with cultural rules or norms about proper and improper behavior. Norms are cultural standards or guidelines that enable individuals to distinguish between appropriate and inappropriate behavior in a given society (N. Kottak 2002). While rules and norms are cultural universals, only state societies, those with established governments, have laws that are formulated, proclaimed, and enforced (see Donovan 2007).

Foragers lacked formal **law** in the sense of a legal code with trial and enforcement, but they did have methods of social control and dispute settlement. The absence of law did not mean total anarchy. As described by E. A. Hoebel (1954) in a classic ethnographic study of conflict resolution, a sparse population of some 20,000 Inuit spanned 6,000 miles (9,500 kilometers) of the Arctic region (Figure 17.1). The most significant social groups were the nuclear family and the band. Personal relationships linked the families and bands. Some bands had headmen. There also were shamans (part-time religious specialists). However, these positions conferred little power on those who occupied them.

Hunting and fishing by men were the primary Inuit subsistence activities. The diverse and abundant plant foods available in warmer areas, where

law
Legal code of a state society, with trial and enforcement.

conflict resolution
Means of settling disputes.

female labor in gathering is important, were absent in the Arctic. Traveling on land and sea in a bitter environment, Inuit men faced more dangers than women did. The traditional male role took its toll in lives, so that adult women outnumbered men. This permitted some men to have two or three wives. The ability to support more than one wife conferred a certain amount of prestige, but it also encouraged envy. (*Prestige* is social esteem, respect, or approval.) If a man seemed to be taking additional wives just to enhance his reputation, a rival was likely to steal one of them. Most Inuit disputes were between men and originated over women, caused by wife stealing or adultery.

A jilted husband had several options. He could try to kill the wife stealer. However, if he succeeded, one of his rival's kinsmen surely would try to kill him in retaliation. One dispute might escalate into several deaths as relatives avenged a succession of murders. No government existed to intervene and stop such a *blood feud* (a murderous feud between families). However, one also could challenge a rival to a song battle. In a public setting, contestants made up insulting songs about each other. At the end of the match, the audience proclaimed the winner. However, if the winner was the man whose wife had been stolen, there was no guarantee she would return. Often she stayed with her abductor.

Thefts are common in societies with marked property differentials, like our own, but thefts are uncommon among foragers. Each Inuit had access to the resources he or she needed to sustain life. Every man could hunt, fish, and make the tools necessary for subsistence. Every woman could obtain the materials needed to make clothing, prepare food, and do domestic work. Inuit men could even hunt and fish in the territories of other local groups. There was no notion of private ownership of territory or animals.

Tribal Cultivators

As is true of foraging bands, there are no totally autonomous tribes in today's world. Still, there are societies, for example, in Papua New Guinea and in South America's tropical forests, in which tribal principles continue to operate. Tribes typically have a horticultural or pastoral economy and are organized into villages and/or descent groups (kin groups whose members trace descent from a common ancestor). Tribes lack socioeconomic stratification (i.e., a class structure) and a formal government of their own. A few tribes still conduct small-scale warfare, in the form of intervillage raiding. Tribes have more effective regulatory mechanisms than foragers do, but tribal societies have no sure means of enforcing political decisions. The main regulatory officials are village heads, "big men," descent-group leaders, village councils, and leaders of pantribal associations (see later in the chapter). All these figures and groups have limited authority.

village head
Local tribal leader with limited authority.

Like foragers, horticulturalists tend to be egalitarian, although some have marked gender stratification: an unequal distribution of resources, power, prestige, and personal freedom between men and women (see the chapter "Gender"). Horticultural villages usually are small, with low population density and open access to strategic resources. Age, gender, and personal traits determine how much respect people receive and how much support they get from others. Egalitarianism diminishes, however, as village size and population density increase. Horticultural villages usually have headmen—rarely, if ever, headwomen.

The Village Head

The Yanomami (Chagnon 1997; Ferguson 1995; Ramos 1995) are Native Americans who live in southern Venezuela and the adjacent part of Brazil. (See this chapter's "Appreciating Diversity" for an update on the Yanomami.) Their tribal society has about 26,000 people living in 200 to 250 widely scattered villages, each with a population between 40 and 250. The Yanomami are horticulturalists who also hunt and gather. Their staple crops are bananas and plantains (a bananalike crop). There are more significant social groups among the Yanomami than exist in a foraging society. The Yanomami have families, villages, and descent groups. Their descent groups, which span more than one village, are patrilineal (ancestry is traced back through males only) and exogamous (people must marry outside their own descent group). However, branches of two different descent groups may live in the same village and intermarry.

Traditionally among the Yanomami the only leadership position has been that of **village head** (always a man). His authority, like that of a foraging band's leader, is severely limited. If a headman wants something done, he must lead by example and persuasion. The headman lacks the right to issue orders.

living anthropology **VIDEOS**

Leadership among the Canela, www.mhhe.com/kottak

This clip features ethnographer Bill Crocker, who has worked among the Canela for more than 40 years, and Raimundo Roberto, a respected ceremonial chief, who has been Crocker's key cultural consultant during that entire time. Raimundo discusses his role in Canela society, mentioning the values of generosity, sharing, and comforting words. How does this clip illustrate differences between leadership in a tribal society and leadership in our own? Does Raimundo have formal authority? Compare him to the Yanomami village head and the band leader discussed in this chapter. The clip also shows a mending ceremony celebrating the healing of a rift that once threatened Canela society.

He can only persuade, harangue, and try to influence public opinion. For example, if he wants people to clean up the central plaza in preparation for a feast, he must start sweeping it himself, hoping his covillagers will take the hint and relieve him.

When conflict erupts within the village, the headman may be called on as a mediator who listens to both sides. He will give an opinion and advice. If a disputant is unsatisfied, the headman has no power to back his decisions and no way to impose punishments. Like the band leader, he is first among equals.

A Yanomami village headman also must lead in generosity. Expected to be more generous than any other villager, he cultivates more land. His garden provides much of the food consumed when his village hosts a feast for another village. The headman represents the village in its dealings with outsiders, including Venezuelan and Brazilian government agents.

The way someone acts as headman depends on his personal traits and the number of supporters he can muster. Napoleon Chagnon (1983/1997) describes how one village headman, Kaobawa, guaranteed safety to a delegation from a village with which a covillager of his wanted to start a war. Kaobawa was a particularly effective headman. He had demonstrated his fierceness in battle, but he also knew how to use diplomacy to avoid offending other villagers. No one in his village had a better personality for the headmanship. Nor (because Kaobawa had many brothers) did anyone have more supporters. Among the Yanomami, when a village is dissatisfied with its headman, its members can leave and found a new village. This happens from time to time and is called village fissioning.

With its many villages and descent groups, Yanomami sociopolitical organization is more complicated than that of a band-organized society. The Yanomami face more problems in regulating relations between groups and individuals. Although a headman sometimes can prevent a specific violent act, intervillage raiding has been a feature of some areas of Yanomami territory, particularly those studied by Chagnon (1997).

It's important to recognize as well that the Yanomami are not isolated from outside events. They live in two nation-states, Venezuela and Brazil, and attacks by outsiders, especially Brazilian ranchers and miners, have plagued them (Chagnon 1997; *Cultural Survival Quarterly* 1989; Ferguson 1995). During a Brazilian gold rush between 1987 and 1991, one Yanomami died each day, on average, from such attacks. By 1991, there were some 40,000 miners in the Brazilian Yanomami homeland. Some Indians were killed outright. The miners introduced new diseases, and the swollen population ensured that old diseases became epidemic. In 1991, the American Anthropological Association reported on the plight of the Yanomami (*Anthropology Newsletter*, September 1991). Brazilian Yanomami were dying at a rate of 10 percent annually, and their fertility rate had dropped to zero. Since then, one Brazilian president

has declared a huge Yanomami territory off limits to outsiders. Unfortunately, local politicians, miners, and ranchers have managed to evade the ban. The future of the Yanomami remains uncertain (see "Appreciating Diversity").

The "Big Man"

Many societies of the South Pacific, particularly on the Melanesian Islands and in Papua New Guinea, had a kind of political leader that we call the big man. The **big man** (almost always a male) was an elaborate version of the village head, but with one significant difference. Unlike the village head, whose leadership is limited to one village, the big man had supporters in several villages. The big man thus was a regulator of regional political organization.

Consider the Kapauku Papuans, who live in Irian Jaya, Indonesia (which is on the island of New Guinea) (see Figure 17.2.). Anthropologist Leopold Pospisil (1963) studied the Kapauku (then 45,000 people), who grow crops (with the sweet potato as their staple) and raise pigs. Their economy is too complex to be described as simple horticulture. Labor-intensive cultivation requires mutual aid in turning the soil before planting. The digging of long drainage ditches, which a big man often helped

big man
Generous tribal entrepreneur with multivillage support.

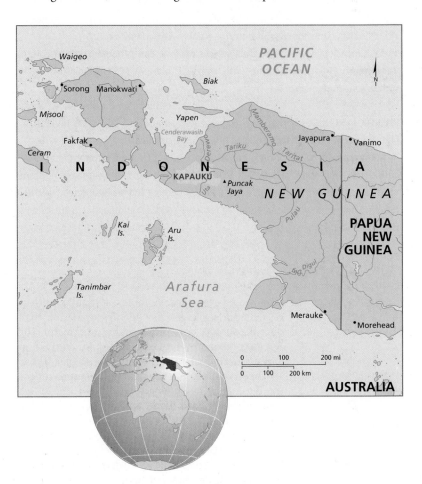

FIGURE 17.2 Location of the Kapauku.

Yanomami Update: Venezuela Takes Charge, Problems Arise

Appreciating the complexity of culture means recognizing that human beings never have lived in isolation from other groups. The cultural practices that link people include marriage, religion (e.g., the missionization described here), trade, travel, exploration, warfare, and conquest. As we see in this account, local people today must heed not only their own customs but also a diversity of laws, policies, and decisions made by outsiders. As you read this account, pay attention to the various interest groups involved and how their goals and wishes might clash. Also consider the various levels of political regulation (local, regional, national, and international) that determine how contemporary people such as the Yanomami live their lives and strive to maintain their health, autonomy, and cultural traditions. Consider as well the effectiveness of Yanomami leaders in dealing with agents of the Venezuelan state.

PUERTO AYACUCHO, Venezuela—Three years after President Hugo Chávez expelled American missionaries from the Venezuelan Amazon, accusing them of using proselytism of remote tribes as a cover for espionage, resentment is festering here over what some tribal leaders say was official negligence. . . .

Some leaders of the Yanomami, one of South America's largest forest-dwelling tribes, say that 50 people in their communities in the southern rain forest have died since the expulsion of the missionaries . . . because of recurring shortages of medicine and fuel, and unreliable transportation out of the jungle to medical facilities.

Mr. Chávez's government disputes the claims and points to more spending than ever on social welfare programs for the Yanomami. The spending is part of a broader plan to assert greater military and social control over expanses of rain forest that are viewed as essential for Venezuela's sovereignty. . . .

In recent interviews here, government officials contended that the Yanomami could be exaggerating their claims to win more resources from the government and undercut its authority in the Amazon. . . .

The Yanomami claims come amid growing concern in Venezuela over indigenous health care after a scandal erupted in August over a tepid official response to a mystery disease that killed 38 Warao Indians in the country's northeast.

"This government makes a big show of helping the Yanomami, but rhetoric is one thing and reality another," said Ramón González, 49, a Yanomami leader from the village of Yajanamateli who traveled recently to Puerto Ayacucho, the capital of Amazonas State, to ask military officials and civilian doctors for improved health care.

"The truth is that Yanomami lives are still considered worthless," said Mr. González. "The boats, the planes, the money, it's all for the criollos, not for us," he said, using a term for nonindigenous Venezuelans. . . .

There are about 26,000 Yanomami in the Amazon rain forest, in Venezuela and Brazil, where they subsist as seminomadic hunters and cultivators of crops like manioc and bananas.

They remain susceptible to ailments for which they have weak defenses, including respiratory diseases and drug-resistant strains of malaria. In Puerto Ayacucho, they can be seen wandering through the traffic-clogged streets, clad in the modern uniform of T-shirts and baggy pants, toting cellphones. . . .

Mr. González and other Yanomami leaders provided the names of 50 people, including 22 children, who they said died from ailments like malaria and pneumonia after the military limited civilian and missionary flights to their villages. . . . The military replaced the missionaries' operations with its own fleet of small planes and helicopters, but critics say the missions were infrequent or unresponsive.

The Yanomami leaders said they made the list public after showing it to health and military

organize, is even more complex. Kapauku cultivation supports a larger and denser population than does the simpler horticulture of the Yanomami. The Kapauku economy required collective cultivation and political regulation of the more complex tasks.

The key political figure among the Kapauku was the big man. Known as a *tonowi*, he achieved his status through hard work, amassing wealth in the form of pigs and other native riches. The achieved status of big man rested on certain characteristics that distinguished him from his fellows. Key attributes included wealth, generosity, eloquence, physical fitness, bravery, supernatural powers, and the ability to gain the support and loyalty of others. Men became big men because they had certain personalities; they did not inherit their status but created it through hard work and good judgment. Wealth resulted from successful pig breeding and trading. As a man's pig herd and prestige grew, he attracted supporters. He sponsored pig feasts in which pork (provided by the big man and his supporters) was distributed to guests, bringing him more prestige and widening his network of support.

The big man's supporters, recognizing his past favors and anticipating future rewards, recognized him as a leader and accepted his decisions as binding.

officials and receiving a cold response. "They told us we should be grateful for the help we're already being given," said Eduardo Mejía, 24, a Yanomami leader from the village of El Cejal.

"The missionaries were in Amazonas for 50 years, creating dependent indigenous populations in some places, so their withdrawal was bound to have positive and negative effects," said Carlos Botto, a senior official with Caicet, a government research institute that focuses on tropical diseases.

"But one cannot forget that the Yanomami and other indigenous groups have learned how to exert pressure on the government in order to receive food or other benefits," he said. "This does not mean there aren't challenges in providing them with health care, but caution is necessary with claims like these."

The dispute has also focused attention on an innovative government project created in late 2005, the Yanomami Health Plan. With a staff of 46, it trains some Yanomami to be health workers in their villages while sending doctors into the jungle to provide health care to remote communities.

"We have 14 doctors in our team, with 11 trained in Cuba for work in jungle areas," said Meydell Simancas, 32, a tropical disease specialist who directs the project from a compound here once owned by New Tribes Mission.

Dr. Simancas said that more than 20 Yanomami had been trained as paramedics, and that statistics showed that doctors had increased immunizations and programs to control malaria and river blindness across Amazonas.

The Yanomami leaders complaining of negligence acknowledged Dr. Simancas's good intentions. But they said serious problems persisted in coordinating access to doctors and medicine with the military, which the Yanomami and government doctors both rely on for travel in and out of the rain forest. . . .

Yanomami leaders point to what they consider to be a broad pattern of neglect and condescension from public officials. . . .

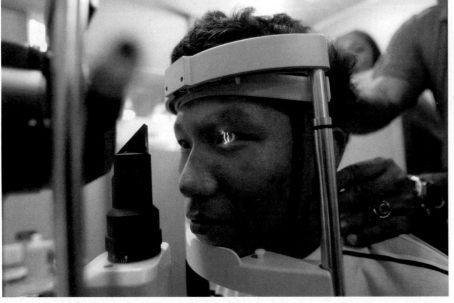

Shown here, as part of a public health outreach program, Julio Guzman, an indigenous Yanomami, has his eyes checked by a Venezuelan government doctor.

The *tonowi* was an important regulator of regional events in Kapauku life. He helped determine the dates for feasts and markets. He initiated economic projects requiring the cooperation of a regional community.

The Kapauku big man again exemplifies a generalization about leadership in tribal societies: If someone achieves wealth and widespread respect and support, he or she must be generous. The big man worked hard not to hoard wealth but to be able to give away the fruits of his labor, to convert wealth into prestige and gratitude. A stingy big man would lose his support. Selfish and greedy big men sometimes were murdered by their fellows (Zimmer-Tamakoshi 1997).

Pantribal Sodalities

Big men could forge regional political organization, albeit temporarily, by mobilizing supporters from several villages. Other principles in tribal societies—such as a belief in common ancestry, kinship, or descent—could be used to link local groups within a region. The same descent group, for example, might span several villages, and its dispersed members might recognize the same leader.

The "big man" persuades people to organize feasts, which distribute pork and wealth. Shown here is such a regional event, drawing on several villages, in Papua New Guinea. Big men owe their status to their individual personalities rather than to inherited wealth or position. Does our society have equivalents of big men?

pantribal sodalities
Nonkin-based groups with regional political significance.

Principles other than kinship also can link local groups, especially in modern societies. People who live in different parts of the same nation may belong to the same labor union, sorority or fraternity, political party, or religious denomination. In tribes, nonkin groups called *associations* or *sodalities* may serve a similar linking function. Often, sodalities are based on common age or gender, with all-male sodalities more common than all-female ones.

Pantribal sodalities are groups that extend across the whole tribe, spanning several villages. Such sodalities were especially likely to develop in situations of warfare with a neighboring tribe. Mobilizing their members from multiple villages within the same tribe, pantribal sodalities could assemble a force to attack or retaliate against another tribe.

The best examples of pantribal sodalities come from the Central Plains of North America and from tropical Africa. During the 18th and 19th centuries, Native American populations of the Great Plains of the United States and Canada experienced a rapid growth of pantribal sodalities. This development reflected an economic change that followed the spread of horses, which had been reintroduced to the Americas by the Spanish, to the area between the Rocky Mountains and the Mississippi River. Many Plains Indian societies changed their adaptive strategies because of the horse. At first they had been foragers who hunted bison (buffalo) on foot. Later they adopted a mixed economy based on hunting, gathering, and horticulture. Finally they changed to a much more specialized economy based on horseback hunting of bison (eventually with rifles).

As the Plains tribes were undergoing these changes, other tribes also adopted horseback hunting and moved into the Plains. Attempting to occupy the same area, groups came into conflict. A pattern of warfare developed in which the members

Natives of the Great Plains of North America originally hunted bison (buffalo) on foot, using the bow and arrow. The introduction of horses and rifles fueled a pattern of horse raiding and warfare. How far had the change gone, as depicted in this painting?

of one tribe raided another, usually for horses. The economy demanded that people follow the movement of the bison herds. During the winter, when the bison dispersed, a tribe fragmented into small bands and families. In the summer, when huge herds assembled on the Plains, the tribe reunited. They camped together for social, political, and religious activities, but mainly for communal bison hunting.

Two activities demanded strong leadership: organizing and carrying out raids on enemy camps (to capture horses) and managing the summer bison hunt. All the Plains societies developed pantribal sodalities, and leadership roles within them, to police the summer hunt. Leaders coordinated hunting efforts, making sure that people did not cause a stampede with an early shot or an ill-advised action. Leaders imposed severe penalties, including seizure of a culprit's wealth, for disobedience.

Many tribes that adopted this Plains strategy of adaptation had once been foragers for whom hunting and gathering had been individual or small-group affairs. They never had come together previously as a single social unit. Age and gender were available as social principles that could quickly and efficiently forge unrelated people into pantribal sodalities.

Raiding of one tribe by another, this time for cattle rather than horses, also was common in eastern and southeastern Africa, where pantribal sodalities also developed. Among the pastoral Masai of Kenya, men born during the same four-year period were circumcised together and belonged to the same named group, an *age set,* throughout their lives. The sets moved through *age grades,* the most important of which was the warrior grade. Members of a set felt a strong allegiance to one another. Masai women lacked comparable set organization, but they also passed through culturally recognized age grades: the initiate, the married woman, and the female elder.

In certain parts of western and central Africa, pantribal sodalities are secret societies, made up exclusively of men or women. Like our college fraternities and sororities, these associations have secret initiation ceremonies. Among the Mende of Sierra Leone, men's and women's secret societies were very influential. The men's group, the Poro, trained boys in social conduct, ethics, and religion and it supervised political and economic activities. Leadership roles in the Poro often overshadowed village headship and played an important part in social control, dispute management, and tribal political regulation. Age, gender, and ritual can link members of different local groups into a single social collectivity in a tribe and thus create a sense of ethnic identity, of belonging to the same cultural tradition.

Nomadic Politics

Herders have varied political systems. Unlike the Masai (just discussed) and other tribal herders, some

Among the Masai of Kenya and Tanzania, men born during the same four-year period were circumcised together. They belonged to the same named group, an age set, throughout their lives. The sets moved through grades, of which the most important was the warrior grade. Here we see the warrior (*ilmurran*) age grade dancing with a group of girls of a lower age grade (*intoyie*). Do we have any equivalents of age sets or grades in our own society?

pastoralists have chiefs and live in nation-states. The scope of political authority among pastoralists expands considerably as regulatory problems increase in densely populated regions (see Salzman 2008). Consider two Iranian pastoral nomadic tribes—the Basseri and the Qashqai (Salzman 1974). Starting each year from a plateau near the coast, these groups took their animals to grazing land 17,000 feet (5,400 meters) above sea level (see Figure 17.3).

The Basseri and the Qashqai shared this route with each other and with several other ethnic groups. Use of the same pastureland at different times of year was carefully scheduled. Ethnic-group movements were tightly coordinated. Expressing this schedule is *il-rah,* a concept common to all Iranian nomads. A group's *il-rah* is its customary path in time and space. It is the schedule, different for each group, of when specific areas can be used in the annual trek.

Each tribe had its own leader, known as the *khan* or *il-khan*. The Basseri *khan*, because he dealt with a smaller population, faced fewer problems in coordinating its movements than did the leaders of the Qashqai. Correspondingly, his rights, privileges, duties, and authority were weaker. Nevertheless, his authority exceeded that of any political figure discussed so far. The *khan's* authority still came from his personal traits rather than from his office. That is, the Basseri followed a particular *khan* not because of a political position he happened to fill but because of their personal allegiance and loyalty to him as a man. The *khan* relied on the support of the heads of the descent groups into which Basseri society was divided.

Among the Qashqai, however, allegiance shifted from the person to the office. The Qashqai had multiple

Political organization is well developed among the Qashqai, who share their nomadic route and strategic resources with several other tribes. Here, Qashqai nomads cross a river in Iran's Fars province.

FIGURE 17.3 Location of the Basseri and Qashqai.

levels of authority and more powerful chiefs or *khans*. Managing 400,000 people required a complex hierarchy. Heading it was the *il-khan*, helped by a deputy, under whom were the heads of constituent tribes, under each of whom were descent-group heads.

A case illustrates just how developed the Qashqai authority structure was. A hailstorm prevented some nomads from joining the annual migration at the appointed time. Although everyone recognized that they were not responsible for their delay, the *il-khan* assigned them less favorable grazing land, for that year only, in place of their usual pasture. The tardy herders and other Qashqai considered the judgment fair and didn't question it. Thus, Qashqai authorities regulated the annual migration. They also adjudicated disputes between people, tribes, and descent groups.

These Iranian cases illustrate the fact that pastoralism often is just one among many specialized economic activities within a nation-state. As part of a larger whole, pastoral tribes are constantly pitted against other ethnic groups. In these nations, the state becomes a final authority, a higher-level regulator that attempts to limit conflict between ethnic groups. State organization arose not just to manage agricultural economies but also to regulate the activities of ethnic groups within expanding social and economic systems (see Das and Poole 2004).

CHIEFDOMS

The first states emerged in the Old World around 5,500 years ago. The first chiefdoms developed perhaps a thousand years earlier, but few survive today. In many parts of the world, the chiefdom was a transitional form of organization that emerged during the evolution of tribes into states. State formation began in Mesopotamia (currently Iran and Iraq). It next occurred in Egypt, the Indus Valley of Pakistan and India, and northern China. A few thousand years later states arose in two parts of the Western Hemisphere—Mesoamerica (Mexico, Guatemala, Belize) and the central Andes (Peru and Bolivia). Early states are known as archaic, or nonindustrial, states, in contrast to modern industrial nation-states. Robert Carneiro defines the state as "an autonomous political unit encompassing many communities within its territory, having a centralized government with the power to collect taxes, draft men for work or war, and decree and enforce laws" (Carneiro 1970, p. 733).

The chiefdom and the state, like many categories used by social scientists, are ideal types. That is, they are labels that make social contrasts seem sharper than they really are. In reality there is a continuum from tribe to chiefdom to state. Some societies had many attributes of chiefdoms but retained tribal features. Some advanced chiefdoms had many attributes of archaic states and thus are difficult to assign to either category. Recognizing this "continuous change" (Johnson and Earle 2000), some anthropologists speak of "complex chiefdoms" (Earle 1987, 1997), which are almost states.

Political and Economic Systems

Geographic areas with chiefdoms included the circum-Caribbean (e.g., Caribbean islands, Panama, Colombia), lowland Amazonia, what is now the southeastern United States, and Polynesia. Chiefdoms created the megalithic cultures of Europe, including the one that built Stonehenge. Bear in mind that chiefdoms and states can fall (disintegrate) as well as rise. Before Rome's expansion, much of Europe was organized at the chiefdom level, to which it reverted for centuries after the fall of Rome in the fifth century C.E. Much of our ethnographic knowledge about chiefdoms comes from Polynesia (Kirch 2000), where they were common at the time of European exploration. In chiefdoms, social relations are mainly based on kinship, marriage, descent, age, generation, and gender—as they are in bands and tribes. This is a basic difference between chiefdoms and states. States bring nonrelatives together and oblige them to pledge allegiance to a government.

Stonehenge, England, and an educational display designed for tourists and visitors. Chiefdoms created the megalithic cultures of Europe, such as the one that built Stonehenge over 5,000 years ago. Between the emergence and spread of food production and the expansion of the Roman empire, much of Europe was organized at the chiefdom level, to which it reverted after the fall of Rome.

Unlike bands and tribes, however, chiefdoms administer a clear-cut and permanent regional political system. Chiefdoms may include thousands of people living in many villages or hamlets. Regulation is carried out by the chief and his or her assistants, who occupy political offices. An **office** is a permanent position, which must be refilled when it is vacated by death or retirement. Because official vacancies are filled systematically, the political system that is the chiefdom endures across the generations, thus ensuring permanent political regulation.

Polynesian chiefs were full-time specialists whose duties included managing the economy. They regulated production by commanding or prohibiting (using religious taboos) the cultivation of certain lands and crops. Chiefs also regulated distribution and consumption. At certain seasons—often on a ritual occasion such as a first-fruit ceremony—people would offer part of their harvest to the chief through his or her representatives. Products moved up the hierarchy, eventually reaching the chief. Conversely, illustrating obligatory sharing with kin, chiefs sponsored feasts at which they gave back some of what they had received. Unlike big men, chiefs were exempt from ordinary work and had rights and privileges unavailable to the masses. Like big men, however, they still returned a portion of the wealth they took in.

Such a flow of resources to and then from a central place is known as *chiefly redistribution*, which offers economic advantages. If different parts of the chiefdom specialized in particular products, chiefly redistribution made those products available to the entire society. Chiefly redistribution also helped stimulate production beyond the basic subsistence level and provided a central storehouse for goods that might become scarce in times of famine (Earle 1987, 1997).

Status Systems

Social status in chiefdoms was based on seniority of descent. Polynesian chiefs kept extremely long genealogies. Some chiefs (without writing) managed to trace their ancestry back fifty generations. All the people in the chiefdom were thought to be related to one another. Presumably, all were descended from a group of founding ancestors.

The status of chief was ascribed, based on seniority of descent. The chief would be the oldest child (usually son) of the oldest child of the oldest child, and so on. Degrees of seniority were calculated so intricately on some islands that there were as many ranks as people. For example, the third son would rank below the second, who in turn would rank below the first. The children of an eldest brother, however, would all rank above the children of the next brother, whose children in turn would outrank those of younger brothers. However, even the lowest-ranking man or woman in a chiefdom

An outdoor portrait of a Maori chief at the Polynesian Cultural Center in Hawaii. Both Hawaii and New Zealand, where the Maori live, were sites of traditional Polynesian chiefdoms. How do chiefs differ from ordinary people?

was still the chief's relative. In such a kin-based context, everyone, even a chief, had to share with his or her relatives. Because everyone had a slightly different status, it was difficult to draw a line between elites and common people. Other chiefdoms calculated seniority differently and had shorter genealogies than did those in Polynesia. Still, the concern for seniority and the lack of sharp gaps between elites and commoners are features of all chiefdoms.

The status systems of chiefdoms, as of states, were associated with differential access to resources. Some men and women had privileged access to power, prestige, and wealth. They controlled strategic resources such as land and water. Earle characterizes chiefs as "an incipient aristocracy with advantages in wealth and lifestyle" (1987, p. 290).

Compared with chiefdoms, archaic states drew a much firmer line between elites and masses, distinguishing at least between nobles and commoners. Kinship ties did not extend from the nobles to the commoners because of stratum endogamy—marriage within one's own group. Commoners married commoners; elites married elites.

The Emergence of Stratification

The status system of a chiefdom differed from that of a state because of the chiefdom's kinship basis. In the context of differential wealth and power, the chiefly type of status system didn't last very long. Chiefs would start acting like kings and try to erode the kinship basis of the chiefdom. In Madagascar they would do this by demoting their more distant relatives to commoner status and banning marriage between nobles and commoners (Kottak 1980). Such moves, if accepted by the society, created separate social strata—unrelated groups that differ in their access to wealth, prestige, and power. (A *stratum* is one of two or more groups that contrast in social status and access to strategic resources. Each stratum includes people of both sexes and all ages.) The creation of separate social strata is called *stratification,* and its emergence signified the transition from chiefdom to state. The presence of stratification is one of the key distinguishing features of a state.

The influential sociologist Max Weber (1922/1968) defined three related dimensions of social stratification: (1) Economic status, or **wealth**, encompasses all a person's material assets, including income, land, and other types of property. (2) Power, the ability to exercise one's will over others—to get what one

A lucky couple enjoys their photocall in Falkirk, Scotland, on July 15, 2011, after winning a record GBP161m ($259m USD) in the EuroMillions Lottery. Are these new multimillionaires likely to gain prestige, or just money, from their luck?

TABLE 17.1 Max Weber's Three Dimensions of Stratification

wealth	=>	economic status
power	=>	political status
prestige	=>	social status

wants—is the basis of political status. (3) **Prestige**—the basis of social status—refers to esteem, respect, or approval for acts, deeds, or qualities considered exemplary. Prestige, or "cultural capital" (Bourdieu 1984), gives people a sense of worth and respect, which they may often convert into economic advantage (Table 17.1).

In archaic states—for the first time in human evolution—there were contrasts in wealth, power, and prestige between entire groups (social strata) of men and women. Each stratum included people of both genders and all ages. The **superordinate** (higher or elite) stratum had privileged access to valued resources. Access to those resources by members of the **subordinate** (lower or underprivileged) stratum was limited by the privileged group.

STATE SYSTEMS

Recap 17.1 summarizes the information presented so far on bands, tribes, chiefdoms, and states. States, remember, are autonomous political units with social strata and a formal government. States tend to be large and populous, and certain statuses, systems, and subsystems with specialized functions are found in all states (see Sharma and Gupta 2006). They include the following:

1. Population control: fixing of boundaries, establishment of citizenship categories, and censusing.

2. Judiciary: laws, legal procedure, and judges.

3. Enforcement: permanent military and police forces.

4. Fiscal: taxation.

In archaic states, these subsystems were integrated by a ruling system or government composed of civil, military, and religious officials (Fried 1960). Let's look at the four subsystems one by one.

Population Control

To keep track of whom they govern, states conduct censuses. A state demarcates boundaries to separate that state from other societies. Customs agents, immigration officers, navies, and coast guards patrol frontiers. States also regulate population through administrative subdivision: provinces, districts, "states," counties, subcounties, and parishes. Lower-level officials manage the populations and territories of the subdivisions.

States often promote geographic mobility and resettlement, severing longstanding ties among people, land, and kin (Smith 2003). Population displacements have increased with globalization and as war, famine, and job seeking churn up migratory currents. People in states come to identify themselves by new statuses, both ascribed and achieved—including residence, ethnicity, occupation, political party, religion, and team or club affiliation—rather than only as members of a descent group or extended family.

States also manage their populations by granting different rights and obligations to citizens and noncitizens. Status distinctions among citizens also are common. Archaic states granted different rights to nobles, commoners, and slaves. In American history prior to the Emancipation Proclamation, there were different laws for enslaved and free people. In European colonies, separate courts judged cases involving only natives and cases involving Europeans. In contemporary America, a military judiciary coexists alongside the civil system.

Judiciary

All states have laws based on precedent and legislative proclamations. Without writing, laws may be preserved in oral tradition. Crimes are violations of the legal code ("breaking the law"), with

prestige
Esteem, respect, or approval.

superordinate
Upper, privileged, group in a stratified society.

subordinate
Lower, underprivileged group in a stratified society.

RECAP 17.1 Economic Basis of and Political Regulation in Bands, Tribes, Chiefdoms, and States

SOCIOPOLITICAL TYPE	ECONOMIC TYPE	EXAMPLES	TYPE OF REGULATION
Band	Foraging	Inuit, San	Local
Tribe	Horticulture, pastoralism	Yanomami, Kapauku, Masai	Local, temporary regional
Chiefdom	Productive horticulture, pastoral nomadism, agriculture	Qashqai, Polynesia, Cherokee	Permanent regional
State	Agriculture, industrialism	Ancient Mesopotamia, contemporary United States and Canada	Permanent regional

focus on GLOBALIZATION

The Political Role of New Media

Global forces often face roadblocks to their international spread. Although the Internet makes possible the instantaneous global transmission of information, many countries censor the Internet and other mass media for political or moral reasons. Cuba makes all unauthorized Internet surfing illegal. Many countries limit access to porn sites. China has a sophisticated censorship system—sometimes called the "Great Firewall of China" (Lynn 2009). China's local search engine, Baidu, which observes Chinese censorship rules, has overtaken Google in the Chinese market. Despite censorship, China now has more people online than there are people in the United States (Lynn 2009).

Censorship can be a barrier to international business. The World Trade Organization (WTO) favors freedom of access to the Internet for commercial reasons: to allow free trade. WTO rules allow member nations to restrict trade to protect public morals or ensure public order, but with the understanding that such restrictions will disrupt trade as little as possible.

If the Internet and other media are used to promote free trade, how about free thought? The media have the capacity to enlighten by providing users with unfamiliar information and viewpoints and by offering a forum for dissident voices. On the other hand, the media also spread and reinforce stereotypes and misinformation, and, in doing so, close people's minds to complexity.

The media also promote fear, which often is manipulated for political reasons. Waves of internationally transmitted images and information can reinforce the perception that the world is a dangerous place, with threats to security and order everywhere. Facebook, Twitter, YouTube, cell-phone and digital cameras, and cable/satellite TV link people across the globe. Constant and instantaneous reporting has blurred the distinction between the international, the national, and the local. Geographic distance is obscured, and risk perception is magnified, by the barrage of "bad news" received daily from so many places. Many people have no idea how far away the disasters and threats really are. Was that suspicious package found in Paris or Pasadena? Did that bomb go off in Mumbai or Michigan? Votes in Athens, Greece or Rome, Italy can affect the American stock market more than votes in Athens or Rome, Georgia.

The political manipulation of media is not new. (Think of book banning and burning, for example. See http://www.adlerbooks.com/banned.html for a list of books that have been banned at some time in the United States.) Would-be guardians of morality and authoritarian regimes always have sought to silence dissident voices. What is new is the potentially instantaneous and global reach of the voices that question authority. New media, including cell phones, Twitter, and YouTube, have been used to muster public opinion against authority figures in places as distant as Cairo, Egypt and Davis, California. Can you think of examples of how new media have been used to question authority?

fiscal
Pertaining to finances and taxation.

---

specified types of punishment. To handle crimes and disputes, all states have courts and judges (see Donovan 2007).

A striking contrast between states and nonstates is intervention in family affairs. Governments step in to halt blood feuds and regulate previously private disputes. States attempt to curb internal conflict, but they aren't always successful. About 85 percent of the world's armed conflicts since 1945 have begun within states—in efforts to overthrow a ruling regime or as disputes over ethnic, religious, or human rights issues (see Barnaby 1984; Chatterjee 2004; Nordstrom 2004; Tishkov 2004).

Enforcement

All states have agents to enforce judicial decisions, for example, to mete out punishment and collect fines. Confinement requires jailers. If there is a death penalty, executioners are needed. Government officials have the power to collect fines and confiscate property. The government attempts to suppress internal disorder (with police) and to guard against external threats (with the military and border officials). As described in this chapter's "Focus on Globalization," censorship is another tool that governments may employ to secure their authority.

Armies help states subdue and conquer neighboring nonstates, but this isn't the only reason state organization has spread. Although states impose hardships, they also offer advantages. They have formal mechanisms designed to protect against external threats and to preserve internal order. When they are successful in promoting internal peace, states enhance production. Their economies can support massive, dense populations, which supply armies and colonists to promote expansion.

Fiscal Systems

States need financial or **fiscal** mechanisms (e.g., taxation) to support government officials and numerous other specialists. As in the chiefdom, the state intervenes in production, distribution, and consumption. The state may require a certain area to produce specific things, or ban certain activities in particular places. Like chiefdoms, states have redistribution, but less of what comes in from the people actually goes back to the people.

In nonstates, people customarily share with their relatives, but citizens also have to turn over a substantial portion of what they produce to the state (the "rent fund" discussed in the previous chapter). Markets and trade usually are under at least some state oversight, with officials overseeing distribution and exchange, standardizing weights and measures, and collecting taxes on goods passing into or through the state. Of the revenues the state collects, it reallocates part for the general good and keeps another part (often larger) for itself—its agents and agencies. State organization doesn't bring more freedom or leisure to the common people, who may be conscripted to build monumental public works. Some projects, such as dams and irrigation systems, may be economically necessary, but residents of archaic states also had to build temples, palaces, and tombs for the elites. Those elites reveled in the consumption of sumptuary goods—jewelry, exotic food and drink, and stylish clothing reserved for, or affordable only by, the rich. Peasants' diets suffered as they struggled to meet government demands. Commoners perished in territorial wars that had little relevance to their own needs. Are any of these observations true of contemporary states?

SOCIAL CONTROL

In studying political systems, anthropologists pay attention not only to the formal institutions but to other forms of social control as well. The concept of social control is broader than "the political." **Social control** refers to "those fields of the social system (beliefs, practices, and institutions) that are most actively involved in the maintenance of any norms and the regulation of any conflict" (N. Kottak 2002, p. 290). Norms, as defined earlier in this chapter, are cultural standards or guidelines that enable individuals to distinguish between appropriate and inappropriate behavior.

Previous sections of this chapter have focused more on formal political organization than on sociopolitical process. We've seen how the scale and strength of political systems have expanded in relation to economic changes. We've examined means of conflict resolution, or their absence, in various types of society. We've looked at political decision making, including leaders and their limits. We've also recognized that all contemporary humans have been affected by states, colonialism, and the spread of the modern world system.

Sociopolitical was introduced as a key concept at the beginning of this chapter. So far, we've focused mainly on the political part of sociopolitical; now we focus on the social part. In this section we'll see that political systems have their informal, social, and subtle aspects along with their formal, governmental, and public dimensions.

Hegemony and Resistance

Antonio Gramsci (1971) developed the concept of **hegemony** for a stratified social order in which subordinates comply with domination by internalizing their rulers' values and accepting the "naturalness" of domination (this is the way things were meant to be). According to Pierre Bourdieu (1977, p. 164), every social order tries to make its own arbitrariness (including its mechanisms of control and domination) seem natural and in everyone's interest. Often promises are made (things will get better if you're patient).

To handle disputes and crimes, all states, including Bermuda, shown here, have courts and judges. Does this photo say anything about cultural diffusion and/or colonialism?

Both Bourdieu (1977) and Michel Foucault (1979) argue that it is easier and more effective to dominate people in their minds than to try to control their bodies. Besides, and often replacing, physical coercion are more insidious forms of social control. These include various techniques of persuading and managing people and of monitoring and recording their beliefs, activities, and contacts.

Hegemony, the internalization of a dominant ideology, is one way in which elites curb resistance and maintain power. Another way is to make subordinates believe they eventually will gain power—as young people usually foresee when they let their elders dominate them. Another way of curbing resistance is to separate or isolate people while supervising them closely, as is done in prisons (Foucault 1979).

Popular resistance is most likely to be expressed openly when people are allowed to assemble. The oppressed may draw courage from their common sentiments and the anonymity of the crowd. Sensing danger, the elites often discourage public gatherings. They try to limit and control holidays, funerals, dances, festivals, and other occasions that might unite the oppressed. For example, in the American South before the Civil War, gatherings of five or more slaves were prohibited unless a white person was present.

Factors that interfere with community formation—such as geographic, linguistic, and ethnic separation—also work to curb resistance. Consequently, southern U.S. plantation owners sought slaves with diverse cultural and linguistic backgrounds. Despite the measures used to divide them, the slaves resisted, developing their own popular culture, linguistic codes, and religious vision. The masters stressed portions of the Bible that stressed compliance (e.g., the book of Job). The slaves, however, preferred the story of Moses

social control
Maintaining social norms and regulating conflict.

hegemony
Social order in which subordinates accept hierarchy as "natural."

and deliverance. The cornerstone of slave religion became the idea of a reversal in the conditions of whites and blacks. Slaves also resisted directly, through sabotage and flight. In many New World areas, slaves managed to establish free communities in the hills and other isolated areas (Price 1973).

Weapons of the Weak

The study of sociopolitical systems also should consider the sentiments and activity that may lurk beneath the surface of evident, public behavior. In public, the oppressed may seem to accept their own domination, even as they question it in private. James Scott (1990) uses "public transcript" to describe the open, public interactions between superordinates and subordinates—the outer shell of power relations. He uses "hidden transcript" to describe the critique of power that proceeds out of sight of the powerholders. In public, the elites and the oppressed may observe the etiquette of power relations. The dominants act like masters while their subordinates show humility and defer.

Often, situations that seem to be hegemonic do have active resistance, but it is individual and disguised rather than collective and defiant. James Scott (1985) uses Malay peasants, among whom he did fieldwork, to illustrate small-scale acts of resistance—which he calls "weapons of the weak." The Malay peasants used an indirect strategy to resist an Islamic tithe (religious tax). Peasants were expected to pay the tithe, usually in the form of

rice, which was sent to the provincial capital. In theory, the tithe would come back as charity, but it never did. Peasants didn't resist the tithe by rioting, demonstrating, or protesting. Instead they used a "nibbling" strategy, based on small acts of resistance. For example, they failed to declare their land or lied about the amount they farmed. They underpaid, or delivered rice contaminated with water, rocks, or mud, to add weight. Because of this resistance, only 15 percent of what was due actually was paid (Scott 1990, p. 89).

Hidden transcripts tend to be expressed publicly at certain times (festivals and Carnavals) and in certain places (e.g., markets). Because of its costumed anonymity, Carnaval (aka Mardi Gras in New Orleans) is an excellent arena for expressing normally suppressed feelings. Carnavals celebrate freedom through immodesty, dancing, gluttony, and sexuality (DaMatta 1991). Carnaval may begin as a playful outlet for frustrations built up during the year. Over time, it may evolve into a powerful annual critique of stratification and domination and thus a threat to the established order (Gilmore 1987). (Recognizing that ceremonial license could turn into political defiance, the Spanish dictator Francisco Franco outlawed Carnaval.)

Shame and Gossip

Many anthropologists have noted the importance of "informal" processes of social control, such as fear, stigma, shame, and gossip, especially in small-scale societies (see Freilich, Raybeck, and Savishinsky 1991). Gossip, which can lead to shame, sometimes is used when a direct or formal sanction is risky or impossible (Herskovits 1937). Margaret Mead (1937) and Ruth Benedict (1946) distinguished between shame as an external sanction (i.e., forces set in motion by others) and guilt as an internal sanction, psychologically generated by the individual. They regarded shame as a more prominent form of social control in non-Western societies and guilt as a more dominant emotional sanction in Western societies. Of course, to be effective as a sanction, the prospect of being shamed or of shaming oneself must be internalized by the individual. In small-scale societies, in a social environment where everyone knows everyone else, most people try to avoid behavior that might spoil their reputations and alienate them from their social network.

Nicholas Kottak (2002) studied political systems, and social control more generally, among the rural Makua of northern Mozambique (Figure 17.4). Social control mechanisms among the Makua extended well beyond the formal political system, as revealed in conversations about social norms and crimes. The Makua talk easily about norm violations, conflicts, and the sanctions that can follow them. Jail, sorcery, and shame are the main sanctions anticipated by the rural Makua.

"Schwellkoepp" or "Swollen Heads" caricature local characters during a Carnaval parade in Mainz, Germany. Because of its costumed anonymity, Carnaval is an excellent arena for expressing normally suppressed speech. Is there anything like Carnaval in your society?

Makua ideas about social control emerged most clearly in discussions about what would happen to someone who stole his or her neighbor's chicken. Most Makua villagers have a makeshift chicken coop in a corner of their home. Chickens leave the coop before sunrise each day and wander around looking for scraps. Villagers may be tempted to steal a chicken when its owner seems oblivious to its whereabouts. The Makua have few material possessions and a meat-poor diet, making free-ranging chickens a real temptation. Their discussions about unsupervised chickens and the occasional chicken theft as community problems clarified their ideas about social control—about why people did *not* steal their neighbor's chickens.

The Makua perceived three main disincentives or sanctions: jail (*cadeia*), sorcery attack (*enretthe*), and shame (*ehaya*). (As used here, a *sanction* refers to a kind of punishment that follows a norm violation.) The main sanctions—sorcery and, above all, shame—came from society rather than from the formal political system. First, sorcery: Once someone discovered his chicken had been stolen, he would, the Makua thought, ask a traditional healer to launch a sorcery attack on his behalf. This would either kill the thief or make him very ill.

According to Nicholas Kottak (2002), the Makua constantly mention the existence of sorcerers and sorcery, although they aren't explicit about who the sorcerers are. They see sorcery as based on malice, which everyone feels at some point. Having felt malice themselves, individual Makua probably experience moments of self-doubt about their own potential status as a sorcerer. The recognize that others have similar feelings. Local theories see sickness,

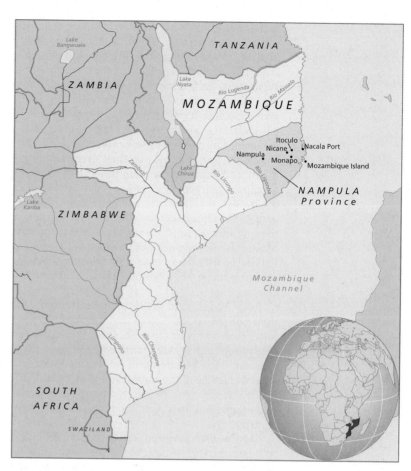

FIGURE 17.4 Location of the Makua and the Village of Nicane in Northern Mozambique.
The Province of Nampula shown here is Makua Territory.

Nicholas Kottak (back center) attends a village meeting among the Makua of northern Mozambique. Two chiefs have called the meeting to renegotiate the boundaries of their political jurisdictions.

social misfortune, and death as caused by malicious sorcery. Life expectancy is short and infant mortality high in a Makua village. Health, life, and existence are far more problematic than they are for most Westerners. Such uncertainty heightens fears relating to sorcery. Any conflict or norm violation is dangerous because it might trigger a sorcery attack. In particular, the Makua see the chicken thief as the inevitable target of a vengeance sorcery attack.

Makua fear sorcery, but they overwhelmingly mentioned shame as the main reason not to steal a neighbor's chicken. The chicken thief, having been discovered, would have to attend a formal, publicly organized village meeting, which would determine the appropriate punishment and compensation. The Makua were concerned not so much with a potential fine as with the intense and enduring shame or embarrassment they would feel as a confirmed chicken thief.

Rural Makua tend to live in one community for their entire lives. Such communities typically have fewer than a thousand people, so that residents can easily keep track of one another's identities and reputations. Tight clustering of homes, markets, and schools facilitates the monitoring process. In this social environment, people try to avoid behavior that might spoil their reputations and alienate them from society.

Shame can be a very powerful sanction. Bronislaw Malinowski (1927) described how Trobriand Islanders might climb to the top of a palm tree and dive to their deaths because they couldn't tolerate the shame associated with public knowledge of some stigmatizing action. Makua villagers tell the story of a man rumored to have fathered a child with his stepdaughter. The political authorities imposed no formal sanctions (e.g., a fine or jail time) on this man, but gossip about the affair circulated widely. The gossip crystallized in the lyrics of a song that groups of young women would perform. After the man heard his name and alleged incestuous behavior mentioned in that song, he hanged himself by the neck from a tree (Kottak 2002). (Previously we saw the role of song in the social control system of the Inuit. We'll see it again in the case of the Igbo women's war, discussed below.)

We see from this discussion that people aren't just citizens of governments, they also are members of society, and social sanctions exist alongside governmental ones. Such sanctions also exemplify other "weapons of the weak," because they often are wielded most effectively by people, for example, women or young people, who have limited access to the formal authority structure, as in the Igbo case, to which we now turn.

The Igbo Women's War

Shame and ridicule—used by women against men—played a key role in a decisive protest movement that took place in southeastern Nigeria in late 1929. This is remembered as the "Aba Women's Riots of 1929" in British colonial history, and as the "Women's War" in Igbo history (see Dorward 1983; Martin 1988; Mba 1982; Oriji 2000; Van Allen 1971). During this two-month "war," at least 25,000 Igbo women joined protests against British officials, their agents, and their colonial policies. This massive revolt touched off the most serious challenge to British rule in the history of what was then the British colony of Nigeria.

In 1914, the British had implemented a policy of indirect rule by appointing local Nigerian men as their agents—known as "warrant chiefs." These chiefs became increasingly oppressive, seizing property, imposing arbitrary regulations, and imprisoning people who criticized them. Colonial administrators further stoked local outrage when they announced plans to impose taxes on Igbo market women. These women were key suppliers of food for Nigeria's growing urban population; they feared being forced out of business by the new tax. Market women were key organizers of the protests.

After hearing about the tax in November 1929, thousands of Igbo women assembled in various towns to protest both the warrant chiefs and the taxes on market women. They used a traditional practice of censoring and shaming men through all-night song-and-dance ridicule (often called "sitting on a man"). This process entailed constant singing and dancing around the houses and offices of the warrant chiefs. The women also would follow the chiefs' every move, forcing the men to pay attention by invading their space. Disturbed by the whole process, wives of the warrant chiefs also pressured their husbands to listen to the protestors' demands.

In Nigeria, contemporary Igbo women collect water from a well standpipe. Political action by organized groups of Igbo women posed the first major challenge to British authority in Nigeria and West Africa more generally during the colonial period.

The protests were remarkably effective. The tax was abandoned, and many of the warrant chiefs resigned, some to be replaced by women. Other women were appointed to the Native courts as judges. The position of women improved in Nigeria, where market women especially remain a powerful political force to this day. Many Nigerian political events in the 1930s, 1940s, and 1950s were inspired by the Women's War, including additional tax protests. This women's war inspired many other protests in regions all over Africa. The Igbo uprising is seen as the first major challenge to British authority in Nigeria and West Africa during the colonial period.

At the beginning of this chapter, power was defined as the ability to exercise one's will over others. It was contrasted with authority—the formal, socially approved use of power (e.g., by government officials). The case of the Igbo women's war shows how women effectively used their social power (through song, dance, noise, and "in-your-face" behavior) to subvert the formal authority structure and, in so doing, gained greater influence within that structure. Can you think of other, perhaps recent, examples?

acing the COURSE

summary

1. Although no ethnographer has been able to observe a sociopolitical system uninfluenced by some state, many anthropologists use a typology that classifies societies as bands, tribes, chiefdoms, or states. Foragers tended to live in egalitarian, band-organized societies. Personal networks linked individuals, families, and bands. Band leaders were first among equals, with no sure way to enforce decisions. Disputes rarely arose over strategic resources, which were open to all.

2. Political authority increased with growth in population size and density and in the scale of regulatory problems. More people mean more relations among individuals and groups to regulate. Increasingly complex economies pose further regulatory problems.

3. Heads of horticultural villages are local leaders with limited authority. They lead by example and persuasion. Big men have support and authority beyond a single village. They are regional regulators, but temporary ones. In organizing a feast, they mobilize labor from several villages. Sponsoring such events leaves them with little wealth but with prestige and a reputation for generosity.

4. Age and gender also can be used for regional political integration. Among North America's Plains Indians, men's associations (pantribal sodalities) organized raiding and buffalo hunting. Such sodalities provide offense and defense when there is intertribal raiding for animals. Among pastoralists, the degree of authority and political organization reflects population size and density, interethnic relations, and pressure on resources.

5. The state is an autonomous political unit that encompasses many communities. Its government collects taxes, drafts people for work and war, and decrees and enforces laws. The state is a form of sociopolitical organization based on central government and social stratification. Early states are known as archaic, or nonindustrial, states, in contrast to modern industrial nation-states.

6. Unlike tribes, but like states, chiefdoms had permanent regional regulation and differential access to resources. But chiefdoms lacked stratification. Unlike states, but like bands and tribes, chiefdoms were organized by kinship, descent, and marriage. Chiefdoms emerged in several areas, including the circum-Caribbean, lowland Amazonia, the southeastern United States, and Polynesia.

7. Weber's three dimensions of stratification are wealth, power, and prestige. In early states—for the first time in human history—contrasts in

wealth, power, and prestige between entire groups of men and women came into being. A socioeconomic stratum includes people of both sexes and all ages. The superordinate—higher or elite—stratum enjoys privileged access to resources.

8. Certain systems are found in all states: population control, judiciary, enforcement, and fiscal. These are integrated by a ruling system or government composed of civil, military, and religious officials. States conduct censuses and demarcate boundaries. Laws are based on precedent and legislative proclamations. Courts and judges handle disputes and crimes. A police force maintains internal order, as a military defends against external threats. A financial or fiscal system supports rulers, officials, judges, and other specialists and government agencies.

9. *Hegemony* describes a stratified social order in which subordinates comply with domination by internalizing its values and accepting its "naturalness."

Situations that appear hegemonic may have resistance that is individual and disguised rather than collective and defiant. "Public transcript" refers to the open, public interactions between the dominators and the oppressed. "Hidden transcript" describes the critique of power that goes on where the powerholders can't see it. Discontent also may be expressed in public rituals such as Carnaval.

10. Broader than the political is the concept of social control—those fields of the social system most actively involved in the maintenance of norms and the regulation of conflict. Sanctions are social as well as governmental. Shame and gossip can be effective social sanctions. In the Igbo women's war, women effectively used their social power (through song, dance, noise, and "in-your-face" behavior) to subvert the formal authority structure and, in so doing, gained greater influence within that structure.

key terms

band 379
big man 383
conflict resolution 381
differential access 379
fiscal 392
hegemony 393
law 381
office 389
pantribal sodalities 386

power 378
prestige 391
social control 393
subordinate 391
superordinate 391
tribe 379
village head 382
wealth 390

test yourself

MULTIPLE CHOICE

1. The anthropological approach to the study of political systems and organization is global and comparative,
   a. but it focuses exclusively on nonstates, leaving the study of states and nation-states to political scientists.
   b. and it includes nonstates as well as the states and nation-states traditionally studied by political scientists.
   c. although this sometimes leads to disciplinary turf wars with other disciplines such as political science and sociology.
   d. but it focuses on people's experiences and leaves the study of institutions of political power to other scholars.
   e. although this area is becoming less and less interesting to study because there are very few new nation-states.

2. Why is the term *sociopolitical organization* preferred over Morton Fried's term *political organization* in discussing the regulation or management of interrelations among groups and their representatives?
   a. The term *sociopolitical* is more politically correct.
   b. Anthropologists and political scientists have an interest in political systems and organization, but they cannot agree on the same terminology.
   c. Fried's definition is much less applicable to nonstates, where it often is difficult to detect any "public policy."
   d. *Sociopolitical* is the term that the founders of anthropology used to refer to the regulation or management of interrelations among groups and their representatives.
   e. The term *political* refers only to contemporary Western states.

3. Which of the following statements about the Inuit song battle is true?
   a. It is sometimes the occasion for a "treacherous feast."
   b. It is a widespread feature of tribal society.
   c. It is a ritualized means of designating hunting lands.
   d. It is a means of resolving disputes so as to forestall open conflict.
   e. It was used to initiate colonial strategies.

4. A band refers to a small kin-based group found among foragers. In this type of political system,
   a. misbehavior was punished by a group of men who had more possessions than anyone else.
   b. band leaders were leaders in name only; sometimes they gave advice or made decisions, but they had no way to enforce their will on others.
   c. there is no way of settling disputes since everybody gets along among equals.
   d. laws dictating proper social norms are passed on through songs from generation to generation.
   e. there is no division of labor based on age and gender.

5. Which of the following factors is responsible for the recent changes in Yanomami tribal society?
   a. the fact that they are being overrun by the more expansion-minded Nilotic peoples
   b. the amassing by "big men" of so much wealth that people have begun to regard them as chiefs
   c. village raiding among tribal groups
   d. sexual dimorphism
   e. the encroachment by gold miners and cattle ranchers

6. Why are pantribal sodalities and age grades described in a chapter on political systems?
   a. They are organizing principles other than those based on kinship that are used to mobilize and link local groups to form alliances.
   b. They are at the core of hegemonic power in nation-states.
   c. They are organizing principles that stress the importance of kinship ties.
   d. They illustrate the importance of knowing one's genealogy.
   e. They are principles that precede the Western, modern concept of friendship.

7. The comparison between the Basseri and the Qashqai, two Iranian nomadic tribes, illustrates that
   a. among tribal sociopolitical organizations, pastoralists are the least likely to interact with other populations in the same space and time.
   b. as regulatory problems increase, political hierarchies become more complex.
   c. as regulatory problems decrease, political hierarchies become more complex.
   d. not all cultures with age grades have age sets.
   e. only groups that assimilate are able to successfully resolve political feuds.

8. In foraging and tribal societies, what is the basis for the amount of respect or status attached to an individual?
   a. personal attributes, such as wisdom, leadership skills, and generosity
   b. prestige inherited from your parents
   c. the number of possessions one owns and the ability to convert them into cash
   d. the amount of territory a person owns
   e. rank ascribed at birth, wives, and children

9. In what kind of society does differential access to strategic resources based on social stratification occur?
   a. chiefdoms
   b. bands
   c. states
   d. clans
   e. tribes

10. Antonio Gramsci developed the concept of hegemony to describe
    a. a stratified social order in which subordinates comply with domination by internalizing their rulers' values and accepting the "naturalness" of domination.
    b. overt sociopolitical strategies.
    c. social controls that induce guilt and shame in the population.
    d. the critique of power by the oppressed that goes on offstage—in private—where the powerholders can't see it.
    e. the open, public interactions between dominators and oppressed—the outer shell of power relations.

FILL IN THE BLANK

1. _____ refers to a group uniting all men or women born during a certain span of time.
2. Among the different types of sociopolitical systems, _____ lack socioeconomic stratification and stratum endogamy although they do exhibit inequality and a permanent political structure.
3. The influential sociologist Max Weber defined three related dimensions of social stratification. They are _____, _____, and _____.
4. _____ is esteem, respect, or approval for culturally valued acts or qualities.
5. Broader than political control, the concept of _____ refers to those fields of the social system (beliefs, practices, and institutions) that are most actively involved in the maintenance of any norms and the regulation of any conflict.

CRITICAL THINKING

1. This chapter notes that the labels "band," "tribe," "chiefdom," and "state" are too simple to account for the full range of political diversity and complexity known to archaeologists and ethnographers. Why not get rid of this typology altogether if it does not accurately describe reality? What is the value, if any, of researchers retaining the use of ideal types to study society?
2. Why shouldn't modern hunter-gatherers be seen as representative of Stone Age peoples? What are some of the stereotypes associated with foragers?
3. What are sodalities? Does your society have them? Do you belong to any? Why or why not?
4. What conclusions do you draw from this chapter about the relationship between population density and political hierarchy?
5. This chapter describes population control as one of the specialized functions found in all states. What are examples of population control? Have you had direct experiences with these controls? (Think of the last time you traveled abroad, registered to vote, paid taxes, or applied for a driver's license.) Do you think these controls are good or bad for society?

Chagnon, N. A.

1997   *Yanomamö,* 5th ed. Fort Worth: Harcourt Brace. Most recent revision of a well-known account of the Yanomami, including their social organization, politics, warfare, and cultural change, and the crises they have confronted.

Dentan, R. L.

2008   *Overwhelming Terror: Love, Fear, Peace, and Violence among the Semai of Malaysia.* Lanham, MD: Rowman & Littlefield. Conflict and change in an egalitarian society.

Ferguson, R. B.

2003   *State, Identity, and Violence: Political Disintegration in the Post–Cold War Era.* New York: Routledge. Political relations, the state, ethnic relations, and violence.

Kamrava, M.

2008   *Understanding Comparative Politics: A Framework for Analysis,* 2nd ed. New York: Routledge. How to study political systems worldwide.

Schwartz, M. J., V. W. Turner, and A. Tuden, eds.

2006   *Political Anthropology.* New Brunswick, NJ: Aldine Transaction. Collection of classic ethnographic case studies of political organization.

Solway, J., ed.

2006   *The Politics of Egalitarianism: Theory and Practice.* New York: Berghahn Books. Studies of egalitarian societies.

Go to our Online Learning Center website at **www.mhhe.com/kottak** for Internet exercises directly related to the content of this chapter.

CHAPTER 18

Gender

How are biology and culture expressed in human sex/gender systems?

How do gender, gender roles, and gender stratification correlate with other social, economic, and political variables?

What is sexual orientation, and how do sexual practices vary cross-culturally?

◀ Women today work increasingly outside the home in varied positions, including soldier. This photo, taken in Deu, Germany in 2001, shows one of the first women recruited into the German army—along with her male counterparts.

understanding OURSELVES

A table (18.1) in this chapter lists activities that are generally done by the men in a society, generally done by the women in a society, or done by either men or women (swing). In this table, you will see some "male" activities familiar to our own culture, such as hunting, butchering, and building houses, along with activities that we consider typically female, such as doing the laundry and cooking. This list may bring to mind as many exceptions as followers of these "rules." Although it is not typical, it certainly is not unheard of for an American woman to hunt large game (think of Sarah Palin) or an American man to cook (think of any male celebrity chef). Celebrities aside, women in our culture increasingly work outside the home in a wide variety of jobs—doctor, lawyer, accountant, professor—traditionally considered men's work. It is not true, however, that women have achieved equity in all types of employment. As of this writing, only 17 out of 100 United States senators are women. Only four women have ever served on the United States Supreme Court.

Ideas about proper gender behavior are changing just as inconsistently as are the employment patterns of men and women. Popular shows like *Sex and the City* feature characters who display nontraditional gender behavior and sexual behavior, while old beliefs, cultural expectations, and gender stereotypes linger. The American expectation that proper female behavior should be polite, restrained, or meek poses a challenge for women, because American culture also values decisiveness and "standing up for your beliefs." When American men and women display similar behavior— speaking their minds, for example—they are judged differently. A man's assertive behavior may be admired and rewarded, but similar behavior by a woman may be labeled "aggressive"—or worse.

Both men and women are constrained by their cultural training, stereotypes, and expectations. For example, American culture stigmatizes male crying. It's okay for little boys to cry, but becoming a man often means giving up this natural expression of joy and sadness. Why shouldn't "big lugs" cry when they feel emotions? American men are trained as well to make decisions and stick to them. In our stereotypes, changing one's mind is more associated with women than with men and may be perceived as a sign of weakness. Men who do it may be seen as "girly." Politicians routinely criticize their opponents for being indecisive, for waffling or "flip-flopping" on issues. What a strange idea—that people shouldn't change their positions if they've discovered there's a better way. Males, females, and humanity may be equally victimized by aspects of cultural training.

Because anthropologists study biology, society, and culture, they are in a unique position to comment on nature (biological predispositions) and nurture (environment) as determinants of human behavior. Human attitudes, values, and behavior are limited not only by our genetic predispositions—which are often difficult to identify—but also by our experiences during enculturation. Our attributes as adults are determined both by our genes and by our environment during growth and development.

SEX AND GENDER

Questions about nature and nurture emerge in the discussion of human sex-gender roles and sexuality. Men and women differ genetically. Women have two X chromosomes, and men have an X and a Y. The father determines a baby's sex because only he has the Y chromosome to transmit. The mother always provides an X chromosome.

The chromosomal difference is expressed in hormonal and physiological contrasts. Humans are sexually dimorphic, more so than some primates, such as gibbons (small tree-living Asiatic apes), and less so than others, such as gorillas and orangutans. **Sexual dimorphism** refers to differences in male and female biology besides the contrasts in breasts and genitals. Women and men differ not just in primary (genitalia and reproductive organs) and secondary (breasts, voice, hair distribution) sexual characteristics but in average weight, height, strength, and longevity. Women tend to live longer than men and have excellent endurance capabilities. In a given population, men tend to be taller and to weigh more than women do. Of course, there is a considerable overlap between the sexes in terms of height, weight, and physical strength, and there has been a pronounced reduction in sexual dimorphism during human biological evolution.

Just how far, however, do such genetically and physiologically determined differences go? What effects do they have on the way men and women act and are treated in different societies? Anthropologists have discovered both similarities and differences in the roles of men and women in different cultures. The predominant anthropological position on sex-gender roles and biology may be stated as follows:

> The biological nature of men and women [should be seen] not as a narrow enclosure limiting the human organism, but rather as a broad base upon which a variety of structures can be built. (Friedl 1975, p. 6)

Although in most societies men tend to be somewhat more aggressive than women are, many of the behavioral and attitudinal differences between the sexes emerge from culture rather than biology. Sex differences are biological, but gender encompasses all the traits that a culture assigns to and inculcates in males and females. "Gender," in other words, refers to the cultural construction of whether one is female, male, or something else.

Given the "rich and various constructions of gender" within the realm of cultural diversity, Susan Bourque and Kay Warren (1987) note that the same images of masculinity and femininity do not always apply. Anthropologists have gathered systematic ethnographic data about similarities and differences involving gender in many cultural settings (Bonvillain 2007; Brettell and Sargent 2009; Mascia-Lees 2010; Mascia-Lees and Black 2000;

The realm of cultural diversity contains richly different social constructions and expressions of gender roles, as is illustrated by these Wodaabe male celebrants in Niger. (Look closely for suggestions of diffusion.) For what reasons do men decorate their bodies in our society?

Nanda 2000; Ward and Edelstein 2009). Anthropologists can detect recurrent themes and patterns involving gender differences. They also can observe that gender roles vary with environment, economy, adaptive strategy, and type of political system. Before we examine the cross-cultural data, some definitions are in order.

Gender roles are the tasks and activities a culture assigns to the sexes. Related to gender roles are **gender stereotypes**, which are oversimplified but strongly held ideas about the characteristics of males and females. **Gender stratification** describes an unequal distribution of rewards (socially valued resources, power, prestige, human rights, and personal freedom) between men and women, reflecting their different positions in a social hierarchy. According to Ann Stoler (1977), the "economic determinants of gender status" include freedom or autonomy (in disposing of one's labor and its fruits) and social power (control over the lives, labor, and produce of others).

In stateless societies, gender stratification often is more obvious in regard to prestige than it is in regard to wealth. In her study of the Ilongots of northern

sexual dimorphism
Marked differences in male and female biology, beyond breasts and genitals.

gender roles
The tasks and activities that a culture assigns to each sex.

gender stereotypes
Oversimplified, strongly held views about males and females.

gender stratification
Unequal distribution of social resources between men and women.

 living anthropology **VIDEOS**

Marginalization of Women, www.mhhe.com/kottak

Despite declarations of equality, half the world's population suffers discrimination. Many cultures favor sons, reinforcing a mindset that women are less than equal. This clip examines the economic, political, social, and cultural devaluation of women. Based on the discussion in this text chapter, is gender discrimination inevitable?

FIGURE 18.1 Location of Ilongots in the Philippines.

Luzon in the Philippines (Figure 18.1), Michelle Rosaldo (1980a) described gender differences related to the positive cultural value placed on adventure, travel, and knowledge of the external world. More often than women, Ilongot men, as headhunters, visited distant places. They acquired knowledge of the external world, amassed experiences there, and returned to express their knowledge, adventures, and feelings in public oratory. They received acclaim as a result. Ilongot women had inferior prestige because they lacked external experiences on which to base knowledge and dramatic expression. On the basis of Rosaldo's study and findings in other stateless societies, Ong (1989) argues that we must distinguish between prestige systems and actual power in a given society. High male prestige may not entail economic or political power held by men over their families. (For more on Rosaldo's contributions to gender studies, see Lugo and Maurer 2000.)

RECURRENT GENDER PATTERNS

Ethnologists compare ethnographic data from several cultures (i.e., cross-cultural data) to discover and explain differences and similarities. Data relevant to the cross-cultural study of gender can be drawn from the domains of economics, politics, domestic activity, kinship, and marriage. Table 18.1 shows cross-cultural data from 185 randomly selected societies on the division of labor by gender.

Remembering the discussion, in the chapter on culture, of universals, generalities, and particularities, the findings in Table 18.1 about the division of labor by gender illustrate generalities rather than universals. That is, among the societies known to ethnography, there is a very strong tendency for men to build boats, but there are exceptions. One was the Hidatsa, a Native American group in which the women made the boats used to cross the Missouri River. (Traditionally, the Hidatsa were village farmers and bison hunters on the North American Plains; they now live in North Dakota.) Another exception: Pawnee women worked wood; this is the only Native American group that assigned this activity to women. (The Pawnee, also traditionally Plains farmers and bison hunters, originally lived in what is now central Nebraska and central Kansas; they now live on a reservation in north central Oklahoma.) Among the Mbuti "pygmies" of Africa's Ituri forest, women hunt—by catching small, slow animals, using their hands or a net (Murdock and Provost 1973).

Exceptions to cross-cultural generalizations may involve societies or individuals. That is, a society like the Hidatsa can contradict the cross-cultural generalization that men build boats by assigning that task to women. Or, in a society where the cultural expectation is that only men build boats, a particular woman or women can contradict that expectation by doing the male activity. Table 18.1 shows that in a sample of 185 societies, certain activities ("swing activities") are assigned to either or both men and women. Among the most important of such activities are planting, tending, and harvesting crops. Some societies customarily assign more farming chores to women, whereas others call on men to be the main farm laborers. Among the tasks almost always assigned to men (Table 18.1), some (e.g., hunting large animals on land and sea) seem clearly related to the greater average size and strength of males. Others, such as working wood and making musical instruments, seem more culturally arbitrary. And women, of course, are not exempt from arduous and time-consuming physical labor, such as gathering firewood and fetching water. In Arembepe, Bahia, Brazil, women routinely transport water in five-gallon tins, balanced on their heads, from wells and lagoons located at long distances from their homes.

Notice that Table 18.1 includes no mention of trade and market activity, in which either men or women, or both, are active. Is Table 18.1 somewhat androcentric in detailing more tasks for men than for women? More than men, women do child care, but the study on which Table 18.1 is based does not break down domestic activities to the same extent that it details work done outside the home. Think about Table 18.1 in terms of today's home and job roles and with respect to the activities done by contemporary women and men. Men still do most of the hunting; either gender can collect the honey

TABLE 18.1   Generalities in the Division of Labor by Gender, Based on Data from 185 Societies

GENERALLY MALE ACTIVITIES	SWING (MALE OR FEMALE) ACTIVITIES	GENERALLY FEMALE ACTIVITIES
Hunting large aquatic animals (e.g., whales, walrus)	Making fire	Gathering fuel (e.g., firewood)
Smelting ores	Body mutilation	Making drinks
Metalworking	Preparing skins	Gathering wild vegetal foods
Lumbering	Gathering small land animals	Dairy production (e.g., churning)
Hunting large land animals	Planting crops	Spinning
Working wood	Making leather products	Doing the laundry
Hunting fowl	Harvesting	Fetching water
Making musical instruments	Tending crops	Cooking
Trapping	Milking	Preparing vegetal food (e.g., processing cereal grains)
Building boats	Making baskets	
Working stone	Carrying burdens	
Working bone, horn, and shell	Making mats	
Mining and quarrying	Caring for small animals	
Setting bones	Preserving meat and fish	
Butchering*	Loom weaving	
Collecting wild honey	Gathering small aquatic animals	
Clearing land	Clothing manufacture	
Fishing	Making pottery	
Tending large herd animals		
Building houses		
Preparing the soil		
Making nets		
Making rope		

*All the activities above "butchering" are almost always done by men; those from "butchering" through "making rope" usually are done by men.

SOURCE: Adapted from G. P. Murdock and C. Provost, "Factors in the Division of Labor by Sex: A Cross-Cultural Analysis," *Ethnology* 12(2) April 1973: 202–225.

from a supermarket, even as most baby-bottom wiping (part of child care and not included in Table 18.1) continues to be in female hands.

Cross-culturally the subsistence contributions of men and women are roughly equal (Table 18.2). But in domestic activities and child care, female labor predominates, as we see in Tables 18.3 and 18.4. Table 18.3 shows that in about half the societies studied, men did virtually no domestic work. Even in societies where men did some domestic chores, the bulk of such work was done by women. Adding together their subsistence activities and their domestic work, women tend to work more hours than men do. Has this changed in the contemporary world?

What about child care? Women tend to be the main caregivers in most societies, but men often play a role. Again there are exceptions, both within and between societies. Table 18.4 uses cross-cultural data to answer the question "Who—men or women—has

TABLE 18.2   Time and Effort Expended on Subsistence Activities by Men and Women*

More by men	16
Roughly equal	61
More by women	23

*Percentage of 88 randomly selected societies for which information was available on this variable.

SOURCE: M. F. Whyte, "Cross-Cultural Codes Dealing with the Relative Status of Women," *Ethnology* 17(2):211–239.

final authority over the care, handling, and discipline of children younger than four years?" Although women have primary authority over infants in two-thirds of the societies, in some societies (18 percent of the total) men have the major say. In the United States and Canada today, some men are primary

TABLE 18.3 Who Does the Domestic Work?*

Males do virtually none	51
Males do some, but mostly done by females	49

*Percentage of 92 randomly selected societies for which information was available on this variable.

SOURCE: M. F. Whyte, "Cross-Cultural Codes Dealing with the Relative Status of Women," *Ethnology* 17(2):211–239.

TABLE 18.4 Who Has Final Authority over the Care, Handling, and Discipline of Infant Children (under Four Years Old)?*

Males have more say	18
Roughly equal	16
Females have more say	66

*Percentage of 67 randomly selected societies for which information was available on this variable.

SOURCE: M. F. Whyte, "Cross-Cultural Codes Dealing with the Relative Status of Women," *Ethnology* 17(2):211–239.

TABLE 18.5 Does the Society Allow Multiple Spouses?*

Only for males	77
For both, but more commonly for males	4
For neither	16
For both, but more commonly for females	2

*Percentage of 92 randomly selected societies.

SOURCE: M. F. Whyte, "Cross-Cultural Codes Dealing with the Relative Status of Women," *Ethnology* 17(2):211–239.

TABLE 18.6 Is There a Double Standard with Respect to PREMARITAL Sex?*

Yes—females are more restricted	44
No—equal restrictions on males and females	56

*Percentage of 73 randomly selected societies for which information was available on this variable.

SOURCE: M. F. Whyte, "Cross-Cultural Codes Dealing with the Relative Status of Women," *Ethnology* 17(2):211–239.

TABLE 18.7 Is There a Double Standard with Respect to EXTRAMARITAL Sex?*

Yes—females are more restricted	43
Equal restrictions on males and females	55
Males punished more severely for transgression	3

*Percentage of 73 randomly selected societies for which information was available on this variable.

SOURCE: M. F. Whyte, "Cross-Cultural Codes Dealing with the Relative Status of Women," *Ethnology* 17(2):211–239.

caregivers despite the cultural fact that the female role in child care remains more prominent. Given the critical role of breast-feeding in ensuring infant survival, it makes sense, for infants especially, for the mother to be the primary caregiver.

There are differences in male and female reproductive strategies. Women give birth, breast-feed,

In many societies women routinely do hard physical labor, as is illustrated by these villagers in India's Bihar State, where women and children work at a brick kiln for income during the summer, after crops have been harvested and before the monsoon rains arrive.

and assume primary responsibility for infant care. Women ensure that their progeny will survive by establishing a close bond with each baby. It's also advantageous for a woman to have a reliable mate to ease the child-rearing process and ensure the survival of her children. (Again, there are exceptions, for example, the Nayars discussed in the chapter "Families, Kinship, and Descent.") Women can have only so many babies during the course of their reproductive years, which begin after menarche (the advent of menstruation) and end with menopause (cessation of menstruation). Men have a longer reproductive period, which can last into the elder years. If they choose to do so, men can enhance their reproductive success by impregnating several women over a longer time span. Cross-culturally, men are much more likely to have multiple mates than women are (see Tables 18.5, 18.6, and 18.7). Among the societies known to ethnography, polygyny (multiple wives) is much more common than polyandry (multiple husbands) (see Table 18.5).

Men mate, within and outside marriage, more than women do. Table 18.6 shows cross-cultural data on premarital sex, and Table 18.7 summarizes the data on extramarital sex. In both cases men are less restricted than women are, although the restrictions are equal in about half the societies studied.

GENDER ROLES AND GENDER STRATIFICATION

Double standards that restrict women sexually or that limit female access to public settings illustrate gender stratification, which also is influenced by economic roles. In one cross-cultural study, Sanday (1974) found that gender stratification decreased when men and women made roughly equal contributions to subsistence. She found that gender stratification was greatest when the women contributed either much more or much less than the men did.

In foraging societies, gender stratification was most marked when men contributed much more to the diet than women did. This was true among the Inuit and other northern hunters and fishers. Among tropical and semitropical foragers, by contrast, gathering usually provides more food than hunting and fishing do. Gathering is generally women's work. Men usually hunt and fish, but women also do some fishing and may hunt small animals. When gathering is prominent, gender status tends to be more equal than it is when hunting and fishing are the main subsistence activities.

Gender status also is more equal when the domestic and public spheres aren't sharply separated. (*Domestic* means within or pertaining to the home.) Strong differentiation between the home and the outside world is called the **domestic–public dichotomy** or the *private–public contrast*. The outside world can include politics, trade, warfare, or work. Often when domestic and public spheres are clearly separated, public activities have greater prestige than domestic ones do. This can promote gender stratification, because men are more likely to be active in the public domain than women are. Cross-culturally, women's activities tend to be closer to home than men's are. Thus, another reason hunter-gatherers have less gender stratification than food producers do is that the domestic-public dichotomy is less developed among foragers.

We've seen that certain gender roles are more sex-linked than others. Men are the usual hunters and warriors. Given such tools and weapons as spears, knives, and bows, men make better hunters and fighters because they are bigger and stronger on the average than are women in the same population (Divale and Harris 1976). The male hunter-fighter role also reflects a tendency toward greater male mobility.

In foraging societies, women are either pregnant or lactating during most of their childbearing period. Late in pregnancy and after childbirth,

Among foragers, gender stratification tends to increase when men contribute much more to the diet than women do—as has been true among the Inuit and other northern hunters and fishers. Shown here, in Foxe Basin, Nunavut (in Canada's Northwest Territories), Inuit hunters load walrus onto their boats.

carrying a baby limits a woman's movements, even her gathering. However, among the Agta of the Philippines (Griffin and Estioko-Griffin 1985), women not only gather; they also hunt with dogs while carrying their babies with them. Still, given the effects of pregnancy and breast-feeding on mobility, it is rarely feasible for women to be the primary hunters (Friedl 1975). Warfare, which also requires mobility, is not found in most foraging societies, nor is interregional trade well developed. Warfare and trade are two public arenas that can contribute to status inequality of males and females among food producers.

domestic–public dichotomy
Work at home versus more valued work outside.

Many jobs that men do in some societies are done by women in others, and vice versa. In West Africa, women play a prominent role in trade and marketing. In Togo, shown here, women dominate textile sales. Is there a textile shop near you? Who runs it?

Reduced Gender Stratification—Matrilineal-Matrilocal Societies

Cross-cultural variation in gender status is related to rules of descent and postmarital residence (Friedl 1975; Martin and Voorhies 1975). Many horticultural societies have **matrilineal descent** (descent traced through females only) and *matrilocality* (residence after marriage with the wife's relatives). In such societies, female status tends to be high (see Blackwood 2000). Matriliny and matrilocality disperse related males, rather than consolidating them. By contrast, patriliny and patrilocality keep male relatives together, an advantage given warfare. Matrilineal-matrilocal systems tend to occur in societies where population pressure on strategic resources is minimal and warfare is infrequent.

Women tend to have high status in matrilineal-matrilocal societies for several reasons. Descent-group membership, succession to political positions, allocation of land, and overall social identity all come through female links. In Negeri Sembilan, Malaysia (Peletz 1988), matriliny gave women sole inheritance of ancestral rice fields. Matrilocality created solidary clusters of female kin. Women had considerable influence beyond the household. In such matrilineal contexts, women are the basis of the entire social structure. Although public authority may be (or may appear to be) assigned to the men, much of the power and decision making may actually belong to the senior women.

A Minangkabau bride and groom in West Sumatra, Indonesia, where anthropologist Peggy Reeves Sanday has conducted several years of ethnographic fieldwork.

Matriarchy

Cross-culturally, anthropologists have described tremendous variation in the roles of men and women, and the power differentials between them. If a patriarchy is a political system ruled by men, what would a matriarchy be? Would a matriarchy be a political system ruled by women, or a political system in which women play a much more prominent role than men do in social and political organization? Anthropologist Peggy Sanday (2002) has concluded that matriarchies exist, but not as mirror images of patriarchies. The superior power that men typically have in a patriarchy isn't matched by women's equally disproportionate power in a matriarchy. Many societies, including the matrilineal Minangkabau of West Sumatra, Indonesia, whom Sanday has studied for decades, lack the substantial power differentials that typify patriarchal systems. Minangkabau women play a central role in social, economic, and ceremonial life and as key symbols. The primacy of matriliny and matriarchy is evident at the village level, as well as regionally, where seniority of matrilineal descent serves as a way to rank villages.

The four million Minangkabau constitute one of Indonesia's largest ethnic groups. Located in the highlands of West Sumatra, their culture is based on the coexistence of matrilineal custom and a nature-based philosophy called *adat*, complemented by Islam, a more recent (16th-century) arrival. The Minangkabau view men and women as cooperative partners for the common good rather than competitors ruled by self-interest. People gain prestige when they promote social harmony rather than by vying for power.

Sanday considers the Minangkabau a matriarchy because women are the center, origin, and foundation of the social order. Senior women are associated with the central pillar of the traditional house, the oldest one in the village. The oldest village in a cluster is called the "mother village." In ceremonies, women are addressed by the term used for their mythical Queen Mother. Women control land inheritance, and couples reside matrilocally. In the wedding ceremony, the wife collects her husband from his household and, with her female kin, escorts him to hers. If there is a divorce, the husband simply takes his things and leaves. Yet despite the special position of women, the Minangkabau matriarchy is not the equivalent of female rule, given the Minangkabau belief that all decision making should be by consensus.

Increased Gender Stratification—Patrilineal-Patrilocal Societies

Martin and Voorhies (1975) link the decline of matriliny and the spread of the **patrilineal-patrilocal complex** (consisting of patrilineality, patrilocality, warfare, and male supremacy) to pressure on resources. (Societies with **patrilineal descent** trace descent through males only. In *patrilocal* societies a woman moves to her husband's village after marriage.) Faced with scarce resources, patrilineal-patrilocal cultivators such as the Yanomami often wage warfare against other villages. This favors patrilocality and patriliny, customs that keep related men together in the same village, where they make strong allies in battle. Such societies tend to have a sharp domestic-public dichotomy, and men tend to dominate the prestige hierarchy. Men may use their public roles in warfare and trade and their greater prestige to symbolize and reinforce the devaluation or oppression of women.

The patrilineal-patrilocal complex characterizes many societies in highland Papua New Guinea. Women work hard growing and processing subsistence crops, raising and tending pigs (the main domesticated animal and a favorite food), and doing domestic cooking, but they are isolated from the public domain, which men control. Men grow and distribute prestige crops, prepare food for feasts, and arrange marriages. The men even get to trade the pigs and control their use in ritual.

In densely populated areas of the Papua New Guinea highlands, male-female avoidance is associated with strong pressure on resources (Lindenbaum 1972). Men fear all female contacts, including sex. They think that sexual contact with women will weaken them. Indeed, men see everything female as dangerous and polluting. They segregate themselves in men's houses and hide their precious ritual objects from women. They delay marriage, and some never marry.

By contrast, the sparsely populated areas of Papua New Guinea, such as recently settled areas, lack taboos on male-female contacts. The image of woman as polluter fades, heterosexual intercourse is valued, men and women live together, and reproductive rates are high.

In some parts of Papua New Guinea, the patrilineal-patrilocal complex has extreme social repercussions. Regarding females as dangerous and polluting, men may segregate themselves in men's houses (such as this one, located near the Sepik River), where they hide their precious ritual objects from women. Are there places like this in your society?

patrilineal descent
Descent traced through men only.

tings, such as Canada and the United States. Cities, with their impersonality and isolation from extended kin networks, are breeding grounds for domestic violence.

We've seen that gender stratification typically is reduced in societies in which women have prominent roles in the economy and social life. When a woman lives in her own village, she has kin nearby to protect her interests. Even in patrilocal polygynous (multiple wives) settings, women often count on the support of their cowives and sons in disputes with potentially abusive husbands. Such settings,

Patriarchy and Violence

Patriarchy describes a political system ruled by men in which women have inferior social and political status, including basic human rights. Barbara Miller (1997), in a study of systematic neglect of females, describes women in rural northern India as "the endangered sex." Societies that feature a full-fledged patrilineal-patrilocal complex, replete with warfare and intervillage raiding, also typify patriarchy. Such practices as dowry murders, female infanticide, and clitoridectomy (removal of the clitoris) exemplify patriarchy, which extends from tribal societies such as the Yanomami to state societies such as India and Pakistan.

Although more prevalent in certain social settings than in others, family violence and domestic abuse of women are worldwide problems. Domestic violence certainly occurs in nuclear family set-

patriarchy
Political system ruled by men.

The women's rights movement has raised awareness of domestic abuse and violence. Brazilian victims of domestic abuse can seek help at special police stations, including this women's police bus in Paracambi, a suburb of Rio de Janeiro.

which can provide a safe haven for women, are retracting rather than expanding in today's world. Isolated families and patrilineal social forms have spread at the expense of matriliny. Many nations have declared polygyny illegal. More and more women, and men, find themselves cut off from their families and extended kin.

With the spread of the women's rights movement and the human rights movement, attention to domestic violence and abuse of women has increased. Laws have been passed, and mediating institutions established. Brazil's female-run police stations for battered women provide an example, as do shelters for victims of domestic abuse in the United States and Canada. But patriarchal institutions do persist in what should be a more enlightened world.

GENDER IN INDUSTRIAL SOCIETIES

The domestic-public dichotomy influences gender stratification in industrial societies, including the United States and Canada. However, gender roles have been changing rapidly in North America. The "traditional" idea that "a woman's place is in the home" developed among middle- and upper-class Americans as industrialism spread after 1900. Earlier, pioneer women in the Midwest and West were recognized as fully productive workers in farming and home industry. Under industrialism, attitudes about gendered work came to vary with class and region. In early industrial Europe, men, women, and children had flocked to factories as wage laborers. Enslaved Americans of both sexes had done grueling work in cotton fields. After abolition, southern African-American women continued working as field hands and domestics. Poor white women labored in the South's early cotton mills. In the 1890s, more than one million American women held menial, repetitious, and unskilled factory positions (Margolis 1984, 2000; Martin and Voorhies 1975). Poor, immigrant, and African-American women continued to work throughout the 20th century.

After 1900, a flood of Europeans migrated to the United States, providing a male labor force willing to work for wages lower than those of American-born men. Immigrant men moved into factory jobs that previously had gone to women. As machine tools and mass production further reduced the need for female labor, the notion that women were biologically unfit for factory work began to gain ground (Martin and Voorhies 1975).

Maxine Margolis (1984, 2000) has shown how gendered work, attitudes, and beliefs have varied in response to American economic needs. For example, wartime shortages of men have promoted the idea that work outside the home is women's patriotic duty. During the world wars, the notion that women are biologically unfit for hard physical labor faded. Inflation and the culture of consumption also have spurred female employment. When demand and/or prices rise, multiple paychecks help maintain family living standards.

The steady increase in female paid employment since World War II also reflects the baby boom and industrial expansion. American culture traditionally has defined clerical work, public school teaching, and nursing as female occupations. With rapid population growth and business expansion after World War II, the demand for women to fill such jobs grew steadily. Employers also found that they could increase their profits by paying women lower wages than they would have to pay to returning male war veterans.

Changes in the economy led to changes in attitudes toward and about women (Margolis 1984, 2000). Economic changes paved the way for the contemporary women's movement, which also was spurred by the publication of Betty Friedan's book *The Feminine Mystique* in 1963 and the founding of NOW, the National Organization for Women, in 1966. The movement in turn promoted expanded work opportunities for women, including the goal of equal pay for equal work. Between 1970 and 2010, the female percentage of the American workforce rose from 38 to 47 percent. Almost half of all Americans who work outside the home are women. Over 65 million women now have paid employment, compared with 73 million men. Women fill more than half (52 percent) of all management/professional jobs (*Statistical Abstract of the United States 2012,* Table 616). And it's not mainly single women working, as once was the case. Table 18.8 presents figures on the increasing cash employment of American wives and mothers, including those with children under six years old.

Note in Table 18.8 that the cash employment of American married men has been falling while that of American married women has been rising. There has been a dramatic change in behavior and attitudes since 1960, when 89 percent of all married men worked, compared with just 32 percent of married women. The comparable figures in 2010 were 76 percent and 61 percent. The ratio of female to male earnings rose from 68 percent in 1989 to 77 percent in 2006, then fell to 72 percent in 2010.

As women increasingly work outside the home, ideas about the gender roles of males and females have changed. Compare your grandparents and your parents. Chances are you have a working mother, but your grandmother was more likely a stay-at-home mom. Your grandfather is more likely than your father to have worked in manufacturing and to have belonged to a union. Your father is more likely than your grandfather to have

TABLE 18.8 Cash Employment of American Mothers, Wives, and Husbands, 1960–2010*

YEAR	PERCENTAGE OF MARRIED WOMEN, HUSBAND PRESENT WITH CHILDREN UNDER SIX	PERCENTAGE OF ALL MARRIED WOMEN†	PERCENTAGE OF ALL MARRIED MEN‡
1960	19	32	89
1970	30	40	86
1980	45	50	81
1990	59	58	79
2010	62	61	76

*Civilian population 16 years of age and older.

†Husband present.

‡Wife present.

SOURCE: *Statistical Abstract of the United States 2012,* Table 597, p. 384; Table 599, p. 385. http://www.census.gov/prod/2011pubs/12statab/labor.pdf.

shared child care and domestic responsibilities. Age at marriage has been delayed for both men and women. College educations and professional degrees have increased. What other changes do you associate with the increase in female employment outside the home?

Today's jobs aren't especially demanding in terms of physical labor. With machines to do the heavy work, the smaller average body size and lesser average strength of women are no longer impediments to blue-collar employment. The main reason we don't see more modern-day Rosies working alongside male riveters is that the U.S. workforce itself has been abandoning heavy-goods manufacture. In the 1950s, two-thirds of American jobs were blue-collar, compared with less than 15 percent today. The location of those jobs has shifted within the world capitalist economy. Third World countries, with their cheaper labor costs, produce steel, automobiles, and other heavy goods less expensively than the United States can, but the United States excels at services. The American mass education system has many inadequacies, but it does train millions of people for service- and information-oriented jobs.

The Feminization of Poverty

Alongside the economic gains of many American women stands an opposite extreme: the feminization of poverty. This refers to the increasing representation of women (and their children) among America's poorest people. Women head over half of U.S. households with incomes below the poverty line. Feminine poverty has been a trend in the United States since World War II, but it has accelerated recently. In 1959, female-headed households accounted for just one-fourth of the American poor. Since then, that figure has more than doubled.

During the world wars, the notion that women were biologically unfit for hard physical labor faded. World War II's Rosie the Riveter—a strong, competent woman dressed in overalls and a bandanna—was introduced as a symbol of patriotic womanhood. Is there a comparable poster woman today? What does her image say about modern gender roles?

focus on GLOBALIZATION

The Global Gender Gap Index

The World Economic Forum, based in Geneva, Switzerland, began publishing its annual Global Gender Gap Index in 2006 (see Hausmann, Tyson, and Zahidi 2011). This index is designed to measure gender-based disparities and to track progress in reducing them. It ranks 135 countries based on the size of the gap between males and females in four major categories: economic opportunity and participation, educational attainment, health and survival, and political empowerment.

The indexed countries represent over 90 percent of the world's population, and most of them have made progress in closing the gender gap. Globally, 96 percent of the health/survival gap and 93 percent of the education gap between women and men have been closed. However, only 59 percent of the economic gap, and a paltry 18 percent of the political gap has been closed.

Clearly, women's political gains have lagged their gains in health and education. Although women played key roles in the uprising that launched the Arab Spring in 2011, their future as political leaders in Middle Eastern countries remains doubtful. Worldwide, only about twenty women serve today as elected heads of government (e.g., presidents, chancellors, or prime ministers). In ministries, parliaments, and houses of congress the global average is less than 20 percent female.

What regions have done the most to correct gender-based inequality? North America leads, followed closely by Europe and Central Asia. Those regions have closed over 70 percent of their gender gaps. Latin America, Asia, and Africa come next—between 60 percent and 70 percent. The Middle East/North Africa ranks last, having closed just 58 percent of its gender gap.

Four Nordic countries consistently have held the top four positions in the index: Iceland, Norway, Finland, and Sweden. Although no country has yet achieved full gender equality, these four countries have closed over 80 percent of their gender gaps. The lowest-ranking country, Yemen, has closed less than half.

The United States ranked 17th on the Global Gender Gap Index in 2011, up from 19th place in 2010. The report found no gender gap in American educational attainment. U.S. literacy rates are high for both genders, and rates of female enrollment are high in primary, secondary, and tertiary education. The United States was 6th in the world in economic participation and opportunity, reflecting its high rate of female labor force participation. On the other hand, the United States ranked only 68th in terms of equal pay for equal work. The United States did rise in the political empowerment rankings—from 66th place in 2006 to 39th place in 2011.

Based on the four sets of criteria surveyed, what progress has been made globally in closing the gender gap? By 2011, 18 percent of the global political empowerment gap had been closed, versus 14 percent in 2006. In 2011, 59 percent of the economic participation gap had been closed, versus 56 percent in 2006. In 2011, 93 percent of the educational achievement gap had been closed, up a bit from 92 percent in 2006. On health and survival, however, there was a small decline between 2006 and 2011, from 97 percent to 96 percent.

A country's gender equality is correlated with its overall economic development and its global competitiveness. Because women represent about half of any national talent base, a country's long-run competitiveness depends significantly on the opportunities and accomplishments it allows its women. There's still a lot of progress to be made.

Married couples are much more secure economically than single mothers are. The data in Table 18.9 demonstrate that the average income for married-couple families is more than twice that of families maintained by a woman. The average one-earner family maintained by a woman had an annual income of $32,597 in 2009. This was less than one-half the mean income ($71,830) of a married-couple household.

The feminization of poverty isn't just a North American phenomenon. The percentage of single-parent (usually female-headed) households has been increasing worldwide. The figure ranges from about 10 percent in Japan, to below 20 percent in certain South Asian and Southeast Asian countries, to almost 50 percent in certain African countries and the Caribbean (Buvinic 1995, *Statistical Abstract of the United States 2012*, Table 1337). The percentage of single-parent households rose in every nation listed in Table 18.10 between 1980–81 and 2009. The United States maintains the largest percentage of single-parent households (29.5 percent), followed by the United Kingdom (25 percent), Canada (24.6 percent), Ireland (22.6 percent), and Denmark (21.7 percent). The rate of increase in single-parent households over the past 30 years has been highest in Ireland, where it tripled, from 7.2 to 22.6 percent.

Globally, households headed by women tend to be poorer than are those headed by men. In one study, the percentage of single-parent families considered poor was 18 percent in Britain, 20 percent in Italy, 25 percent in Switzerland, 40 percent in Ireland, 52 percent in Canada, and 63 percent in the United States (Buvinic 1995).

It is widely believed that one way to improve the situation of poor women is to encourage them to organize. New women's groups can in some cases revive or replace traditional forms of social organization that have been disrupted. Membership in a group can help women to mobilize resources, to rationalize production, and to reduce the risks and costs associated with credit (Dunham 2009). Organization also allows women to develop self-confidence and to decrease dependence on others. Through such organization, poor women throughout the world are working to determine their own needs and priorities, and to change things so as to improve their social and economic situation (Buvinic 1995). This chapter's "Focus on Globalization" describes an index designed to measure, country by country, gender-based disparities and to track progress in reducing them.

Work and Happiness

Table 18.11 shows female labor force participation in various countries—condensed from 30 countries for which data were available—in 2008. The United States, with 69.3 percent of its women employed that year, ranked thirteenth, while Canada (74.4 percent)

TABLE 18.9 Median Annual Income of U.S. Households, by Household Type, 2009

	NUMBER OF HOUSEHOLDS (1,000s)	MEDIAN ANNUAL INCOME (DOLLARS)	PERCENTAGE OF MEDIAN EARNINGS COMPARED WITH MARRIED-COUPLE HOUSEHOLDS
All households	117,538	49,777	69
Family households	78,833	61,265	85
Married-couple households	58,410	71,830	100
Male earner, no wife	5,580	48,084	67
Female earner, no husband	14,843	32,597	45
Nonfamily households	38,705	30,444	42
Single male	18,263	36,611	51
Single female	20,442	25,269	35

SOURCE: *Statistical Abstract of the United States 2012,* Table 692, p. 453. http://www.census.gov/prod/2011pubs/12statab/income.pdf.

TABLE 18.10 Percentage of Single-Parent Households, Selected Countries, 1980–81 and 2009.

COUNTRY	1980–81	2009
United States	19.5	29.5
United Kingdom	13.9	25.0
Canada	12.7	24.6
Ireland	7.2	22.6
Denmark	13.4	21.7
France	10.2	19.8
Japan	4.9	10.2

SOURCE: *Statistical Abstract of the United States 2010,* Table 1301.

ranked sixth. Iceland topped the list, with 82.5 percent of its women in the work force. Turkey was lowest; only 26.7 percent of its women were employed.

In 2010 Gallup conducted a survey of the world's 132 happiest countries, based on various measures, including the percentages of people in that country who were thriving, and suffering. Respondents also were asked to rate their own lives on a scale from zero (worst possible) to 10 (best possible). Denmark was the world's happiest nation; Canada came in sixth; and the United States, twelfth.

Interestingly, we can detect a correlation between the two rankings–of happiness and of women's work outside the home. We see in Table 18.11 that of the

TABLE 18.11 Female Labor Force Participation by Country, 2008

COUNTRY	PERCENTAGE OF WOMEN IN LABOR FORCE	RANK AMONG WORLD'S 15 "HAPPIEST COUNTRIES"
Iceland	82.5	*
Sweden	78.2	9
Norway	77.4	3
Denmark	77.3	1
Switzerland	76.6	7
Canada	74.4	6
Finland	74.0	2
New Zealand	72.0	8
Netherlands	72.6	4
United Kingdom	70.2	*
Australia	69.9	11
Germany	69.7	*
United States	69.3	12
Turkey (lowest in table)	26.7	*

*These countries were not among the 15 "happiest countries."

SOURCE: *Statistical Abstract of the United States 2010,* Table 1330; Huffington Post, http://www.huffingtonpost.com/2010/07/03/worlds-happiest-countries_n_633814.

Denmark, which has a high rate of workplace women, a rising birthrate, and readily available child care, is rated the world's happiest country. The genetics researcher shown here is the mother of a toddler.

South Africa's Caster Semenya celebrates her gold medal run in the final of the Women's 800m during the World Athletics Championships in Berlin in August 2009. Following that victory, questions were raised about her gender, and she was subjected to gender testing. She was sidelined for eleven months while the tests were reviewed before being cleared to run again in 2010.

thirteen countries with greatest female labor force participation, ten ranked among the world's happiest (See Levy 2010). What factors might explain this correlation? Why, as more women work outside the home, might a country's population achieve a greater sense of well-being? More money? More taxes? More social services? More personal freedom? We report; you decide!

BEYOND MALE AND FEMALE

Gender is socially constructed, and societies may recognize more than two genders. The contemporary United States, for example, includes individuals who self-identify using such labels as "transgender," "intersex," "third gender," and "transsexual." Such persons contradict dominant male/female gender distinctions by being part male and female, or neither male nor female. Because people who self-identify as "transgender" are increasingly visible, we must be careful about seeing "masculine " and "feminine" as absolute and binary categories.

Sex, we have seen, is biological, whereas gender is socially constructed. Transgender is a social category that includes individuals who *may or may not* contrast biologically with ordinary males and females. Within the transgender category, intersex people (see below) usually contrast biologically with ordinary males and females, but *transgender also includes people whose gender identity has no apparent biological roots*. The term **intersex** encompasses a group of conditions involving a discrepancy between the external genitals (penis, vagina, etc.) and the internal genitals (testes, ovaries, etc.). The older term for this condition, *hermaphroditism*, combined the names of a Greek god and goddess. Hermes was a god of male sexuality (among other things) and Aphrodite a goddess of female sexuality, love, and beauty.

The causes of intersex are varied and complex (Kaneshiro 2009): (1) An XX Intersex person has the chromosomes of a woman (XX) and normal ovaries, uterus, and fallopian tubes, but the external genitals appear male. Usually this results from a female fetus having been exposed to an excess of male hormones before birth. (2) An XY Intersex person has the chromosomes of a man (XY), but the external genitals are incompletely formed, ambiguous, or female. The testes may be normal, malformed, or absent. (3) A True Gonadal Intersex person has both ovarian and testicular tissue. The external genitals may be ambiguous or may appear to be female or male. (4) Intersex also can result from an unusual chromosome combination, such as X0 (only one X chromosome), XXY, XYY, and XXX. In the last three cases there is an extra sex chromosome, either an X or a Y. These chromosomal combinations don't typically produce a discrepancy between internal and external genitalia, but there may be problems with sex hormone levels and overall sexual development.

The XXY configuration, known as *Klinefelter's syndrome*, is the most common unusual sex chromosome combination and the second most common condition (after Down syndrome) caused by the presence of extra chromosomes in humans. Effects of Klinefelter's occur in about 1 of every 1,000 males. One in every 500 males has an extra X chromosome but lacks the main symptoms—small testicles and reduced fertility. With XXX, also known as *triple X syndrome*, there is an extra X chromosome in each cell of a human female. Triple X occurs in about 1 of every 1,000 female births. There usually is no physically distinguishable difference between triple X women and other women. The same is true of XYY compared with other males.

Turner syndrome encompasses several conditions, of which 0X (absence of one sex chromosome) is most common. In this case, all or part of one of the sex chromosomes is absent. Typical females have two X chromosomes, but in Turner syndrome, one of those chromosomes is missing or abnormal. Girls with Turner syndrome typically are sterile because of nonworking ovaries and amenorrhea (absence of a menstrual cycle).

Biology, remember, isn't destiny; people construct their identities in society. Many individuals affected by one of the biological conditions just described see themselves simply as male or female, rather than transgender. Self-identified **transgender** people tend to be individuals whose gender identity contradicts their biological sex at birth and the gender identity that society assigned to them in infancy. The transgender category is diverse; it includes individuals with varied perceptions of self and manner of gender performance. Some lean male; some, female; and some toward neither of the dominant genders.

Fear and ignorance related to diversity in gender fuels discrimination, principally because outsiders perceive transgender as a homogeneous and stigmatized category. In fact, there is nothing new or abnormal about diverse gender roles and identities, as the anthropological record attests. Gender variance is a human phenomenon that has taken many forms across societies and cultures.

The historical and ethnographic records reveal the malleability of gender categories and roles (Herdt 1994). Consider, for example, the *eunuch* or "perfect servant" (a castrated man who served as a safe attendant to harems in Byzantium [Tougher 2008]). Acknowledgement and accommodation of *hijras* as a third sex/gender in Indian society indicates that certain societal requirements necessitated the castration of some men who then filled special social roles (Nanda 1998). Roscoe writes of the "Zuni man-woman" or *berdache* in the 19th century (see also Lowie 1935). A berdache was a male who

adopted social roles traditionally assigned to women, and through performance of a third gender contributed to the social and spiritual well-being of the community as a whole (Roscoe 1992; 2000). Some Balkan societies included "sworn virgins," born females who assumed male gender roles and activities to meet societal needs when there was a shortage of men (Gremaux 1993). Among the Gheg tribes of North Albania, "virginal transvestites" were biologically female, but locals consider them "honorary men" (Shryock 1988). Albanian adolescent girls have chosen to become men, remain celibate, and live among men, with the support of their families and villagers (Young 2000.) And consider Polynesia. In Tonga the term *fakaleitis* describes males who behave like women, thereby contrasting with mainstream Tongan men who display masculine characteristics. Similar to the fakaleitis of Tonga, Samoan *fa'afafine* and Hawaiian *mahu* refer to men who adopt feminine attributes, behaviors, and visual markers.

This chapter's "Appreciating Anthropology" describes how *transvestites* (men dressing as women) form a third gender in relation to Brazil's polarized male-female identity scale. Transvestites, not uncommon in Brazil, are members of one gender (usually males) who dress as another (female). At the time of the case described in "Appreciating Anthropology," a Brazilian man who wished to be changed surgically into a woman (transgendered) could not obtain the necessary operation in Brazil. Some men, including Roberta Close, as described

transgender
Describing individuals whose gender identity contradicts their biological sex at birth and the gender identity assigned to them in infancy.

Neither man nor woman, hijras constitute India's third gender. Many hijras get their income from performing at ceremonies, begging, or prostitution. The beauty contest shown here was organized by an AIDS prevention and relief organization that works with the local hijra community.

Hidden Women, Public Men—Public Women, Hidden Men

Generations of anthropologists have applied their field's comparative, cross-cultural, and biocultural approaches to the study of sex and gender. To some extent at least, gender, sexual preferences, and even sexual orientation are culturally constructed. Here I describe a case in which popular culture and comments by ordinary Brazilians about beauty and sex led me to an analysis of some striking gender differences between Brazil and the United States.

For several years, one of Brazil's top sex symbols was Roberta Close, whom I first saw in a furniture commercial. Roberta ended her pitch with an admonition to prospective furniture buyers to accept no substitute for the advertised product. "Things," she warned, "are not always what they seem."

Nor was Roberta. This petite and incredibly feminine creature was actually a man. Nevertheless, despite the fact that he—or she (speaking as Brazilians do)—is a man posing as a woman,

Roberta won a secure place in Brazilian mass culture. Her photos decorated magazines. She was a panelist on a TV variety show and starred in a stage play in Rio with an actor known for his supermacho image. Roberta even inspired a well-known, and apparently heterosexual, pop singer to make a video honoring her. In it, she pranced around Rio's Ipanema Beach in a bikini, showing off her ample hips and buttocks.

The video depicted the widespread male appreciation of Roberta's beauty. As confirmation, one heterosexual man told me he had recently been on the same plane as Roberta and had been struck by her looks. Another man said he wanted to have sex with her. These comments, it seemed to me, illustrated striking cultural contrasts about gender and sexuality. In Brazil, a Latin American country noted for its machismo, heterosexual men did not feel that attraction toward a transvestite blemished their masculine identities.

Roberta Close can be understood in relation to a gender-identity scale that jumps from

extreme femininity to extreme masculinity, with little in between. Masculinity is stereotyped as active and public, femininity as passive and domestic. The male-female contrast in rights and behavior is much stronger in Brazil than it is in North America. Brazilians confront a more rigidly defined masculine role than North Americans do.

The active-passive dichotomy also provides a stereotypical model for male-male sexual relations. One man is supposed to be the active, masculine (inserting) partner, whereas the other is the passive, effeminate one. The latter man is derided as a *bicha* (intestinal worm), but little stigma attaches to the inserter. Indeed, many "active" (and married) Brazilian men like to have sex with transvestite prostitutes, who are biological males.

If a Brazilian man is unhappy pursuing either active masculinity or passive effeminacy, there is one other choice—active femininity. For Roberta Close and others like her, the cultural demand of ultramasculinity has yielded to a

---

in "Appreciating Anthropology," traveled to Europe for the procedure. Today transgendered Brazilians are well known in Europe. In France, transvestites regardless of nationality commonly are referred to as "Brésiliennes" (the feminine form of the French word for *Brazilian*), so common are Brazilians among the transvestites in Europe. In Brazil many men do have sexual relations with transvestites, with little stigma attached, as described in "Appreciating Anthropology."

Transvestism is perhaps the most common way of forming genders alternative to male and female. Among the Chukchee of Siberia certain men (usually shamans or religious specialists) copied female dress, speech, and hairstyles and took other men as husbands and sex partners. Female shamans could join a fourth gender, copying men and taking wives.

In the contemporary West, the umbrella category *transgender* encompasses a variety of persons whose gender performance and identity contradict or defy a binary gender structure. Transgender people are productive and contributing members of society, at

least in those sectors to which they have access and when they have relative protection to live as who they are. In recent years, the gay and lesbian rights movement has achieved many successes, including the legalization of same-sex marriage in a few states and the repeal of the "Don't Ask Don't Tell" (DADT) policy of the U.S. armed services. The gay and lesbian rights movement has expanded to include the lesbian, gay, bisexual, and transgender community (LGBT), which works to promote government policies and social practices that protect its members' civil and human rights.

SEXUAL ORIENTATION

Sexual orientation refers to a person's habitual sexual attraction to, and sexual activities with, persons of the opposite sex, *heterosexuality*; the same sex, *homosexuality*; or both sexes, *bisexuality*. *Asexuality*, indifference toward or lack of attraction to either sex, also is a sexual orientation. All four of these forms are

sexual orientation
Sexual attraction to persons of the opposite sex, same sex, or either sex.

performance of ultrafemininity. These men-women form a third gender in relation to Brazil's polarized male-female identity scale.

Transvestites like Roberta are particularly prominent in Rio de Janeiro's annual Carnaval, when an ambience of inversion rules the city. In the culturally accurate words of the American popular novelist Gregory McDonald, who sets one of his books in Brazil at Carnaval time:

> Everything goes topsy-turvy.... Men become women; women become men; grown-ups become children; rich people pretend they're poor; poor people, rich; sober people become drunkards; thieves become generous. Very topsy-turvy. (McDonald 1984, p. 154)

Most notable in this costumed inversion (DaMatta 1991), men dress as women. Carnaval reveals and expresses normally hidden tensions and conflicts as social life is turned upside down. Reality is illuminated through a dramatic presentation of its opposite.

This is the final key to Roberta's cultural meaning. She emerged in a setting in which male-female inversion is part of the year's most popular festival. Transvestites are the pièces de résistance at Rio's Carnaval balls, where they dress as scantily as the real women do. They wear postage-stamp bikinis, sometimes with no tops. Photos of real women and transformed ones vie for space in the magazines. It is often impossible to tell the born women from the hidden men. Roberta Close is a permanent incarnation of Carnaval—a year-

Roberta Close, photographed in 1999, at age 35. In 1989, Close underwent sex reassignment surgery in England. Subsequently she was voted the "Most Beautiful Woman in Brazil."

round reminder of the spirit of Carnavals past, present, and yet to come.

Roberta emerged from a Latin culture whose gender roles contrast strongly with those of the United States. From small village to massive city, Brazilian males are public and Brazilian females are private creatures. Streets, beaches, and bars belong to the men. Although bikinis adorn Rio's beaches on weekends and holidays, there are many more men than women there on weekdays. The men revel in their ostentatiously sexual displays. As they sun themselves and play soccer and volleyball, they regularly stroke their genitals to keep them firm. They are living publicly, assertively, and sexually in a world of men.

Brazilian men must work hard at this public image, constantly acting out their culture's definition of masculine behavior. Public life is a play whose strong roles go to men. Roberta Close, of course, was a public figure. Given that Brazilian culture defines the public world as male, we can perhaps better understand now why a popular Brazilian sex symbol could be a man who excels at performing in public as a woman.

found in contemporary North America and throughout the world. But each type of desire and experience holds different meanings for individuals and groups. For example, an asexual disposition may be acceptable in some places but may be perceived as a character flaw in others. Male-male sexual activity may be a private affair in Mexico, rather than public, socially sanctioned, and encouraged as it was among the Etoro (see pp. 420–421) of Papua New Guinea (see also Blackwood 2010; Blackwood and Wieringa 1999; Herdt 1981, 2006; Kottak and Kozaitis 2012; Lancaster and Di Leonardo 1997; Nanda 2000).

Recently in the United States there has been a tendency to see sexual orientation as fixed and biologically based. There is not enough information at this time to determine the exact extent to which sexual orientation is based on biology. What we can say is that all human activities and preferences, including erotic expression, are at least partially culturally constructed.

In any society, individuals will differ in the nature, range, and intensity of their sexual interests and urges. No one knows for sure why such individual sexual differences exist. Part of the answer appears to be biological, reflecting genes or hormones. Another part may have to do with experiences during growth and development. But whatever the reasons for individual variation, culture always plays a role in molding individual sexual urges toward a collective norm. And such sexual norms vary from culture to culture.

What do we know about variation in sexual norms from society to society, and over time? A classic cross-cultural study (Ford and Beach 1951) found wide variation in attitudes about masturbation, bestiality (sex with animals), and homosexuality. Even in a single society, such as the United States, attitudes about sex differ over time and with socioeconomic status, region, and rural versus urban residence. However, even in the 1950s, prior to the "age of sexual permissiveness" (the pre-HIV period from the mid-1960s through the 1970s), research showed that almost all American men (92 percent) and more than half of American women

FIGURE 18.2 The Location of the Etoro, Kaluli, and Sambia in Papua New Guinea.

The western part of the island of New Guinea is part of Indonesia. The eastern part of the island is the independent nation of Papua New Guinea, home of the Etoro, Kaluli, and Sambia.

(54 percent) admitted to masturbation. In the famous Kinsey report (Kinsey, Pomeroy, and Martin 1948), 37 percent of the men surveyed admitted having had at least one sexual experience leading to orgasm with another male. In a later study of 1,200 unmarried women, 26 percent reported same-sex sexual activities. (Because Kinsey's research relied on nonrandom samples, it should be considered merely illustrative, rather than a statistically accurate representation, of sexual behavior at the time.)

Sex acts involving people of the same sex were absent, rare, or secret in only 37 percent of 76 societies for which data were available in the Ford and Beach study (1951). In the others, various forms of same-sex sexual activity were considered normal and acceptable. As an example, consider the Sudanese Azande, who valued the warrior role (Evans-Pritchard 1970). Prospective warriors—young men aged 12 to 20—left their families and shared quarters with adult fighting men, who had sex with them. The younger men were considered temporary brides of the older men and did the domestic duties of women. Upon reaching warrior status, these young men took their own younger male brides. Later, retiring from the warrior role, Azande men married women. Flexible in their sexual expression, Azande males had no difficulty shifting from sex with older men (as male brides), to sex with younger men (as warriors), to sex with women (as husbands) (see Murray and Roscoe 1998).

An extreme example of tension involving male-female sexual relations in Papua New Guinea is provided by the Etoro (Kelly 1976), a group of 400 people who subsist by hunting and horticulture in the Trans-Fly region (Figure 18.2). The Etoro illustrate the power of culture in molding human sexuality. The following account, based on ethnographic field work by Raymond C. Kelly in the late 1960s, applies only to Etoro males and their beliefs. Etoro cultural norms prevented the male anthropologist who studied them from gathering comparable information about female attitudes. Note, also, that the activities described have been discouraged by missionaries. Since there has been no restudy of the Etoro specifically focusing on these activities, the extent to which these practices continue today is unknown. For this reason, I'll use the past tense in describing them.

Etoro opinions about sexuality were linked to their beliefs about the cycle of birth, physical growth, maturity, old age, and death. Etoro men believed that semen was necessary to give life force to a fetus, which was, they believed, implanted in a woman by an ancestral spirit. Sexual intercourse during pregnancy nourished the growing fetus. The Etoro believed that men had a limited lifetime supply of semen. Any sex act leading to ejaculation was seen as draining that supply, and as sapping a man's virility and vitality. The birth of children, nurtured by semen, symbolized a necessary sacrifice that would lead to the husband's eventual death. Heterosexual intercourse, required only for reproduction, was discouraged. Women who wanted too much sex were viewed as witches, hazardous to their husbands' health. Etoro culture allowed heterosexual intercourse only about 100 days a year. The rest of the time it was tabooed. Seasonal birth clustering shows the taboo was respected.

So objectionable was male-female sex that it was removed from community life. It could occur neither in sleeping quarters nor in the fields. Coitus could happen only in the woods, where it was risky because poisonous snakes, the Etoro claimed, were attracted by the sounds and smells of male-female sex.

Although coitus was discouraged, sex acts between men were viewed as essential. Etoro believed that boys could not produce semen on their own. To grow into men and eventually give life force to their children, boys had to acquire semen orally from older men. From the age of 10 until adulthood, boys were inseminated by older men. No taboos were attached to this. Such oral insemination could proceed in the sleeping area or garden. Every three years, a group of boys around the age of 20 was formally initiated into manhood. They went to a secluded mountain lodge, where they were visited and inseminated by several older men.

Male-male sex among the Etoro was governed by a code of propriety. Although sexual relations between older and younger males were considered culturally essential, those between boys of the same age were discouraged. A boy who took semen from other youths was believed to be sapping their life force and stunting their growth. A boy's rapid physical development might suggest that he was getting semen from other boys. Like a sex-hungry wife, he might be shunned as a witch.

These sexual practices among the Etoro rested not on hormones or genes but on cultural beliefs and traditions. The Etoro were an extreme example of a male-female avoidance pattern that has been widespread in Papua New Guinea and in patrilineal-patrilocal societies. The Etoro shared a cultural pattern, which Gilbert Herdt (1984, 2006) calls "ritualized homosexuality," with some fifty other tribes in Papua New Guinea, especially in that country's Trans-Fly region. These societies illustrate one extreme of a male-female avoidance pattern that is widespread in Papua New Guinea and indeed in many patrilineal-patrilocal societies.

Flexibility in sexual expression seems to be an aspect of our primate heritage. Both masturbation and same-sex sexual activity exist among chimpanzees and other primates. Male bonobos (pygmy chimps) regularly engage in a form of mutual masturbation known as "penis fencing." Female bonobos get sexual pleasure from rubbing their genitals against those of other females (de Waal 1997). Our primate sexual potential is molded by culture, the environment, and reproductive necessity. Heterosexual coitus is practiced in all human societies—which, after all, must reproduce themselves—but alternatives are also widespread (Rathus, Nevid, and Fichner-Rathus 2013). Like gender roles and attitudes more generally, the sexual component of human personality and identity—just how we express our "natural" sexual urges—is a matter that culture and environment direct and limit.

acing the COURSE

1. *Gender roles* are the tasks and activities that a culture assigns to each sex. *Gender stereotypes* are oversimplified ideas about attributes of males and females. *Gender stratification* describes an unequal distribution of rewards by gender, reflecting different positions in a social hierarchy. Cross-cultural comparison reveals some recurrent patterns involving the division of labor by gender and gender-based

summary

differences in reproductive strategies. Gender roles and gender stratification also vary with environment, economy, adaptive strategy, level of social complexity, and degree of participation in the world economy.

2. When gathering is prominent, gender status is more equal than it is when hunting or fishing dominates the foraging economy. Gender status is more equal when the domestic and public spheres aren't sharply separated. Foragers lack two public arenas that contribute to higher male status among food producers: warfare and organized interregional trade.

3. Gender stratification also is linked to descent and residence. Women's status in matrilineal societies tends to be high because overall social identity comes through female links. Women in many societies, especially matrilineal ones, wield power and make decisions. Scarcity of resources promotes intervillage warfare, patriliny, and patrilocality. The localization of related males is adaptive for military solidarity. Men may use their warrior role to symbolize and reinforce the social devaluation and oppression of women. Patriarchy describes a political system ruled by men in which women have inferior social and political status, including basic human rights.

4. Americans' attitudes toward gender vary with class and region. When the need for female labor declines, the idea that women are unfit for many jobs increases, and vice versa. Factors such as war, falling wages, and inflation help explain female cash employment and Americans' attitudes toward it. Countering the economic gains of many American women is the feminization of poverty. This has become a global phenomenon, as impoverished female-headed households have increased worldwide.

5. Societies may recognize more than two genders. The term *intersex* describes a group of conditions, including chromosomal configurations, that may produce a discrepancy between external and internal genitals. Transgender individuals may or may not contrast biologically with ordinary males and females. Self-identified transgender people tend to be individuals whose gender identity contradicts their biological sex at birth and the gender identity that society assigned to them in infancy.

6. There has been a recent tendency to see sexual orientation as fixed and biologically based. But to some extent, at least, all human activities and preferences, including erotic expression, are influenced by culture. Sexual orientation stands for a person's habitual sexual attraction to, and activities with, persons of the opposite sex, *heterosexuality;* the same sex, *homosexuality;* or both sexes, *bisexuality.* Sexual norms vary widely from culture to culture.

key terms

domestic–public dichotomy 409
gender roles 405
gender stereotypes 405
gender stratification 405
intersex 416
matrilineal descent 410

patriarchy 411
patrilineal descent 411
patrilineal-patrilocal complex 411
sexual dimorphism 405
sexual orientation 418
transgender 417

test yourself

MULTIPLE CHOICE

1. "The biological nature of men and women [should be seen] not as a narrow enclosure limiting the human organism, but rather as a broad base upon which a variety of structures can be built."

   a. This statement reflects an idea that is a cultural generality, but not a cultural universal.

   b. This passage reflects the predominant anthropological position on sex-gender roles and biology.

   c. The basic assumptions in this passage are threatened by new medical technologies.

   d. This passage is culturally ethnocentric.

   e. This statement reflects ideas on gender and sex that ignore over fifty years of ethnographic evidence.

2. Traditionally among the Hidatsa, women made boats. Pawnee women worked wood. Among the Mbuti "pygmies," women hunt. Cases such as these suggest that

   a. swing activities usually are done by women.

   b. biology has nothing to do with gender roles.

   c. anthropologists are overly optimistic about finding a society with perfect gender equality.

d. patterns of division of labor by gender are cultural generalities—not universals.

e. exceptions to cross-cultural generalization are actually the rule.

3. Among foragers

a. men excel in the harsh life and therefore accrue much more prestige than women.

b. warfare makes men dominant over women.

c. the status of women falls when they provide most of the food.

d. the lack of a clear public-private dichotomy is associated with relatively mild gender stratification.

e. men and women are completely equal; there is no gender inequality.

4. Which of the following statements about the domestic-public dichotomy is true?

a. It is very clearly demarcated among foragers.

b. It is not significant in urban industrial societies.

c. It is stronger in India and Pakistan than among foragers.

d. It is reinforced in American society by women working both inside and outside the home.

e. It is not present in the modern industrial states of the Western world.

5. Which of the following is *not* part of the patrilineal-patrilocal complex?

a. patrilineality

b. patrilocality

c. warfare

d. male supremacy

e. reduced gender stratification

6. In what kind of society do anthropologists most typically find forced female genital operations, intervillage raiding, female infanticide, and dowry?

a. patrilineal-patrilocal

b. matrilineal-patrilocal

c. matrilineal-matrilocal

d. patrilineal-matrilocal

e. patrilineal-neolocal

7. The "traditional" idea that "a woman's place is in the home"

a. developed among middle- and upper-class Americans as industrialism spread after 1900.

b. is actually a cultural universal.

c. accurately reflects the worldwide sexual division of labor.

d. is based in the preindustrial era and began to disappear as women moved into the factories in the 1900s.

e. was part of the Pledge of Allegiance until it was challenged in the early 1800s.

8. What have recent cross-cultural studies of gender roles demonstrated?

a. The gender roles of men and women are largely determined by their biological capabilities—such as relative strength, endurance, and intelligence.

b. Women are subservient in nearly all societies because their subsistence activities contribute much less to the total diet than do those of men.

c. Foraging, horticultural, pastoral, and industrial societies all have similar attitudes toward gender roles.

d. The relative status of women is variable, depending on factors such as subsistence strategy, the importance of warfare, and the prevalence of a domestic-public dichotomy.

e. Changes in the gender roles of men and women usually are associated with social decay and anarchy.

9. Which of the following statements about transgender/intersex is true?

a. Unusual chromosomal combinations, such as XXX, always show up phenotypically.

b. It is possible to have three sex chromsomes but not to have just one sex chromsome.

c. Genders beyond male and female usually are based on genetic differences.

d. Transgender is a social category that includes individuals who may or may not contrast biologically with ordinary males and females.

e. Outside the United States, women are more likely than men are to change their gender—because women usually have less power and seek it in gender transformation.

10. All of the following are key ideas to take away from this chapter's discussion of sexual orientation *except:*

a. Different types of sexual desires and experiences hold different meanings for individuals and groups.

b. In a society, individuals will differ in the nature, range, and intensity of sexual interests and urges.

c. Culture always plays a role in molding individual sexual urges toward a collective norm and these norms vary from culture to culture.

d. Asexuality, indifference toward, or lack of attraction to either sex, is also a sexual orientation.

e. There is conclusive scientific evidence that sexual orientation is genetically determined.

FILL IN THE BLANK

1. Sex differences are biological, while _____ refers to the cultural construction of whether one is female, male, or something else.

2. _____ refer to the tasks and activities that a culture assigns to the sexes.

3. In general, the status of women is higher in societies with _____ descent than in those with _____ descent.

4. _____ refers to an unequal distribution of socially valued resources, power, prestige, and personal freedom between men and women.

5. _____ refers to a group of conditions involving a discrepancy between the external genitals (penis, vagina, etc.) and the internal genitals (testes, ovaries, etc.).

CRITICAL THINKING

1. How are sexuality, sex, and gender related to one another? What are the differences between these three concepts? Provide an argument about why anthropologists are uniquely positioned to study the relationships between sexuality, sex, and gender in society.

2. Using your own society, give an example of a gender role, a gender stereotype, and gender stratification.

3. What is the feminization of poverty? Where is this trend occurring, and what are some of its causes?

4. Is intersex the same as transgender? If not, how do they differ? How might biological, cultural, and personal factors influence gender identity?

5. This chapter describes Raymond Kelly's research among the Etoro of Papua New Guinea. What were his findings regarding Etoro male-female sexual relations? How did Kelly's own gender affect some of the content and extent of his study? Can you think of other research projects where the ethnographer's gender would have an impact?

Blackwood, E., and S. Wieringa, eds.
1999   *Female Desires: Same-Sex Relations and Trans-gender Practices across Cultures.* New York: Columbia University Press. Lesbianism and male homosexuality in cross-cultural perspective.

Bonvillain, N.
2007   *Women and Men: Cultural Constructs of Gender,* 4th ed. Upper Saddle River, NJ: Prentice Hall. A cross-cultural study of gender roles and relationships, from bands to industrial societies.

Brettell, C. B., and C. F. Sargent, eds.
2009   *Gender in Cross-Cultural Perspective,* 5th ed. Upper Saddle River, NJ: Pearson/Prentice Hall. Articles on variation in gender systems across cultures.

Kimmel, M. S., and M. A. Messner, eds.
2013   *Men's Lives,* 9th ed. Boston: Pearson/Allyn & Bacon. The study of men in society and concepts of masculinity in the United States.

Mascia-Lees, F.
2010   *Gender & Difference in a Globalizing World: Twenty-first Century Anthropology.* Long Grove: IL: Waveland. A thorough and biocultural survey of gender in today's world.

Rathus, S. A., J. S. Nevid, and J. Fichner-Rathus
2010   *Human Sexuality in a World of Diversity,* 8th ed. Boston: Pearson/Allyn & Bacon. Multicultural and ethnic perspectives.

Ward, M. C., and M. Edelstein
2009   *A World Full of Women,* 5th ed. Boston: Allyn & Bacon. A global and comparative approach to the study of women.

suggested additional readings

internet exercises

Go to our Online Learning Center website at **www.mhhe.com/kottak** for Internet exercises directly related to the content of this chapter.

CHAPTER 19

Families, Kinship, and Descent

Why and how do anthropologists study kinship?

How do families and descent groups differ, and what are their social correlates?

How is kinship calculated, and how are relatives classified, in various societies?

◀ In Lahore, Pakistan, families enjoy the atmosphere at Gawal Mandi "Food Street," a night market serving up some of the best food in the city.

understanding OURSELVES

Although it still is something of an ideal in our culture, the nuclear family (mother, father, and biological children) now accounts for fewer than one-fourth of all American households. Such phrases as "love and marriage," "marriage and the family," and "mom and pop" no longer apply to a majority of American households. What kind of family raised you? Perhaps it was a nuclear family. Or maybe you were raised by a single parent, with or without the help of extended kin. Perhaps your extended kin acted as your parents. Or maybe you had a stepparent and/or step- or half-siblings in a blended family. Maybe your family matches none of these descriptions, or fits different descriptions at different times.

Although contemporary American families may seem amazingly diverse, other cultures offer family alternatives that Americans might have trouble understanding. Imagine a society in which someone doesn't know for sure, and doesn't care much about, who his actual mother was. Consider Joseph Rabe, a Betsileo man who was my field assistant in Madagascar. Rabe, who had been raised by his aunt—his father's sister—told me about two sisters, one of whom was his mother and the other his mother's sister. He knew their names, but he didn't know which was which. Illustrating an adoptive pattern common among the Betsileo, Rabe was given as a toddler to his childless aunt. His mother and her sister lived far away and died in his childhood (as did his father), and so he didn't really know them. But he was very close to his father's sister, for whom he used the term for mother. Indeed, he had to call her that because the Betsileo have only one kin term, *reny*, for mother, mother's sister, and father's sister. (They also use a single term, *ray*, for father and all uncles.) The difference between "real" (biologically based) and socially constructed kinship didn't matter to Rabe.

Contrast the Betsileo case with Americans' attitudes about kinship and adoption. On family-oriented radio talk shows, I've heard hosts distinguish between "birth mothers" and adoptive mothers, and between "sperm daddies" and "daddies of the heart." The latter may be adoptive fathers, or stepfathers who have "been like fathers" to someone. American culture tends to promote the idea that kinship is, and should be, biological. It's increasingly common for adopted children to seek out their birth parents (which used to be discouraged as disruptive), even after a perfectly satisfactory upbringing in an adoptive family. The American emphasis on biology for kinship is seen also in the recent proliferation of DNA testing. Viewing our beliefs through the lens of cross-cultural comparison helps us appreciate that kinship and biology don't always converge, nor do they need to.

FAMILIES

The kinds of societies anthropologists have studied traditionally, including many examples considered in this chapter, have stimulated a strong interest in families, along with larger systems of kinship, descent, and marriage. Cross-culturally, the social construction of kinship illustrates considerable diversity.

Understanding kinship systems has become an essential part of anthropology because of the importance of those systems to the people we study. We are ready to take a closer look at the systems of kinship and descent that have organized human life during much of our history.

Ethnographers quickly recognize social divisions—groups—within any society they study. During fieldwork, they learn about significant groups by observing their activities and composition. People often live in the same village or neighborhood, or work, pray, or celebrate together because they are related in some way. To understand the social structure, an ethnographer must investigate such kin ties. For example, the most significant local groups may consist of descendants of the same grandfather. These people may live in neighboring houses, farm adjoining fields, and help each other in everyday tasks. Other sorts of groups, based on different or more distant kin links, get together less often.

The nuclear family is one kind of kin group that is widespread in human societies. The nuclear family consists of parents and children, normally living together in the same household. Other kin groups include extended families (families consisting of three or more generations) and descent groups—lineages and clans. Such groups are not usually residentially based as the nuclear family is. Extended family members get together from time to time, but they don't necessarily live together. Branches of a given descent group may reside in several villages and rarely assemble for common activity. **Descent groups,** which are composed of people claiming common ancestry, are basic units in the social organization of nonindustrial food producers.

Nuclear and Extended Families

A nuclear family lasts only as long as the parents and children remain together. Most people belong to at least two nuclear families at different times in their lives. They are born into a family consisting of their parents and siblings. When they reach adulthood, they may marry and establish a nuclear family that includes the spouse and eventually the children. Since most societies permit divorce, some people establish more than one family through marriage.

Anthropologists distinguish between the **family of orientation** (the family in which one is born and grows up) and the **family of procreation** (formed when one marries and has children). From the individual's point of view, the critical relationships are with parents and siblings in the family of orientation and with spouse and children in the family of procreation.

In most societies, relations with nuclear family members (parents, siblings, and children) take precedence over relations with other kin. Nuclear family organization is very widespread but not universal, and its significance in society differs greatly from one place to another. In a few societies, such as the classic Nayar case described below, nuclear families are rare or nonexistent. In others, the nuclear family plays no special role in social life. Other social units—most notably descent groups and extended families—can assume many of the functions otherwise associated with the nuclear family.

Consider an example from the former Yugoslavia. Traditionally, among the Muslims of western Bosnia (Lockwood 1975), nuclear families lacked autonomy.

Siblings play a prominent role in child rearing in many societies. Here, in China's Yunnan province, two sisters give their younger brother a drink of water from a folded leaf. Do your siblings belong to your family of orientation or your family of procreation?

descent group
Group based on belief in shared ancestry.

family of orientation
Nuclear family in which one is born and grows up.

family of procreation
Nuclear family established when one marries and has children.

Several such families were embedded in an extended family household called a *zadruga*. The *zadruga* was headed by a male household head and his wife, the senior woman. It also included married sons and their wives and children, and unmarried sons and daughters. Each nuclear family had a sleeping room, decorated and partly furnished from the bride's trousseau. However, possessions—even clothing items—were freely shared by *zadruga* members. Even trousseau items could be appropriated for use by other *zadruga* members. Such a residential unit is known as a *patrilocal* extended family, because each couple resides in the husband's father's household after marriage.

The *zadruga* took precedence over its component units. Social interaction was more usual among women, men, or children than between spouses or between parents and children. Larger households ate at three successive settings: for men, women, and children. Traditionally, all children over twelve slept together in boys' or girls' rooms. When a woman wished to visit another village, she sought the permission of the male *zadruga* head. Although men usually felt closer to their own children than to those of their brothers, they were obliged to treat them equally. Children were disciplined by any adult in the household. When a nuclear family broke up, children under seven went with the mother. Older children could choose between their parents. Children were considered part of the

household where they were born even if their mother left. One widow who remarried had to leave her five children, all over seven, in their father's *zadruga,* headed by his brother.

Another example of an alternative to the nuclear family is provided by the Nayars (or Nair), a large and powerful caste on the Malabar Coast of southern India (Figure 19.1). Their traditional kinship system was matrilineal (descent traced only through females). Nayar lived in matrilineal extended family compounds called *tarawads.* The *tarawad* was a residential complex with several buildings, its own temple, granary, water well, orchards, gardens, and land holdings. Headed by a senior woman, assisted by her brother, the *tarawad* housed her siblings, sisters' children, and other matrikin—matrilineal relatives (Gough 1959; Shivaram 1996).

Traditional Nayar marriage seems to have been hardly more than a formality—a kind of coming-of-age ritual. A young woman would go through a marriage ceremony with a man, after which they might spend a few days together at her *tarawad.* Then the man would return to his own *tarawad,* where he lived with his sisters, mother, aunts, and other matrikin. Nayar men belonged to a warrior class, who left home regularly for military expeditions, returning permanently to their *tarawad* on retirement. Nayar women could have multiple sexual partners. Children became members of the mother's *tarawad;* they were not considered to be relatives of their biological father. Indeed, many Nayar children didn't even know who their genitor was. Child care was the responsibility of the *tarawad.* Nayar society therefore reproduced itself biologically without the nuclear family.

FIGURE 19.1 Location of the Nayars in India's Kerala province.

This just-married Khasi couple poses (in 1997) in India's northeastern city of Shillong. The Khasis are matrilineal, tracing descent through women and taking their maternal ancestors' surnames. Women choose their husbands, family incomes are pooled, and extended family households are managed by older women.

Industrialism and Family Organization

For many North Americans, the nuclear family is the only well-defined kin group. Family isolation arises from geographic mobility, which is associated with industrialism. Born into a family of orientation, we leave home for work or college, and the break with parents is under way. Eventually most North Americans marry and start a family of procreation. Because less than 3 percent of the U.S. population now farms, most people aren't tied to the land. We can move to places where jobs are available.

Married couples often live hundreds of miles from their parents. Their jobs have determined where they live (see Descartes and Kottak 2009). Such a postmarital residence pattern is called **neolocality**: Married couples establish a new place of residence—a "home of their own." Among middle-class North Americans, neolocal residence is both a cultural preference and a statistical norm. Most middle-class Americans eventually do establish households and nuclear families of their own.

Within stratified nations, value systems vary to some extent from class to class, and so does kinship. There are significant differences between middle-class and poorer North Americans. For example, in the lower class the incidence of *expanded family households* (those that include nonnuclear relatives) is greater than it is in the middle class. When an expanded family household includes three or more generations, it is an **extended family household,** such as the *zadruga*. Another type of expanded family is the *collateral household,* which includes siblings and their spouses and children.

The higher proportion of expanded family households among poorer Americans has been explained as an adaptation to poverty (Stack 1975). Unable to survive economically as nuclear family units, relatives band together in an expanded household and pool their resources. Adaptation to poverty causes kinship values and attitudes to diverge from middle-class norms (see Hansen 2005). Thus, when North Americans raised in poverty achieve financial success, they often feel obligated to provide financial help to a wide circle of less fortunate relatives. This chapter's "Appreciating Diversity" shows how poor Brazilians use kinship, marriage, and fictive kinship as a form of social security.

Changes in North American Kinship

Although the nuclear family remains a cultural ideal for many Americans, Table 19.1 and Figure 19.2 show that nuclear families accounted for only 21 percent of American households in 2010. Other domestic arrangements now outnumber the "traditional" American household about five to one. There are several reasons for this changing household

An extended family of *cocoteros*, workers on a coconut plantation in the rural town of Barigua in eastern Cuba. Try to guess what the relationships among them might be.

composition. Women increasingly are joining men in the cash workforce. This often removes them from their family of orientation while making it economically feasible to delay marriage. Furthermore, job demands compete with romantic attachments. The median age at first marriage for American women rose from 21 years in 1970 to 26.5 in 2011. For men the comparable ages were 23 and 28.7 (U.S. Census Bureau 2011).

Also, the U.S. divorce rate has risen, making divorced Americans much more common today than they were in 1970. Between 1970 and 2010 the number of divorced Americans more than quintupled— 23.7 million in 2010 versus 4.3 million in 1970.

neolocality
Living situation in which couple establishes new residence.

extended family household
Household with three or more generations.

One among many kinds of American family: A single mother (by choice) bakes cupcakes with her twin daughters at their home in Brooklyn, New York. What do you see as the main differences between nuclear families and single-parent families?

Social Security, Kinship Style

In all societies people care for others. Sometimes, as in our own state-organized society, social security is a function of government as well as of the individual and the family. In other societies, such as Arembepe, as described here, social security is part of systems of kinship, marriage, and fictive kinship.

My book *Assault on Paradise,* 4th edition (Kottak 2006), describes social relations in Arembepe, the Brazilian fishing community I've studied for many years. When I first studied Arembepe, I was struck by how similar its social relations were to those in the egalitarian, kin-based societies anthropologists have studied traditionally. The twin assertions "We're all equal here" and "We're all relatives here" were offered repeatedly as Arembepeiros' summaries of the nature and basis of local life. Like members of a clan (who claim to share common ancestry, but who can't say exactly how they are related), most villagers couldn't trace precise genealogical links to their distant kin. "What difference does it make, as long as we know we're relatives?"

As in most nonindustrial societies, close personal relations were either based or modeled on kinship. A degree of community solidarity was promoted, for example, by the myth that everyone was kin. However, social solidarity was actually much *less* developed in Arembepe than in societies with clans and lineages—which use genealogy to include some people, and *exclude* others from membership, in a given descent group. Intense social solidarity demands that some people be excluded. By asserting they all were related—that is, by excluding no one—Arembepeiros were actually weakening kinship's potential strength in creating and maintaining group solidarity.

Rights and obligations always are associated with kinship and marriage. In Arembepe, the closer the kin connection and the more formal the marital tie, the greater the rights and obligations. Couples could be married formally or informally. The most common union was a stable common-law marriage. Less common, but with more prestige, was legal (civil) marriage, performed by a justice of the peace and conferring inheritance

rights. The union with the most prestige combined legal validity with a church ceremony.

The rights and obligations associated with kinship and marriage constituted the local social security system, but people had to weigh the benefits of the system against its costs. The most obvious cost was this: Villagers had to share in proportion to their success. As ambitious men climbed the local ladder of success, they got more dependents. To maintain their standing in public opinion, and to guarantee that they could depend on others in old age, they had to share. However, sharing was a powerful leveling mechanism. It drained surplus wealth and restricted upward mobility.

How, specifically, did this leveling work? As is often true in stratified nations, Brazilian national cultural norms are set by the upper classes. Middle- and upper-class Brazilians usually marry legally and in church. Even Arembepeiros knew this was the only "proper" way to marry. The most successful and ambitious local men copied the behavior of elite Brazilians. By doing so, they hoped to acquire some of their prestige.

TABLE 19.1 Changes in Family and Household Organization in the United States, 1970 versus 2010

	1970	2010
Numbers:		
Total number of households	63 million	118 million
Number of people per household	3.1	2.6
Percentages:		
Married couples living with children	40%	21%
Family households	81%	67%
Households with five or more people	21%	10%
People living alone	17%	27%
Percentage of single-mother families	5%	11%
Percentage of single-father families	0%	3%
Households with own children under 18	45%	30%

SOURCES: From U.S. Census data in J. M. Fields, "America's Families and Living Arrangements: 2003," *Current Population Reports,* P20-553, November 2004, http://www.census.gov/prod/2004pubs/p20-553.pdf, p. 4; J. M. Fields and L. M. Casper, "America's Families and Living Arrangements: Population Characteristics, 2000," *Current Population Reports,* P20-537, June 2001, http://www.census.gov/prod/2001pubs/p20-537.pdf; U.S. Census Bureau, *Statistical Abstract of the United States 2012,* Tables 59, 62, http://www.census.gov/prod/2011pubs/12statab/pop.pdf.compendia/statab/2009edition.html.

However, legal marriage drained individual wealth, for example, by creating a responsibility to help one's in-laws financially. Such obligations could be regular and costly. Obligations to kids also increased with income, because successful people tended to have more living children. Children were valued as companions and as an eventual economic benefit to their parents. Boys especially were prized because their economic prospects were so much brighter than those of girls.

Children's chances of survival surged dramatically in wealthier households with better diets. The normal household diet included fish—usually in a stew with tomatoes, onions, palm oil, vinegar, and lemon. Dried beef replaced fish once a week. Roasted manioc flour was the main source of calories and was eaten at all meals. Other daily staples included coffee, sugar, and salt. Fruits and vegetables were eaten in season. Diet was one of the main contrasts between households. The poorest people didn't eat fish regularly; often they subsisted on manioc flour, coffee, and sugar. Better-off households supplemented the staples with milk, butter, eggs, rice, beans, and more ample portions of fresh fish, fruits, and vegetables.

Adequate incomes bought improved diets and provided the means and confidence to seek out better medical attention than was locally available. Most of the children born in the wealthier households survived. But this meant more mouths to feed, and (since the heads of such households usually wanted a better education for their children) it meant increased expenditures on schooling. The correlation between economic success and large families was a siphoner of wealth that restricted individual economic advance. Tomé, a fishing entrepreneur, envisioned a life of constant hard work if he was to feed, clothe, and educate his growing family. Tomé and his wife had never lost a child. But he recognized that his growing family would, in the short run, be a drain on his resources. "But in the end, I'll have successful sons to help their mother and me, if we need it, in our old age."

Arembepeiros knew who could afford to share with others; success can't be concealed in a small community. Villagers based their expectations of others on this knowledge. Successful people had to share with more kin and in-laws, and with more distant kin, than did poorer people. Successful captains and boat owners were expected to buy beer for ordinary fishermen; store owners had to sell on credit. As in bands and tribes, any well-off person was expected to exhibit a corresponding generosity. With increasing wealth, people also were asked more frequently to enter ritual kin relationships. Through baptism—which took place twice a year when a priest visited, or which could be done outside—a child acquired two godparents. These people became the coparents (*compadres*) of the baby's parents. The fact that ritual kinship obligations increased with wealth was another factor limiting individual economic advance.

We see that kinship, marriage, and ritual kinship in Arembepe had costs and benefits. The costs were limits on the economic advance of individuals. The primary benefit was social security—guaranteed help from kin, in-laws, and ritual kin in times of need. Benefits, however, came only after costs had been paid—that is, only to those who had lived "proper" lives, not deviating too noticeably from local norms, especially those about sharing.

(Note, however, that each divorce creates two divorced people.) Table 19.2 shows the ratio of divorces to marriages in the United States for selected years between 1950 and 2010. A major jump in the divorce rate took place between 1960 and 1980. During that period the ratio of divorces to marriages doubled. Between 1980 and 2000, the ratio hovered around 50 percent. That is, each year there were about half as many new divorces as there were new marriages. Since 2000 the rate has drifted up, to 55 percent in 2010.

The rate of growth in single-parent households also has outstripped population growth, almost tripling from fewer than 4 million in 1970 to 10.6 million in 2010. (The overall American population in 2010 was 1.5 times its size in 1970.) The percentage (23.1 percent) of children living in fatherless (mother-headed, no resident dad) households in 2010 was more than twice the 1970 rate, while the percentage (3.4 percent) in motherless (father-headed, no resident mom) homes increased four-fold. About 56 percent of American women and 59 percent of American men were currently married in 2009, versus 60 and 65 percent, respectively, in 1970 (Fields 2004; Fields and Casper 2001; *Statistical Abstract of the United States 2012*). However, census data reveal that more American women now live without a husband than with one. By 2005, 51 percent of women said they were living without a spouse, compared with 35 percent in 1950 and 49 percent in 2000 (Roberts et al. 2007). To be sure, contemporary Americans maintain social lives through work, friendship, sports, clubs, religion, and organized social activities. However, the growing isolation from kin that these figures suggest may well be unprecedented in human history.

Table 19.3 documents similar changes in family and household size in the United States and Canada between 1980 and 2010. Those figures confirm a general trend toward smaller families and living units in North America. This trend is also detectable in Western Europe and other industrial nations.

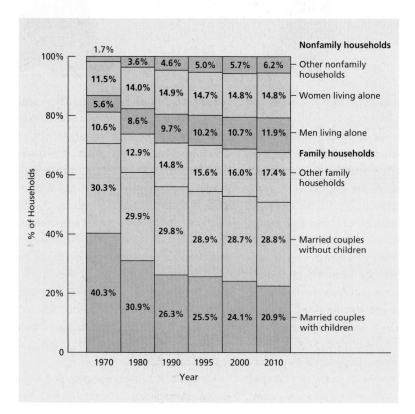

FIGURE 19.2 Households by Type: Selected Years, 1970 to 2010 (Percent Distribution).

SOURCES: J. M. Fields, "America's Families and Living Arrangements: 2003," *Current Population Reports*, P20-553, November 2004, http://www.census.gov/prod/2004pubs/p20-553.pdf, p. 4; *Statistical Abstract of the United States 2012*, Table 59, 62 http://www.census.gov/prod/2011pubs/12statab/pop.pdf.

TABLE 19.3 Household and Family Size in the United States and Canada, 1980 versus 2010

	1980	2010
Average family size:		
United States	3.3	3.1
Canada	3.4	3.0
Average household size:		
United States	2.9	2.6
Canada	2.9	2.6

SOURCES: J. M. Fields, "America's Families and Living Arrangements: 2003," *Current Population Reports*, P20-553, November 2004, http://www.census.gov/prod/2004pubs/p20-553.pdf, pp. 3–4; *Statistics Canada*, 2006 Census, http://www12.statcan.ca/english/census06/data/topics/; *Statistical Abstract of the United States 2012*, Table 62, http://www.census.gov/prod/2011pubs/12statab/pop.pdf.

The entire range of kin attachments is narrower for North Americans, particularly those in the middle class, than it is for nonindustrial peoples. Although we recognize ties to grandparents, uncles, aunts, and cousins, we have less contact with, and depend less on, those relatives than people in other cultures do. We see this when we answer a few questions: Do we know exactly how we are related to all our cousins? How much do we know about our ancestors, such as their full names and where they lived? How many of the people with whom we associate regularly are our relatives?

Differences in the answers to these questions by people from industrial and those from nonindustrial societies confirm the declining importance of kinship in contemporary nations. Immigrants are often shocked by what they perceive as weak kinship bonds and lack of proper respect for family in contemporary North America. In fact, most of the people whom middle-class North Americans see every day are either nonrelatives or members of the nuclear family. On the other hand, Stack's (1975) study of families in a ghetto area of a midwestern city showed that sharing with nonnuclear relatives is an important strategy that the urban poor use to adapt to poverty (see also Willie and Reddick 2009).

One of the most striking contrasts between the United States and Brazil, the two most populous nations of the Western Hemisphere, is in the meaning and role of the family. Contemporary North American adults usually define their families as consisting of their husbands or wives and their children. However, when middle-class Brazilians talk about their families, they mean their parents, siblings, aunts, uncles, grandparents, and cousins. Later they add their children, but rarely the husband or wife, who has his or her own family. The children are shared by the two families. Because middle-class Americans lack an extended family support system, marriage assumes more importance. The husband–wife relationship is supposed to take precedence over either spouse's relationship with his or her own parents. This places a significant strain on North American marriages.

Living in a less mobile society, Brazilians stay in closer contact with their relatives, including members of the extended family, than North Americans do. Residents of Rio de Janeiro and São Paulo, two of

TABLE 19.2 Ratio of Divorces to Marriages per 1,000 U.S. Population, Selected Years, 1950–2010

1950	1960	1970	1980	1990	2000	2010
23%	26%	33%	50%	48%	49%	55%

SOURCE: *Statistical Abstract of the United States 2009*, Table 77, p. 63; *Statistical Abstract of the United States 2012*, Table 132, http://www.census.gov/prod/2011pubs/12statab/pop.pdf

South America's largest cities, are reluctant to leave those urban centers to live away from family and friends. Brazilians find it hard to imagine, and unpleasant to live in, social worlds without relatives. Contrast this with a characteristic American theme: learning to live with strangers.

The Family among Foragers

Populations with foraging economies are far removed from industrial societies in terms of social complexity, but they do feature geographic mobility, which is associated with nomadic or seminomadic hunting and gathering. Here again the nuclear family is often the most significant kin group, although in no foraging society is the nuclear family the only group based on kinship. The two basic social units of traditional foraging societies are the nuclear family and the band.

Unlike middle-class couples in industrial nations, foragers don't usually reside neolocally. Instead, they join a band in which either the husband or the wife has relatives. However, couples and families may move from one band to another several times (see Hill, Walker et al. 2011). Although nuclear families are ultimately as impermanent among foragers as they are in any other society, they are usually more stable than bands are.

Many foraging societies lacked year-round band organization. The Native American Shoshoni of the Great Basin in Utah and Nevada (Figure 19.3) provide an example. The resources available to the Shoshoni were so meager that for most of the year families traveled alone through the countryside hunting and gathering. In certain seasons families assembled to hunt cooperatively as a band; after just a few months together they dispersed (see Fowler and Fowler 2008).

In neither industrial nor foraging societies are people tied permanently to the land. The mobility and the emphasis on small, economically self-sufficient family units promote the nuclear family as a basic kin group in both types of societies.

DESCENT

We've seen that the nuclear family is important in industrial nations and among foragers. The analogous group among nonindustrial food producers is the descent group, a permanent social unit whose members say they have ancestors in common. Descent-group members believe they share, and descend from, those common ancestors. The group endures even though its membership changes, as members are born and die, move in and move out. Often, descent-group membership is determined at birth and is lifelong. In this case, it is an ascribed status.

Descent Groups

Descent groups frequently are exogamous (members must seek their mates from other descent groups). Two common rules serve to admit certain people as

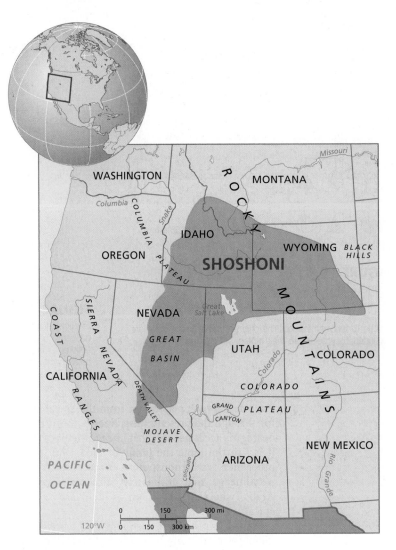

FIGURE 19.3 Location of the Shoshoni.

descent-group members while excluding others. With a rule of *matrilineal descent,* people join the mother's group automatically at birth and stay members throughout life. With *patrilineal descent,* people automatically have lifetime membership in the father's group. (In Figures 19.4 and 19.5, which show matrilineal and patrilineal descent groups, respectively, the triangles stand for males and the circles for females.) Matrilineal and patrilineal descent are types of **unilineal descent.** This means the descent rule uses one line only, either the male or the female line.

Descent groups may be **lineages** or **clans.** Common to both is the belief that members descend from the same *apical ancestor.* That person stands at the apex, or top, of the common genealogy. For example, Adam and Eve, according to the Bible, are the apical ancestors of all humanity. Since Eve is said to have come from Adam's rib, Adam stands as the original apical ancestor for the patrilineal genealogies laid out in the Bible.

How do lineages and clans differ? A lineage uses *demonstrated descent.* Members can name their

unilineal descent
Matrilineal or patrilineal descent.

lineage
Unilineal descent group based on demonstrated descent.

clan
Unilineal descent group based on stipulated descent.

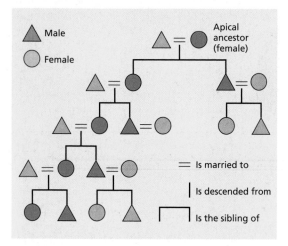

FIGURE 19.4 A Matrilineage Five Generations Deep.

Matrilineages are based on demonstrated descent from a female ancestor. Only the children of the group's women (blue) belong to the matrilineage. The children of the group's men are excluded; they belong to their mother's matrilineage.

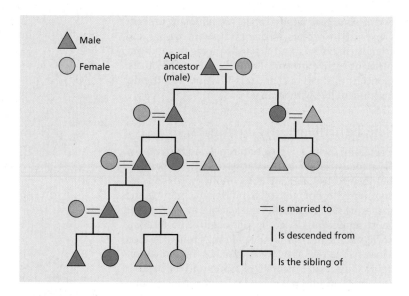

FIGURE 19.5 A Patrilineage Five Generations Deep.

Lineages are based on demonstrated descent from a common ancestor. With patrilineal descent, children of the group's men (blue) are included as descent-group members. Children of the group's female members are excluded; they belong to their father's patrilineage. Also notice lineage exogamy.

forebears in each generation from the apical ancestor through the present. (This doesn't mean the genealogy is accurate, only that lineage members think it is.) In the Bible the litany of men who "begat" other men is a demonstration of descent for a large patrilineage that ultimately includes Jews and Arabs (who share Abraham as their last common apical ancestor).

Unlike lineages, clans use *stipulated descent.* Clan members merely say they descend from the apical ancestor. They don't try to trace the actual genealogical links between themselves and that ancestor. The Betsileo of Madagascar have both clans and lineages. Descent may be demonstrated for the most recent eight to ten generations, then stipulated for the more remote past—sometimes with mermaids and vaguely defined foreign royalty mentioned among the founders (Kottak 1980). Like the Betsileo, many societies have both lineages and clans. In such a case, clans have more members and cover a larger geographic area than lineages do. Sometimes a clan's apical ancestor is not a human at all but an animal or plant (called a *totem*). Whether human or not, the ancestor symbolizes the social unity and identity of the members, distinguishing them from other groups.

The economic types that usually have descent-group organization are horticulture, pastoralism, and agriculture, as discussed in the chapter "Making a Living." Such societies tend to have several descent groups. Any one of them may be confined to a single village, but they usually span more than one village. Any branch of a descent group that lives in one place is a *local descent group.* Two or more local branches of different descent groups may live in the same village. Descent groups in the same village or different villages may establish alliances through frequent intermarriage.

Lineages, Clans, and Residence Rules

As we've seen, descent groups, unlike nuclear families, are permanent units, with new members gained and lost in each generation. Members have access to the lineage estate, where some of them must live, in order to benefit from and manage that estate across the generations. To endure, descent groups need to keep at least some of their members at home. An easy way to do this is to have a rule about who belongs to the descent group and where they should live after they get married. Patrilineal and matrilineal descent, and the postmarital residence rules that usually accompany them, ensure that about half the people born in each generation will live out their lives on the ancestral estate. Neolocal residence, which is the rule for most middle-class Americans, isn't very common outside modern North America, Western Europe, and the European-derived cultures of Latin America and modern Australia and New Zealand.

Much more common is *patrilocality:* A married couple moves to the husband's father's community, so that the children will grow up in their father's village. Patrilocality is associated with patrilineal descent. This makes sense. If the group's male members are expected to exercise their rights in the ancestral estate, it's a good idea to raise them on that estate and to keep them there after they marry.

A less common postmarital residence rule, associated with matrilineal descent, is *matrilocality:* Married couples live in the wife's mother's community, and their children grow up in their mother's village.

Together, patrilocality and matri-locality are known as *unilocal* rules of postmarital residence.

Ambilineal Descent

The descent rules examined so far admit certain people as members while excluding others. A unilineal rule uses one line only, either the female or the male. Besides the unilineal rules, there is another descent rule called nonunilineal or **ambilineal** descent. As in any descent group, membership comes through descent from a common ancestor. However, ambilineal groups differ from unilineal groups in that they do not *automatically* exclude either the children of sons or those of daughters. People can choose the descent group they join (e.g., that of their father's father, father's mother, mother's father, or mother's mother). People also can change their descent-group membership, or belong to two or more groups at the same time.

Unilineal descent is a matter of ascribed status; ambilineal descent illustrates achieved status. With unilineal descent, membership is automatic; no choice is permitted. People are born members of their father's group in a patrilineal society or of their mother's group in a matrilineal society. They are members of that group for life. Ambilineal descent permits more flexibility in descent-group affiliation.

Before 1950, descent groups were generally described simply as patrilineal or matrilineal. If the society tended toward patrilineality, the anthropologist classified it as a patrilineal rather than an ambilineal group. The treatment of ambilineal descent as a separate category was a formal recognition that many descent systems are flexible—some more so than others.

Family versus Descent

There are rights, duties, and obligations associated with kinship and descent. Many societies have both families and descent groups. Obligations to one may conflict with obligations to the other—more so in matrilineal than in patrilineal societies. In the latter, a woman typically leaves home when she marries and raises her children in her husband's community. After leaving home, she has no primary or substantial obligations to her own descent group. She can invest fully in her children, who will become members of her husband's group. In a matrilineal society things are different. A man has strong obligations both to his family of procreation (his wife and children) and to his closest matrikin (his sisters and their children). The continuity of his descent group depends on his sisters and their children, since descent is carried by females, and he has descent-based obligations to look out for their welfare. He also has obligations to his wife and children. If a man is sure his wife's children are his own, he has more incentive to invest in them than is the case if he has doubts.

Compared with patrilineal systems, matrilineal societies tend to have higher divorce rates and greater

Most societies have a prevailing opinion about where couples should live after they marry; this is called a postmarital residence rule. A common rule is patrilocality: the couple lives with the husband's relatives, so that children grow up in their father's community. The top image, taken in 2001, shows a 13-year-old Muslim bride (veiled in pink) in the West African country of Guinea Bissau. On the last day of her three-day wedding ceremony, she will collect laundry from her husband's family, wash it with her friends, and be taken to his village on a bicycle. In the bottom image, in Lendak, Slovakia, women transport part of the bride's dowry to the groom's house.

female promiscuity (Schneider and Gough 1961). According to Nicholas Kottak (2002), among the matrilineal Makua of northern Mozambique, a husband is concerned about his wife's potential promiscuity. A man's sister also takes an interest in her brother's wife's fidelity; she doesn't want her brother wasting time on children who may not be his, thus diminishing his investment as an uncle (mother's brother) in her children. A confessional ritual that is part of the Makua birthing process demonstrates the sister's allegiance

ambilineal
Flexible descent rule, neither patrilineal nor matrilineal.

When Are Two Dads Better than One?— When the Women Are in Charge

Like race, kinship is socially constructed. Cultures develop their own explanations for biological processes, including the role of insemination in the creation and growth of a human embryo. Scientifically informed people know that fertilization of an ovum by a single sperm is responsible for conception. But other cultures, including the Barí and their neighbors, hold different views about procreation. In some societies it is believed that spirits, rather than men, place babies in women's wombs. In others it is believed that a fetus must be nourished by continuing insemination during pregnancy.

There are cultures, including the Barí and others described here, in which people believe that multiple men can create the same fetus. When a baby is born, the Barí mother names the men she recognizes as fathers, and they help her raise the child. In the United States, having two dads may be the result of divorce,

remarriage, stepparenthood, or a same-sex union. In the societies discussed here, multiple (partible) paternity is a common and beneficial social fact.

[Among] the Barí people of Venezuela, . . . multiple paternity is the norm. . . . In such societies, children with more than one official father are more likely to survive to adulthood than those with just one Dad. . . . The findings have . . . been published in a book, *Cultures of Multiple Fathers: The Theory and Practice of Partible Paternity in Lowland South America* [Beckerman and Valentine 2002], that questions accepted theories about social organization, the balance of power between the sexes and human evolution.

[The book] . . . draws on more than two decades of fieldwork among South American tribal peoples. The central theme . . . is the concept of partible paternity—the widespread belief that fertilization is not a one-time event and that

The Barí of Venezuela believe that a child can have multiple fathers.

to her brother. When a wife is deep in labor, the husband's sister, who attends her, must ask, "Who is the real father of this child?" If the wife lies, the Makua believe the birth will be difficult, often ending in the death of the woman and/or the baby. This ritual serves as an important social paternity test. It is in both the husband's and his sister's interest to ensure that his wife's children are indeed his own.

KINSHIP CALCULATION

In addition to studying kin groups, anthropologists are interested in **kinship calculation:** the system by which people in a society reckon kin relationships. To study kinship calculation, an ethnographer must first determine the word or words for different types of "relatives" used in a particular language and then ask questions such as, "Who are your relatives?" Like race and gender (discussed in other chapters), kinship is culturally constructed. This means that some genealogical kin are considered to be relatives whereas others are not. It also means that even people who aren't

genealogical relatives can be constructed socially as kin. Read this chapter's "Appreciating Anthropology," which describes ethnographic findings about the Barí of Venezuela. The Barí recognize multiple fathers, even though biologically there can be only one actual genitor. Cultures develop their own explanations for biological processes, including the role of insemination in the creation and growth of a human embryo.

Through questioning, the ethnographer discovers the specific genealogical relationships between "relatives" and the person who has named them— the **ego**. *Ego* means I (or *me*) in Latin. It's who you, the reader, are in the kin charts that follow. It's your perspective looking out on your kin. By posing the same questions to several local people, the ethnographer learns about the extent and direction of kinship calculation in that society. The ethnographer also begins to understand the relationship between kinship calculation and kin groups: how people use kinship to create and maintain personal ties and to join social groups. In the kinship charts that follow, the gray square labeled "ego" identifies the person whose kinship calculation is being examined.

more than one father can contribute to the developing embryo. . . .

The authors have discovered a strong correlation between the status of women in the society and the benefits of multiple paternity. . . . Among the Barí, 80% of children with two or more official dads survive to adulthood, compared with 64% with one father. This contrasts with male-dominated cultures such as the neighboring Curripaco, where children of doubtful parentage are outcast and frequently die young.

Explaining the significance of this discovery, Paul Valentine said: "The conventional view of the male-female bargain is that a man will provide food and shelter for a woman and her children if he can be assured that the children are biologically his. Our research turns this idea on its head. . . . In societies where women control marriages and other aspects of social life, both men and women have multiple partners and spread the responsibilities of child rearing." It is of course scientifically impossible to have more than one biological father, but aboriginal peoples in South America, Africa and Australasia [Australia and Asia] believe that it takes more than one act of intercourse to make a baby. In some of these societies, nearly all children have multiple fathers. In others, while partible paternity is accepted, socially the child has only one father. However, in the middle are groups where some children do have multiple fathers and some do not. In this case, the children can be compared to see how having more than one father benefits the children—and generational studies show that the children do benefit from the extra care.

When a child is born among the Barí, the mother publicly announces the names of the one or more men she believes to be the fathers, who, if they accept paternity, are expected to provide care for the mother and child. . . . "In small egalitarian societies, women's interests are best served if mate choice is a non-binding, female decision; if a network of multiple females to aid or substitute for a woman in her mothering responsibilities exists; if multiple men support a woman and her children; and if a woman is shielded from the effects of male sexual jealousy." . . .

In cultures where women choose their mates, women have broad sexual freedom and partible paternity is accepted, women clearly have the upper hand. In Victorian-style societies where women's sexual activity is controlled by men, marriage is exclusive and male sexual jealousy is a constant threat, men have the upper hand. In between is a full range of combinations and options, all represented in the varying South American cultures. . . .

Robert Carneiro, curator at the American Museum of Natural History, said: "Rarely does a book thrust open a door, giving us a striking new view. It has long been known that . . . peoples around the world believe that one act of sexual intercourse is not enough for a child to be born. Now for the first time we have a volume that deals with the consequences and ramifications of this belief, and it does so in exhaustive and fascinating detail." . . .

SOURCE: Patrick Wilson, "When Are Two Dads Better Than One? When the Women Are in Charge," http://alphagalileo.org (June 12, 2002). Reprinted by permission of the University of East London, UK.

Genealogical Kin Types and Kin Terms

At this point, we may distinguish between *kin terms* (the words used for different relatives in a particular language) and *genealogical kin types*. We designate genealogical kin types with the letters and symbols shown in Figure 19.6. *Genealogical kin type* refers to an actual genealogical relationship (e.g., father's brother) as opposed to a kin term (e.g., *uncle*).

Kin terms reflect the social construction of kinship in a given culture. A kin term may (and usually does) lump together several genealogical relationships. In English, for instance, we use *father* primarily for one kin type: the genealogical father. However, *father* can be extended to an adoptive father or stepfather—and even to a priest. *Grandfather* includes mother's father and father's father. The term *cousin* lumps together several kin types. Even the more specific *first cousin* includes mother's brother's son (MBS), mother's brother's daughter (MBD), mother's sister's son (MZS), mother's sister's daughter (MZD), father's brother's son (FBS), father's brother's daughter (FBD), father's sister's son (FZS), and father's sister's daughter (FZD). *First cousin* thus lumps together at least eight genealogical kin types.

Uncle encompasses mother's and father's brothers, and *aunt* includes mother's and father's sisters. We also use *uncle* and *aunt* for the spouses of our "blood" aunts and uncles. We use the same term for mother's brother and father's brother because we perceive them as being the same sort of relative. Calling them *uncles*, we distinguish between them and another kin type, F, whom we call *Father, Dad,* or *Pop*. In many societies, however, it is common to call a father and a father's brother by the same term. Later we'll see why.

In the United States and Canada, the nuclear family continues to be the most important group based on kinship. This is true despite an increased incidence of single parenthood, divorce, and remarriage. The nuclear family's relative isolation from other kin groups in modern nations reflects geographic mobility within an industrial economy with sale of labor for cash.

It's reasonable for North Americans to distinguish between relatives who belong to their nuclear families and those who don't. We are more likely to grow up

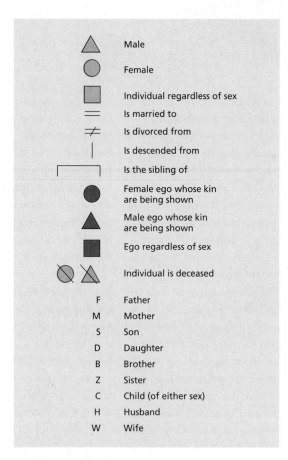

	Male
	Female
	Individual regardless of sex
	Is married to
	Is divorced from
	Is descended from
	Is the sibling of
	Female ego whose kin are being shown
	Male ego whose kin are being shown
	Ego regardless of sex
	Individual is deceased
F	Father
M	Mother
S	Son
D	Daughter
B	Brother
Z	Sister
C	Child (of either sex)
H	Husband
W	Wife

FIGURE 19.6 Kinship Symbols and Genealogical Kin Type Notation.

bilateral kinship calculation
Kin ties calculated equally through men and women.

A neolocal American nuclear family in front of their home. The nuclear family's relative isolation from other kin groups in modern nations reflects geographic mobility within an industrial economy with sale of labor for cash.

with our parents than with our aunts and uncles. We tend to see our parents more often than we see our uncles and aunts, who may live in different towns and cities. We often inherit from our parents, but our cousins have first claim to inherit from our aunts and uncles. If our marriage is stable, we see our children daily as long as they remain at home. They are our heirs. We feel closer to them than to our nieces and nephews.

American kinship calculation and kin terminology reflect these social features. Thus, the term *uncle* distinguishes between the kin types MB and FB on the one hand and the kin type F on the other. However, this term also lumps kin types together. We use the same term for MB and FB, two different kin types. We do this because American kinship calculation is **bilateral**—traced equally through males and females, for example, father and mother. Both kinds of uncle are brothers of one of our parents. We think of both as roughly the same kind of relative.

"No," you may object, "I'm closer to my mother's brother than to my father's brother." That may be. However, in a representative sample of Americans, we would find a split, with some favoring one side and some favoring the other. We'd actually expect a bit of *matrilateral skewing*—a preference for relatives on the mother's side. This occurs for many reasons. When contemporary children are raised by just one parent, it's much more likely to be the mother than the father. Also, even with intact marriages, the wife tends to play a more active role in managing family affairs, including family visits, reunions, holidays, and extended family relations, than the husband does. This would tend to reinforce her kin network over his and thus favor matrilateral skewing.

Bilateral kinship means that people tend to perceive kin links through males and females as being similar or equivalent. This bilaterality is expressed in interaction with, living with or near, and rights to inherit from relatives. We don't usually inherit from uncles, but if we do, there's about as much chance that we'll inherit from the father's brother as from the mother's brother. We usually don't live with an aunt, but if we do, it might be either the mother's sister or the father's sister.

KINSHIP TERMINOLOGY

People perceive and define kin relations differently in different societies. In any culture, kinship terminology is a classification system, a taxonomy or typology. It is a *native taxonomy,* developed over generations by the people who live in a particular society. A native classification system is based on how people perceive similarities and differences in the things being classified.

However, anthropologists have discovered that there are a limited number of patterns in which people classify their kin. People who speak very different languages may use exactly the same system of kinship terminology. This section examines the four main ways of classifying kin on the parental generation: lineal, bifurcate merging, generational, and bifurcate collateral. We also consider the social correlates of these classification systems. (Note that each of the systems described here applies to the parental generation. There also are differences in kin terminology on ego's generation. These systems involve the classification of siblings and cousins. There are six such systems, called Eskimo, Iroquois, Hawaiian, Crow, Omaha, and Sudanese cousin terminology, after societies that traditionally used them. You can see them diagrammed and discussed at the following websites: http://anthro.palomar.edu/kinship/kinship_5.htm; http://anthro.palomar.edu/kinship/kinship_6.htm; http://www.umanitoba.ca/faculties/arts/anthropology/tutor/kinterms/termsys.html.)

A **functional explanation** will be offered for each system of kinship terminology, such as lineal, bifurcate merging, and generational terminology. Functional explanations attempt to relate particular customs (such as the use of kin terms) to other features of a society, such as rules of descent and postmarital residence. Certain aspects of a culture are *functions* of others. That is, they are correlated variables, so that when one of them changes, the others inevitably change too. For certain terminologies, the social correlates are very clear.

Kin terms provide useful information about social patterns. If two relatives are designated by the same term, we can assume that they are perceived as sharing socially significant attributes. Several factors influence the way people interact with, perceive, and classify relatives. For instance, do certain kinds of relatives customarily live together or apart? How far apart? What benefits do they derive from each other, and what are their obligations? Are they members of the same descent group or of different descent groups? With these questions in mind, let's examine systems of kinship terminology.

Lineal Terminology

Our own system of kinship classification is called the *lineal system* (Figure 19.7). The number 3 and the color light blue stand for the term *uncle*, which we apply both to FB and to MB. **Lineal kinship terminology** is found in societies such as the United States and Canada in which the nuclear family is the most important group based on kinship.

Lineal kinship terminology has absolutely nothing to do with lineages, which are found in very different social contexts. (What contexts are those?) Lineal kinship terminology gets its name from the fact that it distinguishes lineal relatives from collateral relatives. What does that mean? A **lineal relative** is an ancestor or descendant, anyone on the direct *line* of descent that leads to and from ego (Figure 19.8). Thus, lineal relatives are one's parents, grandparents, great-grandparents, and other direct forebears. Lineal relatives also include children, grandchildren, and

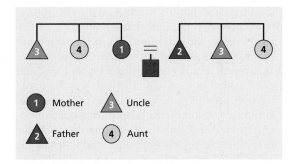

FIGURE 19.7 Lineal Kinship Terminology.

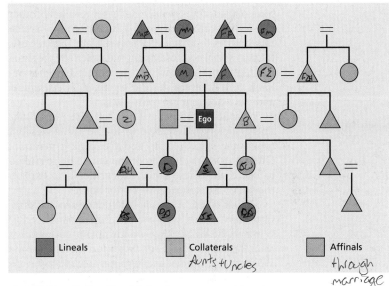

FIGURE 19.8 The Distinctions among Lineals, Collaterals, and Affinals as Perceived by Ego.

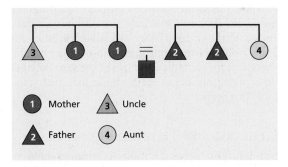

FIGURE 19.9 Bifurcate Merging Kinship Terminology.

great-grandchildren. **Collateral relatives** are all other kin. They include siblings, nieces and nephews, aunts and uncles, and cousins (Figure 19.8). **Affinals** are relatives by marriage, whether of lineals (e.g., son's wife) or of collaterals (sister's husband).

Bifurcate Merging Terminology

Bifurcate merging kinship terminology (Figure 19.9) *bifurcates*, or splits, the mother's side and

functional explanation
One based on correlation or co-occurrence of social variables.

lineal kinship terminology
Four parental kin terms: M, F, FB=MB, and MZ=FZ.

lineal relative
Ego's direct ancestors and descendants.

collateral relative
Relative outside ego's direct line, e.g., B, Z, FB, MZ.

affinals
Relatives by marriage.

bifurcate merging kinship terminology
Four parental kin terms: M=MZ, F=FB, MB, and FZ each stands alone.

the father's side. But it also *merges* same-sex siblings of each parent. Thus, mother and mother's sister are merged under the same term (1), while father and father's brother also get a common term (2). There are different terms for mother's brother (3) and father's sister (4).

People use this system in societies with unilineal (patrilineal and matrilineal) descent rules and unilocal (patrilocal and matrilocal) postmarital residence rules. When the society is unilineal and unilocal, the logic of bifurcate merging terminology is fairly clear. In a patrilineal society, for example, father and father's brother belong to the same descent group, gender, and generation. Since patrilineal societies usually have patrilocal residence, the father and his brother live in the same local group. Because they share so many attributes that are socially relevant, ego regards them as social equivalents and calls them by the same kinship term—2. However, the mother's brother belongs to a different descent group, lives elsewhere, and has a different kin term—3.

What about mother and mother's sister in a patrilineal society? They belong to the same descent group, the same gender, and the same generation. Often they marry men from the same village and go to live there. These social similarities help explain the use of the same term—1—for both.

Similar observations apply to matrilineal societies. Consider a society with two matrilineal clans, the Ravens and the Wolves. Ego is a member of his mother's clan, the Raven clan. Ego's father is a member of the Wolf clan. His mother and her sister are female Ravens of the same generation. If there is matrilocal residence, as there often is in matrilineal societies, they will live in the same village. Because they are so similar socially, ego calls them by the same kin term—1.

The father's sister, however, belongs to a different group, the Wolves; lives elsewhere; and has a different kin term—4. Ego's father and father's brother are male Wolves of the same generation. If they marry women of the same clan and live in the same village, this creates additional social similarities that reinforce this usage.

Generational Terminology

generational kinship terminology

Just two parental kin terms: M=MZ=FZ and F=FB=MB.

Like bifurcate merging kinship terminology, **generational kinship terminology** uses the same term for parents and their siblings, but the lumping is more complete (Figure 19.10). With generational terminology, there are only two terms for the parental *generation*. We may translate them as "father" and "mother," but more accurate translations would be "male member of the parental generation" and "female member of the parental generation."

Generational kinship terminology does not distinguish between the mother's and father's sides. It does not bifurcate, but it certainly does merge. It uses just one term for father, father's brother, and mother's brother. In a unilineal society, these three kin types would never belong to the same descent

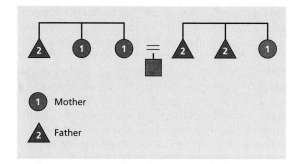

FIGURE 19.10 Generational Kinship Terminology.

group. Generational kinship terminology also uses a single term for mother, mother's sister, and father's sister. Nor, in a unilineal society, would these three ever be members of the same group.

Nevertheless, generational terminology suggests closeness between ego and his or her aunts and uncles—much more closeness than exists between Americans and these kin types. How likely would you be to call your uncle "Dad" or your aunt "Mom"? We'd expect to find generational terminology in societies in which extended kinship is much more important than it is in our own but in which there is no rigid distinction between the father's side and the mother's side.

It's logical, then, that generational kin terminology is found in societies with ambilineal descent, where descent-group membership is not automatic. People may choose the group they join, change their descent-group membership, or belong to two or more descent groups simultaneously. Generational terminology fits these conditions. The use of intimate kin terms signals that people have close personal relations with all their relatives of the parental generation. People exhibit similar behavior toward their aunts, uncles, and parents. Someday they'll have to choose a descent group to join. Furthermore, in ambilineal societies, postmarital residence is usually ambilocal. This means that the married couple can live with either the husband's or the wife's group.

Significantly, generational terminology also characterizes certain foraging bands, including Kalahari San groups and several native societies of North America. Use of this terminology reflects certain similarities between foraging bands and ambilineal descent groups. In both societies, people have a choice about their kin-group affiliation. Foragers always live with kin, but they often shift band affiliation and so may be members of several different bands during their lifetimes. Just as in food-producing societies with ambilineal descent, generational terminology among foragers helps maintain close personal relationships with several parental-generation relatives whom ego may eventually use as a point of entry into different groups. Recap 19.1 lists the types of kin group, the postmarital residence rule, and the economy associated with the four types of kinship terminology.

KINSHIP TERMINOLOGY	KIN GROUP	RESIDENCE RULE	ECONOMY
Lineal	Nuclear family	Neolocal	Industrialism, foraging
Bifurcate merging	Unilineal descent group— patrilineal or matrilineal	Unilocal—patrilocal or matrilocal	Horticulture, pastoralism, agriculture
Generational	Ambilineal descent group, band	Ambilocal	Agriculture, horticulture, foraging
Bifurcate collateral	Varies	Varies	Varies

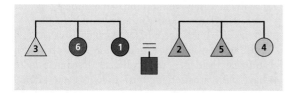

FIGURE 19.11 Bifurcate Collateral Kinship Terminology.

Bifurcate Collateral Terminology

Of the four kin classification systems, **bifurcate collateral kinship terminology** is the most specific. It has separate terms for each of the six kin types of the parental generation (Figure 19.11). Bifurcate collateral terminology isn't as common as the other types. Many of the societies that use it are in North Africa and the Middle East, and many of them are offshoots of the same ancestral group.

Bifurcate collateral terminology also may be used when a child has parents of different ethnic backgrounds and uses terms for aunts and uncles derived from different languages. Thus, if you have a mother who is Latina and a father who is Anglo, you may call your aunts and uncles on your mother's side "tia" and "tio," while calling those on your father's side "aunt" and "uncle." And your mother and father may be "Mom" and "Pop." That's a modern form of bifurcate collateral kinship terminology.

bifurcate collateral kinship terminology
Six separate parental kin terms: M, F, MB, MZ, FB, and FZ.

acing the **COURSE**

1. In nonindustrial societies, kinship, descent, and marriage organize social and political life. In studying kinship, we must distinguish between kin groups, whose composition and activities can be observed, and kinship calculation—how people identify and designate their relatives.

2. One widespread kin group is the nuclear family, consisting of a married couple and their children. There are functional alternatives to the nuclear family. That is, other groups may assume functions usually associated with the nuclear family. Nuclear families tend to be especially important in foraging

summary

and industrial societies. Among farmers and herders, other kinds of kin groups often overshadow the nuclear family.

3. In contemporary North America, the nuclear family is the characteristic kin group for the middle class. Expanded households and sharing with extended family kin occur more frequently among the poor, who may pool their resources in dealing with poverty. Today, however, even in the American middle class, nuclear family households are declining as single-person households and other domestic arrangements increase.

4. The descent group is a basic kin group among nonindustrial food producers (farmers and herders). Unlike families, descent groups have perpetuity—they last for generations. Descent-group members share and manage a common estate: land, animals, and other resources. There are several kinds of descent groups. Lineages are based on demonstrated descent; clans, on stipulated descent. Descent rules may be unilineal or ambilineal. Unilineal (patrilineal and matrilineal) descent is associated with unilocal (respectively, patrilocal and matrilocal) postmarital residence. Obligations to one's descent group and to one's family of procreation may conflict, especially in matrilineal societies.

5. A kinship terminology is a classification of relatives based on perceived differences and similarities. Comparative research has revealed a limited number of ways of classifying kin. Because there are correlations between kinship terminology and other social practices, we often can predict kinship terminology from other aspects of culture. The four basic kinship terminologies for the parental generation are lineal, bifurcate merging, generational, and bifurcate collateral. Many foraging and industrial societies use lineal terminology, which is associated with nuclear family organization. Cultures with unilocal residence and unilineal descent tend to have bifurcate merging terminology. Generational terminology correlates with ambilineal descent and ambilocal residence.

key terms

affinals 441
ambilineal 437
bifurcate collateral kinship terminology 443
bifurcate merging kinship terminology 441
bilateral kinship calculation 440
clan 435
collateral relative 441
descent group 429
ego 438
extended family household 431

family of orientation 429
family of procreation 429
functional explanation 441
generational kinship terminology 442
kinship calculation 438
lineage 435
lineal kinship terminology 441
lineal relative 441
neolocality 431
unilineal descent 435

test yourself

MULTIPLE CHOICE

1. Why is a focus on the nuclear family characteristic of many modern nations? Because
   a. the nuclear family is the most common family arrangement in industrialized societies.
   b. isolation from the extended family arises from geographic mobility that is characteristic of many industrialized societies.
   c. modernity is associated with smaller and more exclusive households, especially among the urban poor.
   d. higher incomes have made it possible for most adults to achieve the American cultural ideal of a nuclear family.
   e. the nuclear family is the most developed form of domestic arrangement.

2. The nuclear family is the most common kin group in what kinds of societies?
   a. tribal societies and chiefdoms
   b. ambilineal and collateral
   c. lineages and clans

d. industrial middle class and foraging bands

e. patrilocal and matrilocal

3. Which of the following statements about the nuclear family is *not* true?

   a. The nuclear family is a cultural universal.

   b. In the United States, nuclear families accounted for just 21 percent of households in 2010.

   c. A family of orientation may be a nuclear family.

   d. A family of procreation may be a nuclear family.

   e. Most people belong to at least two nuclear families during their lives.

4. What does the classification of a descent group as either a lineage or a clan indicate?

   a. A lineage uses demonstrated descent while a clan uses stipulated descent.

   b. Descent is always achieved.

   c. How individuals define and think about relationships of descent is culturally universal.

   d. Only in lineages do members descend from an apical ancestor.

   e. Members of lineages do not like to rely on their memory to know who their ancestors are.

5. Like race, kinship is culturally constructed. This means that

   a. the educational system is failing to educate people about real, biologically based human relations.

   b. like race, kinship is a fiction, with no real social consequence.

   c. it is a phenomenon separated from other real aspects of society, such as economics and politics.

   d. studies of kinship tell us little about people's actual experiences.

   e. people perceive and define kin relations differently in different cultures, although anthropologists have discovered a limited number of patterns in which people classify their kin.

6. Anthropologists are interested in kinship calculation,

   a. but only if it changes demographics from decade to decade.

   b. which means how people evaluate the worth of anthropological research.

   c. and then they do their best to impose their etic perspective on people's emic views.

   d. which means how people apply mathematical principles to determine degrees of relatedness with the ancestors of anatomically modern humans.

   e. which means the system by which people in a society reckon kin relationships.

7. In any culture, kinship terminology is a classification system, a taxonomy or typology. More generally, a taxonomic system

   a. is most accurate when based on Western science.

   b. is based on how people perceive similarities and differences in the things being classified.

   c. only makes any sense to those who study it for years.

   d. usually changes with every generation.

   e. applies best to nonliving things.

8. What is another name for a person's "in-laws"?

   a. family of orientation

   b. merging relatives

   c. affinals

   d. collaterals

   e. lineals

9. In this chapter, a functional explanation is offered for various systems of kinship terminology. What does a functional explanation suggest about a system of kinship terminology?

   a. Kinship terminology becomes a system only when it *functions* properly.

   b. Certain kinship terms are what *cause* certain patterns of behavior.

   c. A functional explanation accurately *predicts* what types of kinship terminology will develop in future generations if enough data about the system are collected.

   d. A functional explanation attempts to *correlate* particular customs (in this case kinship terms) to other features of society.

   e. A functional explanation *distinguishes* genealogical kin types from kin terms.

10. In a bifurcate merging kinship terminology, which of the following pairs would be called by the same term?

   a. MZ and MB

   b. M and MZ

   c. MF and FF

   d. M and F

   e. MB and FB

FILL IN THE BLANK

1. The family of _____ is the name of the family in which a child is raised, while the family of _____ is the name of the family established when one marries and has children.
2. _____ refers to the postmarital residence pattern in which the married couple is expected to establish its own home.
3. A _____ refers to a unilineal descent group whose members demonstrate their common descent from an apical ancestor.
4. In _____ kinship calculation, kin ties are traced equally through males and females.
5. In a bifurcate merging kinship terminology, _____ and _____ relatives are merged.

CRITICAL THINKING

1. Why is kinship so important to anthropologists? How might the study of kinship be useful for research in fields of anthropology other than cultural anthropology?
2. What are some examples of alternatives to nuclear family arrangements considered in this chapter? What may be the impact of new (and increasingly accessible) reproductive technologies on domestic arrangements?
3. Although the nuclear family remains the cultural ideal for many Americans, other domestic arrangements now outnumber the "traditional" American household about five to one. What are some reasons for this? Do you think this trend is good or bad? Why?
4. To what sorts of family or families do you belong? Have you belonged to other kinds of families? How do the kin terms you use compare with the four classification systems discussed in this chapter?
5. Cultures with unilocal residence and unilineal descent tend to have bifurcate merging terminology, while ambilineal descent and ambilocal residence correlate with generational terminology. Why does this make sense? What are some examples of each case?

Carsten, J.
2004   *After Kinship.* New York: Cambridge University Press. Rethinking anthropological approaches to kinship for the modern world.

Descartes, L., and C. P. Kottak
2009   *Media and Middle Class Moms: Images and Realities of Work and Family.* New York: Routledge. The role of the media in American family life.

Hansen, K. V.
2005   *Not-So-Nuclear Families: Class, Gender, and Networks of Care.* New Brunswick, NJ: Rutgers University Press. Support networks based in class, gender, and kinship.

Parkin, R., and L. Stone, eds.
2004   *Kinship and Family: An Anthropological Reader.* Malden, MA: Blackwell. Up-to-date reader.

Stacey, J.
2011   *Unhitched: Love, Marriage, and Family Values from West Hollywood to Western China.* New York: New York University Press. Profiles unfamiliar cultures of contemporary love, marriage, and family values from around the world.

Willie, C. V., and R. J. Reddick
2009   *A New Look at Black Families,* 6th ed. Lanham, MA: Rowman and Littlefield. Family experience in relation to socioeconomic status, presented through case studies.

Go to our Online Learning Center website at **www.mhhe.com/kottak** for Internet exercises directly related to the content of this chapter.

CHAPTER 20

Marriage

How is marriage defined and regulated, and what rights does it convey?

What role does marriage play in creating and maintaining group alliances?

What forms of marriage exist cross-culturally, and what are their social correlates?

◀ Part of a wedding ceremony in Khartoum, Sudan. On women's night, friends gather, and an older woman anoints the bride with oil.

understanding OURSELVES

According to the radio talk show psychologist (and undergraduate anthropology major) Dr. Joy Browne, parents' job is to give their kids "roots and wings." Roots, she says, are the easier part. In other words, it's easier to raise children than to let them go. Has that been true of your parents with respect to you? I've heard comments about today's "helicopter parents" hovering over even their college-aged kids, using cell phones, e-mail, and texting to follow their progeny more closely than in prior generations. Do you have any experience with such a pattern?

It can be difficult to make the transition between the family that raised us (our family of orientation) and the family we form if we marry and have children (our family of procreation). In contemporary America, we usually get a head start by "leaving home" long before we marry. We go off to college or find a job that enables us to support ourselves so that we can live independently, or with roommates. In nonindustrial societies people, especially women, may leave home abruptly when they marry. Often a woman must leave her home village and her own kin and move in with her husband and his relatives. This can be an unpleasant and alienating transition. Many women complain about feeling isolated in their husband's village, where

they may be mistreated by their husband or in-laws, including the mother-in-law.

In contemporary North America, although neither women nor men typically have to adjust to in-laws living nearby full-time, conflicts with in-laws aren't at all uncommon. Just read "Dear Abby" or listen to Dr. Joy Browne (cited previously) for a week. Even more of a challenge is learning to live with our spouse. Marriage always raises issues of accommodation and adjustment. Initially the married couple is just that, unless there are children from a previous marriage. If there are, adjustment issues will involve stepparenthood—and a prior spouse—as well as the new marital relationship. Once a couple has its own child, the family-of-procreation mentality takes over. In the United States family loyalty shifts, but not completely, from the family of orientation to the family that includes spouse and child(ren). Given our bilateral kinship system, we maintain relations with our sons and daughters after they marry, and grandchildren theoretically are as close to one set of grandparents as to the other set. In practice, grandchildren tend to be a bit closer to their mother's than to their father's families. Can you speculate about why that might be? How is it for you? Are you closer to your paternal or maternal grandparents? How about your uncles and aunts on one side or the other? Why is that?

WHAT IS MARRIAGE?

"Love and marriage," "marriage and the family": These familiar phrases show how we link the romantic love of two individuals to marriage and how we link marriage to reproduction and family creation. But marriage is an institution with significant roles and functions in addition to reproduction (see Stockard 2001). What is marriage, anyway?

No definition of marriage is broad enough to apply easily to all societies and situations. A commonly quoted definition comes from *Notes and Queries on Anthropology*:

Marriage is a union between a man and a woman such that the children born to the woman are recognized as legitimate offspring of both partners (Royal Anthropological Institute 1951, p. 111).

This definition isn't universally valid for several reasons. In many societies, marriages unite more than two spouses. Here we speak of *plural marriages,* as when a man weds two (or more) women, or a woman weds a group of brothers—an arrangement called *fraternal polyandry* that is characteristic of certain Himalayan cultures. In the Brazilian community of Arembepe, people can choose among various forms of marital union. Most people live in long-term "common-law" domestic partnerships that are not legally sanctioned. Some have civil marriages, which are licensed and legalized by a justice of the peace. Still others go through religious ceremonies, so that they are united in "holy matrimony," although not legally. And some have both civil and religious ties. The different forms of union permit someone to have multiple spouses (e.g., one common-law, one civil, one religious) without ever getting divorced.

Some societies recognize various kinds of same-sex marriages. In South Sudan, a Nuer woman can marry a woman if her father has only daughters but no male heirs, who are necessary if his patrilineage is to survive. He may ask his daughter to stand as a son in order to take a bride. This daughter will become the socially recognized husband of another woman (the wife). This is a symbolic and social relationship rather than a sexual one. The "wife" has sex with a man or men (whom her female "husband" must approve) until she gets pregnant. The children born to the wife are accepted as the offspring of both the female husband and the wife. Although the female husband is not the actual **genitor,** the biological father, of the children, she is their **pater,** or socially recognized father. What's important in this Nuer case is *social* rather than *biological paternity.* We see again how kinship is socially constructed. The bride's children are considered the legitimate offspring of her female "husband," who is biologically a woman but socially a man, and the descent line continues.

INCEST AND EXOGAMY

In nonindustrial societies, a person's social world includes two main categories—friends and strangers. Strangers are potential or actual enemies. Marriage is one of the primary ways of converting strangers into friends, of creating and maintaining personal and political alliances, relationships of affinity. **Exogamy,** the custom and practice of seeking a mate outside one's own group, has adaptive value because it links people into a wider social network that nurtures, helps, and protects them in times of need. Incest restrictions (prohibitions on sex with relatives) reinforce exogamy by pushing people to seek their mates outside the local group. Most societies discourage sexual contact involving close relatives, especially members of the same nuclear family.

Incest refers to sexual contact with a relative, but cultures define their kin, and thus incest, differently. In other words, incest, like kinship, is socially constructed. Marriage entails sex, so one can marry only someone with whom sex is permitted. Besides kinship, other factors that restrict sexual access include age and the range of sexual acts that are socially tolerated. In the United States the age of consent for sexual activity varies by state between 16 and 18. It is 16 in Canada and 14 in Italy. Cultures and governments routinely try to regulate sexual activity. Until 2003, when the Supreme Court struck them down, several states had sodomy laws, used mainly against gay men who engaged in nonreproductive sex. Most people probably don't know what is legal and what isn't in a given state or country and can get in trouble as a result (e.g., when an 18-year-old has sex with a 17-year-old).

Sex is contested. That is, people in the same culture can disagree and argue about the definition and propriety of particular sexual acts. President Bill Clinton famously asserted "I did not have sexual relations with that women. . . ." Should sexual practices other than heterosexual coitus (oral sex, for example) be considered "sexual relations"? With respect to incest restrictions, what, if any, kind of sexual contact is permissible between a teenager and his or her same-sex or opposite-sex cousin of comparable age? How about step-siblings, half-siblings, and siblings? Some U.S. states permit marriage, and therefore sex, with first cousins, while others ban it. The social construction of kinship, and of incest, is far from simple.

For example, is a first cousin always a relative? Many societies distinguish between two kinds of first cousins: cross cousins and parallel cousins (see Ottenheimer 1996). The children of two brothers or two sisters are **parallel cousins.** The children of a brother and a sister are **cross cousins.** Your mother's sister's children and your father's brother's children are your parallel cousins. Your father's sister's children and your mother's brother's children are your cross cousins.

The American kin term *cousin* doesn't distinguish between cross and parallel cousins, but in many societies, especially those with unilineal descent, the distinction is essential. As an example, consider a community with only two descent groups. This exemplifies what is known as *moiety* organization—from the French *moitié,* which means "half." Descent bifurcates the community so that everyone belongs to one half or the other. Some societies have patrilineal moieties; others have matrilineal moieties.

In Figures 20.1 and 20.2, notice that cross cousins always are members of the opposite moiety and parallel cousins always belong to your (ego's) own moiety. With patrilineal descent (Figure 20.1), people take the father's descent-group affiliation; in a matrilineal society (Figure 20.2), they take the mother's affiliation. You can see from these diagrams that your mother's sister's children (MZC) and your father's brother's children (FBC) always belong to your group. Your cross cousins—that is, FZC and MBC—belong to the other moiety.

Parallel cousins belong to the same generation and the same descent group as ego does, and they

---

genitor
A child's biological father.

pater
One's socially recognized father; not necessarily the genitor.

parallel cousins
Children of two brothers or two sisters.

cross cousins
Children of a brother and a sister.

exogamy
Marriage outside a given group.

incest
Forbidden sexual relations with a close relative.

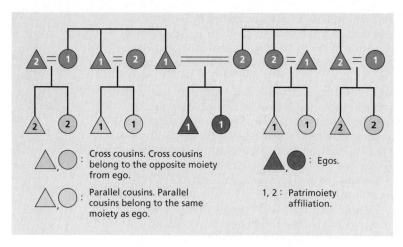

FIGURE 20.1 Parallel and Cross Cousins and Patrilineal Moiety Organization.

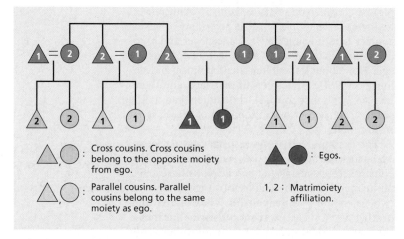

FIGURE 20.2 Matrilineal Moiety Organization.

Among the Yanomami of Brazil and Venezuela (shown here), sex with (and marriage to) cross cousins is proper, but sex with parallel cousins is considered incestuous. With unilineal descent, sex with cross cousins isn't incestuous because cross cousins never belong to ego's descent group.

are like ego's brothers and sisters. They are called by the same kin terms as brothers and sisters are. Defined as close relatives, parallel cousins, like siblings, are excluded as potential mates; cross cousins are not.

In societies with unilineal moieties, cross cousins always belong to the opposite group. Sex with cross cousins isn't incestuous, because they aren't considered relatives. In fact, in many unilineal societies, people must marry either a cross cousin or someone from the same descent group as a cross cousin. A unilineal descent rule ensures that the cross cousin's descent group is never one's own. With moiety exogamy, spouses must belong to different moieties.

Among the Yanomami of Venezuela and Brazil (Chagnon 1997), boys anticipate eventual marriage to a cross cousin by calling her "wife." They call their male cross cousins "brother-in-law." Yanomami girls call their male cross cousins "husband" and their female cross cousins "sister-in-law." Among the Yanomami, as in many societies with unilineal descent, sex with cross cousins is proper but sex with parallel cousins is considered incestuous.

If cousins can be classified as nonrelatives, how about even closer biological kin types? When unilineal descent is very strongly developed, the parent who belongs to a different descent group than your own isn't considered a relative. Thus, with strict patrilineality, the mother is not a relative but a kind of in-law who has married a member of your own group—your father. With strict matrilineality, the father isn't a relative because he belongs to a different descent group.

The Lakher of Southeast Asia (Figure 20.3) are strictly patrilineal (Leach 1961). Using the male ego (the reference point, the person in question) in Figure 20.4, let's suppose that ego's father and mother get divorced. Each remarries and has a daughter by a second marriage. A Lakher always belongs to his or her father's group, all of whose members (one's agnates, or patrikin) are considered relatives, because they belong to the same descent group. Ego can't have sex with or marry his father's daughter by the second marriage, just as in contemporary North America it's illegal for half-siblings to have sex and marry. However, unlike our society, where all half-siblings are restricted, sex between our Lakher ego and his maternal half-sister would be nonincestuous. She isn't ego's relative because she belongs to her own father's descent group rather than ego's. The Lakher illustrate very well that definitions of relatives, and therefore of incest, vary from culture to culture.

INCEST AND ITS AVOIDANCE

We know from primate research that adolescent males (among monkeys) or females (among apes) often move away from the group in which they were born (see Rodseth et al. 1991 and this chapter's "Appreciating Anthropology"). This emigration reduces the frequency of incestuous unions, but it doesn't eliminate them. DNA testing of wild chimps has confirmed incestuous unions between adult sons and their mothers, who reside in the same group. Human behavior with respect to mating with close relatives may express a generalized primate tendency, in which we see both urges and avoidance.

A cross-cultural study of eighty-seven societies (Meigs and Barlow 2002) suggested that incest occurred in several of them. It's not clear, however, whether the authors of the study controlled for the social construction of incest. They report, for example, that incest occurs among the Yanomami, but they may be considering cross-cousin marriage to be incestuous, when it is not so considered by the Yanomami. Indeed it is the preferred form of marriage, not just for the Yanomami but in many tribal societies. Another society in their sample is the Ashanti, for whom the ethnographer Meyer Fortes reports, "In the old days it [incest] was punished by death. Nowadays the culprits are heavily fined" (Fortes 1950, p. 257). This suggests that there really were violations of Ashanti incest restrictions, and that such violations were, and still are, punished. More strikingly,

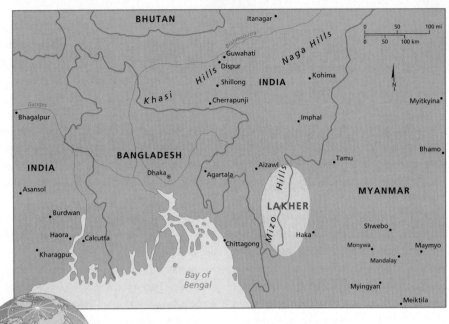

FIGURE 20.3 Location of the Lakher.

among twenty-four Ojibwa individuals from whom he obtained information about incest, A. Irving Hallowell found eight cases of parent–child incest and ten cases of brother–sister incest (Hallowell 1955, pp. 294–95). Because reported cases of actual parent–child and sibling incest are rare in the ethnographic literature, questions about the possibility of social construction arise here, too. In many cultures, including the Ojibwa, people use the same terms for their mother and their aunt, their father and their uncle, and their cousins and siblings. Could the siblings in the Ojibwa case actually have been cousins; and the parents and children, uncles and nieces?

In ancient Egypt, sibling marriage apparently was allowed both for royalty and commoners, in some districts at least. Based on official census records from Roman Egypt (first to third centuries C.E.), 24 percent of all documented marriages in the Arsinoites district were between "brothers" and "sisters." The rates were 37 percent for the city of Arsinoe and 19 percent for the surrounding villages. These figures are much higher than any other documented levels of inbreeding among humans (Scheidel 1997). Again one wonders if the relatives involved were actually as close biologically as the kin terms would imply.

According to Anna Meigs and Kathleen Barlow (2002), for Western societies with nuclear family organization, "father-daughter incest" is much more common with stepfathers than with biological fathers. But is it really incest if they aren't biological relatives? American culture is unclear on this matter.

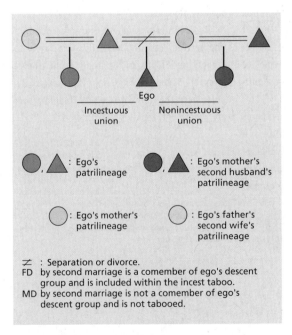

FIGURE 20.4 Patrilineal Descent-Group Identity and Incest among the Lakher.

Come Join My Band, Baby

Based on data from thirty-two recent foraging societies, anthropologists suggest how early hominin society might have diverged from proto-chimpanzee society. Key developments in early human evolution would have been (1) formation of an enduring pair bond between a male and a female and (2) the possibility of both male and female dispersal and movement between bands. Humans uniquely recognize their relatives through both males and females. Recognition of kin in different bands would have enhanced cooperation between bands. As people moved from band to band, they would have shared ideas and inventions through social learning. Although few anthropologists would doubt the central role of cooperation and social learning in human evolution, many would question the use of contemporary and recent hunter-gatherers as models for early hominin social organization.

Anthropologists studying living hunter-gatherers have radically revised their view of how early human societies were structured, a shift that yields new insights into how humans evolved away from apes.

Early human groups, according to the new view, would have been more cooperative and willing to learn from one another than . . . chimpanzees. . . . The advantages of cooperation and social learning then propelled the incipient human groups along a different evolutionary path. . . .

A team of anthropologists led by Kim R. Hill of Arizona State University and Robert S. Walker of the University of Missouri analyzed data from 32 living hunter-gatherer peoples. . . .

Michael Tomasello, a psychologist at the Max Planck Institute for Evolutionary Anthropology in Germany, said the survey provided a strong foundation for the view that cooperative behavior, as distinct from the fierce aggression between chimp groups, was the turning point that shaped human evolution. . . .

The finding corroborates an influential new view of early human origins advanced by Bernard Chapais, a primatologist at the University of Montreal, in his book *Primeval Kinship* (2008). Dr. Chapais showed how a simple development, the emergence of a pair bond between male and female, would have allowed people to recognize their relatives, something chimps can do only to a limited extent. When family members dispersed to other bands, they would be recognized and neighboring bands would cooperate instead of fighting to the death as chimp groups do.

In chimpanzee societies, males stay where they are born and females disperse at puberty to neighboring groups, thus avoiding incest. . . .

Dr. Hill and Dr. Walker find that though it is the daughters who move in many hunter-gatherer societies, the sons leave the home community in many others. In fact, the human pattern of residency is so variable that it counts as a pattern in itself, one that the researchers say is not known for any species of ape or monkey. Dr. Chapais calls this social pattern "bilocality."

Modern humans have lived as hunter-gatherers for more than 90 percent of their existence as a species. If living hunter-gatherers are typical of ancient ones, the new data about their social pattern has considerable bearing on early human evolution. . . .

The new data . . . furnishes the context in which two distinctive human behaviors emerged, those of cooperation and social learning, Dr. Hill said. A male chimp may know in his lifetime just 12 other males, all from his own group. But a hunter-gatherer, because of cooperation between bands, may interact with a thousand individuals in his tribe. Because humans are unusually adept at social learning, including copying useful activities from others, a large social network is particularly effective at spreading and accumulating knowledge.

Knowledge can in fact be lost by hunter-gatherers if a social network gets too small. One group of the Ache people of Paraguay, cut off from its home territory, had lost use of fire when first contacted. Tasmanians apparently forgot various fishing techniques after rising sea levels broke their contact with the Australian mainland 10,000 years ago.

Dr. Chapais said that the new findings "validate and enrich" the model of human social evolution proposed in his book. "If you take the promiscuity that is the main feature of chimp society, and replace it with pair bonding, you get many of the most important features of human society," he said.

Recognition of relatives promoted cooperation between neighboring bands, in his view, allowing people to move freely from one to another. Both sons and daughters could disperse from the home group, unlike chimp society, where only females can disperse. . . .

SOURCE: Nicholas Wade, "New View of How Humans Moved Away from Apes." From *The New York Times*, March 10, 2011. © 2011 The New York Times. All rights reserved. Used by permission and protected by the Copyright Laws of the United States. The printing, copying, redistribution, or retransmission of this Content without express written permission is prohibited. www.nytimes.com

Incest also happens with biological fathers, especially those who were absent or did little caretaking of their daughters in childhood (Williams and Finkelhor 1995). In a carefully designed study, Linda M. Williams and David Finkelhor (1995) found father-daughter incest to be least likely when there was substantial paternal parenting of daughters. This experience enhanced the father's parenting skills and his feelings of nurturance, protectiveness, and identification with his daughter, thus reducing the chance of incest.

A century ago, early anthropologists speculated that incest restrictions reflect an instinctive horror of mating with close relatives (Hobhouse 1915; Lowie 1920/1961). But why, one wonders, if humans really do have an instinctive aversion to incest, would formal restrictions be necessary? No one would want to have sexual contact with a relative. Yet, as social workers, judges, psychiatrists, and psychologists are well aware, incest is more common than we might suppose.

Incest Avoidance

Why do societies discourage incest? Is it because incestuous unions tend to produce abnormal offspring, as the early anthropologist Lewis Henry Morgan (1877/1963) suggested? Laboratory experiments with animals that reproduce faster than humans do (such as mice and fruit flies) have been used to investigate the effects of inbreeding: A decline in survival and fertility does accompany brother–sister mating across several generations. However, despite the potentially harmful biological results of systematic inbreeding, human marriage

Discovered in Egypt's Valley of the Kings, a gold and silver inlaid throne from the tomb of Tutankhamun is now on display in Cairo's Egyptian Museum. Sibling marrage was allowed not only for ancient Egyptian royalty but also for commoners in some regions.

patterns are based on specific cultural beliefs rather than universal concerns about biological degeneration several generations in the future. Biological concerns certainly cannot explain why so many societies promote marriage of cross cousins but not of parallel cousins.

In most societies, people avoid incest by following rules of exogamy, which force them to mate and marry outside their kin group (Lévi-Strauss 1949/1969; Tylor 1889; White 1959). Exogamy is adaptively advantageous because it creates new social ties and alliances. Marrying a close relative, with whom one already is on peaceful terms, would be counterproductive. There is more to gain by extending peaceful relations to a wider network of groups (see "Appreciating Anthropology). Marriage within the group would isolate that group from its neighbors and their resources and social networks, and might ultimately lead to the group's extinction. Exogamy helps explain human adaptive success. Besides its sociopolitical function, exogamy also ensures genetic mixture between groups and thus maintains a successful human species.

How many fingers do this Indian woman and her child have? Such genetically determined traits as polydactylism (extra fingers) may show up when there is a high incidence of endogamy. Despite the biological effects of inbreeding, marriage preferences and prohibitions are based on specific cultural beliefs rather than universal concerns about future biological degeneration.

ENDOGAMY

The practice of exogamy pushes social organization outward, establishing and preserving alliances among groups. In contrast, rules of **endogamy** dictate mating or marriage within a group to which one belongs. Formal endogamic rules are less common but are still familiar to anthropologists. Indeed, most societies *are* endogamous units, although they usually do not need a formal rule requiring people to marry someone from their own society. In our own society, classes and ethnic groups are quasi-endogamous groups. Members of an ethnic or religious group often want their children to marry within that group, although many of them do not do so. The outmarriage rate varies among such groups, with some more committed to endogamy than others are.

Homogamy means to marry someone similar, as when members of the same social class intermarry. In modern societies, there's a correlation between socioeconomic status (SES) and education. People with similar SES tend to have similar educational aspirations, to attend similar schools, and to aim at similar careers. For example, people who meet at an elite private university are likely to have similar backgrounds and career prospects. Homogamous marriage may work to concentrate wealth in social classes and to reinforce the system of social stratification. In the United States, for example, the rise in

female employment, especially in professional careers, when coupled with homogamy, has dramatically increased household incomes in the upper classes. This pattern has been one factor in sharpening the contrast in household income between the richest and poorest quintiles (top and bottom 20 percent) of Americans.

Caste

An extreme example of endogamy is India's caste system, which was formally abolished in 1949, although its structure and effects linger. Castes are stratified groups in which membership is ascribed at birth and is lifelong. Indian castes are grouped into five major categories, or *varna.* Each is ranked relative to the other four, and these categories extend throughout India. Each *varna* includes a large number of subcastes (*jati*), each of which includes people within a region who may intermarry. All the *jati* in a single *varna* in a given region are ranked, just as the *varna* themselves are ranked.

Occupational specialization often sets off one caste from another. A community may include castes of agricultural workers, merchants, artisans, priests, and sweepers. The untouchable *varna,* found throughout India, includes subcastes whose ancestry, ritual status, and occupations are considered so impure that higher-caste people consider even casual contact with untouchables to be defiling.

The belief that intercaste sexual unions lead to ritual impurity for the higher-caste partner has been important in maintaining endogamy. A man who has sex with a lower-caste woman can restore his purity with a bath and a prayer. However, a woman who has intercourse with a man of a lower caste has no such recourse. Her defilement cannot be undone. Because the women have the babies, these differences protect the purity of the caste line, ensuring the pure ancestry of high-caste children. Although Indian castes are endogamous groups, many of them are internally subdivided into exogamous lineages. Traditionally this meant that Indians had to marry a member of another descent group from the same caste.

Royal Endogamy

Royal endogamy, based in a few societies on brother–sister marriage, is similar to caste endogamy. Inca Peru, ancient Egypt, and traditional Hawaii all allowed royal brother–sister marriages. In ancient Peru and Hawaii, such marriages were permitted despite the restrictions on sibling incest that applied to commoners in those societies.

Manifest and Latent Functions
To understand royal brother–sister marriage, it is useful to distinguish between the manifest and latent functions of customs and behavior. The *manifest*

An extreme example of endogamy is India's caste system, which was formally abolished in 1949, although its structure and effects linger. Shown here, a member of the Dalit, or untouchable caste, cleans a sewer drain in a market in Jodhpur, India. The work of sweepers and tanners has been considered so smelly and dirty that they have been segregated residentially.

function of a custom refers to the reasons people in that society give for it. Its *latent function* is an effect the custom has on the society that its members don't mention or may not even recognize.

Royal endogamy illustrates this distinction. Hawaiians and other Polynesians believed in an impersonal force called *mana*. Mana could exist in things or people, in the latter case marking them off from other people and making them sacred. The Hawaiians believed that no one had as much mana as the ruler. Mana depended on genealogy. The person whose own mana was exceeded only by the king's was his sibling. The most appropriate wife for a king was his own full sister. Notice that the brother–sister marriage also meant that royal heirs would be as manaful, or sacred, as possible. The manifest function of royal endogamy in ancient Hawaii was part of that culture's beliefs about mana and sacredness.

Royal endogamy also had latent functions—political repercussions. The ruler and his wife had the same parents. Since mana was believed to be inherited, they were almost equally sacred. When the king and his sister married, their children indisputably had the most mana in the land. No one could question their right to rule. But if the king had taken as a wife someone with less mana than his sister, his sister's children eventually could cause problems. Both sets of children could assert their sacredness and right to rule. Royal sibling marriage therefore limited conflicts about succession by reducing the number of people with claims to rule. The same result would be true in ancient Egypt and Peru.

Other kingdoms, including European royalty, also have practiced endogamy, but based on cousin marriage rather than sibling marriage. In many cases, as in Great Britain, it is specified that the eldest child (usually the son) of the reigning monarch should succeed. This custom is called *primogeniture*. Commonly, rulers have banished or killed claimants who rival the chosen heir.

Royal endogamy also had a latent economic function. By limiting the number of heirs, marriage of relatives helped keep estates intact. Power often rests on wealth, and royal endogamy tended to ensure that royal wealth remained concentrated in the same line.

MARITAL RIGHTS AND SAME-SEX MARRIAGE

The British anthropologist Edmund Leach (1955) observed that, depending on the society, several different kinds of rights are allocated by marriage. According to Leach, marriage can, but doesn't always, accomplish the following:

1. Establish the legal father of a woman's children and the legal mother of a man's.

2. Give either or both spouses a monopoly on the sexuality of the other.

3. Give either or both spouses rights to the labor of the other.

4. Give either or both spouses rights over the other's property.

5. Establish a joint fund of property—a partnership—for the benefit of the children.

6. Establish a socially significant "relationship of affinity" between spouses and their relatives.

The discussion of same-sex marriage that follows will serve to illustrate the six rights just listed by seeing what happens in their absence. What if same-sex marriages, which by and large are illegal in the United States, were legal? Could a same-sex marriage establish legal parentage of children born to one or both partners after the partnership is formed? In the case of a different-sex marriage, children born to the wife after the marriage takes place usually are legally defined as her husband's regardless of whether he is the genitor.

Nowadays, of course, DNA testing makes it possible to establish paternity, just as modern reproductive technology makes it possible for a lesbian couple

This lesbian family is participating in a Gay Pride parade to commemorate the Stonewall uprising of 1968 (Greenwich Village, New York City), when gay patrons fought back against a police raid on the Stonewall Inn. Despite recent advances in gay rights, same-sex marriage remains illegal in most of the United States.

mater
Socially recognized
mother of a child.

to have one or both partners artificially inseminated. When same-sex marriages are legal, the social construction of kinship easily makes both partners parents. If a Nuer woman married to a woman can be the pater of a child she did not father, why can't two lesbians be the **maters** (socially recognized mothers) of a child to whom only one of them gave birth? And if a married different-sex couple can adopt a child who becomes theirs through the social and legal construction of kinship, the same logic could be applied to a gay male or lesbian couple.

Continuing with Leach's list of the rights transmitted by marriage, same-sex marriage could certainly give each spouse rights to the sexuality of the other. Unable to marry legally, gay men and lesbians have used various devices, such as mock weddings, to declare their commitment and desire for a monogamous sexual relationship. In April 2000, Vermont passed a bill allowing same-sex couples to unite legally, with virtually all the benefits of marriage. In June 2003, a court ruling established same-sex marriages as legal in the province of Ontario, Canada. On June 28, 2005, Canada's House of Commons voted to guarantee full marriage rights to same-sex couples throughout that nation. In the United States six states—Massachusetts, Connecticut, Iowa, Vermont, New Hampshire, and New York—allowed same-sex marriage as of 2012. Civil unions for same-sex couples are legal in New Jersey. In reaction to same-sex marriage, voters in at least nineteen U.S. states have approved measures in their state constitutions defining marriage as an exclusively heterosexual union. On November 4, 2008, Californians voted 52 percent to 48 percent to override the right to same-sex marriage,

which the courts had approved earlier that year. Currently that ban is under judicial review.

Legal same-sex marriages can give each spouse rights to the other spouse's labor and its products. Some societies have allowed marriage between members of the same biological sex, who may, however, be considered to belong to a different, socially constructed, gender. As reported in the chapter "Gender," several Native American groups had figures known as *berdaches,* representing a third gender (Murray and Roscoe 1998). These were biological men who assumed many of the mannerisms, behavior patterns, and tasks of women. Sometimes *berdaches* married men, who shared the products of their labor from hunting and filled traditional male roles, as the *berdache* fulfilled the traditional wifely role. Also, in some Native American cultures, a marriage of a "manly-hearted woman" (a third or fourth gender) to another woman brought the traditional male-female division of labor to their household. The manly woman hunted and did other male tasks, while the wife played the traditional female role.

There's no logical reason why same-sex marriage could not give spouses rights over the other's property. But in the United States, the same inheritance rights that apply to male-female couples do not apply to same-sex couples. For instance, even in the absence of a will, property can pass to a widow or a widower without going through probate. The wife or husband pays no inheritance tax. This benefit is not available to gay men and lesbians.

What about Leach's fifth right—to establish a joint fund of property—to benefit the children? Here again, gay and lesbian couples are at a disadvantage.

In Lagos, Nigeria, women work with green vegetables in a bayside market. In parts of Nigeria, prominent market women may take a wife. Such marriage allows wealthy women to strengthen their social status and the economic importance of their households.

If there are children, property is separately, rather than jointly, transmitted. Some organizations do make staff benefits, such as health and dental insurance, available to same-sex domestic partners.

Finally, there is the matter of establishing a socially significant "relationship of affinity" between spouses and their relatives. In many societies, one of the main roles of marriage is to establish an alliance between groups, in addition to the individual bond. Affinals are relatives through marriage, such as a brother-in-law or mother-in-law. For same-sex couples in contemporary North America, affinal relations can be problematic. In an unofficial union, terms like "daughter-in-law" and "mother-in-law" may sound strange. Many parents are suspicious of their children's sexuality and lifestyle choices and may not recognize a relationship of affinity with a child's partner of the same sex.

This discussion of same-sex marriage has been intended to illustrate the different kinds of rights that typically accompany marriage by seeing what may happen when there is a permanent pair-bond without legal sanction. In just six of the United States are such unions fully legal. As we have seen, same-sex marriages have been recognized in different historical and cultural settings. In certain African cultures, including the Igbo of Nigeria and the Lovedu of South Africa, women have been permitted to marry other women. In situations in which women, such as prominent market women in West Africa, are able to amass property and other forms of wealth, they may take a wife. Such marriage allows the prominent woman to strengthen her social status and the economic importance of her household (Amadiume 1987).

MARRIAGE AS GROUP ALLIANCE

Outside industrial societies, marriage often is more a relationship between groups than one between individuals. We think of marriage as an individual matter. Although the bride and groom usually seek their parents' approval, the final choice (to live together, to marry, to divorce) lies with the couple. Contemporary Western societies stress the notion that romantic love is necessary for a good marriage. Increasingly this idea characterizes other cultures as well. The mass media and migration spread to other societies Western ideas about the importance of love for marriage.

Just how widespread is romantic love, and what role should it play in marriage? A study by anthropologists William Jankowiak and Edward Fischer (1992) found romantic ardor to be very common cross-culturally. Previously, anthropologists had tended to ignore evidence for romantic love in other cultures, probably because arranged marriages were so common. Surveying ethnographic data from 166 cultures, Jankowiak and Fischer (1992) found evidence for romantic love in 147 of them—89 percent (see also Jankowiak 1995, 2008). In the other 19 societies, the absence of conclusive evidence may have reflected the ethnographer's oversight rather than an actual absence of romantic feelings.

Even if romance is as ubiquitous as marriage, the two don't necessarily go together. As reported by Marjorie Shostak (1983), Nisa, a !Kung San woman from the Kalahari, contrasted the enduring affection she felt for her husband with the more fleeting passion and excitement she felt for her lovers (see Goleman 1992).

Recent diffusion of Western ideas about the importance of love for marriage has influenced marital decisions in other cultures. Among villagers in the Kangra valley of northern India, as reported by anthropologist Kirin Narayan (quoted in Goleman 1992), even in the traditional arranged marriages, the partners might eventually fall in love. In that area today, however, the media have spread the idea that young people should choose their own spouse based on romantic love, and elopements now rival arranged marriages.

The same trend away from arranged marriages toward love matches has been noted among Native Australians. Traditionally in the Australian Outback, marriages were arranged when children were very young. Missionaries disrupted that pattern, urging that marriage be postponed to adolescence. Before the missionaries, according to anthropologist Victoria Burbank, all girls married before puberty, some as early as age 9; nowadays the average female age at marriage is 17 years (see Burbank 1988). Parents still prefer the traditional arrangement in which a girl's mother chooses a boy from the appropriate kin group. But more and more girls now choose to elope and get pregnant, thus forcing a marriage to someone they love. In the group Burbank studied, most marriages now are love matches (see Burbank 1988; Goleman 1992).

Whether or not they are cemented by passion, marriages in nonindustrial societies remain the concern of social groups rather than mere individuals. The scope of marriage extends from the social to the political. Strategic marriages are tried and true ways of establishing alliances between groups.

People don't just take a spouse; they assume obligations to a group of in-laws. When residence is patrilocal, for example, a woman often must leave the community where she was born. She faces the prospect of spending the rest of her life in her husband's village, with his relatives. She may even have to transfer her major allegiance from her own group to her husband's.

Gifts at Marriage

In societies with descent groups, people enter marriage not alone but with the help of the descent group. Often it is customary for a substantial gift to be given before, at, or after the marriage by the

In this 2009 photo, a bride and groom are escorted back to the bride's home after their wedding ceremony in a village in southwest China's Guizhou Province. Having observed traditional wedding customs of their Miao ethnic group, they are congratulated by fellow villagers and tourists.

lobola
A substantial marital gift from the husband and his kin to the wife and her kin.

dowry
Substantial gifts to husband's family from wife's group.

husband and his kin to the wife and her kin. The BaThonga of Mozambique call such a gift *lobola*, and the custom of giving something like **lobola** is very widespread in patrilineal societies (Radcliffe-Brown 1924/1952). This gift compensates the bride's group for the loss of her companionship and labor. More important, it makes the children born to the woman full members of her husband's descent group. In matrilineal societies, children are members of the mother's group, and there is no reason for a lobola-like gift.

Another kind of marital gift, **dowry**, occurs when the bride's family or kin group provides substantial gifts when their daughter marries. For rural Greece, Ernestine Friedl (1962) has described a form of dowry in which the bride gets a wealth transfer from her mother, to serve as a kind of trust fund during her marriage. Usually, however, the dowry goes to the husband's family, and the custom is correlated with low female status. In this form of dowry, best known from India, women are perceived as burdens. When a man and his family take a wife, they expect to be compensated for the added responsibility.

Although India passed a law in 1961 against compulsory dowry, the practice continues. When the dowry is considered insufficient, the bride may be harassed and abused. Domestic violence can escalate to the point where the husband or his family burn the bride, often by pouring kerosene on her and lighting it, usually killing her. It should be pointed out that dowry doesn't necessarily lead to domestic abuse. In fact, Indian dowry murders seem to be a fairly recent phenomenon. It also has been estimated

that the rate of spousal murders in the contemporary United States may rival the incidence of India's dowry murders (Narayan 1997).

Sati was the very rare practice through which widows were burned alive, voluntarily or forcibly, on the husband's funeral pyre (Hawley 1994). Although it has become well known, *sati* was mainly practiced in a particular area of northern India by a few small castes. It was banned in 1829. Dowry murders and *sati* are flagrant examples of *patriarchy,* a political system ruled by men in which women have inferior social and political status, including basic human rights.

Lobola-like gifts exist in many more cultures than dowry does, but the nature and quantity of transferred items differ. Among the BaThonga of Mozambique, whose name—lobola—I am using for this widespread custom, the gift consists of cattle. Use of livestock (usually cattle in Africa, pigs in Papua New Guinea) for lobola is common, but the number of animals given varies from society to society. We can generalize, however, that the larger the gift, the more stable the marriage. Lobola is insurance against divorce.

Imagine a patrilineal society in which a marriage requires the transfer of about twenty-five cattle from the groom's descent group to the bride's. Michael, a member of descent group A, marries Sarah from group B. His relatives help him assemble the lobola. He gets the most help from his close agnates (patrilineal relatives): his older brother, father, father's brother, and closest patrilineal cousins.

The distribution of the cattle once they reach Sarah's group mirrors the manner in which they were assembled. Sarah's father, or her oldest brother if the

This photo, taken in South Africa, shows the lobola cattle presented at the 2010 wedding of Mandla Mandela (grandson of former South African president Nelson Mandela) and his French wife, Anais Grimaud.

father is dead, receives her lobola. He keeps most of the cattle to use as lobola for his sons' marriages. However, a share also goes to everyone who will be expected to help when Sarah's brothers marry.

When Sarah's brother David gets married, many of the cattle go to a third group: C, which is David's wife's group. Thereafter, they may serve as lobola to still other groups. Men constantly use their sisters' lobola cattle to acquire their own wives. In a decade, the cattle given when Michael married Sarah will have been exchanged widely.

In such societies, marriage entails an agreement between descent groups. If Sarah and Michael try to make their marriage succeed but fail to do so, both groups may conclude that the marriage can't last. Here it becomes especially obvious that such marriages are relationships between groups as well as between individuals. If Sarah has a younger sister or niece (her older brother's daughter, for example), the concerned parties may agree to Sarah's replacement by a kinswoman.

However, incompatibility isn't the main problem that threatens marriage in societies with lobola customs. Infertility is a more important concern. If Sarah has no children, she and her group have not fulfilled their part of the marriage agreement. If the relationship is to endure, Sarah's group must furnish another woman, perhaps her younger sister, who can have children. If this happens, Sarah may choose to stay with her husband. Perhaps she will someday have a child. If she does stay on, her husband will have established a plural marriage.

Most nonindustrial food-producing societies, unlike most foraging societies and industrial nations, allow **plural marriages,** or *polygamy* (see Zeitzen 2008). There are two varieties; one is common, and the other is very rare. The more common variant is **polygyny,** in which a man has more than one wife (see this chapter's "Appreciating Diversity"). The rare variant is **polyandry,** in which a woman has more than one husband. If the infertile wife remains married to her husband after he has taken a substitute wife provided by her descent group, this is polygyny. Reasons for polygyny other than infertility will be discussed shortly.

Durable Alliances

It is possible to exemplify the group-alliance nature of marriage by examining still another common practice: continuation of marital alliances when one spouse dies.

Sororate

What happens if Sarah dies young? Michael's group will ask Sarah's group for a substitute, often her sister. This custom is known as the **sororate** (Figure 20.5). If Sarah has no sister or if all her sisters are already married, another woman from her group may be available. Michael marries her, there is no need to return the lobola, and the alliance continues. The sororate exists in both matrilineal and patrilineal societies. In a matrilineal society with matrilocal postmarital residence, a widower may remain with

plural marriage
More than two spouses simultaneously, aka polygamy.

polygyny
Man has more than one wife at the same time.

polyandry
Woman has more than one husband at the same time.

sororate
Widower marries sister of his deceased wife.

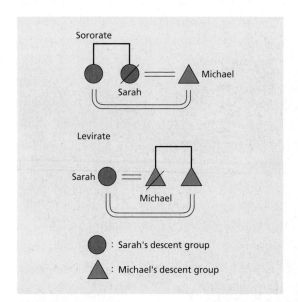

FIGURE 20.5 Sororate and Levirate.

his wife's group by marrying her sister or another female member of her matrilineage.

Levirate

What happens if the husband dies? In many societies, the widow may marry his brother. This custom is known as the **levirate.** Like the sororate, it is a continuation marriage that maintains the alliance between descent groups, in this case by replacing the husband with another member of his group. The implications of the levirate vary with age. One study found that in African societies, the levirate, though widely permitted, rarely involves cohabitation of the widow and her new husband. Furthermore, widows don't automatically marry the husband's brother just because they are allowed to. Often, they prefer to make other arrangements (Potash 1986).

levirate
Widow marries brother of her deceased husband.

DIVORCE

Ease of divorce varies across cultures. What factors work for and against divorce? As we've seen, marriages that are political alliances between groups are more difficult to dissolve than are marriages that are more individual affairs, of concern mainly to the married couple and their children. We've seen that a substantial lobola gift may decrease the divorce rate for individuals and that replacement marriages (levirate and sororate) also work to preserve group alliances. Divorce tends to be more common in matrilineal than in patrilineal societies. When residence is matrilocal (in the wife's place), the wife may simply send off a man with whom she's incompatible.

Among the Hopi of the American Southwest, houses were owned by matrilineal clans, with matrilocal postmarital residence. The household head was the senior woman of that household, which also included her daughters and their husbands and

Courtship among the Dinka, www.mhhe.com/kottak

This clip shows courtship practices among the Dinka, pastoralists of South Sudan. It describes the importance of the gift (in cattle) customarily given by the family of the groom to the family of the bride. According to the Dinka, why are cattle and children similar? The narrator claims there is no room for romance in Dinka courtship. Based on what you see in this clip, do you believe this claim to be true? The clip also illustrates the text's point that marriage in such societies is as much a relation between groups as one between individuals. The Dinka have descent groups. Do you think they are patrilineal or matrilineal? Why? Among the Dinka, what are the barriers to marriage—and to polygyny?

children. A son-in-law had no important role there; he returned to his own mother's home for his clan's social and religious activities. In this matrilineal society, women were socially and economically secure, and the divorce rate was high. Consider the Hopi of Oraibi (Orayvi) pueblo, northeastern Arizona (Levy with Pepper 1992; Titiev 1992). In a study of the marital histories of 423 Oraibi women, Mischa Titiev found that 35 percent had been divorced at least once. Jerome Levy found that 31 percent of 147 adult women had been divorced and remarried at least once. For comparison, of all ever-married women in the United States, only 4 percent had been divorced in 1960, 10.7 percent in 1980, and 13.7 percent in 2010. Titiev characterizes Hopi marriages as unstable. Part of this brittleness was due to conflicting loyalties to matrikin versus spouse.

Hopi piki bread maker Rebecca Namingha mixes blue corn meal and ashes with water. She'll cook the batter on a hot stone. Traditionally among the matrilineal-matrilocal Hopi, women were socially and economically secure, and the divorce rate was high.

Most Hopi divorces appear to have been matters of personal choice. Levy generalizes that, cross-culturally, high divorce rates are correlated with a secure female economic position. In Hopi society women were secure in their home and land ownership and in the custody of their children. In addition, there were no formal barriers to divorce.

Divorce is harder in a patrilineal society, especially when substantial lobola would have to be reassembled and repaid if the marriage failed. A woman residing patrilocally (in her husband's household and community) might be reluctant to leave him. Unlike the Hopi, who let the kids stay with the mother, in patrilineal, patrilocal societies, the children of divorce would be expected to remain with their father, as members of his patrilineage. From the women's perspective this is a strong impediment to divorce.

Political and economic factors complicate the divorce process. Among foragers, different factors tend to favor and oppose divorce. What factors work against durable marriages? Since foragers tend to lack descent groups, the political alliance functions of marriage are less important to them than they are to food producers. Foragers also tend to have minimal material possessions. The process of dissolving a joint fund of property is less complicated when spouses do not hold substantial resources in common. What factors favor marital stability among foragers? In societies where the family is an important year-round unit with a gender-based division of labor, ties between spouses tend to be durable. Also, sparse populations mean few alternative spouses if a marriage doesn't work out. But in band-organized societies, foragers can always find a band to join or rejoin if a marriage doesn't work. And food producers can always draw on their descent-group estate if a marriage fails. With patriliny, a woman often can return home, albeit without her children, and with matriliny, a man can do the same. Descent-group estates are not transferred through marriages, although movable resources such as lobola cattle certainly are.

In contemporary Western societies, when romance fails, so may the marriage. Or it may not fail, if the other rights associated with marriage, as discussed previously in this chapter, are compelling. Economic ties and obligations to kids, along with other factors, such as concern about public opinion, or simple inertia, may keep marriages intact after sex, romance, and/or companionship fade. Also, even in modern societies, royalty, leaders, and other elites may have political marriages similar to the arranged marriages of nonindustrial societies.

In the United States, divorce figures have been kept since 1860. Divorces tend to increase after wars and to decrease when times are bad economically. But with more women working outside the home, economic dependence on the husband as breadwinner is weaker, which no doubt facilitates a decision to divorce when a marriage has major problems.

TABLE 20.1 Changing Divorce Rates (Number per Year) in the United States, 1940 through 2008

YEAR	DIVORCE RATE PER 1,000 POPULATION	DIVORCE RATE PER 1,000 WOMEN AGED 15 AND OLDER
1940	2.0	8.8
1950	2.6	10.3
1960	2.2	9.2
1970	3.5	14.9
1980	5.2	22.6
1990	4.7	20.9
2000	4.2	19.5
2010	3.5	13.7

SOURCE: S. C. Clarke, "Advance Report of Final Divorce Statistics, 1989 and 1990," *Monthly Vital Statistics Report* 43(8, 9), Hyattsville, MD: National Center for Health Statistics; R. Hughes, Jr., "Demographics of Divorce," 1996, http://www.hec.ohiostate.edu/famlife/divorce/demo.htm; *National Vital Statistics Reports* 54(12), 2006, http://www.cdc.gov/nchs/data/nvsr/nvsr54/nvsr54_12.pdf; *Statistical Abstract of the United States* 2012, Tables 56, 78, and 132.

Table 20.1 is based on two measures of the divorce rate. The left column shows the rate per 1,000 people per year in the overall population. The right column shows the annual rate per 1,000 married women over the age of 15, which is the best measure of divorce. In either case, comparing 2000 with 1960, the divorce rate more than doubled. Note that the rate rose slightly after World War II (1950), then declined a decade later (1960). The most notable rate rise occurred between 1960 and 1980. Since then the rate has declined.

Among nations, the United States has one of the world's highest divorce rates. There are several probable causes: economic, cultural, and religious among them. Economically, the United States has a large percentage of gainfully employed women. Work outside the home provides a cash basis for independence, as it also places strains on marriage and social life for both partners. Culturally, Americans tend to value independence and its modern form, self-actualization. Also, Protestantism (in its various guises) is the most common form of religion in the United States. Of the two major religions in the United States and Canada (where Catholicism predominates), Protestantism has been less stringent in denouncing divorce than has Catholicism.

PLURAL MARRIAGES

In contemporary North America, where divorce is fairly easy and common, polygamy (marriage to more than one spouse at the same time) is against the law. Marriage in industrial nations joins individuals, and relationships between individuals can

Five Wives and 55 Children

Diversity in marriage customs has been a prominent topic in anthropology since its origin. Many societies, including Turkey, that once allowed plural marriage have banned it. Polygyny is the form of polygamy (plural marriage) in which a man has more than one wife. Marriage usually is a domestic partnership, but under polygyny secondary wives may or may not reside near the first wife. In this Turkish case the five wives have their own homes. Polygamy has survived in Turkey since the Ottoman period (which ended in 1922), when having several wives was viewed as a symbol of a man's power, wealth, and sexual prowess. Unlike the past, when the practice was customary (for men who could afford it) and not illegal, polygamy can put contemporary women at risk. Because their marriages have no official status, secondary wives who are abused or mistreated have no legal recourse. Like all institutions studied by anthropologists, customs involving plural marriage are changing in the contemporary world and in the context of nation-states and globalization.

ISIKLAR, Turkey, July 6—With his 5 wives, 55 children and 80 grandchildren, 400 sheep, 1,200 acres of land and a small army of servants, Aga Mehmet Arslan would seem an unlikely defender of monogamy.

Though banned, polygamy is widespread in the Isiklar region. Yet if he were young again, said Mr. Arslan, a sprightly, potbellied, 64-year-old Kurdish village chieftain, he would happily trade in his five wives for one.

"Marrying five wives is not sinful, and I did so because to have many wives is a sign of power," he said, perched on a divan in a large cushion-filled room at his house, where a portrait of Turkey's first president, Mustafa Kemal Ataturk, who outlawed polygamy in 1926, is prominently displayed.

"But I wouldn't do it again," he added, listing the challenges of having so many kin—like the need to build each wife a house away from the others to prevent friction and his struggle to remember all of his children's names. "I was uneducated back then, and God commands us to be fruitful and multiply."

Though banned by Ataturk as part of an effort to modernize the Turkish republic and empower women, polygamy remains widespread in this deeply religious and rural Kurdish region of southeastern Anatolia, home to one-third of Turkey's 71 million people. The practice is generally accepted under the Koran.

Polygamy is creating cultural clashes in a country struggling to reconcile the secularism of

Many societies, including Turkey (as described here), that once permitted plural marriage have outlawed it. The Turkish bride shown here does not plan to share her husband. The photo shows the couple on their wedding day in Istanbul. Does polygyny offer any advantages to women?

be severed more easily than can those between groups. As divorce grows more common, North Americans practice *serial monogamy:* Individuals have more than one spouse but never, legally, more than one at the same time. As stated earlier, the two forms of polygamy are polygyny and polyandry. Polyandry is practiced in only a few cultures, notably among certain groups in Tibet, Nepal, and India. Polygyny is much more common.

Polygyny

We must distinguish between the social approval of plural marriage and its actual frequency in a particular society. Many cultures approve of a man's having more than one wife. However, even when polygyny is encouraged, most men are monogamous, and polygyny characterizes only a fraction of the marriages. Why is this true?

One reason is equal sex ratios. In the United States, about 105 males are born for every 100 females. In adulthood, the ratio of men to women equalizes, and eventually it reverses. The average North American woman outlives the average man. In many nonindustrial societies as well, the male-biased sex ratio among children reverses in adulthood.

The custom of men marrying later than women promotes polygyny. Among the Kanuri people of Bornu, Nigeria, men got married between the ages of 18 and 30; women, between 12 and 14 (Cohen 1967).

the republic with its Muslim traditions. It also risks undermining Turkey's drive to gain entry into the European Union.

"The E.U. is looking for any excuse not to let Turkey in, and polygamy reinforces the stereotype of Turkey as a backward country," said Handan Coskun, director of a women's center.

Because polygamous marriages are not recognized by the state—imams who conduct them are subject to punishment—the wives have no legal status, making them vulnerable when marriages turn violent. Yet the local authorities here typically turn a blind eye because the practice is viewed as a tradition....

In Turkey, polygamy experts explain the practice as a hangover from the Ottoman period, when harem culture abounded and having several wives was viewed as a symbol of influence, sexual prowess and wealth.

Remzi Otto, a sociology professor at Dicle University in Diyarbakir, who conducted a survey of 50 polygamous families, said some men took second wives if their first wives could not conceive sons. Some also take widowed women and orphan girls as second wives to give them a social safety net. Love, he added, can also play a role.

"Many men in this region are forced into marriages when they are as young as 13, so finding their own wife is a way to rebel and express their independence," he said.

Isiklar, the remote village where Mr. Arslan is the aga, or chief, can be found at the end of a long dirt road, surrounded by sweeping verdant fields. Most of the local residents share the surname Arslan, which means lion in Turkish and connotes virility.

Mr. Arslan said he regretted his multiple marriages and had forbidden his sons to take more than one wife. He is also educating his daughters. "I have done nothing shameful," he said. "I don't drink. I treat everyone with respect. But having so many wives can create problems."

His biggest headache, he said, stems from jealousy among the wives, the first of whom he married out of love. "My rule is to behave equally toward all of my wives," he said. "But the first wife was very, very jealous when the second wife came. When the third arrived, the first two created an alliance against her. So I have to be a good diplomat."

Mr. Arslan, who owns land, real estate and shops throughout the region, said the financial burden of so many offspring could be overwhelming. "When I go to the shoe shop, I buy 100 pairs of shoes at a time," he said. "The clerk at the store thinks I'm a shoe salesman and tells me to go visit a wholesaler."

He also has trouble keeping track of his children. He recently saw two boys fighting in the street and told them they would bring shame on their families. "Do you not recognize me?" one replied. "I am your son." ...

Women's groups say polygamy is putting women at risk. "These women can be abused, raped, mistreated, and because their marriages are not legal, they have nowhere to turn," said Ms. Coskun, the director of the women's center, which has opened bread-making factories in poor rural areas where women can work and take classes on women's rights....

Back in Isiklar, Mr. Arslan acknowledged that polygamy was an outmoded practice. "God has been giving to me because I am giving to my family," he said. "But if you want to be happy, marry one wife."

The age difference between spouses meant that there were more widows than widowers. Most of the widows remarried, some in polygynous unions. Among the Kanuri of Bornu and in other polygynous societies, widows made up a large number of the women involved in plural marriages (Hart, Pilling, and Goodale 1988). In many societies, including the Kanuri, the number of wives is an indicator of a man's household productivity, prestige, and social position (see "Appreciating Diversity"). The more wives, the more workers. Increased productivity means more wealth. This wealth in turn attracts additional wives to the household. Wealth and wives bring greater prestige to the household and its head.

If a plural marriage is to work, there needs to be some agreement among the existing spouses when another one is to be added, especially if they are to share the same household. In certain societies, the first wife requests a second wife to help with household chores. The second wife's status is lower than that of the first; they are senior and junior wives. The senior wife sometimes chooses the junior one from among her close kinswomen. Among the Betsileo of Madagascar, the different wives always lived in different villages. A man's first and senior wife, called "Big Wife," lived in the village where he cultivated his best rice field and spent most of his time. High-status men with several rice fields and multiple wives had households near each field. They spent most of

This 2009 photo shows South African president Jacob Zuma with his wives Sizakele Khumalo, right, Nompumelo Ntuli, left, and Tobeka Madiba, second left, after giving his annual State of the Nation address. Could a man with three wives be elected president of the United States?

their time with the senior wife but visited the others throughout the year.

Plural wives can play important political roles in nonindustrial states. The king of the Merina, a populous society in the highlands of Madagascar, had palaces for each of his twelve wives in different provinces. He stayed with them when he traveled through the kingdom. They were his local agents, overseeing and reporting on provincial matters. The king of Buganda, the major precolonial state of Uganda, took hundreds of wives, representing all the clans in his nation. Everyone in the kingdom became the king's in-law, and all the clans had a chance to provide the next ruler. This was a way of giving the common people a stake in the government.

These examples show that there is no single explanation for polygyny. Its context and function vary from society to society and even within the same society. Some men are polygynous because they have inherited a widow from a brother (the levirate). Others have plural wives because they seek prestige or want to increase household productivity. Still others use marriage as a political tool or a means of economic advancement. Men and women with political and economic ambitions cultivate marital alliances that serve their aims. In many societies, including the Betsileo of Madagascar and the Igbo of Nigeria, women arrange the marriages.

Like all institutions studied by anthropologists, customs involving plural marriage are changing in the contemporary world and in the context of nation-states and globalization. This chapter's "Appreciating Diversity" focuses on changing marriage customs in Turkey. Traditionally, polygyny has been allowed there for men who could afford multiple wives and many children. Polygyny now is outlawed, but it still is practiced. Because polygynous unions now lack legal status, secondary wives are at risk if their husband mistreats, neglects, or leaves them.

Polyandry

Polyandry is rare and is practiced under very specific conditions. Most of the world's polyandrous peoples live in South Asia—Tibet, Nepal, India, and Sri Lanka. In some of these areas, polyandry seems to be a cultural adaptation to mobility associated with customary male travel for trade, commerce, and military operations. Polyandry ensures there will be at least one man at home to accomplish male activities within a gender-based division of labor. Fraternal polyandry is also an effective strategy when resources are scarce. Brothers with limited resources (in land) pool their resources in expanded (polyandrous) households. They take just one wife. Polyandry restricts the number of wives and heirs. Less competition among heirs means that land can be transmitted with minimal fragmentation.

acing the COURSE

summary

1. Marriage, which usually is a form of domestic partnership, is hard to define. Human behavior with respect to mating with close relatives may express a generalized primate tendency, illustrating both urges and avoidance. But types, risks, and avoidance of incest also reflect specific kinship structures. The avoidance of incest promotes exogamy, which widens social networks, creating friends and allies in different groups.

2. Exogamy extends social and political ties outward. This is confirmed by a consideration of endogamy—marriage within the group. Endogamic rules are common in stratified societies. One extreme example is India, where castes are the endogamous units. Castes are subdivided into exogamous descent groups. Certain ancient kingdoms encouraged royal incest while prohibiting incest by commoners.

3. The discussion of same-sex marriage, which, by and large, is illegal in the United States, illustrates the various rights that go along with different-sex marriages. Marriage establishes the legal parents of children. It gives each spouse rights to the sexuality, labor, and property of the other. And it establishes a socially significant "relationship of affinity" between each spouse and the other spouse's relatives.

4. In societies with descent groups, marriages are relationships between groups as well as between spouses. In patrilineal societies, the groom and his relatives often transfer wealth to the bride and her relatives. As the value of that tranfer increases, the divorce rate declines. Particularly in nonindustrial food-producing societies, marital customs create and maintain group alliances. Examples include the sororate, by which a man marries the sister of his deceased wife, and the levirate, by which a woman marries the brother of her deceased husband.

5. The ease and frequency of divorce vary across cultures. Political, economic, social, cultural, and religious factors affect the divorce rate. When marriage is a matter of intergroup alliance, as is typically true in societies with descent groups, divorce is less common. A large fund of joint property also complicates divorce.

6. Many societies permit plural marriages. The two kinds of polygamy are polygyny and polyandry. The former involves multiple wives; the latter, multiple husbands. Polygyny is much more common than is polyandry.

Some of these rights may be established by same-sex domestic partnerships.

key terms

cross cousins 451
dowry 460
endogamy 456
exogamy 451
genitor 451
incest 451
levirate 462
lobola 460

mater 458
parallel cousins 451
pater 451
plural marriage 461
polyandry 461
polygyny 461
sororate 461

test yourself

MULTIPLE CHOICE

1. This chapter describes the example of marital unions between women among the Nuer of South Sudan. These unions are symbolic and social relationships rather than sexual ones, as in the case of a woman who marries another woman if her father has only daughters but no male heirs. The "wife" can then have sex with another man until she gets pregnant. The resulting children are accepted as the offspring of both the female husband and the wife. Examples like this one highlight

   a. how some societies need a better educational system to teach people about proper kinship relationships.

   b. how some societies suffer from the lack of male fathers.

c. how despite appearances, marriage has little to do with wealth and it is really all about sex.

d. how kinship relationships take different meanings in different social contexts; they are socially constructed.

e. how some societies could benefit from exposure to modernity.

2. How is exogamy adaptive?

a. It increases the likelihood that disadvantageous alleles will find phenotypic expression and thus be eliminated from the population.

b. It impedes peaceful relations among social groups and therefore promotes population expansion.

c. It was an important causal factor in the origin of the state.

d. It is not adaptive; it is just a cultural construction.

e. It increases the number of individuals on whom one can rely in time of need.

3. Who are your cross cousins?

a. the children of your mother's brother or your father's sister

b. the children of your mother's sister or your father's brother

c. your father's cousins' children

d. your mother's cousins' children

e. your cousins of the opposite sex

4. Among the Yanomami, as in many societies with unilineal descent, sex with cross cousins is proper but sex with parallel cousins is considered incestuous. Why?

a. The Yanomami consider parallel cousins to be relatives, whereas cross cousins are actual or potential affinals.

b. Among the Yanomami, the cross cousins are actually the parallel cousins.

c. The Yanomami, as well as members of other societies with unilineal descent, share a gene that impedes them from having sex with parallel cousins.

d. This behavior is a human universal.

e. The Yanomami consider cross cousins closer relatives than all other kin.

5. Most societies discourage incest because

a. of instinctive horror caused by genes.

b. exogamy promotes alliances.

c. they fear biological degeneration.

d. of genetically determined attraction for those most different from ourselves.

e. They don't; all societies permit incest to some degree.

6. Some Polynesian communities believe in the impersonal force called *mana* and that having high levels of mana marks people as sacred. The practice of royal endogamy was one way of making sure that this impersonal force remained within the ruling class. What type of explanation is this?

a. a latent function, the explanation investigators give for people's customs

b. an affinal function that encourages the extension of affinal bonds to an ever-widening circle of people

c. a genetic explanation

d. a manifest function, the explanations people give for their customs

e. an etic explanation

7. Among some Native American groups, figures known as *berdaches* were biological men who assumed the behavior and tasks of women. Sometimes they married men and together they would share the products of each other's labor in the same way that different-sex marriages do. This example illustrates

a. how Arizona is one of many states that recognize same-sex marriages in the United States.

b. how, if legal, same-sex marriages could easily give each spouse rights to the other spouse's labor and its products.

c. the rare social phenomenon of polyandry.

d. how same-sex marriages make good economic sense.

e. how Edmund Leach was wrong to suggest that all societies define marriage similarly.

8. Which of the following statements about divorce is *not* true?

a. Divorce is more common now than it was a century ago.

b. The more substantial the joint property, the more complicated the divorce.

c. Divorce is unique to industrialized nation-states.

d. Divorce is easier in matrilineal than in patrilineal societies.

e. When substantial wealth is transferred at marriage, the divorce rate declines.

9. Which of the following is *not* a form of polygamy?

a. a man who has three wives

b. a woman who has three husbands, all of whom are brothers

c. a man who marries, then divorces, then marries again, then divorces again, then marries again, each time to a different woman

d. a man who has three wives, all of whom are sisters

e. a man who has two wives, one of whom is biologically female, while the other is biologically male, but is regarded as having the spirit of a woman

10. Which of the following statements about marriage is true?
    a. It must involve at least one biological male and at least one biological female.
    b. It involves a woman and the genitor of her children.
    c. It always involves a priest.
    d. Rings must be exchanged.
    e. It is a cultural universal.

FILL IN THE BLANK

1. The term _____ refers to the biological father of a child, while _____ is the term anthropologists use to identify ego's socially recognized father.
2. _____ refers to the culturally sanctioned practice of marrying someone within a group to which one belongs.
3. _____ is a marital exchange in which the bride's family or kin group provides substantial gifts when their daughter marries. This custom is correlated with _____ female status.
4. When a widower marries a sister of his deceased wife, this is called a _____.
5. The custom called _____ occurs when a widow marries a brother of her deceased husband.

CRITICAL THINKING

1. What is homogamy? In countries such as the United States, what are the social and economic implications of homogamy (especially when coupled with other trends such as the rise of female employment)?
2. What is dowry? What customs involving gift giving typically occur with marriage in patrilineal societies? Do you have comparable customs in your society? Why or why not?
3. According to Edmund Leach (1955), depending on the society, several different kinds of rights are allocated by marriage. What are these rights? Which among these rights do you consider more fundamental than others in your definition of marriage? Which ones can you do without? Why?
4. Outside industrial societies, marriage is often more a relationship between groups than one between individuals. What does this mean? What are some examples of this?
5. Divorce tends to be more common in matrilineal than in patrilineal societies. Why?

Multiple Choice: 1. (D); 2. (E); 3. (A); 4. (A); 5. (B); 6. (B); 7. (B); 8. (C); 9. (C); 10. (E); **Fill in the Blank:** 1. genitor, pater; 2. Endogamy; 3. Dowry, low; 4. sororate; 5. levirate

suggested additional readings

Ingraham, C.
   2008   *White Weddings: Romancing Heterosexuality in Popular Culture*, 2nd ed. New York: Routledge. Love and marriage, including the ceremony, in today's United States.
Jankowiak, W. R., ed.
   2008   *Intimacies: Love and Sex across Cultures.* New York: Columbia University Press. Case studies of love, sex, and marriage in different societies.
Levine, N. E.
   1988   *The Dynamics of Polyandry: Kinship, Domesticity, and Population in the Tibetan Border.* Chicago: University of Chicago Press. Case study of fraternal polyandry and household organization in northwestern Nepal.
Malinowski, B.
   2001 (orig. 1927)   *Sex and Repression in Savage Society.* New York: Routledge. Classic study of sex, marriage, and kinship among the matrilineal Trobrianders.
Stockard, J. E.
   2001 *Marriage in Culture: Practice and Meaning across Diverse Soceties.* San Diego, CA: Harcourt. The cases examined here offer a comparative view of marrage.
Zeitzen, M. K.
   2008   *Polygamy: A Cross-Cultural Analysis.* New York: Berg. Comparative case studies and analysis of plural marriage customs.

Go to our Online Learning Center website at **www.mhhe.com/kottak** for Internet exercises directly related to the content of this chapter.

internet exercises

CHAPTER 21

Religion

What is religion, and what are its various forms, social correlates, and functions?

What is ritual, and what are its various forms and expressions?

What role does religion play in maintaining and changing societies?

◀ Worshippers attend a mass on the island of Flores, Indonesia.

understanding OURSELVES

Have you ever noticed how much baseball players spit? Outside baseball—even among other male sports figures—spitting is considered impolite. Football players, with their customary headgear, don't spit, nor do basketball players, who might slip on the court. No spitting by tennis players, gymnasts, or swimmers. Not even Mark Spitz (a swimmer turned dentist). But watch any baseball game for a few innings and you'll see spitting galore. Since pitchers appear to be the spitting champions, the custom likely originated on the mound. It continues today as a carryover from the days when pitchers routinely chewed tobacco, believing that nicotine enhanced their concentration and effectiveness. The spitting custom spread to other players, who unabashedly spew saliva from the outfield to the dugout steps.

For the student of custom, ritual, and magic, baseball is an especially interesting game, to which lessons from anthropology are easily applied. The pioneering anthropologist Bronislaw Malinowski, writing about Pacific Islanders rather than baseball players, noted they had developed all sorts of magic to use in sailing, a hazardous activity. He proposed that when people face conditions they can't control (e.g., wind and weather), they turn to magic. Magic, in the form of rituals, taboos, and sacred objects, is particularly evident in baseball. Like sailing magic, baseball magic serves to reduce psychological stress, creating an illusion of control when real control is lacking.

In several publications about baseball, the anthropologist George Gmelch makes use of Malinowski's observation that magic is most common in situations dominated by chance and uncertainty. All sorts of magical behaviors surround pitching and batting, which are full of uncertainty. There are fewer rituals for fielding, over which players have more control. (Batting averages of .350 or higher are very rare after a full season, but a fielding percentage below .900 is a disgrace.) Especially obvious are the rituals (like the spitting) of pitchers, who may . . . tug their cap between pitches, spit in a particular direction, magically manipulate the resin bag, talk to the ball, or wash their hands after giving up a run. Batters have their rituals, too. It isn't uncommon to see Milwaukee Brewer outfielder Carlos Gomez kiss his bat, which he likes to talk to, smell, threaten—and reward when he gets a hit. Another batter routinely would spit, then ritually touch his gob with his bat, to enhance his success at the plate.

Humans use tools to accomplish a lot, but technology still doesn't let us "have it all." To keep hope alive in situations of uncertainty, and for outcomes we can't control, all societies draw on magic and religion as sources of nonmaterial comfort, explanation, and control. What are your rituals?

WHAT IS RELIGION?

Given the varied nature and worldwide scope of beliefs and behavior labeled "religious," anthropologists know how difficult it is to define **religion.** In his book *Religion: An Anthropological View*, Anthony F. C. Wallace offered this definition: "belief and ritual concerned with supernatural beings, powers, and forces" (1966, p. 5). By "supernatural" he referred to a nonmaterial realm beyond (but believed to impinge on) the observable world. This realm cannot be verified or falsified empirically and is inexplicable in ordinary terms. It must be accepted "on faith." Supernatural beings—deities, ghosts, demons, souls, and spirits—make their homes outside our material world, although they may visit it from time to time. There also are supernatural or sacred forces, some of them wielded by deities and spirits, others that simply exist. In many societies, people believe they can benefit from, become imbued with, or manipulate supernatural forces (see Bowie 2006; Bowen 2008; Crapo 2006; Lambek 2008; Stein and Stein 2008; Warms, Garber, and McGee 2009).

Wallace's definition of religion focuses on presumably universal categories (beings, powers, and forces) within the supernatural realm. For Emile Durkheim (1912/2001), one of the founders of the anthropology of religion, the key distinction was between the sacred and the profane. Like the supernatural for Wallace, Durkheim's "sacred" was the domain set off from the ordinary or the mundane (he used the word "profane"). For Durkheim, every society had its sacred, but that domain was socially constructed; it varied from society to society. Durkheim focused on Native Australian societies, which he believed had preserved the most elementary or basic forms of religion. He noted that their most sacred objects, including plants and animals that served as totems, were not supernatural at all. Rather they were "real world" entities (e.g., kangaroos, grubs) that, over the generations, had acquired special meaning for the social groups that had made them sacred and continued to "worship" them.

Many definitions of religion focus on groups of people who gather together regularly for worship (see Reese 1999). These congregants or adherents internalize common beliefs and a shared system of meaning. They accept a set of doctrines involving the relationship between the individual and divinity, the sacred, or whatever is taken to be the ultimate nature of reality. Anthropologists like Durkheim have stressed the collective, social, shared, and enacted nature of religion, the emotions it generates, and the meanings it embodies. As Michael Lambek (2008, p. 5) remarks, "good anthropology understands that religious worlds are real, vivid, and significant to those who construct and inhabit them." Durkheim (1912/2001) highlighted religious effervescence, the bubbling up of collective emotional intensity generated by worship. Victor Turner (1969/1995) updated Durkheim's notion, using the term **communitas,** an intense community spirit, a feeling of great social solidarity, equality, and togetherness.

The word *religion* derives from the Latin *religare*—"to tie, to bind," but it is not necessary for all members of a given religion to meet together as a common body. Subgroups meet regularly at local congregation sites. They may attend occasional meetings with adherents representing a wider region. And they may form an imagined community with people of similar faith throughout the world.

In studying religion cross-culturally, anthropologists pay attention to religion as a social phenomenon as well as to the meanings of religious doctrines, settings, acts, and events. Verbal manifestations of religious beliefs include prayers, chants, myths, texts, and statements about, including rules of, ethics and morality (see Cunningham 1999; Klass 2003; Moro and Meyers 2010; Stein and Stein 2011). The anthropological study of religion also encompasses notions about purity and pollution (including taboos involving diet and physical contact), sacrifice, initiation, rites of passage, vision quests, pilgrimages, spirit possession, prophecy, study, devotion, and moral actions (Lambek 2008, p. 9).

Like ethnicity and language, religion is associated with social divisions within and between societies and nations. Religion both unites and divides. Participation in common rites may affirm, and thus maintain, the solidarity of a group of adherents. As we know from daily headlines, however, religious difference also may be associated with bitter enmity. In today's world, contacts and confrontations have increased between so-called world religions, such as Christianity and Islam, and the more localized forms of religion that missionaries typically lump together under the disparaging term "paganism." Increasingly, world religions compete for adherents and global power, and ethnic, regional, and class conflicts come to be framed in religious terms. Recent and contemporary examples of religion as a social and political force include the Iranian revolution, the rise of the religious right in the United States, and the spread of Pentecostalism in Korea, Africa, and Latin America.

Long ago, Edward Sapir (1928/1956) argued for a distinction between "a religion" and "religion." The former term would apply only to a formally organized religion, such as the world religions just mentioned. The latter—religion—is universal; it refers to religious beliefs and behavior, which exist in all societies, even if they don't stand out as a separate and clearly demarcated sphere. Indeed, many anthropologists (e.g., Asad 1983/2008) argue that such categories as "religion," "politics," and "the economy" are arbitrary constructs that apply best, and perhaps only, to Western, Christian, and modern societies. In such contexts religion can be seen as a specific domain, separate from politics and the economy. By contrast, in nonindustrial societies, religion typically is more embedded in society. Religious beliefs may help regulate the economy (e.g., astrologers determine when to plant) or permeate politics (e.g., divine right of kings). (Although religion also spills over into politics in the contemporary United States, it isn't supposed to. That is, the legal system views religion and politics as spheres that should be kept separate.)

Anthropologists agree that religion exists in all human societies; it is a cultural universal. However, we'll see that it isn't always easy to distinguish the sacred from the profane and that different societies conceptualize divinity, the sacred, the supernatural, and ultimate realities very differently.

religion
Belief and ritual concerned with supernatural beings, powers, and forces.

communitas
Intense feeling of social solidarity.

EXPRESSIONS OF RELIGION

polytheism
Worship of multiple deities, who control aspects of nature.

monotheism
Worship of an eternal, omniscient, omnipotent, and omnipresent supreme being.

When did religion begin? No one knows for sure. There are suggestions of religion in Neandertal burials and on European cave walls, where painted stick figures may represent shamans, early religious specialists. Nevertheless, any statement about when, where, why, and how religion arose, or any description of its original nature, can only be speculative. Although such speculations are inconclusive, many have revealed important functions and effects of religious behavior. Several theories will be examined now.

Spiritual Beings

mana
Impersonal sacred force, so named in Melanesia and Polynesia.

taboo
Sacred and forbidden; prohibition backed by supernatural sanctions.

animism
Belief in souls or doubles.

Another founder of the anthropology of religion was the Englishman Sir Edward Burnett Tylor (1871/1958). Religion arose, Tylor thought, as people tried to understand conditions and events they could not explain by reference to daily experience. Tylor believed that ancient humans—and contemporary nonindustrial peoples—were particularly intrigued with death, dreaming, and trance. People see images they may remember when they wake up or come out of a trance state. Tylor concluded that attempts to explain dreams and trances led early humans to believe that two entities inhabit the body. One is active during the day, and the other—a double or soul—is active during sleep and trance states. Although they never meet, they are vital to each other. When the double permanently leaves the body, the person dies. Death is departure of the soul. From the Latin for soul, *anima*, Tylor named this belief animism. The soul was one sort of spiritual entity; people remembered various images from their dreams and trances—other spirits. For Tylor, **animism,** the earliest form of religion, was a belief in spiritual beings.

Tylor proposed that religion evolved through stages, beginning with animism. **Polytheism** (the belief in multiple gods) and then **monotheism** (the belief in a single, all-powerful deity) developed later. Because religion originated to explain things, Tylor thought it would decline as science offered better explanations. To an extent, he was right. We now have scientific explanations for many things that religion once elucidated. Nevertheless, because religion persists, it must do something more than explain. It must, and does, have other functions and meanings.

Powers and Forces

In addition to animism—and sometimes coexisting with it in the same society—is a view of the supernatural as a domain of impersonal power, or force, which people can control under certain conditions. (You'd be right to think of *Star Wars*.) Such a conception is particularly prominent in Melanesia, the area of the South Pacific that includes Papua New Guinea and adjacent islands. Melanesians believed in **mana,** a sacred impersonal force existing in the universe. Mana can reside in people, animals, plants, and objects.

Melanesian mana was similar to our notion of good luck. Objects with mana could change someone's luck. For example, a charm or amulet belonging to a successful hunter might transmit the hunter's mana to the next person who held or wore it. A woman might put a rock in her garden, see her yields improve, and attribute the change to the force contained in the rock.

Beliefs in manalike forces are widespread, although the specifics of the religious doctrines vary. Consider the contrast between mana in Melanesia and mana in Polynesia (the islands included in a triangular area marked by Hawaii to the north, Easter Island to the east, and New Zealand to the southwest). In Melanesia, anyone could acquire mana by chance, or by working hard to get it. In Polynesia, however, mana wasn't potentially available to everyone but was attached to political offices. Chiefs and nobles had more mana than ordinary people did.

So charged with mana were the highest chiefs that contact with them was dangerous to commoners. The mana of chiefs flowed out of their bodies. It could infect the ground, making it dangerous for others to walk in the chief's footsteps. It could permeate the containers and utensils chiefs used in eating. Because high chiefs had so much mana, their bodies and possessions were **taboo** (set apart as sacred and off-limits to ordinary people). Because ordinary people couldn't bear as much sacred current as royalty could, when commoners were accidentally exposed, purification rites were necessary.

One function of religion is to explain. As Horton (1993) and Lambek (2008) point out, there are universals in human thought and experience, common conditions and situations that call out for explanation. What happens in sleep and trance, and with

Illustrating polytheism, this section of the East Frieze of the Parthenon (Athens, Greece) shows Poseidon, Apollo, and Artemis. The frieze dates to ca. 447–432 B.C.E.

death?—The soul leaves the body. Why do some people prosper while others fail?—Blame it on such nonmaterial factors as luck, mana, sorcery, or being one of "God's chosen."

The beliefs in spiritual beings (e.g., animism) and supernatural forces (e.g., mana) fit within Wallace's definition of religion given at the beginning of this chapter. Most religions include both spirits and impersonal forces. Likewise the supernatural beliefs of contemporary North Americans include beings (gods, saints, souls, demons) and forces (charms, talismans, crystals, and sacred objects).

Magic and Religion

Magic refers to supernatural techniques intended to accomplish specific aims. These techniques include magical actions, offerings, spells, formulas, and incantations used with deities or with impersonal forces. Magicians employ *imitative magic* to produce a desired effect by imitating it. If magicians wish to harm someone, they may imitate that effect on an image of the victim. Sticking pins in "voodoo dolls" is an example. With *contagious magic*, whatever is done to an object is believed to affect a person who once had contact with it. Sometimes practitioners of contagious magic use body products from prospective victims—their nails or hair, for example. The spell performed on the body product is believed eventually to reach the person (see Stein and Stein 2008). Magic exists in societies with diverse religious beliefs, including animism, mana, polytheism, or monotheism.

Uncertainty, Anxiety, Solace

Religion and magic don't just explain things and help people accomplish goals. They also enter the realm of human feelings. In other words, they serve emotional needs as well as cognitive (e.g., explanatory) ones. For example, supernatural beliefs and practices can help reduce anxiety. Magical techniques can dispel doubts that arise when outcomes are beyond human control. Similarly, religion helps people face death and endure life crises.

Although all societies have techniques to deal with everyday matters, there are certain aspects of people's lives over which they lack control. When people face uncertainty and danger, according to Malinowski, they turn to magic.

> [H]owever much knowledge and science help man in allowing him to obtain what he wants, they are unable completely to control chance, to eliminate accidents, to foresee the unexpected turn of natural events, or to make human handiwork reliable and adequate to all practical requirements. (Malinowski 1931/1978, p. 39)

As was discussed in this chapter's "Understanding Ourselves," Malinowski found that the Trobriand Islanders used a variety of magical practices when

Illustrating baseball magic, in April 2012, in Phoenix, Arizona, San Francisco Giants relief pitcher Sergio Romo (54) and third baseman Pablo Sandoval (48) go through a pregame ritual before playing the Arizona Diamondbacks. The Diamondbacks went on to defeat the Giants 7-6.

they went on sailing expeditions, a hazardous activity. He proposed that because people can't control matters such as wind, weather, and the fish supply, they turn to magic. People may call on magic when they come to a gap in their knowledge or powers of practical control yet have to continue in a pursuit (Malinowski 1931/1978).

Malinowski noted that it was only when confronted by situations they could not control that Trobrianders, out of psychological stress, turned

magic
Use of supernatural techniques to accomplish specific ends.

Trobriand Islanders prepare a traditional trading canoe for use in the Kula, which is a regional exchange system. The woman brings trade goods in a basket, while the men prepare the long canoe to set sail. Magic is often associated with uncertainty, such as sailing in unpredictable waters.

from technology to magic. Despite our improving technical skills, we can't control every outcome, and magic persists in contemporary societies. As was discussed in "Understanding Ourselves," magic is particularly evident in baseball, where George Gmelch (1978, 2001, 2006) describes a series of rituals, taboos, and sacred objects. Like Trobriand sailing magic, these behaviors serve to reduce psychological stress, creating an illusion of magical control when real control is lacking. Even the best pitchers have off days and bad luck. Gmelch's conclusions confirm Malinowski's that magic is most prevalent in situations of chance and uncertainty, especially pitching and batting.

Passage rites are often collective. A group—such as these initiates in Togo or these Navy trainees in San Diego—passes through the rites as a unit. Such liminal people experience the same treatment and conditions and must act alike. They share communitas, an intense community spirit, a feeling of great social solidarity or togetherness.

According to Malinowski, magic is used to establish control, but religion "is born out of . . . the real tragedies of human life" (1931/1978, p. 45). Religion offers emotional comfort, particularly when people face a crisis. Malinowski saw tribal religions as concerned mainly with organizing, commemorating, and helping people get through such life events as birth, puberty, marriage, and death.

Rituals

Several features distinguish **ritual** behavior from other kinds of behavior (Rappaport 1974, 1999). Rituals are formal—stylized, repetitive, and stereotyped. People perform them in special (sacred) places and at set times. Rituals include liturgical orders—sequences of words and actions invented prior to the current performance of the ritual in which they occur.

These features link rituals to plays, but there are important differences. Actors in plays merely portray something, but ritual performers—who make up congregations—are in earnest. Rituals convey information about the participants and their traditions. Repeated year after year, generation after generation, rituals translate enduring messages, values, and sentiments into action.

Rituals are social acts. Inevitably, some participants are more committed than others are to the beliefs that lie behind the rites. However, just by taking part in a joint public act, the performers signal that they accept a common social and moral order, one that transcends their status as individuals.

Rites of Passage

Magic and religion, as Malinowski noted, can reduce anxiety and allay fears. Ironically, beliefs and rituals also can create anxiety and a sense of insecurity and danger (Radcliffe-Brown 1962/1965). Anxiety may arise because a rite exists. Indeed, participation in a collective ritual (e.g., circumcision of early teen boys, common among East African pastoralists) may produce stress, whose common reduction, once the ritual is completed, enhances the solidarity of the participants.

Rites of passage can be individual or collective. Traditional Native American vision quests illustrate individual **rites of passage** (customs associated with the transition from one place or stage of life to another). To move from boyhood to manhood, a youth temporarily separated from his community. After a period of isolation in the wilderness, often featuring fasting and drug consumption, the young man would see a vision, which would become his guardian spirit. He would return then to his community as an adult.

Contemporary rites of passage include confirmations, baptisms, bar and bat mitzvahs, initiations, weddings, and applying for Social Security and Medicare. Passage rites involve changes in social status, such as from boyhood to manhood and from nonmember to sorority sister. More generally, a rite

LIMINALITY	NORMAL SOCIAL STRUCTURE
Transition	State
Homogeneity	Heterogeneity
Communitas	Structure
Equality	Inequality
Anonymity	Names
Absence of property	Property
Absence of status	Status
Nakedness or uniform dress	Dress distinctions
Sexual continence or excess	Sexuality
Minimization of sex distinctions	Maximization of sex distinctions
Absence of rank	Rank
Humility	Pride
Disregard of personal appearance	Care for personal appearance
Unselfishness	Selfishness
Total obedience	Obedience only to superior rank
Sacredness	Secularity
Sacred instruction	Technical knowledge
Silence	Speech
Simplicity	Complexity
Acceptance of pain and suffering	Avoidance of pain and suffering

SOURCE: Reprinted with permission from Victor W. Turner, *The Ritual Process: Structure and Anti-Structure* (New York: Aldine de Gruyter). Copyright © 1995 by Walter de Gruyter, Inc.

of passage may mark any change in place, condition, social position, or age.

All rites of passage have three phases: separation, liminality, and incorporation. In the first phase, people withdraw from ordinary society. In the third phase, they reenter society, having completed a rite that changes their status. The second or liminal phase is the most interesting. It is the limbo or "time out" during which people have left one status but haven't yet entered or joined the next (Turner 1969/1995).

Liminality always has certain characteristics. Liminal people exist apart from ordinary distinctions and expectations, living in a time out of time. A series of contrasts demarcate liminality from normal social life. For example, among the Ndembu of Zambia, a chief underwent a rite of passage prior to taking office. During the liminal period, his past and future positions in society were ignored, even reversed. He was subjected to a variety of insults, orders, and humiliations.

Passage rites often are collective. Several individuals—boys being circumcised, fraternity or sorority initiates, men at military boot camps, football players in summer training camps, women becoming nuns—pass through the rites together as a group. Recap 21.1 summarizes the contrasts or oppositions between liminality and normal social life. Most notable is a social aspect of collective liminality called communitas (Turner 1967/1974), an intense community spirit, a feeling of great social solidarity, equality, and togetherness. Liminal people experience the same treatment and conditions and must act alike. Liminality may be marked ritually and symbolically by reversals of ordinary behavior. For example, sexual taboos may be intensified, or conversely, sexual excess may be encouraged. Liminal symbols, such as special clothing or body paint, mark the condition as extraordinary—outside and beyond ordinary society and everyday life. Liminality is basic to all passage rites. Furthermore, in certain societies, including our own, liminal symbols may be used to set off one (religious) group from another, and from society as a whole. Such "permanent liminal groups" (e.g., sects, brotherhoods, and cults) are found most characteristically in nation-states. Such liminal features as humility, poverty, equality, obedience, sexual abstinence, and silence (see Recap 21.1) may be required for all sect or cult members. Those who join such a group agree to its rules. As if they were undergoing a passage rite—but in this case a never-ending one—they may have to abandon their previous possessions and social ties, including those with family members. Is liminality compatible with Facebook?

Members of a sect or cult often wear uniform clothing. Often they adopt a common hairstyle (shaved head, short hair, or long hair). Liminal groups submerge the individual in the collective.

liminality
The in-between phase of a passage rite.

This may be one reason why Americans, whose core values include individuality and individualism, are so fearful and suspicious of "cults."

Not all collective rites are rites of passage. Most societies observe occasions on which people come together to worship or celebrate and, in doing so, affirm and reinforce their solidarity. Rituals such as the totemic ceremonies described below are *rites of intensification*: They intensify social solidarity. The ritual creates communitas and produces emotions (the collective spiritual effervescence described by Durkheim 1912/2001) that enhance social solidarity.

Totemism

Totemism was a key ingredient in the religions of the Native Australians. **Totems** could be animals, plants, or geographical features. In each tribe, groups of people had particular totems. Members of each totemic group believed themselves to be descendants of their totem. They customarily neither killed nor ate it, but this taboo was lifted once a year, when people assembled for ceremonies dedicated to the totem. These annual rites were believed to be necessary for the totem's survival and reproduction.

Totemism uses nature as a model for society. The totems usually are animals and plants, which are part of nature. People relate to nature through their totemic association with natural species. Because each group has a different totem, social differences mirror natural contrasts. Diversity in the natural order becomes a model for diversity in the social order. However, although totemic plants and animals occupy different niches in nature, on another level they

are united because they all are part of nature. The unity of the human social order is enhanced by symbolic association with and imitation of the natural order (Durkheim 1912/2001; Lévi-Strauss 1963; Radcliffe-Brown 1962/1965).

Totemism is one form of **cosmology**—a system, in this case a religious one, for imagining and understanding the universe. Claude Lévi-Strauss, a prolific French anthropologist and a key figure in the anthropology of religion, is well known for his studies of myth, folklore, totemism, and cosmology. Lévi-Strauss believed that one role of religious rites and beliefs is to affirm, and thus maintain, the solidarity of a religion's adherents. Totems are sacred emblems symbolizing common identity. This is true not just among Native Australians, but also among Native American groups of the North Pacific Coast of North America, whose totem poles are well known. Their totemic carvings, which commemorated, and told visual stories about, ancestors, animals, and spirits, were also associated with ceremonies. In totemic rites, people gather together to honor their totem. In so doing, they use ritual to maintain the social oneness that the totem symbolizes.

Totemic principles continue to demarcate groups, including clubs, teams, and universities, in modern societies. Badgers and Wolverines are animals, and (it is said in Michigan) Buckeyes are some kind of nut (more precisely, buckeye nuts come from the buckeye tree). Differences between natural species (e.g., Lions, and Tigers, and Bears) serve to distinguish sports teams, and even political parties (donkeys and elephants). Although the modern context is more secular, one can still witness, in intense college football rivalries, some of the effervescence Durkheim noted in Australian totemic religion and other rites of intensification.

RELIGION AND CULTURAL ECOLOGY

Another domain in which religion plays a prominent role is cultural ecology. Behavior motivated by beliefs in supernatural beings, powers, and forces may help people survive in their material environment. In this section, we will see how beliefs and rituals may function as part of a group's cultural adaptation to its environment.

Sacred Cattle in India

The people of India revere zebu cattle, which are protected by the Hindu doctrine of *ahimsa*, a principle of nonviolence that forbids the killing of animals generally. Western economic development experts occasionally (and erroneously) cite the Hindu cattle taboo to illustrate the idea that religious beliefs can stand in the way of rational economic decisions. Hindus might seem to be irrationally ignoring a valuable food (beef) because of their cultural or religious traditions. The

cosmology
A system, often religious, for imagining and understanding the universe.

totem
An animal, plant, or geographic feature associated with a specific social group, to which that totem is sacred or symbolically important.

Sacred cows take their time during rush hour in Varanasi, India. India's zebu cattle are protected by the doctrine of *ahimsa*, a principle of nonviolence that forbids the killing of animals generally. This Hindu doctrine puts the full power of organized religion behind the command not to destroy a valuable resource even in times of extreme need.

economic developers also comment that Indians don't know how to raise proper cattle. They point to the scraggly zebus that wander about town and country. Western techniques of animal husbandry grow bigger cattle that produce more beef and milk. Western planners lament that Hindus are set in their ways. Bound by culture and tradition, they refuse to develop rationally.

However, these assumptions are both ethnocentric and wrong. Sacred cattle actually play an important adaptive role in an Indian ecosystem that has evolved over thousands of years (Harris 1974, 1978). Peasants' use of cattle to pull plows and carts is part of the technology of Indian agriculture. Indian peasants have no need for large, hungry cattle of the sort that economic developers, beef marketers, and North American cattle ranchers prefer. Scrawny animals pull plows and carts well enough but don't eat their owners out of house and home. How could peasants with limited land and marginal diets feed supersteers without taking food away from themselves?

Indians use cattle manure to fertilize their fields. Not all the manure is collected, because peasants don't spend much time watching their cattle, which wander and graze at will during certain seasons. In the rainy season, some of the manure that cattle deposit on the hillsides washes down to the fields. In this way, cattle also fertilize the fields indirectly. Furthermore, in a country where fossil fuels are scarce, dry cattle dung, which burns slowly and evenly, is a basic cooking fuel.

Far from being useless, as the development experts contend, sacred cattle are essential to Indian cultural adaptation. Biologically adapted to poor pasture land and a marginal environment, the scraggly zebu provides fertilizer and fuel, is indispensable in farming, and is affordable for peasants. The Hindu doctrine of *ahimsa* puts the full power of organized religion behind the command not to destroy a valuable resource even in times of extreme need.

SOCIAL CONTROL

Religion means a lot to people. It helps them cope with uncertainty, adversity, fear, and tragedy. It offers hope that things will get better. Lives can be transformed through spiritual healing. Sinners can repent and be saved—or they can go on sinning and be damned. If the faithful truly internalize a system of religious rewards and punishments, their religion becomes a powerful influence on their attitudes and behavior, and what they teach their children.

Many people engage in religious activity because it works for them. Prayers get answered. Faith healers heal. Native Americans in southwestern Oklahoma use faith healers at high monetary costs, not just because it makes them feel better about the uncertain, but because it works (Lassiter 1998). Each year legions of Brazilians visit a church, Nosso Senhor do Bomfim, in the city of Salvador, Bahia. They vow to repay "Our Lord" (Nosso Senhor) if healing happens.

Showing that the vows work, and are repaid, are the thousands of *ex votos*, plastic impressions of every conceivable body part, that adorn the church, along with photos of people who have been cured.

Religion can work by getting inside people and mobilizing their emotions—their joy, their wrath, their certainty, their righteousness. People can feel a deep sense of shared joy, meaning, experience, communion, belonging, and commitment to their religion. The power of religion affects action. When religions meet, they can coexist peacefully, or their differences can be a basis for enmity and disharmony, even battle. Religious fervor has inspired Christians on crusades against the infidel and has led Muslims to wage holy wars against non-Islamic peoples. Throughout history, political leaders have used religion to promote and justify their views and policies.

How may leaders mobilize communities and, in so doing, gain support for their own policies? One way is by persuasion; another is by instilling hatred or fear. Consider witchcraft accusations. Witch hunts can be powerful means of social control by creating a climate of danger and insecurity that affects everyone, not just the people who are likely targets. No one wants to seem deviant, to be accused of being a witch. Witch hunts often take aim at people who can be accused and punished with least chance of retaliation. During the great European witch craze, during the 15th, 16th, and 17th centuries (Harris 1974), most accusations and convictions were against poor women with little social support.

Witchcraft accusations often are directed at socially marginal or anomalous individuals. Consider the Betsileo of Madagascar, who believe that married men should live in their father's village. Marcel contradicts this rule by residing in his mother's village. People like Marcel who violate cultural norms have to be particularly careful about how they act. Just a bit of unusual behavior (e.g., staying up late at night) can fuel suspicion that they are engaging in witchcraft; they may be avoided or ostracized as a result. In peasant communities, people who stand out economically, especially if they seem to be benefiting at the expense of others, often face witchcraft accusations, leading to social ostracism or punishment. In this case witchcraft accusation becomes a **leveling mechanism,** a custom or social action that operates to reduce status differences and thus to bring standouts in line with community norms—another form of social control.

To ensure proper behavior, religions offer rewards (e.g., the fellowship of the religious community) and punishments (e.g., the threat of being cast out or excommunicated). Religions, especially the formal, organized ones typically found in state societies, often prescribe a code of ethics and morality to guide behavior. The Judaic Ten Commandments laid down a set of prohibitions against killing, stealing, adultery, and other misdeeds. Crimes are breaches of secular laws, as sins are breaches of religious strictures. Some rules (e.g., the Ten Commandments) proscribe or

leveling mechanism
Custom that brings standouts back in line with community norms.

prohibit behavior; others prescribe behavior. The Golden Rule, for instance, is a religious guide to do unto others as you would have them do unto you. Moral codes are ways of maintaining order and stability. Codes of morality and ethics are constantly reinforced in religious sermons, catechisms, and the like. They become internalized psychologically. They guide behavior and produce regret, guilt, shame, and the need for forgiveness, expiation, and absolution when they are not followed.

KINDS OF RELIGION

Religion is a cultural universal. But religions exist in particular societies, and cultural differences show up systematically in religious beliefs and practices. For example, the religions of stratified, state societies differ from those of societies with less marked social contrasts—societies without kings, lords, and subjects. What can a given society afford in terms of religion? Churches, temples, and other full-time religious establishments, with their monumental structures and hierarchies of officials, must be supported in some consistent way, such as by tithes and taxes. What kinds of societies can support such hierarchies and architecture?

All societies have religious figures—those believed capable of mediating between humans and the supernatural. More generally, all societies have medico-magico-religious specialists. Modern societies can support both priesthoods and health care professionals. Lacking the resources for such specialization, foraging societies typically have only part-time specialists, who often have both religious and healing roles. **Shaman** is the general term encompassing curers ("witch doctors"), mediums, spiritualists, astrologers, palm readers, and other independent diviners. In foraging societies, shamans usually are part-time; that is, they also hunt or gather.

The annual totemic ceremonies of Native Australians temporarily brought together foragers who had to disperse most of the year to hunt and gather for subsistence. Given seasonal harvests of fish and other resources in a rich natural environment, foraging tribes on the North Pacific Coast of North America could host ceremonies like the potlatch described in the chapter "Making a Living." However, community rituals including harvest ceremonies and collective rites of passage are much more common in farming and herding societies than among foragers.

Societies with productive economies (based on agriculture and trade) and large, dense populations—that is, nation-states—can support full-time religious specialists—professional priesthoods. Like the state itself, priesthoods are hierarchically and bureaucratically organized. Anthony Wallace (1966) describes the religions of such stratified societies as "ecclesiastical" (pertaining to an established church and its hierarchy of officials) and Olympian, after Mount Olympus, home of the classical Greek gods. In such religions, powerful anthropomorphic gods have specialized functions, for example, gods of love, war, the sea, and death. Such *pantheons* (collections of deities) were prominent in the religions of many nonindustrial nation-states, including the Aztecs of Mexico, several African and Asian kingdoms, and classical Greece and Rome.

Greco-Roman religions were polytheistic, featuring many deities. In monotheism, all supernatural phenomena are believed to be manifestations of, or under the control of, a single eternal, omniscient, omnipotent, and omnipresent being. In the ecclesiastical monotheistic religion known as Christianity, a single supreme being is manifest in a trinity. Robert Bellah (1978) viewed most forms of Christianity as examples of "world-rejecting religion." According to Bellah, the first world-rejecting religions arose in ancient civilizations, along with literacy and a specialized priesthood. These religions are so named because of their tendency to reject the natural (mundane, ordinary, material, secular) world and to focus instead on a higher (sacred, transcendent) realm of reality. The divine is a domain of exalted morality to which humans can only aspire. Salvation through fusion with the supernatural is the main goal of such religions.

Protestant Values and Capitalism

Notions of salvation and the afterlife dominate Christian ideologies. However, most varieties of Protestantism lack the hierarchical structure of earlier monotheistic religions, including Roman Catholicism. With a diminished role for the priest (minister), salvation is directly available to individuals. Regardless of their social status, Protestants have unmediated access to the supernatural. The individualistic focus of Protestantism offers a close fit with capitalism and with American culture.

In his influential book *The Protestant Ethic and the Spirit of Capitalism* (1904/1958), the social theorist Max Weber linked the spread of capitalism to the values preached by early Protestant leaders. Weber saw European Protestants (and eventually their American descendants) as more successful financially than Catholics. He attributed this difference to the values stressed by their religions. Weber saw Catholics as more concerned with immediate happiness and security. Protestants were more ascetic, entrepreneurial, and future oriented, he thought.

Capitalism, said Weber, required that the traditional attitudes of Catholic peasants be replaced by values befitting an industrial economy based on capital accumulation. Protestantism placed a premium on hard work, an ascetic life, and profit seeking. Early Protestants saw success on earth as a sign of divine favor and probable salvation. According to some Protestant credos, individuals could gain favor with God through good works. Other sects stressed predestination, the idea that only a few mortals have been selected for eternal life and that people cannot change their fates. However, material success, achieved

shaman
A part-time magico-religious practitioner.

living anthropology **VIDEOS**

Ritual Possession, www.mhhe.com/kottak

The central figure in this clip is Nana Kofi Owusu, a senior priest-healer among Ghana's Bono people. The Bono believe in a hierarchy of deities and spirits. The highest god is linked to ordinary people through lower-level deities and spirits and the priest-healers and others who receive spirits. Nana Owusu serves as the guardian of various shrines, including one principal one, which he keeps and honors in a separate room of his house and wears on his head during ceremonies. Among the Bono is it only men who receive spirits, or can women receive them, too? How is succession established for the position of priest-healer—how did Nana Owusu achieve this status? According to the professor shown in the clip, do people usually know it when they are possessed?

TABLE 21.1 Religions of the World, by Estimated Number of Adherents, 2005

Christianity	2.1 billion
Islam	1.3 billion
Secular/Nonreligious/Agnostic/Atheist	1.1 billion
Hinduism	900 million
Chinese traditional religion	394 million
Buddhism	376 million
Primal-indigenous	300 million
African traditional and diasporic	100 million
Sikhism	23 million
Juche	19 million
Spiritism	15 million
Judaism	14 million
Baha'i	7 million
Jainism	4.2 million
Shinto	4 million
Cao Dai	4 million
Zoroastrianism	2.6 million
Tenrikyo	2 million
Neo-Paganism	1 million
Unitarian-Universalism	800 thousand
Rastafarianism	600 thousand
Scientology	500 thousand

SOURCE: Adherents.com. 2005. http://www.adherents.com/Religions_By_Adherents.html. Reprinted by permission of Preston Hunter, adherents.com.

through hard work, could be a strong clue that someone was predestined to be saved.

Weber also argued that rational business organization required the removal of industrial production from the home, its setting in peasant societies. Protestantism made such a separation possible by emphasizing individualism: Individuals, not families or households, would be saved or not. Interestingly, given the connection that is usually made with morality and religion in contemporary American discourse about family values, the family was a secondary matter for Weber's early Protestants. God and the individual reigned supreme.

Today, of course, in North America as throughout the world, people of many religions and with diverse worldviews are successful capitalists. Furthermore, traditional Protestant values often have little to do with today's economic maneuvering. Still, there is no denying that the individualistic focus of Protestantism was compatible with the severance of ties to land and kin that industrialism demanded. These values remain prominent in the religious background of many of the people of the United States.

WORLD RELIGIONS

Information on the world's major religions is provided in Table 21.1 (number of adherents) and Figure 21.1 (percentage of world population). Based on people's claimed religions, Christianity is the world's largest, with some 2.1 billion adherents. Islam, with some 1.3 billion practitioners, is next, followed by Hinduism, then Chinese traditional religion (also known as Chinese folk religion or Confucianism), and Buddhism. More than a billion people claim no official religion, but only about a fifth of them are self-proclaimed atheists. Worldwide, Christianity's growth rate of 2.3 percent just matches the rate of world population increase (Adherents.com 2002;

Ontario Consultants 2001). Islam is growing at a faster pace, about 2.9 percent annually. This chapter's "Appreciating Diversity" examines how Islam has spread by adapting successfully to many national and cultural differences, including the presence of other religions that were already established in the areas to which Islam has spread (see also Ahmed 2007, 2008; Kamrava 2011; Shryock 2010).

Within Christianity, there is variation in the growth rate. There were an estimated 680 million "born-again" Christians (i.e., Pentecostals and Evangelicals) in the world in 2001, with an annual worldwide growth rate of 7 percent, versus just 2.3 percent for Christianity overall. (This would translate into 1.15 billion Pentecostals and Evangelicals by 2013.) The global growth rate of Roman Catholics has been estimated at only 1.3 percent, compared with a Protestant growth rate of 3.3 percent per year (Winter 2001). Much of this explosive growth, especially in Africa, is of a type of Protestantism that would be scarcely recognizable to most Americans, given its incorporation of many animistic elements. (See this chapter's "Focus on Globalization" for more on the spread of evangelical Protestantism.)

Spreading Evangelical Protestantism

Evangelical Protestantism originated in Europe and North America, but it has become a rapidly spreading global phenomenon. A century ago, more than 90 percent of the world's approximately 80 million Evangelicals lived in Europe and North America (Pew Research Center 2011). Today, estimates of the number of Evangelicals worldwide range from 400 million to over 1 billion, most of them living outside Europe and North America.

In discussions of globalization, many scholars find it useful to distinguish between the "Global South" and the "Global North." The former consists of developing countries in sub-Saharan Africa, the Middle East and North Africa, Latin America, and most of Asia. The "Global North" includes Europe, North America, Australia, New Zealand, and Japan.

The growth of Evangelical Protestantism has been most explosive in the Global South. One example is Brazil—traditionally (and still) the world's most Catholic country. When Pope John Paul II visited Brazil in 1980, 89 percent of its population claimed to be Roman Catholic. Since then, Evangelical Protestantism has spread like wildfire. Evangelicals now represent at least 15 percent of Brazil's more than 200 million people.

Evangelical Protestantism stresses conservative morality, the authority of the Bible, and a personal ("born again") conversion experience. Most Brazilian Evangelicals are Pentecostals, who add glossolalia (speaking in tongues) and beliefs in faith healing, exorcism, and miracles. São Paulo, Brazil's largest city, has been called the Pentecostal world capital, with over 4 million adherents.

Peter Berger (2010) suggests that modern Pentecostalism may be the fastest-growing religion in human history and focuses on its social dimensions. Based on my own experience in Brazil, I would agree with Berger that new Pentecostals tend to come from underprivileged, poor, and otherwise marginalized groups in areas undergoing rapid social change. Pentecostalism can promote strong communities, while offering practical and psychological support to people whose circumstances are changing (Berger 2010).

The British sociologist David Martin (2010) argues that Pentecostalism is spreading because its adherents embody Max Weber's Protestant ethic—valuing self-discipline, hard work, and saving. A contrary view sees Pentecostalism as a kind of cargo cult, based on belief in the efficacy of magic and ritual activity (Freston 2008; Meyer 1999). Berger (2010) suggests that the millions of Pentecostals in the world today probably include both types—Weberian Protestants working to produce material wealth as a sign of their salvation, and less industrious types who have faith that magic and ritual will bring them good fortune.

Additional information about where Evangelical Protestantism is spreading and the attitudes of its leaders comes from the Pew Research Center (2011), which surveyed 2,196 Evangelical leaders from 166 countries and territories. They were attending a conference on World Evangelization held in Cape Town, South Africa in October 2010. Conference participants were asked to rate the prospects for Evangelical Christianity in their home countries, to give their views on what it means to be an Evangelical, and to describe their beliefs on theological, social, and political issues.

Leaders from the Global South were more optimistic than those from the Global North that Evangelical Protestantism would increase its influence in their countries. Leaders from the United States were especially pessimistic, with 82 percent saying Evangelicals are losing influence in their country. Global South participants tended to be more conservative overall than those from the Global North. The former were more likely to take the Bible literally and even to favor granting it legal authority in their countries.

Evangelical leaders from the Middle East were the most likely to regard conflict between religions as a problem. Ninety percent of those living in Muslim-majority countries called the influence of Islam a major threat, compared with just 41 percent of leaders from other countries. On the other hand, leaders from Muslim-majority countries tended to have more positive opinions of Muslims than others did.

Overall, conference participants saw secularism, consumerism, materialism, and popular culture as the greatest threats they face today. They were not wrong: These other aspects of globalization do offer competition to the spread of religion.

In São Paulo, Brazil, evangelicals pray inside the Bola de Neve Church. Popular with youths, this church sponsors activities including surfing, skating, and rock and roll and reggae music with religious lyrics.

Table 21.2 classifies eleven world religions according to their degree of internal unity and diversity. Listed first are the most cohesive/unified groups. Listed last are the religions with the most internal diversity. The list is based mainly on the degree of doctrinal similarity among the various subgroups. To a lesser extent it reflects diversity in practice, ritual, and organization. (The list includes the majority manifestations of each religion, as well as subgroups that the larger branches may label "heterodox.") How would you decide whether a value judgment is implied by this list? Is it better for a religion to be highly unified, cohesive, monolithic, and lacking in internal diversity, or to be fragmented, schismatic, multifaceted, and abounding in variations on the same theme? Over time such diversity can give birth to new religions; for example, Christianity arose from Judaism, Buddhism from Hinduism, Baha'i from Islam, and Sikhism from Hinduism. Within Christianity, Protestantism developed out of Roman Catholicism.

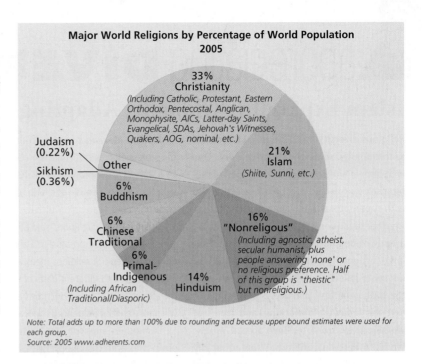

Major World Religions by Percentage of World Population 2005

Note: Total adds up to more than 100% due to rounding and because upper bound estimates were used for each group.
Source: 2005 www.adherents.com

FIGURE 21.1 Major World Religions by Percentage of World Population, 2005.

SOURCE: Adherents.com. 2005. http://www.adherents.com/Religions_By_Adherents.html. Reprinted by permission of Preston Hunter, adherents.com.

RELIGION AND CHANGE

Religious fundamentalists seek order based on strict adherence to purportedly traditional standards, beliefs, rules, and customs. Christian and Islamic fundamentalists recognize, decry, and attempt to redress change, yet they also contribute to change (Antoun 2008). In a worldwide process, new religions challenge established churches. In the United States, for example, conservative Christian TV hosts have become influential broadcasters and opinion shapers. In Latin America, Evangelical Protestantism is winning millions of converts from Roman Catholicism.

Like political organization, religion helps maintain social order. And like political mobilization, religious energy can be harnessed not just for change but also for revolution. Reacting to conquest or to actual or perceived foreign domination, for instance, religious leaders may seek to alter or revitalize their society. In an "Islamic Revolution," for example, Iranian ayatollahs marshaled religious fervor to create national solidarity and radical change. We call such movements nativistic movements (Linton 1943) or revitalization movements (Wallace 1956).

Revitalization Movements

Revitalization movements are social movements that occur in times of change, in which religious leaders emerge and undertake to alter or revitalize a society. Christianity originated as a revitalization movement. Jesus was one of several prophets who preached new religious doctrines while the Middle East was under Roman rule. It was a time of social unrest, when a foreign power ruled the land. Jesus inspired a new, enduring, and major religion. His contemporaries were not so successful.

The Handsome Lake religion arose around 1800 among the Iroquois of New York State (Wallace 1970). Handsome Lake, the founder of this revitalization movement, was a leader of one of the Iroquois tribes. The Iroquois had suffered because of their support of the British against the American colonials (and for other reasons). After the colonial

TABLE 21.2 Classical World Religions Ranked by Internal Religious Similarity

MOST UNIFIED
Baha'i
Zoroastrianism
Sikhism
Islam
Jainism
Judaism
Taoism
Shinto
Christianity
Buddhism
Hinduism
MOST DIVERSE

SOURCE: Adherents.com. 2001. http://www.adherents.com/Religions_By_Adherents.html. Reprinted by permission of Preston Hunter, adherents.com.

revitalization movements
Movements aimed at altering or revitalizing a society.

Islam Expanding Globally, Adapting Locally

Religious diversity has been a key interest of anthropology since the 19th century. One well-known anthropological definition of religion stresses beliefs and behavior concerned with supernatural beings, powers, and forces. Another definition focuses on congregants— a body of people who gather together regularly for worship, and who accept a set of doctrines involving the relationship between the individual and divinity. Some religions, and the beliefs, affirmations, and forms of worship they promote, have spread widely. We learn here how Islam has spread rapidly by adapting locally to various nations and cultures. In this process, although certain fundamentals endure, there is also room for considerable diversity. Local people always assign their own meanings to the messages and social forms, including religion, they receive from outside. Such meanings reflect their cultural backgrounds and experiences. Islam has adapted successfully to many cultural differences, including linguistic practices, architectural styles, and the presence of other religions, such as Hinduism, already established in that area.

One in every five people worldwide is a Muslim, some 1.3 billion believers. Islam is the world's fastest growing religion and it has spread across the globe.

Muslims everywhere agree on the Shahadah, the profession of faith: "There is no God but Allah; Mohammed is the prophet of Allah." But Islam is far from homogeneous—the faith reflects the increasingly diverse areas in which it is practiced.

"Islam is a world religion," said Ali Asani, a Harvard professor of Indo-Muslim Languages and Culture. "When . . . religious ideas and concepts are transferred to different parts of the world . . . the expressions of those doctrines and theology will necessarily be influenced by local culture."

Sometimes such regional distinctions are obvious to even casual observers. Mosques, for example, all share common features—they face Mecca and have a mihrab, or niche, that indicates that direction. Yet they also boast unique architectural elements and decor that suggest whether their location is Iran, Africa, or China. The houses of worship provide what Asani calls "a visual reminder of cultural diversity." Other easily grasped regional distinctions have their origins at the level of language. While Arabic is Islam's liturgical language, used for prayer, most Muslims' understanding of their faith occurs in their local language.

"Languages are really windows into culture," Asani explains. "So very often what you find is that theological Islamic concepts get translated into local idioms." . . .

Some Islamic fundamentalists might frown upon the diversity caused by local characteris-

tics, but such are the predominant forms of Islam. "Rather than discussing Islam, we might more accurately talk about 'Islams' in different cultural contexts," Asani said. "We have Muslim literature from China, for example, where Islamic concepts are understood within a Confucian framework."

In the region of Bengal, now part of the nation of Bangladesh and the Indian state of West Bengal, a popular literary tradition created a context for the arrival of Islam. The concept of the avatar is important to the Hindu tradition, in which these deities become incarnate and descend to Earth to guide the righteous and fight evil.

"What you find in 16th century Bengal is the development of what you might call 'folk literature' where the Islamic idea of the prophet becomes understood within the framework of the avatar," Asani said. "So you have bridges being built between religious traditions as concepts resonate against each other."

This example is quite different from conditions in pre-Islam Arabia, at the time of Mohammed, where the poet held a special place in society. "If you consider the Koran, the word means 'recitation' in Arabic, and it's primarily an oral scripture, intended to be recited aloud and heard; to be performed," Asani said. "Viewed from a literary perspective, its form and structure relate very well to the poetic traditions of pre-Islamic Arabia. It's an example where the format

victory and a wave of immigration to their homeland, the Iroquois were dispersed on small reservations. Unable to pursue traditional horticulture and hunting in their homeland, they became heavy drinkers and quarreled among themselves.

Handsome Lake was a heavy drinker who started having visions from heavenly messengers. The spirits warned him that unless the Iroquois changed their ways, they would be destroyed. His visions offered a plan for coping with the new order. Witchcraft, quarreling, and drinking would end. The Iroquois would

copy European farming techniques, which, unlike traditional Iroquois horticulture, stressed male rather than female labor. Handsome Lake preached that the Iroquois should also abandon their communal longhouses and matrilineal descent groups for more permanent marriages and individual family households. The teachings of Handsome Lake produced a new church and religion, one that still has members in New York and Ontario. This revitalization movement helped the Iroquois adapt to and survive in a modified environment. They eventually gained a

of revelation was determined by the culture. In pre-Islamic Arabia the poet was often considered to be inspired in his poetic compositions by jinn from another world. So when the Prophet Muhammed began receiving revelations which were eventually compiled into the Koran, he was accused of being a poet, to which he responded 'I'm not a poet but a prophet.'" . . .

Islam came to Indonesia with merchants who were not theologians but simply practicing Muslims who people looked to as an example. There were also Sufi teachers who were quite willing to create devotional exercises that fit the way peo-

ple in Sumatra or Java already practiced their faith. The two largest Muslim groups in Indonesia today, and perhaps in the world, are Muhammadyya and Nahdlatul Ulama. Each of them has over 30 million members, and each began as a local reform movement rooted in the promotion of a more modern education within the framework of Islam. . . .

A large number of Muslims, of course, don't live in Islamic nations at all but as minorities in other countries. The emergence of some minority Muslim communities has been an interesting and important development of the last 25 to 30 years.

Some relatively small communities can have a large impact. The European Muslim populations, for example, have a high component of refugee intellectuals. They've had an effect on their adopted countries, and also on the rest of the Islamic world. . . .

In South Africa the Muslim community is less than three percent of the population—but it's highly visible and highly educated. In the days of apartheid they had the advantage of being an intermediary, a community that was neither black nor white. By the 1980s the younger Muslim leadership became very opposed to apartheid on Islamic grounds and on basic human rights grounds. Muslims became quite active in the African National Congress (ANC). Though they were only a small minority when apartheid was destroyed, a number of Muslims became quite visible in the new South African regime—and throughout the larger Muslim world.

Encompassing both Islamic states and minority communities, Islam is the world's fastest growing religion and an increasingly common topic of global conversation. Yet much of the discourse paints the faith with a single brush. As more people become familiar with Islam around the world it may be well for them to first ask, as Professor Asani suggests: "Whose Islam? Which Islam?"

Reciting a Salah Muslim prayer at the Umayyad mosque in Damascus, Syria.

SOURCE: Brian Handwerk, "Islam Expanding Globally, Adapting Locally," *National Geographic News*, October 24, 2003. http://news.nationalgeographic.com. © 2003 National Geographic Society. Reprinted with permission.

reputation among their non-Indian neighbors as sober family farmers.

Syncretisms

Especially in today's world, religious expressions emerge from the interplay of local, regional, national, and international cultural forces. **Syncretisms** are cultural mixes, including religious blends, that emerge from acculturation—the exchange of cultural features when cultures come into continuous

firsthand contact. One example of religious syncretism is the mixture of African, Native American, and Roman Catholic saints and deities in Caribbean *vodun*, or "voodoo," cults. This blend also is present in Cuban *santeria* and in *candomblé*, an "Afro-Brazilian" cult. Another syncretism is the blend of Melanesian and Christian beliefs in cargo cults.

Like the Handsome Lake religion just discussed, cargo cults are revitalization movements. Such movements may emerge when natives have regular contact with industrial societies but lack their

syncretisms
Cultural, especially religious, mixes, emerging from acculturation.

wealth, technology, and living standards. Some such movements attempt to explain European domination and wealth and to achieve similar success magically by mimicking European behavior and manipulating symbols of the desired lifestyle. The syncretic **cargo cults** of Melanesia and Papua New Guinea weave Christian doctrine with aboriginal beliefs (Figure 21.2). They take their name from their focus on cargo: European goods of the sort natives have seen unloaded from the cargo holds of ships and airplanes.

In one early cult, members believed that the spirits of the dead would arrive in a ship. These ghosts would bring manufactured goods for the natives and would kill all the whites. More recent cults replaced ships with airplanes (Worsley 1959/1985). Many cults have used elements of European culture as sacred objects. The rationale is that Europeans use these objects, have wealth, and therefore must know the "secret of cargo." By mimicking how Europeans use or treat objects, natives hope also to come upon the secret knowledge needed to gain cargo.

For example, having seen Europeans' reverent treatment of flags and flagpoles, the members of one cult began to worship flagpoles. They believed the flagpoles were sacred towers that could transmit messages between the living and the dead. Other natives built airstrips to entice planes bearing canned goods, portable radios, clothing, wristwatches, and motorcycles. Near the airstrips they made effigies of towers, airplanes, and radios. They talked into the cans in a magical attempt to establish radio contact with the gods.

Some cargo cult prophets proclaimed that success would come through a reversal of European domination and native subjugation. The day was near, they preached, when natives, aided by God, Jesus, or native ancestors, would turn the tables. Native skins would turn white, and those of Europeans would turn brown; Europeans would die or be killed.

As syncretisms, cargo cults blend aboriginal and Christian beliefs. Melanesian myths told of ancestors shedding their skins and changing into powerful beings and of dead people returning to life. Christian missionaries, who had been in Melanesia since the late 19th century, also spoke of resurrection. The cults' preoccupation with cargo is related to traditional Melanesian big man systems. In the chapter "Political Systems," we saw that a Melanesian big man had to be generous. People worked for the big man, helping him amass wealth, but eventually he had to give a feast and give away all that wealth.

Because of their experience with big man systems, Melanesians believed that all wealthy people eventually had to give their wealth away. For decades, they had attended Christian missions and worked on plantations. All the while they expected Europeans to return the fruits of their labor as their own big men did. When the Europeans refused to distribute the wealth or even to let natives know the

cargo cults
Postcolonial, acculturative religious movements in Melanesia.

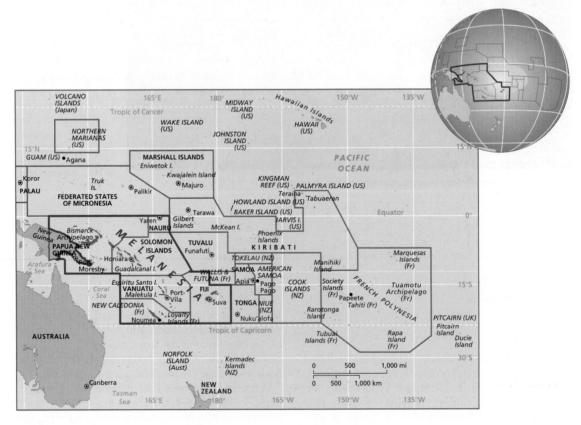

FIGURE 21.2 Location of Melanesia.

secret of its production and distribution, cargo cults developed.

Like arrogant big men, Europeans would be leveled, by death if necessary. However, natives lacked the physical means of doing what their traditions said they should do. Thwarted by well-armed colonial forces, natives resorted to magical leveling. They called on supernatural beings to intercede, to kill or otherwise deflate the European big men and redistribute their wealth.

Cargo cults are religious responses to the expansion of the world capitalist economy. However, this religious mobilization had political and economic results. Cult participation gave Melanesians a basis for common interests and activities and thus helped pave the way for political parties and economic interest organizations. Previously separated by geography, language, and customs, Melanesians started forming larger groups as members of the same cults and followers of the same prophets. The cargo cults paved the way for political action through which the indigenous peoples eventually regained their autonomy.

A cargo cult in Vanuatu. Boys and men march with spears, imitating British colonial soldiers. Does anything in your own society remind you of a cargo cult?

Antimodernism and Fundamentalism

Antimodernism describes the rejection of the modern in favor of what is perceived as an earlier, purer, and better way of life. This viewpoint grew out of disillusionment with Europe's Industrial Revolution and subsequent developments in science, technology, and consumption patterns. Antimodernists typically consider technology's use today to be misguided, or think technology should have a lower priority than religious and cultural values.

Religious fundamentalism, a form of contemporary antimodernism, can be compared to the revitalization movements discussed previously. **Fundamentalism** describes antimodernist movements in various religions. Ironically, religious fundamentalism is itself a modern phenomenon, based on a strong feeling among its adherents of alienation from the perceived secularism of the surrounding (modern) culture. Fundamentalists assert an identity separate from the larger religious group from which they arose. Their separation reflects their belief that the founding principles on which the larger religion is based have been corrupted, neglected, compromised, forgotten, or replaced with other principles. Fundamentalists advocate strict fidelity to the "true" religious principles of the larger religion.

Fundamentalists also seek to rescue religion from absorption into modern, Western culture, which they see as already having corrupted the mainstream version of their religion—and others. Fundamentalists establish a "wall of virtue" against alien religions as well as against the modernized, compromised version of their own religion. In Christianity, fundamentalists are "born again," as opposed to "mainline,"

"liberal," or "modernist" Protestants. In Islam they are *jama'at* (in Arabic, enclaves based on close fellowship) engaged in *jihad* (struggle) against a Western culture hostile to Islam and the God-given (*shariah*) way of life. In Judaism they are *Haredi*, "Torah-true" Jews. All such groups see a sharp divide between themselves and other religions, and between a "sacred" view of life and the "secular" world and "nominal religion" (see Antoun 2001).

Fundamentalists strive to protect a distinctive doctrine and way of life and of salvation. A strong sense of community is created, focused on a clearly defined religious way of life. The prospect of joining such a community may appeal to people who find little that is distinctive or vital in their previous religious identity. Fundamentalists get their converts, mainly from their larger religion, by convincing them of its inauthenticity. Many fundamentalists are politically aware citizens of nation-states. Often they believe that government processes and policies must recognize the way of life set forth in scripture. In their eyes, the state should be subservient to God.

A New Age

Fundamentalists may or may not be correct in seeing a rise in secularism in contemporary North America. Between 1990 and 2008, the number of Americans giving no religious preference grew from 7 to 16 percent. In Canada the comparable figure rose from 12 to 17 percent between 1991 and 2001 (Table 21.3). Of course, people who lack a religious preference aren't necessarily atheists. Many of them are believers who don't belong to a church. According to U.S. Census Bureau figures for 2008, 3.6 million Americans (around 1 percent of the population) self-identified

antimodernism
Rejecting the modern for a presumed earlier, purer, better way.

fundamentalism
Advocating strict fidelity to a religion's presumed founding principles.

On August 27, 2011, this flashmob meditation session was held in London's (England) Trafalgar Square. Does this performance illustrate secular religion?

trends and forms of spiritualism. Some Americans have turned to charismatic Christianity. In the United States and Australia, respectively, some people who are not Native Americans or Native Australians have appropriated the symbols, settings, and purported religious practices of Native Americans and Native Australians, for New Age religions. Many natives have strongly protested the use of their sacred symbols and places by such groups.

New religious movements have varied origins. Some have been influenced by Christianity; others, by Eastern (Asian) religions; still others, by mysticism and spiritualism. Religion also evolves in tandem with science and technology. For example, the Raelian Movement, a religious group centered in Switzerland and Montreal, promotes cloning as a way of achieving "eternal life." Raelians believe that extraterrestrials called "Elohim" artificially created all life on earth. The group has established a company called Valiant Venture Ltd., which offers infertile and homosexual couples the opportunity to have a child cloned from one of the spouses (Ontario Consultants on Religious Tolerance 1996).

In the United States, the official recognition of a religion entitles it to a modicum of respect, and certain benefits, such as exemption from taxation on its income and property (as long as it does not engage in political activity). Not all would-be religions receive official recognition. For example, Scientology is recognized as a church in the United States but not in Germany.

SECULAR RITUALS

In concluding this discussion of religion, we may recognize some problems with the definition of religion given at the beginning of this chapter. The first problem: If we define religion with reference to supernatural beings, powers, and forces, how do we classify ritual-like behavior that occurs in secular contexts? Some anthropologists believe there are both sacred and secular rituals. Secular rituals include formal, invariant, stereotyped, earnest, repetitive behavior and rites of passage that take place in nonreligious settings.

as atheists or agnostics. Even fewer (about 90,000 in 2008) called themselves "secular" or "humanists." Still, atheists and secular humanists do exist, and they, too, are organized.

Like members of religious groups, they use varied media, including print and the Internet, to communicate among themselves. Just as Buddhists can peruse *Tricycle: The Buddhist Review,* secular humanists can find their views validated in *Free Inquiry,* a quarterly identifying itself as "the international secular humanist magazine." Secular humanists speak out against organized religion and its "dogmatic pronouncements" and "supernatural or spiritual agendas" and the "obscurantist views" of religious leaders who presume "to inform us of God's views" by appealing to sacred texts (Steinfels 1997).

Is American society really growing more secular? A considerable body of sociological research suggests that levels of American religiosity haven't changed much over the past century (see Finke and Stark 2005). To be sure, there are new religious

TABLE 21.3 Religious Composition of the Populations of the United States, 1990 and 2008, and Canada, 1991 and 2001

| | UNITED STATES | | CANADA | |
	1990	2008	1991	2001
Protestant	60%	54%	36%	29%
Catholic	26	26	46	44
Jewish	2	1	1	1
Other	5	3	4	9
None given	7	16	12	17

SOURCE: *Statistical Abstract of the United States 2012,* Table 75, p. 61, http://www.census.gov/compendia/statab/2012/tables/12s0075. pdf; *Census of Canada,* 2001. http://www40.statcan.ca/101/cst01/demo30a.htm?sdi=religion.

A second problem: If the distinction between the supernatural and the natural is not consistently made in a society, how can we tell what is religion and what isn't? The Betsileo of Madagascar, for example, view witches and dead ancestors as real people who play roles in ordinary life. However, their occult powers are not empirically demonstrable.

A third problem: The behavior considered appropriate for religious occasions varies tremendously from culture to culture. One society may consider drunken frenzy the surest sign of faith, whereas another may inculcate quiet reverence. Who is to say which is "more religious"?

It is possible for apparently secular settings, things, and events to acquire intense meaning for individuals who have grown up in their presence. For example, identities and loyalties based on fandom, football, baseball, and soccer can be powerful indeed. Rock stars and bands can mobilize many. A World Series win led to celebrations across a "Red Sox nation." Italians and Brazilians are rarely, if ever, as nationally focused and emotionally unified as they are when their teams are competing in the World Cup. The collective effervescence that Durkheim found so characteristic of religion can equally well describe what Brazilians experience when their country wins a World Cup.

In the context of comparative religion, the idea that the secular can become sacred isn't surprising. Long ago, Durkheim (1912/2001) pointed out that almost everything, from the sublime to the ridiculous, has in some societies been treated as sacred. The distinction between sacred and profane doesn't depend on the intrinsic qualities of the sacred symbol. In Australian totemic religion, for example, sacred beings include such humble creatures as ducks, frogs, rabbits, and grubs, whose inherent qualities could hardly have given rise to the religious sentiment they inspire.

Many Americans believe that recreation and religion are separate domains. From my fieldwork in Brazil and Madagascar and my reading about other societies, I believe that this separation is both ethnocentric and false. Madagascar's tomb-centered ceremonies are times when the living and the dead are joyously reunited, when people get drunk, gorge themselves, and enjoy sexual license. Perhaps the gray, sober, ascetic, and moralistic aspects of many religious events in the United States, in taking the "fun" out of religion, force us to find our religion in fun.

acing the **COURSE**

summary

1. Religion, a cultural universal, consists of belief and behavior concerned with supernatural beings, powers, and forces. Religion also encompasses the feelings, meanings, and congregations associated with such beliefs and behavior. Anthropological studies have revealed many aspects and functions of religion.

2. Tylor considered animism—the belief in spirits or souls—to be religion's earliest and most basic form. He focused on religion's explanatory role, arguing that religion would eventually disappear as science provided better explanations. Besides animism, yet another view of the supernatural also occurs in nonindustrial societies. This sees the supernatural as a domain of raw, impersonal power or force (called mana in Polynesia and Melanesia). People can manipulate and control mana under certain conditions.

3. When ordinary technical and rational means of doing things fail, people may turn to magic. Often they use magic when they lack control over outcomes. Religion offers comfort and psychological security at times of crisis. However, rites also can create anxiety. Rituals are formal, invariant, stylized, earnest

acts in which people subordinate their particular beliefs to a social collectivity. Rites of passage have three stages: separation, liminality, and incorporation. Such rites can mark any change in social status, age, place, or social condition. Collective rites often are cemented by communitas, a feeling of intense solidarity.

4. Besides their psychological and social functions, religious beliefs and practices play a role in the adaptation of human populations to their environments. The Hindu doctrine of *ahimsa*, which prohibits harm to living things, makes cattle sacred and beef a tabooed food. The taboo's force stops peasants from killing their draft cattle even in times of extreme need.

5. Religion establishes and maintains social control through a series of moral and ethical beliefs, and real and imagined rewards and punishments, internalized in individuals. Religion also achieves social control by mobilizing its members for collective action. Religion helps maintain social order, but it also can promote change. Revitalization movements blend old and new beliefs and have helped people adapt to changing conditions.

6. Protestant values have been important in the United States, as they were in the rise and spread of capitalism in Europe. The world's major religions vary in their growth rates, with Islam expanding more rapidly than Christianity. There is growing religious diversity in the United States and Canada. Fundamentalists are antimodernists who claim an identity separate from the larger religious group from which they arose; they advocate strict fidelity to the "true" religious principles on which the larger religion was founded. Religious trends in contemporary North America include rising secularism and new religions, some inspired by science and technology, some by spiritism. There are secular as well as religious rituals.

key terms

animism 474
antimodernism 487
cargo cults 486
communitas 473
cosmology 478
fundamentalism 487
leveling mechanism 479
liminality 477
magic 475
mana 474

monotheism 474
polytheism 474
religion 472
revitalization movements 483
rites of passage 476
ritual 476
shaman 480
syncretisms 485
taboo 474
totem 478

test yourself

MULTIPLE CHOICE

1. According to Sir Edward Tylor, the founder of the anthropology of religion, what is the sequence through which religion evolved?
   a. animism, polytheism, monotheism
   b. communitas, polytheism, monotheism
   c. mana, polytheism, monotheism
   d. animism, cargo cults, monotheism
   e. polytheism, animism, monotheism

2. Which of the following describes the concept of mana, a sacred impersonal force existing in the universe, as was used in Polynesia and Melanesia?
   a. In Polynesia and Melanesia, mana was taboo.
   b. The concept of mana was absent in societies with differential access to strategic resources.

   c. In Melanesia, where mana was similar to the notion of luck, anyone could get it; but in Polynesia, mana was attached to political elites.
   d. Most anthropologists agree that mana was the most primitive religious doctrine in Polynesia and Melanesia.
   e. In both cases mana was concerned with supernatural beings rather than with powers or forces.

3. What is the irony that this chapter highlights when describing rites of passage?
   a. Despite their prevalence during the time that Victor Turner did his research, rites of passage have disappeared with the advent of modern life.
   b. Participants in rites of passage are tricked into believing that there was a big change in their lives.

c. Rites of passage only make worse the anxieties caused by other aspects of religion.

d. Beliefs and rituals can both diminish and create anxiety and a sense of insecurity and danger.

e. Rites of passage would be effective in diminishing anxiety and fear if they did not involve the liminal phase.

4. What is typically observed during the liminal phase of a rite of passage?

a. intensification of social hierarchy

b. symbolic reversals of ordinary behavior

c. formation of a ranking system

d. use of secular language

e. no change in the social norms

5. The anthropological analysis of the Hindu practice of *ahimsa* suggests that

a. religion is a realm of behavior in which people do *not* try to behave rationally (i.e., maximize profit and minimize loss).

b. the economic principle known as generalized reciprocity is the basis of Hinduism.

c. beliefs about the supernatural can function as part of a group's adaptation to the environment.

d. religious beliefs often impede evolutionary progress by encouraging wasteful energy expenditure.

e. antagonism between the sexes characterizes primitive religious practice.

6. Which of the following is true about religion and social control?

a. It is not uncommon for political leaders to use religion to justify social control.

b. Religion is used for social control mainly by Muslim clerics who dominate the political sphere of their society.

c. Social control measures typically have little or no interest in women.

d. Leveling mechanisms, such as witchcraft accusations, are the primary means of social control in state-organized societies.

e. Social control exists mainly in tribal societies.

7. In his influential book *The Protestant Ethic and the Spirit of Capitalism* (1904/1958), Max Weber argues that

a. communal religion was the perfect breeding ground for elements of capitalism.

b. the spirit of capitalism was a result of the rise of the concept of the modern antireligious self.

c. the rise of capitalism required the spread of the shamanistic ethic of individualism.

d. the rise of capitalism required overcoming idiosyncratic belief systems and placing Catholic values in their place.

e. the rise of capitalism required that the traditional attitudes of Catholic peasants be replaced by values fitting an industrial economy based on capital accumulation.

8. The syncretic religions that mix Melanesian and Christian beliefs known as cargo cults are

a. a religious response to the expansion of the world capitalist economy, often with political and economic consequences.

b. culturally defined activities associated with the transition from one place or stage of life to another.

c. cultural acts that mock the widespread but erroneous belief of European cultural supremacy.

d. just like religious fundamentalisms in that they are ancient cultural phenomena enjoying a rebirth in current world affairs.

e. antimodernist movements that reject anything Western.

9. All of the following are true about religious fundamentalism *except this fact*:

a. It seeks to rescue religion from absorption into modern Western culture.

b. It is a very modern phenomenon.

c. It is a form of animism.

d. It is based on a strong feeling among adherents of alienation from the perceived secularism of the surrounding (modern) culture.

e. It is a form of antimodernism.

10. Is American society really growing more secular? On this question, a considerable body of sociological research suggests that

a. it is becoming more secular because scientific education in schools is improving.

b. this question cannot be answered accurately because people typically lie about their religious affiliations in surveys.

c. it is becoming more religious because more and more people feel their national identity threatened due to rising levels of migration from non-Christian countries.

d. levels of American religiosity haven't changed much over the past century.

e. it is becoming more secular because less people go to church.

FILL IN THE BLANK

1. According to Tylor, _____, a belief in spiritual beings, was the earliest form of religion.
2. _____ magic is based on the belief that whatever is done to an object will affect a person who once had contact with it.
3. The term _____ refers to an intense feeling of solidarity that characterizes collective liminality.
4. A _____ refers to a custom or social action that operates to reduce differences in wealth and bring standouts in line with community norms.
5. A _____ is a cultural, especially a religious, mix, emerging from acculturation.

CRITICAL THINKING

1. How did anthropologist Anthony Wallace define religion? After reading this chapter, what problems do you think there are with his definition?
2. Describe a rite of passage you (or a friend) have been through. How did it fit the three-stage model given in the text?
3. From the news or your own knowledge, can you provide additional examples of revitalization movements, new religions, or liminal cults?
4. Religion is a cultural universal. But religions are parts of particular cultures, and cultural differences show up systematically in religious beliefs and practices. How so?
5. This chapter notes that many Americans see recreation and religion as separate domains. Based on my fieldwork in Brazil and Madagascar and my reading about other societies, I believe that this separation is both ethnocentric and false. Do you agree with this? What has been your own experience?

Multiple Choice: 1. (A); 2. (C); 3. (D); 4. (B); 5. (C); 6. (A); 7. (E); 8. (A); 9. (C); 10. (D); **Fill in the Blank:** 1. animism; 2. Contagious; 3. *communitas*; 4. leveling mechanism; 5. syncretism

Bowie, F.
  2006 *The Anthropology of Religion: An Introduction.*
  Malden, MA: Blackwell. Surveys classic and recent
  work in the anthropology of religion, including the
  politics of religious identity.
Crapo, R. H.
  2003 *Anthropology of Religion: The Unity and Diversity of Religions.* Boston: McGraw-Hill. Examines
  religious universals and variation.
Lambek, M.
  2008 *A Reader in the Anthropology of Religion.*
  Malden, MA: Blackwell. Excellent annotated reader.

Hicks, D., ed.
  2010 *Ritual and Belief: Readings in the Anthropology
  of Religion,* 3rd ed. Lanham, MD: AtlaMira. Up-to-
  date reader, with useful annotation.
Moro, P. A., and J. E. Meyers, eds.
  2010 *Magic, Witchcraft, and Religion: An Anthropological Study of the Supernatural,* 8th ed. Boston:
  McGraw-Hill. A comparative reader covering
  Western and non-Western cultures.
Stein, R. L., and P. L. Stein
  2011 *The Anthropology of Religion, Magic, and
  Witchcraft,* 3rd ed. Upper Saddle River, NJ: Pearson
  Prentice Hall. Readings on religion and culture.

suggested additional readings

Go to our Online Learning Center website at **www.mhhe.com/kottak** for Internet
exercises directly related to the content of this chapter.

internet exercises

CHAPTER 22

Arts, Media, and Sports

What are the arts, and how have they varied historically and cross-culturally?

How does culture influence the media, and vice versa?

How are culture and cultural contrasts expressed in sports?

◀ The Olympics unite arts, media, and sports. This ArcelorMittal Orbit Sculpture was constructed for London's Olympic Park. The sculpture, made mostly of recycled steel, stands 114.5 meters (376 ft) high. Can you see the five Olympic rings within it?

understanding OURSELVES

Imagine a TV broadcast attracting over 70 percent of a nation's viewers. That has happened repeatedly in Brazil as a popular *telenovela* draws to a close. (*Telenovelas* are prime-time serial melodramas that run for about 150 episodes, then end.) It happened in the United States in 1953, when 72 percent of all sets were tuned to *I Love Lucy* as Lucy Ricardo went to the hospital to give birth to Little Ricky. It happened even more impressively in 1956, when 83 percent of all sets tuned to *The Ed Sullivan Show* to watch Elvis Presley's TV debut. A single broadcast's largest audience share in more recent years occurred in 1983 when 106 million viewers and 77 percent of all sets watched the final episode of *M*A*S*H*. In the 21st century, three successive Super Bowls (2010, 2011, and 2012) topped the viewership, but not nearly the audience share, of the *M*A*S*H* finale. Madonna's half-time show did even better than the 2012 Super Bowl itself, attracting 114 million viewers.

One notable development in the United States over the past few decades has been a shift from mass culture to segmented cultures. An increasingly differentiated nation recognizes, even celebrates, diversity. The mass media join—and intensify—this trend, measuring and catering to various "demographics." Products and messages are aimed less at the masses than at particular segments—*target audiences.*

As one example, consider the evolution of sports coverage. From 1961 to 1998 ABC offered a weekly sports anthology titled *Wide World of Sports*. On a given Saturday afternoon Americans might see bowling, track and field, skating, college wrestling, gymnastics, curling, swimming, diving, or another of many sports. It was like having a mini-Olympics running throughout the year. Today, dozens of specialized sports channels cater to every taste. Think of the choices now available though cable and satellite, websites, the iPhone, the iPad, Netflix, DVDs, DVRs, and the remote control. Target audiences now have access to a multiplicity of channels, featuring all kinds of music, sports, games, news, comedy, science fiction, soaps, movies, cartoons, old TV sitcoms, Spanish-language programs, nature shows, travel shows, adventure shows, histories, biographies, and home shopping. News channels (e.g., Fox News or MSNBC) even cater to particular political interests. Although exciting Super Bowl matches still generate large audience shares, I doubt that if Elvis Presley and Michael Jackson returned from the dead for a sing-off on broadcast TV, it would get half the available audience. It seems likely there is a connection between these media developments and the "special interests" about which politicians perpetually complain. Do you think people might agree more—and Americans be less polarized—if everyone still watched the same TV programs? After all, who didn't love Lucy?

WHAT IS ART?

The **arts** include music, performance arts, visual arts, and storytelling and literature (oral and written). These manifestations of human creativity sometimes are called **expressive culture.** People express themselves in dance, music, song, painting, sculpture, pottery, cloth, storytelling, verse, prose, drama, and comedy. Many cultures lack terms that can be translated easily as "art" or "the arts." Yet even without a word for art, people everywhere do associate an aesthetic experience—a sense of beauty, appreciation, harmony, pleasure—with sounds, patterns, objects, and events that have certain qualities. The Bamana people of Mali have a word (like "art") for something that attracts your attention and guides your thoughts (Ezra 1986). Among the Yoruba of Nigeria, the word for art, *ona*, encompasses the designs made on objects, the art objects themselves, and the profession of the creators of such patterns and works. For two Yoruba lineages of leather workers, Otunisona and Osiisona, the suffix *-ona* in their names denotes art (Adepegba 1991).

A dictionary defines **art** as "the quality, production, expression, or realm of what is beautiful or of more than ordinary significance; the class of objects subject to aesthetic criteria" (*The Random House College Dictionary* 1982, p. 76). According to the same dictionary, **aesthetics** involves "the qualities perceived in works of art . . .; the . . . mind and emotions in relation to the sense of beauty" (p. 22). However, a work of art can attract attention and have special significance without being considered beautiful. Pablo Picasso's *Guernica*, a famous painting of the Spanish Civil War, comes to mind as a scene that, while not beautiful, is indisputably moving and thus a work of art.

As George Mills (1971) notes, many cultures lack the roles of "art lover" or "patron of the arts" because art isn't viewed as a separate, special activity. But this doesn't stop individuals from being moved by sounds, patterns, objects, and events in a way that we would call aesthetic. Our own society does provide a fairly well-defined role for the connoisseur of the arts. We also have sanctuaries—concert halls, theaters, museums—where people can go to be aesthetically pleased and emotionally moved by objects and performances.

Western culture tends to compartmentalize art as something apart from everyday life and ordinary culture. This reflects a more general modern separation of institutions like government and the economy from the rest of society. All these fields are considered distinct domains and have their own academic specialists. In non–Western societies the production and appreciation of art are part of everyday life, as popular culture is in our own society. When featured in Western museums, non–Western art often is treated in the same way as "fine art"—that is, separated from its living sociocultural context.

This chapter will not attempt to do a systematic survey of all the arts, or even their major subdivisions. Rather, the general approach will be to examine topics and issues that apply to expressive culture generally. "Art" will be used to encompass all the arts, including print and film narratives, not just the visual ones. In other words, the observations to be made about "art" are intended to apply to music, theater, film, television, books, stories, and lore, as well as to painting and sculpture. In this chapter, some arts and media inevitably receive more attention than others do. Bear in mind, however, that expressive culture encompasses far more than the visual arts. Also included are jokes, storytelling, theater, dance, children's play, games, and festivals, and anthropologists have written about all of these.

That which is aesthetically pleasing is perceived with the senses. Usually, when we think of art, we have in mind something that can be seen or heard. But others might define art more broadly to include things that can be smelled (scents, fragrances), tasted (recipes), or touched (cloth textures). How enduring must art be? Visual works and written works, including musical compositions, may last for centuries. Can a single noteworthy event, such as a feast, which is not in the least eternal, except in memory, be a work of art?

Art and Religion

Some of the issues raised in the discussion of religion also apply to art. Definitions of both art and religion mention the "more than ordinary" or the "extraordinary." Religious scholars may distinguish between the sacred (religious) and the profane (secular). Similarly, art scholars may distinguish between the artistic and the ordinary.

If we adopt a special attitude or demeanor when confronting a sacred object, do we display something similar when experiencing a work of art? According to the anthropologist Jacques Maquet (1986), an artwork is something that stimulates and sustains contemplation. It compels attention and reflection. Maquet stresses the importance of the object's form in producing such contemplation. But other scholars stress feeling and meaning in addition to form. The experience of art involves feeling, such as being moved, as well as appreciation of form, such as balance or harmony.

Many of the high points of Western art had religious inspiration, or were done in the service of religion. Consider *The Creation of Adam* (and other frescoes painted from 1508 to 1512) by Michelangelo, on the ceiling of the Sistine Chapel in Vatican City, Rome, Italy.

arts
Include visual arts, literature (written and oral), music, and performance arts.

expressive culture
Dance, music, painting, sculpture, pottery, cloth, stories, drama, comedy, etc.

art
Object, event, or other expressive form that evokes an aesthetic reaction.

aesthetics
The appreciation of qualities perceived in art.

Such an artistic attitude can be combined with and used to bolster a religious attitude. Much art has been done in association with religion. Many of the high points of Western art and music had religious inspiration, or were done in the service of religion, as a visit to a church or a large museum will surely illustrate. Bach and Handel are as well known for their church music as Michelangelo is for his religious painting and sculpture. The buildings (churches and cathedrals) in which religious music is played and in which visual art is displayed may themselves be works of art. Some of the major architectural achievements of Western art are religious structures.

Art may be created, performed, or displayed outdoors in public or in special indoor settings, such as a theater, concert hall, or museum. Just as churches demarcate religion, museums and theaters set art off from the ordinary world, making it special, while inviting spectators in. Buildings dedicated to the arts help create the artistic atmosphere. Architecture may accentuate the setting as a place for works of art to be presented.

The settings of rites and ceremonies, and of art, may be temporary or permanent. State societies have permanent religious structures: churches and temples. So, too, may state societies have buildings and structures dedicated to the arts. Nonstate societies tend to lack such permanently demarcated settings. Both art and religion are more "out there" in society. Still, in bands and tribes, religious settings can be created without churches. Similarly, an artistic atmosphere can be created without museums. At particular times of the year, ordinary space can be set aside for a visual art display or a musical performance.

The French artist known as JR specializes in transforming urban space into art. The image shown here is part of a large-scale 2008–2009 art project, titled "Women Are Heroes," in Rio de Janeiro, Brazil. Here we see a woman's face on steep steps in Rio's Favela Morro da Providencia. (See http://www.jr-art.net/projects/women-are-heroes-brazil for more images.)

Such special occasions parallel the times set aside for religious ceremonies. In fact, in tribal performances, the arts and religion often mix. For example, masked and costumed performers may imitate spirits. Rites of passage often feature special music, dance, song, bodily adornment, and other manifestations of expressive culture.

In the chapter "Making a Living," we looked at the potlatching tribes of the North Pacific Coast of North America. Erna Gunther (1971) showed how various art forms combined among those tribes to create the visual aspects of ceremonialism. During the winter, spirits were believed to pervade the atmosphere. Masked and costumed dancers represented the spirits. They dramatically reenacted spirit encounters with human beings, which are part of the origin myths of villages, clans, and lineages. In some areas, dancers devised intricate patterns of choreography. Their esteem was measured by the number of people who followed them when they danced.

In any society, art is produced for its aesthetic value as well as for religious purposes. According to Schildkrout and Keim (1990), non-Western art is usually, but wrongly, assumed to have an inevitable connection to ritual. In fact, non-Western societies have art for art's sake just as Western societies do. Even when acting in the service of religion, there is room for individual creative expression (see Osborne and Tanner 2007). In the oral arts, for example, the audience is much more interested in the delivery and performance of the artist than in the particular god for whom the performer may be speaking.

Locating Art

Aesthetic value is one way of distinguishing art. Another way is to consider placement. If something is displayed in a museum, or in another socially accepted artistic setting, someone at least must think it's art. Although tribal societies typically lack museums, they may maintain special areas where artistic expression takes place. One example, discussed below, is the separate space in which ornamental burial poles are manufactured among the Tiwi of North Australia.

Art has been defined as involving that which is beautiful and of more than ordinary significance. But isn't beauty in the eye of the beholder? Don't reactions to art differ among spectators? And, if there can be secular ritual, can there also be ordinary art? The boundary between what's art and what's not is blurred. The American artist Andy Warhol is famous for transforming Campbell's soup cans, Brillo pads, and images of Marilyn Monroe into art. Many recent artists (see photo on the left) have tried to erase the distinction between art and ordinary life by converting the everyday into a work of art.

If something is mass produced or industrially modified, can it be art? Prints made as part of a series certainly may be considered art. Sculptures that are created in clay, then fired with molten metal, such as bronze, at a foundry also are art. But how does one know if a film is art? Is *Star Wars* art? How about *Citizen Kane*? When a book wins a National Book Award, is it immediately elevated to the status of art? What kinds of prizes make art? Objects never intended as art, such as an Olivetti typewriter, may be transformed into art by being placed in a museum, such as New York's Museum of Modern Art. Jacques Maquet (1986) distinguishes such "art by transformation" from art created and intended to be art, which he calls "art by destination."

In state societies, we have come to rely on critics, judges, and experts to tell us what's art and what isn't. A play titled *Art* is about conflict that arises among three friends when one of them buys an all-white painting. They disagree, as people often do, about the definition and value of a work of art. Such variation in art appreciation is especially common in contemporary society, with its professional artists and critics and great cultural diversity. We'd expect more uniform standards and agreement in less diverse, less stratified societies.

To be culturally relativistic, we need to avoid applying our own standards about what art is to the products of other cultures. Sculpture is art, right? Not necessarily. Previously, we challenged the view that non-Western art always has some kind of connection to religion. The Kalabari case to be discussed now makes the opposite point: that religious sculpture is not always art.

Among the Kalabari of southern Nigeria (Figure 22.1), wooden sculptures are carved not for aesthetic reasons but to serve as "houses" for spirits (Horton 1963). These sculptures are used to control the spirits of Kalabari religion. The Kalabari place such a carving, and thus localize a spirit, in a cult house into which the spirit is invited. Here, sculpture is done not for art's sake but as a means of manipulating spiritual forces. The Kalabari do have standards for the carvings, but beauty isn't one of them. A sculpture must be sufficiently complete to represent its spirit. Carvings judged too crude are rejected by cult members. Also, carvers must base their work on past models. Particular spirits have particular images associated with them. It's considered dangerous to produce a carving that deviates too much from a previous image of the spirit or that resembles another spirit. Offended spirits may retaliate. As long as they observe these standards of completeness and established images, carvers are free to express themselves. But these images are considered repulsive rather than beautiful. And they are not manufactured for artistic but for religious reasons.

Art and Individuality

Those who work with non-Western art have been criticized for ignoring the individual and focusing too much on the social nature and context of art. When art objects from Africa or Papua New Guinea are displayed in museums, generally only the name of the tribe and of the Western donor are given, rather than that of the individual artist. It's as though skilled individuals don't exist in non-Western societies. The impression is that art is collectively produced. Sometimes it is; sometimes it isn't.

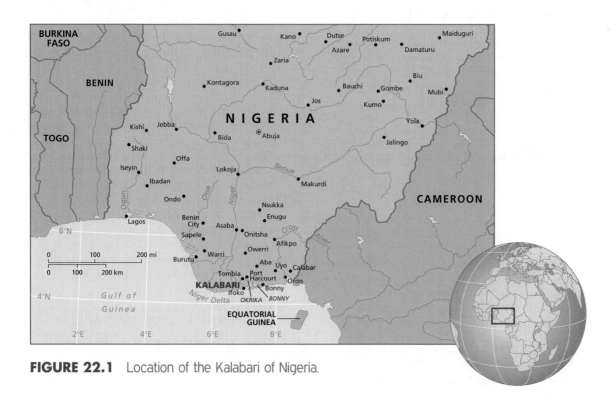

FIGURE 22.1 Location of the Kalabari of Nigeria.

To some extent, there *is* more collective production of art in non-Western societies than in the United States and Canada. According to Hackett (1996), African artworks (sculpted figures, textiles, paintings, or pots) generally are enjoyed, critiqued, and used by communities or groups, rather than being the prerogative of the individual alone. The artist may receive more feedback during the creative process than the individual artist typically encounters in our own society. Here, the feedback often comes too late, after the product is complete, rather than during production, when it can still be changed.

During his fieldwork among Nigeria's Tiv people, Paul Bohannan (1971) concluded that the proper study of art there should pay less attention to artists and more attention to art critics and products. There were few skilled Tiv artists, and such people avoided doing their art publicly. However, mediocre artists would work in public, where they routinely got comments from onlookers (critics). Based on critical suggestions, an artist often changed a design, such as a carving, in progress. There was yet another way in which Tiv artists worked socially rather than individually. Sometimes, when an artist put his work aside, someone else would pick it up and start working on it. The Tiv clearly didn't recognize the same kind of connection between individuals and their art that we do. According to Bohannan, every Tiv was free to know what he liked and to try to make it if he could. If not, one or more of his fellows might help him out.

In Western societies, artists of many sorts (e.g., writers, painters, sculptors, actors, classical and rock musicians) have reputations for being iconoclastic and antisocial. Social acceptance may be more important in the societies anthropologists have traditionally studied. Still, there are well-known individual artists in non-Western societies. They are recognized as such by other community members and perhaps by outsiders as well. Their artistic labor may even be conscripted for special displays and performances, including ceremonies, or palace arts and events.

To what extent can a work of art stand apart from its creator? Haapala (1998) argues that artists and their works are inseparable. "By creating works of art a person creates an artistic identity for himself. He creates himself quite literally into the pieces he puts into his art. He exists in the works he has created." In this view, Picasso created many Picassos, and exists in and through those works of art.

Sometimes little is known or recognized about the individual artist responsible for an enduring artwork. We are more likely to know the name of the recording artist than that of the writer of the songs we most commonly remember and perhaps sing. Sometimes we fail to acknowledge art individually because the artwork was collectively created. To whom should we attribute a pyramid or a cathedral? Should it be the architect, the ruler or leader who commissioned the work, or the master builder who implemented the design? A thing of beauty may be a joy forever even if we don't credit its creator(s).

The Work of Art

Some may see art as a form of expressive freedom, as giving free rein to the imagination and the human need to create or to be playful. But consider the word *opera.* It is the plural of *opus,* which means a work. For the artist, at least, art is work, albeit creative work. In nonstate societies, artists may have to hunt, gather, herd, fish, or farm in order to eat, but they still manage to find time to work on their art. In state societies, at least, artists have been defined as specialists—professionals who have chosen careers as artists, musicians, writers, or actors. If they manage to support themselves from their art, they may be full-time professionals. If not, they do their art part-time, while earning a living from another activity. Sometimes artists associate in professional groups such as medieval guilds or contemporary unions. Actors Equity in New York, a labor union, is a modern guild, designed to protect the interests of its artist members.

Just how much work is needed to make a work of art? In the early days of French impressionism, many experts viewed the paintings of Claude Monet and his colleagues as too sketchy and spontaneous to be true art. Established artists and critics were accustomed to more formal and classic studio styles. The French impressionists got their name from their sketches—*impressions* in French—of natural and social settings. They took advantage of technological innovations, particularly the availability of oil paints in tubes, to take their palettes, easels, and canvases into the field. There they made the pictures of changing light and color that hang today in so many museums, where they are now fully recognized as art. But before impressionism became an officially recognized "school" of art, its works were perceived by its critics as crude and unfinished. In terms of community standards, the first impressionist paintings were evaluated as harshly as were crude and incomplete Kalabari wood carvings of spirits, as discussed previously.

For familiar genres, such as painting or music, societies tend to have standards by which they judge whether an artwork is complete or fully realized. Most people would doubt, for instance, that an all-white painting could be a work of art. Standards may be maintained informally in society, or by specialists, such as art critics. It may be difficult for unorthodox or renegade artists to innovate. But, like the impressionists, they may eventually succeed. Some societies tend to reward conformity, an artist's skill with traditional models and techniques. Others encourage breaks with the past, innovation.

ART, SOCIETY, AND CULTURE

Around 100,000 years ago, some of the world's first artists occupied Blombos Cave, located on a high cliff facing the Indian Ocean at the tip of what is now South Africa. They hunted game and ate fish from the waters below them. In terms of body and brain size, these ancient Africans were anatomically modern humans. They also were turning animal bones into finely worked tools and weapon points. Furthermore, they were engraving artifacts with symbolic marks—manifestations of abstract and creative thought and, presumably, communication through language (Wilford 2002*b*).

A group led by Christopher Henshilwood of South Africa has analyzed bone tools and other artifacts from Blombos Cave, along with the mineral ocher which may have been used for body painting. The most impressive bone tools are three sharp instruments. The bone appears first to have been shaped with a stone blade, then finished into a symmetrical shape and polished for hours. According to Henshilwood (quoted in Wilford 2002*b*), "It's actually unnecessary for projectile points to be so carefully made. It suggests to us that this is an expression of symbolic thinking. The people said, 'Let's make a really beautiful object . . .' Symbolic thinking means that people are using something to mean something else. The tools do not have to have only a practical purpose. And the ocher might be used to decorate their equipment, perhaps themselves."

In Europe, art goes back more than 30,000 years, to the Upper Paleolithic period in western Europe (see Conkey et al. 1997). Cave paintings, the best-known examples of Upper Paleolithic art, were separated from ordinary life and social space. Those images were painted in true caves, located deep in the bowels of the earth. They may have been painted as part of some kind of rite of passage involving retreat from society. Portable art objects carved in stone, bone, and ivory, along with musical whistles and flutes, also confirm artistic expression throughout the Upper Paleolithic (see Lesure 2011). Art usually is more public than the cave paintings. Typically, it is exhibited, evaluated, performed, and appreciated in society. It has spectators or audiences. It isn't just for the artist.

Ethnomusicology

Ethnomusicology is the comparative study of the musics of the world and of music as an aspect of culture and society. The field of ethnomusicology thus unites music and anthropology. The music side involves the study and analysis of the music itself and the instruments used to create it. The anthropology side views music as a way to explore a culture, to determine the role—historic and contemporary— that music plays in that society, and the specific social and cultural features that influence how music is created and performed.

Ethnomusicology studies non-Western music, traditional and folk music, and even contemporary popular music from a cultural perspective. To do this there has to be fieldwork—firsthand study of particular forms of music, their social functions and cultural meanings, within particular societies. Ethnomusicologists talk with local musicians, make

This musician living in the Central African Republic carved this instrument himself.

recordings in the field, and learn about the place of musical instruments, performances, and performers in a given society (Kirman 1997). Nowadays, given globalization, diverse cultures and musical styles easily meet and mix. Music that draws on a wide range of cultural instruments and styles is called World Fusion, World Beat, or World Music—another topic within contemporary ethnomusicology.

Because music is a cultural universal, and because musical abilities seem to run in families, it has been suggested that a predisposition for music may have a genetic basis (Crenson 2000). Could a "music gene" that arose tens, or hundreds, of thousands of years ago have conferred an evolutionary advantage on those early humans who possessed it? The fact that music has existed in all known cultures suggests that it arose early in human history. Providing direct evidence for music's antiquity is an ancient carved bone flute from a cave in Slovenia. This "Divje babe flute," the world's oldest known musical instrument, dates back more than 43,000 years.

Exploring the possible biological roots of music, Sandra Trehub (2001) notes striking similarities in the way mothers worldwide sing to their children— with a high pitch, a slow tempo, and a distinctive tone. All cultures have lullabies, which sound so much alike they cannot be mistaken for anything else (Crenson 2000). Trehub speculates that music might have been adaptive in human evolution because musically talented mothers had an easier time calming their babies. Calm babies who fell asleep easily and rarely made a fuss might have been more likely to survive to adulthood. Their cries would not attract predators; they and their mothers would get more rest; and they would be less likely to be mistreated. If a gene conferring musical ability appeared early in human evolution, given a selective advantage, musical adults would pass their genes to their children.

ethnomusicology
Comparative study of music as an aspect of culture and society.

Music would seem to be among the most social of the arts. Usually it unites people in groups. Indeed, music is all about groups—choirs, symphonies, ensembles, and bands. Could it be that early humans with a biological penchant for music were able to live more effectively in social groups—another possible adaptive advantage? Even master pianists and violinists are frequently accompanied by orchestras or singers. Alan Merriam (1971) describes how the Basongye people of the Democratic Republic of Congo (Figure 22.2) use three features to distinguish between music and other sounds, which are classified as "noise." First, music always involves humans. Sounds emanating from non-human creatures, such as birds and animals, are not music. Second, musical sounds must be organized. A single tap on the drum isn't music, but drummers playing together in a pattern is. Third, music must continue. Even if several drums are struck together simultaneously, it isn't music. They must go on playing to establish some kind of sound pattern. For the Basongye, then, music is inherently cultural (distinctly human) and social (dependent on cooperation).

Originally coined for European peasants, **folk** art, music, and lore refer to the expressive culture of ordinary people, as contrasted with the "high" art or "classic" art of the European elites. When European folk music is performed (see photo on p. 503), the combination of costumes, music, and often song and dance is supposed to say something about local culture and about tradition. Tourists and other outsiders often perceive rural and folk life mainly in terms of such performances. Community residents themselves often use such performances to display and enact their local culture and traditions for outsiders.

In Planinica, a Muslim village in (prewar) Bosnia, Yvonne Lockwood (1983) studied folksong, which could be heard there day or night. The most active singers were unmarried females age 16 to 26 (maidens). Lead singers, those who customarily began and led songs, had strong, full, clear voices with a high range. Like some of their counterparts in contemporary North America (but in a much milder fashion), some lead singers acted unconventionally. One was regarded as immodest because of her risqué lyrics. Another smoked (usually a man's habit) and liked to wear men's trousers. Local criticism aside, she was thought to be witty and to improvise songs better than others did.

The social transition from girl to maiden (marriageable female) was signaled by active participation in public song and dance. Adolescent girls were urged to sing along with women and performing maidens. This was part of a rite of passage by which a little girl (dite) became a maiden (cura). Marriage, in contrast, moved most women from the public to the private sphere; public singing generally stopped. Married women sang in their own homes or among other women. Only occasionally would they join maidens in public song, but they never called attention to themselves by taking the lead. After age 50 wives tended to stop singing, even in private.

For women, singing thus signaled a series of transitions between age grades: girl to maiden (public singing), maiden to wife (private singing), and wife to elder (no more singing). Lockwood describes how one recently married woman made her ritual first visit after marriage to her family of origin. (Postmarital residence was patrilocal.) Then, as she was leaving to return to her husband's village, for "old times' sake" she led the village maidens in song. She used her native daughter status to behave like a maiden this one last time. Lockwood calls it a nostalgic and emotional performance for all who attended.

Singing and dancing were common at *prelos* attended by males and females. In Planinica the Serbo-Croatian word *prelo*, usually defined as "spinning bee," meant any occasion for visiting. *Prelos* were especially common in winter. During the summer, villagers worked long hours, and *prelos* were few. The *prelo* offered a context for play, relaxation, song, and dance. All gatherings of maidens, especially *prelos*, were occasions for song. Married women encouraged them to sing, often suggesting specific songs. If males were also present, a singing duel might occur, in which maidens and young men teased each other. A successful *prelo* was well attended, with much singing and dancing.

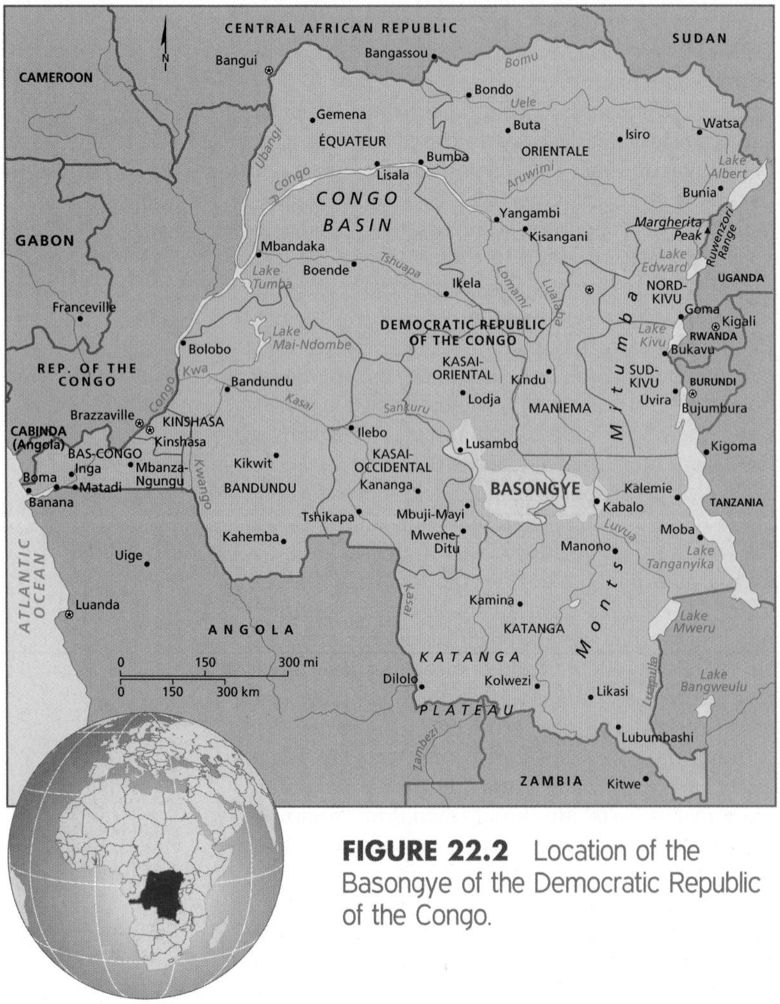

folk
Of the people; e.g., the art, music, and lore of ordinary people.

FIGURE 22.2 Location of the Basongye of the Democratic Republic of the Congo.

In this 2011 photo, musicians play carcaba (iron castanets) and gambri (guitar) in the Kasbah, Tangier, Morocco. For whose pleasure do you suppose this performance is being given? Nowadays, such performances attract tourists as well as local people.

Public singing was traditional in many other contexts among prewar Bosnian Muslims. After a day of cutting hay on mountain slopes, parties of village men would congregate at a specific place on the trail above the village. They formed lines according to their singing ability, with the best singers in front and the less talented ones behind. They proceeded to stroll down to the village together, singing as they went, until they reached the village center, where they dispersed. According to Lockwood, whenever an activity of work or leisure brought together a group of maidens or young men, it rarely ended without public song. It would not be wrong to trace the inspiration for parts of *Snow White* and *Shrek* (the movies) back to the European countryside.

Representations of Art and Culture

Art can stand for tradition, even when traditional art is removed from its original (rural) context. The creative products and images of folk, rural, and non-Western cultures are increasingly spread—and commercialized—by the media and tourism. A result is that many Westerners have come to think of "culture" in terms of colorful customs, music, dancing, and adornments: clothing, jewelry, and hairstyles.

A bias toward the arts and religion, rather than more mundane, less photogenic, economic and social tasks, shows up on TV's Discovery Channel, and even in many anthropological films (see Grimshaw and Ravetz 2009). Many ethnographic films start off with music, often drumbeats: "Bonga, bonga, bonga, bonga. Here in (supply place name), the people are

very religious." We see in such presentations the previously critiqued assumption that the arts of nonindustrial societies usually have a link with religion. The (usually unintended) message is that non-Western peoples spend much of their time wearing colorful clothes, singing, dancing, and practicing religious rituals. Taken to an extreme, such images portray culture as recreational and ultimately not serious, rather than as something that ordinary people live every day of their lives—not just when they have festivals.

Art and Communication

Art also functions in society as a form of communication between artist and community or audience. Sometimes, however, there are intermediaries between the artist and the audience. Actors, for example, are artists who translate the works and ideas of other artists (writers and directors) into the performances that audiences see and appreciate. Musicians play and sing compositions of other people along with music they themselves have composed. Using music written by others, choreographers plan and direct patterns of dance, which dancers then execute for audiences.

How does art communicate? We need to know what the artist intends to communicate and how the audience reacts. Often, the audience communicates right back to the artist. Live performers, for instance, get immediate feedback, as may writers and directors by viewing a performance of their own work. Artists expect at least some variation in reception. In contemporary societies, with increasing diversity in the audience, uniform reactions are rare. Contemporary artists, like businesspeople, are well aware that they have target audiences. Certain segments of the population are more likely to appreciate certain forms of art than other segments are.

Art can transmit several kinds of messages. It can convey a moral lesson or tell a cautionary tale. It can teach lessons the artist, or society, wants told. Like the rites that induce, then dispel, anxiety, the tension and resolution of drama can lead to **catharsis,** intense emotional release, in the audience. Art can move emotions, make us laugh, cry, feel up or down. Art appeals to the intellect as well as to the emotions. We may delight in a well-constructed, nicely balanced, well-realized work of art.

Often, art is meant to commemorate and to last, to carry an enduring message. Like a ceremony, art may serve a mnemonic function, making people remember. Art may be designed to make people remember either individuals or events, such as the AIDS epidemic that has proved so lethal in many world areas, or the cataclysmic events of September 11, 2001.

catharsis
Intense emotional release.

Art and Politics

What is art's social role? To what extent should art serve society? Art can be self-consciously prosocial. It can be used to either express or challenge community sentiment and standards. Art enters the political arena. Decisions about what counts as a work of art, or about how to display art, may be political and controversial. Museums have to balance concern over community standards with a wish to be as creative and innovative as the artists and works they display.

Much art that is valued today was received with revulsion in its own time. Children were prohibited from seeing paintings by Matisse, Braque, and Picasso when those works first were displayed in New York in the Armory Show of 1913. The *New York Times* called that Armory Show "pathological." Almost a century later, the City of New York and then mayor Rudolph Giuliani took the Brooklyn Museum to court over its 1999–2000 "Sensation" exhibit. After religious groups protested Chris Ofili's *Holy Virgin Mary,* a collage that included elephant dung, Giuliani deemed the work sacrilegious. The ensuing court trial prompted anticensorship groups and art advocates to speak out against the mayor's actions. The museum won the case, but Ofili's work again came under attack when a man smuggled paint inside the Brooklyn exhibition and tried to smear it on the *Virgin* (University of Virginia, n.d.). According to art professor Michael Davis, Ofili's collage is "shocking" because it deliberately provokes and intends to jolt viewers into an expanded frame of reference. The mayor's reactions may have been based on the narrow definition that art must be beautiful and an equally limited stereotype of a Virgin Mary as depicted in Italian Renaissance paintings (Mount Holyoke College 1999).

Today, no museum director can mount an exhibit without worrying that it will offend some politically organized segment of society. In the United States there has been an ongoing battle between liberals and conservatives involving the National Endowment for the Arts. Artists have been criticized as aloof from society, as creating only for themselves and for elites, as out of touch with conventional and traditional aesthetic values, even as mocking the values of ordinary people.

The Cultural Transmission of the Arts

Appreciation of the arts depends on cultural background. Watch Japanese tourists in a Western art museum trying to interpret what they are seeing. Conversely, the form and meaning of a Japanese tea ceremony, or a demonstration of origami (Japanese paper folding), will be alien to a foreign observer. Appreciation for the arts must be learned. It is part of enculturation, as well as of more formal education. Robert Layton (1991) suggests that whatever universal principles of artistic expression may exist, they have been put into effect in a diversity of ways in different cultures.

What is aesthetically pleasing depends to some extent on culture. Based on familiarity, music with certain tonalities and rhythm patterns will please some people and alienate others. In a study of Navajo music, McAllester (1954) found that it reflected the overall culture of that time in three main ways: First, individualism was a key Navajo cultural value. Thus, it was up to the individual to decide what to do with his or her physical property, knowledge, ideas, or songs. Second, McAllester found that a general Navajo conservatism also extended to music. The Navajo saw foreign music as

Appreciation for the arts must be learned. Here, three American boys seem intrigued by the painting *Paris on a Rainy Day* at the Chicago Art Institute. How does the placement of art in museums affect art appreciation?

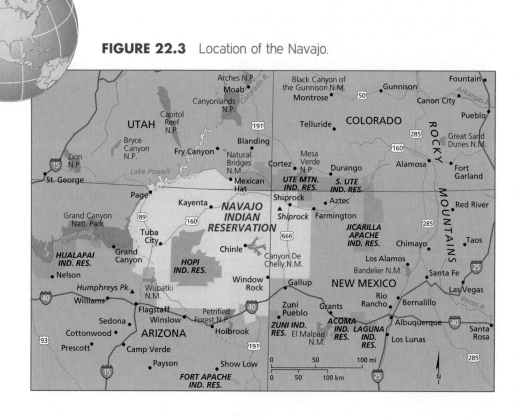

FIGURE 22.3 Location of the Navajo.

dangerous and rejected it. (This second point is no longer true; there are now Navajo rock bands.) Third, a general stress on proper form applied to music. There was, in Navajo belief, a right way to sing every kind of song (see Figure 22.3 for the location of the Navajo).

People learn to listen to certain kinds of music and to appreciate particular art forms, just as they learn to hear and decipher a foreign language. Unlike Londoners and New Yorkers, Parisians don't flock to musicals. Despite its multiple French origins, even the musical *Les Misérables,* a huge hit in London, New York, and dozens of cities worldwide, bombed in Paris. Humor, too, a form of verbal art, depends on cultural background and setting. What's funny in one culture may not translate as funny in another. When a joke doesn't work, an American may say, "Well, you had to be there at the time." Jokes, like aesthetic judgments, depend on context.

At a smaller level of culture, certain artistic traditions may be transmitted in families. In Bali, for example, there are families of carvers, musicians, dancers, and mask makers. Among the Yoruba of Nigeria, two specific lineages are entrusted with important bead embroidery works, such as for the king's crown and the bags and bracelets of priests. The arts, like other professions, often "run" in families. The Bachs, for example, produced not only

living anthropology **VIDEOS**

Art of the Aborigines, www.mhhe.com/kottak

This clip focuses on an aboriginal artist in the community of Galiwinku in northern Australia. Here we have an excellent illustration of how aspects of culture (art, religion, kinship, economics, law) that stand apart in our own society are inseparable in others. The artist makes a string bag, based on a pattern her father originated. She uses knowledge taught to her by her mother, grandmother, and grandfather. According to the narrator, the artist weaves a story of the dreamtime—the mythical past when the world as we know it was created—into the bag, which thus has spiritual as well as artistic and functional significance. How widespread is this art in the community shown here? How was the bag used during gathering? How does the creative act here depict enculturation?

Johann Sebastian but several other noted composers and musicians.

In Chapter 1, anthropology's approach to the arts was contrasted with a traditional humanities focus on "fine arts," as in art history, "Great Books," and classical music. Anthropology has extended the definition of "cultured" well beyond the elitist meaning

Schoolchildren play violins in an orchestra. Does this scene illustrate education, enculturation, or both?

This photo was taken on St. Paul Island, on the Bering Sea coast of Alaska. A traditional Aleut storyteller uses a drum to tell his tale to young Aleut people. Who are the storytellers of your society? How do their narrative techniques and styles differ from the one shown here?

anthropology **ATLAS**

http://www.mhhe.com/anthromaps
Locate the ethnographic site for the Tiwi of North Australia on Map 10.

of "high" art and culture. For anthropologists, everyone acquires culture through enculturation. In academia today, growing acceptance of the anthropological definition of culture has helped broaden the study of the humanities from fine art and elite art to "folk" and non-Western arts, and the creative expressions of popular culture.

This chapter's "Appreciating Anthropology" shows that techniques that anthropologists have used to analyze myths and folktales can be extended to two fantasy films that most of you have seen: *The Wizard of Oz* and *Star Wars*. "Appreciating Anthropology" again highlights the contributions of the French anthropologist Claude Lévi-Strauss (1967) along with the neo-Freudian psychoanalyst Bruno Bettelheim (1975). Both have made important contributions to the study of myths and fairy tales.

In many societies, myths, legends, tales, and the art of storytelling play important roles in the transmission of culture and the preservation of tradition. In the absence of writing, oral traditions may preserve details of history and genealogy, as in many parts of West Africa. Art forms often go together. For example, music and storytelling may be combined for drama and emphasis (see the lower photo), much as they are in films and theater.

At what age do children start learning the arts? In some cultures, they start early. Contrast the photo of the violin class (above left) with the photo of the Aleut gathering (below). The violin scene shows formal instruction. Teachers take the lead in showing students how to play the violin. The Aleut photo shows a more informal local scene in which children are learning about the arts as part of their overall enculturation. Presumably, the violin students are learning the arts because their parents want them to, not necessarily because they have an artistic temperament that they need or wish to express. Sometimes children's participation in arts or performance, including sports, exemplifies forced enculturation. It may be pushed by parents rather than by kids themselves. In the United States, performance, usually associated with schools, has a strong social, and usually competitive, component. Kids perform with their peers. In the process, they learn to compete, whether for a first-place finish in a sports event or for a first chair in the school orchestra or band.

The Artistic Career

In nonindustrial societies, artists tend to be part-time specialists. In states, there are more ways for artists to practice their craft full-time. The number of positions in "arts and leisure" has mushroomed in contemporary societies, especially in North America. Many non-Western societies also offer career tracks in the arts: For example, a child born into a particular family or lineage may discover that he or she is destined for a career in leather working or weaving. Some societies are noted for particular arts, such as dance, wood carving, or weaving.

An artistic career also may involve some kind of calling. Individuals may discover they have a particular talent and find an environment in which that talent is nourished. Separate career paths for artists usually involve special training and apprenticeship. Such paths are more likely in a complex society, where there are many separate career tracks, than in band or tribal societies, where expressive culture is less formally separated from daily life.

Artists need support if they are to devote full time to creative activity. They find support in their families or lineages if there is specialization in the arts involving kin groups. State societies often have patrons of the arts. Usually members of the elite class, patrons offer various kinds of support to aspiring and talented artists, such as court and palace painters, musicians, or sculptors. In some cases, an artistic career may entail a lifetime of dedication to religious art.

Goodale and Koss (1971) describe the manufacture of ornamental burial poles among the Tiwi of North Australia. Temporary separation and detachment from other social roles allowed burial pole artists to devote themselves to their work. The pole artists were ceremonially commissioned as such after a death. They were granted temporary freedom from the daily food quest. Other community members agreed to serve as their patrons. They supplied the artists with hard-to-get materials needed for their work. The artists were sequestered in a work area near the grave. That area was taboo to everyone else.

The arts usually are defined as neither practical nor ordinary. They rely on talent, which is individual, but which must be channeled and shaped in socially approved directions. Inevitably, artistic talent and production pull the artist away from the practical need to make a living. The issue of how to support artists and the arts arises again and again. We've all heard the phrase "struggling artist." But how should society support the arts? If there is state or religious support, something is typically expected in return. There is inevitably some limitation of the artist's "free" expression. Patronage and sponsorship also may result in the creation of art works that are removed from public display. Art commissioned for elites often is displayed only in their homes, perhaps finding its way into museums after their deaths. Church-commissioned art may be closer to the people.

Continuity and Change

The arts go on changing, although certain art forms have survived for thousands of years. The Upper Paleolithic cave art that has survived for more than 30,000 years was itself a highly developed manifestation of human creativity and symbolism, with a long evolutionary history. Monumental architecture, along with sculpture, reliefs, ornamental pottery, and written music, literature, and drama, have survived from early civilizations.

Countries and cultures are known for particular contributions, including art. The Balinese are known for dance; the Navajo for sand paintings, jewelry, and weaving; and the French for making cuisine an art form. We still read Greek tragedies and comedies in college, as we also read Shakespeare and Milton, and view the works of Michelangelo. Greek theater is among the most enduring of the arts. The words of Aeschylus, Sophocles, Euripides, and Aristophanes have been captured in writing and live on. Who knows how many great preliterate creations and performances have been lost?

Classic Greek theater survives throughout the world. It is read in college courses and performed on stages from Athens to New York. In today's world, the dramatic arts are part of a huge "arts and leisure"

In an ancient amphitheatre at Syracuse, Sicily, ancient Greek theater (*Medea*) is being performed for a contemporary audience. Theater is typically a multimedia experience, with visual, aural, and often musical attributes.

A synthesis of new and old theater techniques, including puppetry, is used in this production of the stage play *War Horse* at London's Olivier Theatre.

industry, which links Western and non-Western art forms in a global network that has both aesthetic and commercial dimensions (see Marcus and Myers 1995; Root 1996). Non-Western musical traditions and instruments have joined this network. We've seen that local musicians perform for outsiders, including tourists who increasingly visit their villages. And "tribal" instruments such as the Native Australian didgeridoo, a very long wooden wind instrument, are now exported worldwide. At least one

I'll Get You, My Pretty, and Your Little R2

Techniques that anthropologists have used to analyze myths and folktales can be extended to two fantasy films that most of you have seen. *The Wizard of Oz* has been telecast regularly for decades. The original *Star Wars* remains one of the most popular films of all time. Both are familiar and significant cultural products with obvious mythic qualities. The contributions of the French structuralist anthropologist Claude Lévi-Strauss (1967) and the neo-Freudian psychoanalyst Bruno Bettelheim (1975) to the study of myths and fairy tales permit the following analysis of visual fairy tales that contemporary Americans know well.

Examining the myths and tales of different cultures, Lévi-Strauss determined that one tale could be converted into another through a series of simple operations, for example, by doing the following:

1. Converting the positive element of a myth into its negative.
2. Reversing the order of the elements.
3. Replacing a male hero with a female hero.
4. Preserving or repeating certain key elements.

Through such operations, two apparently dissimilar myths can be shown to be variations on a common structure, that is, to be transformations of each other.

We'll see now that *Star Wars* is a systematic structural transformation of *The Wizard of Oz*. We may speculate about how many of the resemblances were conscious and how many simply reflect a process of enculturation that *Star Wars* writer and director George Lucas shares with other Americans.

The Wizard of Oz and *Star Wars* both begin in arid country, the first in Kansas and the second on the desert planet Tatooine. (Recap 22.1 lists the similarities discussed here.) *Star Wars* converts *The Wizard's* female hero, Dorothy, into a boy, Luke Skywalker. Fairy-tale heroes usually have short, common first names and second names that describe their origin or activity. Thus Luke, who travels aboard spaceships, is a Skywalker, while Dorothy Gale is swept off to Oz by a cyclone (a gale of wind). Dorothy leaves home with her dog, Toto, who is pursued by and has managed to escape from

a woman who in Oz becomes the Wicked Witch of the West. Luke follows his "Two-Two" (R2D2), who is fleeing Darth Vader, the witch's structural equivalent.

Dorothy and Luke each start out living with an uncle and an aunt. However, because of the gender change of the hero, the primary relationship is reversed and inverted. Thus Dorothy's relationship with her aunt is primary, warm, and loving, whereas Luke's relationship with his uncle, though primary, is strained and distant. Aunt and uncle are in the tales for the same reason. They represent home (the nuclear family of orientation), which children (according to American culture norms) must eventually leave to make it on their own. As Bettelheim (1975) points out, fairy tales often disguise parents as uncle and aunt, and this establishes social distance. The child can deal with the hero's separation (in *The Wizard of Oz*) or the aunt's and uncle's deaths (in *Star Wars*) more easily than with the death of or separation from real parents. Furthermore, this permits the child's strong feelings toward his or her real parents to

store in Amsterdam, the Netherlands, specializes in didgeridoos, the only item it carries. Dozens of stores in any world capital hawk "traditional" arts, including musical instruments, from a hundred Third World countries.

American culture values change, experimentation, innovation, and novelty. But creativity also may be based on tradition. The Navajo, for example, can be at once individualistic, conservative, and creative in their attention to traditional form. In some cases and cultures, as with the Navajo, it's not necessary for artists to be innovative as they are being creative. Creativity can be expressed in variations on a traditional form. We see an example of this in this chapter's "Appreciating Anthropology," in which *Star Wars*, despite its specific story and innovative special effects, is shown to share its narrative structure with a previous film and story. Often, artists show fealty to the past,

building on, rather than rejecting, the work of their predecessors.

Just as ingredients and flavors from all over the world are combined in modern cuisine, so too are elements from many cultures and epochs woven into contemporary art and performance. We've seen that the arts typically draw in multiple media. Given the richness of today's media world, multimedia are even more marked.

MEDIA AND CULTURE

Today's mass culture, aka popular culture, features cultural forms that have appeared and spread rapidly because of major changes in the material conditions of contemporary life—particularly work organization, transportation, and communication, including the media. Sports, movies, TV shows, amusement parks, and fast-food restaurants have become

be represented in different, more central characters, such as the Wicked Witch of the West and Darth Vader.

Both films focus on the child's relationship with the parent of the same sex, dividing that parent into three parts. In *The Wizard,* the mother is split into two parts bad and one part good. They are the Wicked Witch of the East, dead at the beginning of the movie; the Wicked Witch of the West, dead at the end; and Glinda, the good mother, who survives. The original *Star Wars* reversed the proportion of good and bad, giving Luke a good father (his own), the Jedi knight who is proclaimed dead at the film's beginning. There is another good father, Ben Kenobi, who is ambiguously dead when the movie ends. Third is the evil father figure, Darth Vader. As the good-mother third survives *The Wizard of Oz,* the bad-father third lives on after *Star Wars,* to strike back in the sequel.

The child's relationship with the parent of the opposite sex also is represented in the two films. Dorothy's father figure is the Wizard of Oz, an initially terrifying figure who later is proved to be a fake. Bettelheim notes that the typical fairy-tale father is disguised as a monster or giant. Or else, when preserved as a human, he is weak, distant, or ineffective. Dorothy counts on the wizard to save her but finds that he makes seemingly impossible demands and in the end is just an ordinary man. She succeeds on her own, no longer relying on a father who offers no more than she herself possesses.

In *Star Wars* (although emphatically not in the later films), Luke's mother figure is Princess Leia. Bettelheim notes that boys commonly fantasize their mothers to be unwilling captives of their fathers. Fairy tales often disguise mothers as princesses whose freedom the boy-hero must obtain. In graphic Freudian imagery, Darth Vader threatens Princess Leia with a needle the size of the witch's broomstick. By the end of the film, Luke has freed Leia and defeated Vader.

There are other striking parallels in the structure of the two films. Fairy-tale heroes often are accompanied on their adventures by secondary characters who personify the virtues needed in a successful quest. Such characters often come in threes. Dorothy takes along wisdom (the Scarecrow), love (the Tin Woodman), and courage (the Lion). *Star Wars* includes a structurally equivalent trio—Han Solo, C3PO, and Chewbacca—but their association with particular qualities isn't as precise. The minor characters also are structurally parallel: Munchkins and Jawas, Apple Trees and Sand People, Flying Monkeys and Stormtroopers. And compare settings—the witch's castle and the Death Star, the Emerald City and the rebel base. The endings also are parallel. Luke accomplishes his objective on his own, using the Force (mana, magical power). Dorothy's goal is to return to Kansas. She does that by tapping her shoes together and drawing on the Force in her ruby slippers.

All successful cultural products blend old and new, drawing on familiar themes. They may rearrange them in novel ways and thus win a lasting place in the imaginations of the culture that creates or accepts them. *Star Wars* successfully used old cultural themes in novel ways. It did that by drawing on *the* American fairy tale, one that had been available in book form since the turn of the 20th century.

powerful elements of national (and international) culture. They provide a framework of common expectations, experiences, and behavior overriding differences in region, class, formal religious affiliation, political sentiments, gender, ethnic group, and place of residence.

Using the Media

Any media-borne image or message can be analyzed in terms of its nature, including its symbolism, and its effects. It also can be analyzed as a text. We usually think of a text as a textbook, like this one, but the term has a more general meaning. **Text** can refer to anything that can be "read"—that is, processed, interpreted, and assigned meaning by anyone exposed to it. In this sense, a text doesn't have to be written. The term may refer to a film, an image, or an event. "Readers"—users of the text—make their own interpretations and derive their own feelings from it. "Readers" of media messages constantly produce their own meanings.

In his book *Understanding Popular Culture* (1989), John Fiske views each individual's use of popular culture as a creative act (an original "reading" of a text). For example, a particular rock star or movie means something different to each fan as well as to each person who really dislikes that star or film. As Fiske puts it, "the meanings I make from a text are pleasurable when I feel that they are my meanings and that they relate to my everyday life in a practical, direct way" (1989, p. 57). All of us can creatively "read" print media, along with music, television, films, celebrities, and other popular culture products (see Fiske and Hartley 2003, Fiske 2011).

Media consumers actively select, evaluate, and interpret media in ways that make sense to them. People use media for all sorts of reasons: to validate beliefs, to

text
Cultural product that is processed and assigned meaning by anyone exposed to it.

RECAP 22.1   *Star Wars* as a Structural Transformation of *The Wizard of Oz*

STAR WARS	THE WIZARD OF OZ
Male hero (Luke Skywalker)	Female hero (Dorothy Gale)
Arid Tatooine	Arid Kansas

Luke follows R2D2:
  R2D2 flees Vader
	Dorothy follows Toto:
	  Toto flees witch

Luke lives with uncle and aunt:
  Primary relationship with uncle
  (same sex as hero)
  Strained, distant relationship with uncle
	Dorothy lives with uncle and aunt:
	  Primary relationship with aunt
	  (same sex as hero)
	  Warm, close relationship with aunt

Tripartite division of same-sex parent:
  2 parts good, 1 part bad father
  Good father dead at beginning
  Good father dead (?) at end
  Bad father survives
	Tripartite division of same-sex parent:
	  2 parts bad, 1 part good mother
	  Bad mother dead at beginning
	  Bad mother dead at end
	  Good mother survives

Relationship with parent of opposite sex
    (Princess Leia Organa):
  Princess is unwilling captive
  Needle
  Princess is freed
	Relationship with parent of opposite sex
	    (Wizard of Oz):
	  Wizard makes impossible demands
	  Broomstick
	  Wizard turns out to be sham

Trio of companions:
  Han Solo, C3PO, Chewbacca
	Trio of companions:
	  Scarecrow, Tin Woodman, Cowardly Lion

Minor characters:
  Jawas
  Sand People
  Stormtroopers
	Minor characters:
	  Munchkins
	  Apple Trees
	  Flying Monkeys

Settings:
  Death Star
  Verdant Tikal (rebel base)
	Settings:
	  Witch's castle
	  Emerald City

Conclusion:
  Luke uses magic to accomplish goal
  (destroy Death Star)
	Conclusion:
	  Dorothy uses magic to accomplish goal
	  (return to Kansas)

indulge fantasies, to find messages unavailable in the local setting, to locate information, to make social comparisons, to relieve frustrations, to chart social courses, and to formulate life plans. Through popular culture, including various media, people may symbolically resist the unequal power relations they face each day in the family, at work, and in the classroom. Popular culture (from hip-hop to comedy) can be used to express discontent and resistance by groups that are or feel powerless or oppressed.

In one town in southern Brazil, Alberto Costa found that women and young adults of both sexes were particularly attracted to *telenovelas,* melodramatic nightly programs often compared to American soap operas, usually featuring sophisticated urban settings (see Kottak 2009). In the small community that Costa studied (as part of a larger study of TV in Brazil in which I participated), young people and women used the more liberal content of *telenovelas* to challenge conservative local norms. In Brazil, traditional information brokers and moral guardians (e.g., older men, elites, intellectuals, educators, and the clergy) tended to be more suspicious and dismissive of the media than were less powerful people—probably because media messages often clashed with their own.

In a more recent study in Michigan, focusing on media use in the context of work and family decision making, Lara Descartes and I (Descartes and Kottak 2009) found that parents selected media messages that supported and reinforced their own opinions and life choices. Varied media images of work and family allowed parents to get a sense of what others were thinking and doing, and to identify or contrast themselves with media figures. Our informants compared themselves with people and situations from the media as well as with people in their own lives. We also found, as in Brazil, that some people (traditionalists) were much more dismissive of, distrustful of, or hostile to media than others were.

When people seek certain messages and cannot easily find them in their home communities, they

For years, India's Bollywood film and TV industry has been an important non–Western center of cultural production. Shown here, an Indian cinema worker mounts a poster for the Oscar-winning movie *Slumdog Millionaire*, which was inspired in part by the Bollywood tradition.

are likely to look somewhere else. The media offer a rich web of external connections (through cable, satellite, the Internet, television, movies, radio, telephones, print, and other sources) that can provide contact, information, entertainment, and potential social validation. In Brazil, greater use of all media (e.g., TV and print) was part of an external orientation, a general wish for information, contacts, models, and support beyond those that were locally and routinely available. This linking role of media probably is less important for people who feel most comfortable in and with their local setting. For some of our informants in Michigan, media offered a welcome gateway to a wider world, while others were comfortable with, and even sought to enhance, their isolation, limiting both media exposure and the outside social contacts of themselves and their children.

Connection to a wider world, real or imagined, is a way to move beyond local standards and expectations, even if the escape is only temporary and vicarious. David Ignatius (2007) describes the escapist value of 19th-century English novels, expressed particularly through their heroines—women who were "passionate seekers," pursuing "free thought and personal freedom," rejecting the "easy comforts and arranged marriages of their class" in their quest for something more. Despite (and/or because of) their independent or rebellious temperaments, characters such as Elizabeth Bennett in Jane Austen's *Pride and Prejudice* almost always found a happy ending. Sympathetic 19th-century readers found such a heroine's success "deeply satisfying" because there were so few opportunities in real life (the local community) to see such behavior and choices (all quotes from Ignatius 2007: A21).

The arts, including mass media, allow us to imagine lifestyles and possibilities beyond our own circumstances and personal experience. We catch occasional glimpses of the rich and famous. Repeatedly we see portrayals of a homogenized upper-middle-class lifestyle. We also see images, often stereotyped, of ethnic contrasts (see this chapter's "Appreciating Diversity").

Another role of the media is to provide social cement—a basis for sharing—as families or friends watch favorite programs or attend such events as games and performances together. The media can provide common ground for much larger groups, nationally and internationally. Brazilians and Italians can be just as excited, at the same moment but with radically different emotions, by a soccer goal scored in a World Cup match. And they can remember the same winning goal or head butt for decades. The common information and knowledge that people acquire through exposure to the same media illustrate *culture* in the anthropological sense. (For other media roles, functions, and effects, see Askew and Wilk 2002, and Ginsburg, Abu-Lughod, and Larkin 2002).

Assessing the Effects of Television

In the Brazilian study mentioned in the last section, and described more fully in Chapter 1, my associates and I studied how TV influences behavior, attitudes, and values. That research is the basis of my book *Prime-Time Society: An Anthropological Analysis of Television and Culture* (updated ed. 2009)—a comparative study of television in Brazil and the United States. Family planning turned out to be one area in which TV has influenced behavior

From Night Fever to Jersey Shore

A conference held in January 2010 at the John D. Calandra Italian American Institute of Queens College, located in Midtown Manhattan, focused on the popular MTV show *Jersey Shore* and the "Guido culture" of its stars. How do the mass media portray and influence ethnic cultures and ethnicity? The following account describes how the 1977 film *Saturday Night Fever* and its lead character, Tony Manero, provide a kind of origin myth for self-identified members of today's Guido culture. Also, portrayals of Italian Americans in *Jersey Shore*, the Sopranos, and other New Jersey–focused TV shows and movies reinforce stereotypes that many Italian Americans find offensive. Finally, *Jersey Shore* itself creates a stereotype of one kind of "urban youth culture" that may be familiar and comfortable for some, but profoundly alienating for many others.

. . . Some Italian-Americans consider "Guido" a slur and have vehemently protested not only the show but also the use of the term. But others, mostly younger Italian-Americans, use it affectionately to refer to a particular life style. . . . As the show's Pauly D put it: "I was born and raised a Guido. It's just a lifestyle, it's being Italian, it's representing family, friends, tanning, gel, everything."

The [conference] attendees [included] scholars, elected officials, representatives from Italian-American organizations and the Consulate General of Italy, [and] a sprinkling of people who . . . called themselves Guidos and Guidettes.

The main speakers [were] Donald Tricarico, a sociologist from Queensborough Community College, and John DeCarlo, a freelance writer, caterer and self-professed Guido from New Jersey. . . .

Professor Tricarico's . . . talk demonstrated . . . that just as *Jersey Shore* denizens have their own lingo, so do academics—a scholarly version of "Yo, bro" and a fist pump. This "urban youth subculture," he said, is "associated with late capitalism," a second generation that "consumes commodified leisure styles," and has created "a bricolage of symbols."

In other words, they are a result of the rising fortunes of young Italian-Americans. Having finally attained leisure time and money, a new generation has carved out a niche for itself in the popular culture.

As New York State Senator Diane J. Savino, a Democrat who represents Staten Island and parts of Brooklyn, explained, "Guido was never a pejorative." It grew out of the 1950s greaser look, she said, and became a way for Italian-Americans who did not fit the larger culture's definition of beauty to take pride in their own heritage and define "cool" for themselves.

When she was growing up, everybody listened to rock; girls were supposed to be skinny, with straight blond hair (like Marcia Brady on *The Brady Bunch*); guys had ripped jeans, sneakers and straggly hair.

Then in 1977 *Saturday Night Fever* was released. "It changed the image for all of us," Ms. Savino said. As Tony Manero, John Travolta wore a white suit, had slicked-back short hair, liked disco music and was hot. "It was a way we could develop our own standard of beauty," she added.

Indeed, Professor Tricarico calls *Saturday Night Fever* the "origin myth" for "Guidos." Think of Tony Manero as their Adam.

Young Italian-Americans, he said, did what other immigrant groups before have done: take a symbol of derision, own it and redefine it their

in Brazil. My colleagues and I got the idea that TV might be encouraging Brazilians to have smaller families from an intriguing article we read in the *New York Times*. Based on interviews with Brazilians, that report suggested that TV (along with other factors) was influencing Brazilians to limit family size. Fortunately, we had the quantitative data to test that hypothesis.

Our findings in Brazil had already confirmed many other studies conducted throughout the world in showing that the strongest predictor of (smaller) family size is a woman's educational level. However, it turned out that two television variables—current viewing level, and especially the number of years of TV presence in the home—were better predictors of (smaller) family size than

were many other potential predictors, including income, class, and religiosity. Furthermore, the contraceptive effects of TV exposure had been totally unplanned.

In the four towns in our study with the longest exposure to television, the average woman had a TV set in her home for 15 years and had 2.3 pregnancies. In the three communities where TV had arrived most recently, the average woman had a home set for 4 years and had 5 pregnancies. Thus, length of site exposure was a useful predictor of reproductive histories. Of course, television exposure at a site is an aspect of that site's increasing overall access to external systems and resources, which usually include improved methods of contraception. But the impact of longer home TV exposure showed up not only

own way. Young African-Americans did that with the "n word," he added, much to the consternation of their elders, and gay people did the same by proudly using the word "queer."...

As for *Jersey Shore*, what Ms. Savino—and pretty much everyone else who spoke—objected to is the way the subculture has "been exploited by MTV." . . . Joseph Sciame, the president of the Italian Heritage & Culture Committee, said the problem was that no matter how many other positive depictions of Italian-Americans there are, "one showing of a program like *Jersey Shore*, and that's what people think all Italian-Americans are like." . . . As another speaker said, "We have a responsibility to make sure people know that's not us."

Mr. DeCarlo, who turns 29 this year, auditioned for *Jersey Shore* and made it to the final tryouts. He wore a black leather jacket, large gold cross around his neck and a pinky ring. His hair was spiked with gel. As the audition process went along, he said it became clear that MTV was more interested in "shocking reality TV mayhem instead of a family culture."...

To Mr. DeCarlo, Guido refers to a culture of family, food, wine, cigars, coffee, gold chains, Cadillacs and a dialect that gives "fuhgeddaboudit" some panache. Neither his style nor his fondness for clubbing means that "I'm looking for a fight," he said.

"A true Guido is someone with dreams, aspirations and goals," he said. Tony Manero "was very flawed, but you rooted for him because you knew he wanted to do something with his life."...

In May 2011, cast members of *Jersey Shore* sightsee in Florence, Italy. How Italian do you think they looked and acted in Italy?

when we compared sites but also within age cohorts, within sites, and among individual women in our total sample.

What social mechanisms were behind these correlations? Family planning opportunities (including contraception) are greater in Brazil now than they used to be. But, as Manoff (1994) notes, based on experience in Africa, Asia, and Latin America, family planning is not assured by the availability of contraceptives. Popular demand for contraception has to be created—often through "social marketing"—that is, planned multimedia campaigns such as that illustrated by the photo on page 514 showing an advertisement for vasectomies in India (see also Manoff 1994). In Brazil, however, there has been little direct use of TV to get people to limit their off-spring. How then has television influenced Brazilians to plan smaller families?

We noticed that Brazilian TV families tend to have fewer children than traditional small-town Brazilians do. Narrative form and production costs limit the number of players in each *telenovela* (nightly soap opera) to about fifty characters. *Telenovelas* usually are gender-balanced and include three-generation extended families of different social classes, so that some of the main characters can "rise in life" by marrying up. These narrative conventions limit the number of young children per TV family. We concluded that people's ideas about proper family size are influenced as they see, day after day, nuclear families smaller than the traditional ones in their towns. Furthermore, the aim of commercial television is to sell products and

Popular demand for birth control often must be created, for example, through multimedia campaigns, illustrated by the poster shown in this photo from India. In Brazil, however, there has been little direct use of TV to get people to limit their offspring. How, then, has television influenced Brazilians to plan smaller families?

lifestyles. Brazilian TV families routinely are shown enjoying consumer goods and lives of leisure, to which viewers learn to aspire. *Telenovelas* may convey the idea that viewers can achieve such lifestyles by emulating the apparent family planning of TV characters. The effect of Brazilian television on family planning seems to be a corollary of a more general, TV-influenced shift from traditional toward more liberal social attitudes, described in Chapter 1. Anthropologist Janet Dunn's (2000) further fieldwork in Brazil has demonstrated how TV exposure actually works to influence reproductive choice and family planning.

SPORTS AND CULTURE

We now turn to the cultural context of sports and the cultural values expressed in them. Because so much of what we know about sports comes from the media, we also are extending our consideration in this section to the pervasive role of the mass media in contemporary life. This section mainly describes how sports and the media *reflect* culture. Sports and the media *influence* culture as well, as we just saw in the discussion of how Brazilian television modifies social attitudes and family planning. Thus, the influence of media (and sports) on culture and vice versa is reciprocal. Chapter 1 discussed how sports participation can modify body types, and how cultural values (about body proportions) cause sports participation by men and women to vary in different cultures.

Football

Football, we say, is only a game, yet it has become a hugely popular spectator sport. On fall Saturdays, millions of people travel to and from college football games. Smaller congregations meet in high school stadiums. Millions of Americans watch televised football. Indeed, nearly half the adult population of the United States watches the Super Bowl, which attracts fans of diverse ages, ethnic backgrounds, regions, religions, political parties, jobs, social statuses, levels of wealth, and genders.

The popularity of football, particularly professional football, depends directly on the mass media, especially television. Is football, with its territorial incursion, hard hitting, and violence, occasionally resulting in injury, popular because Americans are violent people? Are football spectators vicariously realizing their own hostile and aggressive tendencies? The anthropologist W. Arens (1981) has discounted this interpretation. He points out that football is a peculiarly American pastime. Although a similar game is played in Canada, it is less popular there. Baseball has become a popular sport in the Caribbean, parts of Latin America, and Japan. Basketball and volleyball also are spreading. However, throughout most of the world, soccer is the most popular sport. Arens argues that if football were a particularly effective channel for expressing aggression, it would have spread (like soccer and baseball) to many other countries, where people have as many aggressive tendencies and hostile feelings as Americans do. He concludes reasonably that the explanation for football's popularity must lie elsewhere.

Arens contends that football is popular because it symbolizes certain key aspects of American life. In particular, it features teamwork based on specialization and division of labor, which are pervasive features of contemporary life. Susan Montague and Robert Morais (1981) take the analysis a step further. They argue that Americans appreciate football because it presents a miniaturized and simplified version of modern organizations. People have trouble understanding organizational bureaucracies, whether in business, universities, or government. Football, the anthropologists argue, helps us understand how decisions are made and rewards are allocated in organizations.

Montague and Morais link football's values, particularly teamwork, to those associated with business. Like corporate workers, the ideal players are diligent and dedicated to the team. Within corporations, however, decision making is complicated, and workers aren't always rewarded for their dedication and good job performance. Decisions are simpler and rewards are more consistent in football, these anthropologists contend, and this helps explain its popularity. Even if we can't figure out how Exxon-Mobil or Microsoft run, any fan can become an expert on football's rules, teams, scores, statistics, and patterns of play. Even more important, football suggests that the values stressed by business really do pay off. Teams whose members work the hardest, show the most spirit, and best develop and coordinate their talents can be expected to win more often than other teams do.

Illustrating the values of hard work and teamwork in American football, consider some quotes from a story about the selection of New England Patriots quarterback Tom Brady as 2007 Associated Press Male Athlete of the Year. On the value of hard work: "Tom Brady arrives at Gillette Stadium before the sun comes up. As always, there is work to be done, and no time to waste." "You see him here at 6:15 in the morning, lifting weights, watching film and working out." On the value of teamwork: "I play in a team sport," Brady said. "Everybody I play with is responsible for what each of us accomplishes as individuals and for what we all accomplish as a team." (All quotes from Ulman 2007).

What Determines International Sports Success?

Why do countries excel at particular sports? Why do certain nations pile up dozens of Olympic medals while others win only a handful, or none at all? It isn't simply a matter of rich and poor, developed and underdeveloped, or even of governmental or other institutional support of promising athletes. It isn't even a question of a "national will to win," for although certain nations stress winning even more than Americans do, a cultural focus on winning doesn't necessarily lead to the desired result.

Cultural values, social forces, and the media influence international sports success. We can see this by contrasting the United States and Brazil, two countries with continental proportions and large, physically and ethnically diverse populations. Although each is its continent's major economic power, they offer revealing contrasts in Olympic success: In the 2008 Summer Olympics the United States won 110 medals, while Brazil managed only 15.

Through visual demonstration, commentary, and explanation of rules and training, the media can heighten interest in all kinds of sports—amateur and professional, team and individual, spectator and participatory. Americans' interest in sports has been honed over the years by an ever-growing media establishment, which provides a steady stream of matches, games, playoffs, championships, and analyses. Cable and satellite TV offer almost constant sports coverage, including packages for every sport and season. The Super Bowl is a national event. The Olympic games get extensive coverage and attract significant audiences. Brazilian television, by contrast, traditionally has offered much less sports coverage, with no nationally televised annual event comparable to the Super Bowl or the World Series. The World (soccer) Cup, held every four years, is the only sports event that consistently draws huge national audiences.

In international competition, outstanding Brazilian athletes, such as 1984 Olympic silver medalist swimmer Ricardo Prado—or any soccer player in the Olympics or World Cup—represent Brazilians, almost in the same way as Congress is said to represent the people of the United States. A win by a Brazilian team or the occasional nationally known individual athlete is felt to bring respect to the entire nation, but the Brazilian media are strikingly intolerant of losers. When Prado swam for his medal in the finals of the 400 Individual Medley (IM), during prime time on national TV, one newsmagazine observed that "it was as though he was the country with a swimsuit on, jumping in the pool in a collective search for success" (*Isto É* 1984). Prado's own feelings confirmed the magazine, "When I was on the stands, I thought of just one thing: what they'll think of the result in Brazil." After beating his old world record by 1.33 seconds, in a second-place finish, Prado told a fellow team member, "I think I did everything right. I feel like a winner, but will they think I'm a loser in Brazil?" Prado realized as he swam that he was performing in prime time and that "all of Brazil would be watching" (*Veja* 1984a). He complained about having the expectations of an entire country focused on him. He contrasted the situations of Brazilian and American athletes. The United States has, he said, so many athletes that no single one has to summarize the country's hopes (*Veja* 1984a).

Fortunately, Brazil did seem to value Prado's performance, which was responsible for "Brazil's best result ever in Olympic swimming" (*Veja* 1984*a*). Previously the country had won a total of three bronze medals. Labeling Prado "the man of silver," the media never tired of characterizing his main event, the 400 IM, in which he once had held the world record, as the most challenging event in swimming. However, the kind words for Ricardo Prado did not extend to the rest of the Brazilian team. The press lamented their "succession of failures" (*Veja* 1984*a*). (Brazil finally got swimming gold at the 2008 games in Beijing, with Cesar Cielo Filho winning the 50-meter freestyle race.)

Because Brazilian athletes are expected almost to be their country, and because team sports are emphasized, the Brazilian media focus too exclusively on winning. Winning, of course, is also an American cultural value, particularly for team sports, as in Brazil. American football coaches are famous for comments like "Winning isn't everything; it's the only thing" and "Show me a good loser and I'll show you a loser." However, and particularly for sports such as running, swimming, diving, gymnastics, and skating, which focus on the individual, and in which American athletes usually do well, American culture also admires "moral victories," "personal bests," "comeback athletes," and "Special Olympics," and commends those who run good races without finishing first. In amateur and individual sports, American culture tells us that hard work and personal improvement can be as important as winning.

Americans are so accustomed to being told that their culture overemphasizes winning that they may find it hard to believe that other cultures value it even more. Brazil certainly does. Brazilian sports enthusiasts are preoccupied with world records, probably because only a win (as in soccer) or a best time (as in swimming) can make Brazil indisputably, even if temporarily, the best in the world at something. Prado's former world record in the 400 IM was mentioned constantly in the press prior to his Olympic swim. Such a best-time standard also provides Brazilians with a ready basis to fault a swimmer or runner for not going fast enough, when they don't make previous times. One might predict, accurately, that sports with more subjective standards would not be very popular in Brazil. Brazilians like to assign blame to athletes who fail them, and negative comments about gymnasts or divers are more difficult because grace and execution can't be quantified as easily as time can.

Brazilians, I think, value winning so much because it is so rare. In the United States, resources are more abundant, opportunities for achievement more numerous, and poverty less pervasive. American society has room for many winners. Brazilian society is more stratified; a much smaller middle class and elite group comprise perhaps a third of the population. Brazilian sports echo lessons from the larger society: Victories are scarce and reserved for the privileged few.

Being versus Doing

The factors believed to contribute to sports success belong to a larger context of cultural values. Particularly relevant is the contrast between ascribed and achieved status. Individuals have little control over their ascribed statuses (e.g., age, gender); these depend on what one *is* rather than what one *does*. On the other hand, people have more control over their achieved statuses (e.g., student, golfer, tennis player). American culture emphasizes achieved over ascribed status: We are supposed to make of our lives what we will and can. Success comes through achievement. An American's identity emerges as a result of what he or she does.

In Brazil, on the other hand, identity rests on being rather than doing, on what one is from the start—a strand in a web of personal connections, originating in social class and the extended family. Parents, in-laws, and extended kin routinely are tapped for entries to desired settings and positions. Family position and network membership contribute substantially to individual fortune, and all social life is hierarchical. High-status Brazilians don't stand patiently in line as Americans do. Important people expect their business to be attended to immediately, and social inferiors readily yield. Rules don't apply uniformly, but differentially, according to social class. The final resort in any conversation is "Do you know who you're talking to?" The American opposite, reflecting our democratic and egalitarian ethos, is "Who do you think you are?" (DaMatta 1991).

The following description of a Brazilian judo medalist (as reported by *Veja* magazine) illustrates the importance of ascribed status and the fact that in

In this November 6, 2011, photo, New York Giants' Eli Manning, right, is congratulated by New England Patriots' Tom Brady following the Giants' 24-20 victory in Foxborough, Massachusetts.

Swimmers take off in a heat of the Men's 50m Butterfly at the World Swimming Championships in Rome, Italy, on July 26, 2009. Such sports as swimming, diving, and track give special value not only to winning but also to "personal bests" and "comebacks."

Brazilian life victories are regarded as scarce and reserved for the privileged few.

> Middle-weight Olympic bronze medalist Walter Carmona began judo at age six and became a São Paulo champion at twelve . . . Carmona lives in São Paulo with his family (father, mother, siblings) . . . He is fully supported by his father, a factory owner. Walter Carmona's life has been comfortable—he has been able to study and dedicate himself to judo without worries (Veja 1984*b*, p. 61).

Faced with an athlete from a well-off family, American reporters, by contrast, rarely conclude that privilege is the main reason for success. American media almost always focus on some aspect of doing, some special personal triumph or achievement. Often this involves the athlete's struggle with adversity (illness, injury, pain, the death of a parent, sibling, friend, or coach). The featured athlete is presented as not only successful but noble and self-sacrificing as well.

Given the Brazilian focus on ascribed status, the guiding assumption is that one can't do more than what one is. One year the Brazilian Olympic Committee sent no female swimmers to the Summer Olympics because none had made arbitrarily established cutoff times. This excluded a South American record holder, while swimmers with no better times were attending from other countries. No one seemed to imagine that Olympic excitement might spur swimmers to extraordinary efforts.

Achievement-oriented American sports coverage, in stark contrast, dotes on unexpected results, illustrating adherence to the American sports credo originally enunciated by the New York Yankee legend Yogi Berra: "It's not over till it's over." American culture, supposedly so practical and realistic, has a remarkable faith in coming from behind—in unexpected and miraculous achievements.

These values are those of an achievement-oriented society where (ideally) "anything is possible" compared with an ascribed-status society in which it's ended before it's begun. In American sports coverage, underdogs and unexpected results, virtually ignored by the Brazilian media, provide some of the "brightest" moments. Brazilian culture has little interest in the unexpected.

Athletes internalize these values. Brazilians assume that if you go into an event with a top seed time, as Ricardo Prado did, you've got a chance to win a medal. Prado's second-place finish made perfect sense back home because his former world record had been bettered before the race began.

Given the overwhelming value American culture places on work, it might seem surprising that our media devote so much attention to unforeseen results and so little to the years of training, preparation, and competition that underlie Olympic performance. It probably is assumed that hard work is so obvious and fundamental that it goes without saying. Or perhaps the assumption is that by the time athletes actually enter Olympic competition all are so similar (the American value of equality) that only mysterious and chance factors can explain variable success. The American focus on the unexpected applies to losses as well as wins. Such concepts as chance, fate, mystery, and uncertainty are viewed as legitimate reasons for defeat. Runners and skaters fall; ligaments tear; a gymnast "inexplicably" falls off the pommel horse.

Americans thus recognize chance disaster as companion to unexpected success, but Brazilians

Reflecting larger cultural values, Americans usually do well in sports that emphasize individual achievement. "Special Olympics," such as the one shown here in Atlanta, Georgia, commend people who run good races without being the best in the world.

place more responsibility on the individual, assigning personal fault. Less is attributed to factors beyond human control. When individuals who should have performed well don't do so, they are blamed for their failures. It is culturally appropriate in Brazil to use poor health as an excuse for losing. Brazilian athletes routinely mention colds or diarrhea as a reason for a poor performance, or even for withdrawing from a race at the last minute (*Veja* 1984c). Brazilians use health problems as an excuse, whereas Americans use poor health as a challenge that often can be met and bested.

Despite its characteristic focus on doing, American culture does not insist that individuals can fully control outcomes, and it's not as necessary as it is in Brazil for athletes to explain their own failures. The Brazilian media, by contrast, feel it necessary to assign fault for failure—and this usually means blaming the athlete(s). Characteristically, the American media talk much more about the injuries and illnesses of the victors and finishers than those of the losers and quitters. In discussing steroid use by sports figures, Americans have faulted athletes for chemically achieved success, certainly a violation of the American work ethic. Even if one is *doing* drugs, steroid use alters what one *is*. The success of a modified being is illegitimate compared with the achievements of an independently self-made champion.

acing the COURSE

summary

1. Even if they lack a word for "art," people everywhere do associate an aesthetic experience with objects and events having certain qualities. The arts, sometimes called "expressive culture," include the visual arts, literature (written and oral), music, and theater arts. Some issues raised about religion also apply to art. If we adopt a special attitude or demeanor when confronting a sacred object, do we display something similar with art? Much art has been done in association with religion. In tribal performances, the arts and religion often mix. But non-Western art isn't always linked to religion.

2. The special places where we find art include museums, concert halls, opera houses, and theaters. However, the boundary between what's art and what's not may be blurred. Variation in art appreciation is especially common in contemporary society, with its professional artists and critics and great cultural diversity.

3. Those who work with non-Western art have been criticized for ignoring individual artists and for focusing too much on the social context and collective artistic production. Art is work, albeit creative work.

In state societies, some people manage to support themselves as full-time artists. In nonstates artists are normally part-time. Community standards judge the mastery and completion displayed in a work of art. Typically, the arts are exhibited, evaluated, performed, and appreciated in society. Music, which often is performed in groups, is among the most social of the arts. Folk art, music, and lore refer to the expressive culture of ordinary, usually rural, people.

4. Art can stand for tradition, even when traditional art is removed from its original context. Art can express community sentiment, with political goals used to call attention to social issues. Often, art is meant to commemorate and to last. Growing acceptance of the anthropological definition of culture has guided the humanities beyond fine art, elite art, and Western art to the creative expressions of the masses and of many cultures. Myths, legends, tales, and the art of storytelling often play important roles in the transmission of culture. Many societies offer career tracks in the arts; a child born into a particular family or lineage may discover that he or she is destined for a career in leather working or weaving.

5. The arts go on changing, although certain art forms have survived for thousands of years. Countries and cultures are known for particular contributions. Today, a huge "arts and leisure" industry links Western and non-Western art forms in an international network with both aesthetic and commercial dimensions.

6. Any media-borne message can be analyzed as a text, something that can be "read"—that is, processed, interpreted, and assigned meaning by anyone exposed to it. People use media to validate beliefs, indulge fantasies, seek out messages, make social comparisons, relieve frustrations, chart social courses, and resist unequal power relations. The media can provide common ground for social groups. Length of home TV exposure is a useful measure of the impact of television on values, attitudes, and beliefs. The effect of Brazilian television on family planning seems to be a corollary of a more general TV-influenced shift from traditional toward more liberal social attitudes.

7. Much of what we know about sports comes from the media. Both sports and the media reflect and influence culture. Football symbolizes and simplifies certain key aspects of American life and values (e.g., hard work and teamwork). Cultural values, social forces, and the media influence international sports success. In amateur and individual sports, American culture tells us that hard work and personal improvement can be as important as winning. Other cultures, such as Brazil, may value winning even more than Americans do. The factors believed to contribute to sports success belong to a larger context of cultural values. Particularly relevant is the contrast between ascribed and achieved status: being versus doing. An American's identity emerges as a result of what he or she does. In Brazil, by contrast, identity rests on being: what one is from the start—a strand in a web of personal connections, originating in social class and the extended family.

key terms

aesthetics 497
art 497
arts 496
catharsis 504

ethnomusicology 501
expressive culture 496
folk 502
text 509

test yourself

MULTIPLE CHOICE

1. Which of the following statements about the relationship between art and religion is true?
   a. All non-Western art is produced for religious purposes.
   b. All the greatest accomplishments in Western art have been commissioned by formal religions.
   c. Since nonstate societies lack permanent buildings dedicated to art (museums) or religion (temples, churches), there is no link between art and religion in these societies.
   d. Western art today is completely divorced from religion.
   e. All or most societies use creative expression for both religious and secular purposes.

2. How do most Western societies view, erroneously, non-Western art?
   a. as always linked to religion
   b. as purely secular
   c. as purely profane
   d. as the product of individuals
   e. as unimportant

3. The example of the Kalabari wooden sculpture that serves as "house" for spirits makes the point that
   a. sculpture is always art.
   b. religious sculpture is not always art.
   c. the Kalabari do not have standards for carving.

d. non-Westerners have no concept of completeness.

  e. non-Western art always has some kind of connection to religion.

4. To emphasize the dynamic nature of aesthetic values and tastes, this chapter describes how French impressionism was initially

   a. heralded as one of the great innovations of 19th-century painting.

   b. based on abstract sand paintings from French colonies in West Africa.

   c. a throwback to "old school" painting styles.

   d. criticized for being too sketchy and spontaneous to be considered art.

   e. lauded for being at the forefront of high society.

5. Evidence for symbolism in art confirms the emergence of culture in human history. Symbolic thinking means that

   a. other forms of thinking, such as analytical skills, are sacrificed for the sake of aesthetic pleasure.

   b. scientific thought becomes less important in society.

   c. human groups stop making and using tools for practical ends and instead use them for ritual.

   d. people use one thing to mean something else.

   e. some cultural skills are more adaptive than others.

6. Exploring the possible biological roots of music, researchers have speculated that music might have been adaptive in human evolution because

   a. musically talented mothers had an easier time calming their babies (calmer babies attract fewer predators, grant more rest to their moms, and are less likely to be mistreated).

   b. music promotes competition.

   c. music may have made the activities of hunting and gathering more productive.

   d. singing and dancing are correlated with higher rates of pregnancy.

   e. musically talented mothers increased their chances of attracting physically fit and caring male partners.

7. Alberto Costa's findings of what attracted young people and women in Brazil to *telenovelas* is an example of how

   a. American soap operas are more popular in rural Brazil.

   b. popular culture can be used to express discontent, in this case with conservative local norms.

   c. people identify less and less with national TV programs.

   d. cultural norms have not changed during the last fifty years in Brazil.

   e. there has been a rise in conservative attitudes among the younger generation of Brazilians.

8. Brazilians and Italians being just as excited, at the same moment but with radically different emotions, by a soccer goal scored in a World Cup match is an example of

   a. art's ability to provoke catharsis.

   b. how much more Brazilians and Italians value soccer than the English and the Spanish do.

   c. how much is lost in translation.

   d. media's role as a social cement by providing a common ground for people, nationally and internationally.

   e. how much more competitive Brazilians and Italians are in sports compared to everyone else.

9. A study assessing how TV influences behavior, attitudes, and values in Brazil found that smaller family size correlated with the number of years of TV presence in the home. What probable reason did researchers put forth to explain this correlation?

   a. There is no social mechanism that can explain this correlation.

   b. *Telenovelas* may convey the idea that viewers can achieve a different lifestyle (i.e., having fewer children) by emulating the apparent family planning of TV characters.

   c. Greater exposure to TV was correlated to less time engaged in sexual activity.

   d. Women with longer exposures to the moral code of TV characters rejected their extreme liberal ways.

   e. More TV time correlated with higher divorce rates.

10. Cultural values, social forces, and the media influence international sports success. When comparing the United States and Brazil, which of the following is true?

    a. Brazil has much more television sports coverage than the United States.

    b. Americans' interest in sports has been honed much more over the years by an ever-growing media establishment.

    c. The popularity of football among Americans proves that Americans are more violent than Brazilians.

    d. Researchers have found that the increasing popularity of soccer correlates with less interest in teamwork.

    e. Americans are more focused on winning than Brazilians are.

FILL IN THE BLANK

1. The term _____ *culture* is synonymous with the arts.
2. _____ is the study of the musics of the world and of music as an aspect of culture.
3. _____ refers to an intense emotional release.
4. Around _____ years ago, some of the world's first artists occupied Blombos Cave in what is now South Africa. In Europe, evidence of art goes back to about _____ years ago.
5. _____ can refer to anything that can be "read"—that is, processed, interpreted, and assigned meaning, by anyone exposed to it.

CRITICAL THINKING

1. Recall the last time you were in an art museum. What did you like, and why? How much of your aesthetic tastes can you attribute to your education, to your culture? How much do you think responds to your own individual tastes? How can you make the distinction?
2. Think of a musical composition or performance you consider to be art, but whose status as such is debatable. How would you convince someone else that it is art? What kinds of arguments against your position would you expect to hear?
3. Can you think of a political dispute involving art or the arts? What were the different positions being debated?
4. Media consumers actively select, evaluate, and interpret media in ways that make sense to them. People use media for all sorts of reasons. What are some examples? Which are most relevant to the way you consume, and maybe even creatively alter and produce, media?
5. This chapter describes how sports and the media *reflect* culture. Can you come up with examples of how sports and media *influence* culture?

Multiple Choice: 1. (E); 2. (A); 3. (B); 4. (D); 5. (D); 6. (A); 7. (B); 8. (B); 9. (D); 10. (B). **Fill in the Blank:** 1. *expressive*; 2. Ethnomusicology; 3. Catharsis; 4. 70,000, 30,000; 5. Text

Anderson, R. L.
2004 *Calliope's Sisters: A Comparative Study of Philosophies of Art,* 2nd ed. Upper Saddle River, NJ: Prentice Hall. A comparative study of aesthetics in ten cultures.
Askew, K. M., and R. R. Wilk, eds.
2002 *The Anthropology of Media: A Reader.* Malden, MA: Oxford, Blackwell. Useful anthology, with numerous case studies involving media, society, and culture.
Fiske, J.
2011 *Reading the Popular,* 2nd ed. New York: Routledge. Recent update of a classic text on texts.

Sands, R. R., and L. R. Sands, eds.
2010 *The Anthropology of Sport and Human Movement: A Biocultural Perspective.* Lanham, MD: Lexington Books. Sport, movement, and performance in evolutionary and cross-cultural perspective.
Morphy, H., and M. Perkins, eds.
2006 *The Anthropology of Art: A Reader.* Malden, MA: Oxford/Blackwell. Survey of the major issues, with a focus on visual art.
Svasek, M.
2007 *Anthropology, Art, and Cultural Production.* Ann Arbor, MI: Pluto. Up-to-date introduction.

suggested additional readings

Go to our Online Learning Center website at **www.mhhe.com/kottak** for Internet exercises directly related to the content of this chapter.

internet exercises

CHAPTER 23

The World System and Colonialism

When and why did the world system develop, and what is it like today?

When and how did European colonialism develop and how is its legacy expressed in postcolonial studies?

How do colonialism, Communism, neoliberalism, development, and industrialization exemplify intervention philosophies?

◀ In Kebili, Tunisia, two Bedouin men use a laptop in the desert. Might they be uploading a photo of their camel to Facebook?

understanding OURSELVES

In our 21st-century world system, people are linked as never before by modern means of transportation and communication. Descendants of villages that hosted ethnographers a generation ago now live transnational lives. For me, some of the most vivid illustrations of this new transnationalism come from Madagascar. They begin in Ambalavao, a town in southern Betsileo country, where I rented a small house in 1966–1967.

By 1966, Madagascar had gained independence from France, but its towns still had foreigners to remind them of colonialism. Besides my wife and me, Ambalavao had at least a dozen world-system agents, including an Indian cloth merchant, Chinese grocers, and a few French people. Two young men in the French equivalent of the Peace Corps were there teaching school. One of them, Noel, lived across the street from a prominent local family. Since Noel often spoke disparagingly of the Malagasy, I was surprised to see him courting a young woman from this family. She was Lenore, the sister of Leon, a schoolteacher who became my good friend.

My next trip to Madagascar was a brief visit in February 1981. I had to spend a few days in Antananarivo, the capital. There I was confined each evening to the newly built Hilton hotel by a curfew imposed after a civil insurrection. I shared the hotel with a group of Russian military pilots, there to teach the Malagasy to defend their island, strategically placed in the Indian Ocean, against imagined enemies. Later, I went down to Betsileo country to visit Leon, my schoolteacher friend from Ambalavao, who had become a prominent politician. Unfortunately for me, he was in Moscow, participating in a three-month exchange program.

During my next visit to Madagascar, in summer 1990, I met Emily, the 22-year-old daughter of Noel and Lenore, whose courtship I had witnessed in 1967. One of her aunts brought Emily to meet me at my hotel in Antananarivo. Emily was about to visit several cities in the United States, where she planned to study marketing. I met her again just a few months later in Gainesville, Florida. She asked me about her father, whom she had never met. She had sent several letters to France, but Noel had never responded.

Descendants of Ambalavao now live all over the world. Emily, a child of colonialism, has two aunts in France (Malagasy women married to French men) and another in Germany (working as a diplomat). Members of her family, which is not especially wealthy, have traveled to Russia, Canada, the United States, France, Germany, and West Africa. How many of your classmates, including perhaps you, yourself, have recent transnational roots? A descendant of a rural Kenyan village has even been elected president of the United States. How about that.

Although fieldwork in small communities is anthropology's hallmark, isolated groups are impossible to find today. Truly isolated societies probably never have existed. For thousands of years, human groups have been in contact with one another. Local societies always have participated in a larger system, which today has global dimensions—we call it the *modern world system*, by which we mean a world in which nations are economically and politically interdependent.

THE WORLD SYSTEM

The world system and the relations among the countries within it are shaped by the capitalist world economy (see White 2009). A huge increase in international trade during and after the 15th century led to the **capitalist world economy** (Wallerstein 1982, 2004b), a single world system committed to production for sale or exchange, with the object of maximizing profits rather than supplying domestic needs. **Capital** refers to wealth or resources invested in business, with the intent of using the means of production to make a profit.

World-system theory can be traced to the French social historian Fernand Braudel. In his three-volume work *Civilization and Capitalism, 15th–18th Century* (1981, 1982, 1992), Braudel argued that society consists of interrelated parts assembled into a system. Societies are subsystems of larger systems, with the world system the largest. The key claim of **world-system theory** is that an identifiable social system, based on wealth and power differentials, extends beyond individual countries. That system is formed by a set of economic and political relations that has characterized much of the globe since the 16th century, when the Old World established regular contact with the New World (see Bodley 2003).

According to Wallerstein (1982, 2004b), countries within the world system occupy three different positions of economic and political power: core, periphery, and semiperiphery. The geographic center, or **core,** the dominant position in the world system, includes the strongest and most powerful nations. In core nations, "the complexity of economic activities and the level of capital accumulation is the greatest" (Thompson 1983, p. 12). With its sophisticated technologies and mechanized production, the core churns out products that flow mainly to other core countries. Some also go to the periphery and semiperiphery. According to Arrighi (2010), the core monopolizes the most profitable activities, especially the control of world finance.

Semiperiphery and periphery countries have less power, wealth, and influence than the core does. The **semiperiphery** is intermediate between the core and the periphery. Contemporary nations of the semiperiphery are industrialized. Like core nations, they export both industrial goods and commodities, but they lack the power and economic dominance of core nations. Thus Brazil, a semiperiphery nation, exports automobiles to Nigeria (a periphery nation) and auto engines, orange juice extract, coffee, and shrimp to the United States (a core nation). The **periphery** includes the world's least privileged and powerful countries. Economic activities there are less mechanized than are those in the semiperiphery, although some degree of industrialization has reached even periphery nations. The periphery produces raw materials, agricultural commodities, and, increasingly, human labor for export to the core and the semiperiphery (Shannon 1996).

In the United States and Western Europe today, immigration—legal and illegal—from the periphery and semiperiphery supplies cheap labor for agriculture. U.S. states as distant as California, Michigan, and South Carolina make significant use of farm labor from Mexico. The availability of relatively cheap workers from noncore nations such as Mexico (in the United States) and Turkey (in Germany) benefits farmers and business owners in core countries, while also supplying remittances to families in the semiperiphery and periphery. As a result of 21st-century telecommunications technology, cheap labor doesn't even need to migrate to the United States. Thousands of families in India are being supported as American companies "outsource" jobs—from telephone assistance to software engineering—to nations outside the core (see this chapter's "Focus on Globalization").

The Emergence of the World System

By the 15th century Europeans were profiting from a transoceanic trade-oriented economy, and people worldwide entered Europe's sphere of influence. What was new was the trans-Atlantic component of a long history of Old World sailing and commerce. As early as 600 B.C.E., the Phoenicians/Carthaginians sailed around Britain on regular trade routes and circumnavigated Africa. Likewise, Indonesia and Africa have been linked in Indian Ocean trade for at least 2,000 years. In the 15th century Europe established regular contact with Asia, Africa, and eventually the New World (the Caribbean and the Americas). Christopher Columbus's first voyage from Spain to the Bahamas and the Caribbean in 1492 was soon followed by additional voyages. These journeys opened the way for a major exchange of people, resources, products, ideas, and diseases, as the Old and New Worlds were forever linked (Crosby 2003; Diamond 1997; Fagan 1998; Mann 2011). Led by Spain and Portugal, Europeans extracted silver and gold, conquered the natives (taking some as slaves), and colonized their lands.

The frequency and nature of conflict, violence, and warfare vary among the world's cultures. This chapter's "Appreciating Diversity" examines a debate about the origin and characteristics of warfare among Native Americans. Did European contact play a role in fostering increased violence? The *Columbian exchange* is the term for the spread of people, resources, products, ideas, and diseases between eastern and western hemispheres after contact. As you read "Appreciating Diversity," consider the impact of trade, disease, and slave raiding on Native Americans, including conflict and warfare.

Previously in Europe as throughout the world, rural people had produced mainly for their own needs, growing their own food and making clothing, furniture, and tools from local products. Production beyond immediate needs was undertaken to pay taxes and to purchase trade items such as salt and iron. As

capitalist world economy
Profit-oriented global economy based on production for sale.

capital
Wealth invested with the intent of producing profit.

world-system theory
Idea that a discernible social system, based on wealth and power differentials, transcends individual countries.

core
Dominant position in the world system; nations with advanced systems of production.

semiperiphery
Position in the world system intermediate between core and periphery.

periphery
Weakest structural and economic position in the world system.

appreciating DIVERSITY

Bones Reveal Some Truth in "Noble Savage" Myth

Conflict and violence are variable aspects of human diversity. Here we examine an anthropological debate about the origin and nature of warfare and the role of European contact in fostering conflicts among indigenous peoples in the Americas. Violence among Native Americans did increase after contact. As the article begins, it suggests, mistakenly, that Native Americans lived in prehistory and lacked "civilization." In fact, Native Americans developed states and "civilizations" (e.g., Aztec, Maya, Inca) comparable to those of the Old World (e.g., ancient Mesopotamia and Egypt). Native Americans, most notably the Maya, also developed writing, which they used to record their history—rendering the label prehistory inaccurate. As you read, to understand why violence increased after contact, pay attention to the role of trade, disease, and slave raiding.

A romantic-sounding notion dating back more than 200 years has it that people in prehistory, such as Native Americans, lived in peace and harmony.

Then "civilization" showed up, sowing violence and discord. Some see this claim as naive. It even has a derisive nickname, the "noble savage myth." But new research seems to suggest the "myth" contains at least some truth. Researchers examined thousands of Native American skeletons and found that those from after Christopher Columbus landed in the New World showed a rate of traumatic injuries more than 50 percent higher than those from before the Europeans arrived.

"Traumatic injuries do increase really significantly," said Philip L. Walker, an anthropology professor at the University of California at Santa Barbara, who conducted the study with Richard H. Steckel of Ohio State University.

The findings suggest "Native Americans were involved in more violence after the Europeans arrived than before," Walker said. But he emphasized there was also widespread violence before the Europeans came. Nevertheless, he said, "probably we're just seeing the tip of the iceberg" as far as the difference between violence levels before and after. That's because as many as half of bullet wounds miss the skeleton. Thus, the study couldn't detect much firearm violence, though some tribes wiped each other out using European-supplied guns.

The findings shed light on a controversy that has stirred not only living room discussions, but also an intense, sometimes ugly debate among anthropologists.

It involves two opposing views of human nature: Are we hard-wired for violence, or pushed into it?

Anthropologists who believe the latter seized on the findings as evidence for their view. "What it all says to me is that humans aren't demonic. Human males don't have an ingrained

The encounter between Hernán Cortés (1485–1547) and Montezuma II (1466–1520) is the subject of this 1820 painting by Gallo Gallina of Milan, Italy. Cortés went on to conquer Montezuma's Aztec empire.

late as 1650 the English diet, like diets in most of the world today, was based on locally grown starches (Mintz 1985). In the 200 years that followed, however, the English became extraordinary consumers of imported goods. One of the earliest and most popular of those goods was sugar (Mintz 1985).

Sugar cane originally was domesticated in Papua New Guinea, and sugar was first processed in India. Reaching Europe via the Middle East and the eastern Mediterranean, it was carried to the New World by Columbus (Mintz 1985). The climate of Brazil and the Caribbean proved ideal for growing sugar cane, and Europeans built plantations there to supply the growing demand for sugar. This led to the development in the 17th century of a plantation economy based on a single cash crop—a system known as *monocrop* production.

The demand for sugar in a growing international market spurred the development of the trans-Atlantic slave trade and New World plantation economies based on slave labor. By the 18th century, an increased English demand for raw cotton led to rapid settlement of what is now the southeastern United States and the emergence there of

propensity for war. . . . They can learn to be very peaceful, or terribly violent," said R. Brian Ferguson, a professor of anthropology at Rutgers University in Newark. Ferguson contends that before about 10,000 years ago, war was virtually nonexistent. But experts on the opposing side also said the findings fit their views.

"A 50 percent increase is the equivalent of moving from a suburb to the city, in terms of violence," said Charles Stanish, a professor of anthropology at the University of California at Los Angeles. "This shows the Native Americans were like us. Under stress, they fought more." Both sides called the study, which was presented Friday at the annual meeting of the American Association of Physical Anthropologists in Buffalo, a valuable contribution. . . .

Walker and colleagues examined the skeletons of 3,375 pre-Columbian and 1,165 post-Columbian Native Americans, from archaeological sites throughout North and Central America.

The North Americans came mostly from the coasts and the Great Lakes region, Walker said.

Pre-Columbian skeletons showed an 11 percent incidence of traumatic injuries, he said, compared with almost 17 percent for the post-Columbians.

Walker said his findings surprised him. "I wasn't really expecting it," he said. Yet it undeniably suggests violence, he added. Most of the increase consisted of head injuries in young males, "which conforms pretty closely to the pattern you see today in homicides."

The researchers defined "traumatic injury" as anything leaving a mark on the skeleton, such as a skull fracture, a healed broken arm, or an embedded arrow point or bullet.

Walker said that although part of the increased injury rate doubtless stems from violence by whites themselves, it probably reflects mostly native-on-native violence. "In a lot of cases, such as in California, there weren't that many Europeans around—just a few priests, and thousands of Indians," he said.

Walker said the higher injury rate could have many explanations. Increased violence is normally associated with more densely populated, settled life, which Native Americans experienced in modernity, he said. Disease could also touch off war, he said.

"Here in California, there was a lot of inter-village warfare associated with the introduction of European diseases. People would attribute the disease to evil shamanic activity in another village," he said. Ferguson cited other factors. The Europeans often drew natives into their imperial wars, he said.

"Sometimes, the Europeans would enable someone to pursue a preexisting fight more aggressively, by backing one side," he added. Other times, he said, Europeans got natives to conduct slave raids on one another. Natives also fought over control of areas around trading outposts, to become middlemen, he said. "Sometimes that was a life-or-death matter, since it meant the difference between who would get guns or not." Stanish agreed. "Obviously, having an expanding imperial power coming at you is going to exacerbate tensions," he said. . . . They're going to push you somewhere—into other groups."

"You're also going to get competition over access to the Europeans, who are a form of wealth," he added. Native Americans fought over areas rich in fur, which the whites would buy.

Yet Native American warfare was widespread long before that, Stanish said. . . .

Keith F. Otterbein, an anthropology professor at the State University of New York at Buffalo, said the skeleton findings contribute to a balanced, middle-of-the-road view.

"The folks who are saying there was no early warfare—they're wrong, too. There is, in fact, a myth of the peaceful savage," he said. Otterbein said the controversy won't end here; both sides are too ideologically entrenched.

"Underlying the 'noble savage' myth," Stanish said, "is a political agenda by both the far right and far left. The right tries to turn the 'savages' into our little brown brothers, who need to be pulled up. . . . On the left, they have another agenda, that the Western world is bad."

SOURCE: Jack Lucentini, "Bones Reveal Some Truth in 'Noble Savage Myth'," *Washington Post*, April 15, 2002. Reprinted by permission of Jack Lucentini.

another slave-based monocrop production system. Like sugar, cotton was a key trade item that fueled the growth of the world system.

INDUSTRIALIZATION

By the 18th century the stage had been set for the **Industrial Revolution**—the historical transformation (in Europe, after 1750) of "traditional" into "modern" societies through industrialization of the economy. The seeds of industrial society were planted well before the 18th century (Gimpel 1988). For example, a knitting machine invented in England in 1589 was so far ahead of its time that it played a profitable role in factories two and three centuries later. The appearance of cloth mills late in the Middle Ages foreshadowed the search for new sources of wind and water power that characterized the Industrial Revolution.

Industrialization required capital for investment. The established system of transoceanic trade and commerce supplied that capital from the enormous profits it generated. Wealthy people sought investment

Industrial Revolution
(In Europe, after 1750), socioeconomic transformation through industrialization.

From producer to consumer, in the modern world system. The top photo, taken in the Caribbean nation of Dominica, shows the hard labor required to extract sugar using a manual press. In the bottom photo, an English middle-class family enjoys afternoon tea, sweetened with imported sugar. Which of the ingredients in your breakfast today were imported?

opportunities and eventually found them in machines and engines to drive machines. Industrialization increased production in both farming and manufacturing. Capital and scientific innovation fueled invention.

European industrialization developed from (and eventually replaced) the *domestic system* of manufacture (or home-handicraft system). In this system, an organizer-entrepreneur supplied the raw materials to workers in their homes and collected the finished products from them. The entrepreneur, whose sphere of operations might span several villages, owned the materials, paid for the work, and arranged the marketing.

Causes of the Industrial Revolution

The Industrial Revolution began with cotton products, iron, and pottery. These were widely used goods whose manufacture could be broken down into simple routine motions that machines could perform. When manufacturing moved from homes to factories, where machinery replaced handwork, agrarian societies evolved into industrial ones. As factories produced cheap staple goods, the Industrial Revolution led to a dramatic increase in production. Industrialization fueled urban growth and created a new kind of city, with factories crowded together in places where coal and labor were cheap.

The Industrial Revolution began in England rather than in France (Figure 23.1). Why? Unlike the English, the French didn't have to transform their domestic manufacturing system by industrializing. Faced with an increased need for products, with a late 18th-century population at least twice that of Great Britain, France could simply enlarge its domestic system of production by drawing in new homes. Thus, the French were able to increase production *without innovating*—they could grow the existing system rather than having to adopt a new one. To meet mounting demand for staples—at home and in its colonies—England had to industrialize.

As its industrialization proceeded, Britain's population began to increase dramatically. It doubled during the 18th century (especially after 1750) and did so again between 1800 and 1850. This demographic explosion fueled consumption, but British entrepreneurs couldn't meet the increased demand with the traditional production methods. This spurred experimentation, innovation, and rapid technological change.

English industrialization drew on national advantages in natural resources. Britain was rich in coal and iron ore, and had navigable waterways and easily negotiated coasts. It was a seafaring island-nation located at the crossroads of international trade. These features gave Britain a favored position for importing raw materials and exporting manufactured goods. Another factor in England's industrial growth was the fact that much of its 18th-century colonial empire was occupied by English settler families who looked to the mother country as they tried to replicate European civilization in the New World. These colonies bought large quantities of English staples.

It also has been argued that particular cultural values and religion contributed to industrialization. Many members of the emerging English middle class were Protestant nonconformists. Their beliefs and values encouraged industry, thrift, the dissemination of new knowledge, inventiveness, and willingness to accept change (Weber 1904/1958).

SOCIOECONOMIC EFFECTS OF INDUSTRIALIZATION

The socioeconomic effects of industrialization were mixed. English national income tripled between 1700 and 1815 and increased 30 times more by 1939. Standards of comfort rose, but prosperity was uneven.

At first, factory workers got wages higher than those available in the domestic system. Later, owners started recruiting labor in places where living standards were low and labor (including that of women and children) was cheap.

Social ills worsened with the growth of factory towns and industrial cities, amid conditions like those Charles Dickens described in *Hard Times*. Filth and smoke polluted the 19th-century cities. Housing was crowded and unsanitary, with insufficient water and sewage disposal facilities. People experienced rampant disease and rising death rates. This was the world of Ebenezer Scrooge, Bob Cratchit, Tiny Tim—and Karl Marx.

Industrial Stratification

The social theorists Karl Marx and Max Weber focused on the stratification systems associated with industrialization. From his observations in England and his analysis of 19th-century industrial capitalism, Marx (Marx and Engels 1848/1976) saw socioeconomic stratification as a sharp and simple division between two opposed classes: the bourgeoisie (capitalists) and the proletariat (propertyless workers). The bourgeoisie traced its origins to overseas ventures and the world capitalist economy, which had transformed the social structure of northwestern Europe, creating a wealthy commercial class.

Industrialization shifted production from farms and cottages to mills and factories, where mechanical power was available and where workers could be assembled to operate heavy machinery. The

The Art of Stocking-Frame-Work-Knitting.

Engraved for the Universal Magazine 1750, for J. Hinton at the Kings Arms in S. Pauls Church Yard London.

In the home-handicraft, or domestic, system of production, an organizer supplied raw materials to workers in their homes and collected their products. Family life and work were intertwined, as in this English scene. Is there a modern equivalent to the domestic system of production?

bourgeoisie were the owners of the factories, mines, large farms, and other means of production. The **working class,** or **proletariat,** consisted of people who had to sell their labor to survive. With the decline of subsistence production and with the

bourgeoisie
Owners of the means of production.

working class, or proletariat
People who must sell their labor to survive.

Large paintings of Karl Marx (1818–1883) on display in Tiananmen Square, Beijing, China.

FIGURE 23.1 Location of England (United Kingdom) and France.

rise of urban migration and the possibility of unemployment, the bourgeoisie came to stand between workers and the means of production.

Industrialization hastened the process of *proletarianization*—the separation of workers from the means of production. The bourgeoisie also came to dominate the means of communication, the schools, and other key institutions. *Class consciousness* (recognition of collective interests and personal identification with one's economic group) was a vital part of Marx's view of class. He saw bourgeoisie and proletariat as socioeconomic divisions with radically opposed interests. Marx viewed classes as powerful collective forces that could mobilize human energies to influence the course of history. On the basis of their common experience, workers would develop class consciousness, which could lead to revolutionary

change. Although no proletarian revolution was to occur in England, workers did develop organizations to protect their interests and increase their share of industrial profits. During the 19th century, trade unions and socialist parties emerged to express a rising anticapitalist spirit. The concerns of the English labor movement were to remove young children from factories and limit the hours during which women and children could work. The profile of stratification in industrial core nations gradually took shape. Capitalists controlled production, but labor was organizing for better wages and working conditions. By 1900 many governments had factory legislation and social-welfare programs. Mass living standards in core nations rose as population grew.

In today's capitalist world system the class division between owners and workers is now worldwide.

However, publicly traded companies complicate the division between capitalists and workers in industrial nations. Through pension plans and personal investments, many American workers now have some proprietary interest in the means of production. They are part-owners rather than propertyless workers. The key difference is that the wealthy have *control* over these means. The key capitalist now is not the factory owner, who may have been replaced by thousands of stockholders, but the CEO or the chair of the board of directors, neither of whom may actually own the corporation.

Modern Stratification Systems

Modern stratification systems aren't simple and dichotomous. They include (particularly in core and semiperiphery nations) a middle class of skilled and professional workers. Gerhard Lenski (1966) argued that social equality tends to increase in advanced industrial societies. The masses improve their access to economic benefits and political power. In Lenski's scheme, the shift of political power to the masses reflects the growth of the middle class, which reduces the polarization between owning and working classes. The proliferation of middle-class occupations creates opportunities for social mobility. The stratification system grows more complex (Giddens 1981).

The complexity of their stratification system has gone largely unnoticed by many Americans, who think of themselves as middle class. The perception of the American middle class as a vast undifferentiated group helps mask the substantial differences in income and wealth that set off the richest from the poorest Americans. That gap has been widening. According to U.S. Census data from 1970 to 2009, the top (richest) quintile (fifth) of American households increased its share of national income by 16 percent, while all other quintiles fell. The percentage share of the lowest fifth fell most dramatically—17 percent. In 2009 the top fifth got 50.3 percent of all national income, while the lowest fifth got only 3.4 percent. Comparable figures in 1970 were 43.3 percent and 4.1 percent. The 2009 ratio was 15:1, versus 14:1 in 2000 and 11:1 in 1970. In other words, by 2009 the richest fifth of American households, with a mean annual income of $170,844, had become 15 times wealthier than the poorest fifth, whose mean annual income was only $11,552 (DeNavas-Walt, Proctor, and Smith 2010).

When we consider wealth (investments, property, possessions, etc.) rather than income, the contrast is even more striking: the top 1 percent of American households hold over one-third (35.6 percent) of the nation's wealth (Allegretto 2011). Their net worth was 225 times greater than the median or typical household's net worth in 2009 (Figure 23.2). This is the highest ratio on record. The top 1 percent owns more than the bottom 90 percent combined (Witt 2011, p. 229).

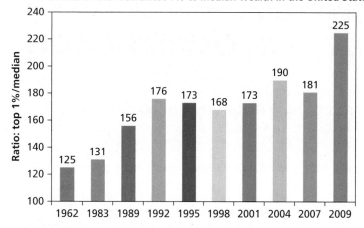

The ratio of the wealthiest 1% to median wealth in the United States

FIGURE 23.2 The Ratio of the Wealthiest 1 Percent to Median Wealth in the United States.

SOURCE: Allegretto, S. A. 2011 The State of Working America's Wealth, Briefing Paper no. 292, Economic Policy Institute, March 23. http://www.epi.org/page/-/BriefingPaper292.pdf.

The Great Recession of December 2007–June 2009 increased inequality. While all Americans were affected, the poor suffered more than the rich did. The percentage of households with zero or negative net worth shot up from 18.6 percent in 2007 to about 25 percent two years later. Between 2007 and 2009, household wealth shrank by 16 percent for the richest fifth of Americans and by 25 percent for the bottom 80 percent. Because of this disparity, the share of household wealth owned by the richest fifth rose by 2.2 percentage points to 87.2 percent. The bottom

This October 15, 2011, demonstration in Philadelphia was one of many that were held in the United States and Canada in support of the Occupy Wall Street demonstration in New York City.

Where in the World Are the Jobs?

Max Weber (1864–1920). Did Weber improve on Marx's view of stratification?

Throughout the world, young people are abandoning traditional subsistence pursuits and seeking cash. A popular song once asked, "How're you gonna keep 'em down on the farm after they've seen Paree." Nowadays most people have seen Paree (Paris, that is), along with other world capitals, maybe not in person, but in print or on-screen images. Young people today are better educated and wiser in the ways of the world than ever before. Increasingly they are exposed to the material and cultural promises of a better life away from the farm. They seek paying jobs, but work is scarce, spurring migration within and across national boundaries. If they can't get cash legally, they seek it illegally.

For the past few years work also has been scarce in the industrial world, including the United States and Western Europe. As the United States struggled to recover from the "Great Recession" of 2007–2009, its stock market (Dow Jones Industrial Average) doubled, from a low of 6457 in March 2009 to around 13,000 three years later. During much of that time, however, increasingly profitable corporations held onto their cash, rather than using it to hire new workers. The goal of capitalism, after all, is profitability. In our global economy, the maximization of profit doesn't necessarily result from hiring workers who are fellow citizens. To reduce labor costs, jobs continue to be outsourced, and machines continue to replace people. Increasingly, corporations offer their customers incentives to bypass humans. Through the Internet we can buy plane tickets (bye bye travel agents), print boarding passes, reserve hotel rooms, move money, and pay bills online. Internet giant Amazon.com threatens to send not only "mom and pop" stores but even once powerful chains like Barnes and Noble, Sears, and Radio Shack into oblivion—and their workers to the unemployment line. Nowadays, when one does manage to speak to an actual human, that person is as likely to be in Mumbai or Manila as Minneapolis or Miami.

What can workers do? Historically, collective bargaining has been the answer, and unions still bring benefits to their workers. Median weekly earnings for American union members—$917 in 2010—remain higher than those of nonunion workers—$717 (Greenhouse 2011). But effective unions have been national or local—not global like today's job market. How likely is it that a worker in Mumbai would strike in sympathy with one in Detroit?

Companies claim, with some justification, that labor unions limit their flexibility, adaptability, and profitability. In the United States, corporations and the politicians they work to elect have become more open about their opposition to unions and more aggressive in limiting workers' rights to organize and recruit. Union membership in the United States has reached its lowest point in more than seventy years. The unionized percentage of the American workforce fell to 11.9 percent in 2010, compared with 20.1 percent in 1983, and a high of 35 percent during the mid-1950s. The number of unionized private sector workers stood at 7.1 million in 2010, versus a larger share—7.6 million workers—in the public sector (Greenhouse 2011). One cause of declining union membership has been a reduction in public sector (government) jobs (which are more likely to be unionized than private sector jobs) because of austerity measures imposed by politicians. From Greece to the United Kingdom, such austerity measures have been spreading internationally, reducing employment and workers' benefits.

80 percent gave up those 2.2 percentage points, keeping just 12.8 percent of all wealth. By 2009, the top 1 percent of wealth-owning households owned 35.6 percent of all net worth. That top 1 percent held an even larger share—42.4 percent—of financial assets (e.g., stocks and bonds) that provide direct financial returns. In 2009 the bottom 90 percent of income-earning households controlled just 25 percent of all net worth and 17.3 percent of direct financial returns (Allegretto 2011). Recognition of such disparities, and that the rich were getting richer and the poor, poorer, led to the Occupy movement of 2011. That movement began on Wall Street and quickly spread to many other cities in the United States and Canada.

Max Weber faulted Karl Marx for an overly simple and exclusively economic view of stratification. As we saw in the chapter "Political Systems," Weber (1922/1968) defined three dimensions of social stratification: wealth, power, and prestige. Although, as Weber showed, wealth, power, and prestige are separate components of social ranking, they tend to be correlated. Weber also believed that social identities based on ethnicity, religion, race, nationality, and other attributes could take priority over class (social identity based on economic status). In addition to class contrasts, the modern world system *is* cross-cut by collective identities based on ethnicity, religion, and nationality (Shannon 1996). Class conflicts tend to occur within nations, and nationalism has prevented global class solidarity, particularly of proletarians (see "Focus on Globalization").

Although the capitalist class dominates politically in most countries, growing wealth has made it easier for core nations to grant higher wages (Hopkins and Wallerstein 1982). However, the improvement in core workers' living standards wouldn't have occurred without the world system. The wealth that flows from periphery and semiperiphery to core has helped core capitalists maintain their profits while satisfying the demands of core workers. In the periphery and semiperiphery, wages and living standards are lower. The current *world stratification system* features a substantial contrast between both capitalists and workers in the core nations, on the one hand, and workers on the periphery, on the other.

COLONIALISM

World-system theory stresses the existence of a global culture. It emphasizes historical contacts, linkages, and power differentials between local people and international forces. The major forces influencing cultural interaction during the past 500 years have been commercial expansion, industrial capitalism, and the dominance of colonial and core nations (Wallerstein 1982, 2004b; Wolf 1982). As state formation had done previously, industrialization accelerated local participation in larger networks. According to Bodley (2012), perpetual expansion is a distinguishing feature of industrial economic systems. Bands and tribes were small, self-sufficient, subsistence-based systems. Industrial economies, by contrast, are large, highly specialized systems in which market exchanges occur with profit as the primary motive (Bodley 2012).

During the 19th century European business interests initiated a concerted search for markets. This process led to European imperialism in Africa, Asia, and Oceania. **Imperialism** refers to a policy of extending the rule of a country or empire over foreign nations and of taking and holding foreign colonies. Imperialism goes back to early states, including Egypt in the Old World and the Incas in the New. A Greek empire was forged by Alexander the Great, and Julius Caesar and his successors spread the Roman empire. More recent examples include the British, French, and Soviet empires (Scheinman 1980).

During the second half of the 19th century, European imperial expansion was aided by improved transportation, which facilitated the colonization of vast areas of sparsely settled lands in the interior of North and South America and Australia. The new colonies purchased masses of goods from the industrial centers and shipped back wheat, cotton, wool, mutton, beef, and leather. The first phase of European colonialism had been the exploration and exploitation of the Americas and the Caribbean after Columbus. A new second phase began as European nations competed for colonies between 1875 and 1914, setting the stage for World War I.

Colonialism is the political, social, economic, and cultural domination of a territory and its people by a foreign power for an extended time (see Bremen and Shimizu 1999; Stoler, McGranahan, and Perdue 2007). If imperialism is almost as old as the state, colonialism can be traced back to the Phoenicians, who established colonies along the eastern Mediterranean 3,000 years ago. The ancient Greeks and Romans were avid colonizers as well as empire builders.

The first phase of modern colonialism began with the European "Age of Discovery"—of the Americas and of a sea route to the Far East. After 1492, the Spanish, the original conquerors of the Aztecs and the Incas, explored and colonized widely in the New World—the Caribbean, Mexico, the southern portions of what was to become the United States, and Central and South America. In the Pacific, Spain extended its rule to the Philippines and Guam. The Portuguese empire included Brazil, South America's largest colonial territory; Angola and Mozambique in Africa; and Goa in South Asia. Rebellions and wars aimed at independence ended the first phase of European colonialism by the early 19th century. Brazil declared independence from Portugal in 1822. By 1825 most of Spain's colonies were politically independent. Spain held onto Cuba and the Philippines until 1898, but otherwise withdrew from the colonial field. During the first phase of colonialism, Spain and Portugal, along with Britain and France, were major colonizing nations. The latter two (Britain and France) dominated the second phase.

British Colonialism

At its peak about 1914, the British empire covered a fifth of the world's land surface and ruled a fourth of its population (see Figure 23.3). Like several other European nations, Britain had two stages of colonialism. The first began with the Elizabethan voyages of the 16th century. During the 17th century, Britain acquired most of the eastern coast of North America, Canada's St. Lawrence basin, islands in the Caribbean, slave stations in Africa, and interests in India.

The British shared the exploration of the New World with the Spanish, Portuguese, French, and Dutch. The British by and large left Mexico, along with Central and South America, to the Spanish and the Portuguese. The end of the Seven Years' War in 1763 forced a French retreat from most of Canada and India, where France previously had competed with Britain (Cody 1998; Farr 1980).

The American Revolution ended the first stage of British colonialism. A second colonial empire, on which the "sun never set," rose from the ashes of the first. Beginning in 1788, but intensifying after 1815, the British settled Australia. Britain had acquired Dutch South Africa by 1815. The establishment of Singapore in 1819 provided a base for a British trade network that extended to much of South Asia and along the coast of China. By this time, the empires of Britain's traditional rivals, particularly Spain, had been severely diminished in scope. Britain's position as imperial power and the world's leading industrial nation was unchallenged (Cody 1998; Farr 1980).

imperialism
Policy aimed at seizing and ruling foreign territory and peoples.

colonialism
Long-term foreign control of a territory and its people.

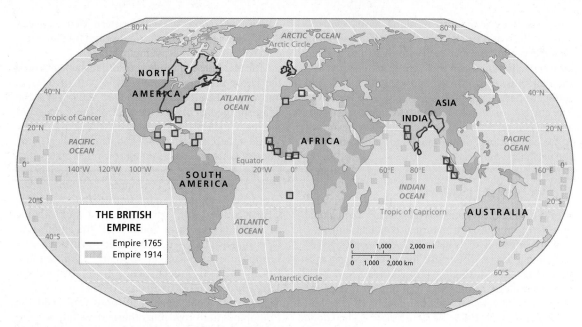

FIGURE 23.3 Map of British Empire in 1765 and 1914.

SOURCE: From the *Academic American Encyclopedia,* Vol. 3, p. 496. 1998 Edition. Copyright © 1998 by Grolier Incorporated. Reprinted with permission.

During the Victorian Era (1837–1901), as Britain's acquisition of territory and of further trading concessions continued, Prime Minister Benjamin Disraeli implemented a foreign policy justified by a view of imperialism as shouldering "the white man's burden"— a phrase coined by the poet Rudyard Kipling. People in the empire were seen as incapable of governing themselves, so that British guidance was needed to civilize and Christianize them. This paternalistic and racist doctrine served to legitimize Britain's acquisition and control of parts of central Africa and Asia (Cody 1998).

After World War II, the British empire began to fall apart, with nationalist movements for independence. India became independent in 1947, as did the Republic of Ireland in 1949. Decolonization in Africa and Asia accelerated during the late 1950s. Today, the ties that remain between Britain and its former colonies are mainly linguistic or cultural rather than political (Cody 1998).

French Colonialism

French colonialism also had two phases. The first began with the explorations of the early 1600s. Prior to the French revolution in 1789, missionaries, explorers, and traders carved out niches for France in Canada, the Louisiana Territory, several Caribbean islands, and parts of India, which were lost along with Canada to Great Britain in 1763 (Harvey 1980).

The foundations of the second French empire were established between 1830 and 1870. In Great Britain the sheer drive for profit led expansion, but French colonialism was spurred more by the state, church, and armed forces than by pure business interests. France acquired Algeria and part of what eventually became Indochina (Cambodia, Laos, and Vietnam). By 1914 the French empire covered 4 million square miles and included some 60 million people (see Figure 23.4). By 1893 French rule had been fully established in Indochina. Tunisia and Morocco became French protectorates in 1883 and 1912, respectively (Harvey 1980).

To be sure, the French, like the British, had substantial business interests in their colonies, but they

On January 1, 1900, a British officer in India receives a pedicure from a servant. What does this photo say to you about colonialism? Who gives pedicures in your society?

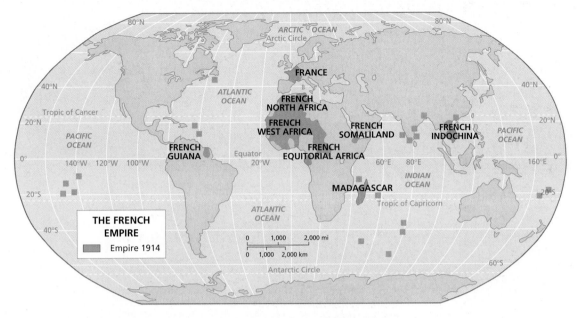

FIGURE 23.4 Map of the French Empire at Its Height around 1914.

SOURCE: From the *Academic American Encyclopedia,* Vol. 8, p. 309. 1998 Edition. Copyright © 1998 by Grolier Incorporated. Reprinted with permission.

also sought, again like the British, international glory and prestige. The French promulgated a *mission civilisatrice,* their equivalent of Britain's "white man's burden." The goal was to implant French culture, language, and religion, Roman Catholicism, throughout the colonies (Harvey 1980).

The French used two forms of colonial rule: *indirect rule,* governing through native leaders and established political structures, in areas with long histories of state organization, such as Morocco and Tunisia; and *direct rule* by French officials in many areas of Africa, where the French imposed new government structures to control diverse societies, many of them previously stateless. Like the British empire, the French empire began to disintegrate after World War II. France fought long—and ultimately futile—wars to keep its empire intact in Indochina and Algeria (Harvey 1980).

Colonialism and Identity

Many geopolitical labels in the news today had no equivalent meaning before colonialism. Whole countries, along with social groups and divisions within them, were colonial inventions. In West Africa, for example, by geographic logic, several adjacent countries could be one (Togo, Ghana, Ivory Coast [Côte d'Ivoire], Guinea, Guinea-Bissau, Sierra Leone, Liberia). Instead, they are separated by linguistic, political, and economic contrasts promoted under colonialism (Figure 23.5).

Hundreds of ethnic groups and "tribes" are colonial constructions (see Ranger 1996). The Sukuma of Tanzania, for instance, were first registered as a single tribe by the colonial administration. Then

missionaries standardized a series of dialects into a single Sukuma language into which they translated the Bible and other religious texts. Thereafter, those texts were taught in missionary schools and to European foreigners and other non-Sukuma speakers. Over time this standardized the Sukuma language and ethnicity (Finnstrom 1997).

As in most of East Africa, in Rwanda and Burundi farmers and herders live in the same areas and speak the same language. Historically they have shared the same social world, although their social organization is "extremely hierarchical," almost "castelike" (Malkki 1995, p. 24). There has been a tendency to see the pastoral Tutsis as superior to the agricultural Hutus. Tutsis have been presented as nobles, Hutus as commoners. Yet when distributing identity cards in Rwanda, the Belgian colonizers simply identified all people with more than ten head of cattle as Tutsi. Owners of fewer cattle were registered as Hutus (Bjuremalm 1997). Years later, these arbitrary colonial registers were used systematically for "ethnic" identification during the mass killings (genocide) that took place in Rwanda in 1994 (as portrayed vividly in the film *Hotel Rwanda*).

Postcolonial Studies

In anthropology, history, and literature, the field of postcolonial studies has gained prominence since the 1970s (see Ashcroft, Griffiths, and Tiffin 1989; Cooper and Stoler 1997). **Postcolonial** refers to the study of the interactions between European nations and the societies they colonized (mainly after 1800). In 1914, European empires, which broke up after World War II, ruled more than 85 percent of the

postcolonial
Describing relations between European nations and areas they colonized and once ruled.

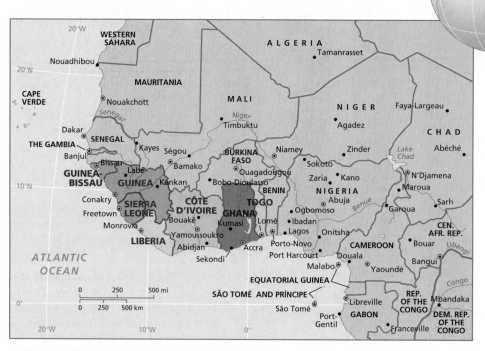

FIGURE 23.5 Small West African Nations Created by Colonialism.

world (Petraglia-Bahri 1996). The term *postcolonial* also has been used to describe the second half of the 20th century in general, the period succeeding colonialism. Even more generically, "postcolonial" may be used to signify a position against imperialism and Eurocentrism (Petraglia-Bahri 1996).

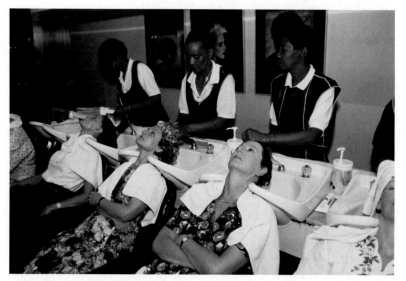

Black workers wash the hair of white customers at a hair salon in Johannesburg's (South Africa) exclusive Hyde Park shopping center. What story does the photo tell you?

The former colonies (*postcolonies*) can be divided into settler, nonsettler, and mixed (Petraglia-Bahri 1996). The settler countries, with large numbers of European colonists and sparser native populations, include Australia and Canada. Examples of nonsettler countries include India, Pakistan, Bangladesh, Sri Lanka, Malaysia, Indonesia, Nigeria, Senegal, and Madagascar. All these had substantial native populations and relatively few European settlers. Mixed countries include South Africa, Zimbabwe, Kenya, and Algeria. Such countries had significant European settlement despite having sizable native populations.

Given the varied experiences of such countries, "postcolonial" has to be a loose term. The United States, for instance, was colonized by Europeans and fought a war for independence from Britain. Is the United States a postcolony? It usually isn't perceived as such, given its current world power position, its treatment of Native Americans (sometimes called internal colonization), and its annexation of other parts of the world (Petraglia-Bahri 1996). Research in postcolonial studies is growing, permitting a wide-ranging investigation of power relations in varied contexts. Broad topics in the field include the formation of an empire, the impact of colonization, and the state of the postcolony today (Petraglia-Bahri 1996).

DEVELOPMENT

During the Industrial Revolution, a strong current of thought viewed industrialization as a beneficial process of organic development and progress. Many economists still assume that industrialization increases production and income. They seek to create in Third World ("developing") countries a process like the one that first occurred spontaneously in 18th-century Great Britain.

We have seen that Britain used the notion of a white man's burden to justify its imperialist expansion and that France claimed to be engaged in a *mission civilisatrice*, a civilizing mission, in its colonies. Both these ideas illustrate an **intervention philosophy**, an ideological justification for outsiders to guide native peoples in specific directions. Economic development plans also have intervention philosophies. John Bodley (1988) argues that the basic belief behind interventions—whether by colonialists, missionaries, governments, or development planners—has been the same for more than 100 years. This belief is that industrialization, modernization, Westernization, and individualism are desirable evolutionary advances and that development schemes that promote them will bring long-term benefits to local people. In a more extreme form, intervention philosophy may pit the assumed wisdom of enlightened colonial or other First World planners against the purported conservatism, ignorance, or "obsolescence" of "inferior" local people.

Neoliberalism

One currently prominent intervention philosophy is neoliberalism. This term encompasses a set of assumptions that have become widespread during the last thirty years. Neoliberal policies are being implemented in developing nations, including postsocialist societies (e.g., those of the former Soviet Union). **Neoliberalism** is the current form of the classic economic liberalism laid out in Adam Smith's famous capitalist manifesto *The Wealth of Nations*, published in 1776, soon after the Industrial Revolution. Smith

The face of the Scottish economist Adam Smith aptly appears on this English 20-pound banknote. In his famed capitalist manifesto, *The Wealth of Nations*, published in 1776, Smith advocated "free" enterprise and competition, with the goal of generating profits.

living anthropology **VIDEOS**

Globalization, www.mhhe.com/kottak

This clip draws parallels between the 1890s and today, mentioning advances in technology that took place through the discoveries and efforts of Bell, Edison, Carnegie, and Morgan. Back then, laissez-faire economic policies allowed the barons of industry to increase profits and grow wealthy. The United States moved from semiperiphery to core. The clip mentions sweatshops, child labor, and low wages as the downside of capitalism. Today, transnational corporations increasingly operate internationally, beyond the boundaries of uniform national laws. This creates new business opportunities but also new legal, ethical, and moral challenges. What's the technological basis of the global village described in the clip? The clip suggests that because the world is so tightly integrated, events in Asia can have immediate ripple effects in the West. Can you think of any examples?

intervention philosophy
Ideological justification for outsiders to guide or rule native peoples.

advocated laissez-faire (hands-off) economics as the basis of capitalism: The government should stay out of its nation's economic affairs. Free trade, Smith thought, was the best way for a nation's economy to develop. There should be no restrictions on manufacturing, no barriers to commerce, and no tariffs. This philosophy is called "liberalism" because it aimed at liberating or freeing the economy from government controls. Economic liberalism encouraged "free" enterprise and competition, with the goal of generating profits. (Note the difference between this meaning of *liberal* and the one that has been popularized on American talk radio, in which "liberal" is used— usually as a derogatory term—as the opposite of "conservative." Ironically, Adam Smith's liberalism is today's capitalist "conservatism.")

Economic liberalism prevailed in the United States until President Franklin Roosevelt's New Deal during the 1930s. The Great Depression produced a turn to Keynesian economics, which challenged liberalism. John Maynard Keynes (1927, 1936) insisted that full employment was necessary for capitalism to grow, that governments and central banks should intervene to increase employment, and that government should promote the common good.

Especially since the fall of Communism (1989–1991), there has been a revival of economic liberalism, now known as neoliberalism, which has been spreading globally. Around the world, neoliberal policies have been imposed by powerful financial institutions such as the International Monetary Fund (IMF), the World Bank, and the Inter-American Development Bank (see Edelman and Haugerud 2005). Neoliberalism entails open (tariff- and barrier-free) international trade and investment. Profits are sought through lowering of costs, whether through

neoliberalism
Principle that governments shouldn't regulate private enterprise; free market forces should rule.

improving productivity, laying off workers, or seeking workers who accept lower wages. In exchange for loans, the governments of postsocialist and developing nations have been required to accept the neoliberal premise that deregulation leads to economic growth, which will eventually benefit everyone through a process sometimes called "trickle down." Accompanying the belief in free markets and the idea of cutting costs is a tendency to impose austerity measures that cut government expenses. This can entail reduced public spending on education, health care, and other social services, as has happened recently with imposed austerity in Greece.

THE SECOND WORLD

The labels "First World," "Second World," and "Third World" represent a common, although ethnocentric, way of categorizing nations. The *First World* refers to the "democratic West"—traditionally conceived in opposition to a "Second World" ruled by "Communism." The *Second World* refers to the former Soviet Union and the socialist and once-socialist countries of Eastern Europe and Asia. Proceeding with this classification, the "less developed countries" or "developing nations" make up the *Third World*.

Communism

The two meanings of communism involve how it is written, whether with a lowercase (small) or an uppercase (large) *c*. Small-*c* **communism** describes a social system in which property is owned by the community and in which people work for the common good. Large-*C* **Communism** was a political movement and doctrine seeking to overthrow capitalism and to establish a form of communism such as that which prevailed in the Soviet Union (USSR) from 1917 to 1991. The heyday of Communism was a forty-year period from 1949 to 1989, when more Communist regimes existed than at any time before or after. Today only five Communist states remain— China, Cuba, Laos, North Korea, and Vietnam, compared with twenty-three in 1985.

Communism, which originated with Russia's Bolshevik Revolution in 1917, and took its inspiration from Karl Marx and Friedrich Engels, was not uniform over time or among countries. All Communist systems were *authoritarian* (promoting obedience to authority rather than individual freedom). Many were *totalitarian* (banning rival parties and demanding total submission of the individual to the state). Several features distinguished Communist societies from other authoritarian regimes (e.g., Spain under Franco) and from socialism of a social demo-

communism
Political system in which property is owned by the community; people working for the common good.

Communism
Political movement aimed at replacing capitalism with Soviet-style communism.

anthropology ATLAS

http://www.mhhe.com/anthromaps Map 17 represents an attempt to assess and display the quality of life by country, based on economic, social, and demographic data.

cratic type. First, the Communist Party monopolized power in every Communist state. Second, relations within the party were highly centralized and strictly disciplined. Third, Communist nations had state ownership, rather than private ownership, of the means of production. Finally, all Communist regimes, with the goal of advancing communism, cultivated a sense of belonging to an international movement (Brown 2001).

Social scientists have tended to refer to such societies as socialist rather than Communist. Today research by anthropologists is thriving in *postsocialist* societies—those that once emphasized bureaucratic redistribution of wealth according to a central plan (Verdery 2001). In the postsocialist period, states that once featured planned economies have been following the neoliberal agenda, by divesting themselves of state-owned resources in favor of privatization and marketization. Some of them have moved toward formal liberal democracy, with political parties, elections, and a balance of powers (Grekova 2001).

Postsocialist Transitions

Neoliberal economists assumed that dismantling the Soviet Union's planned economy would raise gross domestic product (GDP) and living standards. The goal was to enhance production by substituting a decentralized market system and providing incentives through privatization. In October 1991, Boris Yeltsin, who had been elected president of Russia that June, announced a program of radical market-oriented reform, pursuing a changeover to capitalism. Yeltsin's program of "shock therapy" cut subsidies to farms and industries and ended price controls. Since then, postsocialist Russia has faced many problems. The anticipated gains in productivity did not materialize. After the fall of the Soviet Union, Russia's GDP fell by half. Poverty increased, with a quarter of the population sinking below the poverty line. Life expectancy and the birth rate declined. Another problem to emerge in the postsocialist transition is corruption. Since 1996, the World Bank and other international organizations have launched anticorruption programs worldwide. *Corruption* is defined as the abuse of public office for private gain (see Dumas, Wedel, and Callman 2010).

The World Bank's approach to corruption assumes a clear and sharp distinction between the state (the public or official domain) and the private sphere, and that the two should be kept separate. The idea that the public sphere can be separated neatly from the private sphere is ethnocentric. According to Janine Wedel (2002), postsocialist states provide rich contexts in which to explore variability in relations between public and private domains. Alexei Yurchak (2002, 2006) describes two spheres that operate in Russia today; these spheres do not mesh neatly with the assumption of a public–private split.

He calls them the official–public sphere and the personal–public sphere, referring to domains that coexist and sometimes overlap. State officials may respect the law (official–public), while also working with informal or even criminal groups (personal–public). Officials switch from official–public to personal–public behavior all the time in order to accomplish specific tasks.

In an illustrative case from Poland, a man selling an apartment he had inherited was to pay a huge sum in taxes. He visited the state tax office, where a bureaucrat informed him of how much he was being assessed (official–public). She also told him how to avoid paying it (personal–public). He followed her advice and saved a lot of money. The man didn't know the bureaucrat personally. She didn't expect anything in return, and he didn't offer anything. She said she routinely offers such help.

In postsocialist societies, what is legal (official–public) and what is considered morally correct don't necessarily correspond. The bureaucrat just described seemed still to be operating under the old communist notion that state property (tax dollars in this case) belongs both to everyone and to no one. For further illustration of this view of state property, imagine two people working in the same state-owned construction enterprise. To take home for private use materials belonging to the enterprise (i.e., to everyone and no one) is morally acceptable. No one will fault you for it because "everyone does it." However, if a fellow worker comes along and takes materials someone else had planned to take home, that would be stealing and morally wrong (Wedel 2002). In evaluating charges of corruption, anthropologists point out that property notions and spheres of official action in postsocialist societies are in transition.

THE WORLD SYSTEM TODAY

The spread of industrialization continues today, although nations have shifted their positions within the world system. Recap 23.1 summarizes those shifts. By 1900, the United States had become a core nation within the world system and had overtaken Great Britain in iron, coal, and cotton production.

Before and after Communism. Above: on May Day (May 1, 1975), large photos of Politburo members (Communist Party leaders) adorn buildings in Moscow. Below: in 2010, a Burger King outlet opens at a shopping mall in Moscow. Burger King started opening its outlets in Russia nearly two decades after McDonald's, looking to capitalize on new markets' growing appetite for fast food.

RECAP 23.1	Ascent and Decline of Nations Within the World System	
PERIPHERY TO SEMIPERIPHERY	**SEMIPERIPHERY TO CORE**	**CORE TO SEMIPERIPHERY**
United States (1800–1860)	United States (1860–1900)	Spain (1620–1700)
Japan (1868–1900)	Japan (1945–1970)	
Taiwan (1949–1980)	Germany (1870–1900)	
S. Korea (1953–1980)		

SOURCE: Thomas R. Shannon, *An Introduction to the World-System Perspective*, 2nd ed., p. 147. Copyright © 1989, 1996 by Westview Press, Inc. Reprinted by permission of Westview Press, a member of the Perseus Books Group.

Is Mining Sustainable?

How can anthropologists help the people they study? The spread of industrialization, illustrated by the mining described here, has contributed to the destruction of indigenous economies, ecologies, and populations. Today, multinational conglomerates, along with nations such as Papua New Guinea, are repeating—at an accelerated rate—the process of resource depletion that started in Europe and the United States during the Industrial Revolution. Fortunately, however, today's world has some environmental watchdogs, including anthropologists, that did not exist during the first centuries of the Industrial Revolution. Described here is a conundrum confronting a major university. Is a firm whose operations have destroyed the landscapes and livelihoods of indigenous peoples a proper advisor for an institute devoted to ecological sustainability?

In the 1990s, the giant mining company now known as BHP Billiton drew worldwide condemnation for the environmental damage caused by its copper and gold mine in Papua New Guinea. Its mining practices destroyed the way of life of thousands of farming and fishing families who lived along and subsisted on the rivers polluted by the mine, and it was only after being sued in a landmark class-action case that the company agreed to compensate them.

Today several activists and academics who work on behalf of indigenous people around the world say the company continues to dodge responsibility for the problems its mines create for communities in undeveloped parts of the world.

Yet at the University of Michigan at Ann Arbor, BHP Billiton enjoys a loftier reputation: It is one of 14 corporate members of an External Advisory Board for the university's new Graham Environmental Sustainability Institute.

Critics at and outside the university contend that Michigan's decision to enlist BHP Billiton as an adviser to an institute devoted to sustainability reflects badly on the institution and allows the company to claim a mantle of environmental and social responsibility that it does not deserve.

The institute's director says he is satisfied that the company is serious about operating in a more sustainable way. . . .

The arguments echo the discussions about corporate "greenwashing" that have arisen at Stanford University and the University of California at Berkeley over major research grants from ExxonMobil and BP, respectively, and more recently, the debate at the Smithsonian Institution among its trustees over whether to accept a gift from the American Petroleum Institute for a museum exhibition about oceans. (The gift was withdrawn in November.)

For one BHP Billiton critic at Michigan, the issue is personal. Stuart Kirsch, an associate professor of anthropology, has spent most of his academic career documenting the damage caused by BHP Billiton's Ok Tedi mine in Papua New Guinea. . . .

Mr. Kirsch, who first visited some of the affected communities as a young ethnographer in 1987, became involved in the class-action lawsuit brought against the company and helped villagers participate in the 1996 legal settlement. "I put my career on hold while being an activist," he says.

He subsequently published several papers related to his work with the Yonggom people as they fought for recognition and compensation from mine operators—scholarship that helped him win tenure this year—and he remains involved with the network of activists and academics who follow mining and its impact on undeveloped communities around the world. . . .

The company's practices polluted the Ok Tedi and Fly Rivers and caused thousands of people to leave their homes because the mining-induced flooding made it impossible for them to grow food to feed themselves, says Mr. Kirsch.

BHP Billiton, based in Australia, later acknowledged that the mine was "not compatible with our environmental values," and spun it off to an independent company that pays all of its mining royalties to the government of Papua New Guinea.

But Mr. Kirsch says that in doing so, the company skirted responsibility for ameliorating the damage it caused. BHP Billiton says it would have preferred to close the mine, but the Papua New Guinea government, in need of the mine

---

In a few decades (1868–1900), Japan had changed from a medieval handicraft economy to an industrial one, joining the semiperiphery by 1900 and moving to the core between 1945 and 1970. India and China have joined Brazil as leaders of the semiperiphery. Figure 23.6 is a map showing the modern world system.

Twentieth-century industrialization added hundreds of new industries and millions of new jobs. Production increased, often beyond immediate demand, spurring strategies, such as advertising, to sell everything industry could churn out. Mass production gave rise to a culture of consumption, which valued acquisitiveness and conspicuous consumption (Veblen 1934).

Industrialization entailed a shift from reliance on renewable resources to the use of fossil fuels. Fossil fuel energy, stored over millions of years, is being depleted rapidly to support a previously unknown and probably unsustainable level of consumption (Bodley 2012).

Table 23.1 compares energy consumption in various types of cultures. Americans are the world's foremost consumers of nonrenewable resources.

revenues, pressed to keep it open. The deal freed BHP Billiton from any future liabilities for environmental damage.

"They didn't clean it up; they didn't take responsibility for the damage they had done," Mr. Kirsch says of the company. With that record, "it's supposed to provide education to the University of Michigan?" . . .

Illtud Harri, a BHP Billiton spokesman, says the company regrets its past with Ok Tedi but considers its pullout from the mine "a responsible exit" that left in place a system that supports educational, agricultural, and social programs for the people of the community.

He says the company also aims for the most ethical standards in its projects. The company

mines only when it can fully comply with the host country's environmental laws. In places where those regulatory requirements fall below the company's, "we will always be guided by our higher standards," he says.

Mr. Talbot, the interim director of the two-year-old sustainability institute, says . . . "We intentionally selected a cross-sector group of organizations" for the advisory board from a list of about 140 nominees, . . . and several companies that "weren't making any serious efforts" toward sustainability were rejected. . . .

BHP Billiton, a company formed from the 2001 merger of the Australian mining enterprise Broken Hill Proprietary Company with London-

based Billiton, is now the world's largest mining company, with more than 100 operations in 25 countries. . . .

The BHP Billiton charter includes a statement that the company has "an overriding commitment to health, safety, environmental responsibility, and sustainable development." But its critics say the company continues to play a key role in mining projects with questionable records on environmental and human rights, even though in many of those cases, it is not directly responsible. . . .

Mr. Kirsch, who is now on leave from Michigan to write a book, says he is planning to press for an open forum at the university that includes environmental scientists, indigenous people affected by the Ok Tedi mine, and company officials themselves.

BHP Billiton has the resources to present itself as the "golden boy," but, says Mr. Kirsch, "it's much harder to see the people on the Ok Tedi and Fly rivers."

A forum could help to right that imbalance, he says. "Let the students and faculty decide whether this is an appropriate company to advise the University of Michigan," says Mr. Kirsch. "It would be an educational process for everyone involved."

This photo of the Ok Tedi copper mine, taken February 10, 2002, shows the ecological devastation of the native landscape.

SOURCE: Goldie Blumenstyk, "Mining Company Involved in Environmental Disaster Now Advises Sustainability Institute at U. of Michigan," *Chronicle of Higher Education*, Vol. 54, Issue 15 (December 7, 2007), p. A22. Copyright 2007, The Chronicle of Higher Education. Reprinted with permission.

In terms of energy consumption, the average American is about thirty-five times more expensive than the average forager or tribesperson. Since 1900, the United States has tripled its per capita energy use. It also has increased its total energy consumption thirtyfold.

Table 23.2 compares energy consumption, per capita and total, in the United States and selected other countries. The United States represents 20.4 percent of the world's annual energy consumption, compared with China's 17.3 percent, but the average American consumes five times the energy used by

the average Chinese, and nineteen times the energy used by the average inhabitant of India.

Industrial Degradation

Industrialization and factory labor now characterize many societies in Latin America, Africa, the Pacific, and Asia. One effect of the spread of industrialization has been the destruction of indigenous economies, ecologies, and populations, as we see in this chapter's "Appreciating Anthropology." Two centuries ago, as industrialization was developing, fifty million people

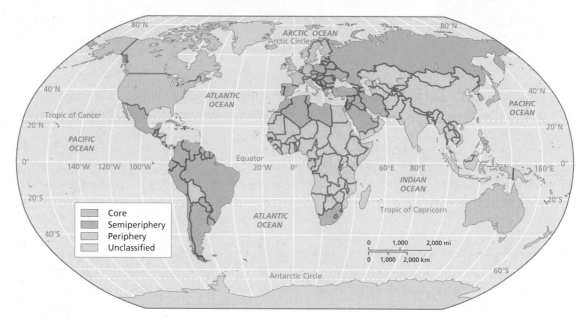

FIGURE 23.6 The World System in 2000.

still lived in politically independent bands, tribes, and chiefdoms. Occupying vast areas, those nonstate societies, although not totally isolated, were only marginally affected by nation-states and the world capitalist economy. In 1800 bands, tribes, and chiefdoms controlled half the globe and 20 percent of its population (Bodley 1988). Industrialization tipped the balance in favor of states.

As industrial states have conquered, annexed, and "developed" nonstates, there has been genocide on a grand scale. *Genocide* refers to a deliberate policy of exterminating a group through warfare or murder. Examples include the Holocaust, Rwanda in

TABLE 23.1 Energy Consumption in Various Contexts

TYPE OF SOCIETY	DAILY KILOCALORIES PER PERSON
Bands and tribes	4,000–12,000
Preindustrial states	26,000 (maximum)
Early industrial states	70,000
Americans in 1970	230,000
Americans in 1990	275,000

SOURCE: John H. Bodley, *Anthropology and Contemporary Human Problems* (Mountain View, CA: Mayfield Publishing, 1985). Reprinted by permission of the author.

TABLE 23.2 Energy Consumption in Selected Countries, 2008

	TOTAL	PER CAPITA
World	493.0*	74[†]
United States	100.6	330
China	85.1	65
Russia	30.4	216
India	20.0	18
Germany	14.4	174
Canada	14.0	422
France	11.3	180
United Kingdom	9.3	151

*462.8 quadrillion (462,800,000,000,000,000) Btu.
[†]70 million Btu.

SOURCE: Based on data in *Statistical Abstract of the United States, 2012* (Table 1383), p. 864.

Copsa Mica, Romania, may well be the world's most polluted city. A factory belches out smoke that leaves its mark on these boys' faces, food, and lungs. What's the term for such environmental devastation?

1994, and Bosnia in the early 1990s. Bodley (1988) estimates that an average of 250,000 indigenous people perished annually between 1800 and 1950. Besides warfare, the causes included foreign diseases (to which natives lacked resistance), slavery, land grabbing, and other forms of dispossession and impoverishment.

Many native groups have been incorporated within nation-states, in which they have become ethnic minorities. Some such groups have been able to recoup their population. Many indigenous peoples survive and maintain their ethnic identity despite having lost their ancestral cultures to varying degrees (partial ethnocide). And many descendants of tribespeople live on as culturally distinct and self-conscious colonized peoples, many of whom aspire to autonomy. As the original inhabitants of their territories, they are called **indigenous peoples** (see Maybury-Lewis 2002).

Around the world many contemporary nations are repeating—at an accelerated rate—the process of resource depletion that started in Europe and the United States during the Industrial Revolution. Fortunately, however, today's world has some environmental watchdogs that did not exist during the first centuries of the Industrial Revolution. Given national and international cooperation and sanctions, the modern world may benefit from the lessons of the past (see Hornborg, McNeill, and Martinez-Alier 2007). This chapter's "Appreciating Anthropology" shows how anthropologists can help local people fight the environmental degradation, in this case from mining, that often accompanies the spread of industrialization. Also raised in "Appreciating Anthropology" is the question of whether a corporation whose operations endanger indigenous peoples is a proper advisor for an institute devoted to ecological sustainability.

indigenous peoples
Original inhabitants of particular areas.

acing the COURSE

summary

1. Local societies increasingly participate in wider systems—regional, national, and global. The capitalist world economy depends on production for sale, with the goal of maximizing profits. The key claim of world-system theory is that an identifiable social system, based on wealth and power differentials, extends beyond individual countries. That system is formed by a set of economic and political relations that has characterized much of the globe since the 16th century. World capitalism has political and economic specialization at the core, semiperiphery, and periphery.

2. Columbus's voyages opened the way for a major exchange between the Old and New Worlds. Seventeenth-century plantation economies in the Caribbean and Brazil were based on sugar. In the 18th century, plantation economies based on cotton arose in the southeastern United States.

3. The Industrial Revolution began in England around 1750. Transoceanic commerce supplied capital for industrial investment. Industrialization hastened the separation of workers from the means of production. Marx saw a sharp division between the bourgeoisie and the proletariat. Class consciousness was a key feature of Marx's view of this stratification. Weber believed that social solidarity based on ethnicity, religion, race, or nationality could take priority over class. Today's capitalist world economy maintains the contrast between those who own the means of production and those who don't, but the division is now worldwide. There is a substantial contrast between not only capitalists but workers in the core nations versus workers on the periphery.

4. Imperialism is the policy of extending the rule of a nation or empire over other nations and of taking and holding foreign colonies. Colonialism is the domination of a territory and its people by a foreign power for an extended time. European colonialism had two main phases. The first started in 1492 and

lasted through 1825. For Britain this phase ended with the American Revolution. For France it ended when Britain won the Seven Years' War, forcing the French to abandon Canada and India. For Spain it ended with Latin American independence. The second phase of European colonialism extended approximately from 1850 to 1950. The British and French empires were at their height around 1914, when European empires controlled 85 percent of the world. Britain and France had colonies in Africa, Asia, Oceania, and the New World.

5. Many geopolitical labels and identities that were created under colonialism had little or nothing to do with existing social demarcations. The new ethnic or national divisions were colonial inventions, sometimes aggravating conflicts.

6. Like colonialism, economic development has an intervention philosophy that provides a justification for outsiders to guide native peoples toward particular goals. Development usually is justified by the idea that industrialization and modernization are desirable evolutionary advances. Neoliberalism revives and extends classic economic liberalism: the idea that governments should not regulate private enterprise and that free market forces should rule. This intervention philosophy currently dominates aid agreements with postsocialist and developing nations.

7. Spelled with a lowercase *c*, communism describes a social system in which property is owned by the community and in which people work for the common good. Spelled with an uppercase *C*, Communism indicates a political movement and doctrine seeking to overthrow capitalism and to establish a form of communism such as that which prevailed in the Soviet Union from 1917 to 1991. The heyday of Communism was between 1949 and 1989. The fall of Communism can be traced to 1989–1990 in eastern Europe and 1991 in the Soviet Union. Postsocialist states have followed the neoliberal agenda, through privatization, deregulation, and democratization.

8. By 1900 the United States had become a core nation. Mass production gave rise to a culture that valued acquisitiveness and conspicuous consumption. One effect of industrialization has been the destruction of indigenous economies, ecologies, and populations. Another has been the accelerated rate of resource depletion.

key terms

bourgeoisie 529

capital 525

capitalist world economy 525

colonialism 533

communism 538

Communism 538

core 525

imperialism 533

indigenous peoples 543

Industrial Revolution 527

intervention philosophy 537

neoliberalism 537

periphery 525

postcolonial 535

semiperiphery 525

working class, or proletariat 529

world-system theory 525

test yourself

MULTIPLE CHOICE

1. The modern world system is
   a. a system in which ethnic groups are increasingly isolated from the economic and political influence of nation-states.
   b. a theory that was popular in the 1980s but has since been replaced with the capitalist world economy.
   c. Karl Marx's theory of social stratification.
   d. a system of global dimensions in which nations are economically and politically interdependent.
   e. Max Weber's theory of the emergence of capitalism.

2. Which of the following statements about world system theory is *not* true?
   a. According to Wallerstein, countries within the world system occupy three different positions of economic and political power: core, periphery, and semiperiphery.
   b. It sees society as consisting of parts assembled into an interrelated system.
   c. It applies mainly to non-Western societies.
   d. It claims that a set of economic and political interconnections has characterized much of the globe since the 16th century.
   e. It is based on political and economic specialization and interdependence.

3. The increasing dominance of world trade has led to
   a. diminishing rates of poverty, social stratification, and environmental degradation.
   b. the disintegration of national boundaries and the free and fair flow of people and resources all around the globe.
   c. the capitalist world economy, a single world system committed to production for sale or exchange, with the object of maximizing profits rather than supplying domestic needs.
   d. a growing concern by all nation-states for ensuring the livelihood of indigenous peoples living within their borders.
   e. the socialist welfare state, a system that attends to the needs of people who have been displaced by the capitalist world economy.

4. What fueled the European "Age of Discovery"?
   a. a desire to save the souls of the natives
   b. pilgrims fleeing persecution in their European homelands
   c. the feudal kingdoms of East Asia reaching out to establish trade links with Europe, mainly through such Middle Eastern countries as Arabia
   d. European commercial interest in exotic raw materials, such as spices and tropical hardwoods
   e. a seven-year drought in Europe that forced governments to look outside their borders to support their populations

5. Which of the following spurred the growth of a market for sugar in Europe?
   a. the development of the trans-Atlantic slave trade and plantation economies in the Americas
   b. the strengthening of the independent indigenous nations of Mexico and South America
   c. the movement of sugar-producing nations from the periphery to the core of the world system
   d. the spread of capitalism from Papua New Guinea (where sugar was first domesticated) to the rest of the world
   e. the impoverishment of the English rural peasantry

6. From his observations in England and his analysis of 19th-century industrial capitalism, Karl Marx saw socioeconomic stratification as a sharp division between two classes: the bourgeoisie and the proletariat. He also argued that class consciousness comes about as a result of
   a. the continuation of ethnic identities even though ethnic "markers" (distinct clothing styles, etc.) have more or less disappeared.
   b. people recognizing they have a common economic interest and identifying themselves as part of the group that shares that interest.
   c. a growing distinction among religious beliefs in complex industrialized societies.
   d. people extending notions of kinship beyond the boundaries of actual biological relations.
   e. the gradual elaboration of gendered differences first established during the period of peasant subsistence farming.

7. This chapter defines imperialism as the policy of extending the rule of a nation or empire, such as the British empire, over foreign nations and of taking and holding foreign colonies, while *colonialism* refers specifically to
   a. the political, social, economic, and cultural domination of a territory and its people by a foreign power for an extended period of time.
   b. imperial influence that disappears once formal independence is granted to former colonies.
   c. the political, social, economic, and cultural domination of a territory and its people by Europe.
   d. the informal and often benevolent approach to enlightening the non-Western world with Western values.
   e. the same as imperialism, but the modern form of imperialism that was created with the rise of the Industrial Revolution.

8. The Sukuma of Tanzania were first registered as a single tribe by colonial administrators. In Rwanda and Burundi, the distribution of colonial identity cards created arbitrary ethnic divisions. These two cases
   a. suggest that strong ethnic identities are a key ingredient of development.
   b. illustrate that many ethnic groups and tribes are colonial constructions, sometimes inciting and aggravating conflict.
   c. are evidence that colonial administrators were informed about the cultures of their colonial subjects.
   d. show how tribal distinctions are better than ethnic ones because the latter always leads to civil violence.
   e. are examples of the Spanish intervention philosophy that eventually all colonial administrations adopted because of its success in Latin America.

9. Since the fall of Communism (1989–1991), neoliberalism, a revival of the older economic liberalism of Adam Smith,
   a. has emphasized "the common good" over "individual responsibility."
   b. has rejected the imposition of austerity measures on governments, a policy more associated with John Maynard Keynes.
   c. has promoted the involvement of the United Nations to ensure it reaches the social groups most in need.
   d. has been an influential intervention philosophy that has become a popular doctrine of powerful financial institutions.
   e. has rarely been favored as a viable policy by powerful financial institutions and states alike.

10. Industrialization and factory labor now characterize many societies in Latin America, Africa, the Pacific, and Asia. One effect of the spread of industrialization has been
    a. a worldwide decrease in energy consumption because of the use of renewable resources.
    b. the increasing overlap of the official-public and the personal-public spheres.
    c. the destruction of indigenous economies, ecologies, and populations.
    d. the rise of corruption, defined as the abuse of public office for private gain.
    e. the increasing confusion of what is public or private property.

FILL IN THE BLANK

1. _____ refers to wealth or resources invested in business with the intent of producing a profit.

2. Weber faulted Marx for an overly simple and exclusively economic view of stratification. According to Weber, there are three dimensions of social stratification. They are _____, _____, and _____.

3. Britain used the notion of a white man's burden to justify its imperialist expansion. France claimed to be engaged in a civilizing mission in its colonies. These, together with some forms of economic development plans, illustrate an _____, an ideological justification for outsiders to guide native peoples in specific directions.

4. The term _____ is used to describe the relations between European countries and their former colonies in the second half of the 20th century.

5. Spelled with an uppercase C, _____ indicates a political movement and doctrine seeking to overthrow capitalism that originated with Russia's Bolshevik Revolution in 1917. Spelled with a lowercase c, _____ describes a social system in which property is owned by the community and in which people work for the common good.

CRITICAL THINKING

1. According to world-system theory, societies are subsystems of bigger systems, with the world system as the largest. What are the various systems, at different levels, in which you participate?

2. How does world-system theory help explain why companies hire thousands of workers in India, while laying off an equivalent number in Europe and the United States?

3. What were the causes of the Industrial Revolution? Why did it begin in England rather than France? How might this knowledge be relevant for an anthropologist interested in investigating the dynamics of industrialization today?

4. Think of a recent case in which a core nation has intervened in the affairs of another nation. What was the intervention philosophy used to justify the action?

5. This chapter describes the labels "First World," "Second World," and "Third World" as a common, although ethnocentric, way of categorizing nations. Why is it ethnocentric? Do you think there is any reason to keep using these labels, despite their problems? Why or why not?

Arrighi, G.
2010   *The Long Twentieth Century: Money, Power, and the Origins of Our Times*. New York: Verso. Updated edition of an influential work that traces the relationship between capital accumulation and state formation over a 700-year period.

Bodley, J.H.
2012   *Anthropology and Contemporary Human Problems*, 6th ed. Lanham, MD: AltaMira. Overview of major problems of today's industrial world: over-consumption, the environment, resource depletion, hunger, overpopulation, violence, and war.

Diamond, J.M.
2005   *Guns, Germs, and Steel: The Fates of Human Societies*. New York: W. W. Norton. An ecological approach to expansion and conquest in world history.

Mann, C. C.
2011   *1493: Uncovering the New World Columbus Created*. New York: Knopf. Very readable account of major aspects of the Columbian exchange.

Wallerstein, I. M.
2004b   *World-Systems Analysis: An Introduction*. Durham, NC: Duke University Press. Basics of world-system theory from the master of that approach.

Wolf, E. R.
1982   *Europe and the People without History*. Berkeley: University of California Press. In this prize-winning classic, an anthropologist examines the effects of European expansion on tribal peoples and sets forth a world-system approach within anthropology.

suggested additional readings

Go to our Online Learning Center website at **www.mhhe.com/kottak** for Internet exercises directly related to the content of this chapter.

internet exercises

CHAPTER 24

Anthropology's Role in a Globalizing World

What is global climate change, and how can anthropologists study it, along with other environmental threats?

What is cultural imperialism, and what forces work to favor and oppose it?

What are indigenous peoples, and how and why has their importance increased in recent years?

◀ Perito Moreno glacier, in Patagonia, Argentina. In 2009, for the first time ever in winter, part of this glacier collapsed, possibly due to global warming.

understanding OURSELVES

What's your favorite science-fiction movie or TV show? What imagined images of other planets stand out in your memory? Can you visualize *Star Wars'* Death Star, poor old Alderan, Luke's encounter with Yoda on a misty world in the Dagoba system, the two suns of Tatooine? How about *Avatar's* Pandora? Such images may be as familiar to you as those of real planets. Think, too, about how extraterrestrials have been portrayed in movies. On the one hand are ET's harmless plant collectors and *Avatar's* endangered Na'vi. More typical are Earth's would-be conquerors, as shown in *Independence Day*, *Starship Troopers, V*, and a hundred others. Still other films, most notably *The Day the Earth Stood Still* (either the 1951 or the 2008 version), feature omnipotent, omniscient guardians of interplanetary affairs.

If some of our most vivid perceptions of other planets are based in fiction, modern technology makes it easier than ever for us to perceive the Earth as both a planet and our world. Anthropologists can use Google Earth to locate communities they have studied in remote corners of the world. My colleagues and I have even used space images to choose communities to study on Earth. Interested in the causes of deforestation in Madagascar, we examined a series of satellite images taken in successive years to determine areas where the forest cover

had diminished significantly. Then we traveled to Madagascar to study those areas on the ground.

It's interesting to imagine what an alien might "see" in similar images. If these aliens were (as the more benevolent science-fiction movies imagine) interested in studying life on Earth, rather than conquering or controlling its inhabitants, they would have a lot to interpret. In my work abroad (and on the ground) I've been impressed by two major global trends: population increase and the shift from subsistence to cash economies. These trends have led to agricultural intensification, resource depletion (including deforestation), and emigration, and have made it increasingly harder to *not* think globally when asking ourselves who we are.

I'm struck by the growing number of young people who have abandoned traditional subsistence pursuits. They seek jobs for cash, but work is scarce, spurring migration within and across national boundaries. In turn, transnational migration increases cultural diversity in the United States, Canada, and western European countries. Even small towns in the South and Midwest have Chinese restaurants. Pizza and tacos are as American as apple pie. Every day we encounter people whose ancestral countries and cultures have been studied by anthropologists for generations—making cultural anthropology all the more relevant to our daily lives in an increasingly interconnected world.

This chapter applies an anthropological perspective to contemporary global issues. We begin by reviewing different meanings of the term *globalization*. The fact that certain risks now have global implications leads to a discussion of climate change, aka global warming. Next, we return to issues of development, this time alongside an intervention philosophy that seeks to impose global ecological morality without due attention to cultural variation and autonomy. Also considered is the threat that deforestation poses to global biodiversity. The second half of this chapter turns from ecology to the contemporary flows of people, technology, finance, information, images, and ideology that contribute to a global culture of consumption. Globalization promotes intercultural communication, through the media, travel, and migration, which bring people from different societies into direct contact. Finally, we'll consider how such contacts and external linkages influence indigenous peoples, and how those groups have organized to confront and deal with national and global issues, including human, cultural, and political rights.

It would be impossible in a single chapter to do a complete review of all the global issues that are salient today and that anthropologists have studied. Many such issues (e.g., war, displacement, terrorism, NGOs, the media) have been considered in previous chapters, and a series of boxes have "focused on globalization" throughout this book. For timely anthropological analysis of a range of global issues, see recent books by John Bodley (2008, 2012) and Richard Robbins (2011). The global issues these anthropologists consider include, but are not limited to, hunger, international interventions, peacekeeping, global health, water shortages, and sanitation.

GLOBALIZATION

In Chapter 2, we considered two meanings of globalization: (1) Globalization as fact: the spread and connectedness of production, distribution, consumption, communication, and technologies across the world. This is the primary meaning of globalization as used in this book. (2) Globalization as contested ideology and policy: efforts by the International Monetary Fund (IMF), the World Bank, the World Trade Organization (WTO), and other international financial powers to create a global free market for goods and services. This second meaning is political and has generated considerable opposition.

The Globalization of Risk

One key component of globalization is the globalization of risk (Smith and Doyle 2002). Environmental and technological risks have multiplied, as we saw in the discussion of the Ok Tedi mine in "Appreciating Anthropology" in the last chapter. Hazards linked to industrial production or a cyberattack can spread quickly today beyond their point of origin.

Paradoxically, concern about risks often is *more* developed in groups that are *less* endangered objectively. In Brazil, for example, awareness of environmental risks is most developed in places and groups that are most directly influenced by the media and by environmentalism, rather than among those who are most endangered. The mass media hone risk perception. Seeking audience-grabbing stories,

news agencies focus on every conceivable "risk"— from bird flu to the latest tropical depression or suspected terrorist plot. A world filled with ubiquitous "risks," many unseen and of unmeasured magnitude, is a rich domain for magical thought, which can divert attention from more serious problems.

Constant rebroadcasting magnifies risk perception. The rise of the Internet and cable/satellite TV, with its 24-hour newscasting, has blurred the distinction between the global, the national, and the local. Geographical distance is obscured in a barrage of information; a threat in Buffalo or Sacramento is perceived as one nearby, even if one lives in Atlanta. With so much to worry about, how can we be rationally selective? Brazil has many more unregulated ecological hazards than the United States does, but Brazilians worry much less about them. To be sure, Brazilians also are selective in their risk perception. For years, crime, violence, and lack of jobs have been their main worries.

The globalization of risk means that risks no longer are just local or regional. Everyone in the world has a carbon footprint, and each consumer of fossil fuels makes his or her own individual contribution to global climate change, to which we now turn.

anthropology ATLAS

http://www.mhhe.com/anthromaps Map 18 shows the impact of global warming on ocean temperatures.

GLOBAL CLIMATE CHANGE

The year 2010 tied 2005 as the hottest ever recorded by NASA's Goddard Institute for Space Studies (GISS), whose analysis covers 131 years (2011 was the second hottest). Earth's surface temperatures have risen about 1.4°F (0.7°C) since the early 20th century (see Johansen 2008). (This chapter's "Appreciating Diversity" discusses how this warming has affected an indigenous group in Alaska.) About two-thirds of this increase has been since 1978 (Figure 24.1). Scientific measurements confirm

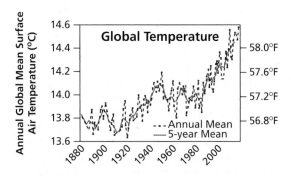

FIGURE 24.1 Global Temperature Change.

Global annual-mean surface air temperature derived from measurements at meteorological stations has increased by 1.4°F (0.7°C) since the early 20th century, with about 0.9°F (0.5°C) of the increase occurring since 1978.

SOURCE: Goddard Institute for Space Studies, from "Understanding and Responding to Climate Change: Highlights of National Academies Reports," http://dels.nas.edu/basc/Climate-HIGH.pdf.

The Plight of Climate Refugees

The United Nations' Intergovernmental Panel on Climate Change estimates that 150 million people worldwide could become environmental refugees by 2050 (York 2009). The Alaskan villagers described here are among the first climate change refugees in the United States. During the past 50 years, the state of Alaska has warmed at more than twice the rate of the rest of the United States (York 2009). Residents of Newtok, Alaska, belong to a federally recognized American Indian tribe. Decades ago, the U.S. government mandated that they (and other Alaskan natives) abandon a nomadic life based on hunting and fishing and settle down in what used to be a winter camp. What obligations does government have to local people whose lives have been disrupted not only by government decree but also by global warming?

NEWTOK, Alaska . . . The earth beneath much of Alaska is not what it used to be. The permanently frozen subsoil, known as permafrost, upon which Newtok and so many other Native Alaskan villages rest is melting, yielding to warming air temperatures and a warming ocean. Sea ice that would normally protect coastal villages is forming later in the year, allowing fall storms to pound away at the shoreline.

Erosion has made Newtok an island, caught between the ever widening Ninglick River and a slough to the north. The village is below sea level, and sinking. Boardwalks squish into the spring muck. Human waste, collected in "honey buckets" that many residents use for toilets, is often dumped within eyeshot in a village where no point is more than a five-minute walk from any other. The ragged wooden houses have to be adjusted regularly to level them on the shifting soil.

Studies say Newtok could be washed away within a decade. Along with the villages of Shishmaref and Kivalina farther to the north, it has been the hardest hit of about 180 Alaska villages that suffer some degree of erosion. Some villages plan to hunker down behind sea walls built or planned by the Army Corps of Engineers, at least for now. Others, like Newtok, have no choice but to abandon their patch of tundra. The corps has estimated that to move Newtok could cost $130 million because of its remoteness, climate and topography. That comes to almost $413,000 for each of the 315 residents. . . .

Newtok's leaders say the corps' relocation estimates are inflated, that they intend to move piecemeal rather than in one collective migration, which they say will save money. But they say government should pay, no matter the

cost—if only there were a government agency charged with doing so. There is not a formal process by which a village can apply to the government to relocate.

"They grossly overestimate it, and that's why federal and state agencies are afraid to step in," said Stanley Tom, the current tribal administrator. . . . "They don't want to spend that much money." Still, Newtok has made far more progress toward moving than other villages, piecing together its move grant by grant.

Through a land swap with the United States Fish and Wildlife Service, it has secured a new site, on Nelson Island, nine miles south. It is safe from the waves on a windy rise above the Ninglick River. They call it Mertarvik, which means "getting water from the spring." They tell their children they will grow up in a place where E. coli does not thrive in every puddle, the way it does here.

With the help of state agencies, it won a grant of about $1 million to build a barge landing at the new site. Bids go out this summer, and construction could be complete next year, providing a platform to unload equipment for building roads, water and sewer systems, houses and a new landing strip. . . .

The administrative leaders of Newtok are mostly men in their 40s, nearly all of them

---

anthropogenic
Caused by humans and their activities.

greenhouse effect
Warming caused by trapped atmospheric gases.

climate change
Global warming, plus changing sea levels, precipitation, storms, and ecosystem effects.

that global warming is not due to increased solar radiation. The causes are mainly **anthropogenic**—caused by humans and their activities. It stands to reason that seven billion people, along with their animals, crops, and machines, have more of an impact on the environment than did the five million or so hunter-gatherers who lived on our planet 12,000 years ago—before the advent of food production.

Because Earth's climate changes constantly, the key question becomes this: How much climate change is due to human activities versus natural climate variability? Most scientists agree that human activities play a major role in global climate change. How can the human factor not be significant given

population growth and rapidly increasing use of fossil fuels, which produce greenhouse gases in the atmosphere?

The **greenhouse effect** is a natural phenomenon that keeps the Earth's surface warm. Greenhouse gases include water vapor (H_2O), carbon dioxide (CO_2), methane (CH_4), nitrous oxide (N_2O), halocarbons, and ozone (O_3). Without them, life as we know it would not exist. Like a greenhouse window, these gases allow sunlight to enter and then prevent heat from escaping the atmosphere. All these gases have increased since the Industrial Revolution. Today, the atmospheric concentration of greenhouse gases has reached its highest level in 400,000 years. It

related. They are widely praised by outsiders for their initiative and determination to relocate.

Yet nearly any place would seem an improvement over Newtok as it exists today, and not all of its problems are rooted in climate change. Some are almost universal to Alaskan villages, which have struggled for decades to reconcile their culture of subsistence hunting and fishing with the expectations and temptations of the world outside.

Excrement dumped from honey buckets is piled on the banks of the slow-flowing Newtok River, not far from wooden shacks where residents take nightly steam baths. An elderly man drains kerosene into a puddle of snowmelt. Children pedal past a walrus skull left to rot, tusks intact, in the mud beside a boardwalk that serves as a main thoroughfare. There are no cars here, just snow machines, boats and all-terrain vehicles

that tear up the tundra. Village elders speak their native Yupik more often than they speak English. They remember when the village was a collection of families who moved with the seasons, making houses from sod, fishing from Nelson Island in the summer, hunting caribou far away in the winter.

Many men still travel with the seasons to hunt and fish. Some will take boats into Bristol Bay this summer to catch salmon alongside commercial fishermen from out of state. But the waterproof jacket sewn from seal gut that Stanley Tom once wore is now stuffed inside a display case at Newtok School next to other relics.

Now Mr. Tom puts on a puffy parka to walk the few hundred feet he travels to work. He checks his e-mail messages to see if there is news from the corps . . . while his brother, Nick, sketches out a budget proposal for a nonprofit corporation to help manage the relocation, presuming the money arrives. *[The projected move to the new site described in this story is proceeding as of 2012].*

SOURCE: William Yardley, "Engulfed by Climate Change, Town Seeks Lifeline." From *The New York Times*, May 27, 2007. © 2007 The New York Times. All rights reserved. Used by permission and protected by the Copyright Laws of the United States. The printing, copying, redistribution, or retransmission of this Content without express written permission is prohibited. www.nytimes.com

Thousands of indigenous people living on the Alaskan tundra derive 90 percent or more of what they eat annually from the land, the rivers, and the Bering Sea. Among them are Stanley and Elizabeth Tom and their children, shown here standing beside the Niutaq River in Newtok, Alaska. The local and regional effects of global warming have made the Toms and their fellow villagers climate change refugees.

will continue to rise—as will global temperatures—without actions to slow it down (National Academy of Sciences 2008, National Research Council 2011).

Scientists prefer the term **climate change** to "global warming." "Climate change" points out that, beyond rising temperatures, there have been changes in sea levels, rainfall patterns, storms, and ecosystem effects. How will climate change affect future regional weather patterns? No one knows for sure, but land areas are predicted to warm more than oceans. The greatest warming probably will occur in higher latitudes, such as Canada, the northern United States, and northern Europe. Climate change may benefit these areas, offering milder winters and

extended growing seasons. However, many more people worldwide probably will be harmed (see Cribb 2010). Already we know that in the Arctic, temperatures have risen almost twice as much as the global average. Arctic landscapes and ecosystems are changing rapidly and perceptibly, as this chapter's "Appreciating Diversity" illustrates.

Coastal communities worldwide can anticipate increased flooding and more severe storms and surges. At risk are people, animals, plants, fresh water supplies, and such industries as tourism and farming. Along with many island nations, Bangladesh, one of the

anthropology **ATLAS**

http://www.mhhe.com/anthromaps
Map 16 shows annual energy consumption around the world.

Methane (CH_4) is a greenhouse gas whose atmospheric concentration has risen due to an increase in various human activities, including livestock raising. Shown here, cattle feeding in Lubbock, Texas. How do cattle produce methane?

world's poorest countries, is projected to lose a significant portion (17.5 percent) of its land, displacing millions of people (National Academy of Sciences 2008).

The world's most distinguished scientists are unified in their support of this core message: Anthropogenic climate change is real, and we need to address it now. The U.S. National Academy of Sciences and National Research Council have issued several reports backing their findings on global climate change (see http://nas-sites.org/americasclimatechoices/sample-page/panel-reports/americas-climate-choices-final-report/). (See also Crate and Nuttall 2008.)

Several factors, known as *radiative forcings*, work to warm and cool the Earth. (Recap 24.1 summarizes them.) Positive forcings, including those due to greenhouse gases, tend to warm the Earth. Negative forcings, such as certain aerosols from industrial processes or volcanic eruptions, tend to cool it. If positive and negative forcings remained in balance, there would be no warming or cooling, but this is not the case today. The positive ones outweigh the negative ones, and the system is out of kilter.

The growing global demand for energy is the single greatest obstacle to slowing climate change. In

RECAP 24.1   What Heats, What Cools, the Earth?

WARMING	
Carbon dioxide (CO_2)	Has natural and human sources; levels increasing due to burning of fossil fuels.
Methane (CH_4)	Has risen due to an increase in human activities, including livestock raising, rice growing, landfill use, and the extraction, handling, and transport of natural gas.
Ozone (O_3)	Has natural sources, especially in the stratosphere, where chemicals have depleted the ozone layer; ozone also produced in the troposphere (lower part of the atmosphere) when hydrocarbons and nitrogen oxide pollutants react.
Nitrous oxide (N_2O)	Has been rising from agricultural and industrial sources.
Halocarbons	Include chlorofluorocarbons (CFCs), which remain from refrigerants in appliances made before CFC ban.
Aerosols	Some airborne particles and droplets warm the planet; black carbon particles (soot) produced when fossil fuels or vegetation are burned; generally have a warming effect by absorbing solar radiation.
COOLING	
Aerosols	Some cool the planet; sulfate (SO_4) aerosols from burning fossil fuels reflect sunlight back to space.
Volcanic eruptions	Emit gaseous SO_2, which, once in the atmosphere, forms sulfate aerosol and ash. Both reflect sunlight back to space.
Sea ice	Reflects sunlight back to space.
Tundra	Reflects sunlight back to space.
WARMING/COOLING	
Forests	Deforestation creates land areas that reflect more sunlight back to space (cooling); it also removes trees that absorb CO_2 (warming).

the United States, about 80 percent of all energy used comes from fossil fuels (petroleum, coal, and natural gas). Alternatives to fossil fuels include nuclear and hydroelectric power and such renewable energy technologies as solar, wind, and biomass generators. Worldwide, energy consumption continues to grow (24 percent between 2000 and 2008) with economic and population expansion. China in particular is rapidly increasing its use of energy, mainly from fossil fuels, and consequently its emissions (Figure 24.2). Between 2000 and 2008 per capita energy consumption more than doubled in China, while declining 7 percent in the United States. China now accounts for over 17 percent of world energy consumption, versus 9 percent in 2000. The U.S. share fell from 25 percent in 2000 to 20 percent in 2008 (*Statistical Abstract of the United States* 2012, Table 1383, p. 864).

ENVIRONMENTAL ANTHROPOLOGY

Anthropology always has been concerned with how environmental forces influence humans and how human activities affect the biosphere and the Earth itself. The 1950s–1970s witnessed the emergence of an area of study known as *cultural ecology* or **ecological anthropology** (see Haenn and Wilk 2006). That field focused on how cultural beliefs and practices helped human populations adapt to their environments, and how people used elements of their culture to maintain their ecosystems (recall the discussion of potlatching in the chapter "Making a Living").

Early ecological anthropologists showed that many indigenous groups did a reasonable job of managing their resources and preserving their ecosystems (see Menzies 2006). Such groups had traditional ways of categorizing resources, regulating their use, and preserving the environment. An **ethnoecology** is any society's set of environmental practices and perceptions—that is, its cultural model of the environment and its relation to people and society. Indigenous ethnoecologies increasingly are being challenged, as migration, media, and commerce spread people, institutions, information, and technology. In the face of national and international incentives to exploit and degrade, ethnoecological systems that once preserved local and regional environments increasingly are ineffective or irrelevant (see Dove, Sajise, and Doolittle 2011).

Anthropologists routinely witness threats to the people they study and their environments. Among such threats are commercial logging, industrial pollution (see last chapter's "Appreciating Anthropology"), and the imposition of external management systems on local ecosystems (see this chapter's "Appreciating Diversity"). Today's ecological anthropology, aka *environmental anthropology,* attempts not only to understand but also to find solutions to

The world's most populous nations, China and India, are rapidly increasing their use of energy, mainly from fossil fuels, and consequently their emissions of CO_2. Pictured here are crowds of cars and buses moving slowly during a serious Beijing traffic jam.

environmental problems. Such problems must be tackled at the national and international levels (e.g., global climate change). Even in remote places, ecosystem management now involves multiple levels. For example, among the Antankarana of northern Madagascar (Gezon 2006), several levels of authority claim the right to use and regulate natural resources and local ecosystems. Actual or would-be regulators there include local communities, traditional leaders (the regional kings or chiefs), provincial and national governments, and the WWF, the Worldwide Fund for Nature (formerly the World Wildlife Fund), an international NGO.

Local people, their landscapes, their ideas, their values, and their traditional management systems face attacks from all sides (see Hornborg, Clark, and Hermele 2011). Outsiders attempt to remake native landscapes and cultures in their own image. The aim of many agricultural development projects, for example, seems to be to make the world as much like a midwestern American agricultural state as possible. Often there is an attempt to impose mechanized farming and nuclear family ownership, even though these institutions may be inappropriate in areas far removed from the midwestern United States. Development projects usually fail when they try to replace indigenous institutions with culturally alien concepts (Kottak 1990*b*).

Global Assaults on Local Autonomy

A clash of cultures related to environmental change may occur when development threatens indigenous

ecological anthropology
Study of cultural adaptations to environments.

ethnoecology
A culture's set of environmental practices and perceptions.

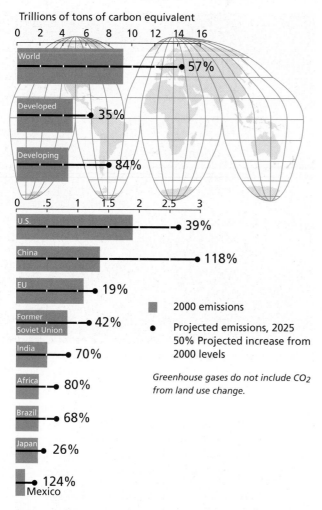

FIGURE 24.2 Projected Emissions of Greenhouse Gases, 2025.

This figure compares CO_2 emissions per nation in 2000 and projections for 2025. In 2000, the largest emitter of CO_2 was the United States, which was responsible for 25 percent of global emissions. In 2025, China and the developing world may significantly increase their CO_2 emissions relative to the United States.

SOURCE: Baumert 2005.

peoples and their environments (as we saw in last chapter's "Appreciating Anthropology"). A second clash of cultures related to environmental change may occur when external regulation aimed at conservation confronts indigenous peoples and their ethnoecologies. Like development projects, conservation schemes may ask people to change their ways in order to satisfy planners' goals rather than local goals. In places as different as Madagascar, Brazil, and the Pacific Northwest of the United States, people have been asked, told, or forced to abandon basic economic activities because to do so is good for "nature" or "the globe." "Good for the globe" doesn't play very well in Brazil, whose Amazon has been a focus of international environmentalist attention. Brazilians complain that outsiders (e.g., Europeans and North Americans) promote "global needs" and

"saving the Amazon" after having destroyed their own forests for economic growth. Well-intentioned conservation plans can be as insensitive as development schemes that promote radical changes without involving local people in planning and carrying out the policies that affect them. When people are asked to give up the basis of their livelihood, they usually resist.

Consider the case of a Tanosy man living on the edge of the Andohahela reserve of southeastern Madagascar. For years he has relied on rice fields and grazing land inside that reserve. Now external agencies are telling him to abandon that land for the sake of conservation. This man is a wealthy *ombiasa* (traditional sorcerer-healer). With four wives, a dozen children, and twenty head of cattle, he is an ambitious, hardworking, and productive peasant. With money, social support, and supernatural authority, he has mounted effective resistance against the park ranger who has been trying to get him to abandon his fields. The *ombiasa* claims he has already relinquished some of his fields, but he is waiting for compensatory land. His most effective resistance has been supernatural. The death of the ranger's young son was attributed to the *ombiasa*'s magic. After that, the ranger became less vigilant in his enforcement efforts.

The spread of environmentalism may expose radically different notions about the "rights" and value of plants and animals versus humans. In Madagascar, many intellectuals and officials complain that foreigners seem more concerned about lemurs and other endangered species than about the people of Madagascar (the Malagasy). As a geographer there remarked to me, "The next time you come to Madagascar, there'll be no more Malagasy. All the people will have starved to death, and a lemur will have to meet you at the airport." Most Malagasy perceive human poverty as a more pressing problem than animal and plant survival.

Still, who can doubt that conservation, including the preservation of biodiversity, is a worthy goal? The challenge for applied ecological anthropology is to devise culturally appropriate strategies for achieving biodiversity conservation in the face of unrelenting population growth and commercial expansion. How does one get people to support conservation measures that may, in the short run at least, diminish their access to resources? Like development plans in general, the most effective conservation strategies pay attention to the needs and wishes of the local people.

Deforestation

Deforestation is a global concern. Forest loss can lead to increased greenhouse gas (CO_2) production, which contributes to global climate change. The destruction of tropical forests also is a major factor in the loss of global biodiversity, since many species, often of limited distribution and including many primates, live in forests. Tropical forests contain at least half of Earth's species while covering just 6 percent of the planet's land surface. Yet tropical forests are disappearing rapidly.

Generations of anthropologists have studied how human economic activities (ancient and modern) affect the environment. Anthropologists know that food producers (farmers and herders) typically do more to degrade the environment than foragers do. Population increase and the need to expand farming caused deforestation in many parts of the ancient Middle East and Mesoamerica (see Hornborg and Crumley 2007). Even today, many farmers think of trees as giant weeds to be removed and replaced with productive fields.

Often, deforestation is demographically driven—caused by population pressure. For example, Madagascar's population is growing at a rate of 3 percent annually, doubling every generation. Population pressure leads to migration, including rural–urban migration. Madagascar's capital, Antananarivo, had just 100,000 people in 1967. The population stands at about 2 million today. Urban growth promotes deforestation if city dwellers rely on fuel wood from the countryside, as is true in Madagascar. As forested watersheds disappear, crop productivity declines. Madagascar is known as the "great red island," after the color of its soil. On that island, the effects of soil erosion and water runoff are visible to the naked eye. From the look of its rivers, Madagascar appears to be bleeding to death. Increasing runoff of water no longer trapped by trees causes erosion of low-lying rice fields near swollen rivers as well as siltation in irrigation canals (Kottak 2007).

Globally, other causes of deforestation include commercial logging, road building, cash cropping, and clearing and burning associated with livestock and grazing. The fact that forest loss has several causes has a policy implication: Different deforestation scenarios require different conservation strategies.

What can be done? On this question applied anthropology weighs in, spurring policy makers to think about new conservation strategies. The traditional approach has been to restrict access to forested areas designated as parks, then employ park guards and punish violators. Modern strategies are more likely to consider the needs, wishes, and abilities of the people (often impoverished) living in and near the forest. Since effective conservation depends on the cooperation of the local people, their concerns must be addressed in devising conservation strategies.

Reasons to change behavior must make sense to local people (see Sillitoe 2007). In Madagascar, the economic value of the forest for agriculture (as an antierosion mechanism and reservoir of potential irrigation water) provides a much more powerful incentive against forest degradation than do such global goals as "preserving biodiversity." Most Malagasy have no idea that lemurs and other endemic species exist only in Madagascar. Nor would such knowledge provide much of an incentive for

A scene from the "great red island" of Madagascar. On that island, the effects of deforestation, water runoff, and soil erosion are visible to the naked eye.

them to conserve the forests if doing so jeopardized their livelihoods.

To curb the global deforestation threat, we need conservation strategies that work. Laws and enforcement may help reduce commercially driven deforestation caused by burning and clear-cutting. But local people also use and abuse forested lands. A challenge for the environmentally oriented applied anthropologist is to find ways to make forest preservation attractive to local people and ensure their cooperation. Applied anthropologists must work to make "good for the globe" good for the people.

anthropology **ATLAS**

http://www.mhhe.com/anthromaps Map 1 shows annual percent of world forest loss. Deforestation is associated with a loss of biodiversity, especially in tropical forests.

INTERETHNIC CONTACT

Since at least the 1920s anthropologists have investigated the changes—on both sides—that arise from contact between industrial and nonindustrial societies. Studies of "social change" and "acculturation" are abundant. British and American ethnographers, respectively, have used these terms to describe the same process. As mentioned, *acculturation* refers to changes that result when groups come into continuous firsthand contact—changes in the cultural patterns of either or both groups (Redfield, Linton, and Herskovits 1936, p. 149).

Acculturation differs from diffusion, or cultural borrowing, which can occur without firsthand contact. For example, most North Americans who eat hot dogs ("frankfurters") have never been to Frankfurt, Germany, nor have most North American Toyota owners or sushi eaters ever visited Japan. Although *acculturation* can be applied to any case of cultural

Applied anthropology uses anthropological perspectives to identify and solve contemporary problems that affect humans. Deforestation is one such problem. Here women take part in a reforestation project in coastal Tanzania near Dar es Salaam.

westernization
The acculturative influence of Western expansion on local cultures worldwide.

cultural imperialism
Spread of one (dominant) culture at the expense of others.

contact and change, the term most often has described **westernization**—the influence of Western expansion on indigenous peoples and their cultures. Thus, local people who wear store-bought clothes, learn Indo-European languages, and otherwise adopt Western customs are called acculturated. Acculturation may be voluntary or forced, and there may be considerable resistance to the process.

Is the global spread of companies like Nike, advertized here in Beijing, China, an example of "cultural imperialism"? Why or why not?

Different degrees of destruction, domination, resistance, survival, adaptation, and modification of native cultures may follow interethnic contact. In the most destructive encounters, native and subordinate cultures face obliteration. When contact with powerful outsiders seriously threatens an indigenous culture, a "shock phase" often follows the initial encounter (Bodley 1988). Outsiders may attack or exploit the native people. Such exploitation may increase mortality, disrupt subsistence, fragment kin groups, damage social support systems, and inspire new religious movements, such as the cargo cults examined in the chapter "Religion" (Bodley 1988). During the shock phase, there may be civil repression backed by military force. Such factors may lead to the group's cultural collapse (*ethnocide*) or physical extinction (*genocide*).

Cultural Imperialism

Cultural imperialism refers to the spread or advance of one culture at the expense of others, or its imposition on other cultures, which it modifies, replaces, or destroys—usually because of differential economic or political influence. Thus, children in the French colonial empire learned French history, language, and culture from standard textbooks also used in France. Tahitians, Malagasy, Vietnamese, and Senegalese learned the French language by reciting from books about "our ancestors the Gauls."

Some commentators think that modern technology, international brands, and the mass media are erasing cultural differences, as homogeneous products reach more people worldwide. But others see a role for modern technology in allowing social groups (local cultures) to express themselves and to survive (Marcus and Fischer 1999). For example, radio, TV, digital media, and increasingly the Internet (e.g., YouTube) constantly bring local happenings to the attention of a larger public. Susan Boyle's rendition of "I Dreamed a Dream" on a British TV show soon became an Internet sensation and made her a global star. Without YouTube, appreciation of Boyle's voice might have been confined to the United Kingdom. Contemporary media play a role in stimulating and organizing local and community activities of many sorts. Think of ways in which this is done by YouTube, Facebook, and Twitter—global networks all.

In Brazil, local practices, celebrations, and performances have changed in the context of outside forces, including the mass media and tourism. In the town of Arembepe, Brazil (Kottak 2006), TV coverage stimulated increased participation in a traditional annual performance, the Chegança. This is a fishermen's danceplay that reenacts the Portuguese discovery of Brazil. Arembepeiros have traveled to the state capital to perform the Chegança before television cameras, for a TV program featuring traditional performances from many rural communities, and cameras have come to Arembepe to record it.

In several towns along the Amazon River, annual folk ceremonies now are staged more lavishly for TV and video cameras. In the Amazon town of Parantíns, for example, boatloads of tourists arriving any time of year are shown a video recording of the town's annual Bumba Meu Boi festival. This is a costumed performance mimicking bullfighting, parts of which have been shown on national TV. This pattern, in which local communities preserve, revive, and intensify the scale of traditional ceremonies to perform for the media and tourists, is expanding. To see whether I could,

I just managed to watch snippets of these annual events in Arembepe and Parantíns on YouTube!

The Brazilian mass media also have helped spread the popularity of holidays like Carnaval and Christmas (Kottak 2009). TV has aided the national spread of Carnaval beyond its traditional urban centers. Still, local reactions to the nationwide broadcasting of Carnaval and its trappings (elaborate parades, costumes, and frenzied dancing) are not simple or uniform responses to external stimuli.

Rather than direct adoption of Carnaval, local Brazilians respond in various ways. Often they don't take up Carnaval itself but modify their local festivities to fit Carnaval images. Others actively spurn Carnaval. One example is Arembepe, where Carnaval has never been important, probably because of its calendrical closeness to the main local festival, which is held in February to honor Saint Francis of Assisi. In the past, villagers couldn't afford to celebrate both occasions. Now, not only do the people of Arembepe reject Carnaval; they also are increasingly hostile to their own main festival. Arembepeiros resent the fact that the Saint Francis festival has become "an outsiders' event," because it draws thousands of tourists to Arembepe each year. The villagers think that commercial interests and outsiders have appropriated Saint Francis.

In opposition to these trends, many Arembepeiros now say they like and participate more in the traditional June festivals honoring Saint John, Saint Peter, and Saint Anthony. In the past, these were observed on a much smaller scale than was the festival honoring Saint Francis. Arembepeiros celebrate them now with a new vigor and enthusiasm, as they react to outsiders and their celebrations, real and televised. The national or the global can become that only if the local cooperates.

In San Gimignano, Italy, boys and young men don medieval costumes and beat drums in a parade through the streets during one of the town's many pageants. Increasingly, local communities perform "traditional" ceremonies for TV and tourists.

MAKING AND REMAKING CULTURE

As they experience globalization, people constantly make and remake culture as they evaluate, and assign their own meanings to, the information, images, and products they receive from outside. Those meanings reflect their cultural backgrounds and experiences.

Indigenizing Popular Culture

indigenized
Modified to fit the local culture.

As global forces enter new communities, they are **indigenized**—modified to fit the local culture. This is true of cultural domains as different as fast food, music, movies, housing styles, science, terrorism, celebrations, and political ideas and institutions (Appadurai 1990; Fiske 2011; Wilk 2006). One classic example is how the movie *Rambo* (the first one in the series) was indigenized by Native Australians. Eric Michaels (1986, 1991) found Rambo to be very popular among aborigines in the deserts of central Australia, who had manufactured their own meanings from the film. Their interpretation was very different from the one imagined by the movie's creators. The Native Australians saw Rambo as someone from the Third World battling the white officer class. This view expressed their resentment about white paternalism and existing race relations. The Native Australians also imagined that there were tribal ties and kin links between Rambo and the prisoners he was rescuing. All this made sense, based on their experience. Native Australians are disproportionately represented in Australia's jails, and their most likely savior would be someone with a personal link to them.

When products and images enter new settings, they are typically indigenized—modified to fit the local culture. Jeans Street, in Bandung, Indonesia, is a strip of stores, vendors, and restaurants catering to young people interested in Western pop culture. How is the poster of *Batman and Robin* indigenized?

A Global System of Images

All cultures express imagination—in dreams, fantasies, songs, myths, and stories. With globalization, however, more people in many more places imagine "a wider set of 'possible' lives than they ever did before. One important source of this change is the mass media. . . ." (Appadurai 1991, p. 197). The United States as a global media center has been joined by Canada, Japan, Western Europe, Brazil, Mexico, Nigeria, Egypt, India, and Hong Kong.

Like print (see Anderson 1991), the electronic mass media can diffuse the cultures of different countries within (and sometimes beyond) their own boundaries, thus enhancing national cultural identity. For example, millions of Brazilians who used to be cut off (by geographic isolation or illiteracy) from urban, national, and international events and information now participate in a larger "mediascape" (Appadurai 1991) through the Internet and especially television (Kottak 1990a, 2009). Many Americans mistakenly think that American programs, when available abroad, inevitably triumph over local products. In fact, this usually doesn't happen when there is appealing local competition.

In Brazil, for example, the most popular network (TV Globo) relies heavily on its own productions, especially *telenovelas* (nightly serial melodramas often compared to American soap operas). Globo plays each night to the world's largest and most devoted audience (perhaps 80 million viewers throughout the nation and beyond—via satellite TV). The programs that attract this horde are made by Brazilians, for Brazilians. Thus, it is not the spread of North American culture through globalization, but a new form of pan-Brazilian national culture, that Globo is propagating. Illustrating once again the importance of cultural fit, we may generalize that programming that is culturally alien won't do very well anywhere if a quality local choice is available. Confirmation comes from many countries, including Japan, Mexico, India, and Nigeria, in all of which national productions are very popular.

The mass media also play a role in maintaining ethnic and national identities among people who lead transnational lives. Arabic-speaking Muslims, including migrants in several countries, follow the TV network Al Jazeera, based in Qatar, which helps reinforce ethnic and religious identities. As groups move, they can stay linked to each other and to their homeland through global media. Diasporas (people who have spread out from an original, ancestral homeland) have enlarged the markets for media, communication, brands, and travel services targeted at specific ethnic, national, or religious groups who now live in various parts of the world.

A Global Culture of Consumption

Another key transnational force is finance. Multinational corporations and other business interests look beyond national boundaries for places in which to invest and from which to draw profits. As Arjun Appadurai (1991, p. 194) puts it, "money, commodities, and persons unendingly chase each other around the world." Residents of many Latin American communities now depend on outside cash, remitted from international labor migration. Also, the economy of the United States is increasingly influenced by foreign investment, especially from Britain, Canada, Germany, the Netherlands, and Japan (Rouse 1991). The American economy also has increased its dependence on foreign labor—through both the immigration of laborers and the export of jobs.

Business, technology, and the media have increased the craving for commodities and images throughout the world (Appadurai 2001; Gottdiener 2000). This has forced nation-states to open to a global culture of consumption. Almost everyone today participates in this culture. Few people have never seen a T-shirt advertising a Western product. American and English rock stars' recordings blast through the streets of Rio de Janeiro, while taxi drivers from Toronto to Madagascar play Brazilian music tapes. Peasants and tribal people participate in the modern world system not only because they have been hooked on cash, but also because their products and images are appropriated by world capitalism (Root 1996). They are commercialized by others (like the Quileute nation in the *Twilight* series of books and movies). Furthermore, indigenous peoples also market their own images and products, through outlets like Cultural Survival (see Mathews 2000).

PEOPLE IN MOTION

The linkages created through globalization have both enlarged and erased old boundaries and distinctions. Arjun Appadurai (1990, p. 1) characterizes today's world as a "translocal" "interactive system" that is "strikingly new." Whether as refugees, migrants, tourists, pilgrims, proselytizers, laborers, businesspeople, development workers, employees of nongovernmental organizations, politicians, terrorists, soldiers, sports figures, or media-borne images, people travel more than ever.

In previous chapters, we saw that foragers and herders are typically seminomadic or nomadic. Today, however, the scale of human movement has expanded dramatically. So important is transnational migration that many Mexican villagers find "their most important kin and friends are as likely to be living hundreds or thousands of miles away as immediately around them" (Rouse 1991). Most migrants maintain their ties with their native land (phoning, Skyping, texting, e-mailing, visiting, sending money, watching home videos or "ethnic TV"). In a sense, they live multilocally—in different places at once. Dominicans in New York City, for example, have been characterized as living "between two islands": Manhattan and the Dominican Republic (Grasmuck and Pessar 1991). Many Dominicans—like migrants from other countries—migrate to the United

Business and the media spur global demand for certain products and brands. The top photo was taken in Beijing, China; the bottom one, in Yangon, Myanmar. What brands and products stand out in the photos?

States temporarily, seeking cash to transform their lifestyles when they return to the Caribbean.

Decisions about whether to risk migration, perhaps illegal, across national boundaries are based on social reasons, such as whether kin already live in the host nation, and economic reasons, in response to ebbs and flows in the global economy. For example, many recent migrants to the United States have chosen to return home because of the recent economic downturn here, as well as more restrictive immigration laws and enforcement policies.

With so many people "in motion," the unit of anthropological study expands from the local community to the **diaspora**—the offspring of an area who have spread to many lands. Anthropologists increasingly follow descendants of the villages we have studied as they move from rural to urban areas and across national boundaries. For an annual meeting of the American Anthropological Association held in Chicago, the anthropologist Robert Kemper

diaspora
Offspring of an area who have spread to many lands.

With so many people on the move, the unit of anthropological study has expanded from the local community to the diaspora. This refers to the offspring of an area (e.g., South Asia) who have spread to many lands, such as this Indian sweets shop owner on Ealing Road in London, UK.

postmodernity
Time of questioning of established canons, identities, and standards.

organized a session of presentations about long-term ethnographic fieldwork. Kemper's own long-time research focus has been the Mexican village of Tzintzuntzan, which, with his mentor George Foster, he has studied for decades. However, their database now includes not just Tzintzuntzan but its descendants all over the world. Given the Tzintzuntzan

Mary Simat, with the Massai Women for Education and Economic Development from Kenya, testifies at the Indigenous Peoples' Global Summit on Climate Change in Anchorage, Alaska, in April 2009. The five-day United Nations–affiliated conference attracted about four hundred people from eighty nations.

diaspora, Kemper was even able to use some of his time in Chicago to visit people from Tzintzuntzan who had established a colony there. In today's world, as people move, they take their traditions and their anthropologists along with them.

Postmodernity describes our time and situation: today's world in flux, these people on the move who have learned to manage multiple identities depending on place and context. In its most general sense, **postmodern** refers to the blurring and breakdown of established canons (rules or standards), categories, distinctions, and boundaries. The word is taken from **postmodernism**—a style and movement in architecture that succeeded modernism, beginning in the 1970s. Postmodern architecture rejected the rules, geometric order, and austerity of modernism. Modernist buildings were expected to have a clear and functional design. Postmodern design is "messier" and more playful. It draws on a diversity of styles from different times and places—including popular, ethnic, and non-Western cultures. Postmodernism extends "value" well beyond classic, elite, and Western cultural forms. *Postmodern* is now used to describe comparable developments in music, literature, and visual art. From this origin, *postmodernity* describes a world in which traditional standards, contrasts, groups, boundaries, and identities are opening up, reaching out, and breaking down.

New kinds of political and ethnic units have emerged along with globalization. In some cases, cultures and ethnic groups have banded together in larger associations. There is a growing pan-Native American identity (Nagel 1996) and an international pantribal movement as well. Thus, in June 1992, the World Conference of Indigenous Peoples met in Rio de Janeiro concurrently with UNCED (the United Nations Conference on the Environment and Development). Along with diplomats, journalists, and environmentalists came 300 representatives of the tribal diversity that survives under globalization—from Lapland to Mali (Brooke 1992; see also Maybury-Lewis 2002; Maybury-Lewis, Macdonald, and Maybury-Lewis 2009). The meeting itself was a global forum, sponsored by the United Nations, perhaps the closest thing Earth has to a planetary council.

INDIGENOUS PEOPLES

The term and concept *indigenous people* gained legitimacy within international law with the creation in 1982 of the United Nations Working Group on Indigenous Populations (WGIP). This group, which meets annually, has representation from all six continents. The draft of the Declaration of Indigenous Rights, produced by the WGIP in 1989, was accepted by the UN for discussion in 1993. Convention 169, an ILO (International Labor Organization) document that supports cultural diversity and indigenous empowerment, was approved in 1989. Such declarations and documents, along with the work of the WGIP, have influenced governments, NGOs, and international agencies, including the World Bank, to express greater concern for, and to adopt policies designed to benefit, indigenous peoples. Social movements worldwide have adopted the term *indigenous people* as a self-identifying and political label based on past oppression but now legitimizing a search for social, cultural, and political rights (de la Peña 2005; Brower and Johnston 2007).

In Spanish-speaking Latin America, social scientists and politicians favor the term *indígena* (indigenous person) over *indio* (Indian)—the colonial term that the Spanish and Portuguese conquerors used to refer to the native inhabitants of the Americas. With the national independence movements that ended Latin American colonialism, the situation of indigenous peoples did not necessarily improve. For the white and *mestizo* (mixed) elites of the new nations, *indios* and their lifestyle were perceived as alien to (European) civilization. But Indians also were seen as redeemable by intellectuals, who argued for social policies to improve their welfare (de la Peña 2005).

Until the mid- to late 1980s, Latin American public discourse and state policies emphasized assimilation and discouraged indigenous identification and mobilization. Indians were associated with a romanticized past but marginalized in the present, except for museums, tourism, and folkloric events. Argentina's Indians were all but invisible. Indigenous Bolivians and Peruvians were encouraged to self-identify as *campesinos* (peasants). The past 30 years have seen a dramatic shift. The emphasis has shifted from biological and cultural assimilation—*mestizaje*—to identities that value difference, especially as indigenous peoples. In Ecuador groups seen previously as Quichua-speaking peasants are classified now as indigenous communities with assigned territories. Other Andean "peasants" have experienced reindigenization as well. Brazil has recognized thirty new indigenous communities in the northeast, a region previously seen as having lost its indigenous population. In Guatemala, Nicaragua, Brazil, Colombia, Mexico, Paraguay, Ecuador, Argentina, Bolivia, Peru, and Venezuela, constitutional reforms have recognized those nations as multicultural (Jackson and Warren 2005). Several national constitutions now recognize the rights of indigenous peoples to cultural distinctiveness, sustainable development, political representation, and limited self-government. In Colombia, for example, indigenous communities have been confirmed as rightful owners of large territories. Their leaders and councils have the same benefits as any local government. Two seats in the Colombian senate are reserved for Indian representatives (de la Peña 2005).

The indigenous rights movement exists in the context of globalization, including transnational movements focusing on human rights, women's rights, and environmentalism. Transnational organizations have helped indigenous peoples to influence legislation. Since the 1980s there has been a

living anthropology **VIDEOS**

Cultural Survival Through History, www.mhhe.com/kottak

In this clip, a genial host tours the village museum built by the local community of San José Magote in Oaxaca, Mexico. The narrator highlights artifacts and exhibits commemorating the site's 3,500-year history, including pottery from an ancient chiefly center, a scale model of a Spanish hacienda, and a portrayal of villagers' successful efforts to return land seized by the Spaniards to community ownership. The clip shows one path to cultural survival. The idea that they are the rightful heirs to the cultural traditions of ancient Mexico is an important part of the identity of the local Zapotec people. How are genealogies used to portray local history? How does the clip link those genealogies to the present? Based on the clip, what roles have women played in Zapotec history?

postmodern
Marked by the breakdown of established canons, categories, distinctions, and boundaries.

postmodernism
Movement after modernism in architecture; now much wider.

general shift in Latin America from authoritarian to democratic rule. Still, inequality and discrimination persist, and there has been resistance to indigenous mobilization, including assassinations of leaders and their supporters. Guatemala, Peru, and Colombia have witnessed severe repression. There have been thousands of indigenous deaths, refugees, and internally displaced persons (Jackson and Warren 2005).

Ceuppens and Geschiere (2005) explore a recent upsurge, in several world areas, of the notion of *autochthony* (being native to, or formed in, the place where found), with an implicit call for excluding strangers. The terms "autochthony" and "indigenous" both go back to classical Greek history, with

La Paz, Bolivia, May 23, 2005: Bolivians claiming an Indian (indigenous) identity rally for indigenous rights and the nationalization of that country's gas resources. In December 2005, Bolivians elected as their president Evo Morales, the candidate of the Indigenous Movement toward Socialism party. The party made further gains in 2006 parliamentary elections.

similar implications. "Autochthony" refers to self and soil. "Indigenous" literally means born inside, with the connotation in classical Greek of being born "inside the house." Both notions stress the need to safeguard ancestral lands (patrimony) from strangers, along with the rights of first-comers to special rights and protection versus later immigrants—legal or illegal (Ceuppens and Geschiere 2005; Hornborg, Clark, and Hermele 2011).

During the 1990s, autochthony became an issue in many parts of Africa, inspiring violent efforts to exclude (European and Asian) "strangers." Simultaneously, autochthony became a key notion in debates about immigration and multiculturalism in Europe. European majority groups have claimed the label *autochthon*. This term highlights the prominence that the exclusion of strangers has assumed in day-to-day politics worldwide (Ceuppens and Geschiere 2005). One familiar example is the United States, as represented in debates over illegal immigration.

Identity in Indigenous Politics

Essentialism describes the process of viewing an identity as established, real, and frozen, to hide the historical processes and politics within which that identity developed. One example would be the ethnic labels "Hutu" and "Tutsi" in Rwanda, as discussed in the chapter "The World System and Colonialism." Those labels actually had nothing to do with ethnicity when they were created. Nation-states have used essentializing strategies (e.g., the Tutsi-Hutu distinction) to perpetuate hierarchies and to justify violence against categories seen as less than fully human.

Identities, emphatically, are not fixed. We saw in the chapter "Ethnicity and Race" that identities are fluid and multiple. People seize on particular, sometimes competing, self-labels and identities. Some Peruvian groups, for instance, self-identify as *mestizos* but still see themselves as indigenous. Identity is a fluid, dynamic process, and there are multiple ways of being indigenous. Neither speaking an indigenous language nor wearing "native" clothing is required. Identities are asserted at particular times and places by particular individuals and groups, and after various kinds of negotiations. Indigenous identity coexists with, and must be managed in the context of, other identity components, including religion, race, and gender. Identities always must be seen as (1) potentially plural, (2) emerging through a specific process, and (3) ways of being someone or something in particular times and places (Jackson and Warren 2005).

No social movement exists apart from the nation that includes it. Nor is any contemporary nation isolated from the world system, globalization, and transnational organization.

THE CONTINUANCE OF DIVERSITY

In our globalizing world, anthropology has a crucial role to play, by promoting a more people-centered vision of social change, one that respects the value of human biological and cultural diversity. The existence of anthropology is itself a tribute to the continuing need to understand similarities and differences among human beings throughout the world. Anthropology teaches us that the adaptive responses of humans can be more flexible than those of other species because our main adaptive means are sociocultural. However, in the face of globalization, the cultural institutions of the past always influence subsequent adaptation, producing continued diversity in the actions and reactions of different groups. With our knowledge and our awareness of our professional responsibilities, let us work to keep anthropology, the study of humankind, the most humanistic of all the sciences.

essentialism
Viewing identities that have developed historically as innate and unchanging.

acing the COURSE

summary

1. Risk perception tends to be greatest in places and among groups that are most directly influenced by the media and by environmentalism, rather than among those who are most endangered. Fueling global warming are human population growth and use of fossil fuels, which produce greenhouse gases. The atmospheric concentration of those gases has increased since the Industrial Revolution, and

especially since 1978. Climate change encompasses global warming along with changing sea levels, precipitation, storms, and ecosystem effects.

2. Anthropology always has been concerned with how environmental forces influence humans and how human activities affect the biosphere. Many indigenous groups did a reasonable job of preserving their ecosystems. An ethnoecology is any society's set of environmental practices and perceptions—that is, its cultural model of the environment in relation to people and society. Indigenous ethnoecologies increasingly are being challenged by global forces that work to exploit and degrade—and that sometimes aim to protect—the environment. The challenge for applied ecological anthropology is to devise culturally appropriate strategies for conservation in the face of unrelenting population growth and commercial expansion.

3. Deforestation is a major factor in the loss of global biodiversity. The global scenarios of deforestation include demographic pressure (from births or immigration) on subsistence economies, commercial logging, road building, cash cropping, fuel wood needs associated with urban expansion, and clearing and burning associated with livestock and grazing. Different deforestation scenarios require different conservation strategies. Applied anthropologists must work to make "good for the globe" good for the people.

4. Different degrees of destruction, domination, resistance, survival, and modification of native cultures may follow interethnic contact. This may lead to a tribe's cultural collapse (ethnocide) or its physical extinction (genocide). *Cultural imperialism* refers to the spread of one culture and its imposition on other cultures, which it modifies, replaces, or destroys—usually because of differential economic or political influence. Some worry that modern technology, including the mass media, is destroying traditional cultures. But others see an important role for new technology in allowing local cultures to express themselves.

5. When forces from global centers enter new societies, they are *indigenized*. Like print, the electronic mass media can help diffuse a national culture within its own boundaries. The media also play a role in preserving ethnic and national identities among people who lead transnational lives. Business, technology, and the media have increased the craving for commodities and images throughout the world, creating a global culture of consumption.

6. People travel more than ever. But migrants also maintain ties with home, so they live multilocally. With so many people "in motion," the unit of anthropological study expands from the local community to the diaspora. *Postmodernity* describes this world in flux, with people on the move who manage multiple social identities depending on place and context. New kinds of political and ethnic units are emerging as others break down or disappear.

7. The term and concept *indigenous people* has gained legitimacy within international law. Governments, NGOs, and international agencies have adopted policies designed to recognize and benefit indigenous peoples. Social movements worldwide have adopted this term as a self-identifying and political label based on past oppression but now signaling a search for social, cultural, and political rights.

8. In Latin America, emphasis has shifted from biological and cultural assimilation to identities that value difference. Several national constitutions now recognize the rights of indigenous peoples. Transnational organizations have helped indigenous peoples influence national legislative agendas. Recent use of the notion of *autochthony* (being native to, or formed in, the place where found) includes a call to exclude strangers, such as recent and illegal immigrants. Identity is a fluid, dynamic process, and there are multiple ways of being indigenous. No social movement exists apart from the nation and world that include it.

key terms

anthropogenic 552
climate change 553
cultural imperialism 558
diaspora 561
ecological anthropology 555
essentialism 564
ethnoecology 555

greenhouse effect 552
indigenized 560
postmodern 562
postmodernism 562
postmodernity 562
westernization 558

test yourself

MULTIPLE CHOICE

1. Scientific measurements confirm that global warming is not due to increased solar radiation. The main reasons for climate change are anthropogenic. This means that
   a. they are caused by humans and their activities.
   b. they are indigenized.
   c. they affect the lives of humans but are caused by normal climate fluctuations.
   d. they are social constructions that politicians and scientists produce to create fear.
   e. they are a natural result of five million years of human evolution.

2. All of the following are true about the greenhouse effect *except* this fact:

   a. Without greenhouse gases—water vapor, carbon dioxide, methane, nitrous oxide, halocarbons, and ozone—life as we know it wouldn't exist.

   b. It is a natural phenomenon that keeps the Earth's surface warm.

   c. Greenhouse gases can remain in the atmosphere for decades, centuries, or longer.

   d. Because it is a natural phenomenon, any increase in the production of greenhouse gases will be solved by nature's own balancing mechanisms.

   e. Today, the atmospheric concentration of greenhouse gases has reached its highest level in 400,000 years.

3. Environmental anthropology

   a. is concerned with ethnoecology—that is, an indigenous society's set of environmental practices and perceptions and how they deviate from the truth that scientists have discovered about nature.

   b. traditionally focused on how indigenous ecologies are incorporated into the environmental policies of nation-states.

   c. attempts not only to understand but also to find solutions to environmental problems.

   d. supports agricultural development projects that help educate people on how to increase mechanized farming and nuclear family ownership.

   e. emerged in the 1950s—but since the 1970s its popularity has waned because environmental problems have become too complex to study from an anthropological perspective.

4. One role for today's environmental anthropologists might be to assess the extent and nature of risk perception in various groups and to harness that awareness to combat environmental degradation. Paradoxically,

   a. risk perception may be *more* developed in groups that are *less* endangered objectively.

   b. the mass media have little to do with risk perception.

   c. risk perception has no effect on actions that can reduce threats to the environment.

   d. the rise of the Internet and cable/satellite TV has accentuated the distinction between the global, the national, and the local, making it easier for environmental anthropologists to study risk perception.

   e. risk perception translates directly into concrete actions to help reduce this source of risk.

5. Which of the following statements about environmentalism is *not* true?

   a. Brazilians complain that First World moralists preach about global needs and saving the Amazon after having destroyed their own forests for First World economic growth.

   b. It began in the Third World in response to the destruction of tropical forests.

   c. Much of the non-Western world sees Western ecological morality as yet another imperialist message.

   d. It can be an intervention philosophy.

   e. Its advocates can be as ethnocentric as are advocates of development.

6. When forces from world centers enter new societies, they are often modified to fit the local culture. Which of the following terms refers to this process?

   a. texting

   b. forced acculturation

   c. essentialization

   d. selective modification

   e. indigenization

7. Which of the following statements about television is true?

   a. Studies show that people reject its messages without much processing or reinterpretation.

   b. It is especially favored by the French because of its role in promoting and exposing the French to other cultures.

   c. It plays a role in allowing people to express themselves and in disseminating local cultures.

   d. American programs usually beat the local competition because of their superior production values and better cutural fit.

   e. It plays no "top-down" role.

8. What term does Arjun Appadurai (1990) use to describe the linkages in the modern world that have both enlarged and erased old boundaries and distinctions?

   a. postmodern

   b. ethnocentric

   c. translocal

   d. essentialized

   e. diasporic

9. What is the term for our contemporary world in flux, with people on the move, in which established groups, boundaries, identities, contrasts, and standards are reaching out and breaking down?

   a. postmodernism

   b. diaspora

   c. hegemony

   d. postmodernity

   e. globalization

10. In Latin America, the drive by indigenous peoples for self-identification has emphasized all of the following *except*
   a. their cultural distinctiveness.
   b. political reforms involving a restructuring of the state.
   c. territorial rights and access to natural resources, including control over economic development.
   d. their political mobilization.
   e. their autochthony, with an implicit call for excluding strangers from their communities.

FILL IN THE BLANK

1. Scientists prefer the term ________ to *global warming*. The former term points out that, beyond rising temperature, there have been changes in sea levels, precipitation, storms, and ecosystem effects.
2. An ________ is any society's set of environmental practices and perceptions—that is, its cultural model of the environment and its relation to people and society.
3. ________ refers to changes that result when groups come into continuous firsthand contact. ________, however, can occur without firsthand contact.
4. ________ refers to the rapid spread or advance of one culture at the expense of others, or its imposition on other cultures.
5. With so many people "in motion" in today's world, the unit of anthropological study expands from the local community to the ________—the offspring of an area who have spread to many lands.

CRITICAL THINKING

1. What does it mean to apply an anthropological perspective to contemporary global issues? Can you come up with an anthropological research question that investigates such issues? Imagine you had a year (and the money!) to carry out this project. How would you spend your time and your resources?
2. The topic of global climate change has been hotly debated during the last few years. Why is there so much debate? Are you concerned about global climate change? Do you think everyone on the planet should be equally concerned and share the responsibility of doing something about it? Why or why not?
3. Consider majority and minority rights in the context of contemporary events involving religion, ethnicity, politics, and law. Should religion be an ascribed or an achieved status? How about ethnicity? Why?
4. Do you now live, or have you ever lived, multilocally? How so?
5. What term do anthropologists use to describe the view that identities have developed historically as innate and unchanging? We know, however, that identities are not fixed; they are fluid and multiple. What does this mean? What implications does this have for understanding indigenous political movements?

Multiple Choice: 1. (A); 2. (D); 3. (C); 4. (A); 5. (B); 6. (E); 7. (C); 8. (C); 9. (D); 10. (E); **Fill in the Blank:** 1. *climate change*; 2. ethnoecology; 3. Acculturation, Diffusion; 4. Cultural imperialism; 5. diaspora

suggested additional readings

Appadurai, A., ed.
2001 *Globalization.* Durham, NC: Duke University Press. The flows that create today's world system.

Bodley, J. H.
2012 *Victims of Progress*, 6th ed. Lanham, MD: AltaMira. Social change, acculturation, and culture conflict involving indigenous peoples.

Dove, M. R., and C. Carpenter, eds.
2008 *Environmental Anthropology: A Historical Reader.* Malden, MA: Blackwell. Development of, and theory and case studies in, environmental anthropology.

Johansen, B. E.
2003 *Indigenous Peoples and Environmental Issues: An Encyclopedia.* Westport, CT: Greenwood. A compendium of knowledge about environmental issues as they affect and reflect local communities.

Maybury-Lewis, D., T. Macdonald, and B. Maybury-Lewis, eds.
2009 *Manifest Destinies and Indigenous Peoples.* Boston: Allyn & Bacon. Contemporary struggles of indigenous peoples: case studies.

Robbins, R. H.
2011 *Global Problems and the Culture of Capitalism*, 5th ed. Boston: Pearson/Allyn & Bacon. Examines issues of domination, resistance, and social and economic problems in today's world.

internet exercises

Go to our Online Learning Center website at **www.mhhe.com/kottak** for Internet exercises directly related to the content of this chapter.

GLOSSARY

Audible pronunciations for many of the following terms are provided in the electronic Glossary on the Online Learning Center at **www.mhhe.com/kottak.**

A. afarensis Early forms of *Australopithecus*, known from Hadar in Ethiopia ("Lucy") and Laetoli in Tanzania; the Hadar remains date to 3.3–3.0 m.y.a.; the Laetoli remains are older, dating to 3.8–3.6 m.y.a.; despite its many apelike features, *A. afarensis* was an upright biped.

A. africanus Gracile *Australopithecus* species (3.0?–2.0? m.y.a.), South Africa; first australopithecine ever discovered.

A. anamensis Earliest known *Australopithecus* species (4.2–3.9 m.y.a.), from Kenya.

A. boisei Late, hyperrobust *Australopithecus* species (2.6?–1.2 m.y.a.), East Africa; coexisted with early *Homo*.

absolute dating Dating techniques that establish dates in numbers or ranges of numbers; examples include the radiometric methods of ^{14}C, K/A, ^{238}U, TL, and ESR dating.

acculturation The exchange of cultural features that results when groups come into continuous firsthand contact; the cultural patterns of either or both groups may be changed, but the groups remain distinct.

Acheulean Derived from the French village of St. Acheul, where these tools were first identified; Lower Paleolithic tool tradition associated with *H. erectus*.

achieved status Social status that comes through talents, choices, actions, and accomplishments, rather than ascription.

adaptive Favored by natural selection in a particular environment.

adaptive strategy Means of making a living; productive system.

aesthetics Appreciation of the qualities perceived in works of art; the mind and emotions in relation to a sense of beauty.

A. garhi Tool-making *Australopithecus* species (2.5 m.y.a..); discovered in Ethiopia.

agency The actions of individuals, alone and in groups, that create and transform culture.

agriculture Nonindustrial systems of plant cultivation characterized by continuous and intensive use of land and labor.

allele A biochemical variant of a particular gene.

Allen's rule Rule stating that the relative size of protruding body parts (such as ears, tails, bills, fingers, toes, and limbs) tends to increase in warmer climates.

ambilineal Principle of descent that does not automatically exclude the children of either sons or daughters.

AMHs See *anatomically modern humans.*

analogies Similarities arising as a result of similar selective forces; traits produced by convergent evolution.

anatomically modern humans (AMHs) Hominins including the Cro-Magnons of Europe (31,000 B.P.) and the older fossils from Skhūl (100,000), Qafzeh (92,000), Herto, and other sites; continue through the present; also known as *H. sapiens sapiens.*

animism Belief in souls or doubles.

anthropogenic Caused by humans and their activities.

anthropoids Members of Anthropoidea, one of the two suborders of primates; monkeys, apes, and humans are anthropoids.

anthropology The study of the human species and its immediate ancestors.

anthropology and education Anthropological research in classrooms, homes, and neighborhoods, viewing students as total cultural creatures whose enculturation and attitudes toward education belong to a larger context that includes family, peers, and society.

anthropometry The measurement of human body parts and dimensions, including skeletal parts (*osteometry*).

antimodernism The rejection of the modern in favor of what is perceived as an earlier, purer, and better way of life.

applied anthropology The application of anthropological data, perspectives, theory, and methods to identify, assess, and solve contemporary social problems.

arboreal Tree-dwelling; arboreal primates include gibbons, New World monkeys, and many Old World monkeys.

archaeological anthropology The study of human behavior and cultural patterns and processes through the culture's material remains.

archaic H. sapiens Early *H. sapiens*, consisting of the Neandertals of Europe and the Middle East, the Neandertal-like hominids of Africa and Asia, and the immediate ancestors of all these hominids; lived from about 300,000 to 28,000 B.P.

Ardipithecus Earliest recognized hominin genus (5.8–4.4 m.y.a), Ethiopia; species are *kadabba* (earlier) and *ramidus* (later).

A. robustus aka *Paranthropus*; robust *Australopithecus* species (2.0?–1.0? m.y.a.), South Africa.

art An object or event that evokes an aesthetic reaction—a sense of beauty, appreciation, harmony, and/or pleasure; the quality, production, expression, or realm of what is beautiful or of more than ordinary significance; the class of objects subject to aesthetic criteria.

arts The arts include the visual arts, literature (written and oral), music, and theater arts.

ascribed status Social status (e.g., race or gender) that people have little or no choice about occupying.

assimilation The process of change that a minority group may experience when it moves to a country where another culture dominates; the minority is incorporated into the dominant culture to the point that it no longer exists as a separate cultural unit.

association An observed relationship between two or more variables.

australopithecines Varied group of Pliocene-Pleistocene hominids. The term is derived from their former classification as members of a distinct subfamily, the Australopithecinae; now they are distinguished from *Homo* only at the genus level.

569

authority The formal, socially approved use of power, e.g., by government officials.

Aztec Last independent state in the Valley of Mexico; capital was Tenochtitlan. Thrived between 1325 and the Spanish Conquest in 1520.

balanced polymorphism Two or more forms, such as alleles of the same gene, that maintain a constant frequency in a population from generation to generation.

balanced reciprocity See *generalized reciprocity*.

band Basic unit of social organization among foragers. A band includes fewer than 100 people; it often splits up seasonally.

behavioral ecology Study of the evolutionary basis of social behavior.

behavioral modernity Fully human behavior based on symbolic thought and cultural creativity.

Bergmann's rule Rule stating that the smaller of two bodies similar in shape has more surface area per unit of weight and therefore can dissipate heat more efficiently; hence, large bodies tend to be found in colder areas and small bodies in warmer ones.

bifurcate collateral kinship terminology Kinship terminology employing separate terms for M, F, MB, MZ, FB, and FZ.

bifurcate merging kinship terminology Kinship terminology in which M and MZ are called by the same term, F and FB are called by the same term, and MB and FZ are called by different terms.

big man Regional figure found among tribal horticulturalists and pastoralists. The big man occupies no office but creates his reputation through entrepreneurship and generosity to others. Neither his wealth nor his position passes to his heirs.

bilateral kinship calculation A system in which kinship ties are calculated equally through both sexes: mother and father, sister and brother, daughter and son, and so on.

biocultural Referring to the inclusion and combination (to solve a common problem) of both biological and cultural approaches—one of anthropology's hallmarks.

biological anthropology The study of human biological variation in time and space; includes evolution, genetics, growth and development, and primatology.

bipedal Upright two-legged locomotion, the key feature distinguishing early hominins from the apes.

Black English Vernacular (BEV) A rule-governed dialect of American English with roots in Southern English. BEV is spoken by African American youth and by many adults in their casual, intimate speech—sometimes called "ebonics."

blade tool The basic Upper Paleolithic tool type, hammered off a prepared core.

bone biology The study of bone as a biological tissue, including its genetics; cell structure; growth, development, and decay; and patterns of movement (*biomechanics*).

bourgeoisie One of Marx's opposed classes; owners of the means of production (factories, mines, large farms, and other sources of subsistence).

broad-spectrum revolution Period beginning around 15,000 B.P. in the Middle East and 12,000 B.P. in Europe, during which a wider range, or broader spectrum, of plant and animal life was hunted, gathered, collected, caught, and fished; revolutionary because it led to food production.

bronze An alloy of arsenic and copper or tin and copper.

call systems Systems of communication among nonhuman primates, composed of a limited number of sounds that vary in intensity and duration. Tied to environmental stimuli.

capital Wealth or resources invested in business, with the intent of producing a profit.

capitalist world economy The single world system, which emerged in the 16th century, committed to production for sale, with the object of maximizing profits rather than supplying domestic needs.

cargo cults Postcolonial, acculturative religious movements, common in Melanesia, that attempt to explain European domination and wealth and to achieve similar success magically by mimicking European behavior.

catharsis Intense emotional release.

chiefdom Form of sociopolitical organization intermediate between the tribe and the state; kin-based with differential access to resources and a permanent political structure.

chromosomes Basic genetic units, occurring in matching (homologous) pairs; lengths of DNA made up of multiple genes.

clan Unilineal descent group based on stipulated descent.

climate change Global warming plus changing sea levels, precipitation, storms, and ecosystem effects.

cline A gradual shift in gene frequencies between neighboring populations.

Clovis Stone technology based on a projectile point that was fastened to the end of a hunting spear; it flourished between 12,000 and 11,000 B.P. in North America.

collateral relative A genealogical relative who is not in ego's direct line, such as B, Z, FB, or MZ.

colonialism The political, social, economic, and cultural domination of a territory and its people by a foreign power for an extended time.

Communism Spelled with an uppercase C, a political movement and doctrine seeking to overthrow capitalism and to establish a form of communism such as that which prevailed in the Soviet Union from 1917 to 1991.

communism Spelled with a lowercase c, describes a social system in which property is owned by the community and in which people work for the common good.

communitas Intense community spirit, a feeling of great social solidarity, equality, and togetherness; characteristic of people experiencing liminality together.

complex societies Nations; large and populous, with social stratification and central governments.

configurationalism View of culture as integrated and patterned.

conflict resolution Means of settling disputes.

convergent evolution Independent operation of similar selective forces; the process by which analogies are produced.

core Dominant structural position in the world system; consists of the strongest and most powerful states with advanced systems of production.

core values Key, basic, or central values that integrate a culture and help distinguish it from others.

correlation An association between two or more variables such that when one changes (varies), the other(s) also change(s) (covaries); for example, temperature and sweating.

cosmology A system, often religious, for imagining and understanding the universe.

Cro Magnon The first fossil find (1868) of an AMH, from France's Dorlogne Valley.

cross cousins Children of a brother and a sister.

crossing over During meiosis, the process by which homologous chromosomes intertwine and exchange segments of their DNA.

cultivation continuum A continuum based on the comparative study of nonindustrial cultivating societies in which labor intensity increases and fallowing decreases.

cultural anthropology The study of human society and culture; describes, analyzes, interprets, and explains social and cultural similarities and differences.

cultural colonialism Internal domination by one group and its culture or ideology over others.

cultural consultants Subjects in ethnographic research; people the ethnographer gets to know in the field, who teach him or her about their culture.

cultural imperialism The rapid spread or advance of one culture at the expense of others, or its imposition on other cultures, which it modifies, replaces, or destroys—usually because of differential economic or political influence.

cultural relativism The position that the values and standards of cultures differ and deserve respect. Anthropology is characterized by methodological rather than moral relativism: In order to understand another culture fully, anthropologists try to understand its members' beliefs and motivations. Methodological relativism does not preclude making moral judgments or taking action.

cultural resource management (CRM) The branch of applied archaeology aimed at preserving sites threatened by dams, highways, and other projects.

cultural rights Doctrine that certain rights are vested in identifiable groups, such as religious and ethnic minorities and indigenous societies. Cultural rights include a group's ability to preserve its culture, to raise its children in the ways of its forebears, to continue its language, and not to be deprived of its economic base by the nation-state in which it is located.

cultural transmission A basic feature of language; transmission through learning.

culture Distinctly human; transmitted through learning; traditions and customs that govern behavior and beliefs.

cuneiform Early Mesopotamian writing that used a stylus (writing implement) to write wedge-shaped impressions on raw clay; from the Latin word for "wedge."

curer Specialized role acquired through a culturally appropriate process of selection, training, certification, and acquisition of a professional image; the curer is consulted by patients, who believe in his or her special powers, and receives some form of special consideration; a cultural universal.

daughter languages Languages developing out of the same parent language; for example, French and Spanish are daughter languages of Latin.

dendrochronology Or tree-ring dating: a method of absolute dating based on the study and comparison of patterns of tree-ring growth.

descent Rule assigning social identity on the basis of some aspect of one's ancestry.

descent group A permanent social unit whose members claim common ancestry; fundamental to tribal society.

development anthropology The branch of applied anthropology that focuses on social issues in—and the cultural dimension of—economic development.

diachronic (Studying societies) across time.

diaspora The offspring of an area who have spread to many lands.

differential access Unequal access to resources; basic attribute of chiefdoms and states. Superordinates have favored access to such resources, while the access of subordinates is limited by superordinates.

diffusion Borrowing of cultural traits between societies, either directly or through intermediaries.

diglossia The existence of "high" (formal) and "low" (informal, familial) dialects of a single language, such as German.

discrimination Policies and practices that harm a group and its members.

disease A scientifically identified health threat caused by a bacterium, virus, fungus, parasite, or other pathogen.

displacement A basic feature of language; the ability to speak of things and events that are not present.

domestic-public dichotomy Contrast between women's role in the home and men's role in public life, with a corresponding social devaluation of women's work and worth.

dominant Allele that masks another allele in a heterozygote.

dowry A marital exchange in which the wife's group provides substantial gifts to the husband's family.

ecological anthropology Study of cultural adaptations to environments.

economizing The rational allocation of scarce means (or resources) to alternative ends (or uses); often considered the subject matter of economics.

economy A population's system of production, distribution, and consumption of resources.

egalitarian society A type of society, most typically found among hunter-gatherers, that lacks status distinctions except those based on age, gender, and individual qualities, talents, and achievements.

ego Latin for *I*. In kinship charts, the point from which one views an egocentric genealogy.

emic The research strategy that focuses on local explanations and criteria of significance.

empire A mature, territorially large, and expansive state; empires are typically multiethnic, multilinguistic, and more militaristic, with a better-developed bureaucracy than earlier states.

enculturation The social process by which culture is learned and transmitted across the generations.

endogamy Rule or practice of marriage between people of the same social group.

essentialism The process of viewing an identity as established, real, and frozen to hide the historical processes and politics within which that identity developed.

ethnic group Group distinguished by cultural similarities (shared among members of that group) and differences (between that group and others); ethnic-group members share beliefs, customs, and norms and, often, a common language, religion, history, geography, and kinship.

ethnicity Identification with, and feeling part of, an ethnic group and exclusion from certain other groups because of this affiliation.

ethnocentrism The tendency to view one's own culture as best and to judge the behavior and beliefs of culturally different people by one's own standards.

ethnocide Destruction of cultures of certain ethnic groups.

ethnoecology Any society's set of environmental practices and perceptions; its cultural model of the environment and its relation to people and society.

ethnography Fieldwork in a particular culture.

ethnology Cross-cultural comparison; the comparative study of ethnographic data, society, and culture.

ethnomusicology The comparative study of the musics of the world and of music as an aspect of culture and society.

ethnosemantics The study of lexical (vocabulary) contrasts and classifications in various languages.

etic The research strategy that emphasizes the ethnographer's rather than the locals' explanations, categories, and criteria of significance.

evolution Belief that species arose from others through a long and gradual process of transformation, or descent with modification.

excavation Digging through the layers of deposits that make up an archaeological or fossil site.

exogamy Rule requiring people to marry outside their own group.

expressive culture The arts; people express themselves creatively in dance, music, song, painting, sculpture, pottery, cloth, storytelling, verse, prose, drama, and comedy.

extended family household Expanded household including three or more generations.

family of orientation Nuclear family in which one is born and grows up.

family of procreation Nuclear family established when one marries and has children.

fiscal Pertaining to finances and taxation.

focal vocabulary A set of words and distinctions that are particularly important to certain groups (those with particular foci of experience or activity), such as types of snow to Eskimos or skiers.

folk Of the people; originally coined for European peasants; refers to the art, music, and lore of ordinary people, as contrasted with the "high" art or "classic" art of the European elites.

food production Cultivation of plants and domestication (stockbreeding) of animals; first developed 10,000 to 12,000 years ago.

fossils Remains (e.g., bones), traces, or impressions (e.g., footprints) of ancient life.

functional explanation Explanation that establishes a correlation or interrelationship between social customs. When customs are functionally interrelated, if one changes, the others also change.

functionalism Approach focusing on the role (function) of sociocultural practices in social systems.

fundamentalism Describes antimodernist movements in various religions. Fundamentalists assert an identity separate from the larger religious group from which they arose; they advocate strict fidelity to the "true" religious principles on which the larger religion was founded.

gender roles The tasks and activities that a culture assigns to each sex.

gender stereotypes Oversimplified but strongly held ideas about the characteristics of males and females.

gender stratification Unequal distribution of rewards (socially valued resources, power, prestige, and personal freedom) between men and women, reflecting their different positions in a social hierarchy.

gene Area in a chromosome pair that determines, wholly or partially, a particular biological trait, such as whether one's blood type is A, B, or O.

genealogical method Procedures by which ethnographers discover and record connections of kinship, descent, and marriage, using diagrams and symbols.

gene flow Exchange of genetic material between populations of the same species through direct or indirect interbreeding.

gene pool All the alleles, genes, chromosomes, and genotypes within a breeding population—the "pool" of genetic material available.

general anthropology The field of anthropology as a whole, consisting of cultural, archaeological, biological, and linguistic anthropology.

generality Culture pattern or trait that exists in some but not all societies.

generalized reciprocity Principle that characterizes exchanges between closely related individuals. As social distance increases, reciprocity becomes balanced and finally negative.

generational kinship terminology Kinship terminology with only two terms for the parental generation, one designating M, MZ, and FZ and the other designating F, FB, and MB.

genetic evolution Change in gene frequency within a breeding population.

genitor Biological father of a child.

genocide Deliberate elimination of a group through mass murder.

genotype An organism's hereditary makeup.

gibbons The smallest apes, natives of Asia; arboreal.

glacials The four or five major advances of continental ice sheets in northern Europe and North America.

globalization The accelerating interdependence of nations in a world system linked economically and through mass media and modern transportation systems.

gracile Opposite of robust; "gracile" indicates that members of *A. africanus* were a bit smaller and slighter, less robust, than members of *A. robustus*.

greenhouse effect Warming from trapped atmospheric gases.

Halafian An early (7500–6500 B.P.) and widespread pottery style, first found in northern Syria; refers to a delicate ceramic style and to the period when the first chiefdoms emerged.

haplogroup A lineage marked by one or more specific genetic mutations.

health care systems Beliefs, customs, and specialists concerned with ensuring health and preventing and curing illness; a cultural universal.

hegemony As used by Antonio Gramsci, a stratified social order in which subordinates comply with domination by internalizing its values and accepting its "naturalness."

Herto Very early (160,000–154,000 B.P.) AMHs found in Ethiopia.

heterozygous Having dissimilar alleles of a given gene.

Hilly Flanks Woodland zone that flanks the Tigris and Euphrates rivers to the north; zone of wild wheat and barley and of sedentism (settled, nonmigratory life) preceding food production.

historical linguistics Subdivision of linguistics that studies languages over time.

historical particularism Idea (Boas) that histories are not comparable; diverse paths can lead to the same cultural result.

holistic Interested in the whole of the human condition: past, present, and future; biology, society, language, and culture.

hominid A member of the taxonomic family that includes humans and the African apes and their immediate ancestors.

hominin A member of the human lineage after its split from ancestral chimps; the term *hominin* is used to describe all the human species that ever have existed, including the extinct ones, and excluding chimps and gorillas.

hominoids Members of the superfamily including humans and all the apes.

Homo habilis Term coined by L. S. B. and Mary Leakey; immediate ancestor of *H. erectus*; lived from about 2.4 to 1.4 m.y.a.

homologies Traits that organisms have jointly inherited from a common ancestor.

homozygous Possessing identical alleles of a particular gene.

honorific A term, such as "Mr." or "Lord," used with people, often by being added to their names, to "honor" them.

horticulture Nonindustrial system of plant cultivation in which plots lie fallow for varying lengths of time.

human rights Doctrine that invokes a realm of justice and morality beyond and superior to particular countries, cultures, and religions. Human rights, usually seen as vested in individuals, would include the right to speak freely, to hold religious beliefs without persecution, and not to be murdered, injured, enslaved, or imprisoned without charge.

hypodescent Rule that automatically places the children of a union or mating between members of different socioeconomic groups in the less privileged group.

hypothesis A suggested but as yet unverified explanation.

illness A condition of poor health perceived or felt by an individual.

imperialism A policy of extending the rule of a nation or empire over foreign nations or of taking and holding foreign colonies.

incest Sexual relations with a close relative.

increased equity A reduction in absolute poverty and a fairer (more even) distribution of wealth.

independent assortment Mendel's law of; chromosomes are inherited independently of one another.

independent invention Development of the same cultural trait or pattern in separate cultures as a result of comparable needs, circumstances, and solutions.

indigenized Modified to fit the local culture.

Industrial Revolution The historic transformation (in Europe, after 1750) of "traditional" into "modern" societies through industrialization of the economy.

informed consent Agreement to take part in research, after the people being studied have been told about that research's purpose, nature, procedures, and potential impact on them.

interglacials Extended warm periods between such major glacials as Riss and Würm.

international culture Cultural traditions that extend beyond national boundaries.

interpretive anthropology (Geertz) The study of a culture as a system of meaning.

intersex Pertaining to a group of conditions reflecting a discrepancy between the external genitals (penis, vagina, etc.) and the internal genitals (testes, ovaries, etc.).

intervention philosophy Guiding principle of colonialism, conquest, missionization, or development; an ideological justification for outsiders to guide native peoples in specific directions.

interview schedule Ethnographic tool for structuring a formal interview. A prepared form (usually printed or mimeographed) that guides interviews with households or individuals being compared systematically. Contrasts with a *questionnaire* because the researcher has personal contact with the local people and records their answers.

IPR Intellectual property rights, consisting of each society's cultural base—its core beliefs and principles. IPR are claimed as a group right—a cultural right—allowing indigenous groups to control who may know and use their collective knowledge and its applications.

key cultural consultant Person who is an expert on a particular aspect of local life.

kinesics The study of communication through body movements, stances, gestures, and facial expressions.

kinship calculation The system by which people in a particular society reckon kin relationships.

language Human beings' primary means of communication; may be spoken or written; features productivity and displacement and is culturally transmitted.

law A legal code, including trial and enforcement; characteristic of state-organized societies.

leveling mechanism A custom or social action that operates to reduce differences in wealth and thus to bring standouts in line with community norms.

levirate Custom by which a widow marries the brother of her deceased husband.

lexicon Vocabulary; a dictionary containing all the morphemes in a language and their meanings.

life history Gathered by an ethnographer, an account of the life of a key consultant or narrator; provides a personal cultural portrait of existence or change in a culture.

liminality The critically important marginal or in-between phase of a rite of passage.

lineage Unilineal descent group based on demonstrated descent.

lineal kinship terminology Parental generation kin terminology with four terms: one for M, one for F, one for FB and MB, and one for MZ and FZ.

lineal relative Any of ego's ancestors or descendants (e.g., parents, grandparents, children, grandchildren) on the direct line of descent that leads to and from ego.

linguistic anthropology The descriptive, comparative, and historical study of language and of linguistic similarities and differences in time, space, and society.

lobola A substantial marital gift from the husband and his kin to the wife and her kin.

longitudinal research Long-term study of a community, region, society, culture, or other unit, usually based on repeated visits.

magic Use of supernatural techniques to accomplish specific aims.

maize Corn; domesticated in highland Mexico.

mana Sacred impersonal force in Melanesian and Polynesian religions.

manioc Cassava; a tuber domesticated in the South American lowlands.

market principle Profit-oriented principle of exchange that dominates in states, particularly industrial states. Goods and services are bought and sold, and values are determined by supply and demand.

mater Socially recognized mother of a child.

matrilineal descent Unilineal descent rule in which people join the mother's group automatically at birth and stay members throughout life.

means (or factors) of production Land, labor, technology, and capital—major productive resources.

medical anthropology Unites biological and cultural anthropologists in the study of disease, health problems, health care systems, and theories about illness in different cultures and ethnic groups.

meiosis Special process by which sex cells are produced; four cells are produced from one, each with half the genetic material of the original cell.

melanin Substance manufactured in specialized cells in the lower layers of the epidermis (outer skin layer); melanin cells in dark skin produce more melanin than do those in light skin.

Mesoamerica Middle America, including Mexico, Guatemala, and Belize.

Mesolithic Middle Stone Age, whose characteristic tool type was the microlith; broad-spectrum economy.

Mesopotamia The area between the Tigris and Euphrates rivers in what is now southern Iraq and southwestern Iran; location of the first cities and states.

metallurgy Knowledge of the properties of metals, including their extraction and processing and the manufacture of metal tools.

mitosis Ordinary cell division; DNA molecules copy themselves, creating two identical cells out of one.

mode of production Way of organizing production—a set of social relations through which labor is deployed to wrest energy from nature by means of tools, skills, and knowledge.

molecular anthropology Genetic analysis, involving comparison of DNA sequences, to determine evolutionary links and distances among species and among ancient and modern populations.

monotheism Worship of an eternal, omniscient, omnipotent, and omnipresent supreme being.

morphology The study of form; used in linguistics (the study of morphemes and word construction) and for form in general—for example, biomorphology relates to physical form.

Mousterian Middle Paleolithic toolmaking tradition associated with Neandertals.

multiculturalism The view of cultural diversity in a country as something good and desirable; a multicultural society socializes individuals not only into the dominant (national) culture but also into an ethnic culture.

multivariate Involving multiple factors, causes, or variables.

mutation Change in the DNA molecules of which genes and chromosomes are built.

m.y.a. Million years ago.

nation Once a synonym for "ethnic group," designating a single culture sharing a language, religion, history, territory, ancestry, and kinship; now usually a synonym for state or *nation-state*.

national culture Cultural experiences, beliefs, learned behavior patterns, and values shared by citizens of the same nation.

nationalities Ethnic groups that once had, or wish to have or regain, autonomous political status (their own country).

nation-state An autonomous political entity; a country like the United States or Canada.

Natufians Widespread Middle Eastern culture, dated to between 12,500 and 10,500 B.P.; subsisted on intensive wild cereal collecting and gazelle hunting and had year-round villages.

natural selection The process by which the forms most fit to survive and reproduce in a given environment do so in greater numbers than others in the same population; more than survival of the fittest, natural selection is differential reproductive success.

Neandertals *H. sapiens neanderthalensis,* representing an archaic *H. sapiens* subspecies that lived in Europe and the Middle East between 130,000 and 28,000 B.P.

negative reciprocity See *generalized reciprocity.*

neoliberalism Revival of Adam Smith's classic economic liberalism, the idea that governments should not regulate private enterprise and that free-market forces should rule; a currently dominant intervention philosophy.

Neolithic New Stone Age, coined to describe techniques of grinding and polishing stone tools; the first cultural period in a region in which the first signs of domestication are present.

neolocality Postmarital residence pattern in which a couple establishes a new place of residence rather than living with or near either set of parents.

nomadism (pastoral) Movement throughout the year by the whole pastoral group (men, women, and children) with their animals; more generally, nomadism is movement throughout the year in pursuit of strategic resources.

norms Cultural standards or guidelines that enable individuals to distinguish between appropriate and inappropriate behavior in a given society.

office Permanent political position.

Oldowan Earliest (2.5 to 1.2 m.y.a.) stone tools; sharp flakes struck from cores (choppers).

opposable thumb A thumb that can touch all the other fingers.

overinnovation Characteristic of projects that require major changes in natives' daily lives, especially ones that interfere with customary subsistence pursuits.

paleoanthropology Study of hominid and human life through the fossil record.

Paleolithic Old Stone Age (from Greek roots meaning "old" and "stone"); divided into Lower (early), Middle, and Upper (late).

paleontology Study of ancient life through the fossil record.

paleopathology Study of disease and injury in skeletons from archaeological sites.

palynology Study of ancient plants through pollen samples from archaeological or fossil sites in order to determine a site's environment at the time of occupation.

pantribal sodality A nonkin-based group that exists throughout a tribe, spanning several villages.

parallel cousins Children of two brothers or two sisters.

particularity Distinctive or unique culture trait, pattern, or integration.

pastoralists People who use a food-producing strategy of adaptation based on care of herds of domesticated animals.

pastoral nomadism See *nomadism (pastoral).*

pater Socially recognized father of a child; not necessarily the genitor.

patriarchy Political system ruled by men in which women have inferior social and political status, including basic human rights.

patrilineal descent Unilineal descent rule in which people join the father's group automatically at birth and stay members throughout life.

patrilineal-patrilocal complex An interrelated constellation of patrilineality, patrilocality, warfare, and male supremacy.

peasant Small-scale agriculturalist living in a state with rent fund obligations.

periphery Weakest structural position in the world system.

phenotype An organism's evident traits, its "manifest biology"—anatomy and physiology.

phenotypical adaptation Adaptive biological changes that occur during the individual's lifetime, made possible by biological plasticity.

phoneme Significant sound contrast in a language that serves to distinguish meaning, as in minimal pairs.

phonemics The study of the sound contrasts (phonemes) of a particular language.

phonetics The study of speech sounds in general; what people actually say in various languages.

phonology The study of sounds used in speech.

physical anthropology See *biological anthropology.*

Pleistocene Epoch of *Homo*'s appearance and evolution; began 1.8 million years ago; divided into Lower, Middle, and Upper.

plural marriage Any marriage with more than two spouses, aka polygamy.

plural society A society that combines ethnic contrasts and economic interdependence of the ethnic groups.

political economy The web of interrelated economic and power relations in society.

polyandry Variety of plural marriage in which a woman has more than one husband.

polygyny Variety of plural marriage in which a man has more than one wife.

polytheism Belief in several deities who control aspects of nature.

population genetics Field that studies causes of genetic variation, maintenance, and change in breeding populations.

postcolonial Referring to interactions between European nations and the societies they colonized (mainly after 1800); more generally, "postcolonial" may be used to signify a position against imperialism and Eurocentrism.

postmodern In its most general sense, describes the blurring and breakdown of established canons (rules, standards), categories, distinctions, and boundaries.

postmodernism A style and movement in architecture that succeeded modernism. Compared with modernism, postmodernism is less geometric, less functional, less austere, more playful, and more willing to include elements from diverse times and cultures; postmodern now describes comparable developments in music, literature, visual art, and anthropology.

postmodernity Condition of a world in flux, with people on the move, in which established groups, boundaries, identities, contrasts, and standards are reaching out and breaking down.

potlatch Competitive feast among Indians on the North Pacific Coast of North America.

power The ability to exercise one's will over others—to do what one wants; the basis of political status.

prejudice Devaluing (looking down on) a group because of its assumed behavior, values, capabilities, attitudes, or other attributes.

prestige Esteem, respect, or approval for acts, deeds, or qualities considered exemplary.

primary states States that arise on their own (through competition among chiefdoms), not through contact with other state societies.

primatology The study of fossil and living apes, monkeys, and prosimians, including their behavior and social life.

productivity A basic feature of language; the ability to use the rules of one's language to create new expressions comprehensible to other speakers.

prosimians The primate suborder that includes lemurs, lorises, and tarsiers.

protolanguage Language ancestral to several daughter languages.

punctuated equilibrium Evolutionary theory that long periods of stasis (stability), during which species change little, are interrupted (punctuated) by evolutionary leaps.

questionnaire Form (usually printed) used by sociologists to obtain comparable information from respondents. Often mailed to and filled in by research subjects rather than by the researcher.

race An ethnic group assumed to have a biological basis.

racial classification The attempt to assign humans to discrete categories (purportedly) based on common ancestry.

racism Discrimination against an ethnic group assumed to have a biological basis.

random genetic drift Change in gene frequency that results not from natural selection but from chance; most evident in small populations.

random sample A sample in which all members of the population have an equal statistical chance of being included.

ranked society A type of society with hereditary inequality but not social stratification; individuals are ranked in terms of their genealogical closeness to the chief, but there is a continuum of status, with many individuals and kin groups ranked about equally.

recessive Genetic trait masked by a dominant trait.

reciprocity One of the three principles of exchange; governs exchange between social equals; major exchange mode in band and tribal societies.

reciprocity continuum A continuum running from generalized (closely related/deferred return) to negative (strangers/immediate return) reciprocity.

redistribution Major exchange mode of chiefdoms, many archaic states, and some states with managed economies.

refugees People who have been forced (involuntary refugees) or who have chosen (voluntary refugees) to flee a country, to escape persecution or war.

relative dating Dating technique, for example, stratigraphy, that establishes a time frame in relation to other strata or materials, rather than absolute dates in numbers.

religion Belief and ritual concerned with supernatural beings, powers, and forces.

remote sensing Use of aerial photos and satellite images to locate sites on the ground.

revitalization movements Movements that occur in times of change, in which religious leaders emerge and undertake to alter or revitalize a society.

rickets Nutritional disease caused by a shortage of vitamin D; interferes with the absorption of calcium and causes softening and deformation of the bones.

rites of passage Culturally defined activities associated with the transition from one place or stage of life to another.

ritual Behavior that is formal, stylized, repetitive, and stereotyped, performed earnestly as a social act; rituals are held at set times and places and have liturgical orders.

robust Large, strong, sturdy; said of skull, skeleton, muscle, and teeth; opposite of gracile.

sample A smaller study group chosen to represent a larger population.

Sapir-Whorf hypothesis Theory that different languages produce different ways of thinking.

science A systematic field of study or body of knowledge that aims, through experiment, observation, and deduction, to produce reliable explanations of phenomena, with reference to the material and physical world.

scientific medicine As distinguished from Western medicine, a health care system based on scientific knowledge and procedures, encompassing such fields as pathology, microbiology, biochemistry, surgery, diagnostic technology, and applications.

sedentism Settled (sedentary) life; preceded food production in the Old World and followed it in the New World.

semantics A language's meaning system.

semiperiphery Structural position in the world system intermediate between core and periphery.

settlement hierarchy A ranked series of communities differing in size, function, and type of building; a three-level settlement hierarchy indicates state organization.

sexual dimorphism Marked differences in male and female biology besides the contrasts in breasts and genitals.

sexual orientation A person's habitual sexual attraction to, and activities with, persons of the opposite sex, heterosexuality; the same sex, homosexuality; or both sexes, bisexuality.

sexual selection Based on differential success in mating, the process in which certain traits of one sex (e.g., color in male birds) are selected because of advantages they confer in winning mates.

shaman A part-time religious practitioner who mediates between ordinary people and supernatural beings and forces.

smelting The high-temperature process by which pure metal is produced from an ore.

social control Those fields of the social system (beliefs, practices, and institutions) that are most actively involved in the maintenance of norms and the regulation of conflict.

sociolinguistics Investigates relationships between social and linguistic variations.

sororate Custom by which a widower marries the sister of his deceased wife.

speciation Formation of new species; occurs when subgroups of the same species are separated for a sufficient length of time.

species Population whose members can interbreed to produce offspring that can live and reproduce.

state Sociopolitical organization based on central government and socioeconomic stratification—a division of society into classes.

state (nation-state) Complex sociopolitical system that administers a territory and populace with substantial contrasts in occupation, wealth, prestige, and power. An independent, centrally organized political unit; a government. A form of social and political organization with a formal, central government and a division of society into classes.

status Any position that determines where someone fits in society; may be ascribed or achieved.

stereotypes Fixed ideas—often unfavorable—about what the members of a group are like.

stratification Characteristic of a system with socioeconomic strata—groups that contrast in regard to social status and access to strategic resources. Each stratum includes people of both sexes and all ages.

stratified Class-structured; stratified societies have marked differences in wealth, prestige, and power between social classes.

stratigraphy Science that examines the ways in which earth sediments are deposited in demarcated layers known as *strata* (singular, *stratum*).

style shifts Variations in speech in different contexts.

subcultures Different cultural traditions associated with subgroups in the same complex society.

subgroups Languages within a taxonomy of related languages that are most closely related.

subordinate The lower, or underprivileged, group in a stratified system.

superordinate The upper, or privileged, group in a stratified system.

superorganic (Kroeber) The special domain of culture, beyond the organic and inorganic realms.

survey research Characteristic research procedure among social scientists other than anthropologists. Studies society through sampling, statistical analysis, and impersonal data collection.

symbol Something, verbal or nonverbal, that arbitrarily and by convention stands for something else, with which it has no necessary or natural connection.

symbolic anthropology The study of society through sampling, statistical analysis, and impersonal data collection.

synchronic (Studying societies) at one time.

syncretisms Cultural mixes, including religious blends, that emerge from acculturation—the exchange of cultural features when cultures come into continuous firsthand contact.

syntax The arrangement and order of words in phrases and sentences.

systematic survey Information gathered on patterns of settlement over a large area; provides a regional perspective on the archaeological record.

taboo Set apart as sacred and off-limits to ordinary people; prohibition backed by supernatural sanctions.

taphonomy The study of the processes that affect the remains of dead animals, such as their scattering by carnivores and scavengers, their distortion by various forces, and their possible fossilization.

taxonomy Classification scheme; assignment to categories (*taxa*; singular, *taxon*).

teosinte Or teocentli, a wild grass; apparent ancestor of maize.

Teotihuacan A.D. 100 to 700; first state in the Valley of Mexico and earliest major Mesoamerican empire.

terrestrial Ground-dwelling; baboons, macaques, and humans are terrestrial primates; gorillas spend most of their time on the ground.

text Any cultural product that can be "read"—that is, processed, interpreted, and assigned meaning by anyone (any "reader") exposed to it.

theory A set of ideas formulated (by reasoning from known facts) to explain something. The main value of a theory is to promote new understanding. A theory suggests patterns, connections, and relationships that may be confirmed by new research.

Thomson's nose rule Rule stating that the average nose tends to be longer in areas with lower mean annual temperatures; based on the geographic distribution of nose length among human populations.

totem An animal, plant, or geographic feature associated with a specific social group, to which that totem is sacred or symbolically important.

transgender A category of varied individuals whose gender identity contradicts their biological sex at birth and the gender identity that society assigned to them in infancy.

transhumance One of two variants of pastoralism; part of the population moves seasonally with the herds while the other part remains in home villages.

tribe Form of sociopolitical organization usually based on horticulture or pastoralism. Socioeconomic stratification and centralized rule are absent in tribes, and there is no means of enforcing political decisions.

tropics Geographic belt extending about 23 degrees north and south of the equator, between the Tropic of Cancer (north) and the Tropic of Capricorn (south).

underdifferentiation Planning fallacy of viewing less developed countries as an undifferentiated group; ignoring cultural diversity and adopting a uniform approach (often ethnocentric) for very different types of project beneficiaries.

uniformitarianism Belief that explanations for past events should be sought in ordinary forces that continue to work today.

unilineal descent Matrilineal or patrilineal descent.

unilinear evolutionism Idea (19th century) of a single line or path of cultural development—a series of stages through which all societies must evolve.

universal Something that exists in every culture.

Upper Paleolithic Blade-toolmaking traditions associated with early *H. sapiens sapiens*; named from their location in upper, or more recent, layers of sedimentary deposits.

urban anthropology Anthropological study of cities and urban life.

variables Attributes (e.g., sex, age, height, weight) that differ from one person or case to the next.

village head A local leader in a tribal society who has limited authority, leads by example and persuasion, and must be generous.

wealth All a person's material assets, including income, land, and other types of property; the basis of economic status.

westernization The acculturative influence of Western expansion on native cultures.

working class, or proletariat Those who must sell their labor to survive; the antithesis of the bourgeoisie in Marx's class analysis.

world-system theory Idea that a discernible social system, based on wealth and power differentials, transcends individual countries.

Zapotec state First Mesoamerican state, in the Valley of Oaxaca.

BIBLIOGRAPHY

Abelmann, N., and J. Lie.
  1995. *Blue Dreams: Korean Americans and the Los Angeles Riots.* Cambridge, MA: Harvard University Press.

Abraham, N., S. Howell, and A. Shryock, eds.
  2011 *Arab Detroit 9/11: Life in the Terror Decade.* Detroit: Wayne University Press.

Adams, R. M.
  1981 *Heartland of Cities.* Chicago: Aldine. 2008 An Interdisciplinary Overview of a Mesopotamian City and its Hinterlands, *Cuneiform Digital Library Journal,* http://cdli.ucla.edu/pubs/cdlj/2008/cdlj2008_001.

Adepegba, C. O.
  1991 The Yoruba Concept of Art and Its Significance in the Holistic View of Art as Applied to African Art. *African Notes* 15: 1–6.

Adherents.com
  2002 Major Religions of the World Ranked by Number of Adherents. http://www.adherents.com/Religions_By_Adherents.html.

Ahmed, A. S.
  2004 *Postmodernism and Islam: Predicament and Promise,* rev. ed. New York: Routledge.
  2007 *Journey into Islam: The Crisis of Globalization.* Washington: Brookings Institution Press.
  2008 *Islam Today: A Short Introduction to the Muslim World.* New York: I. B. Tauris.

Aiello, L., and M. Collard
  2001 Our Newest Oldest Ancestor? *Nature* 410: 526–527.

Akazawa, T.
  1980 *The Japanese Paleolithic: A Techno-Typological Study.* Tokyo: Rippo Shobo.

Akazawa, T., and C. M. Aikens, eds.
  1986 *Prehistoric Hunter-Gatherers in Japan: New Research Methods.* Tokyo: University of Tokyo Press.

Allegretto, S. A.
  2011 The State of Working America's Wealth, Briefing Paper no. 292, Economic Policy Institute, March 23. http://www.epi.org/page/-/BriefingPaper292.pdf

Amadiume, I.
  1987 *Male Daughters, Female Husbands.* Atlantic Highlands, NJ: Zed.
  1997 *Reinventing Africa: Matriarchy, Religion, and Culture.* New York: Zed.

American Anthropological Association,
  Anthropology News. Published nine times annually by the American Anthropological Association, Arlington, VA.

Anderson, B.
  1991 *Imagined Communities: Reflections on the Origin and Spread of Nationalism,* rev. ed. London: Verso.
  2006 *Imagined Communities: Reflections on the Origin and Spread of Nationalism,* rev. ed. New York: Verso.

Anderson, R. L.
  1989 *Art in Small Scale Societies.* Upper Saddle River, NJ: Prentice Hall.
  1996 *Magic, Science, and Health: The Aims and Achievements of Medical Anthropology.* Fort Worth: Harcourt Brace.
  2004 *Calliope's Sisters: A Comparative Study of Philosophy of Art,* 2nd ed. Upper Saddle River, NJ: Prentice Hall.

Anderson-Levitt, K. M., ed.
  2012 *Anthropologies of Education: A Global Guide to Ethnographic Studies of Learning and Schooling.* New York: Berghahn Books.

Anemone, R. L.
  2011 *Race and Human Diversity: A Biocultural Approach.* Upper Saddle River, NJ: Prentice Hall/Pearson.

Angier, N.
  1998. When Nature Discovers the Same Design Over and Over, Lookalike Creatures Spark Evolutionary Debate. *New York Times,* December 15, pp. D1, D6.

  2002 Why We're So Nice: We're Wired to Cooperate. *New York Times,* July 23. http://www.nytimes.com/2002/07/23/health/psychology/23COOP.html.

Annenberg/CPB Exhibits
  2000 "Collapse, Why Do Civilizations Fall?" http://www.learner.org/exhibits/collapse/.

Antoun, R. T.
  2001 *Understanding Fundamentalism: Christian, Islamic, and Jewish Movements.* Walnut Creek, CA: AltaMira.
  2008 *Understanding Fundamentalism: Christian, Islamic, and Jewish Movements.* 2nd ed. Lanham, MD: AltaMira.

Aoki, M. Y., and M. B. Dardess, eds.
  1981 *As the Japanese See It: Past and Present.* Honolulu: University Press of Hawaii.

Appadurai, A.
  1990 Disjuncture and Difference in the Global Cultural Economy. *Public Culture* 2(2): 1–24.
  1991 Global Ethnoscapes: Notes and Queries for a Transnational Anthropology. In *Recapturing Anthropology: Working in the Present,* ed. R. G. Fox, pp. 191–210. Santa Fe: School of American Research Advanced Seminar Series.

Appadurai, A., ed.
  2001 *Globalization.* Durham, NC: Duke University Press.

Appiah, K. A.
  1990 Racisms. In *Anatomy of Racism,* ed. David Theo Goldberg, pp. 3–17. Minneapolis: University of Minnesota Press.

Arens, W.
  1981 Professional Football: An American Symbol and Ritual. In *The American Dimension: Cultural Myths and Social Realities,* 2nd ed., ed. W. Arens and S. P. Montague, pp. 1–10. Sherman Oaks, CA: Alfred.

Arensberg, C.
  1987 Theoretical Contributions of Industrial and Development Studies. In *Applied Anthropology in America,* ed. E. M. Eddy and W. L. Partridge. New York: Columbia University Press.

Arrighi, G.
  2010 *The Long Twentieth Century: Money, Power, and the Origins of Our Times,* new and updated ed. New York: Verso.

Asad, T.
  2008 (orig. 1983) The Construction of Religion as an Anthropological Category. In *A Reader in the Anthropology of Religion,* M. Lambek, ed, pp. 110-226. Malden, MA:Blackwood.

Asfaw, B., T. White, and O. Lovejoy
  1999 *Australopithecus garhi:* A New Species of Early Hominid from Ethiopia. *Science* 284: 629.

Ashcroft, B., G. Griffiths, and H. Tiffin
  1989 *The Empire Writes Back: Theory and Practice in Post-Colonial Literatures.* New York: Routledge.

Askew, K. M., and R. R. Wilk, eds.
  2002 *The Anthropology of Media: A Reader.* Malden, MA: Oxford, Blackwell.

Avert.org
  2010 Worldwide HIV and AIDS Statistics. http://www.avert.org/worldstats.htm

Baer, H. A., M. Singer, and I. Susser
  2003 *Medical Anthropology and the World System.* Westport, CT: Praeger.

Bailey, E. J.
  2000 *Medical Anthropology and African American Health.* Westport, CT: Bergin and Garvey.

Bailey, R. C.
  1990 *The Behavioral Ecology of Efe Pygmy Men in the Ituri Forest, Zaire.* Ann Arbor: Anthropological Papers, Museum of Anthropology, University of Michigan, no. 86.

Bailey, R. C., G. Head, M. Jenike, B. Owen, R. Rechtman, and E. Zechenter
  1989 Hunting and Gathering in Tropical Rain Forests: Is It Possible? *American Anthropologist* 91: 59–82.

Barfield, T.
  2010   *Afghanistan: A Cultural and Political History.* Princeton, NJ: Princeton University Press.

Barlett, P. F., ed.
  1980   *Agricultural Decision Making: Anthropological Contribution to Rural Development.* New York: Academic Press.

Barnaby, F., ed.
  1984   *Future War: Armed Conflict in the Next Decade.* London: M. Joseph.

Barnard, A.
  1979   Kalahari Settlement Patterns. In *Social and Ecological Systems,* ed. P. Burnham and R. Ellen, pp. 131–144. New York: Academic Press.

Barnard, A., ed.
  2004   *Hunter-Gatherers in History, Archaeology and Anthropology.* New York: Oxford University Press.

Barnes, E.
  2005   *Diseases and Human Evolution.* Albuquerque: University of New Mexico Press.

Baro, M., and T. F. Deubel
  2006   Persistent Hunger: Perspectives on Vulnerability, Famine, and Food Security in Sub-Saharan Africa. *Annual Review of Anthropology* 35: 521–538.

Baron, D. E.
  1986   *Grammar and Gender.* New Haven, CT: Yale University Press.
  2009   *A Better Pencil: Readers, Writers, and the Digital Revolution.* New York: Oxford University Press.

Barringer, F.
  1992   New Census Data Show More Children Living in Poverty. *New York Times,* May 29, pp. A1, A12–A13.

Barth, F.
  1968   (orig. 1958) Ecologic Relations of Ethnic Groups in Swat, North Pakistan. In *Man in Adaptation: The Cultural Present,* ed. Yehudi Cohen, pp. 324–331. Chicago: Aldine.
  1969   *Ethnic Groups and Boundaries: The Social Organization of Cultural Difference.* London: Allen and Unwin.

Bartlett, B.
  2010   America's Foreign Owned National Debt. *Forbes,* March 12. http://www.forbes.com/2010/03/11/treasury-securities-national-debt-chinatrade-opinions-columnists-bruce-Bartlett_print.html

Barton, C. M. et al.
  2011   Modeling Human Ecodynamics and Biocultural Interactions in the Late Pleistocene of Western Eurasia. *Human Ecology.* DOI 10.1007/s10745-011-9433-8.

Bar-Yosef, O.
  1987   Pleistocene Connections between Africa and Southwest Asia: An Archaeological Perspective. *African Archaeological Review* 5: 29–38.

Beckerman, S., and P. Valentine
  2002   *Cultures of Multiple Fathers: The Theory and Practice of Partible Paternity in Lowland South America.* Gainesville: University of Florida Press.

Beeman, W.
  1986   *Language, Status, and Power in Iran.* Bloomington: Indiana University Press.

Bell, W.
  1981   Neocolonialism. In *Encyclopedia of Sociology,* p. 193. Guilford, CT: DPG Publishing.

Bellah, R. N.
  1978   Religious Evolution. In *Reader in Comparative Religion: An Anthropological Approach,* 4th ed., ed. W. A. Lessa and E. Z. Vogt, pp. 36–50. New York: Harper & Row.

Bellwood, P. S.
  2005   *The First Farmers: Origins of Agricultural Societies.* Malden, MA: Blackwell.

Benazzi, S., et al.
  2011   Early Dispersal of Modern Humans in Europe and Implications for Neanderthal Behaviour. *Nature* 479: 525–528, November 24. doi:10.1038/nature10617.

Benedict, R.
  1940   *Race, Science and Politics.* New York: Modern Age Books.
  1946   *The Chrysanthemum and the Sword.* Boston: Houghton Mifflin.
  1959   (orig. 1934) *Patterns of Culture.* New York: New American Library.

Bennett, J. W.
  1969   *Northern Plainsmen: Adaptive Strategy and Agrarian Life.* Chicago: Aldine.

Berger, P.
  2010   Pentecostalism—Protestant Ethic or Cargo Cult? Peter Berger's blog, July 29. http://blogs.the-american-interest.com/berger/2010/07/29/pentecostalism-%E2%80%93-protestant-ethic-or-cargo-cult/

Berkeleyan
  1999   Berkeley Researchers Head Team That Discovers New Species of Human Ancestor: Earliest Evidence of Meat-Eating, Early Beings Has Been Unearthed in Ethiopia. April 28–May 4, pp. 27, 32. http://www. berkeley.edu/news/berkeleyan/1999/0428/species.html.

Berlin, B. D., E. Breedlove, and P. H. Raven
  1974   *Principles of Tzeltal Plant Classification: An Introduction to the Botanical Ethnography of a Mayan-Speaking People of Highland Chiapas.* New York: Academic Press.

Berlin, B. D., and P. Kay
  1991   *Basic Color Terms: Their Universality and Evolution,* 2nd ed. Berkeley: University of California Press.
  1999   *Basic Color Terms: Their Universality and Evolution.* Stanford, CA: Center for the Study of Language and Information.

Bernard, H. R.
  1994   *Research Methods in Cultural Anthropology,* 2nd ed. Thousand Oaks, CA: Sage.
  2006   *Research Methods in Anthropology: Qualitative and Quantitative Methods,* 4th ed. Walnut Creek, CA: AltaMira.
  2011   *Research Methods in Anthropology: Qualitative and Quantitative Methods,* 5th ed. Lanham, MD: AltaMira.

Bernard, H. R., ed.
  1998   *Handbook of Methods in Cultural Anthropology.* Walnut Creek, CA: AltaMira.

Beriss, D.
  2004   *Black Skins, French Voices: Caribbean Ethnicity and Activism in Urban France.* Boulder, CO: Westview.

Bettelheim, B.
  1975   *The Uses of Enchantment: The Meaning and Importance of Fairy Tales.* New York: Vintage.

Bicker, A., P. Sillitoe, and J. Pottier, eds.
  2004   *Investigating Local Knowledge: New Directions, New Approaches.* Burlington, VT: Ashgate.

Bilefsky, D.
  2006   Polygamy Fosters Culture Clashes (and Regrets) in Turkey. *New York Times,* July 10.

Binford, L. R.
  1968   Post-Pleistocene Adaptations. In *New Perspectives in Archeology,* ed. S. R. Binford and L. R. Binford, pp. 313–341. Chicago: Aldine.
  1981   *Bones: Ancient Men and Modern Myths.* New York: Academic Press.

Binford, L. R., and S. R. Binford
  1979   Stone Tools and Human Behavior. In *Human Ancestors, Readings from Scientific American,* ed. G. L. Isaac and R. E. F. Leakey, pp. 92–101. San Francisco: W. H. Freeman.

Bird-David, N.
  1992   Beyond "The Original Affluent Society": A Culturalist Reformulation. *Current Anthropology* 33(1): 25–47.

Bjuremalm, H.
  1997   Rättvisa kan skipas i Rwanda: Folkmordet 1994 går att förklara och analysera på samma sätt som förintelsen av judarna. *Dagens Nyheter* [06-03-1997, p. B3].

Blackwood, E.
  2000   *Webs of Power: Women, Kin, and Community in a Sumatran Village.* Lanham, MD: Rowman and Littlefield.
  2010   *Falling into the Lesbi World: Desire and Difference in Indonesia.* Honolulu: University of Hawaii Press.

Blackwood, E., and S. Wieringa, eds.
  1999   *Female Desires: Same-Sex Relations and Transgender Practices across Cultures.* New York: Columbia University Press.

Blanton, R. E.
    1999   *Ancient Oaxaca: The Monte Alban State.* New York: Cambridge University Press.

Blau, S., and D. Ubelaker, eds.
    2008.   *Handbook of Forensic Anthropology and Archaeology.* Walnut Creek, CA: Left Coast Press.

Bloch, M., ed.
    1975   *Political Language and Oratory in Traditional Societies.* London: Academic.

Blommaert, J.
    2010   *Sociolinguistics of Globalization.* New York: Cambridge University Press.

Blum, H. F.
    1961   Does the Melanin Pigment of Human Skin Have Adaptive Value? *Quarterly Review of Biology* 36: 50–63.

Boas, F.
    1966   (orig. 1940) *Race, Language, and Culture.* New York: Free Press.

Boaz, N. T.
    1997   *Eco Homo: How the Human Being Emerged from the Cataclysmic History of the Earth.* New York: Basic Books.
    1999   *Essentials of Biological Anthropology.* Upper Saddle River, NJ: Prentice Hall.

Boaz, N. T., and R. L. Ciochon
    2004   Headstrong Hominids. *Natural History* 113(1): 28–34.

Bocquet-Appel, J.-P., and O. Bar-Yosef
    2008   *The Neolithic Demographic Transition and its Consequences.* New York: Springer.

Bodley, J. H.
    2003   *The Power of Scale: A Global History Approach.* Armonk, NY: M. E. Sharpe.
    2008   *Victims of Progress,* 5th ed. Lanham, MD: AltaMira.
    2012   *Anthropology and Contemporary Human Problems,* 6th ed. Lanham, MD: AltaMira.

Bodley, J. H., ed.
    1988   *Tribal Peoples and Development Issues: A Global Overview.* Mountain View, CA: Mayfield.

Bogaard, A.
    2004   *Neolithic Farming in Central Europe: An Archaeobotanical Study of Crop Husbandry Practices.* New York: Routledge.

Bogin, B.
    2001   *The Growth of Humanity.* New York: Wiley-Liss.

Bolton, R.
    1981   Susto, Hostility, and Hypoglycemia. *Ethnology* 20(4): 227–258.

Bonnichsen, R., and A. L. Schneider
    2000   *Battle of the Bones.* New York Academy of Sciences, *The Sciences,* July/August. http://www.friendsofpast.org/forum/battle.html.

Bono
    2011   A Decade of Progress on AIDS. *New York Times,* November 30, p. 39. http://www.nytimes.com/2011/12/01/opinion/a-decade-of-progress-on-aids.html?scp=1&sq=bono%20world%20aids%20day&st=cse

Bonvillain, N.
    2007   *Women and Men: Cultural Constructs of Gender,* 4th ed. Upper Saddle River, NJ: Prentice Hall.
    2012   *Language, Culture, and Communication: The Meaning of Messages,* 7th ed. Boston: Pearson Prentice Hall.

Bourdieu, P.
    1977   *Outline of a Theory of Practice.* Translated by Richard Nice. Cambridge, UK: Cambridge University Press.
    1982   *Ce Que Parler Veut Dire.* Paris: Fayard.
    1984   *Distinction: A Social Critique of the Judgment of Taste.* Translated by R. Nice. Cambridge, MA: Harvard University Press.

Bourque, S. C., and K. B. Warren
    1987   Technology, Gender and Development. *Daedalus* 116(4): 173–197.

Bowen, J. R.
    2008   *Religion in Practice: An Approach to Anthropology of Religion,* 4th ed. Boston: Pearson/Allyn and Bacon.

Bowie, F.
    2006   *The Anthropology of Religion: An Introduction.* Malden, MA: Blackwell.

Bowler, J. M., H. Johnston, J. M. Olley, J. R. Prescott, R. G. Roberts, W. Shawcross, and N. A. Spooner.
    2003   New Ages for Human Occupation and Climatic Change at Lake Mungo, Australia. *Nature* 421: 837–840.

Brace, C. L.
    1995   *The Stages of Human Evolution,* 5th ed. Englewood Cliffs, NJ: Prentice Hall.
    2005   *"Race" is a Four-Letter Word: The Genesis of the Concept.* New York: Oxford University Press.

Brace, C. L., and F. B. Livingstone
    1971   On Creeping Jensenism. In *Race and Intelligence,* ed. C. L. Brace, G. R. Gamble, and J. T. Bond, pp. 64–75. Anthropological Studies, no. 8. Washington, DC: American Anthropological Association.

Bradley, B. J., D. M. Doran-Sheehy, D. Lukas, C. Boesch, and L. Vigilant
    2004   Dispersed Male Networks in Western Gorillas. *Current Biology* 14: 510–513.

Braidwood, R. J.
    1975   *Prehistoric Men,* 8th ed. Glenview, IL: Scott Foresman.

Braudel, F.
    1981   *Civilization and Capitalism, 15th–18th Century.* Volume I: *The Structure of Everyday Life: The Limits.* Translated by S. Reynolds. New York: Harper & Row.
    1982   *Civilization and Capitalism, 15th–18th Century.* Volume II: *The Wheels of Commerce.* New York: HarperCollins.
    1992   *Civilization and Capitalism, 15th–18th Century.* Volume III: *The Perspective of the World.* Berkeley: University of California Press.

Bremen, J. V., and A. Shimizu, eds.
    1999   *Anthropology and Colonialism in Asia and Oceania.* London: Curzon.

Brenneis, D.
    1988   Language and Disputing. *Annual Review of Anthropology* 17: 221–237.

Brettell, C. B., and C. F. Sargent, eds.
    2009   *Gender in Cross-Cultural Perspective,* 5th ed. Upper Saddle River, NJ: Pearson/Prentice Hall.

Briggs, C. L.
    2005   Communicability, Racial Discourse, and Disease. *Annual Review of Anthropology* 34: 269–291.

Brooke, J.
    1992   Rio's New Day in Sun Leaves Laplander Limp. *New York Times,* June 1, p. A7.

Brookings Institution,
    2010.   *State of Metropolitan America: On the Front Lines of Demographic Transition.* The Brookings Institution Metropolitan Policy Program. http://www.brookings.edu/~/media/Files/Programs/Metro/state_of_metro_america/metro_america_report1.pdf.

Brower, B., and B. R. Johnston
    2007   *Disappearing Peoples? Indigenous Groups and Ethnic Minorities in South and Central Asia.* Walnut Creek, CA: Left Coast Press.

Brown, A.
    2001   Communism. *International Encyclopedia of the Social & Behavioral Sciences,* pp. 2323–2326. New York: Elsevier.

Brown, D.
    1991   *Human Universals.* New York: McGraw-Hill.

Brown, M. F.
    2003   *Who Owns Native Culture?* Cambridge, MA: Harvard University Press.

Brown, P. J., and R. L. Barrett
    2010   *Understanding and Applying Medical Anthropology,* 2nd ed. New York: McGraw-Hill.

Brownstein, R.
    2010   The Gray and the Brown: The Generational Mismatch. *National Journal,* July 24. http://www.nationaljournal.com/njmagazines/cs_20100724_3946php.

Bryant, V. M.
    1999   Review of Piperno, D. R., and D. M. Pearsall, *The Origins of Agriculture in the Lowland Neotropics* (1998), *North American Archaeologist* (26): 245–246.
    2003   Invisible Clues to New World Domestication. *Science* February 14, 299 (5609): 1029–1030.

2007a Artifact: Maize Pollen. *Archaeology* 60(4). www. archaeology.org/0707/etc/artifact.html.

2007b Little Things Mean a Lot: The Search for Starch Grains at Archaeological Sites. *Mammoth Trumpet* 22(4): 3–4, 16.

Burbank, V. K.

1988 *Aboriginal Adolescence: Maidenhood in an Australian Community.* New Brunswick: Rutgers University Press.

Burger, J., M. Kirchner, B. Bramanti, W. Haak, and M. G. Thomas

2007 Absence of the Lactase-Persistence Associated Allele in Early Neolithic Europeans. *Proceedings of the National Academy of Sciences* 104(10): 3736–3741.

Burley, D. V., and W. R. Dickinson

2001 Origin and Significance of a Founding Settlement in Polynesia. *Proceedings of the National Academy of Sciences* 98: 11829–11831.

Burling, R.

1970 *Man's Many Voices: Language in Its Cultural Context.* New York: Harcourt Brace Jovanovich.

Buroway, M.

2000 Introduction. *Global Ethnography: Forces, Connections, and Imaginations in a Postmodern World.* Berkeley: University of California Press.

Buroway, M. et al.

2000 *Global Ethnography: Forces, Connections, and Imaginations in a Postmodern World.* Berkeley: University of California Press.

Butler, R.

2005 World's Largest Cities: [Ranked by City Population]. http://www.mongabay.com/cities_pop_01.htm.

Buvinic, M.

1995 The Feminization of Poverty? Research and Policy Needs. In *Reducing Poverty through Labour Market Policies.* Geneva: International Institute for Labour Studies.

Cachel, S.

2006 *Primate and Human Evolution.* New York: Cambridge University Press.

Callaway, E.

2011 Ancient DNA Reveals Secrets of Human History. *Nature* 476, 136–137.

Campbell, B. G., J. D. Loy, and K. Cruz-Uribe, eds.

2006 *Humankind Emerging*, 9th ed. Boston: Pearson Allyn & Bacon.

Campbell, C. J., ed.

2011 *Primates in Perspective*, 2nd ed. New York: Oxford University Press.

Cann, R. L., M. Stoneking, and A. C. Wilson

1987 Mitochondrial DNA and Human Evolution. *Nature* 325: 31–36.

Carey, B.

2007 Washoe, a Chimp of Many Words Dies at 42. *New York Times,* November 1. http:// www.nytimes.com.

Carlson, T. J. S., and L. Maffi, eds.

2004 *Ethnobotany and Conservation of Biocultural Diversity. Advances in Economic Botany,* v. 15. Bronx, NY: New York Botanical Garden Press.

Carneiro, R. L.

1956 Slash-and-Burn Agriculture: A Closer Look at Its Implications for Settlement Patterns. In *Men and Cultures,* Selected Papers of the Fifth International Congress of Anthropological and Ethnological Sciences, pp. 229–234. Philadelphia: University of Pennsylvania Press.

1968 (orig. 1961) Slash-and-Burn Cultivation among the Kuikuru and Its Implications for Cultural Development in the Amazon Basin. In *Man in Adaptation: The Cultural Present,* ed. Y. A. Cohen, pp. 131–145. Chicago: Aldine.

1970 A Theory of the Origin of the State. *Science* 69: 733–738.

1990 Chiefdom-Level Warfare as Exemplified in Fiji and the Cauca Valley. In *The Anthropology of War,* ed. J. Haas, pp. 190–211. Cambridge, UK: Cambridge University Press.

1991 The Nature of the Chiefdom as Revealed by Evidence from the Cauca Valley of Colombia. In *Profiles in Cultural Evolution,* ed. A. T. Rambo and K. Gillogly, *Anthropological Papers* 85, pp. 167–190. Ann Arbor: University of Michigan Museum of Anthropology.

Carsten, J.

2004 *After Kinship.* New York: Cambridge University Press.

Carter, J.

1988 Freed from Keepers and Cages, Chimps Come of Age on Baboon Island. *Smithsonian,* June, pp. 36–48.

Castells, M.

2001 Information Technology and Global Capitalism. In *On the Edge. Living with Global Capitalism,* W. Hutton and A. Giddens, eds. London: Vintage.

Cavalli-Sforza, L. L., and W. F. Bodmer

1999 *The Genetics of Human Populations.* Mineola, NY: Dover.

Cernea, M. M., ed.

1991 *Putting People First: Sociological Variables in Rural Development,* 2nd ed. New York: Oxford University Press (published for the World Bank).

Ceuppens, B., and P. Geschiere

2005 Autochthony: Local or Global? New Modes in the Struggle over Citizenship and Belonging in Africa and Europe. *Annual Review of Anthropology* 34: 385–407.

Chagnon, N. A.

1997 *Yanomamö,* 5th ed. Fort Worth: Harcourt Brace.

Chambers, E.

1987 Applied Anthropology in the Post-Vietnam Era: Anticipations and Ironies. *Annual Review of Anthropology* 16: 309–337.

Champion, T., and C. Gamble, eds.

1984 *Prehistoric Europe.* New York: Academic Press.

Chang, K. C.

1977 *The Archaeology of Ancient China.* New Haven, CT: Yale University Press.

Chapais, B.

2008 *Primeval Kinship: How Pair Bonding Gave Birth to Human Society.* Cambridge, MA: Harvard University Press.

Chatterjee, P.

2004 *The Politics of the Governed: Reflections on Popular Politics in Most of the World.* New York: Columbia University Press.

Chazan, M.

2011 *World Prehistory and Archaeology*, 2nd ed. Upper Saddle River, NJ: Prentice Hall.

Cheney, D. L., and R. M. Seyfarth

1990 In the Minds of Monkeys: What Do They Know and How Do They Know It? *Natural History,* September, pp. 38–46.

Chibnik, M.

2011 *Anthropology, Economics, and Choice.* Austin: University of Texas Press.

Childe, V. G.

1950 The Urban Revolution, *Town Planning Review* 21: 3–17.

1951 *Man Makes Himself.* New York: New American Library.

Chiseri-Strater, E., and B. S. Sunstein

2012 *Fieldworking: Reading and Writing Research,* 4th ed. Upper Saddle River, NJ: Prentice Hall.

Choi, C. Q.

2011 Savanna, Not Forest, Was Human Ancestors' Proving Ground. *Live Science,* August 3. http://www.livescience. com/15377-savannas-human-ancestors-evolution.html

Chomsky, N.

1955 *Syntactic Structures.* The Hague: Mouton.

Ciochon, R. L.

1983 Hominoid Cladistics and the Ancestry of Modern Apes and Humans. In *New Interpretations of Ape and Human Ancestry,* ed. R. L. Ciochon and R. S. Corruccini, pp. 783–843. New York: Plenum Press.

Ciochon, R. L., J. Olsen, and J. James

1990 *Other Origins: The Search for the Giant Ape in Human Prehistory.* New York: Bantam Books.

Clark, G.

2010 *African Market Women: Seven Life Stories from Ghana.* Indianapolis: Indiana University Press.

Coates, J.

1986 *Women, Men, and Language.* London: Longman.

Coburn, N.

2011 *Bazaar Politics: Power and Pottery in an Afghan Market Town.* Stanford, CA: Stanford University Press.

Cody, D.
1998   British Empire. http://www.victorianweb.org/.

Cohen, M. N., and G. J. Armelagos, eds. 1984 *Paleopathology at the Origins of Agriculture.* New York: Academic Press.

Cohen, P.
2008   The Pentagon Enlists Social Scientists to Study Security Issues. *New York Times,* June 18.

Cohen, R.
1967   *The Kanuri of Bornu.* New York: Harcourt Brace Jovanovich.

Cohen, Y. A.
1974a   *Man in Adaptation: The Cultural Present,* 2nd ed. Chicago: Aldine.
1974b   Culture as Adaptation. In *Man in Adaptation: The Cultural Present,* 2nd ed., ed. Y. A. Cohen, pp. 45–68. Chicago: Aldine.

Colson, E., and T. Scudder
1975   New Economic Relationships between the Gwembe Valley and the Line of Rail. In *Town and Country in Central and Eastern Africa,* ed. David Parkin, pp. 190–210. London: Oxford University Press.
1988   *For Prayer and Profit: The Ritual, Economic, and Social Importance of Beer in Gwembe District, Zambia, 1950–1982.* Stanford, CA: Stanford University Press.

Conard, N. J.
2011   *Neanderthal Lifeways, Subsistence, and Technology.* New York: Springer.

Conkey, M., O. Soffer, D. Stratmann, and N. Jablonski
1997   *Beyond Art: Pleistocene Image and Symbol.* San Francisco: Memoirs of the California Academy of Sciences, no. 23.

Conklin, H. C.
1954   *The Relation of Hanunóo Culture to the Plant World.* Unpublished Ph.D. dissertation, Yale University.

Connah, G.
2004   *Forgotten Africa: An Introduction to Its Archaeology.* New York: Routledge.

Cooper, F., and A. L. Stoler, eds.
1997   *Tensions of Empire: Colonial Cultures in a Bourgeois World.* Berkeley: University of California Press.

Crapo, R. H.
2003   *Anthropology of Religion: The Unity and Diversity of Religions.* Boston: McGraw-Hill.

Crate, S. A., and M. Nuttall
2008   *Anthropology and Climate Change: From Encounters to Actions.* Walnut Creek, CA: Left Coast Press.

Crenson, M.
2000   Music—From the Heart or from the Genes. http://www.cis.vt.edu/modernworld/d/musicgenes.html.

Cresswell, T.
2006   *On the Move: Mobility in the Modern West.* New York: Routledge.

Cribb, J.
2010   *The Coming Famine: The Global Food Crisis and What We Can Do to Avoid It.* Berkeley: University of California Press.

Crick, F. H. C.
1968   (orig. 1962) The Genetic Code. In *The Molecular Basis of Life: An Introduction to Molecular Biology, Readings from Scientific American,* pp. 198–205. San Francisco: W. H. Freeman.

Crosby, A. W., Jr.
2003   *The Columbian Exchange: Biological and Cultural Consequences of 1492.* Westport, CT: Praeger.

Cueppens, B., and P. Geschiere
2005   Autocthony: Local or Global? New Modes in the Struggle over Citizenship and Belonging in Africa and Europe. *Annual Review of Anthropology* 34: 385–407.

Cultural Survival Quarterly
1989   Quarterly journal. Cambridge, MA: Cultural Survival.

Cunningham, G.
1999   *Religion and Magic: Approaches and Theories.* New York: New York University Press.

Dalton, G., ed.
1967   *Tribal and Peasant Economies.* Garden City, NY: Natural History Press.

Dalton, R.
2006   Ethiopia: Awash with Fossils. http://www.nature.com/news/2006/060102/full/439014a.html.

DaMatta, R.
1991   *Carnivals, Rogues, and Heroes: An Interpretation of the Brazilian Dilemma.* Translated from the Portuguese by John Drury. Notre Dame, IN: University of Notre Dame Press.

D'Andrade, R.
1984   Cultural Meaning Systems. In *Culture Theory: Essays on Mind, Self, and Emotion,* ed. R. A. Shweder and R. A. Levine, pp. 88–119. Cambridge, UK: Cambridge University Press.

Darwin, C.
2009   (orig. 1859) *On the Origin of Species.* Alachua, FL: Bridge-Logos.

Darwin, E.
1796   (orig. 1794) *Zoonomia, Or the Laws of Organic Life,* 2nd ed. London: J. Johnson.

Das, V., and D. Poole, eds.
2004   *Anthropology in the Margins of the State.* Santa Fe, NM: School of American Research Press.

Degler, C.
1970   *Neither Black nor White: Slavery and Race Relations in Brazil and the United States.* New York: Macmillan.

de la Peña, G.
2005   Social and Cultural Policies toward Indigenous Peoples: Perspectives from Latin America. *Annual Review of Anthropology* 34: 717–739.

DeLumley, H.
1976   (orig. 1969) A Paleolithic Camp at Nice. In *Avenues to Antiquity, Readings from Scientific American,* ed. B. M. Fagan, pp. 36–44. San Francisco: W. H. Freeman.

DeMarco, E.
1997   New Dig at 9,000-Year-Old City Is Changing Views on Ancient Life. *New York Times,* November 11. http://www.nytimes.com.

Dembski, W. A.
2004   *The Design Revolution: Answering the Toughest Questions about Intelligent Design.* Downers Grove, IL: InterVarsity Press.

DeNavas-Walt, C., B. D. Proctor, and J. C. Smith
2010   *Income, Poverty, and Health Insurance Coverage in the United States: 2009.* U.S. Census Bureau, Current Population Reports, P60-238. U.S. Government Printing Office, Washington, DC, 2010. http://www.census.gov/prod/2010pubs/p60-238.pdf

Dentan, R. K.
1979   *The Semai: A Nonviolent People of Malaya,* fieldwork edition. New York: Harcourt Brace.
2008   *Overwhelming Terror: Love, Fear, Peace and Violence among the Semai of Malaysia.* Lanham, MD: Rowman & Littlefield.

Descartes, L., and C. P. Kottak
2009   *Media and Middle-Class Moms.* New York: Routledge.

De Vos, G. A., and H. Wagatsuma
1966   *Japan's Invisible Race: Caste in Culture and Personality.* Berkeley: University of California Press.

De Vos, G. A., W. O. Wetherall, and K. Stearman
1983   *Japan's Minorities: Burakumin, Koreans, Ainu and Okinawans.* Report no. 3. London: Minority Rights Group.

De Waal, F. B. M.
1995   Bonobo Sex and Society: The Behavior of a Close Relative Challenges Assumptions about Male Supremacy in Human Evolution. *Scientific American,* March, pp. 82–88.
1997   *Bonobo: The Forgotten Ape.* Berkeley: University of California Press.
1998   *Chimpanzee Politics: Power and Sex among Apes.* Baltimore: Johns Hopkins Universty Press.
2001   *The Ape and the Sushi Master: Cultural Reflections by a Primatologist.* New York: Basic Books.
2007   *Chimpanzee Politics: Power and Sex among Apes,* 25th anniversary ed. Baltimore: Johns Hopkins University Press.

Diamond, J. M.
1990   A Pox upon Our Genes. *Natural History,* February, pp. 26–30.
1997   *Guns, Germs, and Steel: The Fates of Human Societies.* New York: W. W. Norton.
2005   (orig. 1997) *Guns, Germs, and Steel: The Fates of Human Societies.* New York: W. W. Norton.

Dickau, R, A. J. Ranere, and R. G. Cooke
2007   Starch Grain Evidence for the Preceramic Dispersals of Maize and Root Crops into Tropical Dry and Humid Forests of

Panama. *Proceedings of the National Academy of Sciences of the United States of America* 104(9): 3651–3656. http://www.pnas.org/cgi/content/full/104/9/3651.

Dillon, S.
  2006   In School across U.S., the Melting Pot Overflows. *New York Times*, August 27. http://www.nytimes.com.

Divale, W. T., and M. Harris
  1976   Population, Warfare, and the Male Supremacist Complex. *American Anthropologist* 78: 521–538.

Donham, D. L.
  2011   *Violence in a Time of Liberation: Murder and Ethnicity at a South African Gold Mine, 1994.* Durham, NC: Duke University Press.

Donovan, J. M.
  2007   *Legal Anthropology: An Introduction.* Lanham, MD: Rowman & Littlefield.

Dorward, D. C., ed.
  1983   *The Igbo "Women's War" of 1929: Documents Relating to the Aba Riots in Eastern Nigeria.* Wakefield, England: East Ardsley, 1983.

Douglas, M.
  1970   *Natural Symbols: Explorations in Cosmology.* London: Barrie and Rockliff, The Crescent Press.

Dove, M. R, and C. Carpenter, eds.,
  2008   *Environmental Anthropology: A Historical Reader.* Malden, MA: Blackwell.

Dove, M. R., P. E. Sajise, and A. A. Doolittle, eds.
  2011   *Beyond the Sacred Forest: Complicating Conservation in Southeast Asia.* Durham, NC: Duke University Press.

Draper, P.
  1975   !Kung Women: Contrasts in Sexual Egalitarianism in Foraging and Sedentary Contexts. In *Toward an Anthropology of Women,* ed. R. Reiter, pp. 77–109. New York: Monthly Review Press.

Dressler, W. W., K. S. Oths, and C. C. Gravlee
  2005   Race and Ethnicity in Public Health Research. *Annual Review of Anthropology* 34: 231–252.

Duffield, M., and V. Hewitt, eds.
  2009   *Empire, Development, and Colonialism: The Past in the Present.* Rochester, NY: James Currey.

Dumas, L. J., J. R. Wedel, and G. Callman
  2010   *Confronting Corruption, Building Accountability: Lessons from the World of International Development Advising.* New York: Palgrave Macmillan.

Dunham, S. A.
  2009   *Surviving Against the Odds: Village Industry in Indonesia.* Durham, NC: Duke University Press.

Dunn, J. S.
  2000   *The Impact of Media on Reproductive Behavior in Northeastern Brazil.* Ph.D. dissertation, Department of Anthropology, University of Michigan, Ann Arbor.

Durkheim, E.
  1951   (orig. 1897) *Suicide: A Study in Sociology.* Glencoe, IL: Free Press.
  2001   (orig. 1912) *The Elementary Forms of the Religious Life.* Translated by Carol Cosman. Abridged with an introduction and notes by Mark S. Cladis. New York: Oxford University Press.

Durrenberger, E. P., and T. D. King, eds.
  2000   *State and Community in Fisheries Management: Power, Policy, and Practice.* Westport, CT: Bergin and Garvey.

Earle, T. K.
  1987   Chiefdoms in Archaeological and Ethnohistorical Perspective. *Annual Review of Anthropology* 16: 279–308.
  1991   *Chiefdoms: Power, Economy, and Ideology.* New York: Cambridge University Press.
  1997   *How Chiefs Come to Power: The Political Economy in Prehistory.* Stanford, CA: Stanford University Press.

Eckert, P.
  1989   *Jocks and Burnouts: Social Categories and Identity in the High School.* New York: Teachers College Press, Columbia University.
  2000   *Linguistic Variation as Social Practice: The Linguistic Construction of Identity in Belten High.* Malden, MA: Blackwell.

Eckert, P., and S. McConnell-Ginet
  2003   *Language and Gender.* New York: Cambridge University Press.

Eckert, P., and J. R. Rickford, eds.
  2001   *Style and Sociolinguistic Variation.* New York: Cambridge University Press.

Edelman, M., and A. Haugerud
  2005   *The Anthropology of Development and Globalization: From Classical Political Economy to Contemporary Neoliberalism.* Malden, MA: Blackwell.

Edwards, D. N.
  2004   *The Nubian Past: An Archaeology of Sudan.* New York: Routledge.

Egan, T.
  2005   A Skeleton Moves frorm the Courts to the Laboratory. *New York Times*, July 19.

Eldredge, N.
  1985   *Time Frames: The Rethinking of Darwinian Evolution and the Theory of Punctuated Equilibria.* New York: Simon & Schuster.

Eldredge, N., and S. Pearson
  2010   *Charles Darwin and the Mystery of Mysteries.* New York: Rb Flash Point/Roaring Brook Press.

Elson, C.
  2007   *Excavations at Cerro Tilcajete: A Monte Alban II Administrative Center in the Valley of Oaxaca.* Memoir 42 of the Museum of Anthropology, University of Michigan, Ann Arbor.

Ember, M., and C. R. Ember
  1997   Science in Anthropology. In *The Teaching of Anthropology: Problems, Issues, and Decisions,* ed. C. P. Kottak, J. J. White, R. H. Furlow, and P. C. Rice, pp. 29–33. Mountain View, CA: Mayfield.

Endicott, K. M., and R. Welsch
  2009   *Taking Sides Clashing Views on Controversial Issues in Anthropology,* 4th ed. Boston, McGraw-Hill.

Ervin, A. M.
  2005   *Applied Anthropology: Tools and Perspectives for Contemporary Practice.* 2nd ed. Boston: Pearson/Allyn & Bacon.

Escobar, A.
  1991   Anthropology and the Development Encounter: The Making and Marketing of Development Anthropology. *American Ethnologist* 18: 658–682.
  1994   Welcome to Cyberia: Notes on the Anthropology of Cyberculture. *Current Anthropology* 35(3): 211–231.
  1995   *Encountering Development: The Making and Unmaking of the Third World.* Princeton, NJ: Princeton University Press.

Evans-Pritchard, E. E.
  1940   *The Nuer: A Description of the Modes of Livelihood and Political Institutions of a Nilotic People.* Oxford: Clarendon Press.
  1970   Sexual Inversion among the Azande. *American Anthropologist* 72: 1428–1433.

Ezekiel, E.
  2011   Foreign Aid Is Not a Rathole. *New York Times*, November 30, 2011. www.nytimes.com. Http://opinionator.blogs.nytimes.com/2011/11/30/foreign-aid-is-not-a-rathole/?scp=3&sq=ezekiel%20emanuel%20december%201&st=cse

Ezra, K.
  1986   *A Human Ideal in African Art: Bamana Figurative Sculpture.* Washington, DC: Smithsonian Institution Press for the National Museum of African Art.

Fagan, B. M.
  1996   *World Prehistory: A Brief Introduction,* 3rd ed. New York: HarperCollins.
  1998   *Clash of Cultures,* 2nd ed. Walnut Creek, CA: AltaMira.
  2010   *People of the Earth: A Brief Introduction to World Prehistory,* 13th ed. Upper Saddle River, NJ: Prentice Hall.
  2011   *World Prehistory: A Brief Introduction,* 8th ed. Boston: Prentice Hall.
  2012   *Archaeology: A Brief Introduction,* 11th ed. Boston: Pearson

Farner, R. F., ed.,
  2004   *Nationalism, Ethnicity, and Identity: Cross-National and Comparative Perspectives.* New Brunswick, NJ: Transaction.

Farr, D. M. L.
  1980   British Empire. *Academic American Encyclopedia,* vol. 3, pp. 495–496. Princeton, NJ: Arete.

Fasold, R. W., and J. Connor-Linton
    2006   *An Introduction to Language and Linguistics.* New York: Cambridge University Press.

Fearon, J. D.
    2003   Ethnic and Cultural Diversity by Country. *Journal of Economic Growth* 8:2 (June 2003):195–222.

Feder, K. L.
    2011a   *Frauds, Myths, and Mysteries: Science and Pseudoscience in Archaeology.* New York: McGraw-Hill.
    2011b   *The Past in Perspective: An Introduction to Human Prehistory,* 5th ed. New York: Oxford University Press.

Feinman, G. M., and J. Marcus, eds.
    1998   *Archaic States.* Santa Fe, NM: School of American Research Press.

Ferguson, R. B.
    1995   *Yanomami Warfare: A Political History.* Santa Fe, NM: School of American Research Press.
    2003   *The State, Identity, and Violence: Political Disintegration in the Post–Cold War Era.* New York: Routledge.

Ferraro, G. P.
    2010   *The Cultural Dimension of International Business,* 6th ed. Upper Saddle River, NJ: Prentice Hall.

Fields, J. M.
    2004   America's Families and Living Arrangements: 2003. U.S. Census Bureau. *Current Population Reports,* P20–553, November. http://www.census.gov.

Fields, J. M., and L. M. Casper
    2001   America's Families and Living Arrangements: Population Characteristics, 2000. U.S. Census Bureau. *Current Population Reports,* P20-537, June 2001. http://www.census.gov/prod/2001pubs/p20-537.pdf.

Finke, R., and R. Stark,
    2005   *The Churching of America, 1776–2005: Winners and Losers in Our Religious Economy.* New Brunswick, NJ: Rutgers University Press.

Finkler, K.
    1985   *Spiritualist Healers in Mexico: Successes and Failures of Alternative Therapeutics.* South Hadley, MA: Bergin and Garvey.

Finnstrom, S.
    1997   Postcoloniality and the Postcolony: Theories of the Global and the Local. http://www.postcolonialweb.org/.

Fisher, A.
    1988a   The More Things Change. *MOSAIC* 19(1):22-33.
    1988b   On the Emergence of Humanness. *MOSAIC* 19(1):34-45.

Fiske, J.
    1989   *Understanding Popular Culture.* Boston: Unwin Hyman.
    2011   *Reading the Popular,* 2nd ed. New York: Routledge.

Fiske, J., and J. Hartley
    2003   *Reading Television,* 2nd ed. New York: Routledge.

Flannery, K. V.
    1969   Origins and Ecological Effects of Early Domestication in Iran and the Near East. In *The Domestication and Exploitation of Plants and Animals,* ed. P. J. Ucko and G. W. Dimbleby, pp. 73–100. Chicago: Aldine.
    1973   The Origins of Agriculture. *Annual Review of Anthropology* 2: 271–310.
    1986   *Guila Naquitz: Archaic Foraging and Early Agriculture in Oaxaca, Mexico.* Orlando, FL: Academic Press.
    1995   Prehistoric Social Evolution. In *Research Frontiers in Anthropology,* C. R. Ember and M. Ember, eds., pp. 1–26. Upper Saddle River, NJ: Prentice Hall.
    1999   Chiefdoms in the Early Near East: Why It's So Hard to Identify Them. In *The Iranian World: Essays on Iranian Art and Archaeology,* ed. A. Alizadeh, Y. Majidzadeh, and S. M. Shahmirzadi. Tehran: Iran University Press.

Flannery, K. V., and J. Marcus
    2000   Formative Mexican Chiefdoms and the Myth of the "Mother Culture." *Journal of Anthropological Archaeology* 19: 1–37.
    2003a   *The Cloud People: Divergent Evolution of the Zapotec and Mixtec Civilizations.* Clinton Corners, NY: Percheron Press.
    2003b   The Origin of War: New 14C Dates from Ancient Mexico. *Proceedings of the National Academy of Sciences of the United States of America,* 100(20): 11801–11805.

Fleisher, M. L.
    2000   *Kuria Cattle Raiders: Violence and Vigilantism on the Tanzania/Kenya Frontier.* Ann Arbor: University of Michigan Press.

Fluehr-Lobban, C.
    2005   *Race and Racism: An Introduction.* Lanham, MD: AltaMira.

Ford, C. S., and F. A. Beach
    1951   *Patterns of Sexual Behavior.* New York: Harper Torchbooks.

Fortes, M.
    1950   Kinship and Marriage among the Ashanti. In *African Systems of Kinship and Marriage,* ed. A. R. Radcliffe-Brown and D. Forde, pp. 252–284. London: Oxford University Press.

Fossey, D.
    1983   *Gorillas in the Mist.* Boston: Houghton Mifflin.

Foster, G. M., and B. G. Anderson
    1978   *Medical Anthropology.* New York: McGraw-Hill.

Foucault, M.
    1979   *Discipline and Punish: The Birth of the Prison.* Translated by Alan Sheridan. New York: Vintage Books, University Press.
    1990   *The History of Sexuality,* vol. 2, *The Use of Pleasure.* Translated by R. Hurley. New York: Vintage.

Fouts, R.
    1997   *Next of Kin: What Chimpanzees Have Taught Me about Who We Are.* New York: William Morrow.

Fowler, C. S., and D. D. Fowler, eds.
    2008   *The Great Basin: People and Place in Ancient Times.* Santa Fe, NM: School for Advanced Research Press.

Frake, C. O.
    1961   The Diagnosis of Disease among the Subanun of Mindanao. *American Anthropologist* 63: 113–132.

Free Dictionary
    2004   Honorific. http://encyclopedia.thefreedictionary.com/Honorific.

Freilich, M., D. Raybeck, and J. Savishinsky
    1991   *Deviance: Anthropological Perspectives.* Westport, CT: Bergin and Garvey.

French, H. W.
    2002   Whistling Past the Global Graveyard. *New York Times,* July 14.

Freston, P., ed.
    2008   *Evangelical Christianity and Democracy in Latin America.* New York: Oxford University Press.

Freud, S.
    1950   (orig. 1918) *Totem and Taboo.* Translated by J. Strachey. New York: W. W. Norton.

Fricke, T.
    1994   *Himalayan Households: Tamang Demography and Domestic Processes,* 2nd ed. New York: Columbia University Press.

Fried, M. H.
    1960   On the Evolution of Social Stratification and the State. In *Culture in History,* ed. S. Diamond, pp. 713–731. New York: Columbia University Press.
    1967   *The Evolution of Political Society: An Essay in Political Anthropology.* New York: McGraw-Hill.

Friedan, B.
    1963   *The Feminine Mystique.* New York: W. W. Norton.

Friedl, E.
    1962   *Vasilika: A Village in Modern Greece:* New York: Holt, Rinehart, and Winston.
    1975   *Women and Men: An Anthropologist's View.* New York: Harcourt Brace Jovanovich.

Friedman, J., ed.
    2003   *Globalization, the State, and Violence.* Walnut Creek, CA: AltaMira.

Friedman, J., and M. J. Rowlands, eds.
    1978   *The Evolution of Social Systems.* Pittsburgh: University of Pittsburgh Press.

Friedman, K. E., and J. Friedman
    2008   *The Anthropology of Global Systems.* Lanham, MD: Altamira.

Frisancho, A. R.
    1993   *Human Adaptation and Accommodation.* Ann Arbor: University of Michigan Press.

Futuyma, D. J.
1998   *Evolutionary Biology.* Sunderland, MA: Sinauer Associates.

Gal, S.
1989   Language and Political Economy. *Annual Review of Anthropology* 18: 345–367.

Galdikas, B. M.
2007   The Vanishing Man of the Forest. *International Herald Tribune,* January 7. http://www.nytimes.com/2007/01/07/opinion/07iht-edgald.4127210.html?_r=1&scp=1&sq=orangutan%20endangered&st=cse.

Gamble, C.
1999   *The Palaeolithic Societies of Europe.* New York: Cambridge University Press.
2008   *Archaeology, the Basics,* 2nd ed. New York: Routledge.

Gardner, R. A., B. T. Gardner, and T. E. Van Cantfort, eds.
1989   *Teaching Sign Language to Chimpanzees.* Albany: State University of New York Press.

Geertz, C.
1973   *The Interpretation of Cultures.* New York: Basic Books.
1983   *Local Knowledge.* New York: Basic Books.
1995   *After the Fact: Two Countries, Four Decades, One Anthropologist.* Cambridge, MA: Harvard University Press.

Geis, M. L.
1987   *The Language of Politics.* New York: Springer-Verlag.

Gellner, E.
1983   *Nations and Nationalism.* Ithaca, NY: Cornell University Press.
1997   *Nationalism.* New York: New York University Press.

General Anthropology: Bulletin of the General Anthropology Division, American Anthropological Association.

Gezon, L. L.
2006   *Global Visions, Local Landscapes: A Political Ecology of Conservation, Conflict, and Control in Northern Madagascar.* Lanham, MD: AltaMira.

Gibbons, A.
2001   The Peopling of the Pacific. *Science* 291: 1735. http://www.familytreedna.com/pdf/Gibbons_Science2001.pdf.

Giddens, A.
1981   *The Class Structure of the Advanced Societies,* 2nd ed. London: Hutchinson.

Gillespie, J. H.
2004   *Population Genetics: A Concise Guide,* 2nd ed. Baltimore: Johns Hopkins University Press.

Gilmore, D. D.
1987   *Aggression and Community: Paradoxes of Andalusian Culture.* New Haven, CT: Yale University Press.

Gilmore-Lehne, W. J.
2000   Pre-Sumerian Cultures: Natufian through Ubaid Eras: 10, 500–3500 B.C.E. http://loki.stockton.edu/~gilmorew/consorti/1bnear.htm.

Gimpel, J.
1988   *The Medieval Machine: The Industrial Revolution of the Middle Ages,* 2nd ed. Aldershot, Hants, England: Wildwood House.

Ginsburg, F. D., L. Abu-Lughod, and B. Larkin, eds.
2002   *Media Worlds: Anthropology on New Terrain.* Berkeley: University of California Press.

Gledhill, J.
2000   *Power and Its Disguises: Anthropological Perspectives on Politics.* Sterling, VA: Pluto Press.

Gmelch, G.
1978   Baseball Magic. *Human Nature* 1(8): 32–40.
2001   *Inside Pitch: Life in Professional Baseball.* Washington, DC: Smithsonian Institution Press.
2006a   *Inside Pitch: Life in Professional Baseball.* Lincoln: University of Nebraska Press.
2006b   *Baseball without Borders: The International Pastime.* Lincoln: University of Nebraska Press

Gmelch, G., and W. Zenner, eds.
2002   *Urban Life: Readings in the Anthropology of the City.* Prospect Heights, IL: Waveland.

Goldberg, D. T., ed.
1990   *Anatomy of Racism.* Minneapolis: University of Minnesota Press.

Goleman, D.
1992   Anthropology Goes Looking for Love in All the Old Places. *New York Times,* November 24, 1992, p. B1.

Goodale, J., and J. D. Koss
1971   The Cultural Context of Creativity among Tiwi. In *Anthropology and Art: Readings in Cross-Cultural Aesthetics,* ed. C. Otten, pp. 182–203. Austin: University of Texas Press.

Goodall, J.
1996   *My Life with the Chimpanzees.* New York: Pocket Books.
2009   *Jane Goodall: 50 Years at Gombe, A Tribute to Five Decades of Wildlife Research, Education, and Conservation.* New York: Stewart, Tabori, and Chang.
2010   *In the Shadow of Man,* new ed. Boston: Mariner Books.

Goodenough, W. H.
1953   *Native Astronomy in the Central Carolines.* Philadelphia: University of Pennsylvania Press.

Gotkowitz, L., ed.
2011   *Histories of Race and Racism: The Andes and Mesoamerica from Colonial Times to the Present.* Durham, NC: Duke University Press.

Gottdiener, M., ed.
2000   *New Forms of Consumption: Consumers, Culture, and Commodification.* Lanham, MD: Rowman and Littlefield.

Gough, E. K.
1959   The Nayars and the Definition of Marriage. *Journal of Royal Anthropological Institute* 89: 23–34.

Gould, S. J.
1999   *Rock of Ages: Science and Religion in the Fullness of Life.* New York: Ballantine Books.
2002   *The Structure of Evolutionary Theory.* Cambridge, MA: Belknap Press of Harvard University Press.

Gowlett, J. A. J.
1993   *Ascent to Civilization: The Archaeology of Early Humans.* New York: McGraw-Hill.

Graeber, D.
2011   *Debt: The First 5,000 Years.* Brooklyn, NY: Melville House.

Gramsci, A.
1971   *Selections from the Prison Notebooks.* Edited and translated by Quenten Hoare and Geoffrey Nowell Smith. London: Wishart.

Grasmuck, S., and P. Pessar
1991   *Between Two Islands: Dominican International Migration.* Berkeley: University of California Press.

Gray, J.
1999   *False Dawn. The Delusions of Global Capitalism,* London: Granta.

Greaves, T. C.
1995   Problems Facing Anthropologists: Cultural Rights and Ethnography. *General Anthropology* 1(2): 1, 3–6.

Green, E. C.
1992   (orig. 1987) The Integration of Modern and Traditional Health Sectors in Swaziland. In *Applying Anthropology: An Introductory Reader,* ed. A. Podolefsky and P. J. Brown, pp. 246–251. Mountain View, CA: Mayfield.

Green, G. M., and R. W. Sussman
1990   Deforestation History of the Eastern Rain Forests of Madagascar from Satellite Images. *Science* 248: 212–215.

Green, R. E., J. Krause, S. E. Ptak, A. W. Briggs, M. T. Ronan, J. F. Simons, L. Du, M. Egholm, J. M. Rothberg, M. Paunovic, and S. Pääbo.
2006   Analysis of one million base pairs of Neanderthal DNA. *Nature* 444: (November 16): 330–336. http://www.nature.com/nature/journal/v444/n7117/full/nature05336.html.

Green, R. E., et al.
2010   A Draft Sequence of the Neandertal Genome. *Science,* 7 May, 328 (5979) pp. 710–722.

Green, T.
2006   Archaeologist Makes the Case for Burying Dominant Theory of First Americans. Austin: University of Texas Research. http://www.utexas.edu/research/impact/collins.html.

Greenhouse, S.
2011   Union Membership in U.S. Fell to a 70-Year Low Last Year. *New York Times,* January 21.

Greiner, T. M.

2003 What Is the Difference between Hominin and Hominid When Classifying Humans? MadSci Network: Evolution. http://www.madsci.org/posts/archives/Apr2003/1050350684.Ev.r.html.

Grekova, M.

2001 Postsocialist Societies. *International Encyclopedia of the Social and Behavioral Sciences,* pp. 11877–11881. New York: Elsevier.

Gremaux, R.

1993 Woman Becomes Man in the Balkans. In *Third Sex Third Gender: Beyond Sexual Dimorphism in Culture and History,* G. Herdt, ed. Cambridge: MIT Press.

Griffin, P. B., and A. Estioko-Griffin, eds.

1985 *The Agta of Northeastern Luzon: Recent Studies.* Cebu City, Philippines: University of San Carlos.

Grimshaw, A.

2009 *Observational Cinema: Anthropology, Film, and the Exploration of Social Life.* Bloomington: Indiana University Press.

Grimshaw, A., and A. Ravetz

2005 *Visualizing Anthropology.* Portland, OR: Intellect.

Gudeman, S., ed.

1998 *Economic Anthropology.* Northampton, MA: E. Elgar.

Gugliotta, G.

2002 Earliest Human Ancestor? Skull Dates to When Apes, Humans Split. *Washington Post,* July 11, p. A01.

2004 New Evidence of Controlled Fire Is Unearthed: Israeli Team's Finds at Ancient Campsite Near Jordan River Suggest Humans Harnessed Blazes 790,000 Years Ago. *Washington Post,* May 10, p. A-10.

2005*a* More Fossil Evidence from "Hobbit" Island. *Washington Post,* October 12, p. A-03.

2005*b* Tools Found in Britain Show Much Earlier Human Existence. *Washington Post,* December 15, p. A-24.

Gunther, E.

1971 Northwest Coast Indian Art. In *Anthropology and Art: Readings in Cross-Cultural Aesthetics,* ed. C. Otten, pp. 318–340. Austin: University of Texas Press.

Gupta, A., and J. Ferguson

1997*b* Beyond "Culture": Space, Identity, and the Politics of Difference. In *Culture, Power, Place: Explorations in Critical Anthropology,* ed. A. Gupta and J. Ferguson, pp. 33–51. Durham, NC: Duke University Press.

Gupta, A., and J. Ferguson, eds.

1997*a* *Anthropological Locations: Boundaries and Grounds of a Field Science.* Berkeley: University of California Press.

1997*b* *Culture, Power, Place: Explorations in Critical Anthropology.* Durham, NC: Duke University Press.

Guyot, J., and C. Hughes

2007 Researchers Find Earliest Evidence for Modern Human Behavior. *Arizona State University Research Magazine.* http://researchmag.asu.edu/2008/02researchers_find_earliest_evid.html.

Haapala, A.

1998 Literature: Invention of the Self. *Canadian Aesthetics Journal* 2. http://www.uqtr.ca/AE/vol_2/haapala.html.

Hackett, R. I. J.

1996 *Art and Religion in Africa.* London: Cassell.

Haenn, N., and R. R. Wilk, eds.

2006 *The Environment in Anthropology: A Reader in Ecology, Culture, and Sustainable Living.* New York: New York University Press.

Hallowell, A. I.

1955 *Culture and Experience.* Philadelphia: University of Pennsylvania Press.

Hancock, G.

2011 *Fingerprints of the Gods.* New York: MJF Books.

Hancock, G., and R. Bauval

1996 *Message of the Sphinx: A Quest for the Hidden Legacy of Mankind.* New York: Three Rivers Press.

Handwerk, B.

2008 Half of Humanity Will Live in Cities by Year's End. *National Geographic News,* March 13. www.nationalgeographic.com/news/pf30472163.html.

Handwerker, W. P.

2009 *The Origins of Cultures: How Individual Choices Make Cultures Change.* Walnut Creek, CA: Left Coast Press.

Hann, C., and K. Hart

2011 *Economic Anthropology: History, Ethnography, Critique.* Malden, MA: Polity Press.

Hann, C., and K. Hart, eds.

2009 *Market and Society: The Great Transformation Today.* New York: Cambridge University Press.

Hansen, K. V.

2005 *Not-So-Nuclear Families: Class, Gender, and Networks of Care.* New Brunswick, NJ: Rutgers University Press.

Harcourt, A. H., D. Fossey, and J. Sabater-Pi

1981 Demography of *Gorilla gorilla. Journal of Zoology* 195: 215–233.

Harlan, J. R., and D. Zohary

1966 Distribution of Wild Wheats and Barley. *Science* 153: 1074–1080.

Harlow, H. F.

1971 *Learning to Love.* San Francisco: Albion.

Harris, M.

1964 *Patterns of Race in the Americas.* New York: Walker.

1970 Referential Ambiguity in the Calculus of Brazilian Racial Identity. *Southwestern Journal of Anthropology* 26(1): 1–14.

1974 *Cows, Pigs, Wars, and Witches: The Riddles of Culture.* New York: Random House.

1978 *Cannibals and Kings.* New York: Vintage.

1989 *Our Kind: Who We Are, Where We Came From, Where We Are Going.* New York: Harper & Row.

2001*a* (orig. 1979) *Cultural Materialism: The Struggle for a Science of Culture.* Walnut Creek, CA: AltaMira.

2001*b* (orig. 1968) *The Rise of Anthropological Theory.* Walnut Creek, CA: AltaMira.

Harris, M., and C. P. Kottak

1963 The Structural Significance of Brazilian Racial Categories. *Sociologia* 25: 203–209.

Harrison, G. G., W. L. Rathje, and W. W. Hughes

1994 Food Waste Behavior in an Urban Population. In *Applying Anthropology: An Introductory Reader,* 3rd ed., ed. A. Podolefsky and P. J. Brown, pp. 107–112. Mountain View, CA: Mayfield.

Harrison, K. D.

2007 *When Languages Die: The Extinction of the World's Languages and the Erosion of Human Knowledge.* New York: Oxford University Press.

2010 *The Last Speakers: The Quest to Save the World's Most Endangered Languages.* Washington: National Geographic.

Hart, C. W. M., A. R. Pilling, and J. C. Goodale

1988 *The Tiwi of North Australia,* 3rd ed. Fort Worth: Harcourt Brace.

Hart, D., and R. W. Sussman

2009 *Man the Hunted: Primates, Predators, and Human Evolution,* expanded ed. Boulder, CO: Westview Press.

Hartl, D. L., and E. W. Jones

2011 *Essential Genetics: A Genomics Perspective,* 5th ed. Boston: Jones and Bartlett.

Harvey, D. J.

1980 French Empire. *Academic American Encyclopedia,* vol. 8, pp. 309–310. Princeton, NJ: Arete.

Hassig, R.

1985 *Trade, Tribute, and Transportation: The Sixteenth-Century Political Economy of the Valley of Mexico.* Norman: University of Oklahoma Press.

Haugerud, A., M. P. Stone, and P. D. Little, eds.

2011 *Commodities aad Globalization: Anthropological Perspectives.* Lanham, MD: Rowman & Littlefield.

Hausfater, G., and S. Hrdy, eds.

1984 *Infanticide: Comparative and Evolutionary Perspectives.* Hawthorne, NY: Aldine.

Hausmann, R., L. D. Tyson, and S. Zahidi

2011 *The Global Gender Gap Report 2011.* Geneva: World Economic Forum.

Hawkes, K., J. O'Connell, and K. Hill

1982 Why Hunters Gather: Optimal Foraging and the Aché of Eastern Paraguay. *American Ethnologist* 9: 379–398.

Hawley, J. S,. ed.

1994 *Sati, the Blessing and the Curse: The Burning of Wives in India.* New York: Oxford University Press.

Hayden, B.
1981   Subsistence and Ecological Adaptations of Modern Hunter/Gatherers. In *Omnivorous Primates: Gathering and Hunting in Human Evolution,* ed. R. S. Harding and G. Teleki, pp. 344–421. New York: Columbia University Press.

Helman, C.
2007   *Culture, Health, and Illness,* 5th ed. New York: Oxford University Press.

Henry, D. O.
1989   *From Foraging to Agriculture: The Levant at the End of the Ice Age.* Philadelphia: University of Pennsylvania Press.
1995   *Prehistoric Cultural Ecology and Evolution: Insights from Southern Jordan.* New York: Plenum Press.

Henry, J.
1955   Docility, or Giving Teacher What She Wants. *Journal of Social Issues* 2: 33–41.

Herdt, G.
1981   *Guardians of the Flutes.* New York: McGraw-Hill.
1994   *Third Sex, Third Gender: Beyond Sexual Dimorphism in Culture and History.* Cambridge, MA: MIT Press.
2006   *The Sambia: Ritual, Sexuality, and Change in Papua New Guinea.* Belmont, CA: Thomson/Wadsworth.

Herdt, G. H., ed.
1984   *Ritualized Homosexuality in Melanesia.* Berkeley: University of California Press.

Herskovits, M.
1937   *Life in a Haitian Valley.* New York: Knopf.

Hess, E.
2008   *Nim Chimsky: The Chimp Who Would Be Human.* New York: Bantam Books.

Heyerdahl, T.
1971   *The Ra Expeditions.* Translated by P. Crampton. Garden City, NY: Doubleday.

Hicks, D., ed.
2010   *Ritual and Belief: Readings in the Anthropology of Religion,* 3rd ed. Boston: McGraw-Hill.

Higham, T., et al.
2011   The Earliest Evidence for Anatomically Modern Humans in Northwestern Europe. *Nature* 479: 521–524, November 24. doi:10.1038/nature10484.

Hill, J. H.
1978   Apes and Language. *Annual Review of Anthropology* 7: 89–112.

Hill, K. R., and A. M. Hurtado
1996   *Aché Life History: The Ecology and Demography of a Foraging People.* New York: Aldine.

Hill, K. R., R. S. Walker, et al.
2011   Co-Residence Patterns in Hunter-Gatherer Societies Show Unique Human Social Structure. *Science* 11 March 2011: 1286-1289. [DOI:10.1126/science.1199071]

Hill-Burnett, J.
1978   Developing Anthropological Knowledge Through Application. In *Applied Anthropology in America,* ed. E. M. Eddy and W. L. Partridge, pp. 112–128. New York: Columbia University Press.

Hinton, A. L., and K. L. O'Neill, eds.
2009   *Genocide: Truth, Memory, and Representation.* Durham, NC: Duke University Press.

Hobhouse, L. T.
1915   *Morals in Evolution,* rev. ed. New York: Holt.

Hoebel, E. A.
1954   *The Law of Primitive Man.* Cambridge, MA: Harvard University Press.
1968   (orig. 1954) The Eskimo: Rudimentary Law in a Primitive Anarchy. In *Studies in Social and Cultural Anthropology,* ed. J. Middleton, pp. 93–127. New York: Crowell.

Holden, A.
2005   *Tourism Studies and the Social Sciences.* New York: Routledge.

Hole, F., K. V. Flannery, and J. A. Neely
1969   *The Prehistory and Human Ecology of the Deh Luran Plain.* Memoir no. 1. Ann Arbor: University of Michigan Museum of Anthropology.

Holst, I., J. E. Moreno, and D. R. Piperno
2007   The Identification of Teosinte, Maize, and *Tripsacum* in Mesoamerica by Using Pollen, Starch Grains, and Phytoliths. *Proceedings of the National Academy of Sciences USA* 104: 17608–17613.

Holtzman, J.
2000   *Nuer Journeys, Nuer Lives.* Boston: Allyn & Bacon.

Hooker, R.
1996   Civilizations in Africa. http://www.wsu.edu:8080/~dee/civafrca/contents.htm.

Hopkins, T., and I. Wallerstein
1982   Patterns of Development of the Modern World System. In *World System Analysis: Theory and Methodology,* by T. Hopkins, I. Wallerstein, R. Bach, C. Chase-Dunn, and R. Mukherjee, pp. 121–141. Thousand Oaks, CA: Sage.

Hornborg, A., B. Clark, and K. Hermele, eds.
2011.   *Ecology and Power: Struggles over Land and Material Resources in the Past, Present and Future.* New York; Routledge.

Hornborg, A., and C. L. Crumley, eds.
2007.   *The World System and the Earth System: Global Socioenvironmental Change and Sustainability since the Neolithic.* Walnut Creek, CA; Left Coast Press.

Hornborg, A., J. R. McNeill, and J. Martinez-Alier, eds.
2007   *Rethinking Environmental History: World-System History and Global Environmental Change.* Lanham, MD: AltaMira.

Horton, R.
1963   The Kalabari Ekine Society: A Borderland of Religion and Art. *Africa* 33: 94–113.
1993   *Patterns of Thought in Africa and the West: Essays on Magic, Religion, and Science.* New York: Cambridge University Press.

Hudjashov, G., T. Kivisilda, P. A. Underhill, P. Endicott, J. J. Sanchez, A. A. Lin, P. Shen, P. Oefner, C. Renfrew, R. Villems, and P. Forster.
2007   Revealing the Prehistoric Settlement of Australia by Y Chromosome and mtDNA Analysis. *Proceedings of the National Academy of Sciences* 104(21): 8726–8730.

Huffington Post
2010   The Most Famous American Brands in Foreign Hands. October 8. http://www.huffingtonpost.com/2010/10/08/american-brands-in-foreig_n_755900.html#s152955&title=Budweiser.

Hunter, M. L.
2005   *Race, Gender, and the Politics of Skin Tone.* New York: Routledge.

Hurtado. A. M., C. A. Lambourne, P. James, K. Hill, K. Cheman, and K. Baca
2005   Human Rights, Biomedical Science, and Infectious Diseases among South American Indigenous Groups. *Annual Review of Anthropology* 34: 639–665.

Ignatius, D.
2007   Summer's Escape Artists. *Washington Post,* July 26. http://www.washingtonpost.com/wp-dyn/content/article/2007/07/25/AR2007072501879.html.

Ingraham, C.
2008   *White Weddings: Romancing Heterosexuality in Popular Culture,* 2nd ed. New York: Routledge.

Inhorn, M. C., and P. J. Brown
1990   The Anthropology of Infectious Disease. *Annual Review of Anthropology* 19: 89–117.

Iqbal, S.
2002   A New Light on Skin Color. *National Geographic Online Extra.* http://magma.nationalgeographic.com/ngm/0211/feature2/online_extra.html.

Isaac, G. L.
1972   Early Phases of Human Behavior: Models in Lower Paleolithic Archaeology. In *Models in Archaeology,* ed. D. L. Clarke, pp. 167–199. London: Methuen.
1978   Food Sharing and Human Evolution: Archaeological Evidence from the Plio-Pleistocene of East Africa. *Journal of Anthropological Research* 34: 311–325.

Isaacson, A.
2012   A Mini-Eden for Endangered Orangutans. *New York Times,* January 6.

Isto É
1984   *Olimpíadas,* August 8.

Jablonski, N. G.
    2006   *Skin: A Natural History.* Berkeley: University of California Press.
Jablonski, N. G., and Chaplin, G.
    2000   The Evolution of Human Skin Coloration. *Journal of Human Evolution* (39): 57–106.
Jackson, J., and K. B. Warren
    2005   Indigenous Movements in Latin America, 1992–2004: Controversies, Ironies, New Directions. *Annual Review of Anthropology* 34: 549–573.
Jankowiak, W. R., ed.
    1995   *Romantic Passion: A Universal Experience?* New York: Columbia University Press.
    2008   *Intimacies: Love and Sex across Cultures.* New York: Columbia University Press.
Jankowiak, W. R., and E. F. Fischer
    1992   A Cross-Cultural Perspective on Romantic Love. *Ethnology* 31(2): 149–156.
Jenks, C.
    2005   *Culture,* 2nd ed. New York: Routledge.
Jiao, T.
    2007   *The Neolithic of Southeast China: Cultural Transformation and Regional Interaction on the Coast.* Youngstown, NY: Cambria Press.
Johansen, B. E.
    2003   *Indigenous Peoples and Environmental Issues: An Encyclopedia.* Westport, CT: Greenwood Press.
    2008   *Global Warming 101.* Westport, CT: Greenwood.
Johanson, D. C., and T. D. White
    1979   A Systematic Assessment of Early African Hominids. *Science* 203: 321–330.
Johanson, D. C., and K. Wong
    2009   *Lucy's Legacy: The Quest for Human Origins.* New York: Harmony Books.
Johnson, A. W.
    1978   *Quantification in Cultural Anthropology: An Introduction to Research Design.* Stanford, CA: Stanford University Press.
Johnson, A. W., and T. Earle
    2000   *The Evolution of Human Societies: From Foraging Group to Agrarian State,* 2nd ed. Stanford, CA: Stanford University Press.
Jolly, C. J., and R. White
    1995   *Physical Anthropology and Archaeology,* 5th ed. New York: McGraw-Hill.
Joralemon, D.
    2010   *Exploring Medical Anthropology,* 3rd ed. Boston: Pearson.
Jordan, A.
    2003   *Business Anthropology.* Prospect Heights, IL: Waveland.
Joyce, R. A.
    2008   *Ancient Bodies, Ancient Lives: Sex, Gender, and Archaeology.* New York: Thames and Hudson.
Kamrava, M.
    2008   *Understanding Comparative Politics; A Framework for Analysis,* 2nd ed. New York: Routledge.
    2011   *The Modern Middle East: A Political History since the First World War,* 2nd ed. Berkeley: University of California Press.
Kamrava, M., ed. *Innovation in Islam: Traditions and Contributions.* Berkeley: University of California Press.
Kan, S.
    1986   The 19th-Century Tlingit Potlatch: A New Perspective. *American Ethnologist* 13: 191–212.
    1989   *Symbolic Immortality: The Tlingit Potlatch of the Nineteenth Century.* Washington, DC: Smithsonian Institution Press.
Kaneshiro, Neil K.
    2009   Intersex. *Medline Plus.* National Institutes of Health, U/S. National Library of Medicine. http://www.nlm.nih.gov/medlineplus/ency/article/001669.htm
Kaufman, S. R., and L. M. Morgan
    2005   The Anthropology of the Beginnings and Ends of Life. *Annual Review of Anthropology* 34: 317–341.
Kearney, M.
    1996   *Reconceptualizing the Peasantry: Anthropology in Global Perspective.* Boulder, CO: Westview Press.

    2004   *Changing Fields of Anthropology: From Local to Global.* Lanham, MD: Rowman and Littlefield.
Kelly, R. C.
    1976   Witchcraft and Sexual Relations: An Exploration in the Social and Semantic Implications of the Structure of Belief. In *Man and Woman in the New Guinea Highlands,* ed. P. Brown and G. Buchbinder, pp. 36–53. Special Publication, no. 8. Washington, DC: American Anthropological Association.
Kennedy, P.
    2010   *Local Lives and Global Transformations: Towards a World Society.* New York: Palgrave Macmillan.
Kent, S.
    1992   The Current Forager Controversy: Real versus Ideal Views of Hunter-Gatherers. *Man* 27: 45–70.
    1996   *Cultural Diversity among Twentieth-Century Foragers: An African Perspective.* New York: Cambridge University Press.
    1998   *Gender in African Prehistory.* Walnut Creek, CA: AltaMira.
Kent, S., and H. Vierich
    1989   The Myth of Ecological Determinism: Anticipated Mobility and Site Organization of Space. In *Farmers as Hunters: The Implications of Sedentism,* ed. S. Kent, pp. 96–130. New York: Cambridge University Press.
Kent, S., ed.
    2002   *Ethnicity, Hunter-gatherers, and the "Other": Association or Assimilation in Africa.* Washington: Smithsonian Institution Press.
Keppel, K. G., J. N. Pearch, and D. K. Wagener
    2002   Trends in Racial and Ethnic-Specific Rates for the Health Status Indicators: United States 1990-98. *Healthy People Statistical Notes No. 23.* Hyattsville, MD: National Center for Health Statistics.
Kershaw, S.
    2005   In Petition to Government, Tribe Hopes for Return to Whaling Past. *New York Times,* September 19.
    2009   For Teenagers, Hello Means 'How About a Hug?' *New York Times,* May 28.
Keynes, J. M.
    1927   *The End of Laissez-Faire.* London: L. and Virginia Woolf.
    1936   *General Theory of Employment, Interest, and Money.* New York: Harcourt Brace.
Kimmel, M. S., and M. A. Messner, eds.
    2013   *Men's Lives,* 9th ed. Boston: Allyn & Bacon.
Kinsey, A. C., W. B. Pomeroy, and C. E. Martin
    1948   *Sexual Behavior in the Human Male.* Philadelphia: W. B. Saunders.
Kirch, P. V.
    2000   *On the Road of the Winds: An Archaeological History of the Pacific Islands Before European Contact.* Berkeley: University of California Press.
Kirman, P.
    1997   An Introduction to Ethnomusicology. http://www.insideworldmusic.com/library/weekly/aa101797.htm.
Kjaerulff, J.
    2010   *Internet and Change: An Ethnography of Knowledge and Flexible Work.* Walnut Creek, CA: Left Coast Press.
Klass, M.
    2003   *Mind over Mind: The Anthropology and Psychology of Spirit Possession.* Lanham, MA: Rowman & Littlefield.
Klein, N.
    2000   *No Logo: Taking Aim at the Brand Bullies.* New York: Picador.
Klein, R. G., with B. Edgar
    2002   *The Dawn of Human Culture.* New York: Wiley.
Kluckhohn, C.
    1944   *Mirror for Man: A Survey of Human Behavior and Social Attitudes.* Greenwich, CT: Fawcett.
Knauft, B.
    2005   *The Gebusi: Life Transformed in a Rainforest World.* Boston: McGraw-Hill.
Kochhar, R., R. Fry, and P. Taylor
    2011   Wealth Gaps Rise to Record Highs between Whites, Blacks, Hispanics. Pew Research Center. *Pew Social and Economic Trends.* http://www.pewsocialtrends.org/2011/07/26/wealth-gaps-rise-to-record-highs-between-whites-blacks-hispanics/

Kottak, C. P.
1980 *The Past in the Present: History, Ecology, and Social Organization in Highland Madagascar.* Ann Arbor: University of
Michigan Press.
1990a *Prime-Time Society: An Anthropological Analysis of
Television and Culture.* Belmont, CA: Wadsworth.
1990b Culture and Economic Development. *American
Anthropologist* 92(3): 723–731.
1991 When People Don't Come First: Some Lessons from
Completed Projects. In *Putting People First: Sociological Variables in Rural Development,* 2nd ed., ed. M. Cernea, pp. 429–464.
New York: Oxford University Press.
1999a *Assault on Paradise: Social Change in a Brazilian
Village,* 3rd ed. New York: McGraw-Hill.
1999b The New Ecological Anthropology. *American
Anthropologist* 101(1): 23–35.
2004 An Anthropological Take on Sustainable Development:
A Comparative Study of Change. *Human Organization* 63(4):
501–510.
2006 *Assault on Paradise: The Globalization of a Little
Community in Brazil,* 4th ed. New York: McGraw-Hill.
2007 Return to Madagascar: A Forty Year Retrospective.
*General Anthropology: Bulletin of the General Anthropology Divi-
sion of the American Anthropological Association* 14(2): 1–10.
2009 *Prime-Time Society: An Anthropological Analysis of Television and Culture,* updated ed. Walnut Creek, CA: Left Coast Press.
Kottak, C. P., L. L. Gezon, and G. Green
1994 Deforestation and Biodiversity Preservation in
Madagascar: The View from Above and Below. CIESIN Human
Dimensions Kiosk. http://www.ciesin.com.
Kottak, C. P., and K. A. Kozaitis
2012 *On Being Different: Diversity and Multiculturalism in
the North American Mainstream,* 4th ed. Boston: McGraw-Hill.
Kottak, N. C.
2002 *Stealing the Neighbor's Chicken: Social Control in Northern Mozambique.* Ph.D. dissertation. Department of Anthropology, Emory University, Atlanta, GA.
Kretchmer, N.
1975 (orig. 1972) Lactose and Lactase. In *Biological Anthropology,
Readings from Scientific American,* ed. S. H. Katz, pp. 310–318.
San Francisco: W. H. Freeman.
Kroeber, A. L.
1923 *Anthropology.* New York: Harcourt, Brace.
1944 *Configurations of Cultural Growth.* Berkeley: University
of California Press.
1987 (orig. 1952) *The Nature of Culture.* Chicago: University of
Chicago Press.
Kuhn, S. L., M. C. Stiner, and D. S. Reese
2001 Ornaments of the Earliest Upper Paleolithic: New Insights from the Levant. *Proceedings of the National Academy of
Sciences of the United States of America* 98(13): 7641–7646.
Kuniholm, P. I.
1995 Dendrochronology, in Science in Archaeology: A Review.
American Journal of Archaeology 99: 79–142.
2004 Home page of the Malcolm and Carolyn Wiener Labora-
tory for Aegean and Near Eastern Dendrochronology at Cornell
University. http://www.arts.cornell.edu/dendro/.
Kuper, L.
2006 *Race, Class, and Power: Ideology and Revolutionary
Change in Plural Societies.* New Brunswick, NJ: Transaction.
Kurtz, D. V.
2001 *Political Anthropology: Power and Paradigms.* Boulder,
CO: Westview Press.
Labov, W.
1972a *Language in the Inner City: Studies in the Black English
Vernacular.* Philadelphia: University of Pennsylvania Press.
1972b *Sociolinguistic Patterns.* Philadelphia: University of
Pennsylvania Press.
2006 *The Social Stratification of English in New York City.*
New York: Cambridge University Press.
Lacey, M.
2005 Remote and Poked: Anthropology's Dream Tribe.
New York Times, December 18. http://www.nytimes.com/2005/
12/18/international/africa/18tribe.html?_r=1&pagewanted=all.

Laguerre, M. S.
1984 *American Odyssey: Haitians in New York.* Ithaca, NY:
Cornell University Press.
1998 *Diasporic Citizenship: Haitian Americans in Transnational
America.* New York: St. Martin's Press.
1999 *The Global Ethnopolis: Chinatown, Japantown, and
Manilatown in American Society.* New York: St. Martin's Press.
Lakoff, R. T.
2004 *Language and Woman's Place.* New York: Harper & Row.
Lambek, M., ed.
2008 *A Reader in the Anthropology of Religion.* Malden, MA:
Blackwell.
Lancaster, R. N., and M. Di Leonardo, eds.
1997 *The Gender/Sexuality Reader: Culture, History, Political
Economy.* New York: Routledge.
Landes, D.
1999 *The Wealth and Poverty of Nations. Why Some Are So
Rich and Some Are So Poor.* London: Abacus.
Lange, M.
2009 *Lineages of Despotism and Development: British Colonial-
ism and State Power.* Chicago: University of Chicago Press.
Largent, F.
2007a Clovis Dethroned: A New Perspective on the First
Americans, Part 1. *Mammoth Trumpet* 22(3): 1–3, 20.
2007b Clovis Dethroned: A New Perspective on the First
Americans, Part 2. *Mammoth Trumpet* 22(4): 1–2, 13.
Larsen, C. S.
2000 *Skeletons in Our Closet: Revealing Our Past through
Bioarchaeology.* Princeton, NJ: Princeton University Press.
2011 *Our Origins: Discovering Physical Anthropology.*
New York: W. W. Norton.
Larson, A.
1989 Social Context of Human Immunodeficiency Virus Trans-
mission in Africa: Historical and Cultural Bases of East and Central
African Sexual Relations. *Review of Infectious Diseases* 11: 716–731.
Lassiter, L. E.
1998 *The Power of Kiowa Song: A Collaborative Ethnography.*
Tucson: University of Arizona Press.
Layton, R.
1991 *The Anthropology of Art,* 2nd ed. New York: Cambridge
University Press.
Leach, E. R.
1955 Polyandry, Inheritance and the Definition of Marriage.
Man 55: 182–186.
1961 *Rethinking Anthropology.* London: Athlone Press.
1970 (orig. 1954) *Political Systems of Highland Burma: A Study
of Kachin Social Structure.* London: Athlone Press.
1985 *Social Anthropology.* New York: Oxford University Press.
Leadbeater, C.
1999 *Europe's New Economy.* London: Centre for European
Reform.
Leakey, M. G., C. S. Feibel, I. McDougall, and A. Walker
1995 New Four-Million-Year-Old Hominid Species from
Kanapoi and Allia Bay, Kenya. *Nature* 376: 565–571.
Lee, R. B.
1974 (orig. 1968) What Hunters Do for a Living, or, How to Make
Out on Scarce Resources. In *Man in Adaptation: The Cultural
Present,* 2nd ed., ed. Y. A. Cohen, pp. 87–100. Chicago: Aldine.
1979 *The !Kung San: Men, Women, and Work in a Foraging
Society.* New York: Cambridge University Press.
1984 *The Dobe !Kung.* New York: Holt, Rinehart and Winston.
2003 *The Dobe Ju/'hoansi,* 3rd ed. Belmont, CA: Wadsworth.
Lee, R. B., and R. H. Daly
1999 *The Cambridge Encyclopedia of Hunters and Gatherers.*
New York: Cambridge University Press.
Leman, J.
2001 *The Dynamics of Emerging Ethnicities: Immigrant and In-
digenous Ethnogenesis in Confrontation.* New York: Peter Lang.
Lemonick, M. D., and A. Dorfman
1999 Up from the Apes: Remarkable New Evidence Is Filling
In the Story of How We Became Human. *Time* 154(8): 5–58.
Lenski, G.
1966 *Power and Privilege: A Theory of Social Stratification.*
New York: McGraw-Hill.

Lesure, R. G.
    2011   *Interpreting Ancient Figurines: Context, Comparison, and Prehistoric Art.* New York: Cambridge University Press.

Levine, N. E.
    1988   *The Dynamics of Polyandry: Kinship, Domesticity, and Population on the Tibetan Border.* Chicago: University of Chicago Press.

Levinson, B. A. U., and M. Pollock, eds.
    2011   *A Companion to the Anthropology of Education.* Malden, MA: Blackwell.

Lévi-Strauss, C.
    1963   *Totemism.* Translated by R. Needham. Boston: Beacon Press.
    1967   *Structural Anthropology.* New York: Doubleday.
    1969   (orig. 1949) *The Elementary Structures of Kinship.* Boston: Beacon Press.

Levy, F.
    2010   The World's Happiest Countries. *Forbes,* July 14. http://www.forbes.com/2010/07/14/world-happiest-countries-lifestyle-realestate-gallup.html

Levy, J. E., with B. Pepper
    1992   *Orayvi Revisited: Social Stratification in an "Egalitarian" Society.* Santa Fe, NM: School of American Research Press; Seattle: University of Washington Press.

Lewellen, T. C.
    2002   *The Anthropology of Globalization: Cultural Anthropology Enters the 21st Century.* Wesport, CT: Bergin and Garvey.
    2003   *Political Anthropology: An Introduction,* 3rd ed. Westport, CT: Praeger.
    2010   Groping toward Globalization: In Search of Anthropology without Boundaries. *Reviews in Anthropology* 31(1): 73–89.

Lewis, B., W. A. R. Jurmain, and L. Kilgore
    2007   *Understanding Physical Anthropology and Archaeology,* 9th ed. Belmont, CA: Thomson.

Lie, J.
    2001   *Multiethnic Japan.* Cambridge, MA: Harvard University Press.

Lieberman, P.
    1998   *Eve Spoke: Human Language and Human Evolution.* New York: W. W. Norton.

Lindenbaum, S.
    1972   Sorcerers, Ghosts, and Polluting Women: An Analysis of Religious Belief and Population Control. *Ethnology* 11: 241–253.

Linton, R.
    1943   Nativistic Movements. *American Anthropologist* 45: 230–240.

Little, K.
    1971   *Some Aspects of African Urbanization South of the Sahara. McCaleb Modules in Anthropology.* Reading, MA: Addison-Wesley.

Livingstone, F. B.
    1969   Gene Frequency Clines of the *b* Hemoglobin Locus in Various Human Populations and Their Similarities by Models Involving Differential Selection. *Human Biology* 41: 223–236.

Lockwood, W. G.
    1975   *European Moslems: Economy and Ethnicity in Western Bosnia.* New York: Academic Press.

Lockwood, Y. R.
    1983   *Text and Context: Folksong in a Bosnian Muslim Village.* Columbus, OH: Slavica.

Loomis, W. F.
    1967   Skin-Pigmented Regulation of Vitamin-D Biosynthesis in Man. *Science* 157: 501–506.

Loveday, L.
    1986   Japanese Sociolinguistics: An Introductory Survey. *Journal of Pragmatics* 10: 287–326.
    2001   *Explorations in Japanese Sociolinguistics.* Philadelphia: J. Benjamins.

Lowie, R. H.
    1935   *The Crow Indians.* New York: Farrar and Rinehart.
    1961   (orig. 1920) *Primitive Society.* New York: Harper & Brothers.

Lugo, A., and B. Maurer
    2000   *Gender Matters: Rereading Michelle Z. Rosaldo.* Ann Arbor, University of Michigan Press.

Lyell, C.
    1969   (orig. 1830–37) *Principles of Geology.* New York: Johnson.

Lynn, J.,
    2009.   Internet Censorship Seen Liable to WTO Challenge. *Reuters,* November 6. http://www.reuters.com/article/idUS-TRE5A520220091106.

Lyotard, J. F.
    1993   *The Postmodern Explained.* Translated by J. Pefanis, M. Thomas, and D. Barry. Minneapolis: University of Minnesota Press.

MacKinnon, J.
    1974   *In Search of the Red Ape.* New York: Ballantine.

Madra, Y. M.
    2004   Karl Polanyi: Freedom in a Complex Society. *Econ-Atrocity Bulletin: In the History of Thought.* http://www.fguide.org/Bulletin/polanyi.htm.

Malinowski, B.
    1927   *Sex and Repression in Savage Society.* London and New York: International Library of Psychology, Philosophy and Scientific Method.
    1929a   Practical Anthropology. *Africa* 2: 23–38.
    1944   *A Scientific Theory of Culture, and Other Essays.* Chapel Hill: University of North Carolina Press.
    1961   (orig. 1922) *Argonauts of the Western Pacific.* New York: Dutton.
    1978   (orig. 1931) The Role of Magic and Religion. In *Reader in Comparative Religion: An Anthropological Approach,* 4th ed., ed. W. A. Lessa and E. Z. Vogt, pp. 37–46. New York: Harper & Row.
    2001   (orig. 1927) *Sex and Repression in Savage Society.* Chicago: University of Chicago Press.

Malkin, C.
    2004   Earliest Primate Discovered in China. *Science Now,* January 5. American Association for the Advancement of Science. http://cmbi.bjmu.edu.cn/news/0401/13.htm.

Malkki, L. H.
    1995   *Purity and Exile: Violence, Memory, and National Cosmology among Hutu Refugees in Tanzania.* Chicago: University of Chicago Press.

Mann, Charles C.
    2011   *1493: Uncovering the New World Columbus Created.* New York: Knopf.

Manoff, Richard K.
    1994   How Family Planning Came to Bangladesh. Letter to the Editor. *New York Times,* Sunday, January 16, pp. 4–16.

Maquet, J.
    1964   Objectivity in Anthropology. *Current Anthropology* 5: 47–55.
    1986   *The Aesthetic Experience: An Anthropologist Looks at the Visual Arts.* New Haven, CT: Yale University Press.

Marcus, G. E., and M. M. J. Fischer
    1986   *Anthropology as Cultural Critique: An Experimental Moment in the Human Sciences.* Chicago: University of Chicago Press.
    1999   *Anthropology as Cultural Critique: An Experimental Moment in the Human Sciences,* 2nd ed. Chicago: University of Chicago Press.

Marcus, G. E., and F. R. Myers, eds.
    1995   *The Traffic in Culture: Refiguring Art and Anthropology.* Berkeley: University of California Press.

Marcus, J.
    1989   From Centralized Systems to City-States: Possible Models for the Epiclassic. In *Mesoamerica after the Decline of Teotihuacan: A.D. 700–900,* ed. R. A. Diehl and J. C. Berlo, pp. 201–208. Dumbarton Oaks: Washington, D.C.
    1992   *Mesoamerican Writing Systems: Propaganda, Myth, and History in Four Ancient Civilizations.* Princeton, NJ: Princeton University Press.

Marcus, J., and K. V. Flannery
    1996   *Zapotec Civilization: How Urban Society Evolved in Mexico's Oaxaca Valley.* New York: Thames and Hudson.

Marean, C. W. et al.
    2007   Early Human Use of Marine Resources and Pigment in South Africa during the Middle Pleistocene. *Nature* 449: 905–908 (18 October), doi:10.1038/nature06204.

Margolis, M.
1984 *Mothers and Such: American Views of Women and How They Changed.* Berkeley: University of California Press.
1994 *Little Brazil: An Ethnography of Brazilian Immigrants in New York City.* Princeton, NJ: Princeton University Press.
2000 *True to Her Nature: Changing Advice to American Women.* Prospect Heights, IL: Waveland.

Marshack, A.
1972 *Roots of Civilization.* New York: McGraw-Hill.

Martin, D.
1990 *Tongues of Fire: The Explosion of Protestantism in Latin America.* Cambridge, MA: Blackwell.

Martin, E.
1992 The End of the Body? *American Ethnologist* 19: 121–140.

Martin, K., and B. Voorhies
1975 *Female of the Species.* New York: Columbia University Press.

Martin, S. M.
1988 *Palm Oil and Protest: An Economic History of the Ngwa Region, South-Eastern Nigeria, 1800–1980.* New York: Cambridge University Press.

Marx, K., and F. Engels
1976 (orig. 1848) *Communist Manifesto.* New York: Pantheon.

Mascia-Lees, F.
2010 *Gender & Difference in a Globalizing World: Twenty-First Century Anthropology.* Long Grove, IL: Waveland.

Mascia-Lees, F., and N. J. Black
2000 *Gender and Anthropology.* Prospect Heights, IL: Waveland.

Mathews, G.
2000 *Global Culture/Individual Identity: Searching for Home in the Cultural Supermarket.* New York: Routledge.

Maugh, T. H., III
2007 One Language Disappears Every 14 Days; about Half of the World's Distinct Tongues Could Vanish This Century, Researchers Say. *Los Angeles Times,* September 19.

Maybury-Lewis, D.
2002 *Indigenous Peoples, Ethnic Groups, and the State,* 2nd ed. Boston: Allyn & Bacon.

Maybury-Lewis, D., T. Macdonald, and B. Maybury-Lewis, eds.
2009 *Manifest Destinies and Indigenous Peoples.* Cambridge, MA: David Rockefeller Center for Latin American Studies and Harvard University Press.

Mayell, H.
2003 Orangutans Show Signs of Culture, Study Says. *National Geographic News,* January 3. http://www.nationalgeographic.com/news/2002/12/1220_021226_orangutan.html.
2004a Wild Orangs, Extinct by 2023? *National Geographic News,* March 9. http://news.nationalgeographic.com/news/2003/09/0930_030930_orangutanthreat.html.
2004b Is Bead Find Proof Modern Thought Began in Africa? *National Geographic News,* March 31. http://news.nationalgeographic.com/news/2004/03/0331_040331_ostrichman.html.
2004c Three High-Altitude Peoples, Three Adaptations to Thin Air. *National Geographic News,* February 25.

Mayer, E.
2001 *What Evolution Is.* New York: Basic Books.

Mba, N. E.
1982 *Nigerian Women Mobilized: Women's Political Activity in Southern Nigeria, 1900–1965.* Berkeley: University of California Press, 1982.

Mayr, E.
2001 *What Evolution Is.* New York: Basic Books.

McAllester, D. P.
1954 *Enemy Way Music: A Study of Social and Esthetic Values as Seen in Navaho Music.* Cambridge, MA: Peabody Museum of American Archaeology and Ethnology, Papers 41(3).

McBrearty, S., and A. S. Brooks
2000 The Revolution That Wasn't: A New Interpretation of the Origin of Modern Human Behavior. *Journal of Human Evolution* 39: 453–563.

McBrearty, S., and C. Stringer
2007 The Coast in Colour. *Nature* 449: 793–794.

McCaskie, T. C.
1995 *State and Society in Pre-Colonial Asante.* New York: Cambridge University Press.

McConnell-Ginet, S.
2010 *Gender, Sexuality, and Meaning: Linguistic Practice and Politics.* New York: Oxford University Press.

McDonald, G.
1984 *Carioca Fletch.* New York: Warner Books.

McDougall, I., F. H. Brown, and J. G. Fleagle
2005 Stratigraphic Placement and Age of Modern Humans from Kibish, Ethiopia. *Nature* 433: 733–736.

McElroy, A., and P. K. Townsend
2009 *Medical Anthropology in Ecological Perspective,* 5th ed. Boulder, CO: Westview Press.

McGee, R. J., and R. L. Warms.
2012 *Anthropological Theory: An Introductory History,* 5th ed. New York: McGraw-Hill.

Mead, M.
1937 *Cooperation and Competition among Primitive Peoples.* New York: McGraw-Hill.
1950 (orig. 1935) *Sex and Temperament in Three Primitive Societies.* New York: New American Library.
1961 (orig. 1928) *Coming of Age in Samoa.* New York: Morrow Quill.

Meadow, R., ed.
1991 *Harappa Excavations 1986–1990: A Multidisciplinary Approach to Third Millennium Urbanism.* Monographs in World Archeology, no. 3. Madison, WI: Prehistory Press.

Meadow, R. H., and J. M. Kenoyer
2000 The Indus Valley Mystery: One of the World's First Great Civilizations Is Still a Puzzle. *Discovering Archaeology,* April, pp. 38–43.

Meigs, A., and K. Barlow
2002 Beyond the Taboo: Imagining Incest. *American Anthropologist* 104(1): 38–49.

Menzies, C. R., ed.
2006 *Traditional Ecological Knowledge and Natural Resource Management.* Lincoln: University of Nebraska Press.

Mercader, J.
2009 Mozambican Grass Seed Consumption During the Middle Stone Age. *Science* 326 (5960): 1680–1683.

Mercader, J., M. Panger, and C. Boesch
2002 Excavation of a Chimpanzee Stone Tool Site in the African Rainforest. *Science* 296: 1452–1455.

Merriam, A.
1971 The Arts and Anthropology. In *Anthropology and Art: Readings in Cross-Cultural Aesthetics,* ed. C. Otten, pp. 93–105. Austin: University of Texas Press.

Meyer, B.
1999 *Translating the Devil: Religion and Modernity among the Ewe in Ghana.* Trenton, NJ: Africa World Press.

Michaels, E.
1986 Aboriginal Content. Paper presented at the meeting of the Australian Screen Studies Association, December, Sydney.
1991 Aboriginal Content: Who's Got It–Who Needs It? *Visual Anthropology* 4: 277–300.

Miles, H. L.
1983 Apes and Language: The Search for Communicative Competence. In *Language in Primates,* ed. J. de Luce and H. T. Wilder, pp. 43–62. New York: Springer-Verlag.

Miller, B. D.
1997 *The Endangered Sex: Neglect of Female Children in Rural North India.* New York: Oxford University Press.

Miller, J. n.d. Alaskan Tlingit and Tsimtsian. Seattle: University of Washington Libraries, Digital Collections. http://content.lib.washington.edu/aipnw/miller1.html.

Miller, L.
2004 The Ancient Bristlecone Pine, Dendrochronology. http://www.sonic.net/bristlecone/dendro.html.

Miller, N., and R. C. Rockwell, eds.
1988 *AIDS in Africa : The Social and Policy Impact.* Lewiston, NY: Edwin Mellen.

Mills, G.
1971 Art: An Introduction to Qualitative Anthropology. In *Anthropology and Art: Readings in Cross-Cultural Aesthetics,* ed. C. Otten, pp. 66–92. Austin: University of Texas Press.

Mintz, S. W.
1985 *Sweetness and Power: The Place of Sugar in Modern History*. New York: Viking Penguin.

Mitani, J. C.
2011 Fearing a Planet Without Apes. *New York Times,* August 20.

Mitani, J. C., and D. P. Watts
1999 Demographic Influences on the Hunting Behavior of Chimpanzees. *American Journal of Physical Anthropology* 109: 439–454.

Mitchell, J. C.
1966 Theoretical Orientations in African Urban Studies. In *The Social Anthropology of Complex Societies,* ed. M. Banton, pp. 37–68. London: Tavistock.

Molnar, S.
2006 *Human Variation: Races, Types, and Ethnic Groups,* 6th ed. Upper Saddle River, NJ: Prentice Hall.

Montague, S., and R. Morais
1981 Football Games and Rock Concerts: The Ritual Enactment. In *The American Dimension: Cultural Myths and Social Realities,* 2nd ed., ed. W. Arens and S. B. Montague, pp. 33–52. Sherman Oaks, CA: Alfred.

Montgomery, S.
1991 *Walking with the Great Apes: Jane Goodall, Dian Fossey, Biruté Galdikas*. Boston: Houghton Mifflin.

Mooney, A.
2011 *Language, Society, and Power*. New York: Routledge.

Moore, J. D.
2009 *Visions of Culture: An Introduction to Anthropological Theories and Theorists,* 3rd ed. Lanham, MD: AltaMira.

Moran, L.
1993 Evolution Is a Fact and a Theory. The Talk Origins Archive. http://www.talkorigins.org/faqs/evolution-fact.html.

Morgan, L. H.
1963 (orig. 1877) *Ancient Society*. Cleveland: World Publishing.
1966 (orig. 1851) *League of the Ho-dé-no-sau-nee or Iroquois*. New York: B. Franklin.
1997 (orig. 1870) *Systems of Consanguinity and Affinity of the Human Family*. Lincoln: University of Nebraska Press.

Morkot, R.
2005 *The Egyptians: An Introduction*. New York: Routledge.

Moro, P. A., and J. E. Myers
2010 *Magic, Witchcraft, and Religion: A Reader in the Anthropology of Religion,* 8th ed. New York: McGraw-Hill.

Morphy, H., and M. Perkins, eds.
2006 *The Anthropology of Art: A Reader*. Malden, MA: Oxford, Blackwell.

Motseta, S.
2006 Botswana Gives Bushmen Tough Conditions. *Washington Post,* December 14. http://www.washingtonpost.com/wp-dyn/content/article/2006/12/14/AR2006121401008.html.

Mounier, A., S. Condemi, and G. Manzi
2011 The Stem Species of Our Species: A Place for the Archaic Human Cranium from Ceprano, Italy. *PLoS ONE* 6(4): e18821. doi:10.1371/journal.pone.0018821.

Mount Holyoke College
1999 Dung-Covered Madonna Sparks Controversy; Art Professor Michael Davis Takes a Look. *College Street Journal* 13(6), October 8. http://www.mtholyoke.edu/offices/comm/csj/991008/madonna.html.

Moyá-Solá, S., et al.
2004 *Pierolapithecus catalaunicus:* A New Middle Miocene Great Ape from Spain. *Science* 306(5700): 1339–1344.

Muhlhausler, P.
1986 *Pidgin and Creole Linguistics*. London: Blackwell.

Mukhopadhyay, C. C., R. Henze, and Y. T. Moses
2007 *How Real Is Race? A Sourcebook on Race, Culture, and Biology*. Lanham, MD: AltaMira.

Mullaney, T.
2011 *Coming to Terms with the Nation: Ethnic Classification in Modern China*. Berkeley: University of California Press.

Murchison, J. M.
2010 *Ethnography Essentials: Designing, Conducting, and Presenting Your Research*. San Francisco: Jossey Bass.

Murdock, G. P., and C. Provost
1973 Factors in the Division of Labor by Sex: A Cross-Cultural Analysis. *Ethnology* 12(2): 203–225.

Murray, S. O., and W. Roscoe, eds.
1998 *Boy-Wives and Female Husbands: Studies in African Homosexualities*. New York: St. Martin's Press.

Mydans, S.
1992a Criticism Grows over Aliens Seized During Riots. *New York Times,* May 29, p. A8.
1992b Judge Dismisses Case in Shooting by Officer. *New York Times,* June 4, p. A8.

Nadeem, S.
2011 *Dead Ringers: How Outsourcing Is Changing the Way Indians Understand Themselves*. Princeton, NJ: Princeton University Press.

Nafte, M.
2009 *Flesh and Bone: An Introduction to Forensic Anthropology,* 2nd ed. Durham, NC: Carolina Academic Press.

Nagel, J.
1996 *American Indian Ethnic Renewal: Red Power and the Resurgence of Identity and Culture*. New York: Oxford University Press.

Nanda, S.
1998 *Neither Man nor Woman: The Hijras of India*. Belmont, CA: Thomson/Wadsworth.
2000 *Gender Diversity: Crosscultural Variations*. Prospect Heights, IL: Waveland.

Narayan, K.
1997 *Mondays on the Dark Night of the Moon: Himalayan Foothill Folktales*. New York: Oxford University Press.

National Academy of Sciences
2008 Understanding and Responding to Climate Change: Highlights of National Academies Reports. http://dels.nas.edu/dels/rpt_briefs/climate_change_2008_final.pdf.

National Research Council
2011 America's Climate Choices. http://nas-sites.org/americasclimatechoices/sample-page/panel-reports/americas-climate-choices-final-report/

Newman, M.
1992 Riots Bring Attention to Growing Hispanic Presence in South-Central Area. *New York Times,* May 11, p. A10.

New York Times
2005 Intelligent Design Derailed. Editorial Desk, December 22. http://www.nytimes.com/2005/12/22/opinion/22thur1.html?ex=1292907600&en=af56b21719a9dd8f&ei=5090&partner=rssuserland&emc=rss.

Ni, X., W. Wang, Y. Hu, and C. Li
2004 A Euprimate Skull from the Early Eocene of China. *Nature* 427: 65–68.

Nolan, R. W.
2002 *Development Anthropology: Encounters in the Real World*. Boulder, CO: Westview Press.
2003 *Anthropology in Practice*. Boulder, CO: Lynne Rienner.

Nordstrom, C.
2004 *Shadows of War: Violence, Power, and International Profiteering in the Twenty-First Century*. Berkeley: University of California Press.

Nugent, D., and J. Vincent, eds.
2004 *A Companion to the Anthropology of Politics*. Malden, MA: Blackwell.

Nunn, N., and N. Qian
2010 The Colombian Exchange: A History of Disease, Food, and Ideas. *Journal of Economic Perspectives* 24(2): 163–188.

Nuwer, R.
2011 Reading Bones to Identify Genocide Victims. *New York Times,* November 18.

Nystrom, P., and P. Ashmore
2008 *The Life of Primates*. Upper Saddle River, NJ: Pearson Prentice Hall.

O'Connell, J. F., and J. Allen
2004 Dating the colonization of Sahul (Pleistocene Australia–New Guinea): A review of recent research. *Journal of Archaeological Science* 31: 835–853.

Omohundro, J. T.
2001 *Careers in Anthropology,* 2nd ed. Boston: McGraw-Hill.

Ong, A.

1987 *Spirits of Resistance and Capitalist Discipline: Factory Women in Malaysia.* Albany: State University of New York Press.

1989 Center, Periphery, and Hierarchy: Gender in Southeast Asia. In *Gender and Anthropology: Critical Reviews for Research and Teaching,* ed. S. Morgen, pp. 294–312. Washington, DC: American Anthropological Association.

2006 *Neoliberalism as Exception: Mutations in Citizenship and Sovereignty.* Durham, NC: Duke University Press.

2010 *Spirits of Resistance and Capitalist Discipline: Factory Women in Malaysia,* 2nd ed. Albany: State University of New York Press.

Ong, A., and S. J. Collier, eds.

2005 *Global Assemblages: Technology, Politics, and Ethics as Anthropological Problems.* Malden, MA: Blackwell.

Ontario Consultants on Religious Tolerance

1996 Religious Access Dispute Resolved. Internet Mailing List, April 12.

1997 Swiss Cult Promotes Cloning.

2001 Religions of the World: Number of Adherents; Rates of growth. http://www.religioustolerance.org/worldrel.htm.

Oriji, J. N.

2000 Igbo Women From 1929–1960. *West Africa Review* 2: 1.

Ortner, S. B.

1984 Theory in Anthropology Since the Sixties. *Comparative Studies in Society and History* 126(1): 126–166.

Osborne, R., and J. Tanner, eds.

2007 *Art's Agency and Art History.* Malden, MA: Blackwell.

Ottenheimer, M.

1996 *Forbidden Relatives: The American Myth of Cousin Marriage.* Champaign–Urbana: University of Illinois Press.

Otterbein, K. F.

2004 *How War Began.* College Station: Texas A&M University Press.

Owen, J.

2006 "Lucy's Baby"—World's Oldest Child—Found by Fossil Hunters. *National Geographic News,* September 20. http://news.nationalgeographic.com/news/2006/09/060920-lucys-baby.html.

Pappas, St.

2011 Paleo CSI: Early Hunters Left Mastodon Murder Weapon Behind. *Live Science.* October 20. http://www.livescience.com/16641-early-american-hunters-mastodon.html.

Park, M. A.

2010 *Biological Anthropology,* 6th ed. Boston: McGraw-Hill.

Parkin, R., and L. Stone, eds.

2004 *Kinship and Family: An Anthropological Reader.* Malden, MA: Blackwell.

Parsons, J. R.

1974 The Development of a Prehistoric Complex Society: A Regional Perspective from the Valley of Mexico. *Journal of Field Archaeology* 1: 81–108.

1976 The Role of Chinampa Agriculture in the Food Supply of Aztec Tenochtitlan. In *Cultural Change and Continuity: Essays in Honor of James Bennett Griffin,* ed. C. E. Cleland, pp. 233–262. New York: Academic Press.

Parzinger, H., et al.

2006 Declaration (on the Bosnia pyramid hoax). *The European Archaeologist.* December 11. http://www.e-a-a.org/statement.pdf.

Patterson, F.

1978 Conversations with a Gorilla. *National Geographic,* October, pp. 438–465.

1999 *Koko-love! Conversations with a Signing Gorilla.* New York: Dutton.

Paul, R.

1989 Psychoanalytic Anthropology. *Annual Review of Anthropology* 18: 177–202.

Paulson, T. E.

2005 Chimp, Human DNA Comparison Finds Vast Similarities, Key Differences. *Seattle Post-Intelligencer Reporter,* September 1, 2005. http://seattlepi.nwsource.com/local/238852_chimp01.html.

Peletz, M.

1988 *A Share of the Harvest: Kinship, Property, and Social History among the Malays of Rembau.* Berkeley: University of California Press.

Peters, J. D.

1997 Seeing Bifocally: Media, Place, Culture. In *Culture, Power, Place: Explorations in Critical Anthropology,* ed. A. Gupta and J. Ferguson, pp. 75–92. Durham, NC: Duke University Press.

Peters-Golden, H.

2012 *Culture Sketches,* 6th ed. Boston: McGraw-Hill.

Petraglia-Bahri, D.

1996 Introduction to Postcolonial Studies. http://www.emory.edu/ENGLISH/Bahri/.

Pew Research Center

2011 The Pew Forum on Religion and Public Life. http://www.pewforum.org/uploadedFiles/Topics/Religious_Affiliation/Christian/Evangelical_Protestant_Churches/Global%20Survey%20of%20Evan.%20Prot.%20Leaders.pdf.

Piddocke, S.

1969 The Potlatch System of the Southern Kwakiutl: A New Perspective. In *Environment and Cultural Behavior,* ed. A. P. Vayda, pp. 130–156. Garden City, NY: Natural History Press.

Piperno, D. R.

2001 On Maize and the Sunflower. *Science* 292(5525): 2260–2261.

Piperno, D. R., and D. M. Pearsall

1998 *The Origins of Agriculture in the Lowland Neotropics.* San Diego: Academic Press.

Piperno, D. R., and K. E. Stothert

2003 Phytolith Evidence for Early Holocene *Cucurbita* Domestication in Southwest Ecuador. *Science* 299(5609): 1054–1057.

Podolefsky, A., and P. J. Brown, eds.

1992 *Applying Anthropology: An Introductory Reader,* 2nd ed. Mountain View, CA: Mayfield.

2007 *Applying Anthropology: An Introductory Reader,* 8th ed. Boston: McGraw-Hill.

Pohl, M. E. D., D. R. Piperno, K. O. Pope, and J. G. Jones

2007 Microfossil Evidence for Pre-Columbian Maize Dispersals in the Neotropics from San Andrés, Tabasco, Mexico. *Proceedings of the National Academy of Sciences of the United States of America* 104(29): 11874–11881. April 10.10.1073/pnas.0701425104.

Polanyi, K.

1968 *Primitive, Archaic and Modern Economies: Essays of Karl Polanyi.* Edited by G. Dalton. Garden City, NY: Anchor Books.

Pollock, S.

1999 *Ancient Mesopotamia: The Eden That Never Was.* Cambridge, UK: Cambridge University Press.

Pospisil, L.

1963 *The Kapauku Papuans of West New Guinea.* New York: Harcourt Brace Jovanovich.

Potash, B., ed.

1986 *Widows in African Societies: Choices and Constraints.* Stanford, CA: Stanford University Press.

Price, R., ed.

1973 *Maroon Societies.* New York: Anchor Press, Doubleday.

Price, T. D., and G. M. Feinman

2010 *Images of the Past,* 6th ed. Boston: McGraw-Hill.

Radcliffe-Brown, A. R.

1952 (orig. 1924) The Mother's Brother in South Africa. In A. R. Radcliffe-Brown, *Structure and Function in Primitive Society,* pp. 15–31. London: Routledge & Kegan Paul.

1965 (orig. 1962) *Structure and Function in Primitive Society.* New York: Free Press.

Raffaele, P.

2010 *Among the Great Apes: Adventures on the Trail of Our Closest Relatives.* New York: Smithsonian, Harper.

Rak, Y.

1986 The Neandertal: A New Look at an Old Face. *Journal of Human Evolution* 15(3): 151–164.

Ramachandran, S., and N. Rosenberg

2011 A Test of the Influence of Continental Axes of Orientation on Patterns of Human Gene Flow. *Journal of Physical Anthropology* 146(4): 515–529.

Ramos, A. R.

1995 *Sanumá Memories : Yanomami Ethnography in Times of Crisis.* Madison, WI: University of Wisconsin Press.

Random House College Dictionary 1982, revised ed. New York: Random House.

Ranger, T. O.
 1996   Postscript. In *Postcolonial Identities,* ed. R. Werbner and T. O. Ranger. London: Zed.

Rappaport, R. A.
 1974   Obvious Aspects of Ritual. *Cambridge Anthropology* 2: 2–60.
 1999   *Holiness and Humanity: Ritual in the Making of Religious Life.* New York: Cambridge University Press.

Rathje, W. L., and C. Murphy
 2001   *Rubbish!: The Archaeology of Garbage.* Tucson: University of Arizona Press.

Rathus, S. A., J. S. Nevid, and J. Fichner-Rathus
 2013   *Human Sexuality in a World of Diversity,* 9th ed. Boston: Allyn & Bacon.

Reader, J.
 2011   *Missing Links: In Search of Human Origins.* New York: Oxford University Press.

Redfield, R.
 1941   *The Folk Culture of Yucatan.* Chicago: University of Chicago Press.

Redfield, R., R. Linton, and M. Herskovits
 1936   Memorandum on the Study of Acculturation. *American Anthropologist* 38: 149–152.

Reese, W. L.
 1999   *Dictionary of Philosophy and Religion: Eastern and Western Thought.* Amherst, NY: Humanities Books.

Reiter, R., ed.
 1975   *Toward an Anthropology of Women.* New York: Monthly Review Press.

Relethford, J. H.
 2010   *The Human Species: An Introduction to Biological Anthropology,* 8th ed. Boston: McGraw-Hill.
 2012   *Human Population Genetics.* Hoboken, NJ: Wiley-Blackwell.

Renfrew, C., and P. Bahn
 2008   *Archaeology: Theories, Methods, and Practice,* 5th ed. London: Thames and Hudson.
 2010   *Archaeology Essentials: Theories, Methods, and Practice,* 2nd ed. London: Thames and Hudson.

Renfrew, C., and P. Bahn, eds.
 2005   *Archaeology: The Key Concepts,* New York: Routledge.

Rice, P.
 2002.   Paleoanthropology 2001—Part II. *General Anthropology* 8(2): 11–14.

Rickford, J. R.
 1997   Suite for Ebony and Phonics. http://www.stanford.edu/~rickford/papers/SuiteForEbonyandPhonics.html (also published in *Discover,* December 1997).
 1999   *African American Vernacular English: Features, Evolution, Educational Implications.* Malden, MA: Blackwell.

Rickford, J. R., and R. J. Rickford
 2000   *Spoken Soul: The Story of Black English.* New York: Wiley.

Rilling, J. K., D. A. Gutman, T. R. Zeh, G. Pagnoni, G. S. Berns, and C. D. Kilts
 2002   A Neural Basis for Social Cooperation. *Neuron* 35: 395–405.

Roach, J.
 2007   "Hobbit" Human Was Unique Species, Wrist Bones Suggest. *National Geographic News,* September 20. http://news.nationalgeographic.com/news/pf/65255655.html.

Robbins, R.
 2011   *Global Problems and the Culture of Capitalism,* 5th ed. Boston: Pearson/Allyn & Bacon.

Roberts, D. F.
 1953   Body Weight, Race and Climate. *American Journal of Physical Anthropology* 11: 533–558.
 1986   *Genetic Variation and Its Maintenance: With Particular Reference to Tropical Populations.* New York: Cambridge University Press.

Roberts, S., A. Sabar, B. Goodman, and M. Balleza
 2007   51% of Women Are Now Living Without Spouse. *New York Times,* January 16. http://www.nytimes.com.

Robertson, J.
 1992   Koreans in Japan. Paper presented at the University of Michigan Department of Anthropology, Martin Luther King Jr. Day Panel, January. Ann Arbor: University of Michigan Department of Anthropology (unpublished).

Rodseth, L., R. W. Wrangham, A. M. Harrigan, and B. Smuts
 1991   The Human Community as a Primate Society. *Current Anthropology* 32: 221–254.

Root, D.
 1996   *Cannibal Culture: Art, Appropriation, and the Commodification of Difference.* Boulder, CO: Westview Press.

Rosaldo, M. Z.
 1980a   *Knowledge and Passion: Notions of Self and Social Life.* Stanford, CA: Stanford University Press.
 1980b   The Use and Abuse of Anthropology: Reflections on Feminism and Cross-Cultural Understanding. *Signs* 5(3): 389–417.

Rosaldo, M. Z., and L. Lamphere, eds.
 1974   *Woman, Culture, and Society.* Stanford, CA: Stanford University Press.

Roscoe, W.
 1991   *The Zuni Man-Woman.* Albuquerque: University of New Mexico Press.
 1998   *Changing Ones: Third and Fourth Genders in Native North America.* New York: St. Martin's Press.

Rosenberg, K. R., and W. R. Trevathan
 2001   The Evolution of Human Birth. *Scientific American* 285(5): 60–65.

Rothman, J. M., D. Raubenheimer, and C. A. Chapman
 2011   Nutritional Geometry: Gorillas Prioritize Non-Protein Energy While Consuming Surplus Protein. *Biology Letters* 7: 847–849. London: The Royal Society. sbi.royalsocietypublishing.org.

Rothstein, E.
 2006   Protection for Indian Patrimony That Leads to a Paradox. *New York Times,* March 29.

Rouse, R.
 1991   Mexican Migration and the Social Space of Postmodernism. *Diaspora* 1(1): 8–23.

Royal Anthropological Institute
 1951   *Notes and Queries on Anthropology,* 6th ed. London: Routledge and Kegan Paul.

Ryan, S.
 1990   *Ethnic Conflict and International Relations.* Brookfield, MA: Dartmouth.
 1995   *Ethnic Conflict and International Relations,* 2nd ed. Brookfield, MA: Dartmouth.

Ryang, S., and J. Lie
 2009   *Diaspora Without Homeland: Being Korean in Japan.* Berkeley: University of California Press.

Rylko-Bauer, B., M. Singer, and J. Van Willigen
 2006   Reclaiming Applied Anthropology: Its Past, Present, and Future. *American Anthropologist* 108(1): 178–190.

Sabloff, J. A.
 2008   *Archaeology Matters: Action Archaeology in the Modern World.* Walnut Creek, CA: Left Coast Press.

Sack, K.
 2011   In Tough Times, a Boom in Cremations as a Way to Save Money. *New York Times,* December 8. http://www.nytimes.com/2011/12/09/us/in-economic-downtown-survivors-turning-to-cremations-over-burials.html?scp=1&sq=cremations&st=cse.

Sadig, A. M.
 2010   *The Neolithic of the Middle Nile Region: An Archeology of Central Sudan and Nubia.* East Lansing, MI: Michigan State University Press.

Sahlins, M. D.
 1961   The Segmentary Lineage: An Organization of Predatory Expansion. *American Anthropologist* 63: 322–345.
 1968   *Tribesmen.* Englewood Cliffs, NJ: Prentice Hall.
 1972   *Stone Age Economics.* Chicago: Aldine-Atherton.
 2004   (orig. 1972) *Stone Age Economics.* New York: Routledge.
 2011   (orig. 1972) *Stone Age Economics.* New Brunswick, NJ: Transaction.

Salzman, P. C.
 1974   Political Organization among Nomadic Peoples. In *Man in Adaptation: The Cultural Present,* 2nd ed., ed. Y. A. Cohen, pp. 267–284. Chicago: Aldine.
 2004   *Pastoralists: Equality, Hierarchy, and the State.* Boulder, CO: Westview Press.
 2008   *Culture and Conflict in the Middle East.* Amherst, NY: Humanity Books.

Salzmann, Z., J. M. Stanlaw, and N. Adachi
2012 *Language, Culture, and Society: An Introduction to Linguistic Anthropology,* 5th ed. Boulder, CO: Westview Press.

Sanday, P. R.
1974 Female Status in the Public Domain. In *Woman, Culture, and Society,* ed. M. Z. Rosaldo and L. Lamphere, pp. 189–206. Stanford, CA: Stanford University Press.
2002 *Women at the Center: Life in a Modern Matriarchy.* Ithaca, NY: Cornell University Press.

Sands, R. R., and L. R. Sands, eds.
2010 *The Anthropology of Sport and Human Movement: A Biocultural Perspective.* Lanham, MD: Lexington Books.

Santley, R. S.
1985 The Political Economy of the Aztec Empire. *Journal of Anthropological Research* 41(3): 327–337.

Sapir, E.
1931 Conceptual Categories in Primitive Languages. *Science* 74: 578–584.
1956 (orig. 1928) The Meaning of Religion. In E. Sapir, *Culture, Language and Personality: Selected Essays.* Berkeley: University of California Press.

Schaefer, R.
2013 *Race and Ethnicity in the United States,* 7th ed. Upper Saddle River, NJ: Prentice Hall.

Schaik, C. V.
2004 *Among Orangutans: Red Apes and the Rise of Human Culture.* Tucson: University of Arizona Press.

Scheidel, W.
1997 Brother-Sister Marriage in Roman Egypt. *Journal of Biosocial Science* 29(3): 361–371.

Scheinman, M.
1980 Imperialism. *Academic American Encyclopedia,* vol. 11, pp. 61–62. Princeton, NJ: Arete.

Schildkrout, E., and C. A. Keim
1990 *African Reflections: Art from Northeastern Zaire.* Seattle: University of Washington Press.

Schneider, D. M.
1967 Kinship and Culture: Descent and Filiation as Cultural Constructs. *Southwestern Journal of Anthropology* 23: 65–73.
1968 *American Kinship: A Cultural Account.* Englewood Cliffs, NJ: Prentice Hall.

Schneider, D. M., and K. Gough, eds.
1961 *Matrilineal Kinship.* Berkeley: University of California Press.

Scholte, J. A.
2000 *Globalization: A Critical Introduction.* New York: St. Martin's Press.

Schultz, S., C. Opie, and Q. D. Atkinson
2011 Stepwise Evolution of Stable Sociality in Primates. *Nature* 479: 229–222, November 11. http://www.nature.com/nature/journal/v479/n7372/full/nature10601.html.

Schwartz, J.
2006 Archaeologist in New Orleans Finds a Way to Help the Living. *New York Times,* January 3.

Schwartz, M. J., V. W. Turner, and A. Tuden, eds.
2011 *Political Anthropology.* New Brunswick, NJ: Aldine Transaction.

Schweingruber, F. H.
1988 *Tree Rings: Basics and Applications of Dendrochronology.* Hingham, MA: Kluwer Academic.

Scott, J.
2002 Prehistoric Human Footpaths Lure Archaeologists Back to Costa Rica. University of Colorado Press Release, May 20. http://www.eurekalert.org/pub_releases/2002-05/uoca-phf052002.php.

Scott, James C.
1990 *Domination and the Arts of Resistance.* New Haven, CT: Yale University Press.

Scott, Janny
2009 A Free-Spirited Wanderer Who Set Obama's Path. *New York Times,* May 14. http://www.nytimes.com/2008/03/14/us/politics/14obama.html?pagewanted=all.
2011 *A Singular Woman: The Untold Story of Barack Obama's Mother.* New York: Riverhead Books.

Scudder, T., and E. Colson
1980 *Secondary Education and the Formation of an Elite: The Impact of Education on Gwembe District, Zambia.* London: Academic Press.

Scupin, R.
2012 *Race and Ethnicity: The United States and the World,* 2nd ed. Upper Saddle River, NJ: Prentice Hall.

Sebeok, T. A., and J. Umiker-Sebeok, eds.
1980 *Speaking of Apes: A Critical Anthropology of Two-Way Communication with Man.* New York: Plenum Press.

Senut, B., M. Pickford, D. Gommery, P. Mein, K. Cheboi, and Y. Coppens
2001 First Hominid from the Miocene (Lukeino Formation, Kenya). *Comptes Rendus de l'Academie des Sciences, Series IIA—Earth and Planetary Science* 332(30): 137–144.

Service, E. R.
1962 *Primitive Social Organization: An Evolutionary Perspective.* New York: McGraw-Hill.
1966 *The Hunters.* Englewood Cliffs, NJ: Prentice Hall.

Shannon, T. R.
1989 *An Introduction to the World-System Perspective.* Boulder, CO: Westview Press.
1996 *An Introduction to the World-System Perspective,* 2nd ed. Boulder, CO: Westview Press.

Sharma, A., and A. Gupta, eds.
2006 *The Anthropology of the State: A Reader.* Malden, MA: Blackwell.

Shermer, M.
2002 *In Darwin's Shadow: The Life and Science of Alfred Russel Wallace.* New York: Oxford University Press.

Sherwood, R. J., S. C. Ward, and A. Hill
2002 The Taxonomic Status of the Chemeron Temporal (KNM-BCI). *Science Direct,* February 27. http://www.sciencedirect.com.

Shivaram, C.
1996 Where Women Wore the Crown: Kerala's Dissolving Matriarchies Leave a Rich Legacy of Compassionate Family Culture. *Hinduism Today* 96(2). http://www.hinduism-today.com/archives/1996/2/1996-2-03.shtml.

Shore, B.
1996 *Culture in Mind: Meaning, Construction, and Cultural Cognition.* New York: Oxford University Press.

Shostak, M.
1983 *Nisa, the Life and Words of a !Kung Woman.* New York: Vintage Books.
2000 *Return to Nisa.* Cambridge, MA: Harvard University Press.

Shreeve, J.
1992 The Dating Game: How Old Is the Human Race? *Discover* 13(9): 76–83.

Shryock, A.
1988 Autonomy, Entanglement, and the Feud: Prestige Structures and Gender Values in Highland Albania. *Anthropological Quarterly* 61(3): 113–118.

Shryock, A., ed.
2010 *Islamophobia/Islamophilia: Beyond the Politics of Enemy and Friend.* Bloomington: Indiana University Press.

Silberbauer, G.
1981 *Hunter and Habitat in the Central Kalahari Desert.* New York: Cambridge University Press.

Sillitoe, P., ed.
2007 *Local Science versus Global Science: Approaches to Indigenous Knowledge in International Development.* New York: Berghahn Books.

Simmons, A. H.
2007 *The Neolithic Revolution in the Near East: Transforming the Human Landscape.* Tucson: University of Arizona Press.

Simons, E. L., and P. C. Ettel
1970 *Gigantopithecus. Scientific American,* January, pp. 77–85.

Singer, M.
2008 *Drugging the Poor: Legal and Illegal Drugs and Social Inequality.* Long Grove, IL: Waveland.

Singer, M., and H. Baer
2007 *Introducing Medical Anthropology: A Discipline in Action.* Lanham, MD: AltaMira.

Smart, A., and J. Smart
  2003   Urbanization and the Global Perspective. *Annual Review of Anthropology* 32: 263–285.
Smith, A.
  2008   (orig. 1776) *An Inquiry into the Nature and Causes of the Wealth of Nations: A Selected Edition.* New York: Oxford University Press.
Smith, B. D.
  1995   *The Emergence of Agriculture.* New York: Scientific American Library, W. H. Freeman.
Smith, C. S.
  2006   Some See a 'Pyramid' to Hone Bosnia's Image. Others See a Big Hill. *New York Times,* May 15.
Smith, M. K., and M. E. Doyle
  2002   'Globalization' *The Encyclopedia of Informal Education.* http://www.infed.org/biblio/globalization,.htmhttp://www.infed.org/biblio/globalization.htm
Smitherman, G.
  1986   *Talkin and Testifyin: The Language of Black America.* Detroit: Wayne State University Press.
Solheim, W. G. II
  1976   (orig. 1972) An Earlier Agricultural Revolution. In *Avenues to Antiquity, Readings from Scientific American,* ed. B. M. Fagan, pp. 160–168. San Francisco: W. H. Freeman.
Solway, J., ed.
  2006   *The Politics of Egalitarianism.* New York: Berghahn Books.
Solway, J., and R. Lee
  1990   Foragers, Genuine and Spurious: Situating the Kalahari San in History (with CA treatment). *Current Anthropology* 31(2): 109–146.
Sotomayor, S.
  2009   A Latina Judge's Voice. The Judge Mario G. Olmos Memorial Lecture, delivered at the University of California, Berkeley, School of Law in 2001; published in the spring 2002 issue of the *Berkeley La Raza Law Journal,* republished by the *New York Times* on May 14, 2009.
Spencer, C. S.
  2003   War and Early State Formation in Oaxaca, Mexico. *Proceedings of the National Academy of Sciences of the United States of America* 100(20): 11185–11187. http://www.pnas.org/cgi/doi/10.1073/pnas.2034992100.
Spickard, P., ed.
  2004   *Race and Nation: Ethnic Systems in the Modern World.* New York: Routledge.
Spindler, G. D., ed.
  2000   *Fifty Years of Anthropology and Education, 1950–2000: A Spindler Anthology.* Mahwah, NJ: Erlbaum.
  2005   *New Horizons in the Anthropology of Education.* Mahwah, NJ: Erlbaum.
Spindler, G. D., and L. Hammond, eds.
  2006   *Innovations in Educational Ethnography: Theory, Methods, and Results.* Mahwah, NJ: L. Erlbaum Associates.
Spiro, M. E.
  1993   *Oedipus in the Trobriands.* New Brunswick, NJ: Transaction.
Spoor, F., M. G. Leakey, P. N. Gathongo, F. H. Brown, S. C. Anton, I. McDougall, C. Kiarie, F. K. Manthi, and L. N. Leakey
  2007   Implications of New Early Homo Fossils from Ileret, East of Lake Turkana, Kenya. *Nature* 448 (7154): 688–691. http://news.nature.com//news/2007/070806/070806-5.html.
Srivastava, J., N. J. H. Smith, and D. A. Forno
  1999   *Integrating Biodiversity in Agricultural Intensification: Toward Sound Practices.* Washington, DC: World Bank.
Stacey, J.
  2011   *Unhitched: Love, Marriage, and Family Values from West Hollywood to Western China.* New York: New York University Press.
Stack, C. B.
  1975   *All Our Kin: Strategies for Survival in a Black Community.* New York: Harper Torchbooks.
Statistical Abstract of the United States. Washington, DC: U.S. Bureau of the Census, U.S. Government Printing Office.
  2012   *Statistical Abstract of the United States,* 2012. http://www.census.gov/prod/www/statistical-abstract.html.

Statistics Canada
  2001*a*   1996 Census. Nation Tables. http://www.statcan.ca/english/census96/nation.htm.
Steegman, A. T., Jr.
  1975   Human Adaptation to Cold. *In Physiological Anthropology,* ed. A. Damon, pp. 130–166. New York: Oxford University Press.
Stein, R. L., and P. L. Stein, eds.
  2008   *The Anthropology of Religion, Magic, and Witchcraft,* 2nd ed. Boston: Pearson.
  2011   *The Anthropology of Religion, Magic, and Witchcraft,* 3rd ed. Upper Saddle River, NJ: Pearson Prentice Hall.
Steinfels, P.
  1997   Beliefs: Cloning, as Seen by Buddhists and Humanists. *New York Times,* July 12. http://www.nytimes.com.
Stevens, W. K.
  1992   Humanity Confronts Its Handiwork: An Altered Planet. *New York Times,* May 5, pp. B5–B7.
Stevenson, D.
  2003   *Cities and Urban Cultures.* Philadelphia: Open University Press.
Steward, J. H.
  1955   *Theory of Culture Change.* Urbana: University of Illinois Press.
  1956   *The People of Puerto Rico: A Study in Social Anthropology.* Urbana: University of Illinois Press.
Stockard, J. E.
  2001   *Marriage in Culture: Practice and Meaning Across Diverse Societies.* San Diego, CA: Harcourt.
Stoler, A.
  1977   Class Structure and Female Autonomy in Rural Java. *Signs* 3: 74–89.
Stoler, A. L.
  1995   *Race and the Education of Desire: Foucault's History of Sexuality and the Colonial Order of Things.* Durham, NC: Duke University Press.
  2002   *Carnal Knowledge and Imperial Power: Race and the Intimate in Colonial Rule.* Berkeley: University of California Press.
Stoler, A. L., C. McGranahan, and P. C. Perdue, eds.
  2007   *Imperial Formations.* Santa Fe, NM: School for Advanced Research Press.
Strachan, T., and A. P. Read
  2004   *Human Molecular Genetics,* 3rd ed. New York: Garland Press.
Strathern, A., and P. J. Stewart
  2010   *Kinship in Action: Self and Group.* Boston: Prentice Hall.
Strier, K. B.
  2011   *Primate Behavioral Ecology,* 4th ed. Boston: Allyn & Bacon.
Sunderland, P. L., and R. M. Denny
  2007   *Doing Anthropology in Consumer Research.* Walnut Creek, CA: Left Coast Press.
Sunstein, B. S., and E. Chiseri-Strater
  2012   *Fieldworking: Reading and Writing Research,* 4th ed. Boston: Bedford/St. Martins.
Susman, R. L.
  1987   Pygmy Chimpanzees and Common Chimpanzees: Models for the Behavioral Ecology of the Earliest Hominids. In *The Evolution of Human Behavior: Primate Models,* ed. W. G. Kinzey, pp. 72–86. Albany: State University of New York Press.
Suttles, W.
  1960   Affinal Ties, Subsistence, and Prestige among the Coast Salish. *American Anthropologist* 62: 296–395.
Svasek, M.
  2007   *Anthropology, Art, and Cultural Production.* Ann Arbor, MI: Pluto Press.
Tague, R. G., and C. O. Lovejoy
  1986   The Obstetric Pelvis of A. L. 288-1 (Lucy). *Journal of Human Evolution* 15: 237–255.
Tanaka, J.
  1980   *The San Hunter-Gatherers of the Kalahari.* Tokyo: University of Tokyo Press.
Tannen, D.
  1990   *You Just Don't Understand: Women and Men in Conversation.* New York: Ballantine.
  2005   *Conversational Style: Analyzing Talk Among Friends,* new ed. New York: Oxford University Press.

Tannen, D., ed.
1993   *Gender and Conversational Interaction.* New York: Oxford University Press.

Taylor, C.
1987   Anthropologist-in-Residence. In *Applied Anthropology in America,* 2nd ed., ed. E. M. Eddy and W. L. Partridge. New York: Columbia University Press.
1996   *The Black Churches of Brooklyn.* New York: Columbia University Press.

Terrace, H. S.
1979   *Nim.* New York: Knopf.

Terrell, J. E.
1998   The Prehistoric Pacific. *Archaeology* 51(6). Archaeological Institute of America. http://www.archaeology. org/ 9811/abstracts/pacific.html.

Thompson, W.
1983   Introduction: World System with and without the Hyphen. In *Contending Approaches to World System Analysis,* ed. W. Thompson, pp. 7–26. Thousand Oaks, CA: Sage.

Thomson, A., and L. H. D. Buxton
1923   Man's Nasal Index in Relation to Certain Climatic Conditions. *Journal of the Royal Anthropological Institute* 53: 92–112.

Tice, K.
1997   Reflections on Teaching Anthropology for Use in the Public and Private Sector. In *The Teaching of Anthropology: Problems, Issues, and Decisions,* ed. C. P. Kottak, J. J. White, R. H. Furlow, and P. C. Rice, pp. 273–284. Mountain View, CA: Mayfield.

Tishkoff, S. A. et al.
2007   Convergent Adaptation of Human Lactase Persistence in Africa and Europe. *Nature Genetics* 39(1): 31–40.

Tishkov, V. A.
2004   *Chechnya: Life in a War-Torn Society.* Berkeley: University of California Press.

Titiev, M.
1992   *Old Oraibi: A Study of the Hopi Indians of Third Mesa.* Albuquerque: University of New Mexico Press.

Toner, R.
1992   Los Angeles Riots Are a Warning, Americans Fear. *New York Times,* May 11, pp. A1, A11.

Toth, N.
1985   The Oldowan Reassessed: A Close Look at Early Stone Artifacts. *Journal of Archaelogical Science* 2: 101–120.

Tougher, S.
2008   *The Eunuch in Byzantine History and Society.* New York: Routledge.

Trehub, S. E.
2001   Musical Predispositions in Infancy. *Annals of the New York Academy of Sciences* 930(1): 1–16.

Trevathan, W. R., E. O. Smith, and J. McKenna
2008   *Evolutionary Medicine and Health.* New York: Oxford University Press.

Trigger, B. G.
2003   *Understanding Early Civilizations: A Comparative Study.* Cambridge, UK: Cambridge University Press.

Trivedi, B. P.
2001   Scientists Identify a Language Gene. *National Geographic News,* October 4. http://news.nationalgeographic.com/news/2001/10/1004_TVlanguagegene.html.

Trudgill, P.
2000   *Sociolinguistics: An Introduction to Language and Society,* 4th ed. New York: Penguin.
2010   *Investigations in Sociohistorical Linguistics: Stories of Colonisation and Contact.* New York: Cambridge University Press.

Turnbull, C.
1965   *Wayward Servants: The Two Worlds of the African Pygmies.* Garden City, NY: Natural History Press.

Turner, V. W.
1967   *The Forest of Symbols: Aspects of Ndembu Ritual.* Ithaca, NY: Cornell University Press.
1995   (orig. 1969) *The Ritual Process.* Hawthorne, NY: Aldine.
1996   (orig. 1957) *Schism and Continuity in an African Society: A Study of Ndembu Village Life.* Washington, DC: Berg.

Tylor, E. B.
1889   On a Method of Investigating the Development of Institutions: Applied to Laws of Marriage and Descent. *Journal of the Royal Anthropological Institute* 18: 245–269.
1958   (orig. 1871) *Primitive Culture.* New York: Harper Torchbooks.

Ulijaszek, S. J., and H. Lofink
2006   Obesity in Biocultural Perspective. *Annual Review of Anthropology* 35: 337–360.

Ulman, H.
2007   Brady an Easy Winner of AP Male Athlete. *Associated Press,* December 22. http://abcnws.go.com/sports/wireStory?id=4042479.

University of Virginia n.d. American Studies Program, Armory Show of 1913. http://xroads.virginia.edu/~MUSEUM/Armory/ofili.html.

Van Allen, J.
1971   *"Aba Riots" or "Women's War"?: British Ideology and Eastern Nigerian Women's Political Activism.* Waltham, MA: African Studies Association.

Van Cantfort, T. E., and J. B. Rimpau
1982   Sign Language Studies with Children and Chimpanzees. *Sign Language Studies* 34: 15–72.

Van der Elst, D., and P. Bohannan
2003   *Culture as Given, Culture as Choice,* 2nd ed. Prospect Heights, IL: Waveland.

Vayda, A. P.
1968 (orig. 1961)   Economic Systems in Ecological Perspective: The Case of the Northwest Coast. In *Readings in Anthropology,* 2nd ed., vol. 2, ed. M. H. Fried, pp. 172–178. New York: Crowell.

Veblen, T.
1934   *The Theory of the Leisure Class: An Economic Study of Institutions.* New York: The Modern Library.

Veja 1984*a*   *Olimpíadas,* August 8, pp. 36–50.
1984*b*   *Vitórias no Tatame.* August 15, p. 61.
1984*c*   *Brasil de Ouro e de Prata.* August 15, p. 48. BBC News.

Vekua, A., D. Lordkipanidze, and G. P. Rightmire
2002   A Skull of Early Homo from Dmanisi, Georgia. *Science,* July 5, pp. 85–89.

Verdery, K.
2001   Socialist Societies: Anthropological Aspects. *International Encyclopedia of the Social & Behavioral Sciences,* pp. 14496–14500. New York: Elsevier.

Vidal, J.
2003   Every Third Person Will Be a Slum Dweller Within 30 Years, UN Agency Warns: Biggest Study of World's Cities Finds 940 Million Already Living in Squalor. *The Guardian,* October 4. http://www.guardian.co.uk/international/story/0,3604,1055785,00.html.

Vigil, J. D.
2003   Urban Violence and Street Gangs. *Annual Review of Anthropology* 32: 225–242.
2010   Gang Redux: A Balanced Anti-Gang Strategy. Long Grove, IL: Waveland.
2012   *From Indians to Chicanos; The Dynamics of Mexican-American Culture,* 3rd ed. Boulder, CO: Westview.

Vincent, J.
1990   *Anthropology and Politics: Visions, Traditions, and Trends.* Tucson: University of Arizona Press.

von Cramon-Taubadel, N.
2011   Global Human Mandibular Variation Reflects Differences in Agricultural and Hunter-Gatherer Subsistence Strategies. *Proceedings of the National Academy of Sciences,* 108(49): 19546–19551.

Von Daniken, E.
1971   *Chariots of the Gods: Unsolved Mysteries of the Past.* New York: Bantam.

Wade, N.
2004   New Species Revealed: Tiny Cousins of Humans. *New York Times,* October 28, national edition, pp. A1, A6.
2007   Fossil DNA Expands Neanderthal Range. *New York Times,* October 2. www.nytimes.com.
2011*a*   New Fossils May Redraw Human Ancestry. *New York Times,* September 8. http://www.nytimes.com/2011/09/09/science/09fossils.html.
2011*b*   New View of How Humans Moved Away from Apes. *New York Times,* March 10.

Wade, P.

2002   *Race, Nature, and Culture: An Anthropological Perspective.* Sterling, VA: Pluto Press.

2010   *Race and Ethnicity in Latin America,* 2nd ed. New York: Pluto Press.

Wallace, A. F. C.

1956   Revitalization Movements. *American Anthropologist* 58: 264–281.

1966   *Religion: An Anthropological View.* New York: McGraw-Hill.

1970   *The Death and Rebirth of the Seneca.* New York: Knopf.

Wallerstein, I. M.

1982   The Rise and Future Demise of the World Capitalist System: Concepts for Comparative Analysis. In *Introduction to the Sociology of "Developing Societies,"* ed. H. Alavi and T. Shanin, pp. 29–53. New York: Monthly Review Press.

2000   *The Essential Wallerstein.* New York: New Press, W. W. Norton.

2004   *World-Systems Analysis: An Introduction.* Durham, NC: Duke University Press.

Ward, C. V., W. H. Kimbel, and D. C. Johanson

2011   Complete Fourth Metatarsal and Arches in the Foot of *Australopithecus afarensis. Science* 331(6018): 750–753.

Ward, M. C., and M. Edelstein

2009   *A World Full of Women,* 5th ed. Needham Heights, MA: Allyn & Bacon.

Warms, R., J. Garber, and R. J. McGee, eds.

2009   *Sacred Realms: Readings in the Anthropology of Religion,* 2nd ed. New York: Oxford University Press.

Waters, M. R., and T. W. Stafford, Jr.

2007   Redefining the Age of Clovis: Implications for the Peopling of the Americas. *Science,* February 23, 315: 1122–1126. 10.1126/science.1137166.

Waters, M. R. et al.

2011   Pre-Clovis Mastodon Hunting 13,800 Years Ago at the Manis Site, Washington. *Science* 334(6054): 351–353. DOI: 10.1126/science.1207663.

Watson, J. D.

1970   *Molecular Biology of the Gene.* New York: Benjamin.

Watson, P. J.

1983   The Halafian Culture: A Review and Synthesis. In *The Hilly Flanks and Beyond: Essays on the Prehistory of Southwestern Asia,* ed. T. C. Young, Jr., P. E. L. Smith, and P. Mortensen. *Studies in Ancient Oriental Civilization* 36: 231–250. Oriental Institute, University of Chicago.

Watzman, H.

2006   The Echoes of Ancient Humans. *Chronicle of Higher Education,* January 27. http://chronicle.com/weekly/v52/i21/21a01601.htm.

Weber, M.

1958   (orig. 1904) *The Protestant Ethic and the Spirit of Capitalism.* New York: Scribner.

1968   (orig. 1922) *Economy and Society.* Translated by E. Fischoff et al. New York: Bedminster Press.

Webster's New World Encyclopedia

1993   College Edition. Englewood Cliffs, NJ: Prentice Hall.

Wedel, J.

2002   Blurring the Boundaries of the State-Private Divide: Implications for Corruption. Paper presented at the European Association of Social Anthropologists (EASA) Conference in Copenhagen, August 14–17. http://www.anthrobase.com/Txt/W/Wedel_J_01.htm.

Weiner, A.

1988   *The Trobrianders of Papua New Guinea.* New York: Holt, Rinehart and Winston.

Weiner, J.

1994   *The Beak of the Finch: A Story of Evolution in Our Time.* New York: Knopf.

Weiner, J. S.

1954   Nose Shape and Climate. *American Journal of Physical Anthropology* 12: 1–4.

Weiss, H.

2005   *Collapse.* New York: Routledge.

Weiss, K. M., and A. Buchanan

2004   *Genetics and the Logic of Evolution.* Hoboken, NJ: Wiley-Liss.

Wendorf, F., and R. Schild

2000   Late Neolithic Megalithic Structures at Nabta Playa (Sahara), Southwestern Egypt. http://www.comp-archaeology.org/WendorfSAA98.html.

Wenke, R. J., and D. I. Olszewski

2007   *Patterns in Prehistory: Mankind's First Three Million Years,* 5th ed. New York: Oxford University Press.

White, L. A.

1949   *The Science of Culture: A Study of Man and Civilization.* New York: Farrar, Strauss.

1959   *The Evolution of Culture: The Development of Civilization to the Fall of Rome.* New York: McGraw-Hill.

2009   *Modern Capitalist Culture,* abridged ed. Walnut Creek, CA: Left Coast Press.

White, T. D., M. T. Black, and P. A. Folkens

2012   *Human Osteology,* 3rd ed. San Diego: Academic Press.

Whiteford, L. M., and R. T. Trotter II

2008   *Ethics for Anthropological Research and Practice.* Long Grove, IL: Waveland.

Whiting, J. M.

1964   Effects of Climate on Certain Cultural Practices. In *Explorations in Cultural Anthropology: Essays in Honor of George Peter Murdock,* ed. W. H. Goodenough, pp. 511–544. New York: McGraw-Hill.

Whorf, B. L.

1956   A Linguistic Consideration of Thinking in Primitive Communities. In *Language, Thought, and Reality: Selected Writings of Benjamin Lee Whorf,* ed. J. B. Carroll, pp. 65–86. Cambridge, MA: MIT Press.

Whyte, M. F.

1978   Cross-Cultural Codes Dealing with the Relative Status of Women. *Ethnology* 17(2): 211–239.

Wilford, J. N.

2000   Ruins Alter Ideas of How Civilization Spread. *New York Times,* May 23. http://www.nytimes.com.

2001a   Skull May Alter Experts' View of Human Descent's Branches. *New York Times,* March 22, late edition, final, section A, p. 1, column 1. http://www.nytimes.com.

2002a   Seeking Polynesia's Beginnings in an Archipelago of Shards. *New York Times,* January 8, Science Desk.

2002b   When Humans Became Human. *New York Times,* February 26, late edition, final, section F, p. 1, column 1. http://www.nytimes.com.

2007a   Fossils in Kenya Challenge Linear Evolution. *New York Times,* August 9, p. A6.

2007b   Fossils Reveal Clues on Human Ancestors. *New York Times,* September 20. www.nytimes.com.

2007c   Squash Seeds Show Andean Cultivation Is 10,000 Years Old, Twice as Old as Thought. *New York Times,* June 29.

2008   Genetic Study Bolsters Columbus Link to Syphilis. *New York Times,* January 15.

2009a   Fossil Skeleton From Africa Predates Lucy. *New York Times,* October 2, pp. A1, A6.

2009b   Feet Offer Clue about Tiny Hominid. *New York Times,* May 9. http://www.nytimes.com.

2011a   Fossil Teeth Put Humans in Europe Earlier Than Though. *New York Times,* November 2.

2011b   In African Cave, Signs of an Ancient Paint Factory. *New York Times,* October 13.

2011c   Earliest Signs of Advanced Tools Found. *New York Times,* August 31. http://www.nytimes.com.

Wilk, R. R.

2006   *Fast Food/Slow Food: The Cultural Economy of the Global Food System.* Lanham, MD: AltaMira.

Wilk, R. R., and L. Cliggett

2007   *Economies and Culture: Foundations of Economic Anthropology.* Boulder, CO: Westview.

Williams, B.

1989   A Class Act: Anthropology and the Race to Nation across Ethnic Terrain. *Annual Review of Anthropology* 18:401–444.

Williams, L. M., and D. Finkelhor

1995   Paternal Caregiving and Incest: Test of a Biosocial Model. *American Journal of Orthopsychiatry* 65(1): 101–113.

Willie, C. V., and R. J. Reddick
  2009   A *New Look at Black Families*, 6th ed. Lanham, MD: Rowman & Littlefield.
Wilmsen, E. N.
  1989   *Land Filled with Flies: A Political Economy of the Kalahari*. Chicago: University of Chicago Press.
Wilson, D. S.
  2002   *Darwin's Cathedral: Evolution, Religion, and the Nature of Society*. Chicago: University of Chicago Press.
Wilson, M. L., and R. W. Wrangham
  2003   Intergroup Relations in Chimpanzees. *Annual Review of Anthropology* 32: 363–392.
Winslow, J. H., and A. Meyer
  1983   The Perpetrator at Piltdown. *Science* 83 (September): 33–43.
Winter, R.
  2001   Religions of the World: Number of Adherents; Names of Houses of Worship; Names of Leaders; Rates of Growth. http://www.religioustolerance.org/worldrel.htm.
Witt,
  2011   *Soc*, 2nd ed. Boston: McGraw-Hill.
Wolchover, N.
  2011   The Original Human Language Like Yoda Sounded. *Life's Little Mysteries*, October 13. http://www.lifeslittlemysteries. om/1836-original-human-language-yoda.html.
Wolf, E. R.
  1966   *Peasants*. Englewood Cliffs, NJ: Prentice Hall.
  1982   *Europe and the People Without History*. Berkeley: University of California Press.
  1999   *Envisioning Power: Ideologies of Dominance and Crisis*. Berkeley: University of California Press.
Wolf, E. R., with S. Silverman
  2001   *Pathways of Power: Building an Anthropology of the Modern World*. Berkeley: University of California Press.
Wolpoff, M. H.
  1980   *Paleoanthropology*. Boston: McGraw-Hill.
  1999   *Paleoanthropology*, 2nd ed. New York: McGraw-Hill.
Wood, B.
  2011   *Human Evolution*. New York: Sterling Books.
Wood, B., ed.
  2011   *Wiley-Blackwell Encyclopedia of Human Evolution*. Hoboken, NJ: Wiley-Blackwell.
Worsley, P.
  1985   (orig. 1959) Cargo Cults. In *Readings in Anthropology* 85/86. Guilford, CT: Dushkin.
Wrangham, R., W. McGrew, F. de Waal, and P. Heltne, eds.
  1994   *Chimpanzee Cultures*. Cambridge, MA: Harvard University Press.

Wright, H. T.
  1977   Recent Research on the Origin of the State. *Annual Review of Anthropology* 6: 379–397.
Wright, H. T., and G. A. Johnson
  1975   Population, Exchange, and Early State Formation in Southwestern Iran. *American Anthropologist* 77: 267–289.
  1994   Prestate Political Formations. In *Chiefdoms and Early States in the Near East: The Organizational Dynamics of Complexity*, ed. G. Stein and M. S. Rothman, *Monographs in World Archaeology* 18: 67–84. Madison, WI: Prehistory Press.
Yellen, J. E., A. S. Brooks, and E. Cornelissen
  1995   A Middle Stone Age Worked Bone Industry from Katanda, Upper Semliki Valley, Zaire. *Science* 268: 553–556.
Yetman, N., ed.
  1991   *Majority and Minority: The Dynamics of Race and Ethnicity in American Life*, 5th ed. Boston: Allyn & Bacon.
  1999   *Majority and Minority: The Dynamics of Race and Ethnicity in American Life*, 6th ed. Boston: Allyn & Bacon.
York, A.
  2009   Alaskan Village Stands on Leading Edge of Climate Change, *Mother Nature Network*, August 19. http://news21. jomc.unc.edu/index.php/stories/alaska.html.
Young, A.
  2000   *Women Who Become Men: Albanian Sworn Virgins*. New York: Berg.
Yurchak, A.
  2002   Entrepreneurial Governmentality in Postsocialist Russia. In *The New Entrepreneurs of Europe and Asia*, ed. V. Bonnell and T. Gold, p. 301. Armonk, NY: M. E. Sharpe.
  2006   *Everything Was Forever Until It Was No More: The Last Soviet Generation*. Princeton, NJ: Princeton University Press.
Zeder, Melinda A.
  1997   The American Archaeologist: Results of the 1994 SAA Census. *SAA Bulletin* 15(2): 12–17.
Zeitzen, M. K.
  2008   *Polygamy: A Cross-Cultural Analysis*. New York: Berg.
Zimmer, C.
  2010   Siberian Fossils Were Neanderthals' Eastern Cousins, DNA Reveals. *New York Times*, December 22. http://www. nytimes.com/2010/12/23/science/23ancestor.html.
Zimmer-Tamakoshi, L.
  1997   The Last Big Man: Development and Men's Discontents in the Papua New Guinea Highlands. *Oceania* 68(2):107–122.

PHOTO CREDITS

CHAPTER 1

Page 2: Detail of photo by Martin Roemers/Panos Pictures; p. 6: Punchstock/Brand X Pictures; p. 8: Smithsonian Institution; p. 9: John Biever/Sports Illustrated/Getty Images; p. 10: Stephane De Sakutin/AFP/Getty Images; p. 12: Peter Bennett/Eyevine/Digital Railroad; p. 15: National Geographic Society; p. 17: Obama Presidential Campaign/AP p. 18: Ton Koene; p. 19: Ricardo Funari/BrazilPhotos/Alamy

CHAPTER 2

p. 24: Chel Beeson/Getty Images; p. 28: Ingram Publishing; p. 29 [left]: William Gottlieb/Corbis; p. 29 [right]: ER Productions Ltd/Blend Images LLC; p. 30: Francesco Broli/The New York Times/Redux Pictures; p. 33: Kenneth Garrett/National Geographic Society; p. 34: OSF/Clive Bromhall/AnimalsAnimals; p. 35 [top]: Hideo Haga/HAGA/The Image Works; p. 35 [bottom]: Carl D. Walsh/Aurora Photos; p. 37: Elizabeth Dalziel/AP; p. 39 [top]: Dan Levine/AFP/Getty Images; p. 39 [bottom]: Dan Levine/AFP/Getty Images; p. 41: Joao Silva/Picturenet; p. 42: Wu Changqing-Imaginechina/AP; p. 43: Travel Pictures/Alamy

CHAPTER 3

p. 48: Mark Edwards/Still Pictures; p. 51: Will & Deni McIntyre/Corbis; p. 52: Eric Stover; p. 53: Charles Harbutt/Actuality; p. 54: Mike Yamashita/Woodfin Camp & Associates; p. 55 Sean Sprague/The Image Works; p. 56: Betty Press/Woodfin Camp & Associates; p. 57: PNC/Brand X Pictures/Getty Images; p. 59: Joe Amon/The Denver Post/AP; p. 60: Carl D. Walsh/Aurora Photos; p. 61: Courtesy Melville J. Herskovits Library of African Studies, Northwestern University; p. 62: UNEP; p. 64: Photo courtesy Intel Corporation

CHAPTER 4

p. 70: Javier Trueba/Madrid Scientific Films/Photo Researchers, Inc.; p. 74 [top left]: Courtesy of Dolores R. Piperno, National Museum of Natural History; p. 74 [top center]: Courtesy of Dolores R. Piperno, National Museum of Natural History; p. 74 [top right]: Courtesy of John G. Jones, Washington State University; p. 74 [bottom] Axel Fassio/Aurora/Getty Images; p. 77: Kenneth Garrett/National Geographic Society; p. 79: Cheryl Gerber/AP; p. 80: Jonathan Blair/Corbis; p. 81 [top]: Leonardo L.T. Rhodes/Earth Scenes/Animals Animals; p. 81 [bottom]: Courtesy of Professor Christopher Henshilwood and Professor Francesco d'Errico, University of Bergen, Norway; p. 82 [left]: Nigel Pavitt/ John Warburton-Lee Photography Ltd/Aurora Photos; p. 82 [right]: Charles V. Angelo/ Photo Researchers, Inc.; p. 83: Jim Sugar/Corbis; p. 84: Dr. Alan Boyde/Visuals Unlimited/Corbis; p. 85: Francis Demange/Gamma-Rapho/Getty Images; p. 86[left]: Harley Soltes/ The New York Times/Redux Pictures; p. 86[right]: Harley Soltes/The New York Times/Redux Pictures

CHAPTER 5

p. 90: Bob Sacha; p. 92: © Graham Dunn/Alamy; p. 93: Noah's Ark By Edward Hicks, 1846, 26½ × 30½, Oil on canvas, Philadelphia Museum of Art, Bequest of Lisa Norris Elkins; p. 95 [top] The Natural History Museum/The Image Works; p. 95 [bottom] Julia Margaret Cameron; p. 97 National Library of Medicine; p. 100: Dr. Gopal Mujrti/Phototake; p. 102: Teake Zuidema/The Image Works; p. 103: Cathy & Gordon Illg/Animals Animals; p. 104: Holly Wilmeth/Aurora Photos; p. 106: John Robinson/Africa Media Online/The Image Works

CHAPTER 6

p. 112: Gary Houlder/Getty Images; p. 115: Paul Grebliunas/Tony Stone/Getty Images; p. 116 [top left]: Sabine Vielmo; p. 116 [bottom left]: Darrell Gulin/Corbis; p. 116 [top right]: Thomas Cockrem/Alamy; p. 117: Steve McCurry/Magnum Photos; p. 118: William D. Bachman/Photo Researchers, Inc.; p. 121: Brent Frazee/Kansas City Star/MCT/Getty Images; p. 122 [top]: Jan Spieczny/Peter Arnold, Inc./Getty Images; p. 122 [bottom]: MCT/Getty Images; p. 123 [top]: Tony Camerano/AP; p. 123 [bottom]: National Library of Medicine; p. 125 [top]: Robert Caputo/Stock, Boston; p. 125 [bottom]: Bryan & Cherry Alexander/Arctic Photo; p. 127: Claudia Lopez/Aurora Photos

CHAPTER 7

p. 132: Paul Souders/Getty Images; p. 138 [top] Denver Museum of Nature & Science; p. 138 [bottom]: Tom McHugh/Photo Researchers, Inc.; p. 139: Frans Lanting/Corbis; p. 140: Karen Kasmauski/National Geographic Society; p. 141: Holger Ehlers/Alamy; p. 143: Irwin Fedriansyah/AP; p. 144 [top]: The Dian Fossey Gorilla Fund International, www.gorillafund.org; p. 144 [bottom]: Michael Nichols/National Geographic/Getty Images; p. 145: Purestock/Getty Images; p. 148 [left]: Tom McHugh/Photo Researchers, Inc.; p. 148[right]: Roland Seitre; p. 149: Russell Ciochon, University of Iowa; p. 151: Luis Gene/ AFP/Getty Images

CHAPTER 8

p. 156: Alexander Joe/AFP/Getty Images; p. 159: National History Museum, London; p. 160: AFP/Corbis; p. 162: Tim White; p. 163 [top]: David Brill; p. 163 [bottom]: Tim White; p. 164: Kenneth Garrett; p. 165: John Reader/Science Photo Library/Photo Researchers, Inc.; p. 167: Lionel Bret/Photo Researchers, Inc.; p. 170 [left]: National History Museum, London; p. 170 [right]: National History Museum, London; p. 171: Luba Dmytryk/National Geographic Society; p. 172 : Des Bartlett/Photo Researchers, Inc.; p. 173: Alexander Joe/Agence France-Presse/Getty Images; p. 174 [all]: Peter Bostrom

CHAPTER 9

p. 178: Frank Franklin II/AP; p. 181: Kenneth Garrett; p. 182: The Natural History Museum, London; p. 183 Kenneth Garrett/National Geographic Society; p. 184 [left]: David L. Brill; p. 184 [center]: John Reader/Photo Researchers, Inc.; p. 184[right]: The Natural History Museum, London; p. 185: Kenneth Garrett; p. 188 [top to bottom]: Courtesy Hisao Baba; p. 190: Conrad P. Kottak; p. 191 [top]: The Natural History Museum, London; p. 191 [bottom]: The Natural History Museum, London; p. 193 [middle]: Philippe Plailly /Photo Researchers, Inc.; p. 193 [bottom]: Dr. Peter Brown

CHAPTER 10

p. 198: French Ministry of Culture and Communication, Regional Direction for Cultural Affairs, Rhone-Alpes Region, Region Department of Archaeology; p. 201: Luba Dmytryk/National Geographic Society; p. 202 [top]: The Natural History Museum, London; p. 202 [bottom]: Courtesy Professor William Calvin, University of Washington School of Medicine; p. 206 [left]: Lindsay Hebberd/Woodfin Camp & Associates; p. 206 [right]: Toby Canham/Pressnet/Topham/The Image Works; p. 207: Anna Zieminski/AFP/Getty Images; p. 208 [left]: Visual Arts Library of London/Alamy; p. 208 [right]: DEA/A. DAGLI ORTI/De Agostini/Getty Images; p. 211: JM Labat/Photo Researchers, Inc.; p. 213: Published by permission of Traditional Owners, photo Prof. J.M. Bowler; p. 215 [top]: Robert Frerck/Odyssey Productions; p. 215 [bottom]: Roger Green, Anthropology Photographic Archive, University of Auckland; p. 217: Gianni Dagli Orti/Corbis; p. 218 [left]: Gonzalez/laif/Aurora Photos; p. 218 [right]: Albrecht G. Schaefer/Corbis

CHAPTER 11

p. 222: Philippe Lissac/Godong/Corbis; p. 225: Gustavo Tomsich/Corbis; p. 226: Erich Lessing/Art Resource, NY; p. 228: dbimages/Alamy; p. 230: A. Tovy/Robertstock/IPN Stock; p. 231: Chad Ehlers/Alamy; p. 233: Craig Lovell/Corbis; p. 234: Ron Giling/Lineair/Still Pictures; p. 235: Mariana Bazo/Reuters/Corbis; p. 236: Marco Ugarte/AP; p. 237: Schalkwijk/Art Resource, NY; p. 240: Frans Lemmens/Lonely Planet Images

CHAPTER 12

p. 246: Jeffrey Becom/Lonely Planet Images; p. 251: Roger Wood/Corbis; p. 252: Donald C. & Priscilla Alexander Eastman/Lonely Planet Images; p. 254: Ancient Art and Architecture Collection Ltd./Bridgeman Art Library; p. 255: Robert Grossman; p. 257: David Coventry/National Geographic Society p. 258 [left]: Erich Lessing/Art Resource, NY; p. 258 [right]: Barry Iverson/Woodfin Camp & Associates; p. 259: Georg Gerster/Photo Researchers, Inc.; p. 261: Ancient Art & Architecture Collection Ltd ©AAAC/Topham/The

Image Works; p. 262: Robert Frerck/Odyssey Productions; p. 263: DEA/ G. Dagliorti/Getty Images; p. 265: Fehim Demir/epa/Corbis; p. 266: Jacques Jangoux; p. 267: DreamPictures/The Image Bank/ Getty Images

CHAPTER 13
p. 272: Ron Giling/Lineair/Still Pictures; p. 277: Conrad P.Kottak; p. 278: Lawrence Migdale/Photo Researchers, Inc.; p. 279: Peggy &Yoran Kahana; p. 281: Christopher M. O'Leary; p. 282: Imaginechina/Corbis; p. 284: Marco Di Lauro/Getty Images; p. 285: Lacrosse Game (36.366.1), watercolor by Ernest Smith, 1936, courtesy of the Rochester Museum & Science Center, Rochester, NY; p. 287 [left]: National Anthropological Archives/Smithsonian Institution; p. 287 [right]: Used with permission of Dr. Aaron Glass and U'mista Cultural Centre in Alert Bay, BC; p. 288 [top]: Mary Evans Picture Library/The Image Works; p. 288 [bottom]: Courtesy Dr. Falco Pfalzgraf, University of London; p. 289 [left]: Ruth Benedict stamp © 1995 United States Postal Service. All Rights Reserved. Used with Permission; p. 289 [right]: United States Postal Service; p. 290 [top]: AP; p. 290 [bottom]: Courtesy University of Florida; p. 292: Courtesy Oxford University; p. 293 [left]: Eric Mansfield; p. 293 [right]: Laura Pedrick/Redux Pictures

CHAPTER 14
p. 300: Raminder Pal Singh/epa/Corbis; p. 303: Michael Nichols/ Magnum Photos; p. 304: Michael Nichols/National Geographic Society; p. 306: Keenpress/National Geographic Society/Corbis; p. 308: Lonny Shavelson; p. 309: Corbis RF; p. 310: Dirk Shadd/St. Petersburg Times/Zuma Press; p. 313: Namas Bhojani/The New York Times/ Redux Pictures p. 314: Photofest; p. 315: Jim Goldberg/Magnum Photos; p. 316: Safeconcerts/Retna/Photoshot/Newscom; p. 318: Lucas Film/Topham/The Image Works p. 319: Chris Rainier/Enduring Voices Project

CHAPTER 15
p. 324: Ted S. Warren/AP; p. 329: David Alan Harvey/Magnum Photos; p. 331: Peter Turnley/Corbis; p. 332: Albert L. Ortega/ Wireimage/Getty Images; p. 334: P.J. Griffiths/Magnum Photos; p. 335 [all]: Conrad P. Kottak; p. 338: Pierre Merimee/Corbis; p. 339: Ed Kashi/VII; p. 340: James Marshall/CORB/Age Fotostock; p. 341: Tyrone Turner/National Geographic Society; p. 342: Art Chen Soon Ling/UNEP; p. 343[left]: Bradley Mayhew/Lonely Planet Images; p. 343[right] Zarip Toroyev/AP

CHAPTER 16
p. 348: Andrew McConnell/Panos Pictures; p. 352: Frans Lanting/ Corbis; p. 354: Archie Mokoka/AP; p. 355: Dominique Halleux/Bios Photo; p. 357: Damon Winter/The New York Times/Redux Pictures; p. 358: Michele Falzone/JAI/Corbis; p. 360 [top]: B.K.Bangash/AP; p. 360 [bottom]: Patrick Pleul/dpa/Corbis; p. 362: Frans Lanting; p. 363: Paula Bronstein/Getty Images; p. 364: Geoffrey Robinson/Rex Features/AP; p. 367: Carl D. Walsh/Aurora Photos; p. 368: John Eastcott/Yva Momatiuk/Woodfin Camp & Associates; p. 370 [top]: American Museum of Natural History; p. 370 [bottom]: James Storm/ Storm Photo; p. 371: Robin Hammond/Panos Pictures

CHAPTER 17
p. 376: Rudi Meisel/VISUM/The Image Works; p. 379: Susan See Photography; p. 380: Joy Tessman/National Geographic Society; p. 385: Edwin Montilva/Corbis; p. 386 [top]: Burt Glinn/Magnum Photos; p. 386 [bottom]: Library of Congress; p. 387: Douglas Kirkland; p. 388: Mike Schneps; p. 389: John A. Novak/Earth Scenes/Animals-Animals; p. 390 [left]: Jeff Greenberg/PhotoEdit; p. 390 [right]: Wattie Cheung/AFP/Getty Images; p. 393: Catherine Karnow/Woodfin Camp & Associates; p. 394: Daniel Roland/AP; p. 395: Nicholas C. Kottak; p. 396: Eye Ubiquitous/SuperStock

CHAPTER 18
p. 402: Sebastian Bolesch; p. 405: Ziva Santop; p. 408: Chris Stowers/ Panos Pictures; p. 409 [top]: Paul Nicklen/National Geographic

Society; p. 409 [bottom]: Wendy Stone; p. 410: Lindsay Hebberd/ Corbis; p. 411 [top]: George Holton/Photo Researchers, Inc.; p. 411 [bottom]: Linda Forsell; p. 413: National Archives; p. 416 [top]: Karsten Schoene/laif/Redux Pictures; p. 416 [bottom]: David J. Phillip/ AP; p. 417: Sinopictures/Maciej Dakowicz/Photolibrary; p. 419: Globo/Getty Images

CHAPTER 19
p. 426: Daryl Visscher/Redux Pictures; p. 429: Eastcott-Momatiuk/ The Image Works; p. 430: Reuters/Corbis; p. 431 [top]: Robert Harding World Imagery; p. 431 [bottom]: Katja Heinemann/Aurora Photos; p. 437 [top]: Ami Vitale/Alamy; p. 437 [bottom]: John Eastcott/ Yva Momatiuk/Stock, Boston; p. 438: Stephen Beckerman, Penn State University; p. 440: Ariel Skelley/Blend Images LLC

CHAPTER 20
p. 448: Michael Freeman/Corbis; p. 452: Universal Images Group/ Getty Images; p. 455 [left]: Kenneth Garrett; p. 455 [right]: DPA/The Images Works; p. 456: Jake Norton/Alamy; p. 457: Joel Gordon; p. 458: James Marshall/The Image Works; p. 460: Qin Gang/Xinhua Press/Corbis; p. 461: Bonile Bam/Gallo Images/Alamy; p. 462: Angel Wynn/DanitaDelimont.com; p. 464: Kayhan Ozer/Reuters/Landov; p. 466: Mike Hutchings/AP

CHAPTER 21
p. 470: Tom Cockrem/Lonely Planet Images; p. 474: Gianni Dagli Orti/Corbis; p. 475 [top]: Chris Pondy/Icon SMI/Corbis; p. 475 [bottom]: Peter Essick/Aurora Photos; p. 476 [top]: Thierry Secretan/Cosmos/Woodfin Camp & Associates; p. 476: Joe McNally/ IPN Stock; p. 478: Mark Henley/Impact/HIP/The Image Works; p. 482: Caetano Barreira/X01990/Reuters/Corbis; p. 485: Holger Leue/Lonely Planet Images; p. 487: Kal Muller/Woodfin Camp & Associates; p. 488: Behzad/Demotix/Corbis

CHAPTER 22
p. 494: Tim Hales/AP/Corbis; p. 497: Alex Segre/Alamy; p. 498: JR/ Aurora Photos; p. 501: John Moss/Photo Researchers, Inc.; p. 503: Nico Tondini/Robert Harding World Imagery/Corbis; p. 504: Robert Frerck/Corbis; p. 506 [top]: Richard Mittleman/Alamy; p. 506 [bottom]: Yva Momatiuk & John Eastcott/Woodfin Camp & Associates; p. 507 [top]: Ingolf Pompe/AgeFotostock; p. 507 [bottom]: Elliott Franks/ArenaPal/The Image Works; p. 511: Deshakalyan Chowdhury/ AFP/Getty Images; p. 513: Splash News/Corbis; p. 514: Namit Arora (www.shunya.net); p. 516: Charles Krupa/AP; p. 517: Tim Clayton/ Corbis; p. 518: Robert W. Ginn/Alamy

CHAPTER 23
p. 522: Philippe Lissac/ Godong/Corbis; p. 526: Archives Charmet/ Bridgeman Art Library; p. 528 [top]: Bruce Dale/ National Geographic Society; p. 528 [bottom]: Henglein and Steets/cultura/ Corbis; p. 529 [top]: The Image Works; p. 529 [bottom]: Michael Nichols/National Geographic Society; p. 531: Alex Brandon/AP; p. 532: Library of Congress Prints and Photographs Division, LC-USZ62-74580; p. 534: Hulton Archive/Getty Images; p. 536: Gideon Mendel/Corbis; p. 537: Chris Leslie Smith/Photo Edit, Inc.; p. 539 [top]: Bettmann/Corbis; p. 539 [bottom]: Misha Japaridze/AP; p. 541: Friedrich Stark; p. 542: V. Leloup/Gamma Presse

CHAPTER 24
p. 548: Javier Etcheverry/Alamy; p. 553: Monica Almeida/New York Times Photo/Redux Pictures; p. 554: Royalty-Free/Corbis; p. 555: STR/AFP/Getty Images; p. 557: UNEP-Topham/The Image Works; p. 558 [top]: Ed Parker/Photographersdirect/Chris Fairclough Worldwide Ltd.; p. 558 [bottom]: Imaginechina/AP; p. 559: Paul Seheult/Eye Ubiquitous/Corbis; p. 560: Andres Hernandez/Getty Images; p. 561 [top]: Pete Saloutos/UpperCut Images/Getty Images; p. 561 [bottom]: Sakchai Lalit/AP Photo; p. 562 [top]: Ken Straiton/ Corbis; p. 562 [bottom]: Al Grillo/AP; p. 563: Jose Luis Quintana/ Reuters/Corbis

NAME INDEX

SUBJECT INDEX

enculturation, 5, 27–28, 29, 292. *See also* microenculturation
children and, 57
performance and, 506
enculturative agents, 26, 28
endogamy, 456–457, 467. *See also* caste endogamy; royal endogamy; stratum endogamy
Enduring Voices Project, 319
energy consumption
in China, 541, 555, 555f
growing demand for, 554–555, 555f
in India, 541, 555f
in selected countries, 542t
by United States, 540–541, 542t, 555
in various contexts, 542t
England
colonialism and, 533–534, 534f
Industrial Revolution in, 528, 543
industrial stratification in, 529–531
location of, 530f
national income of, 528–529
natural resources of, 528
environment. *See also* geography
adaptation and, 105–106
degradation of, 240–241
fitness and, 105–106
heredity and, 12–13
of *Homo*, 190
intensification and, 359
sudden change in, 108
zones of, 226–228
environmental anthropology, 555–557
environmental circumscription, 249–250
Environmental Protection Agency, 50
environmentalism, spread of, 556, 564
Eocene epoch, 146, 147f, 148, 152
epidemic diseases, 60
equity, 54–55
Eridu, 255
Eskimo. *See* Inuit
Eskimo kinship terminology, 441
ESR. *See* electron spin resonance
essentialism, 564
ethical issues, in anthropology, 85–87, 283–285, 297
ethnic cleansing, 343f
ethnic conflict, roots of, 340–344
ethnic expulsion, 342, 344t, 345
ethnic groups, 330, 344, 345
ethnicity and, 327–328
in United States, 339f
ethnic identity, multiculturalism and, 338–340
ethnic interactions, types of, 344t
ethnic tolerance, accommodation and, 337–340
ethnicity, 114, 326, 344–345. *See also* interethnic contact
ethnic groups and, 327–328
mass culture and, 512–513
race and, 328–330
ethnoastronomy, 309
ethnobotany, 309
ethnocentrism, 26, 37, 44
ethnocide, 342, 344t, 345, 558, 565
ethnoecology, 555, 565
ethnographic method, 51
ethnographic techniques, 275–282
ethnography, 9, 11t, 14, 64–65, 274
field techniques of, 275–282
as quantitative and qualitative, 278
specialization of, 296
survey research and, 282, 283t
ethnological theories, 15

ethnology, 9–10, 11t, 15, 21
ethnomedicine, 40, 309
ethnomusicology, 13, 501–503
ethnosemantics, 309
etic approach, 279, 296
Etoro sexual practices, 420–421
eunuch, 417
euprimate, 148
Europe
AMH in, 204, 209
archaic *Homo sapiens* in, 190
Homo erectus in, 190
Neolithic in, 231–233
Europe and the People without History (Wolf, E.), 294
European imperial expansion, 533–536
Evangelical Protestantism, 482
evolution, 15, 92–95. *See also* convergent evolution; general evolution; genetic evolution; macroevolution; microevolution; modern synthesis; multilinear evolution; unilinear evolutionism
of cooperation, 76
forces of, 194
of giraffe necks, 94–95
of hominins, 160
intelligent design versus, 96–97
key developments in, 454
mutations and, 101
of Neandertals, 189
of primates, 146
The Evolution of Culture (White, L.), 290
evolutionary theory, 15
evolutionism, 285–286, 297. *See also* neoevolutionism
excavation, 11, 75, 77–78, 87
archaeology and, 274
biological anthropology and, 274
exchange, 373
cross-cultural, 366–367
distribution and, 366–372
principles, 369–372
exogamy, 34, 355, 382, 455–456, 467
in descent groups, 435
incest and, 451–452
expanded family household, 431, 431f
experimental archaeology, 78
explicandum, 16
expressive culture, 200, 496–497, 518
extended families, 430
patrilocal, 429
extended family household, 431
extinction. *See also* mass extinctions
of dinosaurs, 108, 180
extra-linguistic forces, 312–315
extramarital sex, 408t

F

fa'afafine, 417
facial features, natural selection and, 123–124
fact, theory and, 94–95, 97
factors. *See* alleles; genes
factors of production. *See* means of production
fakaleitis, 417
family, 135f, 428–429, 432–433. *See also* expanded family household; extended families; extended family household; nuclear family; siblings; single-parent households
in Brazil, 434–435
changes in, 432t
in China, 430

descent versus, 437–438
foraging and, 435
industrialism and, 431
isolation of, 431
poverty and, 431
size of, 434t
in United States, 434
family of orientation, 429, 431
transition from, 450
family of procreation, 429, 431
transition to, 450
family planning
television viewing and, 511–513, 514f, 519
women's education and, 512
farming, 210, 238, 241. *See also* agriculture; dry farming; food production; hydraulic agriculture
in Americas, 233–237, 242
in China, 231–233, 231f
in Middle East, 226–234, 241–242
spread of, 229–230
Federal Emergency Management Agency (FEMA), 78
FEMA. *See* Federal Emergency Management Agency
female genital modification (FGM), 40, 411
female infanticide, 411
The Feminine Mystique (Friedan), 412
fertility figure. *See* Venus of Willendorf
FGM. *See* female genital modification
fictive kinship, 355
field language, 276–277
field notes, 275
fieldwork, 524
filariasis, 121–122
Fingerprints of the Gods (Hancock), 264
fire
as adaptation, 186
controlled use of, 186, 194
First World, 538
fiscal, 392
fiscal systems, 392–393, 398
fitness, 15
behavioral ecology and, 145–146, 152
environment and, 105–106
inclusive, 146
of individual, 146
fixation, 106
flake tool, 174, 174f, 185. *See also* Levallois technique
flotation, 78
fluorine absorption analysis, 81
focal vocabulary, 308–309
for hockey, 309t, 310f
folate
role of, 119–120
spermatogenesis and, 120
UV radiation and, 120
folk, 502
folk art, 506
folklore, 13
folktale analysis, 508–509
food production, 7, 122, 210, 224–225, 231. *See also* agriculture; animal domestication; domestication; farming; plant cultivation
advent of, 350
climate change and, 227
costs and benefits of, 239–242, 240f, 241t
disease and, 240
existence of, 355
foraging compared to, 239–241, 241t
geography and, 238–239
invention of, 232f, 232t, 234–235, 242

labor demands of, 239–240, 240f
in Mesoamerica, 262f
Middle Eastern, 226–227
in Old World, 230–233
Old World versus New World, 233
state and, 229–230, 265
transition to, 226
football, 514–515
foraging, 7, 236–237, 242, 351, 353, 361t, 372, 391t. *See also* hunter-gatherers; hunting-gathering
correlates of, 354–355
egalitarianism and, 355
family and, 435
food production compared to, 239–241, 241t
insurance and, 368
kinship and, 435, 442
labor demands of, 239–240, 240f
mobility and, 354–355
by Native Americans, 352
social distinctions among, 355
then and now, 353t
foraging bands, 380–382
gender stratification among, 409, 409f
foramen magnum, 161, 169f
forces, powers and, 474–475
forensic anthropology, 51–52, 51t, 84
Forest of Symbols (Turner, V.), 292
formative, 226
fossil fuel energy, 540
alternatives to, 555
growing demand for, 555
fossil record, 80, 87
jumps in, 107
fossils, 75, 93. *See also* Skhūl fossils
of AMHs, 204
from Australia, 213f
chances for, 80, 81f
of hominids, 161t
of hominins, 161t
of hominoids, 161t
of *Homo*, 189t
four-field anthropology, 8–9, 286, 295–297
FOXP2, 305
France
colonialism and, 533–535, 535f
location of, 530f
fraternal polyandry, 451, 466
Frauds, Myths, and Mysteries: Science and Pseudoscience in Archaeology (Feder), 264
free trade advocates, 42–43
functionalism, 287–289, 297
fundamentalism
antimodernism and, 487
Christianity and, 487

G

Gabon, 150
gametes, 99–100
gang demographics, 59
gang significance, 59f
gang violence, 59
garbology, 11–12, 50, 84
The Gates (installation art piece), 498f
gathering. *See also* hunting-gathering
cultivation and, 10
women and, 409
gay and lesbian rights movement, 418
Gê people, 356
gender. *See also* global gender gap index; transgender
in Brazil, 417–419
construction of, 416, 418

discrimination, 405, 417
division of labor and, 355, 357f, 361–362, 406, 421–422
human behavior and, 404
in industrial societies, 412–416
language and, 308
multiple negation and, 311t
proper behavior according to, 404
recurrent patterns of, 406–409
sex and, 405–406, 416
speech and, 311
status and, 405–406, 409, 422
gender roles, 274, 405, 421–422
gender stratification and, 409–412
modern, 413, 413f
gender stereotypes, 421. *See also* stereotypes
gender stratification, 405–406, 421–422
among foraging bands, 409, 409f
gender roles and, 409–412
increased, 411
reduced, 410
gene flow, 106f, 109
alleles and, 106–107
gene pool, 101
genealogical kin types
kinship terminology and, 439–440
notation of, 440f
genealogical method, 275, 278, 296
general anthropology, 8–9
general evolution, 290
general principal. *See* law (scientific principle)
generalities
domination and, 35
among humans, 34–35
universals and, 34–35, 44
generalized reciprocity, 368–369
generation gap, 6. *See also* cultural generation gap
generational kinship terminology, 442–443, 442f, 443t
genes, 92, 96–98
disease and, 121–123
genetic clocks, 84, 203
genetic drift. *See* random genetic drift
genetic evolution, population genetics and, 101–107
genetic markers
long-term, 117
phenotype and, 117
genetics, 12, 96–99. *See also* biochemical genetics; molecular genetics; population genetics
genitor, 451
genocide, 52, 342, 343f, 344t, 345, 558, 565
in Bosnia, 543
in Rwanda, 535, 542
genome. *See also* human genome
of Australian Aborigines, 118
genotype, 98, 101
phenotype and, 335
race and, 331, 332f
genus/genera, 135, 135f
geography, 239f
food production and, 238–239
variation and, 13
geological time scale, 147f
Georgia, Republic of
Homo erectus in, 187, 195
refugee camp near, 343f
German Roma people, 431f
Gheg tribes, 417

gibbons, 140, 150
bipedalism in, 141f
limb ratio of, 141f
sexual dimorphism in, 152
Gigantism, 194
Gigantopithecus, 149f, 151–152
GISS. *See* NASA's Goddard Institute for Space Studies
glacials, 188–189. *See also* Mindel glacial; Riss glacial; Würm glacial
retreat of, 210–211, 219, 224
global communication speed, 43
global forces, 8
global gender gap index, 414
global network scale, 43
global warming, 552, 564. *See also* climate change; greenhouse effect; temperature
globalization, 10, 42f, 58, 210, 550. *See also* Columbian exchange; modern world system
as contested ideology, 551
disease and, 104, 124
of economy, 364
effects of, 42
as fact, 551
health problems and, 62
of Internet, 312–313
of jobs, 532
links created though, 561
meanings of, 42–44
migration and, 340
opposition to, 42–43
religion and, 482
of risk, 551
glossolalia, 482
Gombe Stream National Park, Tanzania, 33, 144f, 145
Google, Indian users of, 312–313, 313f
gorillas (*Gorilla gorilla*), 32, 140–141, 144f, 150, 152
chimpanzees compared to, 143–144
cranial capacity of, 171
feeding habits of, 142
language capacity of, 304–305
sexual dimorphism in, 142, 152
zoo display of, 132f, 134
gossip, 394–396, 398
gracile, 169
robust and, 170
skull form of, 171f
grain axis, 229, 229f
Gran Dolina, Atapuerca, Spain, 70f
grasping, 32, 137
grave goods, 256, 257f
great apes. *See* apes
Great Apes Conservation Act, 150
Great Apes Conservation Fund, 150
Great Britain. *See* England
Great Chain of Being, 330
Great Depression, 537
Great Rift Valley, Africa, 82f
potassium-argon dating of, 82
Greco-Roman religions, 480
Greek theater, art and, 507, 507f
greenhouse effect, 552
greenhouse gases, 552–553, 564–565
deforestation and, 556
projected emissions of, 556f
grooming, 32
guanine, 99
guenon, 139f
guilt, 394
Gullah, 308
Gwembe District, Zambia, 280, 280f

H

H1N1 virus, 104–105, 104f, 124
habitat destruction, 150
Hadar jawbone, 173
Halafian, 254, 268
halocarbons, 552, 554t
Hammamet, Tunisia, 80
hand ax, 185, 185f, 186f
Handsome Lake religion,
    483–485
haplogroup, 84, 117, 214
happiness, work and, 415–416, 416f
Harappan state, 259–260
Hard Times (Dickens), 529
Hawaiian kinship terminology, 441
headman, 382–383
health care systems, 60, 61
health interventions, 62
health problems
    globalization and, 62
    industrialization and, 62
hegemony, 295, 393–394, 398
hemoglobin, 103–106
    high altitude adaptation and, 126
herding, 241. *See also* pastoralism
    in Middle East, 226–233
heredity, 96–97
    contributions to, 100
    environment and, 12–13
hermaphroditism, 416
Herto, 201
Herto skulls, 201
heterosexuality, 418, 421–422
heterozygous cross, 98, 98f
Hidatsa women, 406
hidden transcript, 394, 398
high-altitude adaptations, 4–7, 5t
    differing mechanisms of, 125–127
    hemoglobin and, 126
hijras, 417, 417f
Hilly Flanks, 226–228, 227f, 242
Hinduism, 481, 481t, 483f, 483t
Hispanics/Latinos, 329, 329f
    in United States, 328, 328t
historical archaeology, 78
historical linguistics, 13, 316–320
historical particularism, 286–287
HIV infection
    in Africa, 60–61
    circumcision and, 61
    global rates of, 60–61
    prostitution and, 60–61
holism, 5, 13
holistic science, 5
Holocaust, 331, 542
Holocene epoch, 146, 147f, 152
home-handicraft system, 528, 529f
Hominid, 136–137, 160
Hominidae, 32, 136
hominids, 32
    feet of, 33f
    fossils of, 161t
    phylogenetic tree for hominins, apes
        and, 165f
    social organization of, 134
hominini, 137
hominins, 32
    diversity of, 76
    earliest, 160–164
    evolution of, 160
    features of, 175
    fossils of, 161t
    phylogenetic tree for hominids, apes
        and, 165f
    stone tools of, 33

Hominoidea, 135, 136t, 140
hominoids
    fossils of, 161t
    in Miocene epoch, 149–151
Homo, 5, 28
    ancestors of, 171
    australopithecines compared with,
        167t, 171–174
    Australopithecus boisei and, 172, 174
    chimpanzee skull and, 169f
    early, 181–183
    efficiency of, 175
    environment of, 190
    fossil summary of, 189t
    hunting by, 170
    limb ratio of, 141f
    range of, 209
Homo antecessor, Homo heidelbergensis
    and, 189–191
Homo erectus, 151, 161t, 172
    adaptive strategies of, 185–187
    in Africa, 187–188, 195
    ancestor of, 173
    body composition of, 185
    brain size of, 189t
    in China, 188
    cranial capacity of, 182–183, 185
    in Europe, 190
    expansion/spread of, 175, 183, 185,
        187, 187f
    in Georgia, 187, 195
    healed fractures of, 184
    Homo habilis and, 181–183
    humans and, 184
    in Indonesia, 187–188
    Lower Paleolithic tools and, 185
    probable maximum distribution
        of, 187f
    sexual dimorphism in, 182–183
    sites of, 187f
    skull form of, 184, 184f, 186, 186f,
        188f, 201f
Homo floresiensis, 194–195
    skull form of, 194f
Homo habilis, 161t, 172, 195
    cranial capacity of, 181
    Homo erectus and, 181–183
    Homo rudolfensis and, 181
    skull form of, 182f
    toolmaking by, 174
Homo heidelbergensis, Homo antecessor
    and, 189–191
Homo rudolfensis, 161t
    Homo habilis and, 181, 181f
Homo sapiens, 96, 128. *See also*
    anatomically modern humans;
    archaic *Homo sapiens*; humans
    chimpanzees compared to, 168f
    cranial capacity of, 171
    dentition of, 173f
    language and, 27
    sexual dimorphism in, 144, 405
    shared common ancestor of, 117
    zoological taxonomy of, 135t
Homo sapiens neanderthalensis, 188. *See
    also* Neandertals
homogamy, 456
homologies, 135
    analogies and, 136–137, 152
homonyms, 315
homophobia, in United States, 26
homosexuality, 418, 422
    of Azande, 420
    of Etoro, 420–421
    ritualized, 421

homozygous cross, 98, 98f
honorifics, 248, 311
Hopi language, 308, 308f
Hopi people, divorce among, 462–463
horticulture, 351, 355–357, 361t, 362,
    372, 382, 391t, 397
    agriculture compared to, 359
    diversity in, 359
households. *See also* collateral household;
        expanded family household;
        extended family household; single-
        parent households
    changes in, 432t
    size of, 434t
    by type, 434f
HTS. *See* Human Terrain System
HTT. *See* Human Terrain Team
hugging, 6–7
human adaptability, diversity and, 4
human behavior. *See also* sexual behavior
    gender and, 404
    as learned, 331
    need fulfillment through, 32
    observation of, 30
    reconstruction of, 76
    religion and, 489
    variation in, 289–290
    women and, 404
human biological plasticity, 12
human condition, 4
human diversity, 4–8, 34–36, 114, 128
    conflict and, 526
    violence and, 526
human ecology, 11
human genetics, 12
human genome, 117
human growth and development, 12
human nature, 8
    plasticity of, 289
human rights, 40, 44
Human Rights Center, 52
Human Terrain System (HTS), 53
    AAA on, 284–285
Human Terrain Team (HTT), 284f
humanistic science, 13
humans, 137. *See also* anatomically
        modern humans; archaic *Homo
        sapiens*; *Homo*; *Homo sapiens*
    attributes of, 5
    bands of, 34
    biological adaptation of, 121–128
    birth in, 72
    chimpanzee pelvis and, 169f
    common ancestor of Neandertals
        and, 204
    cooperation and, 32, 34, 44, 72
    dentition in, 166f
    female pelvis in, 72
    generalities among, 34–35
    genetic uniformity of, 117
    Homo erectus and, 184
    hunting by, 33
    key attributes of, 158–160
    life-cycle events of, 35–36
    limited offspring of, 32–33
    mating in, 34
    particularities among, 34–36
    primate ancestor of, 32
    primates and, 32–34, 44, 134
    skeleton of, 191f
    skull form of, 194f
    sociality and, 72
    universals among, 34–35, 293
Humboldt's woolly monkey, 139f
humor, 505

hunter-gatherers, 34
  effort required of, 352
  health of, 60
  populations among, 75
  worldwide distribution of recent, 351f
hunting
  of apes, 150
  by chimpanzees, 33
  cooperation in, 186
  by *Homo*, 170
  by humans, 33
  by Mbuti, 406
  by Plains Indians, 360, 386f, 397
  significance of, 183
  techniques, 225
hunting-gathering. *See also* foraging;
    hunter-gatherers
  as new strategy, 183
Hutus, 535, 564
hybrid, 97
hydraulic agriculture, 249
hydraulic systems, 249
hyperrobust, 169, 181
hyperventilation, 6–7
hypodescent, 331–334, 345
hypotheses, 15–16, 18, 21
hypoxia, 126

I

ice ages, 127, 210
  end of, 227
ideal culture, 36
identical twins, 101–102, 102f
identity. *See also* brand identity; ethnic
    identity; situational negotiation of
    social identity; social identity
  within anthropology, 296
  colonialism and, 535, 544
  as fluid, 564
  indigenous as, 564
  in regional system, 294
Ifugao, 358
  location, 358f
Igbo women, 396–397
ilia/ilium, 169f. *See also* pelvis
illness, 59. *See also* disease
  causes of, 60–61
  as emic, 279
  poverty and, 62
Ilongot people, 405–406
  location of, 406f
il-rah, 387
imagined communities, nationalities
    and, 337
IMF. *See* International Monetary Fund
imitative magic, 475
immigration, 339, 561–562
  history, 340
  to United States, 412
imperialism, 533, 543. *See also* cultural
    imperialism
impressionism, 500
impulse control, 76
inalienable rights, 40
Inca people, 260, 265
  decimation of, 124
incest
  among Ashanti people, 453
  avoidance, 452–455, 467
  exogamy and, 451–452
  father-daughter, 453, 455
  among Lakher, 453f
  occurrence of, 453
  among Ojibwa people, 453
  among Yanomami, 453

inclusive fitness, 146
increased equity, 54
independent assortment, 108
  contradiction to, 101
  recombination and, 99–100
independent invention, 41–42
  diffusion versus, 287
India
  energy consumption in, 541, 555f
  Google use in, 312–313, 313f
  independence of, 534
  patriarchy in, 409f, 411
  sacred cattle in, 478–479
indígena, 563
indigenized, 560, 565
indigenous, 563
  as identity, 564
indigenous intellectual property rights
    (IPR), 40, 41f, 44
indigenous peoples, 543, 562–565
  of South America, 60
indigenous people's heath, colonialism
    and, 60
indigenous rights movement, 563, 563f
indio, 563
indirect rule, 535
individualism, 26–27, 32
  art and, 499–500
  in Navajo people, 504, 508
individuals
  culture and, 36–41, 291–292
  fitness of, 146
Indo-European languages, 316, 318
Indonesia, 142–143, 150
  Homo erectus in, 187–188
  Islam in, 485
Indus River Valley, 259–260, 268
industrial degradation, 541–543, 542f
industrial economies
  alienation in, 363–365
  perpetual expansion of, 533
industrial melanism, 95, 95f
industrial production, 7
Industrial Revolution, 43, 251, 527
  causes of, 528
  disillusionment with, 487
  in England, 528, 543
industrial societies, gender in, 412–416
industrial stratification, in England,
    529–531
industrialism, 351, 361t, 372, 391t
  family and, 431
industrialization, 14, 58
  effects of, 539–544
  health problems and, 62
  socioeconomic effects of, 528–533
  spread of, 539–541
  transoceanic trade and, 527–528
  view of, 537
infanticide, 146
infectious disease, 129
  mounting risk of, 122
infertility, marriage and, 461
infibulation, 40
informants, 275. *See also* key cultural
    consultants
informed consent, 85, 283
infraorder, 135f
infrastructure, 291
innovation, 50
  indigenous models for, 56–57
  strategies for, 55–57
  success of, 63
insurance, foraging and, 368
intelligent design, evolution vs., 96–97

intensification
  of agriculture, 259, 550
  environment and, 359
  rites of, 478
Inter-American Development Bank, 537
intercommunity feasting, adaptive value
    of, 371–372
interethnic contact, 557, 559
  shock phase of, 558
interglacials, 189
Intergovernmental Panel on Climate
    Change, 356
international culture, 36
International Monetary Fund (IMF),
    42–43, 537, 551
international transaction volume, 43
Internet, 364
  censorship and, 392
interpretive anthropology, 292–293, 297
intersex, 416–417, 422
interstadials, 189
intervention philosophy, 537
interview schedules, 276–278, 296
interviews, 275–278
intrinsic racism, 333
Inuit, 351f, 352, 381–382, 391t
  body composition of, 124, 125f
  location of, 381f
IPR. *See* indigenous intellectual property
    rights
Iron Age, 258t, 259
Iroquois kinship terminology, 441
irrigation systems, 237f, 240, 242,
    357–358, 372. *See also* hydraulic
    systems; pot irrigation
  necessity of, 227
  simple, 229, 230f, 237
  small-scale, 234
  states and, 252, 266–267
Islam, 481, 481t, 483f, 483t, 485f
  in Africa, 485
  expansion of, 484–485, 490
  in Indonesia, 485

J

Janjaweed, 343f
Japan, race in, 333–334, 336, 345
Java man, 187
Jericho, 253–254, 254f
Jomon culture, 225
judiciary, 391, 393f, 398
  enforcement of, 392

K

K/A dating. *See* potassium-argon dating
Kabwe skull, 191
Kalabari people
  art of, 499
  location of, 499f
Kalimantan, 142
Kamayurá people, 356–357, 357f
Kannada, 312
Kanuri people, 464–465
Kanzi, 304f
Kapauku Papuans, 383–385, 391t
  location of, 383f
Kennewick Man, 86, 86f
Kenyanthropus platyops, 161t,
    163–164, 164f
key cultural consultants, 275, 278, 296
key informants, 278
Keynesian economics, 537
khan, authority of, 387–388
Khasi people, 430f
Kibale National Park, Uganda, 33

nature. *See also* human nature
    culture and, 29
    nurture and, 404
    of warfare, 526–527
Navajo people
    art of, 507
    conservatism of, 504–505, 508
    individualism in, 504, 508
    location of, 505f
Nayar people, 34, 430
    location of, 430f
Nazca lines, 74f
Neander valley, 191
Neandertals, 135, 161t, 188. *See also*
    Denisovans; *Homo sapiens
    neanderthalensis*; Shanidar
    Neandertals
    AMHs and, 192–194, 203, 218
    body composition of, 191–192
    cannibalism in, 193
    cold-adapted, 191–192, 195
    common ancestor of humans and, 204
    cranial capacity of, 180, 193
    DNA of, 189, 191, 203
    evolution of, 189
    reconstruction, 192f
    skeleton of, 191f
    skull form of, 186f, 194f, 201f
need fulfillment, through human behavior,
    32
needs functionalism, 288
negative equity, 55
negative reciprocity, 368–369
neglected tropical diseases, 121
négritude, 337
Negroid, 115
Nelson Island, 552
neoevolutionism, 290
neoliberalism, 537–538, 544
Neolithic, 237–239, 242, 258t
    in Africa, 230–231
    in Asia, 231–233
    diet, 238
    in Europe, 231–233
Neolithic Revolution, 210, 226, 251
neolocality, 431, 436, 443t
neural tube defects (NTDs), 120
New Caledonia, 215
new media, political role of, 392
New World domestication, 233–237
New World monkeys. *See* monkeys
Newtok, Alaska, 552–553, 553f
Ngadha people, 195
NGO. *See* nongovernmental organization
night monkey, 139
Nilotes, 116–117
    body composition of, 124, 125f
Nippur, Iraq, 81f
nitric oxide synthesis, 126
nitrous oxide, 552, 554t
Nittano, Japan, 225
noble savage myth, 526–527
noise, music differentiated from, 502
nomadic politics, 387–388
nomadism, 360. *See also* pastoral
    nomadism
nongovernmental organization (NGO), 56f
nonhuman primates
    quadrupedalism and, 72
    study of, 134
nonindustrial societies, production in,
    361–362, 372–373
nonsettler countries, 536
nonunilineal descent. *See* ambilineal
    descent

nonverbal communication, 305–306, 320
norms, 393. *See also* sexual norms
North American kinship changes in,
    431–435, 432t
NTDs. *See* neural tube defects
nuclear family, 34–35, 428–431, 439, 440f
Nuer, same-sex marriage among,
    451, 458
The Nuer (Evans-Pritchard), 288
nurture, nature and, 404
nutrition, 13. *See also* diet

O

Oaxacan people, 262–263, 266f, 563. *See
    also* Monte Albán
observation, 27, 275–276, 296
occipital bun, 183
Oceania, 216f
Oedipus complex, 14
office (political position), 389
official-public sphere, 539
OH5, 182f
OH7, 181
OH9, 184f, 188
OH24, 182f
OH62, 182
Ojibwa people, incest among, 453
Old World, food production in,
    230–233
Old World monkeys. *See* monkeys
Oldowan tools, 174–175, 185
Olduvai Gorge, Tanzania, 33, 82f
Oligocene epoch, 146, 147f, 152
    anthropoids in, 148–149
    climate change in, 149
Olmec heads, 255, 262, 262f
Olmec people, 261–263, 262f
Omaha kinship terminology, 441
Omo 1, 201
Omo 2, 201
On the Origin of Species (Darwin, C.),
    94, 191
opposable thumbs, 32–33, 44, 137
oppression, aftermaths of, 342–344
oral arts, 498
orangutan (*Pongo*), 137, 140, 150
    sexual dimorphism of, 141, 152
    threats to, 142–143
orbitofrontal cortex, 76
order, 135f
origin myth, 512–513. *See also* myth
    analysis
Orrorin tugenensis, 159, 161t, 162, 175
orthograde posture, 139
osteology, 12
osteometry, 84, 85f
osteoporosis, 119
overinnovation, 55–56
ovum, 100
owl monkey, 139
ozone, 552, 554t

P

Pacific, settlement of, 215–218
paganism, 473
paint-pot theory, 96–97
paleoanthropology, 12, 73, 80
Paleocene epoch, 146, 147f, 152
paleoecology, 11
Paleolithic tools, 185
paleontology, 12, 73, 75, 80
paleopathology, 84, 87
Paleozoic era, 108, 146
palynology, 73
pandemic, 61

Panglossian functionalism, conflict
    versus, 288–289
pantribal sodalities, 385–387
Papua New Guinea, 14f, 212f, 219, 420f.
    See also Pacific
    mining in, 540–541
parallel cousins, 451–452
Paranthropus robustus, 169
parental investment, 32–33
    of primates, 138
partible paternity, 438–439, 438f
participant observation, 14, 275–276, 296
particularities, 35f, 44
    among humans, 34–36
pastoral nomadism, 360, 391t
pastoralism, 228f, 351, 359–361, 361t,
    372, 391t, 397. *See also* herding
pastoralists, 359
    diet of, 360
pater, 451
patriarchy, 14, 422
    flagrant examples of, 460
    in India, 409f, 411
    violence and, 411–412
patrilineal descent, 288, 382, 411, 422,
    435, 436f. *See also* kinship
    moiety organization in, 451–452, 452f
patrilineal-patrilocal complex, 411, 411f
patrilocal extended family, 429
patrilocality, 411, 436–437, 437f, 443t
Patterns of Culture (Benedict), 289
Pawnee women, 406
PDAs. *See* public displays of affection
pea plants, 96–99, 98f, 108
peace keeping, specialization and, 362
peasants, 365–366
pebble tools, 174–175, 185, 185f
Peking man, 184f, 188
pelvis. *See also* ilia/ilium
    of *Ardipithecus,* 163
    of australopithecines, 167–168
    human versus chimpanzee, 169f
Pentecostalism, 473, 481
    in Brazil, 482
    growth of, 488f
People of Puerto Rico (Steward, J.), 294
performance
    of art, 498
    enculturation and, 506
    linguistic, 310
periphery, 525, 532–533, 538t
personalistic disease theories, 61, 66
personal-public sphere, 538
personhood, 62, 64
phenotype, 98, 101–102, 115
    diversity of, 335f
    genetic markers and, 117
    genotype and, 335
phenotypical adaptation, 125, 129
phoneme, 307
phonemics, 307
phonetics, 307
phonology, 306, 320
phyla/phylum, 135, 135f
phylogenetic trees. *See also* mtDNA
    phylogenetic tree; Y chromosome
    phylogenetic tree
    for apes, hominids, hominins, 165f
    global, 210
phylogenetics, 105
phylogeny, 135
physical anthropology. *See* biological
    anthropology
phytoliths, 73, 74f
pictographic writing, 258f

racial classification, 114–115, 128
  skin color and, 117, 119
  traits and, 116–117
racism, 328. *See also* intrinsic racism
radiative forcings, 554
radiometric dating, 81–82, 87
Raelian Movement, 488
raiding, 383, 387, 397
Rambo (film), 560
random genetic drift, 106, 109
random sample, 282
ranked society, 255, 256t, 268
rapport, 275, 278, 296
real culture, 36
recessive, 96–97, 108
  maladaptive, 102
reciprocity, 373
  egalitarianism and, 368–369
  among Ju/'hoansi, 368–369
reciprocity continuum, 368
recombination, 96
  independent assortment and, 99
Red colobus monkey, 33
red ochre pigment, 200
  as symbol, 206–207, 206f
redistribution, 368, 373. *See also* chiefly
    redistribution
refugees, 342
  climate change and, 552–553, 553f
  ethnic Georgian, 343f
relative dating, 81
religion, 472. *See also* fundamentalism;
    Handsome Lake religion; secularism;
    world religions; *specific religions*
  art and, 497–498, 497f, 518
  change and, 483
  cultural ecology and, 478–479
  diversity and, 484
  expressions of, 474–478
  globalization and, 482
  Greco-Roman, 480
  human behavior and, 489
  kinds of, 480–481
  magic and, 475
  power of, 479
  social control and, 479–480, 490
  in United States, 488t
  as universal, 473
remote sensing, 74, 87
Rendille tribe, 31
rent fund, 365–366, 373, 392
repatriation, 342
replacement fund, 365, 373
reproductive success, 15
  differential, 145
research methods. *See also* longitudinal
    research; problem-oriented research;
    survey research; team research
  in archaeology, 73–78
  in biological anthropology, 73–78
residence rules, 436–437
  kinship terminology and, 443t
resistance. *See also* popular resistance
  festivals as, 394, 398
  slavery and, 393–394
  small-scale acts of, 394
resources. *See also* differential access
  depletion of, 543, 550
respondents, 282
revitalization movements, 483–485, 490.
    See also cargo cults
rhinarium, 148
ribonucleic acid. *See* RNA
rice, 222f, 231–233, 242
rickets, 119

The Rise of Anthropological Theory
    (Harris, M.), 291
Riss glacial, 190
rites of intensification, 478
rites of passage, 476, 476f, 478, 490
  art and, 498
  phases of, 477
ritual, 476
river valley states, 259, 260f
RNA (ribonucleic acid), 99–100
robust, 169
  gracile and, 170
  skull form of, 171f
Rodentia, 136
Roma people, 331f. *See also* German
    Roma people
Roman Catholicism, 27–28, 36, 37f,
    480, 535
  in Brazil, 482
  divorce and, 463
  growth rate of, 481
Romance languages, 316
royal endogamy, 456–457
rural, urban versus, 58–59
Russia, modern, 538–539
Rwandan genocide, 535, 542

S

sacred, profane and, 473, 489
sagittal crest, 170, 171f
Sahel, 261
Sahelanthropus tchadensis, 159, 160–161,
    160f, 161t, 175
Sahul, 212–213, 212f, 219
Salish people, 370f, 371
Samburu tribe, 31, 122f
same-sex marriage
  in Canada, 458
  marital rights and, 457–459
  in Nigeria, 458f, 459
  among Nuer, 451, 458
  in United States, 458–459, 467
Samoan immigrants, 59
sample, 282
sampling, 14, 282
  random, 18
  total, 277
San people, 116, 351f, 352–354, 354f, 368,
    380–381, 380f, 391t. *See also*
    Basarwa people; Dobe Ju/'hoansi
  body size of, 124
  hoodia plant and, 41f
  kinship terminology of, 442
  location of, 369f
sanctions, 395, 398
Sangiran 2, 184f, 188
Sangiran 17, 188, 188f
santeria, 485
Sapir-Whorf hypothesis, 308
sati, 460
savagery, 285–286
scarcity, Betsileo people and, 366–367
*Schism and Continuity in an African
    Society* (Turner, V.), 292
schistosomiasis, 60, 121
science, 16. *See also* scientific method
  anthropological theory and, 291
  challenges to, 296
  determinism and, 291
  diachronic, 288
  goal of, 95
  holistic, 5
  humanistic, 13
  political, 9
  synchronic, 288

The Science of Culture (White, L.), 291
scientific medicine, 62
scientific method, 15–20, 18t, 21
scientific theory. *See* theory
*Scientific Theory of Culture, and Other
    Essays* (Malinowski), 291
Scientology, 488
scrapers, 192, 192f, 209
SE. *See* Standard American English
sea ice, 554t
Second World, 538–539
sectorial fallowing, 359
secularism
  in Canada, 487
  rise of, 487–488, 490
  rituals of, 488–489
  in United States, 487–488
sedentism, 227–228, 237–238
  agriculture and, 359
  cultivation and, 122, 226
  increase in, 380
segmented culture, mass culture and, 496
segregation, 341
selection. *See* directional selection;
    natural selection; sexual selection;
    stabilizing selection
selective agents, microbes as, 122
self-determination, 40
Semai people, 369
semantics, 309
semiperiphery, 525, 532–533, 539t
Serce Liman Bay, Mugla province,
    Turkey, 80f
serial monogamy, 464
settlement. *See also* mixed countries;
    nonsettler countries; settler
    countries
  of Americas, 213–215, 215f
  of Australia, 211–213
  of Pacific, 215–218
settlement hierarchy, 266
settlement levels, 11
settlement patterns, social complexity
    and, 75
settler countries, 536
sex, gender and, 405–406, 416
*Sex and Temperament in Three Primitive
    Societies* (Mead), 290
sex cells, 99
sexual behavior, as contested, 451
sexual dimorphism, 139–140
  in *Australopithecus afarensis,* 167
  in *Australopithecus africanus,* 170
  in chimpanzees, 144, 152
  in gibbons, 152
  in gorillas, 142, 152
  in *Homo erectus,* 182–183
  in *Homo sapiens,* 144, 405
  in orangutans, 141, 152
  of Proconsul, 149
sexual norms, 419–420
sexual orientation, 418, 420, 422
  flexibility in, 421
  in United States, 419
sexual reproduction, 96
sexual selection, 103, 103f
sexually transmitted diseases (STDs), 60
shamans, 61, 381, 480. *See also* curer
shame, 394–396, 398
Shang dynasty, 260, 268
  art of, 261
Shanidar Neandertals, 191
sharing, 34, 44
  as leveling mechanism, 432–433
Shasavan people, 360f

shell ornaments, 208
shifting cultivation, 356
shivering, 32
Shoshoni people, location of, 435f
Shoshonius, 138f
siamangs, 140, 152
siblings, 429f
  marriage of, 453
sickle-cell anemia, 95, 103–106, 103f,
    108–109, 240
  adaptive value of, 121
El Sidrón, 189, 193
Sierra Leone, life expectancy in, 60
sign language, 304–305
  in apes, 303
silent trade, Mbuti people and, 369
silverback, 142–143
Sima de los Huesos, 189
single-parent households, 415t, 431f, 440
  increase in, 433
*A Singular Woman: The Untold Story
    of Barack Obama's Mother* (Scott),
    16–17
site identification, 75
situational negotiation of social identity,
    326–328
skeletal biology. *See* bone biology
Skhūl fossils, 202
skin color, 118
  geographic distribution of, 119–120
  natural selection and, 119, 120t
  racial classification and, 117, 119
  variation in, 119–121
skull form
  of AMH, 201f, 202f
  of archaic *Homo sapiens,* 201f
  of *Australopithecus afarensis,* 159, 171f
  of *Australopithecus africanus,* 170f, 171f
  of *Australopithecus boisei,* 170f,
      171f, 182f
  of *Australopithecus robustus,* 171f
  changes in, 117
  of graciles, 171f
  of *Homo erectus,* 184, 184f, 186, 186f,
      188f, 201f
  of *Homo floresiensis,* 194f
  of *Homo habilis,* 182f
  Homo versus chimpanzee, 169f
  of humans, 194f
  of Neandertals, 186f, 194f, 201f
  of robusts, 171f
slash-and-burn horticulture, 355, 355f
slavery
  of African Americans, 11, 124
  Brazil and, 335, 345
  race and, 330
  resistance and, 393–394
smallpox, 114, 123f, 240
  ABO blood group system and,
    122–123
smelting, 259, 269
Smilodectes, 148f
soccer, 514. *See also* World Cup soccer
social anthropology. *See* cultural
    anthropology
social competition, 208
social complexity, settlement patterns and,
    75
social control, 295, 393, 398
  informal, 394–396
  religion and, 479–480, 490
  song as, 382, 396–397
social facts, 292
social fund, 365, 373
social identity, 282

social indicators, 282–283
social stratification, 240, 248, 252–253,
    255, 256t, 268. *See also* gender
    stratification; industrial
    stratification; stratified
  complexity of, 531
  dimensions of, 390–391, 391t, 397, 532
  emergence of, 390–391
  modern, 531–533
sociality, 32
  humans and, 72
  of primates, 138
  subsistence and, 350
society, 5. *See also* complex societies;
    egalitarianism; industrial societies;
    nonindustrial societies; plural
    society; ranked society; social
    stratification
  art and, 500–508
  complexity in, 11
  economy and, 363
  multiple spouses allowed by, 408t
  units of, 354
sociocultural anthropology. *See* cultural
    anthropology
sociolinguistics, 13, 310–316, 320
sociology, 21, 297
  cultural anthropology and, 13–14
sociopolitical organization, 379, 391t
sodalities, 386. *See also* pantribal
    sodalities
Solomon Islands, 216, 216f
song, as social control, 382, 396–397
sorcery, 395–396
sororate marriages, 461–462, 462f
soul loss, 61
South America, indigenous populations
    of, 60
South Ossetia, 343f
Spanish empire, 533
specialization, peace keeping and, 362
speciation, 107–108
species, 107, 135, 135f
speech, 302–303
  evaluations, 313–314
  gender and, 311
  sounds, 306–307
  uneducated, 311–312, 314f
spermatogenesis, folate and, 120
spina bifida, 120, 121f
spirit possession, 364–365
spiritual beings, 474
splitter, lumpers and, 164
sports. *See also specific sports*
  in Brazil, 515–516
  coverage of, 496
  culture and, 514–518
  international success of, 515–518
  magic and, 470f, 472, 475f, 476
  media and, 515
  values in, 515–519
  winning in, 515–516
stabilizing selection, 103–106
Standard American English (SE),
    310–311
  BEV compared to, 315–316
  symbolic capital of, 316
  total phonemes in, 307
  vowel phonemes in, 307f
Star Wars (film), 508–509, 510t
starch grain analysis, 73–74
state formation, 268
  agriculture and, 359
  emergence of, 388
  in Mesoamerica, 261–266

in Middle East, 253–259, 253f
  warfare and, 263–265
states, 336, 379, 388, 391t, 397. *See also*
    Harappan state; primary states; river
    valley states; Zapotec state
  in Africa, 260–261
  art and, 500, 519
  attributes of, 252–253
  collapse of, 266–268
  decision making in, 263
  early, 259–266
  empires and, 252
  expansion of, 263
  food production and, 229–230, 265
  irrigation and, 252, 266–267
  in Mesoamerica, 261–266
  origin of, 248–250, 251f
  property of, 539
  rise of, 257–259
  systems of, 391–393
  threats to, 269
  writing and, 258
statistical techniques, 14
status, 248, 390–391, 391t. *See also*
    achieved status; ascribed status
  burials and, 256
  differentiation, 255, 268
  gender and, 405–406, 409, 422
  language and, 311–316, 315f, 320
  prestige and, 327
  shifting, 327–328
  of women, 439
status systems, 389–390
STDs. *See* sexually transmitted diseases
stereoscopic vision, 137
stereotypes, 341. *See also* gender
    stereotypes
  of men, 404
  of women, 404
stipulated descent, 436
stone bladelets, 206, 206f
stone tools. *See also* Acheulean tools;
    bone tools; chopper core; choppers;
    Clovis tradition; cores; denticulate
    tool; flake tool; Levallois technique;
    Middle Paleolithic tools; Mousterian
    tools; Oldowan tools; Paleolithic
    tools; pebble tools; Upper Paleolithic
    tools
  Australopithecus garhi and, 174–175
  of hominins, 33
Stonehenge, 389f
Stonewall uprising, 457f
storytelling
  of Aleut people, 506f
  art of, 506, 519
  music and, 506
stratification. *See* gender stratification;
    industrial stratification; social
    stratification
stratified, 334. *See also* social
    stratification
stratigraphy, 77, 81, 81f, 87
stratum, 390
stratum endogamy, 390
structural functionalism, 288
structuralism, 293
structure, 291
style shifts, 310
subarctic Indians, 351f
subculture, 37
subgroups, 316
suborder, 135f
subordinate, 391
  superordinate interactions with, 394

universal grammar, 308
universals
   generalities and, 34–35, 44
   among humans, 34–35
   music as, 501
   religion as, 473
Upper Paleolithic tools, 209
   AMHs and, 185
Ur, 255
   temple tower at, 259f
uranium series dating, 82, 83t
urban, rural versus, 58–59
urban anthropology, 58–59, 65
urban living, 58
urban planning, 58–59
urban revolution, 251
urban youth subculture, 512–513
urbanization, in LDCs, 58
Uruk, 253, 255, 259
Uruk period, 257, 268
USAID. *See* U.S. Agency for International
   Development
UV radiation, 119, 128
   folate and, 120

V

variables, 21, 282. *See also* dependent
      variable; predictor variable
   multiple, 18–20
variation, 8, 20, 108
   culture and, 289–290
   geography and, 13
   in human behavior, 289–290
   natural selection and, 94
   within races, 330
   reduction in, 102–103
   in skin color, 119–121
   transmission of, 12
Venus of Willendorf, 208f
vernacular, 315. *See also* Black English
      Vernacular
vertical economy, 228, 238
Vietnam War, 53
village fissioning, 383
village head, 382
violence. *See also* domestic violence
   human diversity and, 526
   patriarchy and, 411–412
virginal transvestites, 417
virgins, sworn, 417
Virunga Mountains, Rwanda, 144f
vision, depth and color, 32. *See also*
      stereoscopic vision
vitamin D
   disease and, 119
   role of, 119
vocabulary. *See* focal vocabulary
volcanic eruptions, 554, 554t
voodoo, 485

W

Wallace's Line, 212f
Warao Indians, 384

warfare, 249–250, 268. *See also*
      Vietnam War
   among Native Americans, 525
   nature of, 526–527
   origin of, 526–527
   among Plains Indians, 386–387, 386f
   state formation and, 263–265
   Yanomami people and, 411
warrior grade, 387, 387f
Washoe, 303
wealth, 389
   diet and, 433
   disparities, 55
   prestige and, 371–372, 390–391,
      390f, 391t
   in United States, 531–532, 531f
The Wealth of Nations (Smith), 537, 537f
wedding, 448f. *See also* marriage
weretigers, 364–365
Western culture, art in, 497
Western folk taxonomy, 62
western lowland gorilla. *See* gorillas
Western medicine, 61–62
westernization, 558
WGIP. *See* United Nations Working
      Group on Indigenous Populations
whaling, 38–39
wheat, 227–229, 229f, 238
When Languages Die (Harrison),
      319 WHO. *See* World Health
      Organization
witchcraft accusations, 479
The Wizard of Oz (film), 508–509, 510t
Wodaabe male celebrants, 405f
women. *See also* Agta women; American
      women; female genital modification;
      female infanticide; Hidatsa women;
      Igbo women; Pawnee women
   activities of, 404, 406–407, 407t
   in Arembepe, Bahia, Brazil, 406
   behavior of, 404
   careers of, 29f, 32, 402f, 404, 412–414
   cash employment of, 412–413,
      413t, 431
   child care by, 407–408
   domestic work by, 408t
   education of, 512
   family planning and, 512
   gathering and, 409
   human behavior and, 404
   organization of, 414–415
   pelvis of, 72
   physical labor of, 408f, 412, 413f
   poverty and, 414–415, 422
   promiscuity of, 437–438
   reproductive strategies of, 408
   singing by, 502–503
   social transition of, 502–503
   status of, 439
   stereotypes of, 404
   subsistence and, 407, 407t, 409
   wages of, 412
   work force participation of, 415t

woolly spider monkey, 139f
word order, 306, 318
work, happiness and, 415–416, 416f
work ethic, 32
working class, 529. *See also* proletariat
World Bank, 42–43, 50, 537, 551
world capitalism, 43, 543
World Cup soccer, 10, 37, 515
World Health Organization (WHO), 121
World Malaria Report, 121
world religions, 481–482, 481t, 483f
   internal unity and diversity of, 483t
world system. *See* modern world system
World Trade Organization (WTO), 42,
      392, 551
   opponents of, 43
world-system theory, 294, 525, 533, 543
writing, 268, 302. *See also* cuneiform
      writing; pictographic writing
   of Maya, 526
   states and, 258
WT15,000, 182, 183f
WTO. *See* World Trade Organization
Würm glacial, 189, 191, 194f, 195,
      202, 210

X

X chromosome, 100f
Xingu National Park, 356–357

Y

Y chromosome, 100f, 203, 210
Y chromosome phylogenetic tree,
      117, 210
Yanomami Health Plan, 385
Yanomami people, 362, 382–385, 391t
   incest among, 453
   marriage of, 452
   warfare and, 411
yaws, 104–105
Yonggom people, 540
Yoruba people, 497
   art of, 505

Z

zadruga, 429–431
Zapotec people, 563
Zapotec state, 263–265, 269
ziggurat, 259f
Zinjanthropus boisei, 170f
zoological taxonomy
   classificatory units of, 135f
   of *Homo sapiens*, 135t
zoology, 12–13
Zoonomia (Darwin, E.), 94
zygote, 100

MAP ATLAS

CONTENTS

MAP 1
Annual Percent of World Forest Loss, 1990–2000

Deforestation is a major environmental problem. In the tropics, large corporations clear forests seeking hardwoods for the global market in furniture and fine woods. As well, the agriculturally driven clearing of the great rain forests of the Amazon Basin, west and central Africa, Middle America, and Southeast Asia has drawn public attention. Reduced forest cover means the world's vegetation system will absorb less carbon dioxide, resulting in global warming. Of concern, too, is the loss of biodiversity (large numbers of plants and animals), the destruction of soil systems, and disruptions in water supply that accompany clearing.

QUESTIONS

Look at Map 1, "Annual Percent of World Forest Loss, 1990–2000."

1. On what continents do you find stable or increased forest cover?

2. Are there areas of Africa with stable or increased forest cover? Where are they? What might the reasons be for this lack of deforestation?

3. How does deforestation in India compare with the area to its east, which includes mainland and insular Southeast Asia?

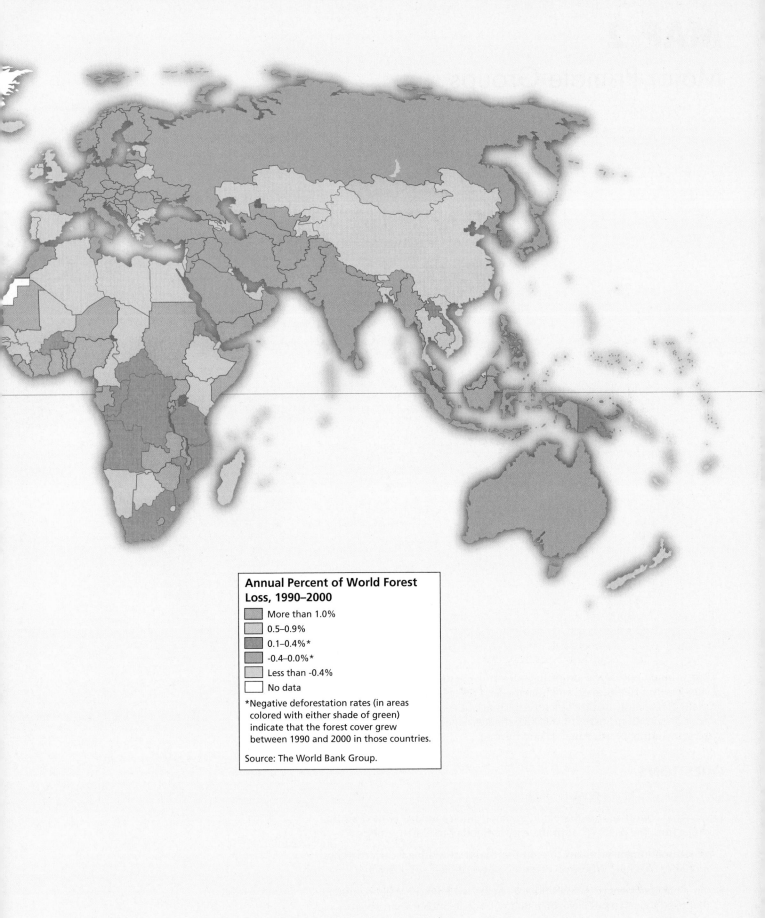

Annual Percent of World Forest Loss, 1990–2000

More than 1.0%

0.5–0.9%

0.1–0.4%*

-0.4–0.0%*

Less than -0.4%

No data

*Negative deforestation rates (in areas colored with either shade of green) indicate that the forest cover grew between 1990 and 2000 in those countries.

Source: The World Bank Group.

MAP 2
Major Primate Groups

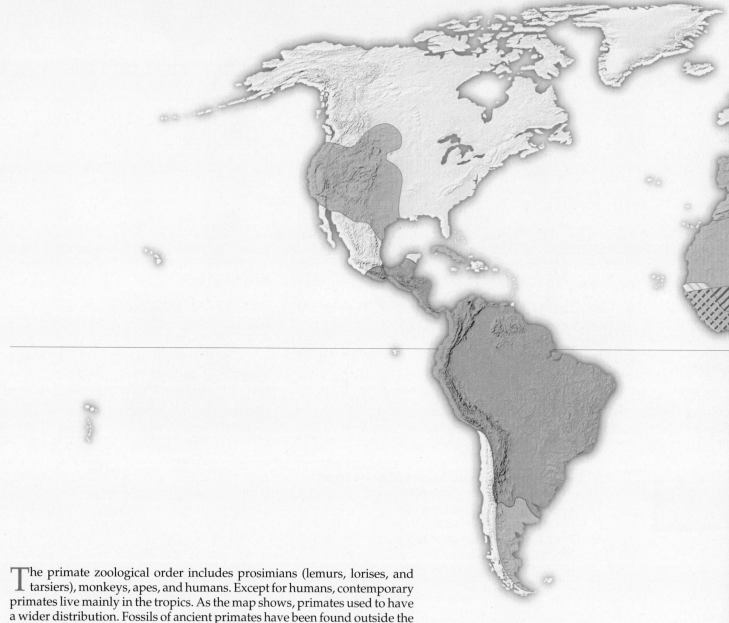

The primate zoological order includes prosimians (lemurs, lorises, and tarsiers), monkeys, apes, and humans. Except for humans, contemporary primates live mainly in the tropics. As the map shows, primates used to have a wider distribution. Fossils of ancient primates have been found outside the tropics, including North America and Europe.

QUESTIONS

Look at Map 2, "Major Primate Groups."

1. On what continents are there nonhuman primates today? How does this differ from the past? What primate thrives today in North America?

2. What nonhuman primates live on the island of Madagascar? Are they monkeys or what? Where do other members of their suborder live?

3. On what continents can you find apes in the wild today? What continent that used to have apes lacks them today (except, of course, in zoos).

Major Primate Groups

- New World Monkeys (living)
- Old World Monkeys (living)
- Prosimians (living)
- Apes (living)
- Fossil only

MAP 3
Evolution of the Primates

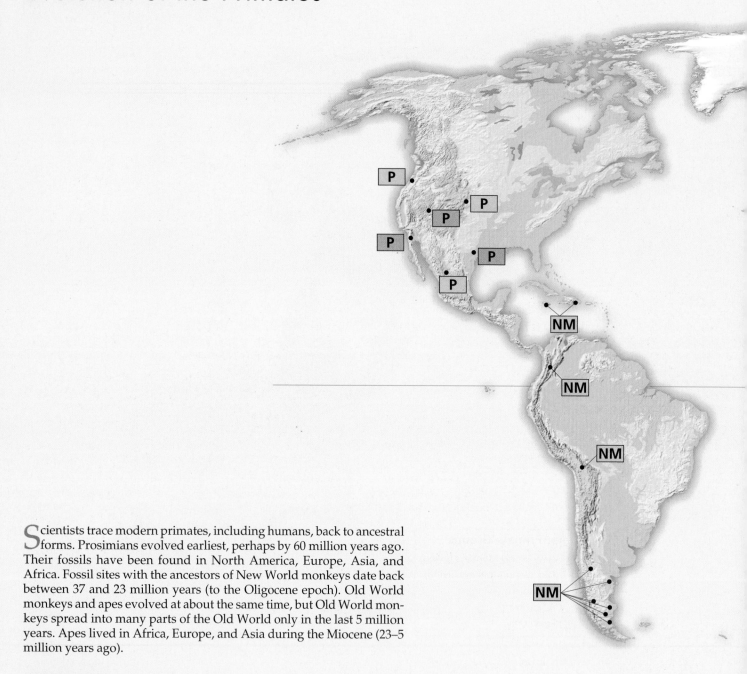

Scientists trace modern primates, including humans, back to ancestral forms. Prosimians evolved earliest, perhaps by 60 million years ago. Their fossils have been found in North America, Europe, Asia, and Africa. Fossil sites with the ancestors of New World monkeys date back between 37 and 23 million years (to the Oligocene epoch). Old World monkeys and apes evolved at about the same time, but Old World monkeys spread into many parts of the Old World only in the last 5 million years. Apes lived in Africa, Europe, and Asia during the Miocene (23–5 million years ago).

QUESTIONS

Look at Map 3, "Evolution of the Primates."

1. What continent(s) had the first primates? What kinds of primates were those?

2. On what continent has the evolution of primates been most continuous? Does this have implications for human evolution?

3. Which continent with several of the earliest primates has the fewest nonhuman primates today?

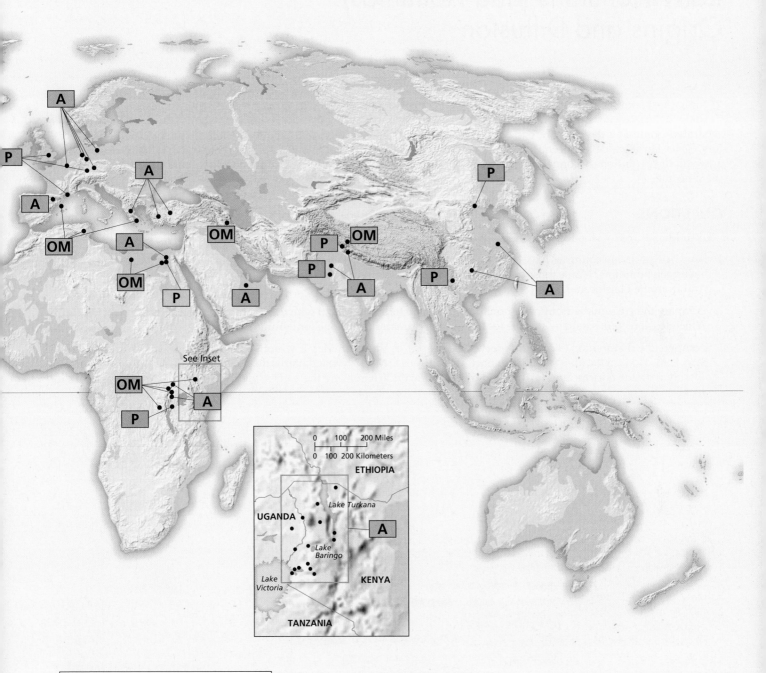

Evolution of the Primates

	Eocene: 57–37 million years ago
	Oligocene: 37–23 million years ago
	Miocene: 23–5 million years ago

OM	Old World monkeys
NM	New World monkeys
P	Prosimians
A	Apes

(Inset map)

0   100   200 Miles
0   100   200 Kilometers

ETHIOPIA

UGANDA   Lake Turkana

A

Lake Baringo

Lake Victoria   KENYA

TANZANIA

MAP 4
Early Hominins (and Hominids): Origins and Diffusion

The earliest hominins, including the ancestors of modern humans, evolved in Africa around 6 million years ago. Many sites date to the late Miocene (8–5 million years ago) when the lines leading to modern humans, chimps, and gorillas may have separated. Some sites dating to the end of the Pliocene epoch (5–1.8 million years ago) contain fossil remains of human ancestors, *Homo*. During the Pleistocene Era(1.8 million–11,000 years ago), humans spread all over the world. Scholars don't always agree on the evolutionary connections between the different fossils, as indicated in the question marks and broken lines on the time line.

QUESTIONS

Look at Map 4, "Early Hominins (and Hominids): Origins and Diffusion."

1. How many African countries have early hominin or hominid sites? Which countries contain sites of hominids that may not have been hominins? Name those two sites. How many African countries have sites from the Miocene? From the Pliocene? And from the Pleistocene?

2. Compare the African distribution of nonhuman primate fossils in Map 3 with the distribution of early hominins in Map 4. Which fossil record is better—the one for nonhuman primates or the one for hominins?

3. Compare the distribution of contemporary African apes, as shown in Map 2, with the distribution of early hominin sites in Map 4. Also look at the distribution of extinct African apes in Map 3. What patterns do you notice? Where did early hominins overlap with the African apes (extinct and contemporary)? Where were there apes but no known early hominins, and vice versa?

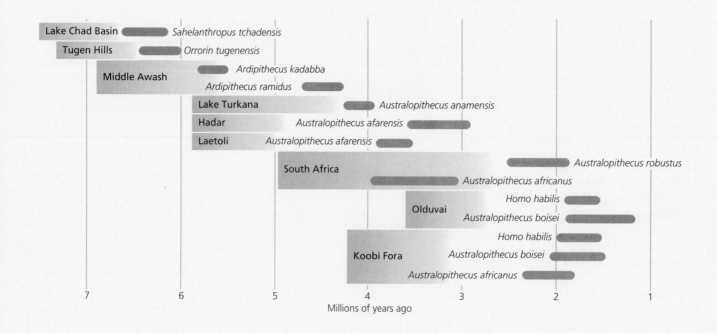

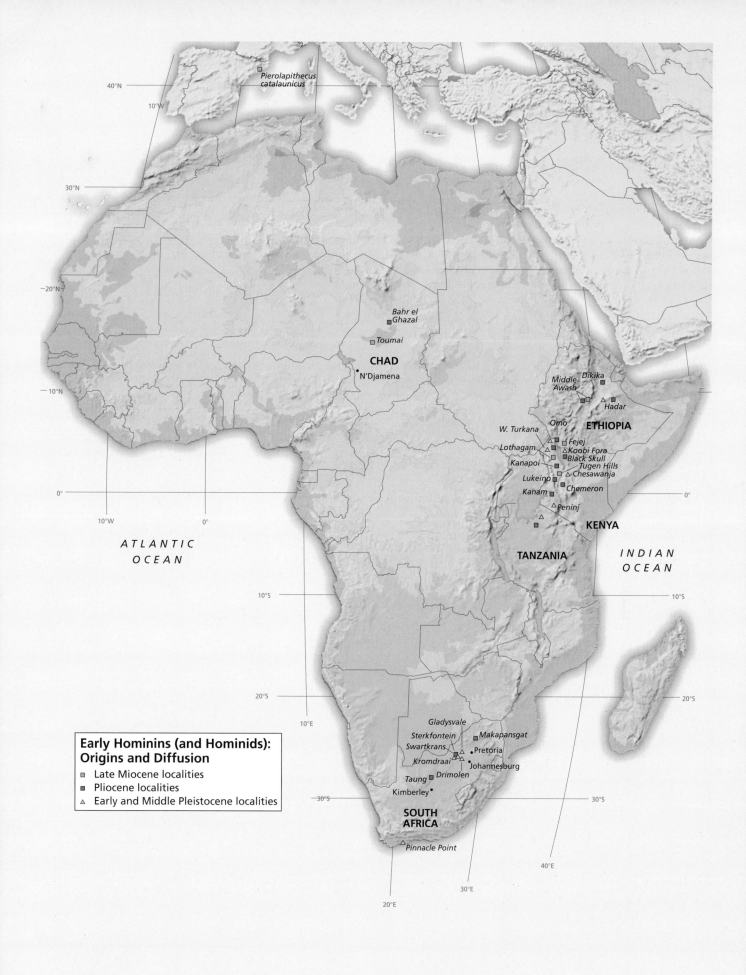

Pierolapithecus
catalaunicus

40°N

10°W

30°N

10°W

20°N

Bahr el
Ghazal

Toumai

CHAD

10°N

N'Djamena

Middle
Awash

Dikika

Hadar

W. Turkana   Omo

ETHIOPIA

Fejej

Lothagam

Koobi Fora

Black Skull

Kanapoi

Tugen Hills

Lukeino

Chesawanja

Kanam

Chemeron

Peninj

KENYA

0°

0°

10°W

0°

ATLANTIC
OCEAN

INDIAN
OCEAN

TANZANIA

10°S

10°S

10°E

20°S

20°S

10°E

Gladysvale

Sterkfontein

Makapansgat

Swartkrans

Pretoria

Kromdraai

Johannesburg

Taung   Drimolen

Early Hominins (and Hominids):
Origins and Diffusion

▫ Late Miocene localities
▪ Pliocene localities
△ Early and Middle Pleistocene localities

Kimberley

30°S

30°S

SOUTH
AFRICA

Pinnacle Point

30°E

40°E

20°E

MAP 5
The Emergence of Modern Humans

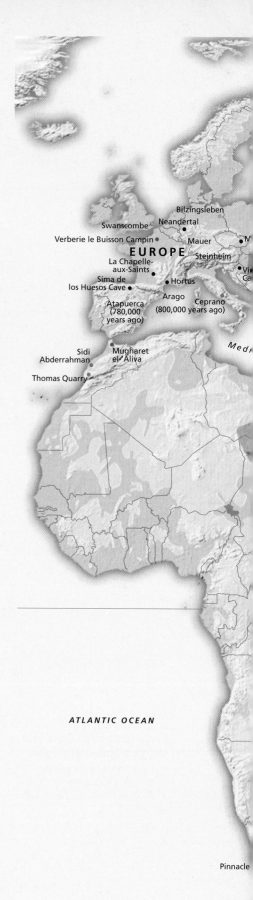

Early forms of *Homo* (*H.*) *erectus*, sometimes called *H. ergaster*, have been found in East Africa and the former Soviet Georgia. By 1.7 million years ago, *H. erectus* had spread from Africa into Asia, including Indonesia, and eventually Europe. The *H. erectus* period may have lasted until 300,000 years ago. Other archaic forms of *Homo*, including fossils sometimes called *H. antecessor* and *H. heidelbergensis*, have been found in various parts of the Old World.

QUESTIONS

Look at Map 5, "The Emergence of Modern Humans."

1. Locate the site of Dmanisi (Georgia). Locate the site of Nariokotome (East Turkana, Kenya). These are sites where similarly dated early remains of *Homo erectus* (or *Homo ergaster*) have been found. Find two additional sites where hominins with similar dates (1.8–1.6 m.y.a.) have been found.

2. Considering Africa and Asia, name five sites (other than Dmanisi and Nariokotome) where *Homo erectus* fossils have been found.

3. Locate Heidelberg (Mauer) and Ceprano. What kinds of hominin fossils have been found there?

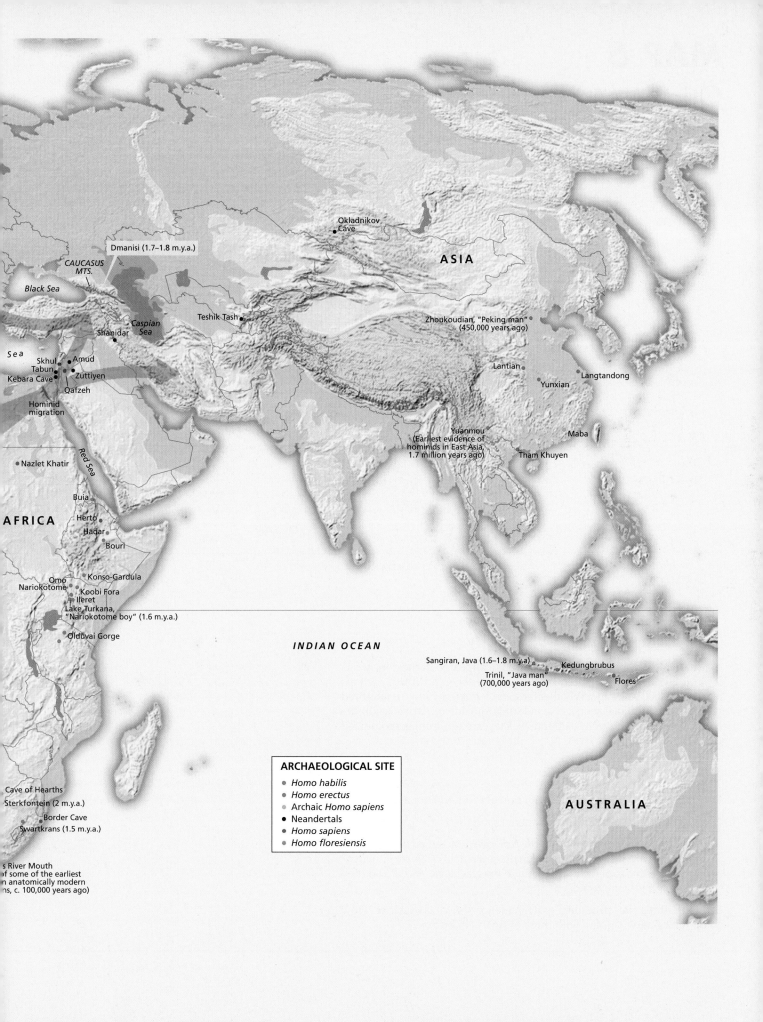

Okladnikov
Cave

ASIA

Dmanisi (1.7–1.8 m.y.a.)

*CAUCASUS
MTS.*

Black Sea

*Caspian
Sea*

Teshik Tash

Shanidar

Zhoukoudian, "Peking man"
(450,000 years ago)

Sea

Skhul
Tabun
Kebara Cave
Zuttiyen
Qafzeh

Amud

Lantian

Langtandong

Yunxian

Hominid
migration

Red Sea

Nazlet Khatir

Buia

AFRICA

Herto
Hadar

Bouri

Konso-Gardula

Omo
Nariokotome

Koobi Fora
Ileret
Lake Turkana,
"Nariokotome boy" (1.6 m.y.a.)

Olduvai Gorge

Yuanmou
(Earliest evidence of
hominids in East Asia,
1.7 million years ago)

Tham Khuyen

Maba

INDIAN OCEAN

Sangiran, Java (1.6–1.8 m.y.a)

Trinil, "Java man"
(700,000 years ago)

Kedungbrubus

Flores

Cave of Hearths
Sterkfontein (2 m.y.a.)
Border Cave
Swartkrans (1.5 m.y.a.)

AUSTRALIA

s River Mouth
f some of the earliest
n anatomically modern
s, c. 100,000 years ago)

ARCHAEOLOGICAL SITE

- *Homo habilis*
- *Homo erectus*
- Archaic *Homo sapiens*
- Neandertals
- *Homo sapiens*
- *Homo floresiensis*

MAP 6
Origins and Distribution of Modern Humans

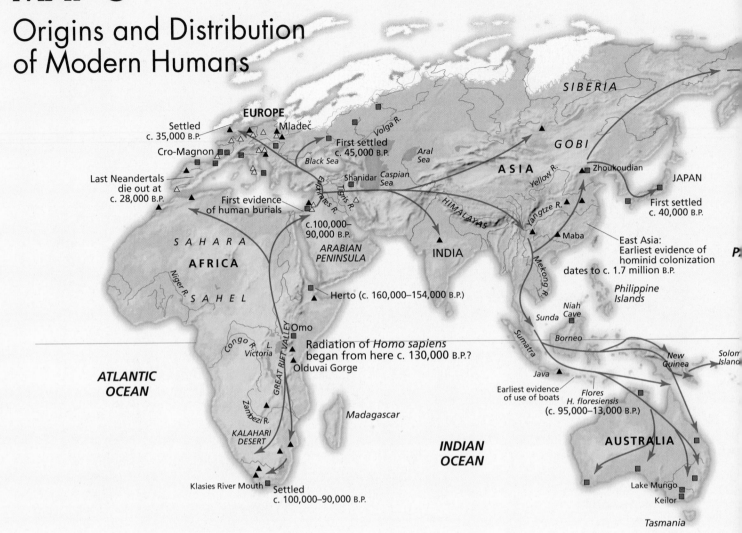

EUROPE

Settled c. 35,000 B.P.

Mladeč

Cro-Magnon

Last Neandertals die out at c. 28,000 B.P.

First evidence of human burials

c.100,000–90,000 B.P.

Volga R.

Black Sea

First settled c. 45,000 B.P.

Aral Sea

Euphrates R.

Tigris R.

Shanidar

Caspian Sea

SAHARA

AFRICA

Niger R.

SAHEL

ARABIAN PENINSULA

Herto (c. 160,000–154,000 B.P.)

Congo R.

L. Victoria

GREAT RIFT VALLEY

Omo

Radiation of *Homo sapiens* began from here c. 130,000 B.P.?

Olduvai Gorge

Zambezi R.

KALAHARI DESERT

Klasies River Mouth

Settled c. 100,000–90,000 B.P.

ATLANTIC OCEAN

Madagascar

INDIAN OCEAN

ASIA

SIBERIA

GOBI

Zhoukoudian

JAPAN

First settled c. 40,000 B.P.

Yellow R.

HIMALAYAS

Yangtze R.

Maba

East Asia: Earliest evidence of hominid colonization dates to c. 1.7 million B.P.

Mekong R.

INDIA

Philippine Islands

Niah Cave

Sunda

Borneo

Sumatra

New Guinea

Solom Island

Java

Earliest evidence of use of boats

Flores H. floresiensis (c. 95,000–13,000 B.P.)

AUSTRALIA

Lake Mungo

Keilor

Tasmania

A natomically modern humans (AMHs), appeared earliest in Africa (at Herto?) and migrated into the rest of the Old World, perhaps around 130,000 years ago. Whether these early modern humans interbred with archaic humans, such as Neandertals, outside of Africa is still debated. Sometime between 25,000 and 9,000 years ago, humans colonized the New World.

QUESTIONS

Look at Map 6, "Origins and Distribution of Modern Humans."

1. When and from where was Australia first settled?

2. When and from where was North America first settled? How many migrations are shown as figuring in the settlement of North America? How were these migrations related to the glacial ice cover? Did they all follow the same route?

3. Locate three sites providing early evidence of AMHs in Africa. How do their dates compare with those of AMHs in Europe?

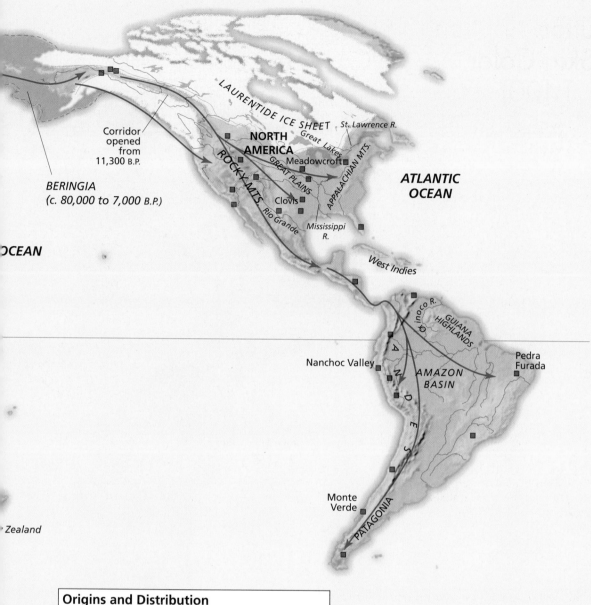

BERINGIA
(c. 80,000 to 7,000 B.P.)

Corridor
opened
from
11,300 B.P.

LAURENTIDE ICE SHEET

St. Lawrence R.
Great Lakes

NORTH
AMERICA

ROCKY MTS.

GREAT PLAINS

Meadowcroft

APPALACHIAN MTS.

ATLANTIC
OCEAN

Clovis

Rio Grande

Mississippi
R.

West Indies

OCEAN

Orinoco R.

GUIANA
HIGHLANDS

Pedra
Furada

Nanchoc Valley

A
N
D
E
S

AMAZON
BASIN

Zealand

Monte
Verde

PATAGONIA

**Origins and Distribution
of Modern Humans**

↰ Possible settlement direction

▲ Archaic *Homo sapiens* (c. 650,000–28,000 B.P.)

△ Neandertals (c. 130,000–28,000? B.P.)

▪ Modern *Homo sapiens* (c. 130,000 B.P.–present)

☐ Areas covered by ice in late
Pleistocene era (18,000 B.P.)

▨ Beringia

MAP 7
The Distribution of Human Skin Color (Before C.E. 1400)

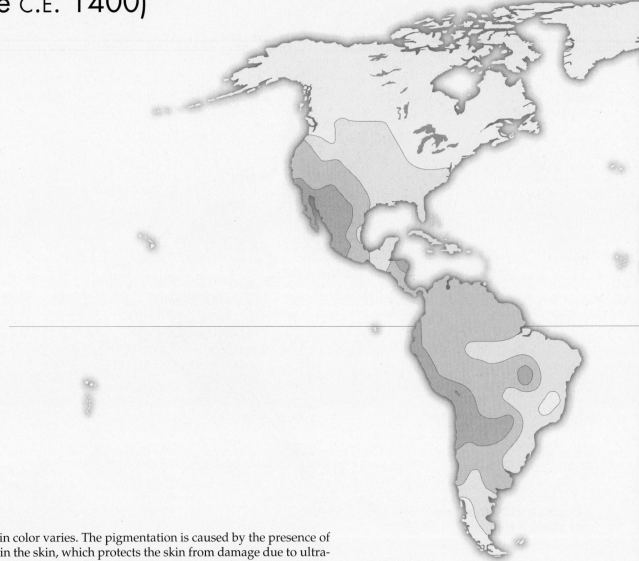

Human skin color varies. The pigmentation is caused by the presence of melanin in the skin, which protects the skin from damage due to ultraviolet radiation. In areas with much UV radiation, people biologically adapted to their environments by increased melanin production.

QUESTIONS

Look at Map 7, "The Distribution of Human Skin Color (Before C.E. 1400)."

1. Where are the Native Americans with the darkest skin color located? What factors help explain this distribution?

2. In both western and eastern hemispheres, is the lightest skin color found in the north or the south? Outside Asia, where do you find skin color closest to northern Asian skin color? Is this surprising given what you have read about migrations and settlement history?

3. Where are skin colors darkest? How might you explain this distribution?

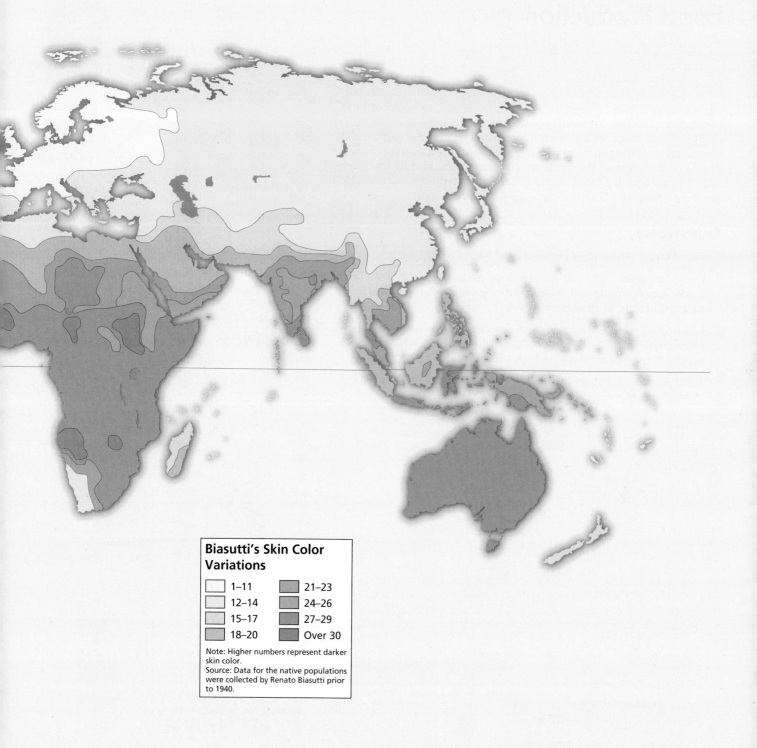

Biasutti's Skin Color Variations

☐ 1–11	☐ 21–23	
☐ 12–14	☐ 24–26	
☐ 15–17	☐ 27–29	
☐ 18–20	☐ Over 30	

Note: Higher numbers represent darker skin color.
Source: Data for the native populations were collected by Renato Biasutti prior to 1940.

MAP 8
The Origin and Spread of Food Production

The Neolithic, or New Stone Age, refers to the period of early farming settlements when people who had been foragers shifted to food production. This pattern of subsistence was based on the domestication of plants and animals. Through domestication, people transformed plants and animals from their wild state to a form more useful to humans. The Neolithic began in the fertile crescent area of the Middle East over 10,000 years ago. It spread to the Levant and Mediterranean, finally reaching Britain and Scandinavia around 5,000 years ago.

QUESTIONS

Look at Map 8, "The Origin and Spread of Food Production."

1. Considering the map and the timeline, name three regions where cattle were domesticated. Based on the timeline, what animals were domesticated in North America?

2. Did Ireland receive Middle Eastern domesticates? What is the origin of the "Irish potato," or white potato (see the timeline), which became, much later, the caloric basis of Irish subsistence?

3. Besides cattle, what animals were domesticated more than once? Where were those areas of domestication?

ATLANTIC OCEAN

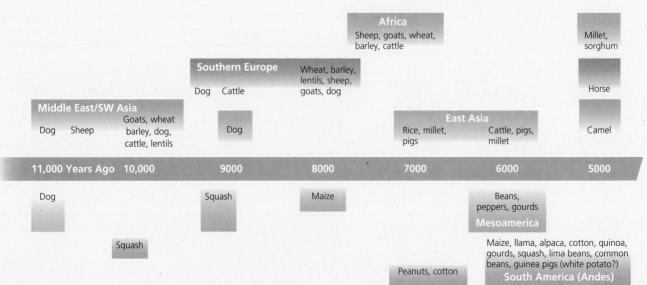

					Africa		Millet, sorghum
					Sheep, goats, wheat, barley, cattle		
		Southern Europe	Wheat, barley, lentils, sheep, goats, dog				Horse
		Dog	Cattle				
Middle East/SW Asia					East Asia		Camel
		Goats, wheat barley, dog, cattle, lentils			Rice, millet, pigs	Cattle, pigs, millet	
Dog	Sheep		Dog				
11,000 Years Ago	10,000	9000	8000	7000	6000	5000
Dog		Squash	Maize		Beans, peppers, gourds	
					Mesoamerica	
	Squash				Maize, llama, alpaca, cotton, quinoa, gourds, squash, lima beans, common beans, guinea pigs (white potato?)	
				Peanuts, cotton	South America (Andes)	

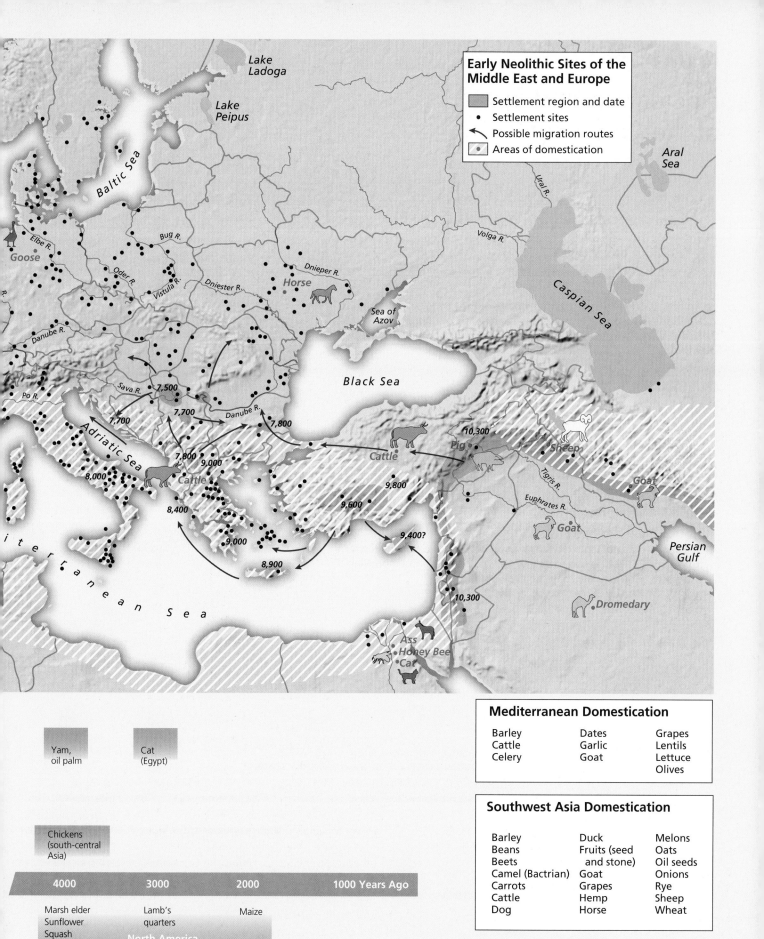

Lake Ladoga

Lake Peipus

Baltic Sea

Aral Sea

Early Neolithic Sites of the Middle East and Europe

- Settlement region and date
- • Settlement sites
- → Possible migration routes
- ⫶ Areas of domestication

Elbe R.

Goose

Bug R.

Oder R.

Vistula R.

Dniester R.

Dnieper R.

Horse

Sea of Azov

Ural R.

Volga R.

Caspian Sea

Danube R.

Po R.

Sava R.

7,500

7,700

7,700

Danube R.

7,800

Black Sea

Cattle

Pig

10,300

Sheep

Adriatic Sea

7,800

9,000

Cattle

Goat

8,000

8,400

9,800

Tigris R.

9,000

9,600

Goat

Euphrates R.

9,400?

Persian Gulf

M e d i t e r r a n e a n   S e a

8,900

10,300

Dromedary

Ass
Honey Bee
Cat

Yam, oil palm

Cat (Egypt)

Mediterranean Domestication

Barley	Dates	Grapes
Cattle	Garlic	Lentils
Celery	Goat	Lettuce
		Olives

Southwest Asia Domestication

Barley	Duck	Melons
Beans	Fruits (seed	Oats
Beets	and stone)	Oil seeds
Camel (Bactrian)	Goat	Onions
Carrots	Grapes	Rye
Cattle	Hemp	Sheep
Dog	Horse	Wheat

Chickens (south-central Asia)

| 4000 | 3000 | 2000 | 1000 Years Ago |

Marsh elder
Sunflower
Squash

Lamb's quarters

Maize

North America

White potato

MAP 9
Ancient Civilizations of the Old World

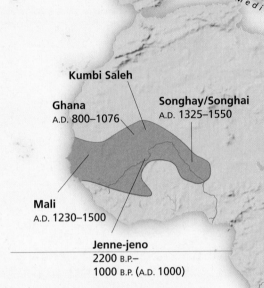

Kumbi Saleh

Ghana
A.D. 800–1076

Songhay/Songhai
A.D. 1325–1550

A rchaic states developed in many parts of the Old World at different periods. The earliest civilizations, such as Mesopotamia, Egypt, and the Indus Valley, are generally placed at about 5500 B.P. States developed later in Asia, Africa, and the Americas (see Map 13).

Mali
A.D. 1230–1500

Jenne-jeno
2200 B.P.–
1000 B.P. (A.D. 1000)

QUESTIONS

Look at Map 9, "Ancient Civilizations of the Old World."

1. What contemporary nations would you have to visit if you wanted to see all the places where ancient civilizations developed in the Old World? Would some countries be off limits for political reasons? How do you think such limitations have affected the archaeological record?

2. Of the ancient states shown on Map 9, which developed latest? Why do you think the first states developed when and where they did?

3. In which of the ancient states shown on Map 9 were Middle Eastern domesticates basic to the economy? In which states shown on Map 9 were other domesticates basic to the economy?

ATLANTIC OCEAN

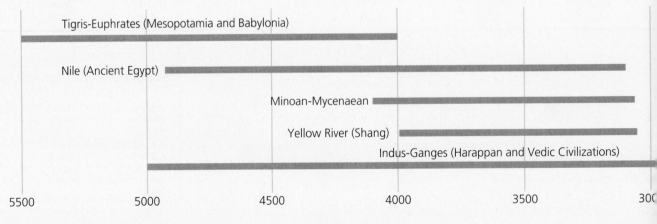

Tigris-Euphrates (Mesopotamia and Babylonia)

Nile (Ancient Egypt)

Minoan-Mycenaean

Yellow River (Shang)

Indus-Ganges (Harappan and Vedic Civilizations)

5500   5000   4500   4000   3500   300

Years (B.P.)

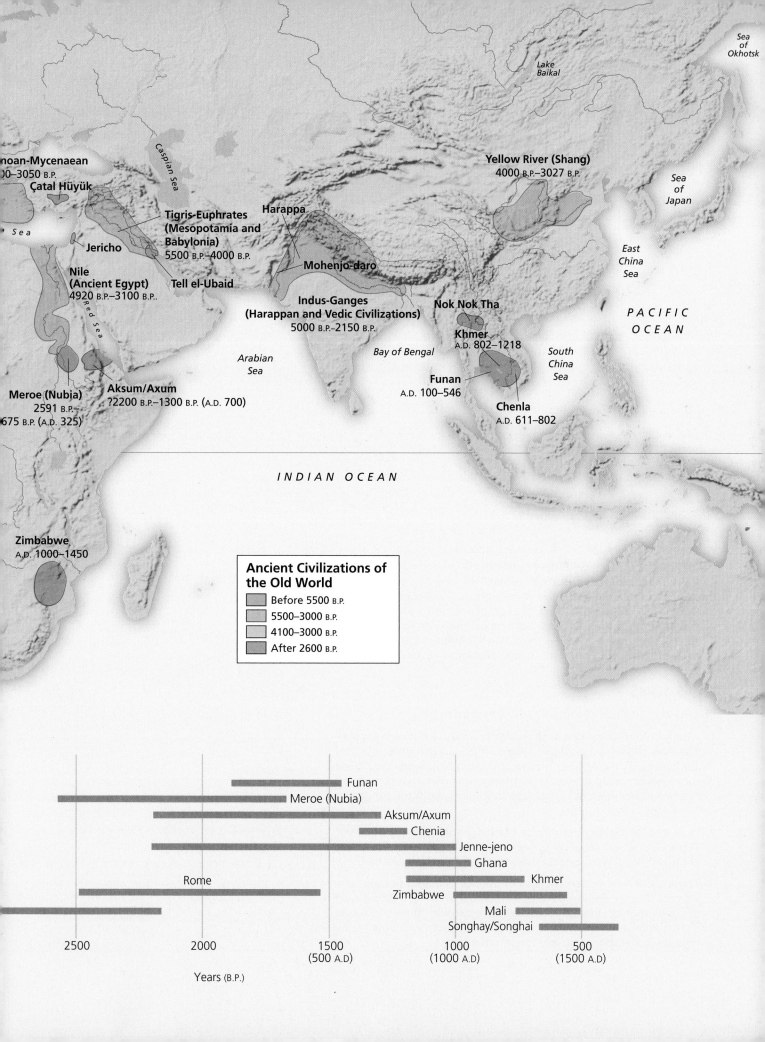

Minoan-Mycenaean
...0–3050 B.P.

Çatal Hüyük

Sea

Jericho

Tigris-Euphrates
(Mesopotamia and
Babylonia)
5500 B.P.–4000 B.P.

Harappa

Nile
(Ancient Egypt)
4920 B.P.–3100 B.P.

Tell el-Ubaid

Mohenjo-daro

Caspian Sea

Yellow River (Shang)
4000 B.P.–3027 B.P.

Lake
Baikal

Sea
of
Okhotsk

Sea
of
Japan

East
China
Sea

Indus-Ganges
(Harappan and Vedic Civilizations)
5000 B.P.–2150 B.P.

Nok Nok Tha

Khmer
A.D. 802–1218

Funan
A.D. 100–546

Chenla
A.D. 611–802

*Arabian
Sea*

Bay of Bengal

*South
China
Sea*

PACIFIC
OCEAN

Meroe (Nubia)
2591 B.P.–
...675 B.P. (A.D. 325)

Aksum/Axum
?2200 B.P.–1300 B.P. (A.D. 700)

Red Sea

INDIAN OCEAN

Zimbabwe
A.D. 1000–1450

**Ancient Civilizations of
the Old World**

Before 5500 B.P.
5500–3000 B.P.
4100–3000 B.P.
After 2600 B.P.

Funan
Meroe (Nubia)
Aksum/Axum
Chenia
Jenne-jeno
Ghana
Khmer
Rome
Zimbabwe
Mali
Songhay/Songhai

2500
2000
1500
(500 A.D)
1000
(1000 A.D)
500
(1500 A.D)

Years (B.P.)

MAP 10
Ethnographic Study Sites Prior to 1950

The development of anthropology as a scientific discipline can be traced to the middle to late part of the 19th century. In cultural anthropology, ethnographic field work became usual and common during the early 20th century. American ethnographers turned to the study of Native Americans, while European anthropologists often studied people living in world areas, such as Africa, which had been conquered and/or colonized by the anthropologist's nation of origin.

QUESTIONS

Look at Map 10, "Ethnographic Study Sites Prior to 1950."

1. Anthropology originated as the scientific study of nonwestern peoples and cultures. Yet Map 10 shows that many anthropological studies conducted prior to 1950 were done in North America. What societies were being studied in North America? Were they considered western or nonwestern? What does this tell us about the concept of "western"?

2. How would you describe the range of ethnographic sites prior to 1950? Were some world areas being neglected, such as the Middle East or mainland Asia? What might be the reasons for such omissions?

3. Think about how changes in transportation and communication have affected the way anthropologists do their research. How might a list of contemporary ethnographic sites contrast with the distribution shown in Map 10. How has longitudinal research been affected by changes in transportation and communication?

Ethnographic Study Sites Prior to 1950

North America
1. Eastern Eskimo
2. Central Eskimo
3. Naskapi
4. Iroquois
5. Delaware
6. Natchez
7. Shawnee
8. Kickapoo
9. Sioux
10. Crow
11. Nez Percé
12. Shoshone
13. Paviotso
14. Kwakiutl
15. Tsimshian
16. Haida
17. Tlingit
18. Navajo
19. Hopi
20. Zuñi
21. Aztec
22. Tzintzuntzan and Cuanajo
23. Maya
24. Cherokee
25. San Pedro

South America
Ecuador
26. Jívaro
Peru
27. Inca
28. Machiguenga
29. Achuara
30. Campa
Bolivia
31. Aymara
Chile
32. Yahgan
Venezuela
33. Yanomamö
Brazil
34. Tapirapé
35. Mundurucu
36. Mehinacu
37. Kuikuru
38. Caingang

Africa
Ghana
39. Ashanti
Nigeria
40. Kadar

Sudan
41. Fur
42. Dinka
43. Nuer
44. Azande
Uganda
45. Bunyoro
46. Ganda
Dem. Rep. of Congo
47. Mbuti
Rwanda
48. Watusi
Kenya
49. Masai
Tanzania
50. Nyakyusa
51. Lovedu
Zambia
52. Ndembu
53. Barotse
Mozambique
54. Bathonga
South Africa
55. !Kung Bushmen
56. Zulu

Asia
Sri Lanka
57. Vedda
58. Sinhalese
India
59. Andaman
60. Nayar
61. Tamil
62. Rajput
Siberia
63. Tungus
Japan
64. Ainu
China
65. Luts'un village
Taiwan
66. Taiwan Chinese
Vietnam
67. Mnong-Gar
Malaya
68. Semai

Pacific
Philippines
69. Tasaday
Indonesia Area
70. Dyaks
71. Alorese
72. Tetum
Australia
73. Tiwi
74. Arunta
75. Murngin
76. Saibai Islanders
New Guinea
77. Arapesh
78. Dani
79. Gururumba
80. Kai
81. Kapauku
82. Mae Enga
83. Kuma
84. Mundugumor
85. Tchambuli
86. Tsembaga Maring
87. Tavade
88. Foré
89. Etoro

Melanesian Islands
90. Manus Islanders
91. New Hanover Islanders
92. Trobriand Islanders
93. Dobuans
94. Rossel Islanders
95. Kaoka
96. Malaita Islanders
97. Espiritu Santo Islanders
98. Tana Islanders
99. Tikopia
100. Sivai
Polynesian Islands
101. Maori
102. Tongans
103. Samoans
104. Mangians
105. Tahitians
106. Hawaiians
Micronesian Islands
107. Truk

MAP 11
Major Families of World Languages

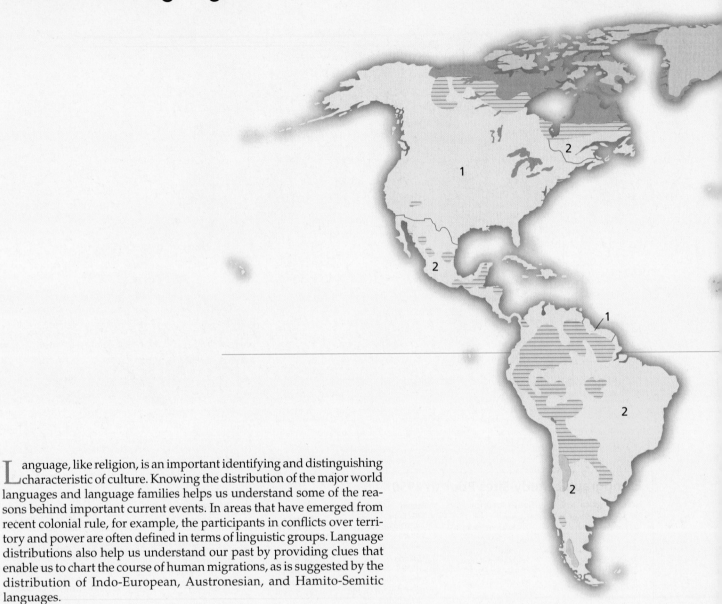

Language, like religion, is an important identifying and distinguishing characteristic of culture. Knowing the distribution of the major world languages and language families helps us understand some of the reasons behind important current events. In areas that have emerged from recent colonial rule, for example, the participants in conflicts over territory and power are often defined in terms of linguistic groups. Language distributions also help us understand our past by providing clues that enable us to chart the course of human migrations, as is suggested by the distribution of Indo-European, Austronesian, and Hamito-Semitic languages.

QUESTIONS

Look at Map 11, "Major Families of World Languages."

1. Name three language families or subfamilies that are spoken on more than one continent. How do you explain this distribution?

2. Where are the Austronesian languages spoken? How might one explain this distribution?

3. What language families are spoken on the African continent? Locate the Niger-Congo language family, of which the Bantu languages comprise a subfamily.

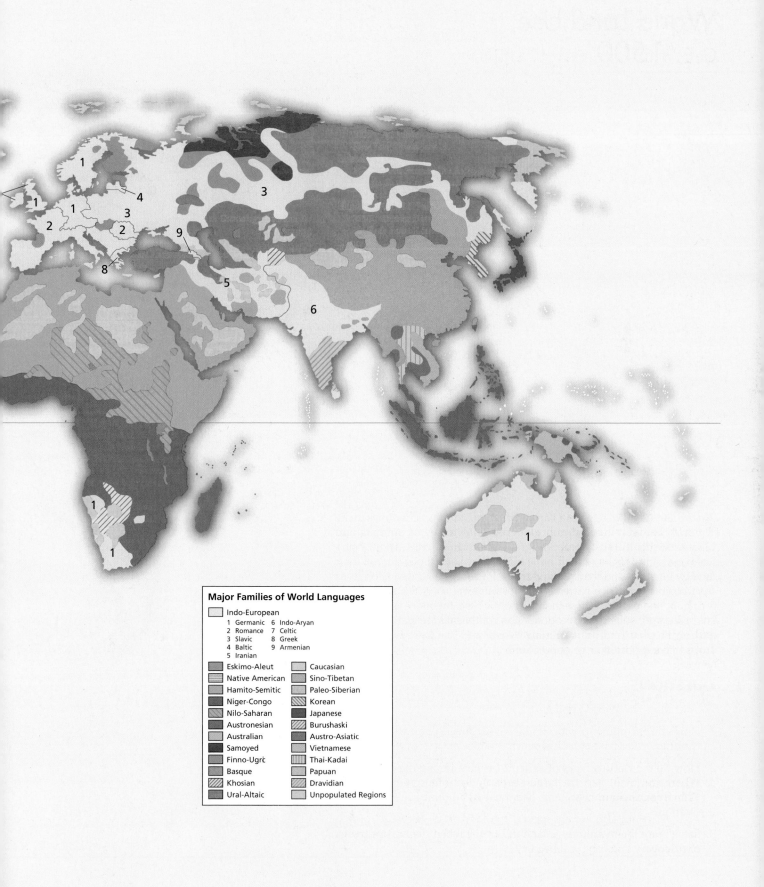

Major Families of World Languages

☐ Indo-European
  1 Germanic 6 Indo-Aryan
  2 Romance   7 Celtic
  3 Slavic   8 Greek
  4 Baltic   9 Armenian
  5 Iranian

Eskimo-Aleut
Native American
Hamito-Semitic
Niger-Congo
Nilo-Saharan
Austronesian
Australian
Samoyed
Finno-Ugric
Basque
Khosian
Ural-Altaic

Caucasian
Sino-Tibetan
Paleo-Siberian
Korean
Japanese
Burushaski
Austro-Asiatic
Vietnamese
Thai-Kadai
Papuan
Dravidian
Unpopulated Regions

MAP 12
World Land Use,
C.E. 1500

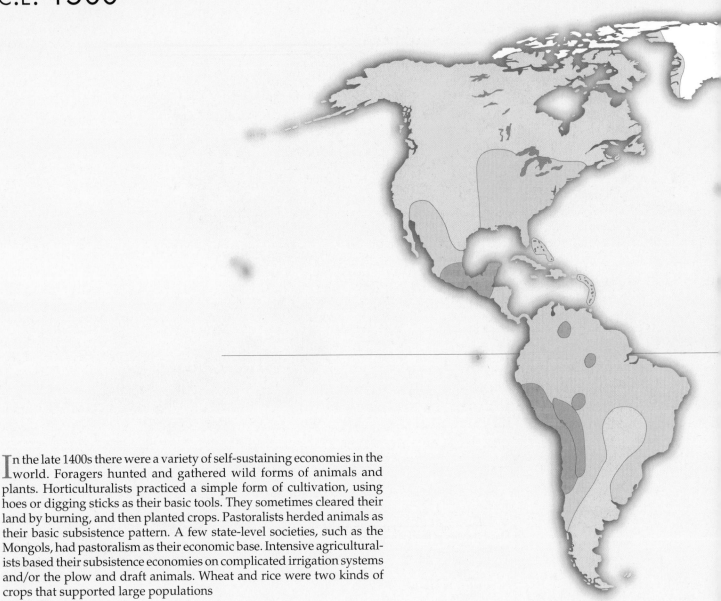

In the late 1400s there were a variety of self-sustaining economies in the world. Foragers hunted and gathered wild forms of animals and plants. Horticulturalists practiced a simple form of cultivation, using hoes or digging sticks as their basic tools. They sometimes cleared their land by burning, and then planted crops. Pastoralists herded animals as their basic subsistence pattern. A few state-level societies, such as the Mongols, had pastoralism as their economic base. Intensive agriculturalists based their subsistence economies on complicated irrigation systems and/or the plow and draft animals. Wheat and rice were two kinds of crops that supported large populations

QUESTIONS

Look at Map 12, "World Land Use, C.E. 1500."

1. Name three continents with significant herding economies. On which continents was pastoralism absent?

2. How do the various types of agriculture vary among the continents? Which continent had the largest area under intensive cultivation? Which continent or continents had the least amount of intensive cultivation?

3. What were the main uses of land in Europe when the European age of discovery and conquest began?

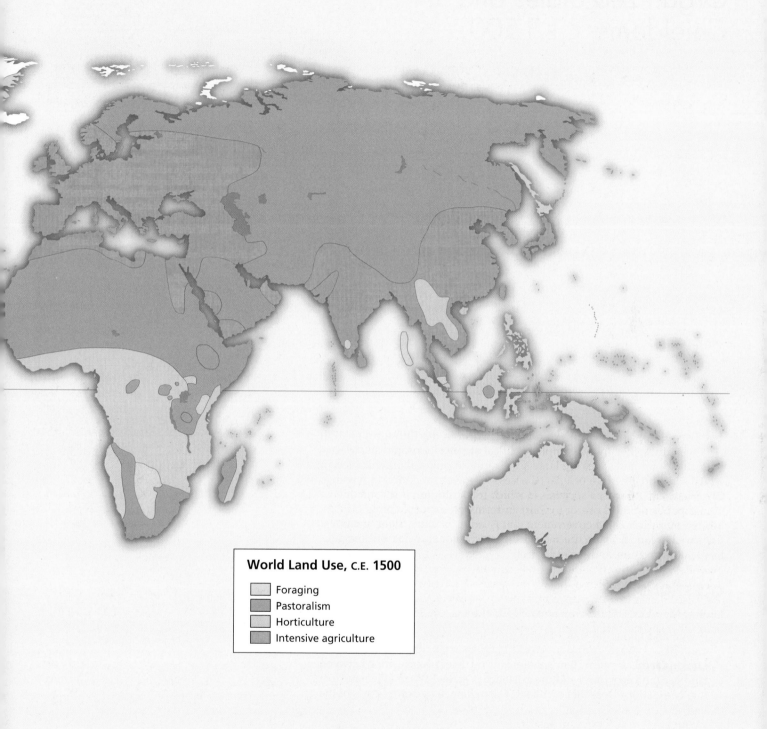

World Land Use, C.E. 1500

Foraging

Pastoralism

Horticulture

Intensive agriculture

MAP 13
Organized States and Chiefdoms, C.E. 1500

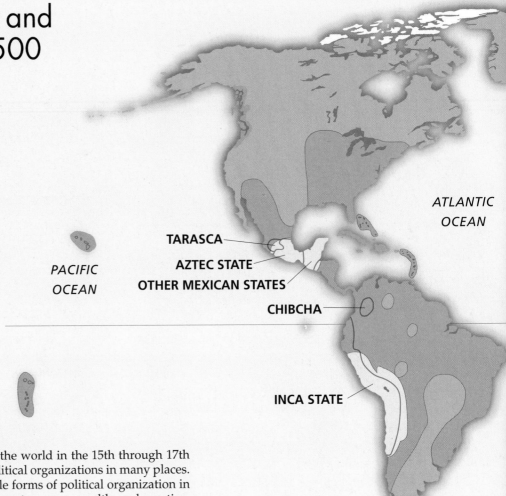

ATLANTIC
OCEAN

PACIFIC
OCEAN

TARASCA

AZTEC STATE

OTHER MEXICAN STATES

CHIBCHA

INCA STATE

When Europeans started exploring the world in the 15th through 17th centuries, they found complex political organizations in many places. Both chiefdoms and states are large-scale forms of political organization in which some people have privileged access to power, wealth, and prestige. Chiefdoms are kin-based societies in which redistribution is the major economic pattern. States are organized in terms of socioeconomic classes, headed by a centralized government that is led by an elite. States include a full-time bureaucracy and specialized subsystems for such activities as military action, taxation, and social control.

QUESTIONS

Look at Map 13, "Organized States and Chiefdoms, C.E. 1500."

1. Locate and name the states that existed in the Western Hemisphere in C.E. 1500. Compare Map 12, "World Land Use: C.E. 1500," with Map13. Looking at the Western Hemisphere, can you detect a correlation between land use (and economy) and the existence of states? What's the nature of that correlation? Does that correlation also characterize other parts of the world?

2. Locate three regions of the world where chiefdoms existed in C.E. 1500. Compare Map 12, "World Land Use: C.E. 1500," with Map 13. Can you detect a correlation between land use (and economy) and the existence of chiefdoms? What's the nature of that correlation?

3. Some parts of the world lacked either chiefdoms or states in C.E. 1500. What are some of those areas? What kinds of political systems did they probably have?

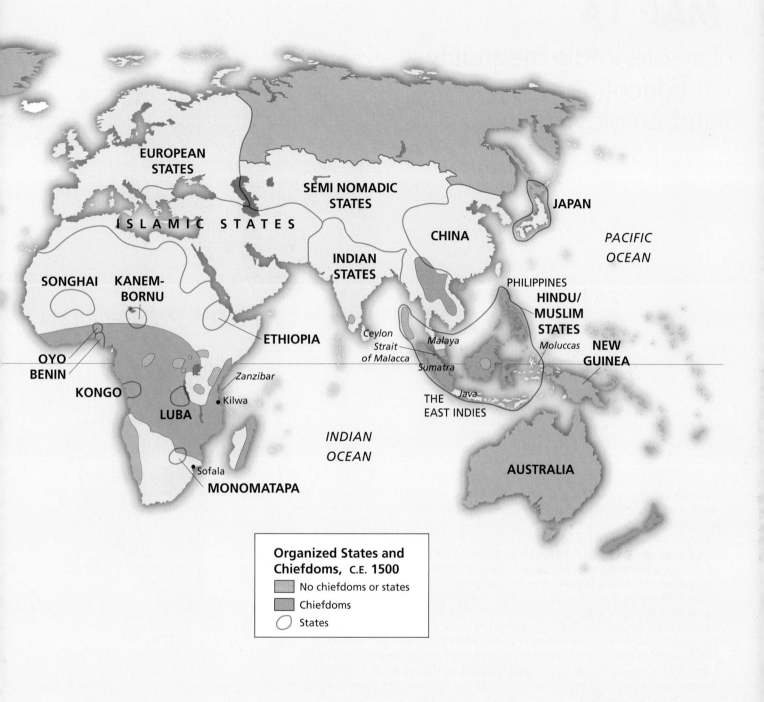

EUROPEAN
STATES

SEMI NOMADIC
STATES

JAPAN

ISLAMIC STATES

CHINA

PACIFIC
OCEAN

SONGHAI

KANEM-
BORNU

INDIAN
STATES

PHILIPPINES

HINDU/
MUSLIM
STATES

NEW
GUINEA

ETHIOPIA

Ceylon
Strait
of Malacca

Malaya

Moluccas

OYO
BENIN

Sumatra

KONGO

Zanzibar

THE
EAST INDIES

Java

LUBA

• Kilwa

INDIAN
OCEAN

• Sofala

MONOMATAPA

AUSTRALIA

**Organized States and
Chiefdoms,** C.E. **1500**

No chiefdoms or states

Chiefdoms

States

MAP 14

Female/Male Inequality in Education and Employment

Inuit

Hidatsa

Iroquois

Pawnee

Arembepe

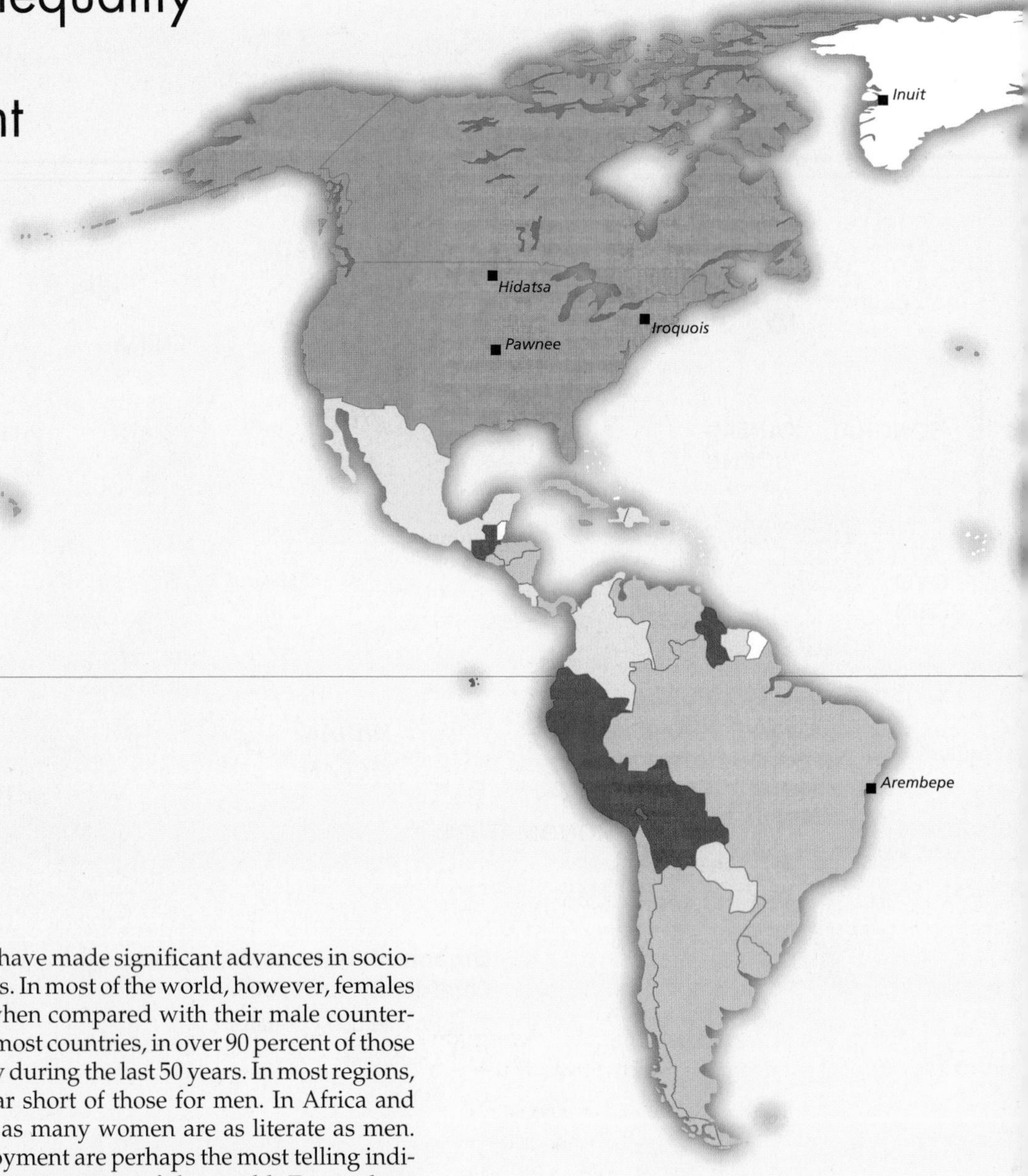

Women in developed countries have made significant advances in socio-economic status in recent years. In most of the world, however, females suffer from significant inequality when compared with their male counterparts. Although women can vote in most countries, in over 90 percent of those countries that right was granted only during the last 50 years. In most regions, literacy rates for women still fall far short of those for men. In Africa and Asia, for example, only about half as many women are as literate as men. Inequalities in education and employment are perhaps the most telling indicators of the unequal status of women in most of the world. Even where women are employed in positions similar to those held by men, they tend to receive less compensation. The gap between rich and poor involves not only a clear geographic differentiation, but a clear gender differentiation as well.

QUESTIONS

Look at Map 14 "Female/Male Inequality in Education and Employment."

1. Locate and name three Third World countries with the same degree of gender-based inequality as the United States and Canada.

2. Two of the world's largest developing nations are coded as having "less inequality." What are they?

3. Most European countries are coded as having "least inequality." Which western European countries are exceptions?

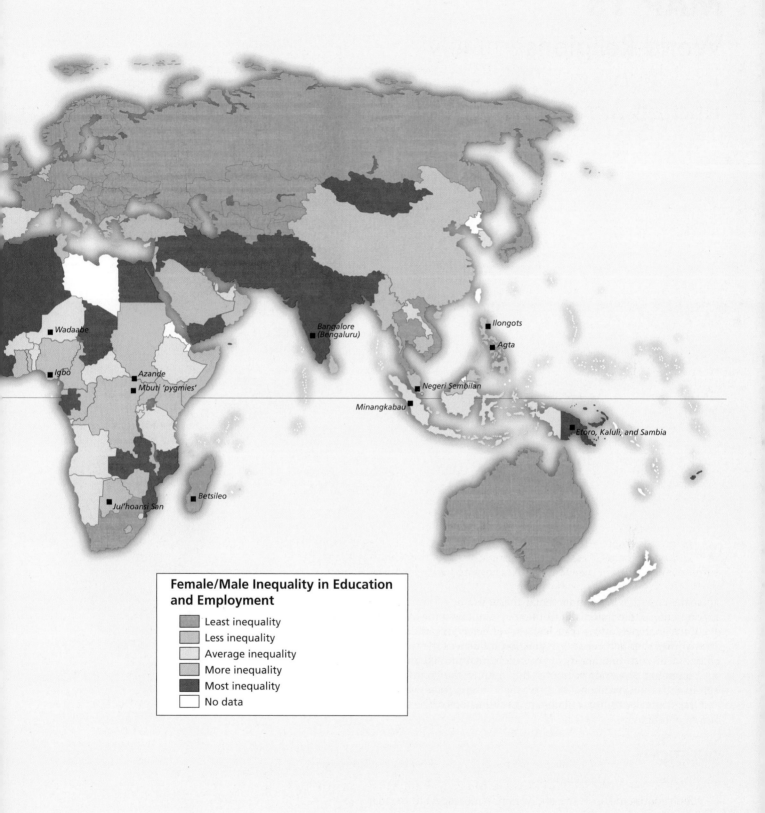

Female/Male Inequality in Education and Employment

- Least inequality
- Less inequality
- Average inequality
- More inequality
- Most inequality
- No data

Wadaabe

Igbo

Azande

Mbuti 'pygmies'

Bangalore (Bengaluru)

Ilongots

Agta

Negeri Sembilan

Minangkabau

Etoro, Kaluli, and Sambia

Betsileo

Ju'hoansi San

MAP 15
World Religions

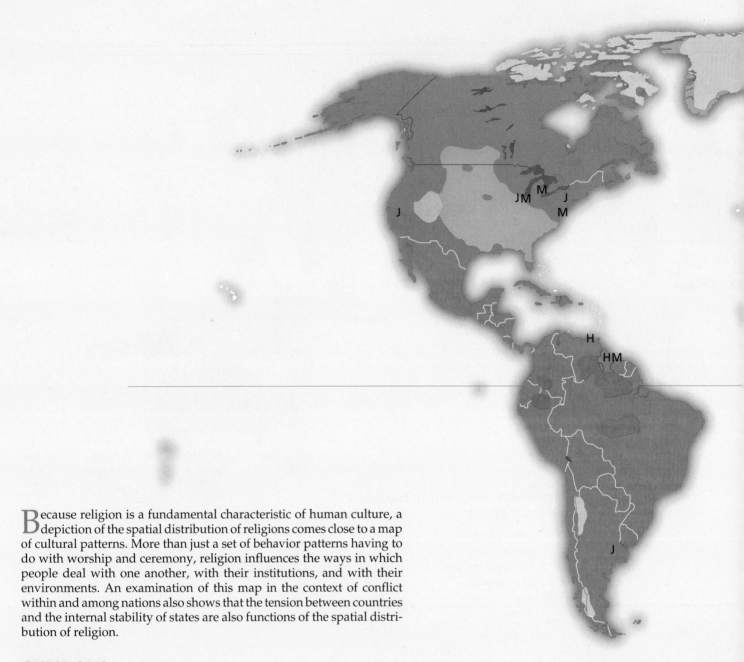

Because religion is a fundamental characteristic of human culture, a depiction of the spatial distribution of religions comes close to a map of cultural patterns. More than just a set of behavior patterns having to do with worship and ceremony, religion influences the ways in which people deal with one another, with their institutions, and with their environments. An examination of this map in the context of conflict within and among nations also shows that the tension between countries and the internal stability of states are also functions of the spatial distribution of religion.

QUESTIONS

Look at Map 15, "World Religions."

1. Which continent has the most diversity with respect to the major religions?

2. Which continent is most Protestant? Why do you think that is the case?

3. Where in the world are "tribal" religions still practiced?

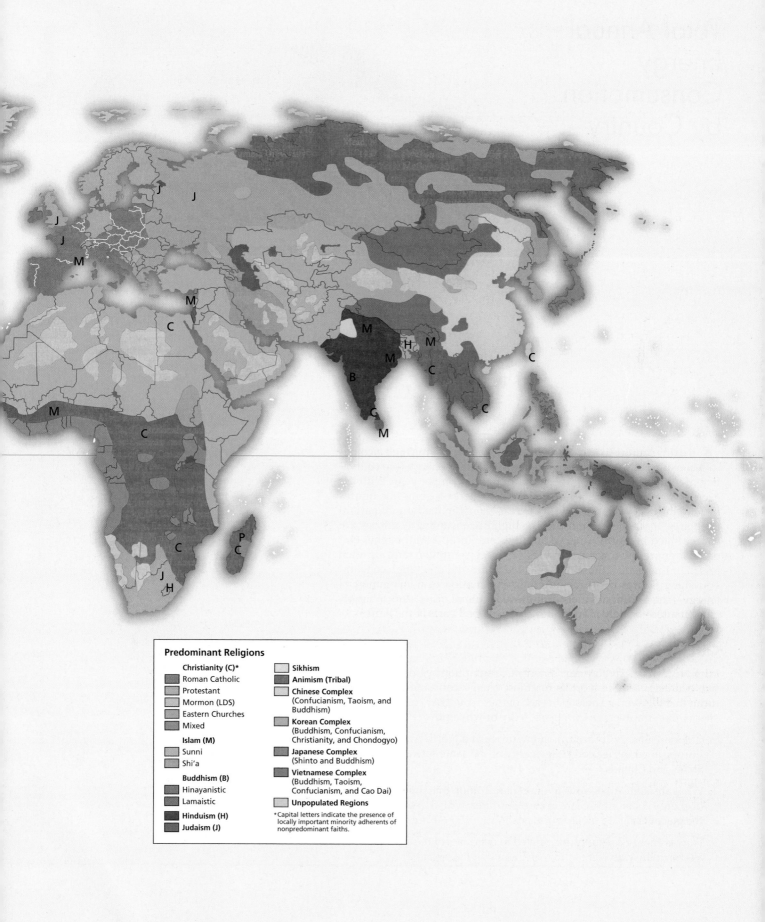

Predominant Religions

Christianity (C)*
 Roman Catholic
 Protestant
 Mormon (LDS)
 Eastern Churches
 Mixed

Islam (M)
 Sunni
 Shi'a

Buddhism (B)
 Hinayanistic
 Lamaistic

Hinduism (H)

Judaism (J)

 Sikhism

Animism (Tribal)

Chinese Complex
(Confucianism, Taoism, and Buddhism)

Korean Complex
(Buddhism, Confucianism, Christianity, and Chondogyo)

Japanese Complex
(Shinto and Buddhism)

Vietnamese Complex
(Buddhism, Taoism, Confucianism, and Cao Dai)

 Unpopulated Regions

*Capital letters indicate the presence of locally important minority adherents of nonpredominant faiths.

MAP 16
Total Annual Energy Consumption by Country

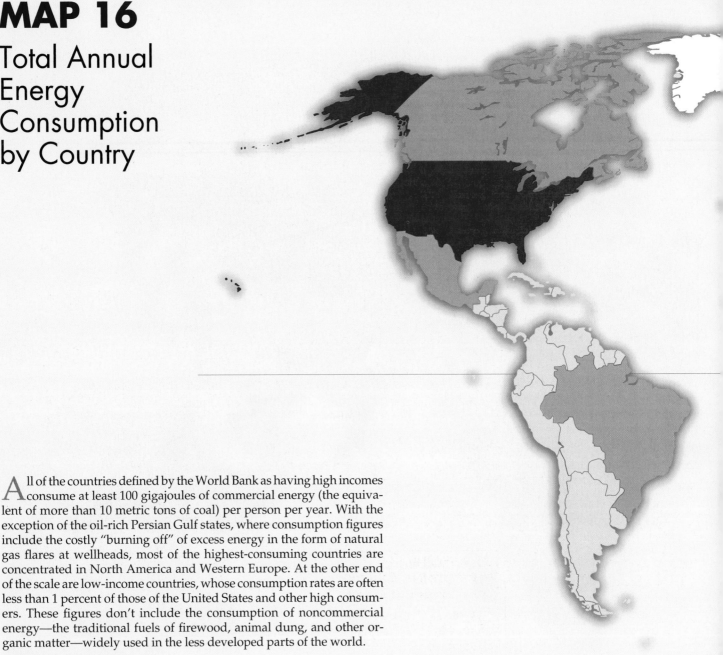

All of the countries defined by the World Bank as having high incomes consume at least 100 gigajoules of commercial energy (the equivalent of more than 10 metric tons of coal) per person per year. With the exception of the oil-rich Persian Gulf states, where consumption figures include the costly "burning off" of excess energy in the form of natural gas flares at wellheads, most of the highest-consuming countries are concentrated in North America and Western Europe. At the other end of the scale are low-income countries, whose consumption rates are often less than 1 percent of those of the United States and other high consumers. These figures don't include the consumption of noncommercial energy—the traditional fuels of firewood, animal dung, and other organic matter—widely used in the less developed parts of the world.

QUESTIONS

Look at Map 16, " Total Annual Energy Consumption by Country." What five countries are the world's foremost energy consumers? Does this mean that the average person in each of these countries consumes more energy than the average European? Why or why not?

1. Compare energy consumption in Europe and North America. Do all European countries consume energy at the same rate as the United States and Canada?

2. What are some exceptions to the generalization that the highest rates of energy consumption are in core countries, with the lowest rates on the periphery?

3. How is energy consumption related to measures of the quality of life, as shown in Map 17?

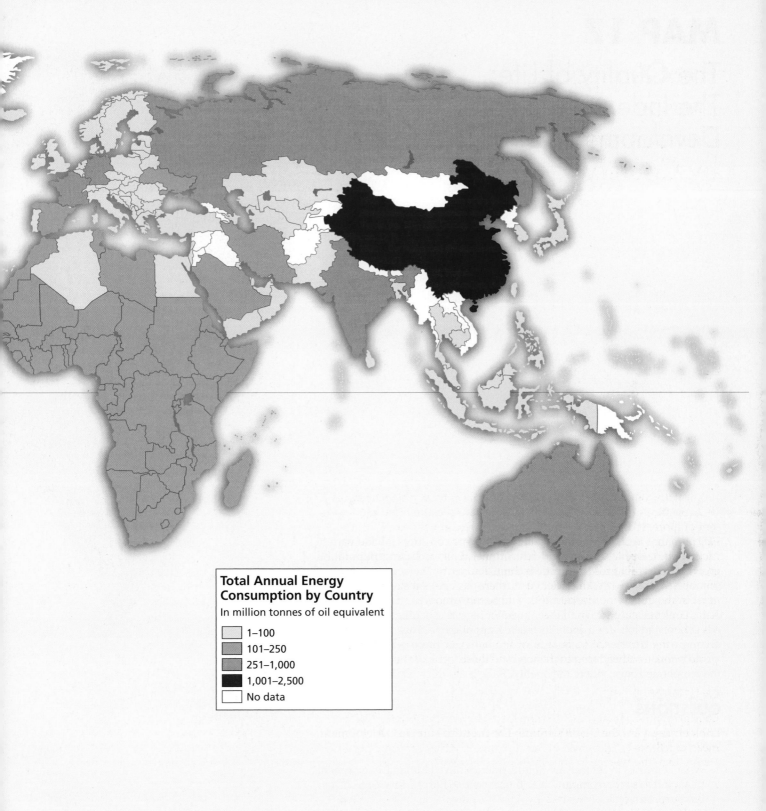

**Total Annual Energy
Consumption by Country**

In million tonnes of oil equivalent

1–100
101–250
251–1,000
1,001–2,500
No data

MAP 17

The Quality of Life: The Index of Human Development, 2007

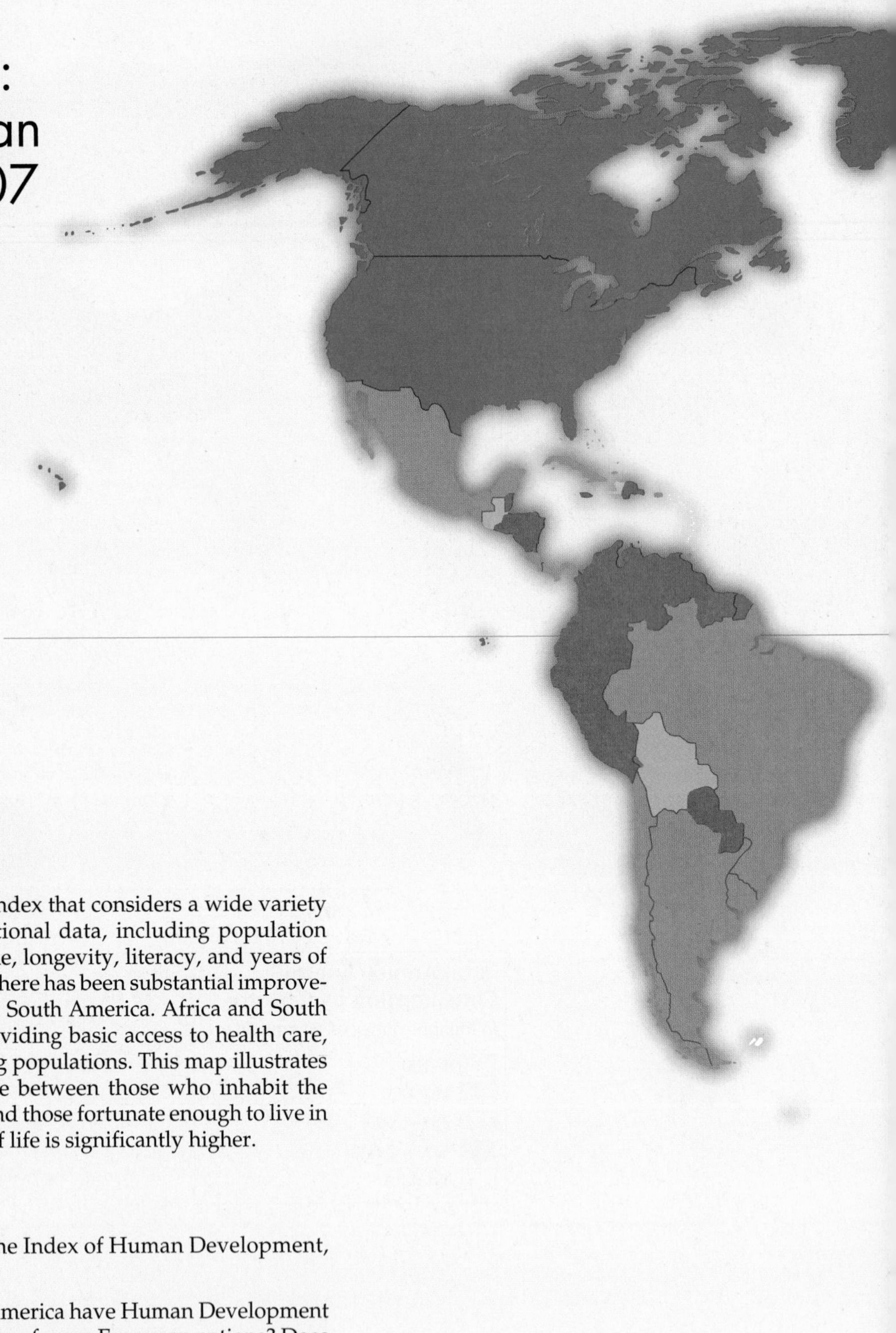

This map is based on a development index that considers a wide variety of demographic, health, and educational data, including population growth, per capita gross domestic income, longevity, literacy, and years of schooling. Compared with earlier years, there has been substantial improvement in the quality of life in Middle and South America. Africa and South Asia, however, face the challenge of providing basic access to health care, education, and jobs for rapidly increasing populations. This map illustrates an enduring difference in quality of life between those who inhabit the world's equatorial and tropical regions and those fortunate enough to live in the temperate zones, where the quality of life is significantly higher.

QUESTIONS

Look at Map 17, "The Quality of Life: The Index of Human Development, 2007."

1. What countries in central and South America have Human Development Index (HDI) scores comparable to those of some European nations? Does this surprise you?

2. Given that Brazil has one of the world's top 10 economies, does its HDI score surprise you? How do Brazil, Mexico, and Venezuela compare in terms of the HDI?

3. Do you notice a correlation between deforestation (Map 1) and quality of life? Does India fit this correlation?

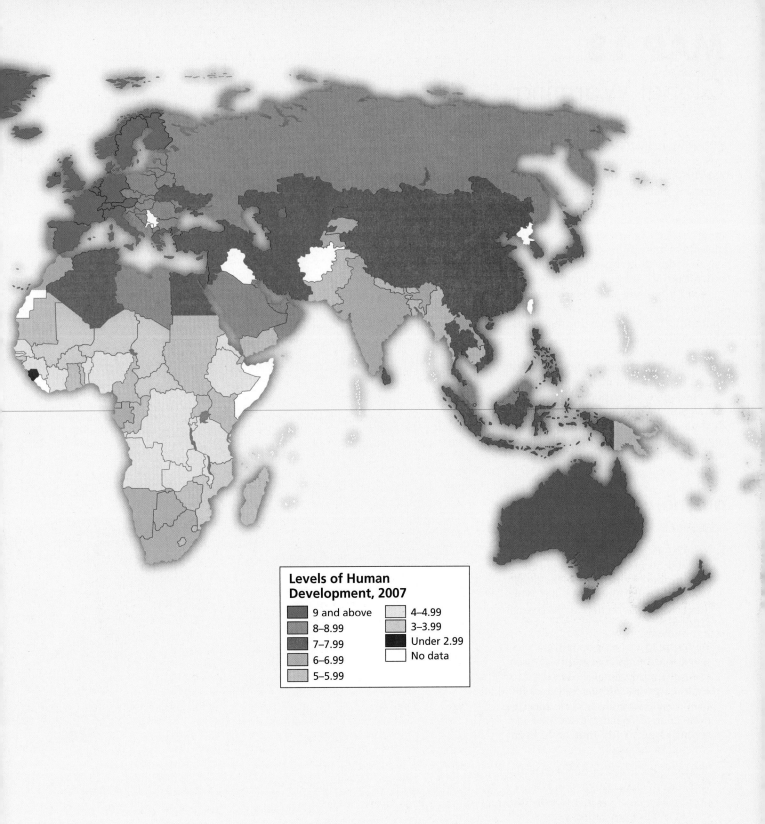

Levels of Human Development, 2007

9 and above

8–8.99

7–7.99

6–6.99

5–5.99

4–4.99

3–3.99

Under 2.99

No data

MAP 18
Global Warming

Since the early 20th century, the Earth's surface temperatures have risen about 1.4° F (0.7° C). Rising temperatures, shrinking glaciers, and melting polar ice provide additional evidence for global warming. Scientists prefer the term climate change to *global warming*. Scientific measurements confirm that global warming is not due to increased solar radiation, but rather are mainly *anthropogenic*—caused by humans and their activities. Because our planet's climate is always changing, the key question becomes: How much global warming is due to human activities versus natural climate variability. Most scientists agree that human activities play a major role in global climate change. Given population growth and rapidly increasing use of fossil fuels, the human factor is significant. The map represents the relative impact of global warming in different regions of the world.

QUESTIONS

Look at Map 18, "Global Warming."

1. Which geographical regions of the world show noticeable effects of global warming? Which show the least? What about the polar regions? Why are certain major sections of the oceans affected?

2. Widespread and long-term trends toward warmer global temperatures and a changing climate are referred to as "fingerprints." Researchers look for them to detect and confirm that climate change. What are some of the recent fingerprints that have been covered in the media?

3. "Harbingers" refer to such events as fires, exceptional droughts, and downpours. They can also include the spread of disease-bearing insects and widespread bleaching of coral reefs. Any and all may be directly or partly caused by a warmer climate. Have you noticed any recent harbingers in the U.S. in the past year? Have they been confined to any specific geographical regions?

Global Warming

- Very low impact
- Low impact
- Medium impact
- Medium high impact
- High impact
- Very high impact

Important Theories

Anthropology: Appreciating Human Diversity provides comprehensive coverage of the major theoretical perspectives at the core of anthropological study. The list below indicates specific text chapters in which these concepts are discussed.

GENERAL APPROACHES

Adaptation: 1, 2, 3, 5, 6, 7, 8, 9, 10, 15, 16, 17, 18, 19, 20, 21, 22, 23, 24

Biocultural approaches: 1, 3, 5, 6, 7, 8, 9, 10, 16, 20, 21, 22, 23

Comparative approaches: 1, 2, 6, 7, 11, 12, 13, 15, 16, 17, 18, 19, 20, 21, 22, 23, 24
    Classification and typologies: 2, 6, 7, 8, 9, 10, 11, 12, 13, 16, 17, 18, 19, 20, 21, 22, 23, 24
    Systemic cross-cultural comparison: 2, 13, 18, 21, 22, 23

Ethnological theory: 1, 2, 3, 13, 15, 18, 19, 20, 21, 22, 23, 24

Ethnography: 1, 2, 3, 13, 16, 17, 18, 19, 20, 21, 22, 23, 24
    Emic and etic approaches: 2, 3, 13, 16, 19, 21, 22, 23, 24
    Longitudinal and multi-sited approaches: 2, 13, 17, 18, 24
    Quantitative and qualitative approaches: 2, 13, 18, 21, 22

Evolutionary theory: 5, 6, 7, 8, 9, 10, 11, 12, 13, 16, 17, 21, 22, 23

Explanation: 1, 2, 3, 5, 6, 7, 8, 9, 10, 11, 12, 13, 15, 16, 17, 18, 19, 20, 21, 22, 23, 24

Holism: 1, 3, 16, 22

Scientific theory: 1, 2, 3, 5, 7, 8, 9, 10, 11, 12, 13, 16, 17, 18, 20, 21, 22, 23, 24

Social theory: 1, 2, 3, 13, 21, 22, 23, 24

SPECIFIC APPROACHES

Colonialism and postcolonial studies: 2, 13, 15, 17, 21, 23, 24

Configurationalism/cultural patterning: 2, 13, 16, 17, 21, 22, 23, 24

Cultural studies and postmodernism: 24

Ecological anthropology: 16, 17, 18, 21, 22, 23

Feminist theory: 3, 13, 18, 23

Functional approaches: 13, 16, 17, 18, 19, 20, 21, 22, 23, 24

Humanistic approaches: 1, 2, 13, 21, 22, 23, 24

Integration and patterning: 2, 3, 13, 15, 17, 21, 22, 23, 24

Interpretive approaches: 2, 13, 17, 21, 22, 24

Political-economy and world-system approaches: 2, 3, 13, 15, 16, 17, 18, 21, 23, 24

Political/legal anthropology and power: 2, 3, 12, 13, 15, 17, 18, 20, 21, 22, 23, 24
    Conflict: 3, 13, 15, 16, 17, 18, 21, 23, 24
    Rise and fall of state, theories for: 12, 16, 23
    Social control: 17, 21, 23, 24

Practice theory: 2, 8, 13, 23, 24
    Culture as contested: 2, 3, 13, 15, 18, 21, 23, 24
    Public and private culture: 2, 17, 21, 22, 23, 24
    Resistance: 2, 3, 15, 17, 21, 23, 24

Psychological approaches: 13, 16, 17, 21, 22, 23, 24

Symbolic approaches: 2, 12, 13, 18, 21, 22, 24

Systemic approaches: 2, 3, 11, 12, 13, 16, 17, 18, 19, 21, 23, 24

Theories of social construction: 2, 15, 18, 19, 20, 21, 22, 23, 24
    Identities: 15, 17, 18, 19, 20, 21, 22, 23, 24
    Native theories (folk classification): 2, 3, 13, 15, 17, 18, 19, 20, 21, 22
    Race and ethnicity: 2, 15, 17, 19, 21, 22, 23, 24
    Social status: 2, 15, 16, 17, 18, 19, 20, 21, 22, 23